Frommer's '96

COMPREHENSIVE TRAVEL GUIDE

England

by Darwin Porter
& Danforth Prince

Macmillan • USA

ABOUT THE AUTHORS

A native of North Carolina, **Darwin Porter** was a bureau chief for the *Miami Herald* when he was 21 and was assigned to write the very first edition of a Frommer guide devoted solely to one European country. Since then, he has written numerous bestselling Frommer guides, notably to England, France, the Caribbean, Italy, and Germany. In 1982, he was joined in his research efforts across England by **Danforth Prince,** formerly of the Paris bureau of the *New York Times,* who has traveled in and written extensively about England.

MACMILLAN TRAVEL

A Simon & Schuster Macmillan Company
1633 Broadway
New York, NY 10019

ISBN 0-02-860634-5
ISSN 1055-5404

Editor: Charlotte Allstrom
Map Editor: Douglas Stallings
Digital cartography by Ortelius Design
Design by Michele Laseau

SPECIAL SALES

Bulk purchases (10+ copies) of Frommer's Travel Guides are available to corporations at special discounts. The Special Sales Department can produce custom editions to be used as premiums and/or for sales promotion to suit individual needs. Existing editions can be produced with custom cover imprints such as corporate logos. For more information write to: Special Sales, Simon & Schuster, 1633 Broadway, New York, NY 10019.

Manufactured in the United States of America

Contents

List of Maps

AN INVITATION TO THE READER

In researching this book, we have come across many wonderful sights, pubs, and restaurants, the best of which we have included here. We are sure that many of you will also discover appealing places as you explore England. Please don't keep them to yourself. Share your experiences, especially if you want to bring to our attention information that has changed since this book was researched. You can address your letters to:

Darwin Porter and Danforth Prince
Frommer's England '96
Macmillan Travel
1633 Broadway
New York, NY 10019

AN ADDITIONAL NOTE

Please be advised that travel information is subject to change at any time. The authors, editors, and publisher cannot be held responsible for the experiences of readers while traveling. Your safety is important to us, however, so we encourage you to stay alert and be aware of your surroundings. Keep a close eye on cameras, purses, and wallets, all favorite targets of thieves and pickpockets.

WHAT THE SYMBOLS MEAN

✪ Frommer's Favorites

Hotels, restaurants, attractions, and entertainment you should not miss.

⑤ Super-Special Values

Hotels and restaurants that offer great value for your money.

The following abbreviations are used for credit cards:

AE	American Express	EU	Eurocard
CB	Carte Blanche	JCB	Japan Credit Bank
DC	Diners Club	MC	MasterCard
DISC	Discover	V	Visa
ER	enRoute		

Getting to Know England

Why go to England? What's its attraction? The England of today has moved far from the prim-and-proper Victorianism of the mid-19th century and is an exciting land of change and experiment. It's not a big country, but 2,500 eventful years have left their mark on its rich tradition, and traveling in England is like experiencing a living, illustrated history book. You can ponder the ancient mystery of Stonehenge, relive the days of Roman Britain when you walk through an excavated villa, and hear in words and place names the linguistic influences of Celtic, Norse, and Norman French as well as Anglo-Saxon.

It's a formidable task to condense the best of England between the covers of a guide—anybody who ever tries to compile a list of the best of anything is usually headed for trouble. However, we'll plunge ahead. The best doesn't have to be the most expensive, so, after familiarizing you with the life of merrie old England, our aim is to stretch your buying power, to show you that you need not always pay top dollar for charm and comfort.

A lot of attention is devoted to the tourist meccas of London, Stratford-upon-Avon, and Oxford. But these ancient cities and towns do not even come close to fully reflecting the complexity and diversity of one of the most culturally rich countries in the world. England defies a clear, logical, coherent plan of sightseeing. It's a patchwork quilt of treasures, with many of the most scenic items tucked away in remote corners—an Elizabethan country estate in Devon, a half-timbered thatched cottage by the sea in Dorset, a regency manor in the Lake District.

1 The Best of England

BEST TRAVEL EXPERIENCES IN ENGLAND

1. **Boat Rides on Lake Windermere.** Inspired by the lyric poetry of such Lake District romantics as the poet William Wordsworth ("hazel bowers/With milk-white clusters hung"), you can board one of the boats at Windermere or Bowness and sail England's most famous lake. That way you'll see the Lake District's scenery, its tilled valleys in the shadow of forbidding peaks, as it was meant to be viewed—from the perspective of the water. Especially

worthy is the round trip from Bowness to Ambleside, at the head of the lake, all the way back around to the village of Lake Side, at the southern tip.

2. **A Night at the Theater.** The torch passed down from Shakespeare is still burning brightly, especially in London but also in all the big cities of England. For some four centuries, the theater tradition in London has flourished—sometimes pestilence, or even excessive taxes, have interrupted performances. Perhaps a rain of blitz bombs sent the actors fleeing from the stage, a gift from an angry Hitler (who had already staked out his private London residence should he win the war). But English theater has always bounced back from disaster. Today, the theater of London is acknowledged as the finest in the world. There are two major subsidized companies, the Royal Shakespeare Company, at the Barbican in London and at Stratford-upon-Avon, and the National Theatre, on the South Bank. The true theater buff will also seek out "fringe" theater—sometimes presented in church cellars or the upstairs rooms of pubs.

3. **Pub Crawling.** Even for those who shun bar-hopping back home, the pursuit of the pint takes on cultural significance in England. Ornate taps fill tankards and mugs in the pubs of England's every village, hamlet, and town. Such names as Eagle Arms, Angel, Pike Eel, the Red Lion, the White Swan, the Bull, and the Royal Oak dot the landscape, their quaint signs beckoning you in. You go not only for the pint but the conviviality, perhaps even the entertainment or (and here you must suspend disbelief) the food. Many pubs serve a delectable Dover sole or some other good dish, not the steak-and-kidney pie that Johnson and Boswell left on their plates during their long-ago travels. Log fires roar in winter, and in summer, drinkers like to stand outside in the bracing air. The pub remains the center of English social life.

4. **Motoring Through the Cotswold Hills.** "In America, you call it driving," said the publican of a mellow old tavern in Stow-on-the-Wold. "Over here we call it motoring." If *driving* means going on a determined point from one place to another, *motoring* is wandering at random, and there's no better place for it than the Cotswolds. Its rolling hills and pasturelands green from nurturing rains, peppered with ivy-covered inns, stone walls, and honey-colored stone cottages whose builders once grew prosperous on wool, the very names of the villages evoke an England of long ago. Bourton-on-the-Water, Upper Slaughter, Chipping Campden, Moreton-in-Marsh, Cirencester, or Wotton-under-Edge—and who can forget Old Sodbury? Less than 100 miles west of London, you have some 500 square miles to explore of an England that romantics fantasize about.

5. **Punting on the Cam.** Although the expression may not mean anything to you, it evokes one of the most pleasurable experiences available in East Anglia. It is "Cantabrigian English" for gliding along in a flat-bottom boat, a long pole (or "punt") pushed into the River Cam's shallow bed, bypassing the weeping willows along the banks, watching the strolling students along the graveled walkways, and taking in the picture-postcard vistas of green lawns along the water's edge. Young men have gone punting along these banks or rested in the grass while contemplating the Theory of Evolution or the Law of Gravity. The ideal time to go punting is on a summer day when you can pack a picnic lunch and find some green grass along the river on which to enjoy your goodies. At graduation time, in June, undergraduates in dinner jackets or long gowns can be seen at night making their way in punts to the university balls.

6. **Touring the Stately Homes.** Although France has its châteaux, and Germany its Rhineland castles, nothing compares with the stately homes of England. Hundreds are open to visitors. Exploring them (and we'll recommend dozens in the pages ahead) is reason enough to come to England. Many of these mansions, which present domestic architectural elements from around the world, date back to the 1400s. The homes are often surrounded by beautiful gardens—perhaps a landscape by Lancelot "Capability" Brown. When the owners got fanciful, they added splashing fountains and miniature pagodas or temples.

7. **The Curio & Antique Hunt.** Whatever you're looking for from the dusty attic of yesterday, England probably has it. It's the place to find that curio or antique you've always dreamed about, and we're talking a Steiff teddy bear, a blunderbuss, an 1890 tin-plate toy train, a postcard ballyhooing the inaugural voyage of the *Titanic,* an aircraft propeller from a downed RAF plane, an eggcup allegedly used by Queen Victoria, a first edition English print from 1700, a Coalbrookdale urn, a theater program from 1926, or the definitive Henry Harper grandfather clock. No one polishes up their antiques, curios, or wanabees quite as brightly as English "old curiosity shop" dealers, some of whom deliberately try to look like characters from Dickens. From auction houses to antique dealers, from flea markets to country fairs, England is for sale, especially Victorian England. Shopping adds zest to the London scene and gives you an extra motive for driving through the countryside. Who knows? You might even come home with a real find! Antique hunters can pick up *Lockson's Guide to Antiques in Britain,* a free pamphlet from the British Tourist Authority. Send a self-addressed, business-size envelope with 32 cents postage to: 531 Fifth Ave., Suite 701, New York, NY 10176-0799.

8. **Walking the Yorkshire Moors.** A trekker's delight, these purple-heathered moors of *Wuthering Heights* fame sprawl across more than 550 square miles and embrace some 1,130 miles of public footpaths where you can breathe the air and experience the exhilaration felt by Emily Brontë's fictional characters. In the east, the park opens onto a cliff-studded coastline. But once you go inland, you'll have only the odd sheep, dramatic scenery, and mist to keep you company. One of the most famous footpaths is Cleveland Way, stretching for more than 100 miles and hugging the coast around most of the circumference of the park. The Esk Valley Walk, another famous trail that draws hundreds of visitors on a summer Sunday, meanders along the flow of the River Esk for some 30 miles, stretching like a snake from the river's source on the moor's "highland" all the way to the sea at Whitby.

BEST HOTELS

1. **The Dorchester,** London *(see page 108).* Acclaimed since its birth in 1931 as one of the world's great hotels, this citadel of luxury is owned by the richest man on earth, the sultan of Brunei. With such an owner, the hotel naturally promotes opulence. After a multimillion-pound restoration, "The Dorch" is more splendid than ever. The rooftop suites, particularly, are dazzling. The Terrace Restaurant, the Grill Room, and the Oriental Room (the most exclusive Chinese eatery in London) all deserve their acclaim.

2. **The Lanesborough,** London *(see page 127).* This temple of luxury, originally constructed of Portland limestone in 1829 in the classical Greek revival style, was once a hospital. A Texas billionaire, Caroline Rose Hunt, transformed it

into a polished, refined citadel of opulent living, where, for example, you're assigned your own personal butler.

3. **Lygon Arms,** Broadway *(see page 543).* Its origins go back to 1532. Charles I used to drop into this fabled inn in the Cotswolds, and even Oliver Cromwell spent a night here, on the eve of the Battle of Worcester. Some of the inn's antiques are listed in *The Dictionary of English Furniture.* Try to get one of the nine rooms in the Tudor Wing, with their tilted oak floors and wooden beams. Number 20, with its massive canopied bed, is our favorite.

4. **Ston Easton Park,** near Bath *(see page 508).* This splendid 1740 Palladian house has been massively and magnificently restored. The hotel's gardens are reason enough to stay here, but the bedrooms, with Chippendale or Hepplewhite four-poster beds, are equally worthy. Check in here for a preview of the "Upstairs, Downstairs" world of the 1700s.

5. **Chewton Glen Hotel,** New Milton, Hampshire *(see page 398).* On the fringe of New Forest between Lymington and Bournemouth, this "hotel/health-and-country club" attracts discriminating clients from around the world. A Relais & Châteaux member, the hotel names its guestrooms after characters in the books of Captain Frederick Marryat, who stayed here in the 1800s. Service, taste, and quality are the hallmarks of this establishment, as reflected by the stunningly designed health club, with its centerpiece swimming pool, the 70 acres of manicured grounds, the period furniture in the rooms, and the first-rate ingredients that go into the meals served in the Marryat Room Restaurant.

6. **Gidleigh Park Hotel,** Chagford, Devon *(see page 440).* Forty acres of grounds in the Teign valley enclose a country-house hotel that is the epitome of gracious living. Every detail suggests the best of rural life: the premier antiques, those big English sofas, fabrics of the highest quality, floral arrangements from the hotel's gardens—all that and a reputation for fine food unequaled in the area.

7. **Thornbury Castle,** near Bristol *(see page 517).* Henry VIII seized this castle for a royal abode, and Mary Tudor lived here for a while. Eventually it was returned to the progeny of its original owner, the duke of Buckingham. This luxurious choice has all the elements associated with English castle living: Tudor portraits, candlelit baronial public rooms, Elizabethan fireplaces, oriel windows, spiral staircases, four-posters, and stone fireplaces. There's even a garden with croquet.

8. **Ettington Park,** Alderminster, 5 miles south of Stratford-upon-Avon on A34 toward Oxford *(see page 562).* From the plant-filled conservatory entrance right up to the spacious, antique-filled bedrooms, you know you're getting something special here. The house is refurbished every year, and guests can soak up Old England country-house living in the tasteful Victorian drawing room or the richly paneled library bar.

9. **Sharrow Bay Country House Hotel,** Lake Ullswater, near Penrith *(see page 640).* One of the gems of England's Lake District, this Relais & Châteaux member is known as much for its cuisine as its accommodations. Some say the team of Brian Sack and Francis Coulson created the original English country-house hotel. The location alone would justify checking in: a 12-acre site with gardens in a national park on bucolic Lake Ullswater, beneath Barton Fell. The lakeside dining room offers panoramic views of the water, and whether it be grilled scallops from the Kyle of Lochalsh or noisettes of English lamb, there is always

something delectable at table here. You also get a little warning: "Cooking Is Art and All Art Is Patience."

BEST HOTEL BUYS

Happiness in a hotel doesn't necessarily mean dropping a lot of money. The following list is a representative sampling of appealing cost-conscious hotels.

1. **Durrants,** London *(see page 136)*. Opposite the Wallace Collection, this mellow hotel goes back two centuries. It's been called "clublike," and there's even a smoking room. The Miller family has owned it for a century.

2. **Wilbraham Hotel,** London *(see page 130)*. An inexpensive choice for Chelsea, this relatively modest hotel was formed by joining a trio of Victorian town houses. The rooms are small and pristine, but the price is right for expensive London, and the area is desirable—right off Sloane Street. Have a drink in The Bar and Buttery and wander back into England of yesterday.

3. **Howfield Manor,** west of Canterbury on the A28 *(see page 339)*. This former manor house outside the cathedral city retains architectural treasures from its days as part of the Priory of St. Gregory. Bedrooms are divided between the original house and a new one. The hotel is filled with character, including solid oak pieces and exposed beams.

4. **Rising Sun Hotel,** Lynmouth *(see page 456)*. At the mouth of the Lyn River—in fact, at the very end of quay—this 14th-century thatched inn has uneven floors and crooked ceilings that are just part of its charm. Snug, cozy, "under-the-eaves" bedrooms guarantee a good night's sleep; or you can rent Shelley's Cottage, where the poet honeymooned with his underage bride. The inn stakes out part of the river for salmon fishing.

5. **Abbey Hotel,** Penzance *(see page 468)*. Owned by Jean Shrimpton, the internationally famous former model, and her husband, Michael Cox, this small-scale hotel is one of charm and quality. Dating from 1660, it occupies the site of a 12th-century abbey overlooking Penzance harbor.

6. **Apsley House,** Bath *(see page 507)*. Away from the city center on the road to Bristol, this 1830 house was supposedly constructed for the duke of Wellington. Its owners, Christopher and Anne Baker, have restored it and created a house of character with an ambience of subdued elegance.

7. **Old Farmhouse,** Lower Swell *(see page 540)*. This was a working farm until the 1960s. A bar-lounge and a restaurant are in the original farmhouse, which dates from the 1500s, and some of the bedrooms are in converted stables. The most desirable accommodations are in the old coach house. A *table d'hôte* dinner of high quality is served in the evening. You can rent a mountain bike and go exploring in the Cotswolds.

8. **Stratford House,** Stratford-upon-Avon *(see page 561)*. Only 100 yards from the River Avon and the Royal Shakespeare Theatre, this little Georgian house has immense charm and an alluring walled garden. Its bedrooms use dark wood and floral fabrics for that English country-house look, and an open fire in the lounge greets visitors on a cold day.

9. **Dean Court Hotel,** York *(see page 655)*. This old building was originally intended to lodge the cathedral clergy of York Minster. A privately owned hotel, the 1850 building lies right beneath the towers of the minster. Converted

into a hotel after World War I, it offers light and airy bedrooms; those at the front open onto cathedral views.

10. **Mermaid Inn,** Rye *(see page 360)*. Perhaps England's most famous smugglers' inn, the Mermaid sheltered Elizabeth I on her visit to Rye in 1573. At the time of the queen's visit, the inn had already been operating for 150 years. Still going strong, it leans heavily on English romance—old-world furnishings, linenfold paneling, four-poster beds, and even a secret staircase. From its door-step, the cobblestone streets of ancient Rye await exploration.

BEST RESTAURANTS

1. **Le Gavroche,** London *(see page 146)*. In this bastion of haute French cuisine, perfection is the rule, and such a lofty state is rarely encountered in a restaurant. For more than a quarter of a century, it has reigned as the apogee of London's great French restaurants. Michel Roux, son of Albert Roux (who founded the restaurant with his brother), is the chef today and serves some of the dishes his father made classic as well as his own innovations.

2. **Bibendum/The Oyster Bar,** London *(see page 177)*. One of the most fashion-able eateries in town, Sir Terence Conran's restaurant in the famous Michelin building emphasizes Mediterranean flavors. The wine list is among the finest in England. Chef Simon Hopkinson always charms and excites the palate. He's considered "big" rather than subtle on flavor.

3. **The Carved Angel,** Dartmouth *(see page 448)*. Its ever-faithful Devon devotees consider dining here an event, an occasion to savor. Its quayside setting, elegant and airy, is ideal for the inspired cuisine of Joyce Molyneux and Nicky Coiley. Part of their secret is their heavy reliance on fresh ingredients.

4. **Le Talbooth,** Dedham *(see page 592)*. In Constable country, this restaurant dis-penses its wares in a half-timbered Tudor building on the banks of the River Stour. Its cuisine has been called "traditional realism."

5. **Miller Howe Hotel,** Windermere *(see page 626)*. In John Tovey's Edwardian country house above Lake Windermere, the chef is renowned for his English cuisine. A reliance on heavy cream sauces has been abandoned in favor of a lighter touch. Seven elaborate vegetables appear on the dinner menu along with the main dishes of the evening.

6. **Epicurean,** in the Hotel on the Park, Cheltenham *(see page 530)*. Chef Patrick McDonald holds forth in a regency terrace building overlooking the fashionable inner promenade. His serious talent is at work in the execution of such dishes as lobster and langoustine ravioli. The enthusiasm for good food based on qual-ity ingredients is infectious here.

7. **Le Manoir Aux Quat' Saisons,** Great Milton, 12 miles southeast of Oxford *(see page 326)*. The countryhouse hotel and restaurant of self-taught Raymond Blanc has led to a TV series for him, as well as cookbooks and a school of cuisine. The seasonal menus are divine.

8. **Marsh Goose,** Moreton-in-Marsh *(see page 542)*. Its devotees call it the best-kept secret in the Cotswolds. Behind honey-colored walls of local stone, Chef Sonya Kidney (yes, that's right) brings flair and individuality to her four-course dinner menus, with about seven or eight choices per course. Her roasted Cotswold lamb with eggplant and tomatoes is worth the trip, but all of her dishes emphasize flavor.

9. **Harvey's Restaurant,** Bristol *(see page 516)*. A contemporary touch brought to classic cuisine makes Ramon Farthing's restaurant an eagerly sought out address in the West Country. The dining room is installed in wine cellars that date from 1796. Service is amiably informal, and imaginative flavors are created from deftly handled, quality ingredients.

10. **La Tante Claire,** London *(see page 172)*. Chef Pierre Koffman's cuisine has been defined as one of "ravishing purity." Beautifully proportioned and impeccably prepared, his legendary pig's trotters with morels is one of his "signature" dishes.

BEST ROMANTIC GETAWAYS

1. **Rye,** Sussex. Originally a Cinque port, today Rye lies inland. Novelist Henry James, who could have lived anywhere in England, chose Rye from 1898 to 1916. Its Mermaid Street is one of the most romantic thoroughfares in southeast England. Stay at The Mermaid Inn, which once hosted Queen Elizabeth I.

2. **Dedham,** Essex. Constable painted *Vale of Dedham* here in one of England's most unspoiled villages. The whole area invites exploration, including nearby Flatford Mill captured on canvas in Constable's *Hay Wain.* Stay at Maison Talbooth and dine at Le Talbooth on nearby Gun Hill.

3. **Grasmere,** in the Lake District. Wordsworth called it "the loveliest spot that man hath ever known." Perhaps an exaggeration, but Grasmere, where Thomas De Quincey wrote *Confessions of an English Opium Eater,* is one of the most romantic villages in one of England's most romantic districts. The ideal romantic place to stay: Michael's Nook, a country-house hotel lying a quarter of a mile from the center of town.

4. **Lyme Regis,** Dorset. *The French Lieutenant's Woman,* starring Meryl Streep, was shot in this typical Dorset coastal town near the home of its author, John Fowles. One of its former admirers was Jane Austen, who set parts of her novel *Persuasion* here. There are no grand hotels, only little town inns for snug, windswept nights near the sea.

5. **Chagford,** Devon. This is Sir Francis Drake country. Surrounded by moors, Chagford is one of the best bases for exploring the often forlorn but romantic north Dartmoor, following in the footsteps of the fictional Lorna Doone. If you're well off, check into Gidleigh Park Hotel. If you're watching the pounds, try Easton Court Hotel, whose rooms have sheltered the likes of Margaret Mead and John Steinbeck.

6. **The Scilly Isles,** off the coast of Cornwall. The isles are warmed by the Gulf Stream, so semitropical plants can thrive there. Known to the Greeks and Romans and rich in Celtic legend, they are idyllic, but their old-fashioned charm is too often missed by tourists racing to see everything in the West Country. Try the New Inn at Tresco, which comprises an interconnected row of 19th-century fisher's cottages.

7. **Bibury,** in the Cotswolds. This village, between Burford and Cirencester, is one of the most romantic in the Cotswolds. Even the poet and artist William Morris, a utopian romancer of Queen Victoria's day, pronounced it "the most beautiful village in England." Check into Bibury Court Hotel, a Jacobean manor house from 1633, with your loved one. Warm yourself by a log-burning fireplace before retreating to your four-poster bed for the night.

BEST MUSEUMS

1. **British Museum,** London. When Sir Hans Sloane died in 1753, he bequeathed to England his vast collection of art and antiquities, all for only 20,000 pounds (and priceless today). Even that figure was only half of what it cost Sloane to accumulate such a vast array of goodies. This formed the nucleus of the collection that would one day embrace everything from the Rosetta stone to the hotly contested Elgin marbles (Greece wants them back). It's all here—two of the four surviving copies of the Magna Carta, a Gutenberg Bible, Shakespeare's First Folio, and much more.

2. **National Gallery,** London. One of the world's greatest collections of western art—every artist from Leonardo to Rembrandt to Picasso—dazzles the eye. The gallery is especially rich in the works of Renaissance artists. In contrast to many of the great national galleries in other European capitals, this artistic treasure-trove was not built upon a royal collection.

3. **Tate Gallery,** London. Two great national collections—some 10,000 works—call this gallery home. Sir Henry Tate, a sugar producer, started the nucleus of the collection, with only 70 or so paintings. But the Tate has grown and grown, and was considerably beefed up when J.M.W. Turner bequeathed some 300 paintings and 19,000 watercolors to England upon his death. Also a repository of the most avant garde modern art, the Tate's collection is so rich it has to be rotated every year.

4. **Fitzwilliam Museum,** Cambridge. Although London dominates the list, there are some outstanding regional museums in England, including this gem near King's College. Exhibits range from paintings by Leonardo da Vinci and Michelangelo to Chinese, Egyptian, and Greek antiquities.

5. **Walker Art Gallery,** Liverpool. One of the finest collections of European and British painting, this gallery deserves to be better known. A nearly complete study of British paintings is displayed there, from Tudor days to the present. The gallery also owns an outstanding collection of pre-Raphaelites.

6. **American Museum,** at Claverton, 2 miles east of Bath. Housed in a neoclassical country house, this collection presents two centuries of American life and styles—including George Washington's mother's recipe for gingerbread.

BEST CATHEDRALS

1. **Westminster Abbey,** London. One of the world's greatest Anglo-French gothic buildings, this minster has witnessed a parade of English history—everything from the crowning of William the Conqueror on Christmas Day 1066 to the World War II blitz. With a couple of exceptions, the kings and queens of England have all been crowned here, and many are buried here.

2. **Canterbury Cathedral,** Canterbury. The object of countless pilgrimages, as described in Chaucer's *Canterbury Tales,* this cathedral replaced one that was destroyed by fire in 1067. A new cathedral, dedicated in 1130, was also destroyed by fire in 1174, when the present structure was built. Its most famous historical event was the murder of Thomas à Becket, whose shrine was an important site for pilgrims until the Reformation.

3. **Salisbury Cathedral,** Salisbury. Considered the most stylistically unified of all cathedrals in England, this edifice was built between 1220 and 1265. Its landmark spire—its most striking feature—was constructed from 1285 to 1320.

Salisbury Cathedral is considered the epitome of the early-English style of architecture.

4. **Winchester Cathedral,** Winchester. Dominating this ancient city and capital of old Wessex, Winchester Cathedral was launched in 1079. In time it became the longest medieval cathedral in England, especially noted for its 12-bay nave. Many famous people are buried here, including the novelist Jane Austen.

5. **Durham Cathedral,** Durham. Completed between 1095 and 1133, this cathedral is a harmonious example of Norman architecture on a broad scale. Its nave, a structure of almost majestic power, is its most characteristic and striking feature. It was one of the harbingers of the pure grace of gothic architecture. Its 13th-century Chapel of the Nine Altars, an outstanding feature, was an early-English addition.

6. **York Minster,** York. The largest gothic cathedral north of the Alps, it is also among the grandest. Its stained glass, the largest single surviving collection of medieval stained glass in England, is its most striking feature. Its unusual octagonal Chapter House has a late-15th-century choir screen by William Hyndeley and a wooden vaulted ceiling.

BEST CASTLES, PALACES & HISTORIC HOMES

1. **Harewood House,** West Yorkshire *(see Chapter 19)*. Edwin Lascelles began constructing this house in 1759, and his "pile" has been called an essay in Palladian architecture. The grand design involved some of the major talents of the day, including Robert Adam, Thomas Chippendale, and Capability Brown, who developed the grounds. A 4¹/₂-acre bird garden features exotic species from all over the world.

2. **Beaulieu Abbey-Palace House,** Beaulieu, in New Forest *(see Chapter 11)*. Palace House is the home of the first lord Montagu. It blends monastic gothic architecture from the Middle Ages with Victorian trappings. For many, the National Motor Museum here is even more fascinating than the house itself. Its collection comprises more than 250 antique vehicles.

3. **Castle Howard,** North Yorkshire *(see Chapter 19)*. This was Sir John Vanbrugh's grand masterpiece, and also the first building he ever designed. Many people will recognize it as the principal location for the popular television series "Brideshead Revisited." The striking entrance is topped by a gilt-and-painted dome. Jonathan Swift commented on Vanbrugh's selection as architect, saying, "Van's genius, without thought or lecture, is hugely turned to Architecture." The park around Castle Howard is sumptuous, one of the most grandiose in Europe.

4. **Blenheim Palace,** Woodstock *(see Chapter 8)*. England's answer to Versailles, this extravagant baroque palace was the home of the 11th duke of Marlborough. It was also the birthplace of Sir Winston Churchill. The structure was designed by Sir John Vanbrugh, of Castle Howard fame. Sarah, the duchess of Marlborough, battled the architects and builders from the beginning, wanting "a clean sweet house and garden be it ever so small." That she didn't get— the structure measures 850 feet from end to end. Capability Brown laid out the gardens.

5. **Windsor Castle,** Windsor *(see Chapter 8)*. The largest inhabited stronghold in the world and the largest castle in England, Windsor Castle has been a royal

abode since William the Conqueror constructed a motte and bailey on the site four years after conquering England. Severely damaged by fire in 1992, it is receiving visitors today to help pay for the restoration. Its major attraction is the great Perpendicular Chapel of St. George's, begun by Edward IV. The chancel is known for its three-tiered stalls, which abound in misericords and ornate carvings (1478–85).

6. **Knole,** Kent *(see Chapter 9)*. Begun in 1456 by the archbishop of Canterbury, this was the childhood home of Vita Sackville-West. It is celebrated for its 365 rooms (one for each day of the year), its 52 staircases (for each week of the year), and its 7 courts (for each day of the week). Knole is one of the largest private houses in England and is considered one of the finest examples of the Tudor style of architecture. It is set in a 1,000-acre deer park where herds of deer roam.

7. **Penshurst Palace,** Penshurst, Kent *(see Chapter 9)*. One of England's most outstanding country homes, this mansion was the former residence of Elizabethan poet Sir Philip Sidney (1554–86). In its day, the house attracted the literati, including Ben Jonson. The original 1346 hall has seen the subsequent addition of Tudor, Jacobean, and neo-gothic wings.

8. **Hever Castle and Gardens,** Kent *(see Chapter 9)*. This was the childhood home of Anne Boleyn, second wife of Henry VIII and mother of Queen Elizabeth I. It was acquired in 1903 by William Waldorf Astor, a multimillionaire American and Anglophile who lavishly restored it and landscaped its grounds. On the outside, it still appears much as it did in Tudor times. A moat and drawbridge "protect" the castle. The garden Astor created follows many styles.

9. **Woburn Abbey,** Woburn *(see Chapter 6)*. A Cistercian abbey for four centuries, Woburn Abbey, the seat of the dukes of Bedford, lies 44 miles north of London. It has been visited by everybody from Queen Victoria to Marilyn Monroe, and that's quite a stretch. Features include Queen Victoria's Bedroom and the Canaletto Room, with 21 perspectives of Venice. The grounds, even more popular than the house, house a Wild Animal Kingdom, the best collection in England after the London Zoo.

10. **Hatfield House,** Hertfordshire *(see Chapter 6)*. Hatfield was the childhood home of Elizabeth I, who was under an oak tree there when she learned she had become queen of England. "It is the Lord's doing and it is marvellous in our eyes." Hatfield is one of the largest and finest country houses in England, complete with antiques, tapestries, paintings, and even the red silk stockings worn by Elizabeth I.

BEST LITERARY SITES

1. **Stratford-upon-Avon** *(see Chapter 16)*. The entire town seems to spin around one literary personality, William Shakespeare. Although the Bard remains a mysterious figure, and there are those who still suggest he didn't even write his plays and poems, the people of Stratford gleefully peddle their literary site. There is Shakespeare's Birthplace, where the son of a glover was born on April 23, 1564. He died in Stratford on the same day, 52 years later. A major attraction is Anne Hathaway's Cottage, in the hamlet of Shottery. Shakespeare married Hathaway when he was only 18 years old.

2. **Haworth,** West Yorkshire *(see Chapter 19)*. This is the second major literary pilgrimage site in England, home of the Brontë Parsonage Museum. It was here

that the famous Brontë sisters lived and spun their web of romance. Here they created their masterpieces, Emily's *Wuthering Heights* and Charlotte's *Jane Eyre* and *Villette*. Anne Brontë also wrote two novels, *The Tenant of Wildfell Hall* and *Agnes Grey*, though neither of them is up to her sisters' work.

3. **Dove Cottage,** Grasmere, in the Lake District *(see Chapter 18).* William Wordsworth lived here with his sister, Dorothy, who commented on the "domestic slip of mountain" behind their cottage. After Wordsworth's marriage to Mary Hutchinson and the birth of their children, Dorothy found the cottage "crammed edgefull." When De Quincey came to visit, he was struck by the simplicity of their lives at Dove Cottage. He assumed tenancy when they moved in 1808 but didn't prove the ideal tenant. First, he tore down their little "moss-hut," or summer house. Later, in 1817, he married his mistress, the already-pregnant Margaret Sympson. Wordsworth didn't object to her pregnancy but opposed the marriage because she was a farmer's daughter. In 1835 De Quincey wrote *Lake Reminiscences,* and Wordsworth expressed himself horrified by it, although he refused to read it.

4. **Keats House,** Hampstead, London *(see Chapter 6).* Most of the poet's brief life was spent in London, where he was born in 1795 in a livery stable run by his father. He moved to Hampstead in 1817, and there he met his fiancée, Fanny Brawne. It was in this house that he coughed blood into his handkerchief. "That drop of blood is my death warrant," he said. "I must die." He left to die in Rome a year later, in 1821.

5. **Samuel Johnson's House,** London *(see Chapter 6).* Born in Lichfield, Staffordshire, in 1709, Johnson knew great poverty in his early life. His famous dictum on London was "When a man is tired of London, he is tired of life." The backwater at No. 7 Gough Square, situated on the north side of Fleet Street, was Johnson's home from 1749 to 1758. Here he worked on his *Rambler* essays and his *Dictionary.* His beloved wife, "Tetty," died there in 1752. Before he died in 1784, Johnson listed (for the sake of his future biographers) more than a dozen addresses where he had lived in London.

BEST AND MOST EVOCATIVE RUINS

1. **Stonehenge,** near Salisbury, Wiltshire *(see Chapter 14).* The most celebrated prehistoric monument in all of Europe, Stonehenge is some 4,000 years old. Despite the "definitive" books written on the subject, its original purpose remains a mystery. Was it an astronomical observatory for a sun-worshipping cult? The romantic theory that Stonehenge was "constructed by the Druids" (and there are still books being published maintaining that!) is, of course, nonsense. The final phase of Stonehenge was completed before the Druids reached Britain in the 3rd century B.C.

2. **Fountains Abbey** (founded 1132), 4 miles southwest of Ripon, in North Yorkshire *(see Chapter 19).* More than any other site, these ruins evoke the monastic life of medieval England. The Cistercian monks constructed "a place remote from all the earth." The site has been awarded World Heritage status. One visits the ruins at the same time as the Studley Royal, whose lavish 18th-century landscaping is one of the few surviving examples of a Georgian green garden.

3. **Kenilworth Castle,** in Warwickshire *(see Chapter 16).* Once the abode of Simon de Montfort, this castle was the setting for Sir Walter Scott's romantic novel,

Kenilworth, first published in 1862, which recounts the supposed murder of Amy Robsart, wife of Robert Dudley, Earl of Leicester. Elizabeth I had presented Kenilworth Castle to her favorite in 1563. The castle was destroyed after the Civil War and is now in ruins. At one time the castle walls enclosed 7 acres.

4. **Avebury,** 7 miles west of Marlborough, Wiltshire *(see Chapter 14)*. Although not as famous as Stonehenge, this is one of Europe's leading prehistoric monuments. Its circle of more than 100 stones—some of them weighing in at 50 tons—is arrayed on a 20-acre site.

5. **Battle,** East Sussex *(see Chapter 10)*. This is the site of the famous Battle of Hastings, fought on October 14, 1066, when the Normans defeated King Harold's English army. A great commemorative abbey was built there by William the Conqueror, the high altar of its church erected over the spot where King Harold fell in battle. The abbey was destroyed at the time of the Dissolution of the Monasteries, in 1538. The place where the altar stood is identified by a plaque. Some ruins and buildings remain, about which Tennyson wrote, "O Garden, blossoming out of English blood."

6. **Glastonbury Abbey,** Glastonbury, Somerset *(see Chapter 14)*. One of the great abbeys of England and once a center of culture and learning, Glastonbury fell quickly into a ruin following the Dissolution of the Monasteries. One story about the abbey, which was always the subject of legend and lore, says that Jesus came there as a child with Joseph of Arimathea. According to another legend, King Arthur was buried at Glastonbury, and this was the site of the fabled Avalon. The abbey's large ruins are open to the public today.

BEST OFFBEAT EXCURSIONS

1. **Caravanning.** Visiting the country lanes of England in a horse-drawn caravan, along valleys and dales with vistas at every turn is one of the finest ways to see England. Many agencies rent this type of caravan, although we prefer Waveney Valley Horse Holidays, Air Station Farm, Fulham Street, St. Mary, Diss, Norfolk 1P21 4QF (☎ 01379/741228). Their caravans are equipped with two double beds, water on board, and gas cooking and lighting—but no refrigerators or bathrooms. Before you start out, the company instructs you on the harnessing and feeding of the horse. You are also provided with a map of the best roads to use, with a listing of stops for watering and grazing the horse as well as to get a bite to eat yourself. The routes are within a 15- to 20-mile radius of the office in Norfolk and are 50 to 60 miles long. Weekly rates range from £246 ($388.70) to £410 ($647.80). The country lanes of Devon are especially recommended for a caravan holiday.

2. **Cruising Inland Waterways.** It's estimated that England has some 2,200 miles of inland waterways, an extensive system that covers the whole country that is relatively free of commercial craft. These waterways flow through landscapes that remind you of Constable's paintings—fens, lakes, nature preserves, beautifully cultivated gardens, and university lawns. Options range from a self-skippered craft to a fully catered cruise with sleeping accommodations. If you're your own skipper, bring along bikes for cycling tours of the hamlets that catch your fancy. You can even rent fishing tackle. Figure on going only about 12 to 15 miles a day, although some "speeders" prefer 20. Supplies are available in many places; otherwise, you can stop at waterside pubs and restaurants. The best source for

information about this type of holiday is British Waterways, Willow Grange, Church Road, Watford, Hertfordshire WD1 3QA (☎ 01923/226422). This company also supplies maps and charts of England's entire waterway system.

3. **The Great Walks of England.** The Country Commission of England has built more than a dozen long-distance footpaths that cut through some of the country's most dramatic scenery. All of these grand walks—some that will create memories for a lifetime—are close enough to country inns, pubs, and hotels for refreshments, food, or overnight stays. Since England is a rainy country, you'll want to be prepared to face the elements. Consult the Ramblers' Association, 1–5 Wandsworth Road, Vauxhall, London SW8 2XX (☎ 0171/582-6878), for its annual *Ramblers' Yearbook*, which is available for £10 ($15.80) and lists some 2,500 bed-and-breakfasts along these footpaths. The most notable walks are Cleveland Way, a 100-mile footpath over moors and dales from Helmsley to Filet, in North Yorkshire; Cotswolds Way, a 100-mile route over wooded valleys and fields from Chipping Campden, in Gloucestershire, to Bath, in Avon; Dales Way, a 78-mile trek through low-lying land from Ilkley, in West Yorkshire, to Bowness-on-Windermere, in Cumbria; and, finally, Hadrian's Wall, near Newcastle, passing castles, forts, turrets, and ruins from Wallsend to Bowness near Carlisle on the Solway Firth.

4. **Cycling Through England.** Britain has some of the best cycling areas in Europe, and the finest of these are covered in *Cycling World* magazine, which sells for £1.80 ($2.85). For a copy, write to Andrew House, 2A Granville Rd., Sidcup, Kent DA14 4BN (☎ 0181/302-6150). If you're interested in cycling holidays in Britain, consider joining the Cyclists' Touring Club, Cotterell House, 69 Meadrow, Godalming, Surrey GU7 3HS (☎ 01483/417217). Some of the best areas for cycling in England include the Lake District (even though it has steep hills), the Peak District (with its Pennine Chain), the Yorkshire Dales (with its deep valleys and dales), and East Anglia (a relatively low-lying terrain through the old Saxon kingdom). East Anglia, with its farms, country villages, thatched homes, church spires, and deserted beaches, remains my favorite. Britain's most ambitious cyclists take the ultimate cycling trip—a three-week trek from Land's End, in Cornwall, all the way to John O'Groats, on the northern coast of Scotland, averaging 50 miles a day. The distance covered is a daunting 1,000 miles.

5. **Camping in Dartmoor National Park.** Some 10 miles west of Exeter and about 7 miles east of Plymouth are the windy moors and green forests of this national park with its haunting atmosphere. Little wonder that this landscape inspired the Sherlock Holmes horror story *The Hound of the Baskervilles.* Wild moors cover most of its 365 square miles. Some prehistoric remains here, including chambered tombs and standing stones, date from 4000 B.C. A tin-mining industry once flourished here, but now only its ruins remain. Guided walks lasting anywhere from 2 to 7 hours and costing from £1.50 to £3 ($2.35–$4.75) depart from several places in the park. Ask at the Dartmoor National Park Tourist Information Centre, Town Hall, Bedford Square, Tavistock PL19 OAE (☎ 01822/612938). If you don't want to camp out, this agency will book bed-and-breakfast accommodations for you in the area. A few official campsites exist, but many campers prefer the open moor for the night. Since the moor is privately owned land, seek permission before camping. Only one night in a single spot is permitted. Campsites include Ashburton Caravan Park, Waterleat,

Ashburton (☎ 01364/652552); River Dart Country Park, Holne Park, Ashburton (☎ 01364/652511), and Yertiz Caravan and Camping Park, Exeter Road, Okehampton (☎ 01837/52281). Most sites are open from April through September, and charges begin at £6 ($9.50) for a two-person tent.

2 The Regions in Brief

England is a part of the United Kingdom, which is made up of England, Wales, Scotland, and Northern Ireland. Only 50,327 square miles, about the same size as New York State, England has an amazing amount of rural land and natural wilderness and an astonishing regional, physical, and cultural diversity. The Pennine Chain is the island's backbone, splitting the country in two, with Lancashire on the west of the divide and Yorkshire on the east. Other highland areas include the Cumbrian Mountains (in the Lake District), with the country's highest peak, 3,210-foot Scafell Pike. Several rivers empty into either the North Sea or the Irish Sea—including the Tyne, at Newcastle, and the Mersey, at Liverpool—but the most famous of all is, of course, the 209-mile Thames, which empties into the English Channel 20 miles downstream from London Bridge.

COTSWOLDS   Touring country par excellence, this is a bucolic land of honey-colored limestone villages where rural England unfolds before you in a timeless tableau, like a storybook picture. In the Middle Ages, wool made the Cotswolders prosperous, but now they put out the welcome mat for tourists. Start at Burford, the traditional gateway to the region, and continue on to Bourton-on-the-Water, Lower and Upper Slaughter, Stow-on-the-Wold, Moreton-in-Marsh, Chipping Campden, and Broadway. Cirencester is the uncrowned capital of the south Cotswolds, and Cheltenham is the still-elegant Regency spa where Margaret Thatcher's political opponents suggested sending her into retirement. Our two favorite villages, where we like to hide out, are Painswick, with its minute cottages, and Bibury, with its cluster of former weavers' cottages, Arlington Row. The inns and pubs of the Cotswolds are famous.

EAST ANGLIA   Fens and salt marshes, villages of thatched cottages—East Anglia is a semicircular geographic bulge northeast of London. The name is applied to four very flat counties: Essex, Cambridgeshire, Norfolk, and Suffolk. Imogen Holst, writing about Benjamin Britten and his Aldeburgh festival (Suffolk) in the "Great Composers" series in 1966, saw it this way: "Even in summer, the gray sea batters itself against the shelf of pebbles, dragging the shingle down with a scrunching, grating, slithering sound. To anyone born on the Suffolk coast, this sound has always meant home." The land of John Constable is still filled with his landscapes. The Fens—that broad expanse of fertile, black soil lying north of Cambridge—remains our favorite district. Go there to see Ely Cathedral. Cambridge, of course, with its colleges and river, is the chief attraction. Alumni have included everyone from Oliver Cromwell to Isaac Newton, from Lord Byron to Charles Darwin. The most important museum is the Fitzwilliam in Cambridge, but visitors also flock to East Anglia for the scenery and its solitary beauty.

EAST MIDLANDS   This area has some of the worst of industrial England, yet there is great natural beauty, plus stately homes you'd like to see. These include Chatsworth in Derbyshire, the seat of the dukes of Devonshire; Sulgrave Manor in Northamptonshire, the ancestral home of George Washington; and Althorp House, also in Northamptonshire, the childhood home of the princess of Wales. The East Midlands embraces Derbyshire, Leicestershire, Lincolnshire,

Northamptonshire, and Nottinghamshire. Lincoln has one of England's great cathedrals, rebuilt in the 13th and 14th centuries. Bostonians like to visit their namesake, the old seaport town of Boston. Nottingham recalls Robin Hood, though the much deforested Sherwood Forest is not what it was in the outlaw's heyday. D.H. Lawrence, who lived at Eastwood, came from this area and fondly recalled it from childhood memories. "It was still the old England of the forest and the agricultural past; there were no motor-cars, the mines were, in a sense, an accident in the landscape, and Robin Hood and his merry men were not very far away."

MIDLANDS AND HEART OF ENGLAND   From this sprawling area came the Industrial Revolution, which made Britain the first industrialized country in the world. This section also gave the world Shakespeare, who was born in Stratford-upon-Avon. One of England's great castles, Warwick Castle, is found here. Events that bring alive again the medieval pageantry, drama, and music of Sir Walter Scott's novel *Kenilworth* are staged in the ruins of Kenilworth Castle. Coventry, heavily bombed in World War II, is visited mainly for its outstanding modern cathedral. The English marshes cut through the old counties of Shropshire and Herefordshire. Ironbridge Gorge was the birthplace of the Industrial Revolution, and the famous Potteries are in Staffordshire. The West Midlands also embrace the so-called "Black Country." Birmingham, nicknamed "Brum," is Britain's largest city after London. While there is talk of a "cultural awakening," the sprawling metropolis is still characterized by its overpass jungles and tacky suburbs. It does have great piles of Victorian architecture. Personally, we think the city has a long way to go.

NORTHEAST AND THE LAKE DISTRICT   Stretching from Liverpool to the Scottish border, northeast England can be a bucolic delight if you steer clear of its industrial pockets. Most people come here to follow in the footsteps of such romantic poets as Wordsworth, who wrote of the beauty of the Lake District. But Chester and Liverpool merit stopovers along the way. We'd recommend that you skip the tawdry resort of Blackpool. It's big, brash, and vulgar, and its beach is polluted. In contrast, the Roman city of Chester is a well-preserved medieval town, known for its encircling wall. And Liverpool, unlike Birmingham, is culturally alive and always intriguing, if only to see where the Beatles came from. Literary Lakeland evokes memories of the Wordsworths, Samuel Taylor Coleridge, John Ruskin, and Beatrix Potter, among others. Windermere makes the best center, but there are many others as well, including Grasmere and Ambleside.

HAMPSHIRE AND WILTSHIRE   Southwest of London, these two counties possess two of England's greatest cathedrals—Salisbury and Winchester—and one of Europe's most significant prehistoric monuments, Stonehenge. But there are even more reasons for visiting. Hampshire is hemmed in by the woodlands and heaths of New Forest in its far west. Portsmouth and Southampton loom large in naval heritage. You might also want to take a ferry over to the Isle of Wight, once Queen Victoria's preferred vacation retreat. In Wiltshire you encounter the beginning of the West Country, with its scenic beauty and monuments—Wilton House, the 17th-century home of the earls of Pembroke, and Old Sarum, the remains of what is believed to have been an Iron Age fortification.

SOUTHEAST   In the land of Charles Lamb, Virginia Woolf, Winston Churchill, Henry James, and countless others, you can pluck the gems from the crowns of Kent, Surrey, and the Sussexes. Here are all the big-name attractions: Brighton, Canterbury, Dover (gateway to the continent), and seemingly limitless country homes and castles—not only Hever and Leeds castles but also Chartwell, the more modest abode where Churchill lived. In small villages, such as Rye and Winchelsea in Sussex, and in interesting towns like Haslemere, you discover the charm of the southeast. Almost all of the Sussex shoreline is built up and seaside towns, such as Eastbourne and Hastings, are often tacky. In fact, although the area's major attraction is Canterbury Cathedral, the Royal Pavilion at Brighton rates as an outstanding, extravagant folly. Teashops, antiques shops (or at least stores calling their wares antiques), pubs, and small inns abound in the area. Surrey is essentially a commuter suburb of London and easily reached for day excursions.

SOUTHWEST   These four counties—Dorset, Somerset, Devon, and Cornwall—are the great vacation centers and retirement havens of England. Dorset, associated with Thomas Hardy, is a land of rolling downs, rocky headlands, well-kept villages, and rich farmlands. Somerset—the Somerset of King Arthur and Camelot—offers such magical towns as Glastonbury. Devon has both Exmoor and Dartmoor, and northern and southern coastlines with such famous resorts as Lyme Regis and such villages as Clovelly. In Cornwall you're never more than 20 miles from the rugged coastline, which ends at Land's End. Among the cities worth visiting in these counties are Bath, with its impressive Roman baths and Georgian architecture; Plymouth, departure point of the *Mayflower;* and Wells, site of a great cathedral.

THAMES VALLEY   England's most famous river runs westward from Kew to its source in the Cotswolds. A land of meadows, woodlands, attractive villages, small market towns, and rolling hillsides, this is one of England's most scenic areas. Many prefer to visit these Thames-side villages by boat, but you might not go for that option after reading Jerome K. Jerome's idyll, *Three Men in a Boat*, which is filled with mishaps. Highlights along the way include Windsor Castle, Elizabeth II's favorite residence, and nearby Eton College, founded by the young Henry VI in 1440. Henley, site of the Royal Regatta, remains our favorite Thames-side town; others are historic Dorchester or Abingdon, and the university city of Oxford, where you can tour its colleges and explore its sights.

YORKSHIRE AND NORTHUMBRIA   Yorkshire will be familiar to fans of the Brontës and James Herriot. York, with its immense cathedral and medieval streets, is the city to visit. Northumbria comprises Northumberland, Cleveland, Durham, and Tyne and Wear (the area around Newcastle). The whole area echoes the ancient border battles between the Scots and English. Hadrian's Wall is a highlight. The great cathedral at Durham is one of Britain's finest examples of Norman church architecture, and Fountains Abbey is among the country's greatest ecclesiastical ruins. Country homes abound; here you find Harewood House and Castle Howard.

3 England Past & Present

Dateline

- 54 B.C. Julius Caesar invades England.
- A.D. 43 Romans conquer England.
- 410 Jutes, Angles, and Saxons form small kingdoms in England.

continues

Britain was probably split off from the continent of Europe some eight millennia ago by continental drift and other natural forces. The early inhabitants, the Iberians, were a small, dark people, later to be identified with stories of fairies, brownies, and "little people." These are the people whose ingenuity and enterprise are believed to have created Stonehenge, but despite that great and mysterious monument little is known about them. They were replaced by the iron-wielding Celts, whose massive invasions around 500 B.C. drove the Iberians back to the Scottish Highlands and Welsh mountains, where some of their descendants still live today.

In 54 B.C. Julius Caesar invaded England, but the Romans did not become established there until A.D. 43. They went as far as Caledonia (now Scotland), where they gave up, leaving that land to "the painted ones," or the warring Picts. The wall built by the Emperor Hadrian across the north of England marked the northernmost reaches of the Roman Empire. During almost four centuries of occupation, the Romans built roads, villas, towns, walls, and fortresses; they farmed the land and introduced first their pagan religions, then Christianity. Agriculture and trade flourished.

When the Roman legions withdrew, around A.D. 410, they left the country open to waves of invasions by Jutes, Angles, and Saxons, who established themselves in small kingdoms throughout the former Roman colony. From the 8th through the 11th centuries, the Anglo-Saxons contended with Danish raiders for control of the land.

By the time of the Norman conquest, the Saxon kingdoms were united under an elected king, Edward the Confessor. His successor was to rule less than a year before the Norman invasion. The date 1066 is familiar to every English schoolchild. It marked an epic event, the only successful military invasion of Britain in history, and one of England's great turning points. King Harold, the last Anglo-Saxon king, was defeated at the Battle of Hastings, and William of Normandy was crowned as William I.

One of William's first acts was to order a survey of the land he had conquered, assessing all property in the nation for tax purposes. This survey was called the Domesday Book, or "Book of Doom," as some pegged it. The resulting document was completed around 1086 and has been a fertile sourcebook for British historians ever since. Norman rule had an enormous impact on English society. All high offices were held by Normans, and the Norman barons were given great grants of lands, and they built Norman-style castles and strongholds throughout the country. French was for centuries the language of the court— few people realize that heroes such as Richard Lionheart probably spoke little or no English.

- **500–1066** Anglo-Saxon kingdoms fight off Viking warriors.
- **1066** William, duke of Normandy, invades England, defeats Harold II at the Battle of Hastings.
- **1154** Henry II, first of the Plantagenets, launches their rule (which lasts until 1399).
- **1215** King John signs the Magna Carta at Runnymede.
- **1337** Hundred Years' War between France and England begins.
- **1485** Battle of Bosworth Field ends the War of the Roses between the Houses of York and Lancaster; Henry VII launches the Tudor dynasty.
- **1534** Henry VIII brings the Reformation to England and dissolves the monasteries.
- **1558** The accession of Elizabeth I ushers in an era of exploration and a renaissance in science and learning.
- **1588** Spanish Armada defeated.
- **1603** James VI of Scotland becomes James I of England, thus uniting the crowns of England and Scotland.
- **1620** Pilgrims sail from Plymouth on the *Mayflower* to found a colony in the New World.
- **1629** Charles I dissolves Parliament, ruling alone.
- **1642–49** Civil War between Royalists and Parliamentarians; the Parliamentarians win.
- **1649** Charles I beheaded, and England is a republic.
- **1653** Oliver Cromwell becomes Lord Protector.

continues

- **1660** Charles II restored to the throne with limited power.
- **1665–66** Great Plague and Great Fire decimate London.
- **1688** James II, a Catholic, is deposed, and William and Mary come to the throne, signing a Bill of Rights.
- **1727** George I, the first of the Hanoverians, assumes the throne.
- **1756–63** In the Seven Years' War, Britain wins Canada from France.
- **1775–83** Britain loses its American colonies.
- **1795–1815** The Napoleonic Wars lead, finally, to the Battle of Waterloo and the defeat of Napoleon.
- **1837** Queen Victoria begins her reign as Britain reaches the zenith of its empire.
- **1901** Victoria dies, and Edward VII becomes king.
- **1914–18** England enters World War I and emerges victorious on the Allied side.
- **1936** Edward VIII abdicates to marry an American divorceé.
- **1939–45** In World War II, Britain stands alone against Hitler from the fall of France in 1940 until America enters the war in 1941; Dunkirk is evacuated in 1940; bombs fall in the blitz of London.
- **1945** Churchill is defeated; the Labor government introduces the welfare state and dismantles the empire.
- **1952** Queen Elizabeth II ascends the throne.

continues

In 1154 Henry II, the first of the Plantagenets, was crowned (r. 1154–1189). Called "one of the most remarkable characters in English history," he ruled a vast empire—not only most of Britain but Normandy, Anjou, Brittany, and Aquitaine in France. Henry was a man of powerful physique, both charming and terrifying. He reformed the courts and introduced the system of common law, which not only still operates in moderated form in England today but also influenced the American legal system. A famous episode in his reign was the murder of Thomas á Becket, Archbishop of Canterbury. Henry, at odds with his archbishop, exclaimed, "Who will rid me of this turbulent priest?" His knights, overhearing and taking him at his word, murdered Thomas in front of the high altar in Canterbury Cathedral.

Henry's wife, Eleanor of Aquitaine, an able and cultured woman, the most famous woman of her time, was a no less colorful character. She accompanied her first husband, Louis VII of France, on the Second Crusade, and it was rumored that there she had a romantic affair with the Saracen leader, Saladin. Domestic and political life did not run smoothly, however, and Henry and Eleanor and their sons were often at odds. The pair have been subjects of many plays and films, including *The Lion in Winter, Becket,* and T. S. Eliot's *Murder in the Cathedral.*

Two of their sons were crowned kings of England. Richard the Lionheart actually spent most of his life outside England, on crusades, or in France. John was forced by his nobles to sign the Magna Carta at Runnymede, in 1215—another date well known to English schoolchildren. The Magna Carta guaranteed that the king was subject to the rule of law and gave certain rights to the king's subjects, beginning a process that eventually led to the development of parliamentary democracy as it is known in Britain today, a process that would have enormous influence on the American colonies many years later. The Magna Carta became known as "the cornerstone of English liberties." The liberties it granted were, of course, only to the barons. It took the rebellion of Simon de Montfort, half a century later, to introduce the notion that the boroughs and burghers should also have a voice and representation.

In 1348 half the population died as the Black Death ravaged England. For half a century, one epidemic or another raged through the land. By the end of the century, the population of Britain had fallen from four million to two million.

England suffered in the Hundred Years War, which went on intermittently for more than a century. By 1371 England had lost much of its land on French soil. Henry V, immortalized by Shakespeare (and made familiar to all moviegoers by Laurence Olivier's and Kenneth Branagh's films) revived England's claims to France, and his victory at Agincourt was notable for making obsolete the forms of medieval chivalry and warfare. After Henry's death in 1422, disputes arose among successors to the crown that resulted in a long period of civil strife, the Wars of the Roses, between the Yorkists, who used a white rose as their symbol, and the Lancastrians with their red rose. The last Yorkist king was Richard III, who got a bad press from Shakespeare, but who is defended to this day as a hero by the people of the city of York. Richard was defeated at Bosworth Field, and the victory introduced to England the first Tudor, the shrewd and wily Henry VII.

- **1973** Britain joins the European Union.
- **1979** Margaret Thatcher becomes prime minister.
- **1982** Britain defeats Argentina in the Falklands War.
- **1990** Thatcher is ousted; John Major becomes prime minister.
- **1991** Britain fights with Allies to defeat Iraq.
- **1992** In this *annus horribilis* of the House of Windsor, several royal marriages collapse, Windsor Castle burns, and the queen becomes a taxpayer.

The Tudors were a different sort of king than the kings that had ruled before them. They introduced into England a strong central monarchy with far-reaching powers. The system worked well under the first three strong and capable Tudor monarchs but began to break down later on when the Stuarts came to the throne.

Henry VIII is surely the most notorious Tudor. Imperious and flamboyant, a colossus among English royalty, he is said to have slammed shut the door on the Middle Ages and introduced the Renaissance to England. He is, of course, best known for his treatment of his six wives and the unfortunate fates that befell five of them. When his first wife, Catherine of Aragon, failed to produce an heir, and his ambitious mistress, Anne Boleyn, became pregnant, he tried to annul his marriage, but the pope refused, and Catherine contested the action. Henry had his marriage with Catherine declared invalid and secretly married Anne Boleyn in 1533.

The events that followed had profound consequences and introduced the religious controversy that was to dominate English politics for the next four centuries. Henry's break with the Roman Catholic Church and the formation of the Church of England, with himself as supreme head, was another turning point in English history. It led eventually to the Dissolution of the Monasteries, civil unrest, and much social dislocation. The confiscation of the church's land and possessions brought untold wealth into the king's coffers and was distributed to a new aristocracy that supported the monarch. In one sweeping gesture Henry destroyed the ecclesiastical culture of the Middle Ages. Among those who were executed for refusing to cooperate with Henry's changes was Sir Thomas More, humanist and international man of letters and author of *Utopia*.

Anne Boleyn bore Henry a daughter, the future Elizabeth I, but failed to produce a male heir. She was brought to trial on a trumped-up charge of adultery and beheaded, and in 1536, Henry married Jane Seymour, who died giving birth to Edward VI. For his next wife, he looked farther afield and chose Anne of Cleves from a flattering portrait, but she proved disappointing—he called her "The Great

Flanders Mare." He divorced her the same year and next picked a pretty young woman from his court—Catherine Howard. She was also beheaded on a charge of adultery, but unlike Anne Boleyn, was probably guilty. Finally, he married an older woman, Catherine Parr, in 1543. She survived him.

Henry's heir, sickly Edward VI (r. 1547–1553), did not live long. He died of consumption—or, as rumor has it, overmedication. He was succeeded by his sister, Mary I (r. 1553–1558), and the trouble Henry had stirred up with the break with Rome came home for the first time. Mary restored the Roman Catholic faith and her persecution of the adherents of the Church of England earned her the name of "Bloody Mary." Some 300 were executed, many burned alive at the stake. She made an unpopular and unhappy marriage with Philip of Spain; despite her bloody reputation, her life was a sad one.

Elizabeth I (r. 1558–1603) came next to the throne, ushering in an era of peace and prosperity, exploration, and a renaissance in science and learning. An entire age was named after her—the Elizabethan Age. She was the last great and grand monarch to rule England, and her passion and magnetism were said to match her father's. Through her era marched Drake, Raleigh, Frobisher, Grenville, Shakespeare, Spenser, Byrd, and Hilliard. During her reign, she had to face the appalling precedent of ordering the execution of a fellow sovereign, Mary Queen of Scots. Her diplomatic skills kept war at bay until 1588, when at the apogee of her reign, the Spanish Armada was defeated. She will be forever remembered as "Good Queen Bess."

The Stuarts ascended the throne in 1603, but though they held it through a century of civil war and religious dissension, they were not as capable as the Tudors in walking the line between the demands of a strong centralized monachy and the rights increasingly demanded by the representatives of the people in Parliament. Charles I, attracted by the French idea of the divine right of the king, considered himself above the law, a mistake the Tudors had never made— Elizabeth, in particular, was clever and careful in her dealings with Parliament. Charles's position was a fatal response to the Puritans and other Dissenters who sought for more power. In 1629 Charles dissolved Parliament, determined to rule without it.

Civil War followed, and the victory went to the Roundheads under Oliver Cromwell. Charles I was put on trial, and was led to his execution, stepping onto the scaffold through the window of his gloriously decorated Banqueting House. His once-proud head rolled on the ground. Oliver Cromwell, the melancholy, unambitious, "clumsy farmer," became England's first and only virtual dictator. He saw his soldiers as God's faithful servants, and promised them rewards in heaven. The English people, however, did not take kindly to this form of government, and after Cromwell's death, Charles II, the dead king's son, returned and was crowned in 1660, but given greatly limited powers.

The reign of Charles II was the beginning of a dreadful decade that saw London decimated by the Great Plague and destroyed by the Great Fire. His successor, James II, attempted to return the country to Catholicism, an attempt that so frightened the powers that be that Catholics were for a long time deprived of their civil rights. James was deposed in the "Glorious Revolution" of 1688 and succeeded by his daughter Mary and her husband, William of Orange, thus securing the Protestant succession that has continued to this day. These tolerant and levelheaded monarchs signed a Bill of Rights, establishing the principle that the monarch reigns not by divine right but by the will of Parliament.

Impressions

"For 'tis a low, newspaper, humdrum, law-suit Country."

—Lord Byron, 1819–24

"England is one of the weird mysteries of God's afterthought."

—Henry Adams, *Letter to John Hay,* December 1900

Queen Anne, Mary's sister, was the last of the Stuarts: She outlived all her children. Her reign (1702–1714) saw the full union of England and Scotland. After her death in 1714, England looked for a Protestant prince to succeed her, and they chose George of Hanover. He was invited to take the throne in 1714 as George I and thus began a 174-year dynasty. He spoke only German and spent as little time as possible in England. He left the running of the government to the English politicians and created the office of prime minister, though it wasn't called that. Under the Hanoverians, the powers of Parliament were extended, and the constitutional monarchy developed as we know it today.

The American colonies were lost under the Hanoverian George III, but British possessions were expanded: Canada was won from the French in the Seven Years' War (1756–63), British control over India was affirmed, and Captain Cook claimed Australia and New Zealand for England. The British became embroiled in the Napoleonic Wars (1795–1815), achieving two of their greatest victories and acquiring two of their greatest heroes: Nelson at Trafalgar and Wellington at Waterloo.

The mid- to late 18th century saw the beginnings of the Industrial Revolution. This event changed the lives of the laboring class, created a wealthy middle class, and transformed England from a rural, agricultural society into an urban, industrial economy. England was now a world-class financial and military power. Male suffrage was extended, though women were to continue under a series of civil disabilities for the rest of the century.

Queen Victoria's reign (1837–1901) coincided with the height of the Industrial Revolution. When she ascended the throne, the monarchy as an institution was in considerable doubt, but her 64-year reign, the longest in tenure in English history, was an incomparable success. The Victorian era was shaped by the growing power of the bourgeosie, the queen and her consort's personal moral stance, and the perceived moral responsibilities of managing a vast empire. During this time, the first trade unions were formed, a public (state) school system developed, and the railroads were built. Benjamin Disraeli persuaded Parliament to declare Victoria empress of India, a most unlikely choice for such a title.

Victoria never recovered from the death of her German husband, Albert. He died from typhoid fever in 1861, and the queen never remarried. Though she had many children, she found them tiresome, but was a pillar of "family values" nonetheless. One historian said her greatest asset was her "relative ordinariness."

Middle-class values ruled Victorian England and were embodied by the queen. The racy England of the past went underground. Our present-day view of England is still influenced by the attitudes of the Victorian era, and we tend to forget that English society in earlier centuries was famous for its rowdiness, sexual licence, and spicy scandal—perhaps the England of the present is only returning to its roots.

Victoria's son Edward VII (r. 1901–1910) was a playboy who had waited too long in the wings. He is famous for mistresses, especially Lillie Langtry, and his love of elaborate dinners. During his brief reign, he, too, had an era named after him, the Edwardian Age. Under Edward the country entered the 20th century, at the height of its imperial power, while at home the advent of the motorcar and the telephone radically changed social life, and the women's suffrage movement began.

World War I marked the end of an era. It had been assumed that peace, progress, prosperity, empire, and even social improvement would continue indefinitely. World War I and the troubled decades of social unrest, political uncertainty, and the rise of nazism and fascism put an end to these expectations.

World War II began in 1939, and soon thereafter Britain had a new and inspiring leader, Winston Churchill, whose mother was an American. Churchill led the nation during its "finest hour." The evacuation of Dunkirk in 1940, the blitz of London, the Battle of Britain, and the D-day invasion of German-occupied France are still remembered by many, and nostalgia for this era when Britain was heroic and was still a great world power shows up in books and frequently on television.

World War II brought many changes to England. Britain lost its empire, and the Labor government, which came into power in 1945, established the welfare state and brought profound social change to Britain.

Upon the death of the "wartime king" George VI, Elizabeth II ascended the throne. Her reign has seen many events. Industrial power, once preeminent in Britain, has eroded, and Britain suffered severe recession. Political power seesawed back and forth between the Conservatives and Labor parties. Margaret Thatcher, who became prime minister in 1979, seriously eroded the welfare state and was ambivalent toward the European Union. Her popularity soared during the successful Falklands War, when Britain seemed to recover for a brief time some of its military glory.

Although the queen has remained steadfast, and punctiliously performed her ceremonial duties, rumors about the royal family abounded, and in the year 1992, which Queen Elizabeth labeled an *annus horribilis,* a devastating fire swept through Windsor Castle, the marriages of several of her children crumbled, and the queen agreed to pay taxes for the first time. Prince Charles and Princess Diana agreed to a separation, and there were ominous rumblings about the future of the House of Windsor. By 1994 and 1995, Britain's economy was improving after several glum years, but Major was coming under increasing criticism as a lackluster prime minister.

The head of state is still a royal, but her duties are only ceremonial, and any political tasks she may perform are only formalities. Real power is in the hands of the prime minister, selected by the ruling party in the House of Commons, and his cabinet. After all that blood and gore, after all those battles and struggles, England emerged as one of the most successful democracies in the world. What would a monarch like Henry II or Henry VIII have thought of all this? They would surely have shouted, "Off with their heads."

4 Architecture & Art

ARCHITECTURE   The most stirring examples of early English architecture are pre-Celtic religious sites, such as Stonehenge. A few well-preserved Roman sites, such as Bath and Verulamium, and a handful of Saxon churches still exist. The most famous Norman architectural examples are the White Tower at the Tower of London and the great romanesque cathedrals of Durham, Norwich, and Ely.

The gothic period in England is usually divided into three parts that span the late 12th to mid-16th centuries: early English, decorated, and Perpendicular—each more lavishly ornamented than the last. Early English lasted from around the mid-12th century until the death of Edward I, in 1307. It was characterized by narrow pointed arches, ribbed vaults, and lancet windows. Salisbury Cathedral, in the city of Salisbury, Wiltshire, is one of the most outstanding examples of this style. Actually, it is the only English cathedral built in one style from start to finish. Other examples include Wells and Lichfield cathedrals and the ruins of the abbeys of Glastonbury and Fountains. The decorated style, a phase of English gothic, began around 1280 and lasted approximately until 1377. Ely Cathedral (1323–30), with its octagon and lantern, is an outstanding example of this style, as are the facades of Exeter Cathedral and York Minster and Lincoln Cathedral's Angel Choir. The Perpendicular style of gothic is peculiarly English. Here attention was paid to vertical lines, and the style's hallmark is paneled decoration all over a structure. Flying buttress and fan-vault roofing were also developed at this time. Exemplary architecture of this period includes the great chapels at Eton, King's College, Cambridge, and St. George's Chapel at Windsor Castle.

Tudor gothic began in 1485, when Henry VII came to the throne. Hampton Court Palace and Bath Abbey are outstanding examples of this style; other fine examples include Penshurst Palace in Kent and such timber-frame buildings as the Guildhall at Lavenham and the Feathers Inn in Ludlow, Shropshire.

The Renaissance came late to England. English architects tended to favor the mannerist approach of Germany and the Low Countries rather than the Italian style, using Flemish gabling and brickwork. Wealthy merchants built lavish mansions, such as Longleat House in Wiltshire, and Hardwick Hall in Derbyshire. The early 17th-century Jacobean period produced highly decorative domestic architecture; Hatfield House in Hertfordshire is a good example. It was Inigo Jones (1573–1652) who brought the formal classicism of the Italian Renaissance to England, and the results can be seen in the Banqueting House in Whitehall and parts of Wilton House in Wiltshire.

This classicism continued to be practiced throughout the 17th century, with baroque and rococo gaining only a foothold. Sir Christopher Wren, the leading 17th-century English architect, redesigned much of London after the Great Fire. He built a new St. Paul's Cathedral and rebuilt 53 churches—two of the most famous are St. Bride's in Fleet Street, and St. Mary-le-Bow. Other Wren masterpieces include the Royal Hospital at Greenwich, the Sheldonian Theatre, in Oxford, and the library at Trinity College, Cambridge.

At the end of his life, Wren was eclipsed by such famous 18th-century architects as Sir John Vanbrugh (1664–1726), creator of Castle Howard and Blenheim Palace, and Sir Nicholas Hawksmoor (ca. 1661–1736). After 1720 the baroque influence declined and the Palladian style took over, especially in domestic architecture. The architects William Kent and Colin Campbell, among others, built great houses surrounded by parkland and natural landscapes. One example is Hokham Hall, where the grounds are dotted with classical sculptures and fountains. Capability Brown was the foremost landscape artist of this period.

In the later 18th century a classical revival took place, led by Sir William Chambers and Robert Adam, whose Syon House, near London, and Kedleston Hall, in Derbyshire, are prime examples. Robert Adam (1728–92), son of a Scottish architect, is a name you'll frequently encounter when touring the stately homes of Britain. After touring Europe, he and his brothers opened a business in London. At that time the landed gentry of England preferred Palladian designs, but Adam was immediately successful in introducing a lighter and more decorative style. He was considered the greatest interior designer in England at the time. Whole terraces and crescents—John Wood the Elder's Royal Crescent, in Bath, for instance—were laid out in the 18th century. Similar schemes can be seen in Cheltenham and Brighton.

In the 19th century building changed as a result of the Industrial Revolution. Factories, railroad stations, concert halls, and theaters were added to the roster of churches and domestic buildings. All kinds of earlier styles—romanesque, Byzantine, gothic were reinterpreted—as glass and iron were introduced. The very technique of building changed as moldings and other internal decorative elements were mass produced. In the late Georgian and regency periods the leading architects were John Nash and Sir John Soane.

Beginning in about 1840 there came the craze for gothic revival that can be seen clearly in the Houses of Parliament, the Law Courts in London, the Natural History Museum, and the controversial Albert Memorial. At the end of the century, architects such as Charles Rennie Mackintosh rejected the overdecoration and heaviness of this Victorian style and sought greater simplicity.

The famous architects of the early 20th century include Sir Edwin Lutyens (1869–1944), who built country houses, the Reuters Building on Fleet Street and other commercial buildings, and laid out such grand schemes as the Whitehall cenotaph. He is also associated, of course, with the grand designs of British Delhi. Modern architecture as we know it really began after World War II. Many early modern buildings were created by immigrants—including Walter Gropius—en route to the United States. Much modern British architecture is blockish and dull (just ask Prince Charles!), with relief provided by such figures as Sir Hugh Casson and Sir Basil Spence.

ART   British art did not really come into its own until the 18th century. In the Middle Ages, most art was religious, and the cathedrals, churches, and monasteries became art galleries of awesome beauty. The depredations of the Dissolution of the Monasteries and Puritan destruction during Civil War meant that little has survived of this period.

Though there were some fine English artists, notably the great miniaturist Nicholas Hilliard and his pupil Isaac Oliver, secular art and artists were largely imported from the Continent—Hans Holbein the Younger in the Tudor period and Van Dyke and Lely during the Stuart period. Grinling Gibbons, employed by Sir Christopher Wren to carve the stalls in St. Paul's, brought sculpture into vogue.

In the 18th century, English painting finally came into its own. William Hogarth (1697–1764), an English painter and engraver, created works that satirized the social customs, hierarchies, and foibles of his era. He is known for his *Marriage à la Mode* (1745). Many Londoners of the time were particularly scandalized by two of his series of engravings, *A Harlot's Progress* and *A Rake's Progress*.

The harbinger of landscape painting, an important development in English art, was Richard Wilson, born in Wales in 1714. As a young man, he was heavily influenced by the French artist Claude Lorraine. He painted his native Welsh mountains set across limpid lakes, although his life was a series of financial struggles.

The giants of landscape painting who followed Wilson included Suffolk-born artist Thomas Gainsborough (1727–1788), who was one of the original members of the Royal Academy of Fine Arts (established in 1768 and still flourishing in Piccadilly). Gainsborough first gained fame as a portraitist: "His touch was as light as the sweep of a cloud and swift as the flash of a sunbeam," wrote the Victorian critic John Ruskin. In his final years, he turned to seascapes and painted idealized pictures of country rustics and children.

Half a century later, John Constable (1776–1837) painted the landscapes of East Anglia. Hayfields, river scenes, church spires, horses and wagons—all of these captured his fantasy and imagination. He wrote of "Light, dews, breezes, bloom, and freshness." His heavy brush strokes and use of paint seem to comprise a technique later employed by the impressionists. He was not appreciated in England, but he won recognition in France after 1824.

A contemporary of Constable's and one of the greatest names in English art, is Joseph Mallord William (J.M.W.) Turner (1775–1851). Ruskin had words for him, too: "He saw that there were more clouds in every sky than had ever been painted, more trees in every forest, more crags on every hillside, and set himself with all his strength to proclaim the great quantity of the universe." Living in Chelsea, and fascinated by the River Thames, Turner painted great cathedrals, country houses, river scenes, and the romantic landscapes of the Lake District and the Yorkshire Dales. He became increasingly fascinated by light, as witnessed in his 1807 painting *Sun Rising Through Vapour*. In the final phase of his life, Turner became more poetic and dreamlike in his paintings. He also produced engravings and thousands of watercolors, 19,000 of which he left to the Tate Gallery in London upon his death.

The multitalented William Blake (1757–1827), English mystic, artist, and poet, made illustrations for the Bible, Milton's *Paradise Lost*, and Robert Blair's *The Grave*, among other works. He is considered one of his era's most evocative catalysts of the exaltation of spirituality through art, using a complex religious symbolism that almost explodes from his illustrations and poetry. He did a series of illustrations, printed from etched copper plates, for his own lyrical poems, including *Songs of Innocence* (1789), now in the Tate Gallery. At the time of his death, he was preparing engravings for Dante's *Divine Comedy*.

The pre-Raphaelite school of painting, a romantic search for beauty, often using idealized medieval or Arthurian themes, was founded by the poet and painter Dante Gabriel Rossetti (1828–1882) in 1848. Notable among the pre-Raphaelite painters was Sir Edward Burne-Jones (1833–1898), who first became known for such large oils as *Le Chant d'Amour* (1877).

One of the most important portrait painters of the 20th century was Augustus John (1878–1961), whose works included portraits of George Bernard Shaw, Tallulah Bankhead, Dylan Thomas, and David Lloyd George. Ben Nicholson became known for semiabstract still lifes and landscapes, sometimes rendered in relief. Graham Sutherland painted in Pembrokeshire and his work decorates the notable modern cathedral of Coventry. Francis Bacon's "bloody meat" portraits disturbed many, and won him both praise and condemnation.

Henry Moore (1898–1986) and Dame Barbara Hepworth (1903–1975) are the towering figures in 20th-century British sculpture. Working in stone and bronze, Moore created abstract, often mammoth, sculptures inspired by organic forms. He is best remembered for his undulating reclining nudes. Many critics consider him the greatest sculptor of the 20th century; others have denounced his work as pointless.

His sometime companion, Dame Barbara Hepworth, also pursued the abstract in sculpture. In her works, hailed for their mastery of texture, she created an interplay of mass and interior space by using painted hollows, voids, and perforations. Much of her work was commissioned, including the United Nations' *Single Form* (1962–63).

For a view of contemporary English art, the galleries of the Tate contain an interesting collection of often controversial modern art, including the paintings of the well-known David Hockney who has had many exhibitions in America.

5 Legendary Heroes

England's preeminent myth is, of course, the Arthurian legend of Camelot and the Round Table. So compelling was this legend that medieval writers treated it as a tale of chivalry, even though the real Arthur, if he lived, probably did so around the time of the Roman or Saxon invasions. Despite its universal adoption throughout Europe, it was in Wales and southern England that the legend initially developed and blossomed. The story was polished and given a literary form for the first time by Geoffrey of Monmouth around 1135. Combining Celtic myth and Christian and classical symbolism (usually without crediting his sources), Geoffrey forged a fictional history of Britain whose form, shape, and elevated values were centered around the mythical King Arthur. Dozens of other storytellers embellished the written and oral versions of the tale. The resulting stewpot described the birth of Arthur, the exploits of the king and his knights, the establishment of a knightly fellowship of the Round Table, and the search for the Holy Grail, the cup Jesus drank from at the Last Supper. This idyllic and noble kingdom was shattered by the adultery of Arthur's queen, Guinevere, with his favorite knight, Lancelot, and the malice of Mordred, Arthur's illegitimate son.

The Arthurian legend has captured the imagination of the British people like no other legend before it. Arthur himself is supposed to still lie sleeping, ready to arise and save Britain in its greatest need. Perhaps only the Bible has been as frequently dissected and analyzed as the Arthurian legend. Some modern historians have traced exploits recounted in the tales to real Viking, Saxon, or even Roman military leaders. The version of the legend by Sir Thomas Malory has become the classic, but there were many others: Edmund Spenser in the Tudor period; in the 17th century, John Milton; in the Victorian Age, Tennyson, William Morris, and Swinburne; and in the 20th century, T.H. White and C.S. Lewis, not to mention the many film treatments.

The other myth that has captured the world's imagination is the legend of Robin Hood, the folk hero of tale and ballad. His slogan, "Take from the rich and give to the poor," fired the imagination of a hardworking, sometimes impoverished English people.

Celebrating their freedom in verdant Sherwood Forest, Robin Hood's eternally youthful band rejoiced in "hearing the twang of the bow of yew and in watching the gray goose shaft as it cleaves the glistening willow wand or brings down the king's proud buck." Life was one long picnic beneath the splendid oaks of a primeval forest, with plenty of ale and flavorful venison poached from the forests of an oppressive king. The clever guerrilla rebellion Robin Hood waged against authority (represented by the haughty, despotic, and overfed sheriff of Nottingham) was punctuated by heroic exploits and a yearning to win justice for the victims of oppression. Later, such historical figures as the Scottish bandit and soldier of fortune Robert MacGregor, known as Rob Roy (1671–1734), were imbued with the heroism and bravado of Robin Hood, and many English reformers drew upon his heroism as they battled the forces of oppression.

6 Lifestyle: Some Aspects, Changes & Differences

The fact that the English have adopted the bulldog as their symbol gives you a clue to their character, at least according to George Orwell, author of *1984* and *Animal Farm*. In 1947 he wrote that millions of Brits "willingly accept as their national emblem the bulldog, an animal noted for its obstinacy, ugliness, and impenetrable stupidity." Orwell, both a socialist and a critic of socialism, had no kindly feelings toward his fellow citizens.

Countless others have attempted to characterize the English, including the writer Arthur Koestler, who described an average Englishman as an "attractive hybrid between an ostrich and a lion: keeping his head in the sand for as long as possible, but when forced to confront reality, capable of heroic deeds."

The Brits have always baffled the Americans, perhaps ever since the latter ceased being Brits and became Americans. Writer Paul Gallico noted: "No one can be as calculatedly rude as the British, which amazes Americans, who do not understand studied insult and can only offer abuse as a substitute."

Of course, an entire book can be written (and many have been) on each of the subjects we're about to review. In our brief space, we want only to pique your interest in the English, and hope you'll go to meet them and form your own opinions about these highly individualistic people with their privacy and reserve, and endless tolerance of eccentricity.

SPEAKING ENGLISH

For an American it can be a minor shock to discover that the English speak English, and Americans speak American. There are enough differences between the two to result in frequent crossed wires and occasional total communication breakdowns, for although the British use words and phrases you think you understand, they often have quite different connotations from their U.S. equivalents.

When the British call someone *mean,* they intend to say *stingy.* And *homely,* meaning ugly, or plain, in America, becomes *pleasant* in England. A c*all* denotes a personal visit, not a phone call. But a person-to-person phone call is a *personal call. To queue up* means to form a line, which they do at every bus stop. And whereas a *subway* is an underground pedestrian passage, the actual subway system is called *the Underground,* or *the tube.* The term *theatre* refers only to the live stage; movie theaters are called *cinemas,* and what's playing in them are *the pictures.* And a *bomb,* which suggests a disaster in America, means a success in England.

In a grocery store, canned goods become *tins,* rutabagas become *swedes,* eggplants become *aubergines,* zucchini are *corgettes,* and endive is *chicory* (to confuse matters, chicory is *endive.*) Both cookies and crackers become *biscuits,* which can be either *dry* or *sweet.* Except graham crackers, that is, which are *digestives.*

The going gets rougher when you're dealing with motor vehicles. The English and Americans share very few words about cars, except for the word *car.* A truck

Impressions

"*England is the paradise of individuality, eccentricity, heresy, anomalies, hobbies and humours.*"

—George Santayana, "The British Character," *Soliloquies in England,* 1892 is called a *lorry*. Gas is *petrol*, windshield is *windscreen*, and bumpers are *fenders*. The hood is the *bonnet*, the trunk is the *boot*, and what you do on the horn is *hoot*.

Luckily, most of us know that an English apartment is a *flat* and an elevator is a *lift*. And you don't rent a room, you *let* it. Although the ground floor is the ground floor, the second floor is the *first floor*. And once you set up housekeeping, you don't vacuum, you *hoover*.

Going clothes shopping? Then you should know that undershirts are called *vests*, and undershorts are *pants* to the English. Long pants are called *trousers*, and their cuffs are called *turn-ups*. Panties are *knickers*, and panty hose are *tights*. Pullover sweaters can be called *jumpers*, and little girls' jumpers are called *pinafores*. If you're looking for diapers, ask for *nappies*.

If you really want a challenge, you can always take on a cockney. Although the cockneys are indigenous Londoners, strictly speaking the label refers only to people born in Cheapside, within sound of the St. Mary-le-Bow church bells.

The exact derivation of the word *cockney* is lost in the mists of antiquity, but it's supposed to have meant an odd fellow. Undoubtedly the oddest feature about the cockneys is the rhyming slang they've concocted over the centuries, a speech pattern based on rhymes that go with particular words and phrases. Take my advice and don't try to delve further, unless you happen to be Professor Higgins—pardon me: Professor 'iggins.

CLASS DIFFERENCES

Any system that appears to be a means of excluding, rather than including, vast members of a country's population is bound to inspire both resentment and ambition. This is the case with Britain's class system, a not-always-subtle hierarchy that is simultaneously celebrated, maligned, and castigated both inside and outside Britain. Well-advised observers of the British scene surmise that the class system of Britain is a firmly entrenched network that will continue even if the privileges and prestige of the royal family are greatly diminished. Of course there are encroachments from virtually all sides. After all, Mick Jagger, that "threat to civilization and the world as we've known it" back in the '60s, can now be seen chatting with Princess Margaret on the Caribbean island of Mustique.

The average visitor to England today, however, will hardly know the class system exists. And before jumping to judgment, here are some facts that might surprise you: Two hundred years ago there were only 115 peers in England, Scotland, and northern Ireland, usually with a power base founded on land ownership and privileges dating back to feudal times. Today there are some 1,700 peers in Britain. This explosion of British titles derives from l9th- and 20th-century policies of elevating to the peerage anyone who contributes in a major way to the well-being of Britain. In recent years this has included a good number of musicians, actors (Laurence Olivier), and film directors (Richard Attenborough). According to Harold Brooks-Baker, publishing director of *Burke's Peerage*, Britain is the only country in the world that has freely granted titles to members of labor unions (whose policies have been anything but aristocratic).

If you're planning the guest list for your next dinner party and find yourself confused about British titles, *Burke's Peerage*, that definitive resource on the importance of virtually everyone in the U.K., can be endlessly helpful. In diminishing order of prestige, the ranking of British titles goes as follows: duke or duchess, marquis or marchioness, earl or countess, and at the bottom of the rung, though still impressive, baron or baroness—the title bestowed on Margaret

Thatcher. Below that are hereditary knights (sirs) and many knights or ladies (dames) whose titles were bestowed for noteworthy but less spectacular achievements, usually in philanthropy, politics, or the arts. Finally there are those landed "lords of the manor" or country gentry that have no titles.

How to interpret the membership rolls, the wigs, the severe demeanors of the House of Lords? Insiders stress that Britain could have an aristocracy without the House of Lords but that the House of Lords could not exist without an aristocracy. Members of the House of Lords must be peers of the realm. Their vote is collectively weighed, with many checks and balances, against the counteracting forces of Parliament's House of Commons. So, the argument goes, the very nature of Britain's legislative process is deeply rooted in the class system, and to get rid of the country's aristocracy would necessitate a radical change in the nature of government.

Oddly enough, snobbery is no more noticeable in Britain than in any other country. Young members of titled families, though attending Eton or other supposed bastions of privilege, expend great effort camouflaging the fact when socializing with friends in the great maw—and social leveler—that is modern London ("I go to school near Windsor"). Much to their credit, and much in opposition to their exclusionary images, Eton and Harrow welcome people from a wide diversity of racial and geographical backgrounds that reflect the far-flung and cosmopolitan nature of Britain's former empire.

The dictum "grammatical correctness is social destiny" is firmly entrenched in Europe and even in the United States. But in England it goes further—accent is social destiny. Though these distinctions are gradually breaking down, those who want to scale the social or professional ladder must acquire the right accent. Contrariwise, members of the British upper class will usually avoid the once prevalent aristocratic speech patterns of the Edwardian Age in favor of those less obviously associated with hereditary power and privilege; in fact, in the rough and tumble settings of the London City—the financial district—perfect diction might well be a hindrance.

So how does a newcomer interpret the many symbols of Britain's class system that appear on all sides? Probably with charity, a sense of bemused sophistication, and even admiration. You'll probably not be admitted to the Royal Enclosure at Ascot, or to White's club in London, at least not on your first visit, or without a sponsor. But in the opinion of Mr. Brooks-Baker, Britain is among the least snobbish countries of the world.

THE ROYALS

When a racy London tabloid reported that eyewitnesses had actually seen Princess Di spot a good-looking young stud at Knightsbridge, lunge for him, toss him in her car, and speed off down the pike with her prize, you knew it was all but over for the House of Windsor. Whether these eyewitnesses saw anything of the sort is highly unlikely, but dishing the dirt on the royals brings millions to Fleet Street coffers. Times have changed: contrast this story to the prolonged press silence about the courtship of King Edward VIII and American divorceé Wallis Warfield Simpson in the 1930s.

Although the Windsors, especially the queen, loathe today's tabloid coverage, the royals set themselves up for it. If only they'd kept their clothes on in public! Princess Di photographed topless on a beach; Fergie frolicking on the Riviera; or "Randy Andy" galloping naked through a Canadian stream in front of a photographer. Only Prince Charles was properly nude in the right place—but at the wrong time—that is, in a men's locker room. The German press gleefully ran uncensored pictures of his royal highness stark naked, although tabs in London modestly covered up the vital parts when they ran the photographs.

No one is sure that Prince Charles will ever inherit the throne, much less with Princess Diana as his queen. Even the most devoted monarchists, however, predict a more scaled-down version of the monarchy—trimmed in size, benefits, and (probably) influence.

Jack Straw, the Labor shadow minister and longtime critic of the monarchy (though not of the queen herself) told me in Shepherd's, a London watering hole used by members of Parliament, that he would like to "see the type of monarchy they have in Norway, or perhaps Sweden. Let the royals shop for groceries like the rest of us. Just like the queen of Denmark. It would signal a classless British society." Even Prince Charles has admitted that a lot of people need to be taken off the royal payroll and the "monarchy scaled back if it is to survive."

PUBS

The pub is integral to the social life of England—it's the neighborhood social club. To meet, to talk, to argue, to catch up on the latest gossip, or to warm yourself from the chill of the weather—are all compelling reasons to visit the local watering hole. Although the pub may conjure up the notion of ales or bottled beer, exceptional pubs sometimes have several hundred whiskies in stock, and perhaps a very good wine list.

Pubs come in all styles, but atmosphere is the key to a good pub. Some are extravagant Victorian gin palaces; others occupy parts of long-gone monasteries or abandoned factories; some are sleek and modern, some are in the country and open onto river banks with weeping willows and white swans floating gracefully by. Of course you can't always drink in a place where Edward VII slipped off with Lillie Langtry, but you can occasionally still find the spot.

The curious names of pubs are legion—Pot Kiln, Shoulder of Mutton, Olde Plough, Beer Engine, Spread Eagle, Phoenix & Firkin. It is said that Cornwall has the largest concentration of good pubs in England, perhaps 30 for every 100,000 souls living there. Devon, Cumbria (embracing the Lake District), Gloucestershire, Oxfordshire, Somerset, and North Yorkshire also have a roster of good pubs, about 25 per 100,000 citizens.

Today pub grub too often means a freezer pack of food prepared at the last minute. However, there are some pub chefs who could have made it in a top restaurant if they had wanted to. The best dishes we've found in our latest rounds include fresh fish and country game, especially venison, pheasant, rabbit, and pigeon.

There are pubs where you can go to to see a striptease show, or a drag act. There are pubs for barristers, pubs for leather queens, pubs for journalists, pubs for factory workers, pubs for punkers, or whatever. Regrettably, many of them do not measure up to one's fantasy of an English pub. Loud jukeboxes, electronic games, and acres of Formica characterize some of the modern pubs. We'll try to steer you clear of those in the following chapters.

BRITS AT PLAY

Many of Britain's national sports are hardly known, much less played, outside that country. Soccer, called football, the most popular British (and European) sport, with about 35 million devotees, is well known in the United States. It is taken so seriously that it has led to widely publicized riots in which people were killed.

Rugby, which supposedly originated at the famous public school in Warwickshire, is less familiar. It's somewhat closer to American football and is primarily an upper- and middle-class game played mainly at the private schools. Welsh rugby, though, is a widely popular sport.

In summer, cricket, "the most English of games," is conducted in a polite and gracious manner by two teams of 11 men who wear white flannels and accept the umpire's judgments without question. From this game came such English phrases as "a sticky wicket" and "it's not cricket." Everyone plays cricket, from the students at Eton to the locals on the village green. An inning is one turn at bat for each side. Games can last from 1 to 5 days, as they do in the International Test Matches. Players bat in pairs from opposite ends of the pitch, a 22-yard-long patch of well-rolled and mowed grass at the center of a large oval field. The bowlers of the opposite team, keeping their arms straight, pitch a small hard ball so that it bounces in front of the batsman. The batsman's object is to hit the ball; the bowler is aiming to knock down the wicket (an assemblage of three upright sticks with a "bail," or crossbar, slotted across the top of them). The intricacies of the game are many, but the whole performance on a sunny weekend afternoon—complete with picnic or afternoon tea—is quintessentially English.

Hunting and shooting are occupations of the English upper class that have been made familiar to us by film and television. Fox hunting brings out the curious British attitude to animals. Brits are great animal lovers, and yet pursue these sports with enthusiasm. Oscar Wilde once characterized fox hunting as ". . . the unspeakable in full pursuit of the uneatable." A section of the public views fox hunting as a cruel sport and loudly protest against it, even organizing groups to disrupt a hunt.

Horse racing is a pastime favored by the royals. The "flat" racing season lasts from late March until November, and the classic race is the Derby run at Epsom Downs in early June. Steeplechasing, a typically English form of racing, involves jumping over fences and hedges, and is more thrilling and certainly more dangerous than "flat" racing. The most famous steeplechase is the Grand National, held annually at Liverpool's Aintree, familiar to any American who has seen the film *National Velvet.*

BRITISH ADVERTISING

Every sociologist in the hemisphere agrees that television (and television advertising) is a good bellwether for popular sentiment. One company aware of the cross-cultural premises of TV as it is broadcast on both sides of the Atlantic is Saatchi & Saatchi Advertising, one of the largest advertising agencies in the world, with massive branches on both sides of the Atlantic. Saatchi's most famous (and influential) British success was their handling of Margaret Thatcher's first electoral campaign, in 1979.

Their point of view on the matter is this: "In terms of marketing, the U.S. and Britain are two distinctly different cultures divided by a common language." There are basic differences in approaching the two markets. The British don't take to schmaltzy presentations in wholesome, family-values style. In product advertising "Brits would probably react favorably," claims a spokesperson, "to humor, to send-ups of the British character, and to subtle forms of satire." Memorable British television ad campaigns include one with John Cleese (famous as the comedic star of the BBC series "Fawlty Towers"), whose pseudo-stuffy style was endlessly popular as a promotional aid for that most-British of products, Schweppes Tonic Water. Several years ago, Saatchi & Saatchi's ad campaign for Irn-Bru cola garnered enthusiastic sales when a 60-second TV spot featured a beach party takeoff on the "Pepsi Generation" themes, complete with lyrics that satirized California beach-community wholesomeness.

The language of British print advertising is often more colorful than it is in America. Here's some copy from an ad for security agents: "Beat the statistics and stockpile your home with acoustic detectors and dynamite-proof safes; employ a private dick to follow your business partner; get your secret documents shredded." Here's one touting an architectural firm: "Contrary to popular superstition, architects are not just a bunch of misguided misanthropes who delight in littering our streets with lumps of rough-hewn concrete and shards of ill-fitting glass. No; whatever your building project, it'll save you time, hassle and money if you contact an architect first."

THE TABLOIDS

London is said to possess the world's best and worst newspapers. The *Guardian* and the *Times*, even the *Financial Times* and the *Independent*, are certainly among the finest newspapers ever published. But the *Star* and the *Sun* are another matter. The latter is not filled with John Major's latest political moves or even how he wouldn't take Clinton's phone calls. Rather, it is filled with racy material about the sex lives of pop stars and television ("telly") personalities. "I don't read the *Sun*," said Albert Hodges. "I buy it for the pictures of the topless models. The wifey won't let me bring it into the flat. I have to look at it on the way home from work." In the best-selling *News of the World*, a Sunday scandal sheet read by 5 million people in Britain, Joan Collins, a favorite subject of yesterday, has lost her throne to the royal family.

In fact, Fleet Street's pressure on the royal family is unrelenting. Some new indiscretion will pop up tomorrow. A late-night phone call from Princess Di to a married man always merits an enormous headline. The gossipy, voyeuristic attention of the tabloids to one family is unprecedented in the history of journalism.

THE BBC

Established in 1927, the British Broadcasting Corporation dominates the airwaves. It broadcasts in 38 languages worldwide. Lord Reith, the first director general, was horrified by American commercial radio, which was then gaining a foothold in Britain. He was anxious to prevent this "free-for-all" dominating British broadcasting. Thus, the BBC was launched on the "high road of Christian morality." In time, however, things changed—the far right denounces many of its broadcasts as "obscene," and during the cold war referred to it as the "Bolshevik Broadcasting Corporation." The far left refers to the corporation as "elitist and a captive of the Conservative movement in Britain." In fact, the BBC is neither one nor the other.

"The secret of the BBC," confided a staffer who preferred to be anonymous, "is that we give the British public what our powers think is good for them." Of course, the BBC can do that because they don't have to feel the heat from advertisers. For years critics of the BBC referred to its programming as "Aunty" in style, perhaps because of too many gardening and knitting programs. David Frost's biting 1960s satire *That Was the Week That Was* did much to remove the "Aunty" label.

The BBC's finest hour (to borrow a term from Churchill) was its coverage of World War II, when it was often right at the center of the action. In fact, it was a little too close to the center in 1940: A bomb exploded inside the BBC studio, but the announcer went on with the program. Talk about the stiff British upper lip.

THE POP MUSIC SCENE

Nothing has equaled the popular enthusiasm that greeted the British musical revolution of the 1960s. Aided by improvements in acoustical technology and the changing sociology of Britain, music was suddenly the passionate interest of millions of youthful Brits, setting the scene for a cultural invasion of American shores that hadn't been seen since the 18th century.

It began with the Beatles—John, Paul, George, and Ringo—whose clean looks and winning innocence won the hearts of every schoolgirl in America. They seemed to be in the vanguard of every cultural and musical movement, and as the '60s progressed, the Beatles didn't simply capitalize on their success or the musical styles that had originally made them popular. Their music evolved with the times and helped shape the cultural and political texture of their era.

The Beatles were the first of many Brits to find North America fertile ground. None was more visible than the Rolling Stones and Mick Jagger, whose sexual antics and destructive/self-destructive behavior made Paul McCartney look like an innocent. The Kinks, though enjoying tremendous musical success in America, despised the "vulgar States" and accused America of trampling the merrie olde English into the musical dustbin. Later, the Who helped elevate British rock to an art form worthy of musical study by launching their "rock opera" *Tommy*. And as the '60s and '70s sped forward, popular taste in Britain splintered further and further into three radically different camps—"the mods," whose identifying trademarks were high-speed motorbikes and loud music; fans who appreciated the Who and their sexual ambiguity; and the "rockers" who favored leather jackets (à la James Dean) and the cultural output of the United States.

As Woodstock made its impact, much of the music and many of the classic bands that youthful America loved originated in Britain. The British musical world of the early '70s produced the "hero of the guitar"—Jimmy Page of Led Zeppelin and Eric Clapton of Cream burst onto the scene. Pink Floyd and Roxy Music introduced us to "art-rock." The music and sexual ambiguity of the talented David Bowie appeared next on the scene, and the word went out that it was okay for two men to make it together, provided those two men were Mick Jagger and David Bowie.

The Sex Pistols startled the music world—so pivotal did their music and challenge to culture seem that British music was divided into "before the Pistols" and "after the Pistols," and punk became a fashion as well as a musical style. Surprises awaited us at every turn. "Ever Fallen in Love?", we later found out, was Pete Shelley's (of the Buzzcocks) ode to a guy. Sexual ambiguity, only suggested by David Bowie, reached its high point in Boy George; here we got painted lips and total androgyny.

After all these years, who's still on the charts? A guy named Elton John, with his "Believe." And in spring 1995, guess who made the charts for the first time in decades? Glenn Miller, with the album *Lost Recordings*.

7 English Cuisine

The late British humorist George Mikes wrote that "the Continentals have good food; the English have good table manners." But the British no longer deserve their reputation for soggy cabbage and tasteless dishes. Contemporary London—and the country as a whole—boasts many fine restaurants and sophisticated cuisine.

MEALS & DINING CUSTOMS   Britain is famous for its enormous breakfast of bacon, eggs, grilled tomato, and fried bread, which, although it has been replaced in places by a continental breakfast, is still to be found. Kipper, or smoked herring, is also a popular breakfast dish. The finest come from the Isle of Man, Whitby, or Lock Fyne, in Scotland. The herrings are split open, placed over oak chips, and slowly cooked to produce a nice pale-brown smoked fish. Lunch, usually eaten between noon and 2pm, is often taken at a pub—or as a sandwich on the run.

Many people still enjoy afternoon tea, which may consist of a simple cup of tea or a formal tea that starts with tiny crustless sandwiches filled with cucumber or watercress and proceeds through scones, crumpets with jam, or clotted cream, followed by cakes and tarts—all accompanied by a proper pot of tea. The tea at Brown's, in London, is quintessentially English, while the Ritz's tea is an elaborate affair, complete with orchestra and dancing. In the country, tea shops abound, and in Devon, Cornwall, and the West Country you'll find the best cream teas; they consist of scones spread with jam and thick, clotted Devonshire cream. A delicious treat, indeed. But it's a misconception to believe that everything stops for tea. People in Britain drink an average of four cups of tea a day. Many younger people prefer coffee.

Dinner is usually served around 8pm, and supper is traditionally a late-night meal, usually eaten after the theater.

THE CUISINE   You don't have to travel around England to sample regional English dishes—you'll find them on many a London menu. On any pub menu you're likely to encounter such dishes as Cornish pasty, cottage pie, or shepherd's pie, traditionally made from the leftovers of the Sunday meal. Or you might find Lancashire hot pot, a stew of mutton, potatoes, kidneys, and onions (sometimes carrots). This concoction was originally put into a deep dish and set on the edge of the stove to cook slowly while the workers spent the day at the local mill. But the most common pub meal is the ploughman's lunch, actually a newly invented old farmworker's tradition that consists of a good chunk of local cheese, a hunk of homemade crusty white or brown bread, some butter, and a pickled onion or two—all washed down with ale.

Among the best-known traditional English dishes, of course, is roast beef and Yorkshire pudding. The beef is often a large sirloin, so named, according to one story, because King James I, then a guest at Houghton Tower, Lancashire, knighted the leg of beef before him. "Arise, Sir Loin," he cried. The flour-based pudding is cooked directly under the joint of that leg, allowing fat from the meat to drop into it. Another dish that makes use of a batter similar to Yorkshire pudding is toad-in-the-hole, in which sausages are cooked in batter. Game, especially pheasant and grouse, is also a staple on British tables.

If you like oysters, try some of the famous Colchester oysters. On the west coast, you'll find a not-to-be-missed delicacy—Morecambe Bay shrimp—and fresh sea-

Impressions

"Even a boiled egg tastes of mutton fat in England."
—Norman Douglas, *Old Calabria*, 1915

food on every menu: cod, haddock, herring, plaice, and Dover sole, the aristocrat of flatfish. Cod and haddock are used in making British fish-and-chips (not always easy to find these days) which the true Briton covers with salt and vinegar.

The East End of London has quite a few interesting old dishes, among them tripe and onions. In winter, Dr. Johnson's favorite tavern, the Cheshire Cheese, on Fleet Street, offers a beefsteak-kidney-mushroom-and-game pudding in a suet case; in summer, there's a pastry case. East Enders can still be seen on Sunday at the Jellied Eel stall by Petticoat Lane, eating eel, cockles (small clams), mussels, whelks, and winkles—all small shellfish eaten with a touch of vinegar. Eel-pie-and-mash shops can still be found in London. They sell what is really a minced-beef pie topped with flaky pastry and served with mashed potatoes and a portion of jellied eel.

The British call desserts "sweets" or "pudding." Trifle is perhaps the most famous of English desserts. A "fool"—a gooseberry fool, for instance—is a light cream dessert whipped up from seasonal fruits. Regional sweets include the northern "flitting" dumpling—dates, walnuts, and syrup mixed with other ingredients and made into a pudding which is easily sliced and carried along when one is "flitting" from place to place. Similarly, hasty pudding, a Newcastle dish, is supposed to have been invented by people in a hurry to avoid the bailiff. It consists of stale bread, to which some dried fruit and milk are added before it is put into the oven.

Cheese is traditionally served after dessert as a savory. There are many regional cheeses, the best known being Cheddar, a good, solid, mature cheese. Others are the semismooth Caerphilly, from a beautiful part of Wales, and Stilton, a blue-veined crumbly cheese that's often enriched with a glass of port.

8   Recommended Books & Recordings

GENERAL & HISTORY   Anthony Sampson's *The Changing Anatomy of Britain* (Random House, 1982) still gives great insight into the idiosyncrasies of English society. Winston Churchill's *History of the English-Speaking Peoples* (Dodd Mead, 1956–58) is a four-volume tour de force, while his *Gathering Storm* (Houghton-Mifflin, 1986) captures London and Europe on the brink of World War II.

Britons: Forging the Nation (1707–1837), by Linda Colley (Yale University Press, 1992). Ms. Colley takes the reader from the Act of Union (formally joining Scotland and Wales to England) up to the adolescent Victoria's succession to the British throne. *Children of the Sun,* by Martin Green (Basic Books, 1976), portrays the "decadent" '20s and the lives of such people as Randolph Churchill, Rupert Brooke, the prince of Wales, and Christopher Isherwood.

Cultural portraits painted by outsiders are often more penetrating than those done by residents. Many visitors have expressed their views on England at different periods. An early 18th-century portrait is offered by K.P. Moritz in his *Journeys of a German in England in 1782* (Holt, Rinehart & Winston, 1965). Moritz traveled from London to the Midlands. Ralph Waldo Emerson recorded his impressions in *English Traits* (1856), as did Nathaniel Hawthorne, in *Our Old Home* (1863). For a marvelously ironic portrait of mid-19th-century Victorian British morals, manners, and society, seek out Taine's *Notes on England* (1872). Henry James's comments on turn-of-the-century England are to be found in his *English Hours.* In *A Passage to England* (St. Martin's, 1959), Nirad Chaudhuri analyzes Britain and the British in a delightful, humorous book.

Cobbet's *Rural Rides* (1830), depicts early 19th-century England. For what's really going on behind that serene Suffolk village scene, read Ronald Blythe's *Akenfield: Portrait of an English Village* (Random House, 1969).

ART & ARCHITECTURE   For opinionated entertainment there's John Betjeman's *Ghastly Good Taste-—the Rise and Fall of English Architecture* (St. Martin's, 1971). Betjeman is well known for his British TV programs on buildings. *A History of English Architecture,* by Peter Kidson, Peter Murray, and Paul Thompson (Penguin, 1979), covers the subject from Anglo-Saxon to modern times. Nikolaus Pevsner's *The Best Buildings of England: An Anthology* (Viking, 1987) and his *Outline of European Architecture* (Penguin, 1960) are both eloquent. *Architecture in Britain 1530–1830,* by John Summerson (Penguin, 1971), concentrates on the great periods of Tudor, Georgian, and Regency architecture. Mark Girouard has written several books on British architecture, including *The Victorian Country House* (Country Life, 1971) and *Life in the English Country House* (Yale University Press, 1978), a fascinating social-architectural history from the Middle Ages to the 20th century, complete with handsome illustrations.

LONDON   *London Perceived,* by novelist and literary critic V.S. Pritchett (Hogarth, 1986), is a witty portrait of the city—its history, art, literature, and life. Virginia Woolf's literary gem *The London Scene: Five Essays* (Random House, 1986) brilliantly depicts the London of the 1930s. *In Search of London,* by H.V. Morton (Methuen, 1988), is filled with anecdotal history and worth reading even though it was written in the 1950s.

In London: The Biography of a City (Penguin, 1980), popular historian Christopher Hibbert paints a very lively portrait. For some real 17th-century history, you can't beat the *Diary of Samuel Pepys* (written 1660–69); and for the flavor of the 18th century, try Daniel Defoe's 3-volume *Tour Thro' the Whole Island of Great Britain,* which was done in 1724–26 and includes a volume on London (Ayer, 1929).

Americans in London, by Brian N. Morton (William Morrow, 1986), is a street-by-street guide to the clubs, homes, and favorite pubs of more than 250 illustrious Americans who made London their temporary home—Mark Twain, Joseph Kennedy, Dwight Eisenhower, and Sylvia Plath. *The Guide to Literary London,* by George Williams (Batsford, 1988), charts a series of literary tours through London from Chelsea to Bloomsbury. *The Capital Companion,* by Peter Gibson (Webb & Bower, 1985), features more than 1,200 alphabetical entries and is filled with facts and anecdotes about the streets of London and their inhabitants.

The Architect's Guide to London, by Renzo Salvadori (Reed International, 1990), documents 100 landmark buildings with photographs and maps. *Nairn's London,* by Ian Nairn (Penguin, 1988), is a stimulating, opinionated discourse on London's buildings. David Piper's *The Artist's London* (Oxford University Press, 1982) does what the title suggests—captures the city that artists have portrayed. In *Victorian and Edwardian London* (Batsford, 1969), John Betjeman expresses his great love of those eras and their great buildings.

BIOGRAPHY   The great biography of Samuel Johnson by his friend James Boswell, whose *Life of Samuel Johnson* (Modern Library College Editions, 1964) was first published in 1791. Antonia Fraser has written several lively biographies of English monarchs and political figures, including Charles II and Oliver Cromwell. Her most recent is *The Wives of Henry VIII* (Knopf, 1992), which tells the sad story of the six women foolish enough to marry the Tudor monarch.

Another great Tudor monarch, Elizabeth I, emerges in a fully rounded portrait by historian Christopher Hibbert: *The Virgin Queen, Elizabeth I, Genius of the Golden Age* (Addison-Wesley, 1992).

The duchess of York (Prince Andrew's estranged wife, "Fergie") captures the era in *Victoria and Albert: A Family Life at Osborne House* (Prentice Hall, 1991), co-written with Benita Stoney. One reviewer said that the authors write about "England's 19th-century rulers not as historical figures but as a loving couple and caring parents."

Another point of view is offered in *Victoria: The Young Queen,* by Monica Charlot (Blackwell, 1991), the first volume in a projected biographical series. This book, praised for its "fresh information," traces the life of Victoria until the death of her husband, Prince Albert, in 1861. Queen Elizabeth II granted Charlot access to the Royal Archives.

In *Elizabeth II, Portrait of a Monarch* (St. Martin's, 1992), Douglas Keay drew on interviews with Prince Philip and Prince Charles to tell a lively story. Other recent works dealing with the royal family take a dimmer view, as exemplified by Anthony Holden's *Tarnished Crown* (Random House, 1993) and A.N. Wilson's *Rise and Fall of the House of Windsor* (W.W. Norton & Company, 1993). Although Wilson's Queen Elizabeth II has performed her role "flawlessly" and Holden's queen is a "ridiculously expensive exercise," both authors take jabs at Prince Charles.

Richard Ellman's magisterial *Oscar Wilde* (Knopf, 1988) reveals, besides Wilde, such Victorian-era personalities as Lillie Langtry, Gilbert and Sullivan, and Henry James. The quintessential English playwright Noël Coward and the London he inhabited are captured in Cole Lesley's *Remembered Laughter* (Knopf, 1977). It includes portraits of Nancy Mitford, Cecil Beaton, John Gielgud, Laurence Olivier and Vivien Leigh, Evelyn Waugh, Rebecca West, and others. *The Lives of John Lennon,* by Albert Goldman (William Morrow, 1988), traces the life of this famous 1960s musician. *Dickens,* by Peter Ackroyd (Harper Perennial, 1992), is in part a study of the novelist's painful childhood. It's a massive volume, tracing everything from the reception of Dickens's first novel, *Pickwick Papers,* to his scandalously deserting his wife.

Other recent releases include *Wild Spirit: The Story of Percy Bysshe Shelley,* by Margaret Morley (Hodder & Stoughton, 1992), a fictionalized biography of the poet; Sally Festing's *Gertrude Jekyll* (Viking, 1992), which paints a portrait of the woman called "the greatest artist in horticulture;" *Anthony Trollope,* by Victoria Glendinning (Knopf, 1993), a provocative portrait of the English novelist; and *Lawrence and the Women: The Intimate Life of D. H. Lawrence,* by Elaine Feinstein (HarperCollins, 1993), which examines this sensitive novelist's involvements with female friends and lovers.

The recent biography *Tennyson,* by Norman Page (New Amsterdam, 1993), was published on the centenary of the poet laureate's death. Humphrey Carpenter's *Benjamin Britten: A Biography* (Charles Scribner's Sons, 1993) examines connections between the composer's music and personal life.

Although no one told the story of Winston Churchill's life more eloquently than he did, a new study by Martin Gilbert has emerged, *Churchill: A Life* (Holt, 1991). This 1,000-page book is a distillation of Gilbert's eight-volume official biography. Historian John Charmley accused Churchill of "appeasement" in his relations with Stalin; the controversy made his *Churchill: The End of Glory—a Political Biography* (Harcourt Brace, 1993) a best-seller in England.

RECORDINGS

The music performed at Elizabeth I's court, including compositions by Thomas Morley (ca. 1557–1602), have been recorded by the Deller Consort; one of their titles is *Now Is the Month of Maying: Madrigal Masterpieces* (Vanguard BG 604).

England's Renaissance church music is best exemplified by English composer William Byrd (1543–1623), listen to his *Cantiones sacrae: 1575,* performed by the Choir of New College, Oxford, and recorded in the New College Chapel for London Records (London CRD 3408).

Henry Purcell's *Dido and Aeneas* is widely available in several performances. For an example of Purcell's orchestral music, listen to *The Virtuoso Trumpet,* performed by trumpeter Maurice André, who is accompanied by the Academy of St. Martin-in-the-Fields, Sir Neville Marriner conducting (RCA Red Seal CRL 3–1430).

John Gay's *The Beggar's Opera,* first performed in 1728, is available in a recording by Britain's National Philharmonic Orchestra and the London Opera Chorus for Polygram Records (London LDR 72008).

The works of the beloved British team of Sir Arthur Sullivan (composer) and Sir W.S. Gilbert (librettist) are widely available. *The Mikado,* performed by the Pro Arte Orchestra and the Glyndebourne Festival Chorus, Sir Malcolm Sargent conducting, is available on Angel Records (3573 B/L).

The compositions of Sir Edward Elgar can be heard on the British Philharmonic Orchestra's recording of the *Pomp and Circumstance* marches, conducted by Andrew Davis (CBS Records/Masterworks IM 37755).

Two fine recordings of England's modern master, Ralph Vaughan Williams, are his Symphony no. 3 ("Pastoral"), performed by the London Symphony Orchestra (Chandos Records CHAN 8594); and his *Sea Symphony,* performed by the London Symphony Orchestra and Chorus, with conductor André Previn and soloists Heather Harper and John Shirley-Quirk (RCA 6237–2RC).

Benjamin Britten's *Ceremony of Carols* performed by the Choir of St. John's College, Cambridge (Argo Records ZRG 5440), and his *Variations for a String Orchestra,* performed by the London Philharmonic Orchestra, with Roger Best, viola (Chandos Records CHAN 8514), are both fine examples of this preeminent British composer. Benjamin Britten's *Song Cycles* (Chandos CHAN–8514), an arrangement of folk songs and poems by William Blake, is performed by baritone Benjamin Luxon and pianist David Willison.

Past Masters (Capitol CDP 7–900–432 and CDP 7–900–442) is a two-volume retrospective collection of Beatles music. Equally important is their milestone album *Sergeant Pepper* (Capitol 2653), which was considered a musical watershed when it was released in 1967.

The Rolling Stones's *Flashpoint* (Sony/CBS Records CK 47–456) is a textbook study of the spirit of rock and roll, with a guest performance by Eric Clapton on a track entitled "Little Red Rooster." Another Rolling Stone great is *Exile on Main Street* (Sony/CBS CGK 40489).

The enigmatic Morrissey is disdainful of British pop culture and fascinated by criminals. He followed his 1992 solo album, *Your Arsenal,* with *Vauxhall and I* (Respire/Sire 45451). He's shifted his obsession from Manchester to his birthplace, the seedy Vauxhall district in south London. The banter of cockney villains appears in the album's recording of "Spring-Heeled Jim."

One 1994 release that won an enthusiastic response from even the most jaded music retailers in Britain came from the emerging rock group Suede. Their album

Nude (Polygram/Sony/Columbia CT 53792) is viewed as a musical exploration of sex and sensibility in the '90s.

A recording of interest to music historians is *All Back Home* (BBC CD844/ REF844), which traces the musical themes of American and Australian folk and blues back to Irish, English, and Scottish roots. The recording includes tracks by Sinead O'Connor, the Everly Brothers, Kate Bush, Bob Dylan, Pete Seeger, the Waterboys, and Thin Lizzy.

Richard Thompson, who performs on *Amnesia* (Capitol C4–48845), has been reviewed as one of the most unusual and iconoclastic of modern British folk performers. He uses guitar, mandolin, and hammer dulcimer in his melodies, and his lyrics showcase political and social satire as well as soulfully nostalgic ballads.

The Pogues's *Rum, Sodomy, and the Lash* (Stiff Records 222701) is folk and rock music with a decidedly funky (sometimes shocking) twist. The half-English, half-Irish group is based in London.

2

Planning a Trip to England

This chapter is devoted to the where, when, and how of your trip—the advance planning required to get it together and take to the road.

After deciding where to go, most people have two fundamental questions: What will it cost? and How do I get there? This chapter will answer both of those questions and also resolve other important issues, such as when to go, what pretrip preparations are needed, where to obtain more information about the destination, and many more.

1 Visitor Information & Entry Requirements

VISITOR INFORMATION
IN THE USA & CANADA

Before you go, you can obtain general information from the following British Tourist Authority Offices.

New York: 551 Fifth Ave., Suite 701, New York, NY 10176-0799 (☎ 212/986-2200).

Toronto: 111 Avenue Rd., Suite 450, Toronto, ON M5R 3J8 (☎ 416/925-6326).

A good travel agent can also provide tourist information. And always check the travel sections of newspapers (such as in the Sunday edition of the *New York Times*) and magazines like *Travel & Leisure* and *Traveler*. If you feel like doing some library work, ask your librarian for a recent edition of *Reader's Guide to Periodical Literature* (a comprehensive index of magazine articles); look up England or a specific city of interest.

ENTRY REQUIREMENTS

DOCUMENTS All U.S. citizens, Canadians, Australians, New Zealanders, and South Africans must have a passport with at least 2 months' remaining validity. No visa is required. The immigration officer will also want proof of your intention to return to your point of origin (usually a round-trip ticket) and visible means of support while you're in Britain. If you're planning to fly from, say, the U.S. or Canada to the U.K. and then on to a country that requires a visa (India, for example), it's wise to secure that visa before your arrival in Britain.

CUSTOMS   For visitors to England, goods fall into two basic categories—purchases made in a non–European Union (EU) country or bought tax free within the EU, and purchases on which tax was paid in the EU. In the former category, limits on imports by individuals (aged 17 and older) include 200 cigarettes, 50 cigars, or 250 grams of loose tobacco; 2 liters of still table wine, 1 liter of liquor (over 22% alcohol content), or 2 liters of liquor (under 22%); and 2 fluid ounces of perfume. In the latter category—items on which tax was paid in the EU—limits are *much* higher: An individual may import 800 cigarettes, 200 cigars, *and* 1 kilogram of loose tobacco; 90 liters of wine, 10 liters of alcohol (over 22%), *and* 110 liters of beer; plus unlimited amounts of perfume.

Returning U.S. citizens who have been away for 48 hours or more are allowed to bring back, once every 30 days, $400 worth of merchandise duty-free. You'll be charged a flat rate of 10% duty on the next $1,000 worth of purchases. Be sure to have your receipts handy. On gifts, the duty-free limit is $50. For more specific guidance, write to the **U.S. Customs Service,** P.O. Box 7407, Washington, DC 20044, requesting the free pamphlet "Know Before You Go."

For a clear summary of Canadian rules, write for the booklet "I Declare," issued by **Revenue Canada,** 875 Heron Rd., Ottawa ON K1A OL5. Canada allows its citizens a $300 exemption, and you are allowed to bring back duty-free 200 cigarettes, 2.2 pounds of tobacco, 40 imperial ounces of liquor, and 50 cigars. In addition, you are allowed to mail gifts to Canada from abroad at the rate of Can$60 a day, provided they are unsolicited and aren't alcohol or tobacco (write on the package: "Unsolicited gift, under $60 value"). All valuables should be declared on the Y-38 Form before departure from Canada, including serial numbers of, for example, expensive foreign cameras that you already own. *Note:* The $300 exemption can be used only once a year and only after an absence of seven days.

The duty-free allowance in Australia is A$400 or, for those under 18, A$200. Personal property mailed back from England should be marked "Australian goods returned" to avoid payment of duty. Upon returning to Australia, citizens can bring in 200 cigarettes or 250 grams of loose tobacco, and 1 liter of alcohol. If you're returning with valuable goods you already own, such as foreign-made cameras, you should file form B263. A helpful brochure, available from Australian consulates or customs offices, is "Customs Information for All Travellers."

New Zealand Customs   The duty-free allowance is NZ$700. Citizens over 17 years of age can bring in 200 cigarettes, or 50 cigars, or 250 grams of tobacco (or a mixture of all three if their combined weight doesn't exceed 250 grams); plus 4.5 liters of wine and beer, or 1.125 liters of liquor. New Zealand currency does not carry import or export restrictions. Fill out a certificate of export, on which you will list the valuables you are taking out of the country; that way, you can bring them back without paying duty. Most questions are answered in a free pamphlet available at New Zealand consulates and customs offices: *New Zealand Customs Guide for Travellers,* Notice no. 4.

MONEY

Before leaving home it's advisable to secure traveler's checks and a small amount of foreign currency to cover costs on arrival overseas. Also take along about $250 in cash.

The British Pound & U.S. Dollar

U.K.£	U.S.$	U.K.£	U.S.$
0.05	0.08	15	23.85
0.10	0.16	20	31.60
0.25	0.40	25	39.50
0.50	0.79	30	47.40
0.75	1.19	35	55.30
1	1.58	40	63.20
2	3.16	45	71.11
3	4.74	50	79.00
4	6.36	55	87.45
5	7.90	60	95.40
6	9.48	65	102.70
7	11.06	70	110.60
8	12.64	75	118.50
9	14.22	100	158.00
10	15.90	125	197.50

CURRENCY/CASH

The British currency is the pound sterling (£), made up of 100 pence (p), which is used throughout the U.K. Notes are issued in £5, £10, £20, and £50 denominations. (A £1 note also circulates in Scotland.) Coins come in 1p, 2p, 5p, 10p, 50p and £1.

At this writing, $1 equals approximately 66p (or £1 = $1.58), and this was the rate of exchange used to calculate the dollar value given in this guide (rounded to the nearest nickel). This rate fluctuates from time to time and may not be the same when you travel to the U.K., so please use the table below only as a general guide.

CURRENCY EXCHANGE

Many hotels in England simply will not accept a dollar-denominated check, and if they do, they'll certainly charge for the conversion. In some cases they'll accept countersigned traveler's checks or a credit card, but if you're prepaying a deposit for hotel reservations, it's cheaper and easier to pay with a check drawn on a British bank.

This can be arranged by a large commercial bank or by a currency specialist such as **Ruesch International,** 825 14th St. NW, Washington, DC 20005 (☎ 202/408-1200 or 800/424-2923), which can perform a wide variety of conversion transactions for individual travelers. To place an order, call and tell them the amount of the sterling-denominated check you need. Ruesch will quote a U.S.-dollar equivalent, adding a $2 fee per check as their service fee. After receiving your dollar-denominated personal check for the agreed-upon amount, Ruesch will mail you a sterling-denominated bank-draft drawn on a British bank and payable to whatever party you specify. Ruesch will also convert checks expressed in foreign currency into U.S. dollars, provide foreign currencies in cash from more than

What Things Cost in London	U.S. $
Taxi from Victoria Station to Paddington Hotel	12.50
Underground from Heathrow Airport to central London	5.25
Local telephone call	0.20
Very expensive double room (at the Dorchester)	355.50
Moderate double room (at Bryanston Court Hotel)	142.20
Inexpensive double room (at Regent Palace Hotel)	121.70
Moderate lunch for one (at Sheekeys)	28.90
Inexpensive lunch for one (at Cheshire Cheese)	15.00
Very expensive dinner for one, without wine (at Le Gavroche)	90.00
Moderate dinner for one, without wine (at Bracewells)	37.00
Inexpensive dinner for one, without wine (at Porter's English Restaurant)	23.60
Pint of beer	2.90
Coca-Cola in a café	1.60
Cup of coffee	1.30
Roll of ASA 100 color film, 36 exposures	8.00
Admission to the British Museum	Free
Movie ticket	7.50
Theater ticket	15.00–52.50

120 countries, and sell traveler's checks payable in either dollars or any of six foreign currencies, including pounds sterling. In addition to its Washington office, Ruesch maintains offices in New York, Los Angeles, Chicago, Atlanta, Boston, and London. Its London office, Ruesch International Ltd., is at 18 Savile Row, London W1X 2AD (☎ 0171/734-2300). Any of these offices can supply drafts and traveler's checks by mail or phone.

TRAVELER'S CHECKS

Traveler's checks are the safest way to carry cash while traveling. Most banks will give you a better exchange rate for traveler's checks than cash. If you can, purchase them in pound denominations. The following are the major issuers of traveler's checks.

American Express (☎ 800/221-7282 in the U.S. and Canada) is one of the largest and most immediately recognized issuers of traveler's checks. The company issues checks denominated in U.S. dollars, Canadian dollars, British pounds sterling, Swiss francs, French francs, German marks, Japanese yen, and Dutch guilders. The vast majority of checks sold in North America are denominated in U.S. dollars. For questions or problems that arise outside the U.S. or Canada, contact any of the company's many regional representatives.

Citicorp (☎ 800/645-6556 in the U.S. and Canada or 813/623-1709 collect from anywhere else in the world), issues checks in U.S. dollars, British pounds, German marks, Japanese yen, and Australian dollars.

What Things Cost in Bath	U.S. $
Taxi from Bath Rail Station to a centrally located hotel	6.30
Local telephone call	0.20
Expensive double (at the Priory Hotel)	244.90
Moderate double (at the Francis Hotel)	150.10
Inexpensive double (at the Sydney Gardens Hotel)	109.00
Inexpensive lunch for one (at Woods)	12.00
Moderate dinner for one, without wine (at The Hole in the Wall)	28.50
Moderate dinner for one, without wine (at The Olive Tree)	30.00
Pint of beer	2.80
Coca-Cola in a café	1.60
Cup of coffee	1.40
Roll of ASA 100 color film, 36 exposures	8.20
Admission to the American Museum	7.90
Movie ticket	6.30
Theater ticket	17.30

Thomas Cook (☎ 800/223-7373 in the U.S. and Canada or 609/987-7300 collect from other parts of the world) issues MasterCard traveler's checks denominated in U.S. dollars, Canadian dollars, French francs, British pounds, German marks, Dutch guilders, Spanish pesetas, Australian dollars, and Japanese yen. Depending on banking laws in the various states, some of the above-mentioned currencies might not be available at every outlet.

Interpayment Services (☎ 800/221-2426 in the U.S. and Canada or 212/858-8500 collect from other parts of the world) sells VISA checks that are issued by a consortium of member banks and the Thomas Cook organization. Traveler's checks are denominated in U.S. or Canadian dollars, British pounds, and German marks.

Issuers sometimes have agreements with groups to sell checks commission free. For example, Automobile Association of America (AAA) clubs sell American Express checks in several currencies without commission.

CREDIT CARDS

Credit cards are useful in England, though one should be warned that many of the low-cost establishments, especially bed-and-breakfasts, do not accept them. VISA is the most widely used card, along with EuroCard (which is the same as MasterCard). American Express is often accepted, mostly in middle- and upper-bracket establishments. Of the "big four," Diners Club is the least accepted.

Credit cards can save your life when you're abroad. With American Express and VISA, for example, you can not only charge purchases but also withdraw sterling from cash machines at many locations in England. Check with your credit-card company before leaving home.

Of course, you may make a purchase with a credit card thinking it will be at a certain rate, only to find that the dollar has declined by the time your bill arrives, and you're actually paying more than you bargained for. Credit-card companies base the rate on the date the charge is posted, not on the date you actually made the transaction—but those are the rules of the game. It can also work in your favor if the dollar rises after you make a purchase.

2 When to Go—Climate, Holidays & Events

CLIMATE British temperatures can range from 30° to 110° Fahrenheit but they rarely drop below 35° or go above 78°. Evenings are cool, even in summer. No Briton will ever really advise you about the weather—it's far too uncertain. If you come here from a hot area, bring some warm clothes. If you're from cooler climes, you should be all right. Note that the British, who consider chilliness wholesome, like to keep the thermostats about 10° below the American comfort level. They are also hopelessly enamored of fireplaces, which warm little but the portion of your anatomy you turn to them. Hotels have central heating but are usually kept just above the goose-bump (in English, "goose pimple") margin.

London's Average Daytime Temperature & Monthly Rainfall

	Jan	Feb	Mar	Apr	May	June	July	Aug	Sept	Oct	Nov	Dec
Temp. °F	40	40	44	49	55	61	64	64	59	52	46	42
Rainfall"	2.1	1.6	1.5	1.5	1.8	1.8	2.2	2.3	1.9	2.2	2.5	1.9

HOLIDAYS England observes New Year's Day, Good Friday, Easter Monday, May Day, spring and summer bank holidays (the last Monday in May and August, respectively), Christmas Day, and Boxing Day (December 26).

ENGLAND CALENDAR OF EVENTS

For more information about these and other events, contact tourist offices in England.

February

- **Jorvik Festival, York.** A 2-week celebration of this historic cathedral city's role as a Viking outpost. For more information, call 01904/621756.

March

✪ **Crufts Dog Show.** The English, they say, love their pets more than their off-spring. Crufts offers an opportunity to observe the nation's pet lovers dote on the 8,000 dogs representing 100 breeds that strut their stuff. It's an emotionally charged event for the English.

   Where: National Exhibition Centre, Birmingham, West Midlands. **When:** Mid-March. **How:** Tickets can be purchased at the door.

April

✪ **The Shakespeare Season.** The Royal Shakespeare Company at Stratford-upon-Avon begins its annual season, presenting a varied program of works by the Bard in his hometown.

   Where: Royal Shakespeare Theater, Waterside (☎ 0789/295623), in Stratford-upon-Avon. **When:** April–January. **How:** Tickets at box office, or else through such agents as Keith Prowse (many locations) in London.

- **Grand National Meeting.** This is the premier steeplechase event in England. It takes place over a 4-mile course at Aintree Racecourse, Aintree, outside Liverpool, Merseyside (☎ 0151/7093631). Early April.

- **Devizes-Westminster International Canoe Race.** A 125-mile race along the Avon River, the Kennet Canal, and the River Thames. No tickets are needed. Call 01372/453976 for more information. April 14–17.

May

- **Chichester Festival Theatre.** Some of the best classic and modern plays are presented at this West Sussex theater from May to October. For tickets and information, contact the Festival Theatre, Oaklands Park, West Sussex PO19 4AP (☎ 01243/781312).
- **Brighton International Festival.** This is England's largest multi-arts festival. Beginning May 5, 1996, and continuing for 24 days, some 400 different cultural events will be staged. For information, write to the Brighton Festival, 21–22 Old Steine, Brighton, Sussex BN1 1EL.
- **Royal Windsor Horse Show,** Home Park, Windsor, Berkshire. The country's major show-jumping presentation, attended by the queen herself. Call 01298/72272 for more information. Mid-May.
- ✪ **Bath International Festival.** One of Europe's most prestigious international festivals of music and the arts. As many as 1,000 performers appear.
  Where: At various venues in Bath, Avon. **When:** Late May to mid-June. **How:** Full details can be obtained from the Bath Festival, Linley House, 1 Pierrepoint Place, Bath BA1 1JY (☎ 01225/463362).
- ✪ **Glyndebourne Festival.** One of England's major cultural events, this festival is centered at a new opera house in Sussex, some 54 miles south of London.
  Where: The 1,200-seat Glyndebourne Opera House. **When:** End of May to late August. **How:** Tickets, which cost £10–£110 ($15.80–$173.80), are available from Glyndebourne Festival Opera Box Office, Lewes, East Sussex BN8 5UU (☎ 01273/813813).

June

- **Derby Day.** Famous horse-racing event at Epsom Downs, Epsom, Surrey. For more details, contact United Racecourse Holdings Ltd., the Racecourse Paddock, Esher, Surrey KT10 9AJ (☎ 01372/470047). Early June.
- **Aldeburgh Festival of Music and the Arts.** The composer Benjamin Britten launched this festival in 1948. For more details, and for the year-round program of events, write to Aldeburgh Foundation, High Street, Aldeburgh, Suffolk IP15 5AX (☎ 01728/452935). June 9–25.
- **Royal Ascot Week.** Ascot Racecourse is open year-round for guided tours, events, exhibitions, and conferences. There are 24 race days throughout the year, with the feature races being the Royal Meeting in June, Diamond Day in July, and the Festival at Ascot in September. For information, contact Ascot Racecourse, Ascot, Berkshire SL5 7JN (☎ 01344/22211).
- **Henley Royal Regatta.** An international rowing competition and premier event on the English social calendar. It takes place at Henley, in Oxfordshire. For more information, call 01491/578034. Late June to early July.

August

- **Cowes Week.** A yachting festival held off the Isle of Wight, in Hampshire. For details, call 01983/291914. Early August.

September
- **Burghley Horse Trials.** This annual event is staged on the grounds of the largest Elizabethan house in England, Burghley House, Stamford, Lincolnshire (☎ 01780/52451). Early September.

October
- **Cheltenham Festival of Literature.** A Cotswold event, featuring readings, book exhibitions, and theatrical performances—all in the famed spa town of Gloucestershire. Call 01242/522878 for more details. Early to mid-October.

November
- **London-Brighton Veteran Car Run.** Begins in London's Hyde Park and ends in the seaside resort of Brighton, in East Sussex. Call 01580/893413 for more details. Early November.

December
- **Christmas.** Observances in all of England's villages, towns, and cities.

LONDON CALENDAR OF EVENTS

January
- **London International Boat Show.** The largest boat show in Europe, held at the Earl's Court Exhibition Centre, Warwick Road. Call 01784/473377 for details. First 2 weeks in January.
- **Charles I Commemoration.** Anniversary of the execution of King Charles I "in the name of freedom and democracy." Hundreds of cavaliers march through central London in 17th-century dress, and prayers are said at Whitehall's Banqueting House. Free. Last Sunday in January.
- **Chinese New Year.** The famous Lion Dancers in Soho perform free. Late January or early February (based on the lunar calendar), and celebrated on the nearest Sunday.

April
- **Easter Parade.** Brightly colored floats and marching bands around Battersea Park offer a full day of activities. Free.

May
- **Outdoor Shakespeare Performances.** If you want to see *Macbeth, Hamlet, Romeo and Juliet,* or any other Shakespeare play, you're advised to "bring a blanket and a bottle of wine." The Bard's works are performed at the Open Air Theatre, Inner Circle, Regent's Park, NW1. Take the tube to Regent's Park or Baker Street. Previews begin in late May and last throughout the summer. Times are Monday, Tuesday, and Friday at 8pm; Wednesday, Thursday, and Saturday at 2:30 and 8pm. Call 0171/486-2431 for more information.
- **Chelsea Flower Show,** Chelsea Royal Hospital. The best of British gardening, with displays of plants and flowers of the season. Tickets are available from overseas reservations agents; contact your local British Tourist Authority Office to find out which agency is handling ticket sales this year, or write to the Chelsea Show Ticket Office, P.O. Box 1426, London W6 0LQ. Late May. Call 0171/630-7422 for more information.

June

- **Epsom Derby Stakes.** Famous horse-racing event at Epsom Downs, Epsom, Surrey. It's the best-known event on the British horse-racing calendar and a chance for men to wear top hats and women, including the queen, to put on silly millinery creations. The "Darby," as it's called here, is run in early June. Grandstand tickets range from £9 to £20 ($14.20 to $31.60). Call 01372/726311 for more information.

- **Grosvenor House Antique Fair.** A very prestigious antiques fair in Grosvenor House. Second week of June.

- **Kenwood Lakeside Concerts.** Annual concerts on the north side of Hampstead Heath, a British tradition of outdoor performances for nearly 50 years. Fireworks displays and laser shows help to enliven the premier musical performances staged here. The audience catches the music as it drifts across the lake from the performance shell. Every Saturday from mid-June to early September.

- **Royal Academy's Summer Exhibition.** This institution, founded in 1768, with Sir Joshua Reynolds as president and Thomas Gainsborough as a member, has for some two centuries sponsored Summer Exhibitions of living painters. Visitors can purchase art at reasonable prices or just browse. Exhibitions are presented daily at Burlington House, Piccadilly Circus, W1. Call 0171/439-7438 for more information. Gala opening of exhibition draws London's artistic elite. June 4–August 13.

- ✪ **Trooping the Colour.** The queen's official birthday parade. Seated in a carriage (no longer on horseback), she inspects her regiments and takes their salute as they parade their colors before her. It's a quintessential British event, with exquisite pageantry and pomp. The young men under the bearskins have been known to pass out from the heat.

  Where: Horse Guards Parade, Whitehall. **When:** A day designated in June (not necessarily the queen's actual birthday). **How:** Tickets for the parade and two reviews, held on preceding Saturdays, are allocated by ballot. Applicants must write between January 1 and the end of February, enclosing a stamped, self-addressed envelope or International Reply Coupon, to the Ticket Office, HQ Household Division, Horse Guards, Whitehall, London SW1X 6AA. Exact dates and ticket prices will be supplied later. The ballot is held in mid-March, and only successful applicants are informed, in April.

- ✪ **Lawn Tennis Championships.** Ever since players took to the grass courts at Wimbledon in 1877, this tournament has drawn a socially prominent crowd. Although the courts are now crowded with all kinds of tennis fans, there's still an excited hush at Centre Court and a certain thrill associated with being there. Savor the strawberries and cream that are part of the experience.

  Where: Wimbledon, SW London. **When:** Late June to early July. **How:** Tickets for Centre and Number One courts are obtainable through a lottery. Write in October to Lawn Tennis Association, P.O. Box 98, Church Road, Wimbledon, London SW19 5AE (☎ 0181/946-2244). Outside court tickets are available daily, but be prepared to wait in line.

July

- **City of London Festival.** An annual art festival throughout the city. Call 071/377-0540 for information. July 3–21.

- **Royal Tournament.** Britain's armed forces put on dazzling displays of athletic and military skills at the Earl's Court Exhibition Centre, Warwick, Road. The tournament has been called "military pomp, show biz, and outright jingoism."

For information and details about performance times and tickets, call 0171/ 373-8141. Late July.

- **The Proms.** A night at "The Proms"—the annual Henry Wood promenade concerts at Royal Albert Hall—attracts music aficionados from around the world. Staged almost daily (except for a few Sundays) these traditional concerts were launched in 1895 and are the principal summer venue for the BBC Symphony Orchestra. Cheering and clapping, Union Jacks on parade, banners and balloons—it's great summer fun. Mid-July through mid-September.

August

- **African-Caribbean Street Fair.** Held for two days in the community of Notting Hill, it's one of the largest annual street festivals in Europe, attracting over half a million people. There's live reggae and soul music plus great Caribbean food. Free. Late August.

October

✪ **Opening of Parliament.** Ever since the 17th century, when the English beheaded Charles I, British monarchs have been denied the right to enter the House of Commons. Instead, the monarch opens Parliament in the House of Lords, reading an official speech that is in fact written by the government. Queen Elizabeth II rides from Buckingham Palace to Westminster in a royal coach accompanied by the Yeoman of the Guard and the Household Cavalry.

> **Where:** Houses of Parliament. **When:** First Monday in October. **How:** The public galleries are open on a first-come, first-served basis.

✪ **Horse of the Year Show.** This is the premier equestrian highlight on the English calendar. Riders fly from every continent to join in this festive display of horsemanship (much appreciated by the Queen herself). The British press call it "an equine extravaganza."

> **Where:** Wembley Arena, Wembley, outside London. **When:** October 3–8. **How:** For more information, call 0181/902-8833.

November

- **Guy Fawkes Night.** Commemorates the anniversary of the "Gunpowder Plot," an attempt to blow up King James I and Parliament. Huge organized bonfires are lit throughout the city, and Guy Fawkes, the plot's most famous conspirator, is burned in effigy. Free. Early November.

✪ **Lord Mayor's Procession and Show.** The queen has to ask permission to enter the square mile in London called the City—and the right of refusal has been jealously guarded by London merchants since the 17th century. Suffice to say that the lord mayor is a powerful character, and the procession from the Guildhall to the Royal Courts is appropriately impressive.

> **Where:** The City. **When:** Second week in November. **How:** You can watch the procession from the street; the banquet is by invitation only.

3 The Active Vacation Planner

More and more, seasoned travelers are looking for fresh, challenging vacation ideas. What follows is not meant to be an exhaustive list, only a place to start.

Caveat: Under no circumstance is the inclusion of an organization in this guide to be interpreted as a guarantee either of its creditworthiness or its competency. Information about the organizations listed below should be followed by your own investigation.

ADVENTURE/WILDERNESS

The following organizations offer tours for the physically fit who want to explore "the wild," or at least country roads, before they disappear forever.

Cyclists's Tourist Club, Cotterell House, 69 Meadrow, Godalming, Surrey GU7 3HS (☎ 01483/417217), sponsors cycling holidays in Britain. Memberships cost £25 ($39.50) a year for adults, £12.50 ($19.75) for those 17 and under. A family with three or more members can obtain a membership for £42 ($66.35). Bicycles are forbidden on most highways, trunk roads, and what the English call "dual carriageways" (two-lane highways). But in town or in the country, the bike is a great way to get around.

English Lakeland Ramblers, 18 Stuyvesant Oval, Suite 1A, New York, NY 10009 (☎ 212/505-1020 or, outside New York, 800/724-8801). This company has designed its walking tours, which last 7 to 9 days, for the average active person in reasonably good physical shape. On its tour of the Lake District, you'll stay and have your meals in a charming 17th-century country inn near Ambleside and Windermere. A minibus takes hikers and sightseers daily to trails and sightseeing points in the region. Experts tell you about the culture and history of the area and highlight its natural wonders.

Outward Bound, at Outward Bound Trust, Chestnut Field, Regent Place, Rugby, Warwickshire CV21 2PJ (☎ 914/424-4000). Outward Bound was founded in 1941 by Kurt Hahn, a German-English educator; it aims to help people "go beyond their self-imposed limits, to use the wilderness as a metaphor for personal growth and self-discovery." Courses in wilderness training incorporate healthy doses of both mountain climbing and boating under challenging conditions. Courses last from 3 days to 3 months. There are now 54 Outward Bound schools and centers throughout the world.

Ramblers' Association, 1–5 Wandsworth Rd., London SW8 2XX (☎ 0171/582-6878), knows more about hiking, or "rambling," as it is called, than anyone else in England. Rambling is one of the most popular British activities. In England and Wales alone there are some 100,000 miles of trails and footpaths—many of them historical, such as the Pennine Way, in Yorkshire. The Ramblers' Association publishes a quarterly magazine that costs £4.99 ($7.90) and lists bed-and-breakfasts near the trails.

Vermont Bicycle Touring, P.O. Box 711, Bristol, VT 05443 (☎ 802/453-4811). Often referred to as the "granddaddy of cycle tour operators," this company offers tours that range from 25 to 40 miles per day. The tours allow for different levels of cycling experience; extra guidance, assistance, and services are always available. A van transports your luggage (and tired cyclists).

Wilderness Travel, Inc., 801 Allston Way, Berkeley, CA 94710 (☎ 510/548-0420 or 800/368-2794). Specializing in walking tours, treks, and inn-to-inn hiking tours of Europe, this company also offers less strenuous walking tours of Cornwall and the Cotswolds that combine transportation with walking sessions of no more than 3 hours at a time.

BOATING

For a new angle on travel in the British Isles, visitors can take boat trips on the network of inland waters threading through the country. You skipper the boat yourself, and the vessels are well equipped, heated, and have all the modern conveniences. Boating holidays make sightseeing easy since you can take your boat right into the center of certain cities, for example, Stratford-upon-Avon, London, or Milton Keynes.

For information and reservations, contact **Weltonfield Narrowboats** at Welton Hythe, Daventry, Northamptonshire, NN11 5LG (☎ 1327/842282). From the beginning of March to the end of October, Weltonfield Narrowboats hires out vessels for extended weekends and longer. The boats come with fully equipped kitchens, bedding, and central heating. You can go anywhere your boat will take you. The boats sleep from two to eight people, and the cost ranges from £258 ($407.65) to £493 ($778.95) for a weekend and from £420 ($663.60) to £986 ($1557.90) for a week. You can also cruise on a "hotelboat," a popular pastime since the early 1960s. These cruises generally last from four nights (called a "short break") to a week. Prices begin at £260 ($410.80) per person for a short break or £345 ($545.10) per person for a week, food included. For more information about holidays on the water, contact the Association of Pleasure Craft Operators, 35A High St., Newport, Shropshire, TF10 8JW (☎ 01952/813572; fax 019521/ 820363).

4 Cultural and Educational Travel Programs & Home Exchanges

EDUCATIONAL/STUDY TRAVEL

What could be more enlightening for students of English literature than to do course work at such renowned universities as Oxford and Cambridge during the week and then to take weekend excursions to the countryside of Shakespeare, Austen, Dickens, and Hardy? While studying at these famed halls of learning, you can live in the dormitories with other students and dine in elaborate halls or the more intimate Fellows' clubs.

Study programs in England are not limited to the liberal arts, or to high school or college students. There's a wide variety of programs from which to choose, and some are designed specifically for teachers and senior citizens (see "For Seniors: Elderhostel" in this chapter). For more information, contact the organizations listed below or those mentioned in the section "For Students" in this chapter.

American Institute for Foreign Study, 102 Greenwich Ave., Greenwich, CT 06830 (☎ 800/727-2437). Affiliated with Richmond College, in London, this organization offers both 10- to 60-day traveling programs for high-school students and academic programs for college students, who can enroll in classes lasting a summer, semester, or full year. There are also programs leading to the British equivalent of an MBA.

Earthwatch, U.S. headquarters at 680 Mt. Auburn St., P.O. Box 403, Watertown, MA 02272 (☎ 617/926-8200). Ecology-minded folks may be interested in the research projects sponsored by this nonprofit organization. Volunteers pay to work with teams during hands-on 2-week programs. Payments made by U.S. volunteers are considered tax-deductible contributions to a scientific project. Earthwatch publishes a bimonthly magazine listing more than 155 unusual opportunities, some of them located in Great Britain. The projects, which range from tracking the migration habits of endangered species to excavating ancient archaeological sites, cost from $700 to $4,300 per person. No special skills are necessary.

IIE (Institute of International Education), U.S. Student Programs Division, 809 United Nations Plaza, New York, NY 10017–3580 (☎ 212/883-8200). This organization is the largest international agency of higher-education exchange in the United States. It administers a variety of academic, training, and grant programs for the U.S. Information Agency (USIA), with special stress on the management of predoctoral Fulbright grants. It is especially helpful in arranging enrollments for U.S. students in summer-school programs.

NRCSA (National Registration Center for Study Abroad), P.O. Box 1393, Milwaukee, WI 53201 (☎ 414/278-0631). This organization offers a $5 catalog outlining 80 to 90 summer schools in Great Britain that offer courses of from 1 to 4 weeks from July through September. Students, teachers, and interested adults can take one course or combine several in England, Scotland, and Wales. Subjects include theater, history, literature, art, castles, architecture, gardens, economics, current events, crafts, and wildlife. NRCSA will register you at the school of your choice and arrange for room and board. Ask them for a free copy of their newsletter.

UNIVAC (University Vacations), 10461 NW 26th St., Miami, FL 33172 (☎ 305/591-1736 or 800/792-0100); in Great Britain, the headquarters in summer is Brasenose College, Oxford OX1 4AJ, England. This organization offers liberal arts programs at Oxford and Cambridge. Courses usually last 7 to 12 days and combine lectures, excursions, and guided walking tours; there's no pressure to prepare papers or take final exams. Adults over 18 are eligible and there are no formal academic requirements. You live at the colleges and eat either in an elaborate dining hall or the more intimate Fellows' dining rooms.

HOMESTAYS/HOME EXCHANGES

Anyone would be enriched by a stay at the home of a friendly Brit. Homestays are an ideal way to gain greater insight into a culture, people, and country. Write to any British Tourist Authority office (see "Visitor Information & Entry Requirements" above in this chapter) and ask for publications listing dozens of agencies and services that provide homestays. (See also "Promoting International Understanding" below in this chapter.)

Another travel alternative is a home exchange, which is not only fun but can save you money. If you'd like to swap your house or apartment for a cottage or flat in England, contact one of the following organizations:

Intervac U.S., P.O. Box 590504, San Francisco, CA 94119 (☎ 415/435-3497 or 800/756-HOME), is part of the largest worldwide exchange network. It publishes four catalogs a year containing some 10,000 homes in 36 countries. Members contact each other directly once the details of their homes are published. The cost is $65 plus postage, which includes three company catalogs that will be mailed to you and the price of listing your home in whichever catalog you select. A fourth catalog costs an extra $19. If you want to publish a photograph of your home, there is an additional $11 charge.

The Invented City, 41 Sutter St., Suite 1090, San Francisco, CA 94104 (☎ 415/673-0347), is an international home-exchange agency. Home-exchange listings are published three times a year, in February, May, and November. A $50 membership fee allows you to list your home and indicate your occupation, hobbies, and when you want to travel.

PROMOTING INTERNATIONAL UNDERSTANDING

It has long been acknowledged that getting to know different peoples is the path to international understanding and peace. Listed below are organizations that foster friendship and goodwill through cultural exchanges, homestays, and educational and work programs. (See also "Homestays/Home Exchanges" above in this chapter.)

Friendship Force, 57 Forsyth St. NW, Suite 900, Atlanta, GA 30303 (☎ 404/522-9490). Founded in Atlanta, Georgia, under the leadership of then-governor Jimmy Carter, Friendship Force exists for the sole purpose of encouraging friendship among disparate peoples around the world. Dozens of branch groups throughout North America meet regularly and arrange group tours, which take advantage of low-cost group rates. Each participant is required to spend 2 weeks in the host country, including 1 week in the home of a local family; most volunteers spend the second week traveling independently. No particular study regimen or work program is prescribed, but participants are asked to behave in a way that reflects well on the United States.

People to People, 501 E. Armour Blvd., Kansas City, MO 64109-2200 (☎ 816/531-4701; fax 816/561-7502). Established by President Eisenhower in the late 1950s, this organization promotes international understanding through education and cultural exchanges. People to People organizes exchanges of adult professionals (in many different fields) for 2- and 3-week programs. There is also a 4-week summer high-school educational program. A summer collegiate study-abroad and internship program offers graduate and undergraduate credit opportunities abroad. Local chapters help arrange homestays and other programs for members. Privileges include travel opportunities, newsletters, and a magazine. Annual fees are $25 for families, $15 for individuals, and $10 for students.

Servas, 11 John St., Suite 407, New York, NY 10038 (☎ 212/267-0252; fax 212/267-0292). A nonprofit, nongovernmental, international, nonreligious network of travelers and hosts, Servas works to build world peace. Members of Servas (which is from Esperanto for "to serve") invite travelers to share living space, usually staying without charge for a visit of 2 nights. Day visits as well as shared meals can also be arranged. Members pay a $55 annual fee and a $25 deposit, fill out an application, and are interviewed for suitability. After they have been approved, they receive directories listing the names and addresses of hosts on six continents.

Work Camps, Volunteers for Peace, 43 Tiffany Rd., Belmont, VT 05730 (☎ 802/259-2759). After World War I, a work-camp program was established to promote "peace and understanding" through combinations of humanitarian work, study, and immersion in foreign cultures. Participants arrange their own travel. The $150 registration fee covers room and board for a 2- or 3-week program. Volunteers for Peace issues a complimentary newsletter. A work-camp directory, which covers 55 countries, is available for a tax-deductible contribution of $12.

OPERA TOURS

The English National Opera and the Royal Opera perform in London 5 or 6 nights each week 11 months a year—everything from the great classics to the light comic operas of Gilbert and Sullivan to new works premiered with flair and imagination. Music lovers might try a tour of England that includes nights at either the splendid London Coliseum or the Royal Opera House, one of the most beautiful theaters in Europe. (See also "The Performing Arts" in Chapter 7.)

In the U.S. probably the best-regarded organizer of music and opera tours is **Dailey-Thorp,** 330 W. 58th St., Suite 610, New York, NY 10019–1817 (☎ 212/307-1515). They can purchase blocks of otherwise-unavailable London opera tickets—along with tickets to the Salzburg Festival, the Bayreuth Festival in

Germany, and events in Vienna, Milan, Paris, Eastern Europe, and elsewhere. Tours range from 7 to 21 days and include first-class accommodations and meals in top-rated European restaurants.

5   Health & Insurance

HEALTH

You will encounter few health problems while traveling in England. The tap water is safe to drink, the milk is pasteurized, and health services are good. Occasionally the change in diet may cause some minor irregularity, so you may want to take some medicine along.

CHRONIC ILLNESS   If you suffer from a chronic illness, talk to your doctor before taking the trip. For such conditions as epilepsy, diabetes or a heart condition, wear a Medic Alert identification tag, which will immediately alert any doctor to your condition and provide the number of Medic Alert's 24-hour hotline so a doctor in a foreign country can obtain your medical records. The cost for a lifetime membership is $35, $45, or $60. In addition, there is a $15 annual fee. Contact the **Medic Alert Foundation,** P.O. Box 1009, Turlock, CA 95381–1009 (☎ 800/432-5378).

PRESCRIPTION DRUGS   Carry all your vital medicine in your carry-on luggage and bring enough prescribed medicines to sustain you during your stay. Bring along copies of your prescriptions that are written in the generic—not brand-name—form.

VACCINATIONS   Vaccinations are required only if you've been in an area where con-tagious disease is prevalent within 14 days prior to your arrival in Great Britain.

FINDING A DOCTOR   If you need a doctor, your hotel can recommend one, or you can contact your embassy or consulate. Before you leave home you can obtain a list of English doctors from the **International Association for Medical Assistance to Travelers (IAMAT).** Contact IAMAT in the United States at 417 Center St., Lewiston, NY 14092 (☎ 716/754-4883); in Canada at 40 Regal Rd., Guelph, ON N1K 1B5 (☎ 519/836-0102); or in Europe at 57 Voirets, 1212 Grand-Lancy Geneva, Switzerland.

INSURANCE

HEALTH   Before leaving home, check to see if your health coverage extends to Europe. If it doesn't or if the coverage is inadequate, consider purchasing short-term travel insurance that will cover medical emergencies. Remember that Medicare covers U.S. citizens traveling in Mexico and Canada only. *Note:* U.S. visitors who become ill while they're in England are only eligible for free *emergency* care. For other treatment, including follow-up care, you will be asked to pay.

PROPERTY   Also check your homeowner's or renter's insurance for off-premises-theft coverage. If you need more coverage, consider a short-term policy.

CANCELLATION CHARGES   If you are traveling as part of a tour or are taking a flight that has cancellation penalties or have prepaid your vacation expenses, you may also want to purchase insurance that covers cancellation. Your credit-card company may provide automatic cancellation coverage.

AUTOMOBILE   If you are going to rent a car in England, check to see whether your automobile insurance, automobile club, or charge card covers personal accident insurance (PAI), collision damage waiver (CDW), or other insurance options. You may be able to avoid additional rental charges if you are already covered.

TRAVEL CLUBS   If you belong to a travel club, ask about insurance coverage or other options that come with your membership.

DOCUMENTATION   To submit any claim, you must have thorough documentation, including all receipts, police reports, and medical records.

Comprehensive Policies

Your best bet may be to purchase a comprehensive travel policy that covers catastrophes and mishaps—trip cancellation, health, emergency assistance, and lost luggage. Many travel agents can sell you a policy (the price is nominal), or you can contact the following companies for more information.

Access America, 6600 W. Broad St., Richmond, VA 23230 (☎ 800/284-8300), offers a comprehensive travel insurance and assistance package, including medical expenses, on-the-spot hospital payments, medical transportation, baggage insurance, trip cancellation or interruption insurance, and collision-damage insurance for a car rental. Their 24-hour hotline connects you to multilingual coordinators who can offer advice and help on medical, legal, and travel problems. Many levels of coverage are available.

Healthcare Abroad (MEDEX), c/o Wallach & Co., P.O. Box 480 (107 W. Federal St.), Middleburg, VA 22117-0480 (☎ 703/687-3166 or 800/237-6615), offers coverage for between 10 and 120 days at $3 per day; this policy includes accident and sickness coverage to the tune of $100,000. Medical evacuation is also included, along with a $25,000 accidental death and dismemberment compensation. Provisions for trip cancellation can also be written into this policy at a nominal cost.

Mutual of Omaha (Tele-Trip), Mutual of Omaha Plaza, Omaha, NE 68175, offers insurance packages priced from $115 per couple for a three-week trip. Included in the packages are travel-assistance services as well as coverage for trip cancellation, trip interruption, flight and baggage delays, accident-related medical costs, accidental death and dismemberment, and medical evacuation costs. A deluxe package that costs $213 per couple offers double the coverage of the standard policy. Holders of major credit cards can make application by phone (☎ 800/228-9792).

Travel Guard International, 1145 Clark Street, Stevens Point, WI 54481 (☎ 800/826-1300), features comprehensive insurance programs that start as low as $44. The program covers everything: trip cancellation and interruption—including bankruptcy and financial default, lost luggage, medical coverage abroad, emergency assistance, accidental death, and 24-hour worldwide emergency hotline.

Travel Insured International, Inc., P.O. Box 280568, East Hartford, CT 06128-0568 (☎ 800/243-3174 in the U.S., 203/528-7663 outside the U.S., between 7:45am and 7pm EST). Trip cancellation and emergency evacuation costs $5.50 for each $100 of coverage. Travel accident and illness insurance goes for $10 for 6 to 10 days, and $500 of insurance for lost, damaged, or delayed luggage is $20 for 10 days. The insurance is underwritten by The Travelers.

6 Tips for Special Travelers

FOR THE DISABLED
IN THE U.S.A.

As you plan your trip, there are many agencies in the United States that can provide information. Knowing in advance which hotels, restaurants, and attractions are wheelchair accessible can save you a lot of frustration—firsthand accounts by other disabled travelers are the best. There are some companies that offer tours specially designed for disabled travelers. The following organizations and publications will help you organize your tour. (See also "In England" below in this chapter.)

"**Air Transportation for Handicapped Persons.**" This free publication, prepared by the U.S. Department of Transportation, can be obtained by writing to Free Advisory Circular no. AC12032, Distribution Unit, U.S. Department of Transportation, Publications Division, M-4332, Washington, DC 20590.

American Foundation for the Blind, 11 Penn Plaza, Suite 300, New York, NY 10001 (☎ 212/502-7000 or 800/232-5463). This is the best information source for the blind.

FEDCAP Rehabilitation Services (formerly known as Federation of the Handicapped), 211 West 14th Street, New York, NY 10011 (☎ 212/727-4200). They offer summer tours for members, who pay a yearly membership fee of $4.

Flying Wheels Travel, 143 West Bridge, P.O. Box 382, Owatoona, MN 55060 (☎ 800/535-6790, or 507/451-5005). This group offers escorted international tours and cruises. It is one of the best organizations serving the needs of the disabled.

A bimonthly publication, *Handicapped Travel Newsletter,* will keep you current on accessible sights worldwide. To order a $15 annual subscription, call 903/677-1260.

The Information Center for Individuals with Disabilities, Fort Point Place, 27–43 Wormwood Street, Boston, MA 02210 (☎ 617/727-5540; fax 617/345-5318). Another good source of information, they have lists of travel agents specializing in tours for the disabled.

Mobility International USA, P.O. Box 10767, Eugene, OR 97440 (☎ 503/343-1284; fax 503/343-6812). This organization answers questions on various destinations and also offers discounts on videos, publications, and programs it sponsors. Its annual fee is $20.

MossRehab Hospital, 1200 W. Tabor Rd., Philadelphia, PA 19141 (☎ 215/456-9603; this service is not a travel agent). To find out about accessibility, call MossRehab. They provide information to telephone callers only.

The Society for the Advancement of Travel for the Handicapped, 347 Fifth Ave., Suite 610, New York, NY 10016 (☎ 212/447-7284; fax 212/725-8253). This organization can provide a list of companies that operate tours for travelers with disabilities. Yearly membership dues are $45 or $25 for senior citizens and students. Send a stamped, self-addressed envelope.

IN ENGLAND

Many London hotels, museums, restaurants, and sightseeing attractions have wheelchair ramps. Disabled people are often granted special discounts (called "concessions") for attractions—and, in some cases, nightclubs—it always pays to ask.

Free information and advice is available from Holiday Care Service, 2 Old Bank Chambers, Station Road, Horley, Surrey RH6 9HW (☎ 01293/774535). The British Tourist Authority sells *London Made Easy* for £2.50 ($3.80); it's a booklet that offers advice and describes facilities for the handicapped. Bookstores often carry *Access in London,* which sells for £4 ($6) and is even more helpful: It lists facilities for the handicapped, among other things.

London's most visible organization for information about physical access to theaters, cinemas, galleries, museums, and restaurants is **Artsline,** 54 Chalton St., London NW1 1HS (☎ 0171/388-2227). Funded by the London Arts Board and staffed mostly by disabled people, it offers free information about wheelchair access, theaters with hearing aids, tourist attractions, and restaurants. Artsline will mail information to North America, but it's even more helpful to contact them after your arrival in London. They're open Monday through Friday from 9:30am to 5:30pm.

Tripscope, The Courtyard, 4 Evelyn Rd., London W4 5JL (☎ 0181/994-9294), cooperates closely with Artsline. It offers travel advice for disabled persons in Britain and elsewhere.

FOR SENIORS

For people aged 60 and older—retired, with the kids on their own, and the mortgage paid off—this is the time to relax and do some globe-trotting. There are people who want your business and are willing to entice you for it. Many organizations offer discounted airfares, accommodations, and car rentals. So be sure to ask for senior-citizen discounts. Educational programs, cruises, and tours specially designed for seniors are also available.

AARP (American Association of Retired Persons), 601 E St. NW, Washington, DC 20049 (☎ 202/434-AARP). This is the best organization for seniors in the United States. Members are offered advice as well as discounts on car rentals and hotels.

Elderhostel, 75 Federal St., Boston, MA 02110–1941 (☎ 617/426-7788). This organization offers an array of university-based summer educational programs for seniors in England and other parts of the world. Most courses last about 3 weeks and are remarkable values—airfare, accommodations in student dormitories or modest inns, meals, and tuition are included. Courses emphasize the liberal arts and include field trips—best of all there's no homework or grades. Participants must be 55 or older. Meals are of the no-frills variety, typical of educational institutions worldwide. The program provides a safe and congenial environment for single "golden girls," who make up some 64% of the enrollment.

SAGA International Holidays, 222 Berkeley St., Boston, MA 02116 (☎ 800/343-0273; fax 617/375-5953). This organization offers inclusive tours and cruises for those 50 and older. Insurance is included in the price of the tours.

For a free copy of "101 Tips for the Mature Traveler," contact **Grand Circle Travel,** 347 Congress St., Suite 3A, Boston, MA 02210 (☎ 617/350-7500 or 800/221-2610; fax 617/350-6206). This travel agency also offers escorted tours and cruises for seniors.

Information is also available from the **National Council of Senior Citizens,** 1331 F St. NW, Washington, DC 20005 (☎ 202/347-8800; fax 202/347-8800). A nonprofit organization, the council charges $12 annually per person/couple, for which you receive a monthly newsletter, part of which is devoted to travel tips. Discounts on hotels and auto rentals are provided.

Mature Outlook, 6001 North Clark Street, Chicago, IL 60660 (☎ 800/ 336-6330); fax 312/764-4871) is a travel organization for people over 50 years of age. Members are offered discounts at ITC-member hotels and will receive a bi-monthly magazine. The $9.95 annual membership entitles you to discounts and, in some cases, free coupons for discounted merchandise from Sears Roebuck & Co. Savings are also offered on selected auto rentals and restaurants.

FOR SINGLE TRAVELERS

Unfortunately for the millions of single Americans, the travel industry is geared to duos, and people who adventure alone often pay a penalty. It pays to travel with someone and split the cost of accommodations; for someone traveling solo, those costs are often more than half the price of a double room. Of course, there are dynamic and action-packed tours and vacations designed for the unattached, as well as companies that will match you with a compatible traveling partner.

Travel Companion, P.O. Box P–833, Amityville, NY 11701 (☎ 516/ 454-0880). This company matches single travelers and like-minded companions. People seeking travel companions fill out a survey of their preferences and needs and receive a listing of potential travel partners. Companions of the same or opposite sex can be requested. Individuals are then listed for 6 months on the company's well-publicized records; the charge is $99 for an eight-month membership. A bimonthly newsletter averaging 40 large pages also gives numer-ous money-saving travel tips of special interest to solo travelers. A sample copy is available for $5. For an application and more information, contact Jens Jurgen at Travel Companion.

Singleworld, 401 Theodore Fremd Ave., Rye, NY 10580 (☎ 914/967-3334 or 800/223-6490). This travel agency operates tours geared to singles. Three basic types of tours are available: a youth-oriented tour for people in their 20s and 30s, jaunts for "all ages," and the over-40 age group. Ask about their London Theater Tour. Annual dues are $25.

Cosmos Tourama, 5310 South Federal Circle, Littleton, CO 80123 (☎ 800/ 221-0090), offers a "guaranteed-share plan"—that is, it agrees to locate a single traveler of the same gender for you to ease the cost of traveling alone.

FOR FAMILIES

Advance planning is the key to any successful overseas vacation, and this is espe-cially true when you're traveling with infants, tots, or teenagers. For little ones, there's the supply of the bottles, food, and diapers that you must at least carry over to England until you can buy more. Recreational activities—splashing around in a pool, running off a little steam in a park—are a welcomed break for most kids. For accommodations, meals, and attractions, be sure to read the "Especially for Kids" features in this guide.

- If you have very small children, discuss your travel plans with your pediatrician. Take along a little first aid kit with thermometer, Band-Aids, and the like.
- On airplanes, a special menu for children must be requested at least 24 hours in advance. If baby food is required, bring your own and ask a flight attendant to warm it to the right temperature.
- Take along a "security blanket." For very young children, this or a favorite book or toy can be a pacifier. For older kids, a baseball cap, a favorite T-shirt, or some good-luck charm can make them feel at home in different surroundings.

- Make advance arrangements for cribs, bottle warmers, or car seats—in England small children aren't allowed to ride in the front seat.
- Ask the hotel if it stocks baby food; if not, take some with you and plan to buy the rest in local groceries.
- Draw up guidelines on bedtime, eating, keeping tidy, being in the sun, even shopping and spending—this will make the vacation more enjoyable.
- Babysitters can be found at most hotels, but insist that the babysitter have at least a rudimentary knowledge of English; this is no longer certainty in England.

Family Travel Times is published 4 times a year by TWYCH (Travel With Your Children) and includes a weekly call-in service for subscribers. Subscriptions ($40 a year) can be ordered from TWYCH, 45 W. 18th St., 7th floor, New York, NY 10011 (☎ 212/206-0688). TWYCH also publishes two nitty-gritty information guides, *Skiing with Children* and *Cruising with Children*, which sell for $29 and $22, respectively, but are discounted to newsletter subscribers. An information packet, including a sample newsletter, is available for $2.

Families Welcome!, 21 W. Colony Place, Suite 140, Durham, NC 27705 (☎ 919/489-2555, or 800/326-0724), a travel company specializing in worry-free vacations for families, offers "City Kids" packages to London, featuring accommodations in family-friendly hotels or apartments. Individually designed family packages can include car rentals, train and ferry passes, and special air prices. A welcome kit contains "insider information" for families traveling in London, such as where to find reliable babysitters, buy Pampers, or locate family friendly restaurants.

FOR STUDENTS

Research is the key for students who want to take advantage of budget travel and study abroad. There are organizations and publications that provide details about programs available specifically to students. (See also "Educational/Study Travel" in this chapter and "Networks and Resources: For Students" in Chapter 3.) Of course, you'll want to carry an International Student Identity Card, which is good for discounts on travel fares and attractions. Youth hostels provide an inexpensive network of accommodations while you're trekking through the country.

Council Travel, 205 E. 42nd St., New York, NY 10017 (☎ 212/661-1414) and at 40 other offices in the United States and 60 offices worldwide; call 800/226-8624 to find the location nearest you. The London office is at West End at 28A Poland St., London W1V 3DB, just off Oxford Circus (☎ 0171/287-3337 for European destinations and 0171/437-7767 for worldwide destinations).

This is America's largest student, youth, and budget-travel group. International Student Identity Cards are available to all bona fide students from any Council Travel office for $16; they entitle the holder to generous travel and other discounts. Discounted air tickets, Eurorail passes, YHA passes, weekend packages, overland safaris, and hostel/hotel accommodations are all bookable from Council Travel.

Council Travel (a subsidiary of the Council on International Educational Exchange) also sells a number of publications for young people considering traveling abroad. These publications include: *Work, Study, Travel Abroad: The Whole World Handbook; Volunteer: The Comprehensive Guide to Voluntary Service in the U.S. and Abroad;* and *Going Places: The High School Students' Guide to Study, Travel, and Adventure Abroad.*

IYHF (International Youth Hostel Federation) at Hostelling International/ American Youth Hostels (HI-AYH), 733 15th St. NW, Suite 840, Washington, DC 20005 (☎ 202/783-6161; or 800/444-6111 in the U.S. and Canada). This organization was formed to provide low-cost overnight accommodations for budget-conscious travelers. Membership costs $25 annually, except for those under 18, who pay $10, and those over 55, who pay $15.

7 Getting There

BY PLANE

While the facts and figures given below are as accurate as research can make them, the fast-moving economics of the airline industry make them very tentative. Always check for the latest flight and fare information.

Airlines compete fiercely on the North America–London route, one of the most heavily traveled in the world, and they offer a confusing barrage of options. The best strategy for securing the lowest fare is to shop around. Above all, remain as flexible about dates as possible. Keep calling the airlines or your travel agent— as the departure date nears, airlines will often discount seats if the flight is not fully booked.

Other general rules to keep in mind are that fares are usually lower during the week (Monday through Thursday noon) and that there are also seasonal fare differences (peak, shoulder, and basic). For transatlantic travel, peak season is summer, basic is winter, and shoulder is in between. Travel during Christmas and Easter weeks is usually more expensive than in the weeks just before or after those holidays.

In every season airlines offer regular first-class, business-class, and economy seating. Most airlines also offer discounted fares, such as the Advance Purchase Excursion (APEX) fare, that carry restrictions (some of them severe) and usually require advance purchase, a minimum stay abroad, and cancellation or alteration penalties.

THE MAJOR AIRLINES

Several airlines fly the enormously popular routes from North America to Great Britain. Below is a list of some of these carriers, arranged alphabetically.

Air Canada (☎ 800/776-3000) flies daily, nonstop to London's Heathrow airport from Vancouver, Montréal, and Toronto. There is frequent direct service from Edmonton, Calgary, Winnipeg, Ottawa, Halifax, and St. John's. All flights provide a smoke-free environment.

American Airlines (☎ 800/624-6262) offers daily flights to London's Heathrow from half a dozen U.S. gateways—New York's JFK (five times daily/ six in June), Chicago's O'Hare (twice daily), and Miami International, Los Angeles International, Philadelphia International, and Boston's Logan (daily).

British Airways (☎ 800/AIRWAYS) offers flights from some 18 U.S. cities to Heathrow and London's other airport, Gatwick, as well as many others to Manchester, Birmingham, and Glasgow. Nearly every flight is nonstop. With more add-on options than any other airline, British Airways can make a visit to Britain cheaper than you might have expected. The 1993 union of some of BA's functions and routings with USAir opened additional North American gateways to BA, improved services, and reduced some of its fares, thus making the airline more competitive. Of particular interest are the "Value Plus," "London on the Town," and "Europe Escorted" packages that include both airfare and heavily discounted hotel accommodations in Britain.

Delta (☎ 800/241-4141). Depending on the day of the week and the season, Delta makes either one or two daily nonstop flights between its headquarters in Atlanta and London's Gatwick. Delta also offers daily, nonstop service to Gatwick from Cincinnati and Miami.

Northwest Airlines (☎ 800/447-4747) This carrier flies nonstop from both Minneapolis and Boston to Gatwick, with connections possible from such other cities as Detroit.

TWA (☎ 800/221-2000) flies nonstop to Gatwick every day from its hub in St. Louis. Connections are possible through St. Louis from most of North America.

United Airlines (☎ 800/241-6522) flies nonstop from New York's JFK to Heathrow between two and three times a day, depending on the season. United also offers nonstop service twice a day from Dulles Airport, in Washington, D.C., and daily service to Heathrow from Newark, San Francisco, Seattle, and Los Angeles.

Virgin Atlantic Airways (☎ 800/862-8621) flies daily to either Heathrow or Gatwick from Boston, Newark, New York's JFK, Los Angeles, and San Francisco. The airline also flies to Gatwick four times a week from Miami, and five times a week from Orlando. Virgin Atlantic also offers flights to London from Chicago through interconnecting service on Kiwi Airlines. Passengers depart from Chicago's Midway airport on Kiwi, then transfer in either Boston or one of the New York–area airports for connections to London. Booking both sections of the itinerary simultaneously is less expensive than if both legs are purchased separately. For information, call Virgin Atlantic or Kiwi (☎ 800/JET-KIWI).

Best-Value Fares

APEX   Generally, your cheapest option on a regular airline is to book an APEX (Advance Purchase Excursion) fare. British Airways, for example, offers three types of APEX fares. The least expensive is a nonrefundable ticket that requires a 21-day advance purchase plus a 7-to-45-day delay before using the return half of your ticket. Passengers who fly midweek (Monday to Thursday) pay less than those who fly in either direction on a weekend (Friday, Saturday, or Sunday). For changes or cancellations in flight dates or destination, penalties range from $150 and up—depending on circumstances.

A slightly more expensive APEX fare offered by BA allows much greater leeway for changing travel plans. It requires a stay abroad that includes at least one Saturday night and allows cancellations or flight changes for a $125 fee; however, you need to book only seven days in advance. Slight variations in price exist for this type of ticket, depending on whether you'll need a maximum stay abroad of 2 months or 12 months. (The option of staying 12 months costs a bit more than the one requiring an earlier return.)

DISCOUNTS   Senior citizens over 60 receive special 10% discounts on British Airways through its Privileged Traveler program. They also qualify for reduced restrictions on APEX cancellations. Discounts are also granted for BA tours and for intra-Britain air tickets if booked in North America. BA also offers youth fares to anyone 12 to 24.

Other Good-Value Choices

BUCKET SHOPS   In the 1960s mainstream airlines in Britain gave this insulting name to resellers of blocks of unsold tickets. More politely referred to as "consolidators," they act as clearinghouses for blocks of tickets that airlines discount and consign during normally slow periods of air travel.

Tickets are usually priced 20% to 35% below the full fare. Payment terms can vary—you may be obliged to purchase 45 days prior to departure or allowed to purchase at the last minute. Regular travel agents sell these tickets, though they usually mark up the ticket by at least 8% to 10%, thereby reducing your discount.

A survey conducted of flyers who use consolidators voiced only one major complaint: Use of such a ticket doesn't qualify you for an advance seat assignment, so you are likely to be assigned a "poor seat" on the plane at the last minute. In the survey flyers estimated their savings at around $200 per ticket. Nearly a third of the passengers reported savings of up to $300 off the regular price. But—and here's the hitch—many people who booked consolidator tickets reported no savings at all as the airlines will sometimes match the consolidator ticket by announcing a promotional fare. The situation is a bit tricky and calls for some careful investigation on your part.

Bucket shops abound from coast to coast. Here are a few recommendations. Look also for their ads in your local newspaper's travel section. They're usually very small and a single column in width.

One of the biggest U.S. consolidators is **Travac,** 989 Sixth Ave., New York, NY 10018 (☎ 212/563-3303 or in the U.S. 800/TRAV-800), which offers discounted seats from the U.S. to most European cities on airlines that include TWA, United, and Delta. Another Travac office is at 2601 East Jefferson St., Orlando, FL 32803 (☎ 407/896-0014).

Or you might try **TFI Tours International,** 34 W. 32nd St., 12th Floor, New York, NY 10001 (☎ 212/736-1140 in New York State or, elsewhere in the U.S., 800/745-8000). This tour company offers services to 177 cities worldwide.

In the Midwest, explore the possibilities of **Travel Avenue,** 10 S. Riverside Plaza, Suite 1404, Chicago, IL 60606 (☎ 800/333-3335), a national agency whose headquarters are here. Its tickets are often cheaper than most shops, and it charges the customer only a $25 fee on international tickets rather than taking the usual $10 commission from an airline. Travel Avenue rebates most of that back to the customer—hence, the lower fares.

In New England, one possibility is **TMI** (Travel Management International), 39 JFK St. (Harvard Square), 3rd Floor, Cambridge, MA 02138 (☎ 800/245-3672). They offer a wide variety of discounts, including youth fares, student fares, and access to other air-related discounts.

Since dealing with an unfamiliar bucket shop can be a bit risky, it's wise to check out a company with the Better Business Bureau.

CHARTER FLIGHTS   For reasons of economy (never for convenience) some travelers opt for charter flights.

Strictly speaking, a charter flight occurs on an aircraft reserved months in advance for a one-time-only transit to some predetermined point. Before paying for a charter, check the restrictions on your ticket or contract. You may be asked to purchase a tour package and pay far in advance. You'll pay a stiff penalty (or forfeit the ticket entirely) if you cancel. Charters are sometimes canceled when the plane doesn't fill up. In some cases, the ticket seller will offer you an insurance policy for your own legitimate cancellation (hospital confinement or death in the family, for example).

There is no way to predict whether a proposed flight to England will cost less on a charter or through a bucket shop. You must investigate at the time of your trip.

One reliable charter-flight operator is **Council Charter,** run by the Council on International Educational Exchange, 205 E. 42nd St., New York, NY 10017 (☎ 212/661-0311 or 800/800-8222), which arranges charter seats on regularly scheduled aircraft.

One of the biggest operators is **Travac,** 989 Sixth Ave., New York, NY 10018 (☎ 212/563-3303 or 800/TRAV-800).

REBATORS   To confuse the situation even more, rebators also compete in the low-airfare market. These outfits pass part of their commission along to the passenger, though many of them assess a fee for their services. Most rebators offer discounts ranging from 10% to 25% plus a $25 handling charge. They are not the same as travel agents but sometimes offer similar services, including discounted accommodations and car rentals.

Travel Avenue, 10 South Riverside Plaza, Suite 1404, Chicago, IL 60606 (☎ 312/876-1116 or 800/333-3335), which specializes in clients in the Midwest, one of the oldest agencies of its kind. It offers cash rebates up front on every airfare over $300. They pride themselves on *not* offering travel counseling. Instead, they sell airline tickets to independent travelers who have already worked out their travel plans. Also available are tour and cruise fares, plus hotel reservations, usually at prices less expensive than what you can find on your own.

Another major rebator is **The Smart Traveller,** 3111 SW 27th Ave., (P.O. Box 330010) Miami, FL 33133 (☎ 305/448-3338, or 800/448-3338; fax 305/443-3544). They also offers discounts on packaged tours.

STANDBY   A favorite of spontaneous travelers with absolutely no scheduled demands on their time, standby fares leave your departure to the whim of fortune and the last-minute availability of a seat. Most airlines don't offer standbys, though some seats are available to London and Vienna.

Virgin Atlantic Airways (☎ 800/862-8621) offers passage from North America to London that can be reserved within 48 hours of the departure time—if seats are available. This type of fare, known as a Late Saver fare, is available year-round, except during the 2 weeks around Christmas and New Year's Day.

TRAVELING AS A COURIER   This cost-cutting technique may not be for everybody. You travel as a passenger and courier, and for this service you'll get a greatly discounted airfare or, in certain rare instances, even a free ticket.

You're allowed only one piece of carry-on luggage; your baggage allowance is used by the courier firm to transport its cargo (which is, by the way, perfectly legitimate). As a courier, you don't actually handle the merchandise you're "transporting" to Europe, you just carry a manifest to present to customs. Upon arrival, an employee of the courier service will reclaim the company's cargo. Incidentally, you fly alone, so don't plan to travel with anybody. (A friend may be able to arrange to fly as a courier the next day.) Most courier services operate from Los Angeles or New York, but some operate out of other cities, such as Chicago or Miami.

Courier services are often listed in the yellow pages or in advertisements in travel sections of newspapers.

To get started, check with **Halbart Express,** 147–05 176th St., Jamaica, NY 11434 (☎ 718/656-8189; open daily 10am–3pm). Another firm to try is **Now Voyager,** 74 Varick St., Suite 307, New York, NY 10013 (☎ 212/431-1616; open daily 10am–6pm). Now Voyager works with several daily flights to London, one of them allowing couriers to stay up to 30 days and bring along a modest amount of luggage.

For $35 a year the **International Association of Air Travel Couriers,** P.O. Box 1349, Lake Worth, FL 33460 (☎ 407/582-8320), will send six issues of its newsletter, *Shoestring Traveler,* and about six issues of *Air Courier Bulletin,* a directory of worldwide air-courier bargains. The organization offers photo identification cards and acts as a troubleshooter if a courier runs into difficulties. The fee also includes access to their 24-hour fax-on-demand system and a computer bulletin board that is updated daily with last-minute flights and bulletin updates.

TRAVEL CLUBS   Another possibility for low-cost air travel is travel clubs, which supply an unsold inventory of tickets at discounts of 20% to 60%. You pay an annual fee and are given a hotline number to find out what discounts are available. Many of these discounts become available several days in advance of the actual departure, sometimes as long as a month in advance. Of course, you're limited to what's available, so you have to be fairly flexible.

Some of the best of these clubs include the following.

Moment's Notice, 425 Madison Ave., New York, NY 10017 (☎ 212/486-0500), charges $25 per year and allows spur-of-the-moment participation in dozens of tours. These tours are geared for impulse purchases and last-minute getaways and offer air and land packages that can represent substantial savings compared to conventional channels. Even nonmembers can call the Moment's Notice hotline (☎ 212/750-9111) to learn what options are available. Most of the company's best-priced tours depart from New Jersey's Newark airport.

For $50 **Sears Discount Travel Club,** 3033 South Parker Rd., Suite 900, Aurora, CO 80014 (☎ 800/255-1487), offers members a catalog (issued four times a year), maps, discounts at selected hotels, and a limited guarantee that equivalent packages will not be undersold by any other travel organization. It also offers a 5% rebate on all airline tickets, tours, hotel accommodations, and car rentals purchased through them. (To collect this rebate, participants are required to fill out some forms and photocopy their receipts and itineraries.)

BY SHIP

OCEAN LINER   The **Cunard Line,** 555 Fifth Ave., New York, NY 10017 (☎ 212/880-7500 or 800/221-4770), boasts that its flagship, *Queen Elizabeth 2,* is the only five-star luxury ocean liner providing regular transatlantic service—some 27 voyages a year between April and December. Many passengers appreciate its graceful introduction to British mores, and no one misses the jet lag.

Fares are extremely complicated, based on the season and the standard and location of the cabin. During the thrift/superthrift season—roughly defined as late autumn or early spring—a trip usually costs at least $2,230 in transatlantic class and around $4,660 in first class. These are per-person, double-occupancy prices. Passengers also pay a $175 port tax. Many packages are offered, including inexpensive airfare from your home city to the port of departure and a return flight to your home city from London on British Airways.

FREIGHTER   If you have time and an adventurous spirit, get a cabin aboard a freighter. It's an offbeat alternative, and often a less expensive one (though a budget accommodation aboard the *QE2* can cost less). No freighter can carry more than 12 passengers because a full-time ship's doctor would be required. Your cabin will be adequate, but don't expect organized activities.

Most freighters dock at Le Havre, Rotterdam, or Bremerhaven, but a few make stops at such unlikely British ports as Felixstowe. Sometimes the final port will change during the crossing, throwing prearranged itineraries into confusion, so you need to be flexible. Passage to Europe from most of North America's Atlantic or Gulf ports takes from 9 to 13 days, depending on the itinerary. Although last-minute berths might suddenly become available, reservations should usually be made at least 6 months in advance. In summer, cabins are often booked as much as a year in advance. Space is more likely to be available in winter.

One of the country's most experienced booking agents for freighter travel is **Anytime, Anywhere Travel,** 91 N. Bedford Rd., Chappaqua, NY 10514 (☎914/ 238-8800). The company can book with several different freighter operators for departures from Houston, Savannah, and New Orleans (among others) that dock in several European cities, including Le Havre (France), Rotterdam (Holland), and Bremerhaven (Germany). The cost is about $1,100 each way, double occupancy, with meals included.

Lykes Brothers Steamship Co., Lykes Center, 300 Poydras St., New Orleans, LA 70130 (☎ 504/528-1400), a maritime shipper, operates 10 vessels equipped to carry between 4 and 12 passengers each. Departures are scheduled from such harbors as Port Elizabeth, N.J.; Wilmington, N.C.; New Orleans; and Galveston, Tex., to such places as Livorno (Italy), Alexandria (Egypt), Felixstowe (England), Le Havre, and Bremerhaven. Lykes does very little to promote or publicize its available berths, and you should not expect the royal treatment as you attempt to book. But a Lykes ship could well be a good alternative to flying to Europe.

Other options are described in *Ford's Freighter Travel Guide,* 19448 Londelius St., Northridge, CA 91324 (☎ 818/701-7414), which is published in May and November and costs $14.95 for a single copy and $20 for a one-year subscription.

BY TRAIN OR CAR FROM CONTINENTAL EUROPE

TRAIN   Britain's isolation from the rest of Europe has led to the development of an independent railway network with different rules and regulations from those observed on the continent. If you're traveling to Britain from the continent, your Eurorail pass will *not* be valid when you get there.

Under the Channel   In 1994 Queen Elizabeth and President François Mitterand officially opened the Channel Tunnel, or Chunnel, and the *Eurostar Express* passenger train began twice-daily service between London and both Paris and Brussels—a 3-hour trip. The $15-billion tunnel, one of the great engineering feats of all time, is the first link between Britain and the continent since the Ice Age.

Rail Europe (☎ 800/94-CHUNNEL) sells direct-service tickets on the *Eurostar* between Paris or Brussels and London. A round-trip fare between Paris and London costs $312 in first class and $248 in second class. You can cut the second-class cost to $152 by making a (nonrefundable) 14-day advance purchase. In London make reservations for *Eurostar* at 01345/300003, in Paris at 44-51-06-02, and in the United States at 800/387-6782.

Eurostar trains arrive and depart from London's Waterloo Station, Paris's Gare du Nord, and Brussels's Central Station.

FERRY/HOVERCRAFT   Sailing ships and ferryboats have long traversed the English Channel bearing supplies, merchandise, and passengers. Today, the major carriers are P&O Channel Lines, Hoverspeed, and Sealink.

P&O Channel Lines (☎ 01233/203388) operates car and passenger ferries between Portsmouth and Cherbourg, France (three departures a day; 4 hours each way); between Portsmouth and Le Havre, France (three a day; 5 hours each way); between Dover and Calais, France (every 90 minutes; 75 minutes each way); and between Felixstowe and Zeebrugge, Belgium (twice a day; 5 hours each way).

P&O's major competitor is **Stena Sealink** (☎ 01233/647047), which carries both passengers and vehicles on its routes. This company is represented in North America by BritRail (☎ 212/575-2667 in New York or 800/677-8585).

By far the most popular route across the Channel is between Calais and Dover. One company, **Hoverspeed,** operates at least 12 hovercraft crossings daily (the trip takes 35 minutes). They also run a SeaCat (a catamaran propelled by jet engines) that takes slightly longer to make the crossing between Boulogne and Folkestone. The SeaCats depart about four times a day on the 55-minute voyage.

Stena Sealink offers conventional ferryboat service between Cherbourg and Southampton (one or two trips a day; 6 to 8 hours) and between Dieppe and Newhaven (four departures daily; 4 hours each way). Stena Sealink's conventional car-ferries between Calais and Dover are very popular; they depart 20 times a day in both directions and take 90 minutes to make the crossing. Typical fares between France and England are as follows: £25 ($39.50) for a one-way adult ticket, £22 ($34.75) for seniors, and £15 ($23.70) for children.

Traveling by Hovercraft or SeaCat cuts the time of your surface journey from the continent to the U.K. A Hovercraft trip is definitely a fun adventure, since the vessel is technically "flying" over the water. A SeaCat crossing from Folkestone to Boulogne is longer in miles but is covered faster than conventional ferryboats make the Calais-Dover crossing. SeaCats also travel from the British mainland to the Isle of Wight, Belfast, and the Isle of Man. For reservations and information call Hoverspeed (☎ 01304/240-241). Typical one-way fares are £26 ($41.10) per person.

CAR   If you plan to take a rented car across or under the Channel, check with the rental company about license and insurance requirements before you leave.

There are many "drive-on, drive-off" car-ferry services across the Channel. The most popular ports in France for Channel crossings are Boulogne and Calais, where you can board Sealink ferries taking you to the English ports of Dover and Folkestone.

There are special Channel Tunnel trains for passenger cars, charter buses, taxis, and motorcycles. Before boarding the train the French call "Le Shuttle," you stop at a toll booth and then pass through customs for both countries at one time. During the 35-minute ride (19 minutes of which are actually in the Chunnel), you stay in a bright, air-conditioned carriage and can remain inside your car or step outside to stretch your legs. When the trip is over, you simply drive off toward your destination. Total travel time between the French and English highway system is about one hour. This car service operates 24 hours a day, 365 days a year; it runs every 15 minutes during peak travel periods and at least once an hour at night.

Duty-free stores, restaurants, and service stations are available to travelers on both sides of the Channel. A bilingual staff is on hand to assist travelers at both the British and French terminals.

ORGANIZED TOURS

Britain's national airline, **British Airways** (☎ 800/AIRWAYS) is Europe's largest tour operator. It books greater numbers of European hotel rooms and has more experience than almost anyone else in the travel industry. BA's selection of tours in the British Isles is gratifyingly extensive and often tailor-made for the specific needs of clients. The company offers a full range of what it calls "designer holidays," each of them planned for participants with sometimes radically different interests. Some of the offerings include carefully structured, tightly scheduled motor-coach tours for clients who feel they need the most channeling, guidance, and well-informed running commentaries.

Equally popular are tours designed for bravely independent souls who need no more than discount vouchers for a rental car and reserved rooms at specific types of hotels. Depending on your tastes and your pocketbook, British Airways can arrange vouchers for discounted accommodations in everything from simple inns above a local pub to suites in the finest aristocratic mansions of England. The company can also arrange a reduced rate on a rented car so you can drive yourself over the hills and through the glens of England without interference from anyone except your chosen companion.

The array of options is huge: Tours can be as straightforward as a 1-day jaunt from London to Canterbury or Brighton (with a return to London in time for a West End play); or they might include short excursions from London to the Edinburgh Music Festival (with difficult-to-obtain tickets included as part of the bargain); or a 9-day all-inclusive tour through the great houses and gardens of England. Clients preferring to travel alone should specify the area of their greatest interest and the dates they intend to visit; then a sales representative can tailor an itinerary specifically for them. (Possibilities for this type of excursion might include the West Country, the Lake District, or perhaps a spate of museum- and theatergoing in London, with discounted rates on stays in a wide assortment of big-city hotels.)

For a free catalog and additional information, call British Airways at the toll-free number listed above *before you book your airline ticket,* since some of the company's available options are contingent upon the purchase of a round-trip transatlantic air ticket.

8 Getting Around

BY PLANE

British Airways (☎ 800/AIRWAYS) flies to more than 20 cities outside London, including Manchester, Glasgow, and Edinburgh. British Airways telephone representatives in North America can give price and schedule information and make reservations for flights, hotels, car rentals, and tours within the U.K. Ask about the British Airways Super Shuttle Saver fares, which can save you up to 50% on travel to certain key British cities. If seats are available on the flight of your choice, no advance reservations are necessary, though to benefit from the lowest prices, passengers must spend a Saturday night away from their point of origin and fly during defined off-peak times. Flights are usually (but not always) restricted to weekdays between 10am and 3:30pm, while most night flights are after 7pm and, in certain cases, on weekends.

Other cost-conscious options include a 14-day round-trip APEX ticket that must be reserved and paid for 14 days in advance, with travel completed within 3 months of departure.

For passengers planning on visiting widely scattered destinations within the U.K., perhaps with a side trip to a city on Europe's mainland, British Airways' Europe Airpass allows discounted travel in a continuous loop to between 3 and 12 cities anywhere on BA's European and domestic air routes. Passengers must end their journey at the same point they begin it and fly exclusively on BA flights. Such a ticket (for instance, from London to Paris, then to Manchester, and finally to London again) will cut the cost of each segment of the itinerary by about 40% to 50% over individually booked tickets. The pass is available for travel to about a dozen of the most-visited cities and regions of Britain, with discounted add-ons available to most of BA's destinations in Europe as well. (Be aware that this Airpass is a value-conscious bargain for round-trip travel between London and Rome, for example, but not very practical for air travel from, say, Rome to Madrid. You'd be better off traveling between points on the continent by full-fare airline ticket, or by train, bus, or car.)

BA's Europe Airpass must be booked and paid for at least 7 days before a passenger's departure from North America. All sectors of the itinerary, including transatlantic passage from North America, must be booked simultaneously. Some changes are permitted in flight dates (but not in destinations) after the ticket is issued. Check with BA for full details and restrictions.

BY TRAIN

Although changes won't be immediately visible to most foreign visitors, readers should expect new developments in British Rail's infrastructure in 1996 and beyond. Although Britain's rail network will remain intact (and, in some cases, be expanded), the British government—in an effort to raise capital and improve rail service—intends to sell some of its routes to independent operators. Each independent franchiser must agree to maintain the switches, tracks, and rail cars according to standards set by British Rail's supervisory board, Railtrack.

Included among the routes being discussed for independent operation are the Gatwick Express, the busy routes between London and Edinburgh, and—in the distant future—certain sales-and-marketing aspects of routes via the Channel Tunnel. None of these changes will affect the existing rituals for issuing rail passes or for selling individual tickets, though by the time of your actual trip, the names of one or another of Britrail's subsidiary companies may have changed. For up-to-date information, any travel agent or ticket vendor can advise you of changes that will affect your trip.

A Eurorail pass is not valid in Great Britain, but there are several special passes for train travel outside London. For railroad information, go to the British Rail/ Sealink office, 4–12 Lower Regent St., SW1 (☎ 0171/928-5151) or to the British Rail Travel centres in the main London railway stations—Waterloo, King's Cross, Euston, and Paddington—each of which deals mainly with its own region.

BRITRAIL PASS   This pass allows unlimited rail travel during a set time period (8 days, 15 days, 22 days, or 1 month). For 8 days, the pass costs $315 in first class,

$230 in "standard"; for 15 days, $515 in first class, $355 in standard; for 22 days, $645 in first class, $445 in standard; and for 1 month, $750 in first class, $520 in standard. Senior citizens (60 and over) qualify for 8-day rates of $295 in first, $209 in standard; for 15 days, $479 in first class, $320 in standard; for 22 days, $585 in first class, $399 in standard; and for 1 month, $675 in first class, $465 in standard. Youth passes (ages 16–25) are sold only in standard class; the price is $189 for 8 days, $280 for 15 days, $355 for 22 days, and $415 for 1 month. Children 5–15 pay half fare, and there's no charge for children age 4 and under.

Americans can obtain a BritRail pass at BritRail Travel International, 1500 Broadway, New York, NY 10036 (☎ 212/575-2667). Canadians can write to 2161 Yonge St., Suite 812, Toronto, ON M4F 386 (☎ 416/484-0571).

BRITRAIL FLEXIPASS　The Flexipass lets you travel anywhere on BritRail. It is particularly good for visitors who want to alternate travel days with blocks of uninterrupted sightseeing time in a particular city or region. Flexipasses can be used for 4 days within any 1-month period and cost $259 in first class and $195 in economy. Seniors pay $235 in first class and $175 in second class; and youths aged 16 to 25 pay $160 to travel economy class. Also available is a Flexipass that allows 8 days of travel within a month and costs $399 in first class, $275 in economy. A senior pass costs $360 in first class, $250 in economy; the youth economy class costs $225.

LONDON EXTRA　If you're planning to confine your explorations of England to day trips from London, London Extra may make better sense than a BritRail pass. It allows unlimited travel to accessible destinations on BritRail's "Network Southeast," which covers the southeast of England and includes many of the most historic and appealing towns and villages of England (for example, Oxford, Cambridge, Dover, Canterbury, Salisbury, and Portsmouth). Frequent trains—41 daily from London to Brighton alone—let you leave early in the morning and return to London in time for the theater or dinner. In addition, this railpass package also includes a London Visitor Travelcard that allows you to use London's public transport system for 3, 4, or 7 days, depending on your ticket.

A 3-day London Extra package in first class costs $105 for adults, $35 for children aged 5 to 15; second class costs $85 for adults and $29 for children. A 7-day London Extra Pass costs $219 for adults and $45 for children in first class and $175 for adults and $35 for children in second class. The pass is also issued in a 4- or 7-day version.

London Extra must be purchased either from your travel agent or BritRail Travel International in the United States or Canada (see addresses above).

BRITAINSHRINKERS TOURS　From early April to the end of October, Britainshrinkers, Ltd., operates a number of escorted, full-day tours that include, in different combinations, visits to Bath, Stonehenge, Stratford-upon-Avon, Oxford, and the Cotswolds. They include train transportation and sightseeing by bus. Tours include some free time to take lunch in a local pub, to shop, and to explore on your own. Tours return to London in time for dinner or the theater. Rates include entrance fees and value-added tax (VAT), but usually not the price of lunch.

Britainshrinkers offers excellent value for the money, and if you use a valid BritRail pass or Flexipass, you can save up to 60% of the cost of each tour you take. Britainshrinkers tours can be purchased from either your travel agent or BritRail in the United States and Canada or in England at BritRail offices (see addresses above).

BY BUS

In Britain, a long-distance touring bus is called a "coach," and "buses" are taken for local transportation. There's an efficient and frequent express motor-coach network—run by National Express and other independent operators—that links most of Britain's towns and cities. Destinations off the main route can be easily reached by stopping and transferring to a local bus. Tickets are relatively cheap—often half the price of rail fare—and it's usually cheaper to purchase a round-trip (or "return") ticket than two one-way fares separately.

Victoria Coach Station, on Buckingham Palace Road (☎ 0171/730-3466), is the departure point for most large coach operators. The coach station is located just 2 blocks from Victoria Station. For credit-card sales (MasterCard and VISA only), call 0171/730-3499 Monday through Saturday from 9am to 7pm. For cash purchases, get there at least 30 minutes before the coach departures.

National Express National Express runs luxurious long-distance coaches that are equipped with hostesses, light refreshments, reclining seats, toilets, and no-smoking areas. Details about all coach services can be obtained by phoning 0171/730-0202 daily from 8am to 10pm. The National Express ticket office at Victoria Station is open from 8am to 7pm.

You might want to consider National Express's **Tourist Trail Pass,** which offers unlimited travel on their network. (You should be aware that this company's service is most extensive in England and Wales.) A 5-day pass costs £79 ($124.80); an 8-day pass, £119 ($188); a 15-day pass, £179 ($282.80).

Green Line For journeys within a 35-mile radius of London, try the Green Line coach service. Their inquiry office is at 4A Fountain Sq., Bulleid Way, SW1 in Victoria (☎ 0181/668-7261).

With a 1-day **Diamond Rover Ticket,** costing £6 ($9.50) for adults and £3 ($4.75) for children, you can visit many of the attractions of Greater London and the surrounding region, including Windsor Castle and Hampton Court. The pass is valid for 1 day on almost all Green Line coaches and country buses Monday through Friday after 9am and all day on Saturday and Sunday.

Green Line has bus routes called Country Bus Lines that circle through the periphery of London. Although they do not usually go directly into the center of the capital, they do hook up with the routes of the Green Line coaches and red buses that do. For information, contact Green Line Country Bus Lines, Lesbourne Road, Reigate, Surrey RH2 7LE (☎ 0181/668-7261).

BY CAR

Many of the most interesting sights on the periphery of London can be reached by train, but if you're planning to get away from the crowds take a day trip or a week's jaunt—and if driving on the left appeals to your sense of adventure—here are some guidelines:

RENTALS The British car-rental market is among the most competitive in Europe. Nevertheless, car rentals are often relatively expensive, unless you avail yourself of one of the promotional deals that are frequently offered by British Airways and others (see below).

London has several rental companies from which to choose (some of which are listed below, in alphabetical order). Most of them will accept your U.S. driver's license, provided you're 23 years old (21 in rare instances) and have had the license for more than a year. Never forget, however, that cars in Britain travel on the left side of the road and have their steering wheels positioned on the "wrong" side of the vehicle.

Many rental companies will grant discounts to clients who reserve their cars in advance (usually 48 hours) through the toll-free reservations offices in the renter's home country. Rentals of a week or more are almost always less expensive, per day, than day rentals.

When you reserve a car, be sure to ask if the price includes the 17.5% Value-Added Tax (VAT), personal accident insurance (PAI), collision-damage waiver (CDW), and any other insurance options. If not, ask what they will cost, because at the end of your rental, they can make a big difference in your bottom line. As in the United States, the CDW and some added insurance are sometimes offered free by certain credit-card companies if you use the card to pay for the rental. Check directly with your credit-card issuer to see if you are covered by your credit card so you can avoid the sometimes unnecessary coverage.

Avis (☎ 800/331-2112) offers a one-day rental of the small but peppy Ford Fiesta with CDW and unlimited mileage for £64 ($101.10) plus taxes. A full week's rental of a similar car, if reserved 14 days in advance, is a much better bargain at £173 ($273.35). The main Avis office is in Mayfair at 8 Balderton St., London W1 (☎ 0171/917-6700; tube: Bond Street).

British Airways (☎ 800/AIRWAYS) offers a relatively inexpensive way to rent a car in Britain through its reservations service. As the U.K.'s largest car renter, BA can offer discounted rates. Depending on size, horsepower, amenities, and season, cars range in price from $20 to $92 per day plus VAT and insurance. Child seats are available free. Understandably, these arrangements are offered only to passengers flying into Britain on BA.

Budget Rent-a-Car (☎ 800/472-3325) maintains 10 offices in London, including at all the major airports and about 100 others throughout the United Kingdom. The busiest London office is near Marble Arch, 89 Wigmore St., W1 (☎ 0171/723-8038; tube: Marble Arch). If you reserve from North America at least 8 business hours prior to pickup, cars will cost from £34 ($53.70) per day for short rentals to about £95 ($150.10) per week (less during promotions). There is unlimited mileage, VAT, and CDW included in the fee.

Hertz (☎ 800/654-3001); in London, 35 Edgware Rd., Marble Arch, London W1 (☎ 0171/402-4242; tube: March Arch). Hertz offers an unlimited-mileage Fiat Uno for £155 ($244.90) per week, including CDW, theft insurance, and VAT.

DRIVING RULES & REQUIREMENTS   In England, as you know, *you drive on the left* and pass on the right. Road signs are clear and the international symbols are unmistakable.

You must present your passport and driver's license when you rent a car in Britain. No special British license is needed. The prudent driver will secure a copy of the *British Highway Code,* available from almost any gas station or newsstand (called a "news stall" in Britain).

Warning: Pedestrians crossings are marked by striped lines (zebra striping) on the road; flashing lights near the curb indicates that drivers must stop and yield the right of way if a pedestrian has stepped out into the zebra zone to cross the street.

ROAD MAPS   The best road map is *The Ordinance Survey Motor Atlas of Great Britain*—whether you're trying to find the fastest route to Manchester or locate some obscure village. Revised annually, it's published by Temple Press and is available at most bookstores, including W&G Foyle, Ltd., 119 Charing Cross Rd., London, WC2 (☎ 0171/439-8501).

BREAKDOWNS　Membership in one of England's two major auto clubs—the Automobile Association (AA) and the Royal Automobile Club (RAC)—can be helpful. Membership, which can be obtained through your car-rental agent, entitles you to free legal and technical advice on motoring matters, as well as a whole range of discounts on automobile products and services.

The AA is located at Norfolk House, Priestly Road, Basingstoke, Hampshire RG24 9NY (☎ 01256/20123). The RAC can be contacted at Spectrum, Bond Street (P.O. Box 700), Bristol, Avon BS99 1RB (☎ 01272/232340).

If your car breaks down on the highway, you can call for 24-hour breakdown service from a roadside phone. The 24-hour number to call for AA is 01800/887766; for RAC it is 01800/828282. All motorways are provided with special emergency phones that are connected to police traffic units, and the police can contact either of the auto clubs on your behalf.

GASOLINE　Called "petrol," gasoline is sold by the liter, with 4.2 liters to a gallon. Prices are much higher than Stateside, and you'll probably have to serve yourself. In some remote areas, stations are few and far between, and many are closed on Sunday.

HITCHHIKING

Frommer's England does not recommend hitchhiking, though it is legal in England—except on motorways. Getting into a car with a stranger can be extremely dangerous, especially for solo travelers. Always exercise caution. Generally, the cleaner and tidier you look, the better your chances for getting a ride. Have a sign with your destination written on it and hold it up for drivers to see. Again, consider the great risk involved before you get into somebody's car. No one—man or woman—should ever contemplate hitchhiking alone.

SUGGESTED ITINERARIES

If you're a first-time visitor to London, see "Suggested Itineraries" in Chapter 6. With London behind your belt, you're set to explore the English countryside. We've divided our explorations into two one-week trips and one two-week trip.

If You Have 1 Week

Day 1　Southeast England lies virtually at London's doorstep. Your major overnight target here is Canterbury, 56 miles to the southeast. On the way there, visit Leeds Castle, 5 miles east of Maidstone on A20. Then follow in the footsteps of Chaucer's characters from *The Canterbury Tales* and reach the city of Canterbury, where you can visit the cathedral in which Thomas à Becket was murdered in 1170. Explore the city's old streets and attractions before settling in for the night.

Day 2　From Canterbury head east to the coast and Sandwich, then go south to Deal. Some 6 miles from Sandwich you'll be at the point where Caesar's legions landed in 55 B.C. After exploring Deal Castle, built in 1540, continue for a mile to the south and visit Walmer Castle, one of Henry VIII's fortifications. Seven miles south along the A258 lies Dover, which has traditionally been Britain's historic gateway to Europe. Spend the night here.

Day 3 After exploring Dover Castle and other attractions, go west through Folkestone, a seaside resort, and across Romney Marsh to the ancient port of Rye (which now lies 2 miles inland because of centuries of silting up). Rye and neighboring Winchelsea, some 3 miles to the southwest, are among the prettiest destinations in southeast England. Definitely plan to pass the night here.

Day 4 In the morning continue southeast to Hastings, a somewhat seedy seaside resort. See the Hastings Embroidery and the castle William the Conqueror built in 1069. You can still reach Battle, site of Battle Abbey, before lunch. After a visit there, follow B2095 and A259 to Pevensey, a former Roman settlement where the troops of William the Conqueror landed. Continue through Wilmington, 7 miles west on A27, and stay on this highway until you reach Lewes. Stop for the night either in Lewes or Alfriston.

Day 5 Leave Lewes and stay on the A27 for 8 miles until you reach Brighton, the major seaside resort in Britain. You can spend most of the day just exploring its Royal Pavilion. Spend the night there.

Day 6 Leave Brighton and take the A27 coastal road to Arundel, 23 miles away. Visit Arundel Castle and have lunch before setting out to explore the Weald and Downland Open Air Museum, outside Singleton. After passing through Singleton, go 8 miles south on A286 until you reach Chichester. Plan an evening at its theater and stay the night in town.

Day 7 On the way back to London stop for the night at Royal Tunbridge Wells, which you can use as a base for exploring some of the most historical properties in Britain: Chartwell (former abode of Winston Churchill); Knole (one of the largest private houses in England); and Penshurst Palace, at Penshurst, 6 miles west of the town of Tonbridge (as opposed to Tunbridge Wells).

Another Trip if You Have 1 Week

Day 1 Begin at Winchester, 64 miles southwest of London. Its greatest monument is its cathedral, but you'll want to walk around and explore its ancient streets as well. In the afternoon drive toward the coast and spend the night in Portsmouth, England's naval capital. Explore its many nautical monuments, including the *Mary Rose*, flagship of the Tudor navy.

Day 2 Stop off for a brief visit at Southampton, 21 miles northwest, from which the *Mayflower* sailed on August 15, 1620. (The vessel had to stop in Plymouth for repairs). Drive eight miles northwest to see Broadlands, just off A3057, home of the Lord Mountbatten—allied commander in Southeast Asia during World War II, the last governor general of India, and confidante of his nephew Prince Charles. Back in Southampton, take the ferry to the Isle of Wight, which Queen Victoria chose as her vacation home. Her mansion is open to the public. Stay at one of the seaside resorts on the island.

Day 3 After returning to Southampton, drive northwest to Salisbury and pass the night. During the day you can see its cathedral and visit Stonehenge, on the outskirts of town.

Day 4 From Salisbury follow the A36 to Lyndhurst, which is the gateway to New Forest. Although you could spend weeks exploring the forest, which was known to the armies of William the Conqueror, you might settle for driving through. Its chief sightseeing attraction is Beaulieu Abbey (which you'll reach after a six-mile drive on the B3056 from Lyndhurst). You can also visit Buckler's Hard, an 18th-century hamlet on the River Beaulieu. Follow the signs to

Lymington, and from there go on A337 to the resort of Bournemouth, 18 miles away. Stay the night there.

Day 5   After a morning in Dorset drive along the southern tier of England, passing through such historic cities as Dorchester for an overnight stop in Lyme Regis. It was featured in the film *The French Lieutenant's Woman*, based on the novel by John Fowles.

Day 6   From Lyme Regis you can continue westward for a night in Plymouth. Along the way, the most interesting places include Torbay (which incorporates Torquay), Dartmouth, and Totnes. Stay the night in Plymouth.

Day 7   From Plymouth, get an early start and drive back toward London, but instead of going through Dorset, cut northeast through Somerset to visit Glastonbury and Wells. And stop for the night in Bath. It would be ideal if you could take three days for this leg of the journey, but you may be pressed for time.

If You Have 2 Weeks

Day 1   After leaving London, head first for Windsor, 21 miles west, and explore its castle and other attractions in the morning. Devote the rest of the day to visiting neighboring Eton and exploring sights in the environs of Windsor (see Chapter 8 for more details). Spend the night in or around Windsor.

Day 2   After leaving the Windsor area, head northwest toward Marlow, with its famed suspension bridge. Continue on the A4155 to Henley, some 7 miles away. Have lunch at the Red Lion Hotel. Some 5 miles to the southwest of Henley, visit Mapledurham House, the Elizabethan mansion of the Blount family on the Thames. Head northwest to Oxford for the night.

Day 3   Explore the major colleges of Oxford in the morning and have lunch at a tavern frequented by students. In the afternoon go 8 miles northwest of Oxford to Woodstock, site of Blenheim Palace, before returning to Oxford for the night.

Days 4–5   Drive northwest from Oxford to Stratford-upon-Avon. You will need all of day 4 and most of day 5 to see its many attractions. On your first night attend a performance of the Royal Shakespeare Company. The following day, continue to explore the attractions of Stratford, but consider visiting a trio of important sights in the vicinity. If you have time for only one, make it Warwick Castle. With more time, consider a visit to Coventry Cathedral, at Coventry, or Sulgrave Manor, ancestral home of George Washington.

Day 6   From Stratford, begin your tour of the Cotswolds. Head south from Stratford to Moreton-in-Marsh and then go on to Stow-on-the-Wold for lunch. Consider getting out of your car and walking between Upper Slaughter and Lower Slaughter. Continue south to Bourton-on-the-Water for an overnight stay.

Day 7   Swing southeast to Burford, often called "the gateway to the Cotswolds," before journeying west again to Bibury for lunch. Head west from Bibury for a quick tour of Cirencester before cutting north to the old spa of Cheltenham for an overnight stop.

Day 8   Leaving Cheltenham, head northeast to Broadway and Chipping Campden. Both towns are celebrated in the Cotswolds, and either one makes an ideal base for exploring the hills.

Day 9   The next morning drive northeast to the historic city of Chester (see Chapter 18, The Northwest). Spend the night there.

Day 10   Continue north from Chester to Liverpool for another night. Liverpool, which has lost its reputation as a seedy, decaying port, has some of the major attractions of the northwest, including a branch of the Tate Gallery and two major cathedrals.

Day 11   Leaving Liverpool continue 55 miles north to Windermere and Bowness, two ideal spots from which to explore the Lake District.

Day 12   Although you can still use Windermere as a base, see as many towns of the Lake District as possible. The most interesting are Coniston, Hawkshead, Rydal, and Ambleside.

Day 13   Head southeast from the Lake District for a night in York (see Chapter 19), the cathedral city and the most interesting tourist site in northeast England.

Day 14   Conclude your visit to England with a morning stopover in Lincoln to see its cathedral. Continue south toward Ely for a look at its ancient cathedral before staying the night in the university town of Cambridge.

9 Tips on Accommodations

CLASSIFICATIONS   Unlike some countries, England doesn't have a rigid hotel-classification system. The tourist board grades hotels by crowns instead of stars. Hotels are judged on their standards, quality, and hospitality, and are rated "approved," "commended," "highly commended," and "deluxe." Five crowns (deluxe) is the highest rating. Depending on their range of facilities, other hotels are rated four, three, two, or one crown. There is even a classification of "listed," with no crowns, and these accommodations are for the most part very modest.

In a five-crown hotel, all rooms must have a private bath; in a four-crown hotel, only 75% have them. In a one-crown hotel, buildings are required to have hot and cold running water in all the rooms. But in "listed" hotels hot and cold running water in the rooms is not mandatory. Crown ratings are posted outside the buildings. However, the system is voluntary, and many hotels do not participate.

Many hotels—especially older ones—still lack private baths for all rooms. However, most have hot and cold running water, and many have modern wings with all the amenities (as well as older sections that are less up-to-date). When making reservations, always ask what section of the hotel you'll be staying in if it has extensions.

All hotels used to include a full English breakfast of bacon and eggs in the room price, but today that is true for only some hotels. The higher the cost of your accommodations, the more likely that you will be charged extra for an English breakfast. A continental breakfast is commonly included, but that usually means just tea or coffee and toast, with extra charges for juice and other items.

PRICE CATEGORIES   In this guide, hotels rated **very expensive** generally charge £195 ($308.10) and up for a double room. Doubles in **expensive** hotels range from about £130 ($205.40) to about £195 ($308.10), though some rooms may be priced higher. **Moderate** hotels offer doubles from about £85 ($134.30) to roughly £130 ($205.40), but some of their special rooms can cost much, much more. Hotels rated **inexpensive** often begin at £49 ($77.40) but could be more. Anything under £49 is considered **"budget"**—at least by English standards. Unless otherwise specified, all rooms include private bath. Parking rates are per night.

RESERVATIONS   Reservations are advised, even in the so-called slow months, from November to April. Tourist travel to London peaks from May to October, when moderate and budget hotels are full. Only the most adventurous show up without a reservation.

It's easiest to reserve with a chain via its North American representatives, but that might not be the type of accommodation you're seeking. For hotels without representatives in North America, write or send a fax. If you write, send an International Reply Coupon, available at post offices. When seeking reservations, give as many alternative dates as possible. If a hotel takes your reservation, you may be asked to send one night's deposit. Many readers have reported great difficulty, or even complete failure, in getting their deposit returned when they were forced to cancel their reservations.

If you call a hotel just before you arrive, you may be lucky enough to secure a room because of a last-minute cancellation. Like airlines, hotels traditionally overbook, counting on last-minute cancellations. When everybody shows up, however, they face irate customers shouting at the desk, waving a confirmed reservation. To avoid this, give the hotel a credit-card number and authorize management to charge you the cost even if you don't show up.

BED & BREAKFASTS   In towns, cities, and villages throughout England, homeowners take in paying guests. Watch for the familiar bed-and-breakfast (B&B) signs. Generally, these are modest family homes, but sometimes they are like small hotels, with as many as 15 rooms. If they're that big, they are more properly classified as guesthouses. B&Bs are the cheapest places you can stay in England and still be comfortable.

Hometours International, P.O. Box 11503, Knoxville, TN 37939 (☎ 615/588-8722 or 800/367-4668), will make bed-and-breakfast reservations in England, Scotland, and Wales. This is the only company to guarantee reservations for more than 400 locations in Britain. Accommodations are paid for in the United States in dollars, and prices start as low as $39 per person per night—though they can go as high as $89 per person in London. The company also offers walking tours of Great Britain, with prices starting as low as $510 for 7 days, including meals. Tours are designed for families, single parents, and singles without children. In addition, Hometours International can arrange for apartments in London. The company also offers cottages in Great Britain that begin at $500 per week.

Another organization that is well equipped to arrange unusual accommodations in Britain is the **Barclay International Group (BIG),** 150 E. 52nd St., New York, NY 10022 (☎ 212/832-3777 or 800/845-6636). They specialize in short-term apartment ("flat") rentals in London and cottages in the English countryside. Considered a viable alternative to traditional hotel stays, they may be appropriate for families, groups of friends, or businesspeople traveling together. Apartments, available for stays as short as 1 night, are usually more luxurious than you imagine; furnished with kitchens, they offer a low-cost alternative to restaurant meals. Apartments suitable for one or two occupants begin, during low season, at around $650 a week (including tax) and can go much higher for deluxe accommodations that offer many hotel-like features and amenities. Some travelers find that they are less expensive than equivalent stays in London hotels. For extended stays in the English countryside, BIG's has country cottages in such areas as the Cotswolds, the Lake District, and Oxford, as well as farther afield in Scotland and Wales.

Reservations for bed-and-breakfast accommodations in London can also be made through the **British Travel Centre** (see "Tourist Information," in Chapter 3).

FARMHOUSES In many parts of the country, farmhouses have one, two, even four rooms set aside for paying guests, who usually arrive in the summer months. They don't have the facilities of most guesthouses, but they have a rustic appeal and charm, especially for motorists, as they tend to lie off the beaten path. Prices are generally lower than bed-and-breakfasts or guesthouses, and sometimes you're offered some good country home cooking (at an extra charge) if you make arrangements in advance. The British Tourist Authority will provide a booklet, *Stay on a Farm,* or you can ask at local tourist offices.

The **Farm Holiday Bureau** (☎ 1203/696909) publishes an annual directory in early December that includes about 1,000 farms and bed-and-breakfasts throughout the United Kingdom. The listings include quality ratings, the number of bedrooms, nearby attractions and activities, and prices as well as line drawings of each property. Also listed are any special details, such as rooms with four-poster beds or activities on the grounds (fishing, for example). Many farms are geared toward children, who can participate in light chores—gathering eggs or just tagging along—for an authentic farm experience. The prices range from £11 to £35 ($17.40 to $55.30) a night and include an English breakfast and usually private facilities. (The higher prices are for stays at mansions and manor houses.)

Another option is the self-catering accommodations, which are usually cottages or converted barns that cost from £80 to £300 ($126.40 to $474) per week. Each property is inspected every year not only by the Farm Holiday Bureau but also by the English Tourist Board. The majority of the properties, excepting those located in the mountains, are open year-round.

If you would like a copy of the directory, call or write to the Farm Holiday Bureau, National Agricultural Centre, Stoneleigh Park, Warwickshire CV8 2LZ (telephone number given above). It costs £7.50 ($11.85) and may be purchased by credit card.

HOLIDAY COTTAGES Throughout England there are fully furnished studios, houses, cottages, "flats" (apartments), even trailers suitable for families or groups that can be rented by the month. The British Tourist Authority and most tourist offices have lists available. *Note:* From October to March rents are sometimes reduced by 50%.

Ask the British Tourist Authority for the free "Apartments in London and Holiday Homes," which lists rental agencies such as **At Home Abroad,** 405 E. 56th St., Apt. 6H, New York, NY 10022 (☎ 212/421-9165; fax 212/752-1591). Interested parties should write or fax a description of their needs, and At Home Abroad will send listings at no charge.

British Travel International, P.O. Box 299, Elkton, VA 22827 (☎ 703/298-2232 or 800/327-6097), represents between 8,000 and 10,000 rental properties in the U.K.—each of which is rented by the week (Saturday to Saturday) and requires a 50% payment in full at the time of booking. They publish a catalog with pictures of their offerings, which is available for a $5 fee that is counted toward a deposit. They have everything from a honey-colored, thatch-roofed cottage in the

Cotswolds to a apartments in a British university city. The company represents about 100 hotels in London whose rates are discounted by 5% to 50%, depending on the season and market conditions, and they have listings of some 4,000 bed-and-breakfast establishments. They are also the North American representative of the U.K.'s largest bus company, National Express.

YOUTH HOSTELS   The Youth Hostels Association (England and Wales) can be contacted at Customer Services Department, YHA, Travelyan House, 8 St. Stephen's Hill, St. Albans, Hertfordshire, AL1 2DY (☎ 01727/855215). It operates a network of 240 youth hostels in major cities, in the countryside, and along the coast. Write or call for a free map showing the locations of each youth hostel and full details, including prices.

10 Tips on Dining

When in England, do as many of the English do and patronize the pubs for lunch. It is the country's dining bargain, where you can wash everything down with some lager if you wish. It's also possible to enjoy pub meals in the evening, when you'll often be able to order dishes (sometimes served in an adjacent dining room) at a fraction of the noontime price.

For major savings, choose the set menu when dining in England. The English have adopted a French expression for this, *table d'hôte*. In some restaurants the set menu costs 30% less than if ordered à la carte. Great deals are available at lunch, though countless restaurants offer set dinners as well.

Many hotels prefer that you book on a half-board basis (room, breakfast, dinner). Invariably, they will quote you a cheaper price for half board than if you book only for breakfast and then order a dinner à la carte in the hotel dining room.

A large English breakfast is sometimes included in the price of the room. If you're in London and going to the theater, you might want to enjoy high tea sometime between 4:30 and 6:30pm. This consists not only of tea but sandwiches and pastries that will fortify you into the evening.

Price Categories   In this guide restaurants are listed as **very expensive** that serve dinner for one without wine for roughly £45 ($71.10). Those charging about £35 to £45 ($55.30 to $71.10) are grouped as **expensive;** those charging about £15 to £35 ($23.70 to $55.30), as **moderate;** and those charging less than about £15 ($23.70), as **inexpensive.**

11 Tips on Shopping

The best buys in England are handcrafts, woolen products (including tweeds, scarves, skirts, sweaters, and tartans), traditional jewelry, and world-renowned pottery and china made by Royal Doulton, Wedgwood, and Royal Worcester. You can also find high-quality posters, art prints, crafts, and art books in many of England's museums, especially those in London.

Bargain hunters arrive in London during a two-week period in January and a one-week period in July, when major department stores such as Selfridges feature sales. Many Europeans cross the English Channel just to take advantage of these sales. Look for advertisements in local newspapers.

Increasingly, flea markets and street markets are the way to shop in England for collectibles and curios. You may have to wade through a lot of junk, but you'll often come upon an attractive souvenir. Try haggling—it works.

FAST FACTS: England

For information on London, refer to "Fast Facts: London," in Chapter 3.

Business Hours With many, many exceptions, business hours are Monday through Friday from 9am to 5pm. The lunch break lasts an hour, but most offices stay open all day. In general, stores are open Monday through Saturday from 9am to 5:30pm. In country towns, there is usually an early closing day (often on Wednesday or Thursday), when the shops close at 1pm. The day varies from town to town.

Camera and Film Film is readily available, especially in large cities. Processing takes about 24 hours, although many places, particularly in London, will do it almost while you wait. There are few restrictions on the use of your camera, except where notices are posted, as in churches, theaters, and certain museums. If in doubt, ask.

Cigarettes Most U.S. brands are available in major towns. *Warning:* More and more places now ban smoking. Make sure you smoke only in the designated smoking areas of theaters and other public places. Some restaurants restrict smoking, as do many bed-and-breakfasts.

Climate See "When to Go," in this chapter.

Crime See "Safety," below.

Currency See "Visitor Information & Entry Requirements" in this chapter.

Customs See "Visitor Information & Entry Requirements" in this chapter.

Dentists Outside London, ask the nearest sympathetic local resident—usually your hotelier—for information.

Doctors Hotels keep lists of local practitioners, for whom you'll have to pay. Outside London, dial 100 and ask the operator for the local police, who will give you the name, address, and telephone number of a doctor in your area. Emergency treatment is free, but if you visit a doctor at his or her "surgery" (office), or if he or she makes a house call to your hotel, you will have to pay. It's wise to take out adequate medical/accident insurance coverage before you leave home.

Documents Required See "Visitor Information & Entry Requirements," in this chapter.

Driving Rules See "Getting Around," in this chapter.

Drug Laws Britain is becoming increasingly severe in enforcing antidrug laws. Persons arrested for possession of even tiny quantities of marijuana have been deported, forced to pay stiff fines, or sentenced to jail for 2 to 7 years. Possession of "white powder" drugs such as heroin or cocaine carry even more stringent penalties.

Drugstores In Britain they're called "chemists." Every police station in the country has a list of emergency chemists. Dial "0" (zero) and ask the operator for the local police, who will give you the name of the one nearest you.

Electricity British electricity is 240 volts AC, 50 cycles, roughly twice the voltage in North America, which is 115 to 120 volts AC, 60 cycles. American plugs don't fit British wall outlets. Always bring suitable transformers and/or adapters (some but definitely not all hotels will supply them). Be warned that you will destroy your American appliances (and possibly start a fire) if you plug them directly into a European electrical outlet without a transformer. Tape recorders, VCRs, and other devices with motors intended to revolve at a fixed number of r.p.m. probably won't work properly even with transformers.

Embassies and Consulates   See "Fast Facts: London," in Chapter 3.

Emergencies   Dial 999 for police, fire, or ambulance. Give your name, address, and telephone number and state the nature of the emergency. Misuse of the 999 service carries a heavy fine. Cardiac arrest, yes—sprained ankle, no. An accident and injury, yes—dented fender, no.

Etiquette   Be normal; be quiet. The British don't like hearing other people's conversations. In pubs you are not expected to buy a round of drinks unless someone has bought you a drink. Don't talk politics or religion in pubs.

Gasoline   See "Getting Around," in this chapter.

Hitchhiking   See "Getting Around," in this chapter.

Holidays   See "When to Go," in this chapter.

Information   See "Visitor Information & Entry Requirements," in this chapter and individual city/regional chapters.

Laundry and Dry Cleaning   Most stores and hotels need 2 days to do the job. London and most provincial towns have launderettes where you can wash and dry your own clothes, but there are no ironing facilities. Many launderettes also have dry-cleaning machines. One-day dry-cleaning service is available.

Legal Aid   The American Services section of the U.S. Consulate (see "Fast Facts: London," in Chapter 3) will give advice if you run into trouble abroad. They can advise you of your rights and even provide a list of attorneys (for which you'll have to pay if services are used). But they cannot interfere on your behalf in the legal processes of Great Britain. For questions about American citizens who are arrested abroad, including ways of getting money to them, telephone the Citizens Emergency Center of the Office of Special Consulate Services in Washington, D.C. (☎ 202/647-5225).

Liquor Laws   The legal drinking age is 18. Children under 16 aren't allowed in pubs, except in certain rooms, and then only when accompanied by a parent or guardian. Don't drink and drive. Penalties are stiff.

In England, pubs can legally be open Monday through Saturday from 11am to 11pm and on Sunday from noon to 10:30pm. Restaurants are also allowed to serve liquor during these hours, but only to people who are dining on the premises. The law allows 30 minutes for "drinking-up time." A meal, incidentally, is defined as "substantial refreshment." And you have to eat and drink sitting down. In hotels, liquor may be served from 11am to 11pm to both residents and nonresidents; after 11pm, only residents, according to the law, may be served.

Lost Property   Report the loss to the nearest police station. For London information, see "Fast Facts: London," in Chapter 3.

Mail   Letters and parcels for you may, as a rule, be addressed to you at any post office except a town suboffice. The words *To Be Called For* or *Poste Restante* must appear in the address. When claiming your mail, always carry some sort of identification. Airmail letters generally take 7 to 10 days to arrive from the United States. Poste restante service is provided solely for the convenience of travelers, and it may not be used in the same town for more than 3 months. It can be redirected, upon request, for a 1-month period, or up to 3 months if so specified on the required application form. Post offices and sub–post offices are centrally located and open Monday through Friday from 9am to 5:30pm and Saturday from 9:30am to noon. Sending an airmail letter to North America costs 39p (60¢), and postcards require a 35p (55¢) stamp. British mailboxes are painted red and carry a royal coat of arms. All post offices accept parcels for mailing, provided they are properly and securely wrapped.

Newspapers   The *Times* is the newspaper of record. The *Telegraph* is white-collar oriented, the *Daily Mail* less so, and the *Guardian* intellectual-liberal. The *International Herald Tribune,* published in Paris, and an international edition of *USA Today* are available daily.

Pets   It is illegal to bring pets to Great Britain—except with veterinary documents, and then most are subject to a 6-month quarantine. Hotels have their own rules, but dogs are usually not allowed in restaurants or public rooms and often not in bedrooms.

Police   Dial 999 if the matter is serious. The British police have a helpful reputation and if the local police cannot help, they will know the address of the person who can. Losses, thefts, and other criminal matters should be reported to the police immediately.

Radio and TV   There are 24-hour radio channels operating throughout the U.K., with mostly pop music and talk shows during the night. TV starts around 6am with breakfast TV and educational programs. Lighter entertainment begins around 4 or 5pm, after the children's programs, and continues until around midnight. There are now four television channels—two commercial and two BBC without commercials.

Religious Services   Times of services are posted outside houses of worship. Almost every creed is catered to in London and other large cities, but in the smaller towns and villages you are likely to find only Anglican (Episcopalian), Roman Catholic, Baptist, and Nonconformist churches.

Restrooms   The signs usually read "Public Toilets." Hotel restrooms are only grudgingly available to nonresidents. Service stations ("garages") also have facilities for customers only, and the key is often kept by the cash register.

Safety   Stay in well-lit areas and out of questionable neighborhoods, especially at night. While Britain is a fairly safe country, every society has its criminals. In Britain, most of the crime perpetrated against tourists is pickpocketing and mugging. These attacks usually occur in such cities as London, Birmingham, or Manchester. Most villages are safe, but, as Miss Marple has proved to you, even that harmless-looking English village isn't that safe.

Shoe Repairs   Many of the large department stores in Britain have "heel bars" where repairs are done while you wait.

Taxes   To encourage energy conservation the British government levies a 25% tax on gasoline ("petrol"). There is also a 17.5% national Value-Added Tax (VAT) that is added to all hotel and restaurant bills, and will be included in the price of many items you purchase. This can be refunded if you shop at stores that participate in the Retail Export Scheme (signs are posted in the window). When you make a purchase, show your passport and request a Retail Export Scheme form (Form VAT 407) and a preaddressed, stamped envelope. Show the VAT form and your sales receipt to British customs when you leave the country. They may also ask to see the merchandise. After customs has stamped it, mail the form back to the shop *before you leave the country*. Your VAT refund will be mailed to you.

Here are three organizing tips to help you through the customs procedures: Keep VAT forms with your passport, pack your purchases in a carry-on bag so you'll have them handy, and allow yourself enough time at your departure point to find a mailbox.

Several readers have reported a scam regarding VAT refunds. The refund forms must be obtained from the retailer on the spot (don't leave the store without one). Some merchants allegedly tell customers they can get a refund form at the airport on their way out of the country. *This is not true.* The form must be completed by the retailer on the spot, or there will be no refund later.

In October 1994, Britain imposed a departure tax: either £5 ($7.90) for flights within Britain and the European Union or £10 ($15.80) for passengers flying elsewhere, including to the United States.

Telephone   British TeleCom is carrying out a massive improvement of its public-phone service. During the transitional period, you may encounter four types of pay phones: The old-style (gray) pay phone is being phased out, but there are many still in use. You will need 10p (15¢) coins to operate such phones; do not use them for overseas calls. They are being replaced by a blue-and-silver push-button model that accepts coins of any denomination. The other two types of phones require cards instead of coins to operate. The Cardphone takes distinctive green cards that are available in four values—£1 ($1.60), £2 ($3.15), £4 ($6.30), £10 ($15.80), and £20 ($31.60). The cards are reusable until the total value has been used up and can be purchased from news agencies and post offices. Finally, the credit-call pay phone operates on credit cards (AE, DC, MC, V) and is most common at airports and large railway stations.

Outside of major cities, phone numbers consist of an exchange code (like an area code) plus a local telephone number. To reach the number, you will need to dial both the exchange code and the number. The exchange codes are usually posted in the call box. If your code is not there, call the operator by dialing 100.

In major cities, phone numbers consist of the exchange code and the local number (seven digits or more). These local digits are all you need to dial if you are calling within the same city. If you're calling elsewhere, you'll also need to dial the exchange code for the city you're calling. Again, you can find these codes on the call box information sheets or by dialing the operator (100).

If you need directory assistance or "information," dial 142 for a number in London. For a number elsewhere in the country, dial 192 and then give the operator the name of the town and then the person's name and address.

To call London from the United States, dial the international code, 44 (Britain's country code), either 0171 or 0181 (London's area codes), and then the seven-digit local telephone number. To call outside London, dial the international code, 44, and then the exchange code and the local telephone number.

To make international calls from England, it's less expensive to dial them yourself from a post office or phone booth than from your hotel room. After you have inserted the coins, dial the international code, then the country code (for the U.S. the code is 1), which is followed by the area code and the local number.

If you're calling collect or need the assistance of an international operator, dial 155. *Caller beware*: some hotels routinely add surcharges of anywhere from 40% to 300% to local, national, and international phone calls made from your hotel room.

Telex and Fax   Both telex and fax are common in hotels and businesses but not elsewhere. If your hotel has telex or fax facilities, they will send a message for you, but you may have to arrange in advance to receive a reply. For telex bureaus, refer to the yellow pages. For information on faxes, dial 100 and ask for the Freefone Intelpost.

Time   England uses Greenwich Mean Time, 5 hours ahead of the U.S. East Coast. British summer time (GMT plus 1 hour) is in effect roughly from the end of March to the end of October.

Tipping   For cab drivers, add about 10% to 15% to the fare shown on the meter. However, if the driver personally loads or unloads your luggage, add 20p (30¢) per bag.

In hotels, porters receive 75p ($1.20) per bag, even if you have only one small suitcase. Hall porters are tipped only for special services. Maids receive £1 ($1.60) per day. In top-ranking hotels the concierge will often submit a separate bill showing charges for newspapers and other items; if he or she has been particularly helpful, tip extra.

Hotels often add a service charge of 10% to 15% to most bills. In smaller bed-and-breakfasts, the tip is not likely to be included. Therefore, tip for special services, such as the waiter who serves you breakfast. If several people have served you in a bed-and-breakfast, you may ask that 10% to 15% be added to the bill and divided among the staff.

In both restaurants and nightclubs, a 15% service charge is added to the bill. To that, add another 3% to 5%, depending on the quality of the service. Waiters in deluxe restaurants and nightclubs are accustomed to the extra 5%, which means you'll end up tipping 20%. If that seems excessive, you must remember that the initial service charge reflected in the fixed price is distributed among all the help. Sommeliers (wine stewards) get about £1 ($1.60) per bottle of wine served. Although tipping in pubs is not common, in cocktail bars the waiter or barmaid usually gets about 75p ($1.20) per round of drinks.

Barbers and hairdressers expect 10% to 15%. Tour guides expect £2 ($3.15), though it's not mandatory. Gas station attendants are rarely tipped. And theater ushers don't expect tips.

Weather   For London, call 0171/246-8091; for Devon and Cornwall, 01392/8091; for the Midlands, 0121/8091.

Yellow Pages   Local phone books have yellow pages at the back of the book. If you can't find what you're looking for, you may not be looking under the proper English equivalent. For example, instead of "drugstore," try "chemist" or "pharmacist."

3 Getting to Know London

Europe's largest city is like a great wheel, with Piccadilly Circus at the hub and dozens of communities branching out from it. Since London is such a conglomeration of sections—each having its own life, hotels, restaurants, and pubs—first-time visitors may be intimidated until they get the hang of it. Most visitors spend all their time in the West End, where most of the attractions are located, except for the historic part of London known as The City, which includes the Tower of London.

London is one of the cities you must visit in your lifetime. Stroll down its streets, patronize its pubs, and visit its world-renowned museums and landmark buildings. It may not be the most beautiful or romantic of the world's cities, but it's near the top of the list as one of the most fascinating.

This chapter will help you get your bearings. It provides a brief orientation and preview of the city's most important neighborhoods and answers questions you'll have about getting around London. It also presents "Fast Facts," a summary of useful information covering everything from babysitters to shoe repairs.

1 Orientation

ARRIVING
By Plane

London is served by four airports. The one you'll arrive at will depend on the airline you're flying and your point of departure.

HEATHROW AIRPORT Heathrow, west of London, in Hounslow (☎ 0181/759-4321), is one of the world's busiest airports. It is divided into four terminals, each of which is relatively self-contained. Terminal 4, the most modern, handles the long-haul and transatlantic operations of British Airways. Most transatlantic flights of U.S. airlines arrive at Terminals 1 or 3. Terminals 1 and 2 receive the intra-European flights of several European airlines.

Getting to Central London There is an Underground (subway) connection from Heathrow Central to the center of London; the trip takes 50 minutes and costs £3.10 ($4.90). There are also airbuses that will take you to central London in about an hour; they cost £6 ($9.50) for adults and £4 ($6.30) for children. A taxi is likely to cost at least £30 ($47.40).

GATWICK   This smaller and more remote airport (☎ 01293/535353 for flight information) lies 25 miles south of London, in West Sussex. Charter flights as well as many scheduled flights arrive here.

Getting to Central London   Trains leave for London every 15 minutes during the day and every hour at night; they cost £8.50 ($13.45) for adults and £4.25 ($6.70) for children under 15. There is also an express Flightline bus (no. 777) from Gatwick to Victoria Station that departs every half hour from 6:30am to 8pm and every hour from 8 to 11pm; it costs £7.50 ($11.85) per person. A taxi from Gatwick to central London usually costs £50 to £60 ($79 to $94.80); however, you must negotiate a fare with the driver before you get into the cab—the meter does not apply since Gatwick lies outside the Metropolitan Police District.

LONDON CITY AIRPORT   Located in the Royal Docklands, about 6 miles east of The City, this airport (☎ 0171/474-5555) is used mainly for STOL (short takeoff and landing) and commuter flights to and from the continent. Most of the passengers you'll see are businesspeople arriving from or leaving for the Common Market countries. Among the STOL and commuter airlines that use this terminal are: Air France; VLM, which has flights to Rotterdam; and London City Airways, which is associated with Sabena and has the Brussels routes.

Getting to Central London   There are three ways to reach the center of London. A blue-and-white bus charges £3 ($4.75) each way to take passengers from the airport to the Liverpool Street Station, where they can connect with rail or Underground transportation to almost any destination. The bus runs every 20 minutes Monday through Friday, and every 30 minutes Saturday and Sunday during the hours the airport is open (approximately 7am to 8:30pm). There's a shuttle bus to Canary Wharf, where trains from the Dockland Line Railway make frequent 10-minute runs to the heart of London's financial district, The City. There, passengers can catch an Underground from the Bank tube stop. London Transport bus no. 473 goes from the City Airport to East London. There, passengers can board any Underground at the Plaistow tube stop.

LONDON STANSTED AIRPORT   Located about 30 miles northeast of the center of London, Stansted—the city's newest airport (☎ 01279/680-500)—often receives flights from the continent.

Getting to Central London   Your best bet is the Stansted Express, a train that will take you from the airport to Liverpool Street Station in just 45 minutes. Tickets cost £10 ($15.80) for adults and £5 ($7.90) for children. Train service is Monday through Friday from 5:30am to 11pm, Saturday from 6:30am to 11pm, and Sunday from 7am to 11pm.

BY TRAIN

Most trains originating in Paris and traveling through the Chunnel arrive at **Waterloo Station.** Visitors from Amsterdam arrive at the **Liverpool Street Station,** and those journeying south by rail from Edinburgh arrive at **King's Cross Station.** Each of these stations is connected to London's vast bus and Underground network, and each has phones, restaurants, pubs, luggage-storage areas, and London Regional Transport Information Centres.

BY CAR

If you're taking a car ferry across the channel, you can quickly connect with a motorway into London. *Remember to drive on the left.* London is encircled by a ring road. Determine which part of the city you wish to enter and follow the signs there. You should confine your driving in London to the *bare minimum*, which means that after you arrive, you need to find a place to park your car during your visit.

Parking is scarce and expensive. Before you arrive in London, call your hotel and inquire if it has a garage (and what the charges are), or else ask the staff for the name and address of a garage close to the hotel.

VISITOR INFORMATION

The British Travel Centre, Rex House, 4–12 Lower Regent St., London SW1 4PQ (tube: Piccadilly Circus), caters to walk-in visitors who arrive to obtain information on all parts of Britain. Telephone information has been suspended—you must come in personally and wait in line. It's often a long wait. On the premises you'll find a British Rail ticket office, a travel agency, a theater-ticket agency, a hotel-booking service, a bookshop, and a souvenir shop—all in one well-equipped and very modern facility. Hours are Monday through Friday from 9am to 6:30pm, Saturday and Sunday from 10am to 4pm, with extended hours on Saturday from June through September.

Equally useful is the London Tourist Board's Tourist Information Centre, forecourt of Victoria Station, SW1 (tube: Victoria), which can help you with almost anything. Staffed by courteous and patient people, the center deals with accommodations in all size and price categories and can handle the whole spectrum of travelers, from singles, students, and family groups to large-scale conventions. It also arranges for travel, tour-ticket sales, and theater reservations, and it has a shop that offers a wide selection of books and souvenirs. The center is open for personal callers at the following times: between Easter and October, daily from 8am to 7pm; November to Easter, Monday to Saturday from 8am to 6pm, Sunday from 9am to 4pm.

The tourist board maintains three other offices: in the basement of one of London's largest department stores, Selfridges, Oxford Street, W1 (tube: Bond Street), open during store hours; at Heathrow Airport's terminals 1, 2, and 3, Underground Concourse; and at the Liverpool Street Railway Station.

The tourist board has a 24-hour recorded information service, "Visitorcall" (☎ 01839/123456), which, for fees of 39p (60¢) or 49p (75¢) per minute (depending on when you call), will play a recorded message about tourist attractions that change every day. The 39p rate is in effect Monday through Friday from 6pm to 8am and Saturday and Sunday all day; at other times the charge is 49p.

For a full information pack on London, write to the London Tourist Board, P.O. Box 151, London E15 2HF.

CITY LAYOUT
Main Districts, Squares & Streets

Fortunately, there is an immense difference between the sprawling vastness of Greater London and the pocket north of the River Thames that might be called "Tourist Territory."

Our London begins at **Chelsea,** on the north bank of the river, and stretches for roughly 5 miles north to **Hampstead.** Its western boundary runs through Kensington, while the eastern boundary lies 5 miles away, at Tower Bridge. Inside this 5-by-5-mile square, you'll find all the hotels and restaurants and nearly all the sights that are usually of interest to visitors.

Make no mistake: This is still a hefty portion of land to cover, and a really thorough exploration of it would take a couple of years. But it has the advantage of being flat and eminently walkable, besides boasting one of the best public transport systems ever devised.

The logical (though not geographical) center of this area is **Trafalgar Square,** which we'll take as our orientation point. Stand there facing the steps of the imposing National Gallery. You're looking northwest. That is the direction of **Piccadilly Circus**—the real core of tourist London—and the maze of streets that make up **Soho.** Farther north runs **Oxford Street,** London's gift to moderately priced shopping, and still farther northwest lies Regent's Park and the zoo.

At your back—that is, south—runs **Whitehall,** which houses or skirts nearly every British government building, from the Ministry of Defence to the official residence of the prime minister, at **10 Downing Street.** In the same direction, a bit farther south, stand the Houses of Parliament and Westminster Abbey.

Flowing southwest from Trafalgar Square is the table-smooth **Mall,** flanked by parks and mansions and leading to Buckingham Palace, the queen's residence. Farther along in the same direction lie **Belgravia** and **Knightsbridge,** the city's plushest residential areas, and south of them lies **Chelsea,** with its chic flavor, plus **King's Road,** principally a boulevard for shopping.

Due west stretches the superb and distinctly high-priced shopping area bordered by **Regent Street** and **Piccadilly Street** (as distinct from the Circus). Farther west lie the equally elegant shops and even more elegant homes of **Mayfair.** Then comes **Park Lane.** On the other side of Park Lane is **Hyde Park,** the biggest park in London and one of the largest in the world.

Charing Cross Road runs north from Trafalgar Square, past **Leicester Square,** and intersects with **Shaftesbury Avenue.** This is London's theater land. A bit farther along, Charing Cross Road turns into a browser's paradise, lined with shops selling new and secondhand books. At last it funnels into **St. Giles Circus.** This is where you enter **Bloomsbury,** site of the University of London, the British Museum, and erstwhile stamping ground of the famed "Bloomsbury group," led by Virginia Woolf.

Northeast of your position lies **Covent Garden,** known for its Royal Opera House and today a major shopping, restaurant, and café district.

Follow **The Strand** eastward from Trafalgar Square and you'll come to **Fleet Street.** Beginning in the 19th century, this corner of London became the most concentrated newspaper district in the world. **Temple Bar** stands where The Strand becomes Fleet Street, and only here do you enter the actual City of London, or "The City." Its focal point and shrine is the Bank of England on **Threadneedle Street,** with the Stock Exchange next door and the Royal Exchange across the street. In the midst of all the hustle and bustle rises **St. Paul's Cathedral,** Sir Christopher Wren's monument to beauty and tranquillity.

At the far eastern fringe of the City looms the **Tower of London,** shrouded in legend, blood, and history and permanently besieged by battalions of visitors.

And this, as far as we can go into it here, concludes the London circle.

FINDING AN ADDRESS London's streets follow no pattern whatsoever, and both their naming and house numbering seem to have been perpetrated by a group of xenophobes with a grudge against foreigners and postal carriers. Don't think, for instance, that Southampton Row is anywhere near Southampton Street or that either of these places has any connection with Southampton Road.

London at a Glance

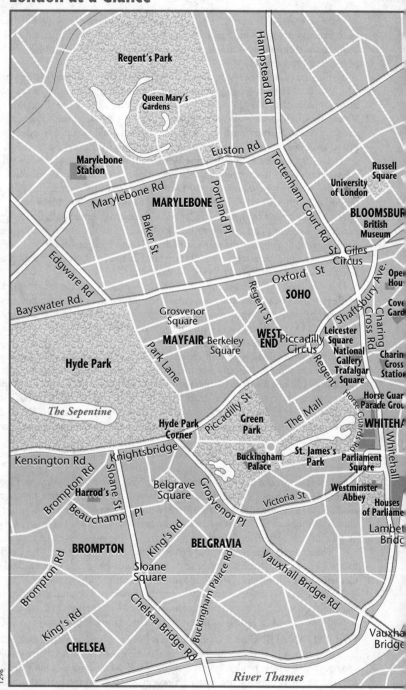

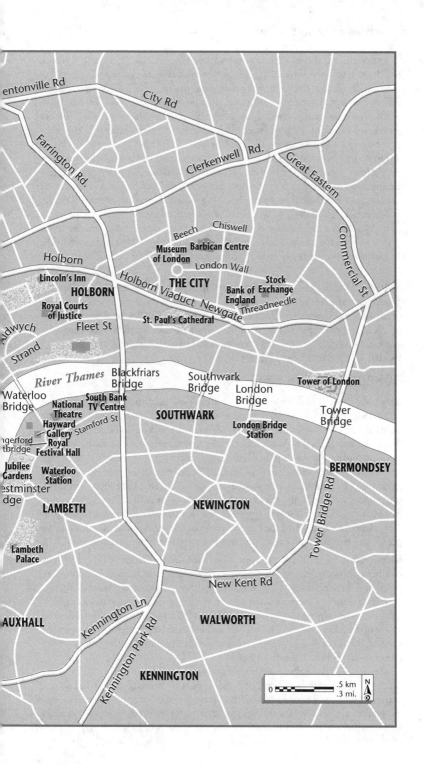

London is checkered with innumerable squares, mews, closes, and terraces, which jut into or cross, overlap, or interrupt whatever street you're trying to follow, usually without the slightest warning. You may be walking along ruler-straight Albany Street and suddenly find yourself flanked by Cumberland Terrace (with a different numbering system). Just keep walking, and after a couple of blocks you're right back on Albany Street (and the original house numbers), but without the faintest idea why the sudden labels have changed.

House numbers run in odds and evens, clockwise and counterclockwise, as the wind blows. *That is, when they exist at all, and frequently they don't.* Many establishments in London, such as the Four Seasons Hotel and Langan's Brasserie, *do not use house numbers,* though a building right next door is numbered. Happily, Londoners are generally glad to assist a bewildered visitor.

Every so often you'll come upon a square that is called a *square* on the south side, a *road* on the north, a *park* on the east, and possibly a *close* on the west side. In this case, it would be advisable to consult a map or ask for directions as you go along.

STREET MAPS   If you're going to explore London in any depth, you'll need a good, detailed street map with an index—not one of those superficial overviews given away free at tourist offices and at many hotels. The best ones are published by *Falk,* and they're available at most newsstands and nearly all bookstores. If you can't find one, go to W.& G. Foyle, Ltd., 113–119 Charing Cross Rd., WC2 (☎ 0171/439-8501; tube: Leicester Square).

NEIGHBORHOODS IN BRIEF

Belgravia   South of Knightsbridge, this has long been the aristocratic quarter of London, rivaling Mayfair in grandness and richness. Although it reached the pinnacle of its prestige during the reign of Queen Victoria, it is still a chic address: The duke and duchess of Westminster, among England's richest citizens, still live at Eaton Square—not in a palace but in an upper-story apartment. Once an area for "duels at dawn" and sheep grazing, Belgravia eventually marked the westward expansion of London. Its centerpiece is Belgrave Square (1825–35). When the townhouses were built, the aristocrats followed—the duke of Connaught, the earl of Essex, even Queen Victoria's mother, the duchess of Kent. On a vacation in 1837, Chopin wrote, "And the English! And the houses! And the palaces! And the pomp, and the carriages! Everything from soap to the razors is extraordinary."

Bloomsbury   This district, a world unto itself, lies northeast of Piccadilly Circus, beyond Soho. Among other things, it is the academic heart of London; here you'll find the University of London, several other colleges, and many bookstores. Despite its student overtones, the section is fairly staid. Its reputation has been fanned by such writers as Virginia Woolf, who lived within its bounds (it figured in her novel *Jacob's Room*). The novelist and her husband, Leonard, were once the unofficial leaders of a group of artists and writers known as the "Bloomsbury group"—nicknamed "Bloomsberries."

The heart of Bloomsbury is Russell Square, and the streets jutting off from the square are lined with hotels and bed-and-breakfasts. Russell Square was laid out between 1800 and 1814, and William Makepeace Thackeray made it the stamping ground of the Osbornes and Sedleys in his novel *Vanity Fair.* Most visitors go to Bloomsbury to see the British Museum, one of the world's greatest repositories of treasures—everything from the Rosetta stone to the Elgin marbles.

Chelsea   A stylish district stretching along the Thames, Chelsea lies south of Belgravia. It begins at Sloane Square, where Gilbert Ledward's Venus fountain plays watery music if the traffic noise doesn't drown it out. Flower sellers hustle their flamboyant blooms here year round. The area has always been a favorite of writers and artists, including Oscar Wilde (who was arrested here), George Eliot, James Whistler, J.M.W. Turner, Henry James, Augustus John, and Thomas Carlyle (whose former home can be visited). Mick Jagger and Margaret Thatcher (not together) have been among recent residents, and Princess Diana and her Sloane Rangers of the 1980s gave it even more fame.

Its major boulevard is King's Road, where Mary Quant launched the miniskirt in the 1960s and the Rolling Stones once lived. It was here that the English punk look began. King's Road runs the entire length of Chelsea, and the best time to visit is on a Saturday, when it's at its liveliest. Originally, the route was the royal carriage route Charles II took to Hampton Court. The hip-hop of King's Road is not typical of upscale Chelsea, which is filled with townhouses and little mews dwellings that only the rich or very successful London professionals can afford. Real estate prices are astronomical.

The City   When the English speak of "The City," they don't mean London. The City is the British equivalent of Wall Street, and the buildings in this district are known all over the world: the Bank of England (on Threadneedle Street); the London Stock Exchange; and the financially troubled Lloyd's of London. This was Londinium, as the Roman conquerors called it in A.D. 43. Landmarks include St. Paul's Cathedral, Christopher Wren's masterpiece, which withstood the London blitz. Some 2,000 years of history unfold at the Museum of London and the Barbican Centre, opened by Queen Elizabeth in 1982 and hailed by her as a "wonder" of the cultural world. At the Guildhall, the first lord mayor of London was installed in 1192.

Covent Garden   The flower, fruit, and "veg" market is long gone (since 1970), but memories of Professor Higgins and his "squashed cabbage leaf," Eliza Doolittle, linger on. Even without the market, Covent Garden is still associated with food, since it accommodates the liveliest group of restaurants, pubs, and cafés in London—outside of Soho. The tradition of food dates from the time when the monks of Westminster Abbey dumped their surplus homegrown vegetables here. In 1670 Charles II granted the earl of Bedford the right to "sell roots and herbs, whatsoever" in the district. The king's mistress, Nell Gwyn, once peddled oranges on Drury Lane. The restored marketplace, with its glass and iron roofs, has been called a "magnificent example of urban recycling." It's not all about food. Inigo Jones built St. Paul's Covent Garden between 1631 and 1633. Jones's "handsomest barn in Europe" was rebuilt after a fire in 1795 and it still attracts actors and artists—everybody from Ellen Terry to Vivien Leigh. The Theatre Royal, Drury Lane was where Nell Gwyn made her debut in 1665, and the Irish actress Dorothea Jordan first caught the eye of the duke of Clarence, later William IV.

The East End   Traditionally one of London's poorest districts, it was nearly bombed out of existence by the Nazis. Hitler, in the words of one commentator at the time, created "instant urban renewal." It is the home of the cockney, surely one of London's most colorful characters. To be a true cockney, one presumably must have been born "within the sound of the Bow Bells," a reference to St. Mary-le-Bow, the church rebuilt by Sir Christopher Wren in 1670. Many immigrants to London have found a home here.

The East End extends eastward from the City walls, encompassing Stepney, Bow, Poplar, West Ham, Canning Town, and other districts. The East End has always been filled with legend and lore. The area beyond the East End, the Docklands, has been called "an emerging third city of London," filled with offices, Thames-side "flats," museums, entertainment complexes, sports centers, shopping malls, and an ever-growing list of restaurants.

Holborn   The old borough of Holborn takes in the heart of legal London—home of the city's barristers, solicitors, and law clerks. Still Dickensian in spirit, the area lets you follow in the Victorian author's footsteps, passing the two Inns of Court and arriving at Bleeding Heart Yard of *Little Dorritt* fame. A 14-year-old Dickens was once employed as a solicitor's clerk at Lincoln's Inn. Old Bailey has stood for English justice down through the years (Fagin went to the gallows from this site in *Oliver Twist*), and everything here seems steeped in history. Even as you're quenching your thirst with a half pint of bitter at the Viaduct Tavern, 126 Newgate St. (tube: St. Paul's), you learn the pub was built over the notorious Newgate Prison (which specialized in death by pressing) and was named after the Holborn Viaduct, the world's first overpass.

Kensington   The Royal Borough lies west of Kensington Gardens and Hyde Park and is traversed by two of London's major shopping streets, Kensington High Street and Kensington Church Street. Since 1689 when asthmatic William III fled Whitehall Palace for Nottingham House (where the air was fresher), the district has enjoyed royal associations. In time Nottingham House became Kensington Palace, and the royals grabbed a chunk of Hyde Park to plant their roses. Queen Victoria was born here. "KP," as the royals say, is still home to Princess Margaret (20 rooms with a view), Prince and Princess Michael of Kent, and the duke and duchess of Gloucester. At the moment the Princess of Wales and her two little princes also reside at Kensington Palace. The Queen permits all these royals to live there free, but insists they pay their own phone, heat, and electricity.

Kensington Gardens has been open to the public ever since George II decreed that "respectably dressed" people would be permitted in on Saturday—provided that servants, soldiers, and sailors were excluded. Kensington Square developed in the footsteps of William III, attracting artists and writers. In time, a maid decided to use Thomas Carlyle's manuscript *The French Revolution* to light a fire, and he had to write it again. Thackeray lived here from 1846 to 1853, during which time he wrote *Vanity Fair*. Over the years Kensington High Street became a Mecca for rich shoppers.

Knightsbridge   One of London's most fashionable neighborhoods, Knightsbridge is a top residential and shopping district, just south of Hyde Park. Harrods, on Brompton Road, is its chief attraction. Founded in 1901, it's been called "the Notre Dame of department stores"—it sells everything from the Rayne pumps preferred by the queen to a Baccharat crystal table valued at £1 million. There's even a department that will arrange your burial. Nearby, Beauchamp Place (pronounced *Beech*-am) is one of London's most fashionable shopping streets, a Regency-era boutique-lined little street with a scattering of restaurants such as San Lorenzo, frequented by Princess Diana and those who'd like to see her. Shops include Bruce Oldfield, at 27 Beauchamp Place, where Princess Diana and even Joan Collins have purchased evening dresses. And, at the end of a shopping day, if Harrods's five restaurants and five bars haven't tempted you, retreat to

Bill Bentley's, at 31 Beauchamp Place, for a dozen oysters washed down with a few glasses of muscatel.

Mayfair Bounded by Piccadilly, Hyde Park, and Oxford and Regent Streets, this is considered the most elegant, fashionable section of London. Luxury hotels exist side by side with Georgian townhouses and swank shops. Grosvenor Square (pronounced *Grov*-nor) is nicknamed "Little America," because it is home to the American Embassy and a statue of Franklin D. Roosevelt. Berkeley (pronounced *Bark*-ley) is home to the English Speaking Union. At least once you'll want to dip into this exclusive section, or perhaps visit Carnaby Street, a block from Regent Street, if you want to remember London from the Swinging '60s. One of the curiosities of Mayfair is Shepherd Market, a tiny village of pubs, two-story inns, book and food stalls, and restaurants—all sandwiched between Mayfair's greatness.

Paddington/Bayswater The Paddington section centers on Paddington Station, north of Kensington Gardens and Hyde Park. It's one of the major centers in London, attracting budget travelers who fill up the bed-and-breakfasts at such places as Sussex Gardens and Norfolk Square. After the first railway was introduced to London, in 1836, it was followed by a circle of sprawling railway terminals, including Paddington Station in 1838. That marked the growth of this somewhat middle-class and prosperous area, now blighted in parts. Just south of Paddington is Bayswater, a sort of unofficial area also filled with a large number of bed-and-breakfasts that attract budget travelers. As London moved west, the area north of Hyde Park known as Tyburnia eventually developed into Bayswater. Inspired by St. Marylebone and elegant Mayfair, terrace houses and spacious squares became home to a relatively prosperous set of Victorians from the mercantile class.

Piccadilly This is the very heart and soul of London, with Piccadilly Circus and its statue of Eros being the virtual gaudy "living room" of London. The circus isn't New York's Times Square yet, but its traffic, neon, and jostling crowds don't do anything to make it fashionable. "Circus" might be an apt word. The Piccadilly thoroughfare was always known as "the magic mile." Traditionally the western road out of town, it was named for the "piccadill," a ruffled collar created by Robert Baker, a tailor in the 1600s. He built a mansion called Piccadilly Hall, and the name is still used today. If you want a little more grandeur, retreat to the Regency promenade of exclusive shops, the Burlington Arcade, designed in 1819. The English gentry—tired of being mud-splashed by horses and carriages along Piccadilly—came here to do their shopping. Some 35 shops, a treasure-trove of goodies, await you. Or make your way to Fortnum and Mason, 181 Piccadilly, the world's most luxurious grocery store, established in 1788. The store sent hams to the duke of Wellington's army, baskets of "tinned" goodies to Florence Nightingale in the Crimea, and packed a "picnic basket" for Stanley when he went looking for Livingstone.

St. James's is often called "Royal London," basking in its association with everybody from the "merrie monarch" Charles II to Elizabeth II, who lives at its most fabled address, Buckingham Palace. Beginning at Piccadilly Circus and moving southwest, it's "frightfully convenient," as the English say. You'll find the American Express office there, on Haymarket, as well as many of London's leading department stores. In this bastion of aristocracy and royalty, a certain pomp still prevails—gentlemen still go to private clubs, and English tradition never dies. The district evokes memories of such figures as Oscar Wilde, George Meredith, and Edward VII.

St. Marylebone   An area that enjoyed famous associations with the likes of Turner and Elizabeth Barrett (waiting for the return of Robert Browning), St. Marylebone lies south of Regent's Park and north of Oxford Street. Many first-time visitors head here to explore Madame Tussaud's waxworks or to walk along Baker Street in the footsteps of Sherlock Holmes. Just north of the district, at Regent's Park, you can visit Queen Mary's Gardens or, in summer, see Shakespeare performed in an open-air theater. Between 1776 and 1780, Robert Adam laid out Portland Place, one of the most characteristic squares; and it was at Cavendish Square that Mrs. Horatio Nelson waited—often in vain—for the return of the admiral. Marylebone Lane and High Street still retain some of their former village atmosphere. Dickens (who seems to have lived everywhere) wrote nearly a dozen books when he resided in St. Marylebone.

Soho   This district is, in a sense, a Jekyll-and-Hyde quarter. In the daytime, it's a paradise for the searcher of spices, continental foods, fruits, fish, and sausages and has at least two street markets offering fruits and vegetables. But at night, it's a dazzle of strip joints, gay clubs, porno movies, and sex emporiums, all intermingled with international restaurants that offer good values. In fact, this section of criss-crossed narrow lanes and crooked streets is the site of many of the city's best foreign restaurants, and Gerrard Street has succeeded in becoming London's first Chinatown.

Soho starts at Piccadilly Circus and spreads out, ending at Oxford Street. One side borders the theater district, on Shaftesbury Avenue. From Piccadilly Circus, walk northeast and you'll come to Soho, to the left of Shaftesbury. This jumbled section can also be approached from the Tottenham Court Road tube station: Walk south along Charing Cross Road and Soho will be to your right.

South Kensington   Lying southeast of Kensington Gardens and Earl's Court, South Kensington is primarily residential and is often called "museumland" because of the many museums located there. They include the Natural History Museum, once part of the British Museum, which has everything from dinosaurs to specimens of Charles Darwin's historic voyage on the HMS *Beagle*. One of the district's chief curiosities is the extravagant Albert Memorial, completed in 1872 by Sir George Gilbert Scott. For sheer excess, the Victorian monument is unequaled in the world.

The Strand and Fleet Street   Beginning at Trafalgar Square, The Strand runs east into Fleet Street and is flanked by theaters, shops, hotels, and restaurants. Ye Olde Cheshire Cheese, serving "ye olde" roast beef; Dr. Johnson's House; Twinings English tea (which the queen herself prefers for her "cuppa")—all these evoke memories of the rich heyday of this district. The Strand runs parallel to the River Thames, and to walk it would be to follow in the footsteps of Charles Lamb, Mark Twain, Henry Fielding, James Boswell, William Thackeray, and Sir Walter Raleigh. The Savoy Theater helped make Gilbert and Sullivan household names. Henry James called The Strand "a tremendous chapter of accidents." Fleet Street has long been London's journalistic hub, and well it should be. William Caxton printed the first book in English here. *The Daily Consort*, the first daily newspaper printed in England, was launched at Ludgate Circus in 1702.

Westminster/Whitehall   Dominated by the Houses of Parliament and Westminster Abbey, this has been the seat of the British government since the days of Edward the Confessor. Even if that power isn't what it used to be, the House of Commons and the House of Lords go about running what's left of the empire. Trafalgar Square, one of the major landmarks, remains a testament to Nelson's naval victory over the French (he died in the moment of his triumph), and the paintings in its landmark National Gallery will restore your soul.

Originally the home of Cardinal Thomas Wolsey, Whitehall was a royal residence for some 160 years—everybody from Henry VIII to James II called it home. It's more of a street today; combined with Parliament Street, it joins Trafalgar Square with Parliament Square. In the district you can visit Churchill's War Rooms and walk down Downing Street to see No. 10, the world's most famous street address. One of its longest tenured occupants, Margaret Thatcher, was Britain's first woman prime minister. No visit would be complete without a call at Westminster Abbey, one of the greatest gothic churches in the world. It has witnessed a panorama of English history, beginning with the coronation of William the Conqueror there on Christmas Day, 1066.

The City of Westminster also encompasses Victoria, an area that takes its unofficial name from bustling Victoria Station, known as "the gateway to the continent."

2 Getting Around

BY PUBLIC TRANSPORTATION

If you know the ropes, transportation within London can be unusually easy and inexpensive. Both the Underground (subway) and bus systems are operated by London Transport—with Travel Information Centres in the Underground stations at King's Cross, Hammersmith, Oxford Circus, St. James's Park, Liverpool Street Station, and Piccadilly Circus, as well as in the British Rail stations at Euston and Victoria and in each of the terminals at Heathrow Airport. They take reservations for London Transport's guided tours and have free Underground and bus maps and other information. A **24-hour telephone information** service is available by calling 0171/222-1234.

London Transport, Travel Information Service, 55 Broadway, London SW1H 0BD, also offers **Travelcards** for use on the bus, Underground, and British Rail service inside Greater London. Available in a number of combinations for adjacent zones, Travelcards can be purchased for periods of from 7 days to a year. A Travelcard allowing travel in two zones for 1 week costs £13.80 ($21.80) for adults and £4.50 ($7.10) for children.

To purchase a Travelcard, you must present a Photocard. If you're 16 years old or older, bring along a passport-type picture of yourself when you buy your Travelcard and the Photocard will be issued free. Child-rate Photocards for Travelcards are issued only at Underground ticket offices or Travel Information Centres; in addition to a passport-type photograph, proof of age is required (a passport or birth certificate, for example). Teenagers (14 or 15) are charged adult fares on all services unless they have one of the cards.

For shorter stays in London, you may want to consider the **One-Day Off-Peak Travelcard.** This Travelcard can be used on most bus, Underground, and British Rail services throughout Greater London Monday through Friday after 9:30am and at any time on weekends and bank holidays. The Travelcard is available at Underground ticket offices, Travel Information Centres, and some newsstands. For two zones, the cost is £2.80 ($4.40) for adults and £1.50 ($2.35) for children aged 5 to 15. Children 4 and under go free.

The **Visitor Travelcard,** allowing unlimited travel on almost the entire London Underground and bus system for up to 7 days, can be purchased in North America (but not in London). Contact a British Tourist Authority office. A 3-day card costs $25 for those 16 and older; $11 for ages 5 through 15. A 4-day card costs $32 for those 16 and older and $13 for children 5 through 15. Finally, a 7-day card costs $49 for those 16 and over and $21 for children 5 through 15. Children 4 and under ride for free.

UNDERGROUND (SUBWAY)

Known locally as "the tube," this is the fastest and easiest (though not the most interesting) way to get from place to place. The tube holds a special place in the hearts of Londoners: During the Blitz thousands of people used it as an air-raid shelter, camping there all night in reasonable safety from the bombs.

All Underground stations are clearly marked with a red circle and blue cross-bar. You descend by stairways, escalators, or huge elevators, depending on the depth. Some Underground stations have complete subterranean shopping arcades and several boast high-tech gadgets, such as push-button information machines.

You pick your station on the large diagram displayed on the wall, which has an alphabetical index to make it easy. You note the color of the line it happens to be on (Bakerloo is brown, Central is red, and so on). By following the colored band, you can see at a glance where—or whether—you'll have to change and how many stops there are to your destination.

If you have British coins, you can get your ticket at one of the vending machines. Otherwise, buy it at the ticket office. You can transfer as many times as you like as long as you stay in the Underground. The flat fare for one trip within the central zone is £1 ($1.60). Trips from the central zone to destinations in the suburbs range from £1 to £4 ($1.60 to $6.30) in most cases.

Note: Be sure to keep your ticket; it must be presented when you get off. If you're caught without a valid ticket, you'll be fined £10 ($15.80) on the spot. If you owe extra money, you'll be asked to pay the difference by the attendant. And if you're out on the town and dependent on the Underground, watch your time carefully; many trains stop running at midnight (11:30pm on Sunday).

BUS

The first thing you learn about London buses is that nobody just gets on them. You "queue up"—that is, form a single-file line at the bus stop. The English do it instinctively, even when there are only two of them. It's one of their eccentricities, and you will grow to appreciate it during rush hour.

The comparably priced bus system is almost as good as the Underground, and you'll have a better view. To find out about current routes, pick up a free bus map at one of London Regional Transport's Travel Information Centres listed above. The map is available only to those who stop by in person; it is not available by mail.

London still has some of the old-style Routemaster buses, with both a driver and conductor. Once you're on the bus, a conductor will pass by your seat. You tell him or her your destination and pay the fare, receiving a ticket in return. This type of bus is being phased out. Newer buses have only a driver. Pay the driver as you enter; later, exit through one of the rear doors. As with the Underground, the fares vary according to the distance traveled. Generally, the cost is 50p to £1.70 (80¢ to $2.70)—less than tube fares. If you travel for two or three stops, the cost is

London Underground

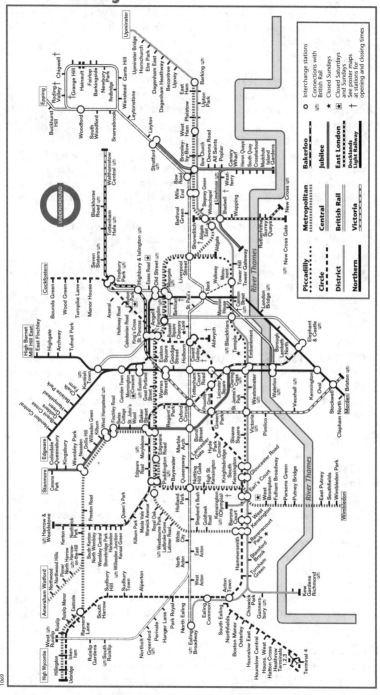

1069

60p (95¢); longer runs within zone 1 cost 80p ($1.25). If you want to be warned when to get off, simply ask the conductor. Call a 24-hour hotline (0171/222-1234) for schedules and fares.

BY TAXI

London cabs are among the best-designed taxis in the world. You can pick one up from a cab station or hail one on the street; if the yellow light on the roof is on, the taxi is free. For a radio cab, you can phone 0171/272-0272 or 0171/253-5000.

FARES   The minimum fare is £1.20 ($1.90) for the first third of a mile or 1 minute and 51 seconds, with increments of 20p (30¢) thereafter, based on distance or time. Each additional passenger is charged 30p (50¢). Passengers pay 10p (15¢) for each piece of luggage in the driver's compartment and any other item more than 2 feet long. Surcharges are imposed after 8pm and on weekends and public holidays. All these tariffs include VAT. Fares usually increase annually. It's recommended that you tip 10% to 15% of the fare.

Warning: If you phone for a cab, the meter starts running when the taxi receives instructions from the dispatcher. So you could find £1 ($1.60) or more already on the meter when you step inside.

Cab Sharing   Permitted in London, cab sharing allows cabbies to offer rides for two to five people. The taxis accepting such riders display a sign on yellow plastic with the words SHARED TAXI. Each of two sharing riders is charged 65% of the fare a lone passenger would be charged. Three people pay 55%, four pay 45%, and five (the seating capacity of all new London cabs) pay 40% of the single-passenger fare.

COMPLAINTS/LOST & FOUND   If you have a complaint about your taxi service, or if you leave something in a cab, phone the **Public Carriage Office,** 15 Penton St., N1 9PU (☎ 0171/230-1631 for complaints; 0171/833-0996 for lost property; tube: Angel Station). To file a complaint, you must have the cab number, which is displayed in the passenger compartment.

BY CAR

See "By Car" in "Getting Around," in Chapter 2, for information on car rentals, a description of driving rules and requirements, and information on gasoline, road maps, and breakdowns.

PARKING   Driving around London is a tricky business. The city is a warren of one-way streets, and parking spots are at a premium. Besides strategically placed, expensive garages, central London also offers metered parking. But be aware that traffic wardens are famous for issuing substantial fines when the meter runs out. The time limit and the cost of metered parking are posted on the meter. Zones marked "Permit Holders Only" are for local residents. If you violate these sacrosanct places, your vehicle is likely to be towed away. A yellow line along the curb indicates "No Parking." A double yellow line signifies "No Waiting." However, at night—meters indicate exact times—and on Sunday, you're allowed to park along a curb with a single yellow line.

BY BICYCLE

You can rent bikes by the day or the week from a number of shops. One of the most popular is On Your Bike, 52–54 Tooley St., London Bridge, SE1 (☎ 0171/ 378-6669; tube: London Bridge). It is open Monday through Friday from 9am to 6pm, on Saturday from 9:30am to 5:30pm. The staff has an inventory of around 60 bikes for men and women. The 10-speed sports bikes, with high seats and low-slung handlebars, are the most popular. They cost £8 ($12.65) per day or £25 ($39.50) per week and require a £50 ($79) deposit. Also popular are the 18-gear mountain bikes, with straight handlebars and oversize gears; designed for rough terrain, they are preferred by many clients for their maneuverability on the roads of "backstreet London." They cost £14 ($22.10) a day or £55 ($86.90) per week and require a deposit of £200 ($316). Deposits are payable by MasterCard or VISA.

ON FOOT

London is too vast and sprawling to explore totally on foot, but if you use public transportation for the long distances and your feet for the narrow crooked lanes, you should do just fine. Remember that cars drive on the left. Always look both ways before stepping off a curb. Vehicles have the right-of-way in London over pedestrians.

FAST FACTS: London

American Express   The main office is at 6 Haymarket, SW1 (☎ 0171/930-4411; tube: Piccadilly Circus). Full services are available Monday through Friday from 9am to 5:30pm and on Saturday from 9am to 4pm. At other times—Saturday from 9am to 6pm and Sunday from 9am to 4pm—only the foreign-exchange bureau is open.

Area Code   London has two area codes—0171 and 0181. The 0171 area code is for central London within a 4-mile radius of Charing Cross (including the City of London, Knightsbridge and Oxford Street, and as far south as Brixton). The 0181 area code is for outer London (including Heathrow Airport, Wimbledon, and Greenwich). Within London, you will need to dial the area code when calling from one of these sections of the city to the other, but not within a section.

Babysitters   Sometimes you can get your hotel to recommend someone, but there are also a number of organizations advertised in the yellow pages that provide registered nurses and carefully screened mothers—as well as trained nannies—as sitters. One such company is Childminders, 9 Paddington St., London W1M 3LA (☎ 0171/935-9763; tube: Baker Street). You pay £4.40 ($6.95) per hour in the daytime and £3.15 to £4.05 ($5 to $6.40) per hour at night. There is a 4-hour minimum, and hotel guests pay a £5 ($7.90) booking fee each time they use a sitter. Universal Aunts, P.O. Box 304, London SW4 0NN (☎ 0171/738-8937), established in 1921, provides child care, mother's helpers, proxy parents, and nannies. Interviews can be arranged in the Clapham or Fulham-Chelsea area. You must call first for an appointment or a booking; details will be supplied over the phone.

Business Hours   Banks are usually open Monday through Friday from 9:30am to 3:30pm. Business offices are open Monday through Friday from 9am to 5pm; the lunch break lasts an hour, but most places stay open during that time. Pubs and bars are allowed to stay open Monday through Saturday from 11am to 11pm, and on Sunday from noon to 10:30pm. Many pubs observe these extended Sunday hours; others prefer to close during the late afternoon (3 to 7pm).

London stores are generally open from 9am to 5:30pm, staying open until 7pm on Wednesday or Thursday. Most central shops close on Saturday around 1pm. However, they do not close for lunch earlier.

Car Rentals See "Getting Around," in Chapter 2.

Currency See "Visitor Information & Entry Requirements" in Chapter 2.

Currency Exchange In general, banks in London provide the best exchange rates, and you're likely to get a better rate for traveler's checks than for cash. At London's airports, there are branch offices of the main banks, but these charge a small fee. There are also bureaux de change at the airports, with offices around London; they charge a fee for cashing traveler's checks and personal U.K. checks and for changing foreign currency into pounds sterling. Some travel agencies, such as American Express and Thomas Cook, also have currency-exchange services.

Dentists For dental emergencies, call Emergency Dental Service (☎ 0171/677-8383), available 24 hours a day.

Doctors In an emergency, contact Doctor's Call (☎ 0181/900-1000). Some hotels also have doctors on call. Medical Express, 117A Harley St., W1 (☎ 0171/499-1991; tube: Regent's Park), is a private British clinic; it's not part of the free British medical establishment. For filling the British equivalent of a U.S. prescription, there is sometimes a surcharge of £20 ($31.60) in addition to the cost of the medication; a British doctor must validate the U.S. prescription. In cases where there is a British equivalent of a mixture, and a chemist does not have to prepare a special medication, there is usually no surcharge. The clinic is open Monday through Friday from 9am to 6pm and on Saturday from 9:30am to 2:30pm.

Drugstores In Britain they're called "chemist shops." Every police station in the country has a list of emergency chemists (dial "0" [zero] and ask the operator for the local police). One of the most centrally located chemists, keeping long hours, is Bliss The Chemist, 5 Marble Arch, W1 (☎ 0171/723-6116; tube: Marble Arch), open daily from 9am to midnight. Every London neighborhood has a branch of the ubiquitous Boots, the leading pharmacist of Britain.

Embassies and High Commissions Passports, visas, whatever your problem, London has representatives in offices from nearly all the countries of the world. The **U.S. Embassy** is at 24 Grosvenor Sq., W1 (☎ 0171/499-9000; tube: Bond Street). However, for passport and visa information, go to the U.S. Passport and Citizenship Unit, 55–56 Upper Brook St., London, W1 (☎ 0171/499-9000, ext. 2563; tube: Marble Arch). Hours are Monday through Friday from 8:30am to noon and from 2 to 4pm. On Tuesday, the office closes at noon.

The **Canadian High Commission,** MacDonald House, 38 Grosvenor Sq., W1 (☎ 0171/629-9492; tube: Bond Street), handles visa and passport problems for Canada. Hours are Monday through Friday from 8:45am to 2pm. The **Australian High Commission** is at Australia House, Strand, WC2 (☎ 0171/379-4334; tube: Charing Cross or Aldwych); it's open Monday through Friday from 10am to 4pm. The **New Zealand High Commission** is at New Zealand House, 80 Haymarket at Pall Mall SW1 (☎ 0171/930-8422; tube: Charing Cross or Piccadilly Circus); it's open Monday through Friday from 10am to noon and 2 to 4pm. The **Irish Embassy** is at 17 Grosvenor Place, SW1

(☎ 0171/235-2171; tube: Hyde Park Corner); it's open Monday through Friday from 9:30am to 5pm.

Emergencies   In London, for police, fire, or an ambulance, dial **999**.

Eyeglasses   Lost or broken? Try Selfridge Opticians on the street level of Selfridges Department Store, 400 Oxford St., W1 (☎ 0171/629-1234, ext. 3353; tube: Bond Street or Marble Arch), open Monday through Saturday from 9:30am to 7pm, on Thursday until 8pm. Contact lenses are also usually available on the same day. Bifocal lenses sometimes take 3 to 5 working days to complete. It's always wise to carry a copy of your eyeglass prescription with you when you travel.

Hairdressers and Barbers   Hairdressers and hairstylists crop up on most major London street corners (a slight exaggeration), and their salons range from grandly imperial refuges of English dowagers to punk-rock citadels of purple hair and chartreuse mascara. One of the most visible—and one of the best—is a branch of Vidal Sassoon, Whiteleys of Bayswater, 151 Queensway, W2 (☎ 0171/792-2741; tube: Bayswater). Unlike some other Sassoon outlets, this one caters to both men and women. The shop is open Monday through Friday from 10am to 7:45pm and Saturday from 9:15am to 6:15pm.

Hospitals   The following offer emergency care in London 24 hours a day, with the first treatment free under the National Health Service: Royal Free Hospital, Pond Street, NW3 (☎ 0171/794-0500; tube: Belsize Park), and University College Hospital, Gower Street, WC1 (☎ 0171/387-9300; tube: Warren Street). Many other London hospitals also have accident and emergency departments.

Hotlines   For police or medical emergencies, dial 999 (no coins required). If you're in some sort of legal emergency, call Release at 0171/729-9904, 24 hours a day. The Rape Crisis Line is 0171/837-1600, also in service 24 hours a day. Samaritans, 46 Marshall St., W1 (☎ 0171/734-2800), maintains a 24-hour crisis hotline that helps with all kinds of trouble, even threatened suicides. The 24-hour AIDS hotline is toll free at 0800/567-123.

Information   See "Visitor Information & Entry Requirements," in Chapter 2, and "Orientation," earlier in this chapter.

Laundry and Dry Cleaning   At Danish Express Laundry, 16 Hinde St., W1 (☎ 0171/935-6306; tube: Bond Street), they will clean, repair, or alter your clothes, even repair shoes. Open Monday through Friday from 8:30am to 5:30pm and on Saturday from 9:30am to 12:30pm, it's one of the best places in London for such services. One of the leading dry cleaners of London is Sketchley, 49 Maddox St., W1 (☎ 0171/629-1292), with more than three dozen branches. And if you're in the vicinity of the Bloomsbury bed-and-breakfasts, you may choose Red and White Laundries, 78 Marchmont St., WC1 (☎ 0171/387-3667; tube: Russell Square), open daily from 6:30am to 8:30pm.

Libraries   London's best collection of periodicals and reference materials is found at the Westminster Reference Library, 35 St. Martin's St., WC2 (☎ 0171/798-2036; tube: Leicester Square), open Monday through Friday from 10am to 7pm and Saturday from 10am to 5pm.

Lost Property   To find lost property, first report to the police and they will advise you where to apply for its return. Taxi drivers are required to hand over property left in their vehicles to the nearest police station. London Regional

Transport's Lost Property Office will try to assist personal callers only at their office at the Baker Street Underground station. For items lost on British Rail, report the loss as soon as possible to the station on the line where the loss occurred. For lost passports, credit cards, or money, report the loss and circumstances immediately to the nearest police station. For lost passports, you should go directly to your embassy or high commission (see "Embassies and High Commissions," above). For lost credit cards, also report to the appropriate organization; the same holds true for lost traveler's checks.

Luggage Storage and Lockers   Places for renting lockers or storing luggage are widely available in London. Lockers can be rented at Heathrow and Gatwick airports and at all major rail stations, including Victoria Station. In addition, there are dozens of independently operated storage companies in the London area. The usual charge is £6 to £10 ($9.50 to $15.80) per item per week. Check the yellow pages for the luggage-storage establishment nearest you.

Maps   See "City Layout" in "Orientation," earlier in this chapter.

Newspapers and Magazines   The *Times* is tops, then the *Telegraph,* the *Daily Mail,* and the *Manchester Guardian,* all London papers carrying the latest news. The *International Herald Tribune,* published in Paris, and an international edition of *USA Today,* beamed via satellite, are available daily. Copies of *Time* and *Newsweek* are also sold at most newsstands. Small magazines, such as *Time Out* and *City Limits,* contain much useful data about the latest happenings in London, including theatrical and cultural events.

Photographic Needs   The Flash Centre, 54 Brunswick Centre, WC1 (☎ 0171/ 837-6163; tube: Russell Square), is considered the best professional photographic equipment supplier in London. You can purchase your film next door at Leeds Film and Hire, which has a wide-ranging stock. Kodachrome is accepted for 48-hour processing.

Police   In an emergency, dial **999** (no coins are needed). You can also go to one of the local police branches in central London, including New Scotland Yard, Broadway, SW1 (☎ 0171/230-1212; tube: St. James's Park).

Post Office   The Main Post Office is at 24 William IV Street, WC2N 4DL (☎ 0171/930-9580; tube: Charing Cross). It operates as three separate businesses: inland and international postal service and banking (open Monday through Saturday from 8:30am to 8pm), philatelic postage stamp sales (open Monday through Friday from 10am to 7pm; Saturday from 10am to 4:30pm), and the post shop, selling greeting cards and stationery (open Monday through Friday from 9am to 6:30pm; Saturday from 9:30am to 5pm). Other post offices and sub–post offices are open Monday through Friday from 9am to 5:30pm and on Saturday from 9am to 12:30pm. Many sub–post offices and some main post offices close for an hour at lunchtime.

Radio   There are 24-hour radio channels operating throughout the U.K., including London. They offer mostly pop music and "chat shows" during the night. Some "pirate" radio stations add more spice to the broadcasting selections. So-called "legal" FM stations are BBC1 (104.8), BBC2 (89.1), BBC3 (between 90 and 92), and the classical station BBC4 (95). There is also the BBC Greater London Radio (94.9) station, with lots of rock; plus LBC Crown (97.3), with much news as well as reports of "what's on" in London. American-style pop-rock is a feature of Capital FM (95.8), and if you like jazz, Jamaican reggae, or salsa, tune in to Choice FM (96.9). Jazz FM (102.2) is not just jazz, but offers sounds of the big-band era, the blues, and whatever.

Religious Services Times of services are posted outside the various places of worship. Almost all major faiths are represented in London. The American Church in London is at 79 Tottenham Court Rd., W1 (☎ 0171/580-2791; tube: Goodge Street). There is a Sunday school for all ages every Sunday from 10 to 10:50am, followed by a worship service from 11am till noon. The American church is an ecumenical, international congregation. The London Tourist Board has a fairly complete list of churches. Protestants ideally might want to attend a Sunday-morning service at either Westminster Abbey (☎ 0171/222-5152) or St. Paul's Cathedral (☎ 0171/248-2705). If you're going to be in London on two separate Sundays, you might go to both landmarks. At Westminster Abbey, Sunday services begin at 8am; other services are at 10am, 11:15am, 3pm, 5:45pm, and 6:30pm. Roman Catholics gravitate to Westminster Cathedral (not to be confused with Westminster Abbey), Ashley Place, SW1 (☎ 0171/798-9055). Masses are conducted there on Sunday at 7am, 8am, 9am, 10:30am, noon, 5:30pm, and 7pm.

Restrooms Often called "loos" by the English, they are usually found at signs saying "Public Toilets." Automatic toilets are found on many streets. They are sterilized after each use. The cost is just 5p (10¢).

Safety See "Fast Facts: England," in Chapter 2.

Shoe Repair Most of the major Underground stations, including the centrally located Piccadilly Circus, have "heel bars"—British for shoe-repair centers. Mostly, these are for quickie jobs. For more extensive repairs, go to one of the major department stores (see "Department Stores" in "Shopping A to Z," in Chapter 7). Otherwise, patronize Jeeves Snob Shop, 8–10 Pont St., SW1 (☎ 0171/235-1101; tube: Knightsbridge).

Smoking Most U.S. brands of cigarettes are available in London. Anti-smoking laws are tougher than ever. Smoking is strictly forbidden in the Underground, including the cars and the platforms. It is allowed only in the back of the uppermost level of double-decker buses and is increasingly frowned upon in many other places.

Taxis See "Getting Around," earlier in this chapter.

Telephone For directory assistance for London, dial 142; for the rest of Britain, dial 192. See "Fast Facts: England," in Chapter 2, for an overview of the telephone system. See also "Area Code," above.

Telex and Fax To send a fax, you can go to the Chesham Executive Centre at 150 Regent St., W1 (☎ 0171/439-6288; tube: Piccadilly Circus). In addition to renting offices by the hour and providing secretarial and stenographic services, the center accepts walk-in business and will send fax messages. The cost of sending a one-page fax from London to anywhere in the world is £2.50 ($3.95), plus VAT and the cost of the phone call. Hours are Monday through Friday from 8:45am to 6pm, Saturday from 9am to noon. See also "Fast Facts: England," in Chapter 2.

Tipping See "Fast Facts: England," in Chapter 2.

Transit Information Phone 0171/222-1234, daily 24 hours.

Water Tap water in London is considered safe to drink, but because the water is different, you might still experience a stomach upset. If in doubt, order mineral water.

Weather Phone 01891/500-401.

3 Networks & Resources

FOR GAY MEN & LESBIANS

London Lesbian and Gay Centre This center contains a bookstore, café, bar, and disco. There is one floor for women only. Located at 67–69 Cowcross St., EC1 (☎ 071/608-1471; tube: Farringdon), it's open Monday and Tuesday from noon to 11pm; Wednesday, Thursday, and Sunday from noon to midnight, and Friday and Saturday from noon to 3am.

Lesbian and Gay Switchboard You can call (☎ 0171/837-7324) 24 hours a day for information about gay-related London activities and advice in general.

The Bisexual Helpline This switchboard (☎ 0181/569-7500) offers useful information, but only Tuesday and Wednesday from 7:30 to 9:30pm. Harassment, gay bashing, and other such matters are handled by Gay and Lesbian Legal Advice (☎ 0171/253-2043) Monday through Friday from 7 to 10pm.

FOR WOMEN

London Rape Crisis Centre This center, P.O. Box 69, WC1 (☎ 0171/837-1600), operates daily from 10am to 10pm. In addition to its counseling services, women are offered medical and legal advice. The center can even arrange to have another woman accompany you to the doctor, clinic, and the police station.

The only feminist bookstore in London is **Silvermoon,** 64–68 Charing Cross Rd., WC2 (☎ 0171/836-7906; tube: Leicester Square). Besides stocking literally thousands of titles by and about women, it sells tapes, videos, jewelry, T-shirts, and other items. It is open Monday through Saturday from 10am to 6:30pm; but on Thursday until 8pm.

FOR STUDENTS

STA Travel This London organization, at 86 Old Brompton Rd., SW7 3LQ (☎ 0171/937-9921; tube: South Kensington), is one of the several that specialize in student discounts and youth fares. It's open Monday through Thursday from 9:30am to 7pm, Friday from 10am to 6pm, and Saturday from 10am to 4pm.

The University of London Student Union Located at 1 Malet St., WC1E 7HY (☎ 0171/580-9551; tube: Goodge Street), this is the largest student union in the world and the best place to learn about student activities in the Greater London area. The union contains a swimming pool, fitness center, gymnasium, general store, sports shop, ticket agency, banks, bars, inexpensive restaurants, live events and discos, an office of STA Travel, and many other facilities. It is open Monday through Friday from 8:30am to 11pm, Saturday from 9am to 11pm, and Sunday from 9:30am to 10:30pm. Bulletin boards at the union provide a rundown on various events being sponsored, some of which it might be possible to attend, whereas others might be "closed door."

London Accommodations

4

London boasts some of the most famous hotels in the world. These include such temples of luxury as Claridge's, Dorchester, the Ritz (where the term "ritzy" originated), Park Lane Hotel, the Savoy, and their recent-vintage rivals, the Four Seasons, the Lanesborough, and the Langham Hilton.

All of these establishments are superlative and none of them is a budget hotel. It is in this bracket that you get the most fantastic contrasts, both in terms of architecture and comfort. Many of London's hotels were built around the turn of the century, which gives them a rather curlicued appearance. But whereas some have gone to no end of pain to modernize their interiors, others have remained at Boer War level, complete with built-in drafts and daisy-strewn wallpaper.

In between, however, you come across up-to-the-minute structures that seem to have been shifted bodily from Los Angeles. These aren't necessarily superior, but they frequently make up in personal service and spaciousness for what they lack in streamlining.

In most but not all of the places listed, there's a service charge ranging from 10% to 15% that's added to the bill. The British government also imposes a VAT (Value-Added Tax) that adds 17.5% to your bill.

In the late '80s and early '90s, the opening of new hotels generated a lot of excitement, as each one seemed to outdazzle the one before. Many charming small-scale hotels emerged—known as *bijou* (jewel) or boutique hotels because of their size and attention to detail. These hotels continue today to pose major competition to the larger, stately establishments built by the Victorians or Edwardians.

By the mid-1990s the excitement had died down, and these new hotels have emerged as a fact of life on the London hotel scene. The recession and rising inflation have taken their toll. There has been no really serious challenge to our list of "the best" in various price categories. This is in complete contrast to the outburst of new and exciting restaurants.

The problem (and it's a serious one) with London hotels is that there are too many expensive ones and not enough of the moderately priced establishments so typical of other European capitals.

In many (but not all) of the hotels listed here, the rates include breakfast, either a full English spread or a smaller continental one.

You should be aware that what is termed "continental breakfast" consists of coffee or tea and some sort of roll or pastry. An "English breakfast" is a fairly lavish meal of tea or coffee, cereal, eggs, toast and jam, and bacon, ham, or sausages.

All hotels, motels, inns, and guesthouses in Britain with four bedrooms or more (including self-catering accommodations) are required to display notices showing minimum and maximum overnight charges. The notice must be displayed in a prominent position in the reception area or at the entrance. The prices shown must include any service charge and may include VAT, and it must be made clear whether or not these items are included. If VAT is not included, it must be shown separately. If meals are provided with the accommodation, this must be made clear, too. If prices are not standard for all rooms, only the lowest and highest prices need to be given.

The prices charged are often astronomical, so resign yourself to paying a lot more in London for a good hotel room than you probably would in many other world-class cities.

RESERVATIONS

Most hotels require at least a day's deposit before they will reserve a room for you. This can be accomplished with an international bank draft or money order, a telephoned instruction in which the number of a valid credit card is transmitted, or, if agreed to in advance, a personal check. Usually you can cancel a room reservation one week ahead of time and get a full refund. Some hotelkeepers will return your money up to three days before the reservation date. But there have also been reports of hotels that will take your deposit and never return it, even if you canceled far in advance. Many budget hotels operate on such a narrow margin of profit that they find just buying stamps for airmail replies too expensive by their standards. Therefore, it's most important that you enclose a prepaid International Reply Coupon, especially if you're writing to a budget hotel.

Because of the low phone charges of calling from North America to London, it might be better to call and speak to the hotel of your choice or (and this grows increasingly more popular every year) send a fax.

July and August are the vacation months in England, when nearly two-thirds of the population strikes out for a long-awaited holiday. Many head for the capital, further exacerbating what is already a crowded hotel situation, particularly at the lower end of the price spectrum.

When summer vacations are over, "the season" in London begins, lasting through October. Therefore, in September and October, as in June, budget hotels are tight—though nothing like what they are in peak months. Many of the West End hotels have vacancies, even in peak season, between 9 and 11am, but by noon they are often packed solid again with fresh arrivals. Therefore, if you arrive without a reservation, begin your search for a room as early in the day as possible. If you arrive late at night—say, on a train from the continent pulling into Victoria Station—you may have to take what you can get, often in a much higher price range than you'd like to pay.

If you're booking into a chain hotel, such as one of the many Hiltons in Britain, you can often call toll free from North America and make reservations over the phone. Whenever such a service is available, we have included the 800 numbers in the hotel description.

TRAVELER'S ADVISORY REGARDING B&BS

If you've arrived in London as a first-time visitor and plan to seek low-cost lodgings, you should know that many of central London's bed-and-breakfast establishments and low-budget hotels are in very poor condition. In fact, since the last edition of this book was researched, we have received more complaints about bed-and-breakfast hotels in London than in any destination on the continent of Europe.

In this chapter, you'll find a list of what we consider adequate bed-and-breakfast lodgings for London, but we present most of them without any particular enthusiasm.

Since it is easy for owners of small budget hotels to fill up their rooms every night—regardless of the condition of the rooms—they have little incentive to improve their services, repair the broken plumbing, or renovate. You'll find far more reasonable and much better places to stay in the budget category once you leave London.

So, be duly warned: Don't expect too much when checking into your typical London bed-and-breakfast. There are a few good ones, but they also tend to be fully booked all year.

WHAT MAKES A LEGEND?

The rich and famous call The Dorchester a "home away from home," and if that is really true it makes one want to visit the sumptuous mansions they must have left behind. Royalty and dignitaries, both domestic and foreign, have been frequent visitors here since the hotel opened in 1931. Princess Elizabeth (now the queen, of course), attended a dinner party here before the announcement of her engagement on July 10, 1947. Prince Philip celebrated his stag night on the eve of his wedding at The Dorchester.

During World War II, several high-ranking government officials moved into the hotel on a semipermanent basis. General Eisenhower, busy with plans for the D-day landings, set up headquarters at the hotel in 1944.

Over the years the hotel was a haven for prominent figures from the literary and art worlds. In addition to hosting the famous Foyles Literary luncheons beginning in the early 1930s, The Dorchester has welcomed such illustrious guests as the poet Cecil Day Lewis and the painter Sir Alfred Munnings. Novelist Somerset Maugham was a frequent guest. Danny Kaye appeared in cabaret at the hotel for £50 ($79) a week in the 1930s and later became a lifelong regular guest. Arriving with a succession of different husbands, including Richard Burton, Elizabeth Taylor always occupied the biggest suite, one that often had to be redecorated after she'd checked out. Sir Ralph Richardson tended to arrive by motorcycle, bringing his crash helmet in to lunch. Alfred Hitchcock viewed The Dorchester as ideal for a murder, given his bent for burying bodies in Hyde Park, across Park Lane. The rich and famous continue to arrive, including Barbra Streisand, Diana Ross, Glenn Close, Michael Jackson, and Karl Lagerfeld.

What's the most unknown fact about the hotel? When The Dorchester Bar was rebuilt in 1938, Harry Craddock, London's most famous barman of the era, produced three of the most popular cocktails of the day—the Martini, Manhattan, and White Lady. He sealed them in phials that were set into the wall of the bar "for posterity." When the bar was reconstructed in 1979, the cocktails, scroll, and recipes were found to be in excellent condition.

1 Mayfair

VERY EXPENSIVE

✪ Claridge's

Brook St., London W1A 2JQ. ☎ **0171/629-8860** or 800/223-6800. Fax 0171/499-2210. 109 rms, 56 suites. A/C TV TEL. £255–£295 ($402.90–$466.10) double; from £550 ($869) suite. Continental breakfast £12.25 ($19.35) extra. AE, DC, MC, V. Tube: Bond St.

Claridge's has been known from the mid-Victorian era under its present name, though an earlier "lodging house" complex occupied much of the hotel's present area as far back as the reign of George IV. It has cocooned royal visitors in an ambiance of discreet elegance since the time of the Battle of Waterloo. Queen Victoria visited Empress Eugénie of France here, and thereafter Claridge's lent respectability to the idea of ladies dining out in public. The hotel took on its present modest exterior in 1898. Inside, art deco decor was added in the 1930s, much of it still existing agreeably along with antiques and TVs. The guestrooms are spacious, many having generous-size baths complete with dressing rooms and numerous amenities. Suites can be connected by private foyers closed away from the main corridors and providing large self-contained units suitable for a sultan and his entourage.

Dining/Entertainment: Excellent food is stylishly served in the intimacy of the Causerie, renowned for its lunch-time smörgåsbord and pretheater suppers, and in the more formal Restaurant, with its English and French specialties. From the Restaurant, the strains of the Hungarian Quartet, a Claridge's institution since 1902, can be heard in the adjacent foyer during lunch and dinner. Both the Causerie and the Restaurant are open daily from noon to 3pm. The Causerie serves evening meals from 5:30 to 11pm, with dinner offered in the Restaurant from 7:30pm to 1am.

Services: 24-hour room service, valet, laundry, babysitting.

Facilities: Hairdresser, car-rental agent, travel and theater desk. Men have use of nearby Bath and Racquets Club (health club), and women can use Berkeley Hotel's Health Club with a rooftop pool and gym. Guests of the hotel with a recognized golf handicap (30 for women, 20 for men) may play unlimited golf (complimentary) at Berkshire's Wentworth Golf Club. Tennis provided at Vanderbilt Club in West London.

✪ The Dorchester

53 Park Lane, London, W1A 2HJ. ☎ **0171/629-8888** or 800/727-9820. Fax 0171/409-0114. 192 rms, 52 suites. A/C MINIBAR TV TEL. £235–£265 ($371.30–$418.70) double; from £350 ($553) suite. VAT extra. Continental breakfast £12.50 ($19.75) extra. AE, DC, MC, V. Tube: Hyde Park Corner or Marble Arch.

A series of socially prominent manor houses and villas had stood on the site of this hotel for as long as anyone could remember, but in 1929, with an increased demand for hotel space in the expensive Park Lane district, a famous mansion—whose inhabitants had been known for everything from great debauchery to great aesthetic skills—was torn down. In its place was erected in 1931 the finest hotel London had seen in many years. Breaking from the neoclassical tradition that contemporary critics felt had forced the hidebound city into one homogenized unit, the most ambitious architects of the era designed a building of reinforced concrete clothed in terrazzo slabs.

Throughout the hotel, you'll find a 1930s interpretation of Regency motifs. The arrangements of flowers and the lavish elegance of the gilded-cage Promenade seem appropriate for a diplomatic reception, yet they convey a kind of sophisticated comfort with which guests from all over the world feel at ease. In the old days, those guests used to include General Eisenhower, Marlene Dietrich, and Bing Crosby; today's roster is likely to list Michael J. Fox, Cher, Tom Cruise, or Michael Jackson.

Owned by the Brunei Investment Agency, who invested $192 million in its make-over, the Dorchester's bedrooms feature linen sheets, all the electronic gadgetry you'd expect from a world-class hotel, and double- and triple-glazed windows to keep the noise out. The bedrooms are filled with plump armchairs and cherry-wood furnishings, and, in many cases, four-poster beds. In mottled gray Italian marble with Lalique-style sconces, even the bathrooms are stylish. The best rooms open onto views of Hyde Park.

Dining/Entertainment: Two of the hotel's restaurants—The Terrace and The Grill—are considered among the finest dining establishments in London, and the Dorchester Bar is a legend. The pink-and-green Terrace is a historic room outfitted in a Regency motif with an overlay of chinoiserie whose combination is especially sumptuous. When referring to its soaring columns capped with gilded palm fronds and mammoth swathes of filigree curtains, one English reviewer referred to it as "pure Cecil B. DeMille." The Terrace still features dancing, a tradition that goes back to the 1930s, when London's "bright young things" patronized the place. Today, unlike yesterday, there is a health-conscious *menu léger* to keep waistlines thin. In addition, the hotel also offers Cantonese cuisine in its Asian restaurant, The Oriental, London's most exclusive and expensive Chinese restaurant, which has been awarded a Michelin star for three years running.

Services: 24-hour room service, laundry, dry cleaning, medical service.

Facilities: One of the best-outfitted health clubs in London, the Dorchester Spa; an exclusive nightclub; barbershop; hairdresser.

✪ Four Seasons Hotel

Hamilton Place, Park Lane, London W1A 1AZ. ☎ **0171/499-0888** or 800/332-3442. Fax 0171/493-1895. 227 rms, 26 suites. A/C MINIBAR TV TEL. £255–£265 ($402.90–$418.70) double; £330–£355 ($521.40–$560.90) conservatory; from £405 ($639.90) suite. English breakfast £15.50 ($24.50) extra. VAT extra. AE, DC, MC, V. Parking £14.50 ($22.90). Tube: Hyde Park Corner.

This deluxe hostelry, a member of the Four Seasons group, has captured the imagination of the glamourmongers of the world ever since it was inaugurated by Princess Alexandra in 1970. Its clientele includes heads of state, superstars, and business executives, among others. Howard Hughes, who could afford anything, chose it as a retreat, but his sprawling eighth-floor suite has since been subdivided into more easily rentable rooms.

Visitors enter a modern reception area, but acres of superbly crafted paneling and opulently conservative decor create the impression that the hotel is far older than it is. A gently inclined grand stairway leads in the grandest manner to a symmetrical grouping of Chinese and European antiques flanked by cascades of fresh flowers.

The rooms are large and beautifully outfitted with well-chosen chintz patterns, reproduction antiques, and plush upholstery, along with dozens of well-concealed electronic extras. Fourteen of the largest rooms house private conservatories.

Dining/Entertainment: The Cocktail Bar is a piano bar that serves drinks in a room where Wellington might have felt at home. A pair of restaurants create a most alluring rendezvous, including the Four Seasons, with views opening onto Park Lane. The finest wines and continental specialties dazzle guests either at lunch or at dinner, with the last order at 10:30pm. The alternative dining choice is the less expensive Lanes Restaurant, rather popular with many members of London's business community. You can obtain refreshments and light snacks from the lounge, which is open from 9am to 1am.

Services: Valet, 24-hour room service, laundry.

Facilities: Shops, theater desk, garden, car-rental agency, concierge, and a health club.

London Hilton on Park Lane

22 Park Lane, London W1Y 4BE. ☎ **0171/493-8000** or 800/445-8667. Fax 0171/493-4957. 396 rms, 50 suites. A/C MINIBAR TV TEL. £195–£285 ($308.10–$450.30) single or double; from £350 ($553) suite. VAT extra. Continental breakfast £7–£14 ($11.05–$22.10) extra. AE, DC, MC, V. Parking £13.50 ($21.35). Tube: Hyde Park Corner.

The tallest building along Park Lane, and indeed one of the tallest structures in London, this hotel created an uproar when it was constructed in 1963. There were persistent allegations that residents of its uppermost floors could spy on the boudoirs of faraway Buckingham Palace.

Now considered a linchpin of the London hotel scene and owned by Britain's Ladbroke chain, the Hilton is graced with large picture windows overlooking London and Hyde Park. Bedrooms are decorated in tastefully restful colors, with fine copies of Georgian furniture.

Dining/Entertainment: Windows on the World restaurant features French/international cuisine and offers panoramic views over London. Reservations far in advance are needed for a window table. An international cuisine is also served in the hotel's Café-Brasserie, and you can order Polynesian food at Trader Vic's downstairs. St. George's Bar is a fashionable rendezvous, and there is dancing to a live band every night in Windows of the World.

Services: 24-hour room service, concierge, laundry and valet, babysitting, massage.

Facilities: Business center, solarium, Hertz Rent A Car desk, theater-ticket booking desk, six executive floors offering private check in and a complimentary continental breakfast.

London Marriott

Grosvenor Sq., London W1A 4AW. ☎ **0171/493-1232** or 800/228-9290. Fax 0171/491-3201. 223 rms, 17 suites. A/C MINIBAR TV TEL. £220 ($347.60) double; from £300 ($474) suite. Children up to 12 stay free in parents' room. English breakfast £12.25 ($19.35) extra. AE, DC, MC, V. Parking £25 ($39.50). Tube: Bond St.

The property was built in a grander era as the very conservative Hotel Europa. After Marriott poured millions of dollars into its refurbishment, only the very best elements, and of course much of the tradition, remained. This triumph of the decorator's art sits proudly behind a red-brick and stone Georgian facade on one of the most distinguished parks in London, Grosvenor Square. Its polite battalions of porters, doormen, and receptionists wait near the entrance along a side street. The American embassy is just a few doors away.

Throughout the hotel's carefully crafted interior, combinations of rose, ivory, and green are consistently used. Its breakfast room is a decorator's dream, filled with a cluster of Chippendale antiques and the kind of chintz that goes perfectly with masses of seasonal flowers. The accommodations are decorated in the Georgian style and have all the electronic extras you'd expect.

Dining/Entertainment: Guests enjoy the Regent Lounge, which is outfitted in an English country style. In the Diplomat, meals are served in an elegant yet comfortable setting. Chef Simon Traynor, one of London's hottest young chefs, serves traditional English cuisine with a twist such as pan-fried cornish crab and prawn cakes on a chive and lemongrass sauce with crispy cabbage.

Services: 24-hour room service, valet, laundry, concierge, babysitting.

Facilities: No-smoking rooms, fitness center, business center.

EXPENSIVE

Brown's Hotel

29–34 Albemarle St., London W1A 4SW. ☎ **0171/493-6020** or 800/225-5843. Fax 0171/ 493-9381. 110 rms, 6 suites. A/C MINIBAR TV TEL. £205–£255 ($323.90–$402.90) double; from £320 ($505.60) suite. Children up to 12 stay free in parents' room. Continental breakfast £11.75 ($18.55) extra. AE, DC, MC, V. Tube: Green Park.

Brown's is highly recommended for those who want a fine hotel among the top traditional choices. This upper-crust, prestigious establishment was created by James Brown, a former manservant of Lord Byron. He and his wife, Sarah, who had been Lady Byron's personal maid, wanted to go into business for themselves. Brown knew the tastes of gentlemen of breeding and wanted to create a dignified, clublike place for them. His dream came true when the hotel, a former townhouse at 23 Dover St., opened in 1837, the year Queen Victoria ascended the throne of England.

Today, Brown's Hotel occupies some 12 historic houses on two streets, in an appropriate location—in Mayfair, just off Berkeley Square. Old-fashioned comfort is dispensed with courtesy. A liveried doorman ushers you to an antique reception desk where you check in. The lounges on the street floor are inviting, including the Roosevelt Room, the Rudyard Kipling Room (the famous author was a frequent visitor here), and the paneled St. George's Bar for the drinking of "spirits."

Dining/Entertainment: Afternoon tea is served in the Albemarle Room. Men are required to wear jackets and ties for teas and for dining in the dining room, which has a quiet dignity and unmatched service. Most meals are à la carte, though there is also a set luncheon menu at £21.50–£24.50 ($33.95–$38.70) and a fixed-price dinner at £29 ($45.80), including service and VAT. Old-time guests wouldn't recognize today's cuisine, under the direction of chef Aidan McCormack, who has brought a more modern British touch to the food. Dover sole has always appeared on the menu, but today you are also likely to get poached red snapper on a bed of crisp cabbage leaves with a saffron sauce.

Services: 24-hour room service, laundry and dry cleaning, babysitting.

Facilities: Men's hairdresser, car-rental agency.

Park Lane Hotel

Piccadilly, London W1Y 8BX. ☎ **0171/499-6321** or 800/223-5652. Fax 01717/499-1965. 310 rms, 48 suites. MINIBAR TV TEL. £185–£210 ($292.30–$331.80) double; from £230 ($363.40) suite. Continental breakfast £10.95 ($17.30). AE, DC, MC, V. Parking £25 ($39.50). Tube: Hyde Park Corner.

This is the most traditional and long-standing of the Park Lane deluxe hotels, proud of its loyal clientele and consistently winning new converts all the time.

Frommer's Best of the Best

BEST B&B   Claverley Hotel *(see page 126)*.   Tranquil and in Knightsbridge, close to Harrods for that special buy, this hotel has won awards as best bed-and-breakfast in London. The awards are deserved. Try fresh salmon kedgeree for breakfast. It's the cook's special.

BEST ENGLISH AMBIANCE   Dukes Hotel *(see page 118)*.   In a gaslit courtyard in back of St. James's Place, the clubby atmosphere of this hotel has the dignity of an elderly duke. From the bread-and-butter pudding served in the dining room to the staff's impeccably correct politeness, it's the epitome of what England used to be.

BEST FOR OPULENCE   The Dorchester *(see page 108)*.   Since it is owned by the world's richest man, the sultan of Brunei, multi-million-pound opulence was the order of the day here—from luxurious bathrooms in white Italian marble to the marble pillared Promenade (one of the finest places for afternoon tea in London). Before jetting off, the sultan left instructions to turn "The Dorch" into the world's greatest hotel. And so they did.

BEST GRAND OLD HOTEL   Park Lane Hotel *(see page 111)*.   This hotel is English to the core. The suites with their art deco bathrooms still have their 1920s decor. No wonder the producers of *Brideshead Revisited* chose the hotel as a site for filming their series. It evokes memories of the grand days of the debutante balls.

BEST DISCREET ADDRESS   Brown's Hotel *(see page 111)*.   If Henry James were alive today, he would check in here. Everything about Brown's has been called "Jamesian." It's quintessentially English and the site of two famous honeymoons—at least: that of Theodore Roosevelt and Edith Carow in 1886 and that of Franklin D. Roosevelt and Eleanor in 1905.

BEST SHABBY GENTILITY   Wilbraham Hotel *(see page 130)*.   Not afraid to be old-fashioned, this hotel remains true to itself—floral wallpaper, old world English politeness, and stately Victoriana. They're so old-fashioned here they still call their lounge "The Bar and Buttery."

Flanked with neighbors who have sold their premises to well-heeled foreigners, the Park Lane is now the last of the Park Lane giants to be privately and staunchly owned by an English family. It was begun in 1913 by an enterprising former member of the Life Guards, who used advanced engineering techniques to construct the foundations and an intricately detailed iron skeleton. When its creator was tragically killed in World War I, local gossips mockingly referred to the echoing and empty shell as "the bird cage." In 1924 one of London's leading hoteliers, Bracewell Smith, completed the construction, and a short time later the Park Lane became one of the leading hotels of Europe.

Today you'll enter an intensely English hotel that sits behind a discreet stone-block facade. One of its gateways, the Silver Entrance, is considered such an art deco marvel that its soaring columns and mirrors have been used as a backdrop in many films, including *Shanghai Surprise,* the U.S. miniseries *The Winds of War,* and the British miniseries *Brideshead Revisited,* P.G. Wodehouses's Jeeves-and-Wooster novels, and Danielle Steel's *Jewels,* to name a few. Designed in a U-shape,

BEST OF THE NEW HOTELS **The Lanesborough** *(see page 127)*. It's new but it's old, originally built in Portland limestone in the classical Greek revival style in 1829. It took a Texas billionaire, Caroline Rose Hunt, of Rosewood Hotels, to pour money into the decrepit old place to the tune of $1.7 million on *each* of the guestrooms. She created this hedonistic temple of luxury even during one of Britain's worst recessions.

BEST FOR BUSINESS **Sheraton Park Tower** *(see page 122)*. For wheeling and dealing in Knightsbridge, this place has a lively business center operating 24 hours a day. While enjoying a panoramic view of Hyde Park, the business client can keep those fax machines ringing.

BEST SMALL HOTEL **The Beaufort** *(see page 123)*. This hotel will charm, lying 200 yards from Harrods on a tree-lined cul-de-sac. Personal service and rural peace combine to make for a winning choice. You're given the key to the front door and made to feel at home.

BEST COUNTRY HOUSE DECOR **Dorset Square Hotel** *(see page 135)*. Tim and Kit (the Kemps, that is) are hoteliers of charm, taste, and sophistication. They were never better than when they spliced two Georgian townhouses together and created this English country-house look with antiques and mahogany bathrooms, right in the heart of London. Gilt-framed paintings and tapestry cushions make you feel warm, cozy, and elegantly refined.

BEST BUY **Aston's Budget Studios** *(see page 133)*. Ms. Shelagh King is a scream and also a delight. This hostess with the mostess welcomes the world to her accommodations, which range widely in price, and well they should—they go from budget lodgings to designer suites. Regardless of how much or how little you pay, Ms. King has a deal for you. Readers love this one.

BEST FOR FAMILIES **Camelot Hotel** *(see page 138)*. For the family on a budget, this pair of 1850 townhouses in Paddington may be simple, but it's on an old tree-filled square. The hotel has sheltered thousands of families from all over the world, welcoming all to its homelike environment.

with a view overlooking Green Park, the Park Lane Hotel offers luxurious and comfortable accommodations, with double-glazed windows, that are among the least expensive of any of the other major Park Lane competitors. Many of the suites offer marble fireplaces and the original marble-sheathed bathrooms. A lot of the rooms have benefited from an impressive refurbishment program—rooms have been enlarged, and the chic decor is designed by the chairman's wife.

Dining/Entertainment: The hotel's restaurant, Bracewells, is recommended in Chapter 5, "London Dining." Bracewells Bar is one of London's most popular cocktail bars, with a talented evening pianist and a decor lined with cinnabar-red Chinese lacquer. Less expensive but still very charming is the Brasserie, serving French cuisine.

Services: 24-hour room service, concierge, valet, babysitting, laundry and dry cleaning.

Facilities: Business center, fitness center, safety-deposit boxes, gift and newspaper shop, barbershop, women's hairdresser, Daniel Ryman Aromatherapy Shop.

2 Piccadilly & St. James's

PICCADILLY

VERY EXPENSIVE

Le Meridien London

21 Piccadilly, London W1V 0BH. ☎ **0171/734-8000** or 800/543-4300. Fax 0171/437-3574. 222 rms, 41 suites. A/C MINIBAR TV TEL. £235–£255 ($371.30–$402.90) double; from £325 ($513.50) suite. English breakfast £12.75($20.15) extra. AE, DC, MC, V. Parking £25 ($39.50). Tube: Piccadilly Circus.

At the time of this hotel's original opening in 1908, the Ionic arcade capping the limestone of its arched neoclassical facade was considered the height of Edwardian extravagance. It was instantly pronounced the grandest hotel in London, but its huge expense soon bankrupted its creator. New owners continued to make the hotel one of the most stylish in the world, receiving such luminaries as Mary Pickford, accompanied by Douglas Fairbanks, and Edward VII. After World War II the hotel sank into a kind of musty obscurity until its lavish refurbishment during the revitalization of the Piccadilly theater district. Today, enjoying its re-incarnation, the hotel is run by the Forte chain. It has enough elaborately detailed plasterwork, stained glass, and limed oak paneling to make any Francophile feel at home, yet offers enough old-world service and style to satisfy even the most discerning British. Except for the intricate beauty of the skylit reception area, the centerpiece of the hotel is the soaring grandeur of the Oak Room Lounge, where gilded carvings and chandeliers of shimmering Venetian glass re-create Edwardian styles. Bedrooms are tasteful, exuding quality, comfort, and style.

Dining/Entertainment: The formal and very elegant Oak Room Restaurant is recommended in Chapter 5, "London Dining." The Terrace Garden Restaurant is less formal, a sun-flooded aerie under the greenhouse walls of the facade's massive Ionic portico. There is, as well, a very British bar sheathed in hardwoods and filled with live piano music.

Services: 24-hour room service, laundry, hairdresser, babysitting.

Facilities: The hotel's Champney's is one of the most exotic health clubs in London, featuring a large pool, saunas, steam baths, aerobic workshops, squash courts, billiard tables, and a private-membership clientele.

Ritz

150 Piccadilly, London W1V 9DG. ☎ **0171/493-8181** or 800/544-7570. Fax 0171/493-2687. 120 rms, 10 suites. MINIBAR TV TEL. £190–£265 ($300.20–$418.70) double; from £495 ($782.10) suite. English breakfast £15 ($23.70) extra. AE, DC, MC, V. Parking £37 ($58.45). Tube: Green Park.

Built in the French Renaissance style in 1906, overlooking the landscapes of Green Park, the Ritz is synonymous with luxury. The original color scheme of apricot, cream, and dusty rose enhances gold-leafed molding, marble columns, and potted palms. The oval Palm Court is dominated by a gold-leafed statue, *La Source*, adorning the fountain.

The bedrooms and suites, each with its own character, radios, and in-house films, are spacious and comfortable. Most are air-conditioned. The well-kept bedrooms often have marble fireplaces and elaborate gilded plasterwork. The decor is often in soft pastel hues.

Dining/Entertainment: It is still the most fashionable place in London to meet for afternoon tea, at which a selection of finger sandwiches, including cucumber and smoked salmon, are served, as well as specially made French pastries, scones, and cake.

The Ritz Restaurant, one of the loveliest dining rooms in the world, has been faithfully restored to its original splendor. Service is efficient yet unobtrusive, and the tables are spaced to allow the most private of conversations, perhaps the reason Edward and Mrs. Simpson dined so frequently at the Ritz.

Services: 24-hour room service, laundry, valet, babysitting.

Facilities: Garden, news kiosk, shopping boutiques, and access to the St. James's Health Club around the corner.

EXPENSIVE

✪ Hotel 22 Jermyn Street

22 Jermyn St., London SW1Y 6HL. ☎ **0171/734-2353** or 800/682-7808. Fax 0171/734-0750. 5 rms, 13 suites. MINIBAR TV TEL. £170 ($268.60) single or double; from £220 ($347.60) suite. English breakfast £13 ($20.55) extra. AE, DC, MC, V. Valet parking £25 ($39.50). Tube: Piccadilly Circus.

Set behind a facade of gray stone with neoclassical embellishments, this structure was originally built in 1870 as an apartment house for English gentlemen doing business in London. Since 1915 it has been administered by three generations of the Togna family, whose most recent scion closed it for a radical restoration in 1990. Now reveling in its new role as a chic and upscale hotel, under the direction of Annette M. Foster, it offers an interior with many plants and the kind of art you might find in an elegant private home. The guestrooms, done in traditional English style, have masses of fresh flowers, chintzes, and furniture.

Services: 24-hour room service, concierge staff, babysitting, laundry, dry cleaning, secretarial services, and a weekly newsletter that keeps guests up to date with restaurants, theater, and exhibitions.

Facilities: Free use of Dictaphones, videophones and fax, two phone lines in each room, a CD-ROM library with access to Internet for patrons, a nearby health club (75 yards away), and the general manager will take you on her morning run.

INEXPENSIVE

Regent Palace Hotel

12 Sherwood St., near Piccadilly Circus, London W1A 4BZ. ☎ **0171/734-7000.** Fax 0171/734-6435. 950 rms (none with bath). TV TEL. £77 ($121.65) double. For stays of two or more nights, £64–£70 ($101.10–$110.60) double, depending on the time of year. All rates include English breakfast. AE, DC, MC, V. Tube: Piccadilly Circus.

Considered a major focal point since it was built in 1915 at the edge of Piccadilly Circus, this is one of the largest hotels in Europe. Today, it's known for its staunch loyalty to its original design, whereby none of the rooms has a private bathroom. (Shared facilities in the hallways are adequate, and each room has a sink with hot and cold running water.) Some clients believe that this huge hotel's design provides a perspective on British life from another era.

The hotel's Original Carvery makes a good place to dine, and The Dome bistro is open for pretheater meals. Drinks are served in the Half Sovereign and the Planters bars. Coffee, sandwiches, and snacks are available in Antonio's Coffee Bar.

There are souvenir and gift shops, an exchange bureau, and a theater-booking agent.

Central London Accommodations

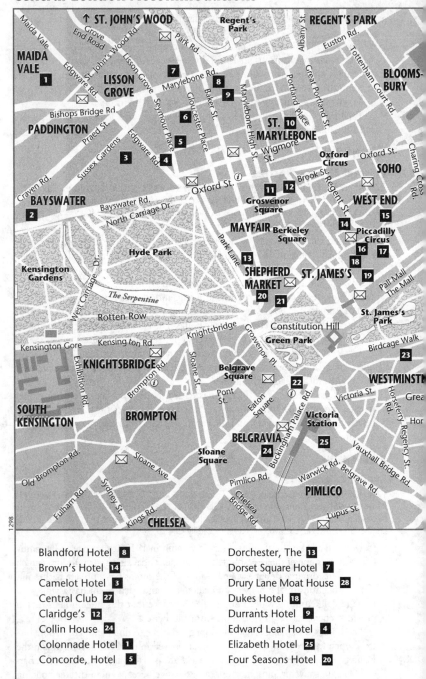

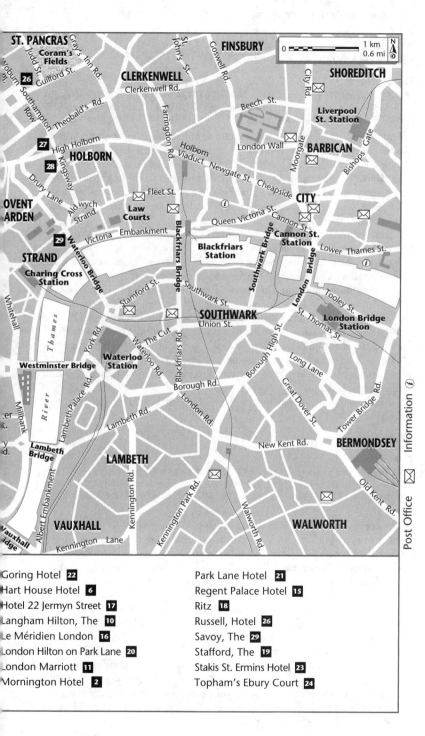

Goring Hotel **22**

Hart House Hotel **6**

Hotel 22 Jermyn Street **17**

Langham Hilton, The **10**

Le Méridien London **16**

London Hilton on Park Lane **20**

London Marriott **11**

Mornington Hotel **2**

Park Lane Hotel **21**

Regent Palace Hotel **15**

Ritz **18**

Russell, Hotel **26**

Savoy, The **29**

Stafford, The **19**

Stakis St. Ermins Hotel **23**

Topham's Ebury Court **24**

Post Office ✉   Information ⓘ

ST. JAMES'S
VERY EXPENSIVE
The Stafford

16–18 St. James's Place, London SW1A 1NJ. ☎ **0171/493-0111** or 800/525-4800. Fax 0171/493-7121. 67 rms, 7 suites. TV TEL. £200–£245 ($316–$387.10) double; from £290 ($458.20) suite. English breakfast £13 ($20.55) extra. AE, DC, MC, V. Tube: Green Park.

Famous for its American Bar and the warmth of its Edwardian decor, the Stafford was built late in the 19th century as a private home on a cul-de-sac off one of the most centrally located and busiest neighborhoods of London. It can be entered via St. James's Place or else via a cobble-covered courtyard that was originally designed as a mews and is known today as the Blue Ball Yard. The Stafford has retained a homelike, country-house atmosphere with touches of antique charm and modern amenities.

The bedrooms and suites are individually decorated and of varying shapes and sizes that correspond to the original function of the building as a private home. A handful of the hotel's newest and plushest accommodations in a restored stable mews require transit across the cobblestones of the mews yard.

Dining/Entertainment: The Stafford Restaurant is an elegant dining room lit with handsome chandeliers and wall sconces and accented with flowers, candles, and white napery. You can lunch or dine on classic international dishes that are made from fresh, select ingredients. A lunch costs from £19.50 ($30.80); a dinner, from £25 ($39.50). The previously mentioned American Bar (actually more like a memento-packed library of an English country house) is an especially cozy attraction. The bar is known for its collection of American university or club ties, badges, and caps.

Services: 24-hour room service, babysitting, concierge, secretarial service, laundry.

EXPENSIVE

Dukes Hotel

35 St. James's Place, London SW1A 1NY. ☎ **0171/491-4840.** Fax 0171/493-1264. 72 rms, 12 suites. A/C TV TEL. £160–£185 ($252.80–$292.30) double; from £210 ($331.80) suite. English breakfast £12.50 ($19.75) extra. AE, DC, MC, V. Parking £37 ($58.45). Tube: Green Park.

Dukes provides elegance without ostentation. A hotel since 1908, it stands in a quiet courtyard off St. James's Street, noted for turn-of-the-century gas lamps. From the hotel it's possible to walk to Buckingham Palace, St. James's Palace, and the Houses of Parliament. Shoppers will be near Bond Street and Piccadilly, and literature buffs will be interested to note that Oscar Wilde lived and wrote at St. James's Place for a time.

Each of the well-furnished and centrally heated bedrooms is decorated in the style of a particular English period, ranging from Regency to Edwardian. All rooms are equipped with en-suite marble bathrooms, telephones, satellite television, private bar, and air-conditioning. Their most recent renovation occurred in 1994.

Dining/Entertainment: Dukes' Restaurant is small, tasteful, and elegant, combining both classic British and continental cuisine. The hotel also has a clublike bar that is known for its rare collection of vintage ports, armagnacs, and cognacs.

Services: 24-hour room service, butler, valet, housekeeping, secretarial, travel reservations and theater booking facilities.

3 Bloomsbury

MODERATE

Hotel Russell

Russell Sq., London WC1 B5BE. ☎ **0171/837-6470** or 800/435-4542. Fax 0171/837-2857. 328 rms, 19 suites. TV TEL. £125 ($197.50) double; from £150 ($237) suite. English breakfast £10.50 ($16.60) extra. AE, DC, MC, V. Tube: Russell Square.

A late Victorian hotel facing the garden of this famous square, and within easy reach of theaters and shopping, the Russell is run by Forte Hotels. The bedrooms, in striking contrast to the ornate Belle Epoque facade, are done in a rather sterile modern, though generally well-maintained, style.

The public rooms have been refurbished and include a main restaurant serving traditional English food. Virginia Woolf's offers grills, pastas, burgers, and salads in a relaxed informal atmosphere. All the dining establishments offer good value.

There is 24-hour room service and laundry.

INEXPENSIVE

Central Club

16–22 Great Russell St., London WC1B 3LR. ☎ **0171/636-7512.** Fax 0171/636-5278. 109 rms. TV TEL. £60.25 ($95.20) double; £18.50 ($29.25) per person in triple or quad. All rates include English breakfast. MC, V. Tube: Tottenham Court Road.

This large and attractive building was designed by Sir Edwin Lutyens, the famous architect, and built around 1932 as a YWCA. Although still vaguely affiliated with YWCA, it now functions as a hotel and accepts men, women, families, and groups traveling together. Each of the simple but comfortable bedrooms has a radio and beverage-making facilities. Included in the rate is use of the lounges, coin-operated laundry facilities, hair salon, gym, solarium, and a coffee shop.

4 The Strand & Covent Garden

THE STRAND

VERY EXPENSIVE

✪ The Savoy

The Strand, London WC2R 0EU. ☎ **0171/836-4343** or 800/63-SAVOY. Fax 0171/240-6040. 154 rms, 48 suites. A/C MINIBAR TV TEL. £205–£275 ($323.90–$434.50) double; from £365 ($576.70) suite. English breakfast £16.25 ($25.70). VAT extra. AE, DC, MC, V. Parking £23 ($36.35). Tube: Charing Cross.

The Savoy is a London landmark, with eight stories behind a facade of light terracotta glazed tiles, rising majestically between the Strand and the Thames. The hotel, opened in 1889, was built by Richard D'Oyly Carte, impresario, for the use of people going to his theater to see the Gilbert and Sullivan operas he staged. Through the Savoy's portals have passed famous personages of yesterday and today, everybody from royalty to stars of stage, screen, TV, and rock. Today the hotel has regained the impeccable hospitality, service, and splendor of its early years.

Forty-eight of the hotel's bedrooms have their own sitting rooms. Each has a different decor, with color-coordinated accessories, and all have comfortable chairs, solid furniture, and large closets. The units offer a blend of antiques—an eclectic combination of such pieces as gilt mirrors, Queen Anne chairs, and Victorian sofas. Guests find fresh flowers and fruit in their rooms on arrival, and at night beds are turned down and a chocolate is placed on the pillows.

Dining/Entertainment: The world-famous Savoy Grill has long been popular with a theatrical clientele. Sarah Bernhardt was among its most celebrated customers in her time. The even-more-elegant River Restaurant is in a prime position, with tables overlooking the Thames; a four-person band plays in the evening for dancing. Also included is the establishment Upstairs, specializing in champagne, Chablis, and seafood. Try fricassee of monkfish with wild rice or salmon kedgeree.

Services: 24-hour room service, nightly turndown, limousine service, same-day laundry and dry cleaning, babysitting.

Facilities: Hairdresser, news kiosk, and a unique Health Club, built on top of the historic Savoy Theatre, that was destroyed by fire in 1990 and rebuilt in 1993. Guests also granted temporary membership in the exclusive Wentworth Club, a golf and country club lying on the outskirts of London (proof of handicap required).

COVENT GARDEN
EXPENSIVE

Drury Lane Moat House

10 Drury Lane, High Holborn, London WC2B 5RE. ☎ **0171/836-6666.** Fax 0171/831-1548. 153 rms, 7 suites. A/C TV TEL. £139 ($219.60) double; from £197 ($311.25) suite. English breakfast from £10.25 ($16.20) extra. VAT extra. AE, DC, MC, V. Parking £15 ($23.70). Tube: Holborn or Covent Garden.

A steel-and-glass structure, originally built in 1978, then later enlarged in the 1980s, with terraced gardens, its own plaza, and individually controlled central heating, the hotel is elegantly decorated in greens and beiges, its extensive planting evoking a garden effect. The well-decorated bedrooms—many for nonsmokers—have hair dryers, in-house videos, radios, trouser presses, and tea/coffee makers.

Dining/Entertainment: Maudie's Bar makes a good pretheater rendezvous, and Maudie's Restaurant is open for lunch and dinner 7 days a week specializing in a French cuisine. Who was the original Maudie? She's Sir Osbert Lancaster's famous arbiter-of-chic cartoon character, Maudie Littlehampton.

Services: 24-hour room service, laundry, baby-listening service.

Facilities: Garage.

5 Westminster & Victoria

WESTMINSTER
MODERATE

Stakis St. Ermins Hotel

Caxton St., London SW1H 0QW. ☎ **0171/222-7888.** Fax 0171/222-6914. 290 rms, 7 suites. MINIBAR TV TEL. £129–159 ($203.80–$251.20) double; from £250 ($395) suite. Children up to 16 stay free in parents' room. Continental breakfast £7.50 ($11.85) extra. AE, DC, MC, V. Tube: St. James's Park.

Many guestrooms are quite sumptuous, with luxurious furnishings that are often elegant and ornate. Other rooms are modernized, tastefully furnished, but often rather compact. Some 55 bedrooms are reserved for nonsmokers.

A turn-of-the-century red-brick building, enlarged with a modern wing, this hotel is ideally located in the heart of Westminster and only a few minutes' walk from Buckingham Palace, the Houses of Parliament, and Westminster Abbey. There is 24-hour room service and laundry service.

The hotel has two restaurants: the Caxton Grill offers an à la carte menu at excellent value, while the Carving Table has a fixed price for lunch and dinner, serving a selection of roast meats, salads, and international dishes. Lunch costs £14.50 ($22.90); dinner, £16.50 ($26.05). The lounge bar serves light snacks 24 hours a day, as well as an afternoon tea every day from 3 to 5:30pm.

VICTORIA
EXPENSIVE

Goring Hotel

15 Beeston Place, Grosvenor Gardens, London SW1W 0JW. ☎ **0171/396-9000.** Fax 0171/ 834-4393. 75 rms, 5 suites. TV TEL. £155–£185 ($244.90–$292.30) double; from £220 ($347.60) suite. English breakfast £12 ($18.95) extra. AE, DC, MC, V. Parking £15 ($23.70). Tube: Victoria Station.

Built in 1910 by Mr. O.R. Goring, this was the first hotel in the world to have central heating and a private bathroom in every bedroom. Located just behind Buckingham Palace, it is situated within easy reach of the royal parks, Victoria Station, the West London air terminals, Westminster Abbey, and the Houses of Parliament.

Today, top-quality service is still provided, this time by the founding father's grandson, George Goring. The rooms here are called apartments. Some of the units are air-conditioned. The charm of a traditional English country home is reflected in the paneled drawing room, where fires burn in the ornate fireplaces on nippy evenings. Nearby is a sun room with a view of the gardens in the rear and a bar situated by the window. All the well-furnished bedrooms have been refurbished with marble bathrooms.

Dining/Entertainment: You can have a three-course luncheon for £21 ($33.20) and dinner for £26 ($41.10). Some of the chef's specialties include a fine duckling pâté, calves' liver with bacon and fried onions, venison, and roast boned best end of lamb.

Services: 24-hour room service, laundry, valet, and free use of local health club.

MODERATE

☺ Topham's Ebury Court

28 Ebury St., London SW1W 0LU. ☎ **0171/730-8147.** Fax 0171/823-5966. 42 rms (23 with bath). TV TEL. £95 ($150.10) double without bath; £115 ($181.70) double with bath. AE, DC, MC, V. Tube: Victoria Station.

Founded in 1937, this hotel was created when five small row houses were interconnected into one coherent whole. With its flower-filled window boxes, the place has a country-house flavor and is brightly painted in turquoise and white. The little reception rooms are informal and decorated with flowery chintzes and attractive antiques. Most rooms have facilities for making coffee and tea. Both laundry and dry-cleaning service are available.

Tophams Restaurant offers traditional English food at both lunch and dinner.

INEXPENSIVE

Collin House

104 Ebury St., London SW1W 9QD. ☎ **0171/730-8031.** Fax 0171/730-8031. 13 rms (8 with bath). £50 ($79) double without bath; £60 ($94.80) double with bath. All rates include English breakfast. No credit cards. Tube: Victoria Station.

Collin House provides a good, clean bed-and-breakfast under the watchful eye of its resident proprietors, Mr. and Mrs. D.L. Thomas. Everything is well maintained in this mid-Victorian townhouse. There are a number of family rooms. The main bus, rail, and Underground terminals are all located about a 5-minute walk from the hotel. Knightsbridge, Piccadilly Circus, Leicester Square, and Oxford Street are easily accessible by tube, bus, or taxi, as are the theaters of the West End.

⑤ Elizabeth Hotel

37 Eccleston Sq., London SW1V 1PB. ☎ **0171/828-6812.** 38 rms (32 with bath or shower), 5 studios and apts (minimum stay of three months). £60 ($94.80) double without bath, £70–£80 ($110.60–$126.40) double with bath or shower; £75 ($118.50) triple without bath, £90 ($142.20) triple with bath or shower; £85 ($134.30) quad without bath, £100 ($158) quad with bath or shower; from £195 ($308.10) weekly studio; from £195 ($308.10) weekly 2-bedroom apt. All rates include English breakfast. No credit cards. Tube: Victoria Station.

The Elizabeth is an unpretentious, privately owned establishment overlooking the gardens of Eccleston Square, which was built by Thomas Cubitt, Queen Victoria's favorite builder. Located behind Victoria Station, it's an excellent place to stay, convenient to Belgravia and Westminster, not far from Buckingham Palace and just a few doors away from a house where Sir Winston Churchill once lived. Most of the accommodations are reached by elevator, and each is individually decorated in a Victorian motif. The original atmosphere of the place has been carefully preserved, as reflected in the furnishings, framed prints, and wallpaper. Some rooms have TVs. If you're going to be in London for a minimum of three months, ask about leasing an apartment.

6 Knightsbridge & Belgravia

KNIGHTSBRIDGE
VERY EXPENSIVE

Sheraton Park Tower

101 Knightsbridge, London SW1X 74N. ☎ **0171/235-8050** or 800/325-3535. Fax 0171/235-8231. 295 rms, 25 suites. A/C MINIBAR TV TEL. £210 ($331.80) double; from £375 ($592.50) suite. VAT extra. English breakfast £14.50 ($22.90) extra. AE, DC, MC, V. Parking £9 ($14.20). Tube: Knightsbridge.

Sheraton Park Tower is not only one of the most convenient hotels in London, virtually at the doorstep of Harrods, but one of the best. Its unusual circular architecture provides a stark but interesting contrast to the well-heeled 19th-century neighborhood around it. From its windows guests have a view of Hyde Park. The front door isn't where you'd expect it—it's discreetly placed in the rear of the building, where taxis can deposit guests more conveniently.

Its busy travertine-covered lobby bustles with scores of international businesspeople, diplomats (the French embassy is across the street), and military persons, who congregate on one of the well-upholstered sofas or amid the Edwardian comfort of the hideaway bar. Back in your room, you'll find such comforts as central

---

Impressions

"Till that day I never noticed one of the worst things about London——the fact that it costs money even to sit down."

—George Orwell, *Down and Out in Paris and London,* 1933

heating, soundproof windows, in-house movies, and a radio, viewbill, voicemail, and in all the executive rooms, fax machines.

Dining/Entertainment: In the Knightsbridge Lounge, near the ground-floor kiosks, afternoon tea is served. The champagne bar offers you the choice of either a glass or a silver tankard filled with the bubbly, along with lobster, club sandwich, or "Bangers and Mash." The Restaurant 101, with its own entrance onto Knightsbridge, is open daily from 7am to 11pm, offering good food; it's ideal for after-theater supper. You can dine on such dishes as crab and salmon ragout, breast of pheasant, or brochette of tiger prawns and scallops.

Services: 24-hour room service, laundry, babysitting.

Facilities: Business center, news kiosk, free access to nearby health club.

EXPENSIVE

Basil Street Hotel

8 Basil St., London SW3 1AH. ☎ **0171/581-3311.** Fax 0171/581-3693. 90 rms (80 with bath or shower), 1 suite. TV TEL. £100 ($158) double without bath, £175 ($276.50) double with bath; £265 ($418.70) suite. English breakfast £11.50 ($18.15) extra. AE, DC, MC, V. Parking £23 ($36.35) at 24-hour nearby garage. Tube: Knightsbridge.

The Basil has long been a favorite little hotel for discerning British who make an annual pilgrimage to London to shop at Harrods and perhaps attend the Chelsea Flower Show. This Edwardian charmer was not ruined by modernization and is preferred by guests who can appreciate a highly individualistic hotel.

There are several spacious and comfortable lounges, appropriately furnished with 18th- and 19th-century decorative accessories. Off the many rambling corridors are smaller sitting rooms. The hotel offers bedrooms that have been modernized and decorated in soft fabrics and harmonious color schemes. The standard of housekeeping is excellent. A three-course table d'hôte luncheon costs £15 ($23.70), and dinner is £20 ($31.60). Candlelight and piano music re-create the atmosphere of a bygone era. The Upstairs Restaurant serves lighter meals and snacks, and the Downstairs Wine Bar offers an excellent selection of wines and inexpensive food. Ideal for a light lunch or afternoon tea, the Parrot Club is a rendezvous reserved only for women.

The Beaufort

33 Beaufort Gardens, London SW3 1PP. ☎ **0171/584-5252** or 212/682-9191. Fax 0171/589-2834. 21 rms, 7 suites. TV TEL. £150–£215 ($237–$339.70) double; £240 ($379.20) junior suite for two. AE, DC, MC, V. Free overnight parking on street. Tube: Knightsbridge.

The Beaufort, located only 200 yards from Harrods, sits behind two Victorian porticoes and an iron fence that was added when the buildings were constructed in the 1870s. The owner combined a pair of adjacent houses, ripped out the old decor, and created an updated ambiance of merit and charm. You register at a small alcove extending off a bay-windowed parlor, and later you climb the stairway used by the queen of Sweden during her stay here several years ago.

Each bedroom features at least one well-chosen painting by a London artist, a modern color scheme, plush carpeting, and a kind of grace throughout. One added advantage of this place is the helpful staff and the direction of its owner, Diana Wallis, a television producer. She created the feeling of a private house in the heart of London, putting earphone radios, flowers, and a selection of books to read in each room.

Dining/Entertainment: Light meals are available from room service; a 24-hour honor bar is also available.

Accommodations from Kensington to Belgravia

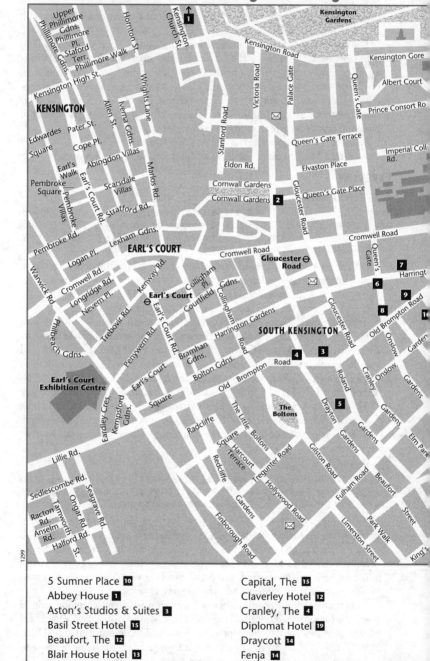

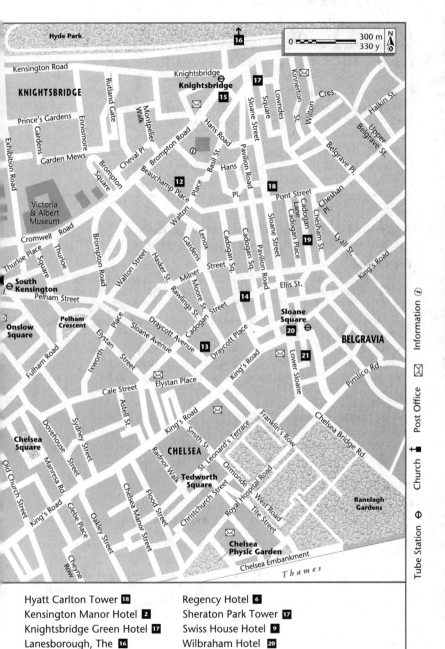

Hyatt Carlton Tower **18**
Kensington Manor Hotel **2**
Knightsbridge Green Hotel **17**
Lanesborough, The **16**
Pelham Hotel **11**
Periquito Hotel Kensington **7**

Regency Hotel **6**
Sheraton Park Tower **17**
Swiss House Hotel **9**
Wilbraham Hotel **20**
Willett **21**

Tube Station ⊖   Church ✝   Post Office ⊠   Information ⓘ

🐱 Family-Friendly Hotels

Sandringham Hotel   *(see p. 140)* Out in Hampstead—children have plenty of room to play on the heath—this hotel offers both triple rooms and family rooms for four or five people.

Hart House Hotel   *(see p. 137)* This small family-run bed-and-breakfast is right in the center of the West End near Hyde Park. Many of its rooms are triples; special family suites with connecting rooms can be arranged.

Blandford Hotel   *(see p. 136)* For the family on a budget, this hotel near Baker Street of Sherlock Holmes fame has a number of triple or family rooms (suitable for four or five guests). Kids can walk to Madame Tussaud's waxworks.

Services: Theater tickets, car rental, sightseeing, babysitting.
Facilities: Access to nearby health club at a nominal charge.

The Capital

22–24 Basil St., London SW3 1AT. ☎ **0171/589-5171** or 800/926-3199. Fax 0171/ 225-0011. 40 rms, 8 suites. A/C MINIBAR TV TEL. £197–£250 ($311.25–$395) double; from £290 ($458.20) suite. AE, DC, MC, V. Parking £15 ($23.70). Tube: Knightsbridge.

The Capital is one of the most personalized hotels in the West End. Small and modern, it's a stone's throw from Harrods. The owner, David Levin, has created a warm townhouse ambiance, the result of an extensive refurbishment program. The elegant fin-de-siècle decoration is matched by the courtesy and professionalism of the staff. The corridors and staircase are all treated as an art gallery, with original oil paintings. The bedrooms are tastefully decorated, many with Ralph Lauren designs.

Dining/Entertainment: The Capital Restaurant is among the finest in London, offering exquisitely prepared main dishes. A fixed-price lunch costs £21.50–£25 ($33.95–$39.50); a set dinner, from £25 ($39.50). You can also order à la carte.

Services: 24-hour room service, laundry.

MODERATE

✪ Claverley Hotel

13–14 Beaufort Gardens, London SW3 1PS. ☎ **0171/589-8541.** Fax 0171/584-3410. 32 rms (29 with bath). TV TEL. £95–£175 ($150.10–$276.50) double with bath. AE, DC, MC, V. All rates include English breakfast. Free parking available on street from 6:30pm– 8:30am. Tube: Knightsbridge.

Located on a quiet cul-de-sac in Knightsbridge, this tasteful hotel is just a few blocks from Harrods. In many ways it's one of the very best hotels in the neighborhood. It's a small, cozy place accented with Georgian-era accessories. The lounge is one of the hotel's most desirable features, with its 19th-century oil portraits, a Regency fireplace, and collection of elegant antiques and leather-covered sofas—much like the ensemble you'd find in a private country house. Here, the hotel serves complimentary tea, coffee, hot chocolate, and cookies 24 hours a day. Awarded the British Tourist Authority's Certificate of Distinction for Bed-and-Breakfast Hotels in 1988, the Claverley continues to maintain the high standards that won it the award. Most rooms have Victorian-inspired wallpaper, wall-to-wall carpeting, and comfortably upholstered armchairs.

Knightsbridge Green Hotel

159 Knightsbridge, London SW1X 7PD. ☎ **0171/584-6274.** Fax 0171/225-1635. 13 rms, 12 suites. TV TEL. £110 ($173.80) double; £125 ($197.50) suite. English breakfast £9.50 ($15) extra. AE, DC, MC, V. Tube: Knightsbridge.

This unusual establishment was constructed a block from Harrods in the 1890s. In 1966, when it was converted into a hotel, the developers were careful to retain the wide baseboards, cove molding, high ceilings, and spacious proportions of the dignified old structure.

None of the accommodations has a kitchen, but the result comes close to apartment-style living. Many of the doubles or twins are suites, each well furnished with access to the second-floor "club room," where coffee and pastries are available throughout the day. Rooms contain trouser press and hair dryer. Many return guests from around the world view this hotel as their "home away from home." Coffee or tea is available all day.

BELGRAVIA
VERY EXPENSIVE

✪ The Lanesborough

1 Lanesborough Place, Hyde Park Corner, London SW1X 7TA. ☎ **0171/259-5599** or 800/999-1828. Fax 0171/259-5606. 49 rms, 46 suites. A/C MINIBAR TV TEL. £245–£310 ($387.10–$489.80) double; from £240 ($379.20) suite. English breakfast £16 ($25.30) extra. AE, DC, MC, V. Parking £3 ($4.75) per hour. Tube: Hyde Park Corner.

Originally built in 1719, as a country house by the second Viscount Lanesborough, it was demolished in 1827. Rebuilt soon after in the neoclassical style as St. George's Hospital, it was famous as the site of one of Florence Nightingale's crusades—she insisted on improvements and enlargements. During the darkest days of World War II, St. George's was one of the most visible beacons of hope as bombs fell on London, and many older Londoners were born or "patched up" within the hospital's severe and medicinal-smelling wards. In 1987, advances in technology had reduced the historic hospital into a hopelessly inefficient medical antique. The medical facilities were moved to newly built quarters in South London, and the grueling task of redefining the building began.

Soon after, a group of hoteliers, the Rosewood Group (famous for their management of such hotels as the Bel-Air in Los Angeles and The Mansion on Turtle Creek in Dallas), received permission from the London Planning Board to upgrade the building into a luxury hotel.

Most of the Georgian details of the historic building were retained. Into the echoing interior were added acres of Regency and neo-gothic details, ornate plasterwork, mahogany paneling, and a well-polished aura similar to what you might have expected in a sumptuously decorated English country house. The bedrooms are as opulent and antique-drenched as you might have expected. Each has electronic sensors to alert the staff as to when a resident is in or out, a VCR, CD and videocassette players, personal safes, fax machines, 24-channel satellite TVs, bathrooms with every conceivable amenity, triple soundproofing, and the services of a personal butler. Security is tight; there are at least 35 surveillance cameras.

Dining/Entertainment: The Conservatory, an elegant restaurant, whose decor was inspired by the Chinese, Indian, and Gothic motifs of the Brighton Pavilion, is open daily from 7am to midnight. The Library Bar, which opens into a Victorian hideaway charmingly named "The Withdrawing Room," re-creates the atmosphere of a private and very elegant London club.

Services: Personal butlers; concierges who can obtain virtually anything.

Facilities: Car-rental kiosk, and exercise equipment (Stairmasters and exercise bicycles) delivered directly to your room whenever you want them.

MODERATE

Diplomat Hotel

2 Chesham St., London SW1X 8DT. ☎ **0171/235-1544.** Fax 0171/259-6153. 27 rms. TV TEL. £105–£140 ($165.90–$221.20) double. All rates include English breakfast buffet. AE, DC, MC, V. Tube: Sloane Sq., Knightsbridge, or Victoria Station.

Part of the Diplomat Hotel's multifaceted allure lies in its status as a small, reasonably priced hotel in an otherwise prohibitively expensive neighborhood filled with privately owned Victorian homes and high-rise first-class hotels. It was originally built in 1882 by one of the neighborhood's most famous architects (Thomas Cubitt) on a wedge-shaped street corner near the site of today's Belgravia Sheraton. You register at a desk framed by the sweep of a partially gilded circular staircase beneath the benign gaze of cherubs looking down from a Regency-era chandelier.

Each of the comfortable high-ceilinged bedrooms boasts well-chosen wallpaper in Victorian-inspired colors, as well as a modern bath equipped with a hair dryer, among other accessories. The staff is very helpful. Each accommodation is named after one of the famous streets in this posh district.

7 Chelsea & Chelsea Harbour

CHELSEA
VERY EXPENSIVE

Hyatt Carlton Tower

2 Cadogan Place, London SW1 X9PY. ☎ **0171/235-1234** or 800/228-9000. Fax 0171/235-9129. 164 rms, 60 suites. A/C MINIBAR TV TEL. £270 ($426.60) single or double; £375 ($592.50) suite. One child up to 18 free in parents' room. English breakfast £14.50 ($22.90) extra. AE, DC, MC, V. Parking £20 ($31.60). Tube: Knightsbridge.

Its location and height made this luxurious hotel a landmark even before Hyatt transformed it into its European flagship. An army of decorators, painters, and antiques dealers turned it into one of the most plushly decorated and best-maintained hotels in the city.

It overlooks one of London's most civilized gardens around which Regency-era townhouses were built as part of an 18th-century planning initiative. The hotel's marble-floored lobby looks a lot like the private salon of an 18th-century merchant, complete with the lacquered and enameled treasures he might have brought back from the Far East. Even the pink-and-blue dragons and flowers that cover the thick wool carpets were made especially for the Hyatt in Hong Kong.

Its bedrooms are opulently outfitted, the beneficiaries of the many millions of dollars that the Hyatt spent on decor. Each features all the modern comforts you'd expect, as well as marble-lined bathrooms, imaginative artwork, and in-house movies.

Dining/Entertainment: After the publicity it once received as "Britain's Tea Place of the Year," the hotel has been viewed as one of the capital's most fashionable corners in which to enjoy a midafternoon pick-me-up. Of course, scones, Devonshire clotted cream, arrays of pastries and delicate sandwiches, and music are all part of the experience. The Rib Room is for relatively informal meals in a warmly atmospheric setting. The Chelsea Room, considered one of the great restaurants of London, is covered separately in Chapter 5, "London Dining." On the upper floor, a neo-Grecian bar serves light meals, and it's also popular as an early rendezvous place during the breakfast buffet.

Services: 24-hour room service, valet and laundry, hairdressing.

Facilities: Chic health club with state-of-the-art exercise equipment, aerobics studio, beauty experts, masseurs, sauna, and solariums.

EXPENSIVE

✪ Draycott

24–26 Cadogan Gardens, London SW3 2RP. ☎ **0171/730-6466.** Fax 0171/730-0236. 24 rms, 5 junior suites. MINIBAR TV TEL. £195 ($308.10) double; £250 ($395) junior suite for two. English breakfast £10.50 ($16.60) extra. AE, DC, MC, V. Tube: Sloane Square.

Located near Sloane Square in the heart of Chelsea, the Draycott opened in 1988 and has become a "secret address" known to fanciers of elegant but small hotels around the world. Here you might rest comfortably in a four-poster bed on fresh, crisp linen, as your champagne cools in a silver bucket. It's that kind of place. Check in with your most prestigious luggage. Out back the view opens onto a well-tended English garden, but inside the tone is set by chintz and a warming fire. Antiques are used discreetly. Staying here is like being a guest in a stately British home. There's even a bowl of apples set out so you can help yourself.

The main allure of the place is in its beautifully furnished bedrooms with private baths. In your room you are likely to find a copy of *An Innkeeper's Diary*, by John Fothergill, but the Draycott doesn't take all his advice seriously—that is, his belief that boring clients should pay a higher tariff. Although there is no restaurant, there is room service that includes perfectly cooked and served breakfasts.

Services: 24-hour room service, laundry, babysitting.

Facilities: Complimentary use of a nearby health club, with sauna and solarium.

Fejna

69 Cadogan Gardens, London SW3 2RB. ☎ **0171/589-7333** or 800/525-4800. Fax 0171/ 581-4958. 13 rms. MINIBAR TV TEL. £130–£195 ($205.40–$308.10) single or double. English breakfast £11.75 ($18.55) extra. AE, DC, MC, V. Free overnight parking available on street; £7 ($11.05) at nearby garage. Tube: Sloane Square.

Fejna is one of the most luxurious bed-and-breakfasts in London, located near the Peter Jones Department Store and the fashionable boutiques of King's Road. It was originally built during the 19th century as a private house and purchased from the estate of Lord Cadogan after World War II. Between 1985 and 1987, the building was completely restored and upgraded into a hotel. The rooms are named after famous writers and painters including, for example, the Turner Room. The bedrooms are decorated in an intensely traditional English style and furnished in part with antiques. The bathrooms, however, are modern, with all the amenities.

Dining/Entertainment: Light meals are available from a room-service menu, backed by a carefully selected wine list.

Services: Room service 7am to 11pm, laundry, shoe cleaning.

Impressions

"London is a roost for every bird."

—Benjamin Disraeli, *Lothair*, 1870

MODERATE

✪ Blair House Hotel

34 Draycott Place, London SW3 2SA. ☎ **0171/581-2323.** Fax 0171/823-7752. 16 rms (all with shower). TV TEL. £90–£98 ($142.20–$154.85) double. All rates include continental breakfast. AE, DC, MC, V. Tube: Sloane Square.

This comfortable hotel is a good, reasonably priced choice in the heart of Chelsea. An old-fashioned building of architectural interest, it has been modified and completely refurbished, with every comfortable room sporting radios and tea- or coffee-making equipment. Breakfast is the only meal served. Babysitting and laundry can be arranged.

INEXPENSIVE

Wilbraham Hotel

1–5 Wilbraham Place (off Sloane St.), London SW1X 9AE. ☎ **0171/730-8296.** Fax 0171/730-6815. 53 rms (40 with bath), 4 suites. TV TEL. £68 ($107.45) double with bath; from £88 ($139.05) suite. English breakfast £5.50 ($8.70) extra. No credit cards. Nearby parking £18 ($28.45). Tube: Sloane Square.

This is a dyed-in-the-wool British hotel set on a quiet residential street just a few hundred yards from Sloane Square. It occupies three Victorian townhouses that have been joined together. The bedrooms are furnished in a traditional style and are well maintained. On the premises is an attractive and old-fashioned lounge, The Bar and Buttery, where you can order drinks, simple lunches, and dinners.

Willett

32 Sloane Gardens, Sloane Sq., London SW1W 8DJ. ☎ **0171/824-8415.** Fax 0171/730-4830. 19 rms. TV TEL. £78–£85 ($123.25–$134.30) double. VAT extra. All rates include English breakfast. AE, DC, MC, V. Tube: Sloane Square.

A 19th-century townhouse opening onto gardens, the Willett is one of the nuggets of Chelsea. It has many architectural flourishes, including a Dutch roof and bay windows. While retaining its traditional charm, the hotel has been fully renovated with new furnishings in all the well-equipped bedrooms and in the public lounge areas. All the rooms have private baths with the larger doubles containing small refrigerators. The breakfast room is especially inviting. In fact, the hotel has rapidly become a favorite address with many discriminating English people who like a townhouse address and who prefer being close to the restaurants, attractions, and good shops of Chelsea.

CHELSEA HARBOUR
VERY EXPENSIVE

Hotel Conrad

Chelsea Harbour, London SW10 0XG. ☎ **0171/823-3000,** 800/HILTONS in the U.S., or 800/268-9275 in Canada. Fax 0171/351-6525. 160 suites. A/C MINIBAR TV TEL. £210–£275 ($331.80–$434.50) double. AE, DC, MC, V. Parking £10 ($15.80). Take the Chelsea Harbour Hoppa Bus C3 from Earl's Court Road and Kensington High Street (Mon–Sat).

Hotel Conrad, one of London's major five-star deluxe hotels, is the first all-suite hotel in Europe. A stunning modern architectural achievement, it's the linchpin of Chelsea Harbour's revitalization, rising high above the many yachts that bob at anchor in London's largest marina. Much of the elegant and comfortable decor inside was designed by David Hicks. The accommodations are streamlined, flooded with sunlight from large windows, and equipped with a full line of toiletries, a hair dryer, and hypoallergenic pillows.

Dining/Entertainment: The hotel's dining and entertainment facilities include the Brasserie, whose stylish and cozy interior overlooks the Thames. The Lounge offers breakfast, light snacks, afternoon tea, and champagne by the glass in the evening (to the accompaniment of live piano music). Drakes Bar, as richly nautical as its name would imply, offers a view of the dozens of neatly moored yachts in the nearby marina.

Services: 24-hour room service, babysitting, luggage storage, laundry.

Facilities: Electronic safety locks, use of fax machines in each suite, personal computer, three phones with two-line capability; a health club with a heated swimming pool, gymnasium, steam rooms, and saunas.

8 Kensington & South Kensington

KENSINGTON
VERY EXPENSIVE

Blakes

33 Roland Gardens, London SW7 3PF. ☎ **0171/370-6701** or 800/926-3173. Fax 0171/373-0442. 41 rms, 9 suites. MINIBAR TV TEL. £150–£300 ($237–$474) double; from £495 ($782.10) suite. English breakfast £16.50 ($26.05) extra. AE, DC, MC, V. Parking £18 ($28.45). Tube: South Kensington or Gloucester Road.

Blakes is one of the best small hotels in London, certainly one of the most sophisticated. The neighborhood may be staunchly middle class, but this hotel is strictly an upper-class bastion of privilege. It's so glamorous, in fact, that guests might see Princess Margaret dining in its basement-level restaurant. The hotel is the creation of a talented actress, Anouska Hempel Weinberg. The richly appointed lobby is furnished with Victorian-era campaign furniture, probably brought back by some empire builder from a sojourn in India, or at least this is the kind of romantic thought it evokes. Bedrooms are highly individualized and come in many sizes. Some contain antiques.

Dining/Entertainment: London's parade of the young and stylish, including "rag trade" types, photographers, and actors, dine downstairs in what is one of the best-reputed restaurants in town. Reservations are strictly observed by a youthful maître d'hôtel. The menu might offer such appetizers as a salad of foie gras with landais truffles and quail eggs on a purée of mushrooms. Main courses include deliciously flavored varieties of teriyaki, poached salmon in a champagne sauce, and roast partridge with juniper berries. None of this, of course, comes cheaply.

Services: 24-hour room service, laundry, babysitting.

Facilities: Access to a nearby health club; an "arrange anything" concierge.

INEXPENSIVE

⑤ Abbey House

11 Vicarage Gate, London W8 4AG. ☎ **0171/727-2594.** 16 rms (none with bath). TV. £55 ($86.90) double; £66 ($104.30) triple; £76 ($120.10) quad. All rates include English breakfast. No credit cards. Tube: Kensington High Street.

Some hotel critics have rated this the best bed-and-breakfast in London. Thanks to renovations, this hotel, which was built in about 1860 on a typical Victorian square, is modern, though many of the original features have been retained. The spacious bedrooms have central heating, electrical outlets for shavers, vanity lights, and hot- and cold-water basins. The hotel offers shared baths, one to each two lodging units. The rooms are each refurbished annually. Considering how well run and maintained the hotel is, it gets top marks for value in this neighborhood.

SOUTH KENSINGTON
EXPENSIVE

✪ Pelham Hotel
15 Cromwell Place, London, SW7 2LA. ☎ **0171/589-8288.** Fax 0171/584-8444. 35 rms, 2 suites. A/C MINIBAR TV TEL. £140–£165 ($221.20–$260.70) double; from £220 ($347.60) suite. English breakfast £10 ($15.80) extra. AE, MC, V. Tube: South Kensington.

This place has charm, style, and class. Privately owned and small, it's one of the nuggets of London, suitable for everyone from your visiting movie star to your individualistic and discerning traveler. Personal service is the hallmark here. Kit and Tim Kemp, *hoteliers extraordinaires,* have made this hotel a gem. It is one of the most stunningly decorated hotels of London, formed from part of a row of early 19th-century terrace houses with a white portico facade. Inside, high ceilings and fine moldings create a backdrop for a luxurious decor, with richly draped fabrics, linens, and silks and a collection of antiques, including Victorian oil paintings. The 18th-century paneling brought from a bank in Suffolk now lines the drawing room, making you feel as if you are in an elegant, private London townhouse. Mrs. Kemp, an inveterate collector, was the hotel decorator, filling Pelham with—among other fine trappings—needlepoint, rugs, and cushions for a homelike warmth.

Dining/Entertainment: The hotel's Kemps Restaurant is one of the finest in South Kensington. An honor bar in the drawing room creates a clublike atmosphere.

Services: "Solve-everything" concierge, room service when you want it, theater-ticket arrangements.

Facilities: Victorian "snuggery" for lounging and reading papers.

MODERATE

The Cranley
10–12 Bina Gardens, London SW5 0LA. ☎ **0171/373-0123** or 800/553-2582 in the U.S. Fax 0171/373-9497. 27 rms, 5 suites. A/C MINIBAR TV TEL. £104–£130 ($164.30–$205.40) single or double; £175–£230 ($276.50–$363.40) suite. All rates include continental breakfast. AE, DC, MC, V. Tube: Gloucester Road.

Originally built as a trio of adjacent townhouses around 1875, the Cranley became a hotel when its Michigan-based owners upgraded the buildings into one of the most charming hotels in South Kensington. Today, each of the high-ceilinged bedrooms has enormous windows, much of the original plasterwork, a scattering of antiques and plush upholstery, and a vivid sense of the 19th century. The public rooms have been described as a stage set for an ultra-English country house. There is no restaurant on the premises, though light snacks are served in the rooms upon request, and breakfast is a light continental affair in one of the public rooms. All but one of the accommodations are equipped with tiny kitchenettes.

5 Sumner Place
5 Sumner Place, London SW7 3EE. ☎ **0171/584-7586.** Fax 0171/823-9962. 14 rms. MINIBAR TV TEL. £85–£95 ($134.30–$150.10) double. All rates include English breakfast. AE, DC, MC, V. Tube: South Kensington.

Winner of the British Tourist Authority award for best bed-and-breakfast in central London in 1991, this carefully restored 1850s Victorian townhouse is a delightful residence. Some of its traditionally furnished bedrooms have minibars, and all have private baths. Each room is immaculately maintained and refreshingly uncluttered. A buffet selection of foods is served within a 19th-century conservatory overlooking a sun terrace. The owners, John and Barbara Palgan, provide the kind of personal attention that makes their many visitors want to return.

The Regency Hotel

100 Queen's Gate, London SW7 5AG. ☎ **0171/370-4595** or 800/328-9898. Fax 0171/370-5555. 198 rms, 11 suites. A/C MINIBAR TV TEL. £105–£120 ($165.90–$189.60) double; £179 ($282.80) luxury suite for two; £199 ($314.40) double suite with Jacuzzi. English breakfast £12.50 ($19.75) extra. AE, DC, MC, V. Tube: Gloucester Road or South Kensington.

The Regency—close to museums, Kensington, and Knightsbridge—takes its name from the historical period of the Prince Regent, later George IV. Located on a street lined with Doric porticoes, six Victorian terrace houses were converted into one stylish, seamless whole by an army of construction engineers and decorators. A Chippendale fireplace, flanked by wing chairs, greets guests near the polished hardwood of the reception area. One of the building's main stairwells has what could be London's most unusual lighting fixture: five Empire chandeliers suspended vertically, one on top of the other. Since its opening, the hotel has hosted everyone from the late Margot Fonteyn to members of the British royal family. The modernized guestrooms are tasteful and elegant.

The hotel's restaurant—the Pavilion Restaurant—serves moderately priced international dishes. Hotel services include 24-hour room service, laundry, and babysitting. At your disposal are the Regency Health Club (with steam rooms, saunas, and a sensory-deprivation tank) and a business center.

INEXPENSIVE

✪ Aston's Budget Studios, Aston's Designer Studios & Suites

39 Rosary Gardens, London SW7 4NQ. ☎ **0171/370-0737** or 800/525-2810. Fax 0171/835-1419. 60 studios and apts (38 with bath). A/C TV TEL. Budget Studios £49–£56 ($77.40–$88.50) double; £70–£85 ($110.60–$134.30) triple; £85–£95 ($134.30–$150.10) quad. Designer Studios £85–£110 ($134.30–$173.80) single or double; £120–£160 ($189.60–$252.80) two-room suite for two to four. AE, DC, MC, V. Tube: Gloucester Road.

Located in a carefully restored row of interconnected Victorian townhouses, this establishment offers a carefree alternative to the traditional hotel—which many readers find well suited for their needs. It features comfortably furnished studios and suites—usually but not always rented by the week—that combine 19th-century nostalgia with the convenience and economy of self-catering, all under the personal management of Ms. Shelagh King. Heavy oak doors and collections of 18th-century hunting scenes give Aston's foyer a traditional atmosphere.

Accommodations are available in several categories of size and luxury: Budget Studios, Designer Studios, and Designer Suites, with accessories and furnishings that are upgraded with each category. Regardless of its price, each unit has lots of convenient extras, which always include—concealed behind doors—a compact but complete kitchenette. The **Budget Studios** have fully serviced bathrooms that are shared with a strictly limited handful of other guests. The **Designer Studios** and two-room **Designer Suites** are decorated with rich fabrics and furnishings, feature marble-sheathed private shower and bathrooms, and have answering machines hooked up to the telephones and a host of electronic accessories well suited to anyone doing business in London. Considering the amenities of this place (which has received very positive feedback from many Frommer readers), the cost of a London holiday here is considerably less than at a more standardized and traditional kind of hotel.

There is laundry service, secretarial service, private catering on request, car and limousine service.

Hotel 167

167 Old Brompton Rd., London SW5 0AN. ☎ **0171/373-0672.** Fax 0171/373-3360. 18 rms. MINIBAR TV TEL. £68–£75 ($107.45–$118.50) double. Extra bed in room £12 ($18.95). All rates include continental breakfast. AE, DC, MC, V. Tube: South Kensington.

Hotel 167 is one of the more fashionable guesthouses in the area, sheltered in a once-private Victorian townhouse, which, including the basement, has four floors of living space. While some of the bedrooms are in the basement, they have big windows for illumination. The decor is quite stylish, with such accents as metal, chrome, and pinewood, in Scandinavian modern and even Japanese styles, and the windows have venetian blinds, not curtains.

Kensington Manor Hotel

8 Emperor's Gate, London SW7 4HH. ☎ **0171/370-7516.** Fax 0171/373-3163. 15 rms, 1 suite. MINIBAR TV TEL. £75–£94 ($118.50–$148.50) double; £120 ($189.60) suite for four. All rates include VAT and English breakfast. AE, DC, MC, V. Tube: Gloucester Road.

Located in a cul-de-sac, this hotel offers warmth and elegance in a stately late Victorian building. Personal service of a high standard is the keynote of this place, including room service, laundry service, and dry cleaning. The bedrooms in this small lodging are individually decorated, each one named after a county of England. A buffet breakfast is served.

9 Earl's Court

INEXPENSIVE

Periquito Hotel Kensington

34–44 Barkston Gardens, London SW5 0EW. ☎ **0171/373-7851.** Fax 0171/370-6570. 75 rms. TV TEL. Sun–Thurs £69 ($109) single or double; Fri–Sat £64 ($101.10) single or double. Breakfast £5–£7 ($7.90–$11.05) extra. AE, DC, MC, V. Parking £8.50–£10 ($13.45–$15.80). Tube: Earl's Court.

When it was first established in 1905, this hotel offered bed-and-breakfast at 5p (8¢) per person; it rapidly expanded to eventually include six adjoining townhouses. By the 1960s, it was the first hotel in London acquired by the then-minor Forte Hotel Group before it went on to become one of the world's largest hotel empires. In 1993 the hotel was bought and radically renovated by a well-recommended British chain, Periquito, noted for its cost-conscious prices. The bedrooms are comfortably contemporary and filled with the bright primary colors for which the chain is known. Each is equipped with cable-connected TV, a coffee maker, and hair dryer. On the premises is a bar and a restaurant, Bistro, Bistro, decorated in a French country-style.

Swiss House Hotel

171 Old Brompton Rd., London SW5 0AN. ☎ **0171/373-2769.** Fax 0171/373-4983. 16 rms (14 with bath). TV TEL. £64 ($101.10) double with bath; £74 ($116.90) triple with bath; £84 ($132.70) quad with bath. All rates include continental breakfast. AE, DC, MC, V. Tube: Gloucester Road.

Swiss House is one of the more desirable bed-and-breakfasts in the Earl's Court area. The hotel is a white-fronted Victorian row house festooned with flowers and vines. The rear windows overlook a communal garden with a view of the London skyline. Like its neighbors, Swiss House has a front-porch portico. Its country-inspired bedrooms are individually designed. Some also have working fireplaces. There's a snack menu, including hot dishes, which can be served in the bedrooms. Traffic is heavy outside, but the windows are double-glazed. Room service is available from noon to 9pm, and babysitting is also offered.

10 St. Marylebone

VERY EXPENSIVE

The Langham Hilton
1 Portland Place, London W1N 4JA. ☎ **0171/636-1000** or 800/445-8667. Fax 0171/ 323-2340. 360 rms, 20 suites. A/C MINIBAR TV TEL. £210–£230 ($331.80–$363.40) double; executive rooms £260–£280 ($410.80–$442.40); £320 ($505.60) suite. English breakfast included with executive rooms and suites; otherwise, £15.20 ($24) extra. AE, DC, MC, V. Parking £19.50 ($30.80). Tube: Oxford Circus.

When this hotel was originally inaugurated in 1865 by the Prince of Wales, its accommodations were considered suitable as the full-time London address for dozens of aristocratic squires seeking respite from their country estates. (Its guests included Antonín Dvořák, Arturo Toscanini, Oscar Wilde, Mark Twain, and Arnold Bennett.) After wartime bombing in 1940, it languished as a dusty office space for the BBC until the early 1990s, when Hilton International took over the premises as a historic and extremely well-located hotel.

Today, the hotel's public rooms reflect the power and majesty of the British Empire at its height in the 19th century. So visible is this painstaking restoration of a great Victorian hotel that Hilton International now considers it its European flagship. The bedrooms, though somewhat less opulent than the public rooms, are well furnished with French provincial furniture and red-oak trim—cozy enclaves from the restaurants, cinemas, and commercial bustle of nearby Leicester Square.

Dining/Entertainment: Afternoon tea is served amid the potted palms of the Edwardian-style Palm Court. Vodka, caviar, and glasses of champagne flow liberally amid the red velvet of the Tsar's Russian Bar and Restaurant, while drinks are served in the Chukka Bar, a green-toned re-creation of a polo player's private club. The most upscale restaurant is a high-ceilinged Victorian fantasy, Memories of the Empire, serving doses of patriotic nostalgia and cuisine from the far corners of the British Commonwealth.

Services: 24-hour room service, concierge.

Facilities: Health club with saunas and Jacuzzis; a business office, with full secretarial services and business equipment.

EXPENSIVE

✪ Dorset Square Hotel
39–40 Dorset Sq., London NW1 6QN. ☎ **0171/723-7874** or 800/553-6674. Fax 0171/ 724-3328. 35 rms, 2 jr. suites. MINIBAR TV TEL. £110–£150 ($173.80–$237) double; £160 ($252.80) junior suite. English breakfast £10 ($15.80) extra. AE, MC, V. Tube: Baker Street or Marylebone.

A grand English country house, the Dorset Square is made up of two Georgian Regency townhouses similar to their neighbors on the small square near Regent's

Park. Hotelier Tim Kemp and his wife, Kit, have transformed the former dwellings into a hotel, with an interior so designed that the public rooms, luxurious bedrooms, and baths still give the impression of being in an elegant private home. The bedrooms are decorated in chintz or printed materials that complement the furniture, a mix of antiques and reproductions. Half the rooms are air-conditioned.

Dining/Entertainment: The hotel restaurant, The Potting Shed, provides simple well-prepared dishes at reasonable prices. In addition to the à la carte menu, a club lunch is featured at £10.50 ($16.60).

Services: 24-hour room service, laundry, babysitting.

MODERATE

Durrants Hotel

George St., London W1H 6BJ. ☎ **0171/935-8131.** Fax 0171/487-3510. 96 rms, 3 suites. TV TEL. £90–£148 ($142.20–$233.85) double; from £200 ($316) suite. English breakfast £8.75 ($13.85) extra. AE, MC, V. Tube: Bond Street.

Established in 1789 off Manchester Square, this historic hotel has a sprawling facade of brown brick highlighted with Georgian detailing. During the 100 years it has been owned by the Miller family, several neighboring houses have been incorporated into the original structure, making a walk through the pine-and-mahogany-paneled public rooms a tour through another century.

You'll find such 18th-century niceties as a letter-writing room sheathed with old paneling and a popular neighborhood pub with Windsor chairs, an open fireplace, and a decor that probably hasn't changed very much in 200 years. The establishment's oldest bedrooms face the front and have slightly higher ceilings than the newer ones. Even the most recent accommodations, however, have elaborate cove moldings, very comfortable furnishings, and a solid feeling of well-being. The in-house restaurant serves full afternoon teas and a satisfying French or traditional and English cuisine in one of the most beautiful Georgian rooms in the neighborhood. The less formal breakfast room is ringed with 19th-century political cartoons by a noted Victorian artist. Laundry service and babysitting are available. There is also 24-hour room service.

INEXPENSIVE

Blandford Hotel

80 Chiltern St., London W1M 1PS. ☎ **0171/486-3103.** Fax 0171/487-2786. 33 rms. TV TEL. £75 ($118.50) double; £145 ($229.10) triple. All rates include English breakfast. AE, DC, MC, V. Tube: Baker Street.

Located only a minute's walk from the tube, this hotel near Baker Street of Sherlock Holmes fame is a find and definitely one of London's better bed-and-breakfasts for the price. Each room has a hair dryer and coffee-making equipment. Five rooms rented as triples are suitable for families. The hotel is family run, and each guest receives personal attention. All rooms have en-suite facilities.

ⓢ Edward Lear Hotel

28–30 Seymour St., London W1H 5WD. ☎ **0171/402-5401.** Fax 0171/706-3766. 31 rms (8 with bath), 4 suites. TV TEL. £49.50 ($78.20) double without bath, £62.50 ($98.75) double with bath; from £72.50 ($114.55) suite. All rates include English breakfast. MC, V. Tube: Marble Arch.

Edward Lear is a popular hotel, made all the more desirable by the bouquets of fresh flowers set up around the public rooms. It's 1 block from Marble Arch in a pair of brick townhouses, both of which date from 1780. The western house was the London home of the 19th-century artist and poet Edward Lear, whose illustrated limericks adorn the walls of one of the sitting rooms. Steep stairs lead up to the bedrooms. The cozy units are fairly small but have all the usual facilities.

Hart House Hotel

51 Gloucester Place, Portman Sq., London W1H 3PE. ☎ **0171/935-2288.** Fax 0171/935-8516. 16 rms (10 with bath). TV TEL. £63 ($99.55) double or twin without bath, £79 ($124.80) double or twin with bath; £80 ($126.40) triple without bath, £89 ($140.60) triple with bath; £95 ($150.10) quad with bath. All rates include English breakfast. AE, MC, V. Tube: Marble Arch or Baker Street.

This is a well-preserved historic building, part of a group of Georgian mansions that were occupied by members of the French nobility living in exile during the French Revolution. Located in the heart of the West End, it is within easy walking distance of many theaters, as well as some of the most sought-after concentrations of shops and public parks in London. Cozy and convenient, the hotel is run by Mr. and Mrs. Bowden and their son Andrew. All bedrooms are clean and comfortable.

Hotel Concorde

50 Great Cumberland Place, London W1H 7FD. ☎ **0171/402-6169.** Fax 0171/724-1184. 28 rms. TV TEL. £72 ($113.75) double; £85 ($134.30) triple. All rates include continental breakfast. AE, DC, MC, V. Parking £18 ($28.45). Tube: Marble Arch.

Owned and run by the Theodore family, this establishment was built as a private house in the 1850s and later converted into a small and stylish hotel. Inside, its reception desk, nearby chairs, and a section of the tiny bar area were at one time parts of a London church. A display case in the lobby has an array of reproduction English silver, each piece of which is for sale. The bedrooms are well maintained and comfortably furnished; this relatively quiet neighborhood is convenient to the attractions and traffic arteries of Marble Arch. The owners maintain 10 apartments in buildings next door and across the street. Each has a kitchen, one to three bedrooms, and, in all cases, only one bathroom. The decor is old-fashioned and most (but not all) apartments have somewhat dowdy furniture. One-bedroom apartments cost £85 ($134.30), two-bedroom apartments rent for £95 ($150.10), and a three-bedroom apartment goes for £105 ($165.90), always with breakfast included.

11 Paddington, Bayswater & Maida Vale

PADDINGTON

MODERATE

Mornington Hotel

12 Lancaster Gate, London W2 3LG. ☎ **0171/262-7361** or 800/528-1234. Fax 0171/706-1028. 68 rms. TV TEL. £93–£113 ($146.95–$178.55) double. All rates include Scandinavian buffet breakfast. AE, DC, MC, V. Tube: Lancaster Gate.

Closely associated with a chain of hotels based in Stockholm, the Mornington brings a touch of Swedish hospitality to the center of London. Just north of Hyde Park and Kensington Gardens, the hotel has been completely redecorated with a Scandinavian-designed interior. The bedrooms are tastefully conceived and comfortable. In the library, visitors can wind down—entertaining their friends or making new ones. In a well-stocked bar you can order snacks and, if you're back in time, afternoon tea. Considering what you get—especially the comfort and service, not to mention a genuine Finnish sauna—the price is competitive for London. The bedrooms are modern and comfortable.

INEXPENSIVE

⑤ Camelot Hotel

45–47 Norfolk Sq., London W2 1RX. ☎ **0171/723-9118.** Fax 0171/402-3412. 44 rms (40 with bath or shower). TV TEL. £71 ($112.20) double with bath; £85 ($134.30) triple with bath; £114 ($180.10) quad with bath. All rates include English breakfast. DC, MC, V. Tube: Paddington.

Originally built in 1850 as a pair of adjacent townhouses, this simple but comfortable hotel stands at the center of an old tree-filled square, about two minutes' walk from Paddington Station. The hotel was refurbished in the late 1980s and now has an elevator. Floral curtains, framed prints, and matching bedspreads create a homelike environment. The comfortable and well-furnished guestrooms have radios and complimentary beverage trays. Families with children are welcome.

BAYSWATER
MODERATE

The Abbey Court

20 Pembridge Gardens, London W2 4DU. ☎ **0171/221-7518.** Fax 0171/792-0858. 22 rms, 3 suites. TV TEL. £130 ($205.40) double or twin; £160 ($252.80) suite with four-poster bed. AE, DC, MC, V. Tube: Notting Hill Gate.

Abbey Court is a small and rather luxurious choice. Situated in a white-fronted mid-Victorian townhouse, it has a flowery patio in front and a conservatory in back. The lobby is graciously decorated with a sunny bay window, flower-patterned draperies, and a comfortable sofa and chairs. You'll find fresh flowers in the reception area and the hallways. Each room offers carefully coordinated fabrics and fine furnishings, mostly 18th- and 19th-century country antiques. Italian-marbled bathrooms are equipped with Jacuzzi bath, shower, and heated towel rails. Light snacks and drinks are available from room service 24 hours a day. Kensington Gardens is a short walk away, as are the antiques stores along Portobello Road.

Pembridge Court Hotel

34 Pembridge Gardens, London W2 4DX. ☎ **0171/229-9977.** Fax 0171/727-4982. 25 rms. TV TEL. £115–£155 ($181.70–$244.90) double. All rates include English breakfast. AE, DC, MC, V. Tube: Notting Hill Gate.

Built in 1852 as a private house, this hotel presents an elegant cream-colored neoclassical facade to a residential neighborhood that has grown increasingly fashionable. Most of the comfortably outfitted bedrooms feature at least one antique, as well as 19th-century engravings and plenty of warmly patterned flowery fabrics. Some of the largest and most stylish rooms are on the top floor, their bathrooms tiled in Italian marble. Others include three deluxe rooms overlooking Portobello Road. The Spencer and Churchill rooms, for example, are decorated in blues and yellows, while the Windsor Room has a contrasting array of tartans. There is 24- hour room service, laundry, and dry cleaning.

In Caps, the hotel's brick-lined restaurant, good Thai, French, and English food and drink, along with a well-chosen array of wines, is served.

MAIDA VALE
MODERATE

Colonnade Hotel

2 Warrington Crescent, London W9 1ER. ☎ **0171/289-2167**. Fax 0171/286-1057. 48 rms.
TV TEL. £90–£120 ($142.20–$189.60) double. All rates include English breakfast.
AE, MC, V. Parking £10 ($15.80). Tube: Warwick Avenue.

The Colonnade, a landmark in the neighborhood since 1938, is built in the Georgian style. For about half a century, it has been run by the Richards family, who maintain its charm and special atmosphere. Rooms suit many tastes, ranging from standard to larger accommodations (16 in all) with four-poster beds. Forty percent of the rooms are air-conditioned. Every bathroom, bedroom, and corridor is centrally heated 24 hours a day from the first chill wind of autumn until the last breath of retreating winter. The hotel also has a highly rated restaurant and bar, Cascades, which is especially known for its fondues in the winter months.

12 Holland Park

VERY EXPENSIVE

✪ Halcyon Hotel

81 Holland Park Ave., London W11 3RZ. ☎ **0171/727-7288**, 800/457-4000 in the U.S.,
or 800/668-8355 in Canada. Fax 0171/229-8516. 43 rms, 19 suites. A/C MINIBAR TV TEL.
£235 ($371.30) double; from £275 ($434.50) suite. English breakfast £12.50 ($19.75)
extra. AE, DC, MC, V. Tube: Holland Park.

As you arrive, you may think at first you're at the wrong address because only a small brass plaque distinguishes the aptly named Halcyon from other buildings on the street. Called "by far the grandest of London's small hotels," the Halcyon was formed by uniting a pair of Victorian mansions originally built in 1860. Today they constitute a hotel of charm, class, fashion, urban sophistication, and much comfort. Since the hotel opened in 1985, its clientele has included a bevy of international film and recording stars who like the privacy and anonymity provided here: the Rolling Stones, Bruce Willis, Sigourney Weaver.

Many of the accommodations are classed as suites, and each unit is lavishly outfitted with the kinds of furnishings and textiles you might find in an Edwardian country house. Several accommodations are filled with such whimsical touches as tented ceilings, and each has all the modern luxuries you'd expect in a hotel of this caliber. The public rooms are inviting oases, with trompe-l'oeil paintings against backgrounds of turquoise. The designer of the hotel was an American, Barbara Thornhill.

Dining/Entertainment: The hotel's superb restaurant, The Room at the Halcyon, is recommended separately in Chapter 5.

Services: Complimentary limousine service, 24-hour room service, babysitting, 1-hour clothes pressing, message-paging system (for which they provide beepers) that extends 20 miles from the hotel.

Facilities: Night safes, business center, membership to Vanderbilt Tennis Club and Lambton Place Health Club.

13 Hampstead

INEXPENSIVE

⑤ Sandringham Hotel

3 Holford Rd., London NW3 1AD. ☎ **0171/435-1569.** Fax 0171/431-5932. 15 rms (all with bath or shower). TV. £74–£85 ($116.90–$134.30) double; £97 ($153.25) triple. All rates include English breakfast. MC, V. Free parking. Tube: Hampstead.

You'd never guess this is a hotel, because it stands on a residential street in one of the best parts of London. The Sandringham Hotel was refurbished in the early 1990s by the energetic American couple who own and operate it. The main lounge is elegant, featuring a Victorian fireplace and a serve-yourself honor bar. The formal dining room overlooks a Japanese garden where in the summer months, afternoon tea is served.

The bedrooms are all individually decorated with lovely antique furnishings and luxurious fabrics with some containing working fireplaces. From the upper rooms, you have a panoramic view over Hampstead Heath to the center of London. Laundry service, babysitting, and room service are available.

14 Airport Hotels

NEAR GATWICK AIRPORT

EXPENSIVE

Gatwick Hilton International Hotel

Gatwick Airport, Gatwick, West Sussex RH6 0LL. ☎ **01293/518080** or 800/445-8667. Fax 01293/528980. 550 rms, 18 suites. A/C TV TEL. £140–£145 ($221.20–$229.10) single or double; from £165 ($260.70) suite. Breakfast £12 ($18.95) extra. AE, DC, MC, V. Parking £5 ($7.90).

The airport's most convenient resting place, this deluxe five-floor hotel is linked to the airport terminal with a covered walkway and offers trolleys to assist with luggage. There is also an electric buggy service between the hotel and the airport for the infirm, the elderly, or anyone with lots of suitcases. The most impressive part of the hotel is the first-floor lobby, which has a glass-covered portico that rises through four floors and contains a scale replica of the De Havilland Moth airplane *Jason*, used by Amy Johnson on her solo flight from England to Australia in 1930. The reception desk is nearby, in an area with a lobby bar and lots of greenery. The rooms are equipped with triple-glazed, soundproofed windows, radios, color TVs, and hair dryers.

Dining/Entertainment: The American-themed restaurant, Amy's, serves buffet breakfasts, lunches, and dinners. The Garden Restaurant, outfitted in an English outdoor theme, serves drinks, full meals, and snacks as well. There's also the Lobby Bar, open 24 hours a day, and a watering hole with a polo-playing theme, The Jockey Bar.

Services: Same-day laundry and dry cleaning (if collected before 9am), up-to-date flight information channel, 24-hour room service, in-house hairdresser, bank, and gift shop.

Facilities: Health club with sauna, steam room, massage room, swimming pool, and gymnasium, Jacuzzi.

NEAR HEATHROW AIRPORT
EXPENSIVE

Sheraton Skyline

A4 Bath Rd., Hayes Middlesex UB3 5BP. ☎ **0181/759-2535** or 800/325-3535 in the U.S. Fax 0181/750-9150. 352 rms, 5 suites. A/C MINIBAR TV TEL. £130–£170 ($205.40–$268.60) double; from £320 ($505.60) suite. English breakfast £12 ($18.95) extra. AE, DC, MC, V. Parking £5 ($7.90).

This hotel's contemporary plushness and array of entertainment and dining facilities attract the experienced traveler, who checks in here either to recover from a long-distance flight or else to avoid London's morning traffic before an early flight the next day. This establishment—more a miniature village than a hotel—was voted the world's best airport hotel sometime during the 1980s. Each room sports a color TV with in-house video movies, massage-style shower, and a radio.

Set behind trees, the hotel operates on an international schedule since business travelers from all over the world check in at all hours. The hotel was designed around an atrium where tropical plants and towering palms thrive beneath a translucent roof. The foundations of a cabana bar are set into the climate-controlled waters of a swimming pool.

Dining/Entertainment: In the Edwardian-style Colony Bar, a fireplace flickers late into the night, and in its adjacent well-upholstered restaurant, the Colony Room, well-prepared food is served beneath massive ceiling timbers and heavy brass chandeliers. A French café offers light meals and full buffet breakfasts, and relax in the Sports Bar offering sports TV channels and giant screen Monday through Friday.

Services: 24-hour room service, laundry, shuttle service to and from four terminals at Heathrow Airport (running every five minutes between 6am and 11:30pm), verification and confirmation of departures from Heathrow.

Facilities: Business center, heated pool, fitness center.

5 London Dining

By the mid-1990s, as we go to press, London has emerged as one of the great food capitals of the world. Chefs, both young and old, have fanned out around the world and have brought items to the London kitchen never seen before, or at least never seen at such an unprecedented rate. These chefs—women and men—have pioneered the new style of cooking called "Modern British," that is forever changing, forever innovative, and forever seeking some new dish or culinary idea.

Time Out, a local magazine, called London a "city of foodies," and dining out is commonplace in spite of the often great expense involved. Food columns in local newspapers in the London of 1996 are read almost as avidly as the astrology column or the latest scandal spinning around the House of Windsor.

Even food that one's mother back in Northampton used to cook has become fashionable again. Yes, we mean British soul food such as faggots, bangers and mash, and Norfolk dumplings and Devizes pie.

Perhaps this has happened because of the minimalist excesses of the 1980s' nouvelle cuisine. You may want to skip the pig's nose with parsley and onion sauce, even though Simpson's is now serving it for breakfast.

If you want to splurge in a big way, you have the London "greats" at your disposal: gourmet havens such as La Tante Claire, Le Gavroche, Chez Nico at Ninety Park Lane, or half a dozen others. The very top restaurants in London rank among those at the top anywhere. Usually they're French, or at least French inspired. However, many chefs also prepare remarkable and inventive English dishes by making use of the very fresh produce available in the country. Wine tends to be very expensive in the leading London restaurants.

If star eateries are too expensive for you, you'll find many more moderately priced restaurants and budget establishments. Among these are public houses, also known variously as the "local," the "watering hole," the "boozer," or the pub. Pubs are a national institution; they represent much more than simply a place in which to drink. For millions of English people the pub is the regular lunchtime rendezvous. For an even-larger number, it also serves as a club, front parlor, betting office, debating chamber, television lounge, or refuge from the family. It is not, by and large, a good "pick-up" spot, but it's very nearly everything else.

At last count, there were some 5,000 to 6,000 pubs in metropolitan London; therefore, our suggestions represent no more than a few random samplings. Perhaps you could try an exploration safari of your own by moving on to possibly greener pastures next door after one drink. If repeated at length, this process becomes a "pub crawl," possibly Britain's most popular national pastime.

Our selections are fine for both women and men, but if you strike out on your own, choose your pubs carefully. Some pubs are what the English call "downright grotty," a dirty, often tough drinking place that attracts what the English refer to as soccer-loving "lager louts." If you're well dressed for the evening and don't want to risk having a drink spilled on you in a crowded pub, a safer bet would be a hotel bar or cocktail lounge.

All restaurants and cafés in Britain are required to display the prices of their food and drink in a place that the customer can see before entering the eating area. If an establishment has an extensive à la carte menu, the prices of a representative selection of food and drink currently available must be displayed as well as the table d'hôte menu, if one is offered. Charges for service and any minimum charge or cover charge must also be made clear. The prices shown must include 17.5% VAT. Most restaurants add a 10% to 15% service charge to your bill. Look at your check to make sure of that. If nothing has been added, leave a 12% to 15% tip.

Finally, there's the matter of location. Once upon a time London had two traditional dining areas: Soho for Italian and Chinese fare, Mayfair and Belgravia for French cuisine. Today the gastronomic legions have conquered the entire heart of the metropolis, and you're likely to find any type of eatery anywhere, from Chelsea to Hampstead. The majority of our selections are in the West End simply because this happens to be most convenient for most visitors.

RESERVATIONS   Nearly all places, except pubs, cafeterias, and fast-food establishments (often chain run), prefer that you make a reservation. Almost invariably, you get a better table if you "book" in advance. Some restaurants absolutely require a reservation, and for a few of the really famous places dedicated diners have been known to reserve tables weeks in advance, even before leaving home (such reservations need to be confirmed when you arrive in London). In the listings below, reservations policies of the various restaurants are noted.

HOURS   Restaurants in London keep widely varied hours, depending on the establishment. In general, lunch is offered from noon to 2pm and dinner is served from 7:30 to 9:30pm. Many restaurants open an hour earlier, and, of course, many others stay open later. Sunday is the typical closing day for London restaurants, but increasingly there are many, many exceptions to that rule.

1 Mayfair & St. James's

MAYFAIR
VERY EXPENSIVE

Chez Nico at Ninety Park Lane
90 Park Lane, W1. ☎ **0171/409-1290.** Reservations required (2 days in advance for lunch, 10 days for dinner). Fixed-price lunch £25 ($39.50) for 3 courses; à la carte dinner £48 ($75.85) for 2 courses, £57 ($90.05) for 3 courses. AE, DC, MC, V. Mon–Fri noon–2pm and 7–11pm; Sat 7–11pm. Closed 10 days around Christmas/New Year's. Tube: Marble Arch. FRENCH.

Frommer's Best of the Best

BEST STEAK, KIDNEY & OYSTER PIE   Oak Room *(see page 146)*.   Some pubs serve a horrible version of this dish —one that even Boswell and Johnson would have turned down. But chef Allen Macheral has adapted this classical dish and made it sublime. It's made *à la française* with braised beef cheeks, kidneys, and oysters topped with puff pastry.

BEST BURGER IN TOWN   Hard Rock Café *(see page 150)*.   Although such an authority as Linda McCartney (Paul's wife) has approved of this café's veggie dishes, most rockers show up for the juicy burgers. Unlike parts of America, they still serve them medium rare here (if you wish). Burgers arrive in a fresh sesame bun with a heap of fries and a salad with such Yankee favorites as Thousand Island or honey mustard. Contrast this offering with that served at the highly touted **Planet Hollywood,** 13 Coventry St., W1, where our recent burgers arrived all pink and watery inside.

BEST JAPANESE RESTAURANT   Suntory *(see page 150)*.   It's still the most famous and still better than a vast array of imitators that have arrived on the scene. One action in the kitchen tells it all. Chefs gently "stroke" the fish first for any irregularities or bruises. If any are found, the fish is discarded. How many kitchens would do that?

BEST BRITISH RESTAURANT   Wiltons *(see page 151)*.   As one reviewer put it, this restaurant has "offered a trough for the toffs since the 18th century." Even the royal family has come here to feast on its renowned poached turbot, those English savories such as angels on horseback (oysters with bacon), whitebait, gull's eggs, and what is reputed to be London's finest game dishes, including grouse and widgeon.

BEST CONTINENTAL RESTAURANT   Le Gavroche *(see page 146)*.   This restaurant pioneered the modern French approach to cuisine in London, or Britain for that matter. The creation of the Roux brothers, the restaurant has lost none of its appeal over the years. If you want to know why, order *pigeonneau de Bresse en vessie aux deux céleris.* Enclosed in a pig's bladder, the whole bird is presented at your table. Skillfully opened, the pigeon is then carved and served on a bed of braised fennel and celery.

BEST AFTER-THEATER CHOICE   The Ivy *(see page 157)*.   Popular for both pre- and after-theater dining, this traditional restaurant is opposite the Ambassador Theatre. The brasserie-type food reflects both English and modern continental influences. You can try longtime favorites such as potted shrimp, tripe and onions, steak frites, or else some more imaginative dishes such as butternut pumpkin salad or a wild mushroom risotto.

BEST AMERICAN RESTAURANT   Joe Allen's *(see page 160)*.   Like a private club, with only a small plaque indicating its entrance, the food here is

No great restaurant in London has changed its location as often as this one, but dedicated habitués from around the world continue to seek out chef Nico Ladenis, regardless of where he moves. In the latest setting in Grosvenor House, more impressive and stylish than ever before, chef Nico remains one of the most talked about chefs of Great Britain—the only one who is a former oil company executive, economist, and self-taught cook.

familiar: Maryland crab cakes, spinach salad, burgers, black bean soup, barbecue ribs, chili, Caesar salad and that famous pecan pie. On our last visit, wasn't that movie legend Lauren Bacall digging into a sirloin steak (rare) with sautéed red onions and steak frites just like she used to cook for Bogie?

BEST ENGLISH ROAST BEEF   Simpson's-in-The-Strand *(see page 160)*.   It may not be good for your health, but roast Scottish beef (they call it "Scotch" here) with Yorkshire pudding is the single most famous English dish served in the old days of the Empire. A time-honored custom since Henry VIII, this dish is the traditional Sunday lunch in Britain. But Simpson's serves it all week and it's a robust affair. Chefs circulate throughout the dining room pushing silver carving wagons, ever ready to cut your choice —rare, medium, or (God forbid) well done.

BEST ATMOSPHERIC PUB   Grenadier *(see page 169)*.   The Duke of Wellington's officers on leave from fighting Napoléon downed many a pint of lager here. Complete with a ghost (allegedly that of an officer flogged to death for cheating at cards), the pub is also a very British restaurant. On Sunday the Bloody Marys are a tradition here.

BEST INDIAN RESTAURANT   Bombay Brasserie *(see page 178)*.   Offering dishes from throughout the subcontinent, this cosmopolitan restaurant tempts with every dish—some fiery hot—ranging from tandoori kitchens to the best of Punjabi fare. Even Goan cuisine is featured. Flavor-packed dishes combine with delicate saucing and a medley of spices create various taste sensations. With Raj pictures and paddle fans, this evocative atmosphere of the old days of the British Empire makes it the most glamorous Indian restaurant in London. Try the mango Bellini to get you going on the road to Bombay.

BEST FOR AFTERNOON TEA   Palm Court, in the Waldorf Hotel *(see page 190)*.   While everyone is putting on their fancy hats and fine apparel and heading for the Ritz for tea (where, chances are, they won't be able to get a table), retreat instead to this grand old hotel, which opened in 1908. At the heart of the hotel, in the palm court the Saturday and Sunday tea dances are a famous London legend. They originated with the famous "Tango Teas" of the '20s and '30s, and have been going strong ever since, interrupted by war and a few other inconveniences. Tea served by a butler in a cutaway is also possible Monday through Friday too.

BEST ENGLISH BREAKFAST   The Fox and Anchor *(see page 186)*.   After the "full house" breakfast at this longtime favorite Smithfield Market Pub, you won't be able to eat until the following morning. It's known for attracting early morning pub crawlers who fancy a pint to get them going for the day. Expect what one local called a "gut-busting" array of breakfast food—everything from black pudding to fried bread and baked beans.

As befits any three-star Michelin restaurant, dinners are memorable in the very best gastronomic tradition of "postnouvelle cuisine," in which the tenets of classical cuisine are creatively and flexibly adapted to local fresh ingredients. The menu, written in English, changes frequently, according to the inspiration of Mr. Ladenis. Specialties include a warm salad of foie gras on toasted brioche with caramelized orange, char-grilled sea bass with a basil purée, fillet of Scottish beef with truffles and foie gras, or Bresse pigeon. Desserts are sumptuous.

✪ Le Gavroche

43 Upper Brook St., W1. ☎ **0171/408-0881.** Reservations required, as far in advance as possible. Appetizers £12.50–£30 ($19.75–$47.40); main courses £12.60–£63 ($19.90–$99.55); fixed-price lunch £55 ($86.90); fixed-price dinner £60 ($90). AE, DC, MC, V. Mon–Fri noon–2pm and 7–11pm. Tube: Marble Arch. FRENCH.

Le Gavroche has long stood for quality French cuisine, perhaps the finest in Great Britain. It's the creation of two Burgundy-born brothers, Michel and Albert Roux. Service is faultless, the ambiance chic and formal without being stuffy. The menu changes constantly, depending on the availability of the freshest produce of the season and, more important, the inspiration of the Roux brothers, who began modestly in London at another location and went on to fame in the culinary world.

Their wine cellar is among the most interesting in London, with many quality burgundies and Bordeaux. Try, if featured, rabbit with herb risotto, papillote of smoked salmon, or tournedos gratinés aux poivres. Desserts are usually called sublime, ranging from a sablé of pears and chocolate to an omelette Rothschild. Most main courses are served on silver trays covered with domes, which are lifted with great flourish. You can enjoy an apéritif upstairs while perusing the menu and enjoying the delectable canapés.

EXPENSIVE

✪ Oak Room

In Le Méridien London, 21 Piccadilly, W1. ☎ **0171/734-8000.** Reservations required. Appetizers £12–£16 ($18.95–$25.30); main courses £22–£39 ($34.75–$61.60); set business lunch £24.50 ($38.70); "menu gourmand" £46 ($72.70). AE, DC, MC, V. Mon–Fri noon–2:30pm and 7–10:30pm; Sat 7–10:30pm. Tube: Piccadilly Circus. FRENCH.

The Oak Room is one of the finest restaurants in London and has been recognized as such with many culinary awards. The setting alone—said to be the most beautiful dining room in the center of London—would be worth the trip. But it's the refined cuisine that's the draw. Lavish in its appointments, this period room where former and current greats of the world have dined has been restored to all its gilded splendor, including the ceiling and the original oak paneling. Averting your eye a moment from this gilded magnificence, you can preview the menu, a creation of French consultant chef Michel Lorain and resident executive chef Allen Macheral. You can select from "Cuisine Créative" or "Cuisine Traditionelle" menus, enjoying such dishes as terrine of poached oysters with a confit of shallots cooked in red wine or cold lasagna of crab meat with a pumpkin and horseradish cream.

MODERATE

✪ Bracewells

In the Park Lane Hotel, Piccadilly, W1. ☎ **0171/499-6321.** Reservations required. Appetizers £6–£12 ($9.50–$18.95); main courses £14–£23 ($22.10–$36.35); 3-course set lunch menu £19.50 ($30.80). AE, DC, MC, V. Mon–Fri 12:30–2:30pm and 7–10:30pm; Sat 7–10:30pm. Tube: Hyde Park Corner or Green Park. BRITISH.

Sheltered by the thick, fortresslike walls of this previously recommended Park Lane Hotel, Bracewells is one of chic London's better-kept secrets. The cuisine, prepared by the highly acclaimed British-born Andrew Bennett, is among the best in the capital, and the decor and the five-star service are worthy of its distinguished clientele. You might begin with a drink among the gilded torchères and comfortable armchairs of Bracewells Bar with canapés of lobster, foie gras, and caviar in the evening. Later you will be ushered into an intimately illuminated room whose Louis XVI paneling was long ago removed from the London home of the American banker and philanthropist John Pierpont Morgan.

The specialties are based on the freshest ingredients, using British recipes and the best of British produce. The menu throughout the year features an array of such dishes as grilled smoked duck and preserved chicken served with apples, or Dublin Bay prawns and asparagus salad with a roast vegetable purée. In addition to traditional grills, such as liver and bacon, dishes prepared at your table include saddle of hare Doivrade (2 courses). Fish dishes featured are lobster with noodles and winter vegetables, and the meat choice might include roast partridge with savoy cabbage and duck liver. A baked artichoke and goat cheese soufflé is one of several vegetarian dishes. Linger over the array of offerings on the dessert trolley or you can always opt for fruit salad that includes an abundance of exotic fruits. It is also reassuring to see traditional hot "puddings" on the menu, including hot cabinet pudding scented with kirsch. There is also an impressive selection of British cheeses ranging from your classic Stilton from Nottinghamshire to a Cerney Ash from Gloucestershire.

The table d'hôte is always worth looking at and represents exceedingly good value. It may for instance, feature starters such as crackington clam pasta followed by braised oxtail and a selection of both hot desserts and those off the trolley. An intelligent selection of wines is recommended to accompany the menu, each of which is available by the glass. The full wine list is a good reflection on the vastness of the hotel's cellars. The sommelier is most helpful.

Gaylord International India Restaurant

16 Albemarle St., W1. ☎ **0171/629-9802.** Appetizers £7–£11 ($11.05–$17.40); main courses £8.25–£10.95 ($13.05–$17.30)); dinner with meat dish £18.95 ($29.95); vegetarian fixed-price lunch or dinner £16.95 ($26.80). AE, DC, MC, V. Daily noon–3pm; Mon–Sat 6–11pm. Tube: Green Park. INDIAN.

Actually there are two Gaylords in London, but this is the newer one and it has established an enviable reputation among local connoisseurs of Indian cuisine. One reason for this is that the Gaylord offers samplings of several regional cooking styles, so that you can feast on Kashmiri and Mughlai as well as on the usual tandoori delicacies. The menu is downright dazzling in its variety. The best idea here is for several people to go and order as many small dishes as possible, so that you can taste a variety. Try the *keema nan* (leavened bread stuffed with delicately flavored minced meat) and certainly the little spiced vegetable pastries known as *samosas*. For a main course, you might choose *goshtaba* (lamb balls cooked in cream and cardamom) or *murg musallam* (diced chicken sautéed herbs, onions, and tomatoes). If you don't like curry, the staff will help you select a meal of any size totally devoid of that spice, but flavored with a great many others. You'll find the manager helpful in guiding you through the less familiar Kashmiri dishes.

Langan's Brasserie

Stratton St. W1. ☎ **0171/493-6437.** Reservations recommended. Appetizers £2.95–£8.50 ($4.65–$13.45); main courses £9.50–£13.95 ($15–$22.05). AE, DC, MC, V. Mon–Fri 12:15–2:45pm and 7–11:30pm; Sat 8pm–12:45am. Tube: Green Park. FRENCH/ENGLISH.

Since its heyday in the early 1980s, when it was among the most hip and sought-after restaurants in London, this upscale brasserie has welcomed an average of 700 diners a day. The 1976 brainchild of the late Peter Langan, in partnership with actor Michael Caine and chef de cuisine Richard Shepherd, it was the first of at least four other London restaurants launched by the same group of entrepreneurs since then. The restaurant sprawls over two noisy, very see-and-be-seen floors, each filled with potted plants, spinning ceiling fans, and a 1930s kind of atmosphere. The menu is defined as "mostly French with a dash of English," and includes a spinach soufflé with anchovy sauce; salad of oyster mushrooms; croustade of quail eggs in a pastry case served with a *duxelle* of mushrooms and hollandaise sauce; Langan's seafood salad; baked fillet of sea bass with walnut oil dressing; and roast crispy duck with applesauce and sage-lemon stuffing. In addition, the menu always features a small, bemused selection of English food prepared as the English would, including sausages with mashed potatoes ("bangers and mash") with a white onion sauce.

Scotts

20 Mount St., W1. ☎ **0171/629-5248.** Reservations required. Appetizers £3.25–£9.50 ($5.15–$15); main courses lunch £8.50–£27.55 ($13.45–$43.55); fixed-price two-course lunch or dinner £15 ($23.70); fixed-price three-course lunch or dinner £18.50 ($29.25). AE, DC, MC, V. Mon–Fri noon–2:45pm and 6–10:45pm; Sat 6–10:45pm. Tube: Green Park. SEAFOOD.

Scotts is considered the most noted restaurant in the world for its oysters, lobster, and caviar. In addition to the regular spacious dining room and cocktail bar, it has a special oyster, lobster, and caviar bar. Its origins are humble, going back to a fishmonger in Coventry Street in 1851. However, its fame rests on its heyday at Piccadilly Circus when the proprietors often entertained Edward VII and his guests in private dining rooms. Scotts has been at its present location since 1967, enjoying a chic address in the neighborhood of the swank Connaught Hotel and Berkeley Square.

The restaurant's chef believes in British produce, and he handles the kitchen with consummate skill and authority. You get top-notch quality and ingredients. Featured are grilled English red mullets with ginger, garlic, and fresh tomato. Dover sole is prepared a variety of ways, though the English prefer it "on the bone," considering filleted fish food for sissies. Starters include home spiced beef with poached leek salad and mustard dressing, oak-smoked salmon with brown soda bread, and a fish soup sporting chunks of Atlantic fish and shellfish served in their own stock. More down-to-earth dishes, such as fish cakes, appear regularly on the luncheon menu.

Quaglino's

16 Bury Street, SW1. ☎ **930-6767.** Reservations recommended. Appetizers £4.95–£9.95 ($7.80–$15.70); main courses £8.95–£22.50 ($14.15–$35.55). Set-price three-course menu (available only at lunch and for dinner between 5:30 and 6:30pm) £12.95 ($20.45). AE, DC, MC, V. Daily noon–3pm and 5:30pm–midnight (till 1am on Fri and Sat). Tube: Green Park. INTERNATIONAL.

It's vast, it's convivial, it's fun, and it was voted best restaurant of the year (1994) by London's *Time Out* magazine. It occupies the premises of a former restaurant, established in 1929 by Giovanni Quaglino from Italy's Piedmont district. Personalities who paraded through these premises in ermine and pearls could fill a between-the-wars roster of Who's Who for virtually every country of Europe.

On Valentine's Day 1993, Sir Terence Conran, noted restaurateur and industrialist, refurbished the place with a vital new decor. Likened to a stylishly decorated waiting room of a railway station, the place was brought into the postmodern age by commissioning eight different artists to individually decorate the octet of massive columns that support the soaring ceiling. (Equivalent in size to what you might have expected within a cathedral, our favorite is the one inspired by the music of The Moody Blues; our least favorite the one decorated in a mélange of smoldering grays.) There's a mezzanine with a bar featuring live jazz every Friday and Saturday night, and an "altar" at the restaurant's back devoted to what might be the most impressive display of crustaceans and shellfish in Britain.

Menu choices have been criticized for their quick preparation and standardized format. Everything seems to be served in bowls, and sometimes the preparation isn't as marvelously subtle as you would expect in more manageably sized eateries. But considering the fact that on some nights up to 800 people might show up here for food, laughter, and gossip, the marvel is that the place functions as well as it does. Come for fun, not for culinary finesse. And consider that the portions are huge, and the *plateau des fruits de mer*, the most expensive dish on the menu —priced at £22.50 ($35.55) per person, with an £11 ($17.40) supplement if you want it garnished with lobster—is worth writing home about. Other choices include chicken soup with cannelloni and bacon; parfait of chicken livers; foie gras; tartlet of crab with saffron; seared salmon with potato pancakes; and grilled rabbit with herb jus, pancetta, and char-grilled vegetables. There's a short list of reasonably priced wines, as well as a much longer and more sophisticated list if you ask for it.

The Veeraswamy

99–101 Regent St., W1. ☎ **0171/734-1401.** Reservations recommended. Appetizers £3–£6.95 ($4.75–$11); main courses £10.50–£16.50 ($16.60–$26.05); lunch buffet £12.95 ($20.45); set menu £20.95–£28.95 ($33.10–$45.75). AE, DC, MC, V. Mon–Sat noon–2:30pm and 6–11:30pm. Tube: Piccadilly Circus. INDIAN.

When it was originally established in 1927 as the first Indian restaurant in Europe, every socialite in London came for the novel experience of tasting the cuisine of Britain's faraway colony. (Its founder, Edward Palmer, who had made a fortune in trading spices, was born in 1860 in India of English parents.) Beautifully restored in the mid-1980s, it is still one of London's leading choices for Indian regional and tribal dishes.

In the kitchen, each chef is a specialist in the cuisine of his region of the subcontinent. Whether from Gujarat or Goa (try the fiery coconut-flavored chicken), the food is often mouth tingling. Vegetarians appreciate the *thalis*, the home-baked breads, and the array of well-seasoned vegetables, which some diners order in combinations as meals unto themselves. The Regent Street business crowd usually opts for the all-you-can-eat lunchtime buffet, while the evening crowd opts for pre- or post-theater dinners, before or after a West End play. (Some diners prefer drinks and appetizers before the play, and then return for their main courses after the play is over—an accommodation that the management here usually schedules gracefully.)

INEXPENSIVE

Brasserie on the Park

In the Park Lane Hotel, Piccadilly, W1. ☎ **0171/499-6321.** Reservations recommended. Appetizers £3.50–£7 ($5.55–$11.05); main courses £4.50–£14.50 ($7.10–$22.90); fixed-price menus £10.95 ($17.30) for two courses. AE, DC, MC, V. Mon–Fri noon–3pm and 6–11pm; Sat noon–11pm; Sun and public holidays noon–11pm. Tube: Hyde Park Corner or Green Park. FRENCH.

Brasserie on the Park in the Park Lane Hotel is bright and breezy, decorated in art deco style to match the hotel's famous ballroom. The à la carte menu features appetizers such as a salad of duck confit, green lentils, lardons of bacon and onions, or oysters served on crushed ice. The main courses feature classic brasserie dishes such as a choice of omelettes to more exotic dishes such as poached brill with seaweed, eggplant confit and saffron potatoes, or beef cooked in a broth of winter vegetables and bone marrow. The special fixed-price menu changes twice weekly (for instance, dishes may include a starter of fish parfait with crab meat followed by roast wild duck with lemon and honey). Popular dishes include such favorites as wild mushroom and herb risotto or tender rump or sirloin steaks. An impressive array of desserts from "double chocolate delight" to traditional bread-and-butter pudding are quite irresistible. The Brasserie offers a choice of wines (available by the glass) that have been carefully selected to complement your chosen dishes. The restaurant frequently holds festivals highlighting specific regions—for example, southwest France, California, and Veneto, in northern Italy.

Hard Rock Café
150 Old Park Lane, W1. ☎ **0171/629-0382.** Reservations not accepted. Appetizers £2.45–£5.25 ($3.85–$8.30); main dishes £5.55–£13.95 ($8.75–$22.05). AE, MC, V. Sun–Thurs 11:30am–12:30am; Fri–Sat 11:30am–1am. Closed Dec 25–26. Tube: Green Park or Hyde Park Corner. AMERICAN.

This is a down-home southern-cum-midwestern American roadside diner with good food at reasonable prices, taped music, and service with a smile. It was established on June 14, 1971, and since then more than 12 million people have eaten there. Almost every night there's a line waiting to get in, as this is one of the most popular places in town with young people, visiting rock-and-film stars, and tennis players from America.

Generous portions are served, and the price of a main dish includes not only a salad but also fries. Their specialties include a smokehouse steak, filet mignon, and a T-bone special. They also offer char-broiled burgers and hot chili. The dessert menu is equally tempting, including homemade apple pie and thick, cold shakes. There's also a good selection of beer.

ST. JAMES'S

Suntory
72–73 St. James's St., SW1. ☎ **0171/409-0201.** Reservations required. Appetizers £4.70–£15.20 ($7.45–$24); main courses £15–£30 ($23.70–$47.40); set lunch £15–£45 ($23.70–$71.10); fixed-price dinner £49.80–£90 ($78.70–$142.20). AE, DC, MC, V. Mon–Sat noon–2pm and 6–10pm. Tube: Green Park. JAPANESE.

Suntory is the most elite, expensive, and best Japanese restaurant in London. Owned and operated by the Japanese distillers and brewers, it offers a choice of dining rooms in a setting evocative of a Japanese manor house. Most first-time visitors prefer the Teppanyaki Dining Room downstairs, where iron grills are set in each table and you share the masterful skills of the high-hatted chef, who is amazingly familiar with a knife. You can also dine in other rooms on such fare as sukiyaki and tempura, perhaps selecting sushi, especially the fresh raw tuna fish delicately sliced. You can also enter one of the private dining rooms, but only if shoeless. Waitresses in traditional dress serve you with all the highly refined ritualistic qualities of the Japanese, including the presentation of hot towels. You may prefer a salad of shellfish and seaweed or a superb squid. Appetizers are artful and delicate, and even the tea is superior.

PUB & WINE BARS

Bubbles

41 N. Audley St., W1. ☎ **0171/491-3237**. Reservations recommended. Appetizers £2.50–
£3.25 ($3.95–$5.15); main courses £6–£12.50 ($9.50–$19.75); fixed-price dinner £14.50
($22.90); fixed-price vegetarian menu £7 ($11.05); glass of wine £2 ($3.15). AE, DC,
MC, V. Daily noon–6pm and 6–10pm. Tube: Marble Arch or Bond Street. ENGLISH/
CONTINENTAL/VEGETARIAN.

Bubbles is an interesting wine bar located between Upper Brook Street and Oxford Street (in the vicinity of Selfridges). The owners attach equal importance to
their food and their impressive wine list. Some selections of wine are sold by the
glass. On the ground floor guests enjoy fine wines but also draft beer and liquor,
along with a limited but well-chosen selection of bar food, such as mussels marinara
and meat and fish salads, including one made with honey-roast ham. Downstairs
is an à la carte restaurant serving both English and continental dishes, including
a selection appealing to vegetarians. Begin, for example, with French onion soup,
followed by roast rack of English lamb or perhaps roast duckling with a lemon-
and-tarragon sauce.

Red Lion

2 Duke of York St., off Jermyn St., SW1. ☎ **0171/930-2030**. Sandwiches £2 ($3.15); fish and
chips £6 ($9.50). No credit cards. Mon–Sat noon–11pm. Tube: Piccadilly Circus. BRITISH.

Ian Nairn (1930–83), a noted British writer on architecture, compared the Red
Lion's spirit to that of Edouard Manet's painting *A Bar at the Folies-Bergère* (see
the collection at the Courtauld Institute Galleries). The menu is composed of a
set number of premade sandwiches, so once they are gone you're out of luck. The
selection usually includes tuna and sweet corn, smoked salmon, and bacon, lettuce,
and tomato. On Fridays and Saturdays homemade fish and chips are also served.
The food is prepared in upstairs kitchens and sent down in a century-old dumb-
waiter; orders are placed at the bar. Wash down your meal with Ind Coope's fine
ales in this little Victorian pub with its early 1900s decorations, one of London's
few remaining gin palaces, with mirrors 150 years old. The house's special beer is
Burton's, an unusual brew made from springwater from the Midlands town of
Bourton-on-Trent.

2 Piccadilly, Leicester Square & Trafalgar Square

PICCADILLY

EXPENSIVE

Wiltons

55 Jermyn St., SW1. ☎ **0171/629-9955**. Reservations required. Appetizers £4.25–£24
($6.70–$37.90); main courses £11.50–£28.50 ($18.15–$45.05). AE, DC, MC, V. Mon–Fri
12:30–2:30pm and 6:30–10:30pm; Sat–Sun 6:30–10:30pm. Closed 2 weeks in Aug. Tube:
Green Park or Piccadilly Circus. BRITISH.

Wiltons is one of the leading exponents of cookery called "as British as a nanny."
In spite of its move into new quarters, its developers re-created the lush ambiance
of the original premises. You might be tempted to have an apéritif or drink in the
bar near the entrance, where photos of the royal family alternate with oil portraits
of the original owners. One of them, the legendary Jimmy Marks, or so it is said,
used to "strike terror into the hearts of newcomers if he took a dislike to them."
However, those days, still fondly recalled by some, are gone forever, and today a

Central London Dining

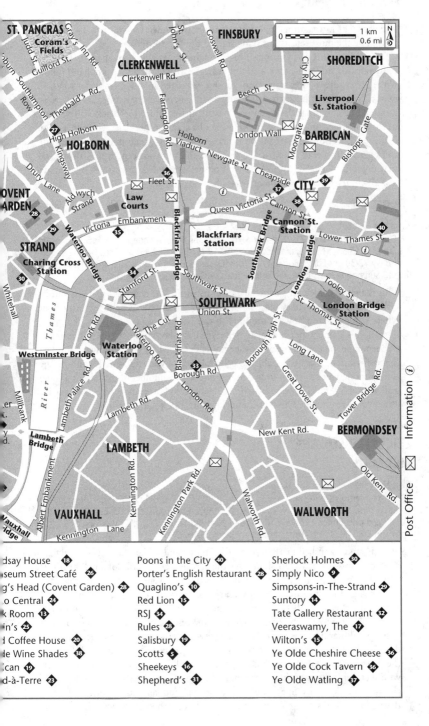

ST. PANCRAS
Coram's Fields
Judd St.
Gray's Inn Rd.
St. John's St.
Coswell Rd.
FINSBURY
City Rd.
SHOREDITCH

0   1 km
    0.6 mi
N

Guilford St.
Southampton Row
Theobald's Rd.
CLERKENWELL
Clerkenwell Rd.
Beech St.
Liverpool St. Station
Bishops Gate

High Holborn
HOLBORN
Kingsway
Drury Lane
Aldwych
Farringdon Rd.
Holborn Viaduct
Newgate St.
London Wall
Moorgate
BARBICAN
Cheapside
CITY

Fleet St.
Law Courts
Strand
Victoria   Embankment
Blackfriars Station
Queen Victoria St.
Cannon St.
Cannon St. Station
Lower Thames St.

COVENT GARDEN
STRAND
Waterloo Bridge
Blackfriars Bridge
Southwark Bridge
London Bridge

Charing Cross Station
Whitehall
Thames
Stamford St.
Southwark St.
SOUTHWARK
Union St.
Tooley St.
St. Thomas St.
London Bridge Station

Westminster Bridge
Waterloo Station
The Cut
Waterloo Rd.
York Rd.
Blackfriars Rd.
Borough Rd.
London Rd.
Borough High St.
Long Lane
Great Dover St.
Tower Bridge Rd.

River Thames
Millbank
Lambeth Palace Rd.
Lambeth Bridge
LAMBETH
Lambeth Rd.
Kennington Rd.
Kennington Park Rd.
New Kent Rd.
BERMONDSEY
Old Kent Rd.

Albert Embankment
Vauxhall Bridge
VAUXHALL
Kennington Lane
Walworth Rd.
WALWORTH

Information (i)
Post Office ⊠

dsay House ⑱
seum Street Café ㉖
g's Head (Covent Garden) ㉘
o Central ㉔
k Room ⑬
in's ㉕
d Coffee House ⑳
de Wine Shades ㊳
can ⑲
d-à-Terre ㉓

Poons in the City ㊵
Porter's English Restaurant ㉘
Quaglino's ⑩
Red Lion ⑮
RSJ ㉞
Rules ㉘
Salisbury ⑲
Scotts ⑤
Sheekeys ⑯
Shepherd's ㉛

Sherlock Holmes ㉚
Simply Nico ⑨
Simpsons-in-The-Strand ㉙
Suntory ⑭
Tate Gallery Restaurant ㉜
Veeraswamy, The ⑰
Wilton's ⑮
Ye Olde Cheshire Cheese ㊱
Ye Olde Cock Tavern ㊱
Ye Olde Watling ㊲

wide array of international guests are warmly welcomed by what we consistently find to be the most sensitive serving staff in the West End.

The thoroughly British menu of this restaurant, which opened in 1941, is known for its fish and game. You might begin with an oyster cocktail and follow with Dover sole, plaice, salmon, or lobster, prepared in any number of ways. In season, you can enjoy such delights as roast partridge, roast pheasant, or roast grouse. The chef might ask you if you want them "blue" or "black," a reference to roasting times. In season, you might even be able to order roast widgeon, a wild, fish-eating river duck. Game is often accompanied by bread sauce (made of milk thickened with bread crumbs). To finish, if you want to seem truly British, you may order a savory such as Welsh rarebit or soft roes or even anchovies. But if that's too much, try the sherry trifle or syllabub.

MODERATE

Greens Restaurant and Oyster Bar

36 Duke St., SW1. ☎ **0171/930-4566.** Reservations recommended for dinner. Appetizers £3.50–£10 ($5.55–$15.80); main courses £9–£18 ($14.20–$28.45). AE, DC, MC, V. Restaurant daily 12:30–2:45pm; Mon-Sat 6–11pm. Oyster bar Mon-Sat 11:30am–3pm and 5:30–11pm; Sun noon–3pm. Tube: Piccadilly Circus or Green Park. SEAFOOD.

This is a good choice for the excellence of its menu, the charm of its staff, and its central location. This busy place has a cluttered entrance leading to a crowded bar where you can stand at what the English call "rat-catcher counters," if the tables are full, to sip fine wines and, from September to May, enjoy oysters. Other foods to encourage the consumption of the wines are quails' eggs, king prawns, smoked Scottish salmon, "dressed" crab, and baby lobsters. If you choose to go on into the dining room, you can select from a long menu with a number of fish dishes or such grilled foods as calves' liver and bacon, kedgeree, and Greens fish cakes with parsley sauce. Desserts include Duke of Cambridge tart, black-currant sorbet, and banana fritters.

LEICESTER SQUARE

MODERATE

Sheekeys

28–32 St. Martin's Court, off Charing Cross Rd., WC2. ☎ **0171/240-2565.** Reservations required. Appetizers £4.95–£14.95 ($7.80–$23.60); main courses £9.95–£25.95 ($15.70–$41); fixed-price lunch £15.95–£18.75 ($25.20–$29.65). AE, DC, MC, V. Mon–Sat 12:30–3pm and 5:30–11:30pm. Tube: Leicester Square. SEAFOOD.

Since it was established in 1896 by an Irish-born vaudevillian, Sheekeys has always been closely associated with London's theater district. A series of small but intimate dining rooms, its walls are almost completely covered with the photographs of British and North American stage-and-screen stars, many of them autographed. A formally dressed staff caters to the culinary needs of a conservative and well-heeled clientele that feels comfortable with the restaurant's sense of tradition and polite good manners. Seafood is the specialty here, one of the few places in London that almost never (and only when specifically requested) fries its food. Instead, the delicate and fresh ingredients are steamed, grilled, or stewed, and then laden with such ingredients as sherry, cream, garlic, lemon, and herbs. The result is usually rich and delicious. Specialties include lobster and langoustine bisque, lobster thermidor, Dover sole prepared in the style of Joseph Sheekey, jellied eels (a British delicacy), fish cakes, and a concoction identified as Sheekeys' fisherman's pie. Desserts include apple tart with calvados.

INEXPENSIVE

✪ Pelican

45 St. Martin's Lane, WC2. ☎ **0171/379-0309.** Reservations recommended on weekdays, required on weekends. In restaurant, appetizers £3.25–£5.95 ($5.15–$9.40); main courses £6.95–£13.95 ($11–$22.05); pretheater suppers £9.95–£11.95 ($15.70–$18.90). In brasserie/wine bar, snacks and platters £3.50–£11.95 ($5.55–$18.90), glass of wine from £2.50 ($3.95). AE, DC, MC, V. Daily noon–12:30am (pretheater supper 5:30–7:30pm). Tube: Charing Cross or Leicester Square. FRENCH/INTERNATIONAL.

More than almost any other restaurant in its neighborhood (adjacent to the English National Opera House), this restaurant vibrates with a constant traffic of clients coming and going to one of the nearby theaters. Set within a long and narrow cream-colored room outfitted with mirrors, framed posters, and art deco accessories, it houses a bustling brasserie and wine bar in front and a genial and somewhat more sedate restaurant in back.

Many patrons who never venture past a position near the front prefer this establishment's venue as a wine bar, enjoying the diversity of vintages, the recorded jazz, and the availability of rapid but well-prepared specials that change every day.

Examples include cream of celery soup, grilled Scotch sirloin steak, and pan-fried veal with Madeira sauce and fresh vegetables. At the restaurant in back, more elaborate meals might include red mullet in a white wine sauce served with root vegetables; goat cheese mousseline with caramelized shallots; and sliced fillet of beef served with a Madeira sauce. Here a pianist adds luster every night after 10pm.

PUB & WINE BAR

Cork & Bottle Wine Bar

44–46 Cranbourn St., WC2. ☎ **0171/734-7807.** Reservations recommended. Appetizers £3.25–£8.95 ($5.15–$14.15); main courses £4.95–£8.95 ($7.80–$14.15); glass of wine from £2.30 ($3.65). AE, DC, MC, V. Mon–Sat 11am–midnight; Sun noon–10:30pm. Tube: Leicester Square. INTERNATIONAL.

Cork & Bottle is just off Leicester Square. The most successful dish is a raised cheese-and-ham pie. It has a cream-cheesy filling, and the well-buttered pastry is crisp—not your typical quiche. (In just one week the bar sold 500 portions of this alone.) The kitchen also offers a chicken and apple salad, Lancashire sausage hot pot, Mediterranean prawns with garlic and asparagus, tandoori chicken, and lamb in ale. The expanded wine list features an excellent selection of Beaujolais crus and wines from Alsace, some 30 selections from "Down Under," 30 champagnes, and a good selection of California labels.

✪ Salisbury

90 St. Martin's Lane, WC2. ☎ **0171/836-5863.** Reservations not accepted. Buffet meal £4.50–£6.50 ($7.10–$10.25); pint of lager £2.11–£2.20 ($3.35–$3.50). AE, DC, MC, V. Mon–Sat 11am–11pm; Sun noon–3pm and 7–10:30pm. Tube: Leicester Square. BRITISH.

Salisbury's glittering cut-glass mirrors reflect the faces of English stage stars (and hopefuls) sitting around the curved buffet-style bar. If you want a less prominent place to dine, choose the old-fashioned wall banquette with its copper-top tables and art nouveau decor. The light fixtures, veiled bronze girls in flowing robes holding up clusters of electric lights concealed in bronze roses, are appropriate. In the saloon, you'll see and hear the Oliviers of yesterday and tomorrow. But don't let this put you off your food. The pub's specialty, an array of homemade pies set out on a buffet table with salads, is really quite good and inexpensive. Food is served from noon until 7:30pm Monday through Saturday.

TRAFALGAR SQUARE
PUB

Sherlock Holmes

10 Northumberland St., WC1. ☎ **0171/930-2644.** Reservations recommended for restaurant. Appetizers £2.75–£5.75 ($4.35–$9.10); main courses £7.75–£13.95 ($12.25–$22.05); fixed-price menus £10.95–£14.95 ($17.30–$23.60); ground-floor snacks £3.25–£4 ($5.15–$6.30). AE, DC, MC, V. Restaurant, Mon–Sat noon–10:30pm; Sun noon–3pm and 7–10pm. Pub, Mon–Sat 11am–11pm; Sun noon–3:30pm and 7–10:30pm. Tube: Charing Cross or Embankment. ENGLISH.

It would be rather strange if Sherlock Holmes were not the old gathering spot for "The Baker Street Irregulars," a once-mighty clan of mystery lovers who met here to honor the genius of Arthur Conan Doyle's most famous fictional character. Upstairs you'll find a re-creation of the living room at 221B Baker St. and such "Holmesiana" as the cobra of "The Adventure of the Speckled Band" and the head of *The Hound of the Baskervilles.* The downstairs is mainly for drinking, but upstairs you can order complete meals with wine. Main dishes are reliable, including roast beef and Yorkshire pudding and the Copper Beeches, grilled butterfly chicken breasts with lemon and herbs. You select a dessert from the trolley. There's also a good snack bar downstairs, with cold meats, salads, cheese, and wine sold by the glass, if you wish.

3 Soho

MODERATE

Alastair Little

49 Frith St., W1. ☎ **0171/734-5183.** Reservations recommended. Appetizers £6–£15 ($9.50–$23.70); main courses £15–£25 ($23.70–$39.50); fixed-price three-course lunch £25 ($39.50). AE, DC, MC, V. Mon–Fri noon–3pm and 6–11:30pm; Sat 6–11:30pm. Tube: Leicester Square. BRITISH.

Housed in a circa-1830 brick-fronted townhouse—which for a brief period is said to have housed the art studio of John Constable—this pleasantly monochromatic restaurant provides an informal and cozy place for a well-prepared lunch or dinner. Owned by the British-Danish-Spanish trio of Alastair Little, Kirsten Pedersen (who directs the dining room), and André-Vega —it features a well-chosen menu with offerings that reflect whatever is available that day from the market. Examples might include roasted sea bass with parsley salad, rack of lamb with rosemary, and Tuscan squab. Dessert might consist of a crème brûlée, tarte tatin with crème fraîche, or a crème caramel. A full complement of wines (mostly California and Australian) might accompany your meal.

Au Jardin des Gourmets

5 Greek St., W1. ☎ **0171/437-1816.** Reservations required. Appetizers £6.85–£10.50 ($10.80–$16.60); main courses £12.50–£16.50 ($19.75–$26.05); fixed-price three-course lunch or dinner £21.50 ($33.95). AE, DC, MC, V. Mon–Fri 12:15–2:30pm and 6:30–11:15pm; Sat 6:30–11:15pm. Tube: Tottenham Court Road. FRENCH.

In an "Ile de France" off Soho Square, devotees of Gallic cuisine have been gathering to enjoy traditional specialties since 1931. Today, Soho Square and Greek

Street have been largely rebuilt and are back in fashion again. The Jardin itself has climbed to a level never previously attained, what with new kitchens and wine cellars, lavatories that can be reached without climbing two floors, and, most important of all, an air-conditioned restaurant that separates smokers and nonsmokers in the two adjacent rooms on the ground floor. There is a comprehensive à la carte menu with such specialties as poached salmon with thinly sliced beet-root, olive oil and raspberry vinegar dressing, noissettes of lamb topped with a foie gras, truffle and madeira sauce, and medallions of venison with juniper berries and sweet and sour red onion compote. The masterful selection of vintage Bordeaux and Burgundies is expertly served.

Bistro Bruno

63 Frith Street, W1. ☎ **0171/734-4545.** Reservations recommended. Appetizers £4–£6.50 ($6.30–$10.25); main courses £11.50–£17 ($18.15–$26.85). AE, DC, MC, V. Mon–Fri noon–2:30pm (last order) and 6:15–11:30pm (last order); Sat 6:15–11:30pm (last order). Tube: Tottenham Court Road. INTERNATIONAL.

Named after its chef and part owner, Bruno Loubet, this is an artfully simple restaurant, with food much more elegant and complicated that its name (bistro) would imply. Within a long and narrow dining room capped with a turquoise ceiling, blue-topped tables, and minimalist accessories, you'll enjoy a menu that changes frequently based on the availability of ingredients and the inspiration of the chef. In many ways, its menu reads like a chic restaurant in France, where combinations of food please the intellect as well as the palate. Menu items include a *boudin blanc* (white sausage) served on a ragout of broad beans; steamed baby sea bass served on a bed of soy and garlic sauce; confit of duck on a corn pancake with grape-flavored chutney; guinea file with rosemary-infused risotto; fillet of skate (stingray) with artichoke hearts; and such creative desserts as fresh strawberries served with green peppercorn ice cream. In 1995, this bistro opened a cost-conscious neighbor in the storefront next door, the Café Bruno, (open throughout the afternoon, Monday to Saturday from noon to 11:30pm) where prices are a bit lower and where the menu is less cerebral and more hearty.

Gay Hussar

2 Greek St., W1. ☎ **0171/437-0973.** Reservations recommended. Appetizers £3.40–£4.75 ($5.35–$7.50); main courses £11.50–£15.50 ($18.15–$24.50); fixed-price lunch £16 ($25.30). AE, DC, MC, V. Mon–Sat 12:30–2:30pm and 5:30–10:45pm. Tube: Tottenham Court Road. HUNGARIAN.

Gay Hussar has been called "the best Hungarian restaurant in the world." The "last of the great Soho restaurants," it's an intimate place, where diners can begin with a chilled wild-cherry soup or a hot, spicy redfish soup in the style of Szeged, in Hungary's southern Great Plain. Main courses are likely to include stuffed cabbage; fish dumplings in dill sauce; half a perfectly done chicken served in mild paprika sauce with cucumber salad and noodles; and, of course, veal goulash with egg dumplings. For dessert, select either raspberry-and-chocolate torte or walnut pancakes.

The Ivy

1–5 West St., WC2. ☎ **0171/836-4751.** Reservations required. Appetizers £4.75–£22.75 ($7.50–$35.95); main courses £6.75–£19.75 ($10.65–$31.20); Sat–Sun lunch £14.50 ($22.90). AE, DC, MC, V. Daily noon–3pm and 5:30pm–midnight (last order). Tube: Leicester Square. ENGLISH.

Effervescent and sophisticated, The Ivy has been intimately associated with the West End theater district since it was originally established in 1911. Since then, its clientele has included prime ministers Lloyd George and Sir Winston Churchill (both of whom knew a lot about viands and wines), Noël Coward, Gracie Fields, Dame Sybil Thorndike, and Rex Harrison. Renovated in the early 1990s, it features a tiny bar near the entrance where guests might be asked to wait until their table is ready and a paneled decor that seems deliberately designed to encourage discreet stargazing. Meals are served until very late, a graceful acknowledgment of the allure of after-theater suppers. Most importantly, the place, with its ersatz 1930s look, is fun, humming, and throbbing with the energy of London's glamour.

Although the menu choices appear deceptively simple, they mask a solid appreciation for fresh ingredients and skillful preparation. They include white asparagus with sea kale and truffle butter; seared scallops with spinach, sorrel, and bacon; and corned beef hash with fried egg. Also included in the offerings are Mediterranean fish soup, a great mixed grill, salads, and such English desserts as sticky toffee and caramelized bread-and-butter pudding.

Lindsay House

21 Romilly St., W1. ☎ **0171/439-0450.** Reservations required. Appetizers £4–£12 ($6.30–$18.95); main courses £12–£15 ($18.95–$23.70); fixed-price lunch £14.75 ($23.30). AE, DC, MC, V. Mon–Sat 12:30–2:30pm and 6pm–midnight; Sun 12:30–2pm and 7–10pm. Closed Dec 25–26. Tube: Leicester Square or Piccadilly Circus. BRITISH.

Lindsay House bases many of its dishes on 18th-century English recipes, though several platters are designated Tudor or nouvelle. Everyone from royalty to film stars, from diplomats to regular people show up here, including an array of discerning Americans. Since the restaurant begins serving dinner early, you might want to consider it for a pretheater dinner before a stage presentation at a Shaftesbury Avenue theater. Owner Roger Wren, who already runs some of the most fashionable restaurants in London (including Waltons of Walton Street, English House, and the English Garden), decided to open this eatery in the heart of Soho. Fireplaces and fresh flowers give it class and style.

The food lives up to the decor. Appetizers, or "first dishes," include wild mushrooms encased in a pastry with rosemary cream sauce. To follow, you might try roast rack of Southdown lamb or steamed chicken glazed with leek and ginger. Desserts include an apple and cinnamon tart with crème fraîche and a traditional bread budding. You might also order a floating island, one of England's best 18th-century confections: light poached meringues floating on a rose-scented custard.

INEXPENSIVE

✪ Chuen Cheng Ku

17 Wardour St., W1. ☎ **0171/437-1398.** Reservations recommended on weekend afternoons. Appetizers £1.75–£8 ($2.75–$12.65); main courses £6.40–£9 ($10.10–$14.20); fixed-price menus £9.50–£30 ($15–$47.40) per person. AE, DC, MC, V. Daily 11am–midnight. Closed Dec 24–25. Tube: Piccadilly Circus or Leicester Square. CHINESE.

This is one of the finest eateries in Soho's "New China," seating 400 diners. A large restaurant on several floors, Chuen Cheng Ku is noted for its Cantonese food and is said to have the longest and most interesting menu in London. Specialties are paper-wrapped prawns, rice in lotus leaves, steamed spareribs in black-bean sauce, and shredded pork with cashew nuts, all served in generous portions. Other featured à la carte dishes include fried oysters with ginger and scallions, sliced duck with chili and black-bean sauce, steamed pork with plum sauce, and Singapore noodles (thin rice noodles, sometimes mixed with curry and pork or shrimp with red-and-green peppers, reflecting a Chinese-Malaysian inspiration). Dumplings are served from 11am to 5:45pm.

PUB

Old Coffee House

49 Beak St., W1. ☎ **0171/437-2197.** Reservations not accepted. Main courses £2.20–£3.95 ($3.50–$6.25); beer from £1.95 ($3.10). No credit cards. Restaurant Mon–Sat noon–3pm. Pub Mon–Sat 11am–11pm; Sun noon–3pm and 7–10:30pm. Tube: Oxford Circus or Piccadilly Circus. BRITISH.

Once honored as "Soho Pub of the Year," the Old Coffee House takes its name from the coffeehouse heyday of 1700s London, when coffee was called "the devil's brew." The pub—heavily decorated with bric-a-brac, including such items as old musical instruments and World War I recruiting posters—still serves pots of filtered coffee. Have your drink at a long, narrow bar, where a lager costs from £1.95 ($3.10), or retreat to the upstairs restaurant, where you can enjoy good pub food at lunch, including such typically English dishes as chicken and leek pie, steak-and-kidney pie, three vegetarian dishes, and scampi and chips. Burgers and fries are always popular.

4 Bloomsbury & Fitzrovia

BLOOMSBURY

MODERATE

Museum Street Café

47 Museum St., W1. ☎ **0171/405-3211.** Reservations required. Lunch £12 ($18.95) for two courses, £15 ($23.70) for three courses; dinner, £17 ($26.85)for two courses, £21 ($33.20) for three courses. MC, V. Mon–Fri 12:30–2:15pm (last order) and 7:15–9:15pm (last order). Tube: Tottenham Court Road. MODERN BRITISH.

In an undistinguished building located within a 2-minute walk from the British Museum, this small-scale but unpretentiously charming dining room was the neighborhood's least appealing "greasy spoon" until it was transformed by Boston-born Gail Koerber and her English partner, Mark Nathan. Today—in a deliberately underfurnished setting filled with simple tables and chairs and lined with primitive paintings—you can sample an array of up-to-date dishes based on the freshness of available ingredients and the inspiration of the chefs. You can enjoy such typical dishes as roasted red pepper soup followed by char-grilled pigeon breast with apple and chestnut sauce or char-grilled swordfish with coriander, soy, and ginger. Dessert might be a lemon and almond tart.

FITZROVIA

MODERATE

Nico Central

35 Great Portland St., W1. ☎ **0171/436-8846.** Reservations required. Lunch appetizers £6.90–£12.20 ($10.90–$19.30); lunch main courses £8–£12 ($12.65–$18.95); fixed-price three-course dinner £26 ($41.10). AE, DC, MC, V. Mon–Fri noon–2pm and 7–11pm; Sat 7–11pm. Tube: Oxford Circus. FRENCH.

In this brasserie, founded and inspired by London's most legendary chef, Nico Ladenis, who now cooks at Chez Nico at Ninety Park Lane (see above), the staff delivers earthy French cuisine. Of course, everything is handled with considerable culinary urbanity. Guests sit on bentwood chairs at linen-covered tables. Nearly a dozen appetizers—called "starters," the pride of the chef—tempt you. The menu changes seasonally according to the inspiration of the chef but might include risotto with cèpes (flap mushrooms) and parmesan; charlotte of goat cheese with a fondue of red peppers; pan-fried foie gras served with brioche and a caramelized orange; braised knuckle of veal; and baked fillet of brill with assorted vegetables.

Pied-à-Terre

34 Charlotte St., W1. ☎ **636-1178.** Reservations recommended. Appetizers £13.50 ($21.35); main courses £23 ($36.35). Fixed-price, two-course lunch £16.50 ($26.05). AE, DC, MC, V. Mon–Fri 12:15–2pm (last order); dinner Mon–Sat 7:15–10:30pm. Tube: Goodge Street. INTERNATIONAL.

Considered a gastronomic restaurant of great desirability, with a subtle and very sophisticated cuisine, this restaurant has deliberately understated its decor in favor of a more intense focus on the food. You'll dine within a strictly (some say rigidly) minimalist decor, where gray and pale-pink walls alternate with metal furniture and focused lighting. At least some of the staff members might be French, as will be the wine list and the inspiration for some, but not all, of the cuisine. Menu items change with the seasons but might include an oyster-and-mushroom broth soup; snails wrapped in a casing of chicken mousse; red mullet with almond sauce; roasted scallops with puréed ginger; fillet of trout with morels and mashed potatoes; sea bass with provençal vegetables floating on a bed of bouillabaisse; fillet of John Dory with peas, covered with foie gras sauce; and fillet of sea bass served with a caviar-flavored hollandaise. Food is beautifully presented, on hand-painted plates, each combining into lush patterns and textures that offset the stylish starkness of the setting.

5 The Strand, Covent Garden & Holborn

THE STRAND
MODERATE

Joe Allen's

13 Exeter St., WC2. ☎ **0171/836-0651.** Reservations required. Appetizers £3.50–£7 ($5.55–$11.05); main courses £5.50–£11 ($8.70–$17.40). No credit cards. Mon–Sat noon–1am; Sun noon–midnight. Tube: Covent Garden or Embankment. AMERICAN.

This fashionable American restaurant attracts primarily theater crowds. It lies north of The Strand in the vicinity of the Savoy Hotel. The restaurant has other branches in Paris and New York. The decor is inspired by the New York branch, with theater posters, red-and-white checked gingham tablecloths, and a menu offering such specialties as black-bean soup, barbecued ribs with black-eyed peas, sirloin steak with sautéed red onions, chili, and pecan pie.

⊗ Simpson's-in-The-Strand

100 The Strand, WC2. ☎ **0171/836-9112.** Reservations required. Appetizers £3.25–£12 ($5.15–$18.95); main courses £14.50 ($22.90); fixed-price lunch £10 ($15.80) for two courses; fixed-price dinner £10 ($15.80) for two courses (6–7pm) only; set breakfasts £8.50–£10 ($13.45–$15.80). AE, DC, MC, V. Mon–Fri 7am–noon; daily noon–2:30pm and 6–11pm. Tube: Charing Cross or Embankment. BRITISH.

Simpson's is more of an institution than a restaurant. Located next to the Savoy Hotel, it has been in business since 1828. All this very Victorian place needs is an empire. It has everything else: Adam paneling, crystal, and an army of grandly formal waiters hovering about. On most first-time visitors' lists, there is this notation: "See the Changing of the Guard, then lunch at Simpson's." One food critic wrote that "nouvelle cuisine here means anything after Henry VIII." However, there is one point on which most diners agree: Simpson's serves the best roasts in London. Huge roasts are trolleyed to your table and you can have slabs of beef carved off and served with traditional Yorkshire pudding. The classic dishes are roast sirloin of beef, roast saddle of mutton with red-currant jelly, roast Aylesbury duckling, and steak, kidney, and mushroom pie. Remember to tip the tailcoated carver, and men should wear a jacket and tie. For a "pudding," you might order the treacle roll and custard or Stilton with vintage port.

Simpsons has started serving fixed-price breakfasts, which means the "trad British brekky" here: black pud, grilled mushrooms, grilled tomatoes, eggs, bacon, sausage, and such lovelies as salmon kedgeree, pig's nose with parsley and onion sauce, kippers, quail eggs with haddock, fried liver, baked beans, fried bread, bubble & squeak, along with stewed fruit, orange juice, coffee, and pastries.

COVENT GARDEN
MODERATE
Christopher's

18 Wellington St., WC2. ☎ **0171/240-4222.** Reservations recommended. In upstairs restaurant, appetizers £5–£12 ($7.90–$18.95); main courses £8–£19 ($12.65–$30). In street-level brasserie, appetizers £4.50–£9 ($7.10–$14.20); main courses £5–£12 ($7.90–$18.95). AE, DC, MC, V. Restaurant, Mon-Fri noon–3pm and 6–11:30pm; Sat 6–11:30pm. Brasserie, Mon-Sat noon–midnight; Sun noon–3:30pm. Tube: Covent Garden. AMERICAN.

This is the most stylish, crowded, and sought-after American restaurant in London, favored by everyone from stage and film stars to the youthful and moneyed successes of London's financial district. It is housed in a Victorian-baroque building that was originally built in 1820 as a papier-mâché factory. After 1864, it was London's first licensed casino.

Many visitors are tempted to remain in the street-level brasserie, where steaks, hamburgers, oysters, and fresh salads are served in a bistro-style setting. Serious drinkers descend into the basement, where a bar awaits, serving pints of lager for around £2.50 ($3.95) each. The establishment's real showcase, however, is the Restaurant, one floor above street level. An elaborate corkscrew-shaped stone staircase beneath a lavishly frescoed ceiling ends at a pair of Italianate dining rooms. There, flavorful and modern American-inspired dishes are served, including smoked tomato soup with fresh pesto, rack of lamb, grilled breast of chicken, and stewed red cabbage with onions. The establishment's owner and namesake is British-born Christopher Gilmour, who spent 11 years in Los Angeles and Chicago trading commodities futures before returning to London with his vision of a smart and sassy urban American restaurant.

Rules

35 Maiden Lane, WC2. ☎ **0171/836-5314.** Reservations recommended. Appetizers £3.50–£5 ($5.55–$7.90); main courses £10–£15.95 ($15.80–$25.20). AE, DC, MC, V. Daily noon–11:30pm. Tube: Covent Garden. ENGLISH.

This could be considered the most quintessentially British restaurant in London. Originally established in 1798 as an oyster bar, and lined with the framed memorabilia of the British Empire at its height, it rambles through a series of Edwardian dining rooms dripping in patriotic nostalgia. In fact, it lays claim to being the oldest restaurant in London still operating on the site of its original premises. Around the turn of the century, Edward VII, portly future king of England, used to arrive here quite frequently with his infamous mistress, Lillie Langtry, before heading up to a private red-velvet dining room on the second floor. Their signed portraits still embellish the yellowing walls, along with that of Charles Dickens, who crafted several of his novels here. Brilliant writer and curmudgeon Graham Greene made a visit to Rules an unchangeable condition of each of his birthdays despite his long-term residence in the south of France. Other artists and actors who appreciated Rules included Thackeray, John Galsworthy, H. G. Wells, Evelyn Waugh, John Barrymore, Clark Gable, and Laurence Olivier.

Today, amid cartoons executed by George Whitelaw in the 1920s, you can order such classic dishes as Irish or Scottish oysters, jugged hare, and Aylesbury duckling in orange sauce. Game dishes are offered year-round. You can order wild Scottish salmon or wild sea trout; wild Highland red deer; or any of an array of such game birds as grouse, snipe, partridge, pheasant, and woodcock. These might be followed by those unusual British savories called angels on horseback (oysters wrapped in bacon and served on toast).

INEXPENSIVE

⊖ Porter's English Restaurant
17 Henrietta St., WC2. ☎ **0171/836-6466.** Reservations recommended. Main courses £6.95–£8 ($11–$12.65); fixed-price menu £15.75 ($24.90). AE, MC, V. Mon–Sat noon–11:30pm; Sun noon–10:30pm. Tube: Covent Garden or Charing Cross. ENGLISH.

This place is owned by the seventh Earl of Bradford, who is a frequent visitor. It has a friendly, informal, and lively atmosphere in comfortable surroundings on two floors. Porter's specializes in classic English pies, including steak and kidney, lamb and apricot, ham, leek, and cheese, and steak, oyster, and clam. Main courses are so generous that the menu wisely eliminates appetizers. Main dishes are served with vegetables of the day or side dishes. The traditional roast beef with Yorkshire pudding is featured on weekends. With whipped cream or custard, the "puddings" come hot or cold, including bread-and-butter pudding or steamed syrup sponge. The English call all desserts puddings, but at Porter's they are the real puddings, as the word is known in the American sense. The bar does quite a few exotic cocktails, and you can also order cider by the half pint or even English wines or traditional English mead. A traditional English tea is also served, costing £3.95 ($6.25) per person.

PUB

Nag's Head
10 James St., WC2. ☎ **0171/836-4678.** Reservations not accepted. Sandwich platters with salad £2.50–£4.95 ($3.95–$7.80); full meal salads £4.25 ($6.70); main courses £4.95 ($7.80); pint of lager £1.80 ($2.85). AE, DC, MC, V. Mon–Sat 11:30am–11pm; Sun noon–3pm and 7:30–10:30pm. Tube: Covent Garden. ENGLISH.

Nag's Head is one of the most famous Edwardian pubs of London. In days of yore, patrons had to make their way through lorries of fruit and flowers for a drink here. Elegantly dressed operagoers in the evening used to mix with cockney cauliflower peddlers at the bar—and 300 years of British tradition happily faded away. With the moving of the market, all that has long ago changed, and the pub is patronized mainly by young people who seem to fill up all the tables every evening, including drinking space around the bar counter. Try a draft Guinness for a change of pace. Lunch is typical pub grub: sandwiches, salads, pork cooked in cider, and garlic prawns. The sandwich platters mentioned above are served only during the lunch hour (noon to 3:30pm); however, snacks are available in the afternoon.

HOLBORN
PUB

Cittie of Yorke

22–23 High Holborn, WC1. ☎ **0171/242-7670.** Reservations not accepted. Appetizers £2.25–£4 ($3.55–$6.30); main courses £4.50–£6 ($7.10–$9.50); glass of wine from £2 ($3.15). AE, MC, V. Mon–Fri 11am–11pm; Sat 11:30am–3pm and 5:30–11pm. Tube: Holborn or Chancery Lane. ENGLISH.

Cittie of Yorke stands near the Holborn Bars, the historic entrance to London marked by dragons holding the coat of arms of The City between their paws. Persons entering and leaving London were checked and paid tolls here. A pub has stood on this site since 1430. This pub's principal hall, believed to have the longest bar counter in England, has handsome screen work, comfortable compartments, a row of large vats, and a high trussed roof. The place is popular with barristers, judges, and employees of London's financial district. Lunchtime rituals include ordering your food at the food counter and physically carrying your choices back to a table. Dinner entails placing your order at the bar—whereupon someone will carry your choice to your table about 10 minutes later. Lunch bustles a bit more frenetically than dinner, when a wider choice of food is available. At any time, you'll have a choice of five hot platters of the day (goulashes, casseroles, lasagna, ham steaks, rump steaks, etc.), plus burgers and sandwiches.

6 The City & Fleet Street

THE CITY
MODERATE

The Hispaniola

Victoria Embankment, Charing Cross, WC2. ☎ **0171/839-3011.** Reservations recommended. Appetizers £2.75–£5.75 ($4.35–$126.40); main courses £6.50–£18.50 ($10.25–$29.25). AE, DC, MC, V. Mon–Fri noon–2pm and 6:30–10pm (last order); Sat 6:30–10pm (last order). Closed Mon, Jan–Apr. Tube: Embankment. ENGLISH/FRENCH.

This large, comfortably outfitted ship was originally built in 1953 to haul passengers around the islands of Scotland. (Until recently, two similar vessels built at the same time carried passengers between Naples, Italy, and the island of Capri.) Stripped of its engine in 1976, the ship is permanently moored to a quay beside the Thames, a few steps from the Embankment underground station. Good food and views of the passing river traffic are part of the waterborne experience on board. Tables are set up on two different levels, and, throughout, a certain elegance prevails. A harpist or an automated piano provides evening music. The menu changes frequently but might include such dishes as queen scallops with chili and sherry dressing, honey roasted pork tenderloin with apple and thyme crumble, salmon steak in a leek and green peppercorn sauce, and several vegetarian dishes.

⊙ Poons in The City

2 Minster Pavement, Minster Court, Mincing Lane, EC3. ☎ **0171/626-0126.** Reservations recommended. Set lunches £20.80–£27.80 ($32.85–$43.90) per person; appetizers £2.60–£6.20 ($4.10–$9.80); main courses £5.80–£8.80 ($9.15–$13.90). AE, DC, MC, V. Mon–Fri noon–11pm. Tube: Monument. CHINESE.

In 1992 Poons opened this branch in the City, less than a 5-minute walk from the Tower of London and close to other City attractions. It is modeled on the Luk Yew Tree House in Hong Kong. Rosewood furniture and the trappings were imported from China.

The menu tempts with both hot and cold hors d'oeuvres, ranging from chicken satay to crispy soft-shell crab to Cantonese chicken. Poons famous Lap Yuk Soom has finely chopped wind-dried bacon. Main courses feature crispy, aromatic duck, prawns with cashew nuts, and barbecued pork. Special dishes can be ordered on 24-hour notice. At the end of the L-shaped restaurant is an 80-seat fast-food area and take-out counter—accessible from Mark Lane—which becomes a relaxing cocktail bar in the evening. The menu here changes every two weeks, and set lunches cost £12.60 ($19.90) per person (minimum of two), with plats du jour such as stir-fried sliced beef or sweet-and-sour chicken going for £4.60 ($7.25).

PUB & WINE BARS

Bow Wine Vaults

10 Bow Churchyard, EC4. ☎ **0171/248-1121.** Reservations recommended. Appetizers £2.50–£4 ($3.95–$6.30); main courses £6.50–£7.95 ($10.25–$12.55); glass of wine from £2.50 ($3.95). AE, DC, MC, V. Restaurant and Grill Bar Mon–Fri 11am–2:45pm. Pub Mon–Fri 11am–11pm. Tube: Bank or St. Paul's. ENGLISH.

Bow Wine Vaults has existed since long before the current wine-bar fad that began in the 1970s and is now a firmly entrenched institution on the London scene. One of the most famous wine bars of London, it attracts cost-conscious diners and drinkers from the financial district who head below ground to its vaulted cellars. Menu choices in the Grill Bar, as it's called, include such traditional fare as deep-fried Camembert, chicken Kiev, and a mixed grill, along with fish. More elegant meals are served in the street-level dining room, called "The Restaurant," which offers an English-inspired menu, including, perhaps, mussels in cider sauce, English wild mushrooms in puff pastry, and individual servings of beef Wellington. Try the steak with brown-butter sauce. Adjacent to the restaurant is a cocktail bar, popular with City employees after work.

The Jamaica Wine House

St. Michael's Alley, off Cornhill, EC3. ☎ **0171/626-9496.** Reservations not accepted. Bar snacks £1–£4 ($1.60–$6.30); lager £1.55–£2 ($2.45–$3.15). AE, DC, MC, V. Mon–Fri 11am–8pm. Tube: Bank. ENGLISH.

The Jamaica Wine House is one of the first coffeehouses to be opened in England, and, reputedly, in the Western world. For years London merchants and daring sea captains came here to lace deals with rum and coffee. Nowadays, the two-level house dispenses beer, ale, lager, and fine wines, among them a variety of ports, to appreciative drinkers. The oak-paneled bar is at street level, attracting a jacket-and-tie crowd of investment bankers, whereas the basement bar is an even cozier retreat. You can order game pie and baked potatoes, toasted sandwiches, and such old English favorites as Lancashire hot pot or shepherd's pie.

Olde Wine Shades

6 Martin Lane, Cannon St., EC4. ☎ **0171/626-6876.** Appetizers £3–£4.40 ($4.75–$6.95); main courses £6–£14 ($9.50–$22.10); glass of wine from £1.90 ($3). AE, MC, V. Mon–Fri 11:30am–3pm and 5–8pm. Closed bank holidays. Tube: Cannon Street. ENGLISH.

Dating from 1663, the Olde Wine Shades survived the Great Fire of 1666 and Hitler's bombs. It is the oldest wine house in The City. Near the Monument (a famous London landmark designed by Christopher Wren to commemorate the Great Fire of 1666), it is decorated with oil paintings and 19th-century political cartoons. It's also one of the many London bars that Dickens used to patronize. There is a restaurant downstairs, and you can order light meals upstairs, including Breton pâté and French bread with ham "off the bone." You can order jacket potatoes filled with cheese, venison pie with a salad garnish, or a large beef salad. Simple fare notwithstanding, men must wear jackets, collars, and ties.

Ye Olde Watling

29 Watling St., EC4. ☎ **0171/248-6252.** Reservations not accepted. Lunch £2.50–£4.95 ($3.95–$7.80); bar snacks from £1.95 ($3.10); beer from £1.70 ($2.70). AE, MC, V. Restaurant Mon–Fri noon–2:30pm. Pub Mon–Fri 11am–10pm. Tube: Mansion House. ENGLISH.

Ye Olde Watling was built after the Great Fire of London. On the ground level is a mellow pub, and upstairs an intimate restaurant where, under oak beams and at trestle tables, you can have a simple choice of English main dishes for lunch. The menu varies daily by including the choice of four hot dishes, such choices as fish and chips, steak-and-kidney pudding, lamb satay, lasagna, fish cakes, and usually a vegetarian dish. All are served with two vegetables or a salad, rice, or potatoes.

FLEET STREET
INEXPENSIVE

✪ Ye Olde Cheshire Cheese

Wine Office Court, 145 Fleet St., EC4. ☎ **0171/353-6170.** Appetizers £2.95–£5 ($4.65–$7.90); main courses £7–£15 ($11.05–$23.70). AE, DC, MC, V. Daily noon–2:30pm and 6–9:30pm. Drinks and bar snacks available daily 11:30am–11pm. Tube: St. Paul's. ENGLISH.

Situated within a recently remodeled, carefully preserved building whose foundation was originally laid in the 13th century, this is one of the most famous of the old City chophouses and pubs. It was established in 1667 and claims to be the spot where Dr. Samuel Johnson (who lived within shouting distance) entertained his admirers with his acerbic wit. Later, many of the ink-stained journalists and scandalmongers of 19th- and early 20th-century Fleet Street made its four-story premises their "local."

Within, you'll find six bars and three dining rooms. The house specialties include "ye famous pudding"—steak, kidney, mushrooms, and game—and Scottish roast beef, with Yorkshire pudding and horseradish sauce. Sandwiches, salads, and such standby favorites as steak-and-kidney pie are also available.

PUB

Ye Olde Cock Tavern

22 Fleet St., EC4. ☎ **0171/353-8570.** Reservations recommended. Appetizers £3–£5.75 ($4.75–$9.10); main courses £8–£12 ($12.65–$18.95); fixed-price two-course lunch £9.95 ($15.70). AE, DC, MC, V. Restaurant Mon–Fri noon–3pm. Pub Mon–Fri 11am–11pm. Tube: Temple or Chancery Lane. ENGLISH.

Dating back to 1549, this tavern boasts a long line of ghostly literary comrades, such as Dickens, who once favored this ancient pub with their presence. Samuel Pepys mentioned the pub in one of his diaries, and Lord Tennyson referred to it in one of his poems, a copy of which is framed and proudly displayed near the front entrance. It's one of the few buildings in London to have survived the Great Fire in 1666. At street level, you can order a pint as well as snack-bar food. You can also order stead-and-kidney pie or a cold chicken-and-beef plate with salad.

At the Carvery upstairs, a meal includes a choice of appetizers, followed by all the roasts you can carve—beef, lamb, pork, or turkey.

7 Westminster & Victoria

WESTMINSTER
MODERATE

Shepherd's

Marsham Court, Marsham St. at the corner of Page St., SW1. ☎ **0171/834-9552.** Reservations recommended. Set meals £18.95 ($29.95) for two courses, £22.95 ($36.25) for three courses. AE, DC, MC, V. Mon–Fri 12:30–2:45pm and 6:30–11:30pm. Tube: Westminster or Pimlico. BRITISH.

Some observers of London's political landscape claim that many of the inner workings of the British government operate from the precincts of this conservative and likable restaurant. Located within the shadow of the Houses of Parliament, 2 blocks north of the Tate Gallery, it enjoys a regular clientele of barristers, members of Parliament, and many of their constituents from the far-flung districts of the British Isles. Since the business of government seems to continue throughout the day and evening, don't imagine that most of the intrigue here occurs at lunchtime; evenings seem just as ripe an hour for parliamentary negotiations, particularly over the restaurant's perennial specialty of roast rib of Scottish beef served with (what else?) Yorkshire pudding. So synchronized is this establishment to the goings-on in Parliament that a Division Bell rings within the dining room, calling MPs back to the House of Commons when it's time to vote.

Ironically, even the decor of the restaurant seems to duplicate that of Parliament, with leather banquettes, sober 19th-century accessories, and a worthy collection of English portraits and landscape paintings.

Menu choices reflect many years of British culinary tradition, but they are prepared intelligently and with fresh ingredients. They include a cream-based mussel stew, hot salmon and potato salad with dill dressing, black pudding with bubble and squeak, roast leg of lamb with mint sauce, fillet of salmon with tarragon and chive butter sauce, a changing array of daily specials based on relatively modern inspiration, and a dessert specialty of crème brûlée that this very English restaurant appropriately identifies as burnt Cambridge cream.

ⓈTate Gallery Restaurant

Millbank, SW1. ☎ **0171/887-8877.** Reservations required 2 days in advance. Appetizers £3.50–£6 ($5.55–$9.50); main courses £8–£16 ($12.65–$25.30). MC, V. Mon–Sat noon–3pm. Tube: Pimlico; bus 77 or 88. ENGLISH.

The restaurant in the Tate Gallery is particularly attractive to wine fanciers, offering what may be the best bargains for superior wines to be found anywhere in the country. It is especially strong on Bordeaux and burgundies. Management keeps the markup on wines in the range of 40% to about 65%, rather than 100% to 200% typically added to the wholesale price at other restaurants. In fact, the prices here are even lower than in most retail wine shops. Wine begins at £10 ($15.80) per bottle or £2.95 ($4.65) per glass. Wine connoisseurs frequently come for lunch, regardless of whatever exhibits may be on view at the museum. If you're looking for food instead of (or in addition to) wine, the restaurant specializes in an English menu that changes about every month. Menu choices might include seafood crêpes; roast duck with spiced apricots; roast English sirloin of beef with Yorkshire pudding; steak, kidney, and mushroom pie; and a selection of vegetarian dishes. At rare intervals, the restaurant also offers dishes inspired by English cuisine of the 17th century, including "hindle wakes" (cold stuffed chicken with prunes) and "pye with fruyt ryfshews" (fruit tart topped with meringue). Access to the restaurant is through the museum's main entrance on Millbank.

VICTORIA
MODERATE

Ken Lo's Memories of China
67–69 Ebury St., SW1. ☎ **0171/730-7734.** Reservations recommended. Appetizers £4.25–£9.75 ($6.70–$15.40); main courses £9.80–£29.50 ($15.50–$46.60); fixed-price lunch £15–£29.50 ($23.70–$46.60); fixed-price dinner £20.50–£29.50 ($32.40–$46.60). AE, DC, MC, V. Mon–Sat noon–2:30pm; daily 7–11:15pm. Tube: Victoria. CHINESE.

Many food critics consider Ken Lo's to be the finest Chinese restaurant in London. It was founded by Ken Lo, whose grandfather was the Chinese ambassador to the Court of St. James (he was knighted by Queen Victoria in 1880). Mr. Lo has written more than 30 cookbooks (including a well-known autobiography) and was once the main figure on his own TV cooking show. His restaurant, which is impeccably staffed and outfitted with an appealing minimalist decor of white with mahogany trim, has been called "a gastronomic bridge between London and China." Menu choices, which derive from broadly divergent regions of China, might include Cantonese quick-fried beef in oyster sauce; lobster with handmade noodles; pomegranate prawn balls; and "bang-bang chicken" (a Szechuan dish), among many others. Although it's owned by the same people, this restaurant should not be confused with another restaurant of the same name (also recommended) in Chelsea Harbour.

Simply Nico
48A Rochester Row, SW1. ☎ **0171/630-8061.** Reservations required. Two-course set lunch £20 ($31.60); three-course set lunch £23.50 ($37.15); three-course fixed-price dinner £25 ($39.50). AE, DC, MC, V. Mon–Fri 12:30–2pm and 6:45–11:15pm; Sat 6:45–11:15pm. Tube: Victoria. FRENCH.

This place was created by Nico Ladenis, the owner of a grander and more expensive restaurant, Chez Nico at Ninety Park Lane (see "Mayfair," above). Run by his sous-chef, Simply Nico is, in the words of Nico, "cheap and cheerful." Wood floors seem to reverberate with the din of contented diners, who pack in here daily at snug tables. The food is often simply prepared and invariably French inspired, with fresh ingredients handled deftly in the kitchen. The fixed-price menu changes frequently. Choices might include such starters as goat cheese with roasted red peppers or poached egg tartlet with hollandaise sauce with marinated puréed mushrooms; main courses might include grilled Scottish beef with horseradish sauce or crispy duck with plum sauce.

WINE BAR

Ebury Wine Bar
139 Ebury St., SW1. ☎ **0171/730-5447.** Reservations recommended. Appetizers £2–£4.50 ($3.15–$7.10); main courses £6.95–£13.50 ($11–$21.35); fixed-price Sunday lunch £9 ($14.20); glass of wine from £2.60 ($4.10). AE, DC, MC, V. Mon–Sat noon–2:45pm and 6–10:30pm; Sun noon–3pm and 7–10pm. Tube: Victoria or Sloane Square. CONTINENTAL.

The Ebury is a wine bar and bistro, convenient for dining or drinking, that attracts a youthful clientele to its often-crowded but always-atmospheric precincts. Wine is sold either by the glass or bottle. You can always get an enticing plat du jour, such as traditional beef Wellington or perhaps one of the grilled fillet steaks.

8   Knightsbridge & Belgravia

KNIGHTSBRIDGE
MODERATE

Fifth Floor at Harvey Nichols

Corner of Knightsbridge at Sloane Street SW1. ☎ **0171/235-5250.** Reservations recommended. Set price menus, £17.50 ($27.65) for two courses, £21.50 ($33.95) for three courses. Appetizers £4.95–£12.50 ($7.80–$19.75); main courses £9.75–£26.50 ($15.40–$41.85). À la carte dishes available at dinner only. AE, DC, MC, V. Mon–Sat noon–3pm and 6:30–11:30pm (last order). Tube: Knightsbridge. BRITISH.

Located on the fifth floor of the flagship store of a chain of clothing emporiums scattered across Britain, this restaurant is probably the most carefully orchestrated of any eatery within any of the large London department stores. There's a simple café near the entrance, which tends to be the domain of shoppers laden with packages looking for a "cuppa" tea and a salad, but serious diners (many from the upscale neighborhoods nearby), usually head directly into the high-ceilinged blue and white restaurant. There, big windows overlook the red-brick Edwardian walls of the Hyde Park Hotel, across the street, and waiters imbue any meal with a polite kind of formality. Menu choices are appropriately fashionable, including such dishes as pan-fried calf's liver with lentils and wild mushrooms; black pudding with mustard and parsley sauce; a salad of marinated grilled leeks and mushrooms with tapenade croûtons; fish cakes of haddock with tartar sauce; shredded duck confit and roulade of fresh figs.

Incidentally, there's a glamorous food emporium (open till 8pm Monday to Saturday) just outside the restaurant's entrance, where ingredients and their variety hint at the culinary splendors to be enjoyed within the restaurant. Although the department store closes at 6pm, a pair of elevators continue to carry restaurant patrons up to the fifth floor even after closing hours at "Harvey Nic's."

San Lorenzo

22 Beauchamp Place, SW3. ☎ **0171/584-1074.** Reservations required. Appetizers £3.50–£9.50 ($5.55–$15); main courses £12.50–£18.50 ($19.75–$29.25). No credit cards. Mon–Sat 12:30–3pm and 7:30–11:30pm. Tube: Knightsbridge. ITALIAN.

Opened in 1987, this is a fashionable restaurant specializing in the cuisines of Tuscany and the Piedmont regions of Italy. Well known for attracting a clientele of painters, writers, photographers, and fashion models, it quickly gained a reputation as one of the favorite dining spots of Princess Diana (business soared as a result). Inside, a series of dining rooms include paintings by, among others, Jonathan Routh, whose tongue-in-cheek depictions of Queen Victoria visiting Jamaica have provoked many an amused commentary throughout the West Indies.

Reliability is the keynote of the cuisine, which includes homemade fettuccine with salmon, carpaccio, risotto with fresh asparagus, bollito misto, fried calamari, veal piccata, grouse, and partridge in white-wine sauce. Regional offerings that are sometimes presented might include salt cod with polenta.

WINE BARS

Bill Bentley's

31 Beauchamp Place, SW3. ☎ **0171/589-5080.** Reservations recommended. Appetizers £2.95–£10 ($4.65–$15.80); main courses £7.50–£16.90 ($11.85–$26.70); glass of wine £2 ($3.15). MC, V. Mon–Sat noon–2:30pm and 6–10:30pm. Tube: Knightsbridge. ENGLISH.

Bill Bentley's stands right on this fashionable restaurant- and boutique-lined block. Its wine list is varied and reasonable, including a good selection of Bordeaux. Many visitors come here just to sample the wines, including some "New World" choices along with popular French selections. In summer, a garden patio is used. If you don't care for the formality of the restaurant, you can order from the wine-bar menu, which begins with half a dozen oysters, or else you can enjoy the chef's fish soup with croûtons and rouille. Main dishes include Bill Bentley's famous fish cakes, served with tomato sauce, and the day's specialties are written on a blackboard. In keeping with contemporary trends in London dining, the menu has been simplified and is rather less expensive than before. The menu is changed frequently, but typical dishes might include avocado, crab and prawn salad as an appetizer, followed by pan-fried calf's liver or a poached stuffed salmon.

BELGRAVIA
MODERATE

Salloos

62–64 Kinnerton St., SW1. ☎ **0171/235-4444.** Reservations recommended. Appetizers £3.50–£5 ($5.55–$7.90); main courses £9.50–£12.50 ($15–$19.75); three-course set lunch £16 ($25.30); four-course set dinner £25 ($39.50). AE, DC, MC, V. Mon–Sat noon–2:30pm and 7–11:30pm. Tube: Hyde Park Corner. PAKISTANI/MUGHLAI.

Considered one of London's most elegant Pakistani restaurants, this small-scale hideaway has only 60 seats and is located in one of London's most fashionably expensive neighborhoods. Amid soothing (that is, dim) lighting that is pierced with spotlights aimed at carefully framed Pakistani embroideries, you can enjoy the specialties, which were developed during the reign of North India's Moghul emperors. A cosmopolitan clientele, seated amid elegant cornices and burnt orange and terra-cotta decor, appreciate such dishes as lamb chops grilled in a tandoori oven; chicken shish kebabs; chicken *karahi* (spicy, with curry); chicken *korma* (moderately spicy and served with yogurt sauce); and a house specialty of *haleem akbari* (shredded lamb cooked in wheat germ with lentils and spices). Salloos is the nickname of the establishment's owner, Muhammad Salahuddin.

PUBS

Grenadier

18 Wilton Row, SW1. ☎ **0171/235-3074.** Reservations recommended. Appetizers £3.50–£8.25 ($5.55–$13.05); main courses £11.15–£18.95 ($17.60–$29.95); glass of wine £2 ($3.15). AE, DC, MC, V. Daily noon–3pm; Mon–Sat 6–11pm; Sun 7–10:30pm. Closed Dec 25–26 and Jan 1. Tube: Hyde Park Corner. ENGLISH.

Tucked away in a mews, Grenadier is one of London's numerous reputedly haunted pubs. Aside from the poltergeist, the basement also houses the original bar and skittles alley used by the duke of Wellington's officers on leave from fighting Napoléon. The scarlet front door of the one-time officers' mess is guarded by a scarlet sentry box and shaded by a vine. The bar is nearly always crowded. Luncheons and dinners are offered daily—even on Sunday, when it is a tradition

Dining from Kensington to Belgravia

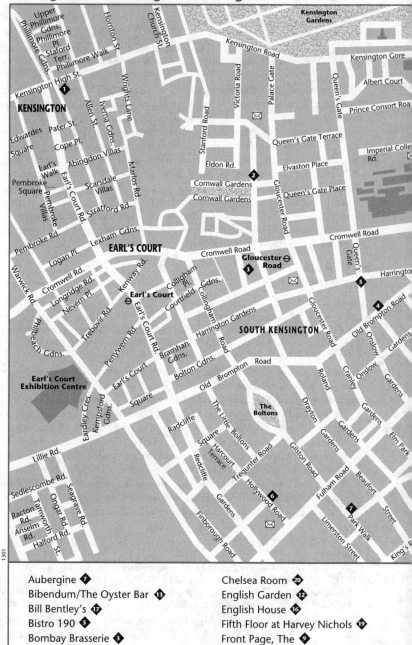

Hilaire ❹	Phoenicia ❶
Joe's ❽	Salloos ㉑
King's Head and Eight Bells ❿	San Lorenzo ⓭
La Tante Claire ⓫	Star Tavern ㉓
Launceton Place Restaurant ❷	Turner's ⓯
Nag's Head, The ㉑	Walton's of Walton Street ⓮

Tube Station ⊖   Church ✝   Post Office ⊠   Information ⓘ

to drink Bloody Marys here. In the stalls along the side, you can order good-tasting fare based on seasonal ingredients. Fillet of beef Wellington is a specialty; other good dishes include pork Grenadier and chicken-and-Stilton roulade. Snacks are available at the bar if you don't want a full meal.

Star Tavern

6 Belgrave Mews West, SW1. ☎ **0171/235-3019.** Reservations not accepted. Lunch pub snacks £2.50–£5 ($3.95–$7.90); dinner pub snacks £3.50–£5.90 ($5.55–$9.30); glass of wine £2.05 ($3.25). No credit cards. Restaurant Mon–Fri noon–2:30pm and 6:30–8:45pm. Pub Mon–Thurs 11:30am–3pm and 5–11pm; Fri 11:30am–11pm; Sat 11:30am–3pm and 6:30–11pm; Sun noon–3pm and 7–10:30pm. Closed Dec 25. Tube: Knightsbridge or Hyde Park Corner. ENGLISH.

Situated in a Georgian mews, the Star Tavern is one of the most colorful pubs in the West End, with a picture-postcard-type facade. In winter it's one of the coziest havens around, with two fireplaces going. Groups of office workers descend after work, staking out their territory. The place is attractive inside, with Victorian walls and banquettes beneath 19th-century Victorian moldings. You can order such dishes as baby spring chicken, sirloin steak, or, perhaps, a vegetable quiche. There is no table service; patrons place their orders at the bar.

9 Chelsea & Chelsea Harbour

CHELSEA
VERY EXPENSIVE

La Tante Claire

68–69 Royal Hospital Rd., SW3. ☎ **0171/352-6045.** Reservations required. Appetizers £19–£25 ($30–$39.50); main courses £24.50–£35 ($38.70–$55.30); fixed-price lunch £25 ($39.50); minimum charge £60 ($94.80) per person. AE, DC, MC, V. Mon–Fri 12:30–2pm and Mon–Fri 7–11pm. Closed Dec 25 and Jan 1. Tube: Sloane Square. FRENCH.

The quality of its cuisine is so legendary that this "Aunt Claire" has become, in the eyes of many critics, the leading choice among the capital's gaggle of French restaurants. It's considered a culinary monument of the highest order. A discreet doorbell, set into the Aegean-blue-and-white facade, prompts an employee to usher you politely inside. There, birch and chrome trim, bouquets of flowers, and a modernized, vaguely Hellenistic decor complement an array of paintings that might have been inspired by Jean Cocteau.

Pierre Koffman is the celebrated chef, creating such specialties as ravioli stuffed with frog meat. Every gastronome in London talks about the pigs' trotters stuffed with morels and the exquisite sauces that complement many of the dishes. These include grilled scallops served on a bed of squid-ink sauce, baked fillet of turbot with cabbage and fresh vegetables cooked in a consommé with preserved duck, or duck in red-wine sauce and confit. For dessert, try a caramelized ice cream soufflé with hazelnuts and a *coulis* of raspberries or the pistachio soufflé.

EXPENSIVE

Aubergine

11 Park Walk, SW10. ☎ **0171/352-3449.** Reservations required. Three-course fixed-price lunch £18–£34 ($28.45–$53.70); fixed-price dinner £34–£44 ($53.70–$69.50). AE, DC, MC, V. Mon–Sat noon–2:30pm and 7–11pm. Tube: South Kensington. FRENCH.

"The Eggplant" is luring savvy diners down to Chelsea, its lower reaches, where Gordon Ramsay, the owner and chef, continues to create excitement. The decor evokes a summer's day, and the tables are placed far enough apart so that you don't have to listen to your fellow diners' conversation. Aubergine is so popular that reservations as far in advance as possible are needed. Even though a visiting movie star or an overpaid decorator might show up, the place is not all hype and publicity. It genuinely delivers a most satisfying menu.

Ramsay has worked with the biggest chefs in London or Paris, including Guy Savoy, Albert Roux, Joël Robuchon, and Marco Pierre White, yet has forged his own style. Begin with —say, cappuccino of haricots blancs with truffle oil, or else a parfait of duck foie gras with a toasted brioche. The watercress soup might be served with poached oysters, and salad of roast wood pigeons is flavored with wild mushrooms. A specialty is red mullet built upon a foundation of eggplant caviar. The fillet of sea bass emerges with braised fennel hearts flavored with tarragon. Guinea *fowl en cocotte* was never lovelier or better tasting than when presented with caramelized sweetbreads, a leek tagliatelle, and a turnip confit. The food has been called "jewel like" to the eye. An assiette of lusciously tempting desserts —offered for at least two diners —gives you an opportunity to sample them in miniature, a taste of this, a taste of that. Most of the wine comes from France, though some bottles come from what some critics in Britain still call "the New World." End with coffee and a selection of delectable *petits fours*.

MODERATE

✪ Chelsea Room

In the Hyatt Carlton Tower, 2 Cadogan Place, SW1. ☎ **0171/235-1234.** Reservations required. Appetizers £4.50–£15 ($7.10–$23.70); main courses £12.50–£28 ($19.75–$44.25); fixed-price lunch £22.50 ($35.55); fixed-price dinner £29.50 ($46.60). AE, DC, MC, V. Mon–Sat 12:30–2:45pm and 7–11pm; Sun 7–10pm. Tube: Sloane Square. FRENCH.

Chelsea Room is a superb restaurant, one of the best in London, situated within one of Hyatt's finest international properties (recommended in Chapter 4, "London Accommodations"). The dining room's combination of haute cuisine, stylish clientele, and elegant decor makes it a much sought-after place for lunch or dinner. It's one floor above the lobby level of the hotel at the end of a paneled hallway reminiscent of something in a private Edwardian house. The color scheme is tasteful and subdued in grays, beiges, and soft greens.

The kitchen is run by maître cuisinier de France Bernard Gaume. Monsieur Gaume has pleased palates at some of the leading and most famous hotels in Europe, including L'Abbaye in Tallories in the French Alps, the Savoy in London, and Hôtel des Bergues in Geneva. His portions are large and satisfying, and their presentation shows his extraordinary flair. Highly professional dishes, original offerings, time-tested classics, and very fresh ingredients are his forte. The menu will change by the time of your visit, but to give you an idea of the cuisine, you might be served sautéed scallops with seafood stock, diced lobster and truffles; fillet of lamb tossed in butter and served with eggplant purée, basil, and tomato; or two small fillets of beef, one with Bordelaise and one with shallot sauce. His desserts require a separate menu, ranging from light chestnut mousse with ginger sauce to chilled hazelnut parfait in a light Cointreau sauce.

English Garden

10 Lincoln St., SW3. ☎ **0171/584-7272.** Reservations required. Appetizers £3.75–£9.95 ($5.95–$15.70); main courses £7.25–£16.75 ($11.45–$26.45); fixed-price set lunch £14.75 ($23.30). AE, DC, MC, V. Mon–Sat 12:30–2:30pm and 7:30–11:30pm; Sun 12:30–2pm and 7–10:30pm. Closed Dec 25–26. Tube: Sloane Square. ENGLISH.

Here in this historic Chelsea townhouse, the decor is pretty and lighthearted. The Garden Room on the ground floor is whitewashed brick with panels of large stylish flowers. The attractive pelmets are in vivid flower colors with stark-white curtains. Rattan chairs in a Gothic theme and candy-pink napery complete the scene. With the domed conservatory roofs and banks of plants, the atmosphere is relaxing and pleasant.

The extensive menu includes lots of salads and fish. Interesting dishes are a checkerboard of freshwater fish, including a steamed fish of the day or roast rack of Welsh lamb with roasted garlic. The chef's daily choices are included in a special luncheon menu. A comprehensive wine list is available, and an excellent French house wine is always available.

English House

3 Milner St., SW3. ☎ **0171/584-3002.** Reservations required. Appetizers £3.75–£9.95 ($5.95–$15.70); main courses £8.50–£15.50 ($13.45–$24.50); fixed-price set lunch £14.75 ($23.30). AE, DC, MC, V. Mon–Sat 12:30–2:30pm and 7:30–11:15pm; Sun 12:30–2pm and 7–10pm. Closed Dec 25–26. Tube: Sloane Square. BRITISH.

This is another design creation of Roger Wren, who did the English Garden, described above. The English House is a tiny restaurant in the heart of Chelsea, where dining is like being a guest in an elegant private house, its decor providing both spectacle and atmosphere. Blues and terra cotta predominate. The walls are clad in a printed cotton depicting a traditional English design of autumn leaves and black currants. The fireplace creates a homelike environment, and the collection of interesting and beautiful furniture adds to the background. Attention has been paid to detail, and even the saltcellars are Victorian in origin.

The food is British, with such succulent offerings as chicken, leek, and lemon pie; poached halibut with orange cream sauce; and grilled fillet of beef with celeriac pancake and port sauce. Summer berries (in season) predominate on the "pudding" menu, including a bowl of fresh berries laced with elderflower syrup. Another offering is a "A Phrase of Apples," the chef's adaptation of a 17th-century recipe for a delectable apple pancake.

PUBS

The Front Page

35 Old Church St., SW3. ☎ **0171/352-0648.** Main courses £2.50–£8 ($3.95–$12.65). MC, V. Restaurant daily noon–2:30pm; Mon–Sat 7–10pm; Sun 7–9:30pm. Pub Mon–Sat 11am–3pm and 5:30–11pm; Sun noon–3pm and 7–11pm. Tube: Sloane Square or South Kensington. CONTINENTAL.

The Front Page is favored by young Chelsea professionals who like the mellow atmosphere provided by its wood paneling, wooden tables, and pews and benches. In one section an open fire burns on cold nights. The pub stands in an expensive residential section of Chelsea and is a good, safe place to go for a drink, with lager beginning at £2 ($3.15). You can also order bottled Budweiser. Check the chalkboard for a listing of the daily specials, which might include hot chicken salad, fish cakes, and smoked salmon and cream cheese bagel. You might begin with a homemade soup du jour.

King's Head and Eight Bells

50 Cheyne Walk, SW3. ☎ **0171/352-1820.** Reservations not accepted. Appetizers £2–£4 ($3.15–$6.30); main courses £3.50–£7.50 ($5.55–$11.85). MC, V. Mon–Sat 11am–11pm; Sun noon–3pm and 7–10:30pm. Tube: Sloane Square. ENGLISH.

This is a historic Thames-side pub. Many distinguished personalities once lived in this area. A short stroll in the neighborhood will take you to the former homes of such people as Carlyle, Swinburne, and George Eliot. In other days, press-gangs used to roam these parts of Chelsea seeking lone travelers to abduct for a life at sea. Today it's popular with stage and TV celebrities as well as writers.

The best English beers are served here, as well as a good selection of reasonably priced wines. A refrigerated display case holds cold dishes and salads, and a hot counter features the homemade specials of the day, including at least one vegetable main dish.

CHELSEA HARBOUR
MODERATE

Ken Lo's Memories of China
Harbour Yard, Chelsea Harbour, SW10. ☎ 0171/352-4953. Reservations recommended. Appetizers £3.50–£9.75 ($5.55–$15.40); main courses £4.50–£29.95 ($7.10–$47.30); fixed-price dinner £13.50–£29.60 ($21.35–$46.75) Mon–Sat; Sun brunch £15 ($23.70). AE, DC, MC, V. Sun–Fri noon–3pm; daily 7pm–12am. Chelsea Harbour Hoppa Bus C3 from Earl's Court Mon–Sat; on Sun, take a taxi. CHINESE.

This restaurant is a slightly less expensive branch of a famous Chinese restaurant with the same name near Victoria Station. This particular branch lies within Chelsea Harbour, a development filled with shops, condominiums, marina facilities, and restaurants. Decorated in shades of beige, the restaurant offers a cuisine that wanders from region to region of China, with an emphasis on fish and seafood. Specialties include Peking duck, steamed sea bass, Mongolian-style barbecued lamb, and chicken in hot black-bean sauce. Especially popular on weekends, it offers a Sunday brunch with live jazz.

INEXPENSIVE

Canteen
Unit G4, Harbour Yard, Chelsea Harbour SW10. ☎ 0171/351-7330. Reservations recommended. Appetizers £6.50 ($10.25); main courses £11.50 ($18.15). Cover charge £1 ($1.60) per person. Three-course set lunch (Sat-Sun only) £17.50 ($27.65). MC, V. Mon-Sat noon–3pm and 6:30pm–midnight (last order); Sun noon–3:30pm and 6:30–10:30pm (last order). Chelsea Harbour Bus C3 from Earl's Court; on Sun, take a taxi. INTER-NATIONAL.

Situated on the ground floor of a three-story office building, some visitors call this the most viable and popular of the several restaurants within the Chelsea Harbour Complex, the multimillion-dollar development of what used to be abandoned piers and wharves southwest of the center of London. You'll dine within a setting influenced by the themes of *Alice in Wonderland,* with a whimsical decor based on depictions of playing cards and harlequins—all very fantastical and the kind of thing that children as well as adults seem to appreciate. Even more attractive are the low prices, where all appetizers and main courses cost the same, though three or four concocted from more expensive raw ingredients are garnished with a small supplement. Menu choices include smoked haddock with poached eggs; gazpacho of crab; Savoy cabbage prepared in the style of Alsace; artichokes stuffed with exotic mushrooms; a papillote of smoked salmon; guinea fowl *en cocotte;* risotto in squid ink; confit of duck in the style of Toulouse; and roast rump of lamb niçoise.

10   Kensington & South Kensington

KENSINGTON
MODERATE

Joe's

126 Draycott Ave., SW3. ☎ **0171/225-2217.** Reservations recommended. Appetizers £4.50–£9.50 ($7.10–$15); main courses £11.95–£13.95 ($18.90–$22.05). AE, DC, MC, V. Mon–Sat noon–3pm and 7–11pm; Sun 10am–5pm. Tube: South Kensington. INTERNATIONAL.

This is one of five London restaurants established by fashion designer Joseph Ettedgui; partly because of its sense of glamour and fun, it is often filled with well-known names on the roster of the British fashion, music, and entertainment industries. (Two fashion-industry names associated with the upper dining room include Vivian West and Elle McPherson.) Amid a split-level decor of pale ashwood paneling and a monochromatic color scheme of beige and honey, you can enjoy such dishes as leek and onion tart with Gorgonzola and mixed greens, fillet of John Dory with celeriac mash and red wine sauce; ricotta tarts, grilled tuna, an eggplant and mussel soup; grilled chicken with onion and pumpkin fritters; and oxtail stew. No one will mind if your meal is composed exclusively of one or more appetizers (the menu is well suited for everyone from slim anorexics, of which there seem to be many, and for heartier appetites as well). There's a bar near the entrance, a cluster of tables for quick meals near the door, and more leisurely (and gossipy) dining available in an area a few steps up from the bar and entrance level.

Launceston Place Restaurant

1A Launceston Place, W8. ☎ **0171/937-6912.** Reservations required. Appetizers £4.50–£9.50 ($7.10–$15); main courses £9–£18 ($14.20–$28.45); set menus £13.50 ($21.35) for two courses, £16.50 ($26.05) for three courses, MC, V. Mon–Sat 12:30–2:30pm and 7–11:30pm; Sun 12:30–3pm. Tube: Gloucester Road. BRITISH.

Launceston Place is situated in an affluent, almost villagelike neighborhood where many Londoners would like to live if they could afford it. The architecturally stylish restaurant comprises a series of uncluttered Victorian parlors illuminated by a rear skylight and decorated with Victorian oils and watercolors, plus contemporary paintings. Since its opening in the spring of 1986, it has been known for its new British cuisine. The menu changes frequently, but you are likely to be served such appetizers as stir-fried squid with lemon, garlic, ginger, and coriander or seared foie gras with grilled sourdough bread and chutney. For a main dish, perhaps it'll be poached smoked haddock with parsley sauce, medallions of pork with mustard sauce, or fillet steak with Bordelaise sauce, garlic, and shallot marmalade.

INEXPENSIVE

ⓈPPhoenicia

11–13 Abingdon Rd., W8. ☎ **0171/937-0120.** Reservations required. Appetizers £2.60–£4.95 ($4.10–$7.80); main courses £7.50–£9.50 ($11.85–$15); buffet lunch £9.95 ($15.70); fixed-price dinner £15.30–£28.30 ($24.15–$44.70). AE, DC, MC, V. Daily noon–midnight; buffet lunch Mon–Sat 12:15–2:30pm. Tube: High Street Kensington. LEBANESE.

Phoenicia is highly regarded, both for the quality of its Lebanese cuisine and its moderate prices. The food is outstanding in its presentation and freshness. For the best value, go for lunch when you can enjoy a buffet of more than a dozen *meze* (appetizers), which are presented in little pottery dishes. Each day at lunch the chef prepares two or three home-cooked dishes to tempt your taste buds, including, for example, chicken in garlic sauce or stuffed lamb with vegetables. Many Lebanese patrons begin their meal with the apéritif "arak," a liqueur some have compared to ouzo. You can select as an appetizer such classic Middle Eastern dishes as hummus or stuffed vine leaves. The kitchen staff bakes its own bread in a clay oven and makes two different types of pizza. Minced lamb, spicy and well flavored, is the ongoing favorite. Various charcoal-grilled dishes are also offered.

SOUTH KENSINGTON
EXPENSIVE

✪ Bibendum/The Oyster Bar

81 Fulham Rd., SW3. ☎ **0171/581-5817.** Reservations required in Bibendum; not accepted in Oyster Bar. Appetizers £4.75–£12 ($7.50–$18.95); main courses £12–£20 ($18.95–$31.60); three-course fixed-price lunch £27 ($42.65); cold shellfish platter in Oyster Bar £22 ($34.75) per person. AE, MC, V. Bibendum Mon–Fri noon–2:30pm and 7–11:15pm; Sat noon–3pm and 7–11:15pm; Sun noon–3pm and 7–10:15pm. Oyster Bar Mon–Sat noon–11pm; Sun noon–3pm and 7–10pm. Tube: South Kensington. MODERN FRENCH/MEDITERRANEAN.

Considered one of the most gastronomically desirable restaurants in the city, this fashionable eatery occupies two floors of a building that is considered one of the art deco masterpieces of London. Built in 1911, it housed the British headquarters of the Michelin tire company. Bibendum, the more visible eatery, is located one floor above street level in a white-tiled art deco–inspired room whose stained-glass windows, streaming sunlight, and chic clientele make meals extremely pleasant. Menu choices are carefully planned interpretations of seasonal ingredients, known for their freshness and simplicity. The menu on the day of your arrival might include red pepper and basil risotto, sautéed squid with aioli and salsa, poached cod with lobster sauce and chives, or breast of duck with garlic and sherry cream sauce.

Simpler meals and cocktails are available on the building's street level, in the Oyster Bar. The bar-style menu and 1930s-style decor stress fresh shellfish presented in the traditional French style on ice-covered platters occasionally adorned with strands of seaweed.

Waltons of Walton Street

121 Walton St., SW3. ☎ **0171/584-0204.** Reservations recommended. Appetizers £4.75–£14 ($7.50–$22.10); main courses £12–£16.75 ($18.95–$26.45); "Simply Waltons" fixed-price lunch £14.75 ($23.30); late-night fixed-price supper £21 ($33.20). AE, DC, MC, V. Mon–Sat 12:30–2:30pm and 7:30–11:30pm Sun 12:30–2:30pm and 7–10:30pm; late-night supper Mon–Sat from 10pm. Tube: South Kensington or Knightsbridge. INTERNATIONAL.

Waltons is elegant and intimate, serving some of the best food in London. A posh rendezvous place, it offers the best-quality fresh produce from local and European markets served with flair in surroundings of silk walls and floral decorations. Its chefs prepare a refined international cuisine, featuring such British dishes as roast breast of Norfolk duck served pink, prime fillet of Scottish beef, and rack of lamb with a herb crust served on a leek purée with a rosemary gravy. Specialties include terrine of squab and grilled pepper with baby spinach; tomato and coriander chutney and raspberry millefeuille; wafers of puff pastry layered with brandy cream and fresh raspberries. Waltons, long a favorite with Harrods' women shoppers, has a reputation for being expensive. However, it has special-value fixed-price menus. The wine list, which features the best champagne list in London, is wide ranging, from Australia to California.

MODERATE

Bistro 190

In the Gore Hotel, 190 Queen's Gate, SW7. ☎ **0171/581-8172.** Reservations recommended. Appetizers £2.65–£6.95 ($4.20–$11); main courses £6.95–£10.50 ($11–$16.60). AE, DC, MC, V. Mon-Sat noon–12:30am; Sun noon–11pm. Tube: Gloucester Road. MEDITERRANEAN.

Located within the airy front room of a hotel, this restaurant features a light Mediterranean cuisine much appreciated by the hip and stylish crowd that comes here. (Many are in the music industry; others are well-known faces in entertainment and media.) Within an artfully simple decor of wooden floorboards, potted plants, lots of framed artworks, and a convivial but gossipy roar that adds a lot to its allure, you can order dishes anytime throughout the afternoon, through until the late hours listed above. Service is not particularly fast, the policy on reservations is confusing, and in the crush of peak dining hours, your waiter may or may not remember the nuances you expressed while placing your order, but the restaurant is nonetheless memorable. Menu choices include such dishes as lamb grilled over charcoal and served with deep-fried basil; salmon fish-cakes with chips; linguini with walnuts and Gorgonzola-flavored cream; a cassoulet of fish with chili toast; Mediterranean chowder with pesto toast; and—if it's available—a dessert (rhubarb crumble) based loosely on old-fashioned British cuisine.

Bombay Brasserie

Courtfield Close, adjoining Bailey's Hotel, SW7. ☎ **0171/370-4040.** Reservations required. Appetizers £3.95–£4.95 ($6.25–$7.80); main courses £11.50–£18 ($18.15–$28.45); buffet lunch £14.95 ($23.60). MC, V. Buffet daily 12:30–3pm; Mon–Sat 7:30pm–midnight; Sun 7:30–11:30pm. Closed Dec 26–27. Tube: Gloucester Road. INDIAN.

By anyone's estimation, this is the finest, most popular, and most talked-about Indian restaurant in London. Established in 1982, with a cavernous trio of rooms, it is staffed with one of the capital's most accommodating teams of Indian waiters, each one willing and very able to advise you on the spice-laden delicacies that thousands of years of Indian culinary tradition have developed. Lattices cover the windows, dhurrie rugs the floors, cooling is by paddle fans, and sepia Raj pictures of imperial Britain at its height adorn the walls.

Before heading in to dinner, you might enjoy a drink amid the wicker chairs of the pink-and-white bar; the atmosphere there has often been compared to Singapore's Raffles. The bartender's specialty is a mango Bellini.

One look at the menu and you're launched on "A Passage to India," a grand culinary tour of the subcontinent: tandoori trout, fish with mint chutney, chicken *tikka* (a dish from the Hindu Kush mountains), and vegetarian meals. One corner of the menu is reserved for Goan cookery, representing that part of India seized from Portugal in 1961. The cookery of North India is represented by Mughlai specialties, including chicken *biryani,* the famous Muslim pilaf dish. Under the category "Some Like It Hot," you'll find such main courses as lamb korma Kashmiri style, a favorite of a frequent customer, Faye Dunaway.

ⓢ Hilaire

68 Old Brompton Rd., SW7. ☎ **0171/584-8993.** Reservations recommended. Two-course fixed-price lunch £16.50 ($26.05); four-course fixed-price dinner £32.50 ($51.35); dinner appetizers £4.50–£16 ($7.10–$25.30); dinner main courses £14.50–£19.50 ($22.90–$30.80). AE, DC, MC, V. Mon–Fri 12:15–2:30pm and 6:30–11:30pm; Sat 6:30–11:30pm. Closed bank holidays. Tube: South Kensington. FRENCH.

✪ Frommer's Favorite Restaurants

Rules *(see page 161)*. One of the oldest and most celebrated restaurants in London—and still going strong—Rules is the best place for that classic English cookery, such as jugged hare, wild duck, grouse, partridge, and wild Highland red deer. At least Edward VII and his mistress Lillie Langtry thought so. The recipes that titillated their palates are still used here. If it's furred or feathered, they've got it in the kitchen.

Porter's English Restaurant *(see page 162)*. Right in the heart of Covent Garden, this restaurant focuses on English cookery for its pies, stews, and steamed "puds." Here you get all those wonderfully British dishes such as bubble & squeak or mushy peas so beloved by John Major. Hot pies with a delicious, dense crust are so filling the restaurant wisely abandons appetizers. Where else can you go these days to get a good Guinness and onion gravy?

Veronica's *(see page 183)*. Behind Queensway fronting Leinister Square, Veronica Shaw has created this little gem devoted to British cookery. Many of her recipes can be traced back to the Tudors, including Henry VIII. Where in London can you still get grilled Wiltshire goat's cheese with elderflower syrup as an appetizer? A recipe from 1664 calls for Cornish scrawled sardines—that is, char-grilled fish coated in a sauce of muscavado and mustard. The Elizabeth bread pudding with Scotch whisky sauce would surely have pleased Elizabeth I.

Hilaire is a jovially cramped restaurant, housed in what was originally a Victorian storefront. Ceiling fans, lemon-yellow walls, and fresh flowers provide the setting within which elegant French specialties are served. Chef Bryan Webb prepares a mixture of classical French and cuisine moderne; thus, this has become one of the most stylish restaurants in London. An apéritif bar, extra tables, and a pair of semi-private alcoves are in the lower dining room. A typical lunch might begin with a red wine risotto with radicchio and sun-dried tomato pesto, followed with sautéed scallops with creamed chicory, and ending with rhubarb sorbet. The menu always reflects the best of the season's offerings, and main courses at dinner might include rack of lamb with tapenade and wild garlic, saddle of rabbit, or grilled tuna with provençal vegetables.

Kemps

In the Pelham Hotel, 15 Cromwell Place, SW7. ☎ **0171/589-8288.** Reservations required. Appetizers £3–£4.75 ($4.75–$7.50); main courses £8.50–£11.50 ($13.45–$18.15); fixed-price lunch £8.95 ($14.15). AE, MC, V. Mon–Sat 12:30–2:30pm; Sun–Fri 7–10:30pm. Tube: South Kensington. ENGLISH.

Kemps is one of the dining "secrets" of London. On the ground floor of this previously recommended elegant little hotel is one of London's finest restaurants. Decorated with a subtle racing motif, the restaurant is accented with subtle lighting, cove moldings, a blue-and-yellow decor, and a large mahogany bar. It provides uniformed and impeccable French service at its limited number of well-attended tables, which are often filled with London luminaries.

Fashion aside, it is the food that attracts diners. The expertly prepared dishes represent an interpretation of modern French cuisine, including salad of char-grilled vegetables and goat cheese on toasted brioche, crab claws served with a poached egg and dandelion greens, and fresh mussels cooked in saffron wine with tagliatelle. For your main course, your selection might be fillet steak served with dauphinoise potato and carrot chips or pan-fried sea bass in a soy sauce with artichokes and new potatoes. Desserts are sumptuous, often presented like portrait miniatures, including a dark chocolate mousse with a white chocolate sauce and orange and walnut tartlet served with custard.

Turner's

87–89 Walton St., SW3. ☎ **0171/584-6711.** Reservations required. Weekday set lunch £9.95–£13.50 ($15.70–$21.35); Sun fixed-price lunch £19.50 ($30.80); set dinner £26.50 ($41.85). AE, DC, MC, V. Mon-Fri 12:30–2:30pm and 7:30–11:15pm; Sat 7:30–11:15pm; Sun 12:30–2:30pm and 7:30–10pm. Closed one week at Christmas. Tube: Knightsbridge. CONTINENTAL.

This restaurant is named after Brian J. Turner, the accomplished London chef who gained fame at many establishments he didn't own, including the Capital Hotel. As one critic aptly put it, his food comes not only fresh from the market that day but also "from the heart." Although Turner grew up in Yorkshire, he surely didn't learn his refined cuisine working in his father's transport "caff" in Leeds.

His cooking has been called "cuisine à la Brian Turner," meaning he doesn't seem to imitate anyone, but he sets his own goals and standards. The establishment's set menus change every day; its à la carte listings at least every season. Examples of cuisine that may or may not be listed by the time of your visit include creamy crab soup, fine chicken liver pâté with foie gras, a terrine of fresh salmon with a dill sauce, roast rack of lamb with herb crust, smoked and roast breast of duck in a port and green peppercorn sauce, or sea bass on a bed of stewed leeks with a bacon dressing.

11 Fulham

MODERATE

Blue Elephant

4–6 Fulham Broadway, SW6. ☎ **0171/385-6595.** Reservations required. Appetizers £5.25–£7.95 ($8.30–$12.55); main courses £6.25–£14.25 ($9.90–$22.50). AE, DC, MC, V. Sun–Fri noon–2:30pm; Mon–Sat 7pm–12:30am; Sun 7–10:30pm. Tube: Fulham Broadway. THAI.

This is the counterpart of the famous L'Eléphant Bleu in Brussels. Located in a converted factory building, London's Blue Elephant has been all the rage since it opened in 1986; in fact, it's the leading Thai restaurant in the capital, where the competition is growing.

In an almost-magical-garden setting of lush tropical foliage, diners are treated to an array of ancient and modern MSG-free Thai food. You can begin with a "floating market" (shellfish in clear broth flavored with chili paste and lemongrass) and go on to a splendid and varied selection of main courses, for which many of the ingredients have been flown in from Thailand. For a main course, you might try roast duck curry served in a clay cooking pot. The most popular choices are the Royal Thai banquet at £25–£28 ($39.50–$44.25) a head and the Sunday buffet at £14.50 ($22.90) per person.

12 Earl's Court, Notting Hill & Holland Park

EARL'S COURT
INEXPENSIVE

Chapter 11

51 Hollywood Rd., SW10. ☎ **0171/351-1663.** Reservations recommended. Appetizers £2.50–£5 ($3.95–$7.90); main courses £6.50–£11 ($10.25–$17.40). AE, DC, MC, V. Mon–Sat 6–11:30pm. Closed Dec 24–26. Tube: Earl's Court. CALIFORNIAN.

Once the best cuisine you could hope to find in this neighborhood was bangers and mash. But today some of the most fashionable members of young London gravitate here, drawn by shops selling some of the most exclusive and costly goods in town. Chapter 11 has a small garden terrace in back, though London's gray skies usually encourage diners to head for the lower dining room instead. The menu is wisely limited, but the dishes are well prepared and based on fresh ingredients. You might begin with butternut pumpkin soup, lobster ricotta ravioli, or a goat cheese soufflé, then follow with Thai prawn curry, grilled tuna steak, grilled rack of lamb with roast garlic and shallots, even a char-grilled hamburger.

NOTTING HILL
EXPENSIVE

Clarke's

124 Kensington Church St., W8. ☎ **0171/221-9225.** Reservations recommended. Fixed-price lunch £22–£26 ($34.75–$41.10); fixed-price dinner £37 ($58.45). MC, V. Mon–Fri 12:30–1:45pm and 7–10pm. Tube: Notting Hill Gate or High Street Kensington. BRITISH.

Named after its owner, English chef Sally Clarke—who is considered one of the finest in London—this is one of the hottest restaurants in Notting Hill Gate. Clarke trained in California at Michael's in Santa Monica and the West Beach Café in Venice (California, that is). In this excellent restaurant, everything is bright and modern, with wood floors, discreet lighting, and additional space in the basement where tables are more spacious and private. Here you get a fixed-price menu with no choice, but the food is so well prepared "in the new style" that diners rarely object. The menu is changed daily. You might begin with an appetizer of apple, Stilton, and celeriac soup, then follow with grilled swordfish with lemon mayonnaise. Desserts are likely to include a baked pear filled with mincemeat, candied orange, and almonds.

HOLLAND PARK
MODERATE

The Room at the Halcyon

In the Halcyon Hotel, 81 Holland Park Ave., W11 ☎ **0171/727-7288.** Reservations required. Appetizers £6–£6.50 ($9.50–$10.25); main courses £14–£18 ($22.10–$28.45); two-course set lunch £18 ($28.45), three-course set dinner £21 ($33.20). AE, DC, MC, V. Mon–Thur noon–2:30pm and 7–10:30pm; Fri noon–2:30pm; Fri-Sat 7–11pm; Sun noon–3pm and 7–10pm. Tube: Holland Park. INTERNATIONAL/ITALIAN.

On the hotel's lower level, the management has installed a restaurant that attracts the rich and famous, including royalty. To reach the restaurant, you pass a medley of colorful and whimsical trompe-l'oeil murals. You might enjoy an apéritif in the pink-tinted bar before heading for a meal in the tastefully uncluttered restaurant. Lattices and a garden view create an image of springtime even in winter.

The menu is highly individualized. One food critic wrote that it "reads like a United Nations of cuisine," though it leans heavily toward Italy. The menu is based on the inspiration of the chef and the vagaries of shopping, since only the freshest ingredients are used. You might begin with spicy chicken soup with lemongrass and coconut milk or terrine of foie gras on spinach with hazelnut oil and green bean salad. Main dishes are likely to feature fillet of brill with leeks, saffron potatoes, a quenelle of caviar, a steamed oyster, and *beurre blanc*; roasted rack of lamb with herbed breadcrumbs, garlic, and rosemary served with creamy garlic potatoes and carrots; or roasted squab with morel mushroom sausage, broad beans, smoked bacon, and sage. There is also a special vegetarian menu.

13   St. Marylebone & Bayswater

ST. MARYLEBONE
MODERATE

Odin's
27 Devonshire St., W1. ☎ **0171/935-7296.** Reservations recommended. Two-course set-price lunch or dinner £20.95 ($33.10); three-course set-price lunch or dinner £22.95 ($36.25). AE, DC, MC, V. Mon–Fri 12:30–2:30pm and 7–11:30pm. Tube: Regent's Park. CONTINENTAL.

Odin's is an elegant restaurant, one of at least four in London that is partially owned by actor Michael Caine. Set adjacent to its slightly less expensive twin, Langan's Bistro (which is recommended separately), it features ample space between tables and an eclectic, air-conditioned decor that was refurbished in 1991. Amid gilt-edged mirrors, evocative paintings, Japanese screens, and art deco accessories, you'll be offered a choice of menu items that changes with the seasons. Typical fare might include an English goat cheese salad served with garlic dressing; pigeon breast with roast new potatoes and onions; grilled Dover sole with a butter sauce; veal with Pommery mustard and tarragon; and fillet of beef with a green peppercorn sauce.

INEXPENSIVE

Langan's Bistro
26 Devonshire St., W1. ☎ **0171/935-4531.** Reservations recommended. Two-course set-price lunch or dinner £15.95 ($25.20); three-course set-price lunch or dinner £17.95 ($28.35). AE, DC, MC, V. Mon–Fri 12:30–3:30pm and 7–11:30pm; Sat 7–11:30pm. Tube: Regent's Park. FRENCH/ENGLISH.

This deliberately unpretentious restaurant has been a busy fixture on the London restaurant scene since the mid-1960s, when it was established by actor Michael Caine and a group of investors. Of the several restaurants within the chain, it's the least expensive, provides the least space between the tables, and is probably the most visually appealing. Set behind a brightly colored storefront on a quiet residential street, it has an interior whose surfaces are richly covered with fanciful clusters of Japanese parasols, rococo mirrors, surrealistic paintings, and old photographs of almost-forgotten subjects.

The French-inspired menu changes with the seasons and might include salmon and broccoli mousse, snails in a garlic butter sauce, poached salmon encased in pastry served with a watercress sauce, sirloin steak with horseradish sauce, and pan-fried squid. The dessert extravaganza is known as "Langan's chocolate pudding."

BAYSWATER
INEXPENSIVE

Ⓢ Veronica's

3 Hereford Rd., W2. ☎ **0171/229-5079**. Reservations required. Appetizers £4.50–£8.50 ($7.10–$13.45); main courses £8.50–£14.50 ($13.45–$22.90); fixed-price menu £11.50 ($18.15). AE, DC, MC, V. Mon–Fri noon–3pm and 6:30pm–midnight; Sat 6:30pm–midnight. Tube: Bayswater or Queensway. ENGLISH.

Called the "market leader in café salons," Veronica's offers some of the finest British cuisine in London at prices you don't mind paying. In fact, it's like a celebration of British food, including some dishes based on recipes used in medieval or Tudor times. For example, your appetizer might be a salad enjoyed by Elizabeth I and called salmagundi, made with crunchy picked vegetables. Another concoction might be watersouchy, a medieval stew crammed with mixed seafood. However, each dish is given today's imaginative interpretation by Veronica Shaw, the owner. One month she'll focus on Scotland; another month, Victorian foods; yet another month, Wales. Many dishes are vegetarian, and everything tastes better when followed with one of the selections of British farmhouse cheeses or a "pudding." The restaurant is brightly and attractively decorated and service is warm and ingratiating.

14 Away from the Center

PIMLICO
MODERATE

Pomegranates

94 Grosvenor Rd., SW1. ☎ **0171/828-6560**. Reservations required. Appetizers £4.75–£5.75 ($7.50–$9.10); main courses £8.75–£15.75 ($13.85–$24.90); fixed-price lunch £9.95–£12.95 ($15.70–$20.45); fixed-price dinner £12.95–£16.95 ($20.45–$26.80). AE, DC, MC, V. Mon–Fri 12:30–2:15pm and 7–11:15pm; Sat 7–11:15pm. Tube: Pimlico. INTERNATIONAL.

This is a basement restaurant by the river in Pimlico. Owner Patrick Gwynn-Jones has traveled far and collected recipes for dishes throughout the world. Asian and Indonesian delicacies vie for space on the fixed-price menus along with European and North American dishes: West Indian curried goat with fried plantains, escargot and wild mushroom pie, Welsh salt duck with white onion sauce, Mexican baked crab with avocado and tequila. The decor is *fin de siècle*, with mirrors and well-laid tables. House wines are reasonably priced, and there is also a good wine list. You have a wide range of choices on the fixed-price menus, which begin with crudités and might end with homemade honey-and-brandy ice cream.

HAMPSTEAD HEATH
INEXPENSIVE

Byron's

3A Downshire Hill, Hampstead NW3. ☎ **0171/435-3544**. Reservations recommended. Appetizers £2.95–£4.50 ($4.65–$7.10); main courses £7.50–11.95 ($11.85–$18.90); set-price lunch £7.50 ($11.85). AE, MC, V. Daily noon–3pm and 6–11pm. Tube: Hampstead. ENGLISH.

Named as an ironic reference to Lord Byron, poet and competitor of John Keats (whose home lies within a 3-minute walk), this is a pleasant restaurant with innovative food. Situated in a semidetached, stone-fronted house that was originally built in the 18th century, it offers a pair of understated dining rooms illuminated with candles. Menu choices, which are updated versions of traditional English recipes, might include a warm salad of duck livers with lentils on a bed of radicchio and chicory; tempura of winter vegetables with a ginger-flavored dipping sauce; potted smoked chicken with prawns, served with anise-flavored biscuits; salt-cured fresh salmon stuffed with chicory mousse and served with a mustard-dill sauce; duck breast with pomegranate sauce; a medley of grilled fish with a fennel-chicory-red-wine sauce; and steamed steak-and-kidney pudding with buttered cabbage. The lunch menu might even offer old-fashioned bangers and mash for dyed-in-the-wool traditionalists. Desserts include a black currant *délice* with cassis-flavored liqueur.

PUB

Spaniards Inn

Spaniards Rd., NW3. ☎ **0171/455-3276.** Appetizers £2.25–£3.50 ($3.55–$5.55); main courses £4.25–£8 ($6.70–$12.65); beer from £1.75 ($2.75). MC, V. Food bar Mon–Fri noon–3pm and 6–9:30pm; Sat noon–9:30pm; Sun noon–9:30pm. Pub Mon–Sat 11am–11pm; Sun noon–3pm and 7–10:30pm. Tube: Hampstead or Golders Green. ENGLISH.

This is a Hampstead Heath landmark, opposite the old tollhouse, a bottleneck in the road where people had to pay the toll to enter the country park of the bishop of London. The notorious highwayman Dick Turpin leaped over the gate on his horse when he was in flight from the law. The pub was originally built in 1585, and the present building dates from 1702. It still has some antique benches, open fires, and cozy nooks in its rooms with their low, beamed ceilings and oak paneling.

The pub serves traditional but above-average food. In summer, customers can sit at slat tables on a terrace in a garden beside a flower-bordered lawn and aviary. Byron, Shelley, Dickens, and Galsworthy patronized the pub. Even Keats may have quaffed a glass here.

CAMDEN TOWN

My Fair Lady

250 Camden High St., NW1. ☎ **0171/485-4433** or 0171/485-6210. Reservations required. Lunch trip £16.95 ($26.80); dinner trip £26.95 ($42.60). MC, V. Dinner trip departs at 8pm Tues–Sat; lunch trip departs at 1pm Sun only. Tube: Camden Town. ENGLISH/FRENCH.

This cruise-while-you-dine establishment, a motor-driven barge, noses through Regent's Canal for three hours, passing through the zoo, Regent's Park, and Maida Hill tunnel before it reaches Robert Browning's Island at Little Venice, where a popular singer-guitarist joins you for the return journey. The menu, which is based on fresh seasonal ingredients, consists of such traditional English fare as prime roast rib of beef, chicken suprême, and fillet of beef.

ST. JOHN'S WOOD
MODERATE

L'Aventure

3 Blenheim Terrace, NW8. ☎ **0171/624-6232.** Reservations required. Three-course fixed-price lunch £18.50 ($29.25); three-course fixed-price dinner £25 ($39.50). AE, DC, MC, V. Sun-Fri 12:30–2:30pm; Mon-Sat 7:30–11pm; Sun 7:30–10pm. Tube: St. John's Wood. FRENCH.

In this leafy cul-de-sac in St. John's Wood, where Edward VII used to slip away with his mistress, Lillie Langtry, this is a cozily chic choice. In an upscale neighborhood, the location is a short stroll from Lord's Cricket Ground and the American School in London. On that rare hot summer night in London, its broad terrace offers outdoor dining. Catherine Parisot, a French woman of charm, now an expatriate living in London, came here on holiday, liked the place so much she stayed and opened this restaurant. The cookery is of a high standard, and in the evening the lights are lowered and candles lit for dinner. Chef Alain Perdrix might offer such tempting appetizers as cream of celeriac soup, cabbage with scallops, and wild mushroom mousse. Main courses perhaps will include fillet of steak with either a shallot or red wine sauce, roast breast of chicken, or salmon roasted on a bed of potatoes and served with oyster mushrooms. A selection of inexpensive French wines accompany the meal.

WATERLOO
MODERATE

RSJ
13A Coin St., SE1. ☎ **0171/928-4554.** Reservations required. Appetizers £3.95–£5.75 ($6.25–$9.10); main courses £9.75–£11.95 ($15.40–$18.90); three-course fixed-price lunch or dinner £15.95 ($25.20). AE, MC, V. Mon–Fri noon–2pm and 6–11pm; Sat 6–11pm. Tube: Waterloo. ENGLISH/FRENCH.

Situated on the traditionally unglamorous south bank of the Thames, this restaurant has such loyal patrons that they travel from many different parts of London to reach it. Others dine here after seeing a program at the South Bank cultural center. Named after a type of construction material (rolled structural joists) used during its restoration, the restaurant occupies the 250-year-old premises of what was originally a stable for the duke of Cornwall. You'll enter from a nondescript street, perhaps order a drink from the stand-up apéritif bar, and be led upstairs to a table in a room that used to be the hayloft. Nigel Wilkinson, the sophisticated owner, personally selects the French wines (especially Loire Valley) that fill his impressive and reasonably priced wine list.

Food, prepared in the tradition of modern British cuisine, includes such specialties as breast of guinea fowl; tagliatelle with wild mushrooms; langous-tine bisque; and roast lamb served with saffron potatoes, French beans, and lamb jus.

ELEPHANT & CASTLE
PUB

The Goose & Firkin
47 Borough Rd., SE1. ☎ **0171/403-3590.** Reservations not accepted. Sandwiches from £1.95 ($3.10); small pies from £1.05 ($1.65); hot platters £2–£3.45 ($3.15–$5.45); glass of wine from £1.83 ($2.90). AE, DC, MC, V. Food Mon–Fri noon–7pm; Sat–Sun noon–3pm. Pub Mon–Fri noon–11pm; Sat–Sun noon–3pm and 7pm–midnight. Tube: Elephant & Castle. ENGLISH.

Established in 1979 on the premises of a much older, unsuccessful pub, this was the first member of a chain, the Goose & Firkin, which later spread throughout the British Isles. The food is a simple assortment of "big baps" (rolls stuffed with ham, turkey, or tuna) or crock pots filled with chili or platters of such pub staples as lasagna. Aside from that, most of the patrons come to drink, converse, and meet with newcomers and other regulars. Goose & Firkin brews its own beer in three special strengths: Goose, Borough Bitter, and the potent Dogbolter. Live music, from either an organist or a guitarist, is presented on Wednesday, Friday, and Saturday from 9 to 11pm.

CLERKENWELL
INEXPENSIVE

The Fox and Anchor
115 Charterhouse St., EC1. ☎ **0171/253-4838.** Reservations required. "The full house" breakfast £6.95 ($11); steak breakfast £4.60–£9.60 ($7.25–$15.15). AE, DC, MC, V. Mon–Fri 7–10:30am and noon–2:15pm. Tube: Farringdon or Barbican. ENGLISH.

For breakfast at its best, try this place, which has been serving traders from the nearby famous Smithfield meat market since the pub was built in 1898. Breakfasts are gargantuan, especially if you order "the full house," which will have at least eight items on your plate, including sausage, bacon, mushrooms, kidney, eggs, beans, white pudding, and a fried slice of bread, to mention just a few, along with unlimited tea or coffee, toast and jam. If you want a more substantial meal, you can order a fillet steak with mushrooms, chips, tomatoes, and salad. Add a Black Velvet (champagne with Guinness) and the day is yours. Of course, in the modern British view, Guinness ruins champagne, but some people order it anyway— just to be traditional. More fashionable is a Bucks fizz, with orange juice and champagne. The Fox and Anchor is noted for its range of fine English ales, all available at breakfast. Butchers from the meat market, spotted with blood, still appear, as do nurses getting off their shift and clerks and tycoons from The City who have been working at bookkeeping chores all night.

EAST END
INEXPENSIVE

Bloom's
90 Whitechapel High St., E1. ☎ **0171/247-6001.** Reservations required. Appetizers £2.50–£3.50 ($3.95–$5.55); main courses £3.90–£8.90 ($6.15–$14.05). AE, DC, MC, V. Sun–Thurs 11am–9:30pm, Fri 11:30am–3pm (until 2pm Dec–Feb). Tube: Aldgate East. KOSHER.

This is London's most famous Jewish restaurant, originally established in 1920. But to reach it, you have to take the tube to the East End near the Tower of London. This large, bustling restaurant is in the back of a delicatessen. The cooking is strictly kosher. Sunday is busy at lunchtime, since many visitors come here after browsing through the used clothing racks and bric-a-brac bins at the nearby Petticoat Lane Sunday market. The cabbage borscht is the traditional opening course, though you may prefer chicken blintzes. Main-dish specialties include sauerbraten and salt (corned) beef. For dessert, the apple strudel is a favorite.

PUB

The Prospect of Whitby
57 Wapping Wall, E1. ☎ **0171/481-1095.** Reservations required. Appetizers £3.50–£8.75 ($5.55–$13.85); main courses £12–£15.95 ($18.95–$25.20); fixed-price menu £8–£27.50 ($12.65–$43.45). AE, DC, MC, V. Restaurant Sun–Fri noon–2pm; Mon–Sat 7–9:45pm. Pub Mon–Sat 11:30am–3pm and 5:30–11pm; Sun noon–3pm and 7–10:30pm. Tube: Wapping. ENGLISH/FRENCH.

The Prospect of Whitby was founded in the days of the Tudors, taking its name from a coal barge that made weekly trips from Yorkshire to London. Come here for a tot, a noggin, or whatever it is you drink and soak up its traditional pubby atmosphere. On the ground floor you can enjoy beer and snacks, or dine in the Pepys Room, which honors the diarist who may—just may—have visited the Prospect in rowdier days, when the seamy side of London deck life held sway here. You can enjoy such dishes as beef and oyster pie, poached salmon in a champagne sauce, and fillet of steak served with a Stilton and wine sauce.

ST. KATHARINE'S DOCK
MODERATE
Dickens Inn by the Tower

St. Katharine's Way, E1. ☎ **0171/488-2208.** Reservations recommended. Pickwick Grill appetizers £2.75–£6.25 ($4.35–$9.90); main courses £8.95–£15.95 ($14.15–$25.20). Tavern Room snacks and platters £3.50–£4.95 ($5.55–$7.80). Pizza restaurant pizzas £4.25–£23 ($6.70–$36.35). AE, DC, MC, V. Restaurant Mon–Sat noon–3:30pm and 6:30–10:30pm; Sun noon–3:30pm and 6:30–9:30pm. Bar Mon-Sat 11am–11pm; Sun noon–3pm and 7–10:30pm. Tube: Tower Hill. ENGLISH.

This three-floor restaurant is housed within the solid brick walls of what was originally (around 1830) a warehouse for the spices then pouring into London from Britain's far-flung empire. Its main decorative allure derives from the massive redwood timbers of its original construction. It is deliberately devoid of carpets, curtains, or anything that might conceal its unusual antique trusses. Large windows permit a sweeping view of the nearby Thames and Tower Bridge.

On the ground level, you'll find a bar and the Tavern Room, serving sandwiches, platters of lasagna or smoked mackerel, steaming bowls of soup or chili, and bar snacks. One floor above street level is a pizza restaurant, serving four sizes of pizza ranging from 12 inches wide to a much-accessorized 18-inch behemoth known as "The Beast." On the next higher floor, you'll find a relatively formal dining room, The Pickwick Grill, serving more elegant meals. Specialties there include roast lamb or roast beef with Yorkshire pudding, fresh seafood, and salads.

INEXPENSIVE
☻ Carvery Restaurant

In the Tower Thistle Hotel, St. Katharine's Way, E1. ☎ **0171/481-2575.** Reservations recommended. Fixed-price menu £15.95 ($25.20). AE, DC, MC, V. Mon–Thur 12:15–2:30pm and 5:30–10:30pm; Fri–Sat 12:15–2:30pm and 5:30–midnight; Sun 12:15–4pm and 5:30–10:30pm. Tube: Tower Hill. ENGLISH.

At the Carvery Restaurant at this modern hotel built overlooking the Thames, you can enjoy some of the most tempting roasts in the Commonwealth.

☻ Family-Friendly Restaurants

Canteen *(see p. 175)*. At Chelsea Harbour, kids and their families dine in a setting influenced by the themes of *Alice in Wonderland,* all whimsical with harlequins and playing cards. The food is international—almost something for every palate.

Ye Olde Cheshire Cheese *(see p. 165)*. Fleet Street's most famous chophouse, established in 1667, is the eternal family favorite. If "ye famous pudding" turns your kid off, the sandwiches and roast beef will tempt instead.

Everything is served buffet style. Before going to the carving table you'll be served either a shrimp cocktail, a bowl of soup, or a cold slice of melon. Then you can choose (rare, medium, or well done) from standing ribs of prime beef with Yorkshire pudding, horseradish sauce, and the drippings; or from tender roast pork with cracklings accompanied by a spiced bread dressing and applesauce; or perhaps the roast spring Southdown lamb with mint sauce—and help yourself to the roast potatoes, the green peas, the baby carrots. Or you may prefer a selection of cold meats and salads from the buffet table. You can end the meal with a choice from the dessert list as well as a large cup of American-style coffee.

BUTLER'S WHARF
MODERATE

Le Pont de la Tour

36d Shad Thames, Butler's Wharf SE1. ☎ **0171/403-8403.** Reservations not accepted in the Bar and Grill; recommended in the Restaurant. Bar and Grill appetizers £2.95–£12.75 ($4.65–$20.15); main courses £8–£14.50 ($12.65–$22.90). Restaurant appetizers £6–£14.50 ($9.50–$22.90); main courses £14.50–£18.50 ($22.90–$29.25); three-course fixed-price lunch £26.50 ($41.85) per person. AE, DC, MC, V. Restaurant Mon–Fri noon–3pm and 6pm–midnight; Sat 6pm–midnight; Sun noon–3pm and 6–11pm. Bar and Grill Mon–Sat noon–midnight; Sun noon–11pm. Tube: Tower Hill or London Bridge. INTERNATIONAL.

The two sections of this restaurant are considered the best established and most interesting of the four or five eateries that occupy a recently developed and much-praised commercial complex that was rescued from urban decay in 1988. Located at the edge of the Thames near Tower Bridge, the complex includes condominiums, rental apartments, offices, and an assortment of food-and-wine shops collectively known as the Gastrodome. Originally constructed of brick and sandstone as a warehouse in the mid-19th century, it's known today as the Butler's Wharf Building. From its windows, diners and shoppers enjoy sweeping views of some of the densest river traffic in Europe.

Although multiple visual and gastronomic diversions are scattered throughout the complex, many patrons prefer the brash hubbub of the Bar & Grill. Its hard surfaces, live entertainment, and choice of cocktails create an animated ambiance in a neighborhood that until recently was not noted for conviviality or warmth. Although such dishes as chicken liver and foie gras parfait, smoked Irish salmon, and langoustine mayonnaise are featured, the culinary star is a heaping platter of fresh shellfish (*fruits de mer*). It's perfect when consumed with a bottle of wine and shared with a friend.

In bold contrast is the large, more formal room known simply as The Restaurant. Filled with white linen, burr oak furniture, and framed reproductions of French cartoons from the 1920s, it offers excellent food and a polite but undeniable English reserve. Menu choices include terrine of foie gras with an onion and raisin confit; sauté of scallops with grilled tomatoes and gremolata; braised lamb shank with roast onions and rosemary; and roast saddle of rabbit with bacon and mustard vinaigrette. Both areas of this restaurant offer additional seating on outdoor terraces overlooking the Thames.

INEXPENSIVE
Butler's Wharf Chop House

36E Shad Thames, SE1. ☎ **0171/403-3404.** Reservations recommended. Set lunch £22.75 ($35.95); dinner appetizers £3.75–£7.50 ($5.95–$11.85); dinner main course £9–£14

($14.20–$22.10). AE, DC, MC, V. Sun-Fri noon–2:45pm (last order); Mon-Sat 6–10:45pm. Tube: Tower Hill. BRITISH.

This is one of four restaurants situated in the renovated warehouse known as Butler's Wharf. Of the four, it's the closest to Tower Bridge, and of the four, it's the one that most aggressively tries to maintain reasonable prices. The complex houses an even cheaper (Italian) restaurant —La Cantina del Ponte — though most people think of that establishment as simply a place for pasta. The complex's more upscale restaurants, Le Pont de la Tour, are separately recommended (see above).

The decor of The Chop House was modeled after that of a large boat house, with russet-colored banquettes, lots of exposed timbers, wood floors, flowers, candles, and big windows overlooking Tower Bridge and the traffic on Britain's most-famous river. Lunchtime crowds include a large number of workers from the City's nearby financial district; evening crowds include many groups of friends and acquaintances dining together under less pressing circumstances. Menu choices are adaptations of British recipes, some (but not all) geared for modern tastes. Examples include Lunesdale breast of duck with pears, cracked pepper, and port wine sauce; a salad of poached codfish with baby spinach; potted crab; roast salmon with a mustard-dill sauce and pickled cucumbers; kidney and oyster pudding; and Dublin bay prawns and salmon wrapped in bacon. There's also a roast of the day; bangers, sausages, and mash; and lamb's kidneys with bubble and squeak and bacon. Dessert might include a double chocolate mousse with Irish coffee sauce or sticky toffee pudding. Drinks might include such stiff-upper-lip choices as Theakston's best bitter, several choices of English wine, and a half-dozen French clarets served by the jug.

15 Afternoon Tea

Brown's Hotel

29–34 Albemarle St., W1. ☎ **0171/493-6020.** Reservations not accepted. Afternoon tea £14.95 ($23.60). AE, DC, MC, V. Daily 3–6pm. Tube: Green Park.

Ranking along with the Ritz Hotel as a chic venue for tea in London, Brown's Hotel offers afternoon tea in its lounge. The room is decorated with English antiques, wall panels, oil paintings, and floral chintz, much like a private English country estate. Give your name to the concierge upon arrival; arrangements will be made for you to be seated on clusters of sofas and settees or at low tables. The regular afternoon tea includes a choice of 10 different teas, sandwiches, and pastries, which are rolled around on a trolley for your selection. Scones with jam and clotted cream are also included. All cakes and pastries are made in the hotel kitchens.

Oak Room Lounge

In Le Méridien London, 21 Piccadilly, W1. ☎ **0171/734-8000.** Reservations recommended. Average tea from £13.50 ($21.35). AE, DC, MC, V. Daily 3–6pm. Tube: Piccadilly Circus or Green Park.

The Oak Room Lounge has been restored to its former Edwardian glory and welcomes nonresidents for the very British tradition of afternoon tea. Formal but unstuffy, the soothing elegance of this oak-paneled room is augmented by comfortable armchairs and background music by a resident harpist. A complete tea includes a selection of sandwiches and tarts. The menu lists a tempting array of more exotic teas, some you may never have tried.

Palm Court

In the Waldorf Hotel, Aldwych, WC2. ☎ **0171/836-2400.** Reservations required. Afternoon tea £13.25 ($20.95); tea dance £20.50 ($32.40). AE, DC, MC, V. Afternoon tea Mon-Fri 3:30–6pm; tea dance Sat-Sun 3:30–6pm. Tube: Covent Garden.

Palm Court combines afternoon tea with afternoon dancing (such as the fox-trot, quickstep, and the waltz). The Palm Court is aptly compared to a 1920s movie set, which is in fact what it's been several times in its long life. Art directors would find it difficult to duplicate such a natural setting. You can order tea on a terrace or in a pavilion the size of a ballroom lit by skylights. On tea-dancing days, the orchestra leader will conduct such favorites as "Ain't She Sweet" and "Yes, Sir, That's My Baby," as a butler in a cutaway inquires if you want a cucumber sandwich. Of course, men must wear jacket and tie.

Palm Court Lounge

In the Park Lane Hotel, Piccadilly, W1. ☎ **0171/499-6321.** Devon cream tea £6.75 ($10.65); afternoon tea £11.25 ($17.80); club sandwich £8.20 ($12.95). AE, DC, MC, V. Daily 24 hours. Tube: Hyde Park Corner or Green Park.

One of the great favorites of London for tea, this place has an atmosphere straight from 1927. Restored to its former charm by John Siddeley, one of the world's leading interior designers, the lounge has a yellow-and-white domed ceiling, torchères, and palms in Compton stoneware jardinieres. A delightful tea of three different types of scones, Devonshire cream, and thick jam, sandwiches, and a selection of cakes with many different types of tea is served daily. Many guests come here after the theater for a sandwich and a drink, as hot food is served 24 hours a day. During the week a pianist plays every afternoon and evening with a trio that plays 1920s music every Sunday afternoon.

✪ Ritz Palm Court

In the Ritz Hotel, Piccadilly, W1. ☎ **0171/493-8181.** Reservations required, at least ten days in advance for weekdays and eight weeks in advance for weekends. Afternoon tea £16.50 ($26.05). AE, DC, MC, V. Daily 2–6pm. Tube: Green Park.

This is the most fashionable place in London to order afternoon tea, and perhaps the hardest to get in without reservations far in advance. The atmosphere is one of marble steps and columns, along with a baroque fountain. It's strictly a setting from the 1920s and 30s. You have your choice of the widest possible variety of teas, served with those delectable little sandwiches on white bread and luscious pastries. Gentlemen are encouraged to wear jackets and ties, and ladies are asked to wear hats. Jeans and sneakers are not acceptable.

London Attractions 6

Dr. Johnson said, "When a man is tired of London, he is tired of life, for there is in London all that life can afford." In this chapter, we'll survey only a fraction of that life: ancient monuments, literary shrines, museums, walking tours, Parliament debates, royal castles, waxworks, palaces, cathedrals, and parks. Some of what we're about to see was known to Johnson and Boswell, even Shakespeare, but much of it is new.

SUGGESTED ITINERARIES

Obviously this list is for the first-time visitor. Presumably, if it's your second or third visit you will want to seek out other highlights. However, such sights as The British Museum can hardly be covered in one visit or perhaps even one lifetime. There are actually people living in London who go to the Museum almost every day, and they are always discovering things they had not seen before.

If You Have 1 Day

Even for those with the tightest of schedules, no first-time visitor should leave London without visiting Westminster Abbey. See the Poets' Corner in the abbey where everybody from Robert Browning to Alfred, Lord Tennyson is buried. After a visit inside, walk over to see Big Ben and the Houses of Parliament. Also see the Changing of the Guard at Buckingham Palace if it's being held and walk over to 10 Downing St., home of the prime minister. Have dinner at one of the little restaurants in Covent Garden. For the ultimate English experience, make it Porter's English Restaurant, owned by the Earl of Bradford. Try one of their classic English pies such as lamb and apricot. For your nightcap, head over to the Red Lion, 2 Duke of York St., in Mayfair *(see page 151)*. Here you can enjoy a lager in the ultimate Victorian pub—a place Oscar Wilde might have chosen for a brandy.

If You Have 2 Days

Spend your first day as above. Devote a good part of the second day to exploring the British Museum, considered the biggest and best in the world. Spend the afternoon visiting the Tower of London and seeing the collection of crown jewels (expect slow-moving lines). Cap

> **? Did You Know?**
>
> - A romance between one of the queen's corgis and one of Princess Margaret's dachshunds produced three royal "dorgis" for the queen.
> - St. Paul's Cathedral is the fifth church dedicated to the patron saint of London to be constructed on the same spot, and the first English cathedral built by one architect.
> - A grocer's daughter from Lincolnshire, Margaret Thatcher, lived at 10 Downing St. longer than any other prime minister.
> - Covent Garden once had so many Turkish baths and brothels it was called "the great square of Venus."
> - The richest man in the world, the sultan of Brunei, owns the landmark art deco Dorchester Hotel. He issued orders to restore it until it was "the greatest hotel in the world."
> - FDR (1882–1945) honeymooned with Eleanor at Brown's Hotel, which had been launched by a manservant of Lord Byron.
> - Nash's Marble Arch (1827), one of the most famous London landmarks, was banned from Buckingham Palace because it was too narrow for the royal coaches to pass through.

your day by boarding one of the London Launches (see below) to experience the city from the river. Go to some really local place for dinner such as Shepherd's, Marsham Court, Marsham Street *(see page 166)*, where you can order roast rib of Scottish beef and Yorkshire pudding with many of the MPs from the House of Commons.

If You Have 3 Days

Spend days 1 and 2 as above. On the third day, go to the National Gallery, facing Trafalgar Square, in the morning. In a lighter vein, enjoy an afternoon at Madame Tussaud's Waxworks. Take our walking tour of St. James's (see below) and try to catch some cultural performance at the South Bank Centre, site of the Royal Festival Hall.

If You Have 5 Days

Spend the first 3 days as above. On the morning of the fourth day, head for The City, the financial district of London in the East End. Your major sightseeing goal here will be Sir Christopher Wren's St. Paul's Cathedral. Take our walking tour of The City and visit such attractions as the Guildhall (The City's city hall). In the late afternoon, head down King's Road in Chelsea to check out the many and varied boutiques, followed by dinner at a Chelsea restaurant.

On the fifth and final day, explore the Victoria and Albert Museum in the morning, then head for the Tate Gallery for lunch at its restaurant. Spend the rest of the afternoon wandering through the gallery enjoying its masterpieces. Finally, see where history was made during the dark days of World War II; visit the Cabinet War Rooms at Clive Steps (see below) where Churchill directed the British operations against the Nazis. In the evening, attend the theater or cram in as many West End shows as you can on the first four nights.

Note: As a rule, and unless otherwise stated, children's prices apply to those aged 16 and under. For senior citizens to obtain available discounts at some attractions, you must be 60 years of age or older. For students to get discounted admissions, wherever granted, they must have a student ID card.

1 The Top Attractions

London is not a city to visit hurriedly. It is so vast, so stocked with treasures that, on a cursory visit, a person will not only miss many of the highlights but also fail to grasp the spirit of London and to absorb its unique flavor. Still, faced with an infinite number of important places to visit and a limited amount of time, the visitor will have to focus on a manageable group.

Here are the top sights of London. Try to see them even if you have to skip all the rest, saving them for next time.

✪ The Tower of London

Tower Hill, on the north bank of the Thames, EC3. ☎ **0171/709-0765.** Admission £7.95 ($12.55) adults, £5.95 ($9.40) students and senior citizens, £5.25 ($8.30) children. Free for children under 5. Family ticket for five (but no more than two adults), £21.95 ($34.70). Mar–Oct Mon–Sat 9am–6pm, Sun 10am–6pm; Nov–Feb Mon–Sat 9am–5pm, Sun 10am–5pm. Closed Dec 24–26, Jan 1. Tube: Tower Hill. Boats: From Westminster Pier.

This ancient fortress continues to pack 'em in because of its macabre associations with all the legendary figures who were imprisoned and/or executed here. James Street once wrote, "There are more spooks to the square foot than in any other building in the whole of haunted Britain. Headless bodies, bodiless heads, phantom soldiers, icy blasts, clanking chains—you name them, the Tower's got them." Many visitors consider the Tower to be the highlight of their sightseeing in London—so schedule plenty of time for it.

The fortress is actually a compound, in which the oldest and finest structure is the White Tower, begun by William the Conqueror. Here you can view the Armouries, which dates from the reign of Henry VIII. A display of instruments of torture and execution will recall some of the most ghastly moments in the history of the Tower. At the Bloody Tower, the Little Princes (Edward V and the Duke of York) were allegedly murdered by their uncle, Richard III. Through Traitors' Gate passed such ill-fated, but romantic, figures as Robert Devereux, known as the second earl of Essex, a favorite of Elizabeth I. At Tower Green, Anne Boleyn and Catherine Howard, two wives of Henry VIII, lost their lives. Many other notable figures have lost their lives at the tower, including Sir Thomas More as well as the 9-day queen, Lady Jane Grey, who was executed at Tower Green. Her husband, Lord Guildford Dudley, was executed at Tower Hill.

To see the **Jewel House,** where the crown jewels are kept, go early in the day during summer because long lines often form. However, a major rebuilding of this structure in 1994 eliminated most waiting time except during peak periods, and its ground level allows easy access for wheelchairs. Ask one of the Yeoman Warders (Beefeaters) in Tudor uniform to tell you how Colonel Blood almost made off with the crown and regalia in the late 17th century. Of the three English crowns, the Imperial State Crown is the most important—in fact, it's probably the most famous crown on earth. Made for Victoria in 1837, it is worn today by Queen Elizabeth when she opens Parliament. Studded with some 3,000 jewels (principally diamonds), it includes the Black Prince's Ruby, worn by Henry V at Agincourt (the 1415 battle where the English defeated the French). Don't miss the 530-carat Star of Africa, a cut diamond on the Royal Sceptre with Cross.

The Much-Abused Portland Vase

One of the most famous exhibits in the British Museum *(see page 197)* is the Portland Vase, a glass vessel imitating the appearance and craftsmanship of cameo-cut vessels of semiprecious stone. The vase is an early and very fine example of Roman glass-blowing, a technique that had been developed only a few decades before the vase was crafted in around 50 B.C. It was discovered in 1582 in a marble sarcophagus in a large burial mound, Monte del Grano, just outside the core of ancient Rome. It was seized by Cardinal Francesco Maria del Monte, who was a ruthless patron of the arts.

Upon his death, del Monte's heirs sold the vase to the Barberini family, who renamed it "Vaso Barberini." Descendants of that fabled family eventually sold the vase in 1780. After a change or two of ownership, it was purchased three years later by Sir William Hamilton, who in turn sold it to the Dowager Duchess of Portland in 1784. The vase was loaned to the British Museum in 1810, and finally purchased by the museum from the Portland family in 1945.

During the interim, however, on February 17, 1845, the vase was smashed into 200 fragments by a young man who called himself William Lloyd. He was taken to the Bow Street police station and under the Willful Damage Act could only be indicted for damaging an object worth £5 or less. He was therefore charged with breaking the glass case, valued at £3. Upon conviction, he was sentenced to a fine of £3 or two months of hard labor. Two days later, an anonymous donor paid the fine, and Lloyd was released. His motive for breaking the vase was never determined.

The task of repairing the vase fell to John Doubleday, a restorer, who completed the task in September 1845. He was paid only about 25 guineas (a guinea is a pound and a shilling) for his effort. Doubleday was unable to incorporate 37 small chips, which were set aside.

In 1948, the vase was reconstructed, but only three of the unused chips were incorporated. As late as 1985, the vase was found to be in "unstable condition." It had to be completely dismantled and reassembled again. This time, the most advanced techniques and the latest epoxy resins were used. Many of Doubleday's old fragments were incorporated. The vase is now supposed to be in fine enough shape to last at least until the late 21st century.

The Tower of London has an evening ceremony called the Ceremony of the Keys. It is the ceremonial locking up of the Tower. The Yeoman Warder will explain to guests the significance of the ceremony. For free tickets, write to the Resident Governor, Queen's House, Tower of London, London EC3N 4AB, and request a specific date, but also list alternative dates. At least 6 weeks' notice is required. All requests must be accompanied by a stamped, self-addressed envelope (British stamps only) or two International Reply Coupons. With ticket in hand, you'll be admitted by a Yeoman Warder at 9:35pm.

There are also the ravens. Six of them, plus two spares, are all registered as official Tower residents and each is fed exactly 6 ounces of rations per day. According to a legend, the Tower of London will stand as long as those black, ominous birds remain in the Tower and so, to be on the safe side, they have one of their wings clipped.

Attractions in The City & Fleet Street

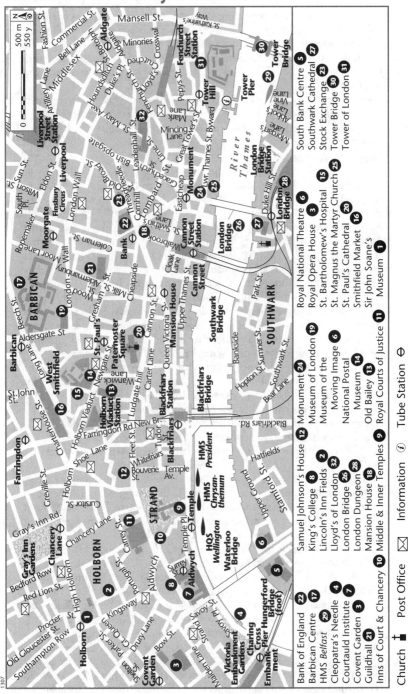

Bank of England	**22**
Barbican Centre	**17**
HMS *Belfast*	**29**
Cleopatra's Needle	**4**
Courtauld Institute	**7**
Covent Garden	**3**
Guildhall	**21**
Inns of Court & Chancery	**10**
Samuel Johnson's House	**12**
King's College	**8**
Lincoln's Inn Fields	**32**
Lloyd's of London	**26**
London Bridge	**28**
London Dungeon	**18**
Mansion House	**9**
Middle & Inner Temples	
Monument	**12**
Museum of London	**24**
Museum of the Moving Image	**6**
National Postal Museum	**14**
Old Bailey	**13**
Royal Courts of Justice	**11**
Royal National Theatre	**6**
Royal Opera House	**3**
St. Bartholomew's Hospital	**15**
St. Magnus the Martyr Church	**25**
St. Paul's Cathedral	**20**
Smithfield Market	**16**
Sir John Soane's Museum	**1**
South Bank Centre	**5**
Southwark Cathedral	**27**
Stock Exchange	**23**
Tower Bridge	**30**
Tower of London	**31**

Church ✝ Post Office ■ Information ⓘ Tube Station Ө

A palace once inhabited by King Edward I in the late 1200s was opened to visitors for the first time in 1993. Above Traitor's Gate, it is the only surviving medieval palace in Britain. Guides are dressed in period costumes. Reproductions of furniture and fittings, including Edward's throne, evoke the era, along with burning incense and candles. Admission to the palace is included in the standard ticket price.

One-hour tours are given by the Yeoman Warders at frequent intervals, starting at 9:30am from the Middle Tower near the main entrance. The tour includes the Chapel Royal of St. Peter and Vincula (St. Peter in Chains). The last guided walk starts about 3:30pm in summer, 2:30pm in winter.

✪ Westminster Abbey

Broad Sanctuary, SW1. ☎ **0171/222-7110.** Admission free to abbey; £1.35 ($2.15) donation suggested. Royal Chapels, Royal Tombs, Coronation Chair, Henry VII Chapel, £4 ($6.30) adults, £1 ($1.60) children; free Wed evenings. Mon-Fri 9:20am-4pm, Sat 9:30am-2pm and 3:45-5pm; Royal Chapels, Wed 6-7:45pm. Tube: Westminster or St. James's Park.

Nearly every figure in English history has left his or her mark on Westminster Abbey. In 1065 the Saxon king, Edward the Confessor, founded the Benedictine abbey and rebuilt the old minster church on this spot, overlooking Parliament Square. The first English king crowned in the abbey was Harold in 1066, before he was killed at the Battle of Hastings later that same year. The man who defeated him, Edward's cousin, William the Conqueror, was also crowned at the abbey; the coronation tradition has continued to the present day, broken only twice (Edward V and Edward VIII). The essentially early English Gothic structure existing today owes more to Henry III's plans than to those of any other sovereign, though many architects, including Wren, have contributed to the abbey.

Built on the site of the ancient lady chapel in the early 16th century, the Henry VII Chapel is one of the loveliest in Europe, with its fan vaulting, Knights of Bath banners, and Torrigiani-designed tomb of the king himself over which has been placed a 15th-century Vivarini painting, *Madonna and Child.* Also buried here are those feuding half-sisters, Elizabeth I and Mary Tudor ("Bloody Mary"). In one end of the chapel, you can stand on Cromwell's memorial stone and view the RAF chapel and its Battle of Britain memorial stained-glass window, unveiled in 1947 to honor the RAF.

You can also visit the most hallowed spot in the abbey, the shrine of Edward the Confessor (canonized in the 12th century). In the saint's chapel is the Coronation Chair, made at the command of Edward I in 1300 to display the Stone of Scone. Scottish kings were once crowned on this stone (in 1950 the Scots stole it back, but it was later returned to its position in the abbey).

Another noted spot in the abbey is the Poets' Corner, to the right of the entrance to the Royal Chapel, with monuments to everybody—Chaucer, Shakespeare, "O Rare Ben Johnson" (his name misspelled), Samuel Johnson, the Brontë sisters, Thackeray, Dickens, Tennyson, Kipling, even the American Longfellow. The most stylized monument is Sir Jacob Epstein's sculptured bust of William Blake. One of the more recent tablets commemorates poet Dylan Thomas.

Statesmen and men of science—such as Disraeli, Newton, Charles Darwin—are also interred in the abbey or honored by monuments. Near the west door is the 1965 memorial to Sir Winston Churchill. In the vicinity of this memorial is the tomb of the Unknown Soldier, commemorating the British dead in World War I. Some totally obscure personages are also buried in the abbey, including an abbey plumber.

Don't overlook the 13th-century chapter house, where Parliament used to meet. And even more fascinating are the treasures in the museum in the Norman *undercroft* (crypt), part of the monastic buildings erected between 1066 and 1100. The collection includes effigies—figures in wax, wood carvings of early English royalty, ancient documents, old religious vestments, the sword of Henry V, and the famous Essex Ring that Elizabeth I is supposed to have given to her favorite earl.

Off the Cloisters, the College Garden is the oldest garden in England, under cultivation for more than 900 years. Surrounded by high walls, flowering trees dot the lawns and park benches provide comfort where you can hardly hear the roar of passing traffic. It is open only on Tuesday and Thursday.

The only time photography is allowed in the abbey is Wednesday evening in the Royal Chapels. On Sunday the Royal Chapels are closed, but the rest of the church is open unless a service is being conducted. For times of services, phone the Chapter Office (☎ 0171/222-5152). Up to six supertours of the abbey are conducted by the vergers Monday through Saturday, beginning at 10am and costing £7 ($11.05) per person.

✪ Houses of Parliament

Westminster Palace, Old Palace Yard, SW1. ☎ **0171/219-4272** for the House of Commons or 0171/219-3107 for the House of Lords. Admission free. House of Lords, open to public Mon–Thurs about 9:30am–2:30pm; also some Fridays (check by phone). House of Commons, open to public Mon, Tues, and Thurs from 2:30pm, Wed from 10am, and Fri from 9:30am. Join line at St. Stephen's entrance. Tube: Westminster.

These are the spiritual opposite of the Tower; they are the stronghold of Britain's democracy, the assemblies that effectively trimmed the sails of royal power. Both Houses (Commons and Lords) are situated in the former royal Palace of Westminster, the king's residence until Henry VIII moved to Whitehall.

The debates are often lively and controversial in the House of Commons (seats are at a premium during crises). Your chance of getting into the House of Lords when it's in session is generally better than for the more popular House of Commons—where even the queen isn't allowed. The old guard of the palace informs me that the peerage speak their minds more freely and are less likely to adhere to party line than their counterparts in the Commons.

The present Houses of Parliament were built in 1840, but the Commons chamber was bombed and destroyed by the Luftwaffe in 1941. The 320-foot tower that houses Big Ben, however, remained standing and the "symbol of London" continues to strike its chimes. Big Ben, incidentally, was named after Sir Benjamin Hall, a cabinet minister distinguished only by his long-windedness.

Except for the Strangers' Galleries, the two Houses of Parliament are closed to tourists. To be admitted to the Strangers' Galleries, join the public line outside the St. Stephen's entrance; often there is a delay before the line is admitted. You might speed matters up by applying at the American embassy or the Canadian High Commission for a special pass. Be aware, though, that the embassy has only four tickets for daily distribution, so you might as well stand in line.

✪ The British Museum

Great Russell St., WC1. ☎ **0171/636-1555.** Admission free. Mon–Sat 10am–5pm, Sun 2:30–6pm (the galleries start to close 10 minutes earlier). Closed Jan 1, Good Friday, early May, Dec 24–26, and bank holidays. Tube: Holborn, Tottenham Court Road, or Russell Square.

The British Museum shelters one of the most comprehensive collections of art and artifacts in the world, including countless treasures of ancient and modern civilizations. Even on a cursory first visit, be sure to see the Asian collections (the finest assembly of Islamic pottery outside the Islamic world), the Chinese porcelain, the Indian sculpture, and the Prehistoric and Romano-British collections. The overall storehouse splits basically into the national collections of antiquities; prints and drawings; coins, medals, and banknotes; and ethnography.

As you enter the front hall, you may want to head first to the Assyrian Transept on the ground floor, where you'll find the winged and human-headed bulls and lions that once guarded the gateways to the palaces of Assyrian kings. Nearby is the Black Obelisk of Shalmaneser III (858–824 B.C.) depicting Jehu, king of Israel, paying tribute. From here you can continue into the angular hall of Egyptian sculpture to see the Rosetta stone, whose discovery led to the deciphering of hieroglyphs.

Also on the ground floor is the Duveen Gallery, housing the Elgin marbles, consisting chiefly of sculptures from the Parthenon, on the Acropolis in Athens.

The classical sculpture galleries house a caryatid from the Erechtheum, also on the Acropolis, a temple started in 421 B.C. and dedicated to Athena and Poseidon. Displayed here, too, are sculptures from the Mausoleum at Halicarnassus (around 350 B.C.).

The Department of Medieval and Later Antiquities has its galleries on the first floor (second floor to Americans), reached by the main staircase. Of its exhibitions, the Sutton Hoo Anglo-Saxon burial ship, discovered in Suffolk, is, in the words of an expert, "the richest treasure ever dug from English soil"; it held gold jewelry, armor, weapons, bronze bowls and cauldrons, silverware, and the inevitable drinking horn of the Norse culture. No body was found, but the tomb is believed to be that of a king of East Anglia who died in the 7th century A.D.

The featured attractions of the upper floor are the Egyptian Galleries, especially the mummies. Egyptian Room 63 is extraordinary, resembling the props for *Cleopatra,* with its cosmetics, domestic utensils, toys, tools, and other work. Items of Sumerian art, unearthed from the Royal Cemetery at Ur (southern Iraq), lie in a room beyond, some dating from about 2500 B.C. In the Iranian room rests "The Treasure of the Oxus," a hoard of riches, perhaps a temple deposit, dating from the 6th to the 3rd century B.C.

See also the galleries of the City of Rome and its Empire, which include exhibitions of art before the Romans. The Portland Vase is one of the most celebrated possessions of the British Museum, having been found in 1582 outside Rome. This vase is the finest example of ancient cameo carving and was made about 25 B.C. It was so named after it was purchased by the duchess of Portland in the 18th century and later sold to the British Museum. The interpretation of the vase remains controversial; there are two main schools of thought: one claiming that the scenes include references to contemporary events such as the birth of the emperor Augustus and the Battle of Actium, the other suggesting that the subjects were drawn from classical mythology, in particular the story of Peleus and Thetis.

In the Manuscript "Saloon" (yes, that's right) are manuscripts of historical and literary interest, including two of the four surviving copies of King John's Magna Carta (1215) and the Lindisfarne Gospels (an outstanding example of the work of Northumbrian artists in the earliest period of English Christianity, written and illustrated about 698 A.D.). Almost every major literary figure, such as Dickens,

Attractions in Mayfair, St. James's, Piccadilly & Covent Garden

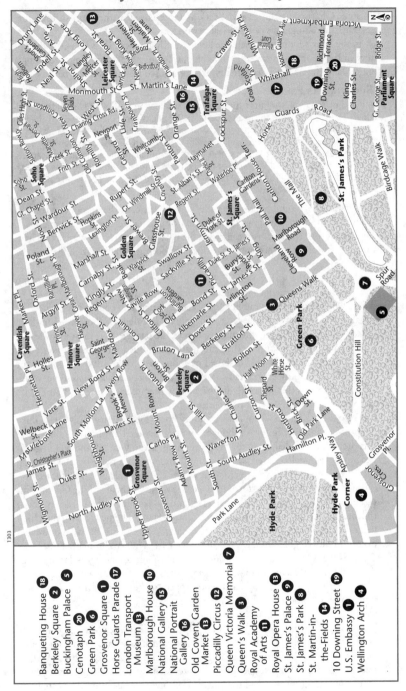

Banqueting House **18**

Berkeley Square **2**

Buckingham Palace **5**

Cenotaph **20**

Green Park **6**

Grosvenor Square **1**

Horse Guards Parade **17**

London Transport Museum **13**

Marlborough House **10**

National Gallery **15**

National Portrait Gallery **16**

Old Covent Garden Market **13**

Piccadilly Circus **12**

Queen Victoria Memorial **7**

Queen's Walk **3**

Royal Academy of Arts **11**

Royal Opera House **13**

St. James's Palace **9**

St. James's Park **8**

St. Martin-in-the-Fields **14**

10 Downing Street **19**

U.S. Embassy **1**

Wellington Arch **4**

1303

Austen, Charlotte Brontë, and Yeats, is represented in the English literature section, plus autographs of historical personages.

In the King's Library—where the library of King George III is housed—the history of the book is illustrated by notable specimens of early printing, including a Gutenberg Bible (1455), the first book ever printed from movable type.

☼ Buckingham Palace

At the end of The Mall (the street running from Trafalgar Sq.). ☎ **0171/930-4832.** Palace tours £8 ($12.65) adults to age 60, £5.50 ($8.70) adults over 60, £4.20 ($6.65) children under 17. (*Warning:* These ticket prices, or even the possibility of public admission to Buckingham Palace, depend entirely on the whim of the queen, since it is her home.) Changing of the guard free. Palace tours: Check tourist information offices, local publications. Changing of the guard: Call Visitorcall at 01839/123-411 for the most up-to-date information about the ceremony. Toll charges range from 39p–69p ($.60–$1.10) per minute. Tube: St. James's Park or Green Park.

This massively graceful building is the official residence of the queen, and you can tell whether Her Majesty is at home by the Royal Standard flying at the masthead. During most of the year, you can't visit the palace unless you're officially invited, but you can do what thousands of others do: peep through the railings into the front yard.

However, in the spring of 1993, Queen Elizabeth II agreed to allow visitors to tour her state apartments and picture galleries, at least for the next 5 years. The palace will be open to the public for 8 weeks in August and September, when the royal family is away on vacation. The queen decided on these Buckingham Palace tours to help defray the massive cost of fire damage at Windsor Castle.

The tours include not only the state apartments, but a number of other rooms used by King George IV and designed by John Nash in the 1800s, including the Throne Room and the grand staircase. The queen's picture gallery has some world-class masterpieces that are rarely if ever seen by the public, including Van Dyck's celebrated equestrian portrait of Charles I.

The red-brick palace was built as a country house for the notoriously rakish duke of Buckingham. In 1762 it was bought by King George III, who (if nothing else) was prolific; he needed room for his 15 children. From then on, the building was expanded, remodeled, faced with Portland limestone, and twice bombed (during the blitz). Today in a 40-acre garden, it stands 360 feet long and has 600 rooms.

Buckingham Palace's most famous spectacle is the Changing of the Guard. This ceremony begins (when it begins) at 11:30am and lasts for half an hour. It's been called the finest example of military pageantry extant. The new guard, marching behind a band, comes from either the Wellington or Chelsea Barracks and takes over from the old guard in the forecourt of the palace. When this martial ceremony occurs is the subject of mass confusion, and you should always check locally to see if one of the world's most famous military rituals is likely to be staged at the time of your visit. This ceremony has been dropped at the last minute and on short notice, leaving thousands of tourists confused, baffled, and perhaps a little angry, feeling they have missed out on a London "must see."

Any schedule announced here is not writ in stone. Officials of the ceremony never announce their plans a year in advance, which poses a dilemma for guide-book writers. In theory at least, the guard is changed daily from about April to mid-July, at which time it goes on its "winter" schedule—that is, changing every other day. The cutback is said to be because of budget constraints. The ceremony might also be abruptly canceled during "uncertain" weather conditions.

Madame Tussaud's

Marylebone Rd., NW1. ☎ **0171/935-6861.** Admission £8.35 ($13.20) adults, £5.25 ($8.30) children under 16. Mon–Fri 10am–5:30pm, Sat–Sun 9:30am–5:30pm (doors open earlier in summer). Closed Dec 25. Tube: Baker Street.

In 1770, an exhibition of life-size wax figures was opened in Paris by Dr. Curtius. He was soon joined by his niece, Strasbourg-born Marie Tussaud, who learned the secret of making lifelike replicas of the famous and the infamous. During the French Revolution, the head of almost every distinguished victim of the guillotine was molded by Madame Tussaud or her uncle.

While some of the figures on display today come from molds taken by Madame Tussaud, who continued to make portraits until she was 81, the exhibition also introduces new images of whoever is *au courant.* An enlarged Grand Hall continues to house years of royalty and old favorites, as well as many of today's heads of state and political leaders. In the Chamber of Horrors, you can have the vicarious thrill of walking through a Victorian London street where special effects include the shadow terror of Jack the Ripper. The instruments and victims of death penalties contrast with present-day criminals portrayed within the confines of prison. You are invited to mingle with the more current stars in the garden party, "meeting" everyone from Arnold Schwarzenegger to Elizabeth Taylor.

"Super Stars" offers the latest technologies in sound, light, and special effects combined with new figures in a celebration of success in the fields of film and sports.

The latest attraction to open here is called "The Spirit of London," a musical show that depicts 400 years of London's history, using special effects that include audio-animatronic figures that move and speak. Visitors take "time-taxis" that allow them to see and hear "Shakespeare" as he writes and speaks lines, to be received by Queen Elizabeth I, and to feel and smell the great fire that started in Pudding Lane in 1666. You'll find a snack bar and gift shops on the premises.

✪ Tate Gallery

Beside the Thames on Millbank, SW1. ☎ **0171/887-8000.** Admission free, except special exhibitions varying from £3 ($4.75) to £5 ($7.90). Mon–Sat 10am–5:50pm, Sun 2–5:50pm. Tube: Pimlico. Bus 77A, C10, or 88.

The Tate houses the best groupings of British paintings from the 16th century on, as well as England's finest collection of modern art (the works of British artists born after 1860), together with foreign art from the impressionists onward. The number of paintings is staggering. Try to schedule at least two visits—the first to see the classic English works, the second to take in the modern collection. Since only a portion of the collections can be displayed at any one time, the works on view change from time to time.

The first giant among English painters, William Hogarth (1697–1764), is almost invariably well represented, particularly by his satirical *O the Roast Beef of Old England* (known as *Calais Gate*). Two other famous 18th-century British painters are Sir Joshua Reynolds (1723–92) and Thomas Gainsborough (1727–88).

In the art of J. M. W. Turner (1775–1851), the Tate possesses its largest collection of the works of a single artist. Most of the paintings and watercolors exhibited here were willed to the nation by Turner. In 1987, a new wing at the Tate, called the Clore Gallery, was opened so that the entire bequest of the artist can be seen.

In a nation of landscape painters, John Constable (1776–1837) stands out. American-born Sir Jacob Epstein became one of England's greatest sculptors, and some of his bronzes are owned and occasionally displayed by the Tate.

The Tate also has the works of many major painters from both the 19th and 20th centuries, including Paul Nash. The drawings of William Blake (1757–1827), the incomparable mystical poet and illustrator of such works as *The Book of Job, The Divine Comedy,* and *Paradise Lost,* attract the most attention.

In the modern collections, the Tate houses works by Matisse, Dalí, Modigliani, Munch, Bonnard, and Picasso.

Truly remarkable is the room devoted to several enormous, somber, but rich abstract canvases by Mark Rothko; the group of paintings and sculptures by Giacometti (1901–66); and the paintings of one of England's best-known modern artists, the late Francis Bacon. Sculptures by Henry Moore and Barbara Hepworth are also occasionally displayed.

Downstairs is the internationally renowned gallery restaurant (see Chapter 5, "London Dining"), with murals by Rex Whistler, as well as a coffee shop.

✪ National Gallery

On the north side of Trafalgar Sq., WC2. ☎ **0171/389-1785.** Admission free. Mon–Sat 10am–6pm, Sun 2–6pm. Closed Jan 1, Good Friday, May Day, Dec 24–26. Tube: Charing Cross, Embankment, or Leicester Square.

In an impressive neoclassical building the National Gallery houses one of the most comprehensive collections of Western paintings, representing all the major schools from the 13th to the early 20th century. The largest part of the collection is devoted to the Italians, including the Sienese, Venetian, and Florentine masters, now housed in the 1991 Sainsbury Wing.

The Sainsbury Wing of the National Gallery also has one of the world's first fully functional multimedia inventories of its contents, the Micro Gallery. Visitors with a particular artistic interest or field of pursuit can key in certain subjects, artist's names, locales, and schools of painting; the computer will produce a cross-referenced series of reports, as well as a map of the National Gallery that pinpoints the location of individual paintings that pertain to the parameters it receives. The system was developed jointly by American Express, Microsoft, and the National Gallery. Except for a core of computers that are reserved in advance for scholarly research, use of the computer terminals is available to members of the general public on a first-come first-served basis. Use of the computers is free, though there's a small charge, usually about £1 ($1.60) for printouts of reports.

Of the early Gothic works, the *Wilton Diptych* (French or English school, late 14th century) is the rarest treasure; it depicts Richard II being introduced to the Madonna and Child by John the Baptist and the Saxon king, Edward the Confessor.

A Florentine gem by Masaccio is displayed, as well as notable works by Piero della Francesca, Leonardo da Vinci, Michelangelo, and Raphael.

Among the 16th-century Venetian masters, the most notable works include a rare *Adoration of the Kings* by Giorgione, *Bacchus and Ariadne* by Titian, *The Origin of the Milky Way* by Tintoretto, and *The Family of Darius Before Alexander* by Veronese.

A number of satellite rooms are filled with works by major Italian masters of the 15th century—such as Andrea Mantegna of Padua, Giovanni Bellini, and Botticelli.

The painters of northern Europe are well represented. For example, there is Jan van Eyck's portrait of G. Arnolfini and his bride, plus Pieter Brueghel the Elder's Bosch-influenced *Adoration.* The 17th-century pauper, Vermeer, is rich on canvas in a *Young Woman at a Virginal.* Fellow Delftite Pieter de Hooch comes on sublimely in a *Courtyard in a House in Delft.*

One of the big drawing cards of the National is its collection of Rembrandts. His *Self-Portrait at the Age of 34* shows him at the pinnacle of his life; his *Self-Portrait at the Age of 63* is more deeply moving and revealing.

Five of the greatest of the homegrown artists—Constable, Turner, Reynolds, Gainsborough, and Hogarth—have masterpieces here, as do three giants of Spanish painting. Velàzquez's portrait of the sunken-faced Philip IV, El Greco's *Christ Driving the Traders from the Temple,* and Goya's portrait of the duke of Wellington (once stolen) and his mantilla-wearing *Doña Isabel de Porcel* are on display.

Other rooms are devoted to early 19th-century French painters, such as Delacroix and Ingres; the later 19th-century French impressionists, such as Manet, Monet, Renoir, and Degas; and postimpressionists such as Cézanne, Seurat, and van Gogh.

The National Gallery has a computer information center where visitors can design a personal tour map. The computer room, located in the Micro Gallery, includes 12 computer work stations that individuals and families can use. The system offers 2,200 paintings to select from, with supporting text for each one. The program includes four indexes that are cross-referenced for your convenience. Using a touch-screen computer, you can design your own personalized tour by selecting a maximum of ten paintings that you would like to view. Once you have made your choices, you print a free personal tour map that shows your selections.

Kensington Palace

The Broad Walk, Kensington Gardens, W8. ☎ **0171/937-9561.** Admission £4.50 ($7.10) adults, £3 ($4.75) children, £3.40 ($5.35) students and senior citizens. Mon–Sat 9am–5pm, Sun 1–5pm. The palace will close from Sept–Apr until 1998 for restoration. Tube: Queensway or Bayswater on the north side of the gardens or High Street Kensington on the south side; then you'll have a long walk.

Home of the state apartments, some of which were used by Queen Victoria—the palace is located at the far western end of Kensington Gardens; the entrance is from the Broad Walk. The palace was acquired by William III (William of Orange) in 1689 and was remodeled by Sir Christopher Wren. George II, who died in 1760, was the last king to use it as a royal residence.

The most interesting chamber to visit is Queen Victoria's bedroom. In this room, on the morning of June 20, 1837, she was aroused from her sleep with the news that she had succeeded to the throne, following the death of her uncle, William IV. As you wander through the apartments, be sure to admire the many fine paintings from the Royal Collection.

A special attraction is the Royal Ceremonial Dress Collection, which shows restored rooms from the 19th century, including Queen Victoria's birth room and a series of room settings with the appropriate court dress of the day, from 1760 to 1950.

The palace gardens, originally the private park of royalty, adjoin Hyde Park and are open to the public for daily strolls around Round Pond, near the heart of Kensington Gardens. Also in Kensington Gardens is the Albert Memorial, honoring Queen Victoria's consort. Facing Royal Albert Hall, the statue reflects the ostentation of the Victorian era.

✪ St. Paul's Cathedral

St. Paul's Churchyard, EC4. ☎ **0171/248-2705.** Cathedral £3 ($4.75) for adults, £2 ($3.15) children (6–16). Galleries £2.50 ($3.95) adults, £1.50 ($2.35) children. Guided tours £3

Attractions from Kensington to Belgravia

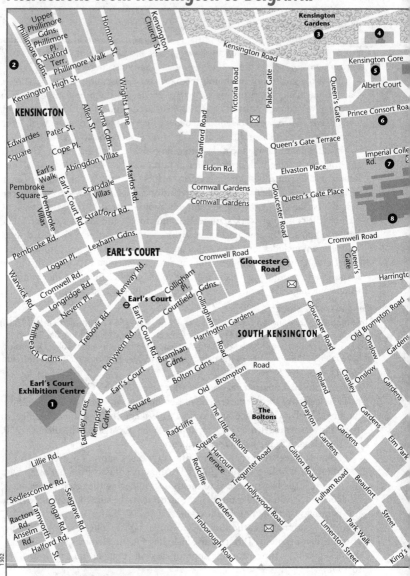

Albert Memorial ④
Belgrave Square ⑲
Thomas Carlyle's House ⑩
Chelsea Embankment ⑫
Chelsea Royal Hospital ⑮
Chelsea's Old Town Hall ⑪
Earl's Court Exhibition Centre ❶

Harrod's ⑳
Holland Park ❷
Holy Trinity Church ⑱
Imperial College ❻
Kensington Gardens ❸
King's Road ⑯
National Army Museum ⑬

Hyde Park

0 ▭▭▭ 300 m
330 y

N

Kensington Road

KNIGHTSBRIDGE

Knightsbridge
Knightsbridge

Prince's Gardens

Rutland Gate

Montpelier Walk

Sloane Square

Lowndes Square

Kinnerton St.

Wilton St.

Cres.

Halkin St.

19

Upper Belgrave St.

Belgrave Pl.

Gardens

Ennismore Gardens

Garden Mews

Cheval Pl.

Brompton Road

Hans Road

Basil St.

Pavilion Road

Sloane Street

Exhibition Road

Brompton Square

Beauchamp Place

Hans Place

Hans Pl.

Pont Street

Cheshan Pl.

Chesham St.

Lyall St.

King's Road

9
Victoria & Albert Museum

Cromwell Road

Walton Place

Lenox Gardens

Cadogan Sq.

Cadogan Lane

Cadogan Place

Thurloe Place

Brompton Road

Walton Street

Hasker St.

Milner St.

Moore St.

Cadogan Street

Cadogan Sq.

Sloane Street

Pavilion Road

Thurloe Square

Thurloe

South Kensington

Pelham Street

Rawlings St.

Street

Ellis St.

Onslow Square

Pelham Crescent

Place

Ixworth Place

Elystan Street

Draycott Avenue

Sloane Avenue

Cadogan Street

Draycott Place

18
Sloane Square
17

BELGRAVIA

Fulham Road

King's Road

16

Lower Sloane

Pimlico Rd.

Cale Street

Elystan Place

Astell St.

King's Road

Smith Street

St. Leonard's Terrace

Franklin's Row

Chelsea Bridge Rd.

Chelsea Square

Dovehouse Street

Sydney Street

Manresa Rd.

Radnor Walk

CHELSEA

Tedworth Square

Ormonde

Royal Hospital Road

15

Ranelagh Gardens

11

Flood Street

Christchurch Street

13
West Road

Old Church Street

King's Road

Glebe Place

Chelsea Manor Street

Oakley Street

Chelsea Physic Garden

Tite Street

14

Cheyne Row

10

12

Chelsea Embankment

T h a m e s

Natural History Museum ❽
Oscar Wilde's Former Home ⓮
Royal Albert Hall ❺
Science Museum ❼
Sloane Square ⓱
Victoria and Albert Museum ❾

Tube Station ⊖   Church ✝   Post Office ⊠   Information ⓘ

($4.75), recorded tours £2.50 ($3.95). Children 5 and under free. Sightseeing Mon–Sat 8:30am–4pm; galleries Mon–Sat 10am–4:15pm. No sightseeing Sun (services only). Tube: St. Paul's.

During World War II, newsreel footage reaching America showed the dome of St. Paul's Cathedral lit by fires caused by bombings all around it. That it survived at all is a miracle since it was badly hit twice during the early years of the Nazi bombardment of London. But St. Paul's is accustomed to calamity, having been burned down three times and destroyed once by invading Norsemen. It was during the Great Fire of 1666 that the old St. Paul's was razed, making way for a new Renaissance structure designed (after many mishaps and rejections) by Sir Christopher Wren and built between 1675 and 1710.

The classical dome of St. Paul's dominates the City's square mile. Inside, the cathedral is laid out like a Greek cross; it houses few art treasures (Grinling Gibbons's choir stalls are an exception) but many monuments—including one to the "Iron Duke" and a memorial chapel to American service personnel who lost their lives in World War II while stationed in the U.K. Encircling the dome is the Whispering Gallery, where discretion in speech is advised. In the crypt lie not only Wren but also the duke of Wellington and Lord Nelson. A fascinating Diocesan Treasury was opened in 1981.

You can climb to the very top of the dome for a spectacular 360° view of London.

Guided tours last 1½ hours and include parts of the cathedral not open to the general public. They take place Monday through Saturday at 11am, 11:30am, 1:30pm, and 2pm. Recorded tours lasting 45 minutes are available throughout the day.

St. Paul's is an Anglican cathedral with daily services at the following times: Matins Monday through Friday at 7:30am, Saturday at 10am, Holy Communion Monday through Saturday at 8am and 12:30pm, and Evensong Monday through Saturday at 5pm. On Sunday, there is Holy Communion at 8 and again at 11:30am, Matins at 10:30am, and Evensong at 3:15pm. Admission charges do not apply if visitors are attending services.

✪ Victoria and Albert Museum

Cromwell Rd., SW7. ☎ **0171/938-8500.** Admission free, but donations of £4.50 ($7.10) suggested for adults, £1 ($1.60) for students and senior citizens. Children under 12 are not asked for a donation. The Victoria and Albert has a lively program of changing exhibitions and displays, so there is always something new to see. Mon noon–5:50pm, Tues–Sun 10am–5:50pm, Jazz Brunch Sun 11am–3pm. Tube: South Kensington.

Located in South Kensington, this museum is one of the liveliest and most imaginative in London. It's named after the queen and her consort but not run in their spirit. The general theme here is the fine and decorative arts, but adhered to in a pleasantly relaxed fashion.

The medieval holdings include many treasures, such as the Eltenberg Reliquary (Rhenish, second half of the 12th century); the Early English Gloucester Candlestick; the Byzantine Veroli Casket, with its ivory panels based on Greek plays; and the Syon Cope, a highly valued embroidery made in England in the early 14th century. The Gothic tapestries, including the Devonshire ones depicting hunting scenes, are displayed in another gallery. An area devoted to Islamic art houses the Ardabil carpet from 16th-century Persia (320 knots per square inch).

The Victoria and Albert houses the largest collection of Renaissance sculpture outside Italy, including a Donatello marble relief, *The Ascension;* a small terra-cotta statue of the Madonna and Child by Antonio Rossellino; a marble group, *Samson and a Philstine,* by Giovanni Bologna; and a wax model of a slave by Michelangelo. The highlight of 16th-century art from the Continent is the marble group *Neptune with Triton* by Bernini. The cartoons by Raphael, which were conceived as designs for tapestries for the Sistine Chapel, are owned by the queen and can also be seen here.

A most unusual, huge, and impressive exhibit is the Cast Courts, life-size plaster models of ancient and medieval statuary and architecture.

The museum has the greatest collection of Indian art outside India. It has Chinese and Japanese galleries as well. In complete contrast are suites of English furniture, metalwork, and ceramics dating beyond the 16th century, and a superb collection of portrait miniatures, including the one Hans Holbein the Younger made of Anne of Cleves for the benefit of Henry VIII, who was again casting around for a suitable wife.

A restaurant serves traditional English snacks and meals, and two museum shops sell gifts, posters, cards, and books.

✪ Trafalgar Square, WC1

One of the landmark squares of London, Trafalgar Square honors one of England's great military heroes, Horatio, Viscount Nelson (1758–1805), who died at the Battle of Trafalgar. Although he suffered from seasickness all his life, he went to sea at the age of 12 and was an admiral at the age of 39. Lord Nelson was a hero of the Battle of Calvi in 1794 where he lost an eye, the Battle of Santa Cruz in 1797 where he lost an arm, and the Battle of Trafalgar in 1805 where he lost his life.

The square today is dominated by a 145-foot granite column, the work of E.H. Baily in 1843. The column looks down Whitehall toward the Old Admiralty, where Lord Nelson's body lay in state. The figure of the naval hero towers 17 feet high, not bad for a man who stood 5 feet 4 inches in real life. The capital is of bronze cast from cannons recovered from the wreck of the *Royal George.* Queen Victoria's favorite animal painter, Sir Edward Landseer, added the four lions at the base of the column in 1868. The pools and fountains were not added until 1939, the last work of Sir Edwin Lutyens.

Political demonstrations still take place at the square and around the column, which has the most aggressive pigeons in London. These birds will even land on your head or perform less desirable stunts. Actually the birds are part of a long feathery tradition, for this site was once used by Edward I (1239–1307) to keep his birds of prey. Called "Longshanks," he came here often before he died of dysentery in 1307. Richard II, who ruled from 1377 to 1399, kept goshawks and falcons here too. By the time of Henry VII, who ruled from 1485 to 1509, the square was used as the site of the royal stables. Sir Charles Barry, who designed the Houses of Parliament, created the present square in the 1830s.

Much of the world focuses on the square via TV cameras on New Year's Eve. It's a wild and raucous time with revelers jumping into the chilly waters of the fountains. In 1986, five people were crushed to death. The giant Christmas tree that is installed here every December is an annual gift from Norway to the British people in appreciation for sheltering their royal family during World War II. Today, street performers, now officially licensed, will entertain you and hope for a token of appreciation for their efforts.

To the southeast of the square, at 36 Craven Street, stands a house once occupied by Benjamin Franklin (1757–74) when he was a general of the Philadelphia

Academy. On the north side of the square rises the National Gallery, constructed in the 1830s. In front of the building is a copy of a statue of George Washington by J.A. Houdon.

To the left of St. Martin's Place is the National Portrait Gallery, a collection of British greats (and not-so-greats)—everyone from Chaucer and Shakespeare to Captain Hook and Nell Gwyn. Also on the square is the landmark St. Martin-in-the-Fields by James Gibbs, with its towering steeple, a resting place of such figures as Sir Joshua Reynolds, William Hogarth, and Thomas Chippendale.

2 More Attractions

ROYAL LONDON

In the Queen's Gallery, entrance on Buckingham Palace Road, SW1 (☎ 0171/799-2331), you can see a sampling of the royal family's art collection. I can't predict what exhibition you're likely to see, since they are changed yearly, but I can tell you that the queen's collection includes an unsurpassed range of royal portraits, including the well-known profile of Henry V; the companion portraits of Elizabeth I as a girl and her half-brother Edward VI; four fine Georgian pictures by Zoffany; two portraits of Queen Alexandra from Sandringham; plus paintings of Queen Elizabeth II and other members of the royal family. Admission to the gallery is £3 ($4.75) for adults, £1.50 ($2.35) for children, and £2 ($3.15) for senior citizens. It's open early March to late December Tuesday through Saturday and bank holidays from 10am to 5pm and on Sunday from 2 to 5pm; closed Monday, except bank holidays. Tube: Green Park, Victoria, or St. James's.

You can get a close look at Queen Elizabeth II's coronation carriage at the Royal Mews, on Buckingham Palace Road, SW1 (☎ 071/799-2331). Her Majesty's State Coach, built in 1761 to the designs of Sir William Chambers, has emblematic and other paintings on the panels and doors executed by Cipriani. The coach, traditionally drawn by eight gray horses, was formerly used by sovereigns when they traveled to open Parliament in person and on other state occasions. Queen Elizabeth used it in 1953 for her coronation and in 1977 for her Silver Jubilee Procession.

Admission is £3 ($4.75) adults, £1.50 ($2.35) children, and £2 ($3.15) senior citizens. Hours are noon to 4pm July through September Wednesday through Friday only. In the off-season months, it is open only on Wednesday and Friday from noon to 4pm. Tube: Green Park, Victoria, or St. James's.

OFFICIAL LONDON

Whitehall, SW1, the seat of the British government, grew up on the grounds of Whitehall Palace and was turned into a royal residence by Henry VIII, who snatched it from its former occupant, Cardinal Wolsey. Whitehall extends south from Trafalgar Square to Parliament Square. Along it you'll find the Home Office, the Old Admiralty Building, and the Ministry of Defence.

Visitors today can see the **Cabinet War Rooms,** the bombproof bunker suite of rooms, just as they were left by Winston Churchill and the British government at the end of World War II. You can see the Map Room with its huge wall maps, the Atlantic map a mass of pinholes (each hole represents at least one convoy). Next door is Churchill's bedroom-cum-office, which has a bed and a desk with two BBC microphones on it for his broadcasts of those famous speeches that stirred the nation.

Attractions in Westminster & Victoria

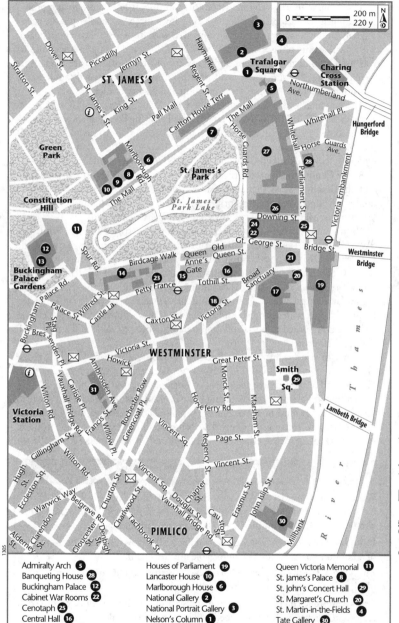

Admiralty Arch ⑤	Houses of Parliament ⑲	Queen Victoria Memorial ⑪
Banqueting House ㉘	Lancaster House ⑩	St. James's Palace ⑧
Buckingham Palace ⑫	Marlborough House ⑥	St. John's Concert Hall ㉙
Cabinet War Rooms ㉒	National Gallery ②	St. Margaret's Church ⑳
Cenotaph ㉕	National Portrait Gallery ③	St. Martin-in-the-Fields ④
Central Hall ⑯	Nelson's Column ①	Tate Gallery ㉚
Clarence House ⑨	New Scotland Yard ⑱	10 Downing St. ㉖
Duke of York Steps ⑦	Parliament Square ㉑	Wellington Barracks ⑭
Foreign Office ㉔	Queen Anne's Gate ⑮	Westminster Abbey ⑰
Home Office ㉓	Queen's Gallery ⑬	Westminster Cathedral ㉛
Horse Guards Parade ㉗		

Post Office ⊠   Information ⓘ

The Transatlantic Telephone Room, its full title, is little more than a broom closet, but it had the Bell Telephone Company's special scrambler phone, called Sig-Saly, and it was where Churchill conferred with Roosevelt. A system of boards with such laconic phrases as "wet," "very wet," "hot and sunny," "dry and dull" was used to indicate weather conditions around the world before maneuvers were planned. All visitors are provided with a step-by-step personal sound guide, providing a detailed account of the function and history of each room.

The entrance to the War Rooms is by Clive Steps at the end of King Charles Street, SW1 (☎ 0171/930-6961), off Whitehall near Big Ben. Visitors receive a cassette-recorded guided tour, and admission is £3.90 ($6.15) for adults and £1.90 ($3) for children. The rooms are open daily from 10am to 5:30pm (last admission at 4:45pm); they're closed on Christmas holidays. Tube: Westminster or St. James's.

At the **Cenotaph** (honoring the dead from two world wars), turn down unpretentious Downing Street to the modest little town house at No. 10, flanked by two bobbies. Walpole was the first prime minister to live here, Churchill the most famous. But Margaret Thatcher was around longer than any of them.

Nearby, north of Downing Street, is the **Horse Guards Building,** Whitehall, SW1 (☎ 0171/414-2396), now the headquarters of the horse guards of the Household Division and London District. There has been a guard change here since 1649, when the site was the entrance to the old Palace of Whitehall. You can watch the Queen's Life Guards ceremony at 11am Monday through Saturday (10am on Sunday). You can also see the hourly smaller change of the guard, when mounted troopers are changed. And at 4pm you can watch the evening inspection, when 10 unmounted troopers and 2 mounted troopers assemble in the courtyard. Tube: Westminster.

Across the street is Inigo Jones's **Banqueting House,** Palace of Whitehall, Horse Guards Avenue, SW1 (☎ 0171/930-4179), site of the execution of Charles I. William and Mary accepted the crown of England here, but they preferred to live at Kensington Palace. The Banqueting House was part of Whitehall Palace, which burned to the ground in 1698, but the ceremonial hall escaped razing. Its most notable feature today is an allegorical ceiling painted by Peter Paul Rubens. Admission to the Banqueting House is £3 ($4.75) for adults, £2 ($3.15) for

---

⭐ Frommer's Favorite London Experiences

Watching the Sun Set at Waterloo Bridge. Waterloo Bridge is the best place in London to watch the sun set over Westminster in the west. The last rays can also be seen bouncing off the City's spires in the East End.

Enjoying a Pub Lunch. Taking lunch in the bustling, overcrowded atmosphere of a London pub is totally uncomfortable but totally fun.

Enjoying a Traditional English Tea. Nothing rounds out an afternoon quite like it—and nothing is more typically British.

Brass Rubbing. You can re-create England's age of chivalry—all those costumed ladies and knights in armor—in medieval brasses. You can spend hours rubbing wax over paper taped over the brass to produce a picture to frame.

A Night at a West End Theater. The West End was the stage for Shakespeare and Marlowe, and today it also can be the stage for next year's Broadway hit.

Attractions in Bloomsbury & Holborn

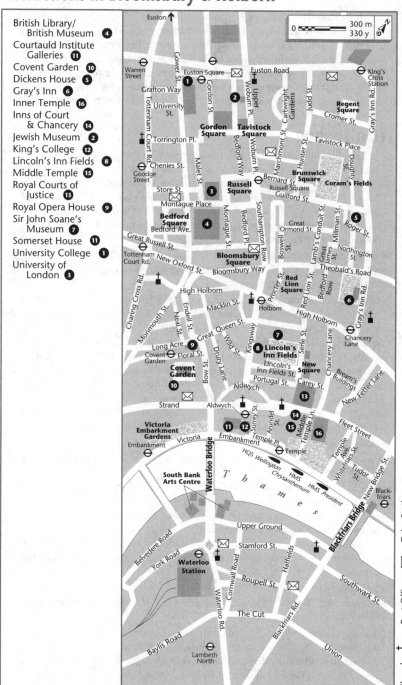

Tube Station ⊖ Post Office ⊠ Church ✝

1304

children, £2.20 ($3.50) for senior citizens and students. It's open Monday through Saturday from 10am to 5pm. Tube: Westminster.

Finally, stroll to Parliament Square for a view of **Big Ben,** the world's most famous timepiece and the symbol of the heart and soul of England. Big Ben is actually the name of the deepest and loudest bell, but it's become the common name for this clock tower on the Houses of Parliament. Opposite, in the gardens of Parliament Square, stands the statue of Churchill by Oscar Nemon. Tube: Westminster.

LEGAL LONDON

The smallest borough in London, bustling Holborn (pronounced HO-burn) is often referred to as Legal London, home of the city's barristers, solicitors, and law clerks. It also embraces the university district of Bloomsbury. Holburn, which houses the ancient Inns of Court—Gray's Inn, Lincoln's Inn, Middle Temple, and Inner Temple—was severely damaged during World War II bombing raids. The razed buildings were replaced with modern offices, but the borough still retains pockets of its former days.

Middle Temple Tudor Hall

Middle Temple Lane, EC4Y. ☎ **0171/353-4355.** Admission free. Hall, Mon–Fri 10:30am–noon and 3–4pm. Tube: Temple.

Going away from the Victoria Embankment, Middle Temple Lane leads between Middle and Inner Temple Gardens in the area known as The Temple, named after the medieval order of the Knights Templar (originally formed by the Crusaders in Jerusalem in the 12th century). It was in the Middle Temple Garden that Henry VI's barons are supposed to have picked the blooms of red and white roses and started the War of the Roses in 1430; today only members of the Temples and their guests are allowed to enter the gardens. But the Middle Temple has a Tudor hall, completed in 1570, that is open to the public. It is believed that Shakespeare's troupe played *Twelfth Night* here in 1602. A table on view is said to come from timber from Sir Francis Drake's *The Golden Hind.*

Temple Church

The Temple, within the precincts of the Inner Temple, EC4. ☎ **0171/353-1736.** Admission free. Wed–Sat 9:30am–4pm. Tube: Temple.

One of three Norman "round churches" left in England, this was first completed in the 12th century—not surprisingly, it has been restored. Look for the knightly effigies and the Norman door, and take note of the circle of grotesque portrait heads, including a goat in a mortar board.

On Inner Temple Lane, about where The Strand becomes Fleet Street going east, is the memorial pillar called **Temple Bar,** which marks the boundary of The City.

Royal Courts of Justice

The Strand, WC2. ☎ **0171/936-6751.** Admission free. Mon–Sat 10am–4:30pm. Tube: Temple.

The Royal Courts of Justice stand north across The Strand. The building, which was completed in 1882 but designed in the 13th-century style, was the home of such courts as admiralty, divorce, probate, chancery, appeals, and Queen's Bench. Leave the Royal Courts building by the rear door and you'll be on Carey Street, not far from New Square.

Lincoln's Inn

Carey St., WC2. ☎ **0171/405-1393.** Admission free. Chapel and garden Mon–Fri noon–2pm. Tube: Holborn or Chancery Lane.

Lincoln's Inn is the oldest of the four Inns of Court, and for more than 500 years has had the power to call to the bar those members who have qualified as barristers (attorneys). Between the City and the West End, Lincoln's Inn comprises 11 acres, including lawns, squares, gardens, a 17th-century chapel, a library, and two halls. One of these, Old Hall, dates from 1490 and has remained almost unaltered with its linen-fold paneling, stained glass, and wooden screen by Inigo Jones. It was once the home of Sir Thomas More, and it was where barristers met, ate, and debated 150 years before the *Mayflower* sailed on its epic voyage. Old Hall set the scene for the opening chapter of Charles Dickens's *Bleak House.* The other hall, Great Hall, remains one of the finest Tudor revival buildings in London, and was opened by Queen Victoria in 1843. It is now the center of the inn and is used for the formal ceremony of calling students to the bar.

Staple Inn

High Holborn St., WC1. Tube: Chancery Lane.

This half-timbered old inn near the Chancery Lane tube stop and eight other former Inns of Chancery are no longer in use in the legal world. Now lined with shops, it was built between 1545 and 1589 and has been rebuilt many times. Dr. Johnson moved here in 1759, the year *Rasselas* was published.

Gray's Inn

Gray's Inn Rd. (entrance on Theobald's Rd.), WC1. ☎ **0171/405-8164.** Admission free. Daily 6am–8pm. Tube: Chancery Lane.

Gray's Inn, north of High Holborn, is the fourth of the ancient Inns of Court still in operation. As you enter, you'll see a late Georgian terrace lined with buildings that, like many of the other houses in the inns, are combined residences and offices. Gray's was restored after suffering heavy damage during World War II bombings. Francis Bacon, scientist and philosopher (1561–1626), was its most eminent tenant. The inn has a rebuilt Tudor Hall, but its greatest attraction is the tree-shaded lawn and handsome gardens, considered the best in the inns. The 17th-century atmosphere exists today only in the square.

Old Bailey (Central Criminal Court)

On the corner of Old Bailey and Newgate St., EC4. ☎ **0171/248-3277.** Admission free. Children under 14 not admitted; ages 14–16 must be accompanied by a responsible adult. No cameras or tape recorders allowed. Mon–Fri 10:30am–1pm and 2–4pm. Tube: Temple, Chancery Lane, or St. Paul's.

This courthouse replaced the infamous Newgate Prison, once the scene of public hangings and other forms of public "entertainment." Entry is strictly on a first-arrival basis, and guests line up outside (where, incidentally, the final public execution took place in the 1860s). Courts 1 to 4, 17, and 18 are entered from Newgate Street, and the balance from Old Bailey (the street). To get here, travel east on Fleet Street, which along the way becomes Ludgate Hill. Cross Ludgate Circus and turn left to the Old Bailey, a domed structure with the figure of *Justice* standing atop it.

Guildhall

King St. in Cheapside, The City, EC2. ☎ **0171/606-3030.** Admission free. May–Sept daily 10am–5pm; Oct–Apr Mon–Sat 10am–5pm. Tube: Bank.

The Civic Hall of the Corporation of London has had a rough time since its beginnings in 1411, notably in the Great Fire of 1666 and the 1940 blitz. The most famous tenants of the rebuilt Guildhall are Gog and Magog, two giants standing over 9 feet high. The present giants are third generation, because the original effigies burned in the London fire and the next set were destroyed in 1940. Restoration has returned the Gothic grandeur to the hall, which is replete with a medieval porch entranceway; monuments to Wellington, Churchill, and Nelson; stained glass commemorating lord mayors and mayors; and banners honoring fishmongers, haberdashers, merchant "taylors," ironmongers, and skinners—some of the major Livery Companies.

MUSEUMS

Sir John Soane's Museum

13 Lincoln's Inn Fields, WC2. ☎ **0171/430-0175.** Admission free. Tues–Sat 10am–5pm; first Tues of each month 6–9pm. Tours given Sat at 2:30pm. Closed Bank holidays. Tube: Chancery Lane or Holborn.

This is the former home of Sir John Soane (1753–1837), an architect who rebuilt the Bank of England (not the present structure). With his multilevels, fool-the-eye mirrors, flying arches, and domes, Soane was a master of perspective and a genius of interior space (his picture gallery, for example, is filled with three times the number of paintings a room of similar dimensions would be likely to hold). Don't miss William Hogarth's satirical series *The Rake's Progress*, which includes his much-reproduced *Orgy* and *The Election*, a satire on mid-18th-century politics. Soane also filled his house with paintings and classical sculpture. Be sure to see the sarcophagus of Pharaoh Seti I, found in a burial chamber in the Valley of the Kings.

Imperial War Museum

Lambeth Rd., SE1. ☎ **0171/416-5000.** Admission £3.90 ($6.15) adults, £1.95 ($3.10) children; free daily 4:30–6pm. Daily 10am–6pm. Closed New Year's Day, Good Friday, first Mon in May, Dec 24–26. Tube: Lambeth North or Elephant & Castle.

Built around 1815, this large domed building, the former Bethlehem Royal Hospital for the Insane (or Bedlam), houses the museum's collections relating to the two world wars and other military operations involving the British and the Commonwealth since 1914. There are four floors of exhibitions, including the Large Exhibits Gallery, a vast area showing historical displays, two floors of art galleries, and a dramatic re-creation of London at war during the blitz. You can see a Battle of Britain Spitfire, the rifle carried by Lawrence of Arabia, and Hitler's political testament, as well as models, decorations, uniforms, photographs, and paintings. It's located just across the Thames.

National Army Museum

Royal Hospital Rd., SW3. ☎ **0171/730-0717.** Admission free. Daily 10am–5:30pm. Closed Jan 1, Good Friday, May bank holiday, Dec 24–26. Tube: Sloane Square.

Located in Chelsea, this museum traces the history of the British land forces, the Indian army, and colonial land forces. The collection starts with the year 1485, the date of the formation of the Yeomen of the Guard. The saga of the forces of the East India Company is also traced, from its beginning in 1602 to Indian independence in 1947. The gory and glory are all here—everything from Florence Nightingale's lamp to the cloak wrapped around the dying Gen. James Wolfe at Québec in 1759. Naturally, there are the "cases of the heroes," mementos of such outstanding men as the duke of Marlborough and the duke of Wellington. But the field soldier isn't neglected either: The Nation in Arms Gallery tells the soldier's story in two world wars, including an exhibit of the British Army in the Far East from 1941 to 1945.

Apsley House

The Wellington Museum, 149 Piccadilly, Hyde Park Corner, W1. ☎ **0171/499-5676.** Admission £3 ($4.75) adults, £1.50 ($2.35) children. Daily 11am–6pm. Closed Jan 1, May Day, Dec 24–26. Tube: Hyde Park Corner.

This former town house of the Iron Duke, the British general (1769–1852) who defeated Napoléon at the Battle of Waterloo and later became prime minister, was opened as a public museum in 1952. The building was designed by Robert Adam and was built in the late 18th century. Wellington once had to retreat behind the walls of Apsley House, fearing an attack from Englishmen outraged by his autocratic opposition to reform. In the vestibule, you'll find a colossal marble statue of Napoléon by Canova—ironic, to say the least; it was presented to the duke by King George IV.

In addition to the famous *Waterseller of Seville* by Velàzquez, the Wellington collection includes works by Correggio, Jan Steen, and Pieter de Hooch. A large porcelain and china collection consists of a magnificent Sèvres porcelain Egyptian service originally made for Empress Joséphine and given to Wellington by Louis XVIII.

Museum of London

150 London Wall, EC2. ☎ **0171/600-3699.** Admission £3.50 ($5.55) adults, £1.75 ($2.75) children. Tues–Sat 10am–5:50pm, Sun noon–5:50pm. Tube: St. Paul's or Barbican.

In London's Barbican district near St. Paul's Cathedral, the Museum of London allows visitors to trace the history of London from prehistoric times to the present—through relics, costumes, household effects, maps, and models. Anglo-Saxons, Vikings, Normans—they're all here, displayed on two floors around a central courtyard. The exhibits are arranged so that visitors can begin and end their chronological stroll through 250,000 years at the main entrance to the museum, and exhibits have quick labels for museum sprinters, more extensive ones for those who want to study, and still deeper details for scholars.

You'll see the death mask of Oliver Cromwell; the Great Fire of London in living color and sound; reconstructed Roman dining rooms with kitchen and utensils; cell doors from Newgate Prison, which was made famous by Charles Dickens; and an amazing shop counter with pre–World War II prices on the items. But the pièce de résistance is the Lord Mayor's coach, built in 1757 and weighing 3 tons. Still used each November in the Lord Mayor's Procession, this gilt-and-red horse-drawn vehicle is like a fairy-tale coach.

The museum, which opened in 1976, overlooks London's Roman and medieval walls and was built at a cost of some $18 million. It's an enriching experience for everybody—at least an hour should be allowed for a full (but still quick) visit. Free lectures on London's history are often given during lunch hours; ask at the entrance hall if one will be given the day you're there. You can reach the museum by going up to the elevated pedestrian precinct at the corner of London Wall and Aldersgate, 5 minutes from St. Paul's. There is also a restaurant, opposite the main entrance.

London Transport Museum

The Piazza, Covent Garden, WC2. ☎ **0171/379-6344.** Admission £4.25 ($6.70) adults, £2.50 ($3.95) children. Sat–Thurs 10am–6pm, Fri 11am–6pm, (last entry at 5:15pm). Closed Dec 24–26. Tube: Covent Garden, Leicester Square, or Charing Cross.

This splendidly restored Victorian building once housed the flower market. Horse buses, motor buses, trams, trolleybuses, railway vehicles, models, maps, posters, photographs, and audiovisual displays illustrate the fascinating evolution of London's transport systems and how they have affected the growth of London. There are also a number of unique working displays: You can put yourself in the driver's seat of a tube train, a tram, and a bus, and also operate full-size signaling equipment. The exhibits include a reconstruction of George Shillibeer's omnibus of 1829, a steam locomotive that ran on the world's first underground railway, and a coach from the first deep-level electric railway. The museum sells a variety of souvenirs of London Transport (see Chapter 7, "London Shopping & After Dark"). It also has a café overlooking Covent Garden Piazza.

Percival David Foundation of Chinese Art

53 Gordon Square, WC1. ☎ **0171/387-3909.** Admission free; donations accepted; £3 ($4.75) for a guided tour. Mon–Fri 10:30am–5pm. Tube: Russell Square, Euston Square. Bus 7, 8, 10, 14, 18, 19, 24, 25, or 27.

Installed in a 19th-century townhouse in the heart of Bloomsbury close to the British Museum, this foundation displays the greatest collection of Chinese ceramics outside China and also offers a library of East Asian and Western books relating to Chinese art and culture. Both were presented to the University of London in 1950 by the late Sir Percival David. There are some 1,700 items of Chinese ceramics, reflecting Chinese court taste dating mainly from the 10th through the 18th centuries. Many of these pieces are not only of exceptional beauty, but bear important inscriptions. Several items in the collection were once owned by Chinese emperors. The foundation possesses an exceptional collection of stonewares from the Song (960–1279) and Yuan (1279–1368) dynasties, including examples of the rare Ru and Guan wares. Among the justly famous blue and white porcelains are two unique temple vases with inscriptions dating from the 15th century onward. A wide variety of polychrome wares are also represented, including examples of the delicate doucai wares from the Chenghua period (1465–87) as well as a remarkable group of 18th-century porcelains traditionally known as Gu yue xuan.

National Postal Museum

King Edward Building, King Edward St., EC1. ☎ **0171/239-5420.** Admission free. Mon–Fri 9:30am–4:30pm. Tube: St. Paul's or Barbican.

This museum houses the most important collection of British Victorian stamps from the Phillips collection, as well as the public record collection of the artwork, essays, and registration sheets of all British stamps. It also features postage stamps from around the world issued since 1878, plus temporary exhibitions.

Royal Air Force Museum

Grahame Park Way, Hendon, NW9. ☎ **081/205-2266.** Admission £5.20 ($8.20) adults, £2.60 ($4.10) children and senior citizens. Daily 10am–6pm. Closed Jan 1, Dec 24–26. Tube: Colindale.

The Royal Air Force Museum, Britain's national museum of aviation, has one of the world's finest collections of historic aircraft and tells the story of flight through the display of more than 60 aircraft. The museum stands on 15 acres of the former airfield at Hendon in North London, and its main aircraft hall occupies two large hangars from World War I. Purpose-built halls house "The Battle of Britain Experience," plus a collection of famous bomber aircraft, including "The Friendly Invasion," commemorating the contribution of the United States Army Air Force to the allied war effort in World War II. Special features of the museum include a flight simulator offering a selection of different flying experiences, film shows, a "sit-in" jet trainer, free demonstrations, and guided tours. There is also a licensed family restaurant. The nearest British Rail station is at Mill Hill Broadway, where bus 303 runs the rest of the way. Access by road is via the A41, the A1, and the M1 (junction 4).

Science Museum

Exhibition Rd., SW7. ☎ **0171/938-8000.** Admission £5 ($7.90) adults, £2.60 ($4.10) children 5–17. Children 4 and under free. Daily 9am–6pm. Tube: South Kensington. Bus 9, 10, 14, 49, 52, 74, 349, and C1.

This museum traces the development of science and industry and their influence on everyday life. The collections are among the largest, most comprehensive, and most significant anywhere. On display is Stephenson's original rocket, the tiny prototype railroad engine. You can also see Whittle's original jet engine and the *Apollo 10* space module. The King George III Collection of scientific instruments is the highlight of a gallery on science in the 18th century.

To help the visitor's understanding of science and technology, there are working models and video displays, including two "hands-on" galleries called Launch Pad and Flight Lab. Health Matters, a permanent gallery on modern medicine, opened in 1994. You can buy souvenirs at the shopping concourse.

Linley Sambourne House

18 Stafford Terrace, W8. ☎ **0181/994-1019.** Admission £3 ($4.75) adults, £2.50 ($3.95) children under 16. Mar–Oct Wed 10am–4pm, Sun 2–5pm. Tube: High Street Kensington.

You'll step back into the days of Queen Victoria when you visit this house, which has remained unchanged for more than a century. Part of a terrace built in the late 1860s, this is a five-story, Suffolk brick structure to which Linley Sambourne, a draftsman who later became a cartoonist for *Punch,* brought his bride. From the moment you step into the entrance hall, you see a mixture of styles and clutter that typified Victorian decor, with a plush portiere, a fireplace valance, stained glass in the backdoor, and a large set of antlers vying for attention. The drawing room alone offers an incredible number of items.

Design Museum

Butler's Wharf, Shad Thames, SE1. ☎ **0171/403-6933.** Admission £4.50 ($7.10) adults, £3.50 ($5.55) children. Mon–Fri 11:30am–6pm; Sat–Sun noon–6pm. Tube: Tower or London Bridge.

This is the only museum in Europe that explains why and how mass-produced objects work and look the way they do and how design contributes to the quality of our lives. The museum comprises: a collection of objects that include cars, furniture, domestic appliances, graphics, and ceramics; the Review, with its changing displays of new products and prototypes from around the world; a library, a shop; a café/bar; and the Blueprint Café, which serves lunch and dinner, plus brunch on Sunday. Located at Butler's Wharf, on the riverbank with views of the Tower Bridge and the river Thames, the Design Museum is a showcase of past and present design.

GALLERIES

National Portrait Gallery

St. Martin's Place, WC2. ☎ **0171/306-0055.** Admission free, except for special exhibitions. Mon–Sat 10am–6pm; Sun noon–6pm. Tube: Charing Cross or Leicester Square.

The National Portrait Gallery was founded in 1856 to collect the likenesses of famous British men and women. Today the collection is the most comprehensive of its kind in the world and constitutes a unique record of the men and women who created (and are still creating) the history and culture of the nation. A few paintings tower over the rest, including Sir Joshua Reynold's portrait of Samuel Johnson ("a man of most dreadful appearance"). Among the best are Nicholas Hilliard's miniature of a handsome Sir Walter Raleigh and a full-length Elizabeth I, along with the Holbein cartoon of Henry VIII (sketched for a family portrait that hung, before it was burned, in the Privy Chamber in Whitehall Palace). You'll also see a portrait of William Shakespeare (with gold earring, no less), which is claimed to be the most "authentic contemporary likeness" of its subject of any work yet known. One of the most unusual pictures in the gallery is a group of the three Brontë sisters painted by their brother Branwell. Famous people of today, including the Baroness Thatcher, are celebrated in two floors of the most recent galleries. Portraits of Paul McCartney, Glenda Jackson, T. S. Eliot, and Iris Murdoch are also exhibited. For a finale, Diana, Princess of Wales, is on the Royal Landing.

The entrance to the museum is around the corner from the National Gallery on Trafalgar Square.

The Wallace Collection

Hertford House, Manchester Sq., W1. ☎ **0171/935-0687.** Admission free. Mon–Sat 10am–5pm; Sun 2–5pm. Closed Jan 1, Good Friday, first Mon in May, Dec 24–26. Tube: Bond Street.

This outstanding collection of artworks bequeathed to the nation by Lady Wallace in 1897 is still displayed in the house of its founders, off Wigmore Street. There are important pictures by artists of all European schools, including Titian, Rubens, van Dyck, Rembrandt, Hals, Velàzquez, Murillo, Reynolds, Gainsborough, and Delacroix. Representing 18th-century France are paintings by Watteau, Boucher, and Fragonard, along with sculpture, furniture, goldsmiths' work, and Sèvres porcelain. Also found are valuable collections of majolica and European and Asian arms and armor. Frans Hals's *Laughing Cavalier* is the most celebrated painting in the collection, but Pieter de Hooch's *A Boy Bringing Pomegranates* and Watteau's *The Music Party* are also well known. Other notable artists include Canaletto, Rembrandt, Gainsborough, and Boucher.

Courtauld Institute Galleries

Somerset House, The Strand, WC2. ☎ **0171/873-2526.** Admission £3 ($4.75)adults, £1.50 ($2.35) children. Mon–Sat 10am–6pm; Sun 2–6pm. Tube: Temple, Covent Garden, or Embankment.

These galleries display a wealth of paintings: the great collection of French impressionist and postimpressionist paintings (masterpieces by Monet, Manet, Degas, Renoir, Cézanne, van Gogh, Gauguin) brought together by the late Samuel Courtauld; the Princes Gate collection of superb old master paintings and drawings, especially those by Rubens, Michelangelo, and Tiepolo; the Gambier-Parry collection of early Italian paintings, ivories, majolica, and other works of art; the Lee collection of old masters; the Roger Fry collection of early 20th century English and French painting; and the Hunter collection of 20th century British painting. The galleries are air-conditioned, and some of the paintings are displayed without glass.

Commonwealth Institute

Kensington High St., W8. ☎ **0171/603-4535.** Admission £1 ($1.60) adults, 50p (80¢) children. Mon–Sat 10am–5pm; Sun 2–5pm. Closed Jan 1, Good Friday, May Day, Dec 24–26. Tube: High Street Kensington, Earl's Court, or Holland Park. Bus 9, 9A, 10, 27, 28, 31, 49, or C1 Hoppa.

Why come just to London when you can visit the Caribbean, climb Mount Kenya, and take a rickshaw across Bangladesh? The history, landscapes, wildlife, and crafts of the Commonwealth countries are presented in this tent-shaped building next to Holland Park. Something's always happening here, from special exhibitions to gallery animations. The Commonwealth Shop is a source for gifts and items, including food and wine from around the world; light refreshments are sold at the Commonwealth Brasserie.

Royal Academy of Arts

Burlington House, Piccadilly, W1. ☎ **0171/439-7438.** Admission price depends on the exhibit. Royal Academy Shop, restaurant, and exhibition, daily 10am–6pm; framing workshop, Mon–Fri 10am–5pm. Tube: Piccadilly Circus or Green Park. Bus 9, 14, 19, 22, or 38.

Founded in 1768, this is the oldest established society in Great Britain devoted solely to the fine arts. The academy is made up of a self-supporting, self-governing body of artists, who conduct art schools, hold exhibitions of the work of living artists, and organize loan exhibits of the arts of past and present periods. A summer exhibition, which has been held annually for an unbroken 225 years, presents contemporary paintings, drawings, engravings, sculpture, and architecture. The academy occupies Burlington House, which was built in Piccadilly in the 1600s and is opposite Fortnum and Mason.

Hayward Gallery

South Bank Centre, Belvedere Rd., SE1. ☎ **0171/928-3144** or 071/261-0127 for recorded information. Admission £5 ($7.90) adults, £3.50 ($5.55) children, £12 ($18.95) family ticket. Thurs–Mon 10am–6pm; Tues–Wed 10am–8pm. Tube: Waterloo.

Opened by Queen Elizabeth II in 1968, this gallery presents a changing program of major contemporary and historical exhibitions. The gallery forms part of the South Bank Centre, which also includes the Royal Festival Hall, the Queen Elizabeth Hall, the Purcell Room, the National Film Theatre, and the National Theatre. The gallery is closed between exhibitions, so check before crossing the Thames.

HAMPSTEAD & HIGHGATE

HAMPSTEAD HEATH

Located about 4 miles north of the center of London, Hampstead Heath consists of hundreds of acres of wild and unfenced royal parkland. On a clear day you can see St. Paul's Cathedral and even the hills of Kent south of the Thames from here. For years, Londoners have come here for kite flying, sunning, fishing in the ponds, swimming, picnicking, and jogging. In good weather, it's also the site of big one-day fairs. Tube: Hampstead.

HAMPSTEAD VILLAGE

When the Underground came to this town in 1907, its attraction as a place to live became widely known, and writers, artists, architects, musicians, and scientists—some from the City—came to join earlier residents. Keats, D. H. Lawrence,

Rabindranath Tagore, Shelley, and Robert Louis Stevenson all once lived here, and Kingsley Amis and John Le Carré still do.

The Regency and Georgian houses in this village are just 20 minutes by tube from Piccadilly Circus. There's a palatable mix of historic pubs, toy shops, and chic boutiques along Flask Walk, a pedestrian mall. The original village, on the side of a hill, still has old roads, alleys, steps, courts, and groves to be strolled through.

Keats House

Wentworth Place, Keats Grove, Hampstead, NW3. ☎ **0171/435-2062.** Admission free; donations welcome. Apr–Oct Mon–Fri 10am–1pm and 2–6pm, Sat 10am–1pm and 2–5pm, Sun 2–5pm; Nov–Mar Mon–Fri 1–5pm, Sat 10am–1pm and 2–5pm, Sun 2–5pm. Tube: Belsize Park or Hampstead. Bus 24 from Trafalgar Square.

The famous poet John Keats lived here for only two years, but that was something like two-fifths of his creative life, because he died in Rome of tuberculosis at the age of 25 (in 1821). In Hampstead, Keats wrote some of his most celebrated odes—including "Ode on a Grecian Urn" and "Ode to a Nightingale." His Regency house is well preserved and is home to the manuscripts of his last sonnet ("Bright star, would I were steadfast as thou art") and a portrait of him on his deathbed in a house on the Spanish Steps in Rome.

Kenwood

Hampstead Lane, NW3. ☎ **0181/348-1286.** Admission free. Apr–Sept daily 10am–6pm; Oct–Mar daily 10am–4pm. Closed Dec 24–25. Tube: Golders Green, then bus 210.

Kenwood was built as a gentleman's country home in the early 18th century. In 1754 it became the seat of Lord Mansfield and was enlarged and decorated by the famous Scottish architect Robert Adam in 1764. In 1927 Lord Iveagh gave it to the nation, along with his art collection. The rooms offer some fine neoclassical furniture, but the main attractions are the works by old masters and British artists. You can see paintings by Rembrandt (*Self-Portrait in Old Age*), Vermeer, Turner, Frans Hals, Gainsborough, Reynolds, Romney, Raeburn, Guardi, and Angelica Kauffmann, plus a portrait of the earl of Mansfield, lord chief justice, who made Kenwood such an important home. A 19th-century family coach that comfortably carried 15 people stands in the Coach House, where there is also a cafeteria.

Fenton House

Windmill Hill, NW3. ☎ **0171/435-3471.** Admission £3.50 ($5.55) adults, £1.75 ($2.75) children, £9 ($14.20) family ticket. Mar Sat–Sun 2–5pm; Apr–Oct Mon–Wed 2–5:30pm, Sat–Sun 11am–5:30pm. Closed Good Friday and Nov–Feb. Tube: Hampstead.

This National Trust property is on the west side of Hampstead Grove, just a short distance north of Hampstead Village. You pass through beautiful wrought-iron gates to reach the red-brick house in a walled garden. Built in 1693, it's one of the earliest, largest, and finest houses in the Hampstead section. The original main staircase, some door frames, and chimneys remain of the early construction. Paneled rooms house furniture, pictures, 18th-century English, German, and French porcelain, and the outstanding Benton-Fletcher collection of early keyboard musical instruments. Exhibits of these date from 1540 to 1805 and include a 17th-century Flemish harpsichord loaned by the Queen Mother, other harpsichords, spinets, clavichords, and a virginal. Occasional concerts are given.

Freud Museum

20 Maresfield Gardens, NW3. ☎ **0171/435-2002.** Admission £2.50 ($3.95) adults, free for children under 12, £1.50 ($2.35) full-time students. Wed–Sun noon–5pm. Tube: Finchley Road.

After he and his family left Nazi-occupied Vienna as refugees, Sigmund Freud lived, worked, and died in this spacious three-story red-brick house in northern London. On view are rooms with original furniture, letters, photographs, paintings, and personal effects of Freud and his daughter, Anna. A focal point of the museum is the study and library, where you can see the famous couch and Freud's large collection of Egyptian, Roman, and Asian antiquities. This domestic and working environment offers a unique perspective on the contribution that Freud made to the understanding of the human mind.

Burgh House

New End Sq., NW3. ☎ **0171/431-0144.** Admission free. House and museum, Wed–Sun noon–5pm; buttery, Wed–Sun 11am–5:30pm. Tube: Hampstead.

A Queen Anne structure built in 1703 in the middle of the village, this was at one time the residence of the daughter and son-in-law of Rudyard Kipling, who often visited here. It's now used for local art exhibits, concerts, recitals, and talks and public meetings on many subjects, and the house is the home of several local societies, including the Hampstead Music Club and the Hampstead Scientific Society.

The Hampstead Museum is also in Burgh House and displays and illustrates the area's local history. It has a room devoted to reproductions by the great artist John Constable, who lived nearby for many years and was buried in the local parish church. There is also a bookstall, well stocked with souvenirs and postcards, plus a licensed buttery (☎ 0171/431-2516), popular for lunch or tea (its prices are the lowest in Hampstead).

HIGHGATE VILLAGE

A stone's throw east of Hampstead Heath, Highgate Village has a number of 16th- and 17th-century mansions, as well as small cottages, lining three sides of the now-pondless Pond Square. Its most outstanding feature, however, is Highgate Cemetery—entered from Swain's Lane, N6 (☎ 0171/340-1834)—the ideal setting for a collection of Victorian sculpture. Once described in the British press as everything from "walled romantic rubble" to "an anthology of horror," the 37-acre burial ground attracts tombstone fanciers. Highgate's most famous grave is that of Karl Marx, who died in Hampstead in 1883; on the tomb is a huge bust of Marx, inscribed with his quotation, "Workers of the world, unite."

The Western Cemetery can be visited only on a guided tour, leaving April through October Monday through Friday at noon, 2pm, and 4pm and on Saturday and Sunday hourly from 11am to 4pm. In winter, tours are conducted Tuesday through Friday at noon, 2pm, and 3pm and on Saturday and Sunday hourly from 11am to 4pm. The Eastern Cemetery can be visited on your own any time Monday through Friday from 10am to 4:45pm, Saturday and Sunday 11am to 4:45pm, April through October. In winter, it is open daily from 10am to 3:45pm. For a tour, a donation of £3 ($4.75) is requested. Tube: Archway, then walk through Waterlow Park.

THE PARKS OF LONDON

London's parklands easily rate as the greatest system of "green lungs" of any large city on the globe. Not as rigidly laid out as the parks of Paris, London's are maintained with a loving care and lavish artistry that puts their American equivalents to shame. Above all, they've been kept safe from land-hungry building firms and city councils. Maybe there's something to be said for inviolate "royal" property, after all. Because that's what most of London's parks are.

Largest of them—and one of the biggest in the world—is **Hyde Park,** W2. With the adjoining Kensington Gardens, it covers 636 acres of central London with velvety lawn interspersed with ponds, flowerbeds, and trees. Hyde Park was once a favorite deer-hunting ground of Henry VIII. Running through the width is a 41-acre lake known as the Serpentine. Rotten Row, a 1 1/2 -mile sand track, is reserved for horseback riding and on Sunday attracts some skilled equestrians.

Kensington Gardens, W2, blending with Hyde Park, border on the grounds of Kensington Palace. These gardens are home to the celebrated statue of Peter Pan, with the bronze rabbits that toddlers are always trying to kidnap. The Albert Memorial is also here.

East of Hyde Park, across Piccadilly, stretch **Green Park** and **St. James's Park,** W1, forming an almost-unbroken chain of landscaped beauty. This is an ideal area for picnics, which you'll find hard to believe was once a festering piece of swamp near the leper hospital. There is a romantic lake, stocked with a variety of ducks and pelicans, descendants of the pair that the Russian ambassador presented to Charles II in 1662.

Regent's Park, NW1, covers most of the district by that name, north of Baker Street and Marylebone Road. Designed by the 18th-century genius John Nash to surround a palace of the prince regent that never materialized, this is the most classically beautiful of London's parks. The core is a rose garden planted around a small lake alive with waterfowl and spanned by humped Japanese bridges. The **open-air theater** and the **London Zoo** are here, and, as in all the local parks, there are hundreds of deck chairs on the lawns in which to sunbathe. The deck-chair attendants, who collect a small fee, are mostly college students on vacation.

MARBLE ARCH & SPEAKERS' CORNER

At the northwest extremity of Mayfair, head for Marble Arch, an enormous *faux pas* that the English didn't try to hide but turned into a monument. Originally it was built by John Nash as the entrance to Buckingham Palace, but it was discovered that it was too small for carriages to pass through. In this part of Hyde Park (Tube: Marble Arch) is the **Speakers' Corner,** where you will see English free speech in action. Everybody from terrorists to orgone theorists mounts the soapbox to speak their minds. The speeches reach their most vehement pitch on Sunday, the best day to visit Marble Arch.

LANDMARK CHURCHES

St. Martin-in-the-Fields, overlooking Trafalgar Square, WC2 (☎ 0171/930-0089), is the Royal Parish Church, dear to the hearts of many English people, especially the homeless. The present classically inspired church, with its famous steeple, dates from 1726; James Gibbs, a pupil of Wren's, is listed as the architect. The first known church on the site dates from the 13th century; among the congregation in years past was George I, who was actually a churchwarden, unique for an English sovereign. From St. Martin's vantage position in the theater district, it has drawn many actors to its door—none more notable than Nell Gwyn, the mistress of Charles II. On her death in 1687, she was buried in the crypt. Throughout the war, many Londoners rode out uneasy nights in the crypt, while Blitz bombs rained down overhead. One, in 1940, blasted out all the windows. Today the crypt has a pleasant restaurant, a bookshop, and a gallery. It is home to London's original Brass Rubbing Centre where visitors are taught this traditional

Attractions in St. Marylebone, Paddington & Bayswater

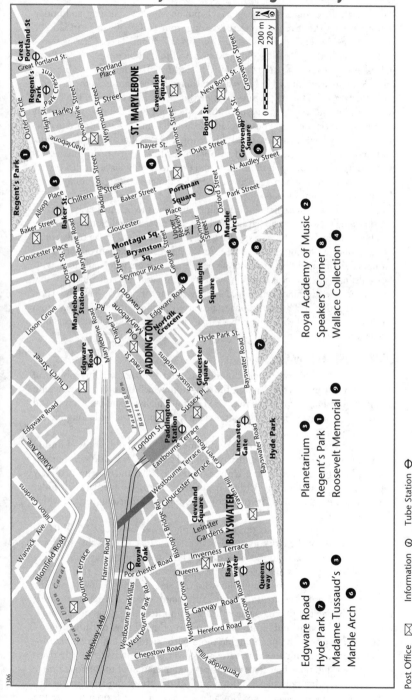

Edgware Road 5
Hyde Park 7
Madame Tussaud's 3
Marble Arch 6

Planetarium 3
Regent's Park 1
Roosevelt Memorial 9

Royal Academy of Music 2
Speakers' Corner 8
Wallace Collection 4

Post Office ⊠   Information ⓘ   Tube Station ⊖

family craft. Free concerts are given at 1:15pm on Monday, Tuesday, and Friday, lasting 50 minutes. Evening concerts, costing from £6 ($9.50) to £15 ($23.70), are presented on Thursday and Saturday nights at 7:30pm. Tube: Charing Cross.

St. Etheldreda's, Britain's oldest Roman Catholic church, lies on Ely Place, Clerkenwell, EC1 (☎ 0171/405-1061), leading off Charterhouse Street at Holborn Circus. Built in 1251, it was mentioned by the Bard in both *Richard II* and *Richard III.* One of the survivors of the Great Fire of 1666, the church was built by and was the property of the diocese of Ely in the days when many bishops had their episcopal houses in London as well as in the actual cathedral cities in which they held their sees. Until this century, the landlord of Ye Olde Mitre public house near Ely Place had to obtain his license from the Justices of Cambridgeshire rather than in London, and even today Ely Place is still a private road, with impressive iron gates and a lodge for the gatekeeper, all administered by six elected commissioners.

St. Etheldreda, whose name is sometimes shortened to St. Awdrey, was a 7th-century king's daughter who left her husband and turned to religion, establishing an abbey on the Isle of Ely. The word *tawdry* comes from the cheap trinkets sold at the annual fair honoring St. Awdrey. St. Etheldreda's is made up of a crypt and an upper church and caters to working people and visitors who come to pray. It has a distinguished musical tradition, with an 11am Latin mass on Sunday. Other mass times are on Sunday at 9am, Monday through Friday at 8am and 1pm, and on Saturday at 9:30am. Lunches are served Monday through Friday from 11:30am to 2pm in the Pantry, with a varied choice of hot and cold dishes. Tube: Farringdon or Chancery Lane.

ALONG THE THAMES

All of London's history and development is linked to this winding ribbon of water—which connects the city with the sea—from which London drew its wealth and its power. For centuries the river was London's highway and main street, and today there is a row of fascinating attractions lying on, across, and alongside the river Thames.

Some of the bridges that span the Thames are household words. **London Bridge,** which, contrary to the nursery rhyme, has never "fallen down," but was dismantled and shipped to the United States in 1971 and was immediately replaced by a new London Bridge; it ran from the Monument (a tall pillar commemorating the Great Fire of 1666) to Southwark Cathedral, parts of which date from 1207.

Its neighbor to the east is the still-standing **Tower Bridge,** E1 (☎ 0171/407-0922), one of the city's most celebrated landmarks and possibly the most photographed and painted bridge on earth. The Tower Bridge was built during 1886–94 with two towers 200 feet apart, joined by footbridges that provide glass-covered walkways for the public, who can enter the north tower, take the elevator to the walkway, cross the river to the south tower, and return to street level. The bridge is a photographer's dream, with interesting views of St. Paul's, the Tower of London, and in the distance, a part of the Houses of Parliament.

You can also visit the main engine room with Victorian boilers and steam-pumping engines, which used to raise and lower the roadway across the river. Among the exhibitions that trace the history and operation of this unique bridge are models showing how the 1,000-ton arms of the bridge can be raised in $1^{1}/_{2}$ minutes to allow ships' passage. Nowadays, electric power is used to raise the bridge, an occurrence that usually happens about once a day, more often in summer. When it's going to open, a bell sounds throughout the bridge and road traffic is stopped. Admission to exhibits is £5 ($7.90) for adults and £3.50 ($5.55) for children. It's open daily from 10am to 4:30pm. Tube: Tower Hill.

The piece of river between the site of the old London Bridge and the Tower Bridge marks the city end of the immense row of docks stretching 26 miles to the coast. Although most of them are no longer in use, they have long been known as the Port of London.

Particular note should be taken of the striking removal of pollution from the Thames during recent decades. The river, so polluted in the 1950s that no marine life could exist in it, can now lay claim to being "the cleanest metropolitan estuary in the world," with many varieties of fish, even salmon, living in its waters.

THAMES FLOOD BARRIER

From time to time throughout centuries, the Thames estuary has brought tidal surges that have on occasion caused disastrous flooding at Woolwich, Hammersmith, Whitehall, Westminster, plus other areas within the river's flood reaches. Furthermore, the flooding peril has increased during this century because of natural causes: the unstoppable rise of tide levels in the Thames; surge tides from the Atlantic; and the down tilt of the country by some 12 inches a century.

All this led to the construction, beginning in 1975, of the Thames Flood Barrier with huge piers linking mammoth rising sector gates, smaller rising sector gates, and falling radial gates, all of which can make a solid steel wall about the height of a five-story building, which completely dams the waters of the Thames, keeping the surge tides from passage up the estuary. The gates are operated every month to remove river silt and be sure they work smoothly.

Since its official opening in 1984, the engineering spectacle has drawn increasing crowds to the site, at a point in the river known as Woolwich Reach in east London, where the Thames is a straight stretch about a third of a mile in width. London Launches (☎ 0171/930-3373) offers trips to the barrier, operating from Westminster Pier. At the Barrier Centre, an audiovisual show depicts the need for the barrier and its operation, and there are also a souvenir shop, a snack bar, and a cafeteria. London Launches leave five times daily from Westminster Pier, with returns from Barrier Pier. Adults pay £5.85 ($9.25)round-trip or £4.15 ($6.55) one-way. Children under 14 are charged £2.95 ($4.65) round-trip or £3 ($4.75) one-way. Senior citizens pay £4.70 ($7.45) round-trip or £3 ($4.75) one-way.

It's also possible to take the boat over and then return by train; the tube stop is Charlton Station. Trains there depart for central London every 30 minutes, and the ride takes only 15 minutes.

The Thames Barrier Visitors' Centre, Unity Way, Woolwich, SE18 (☎ 0181/854-1373), is open Monday through Friday from 10am to 9:30pm and on Saturday and Sunday from 10:30am to 6pm. Admission is £2.55 ($4.05) for adults and £1.55 ($2.45) for children.

FLOATING MUSEUM

HMS *Belfast,* Morgan's Lane, Tooley Street, SE1 (☎ 0171/407-6434), Europe's largest historic warship, is permanently moored on the Thames, opposite the Tower of London. This World War II veteran was among the first to open fire against German fortifications on D-day. It also served with distinction during the Korean War, where it earned the name "that straight-shooting ship" from the United States Navy. By exploring the ship from the bridge right down to the engine and boiler rooms, seven decks below, you can discover how Royal Navy Sailors lived and fought during the past 50 years. Visitors can explore the bridge, operations room, 6-inch gun turrets, living quarters, and galley. HMS *Belfast* is open daily from 10am to 5:45pm in summer and from 10am to 4:45pm in winter. Last boardings are 30 minutes before closing. Admission is £4 ($6.30) for adults, £2 ($3.15) for children, with a discounted ticket of £10 ($15.80) for two adults and two children. Senior citizens and students pay £3 ($4.75). Tube: London Bridge or Tower Hill. A ferry runs daily in summer from Tower Pier (Tower of London) directly to the ship; off-season, the ferry has limited service on weekends and does not run at all from mid-December through January.

LONDON DOCKLANDS

What was once a dilapidated 8 square miles of property surrounded by water—some 55 miles of waterfront acreage within a sailor's cry of London's major attractions—has been reclaimed and restored. Today London Docklands is coming into its own as a leisure, residential, and commercial lure.

Included in this complex are Wapping, the Isle of Dogs, the Surrey and Royal Docks, and more, all with Limehouse at its heart. A visit to the Exhibition Centre on the Isle of Dogs offers an opportunity to see what the Docklands past, present, and future include. Already the area has provided space for overflow from the City of London's square mile, and it looks as though the growth and development is more than promising. A shopping village at Tobacco Dock, a new home at Shadwell Basin for the Academy of St. Martin-in-the-Fields Orchestra, and the London Arena (largest human-made sport-and-leisure complex in the country) at the tip of the Isle of Dogs are being joined by luxury condominiums, offices, hotels, museums, and theaters; these and all the other amenities aimed at making the East End of London a desirable place to live and visit have been or soon will be completed.

The former urban wasteland of deserted warehouses and derelict wharves can be visited by taking the **Docklands Light Railway** that links the Isle of Dogs and London Underground's Tower Hill station, via several new local stations. To see the whole complex, take the railway at the Tower Gateway near Tower Bridge for a short journey through Wapping and the Isle of Dogs. Get off at Island Gardens and pass through the 100-year-old Greenwich Tunnel under the Thames to see the attractions at Greenwich described below in "Easy Excursions from London." A regular waterbus service connects Greenwich with Charing Cross in a river voyage of about half an hour, and other tunnels are planned to link the Docklands with port points and motorways.

3 Especially for Kids

The following attractions are fun places where you can take youngsters without having to worry about their safety. However, you don't need a juvenile escort to have fun visiting them—it's even possible that you'll enjoy them more than any kid around. This is not to say that the other sights listed in this chapter aren't fun for kids—at the British Museum, for example, I've watched group after group of children stand absolutely spellbound in front of the Egyptian mummies, while their parents urge them to come along.

SIGHTS

London Dungeon

28–34 Tooley St., SE1. ☎ **0171/403-0606.** Admission £6.95 ($11) adults, £5.50 ($8.70) children under 14. Apr–Sept daily 10am–5:30pm; Oct–Mar daily 10am–4:30pm. Closed Dec 24–26. Tube: London Bridge.

Situated under the arches of London Bridge Station, the dungeon is a series of tableaux, more grizzly than Madame Tussaud's, that faithfully reproduces the ghoulish conditions of the Middle Ages. The rumble of trains overhead adds to the spine-chilling horror of the place. Bells toll, and there is constant melancholy chanting in the background. Dripping water and live rats (caged!) make for even more atmosphere. The heads of executed criminals were stuck on spikes for on-lookers to observe through glasses hired for the occasion. The murder of Thomas à Becket in Canterbury Cathedral is also depicted. Naturally, there's a burning at the stake, as well as a torture chamber with racking, branding, and fingernail extraction. The Great Fire of London is brought to crackling life by a computer-controlled spectacular that re-creates Pudding Lane, where the fire started.

Of course, this experience may not be to every child's (or adult's) taste. If you survive, there is a souvenir shop selling certificates to testify that you have been through the works.

Natural History Museum

Cromwell Rd., SW7. ☎ **0171/938-9123.** Admission £5 ($7.90) adults, £2.50 ($3.95) children 5–17. Children 4 and under free; free to everyone after 4:30pm Mon–Sat and after 5pm on weekends. Mon–Sat 10am–5:50pm; Sun 11am–5:50pm. Closed Jan 1 and Dec 23–26. Tube: South Kensington.

This is the home of the national collections of living and fossil plants, animals, minerals, rocks, and meteorites, with lots of magnificent specimens on display. Exciting exhibitions designed to encourage people of all ages to enjoy learning about modern natural history include "Human Biology—An Exhibition of Our-selves," "Our Place in Evolution," "Introducing Ecology," "Origin of the Species," "British Natural History," and "Discovering Mammals." What attracts the most attention is the 13,000-square-foot dinosaur exhibit, displaying 14 complete skeletons. The center of the show depicts a trio of ripping, clawing, chewing, moving full-size robotic Deinonychus having a freshly killed Tenontosaurus for lunch.

The Geological Museum, which opened in 1935, has now been engulfed by the Natural History Museum. A gallery connects the two sites. The Geological Museum, though sounding dull, really isn't. It traces the "The Story of Earth," a journey taking you back a billion years, with as much excitement as possible, including erupting volcanos and the re-enactment of an earthquake. Exhibitions offer keen insights into how we obtain light, heat, and power. The mineral col-lection is stunning, including diamonds from Siberia, indigo-blue lapis lazuli from Afghanistan, and even a model of the Koh-i-Noor diamond that Prince Albert himself witnessed cut for The Great Exhibition of 1851. The sheer scope and drama of the place is so overpowering that one visit will hardly do. You get it all here, from a hunk of the moon collected by Apollo astronauts in 1972 to a model of Stonehenge on the second floor. Entrance to the Geological Museum is included in the overall admission to the Natural History Museum.

Bethnal Green Museum of Childhood

Cambridge Heath Rd., E2. ☎ **0181/980-3204.** Admission free. Mon–Thurs and Sat 10am–5:50pm; Sun 2:30–5:50pm. Tube: Bethnal Green.

Here you'll find displays of toys past and present. The variety of dolls alone is staggering, some of them dressed in elaborate period costumes. The dollhouses range from simple cottages to miniature mansions, complete with fireplaces, grand pianos, carriages, furniture, kitchen utensils, and household pets. In addition, the museum displays optical toys, toy theaters, marionettes, puppets, and an exhibit of soldiers and battle toys of both world wars. There is also a display of children's clothing and furniture relating to the social history of childhood.

Rock Circus
London Pavillion, 1 Piccadilly Circus, W1. ☎ **0171/734-7203.** Admission £7.50 ($11.85) adults, £5.50 ($8.70) children ages 15 or under. Family ticket (2 adults, 2 children) £19.95 ($31.50). Sun–Mon and Wed–Thurs 11am–9pm; Tues noon–9pm; Fri–Sat 11am–10pm. Tube: Piccadilly Circus or Leicester Square.

Run by the Tussaud's Group of Madame Tussaud's waxworks, this place tells the story of rock and pop music from the 1950s through the present day, using a combination of wax and "moving" bionic likenesses of all the big names in rock from the past four decades. Very young children might not understand it, but preteens and teenagers will love it. Visitors also get to hear the famous songs from rock history. The highlight of the Rock Circus is a show using Audio Animatronic techniques, in which the Beatles, Elvis Presley, Madonna, Bruce Springsteen, and others perform "live."

ENTERTAINMENT

Unicorn Theatre for Children
The Arts Theatre, 6–7 Great Newport St., WC2. ☎ **0171/379-3280** or 0171/836-3334 for the box office. Tickets £4.50 ($7.10), £6.50 ($10.25), and £7.50 ($11.85) adults or children, depending on seat locations. Performances Sept–June, Sat 11am and 2:30pm, Sun and holidays 2:30pm. Tube: Leicester Square.

Situated in the heart of London's "Theatreland," the Unicorn, founded in 1947 and still going strong, is the city's only theater just for children. The adult actors and actresses present a season of plays for 4- to 12-year-olds each year. A program includes specially commissioned plays, adaptations of old favorites, and entertainment of the highest quality.

Little Angel Theatre
14 Dagmar Passage, Cross St., N1. ☎ **0171/226-1787.** Admission £5–£6.50 ($7.90–$10.25) adults, £4–£5 ($6.30–$7.90) children. Shows, Sat–Sun at 11am and 3pm and during school holidays except summer holidays. Tube: Angel Station (then walk up Upper Street to St. Mary's Church and down the footpath to the left of the church), Highbury and Islington Station; or go by car or taxi to Essex Road and then up to Dagmar Terrace.

Specially constructed for presentation of puppetry in all its forms, this theater is open to the general public and has 400 to 500 performances each year. The theater is the focal point of a loosely formed group of some 20 professional puppeteers who present their own shows or help with performances of the resident company. These vary in style and content from *The Soldier's Tale,* using 8-foot-high figures, to *The Nine Pointed Crown* and *Lancelot the Lion,* written especially for the humble glove puppet. Many of the plays, such as Hans Christian Andersen's *The Little Mermaid* or *The Sleeping Beauty,* are performed with marionettes. You'll be enthralled by the exquisite lighting and the skill with which the puppets are handled.

The theater is beautifully decorated and is well equipped. There's a coffee bar in the foyer and a workshop where the settings and costumes, as well as the puppets, are made. To find out what's playing and to reserve your seats, call the number above. Also, there are many special programs during the Christmas season.

OUTDOOR ACTIVITIES

Battersea Park, SW11 (☎ 0181/871-7530), is a vast patch of woodland, lakes, and lawns on the south bank of the Thames, opposite Chelsea Embankment between Albert Bridge and Chelsea Bridge. Formerly known as Battersea Fields, the present park was laid out in 1852–58 on an old dueling ground (the most famous duel fought here was between Lord Winchelsea and the duke of Wellington in 1829). The park, which measures three-quarters of a mile on each of its four sides, has a lake for boating, a fenced-in deer park with wild birds, and fields for tennis and football (soccer). There's even a children's zoo.

The park's architectural highlight is a Peace Pagoda—built of stone and wood—that was donated in 1986 to the now-defunct Council of Greater London by an order of Japanese monks.

The park, open May through September daily from 7:30am until dusk, is not well serviced by public transportation. The nearest tube is in Chelsea on the right bank (Sloane Square); from there it's a brisk 15-minute walk. If you prefer to ride the bus, take no. 137 from the Sloane Square station, exiting at the first stop after the bus crosses the Thames.

One of the greatest zoos in the world, the **London Zoo,** Regent's Park, NW1 (☎ 0171/722-3333), is more than 150 years old. Run by the Zoological Society of London, the 36-acre garden houses some 8,000 animals, including some of the rarest species on earth. Separate houses are reserved for some species: the insect house (incredible bird-eating spiders, a cross-sectioned ant colony); the reptile house (huge dragonlike monitor lizards and a fantastic 15-foot python); and other additions, such as the Sobell Pavilion for Apes and Monkeys and the Lion Terraces.

Designed for the largest collection of small mammals in the world, the Clore Pavilion has a basement called the Moonlight World, where special lighting effects simulate night for the nocturnal beasties, while rendering them clearly visible to onlookers. You can see all the night rovers in action.

Many families spend an entire day with the animals, watching penguins being fed, enjoying an animal ride in summer, and meeting the young elephants on their walks. There are two fully licensed restaurants—one self-service and the other with waiters.

Zoo admission is £7 ($11.05) for adults, £5 ($7.90) for children 4 to 14, free for children under 4. The zoo is open daily from 10am to 5:30pm (closes at 4pm in winter). Take the tube to Camden Town or bus no. 274 or Z2 in summer only.

Hampstead Heath, the traditional playground of the Londoner, was dedicated "to the use of the public forever" by a special Act of Parliament in 1872. This 800-acre expanse of high heath entirely surrounded by London is a chain of continuous park, wood, and grassland that offers just about every known form of outdoor amusement, with the exception of deep-sea fishing and big-game hunting. There are natural lakes for swimmers who don't mind goose bumps, bridle paths for horseback riders, athletic tracks, hills for kite flying, and a special pond for model yachting. At the shore of Kenwood Lake, in the northern section, is a concert platform devoted to symphony performances on summer evenings. In the northeast corner, in Waterlow Park, ballets, operas, and comedies are staged at the Grass Theatre in June and July. Tube: Hampstead or Belsize Park.

4 Special-Interest Sightseeing

FOR THE LITERARY ENTHUSIAST

See the discussion of Hampstead Village, under "More Attractions," above, for details on Keats's House.

Samuel Johnson's House

17 Gough Sq., EC4. ☎ **0171/353-3745.** Admission £3 ($4.75) adults, £1 ($1.60) children, £2 ($3.15) students and senior citizens. May–Sept, Mon–Sat 11am–5:30pm; Oct–Apr, Mon–Sat 11am–5pm. Tube: Blackfriars (when you come out of the tube station, walk up New Bridge Street and turn left onto Fleet Street; Gough Square is a tiny, hidden square, north of Fleet) or Temple.

Dr. Johnson and his copyists compiled his famous dictionary in this Queen Anne house, where the lexicographer, poet, essayist, and fiction writer lived from 1748 to 1759. Although Johnson also lived at Staple Inn in Holborn and at a number of other houses, the Gough Square house is the only one of his London residences remaining. The 17th-century building has been painstakingly restored, and it's well worth a visit.

Carlyle's House

24 Cheyne Row, SW3. ☎ **0171/352-7087.** Admission £2.90 ($4.60) adults, £1.45 ($2.30) children. Easter–Oct, Wed–Sun 11am–5pm. Tube: Sloane Square. Bus 11, 19, 22, or 39.

From 1834 to 1881 the author of *The French Revolution* and his letter-writing wife took up abode in this modest 1708 terraced house. Furnished essentially as it was in Carlyle's day, the house is located about three-quarters of a block from the Thames, near the Chelsea Embankment and King's Road. It was described by his wife as being "of most antique physiognomy, quite to our humour; all wainscotted, carved and queer-looking, roomy, substantial, commodious, with closets to satisfy any Bluebeard." The second floor features the drawing room of Mrs. Carlyle, but the most interesting chamber is the not-so-soundproof "soundproof" study in the skylit attic. Filled with Carlyle memorabilia—his books, a letter from Disraeli, a writing chair, even his death mask—this is where the author labored over his *Frederick the Great* manuscript.

Cheshire Cheese

Wine Court Office Court, 145 Fleet St., ☎ **0171/353-6170.** Tube: St. Paul's.

The burly figure of G.K. Chesterton, born in London in 1874, was a familiar patron at the Cheshire Cheese. Flamboyant in manner, he was encased in a cloak. That, along with his swordstick, became his trademarks. He was the author of such works as *What's Wrong with the World* (1910) and *The Superstition of Divorce* (1920). Oliver Goldsmith, author of *She Stoops to Conquer* (1773), was also said to have frequented the Cheshire Cheese, as did so many other literary figures of their day. Dr. Johnson, who lived at 17 Gough Square, off Fleet Street, where he completed his dictionary, was also a frequent patron. He must have had some lean nights at the pub because by the time he'd compiled his dictionary he'd already spent his advance of 1,500 guineas.

The Poets' Corner

Westminster Abbey, Broad Sanctuary, SW1. ☎ **0171/222-7110.** Admission and hours same as Westminster Abbey (see above).

When you see the Bard with an arm resting on a stack of books, you know you will have arrived at the Poets' Corner in Westminster Abbey (see above).

Residences of Virginia Woolf

Born in London in 1882, the author, Virginia Woolf, used London as the site of many of her novels and writing, including *Jacob's Room,* published in 1922. Daughter of Sir Leslie Stephen and his wife, Julia Duckworth, the author lived at 22 Hyde Park Gate, off Kensington High Street, west of Royal Albert Hall. Julia died in 1895 and Sir Leslie in 1904.

After the deaths of their parents, the Stephen siblings left Kensington for Bloomsbury, settling in the area around the British Museum. Upper-class Victorians at that time didn't view Bloomsbury as "respectable." From 1905 they lived first at 46 Gordon Square, east of Gower Street and University College. It was here that the nucleus of the Bloomsbury Group was created, which would eventually embrace Clive Bell (husband of Vanessa) and Leonard Woolf, who would become Virginia's husband. Virginia went to live at 29 Fitzroy Square, west of Tottenham Court Road, in a house once lived in by Bernard Shaw. The author lived at several more addresses in Bloomsbury, including one on Brunswick Square, Tavistock Square, and Mecklenburgh Square. However, her homes on those squares have either disappeared or else been altered beyond recognition. It was on those squares, however, that the Bloomsbury Group reached out to include the artists Roger Fry and Duncan Grant. Virginia had also become friends with the economist John Maynard Keyes and the author E.M. Forster. At Tavistock Square (1924–39) and Mecklenburg Square (1939–40) she and Leonard operated Hogarth Press. She published her own early work here, as well as T.S. Eliot's *Waste Land.*

To escape from urban life, Leonard and Virginia purchased Monk's House in the village of Rodmell between Lewes and Newhaven in Sussex. They lived there until 1941 when Virginia drowned herself in nearby Ouse. Her ashes were buried in the garden at Monk's House.

Shakespeare is surrounded with tombstones or memorials to some of the greatest authors in the land. Although Shakespeare himself was buried at Stratford-upon-Avon, many figures less towering than he are buried at the Poets' Corner, including Dickens and Chaucer. Actually, "corner" is a misnomer: the memorial takes up a transept on the south side of the nave. Inscriptions honor Dr. Samuel Johnson, the Brontë sisters, D.H. Lawrence, Lewis Carroll, Edward Lear, Dylan Thomas, and John Masefield. Others were buried here, including Ben Jonson, John Dryden, William Wordsworth, Tennyson, Milton, Kipling, Shelley, Goldsmith, Thackeray, and Hardy, the latter called "the last of the Victorians." Even an American, Henry Wadsworth Longfellow, was interred here.

Dickens's House

48 Doughty St., WC1. ☎ **0171/405-2127.** Admission £3 ($4.75) adults, £2 ($3.15) students, £1 ($1.60) children, £6 ($9.50) families. Mon–Sat 10am–5pm. Tube: Russell Square.

The great English novelist, born in 1812 in what is now Portsmouth, lived here from 1837 to 1839. Unlike some of the London town houses of famous men (Wellington, Sloane), the Bloomsbury house is simple—the embodiment of middle-class restraint. The house has an extensive library, including manuscripts and letters second in importance only to the Forster Collection in the Victoria and

---

⏱ In Their Footsteps

Samuel Johnson (1709–84), lexicographer and savant. The son of an unsuccessful book dealer, Johnson never finished college at Oxford. In 1735, the brilliant author, critic, and conversationalist married Elizabeth Porter, an older woman whom he called Tetty. When he was 28, Johnson came to London. James Boswell, a Scot, helped immortalize him by becoming his biographer.

Accomplishments: His *A Dictionary of the English Language* was by far the best in its field for nearly a century. *Lives of the Poets* stands as a memorial to his genius. **Favorite Haunts:** Ye Olde Cheshire Cheese. **Residences:** His most famous was at 17 Gough Sq. (now a museum). **Resting Place:** Westminster Abbey (Poets' Corner).

Albert Museum. Dickens's drawing room on the first floor has been reconstructed, as have the stillroom, washhouse, and wine cellar in the basement.

FOR VISITING AMERICANS

Despite the fact that they fought two wars against each other, no two countries have stronger links than America and Britain. The common heritage cuts right across political and economic conflicts.

In London, mementos of this heritage virtually crowd in on you. Stand in front of the National Gallery and you'll find a bronze statue of George Washington gazing at you over Trafalgar Square.

Visit **Westminster Abbey** and you'll see a memorial tablet to President Franklin D. Roosevelt, a bust of Longfellow in the Poets' Corner, and the graves of Edward Hyde and James Oglethorpe.

Grosvenor Square, in the heart of the West End, is known as "Little America." Watched over by a statue of FDR, it is the site of the present U.S. embassy and the home of John Adams when he was minister to Britain.

Norfolk House, St. James's Square, was General Eisenhower's headquarters during World War II, the spot from which he directed the Allies in the Normandy landing in 1944.

At 36 Craven St., just off the Strand, stands **Benjamin Franklin's London residence.** And in **St. Sepulchre,** at Holborn Viaduct, is the grave of Capt. John Smith of Pocahontas fame—who had been prevented from sailing on the Mayflower because the other passengers considered him an "undesirable character."

The most moving reminder of national links is the American Memorial Chapel at **St. Paul's Cathedral.** It commemorates the 28,000 U.S. service personnel who lost their lives while based in Britain during World War II. The Roll of Honor with their names was handed over by General Eisenhower on the Fourth of July 1951, and the chapel—with the roll encased in glass—has become an unofficial pilgrimage place for visiting Americans.

5 Walking Tours

The best way to discover London is on foot, using your own shoe leather. This section is organized into a series of walking tours of some major attractions and districts.

WALKING TOUR
Westminster/Whitehall

Start: Tate Gallery. Tube: Pimlico.
Finish: Trafalgar Square. Tube: Charing Cross or Leicester Square.
Time: About 3 hours, excluding interior visits.
Best Times: Monday through Thursday, when Parliament is in session.
Worst Times: Evenings or Sunday, when the district becomes almost deserted except for fast-moving traffic.

Begin your tour in front of the grand Palladian entrance to one of the finest art museums in the world, the:

1. Tate Gallery. Built in 1897 and donated to London by the scion of a sugar manufacturer, it's jammed with the works of virtually every great painter in British history (see "The Top Attractions," above). Return to browse the collections at your leisure, but for the moment, turn north along the west bank of the Thames (the embankment here is known as Millbank), the river that made British history, with the Houses of Parliament looming skyward ahead of you. At the first left-hand turn after the first bridge you'll see (Lambeth Bridge), turn inland onto Dean Stanley Street, which in a block will lead to the symmetrical elegance of:

2. Smith Square, whose centerpiece is St. John's Church. Designed with a highly personalized kind of neoclassicism by Thomas Archer in 1728, it was heavily damaged by bombs in 1941. Rebuilt (but not reconsecrated), it now serves as concert hall for some of the greatest musicians of the Western world.

Retrace your steps back to the Thames, turn left (north) toward the neo-gothic regularity of the Houses of Parliament, and enter the verdant triangular park before its southern entrance. A tranquil oasis rich with sculpture is the:

3. Victoria Tower Garden, which has a 1915 replica of Rodin's 1895 masterpiece *The Burghers of Calais* and A.G. Walker's monument to Emmeline Pankhurst, the early 20th-century leader of the British suffragettes who was frequently imprisoned for her actions and beliefs. Near the northern perimeter to the garden, turn left onto Great College Street and walk about a block, noticing on your right the:

4. Abbey Garden. Continuously cultivated over the past 900 years, and associated with nearby Westminster Abbey, it's the oldest garden in England, rich with lavender and ecclesiastical ruins. Even if the gate is locked, parts of this charming historic oddity are visible from the street outside.

Retrace your steps along Great College Street to Millbank (which on some maps at this point might be referred to as Abingdon Street), turning left (north), remaining on the opposite side of Millbank from the Houses of Parliament. The tower on your left, completed in 1366 by Edward III for the storage of treasure, is the:

5. Jewel Tower, all that remains of the domestic portions of the once-mighty Palace of Westminster. It houses a small museum showing the dramas connected with the construction of the Houses of Parliament. Exiting from the Jewel Tower, continue north along Millbank (Abingdon Street) for 2 blocks, passing on your left the semicircular apse of the rear side of one of Britain's most densely packed artistic and cultural highlights:

6. Westminster Abbey. The spiritual heart of London, completed in 1245, and steeped in enough tradition, sorrow, majesty, and blood to merit an entire volume of its own, this is one of the most majestic and most-visited sights in Europe. Turn left, skirting the building's northern flank, and enter via its western facade.

After you visit, leave the abbey through the Cloisters, emerging into Dean's Yard, site of Westminster School. Look for an arch straight ahead and on the right. It leads back to the west door of the abbey and to:

7. **The Sanctuary,** which consists of two streets, called Broad Sanctuary and Little Sanctuary. In medieval days, the Sanctuary was actually a jumbled mass of buildings and narrow winding lanes. Enclosed by the precinct wall of Westminster, this complex offered a haven for the downcast and the odd political refugee. In time, the Sanctuary was said to shelter a "mire of cutthroats, whores, pickpockets, and murderers." It became so disease ridden and crime oriented that James I shut it down. Although the slums this place generated lasted for hundreds of years, urban renewal has been successful in removing the final traces of this once-notorious haven.

After a walk around, look to your right, just beyond the abbey's north transept, to see the much-restored:

8. **St. Margaret's Church.** Built between 1504 and 1523, it contains the body of the colonizer of Virginia, Sir Walter Raleigh (who was beheaded just outside its front entrance), and served as the site for the marriages of both John Milton (1656) and Sir Winston Churchill (1908). Considered the parish church for the British House of Commons, it has a noteworthy collection of stained-glass windows.

When you exit from St. Margaret's, the neo-gothic bulk of the:

9. **Houses of Parliament** will almost overwhelm you. Built between 1840 and 1860 as the result of a competition won by architects Sir Charles Barry and Augustus Pugin (both of whom suffered several nervous breakdowns and eventual early deaths as a result of the overwork and stress it caused them), it covers 8 acres and has what might be the greatest volume of ornate stonework of any building in the world. Your tour of the interior (which you might want to reserve for another day) begins at the base of Big Ben (its clock tower and tallest feature), near the building's northwest corner. One of Parliament's best views can be enjoyed from a position on the:

10. **Westminster Bridge.** Built in 1862 in the then-popular cast iron, and one of the most ornate bridges in London, it gives, from midway across its span, some of the best views of Parliament anywhere. To reach the bridge, turn right on Bridge Street from your position in front of the misnamed but very visible Big Ben clock tower. Note at the western base of the bridge, aptly named Westminster Pier, the departure point for many boat trips down the Thames.

Retrace your footsteps along Bridge Street, passing by Big Ben, and take the second right-hand turn along the busy Parliament Street. Take the first left along King Charles Street, where, on the left-hand side, you'll reach the:

11. **Cabinet War Rooms,** Clive Steps, King Charles Street. Set 17 feet underground to protect its occupants from Nazi air raids, this unpretentious handful of rooms was the meeting place for Churchill's cabinet during World War II and the originating point of many of his most stirring speeches. A half dozen of the rooms are open for visits.

Retrace your steps back to Parliament Street, turning left (north). Within 2 blocks, turn left at:

Walking Tour — Westminster/Whitehall

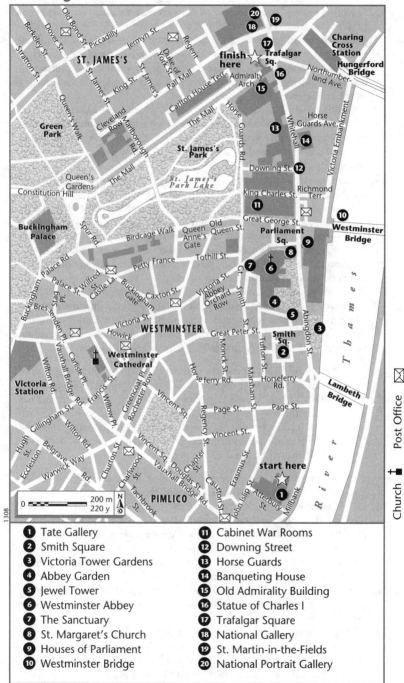

1 Tate Gallery	**11** Cabinet War Rooms
2 Smith Square	**12** Downing Street
3 Victoria Tower Gardens	**13** Horse Guards
4 Abbey Garden	**14** Banqueting House
5 Jewel Tower	**15** Old Admirality Building
6 Westminster Abbey	**16** Statue of Charles I
7 The Sanctuary	**17** Trafalgar Square
8 St. Margaret's Church	**18** National Gallery
9 Houses of Parliament	**19** St. Martin-in-the-Fields
10 Westminster Bridge	**20** National Portrait Gallery

✝ Church   ⊠ Post Office

12. Downing Street. Though security precautions against terrorist activities might prevent you from passing too close, no. 10 along this street is the much-publicized official residence of the British prime minister, no. 11 the official residence of the chancellor of the Exchequer, and no. 12 the office of the chief government whip, the member of Parliament responsible for maintaining discipline and cooperation among majority party members in Parliament's House of Commons.

Continue north along Parliament Street, which, near Downing Street, changes its name to Whitehall. At this point, both sides of the street will be lined with the administrative soul of Britain, buildings that influence politics around the world and whose grandiose architecture is suitably majestic. One of the most noteworthy of these is the:

13. Horse Guards. Completed in 1760 and designed by William Kent, it's one of the most symmetrically imposing of the many buildings along Whitehall and the venue of a ceremony (held Monday through Saturday at 11am and on Sunday at 10am) known as the Mounting of the Guard (which is the first step of an equestrian ceremony that continues with the changing of the Guard in front of Buckingham Palace on days when that ceremony takes place).

Across the avenue rises the pure proportions of one of London's most superlative examples of Palladian architecture, the:

14. Banqueting House. Commissioned by James I, and designed by Inigo Jones in the early 1600s, it's considered one of the most aesthetically and mathematically perfect buildings in England. It has a mural by Peter Paul Rubens, and its facade was the backdrop for perhaps the most disturbing and unsettling execution in British history, that of King Charles I by Parliament.

☕ **TAKE A BREAK**   One of the most famous pubs of London, beloved of parliamentarians throughout England, **the Clarence Pub,** at 53 Whitehall St., W1 (☎ 0171/930-4808), was originally opened in the 18th century and has been cosseting the taste buds of government administrators ever since. With gaslights, oak ceiling beams, antique farm implements dangling from the ceiling, and battered wooden tables ringed with churchlike pews, it offers at least half a dozen choices of real ale and pub grub.

After your drinks with members of Parliament, notice the building that sits almost directly across Whitehall from the pub, the:

15. Old Admiralty Building, at Spring Gardens. Designed in 1725 by Sir Thomas Ripley, and strictly closed except for official business, it served for almost two centuries (until it was replaced by newer quarters between the wars) as the administrative headquarters of the British navy.

Continue walking north until you see what might be the finest and most emotive equestrian statue in London, the:

16. Statue of Charles I. Isolated on an island in the middle of a sea of speeding traffic, it commemorates one of the most tragic kings of British history and the beginning of:

17. Trafalgar Square. Centered around a soaring monument to the hero of the Battle of Trafalgar, Lord Nelson, who defeated Napoléon's navy off the coast of Spain in 1805, it is the single grandest plaza in London. Against the square's northern perimeter rises the grandly neoclassical bulk of the:

18. National Gallery, whose works cannot possibly be cataloged here, but which definitely merits a detailed tour of its own.

The church that flanks the eastern edge of Trafalgar Square is one of London's most famous:

19. St. Martin-in-the-Fields, the home of one of London's greatest chamber orchestras. Designed in the style of Sir Christopher Wren in 1726 by James Gibbs, it has a Corinthian portico and a steeple whose form has inspired the architects of many American churches. It was the christening place of English King Charles II, and the burial place of his infamous but fun-loving mistress, Nell Gwyn.

Finally, for an overview of the faces that altered the course of Britain and the world, walk to the right-hand (east) side of the previously mentioned National Gallery, where the greatest repository of portraits in Europe awaits your inspection at the:

20. National Portrait Gallery, at 2 St. Martin's Place. They're all here—kings, cardinals, mistresses, playwrights, poets, coquettes, dilettantes, and other historical personages. Their assemblage in one gallery celebrates the subject of each painting rather than the artist who created it.

WALKING TOUR
The City

Start: The southern terminus of London Bridge. Tube: Monument.
Finish: St. Paul's Cathedral. Tube: St. Paul's.
Time: About 3 hours, excluding interior visits.
Best Times: Weekday mornings, when the financial district is functioning but its churches are the most unvisited.
Worst Times: Weekends, when the district is almost deserted.

Our tour begins on the southern edge of the Thames, directly to the west of one of the world's most famous bridges. Facing the Thames rises the bulk of:

1. Southwark Cathedral. When it was built in the 1200s, it was an outpost of the faraway diocese of Winchester. Deconsecrated after Henry VIII's Reformation, it later sheltered bakeries and pigpens. Much of what you'll see is a result of a sorely needed 19th-century rebuilding, but a view of its Gothic interior, with its multiple commemorative plaques, gives an idea of the religious power of London's medieval church. After your visit, walk across the famous masonry of:

2. London Bridge. Originally designed by Henry de Colechurch under the patronage of Henry II in 1176—but replaced several times since, the last time in 1971—it's probably the most famous bridge in the world. Until as late as 1729, it was the only bridge across the Thames. During the Middle Ages, it was lined with shops and houses crowded close upon its edges, and served for centuries as the showplace for the severed heads—preserved in tar—of enemies of the British monarchs. (The most famous of these included the head of Sir Thomas More, the highly vocal lord chancellor of England.) From Southwark Cathedral, cross the bridge. At its northern end, notice the first street that descends to the right (east), Monument Street. Detour down it a short distance to read the commemorative plaques attached to the:

3. Monument. Commemorating the Great Fire of 1666, this soaring Doric column is appropriately capped with a carved version of a flaming urn. The disaster that it memorializes erupted in a bakery in nearby Pudding Lane, raged for 4 days and nights, and destroyed 80% of the City. A cramped and foreboding set of stairs spirals up to the top's view over the cityscape so heavily influenced after the fire by architect Sir Christopher Wren.

Retrace your steps toward London Bridge, but before you actually step onto it, detour to the left (south, toward the river) at Monument Street's first intersection, Fish Hill Street. Set near the edge of the water, within its shadow of the bridge, is one of Wren's many churches:

4. **St. Magnus the Martyr.** Completed in 1685 (with its tower added in 1705), it has a particularly magnificent interior that at one time was devoted to the neighborhood's many fishmongers.

After your visit, continue walking east along Lower Thames Street. At the corner of Idol Lane (the fifth narrow street on your left), turn left to see the bombed-out remains of another of Sir Christopher Wren's churches:

5. **St. Dunstan-in-the-East.** Its unexpectedly verdant garden, the only part of the complex that regenerated itself after the Nazi blitz of World War II, offers a comforting oasis amid a sea of traffic and masonry. After your visit, continue walking north. Where Idol Lane dead-ends at Great Tower Street, look straight ahead to the spire of another of Wren's churches, this one in substantially better shape:

6. **St. Margaret Pattens.** Built between 1684 and 1689, it has much of its original paneling and interior fittings and a narrow and slender spire that inspired, in one form or another, many later churches. After your visit, walk to the west side of the church and take Rood Lane north 1 block to Fenchurch. Go left (west) for 2 blocks, then right on Gracechurch Street, into the dusky and narrow streets of Europe's largest financial capital. Within a very short walk, on your right, you'll reach the Victorian arcades of one of the neighborhood's most densely packed shopping centers:

7. **Leadenhall.** Designed in 1881 by Horace Jones, it has all the accouterments you'd need for either a picnic or a full gourmet dinner. Browse at will, but once you've finished return to Gracechurch Street, walk north about a block, then go right (east) on Leadenhall Street. Take the second right-hand (south) turn on Lime Street, where you can admire the soaring and iconoclastically modern:

8. **Lloyd's of London Building.** Designed by Richard Rogers in 1986, this is the most recent home of a company originally founded in the 1680s as a marine insurance market. This is the most famous though financially troubled insurer in the world, with a hypermodern headquarters built atop the heart of the ancient Roman community (Londinium) whose builders launched London's destiny more than 2,000 years ago. Note that within just a few blocks of your position are headquartered the London Metal Exchange, the London Futures and Options Exchange, and hundreds of financial institutions whose clout is felt as far away as the Pacific Basin.

Emerge from Lime Street back onto Leadenhall, where you turn left, then take the first right on Bishopsgate, then the second right-hand turn into an alleyway known as Great St. Helen's. Near its end, you'll find the largest surviving medieval church in London:

9. **St. Helen Bishopsgate.** Begun in the 1400s, it was dedicated to St. Helen, according to legend the British mother of the Roman emperor Constantine. Fashionable during the Elizabethan and Jacobean periods, its monuments, memorials, and grave markers are especially interesting.

Walking Tour — The City

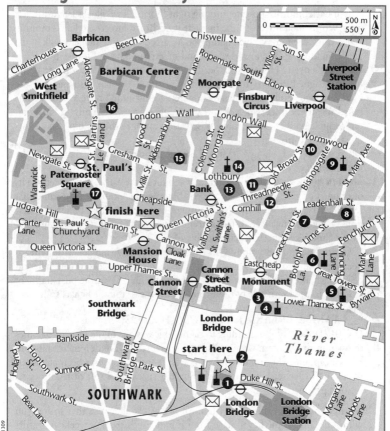

1	Southwark Cathedral	**10**	NatWest Tower
2	London Bridge	**11**	London Stock Exchange
3	Monument	**12**	Royal Exchange
4	St. Magnus the Martyr	**13**	Bank of England
5	St. Dunstan-in-the-East	**14**	St. Margaret's, Lothbury
6	St. Margaret Pattens	**15**	Guildhall
7	Leadenhall	**16**	Museum of London
8	Lloyd's of London Building	**17**	St. Paul's Cathedral
9	St. Helen Bishopsgate		

Exit back onto Bishopsgate, turning right (north). Two blocks later, turn left onto Wormwood Street. At the first left (Old Broad Street), go left. Towering above you—the most visible building on its street—rises the modern bulk of the tallest building in Britain and the second-tallest building in Europe, the:

10. NatWest Tower. Housing the headquarters of National Westminster Bank, it was designed in 1981 by Richard Seifert. Its floor plan is shaped like the NatWest logo. Built upon massive concrete foundations above a terrain composed mostly of impervious clay, it was designed to sway gently in the wind. Unfortunately, there is no public observation tower in the building, so visitors must admire it from afar.

Continue south along Old Broad Street, noticing on your right the bulky headquarters of the:

11. London Stock Exchange. The center was built in the early 1960s to replace its outmoded original quarters. Its role has become much quieter (and somewhat redundant) since 1986, when the nature of most of the City's financial operations changed from a face-to-face agreement between brokers to a computerized clearinghouse conducted electronically.

Continue southwest along Old Broad Street until it merges with Threadneedle Street. Cross over Threadneedle Street, jog a few paces to your left, and head south along the narrow confines of Finch Lane. Cross the busy traffic of Cornhill to the south side of the street. Follow it east to St. Michael's Alley.

☕ **TAKE A BREAK   Jamaica Wine House,** St. Michael's Alley, EC3 (☎ 0171/626-9496). According to claims, this was one of the first coffeehouses to open in the Western world. Historically favored by London merchants and the sea captains who imported their goods, it today dispenses beer, ale, lager, wine, and other refreshments, including bar snacks and soft drinks from its historic precincts.

After you leave, explore the labyrinth of narrow alleyways that shelter you within an almost medieval maze from the district's roaring weekday traffic. Eventually, however, head for the major boulevard (Cornhill), a few steps north of the site of your earlier refueling stop. There, near the junction of five major streets, rises the:

12. Royal Exchange. Designed by William Tite in the early 1840s, its imposing neoclassical pediment is inset with Richard Westmacott's sculpture of a victorious *Commerce.* Launched by a partnership of merchants and financiers during the Elizabethan Age, its establishment was a direct attempt to lure European banking and trading functions from Antwerp (then the financial capital of northern Europe) to London. Separate markets and auction facilities for raw materials were conducted in frenzied trading here until 1982, when the building became the headquarters of the London International Financial Futures Exchange (LIFFE).

On the opposite side of Threadneedle Street rises the massive bulk of the:

13. Bank of England. Originally established "for the Publick Good and Benefit of Our People" in a charter granted in 1694 by William and Mary, it's a treasure-trove both of gold bullion, British banknotes, and historical archives. The only part of this massive building open to the public is the Bank of Eng-land Museum, whose entrance is on a narrow side street, Bartholomew Lane (☎ 0171/601-4878). Open Monday through Friday from 10am to 5pm. Entrance is free.

From the Bank of England, walk northwest along Prince's Street to the intersection of Lothbury. From the northeast corner of the intersection rises another church designed and built by Sir Christopher Wren between 1686 and 1690:

14. St. Margaret's, Lothbury. Filled with statues of frolicking cupids, elaborately carved screens, and a soaring eagle near the altar, it's worth a visit inside.

After you exit, cross Prince's Street and head west on Gresham Street. After traversing a handful of alleyways, you'll see on your right the gardens and the grandly historical facade of the:

15. Guildhall. The power base for the lord mayor of London since the 12th century (and rebuilt, adapted, and enlarged many times since), it was the site of endless power negotiations throughout the Middle Ages between the English kings (headquartered outside the City of Westminster) and the guilds, associations, and brotherhoods of The City's merchants and financiers. Today, the rituals associated with the lord mayor are almost as elaborate as those of the monarchy itself. The medieval crypt of the Guildhall is the largest in London, and its east facade was rebuilt by Sir Christopher Wren after the Great Fire of 1666.

After your visit to the Guildhall, continue walking west on Gresham, and take the second right-hand turn onto Wood Street. Walk 2 blocks north to London Wall, go left for about a block, where you'll see the modern facade of the:

16. Museum of London. Here in new quarters built in 1975, it presents an assemblage of London memorabilia gathered from several earlier museums, as well as one of the best collections of period costumes in the world. Built on top of the Western Gate of the ancient Roman colony of Londinium, it is especially strong on archaeological remnants unearthed during centuries of London building. There are also tableaux portraying the Great Fire and Victorian prison cells.

After your visit to the museum, head south on Aldersgate, whose name soon changes to St. Martins-le-Grand. After you cross Newgate Street, you'll see before you the enormous and dignified dome of one of Europe's most famous and symbolic churches:

17. St. Paul's Cathedral. Considered the masterpiece of Sir Christopher Wren, and the inspiration for the generation of Londoners who survived the firebombing of World War II, it was the scene of the state funerals of Nelson, Wellington, and Churchill, and the wedding celebration of Prince Charles and Princess Diana. It is the only church in England built with a dome, the country's only church in the English baroque style, and the first English cathedral to be designed and built by a single architect. Designated as the cathedral church for the sprawling diocese of London, its role as a church for Londoners contrasts distinctly with the national role of the Royal Church of Westminster Abbey.

WALKING TOUR
St. James's

Start:	The Admiralty Arch. Tube: Charing Cross.
Finish:	Buckingham Palace. Tube: St. James's Park or Green Park.
Time:	About 2 hours, not including stops.
Best Times:	Before 3pm, after which the setting sun might glare into your eyes.
Worst Times:	After dark.

Begin your tour near the southwest corner of Trafalgar Square, at the monumental eastern entrance of the:

1. **Admiralty Arch.** Commissioned by Queen Victoria's son King Edward VII (who died before it was completed), it was designed in 1911 by Sir Aston Webb. Piercing its center are a quintet of arches faced with Portland stone, whose assemblage marks the first (and widest) stage of a majestic processional route leading from Buckingham Palace eastward to St. Paul's Cathedral. The centermost of the five arches is opened only for ceremonial occasions, the two side arches are for vehicular traffic, and the two smallest arches are for pedestrians.

Pass beneath the arch and enter the wide panoramic thoroughfare that leads to Buckingham Palace. With your back to the Admiralty Arch, you'll see the wide and verdant expanse of:

2. **The Mall,** the only deliberately planned avenue in London. Designed by Sir Aston Webb in 1910 as a memorial to the recently departed Queen Victoria, and lined with plane trees, it was originally the garden of the nearby Palace of St. James's and was used for the aristocratic game *paille maille* (a precursor of croquet) by the courtiers of Charles II. On Sunday, the Mall often becomes a pedestrian extension of the adjacent expanse of St. James's Park. The Mall's wide boundaries are a favorite exercise area for London's equestrians and their mounts. Immediately to your left (keeping your back to the arch) are the interconnected buildings of the:

3. **New and Old Admiralties.** Considered one of the most important nerve centers of the British military, they have seen their share of drama since they were originally built and enlarged.

As you stroll in a southwesterly direction down the Mall, the right-hand side will reveal one of the most regal ensembles of town houses in London, the:

4. **Carlton House Terrace.** These buildings replaced the once-palatial home of the 18th-century prince regent, who later became George III. He built (and subsequently demolished) at staggering expense what was considered the most beautiful private home in Britain. Only the columns were saved; they were later recycled into the portico of Trafalgar Square's National Gallery. The subsequent row of ivory-colored neoclassical town houses was one of Nash's last works before he died, much maligned, at the center of a financial scandal in 1835. Today, in addition to art galleries and cultural institutions, the Terrace houses the headquarters of one of the most highly reputed scientific bodies in the world, the Royal Society.

Midway along the length of Carlton House Terrace, its evenly symmetrical neoclassical expanse is pierced with the:

5. **Duke of York Steps and Duke of York Monument**. Built in honor of the second son of George III, the massive sculpture was funded by withholding one day's pay from every soldier in the British Empire. The resulting column was chiseled from pink granite, and the statue was created by Sir Richard Westmacott in 1834. Contemporary wits, knowing that the duke died owing massive debts to his angry creditors, joked that placing his effigy on a column was the only way to keep him away from their grasp. This soaring column and monument (the statue weighs 7 tons) dominates:

6. **Waterloo Place,** the square before it. Considered one of the most prestigious pieces of urban planning in London, it reeks with both aristocratic elegance and nostalgia for England's grand military victories over Napoléon. No. 107

Walking Tour — St. James's

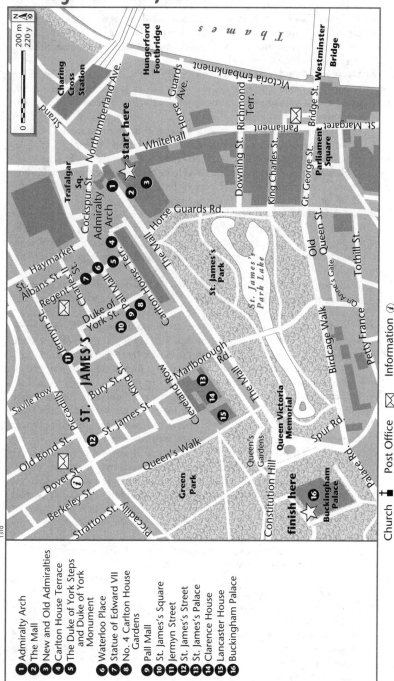

1 Admiralty Arch
2 The Mall
3 New and Old Admiralties
4 Carlton House Terrace
5 The Duke of York Steps and Duke of York Monument
6 Waterloo Place
7 Statue of Edward VII
8 No. 4 Carlton House Gardens
9 Pall Mall
10 St. James's Square
11 Jermyn Street
12 St. James's Street
13 St. James's Palace
14 Clarence House
15 Lancaster House
16 Buckingham Palace

Church ✝   Post Office ⊠   Information ⓘ

Waterloo Place (designed in 1830 and considered one of the finest examples of early 19th-century neoclassical architecture in London) is the headquarters for one of the most distinguished men's clubs in Britain, the Athenaeum Club.

Notice, within Waterloo Place, the:

7. Statue of Edward VII. It was crafted in 1921 by Sir Bertram Mackennal in honor of the man who gave the world the Edwardian Age and much of the grand neighborhood to the northeast of Buckingham Palace. The son of the long-lived Victoria, he ascended the throne at the age of 60, only 9 years before his death. As if to balance the position of his statue, a statue dedicated to the victims of the Crimean War, part of which honors Florence Nightingale, stands at the opposite end of Waterloo Place.

History buffs will appreciate Carlton House Gardens, which run into Carlton House Terrace's western end. Lovers of France and French history especially appreciate the plaques that identify the facade of:

8. No. 4 Carlton House Gardens. These were the London headquarters of Charles de Gaulle's French government-in-exile and site of many of his French-language radio broadcasts to the French Underground during World War II. (Another facade of this same building faces the Mall, on the opposite side of the block.)

One of the streets intersecting Waterloo Place is an avenue rich in the head-quarters of many exclusive private clubs. Not to be confused with the longer and broader expanse of the Mall, this is:

9. Pall Mall. Despite its variant pronunciation in different parts of the empire, Londoners usually pronounce it *pell-mell*. Membership in many of these clubs is prestigious, with waiting lists of up to a decade for the best of them.

Walk west a block along Pall Mall (beware of the speeding one-way traffic), and take the first right (north) turn into the elegant 18th-century precincts of:

10. St. James's Square. Laid out in the 1660s, it was built on land donated by the first earl of St. Albans, Henry Jermyn, a friend of the widow of Charles I and of the future king Charles II. It was originally designed with very large private houses on all sides, probably with artistic input by Sir Christopher Wren, for noble families who wanted to live near the seat of royal power at nearby St. James's Palace. Buildings of the square of special interest include no. 10 (Chatham House), private residence of three British prime ministers, the last of which was Queen Victoria's nemesis, William Gladstone. At no. 32, General Eisenhower and his subordinates planned the 1942 invasion of North Africa and the 1944 Allied invasion of Normandy. At no. 16, the announcement of the climactic defeat by Wellington of Napoléon's forces at Waterloo was delivered (along with the captured eagle-shaped symbols of Napoléon's army) by a blood-stained officer, Major Percy, to the British regent.

Circumnavigate the square, eventually exiting at its northern edge via Duke of York Street. One block later, turn left onto:

11. Jermyn Street, perhaps the most prestigious shopping street in London. Expensive, upscale, with shop attendants who are usually very, very polite, the street offers shops whose windows and displays show a mixture of what is considered inviolable British tradition mingled with the perceived necessities for The Good Life.

TAKE A BREAK Much about the facade and paneled decor of **Green's Champagne and Oyster Bar**—at 36 Duke St., SW1 (☎ 0171/930-4566)—

might remind you of the many men's clubs you've already passed within the surrounding neighborhood. This one, however, welcomes nonmembers and a healthy dose of the clientele is female. There's a battered bar for the consumption of glasses of wine, platters of oysters, dollops of caviar, shrimp, or crabmeat (which you can consume either standing at the bar or sitting at a table), and a wide variety of English-inspired appetizers and main courses. The place is especially popular at lunch time.

Exit from Duke Street onto Jermyn Street, turn right (west), and continue to enjoy the shops. Two blocks later, turn left onto:

12. St. James's Street. As you have by now grown to expect, it has its share of private clubs, the most fashionable of which is, arguably, White's, at no. 37. Its premises were designed in 1788 by James Wyatt. Prince Charles celebrated his stag party here with friends the night before his marriage to Diana. Past members include Evelyn Waugh (who received refuge here from his literary "hounds of modernity"). Even if you're recommended for membership (which is unlikely), the waiting list is 8 years.

At the bottom (south end) of St. James's Street is one of the most historic buildings of London:

13. St. James's Palace. Birthplace of many British monarchs, it served as the principal royal residence from 1698 (when Whitehall Palace burned down) until the ascent of Queen Victoria (who moved into Buckingham Palace) in 1837. Originally enlarged from a Tudor core built by Henry VIII for one of his ill-fated queens, it was altered by Sir Christopher Wren in 1703. The palace, rich in history and connotation, gave its name to the entire neighborhood you've just surveyed. After your visit, walk southwest along Cleveland Row, then turn left (southeast) onto Stable Yard Row. On your left rises the side of:

14. Clarence House. Designed in 1829 by John Nash, it's the official London home of the Queen Mother. On the opposite side of Stable Yard Row rises the side of the very formal:

15. Lancaster House. Designed in 1827 by Benjamin Wyatt, it has, during its lifetime, been known variously as York House and Stafford House. Chopin performed his ballads and nocturnes for Queen Victoria here and Edward VIII lived here during his tenure as the Prince of Wales. Heavily damaged by World War II bombings, it has been gracefully restored, furnished in the French Louis XV style, and now serves as a setting for state receptions and dinners.

Within a few steps, when you arrive at the multiple plane trees of the Mall, turn right for a vista of the front of:

16. Buckingham Palace. The official London residence of every British monarch since Victoria, it exerts a pull and allure that is mystical, magical, carefully cultivated, and vital.

WALKING TOUR
Chelsea

Start: Chelsea Embankment at the Battersea Bridge. Tube: Sloane Square.
Finish: Chelsea's Old Town Hall or any nearby pub. Tube: Sloane Square.
Time: 2 hours, not counting stops, pub time, or visits.

Best Times: Anytime, except rainy days.
Worst Times: Any rainy day.

Begin your tour above the massive masonry buttresses known as the Chelsea Embankment, at the northern terminus of the:

1. **Battersea Bridge,** which will align and orient you to an understanding of Chelsea's vital link to the Thames. Here begins a beautiful walk eastward through a historic neighborhood marred only by the roar of the riverside traffic. Across the water rises the district of Battersea, a rapidly gentrifying neighborhood.

The street beside the Thames will soon be identified as Cheyne Walk. Rich with Georgian and Victorian architecture (and some of the most expensive houses of a very expensive neighborhood), it is considered an architectural treasure house. Although the bulk of your exploration along this street will be eastward, for the moment detour from the base of Battersea Bridge westward to:

2. **Turner's House,** at 119 Cheyne Walk. Its tall and narrow premises sheltered England's greatest painter, J. M. W. Turner (1775–1851), during the last years of his life. Although contemporary with the French impressionists, he painted in a style distinctly and originally different, and his work is uniquely recognizable by its use of shimmering colors. When he died in one of this house's bedrooms, his very appropriate final words were "God is Light."

Just to the east of Turner's House, at nos. 96–100 Cheyne Walk, is a building considered one of Chelsea's most beautiful:

3. **Lindsey House,** completed in the 1670s. Built by the Swiss-born physician to two British kings (James I and Charles II), it became the British headquarters of the Moravian church around 1750. Later divided and sold as four separate residences, it housed the American-born painter James Whistler (at no. 96 between 1866 and 1879). The gardens of no. 99 and no. 100 were designed by Britain's most celebrated Edwardian architect, Sir Edwin Lutyens (1869–1944).

At this point, retrace your steps eastward to Battersea Bridge and begin what will become a long eastward ramble along Cheyne Walk. Midway between the heavy traffic of Beaufort Street and the much quieter Danvers Street, you'll see:

4. **Crosby Hall.** Designated by no identifying street number, its original brick-and-stone construction (resembling a chapel) is prefaced with a modern wing of gray stone added in the 1950s. It was originally built in the early 1400s and owned successively by King Richard III and Sir Thomas More. It was transported in the early 1900s stone by stone from Bishopsgate, partly under the financial incentive of American-born Nancy Astor. Today it provides apartments and dining facilities for the British Federation of University Women. Parts of its interior (which offers paintings by Holbein, a trussed roof, and some Jacobean furniture) are open and free to the public daily except Sunday morning, from 10am to noon and from 2:15 to 5pm.

Continue walking east on Cheyne Walk. After crossing both Danvers Street and Old Church Street, turn left on Old Church Street and walk a few steps to reach:

5. **Chelsea Old Church,** the parish church of Sir Thomas More. Its beauty is diminished only by the masses of traffic outside and the fact that it and its neighborhood were heavily damaged by Nazi bombs during World War II. Painstakingly repaired, it has a chapel partly designed by Hans Holbein, an urn containing the earthly remains of a man who owned most of Chelsea during the

Walking Tour — Chelsea

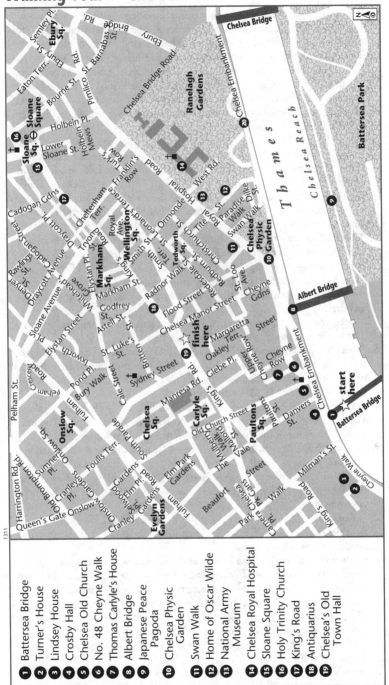

1. Battersea Bridge
2. Turner's House
3. Lindsey House
4. Crosby Hall
5. Chelsea Old Church
6. No. 48 Cheyne Walk
7. Thomas Carlyle's House
8. Albert Bridge
9. Japanese Peace Pagoda
10. Chelsea Physic Garden
11. Swan Walk
12. Home of Oscar Wilde
13. National Army Museum
14. Chelsea Royal Hospital
15. Sloane Square
16. Holy Trinity Church
17. King's Road
18. Antiquarius
19. Chelsea's Old Town Hall

Church ✝   Underground ⊖

1700s, Sir Hans Sloane, and a plaque commemorating the life of American novelist Henry James, a longtime Chelsea resident, who died nearby in 1916. The building's Lawrence Chapel is reputed to have been the scene of Henry VIII's secret marriage to Jane Seymour several days before their official marriage in 1536.

Continue walking east along Cheyne Walk. In about a block, the pavement will branch to form a verdant copse of trees and lawn, behind which stand some of the most expensive and desirable town houses of Chelsea. Occupants of these elegantly proportioned buildings have included some very famous people, such as Mick Jagger, who purchased:

6. **No. 48 Cheyne Walk.** Jagger's neighbors included guitarist Keith Richard, publishing magnate Lord Weidenfeld, and the grandson of oil industry giant Paul Getty, Jr. Artistic denizens of an earlier age included George Eliot who lived part of her life and died at no. 19. The star of the pre-Raphaelite movement, Dante Gabriel Rossetti, lived in what is considered the street's finest building, no. 16.

Branch inland from the Thames, heading north along Cheyne Row, where, after a short walk, at no. 5 Cheyne Row, you'll see:

7. **Thomas Carlyle's House.** Considered one of the most interesting houses in London, particularly to literary enthusiasts, it is one of the neighborhood's few houses that's open to the public. The former home of "the sage of Chelsea" and his wife, Jane, it offers a fascinating insight into the Victorian era. Notice the small gravestone in the garden marking the burial place of the author's favorite dog.

After your visit, retrace your steps to Cheyne Walk and continue walking east. The lacy iron bridge that looms into view is the:

8. **Albert Bridge.** Matched only by the Tower Bridge and the Westminster Bridge, this is one of the most photographed bridges in London. Created at the height of the Victorian fascination with the multiple possibilities of cast iron, it was designed in 1873 by R. M. Ordish.

Continue walking east beneath the trees of Cheyne Walk, heading inland along Royal Hospital Road. Before you leave the banks of the Thames, however, look across the river and try to see the Buddhist-inspired:

9. **Japanese Peace Pagoda.** It was crafted by 50 Japanese nuns and monks and has a massive statue of Buddha covered in gold leaf. The statue was unveiled in 1985. Set at the riverside edge of Battersea Park, according to plans by the Buddhist leader Nichidatsu Fugii, it was offered to Britain by the Japanese government.

Continue walking northeast along Royal Hospital Road. The turf on your right (its entrance is at 66 Royal Hospital Rd.) belongs to the oldest surviving botanic garden in Britain, the:

10. **Chelsea Physic Garden (also known as the Chelsea Botanic Garden).** Established in 1673 on 4 acres of riverfront land that belonged to Charles Cheyne, it was founded by the Worshipful Society of Apothecaries, and later funded permanently by Sir Hans Sloane, botanist and physician to George II, in 1722. The germ of what later became international industries began in the earth of these gardens, greenhouses, and botanical laboratories.

Continue your walk northeast along Royal Hospital Road and turn right at the first cross street onto:

11. **Swan Walk.** Known for its 18th-century row houses, it's an obscure yet charming part of Chelsea. Walk down it, taking your first left onto Dilke Street. At its dead end, turn left onto Tite Street. (From here, your view of the Japanese

Peace Pagoda on the opposite bank of the Thames might be even better than before.) At 34 Tite St. you'll see a plaque commemorating the:

12. Home of Oscar Wilde, where Wilde wrote many of his most charming plays, including *The Importance of Being Earnest* and *Lady Windermere's Fan.* After Wilde was arrested and imprisoned during the most famous trial for homosexuality in British history, the house was sold to pay his debts. The plaque was presented in 1954, a century after Wilde's birth. A few steps away on the same street lie houses that once belonged to two of America's most famous expatriates. No. 31 was the home and studio of John Singer Sargent and no. 35 was the home of James McNeill Whistler.

At the end of Tite Street, turn right onto Royal Hospital Road. Within a block, you'll reach the fortresslike premises of the:

13. National Army Museum. It has galleries devoted to weapons, uniforms, and art, with dioramas of famous battles and such memorabilia as the skeleton of Napoléon's favorite horse.

Next door to the museum, a short distance northeast, is the building that houses the world's most famous horticultural exhibition, the Chelsea Flower Show, held every year on the vast premises of the:

14. Chelsea Royal Hospital. Designed in 1682 in the aftermath of the Great Fire of London by Sir Christopher Wren (and considered, after St. Paul's cathedral, his masterpiece) it may have been built to compete with Louis XIV's construction of Les Invalides in Paris. Both were designed as a home for wounded or aging soldiers, and both are grandiose and immense.

Pass the Royal Hospital and turn left (northeast) 4 blocks later at Chelsea Bridge Road. This street's name changes in about a block to Lower Sloane Street and leads eventually to:

15. Sloane Square. Considered the northernmost gateway to Chelsea, it was laid out in 1780 on land belonging to Sir Hans Sloane. His collection of minerals, fossils, and plant specimens was the core of what eventually became the British Museum. Detour half a block north of Sloane Square (its entrance is on Sloane Street) to visit:

16. Holy Trinity Church, known as a triumph of the late 19th century's arts-and-crafts movement. Completed in 1890, its windows are by William Morris, who followed designs by Burne-Jones and embellishments in the pre-Raphaelite style.

Exit from Sloane Square's southwestern corner and stroll down:

17. King's Road, one of the most variegated and interesting commercial streets in London. It's filled with antiques stores, booksellers, both stylish and punk clothiers, restaurants, coffeehouses, tearooms, and die-hard adherents of the "Sloane Ranger" mystique. Dozens of possibilities for food, sustenance, and companionship exist.

🍵 **TAKE A BREAK**   Luring the homesick Yankee, **Henry J. Bean's (But His Friends All Call Him Hank) Bar & Grill**—195–197 King's Rd. (☎ 0171/352-9255)—has been compared to a "Cheers"-style bar. Big burgers and meaty dogs are part of the American fare, and you can order such drinks as a Tequila Sunrise. In summer, you can eat and drink in the rose garden in back. Happy hour with reduced drink prices is daily from 5:30 to 7:30pm.

After your break (which can be enjoyed at any of the neighborhood's other pubs and cafés along the way), continue walking southwest along King's Road.

Midway between Shawfield Street and Flood Street lies a warren of antiques sellers, all clustered together into a complex known as:

18. Antiquarius, at 131–141 King's Rd., SW3. Browse at will; maybe you'll buy an almost heirloom or perhaps at least something of lasting value.

As you continue down King's Road, you'll see oval-shaped blue-and-white plaques identifying buildings of particular interest. One to watch for is:

19. Chelsea's Old Town Hall. Set on the southern side of King's Road, midway between Chelsea Manor and Oakley Street, its Georgian grandeur makes it the favorite hangout of everyone from punk rockers to soon-to-be-married couples applying for a marriage license. Many wedding parties are photographed in front of it.

The energetic and/or still curious might transform the finale of this walking tour into a pub crawl, as the neighborhood is filled with many enticing choices.

6 Organized Tours

In addition to touring London by foot or tube, you can take one of several coach tours to see the sights, plus there are dozens of fascinating trips offered along the Thames.

BUS TOURS

For the first timer, the quickest and most economical way to bring the big city into focus is to take a bus tour. One of the most popular is called **"The Original London Sightseeing Tour,"** taking only $1^1/_2$ hours. London unfolds from a traditional double-decker bus, with live commentary by a guide. The sightseeing tour costs £10 ($15.80) for adults, £5 ($7.90) for children under 16. The tour plus Madame Tussaud's goes from £17 ($26.85) for adults and £9 ($14.20) for children. Tickets can be purchased on the bus or from any London Transport or London Tourist Board Information Centre where you can receive a discount. The concierges of most central London or airport hotels also sell these tickets.

Departures are from various convenient points within the city, which you can decide upon when you purchase your ticket. For information or ticket purchases on the phone, call 0181/877-1722. It's also possible to write for tickets: London Coaches, Jews Row, London SW18 1TB. You might prefer the London Plus ticket, allowing you to hop on and off guided tour buses all day long, spending time going inside various sights that attract you. The London Plus Hop On/Hop Off ticket costs £10 ($15.80) for adults and £5 ($7.90) for children.

A double-decker air-conditioned coach in the discreet green-and-gold livery of **Harrods** takes sightseeing tours around London's attractions. The first departure from door no. 8 of Harrods on Brompton Road is at 10:30am and there are also tours at 1:30 and 4pm. Tea, coffee, and orange juice are served on board. The two-hour tour costs £18 ($28.45) for adults, £10 ($15.80) for children under 14. All-day excursion tours to Bath, Windsor, Stratford-upon-Avon, plus around all of London are available. You can purchase tickets at Harrods Coach Tours, lower ground floor (☎ 0171/581-3603). Tube: Knightsbridge.

The Big Bus Company Ltd., Waterside Way, London SW17 (☎ 0181/944-7810), is an alternative choice, operating since 1991. This company operates 90-minute tours every 30 minutes departing daily in summer from 9am to 6pm (reduced in the off-season to daily from 9:10am to 3;50pm). Tours cover all the highlights, ranging from the Houses of Parliament and Westminster Abbey to the Tower of London and Buckingham Palace (exterior looks only). Live commentary is provided. Departure points are Marble Arch by Speakers Corner, Green Park by the Ritz Hotel, and Victoria Station (Buckingham Palace Road by the Royal Westminster Hotel). The cost is £8 ($12.65) for adults, £5 ($7.90) for children.

BOAT TRIPS

Touring boats operate on the Thames all year and can take you to various places within Greater London. Main embarkation points are Westminster Pier, Charing Cross Pier, and Tower Pier—a system that enables you, for instance, to take a "water taxi" from the Tower of London to Westminster Abbey. Not only are the boats energy saving, bringing you painlessly to your destination, but they also permit you to sit back in comfort as you see London from the river.

Several companies operate motor launches, offering panoramic views of one of Europe's most historic waterways en route.

The busiest of the companies concerns itself only with downriver traffic from Westminster Pier to such destinations as Greenwich. Between April and September, the most popular excursion departs for Greenwich (a 50-minute ride) at 30-minute intervals between 10:30am and 4pm. Between October and March, boats depart from Westminster Pier at hourly intervals, daily between 10:30am and 3:30pm. Regardless of the season, one-way fares cost £4.80 ($7.60) for adults, £2.40 ($3.80) for children under 16. Round-trip fares cost £5.80 ($9.15) for adults, £3 ($4.75) for children. For information and ticket sales, contact the **Westminster-Greenwich Thames Passenger Boat Service,** Westminster Pier, Victoria Embankment, SW1 (☎ 0171/930-4097; Tube: Westminster).

A second, completely independent network of companies offers boat trips upriver to as far away as Hampton Court. Passage is offered only between early April and late September, with only a limited number of departures per day on ships operated by several different shipping and passenger lines. Passage from Westminster Pier to Hampton Court requires about 4 hours each way. For information and reservations, call **Westminster Passenger Service Association** (Upstream Division), Westminster Pier, Victoria Embankment, SW1 (☎ 0171/930-2062).

CANAL CRUISES   The London canals were once major highways. Since the Festival of Britain in 1951, some of the traditional painted canal boats have been resurrected for Venetian-style trips through these waterways. One of them is *Jason,* which takes you on a 90-minute trip from Blomfield Road in Little Venice through the long Maida Hill tunnel under Edgware Road, through Regent's Park, passing the mosque, the London Zoo, Lord Snowdon's Aviary, past the Pirate's Castle to Camden Lock, and returns to Little Venice.

The season begins on April 1 and lasts through October. During April, May, and September, the boat runs at 10:30am, 12:30pm, and 2:30pm. In June, July, and August, there is an additional trip on weekends during the afternoon, but always telephone first; in October the boat runs at 12:30 and 2:30pm only.

There is a canal-side restaurant/café at Jason's moorings where lunches, dinners, and teas are freshly made to order and food can also be ordered for the boat trips. The round-trip fare is £5.25 ($8.30) for adults and £3.75 ($5.95) for children. For reservations, get in touch with **Jason's Trip,** opposite 60 Blomfield Rd., Little Venice, London W9 (☎ 0171/286-3428). Tube: Warwick Avenue.

WALKING TOURS

ORGANIZED LONDON WALKS   John Wittich, of **J. W. Promotions,** 66 St. Michael's St., W2 (☎ 0171/262-9572), started walking tours of London in 1960. He is a Freeman of the City of London and a member of two of the ancient guilds of London, as well as the author of several books on London walks. There's no better way to search out the unusual, the beautiful, and the historic than to take a walking tour. The company concentrates on personal walking tours for families and groups who have booked in advance. John Wittich conducts all tours. The cost for a walking tour of 1 1/2 to 2 hours is £15 ($23.70) for one or two adults, with £10 ($15.80) per hour assessed for extended walks. A whole-day guided tour costs £60 ($94.80).

Of the companies operating a daily program of regularly scheduled public walks, **The Original London Walks,** 87 Messina Ave., NW6 (☎ 0171/624-3978 or 0171/794-1764), is the best, hands down. Their hallmarks are a variety of routes, reliability, reasonably sized groups, and—above all—superb guides. The guides include the renowned crime historian Donald Rumbelow ("internationally recognized as the leading authority on Jack the Ripper"), a distinguished BBC producer, the foremost authority on the Regent's Canal, the author of the classic guidebook *London Walks,* a London Historical Society officer, and several prominent actors and actresses (including the classical actor Edward Petherbridge). They offer more than 60 walks a week, year-round. Their repertory ranges from Greenwich to Ghost Walks; Beatles to Bloomsbury; Dickens to Docklands; Hampstead to Hidden London; Old Westminster to the Old Jewish Quarter; Legal London to Little Venice to the London Nobody Knows; Covent Garden to Camden Town; Shakespeare to Soho; the Famous Square Mile to the Footsteps of Sherlock Holmes; the "Undiscovered City" to the "Secret Village"; and "Aristocratic London" to "Along the Thames." Walks cost £4 ($6.30) for adults or £3 ($4.75) for students and senior citizens. Children go free. No reservations needed.

7 Sports & Recreation

SPORTS

London can be as exciting for sports enthusiasts as for theater fans. That is, if they happen to be *British* sports enthusiasts. The trouble is that Britain's two main sporting obsessions—soccer and cricket, respectively—are generally unknown and incomprehensible to the average American visitor.

Soccer is the national winter sport. The London teams that set British pulses racing—Arsenal, Chelsea, Tottenham Hotspurs—sound like so many brands of cheese spread to a Statesider.

In summer, the national passion turns to cricket, played either at Lord's, St. John's Wood Road, NW8 (☎ 0171/289-1611; Tube: St. John's Wood), in north London; or at the somewhat less prestigious Oval Cricket Ground, The Oval, Kennington, London SE11 (☎ 0171/582-6660; tube: The Oval), in south London. During the international test matches between Britain and Australia, the West Indies, India, or New Zealand (equivalent in importance to the World Series in the U.S.), the country goes into a collective trance, with everyone glued to the nearest radio or TV describing the event.

Tennis fans from around the world focus on Wimbledon for two weeks (beginning around late June). Here you'll see some of the world's greatest tennis players in action, while enjoying the traditional snack of strawberries and cream. The famous annual championships span roughly the last week in June to the first week in July, with matches lasting from about 2pm till dark. (The gates open at 10:30am.) Although the British founded the All England Lawn Tennis & Croquet Club back in 1877, they haven't produced a world champion in ages. Most tickets range in price from a low of £8 ($12.65) to £50 ($79). For information during the tournament, call 0181/944-1066 for recorded information. For details send a self-addressed stamped envelope (only from September through December) to the All England Lawn Tennis & Croquet Club, P.O. Box 98, Church Road, Wimbledon, SW19 5AE. To reach Wimbledon, take the tube to Southfields.

Within easy reach of central London, there are horse-racing tracks at Kempton Park, Sandown Park, and the most famous of them all, Epsom, where the Derby is the main feature of the meeting in early June. Racing takes place both midweek and on weekends, but not continuously. Sometimes during the summer there are evening race meets, so you should contact United Racecourses Ltd., The Grandstand, Epsom, Surrey (☎ 01372/726311), for information on the next races at Epsom, Sandown Park, or Kempton Park. You can drive yourself or, if you want to travel by rail, call 0171/928-5100 in London for details on train service. Bus no. 406 from Victoria Coach Station also goes there.

Finally, we come to a spectacle for which it is difficult to find a comprehensive tag—the Royal Tournament, which some viewers describe as a series of indoor parades paying homage to the traditions and majesty of the British armed forces. Performed every year in late July, usually for a $2^{1}/_{2}$-week run, it's a long-running spectacle that has been viewed enthusiastically by thousands. The show includes massed bands presenting stirring music, the Royal Navy field-gun competition, the Royal Air Force with their dogs, the Royal Marines in action, the King's Troop Royal Horse Artillery, the Household Cavalry, and a series of visiting military-style exhibitions from throughout the British Commonwealth.

There are two performances Tuesday through Saturday, at 2:30 and 7:30pm, at the Earl's Court Exhibition Centre, Warwick Road, SW5. There are no evening performances on Sunday; and no matinees on Monday. Seats cost from £5 ($7.90) to £24 ($37.90), with discounts of around 20% for children 5 to 14 and senior citizens over 65. For tickets and other information, write to the Royal Tournament Exhibition Centre, Warwick Road (without number), London SW5 9TA (☎ 0171/373-8141; Tube: Earl's Court Station). For any other information, contact the Royal Tournament Horse Guards, Wellington Barracks, Birdcage Walk, London SW1E 6HQ (☎ 0171/799-2323; tube: Westminster).

RECREATION

HORSEBACK RIDING LESSONS   The Ross Nyde Riding School, 8 Bathurst Mews W2 (☎ 0171/262-3791; tube: Lancaster Gate), is the only public stable in Hyde Park. The school has 16 horses that are reliable and not easily disturbed by traffic or other disruptions. It's recommended that you go riding early in the morning to avoid crowds in the park. The stable opens at 7am with rides leaving each hour during the week until dark except on Monday when it is closed. On the weekend, scheduled rides are 10 and 11am Saturday and Sunday; 2 and 3pm Saturday; and 1:30 and 2:30pm on Sunday. The cost of a group lesson is £25 ($39.50) and £30 ($47.40) for a private lesson.

ICE SKATING   The Queen's Ice Skating Club, 17 Queensway, Bayswater W2 (☎ 0171/229-0172; tube: Queensway or Bayswater), is London's only serious ice venue. The admission charge is £5 ($7.90) for adults and £3.50 ($5.55) for children. You can rent a pair of skates for £1.50 ($2.35) and lessons cost £5.50 ($8.70) for 15 minutes. The club is open Sunday through Thursday from 10am to 4:30pm and 7:30 to 10:30pm. On Friday and Saturday evenings, it is open from 7:30 to 11pm for disco night and there are a DJ and flashing lights for your entertainment while you skate.

SWIMMING   Brittania Leisure Centre, 40 Hyde Rd., N1 (☎ 0171/729-4485; tube: Old Street), is a sports-and-recreation center operated and paid for by the eastern borough of Hackney. Although it isn't the largest publicly funded sports-and-recreation facility in London, it is one of the most modern, built in two stages between 1982 and 1988. It has a swimming pool with a wave machine, fountains, badminton-and-squash courts, and soccer-and-volleyball fields. Admission is 60p (95¢) for adults and 30p (45¢) for children. The complex is open Monday through Friday from 9am to 10pm and on Saturday and Sunday from 9am to 6pm.

HEALTH & FITNESS CENTERS   Jubilee Hall Sports Centre, 30 The Piazza, Covent Garden, WC2 (☎ 0171/836-4835; tube: Covent Garden), is the result of a radical makeover during the 1980s of a Victorian-era fish-and-flower market into a modern gym. Today, it's one of the best and most centrally located sports centers in London, with the capital's largest weight room and an avid corps of bodybuilding regulars. It also offers badminton, basketball, aerobics, gymnastics, martial arts, self-defense training (for women), and weight training. Maintained by the City of Westminster, it is open Monday through Friday from 6:30am to 10pm and on Saturday and Sunday from 10am to 5pm. The admission is £6 ($9.50) for use of the weight room and £5 ($7.90) for participation in an aerobics class.

8   Easy Excursions from London

It would be sad to leave England without ever having ventured into the country-side, at least for a day. The English are the greatest excursion travelers in the world, forever dipping into their own rural areas to discover ancient abbeys, 17th-century village lanes, shady woods for picnic lunches, and stately mansions. From London, it's possible to take advantage of countless tours—coach, boat, or a do-it-yourself method on bus or train. On many trips, you can combine two or more methods of transportation; for example, you can go to Windsor by boat and return by coach or train.

I highly recommend the previously described Green Line Coaches, operated by London Country Bus Services Ltd. (see "Getting Around," in Chapter 2).

For longer tours, say, to Stratford-upon-Avon, you'll find the trains much more convenient. Often you can take advantage of the many bargain tickets outlined in Chapter 2 under "Getting Around." For further information about trains to a specific location, go to the British Rail offices on Lower Regent Street.

✪ HAMPTON COURT PALACE

On the north side of the Thames, 13 miles west of London in East Molesey, Surrey (☎ 0181/781-9500), this 16th-century palace of Cardinal Wolsey can teach us a lesson: Don't try to outdo your boss—particularly if he happens to be Henry VIII. The rich cardinal did just that, and he eventually lost his fortune, power, and prestige and ended up giving his lavish palace to the Tudor monarch. Henry took over, even outdoing the Wolsey embellishments. The Tudor additions included the Anne Boleyn gateway, with its 16th-century astronomical clock that even tells the high-water mark at London Bridge. From Clock Court, you can see one of Henry's major contributions, the aptly named great hall, with its hammer-beam ceiling. Also added by Henry were the tiltyard, a tennis court, and kitchen.

To judge from the movie *A Man for All Seasons,* Hampton Court had quite a retinue to feed. Cooking was done in the great kitchens. Henry cavorted through the various apartments with his wife of the moment—everybody from Anne Boleyn to Catherine Parr (the latter reversed things and lived to bury her erstwhile spouse). Charles I was imprisoned here at one time and temporarily managed to escape his jailers.

Although the palace enjoyed prestige and pomp in Elizabethan days, it owes much of its present look to William and Mary—or rather to Sir Christopher Wren, who designed and had built the Northern or Lion Gates, intended to be the main entrance to the new parts of the palace. The fine wrought-iron screen at the south end of the south gardens was made by Jean Tijou around 1694 for William and Mary. You can parade through the apartments today, filled as they are with porcelain, furniture, paintings, and tapestries. The King's Dressing Room is graced with some of the best art, mainly paintings by old masters on loan from Queen Elizabeth II. Finally, be sure to inspect the royal chapel (Wolsey wouldn't recognize it). To confound yourself totally, you may want to get lost in the serpentine shrubbery maze in the garden, also the work of Sir Christopher Wren.

The gardens—including the Great Vine, King's Privy Garden, Great Fountain Gardens, Tudor and Elizabethan Knot Gardens, Board Walk, Tiltyard, and Wilderness—are open daily year-round from 7am until dusk (but not later than 9pm) and can be visited free. The cloisters, courtyards, state apartments, great kitchen, cellars, and Hampton Court exhibition are open mid-March to mid-October daily from 9:30am to 6pm, and mid-October to mid-March daily from 9:30am to 4:30pm. The Tudor tennis court and banqueting house are open the same hours as above, but only from mid-March to mid-October. Admission to all these attractions is £7 ($11.05) for adults, £5.30 ($8.35) for students and senior citizens, and £4.70 ($7.45) for children 5 to 15 (children under 5, free). A family ticket sells for £19.30 ($30.50).

A garden café and restaurant is in the Tiltyard Gardens.

☺ In Their Footsteps

Sir Walter Raleigh (1554–1618) Known for his charm and dashing personality, he was the favorite of Elizabeth I until he was accused of having an affair with one of her maids of honor.

Accomplishments: He wrote many prose works, notably *A History of the World,* but perhaps is best remembered for introducing tobacco and the potato to England. He sponsored various colonization projects in America. **Least Favorite Haunt:** The Tower of London, where he was imprisoned on trumped-up charges of plotting against the king. He stayed there for 13 years. **Resting Place:** St. Margaret's Church in London.

Scandal in St. James's

Recent scandals concerning the House of Windsor are but a familiar refrain in the long saga of royal indiscretions. Take the Stuarts, for example. Some of those kings with a roving eye for a shapely leg would make the Windsors look like virginal church deacons.

Everybody, of course, has heard of Nell Gwyn, mistress of Charles II. The diarist Samuel Pepys pronounced her, "Pretty, witty Nell." A blue plaque marks the spot at 79 Pall Mall where Gwyn lived for 16 years, the only plaque in London honoring the former abode of a royal mistress. It was at this address that Gwyn gave birth to her first son by the king. She threatened to toss the infant out the window unless he was granted a title. This illegitimate boy became the Earl of Burford.

Back in the heyday of St. James's Palace, there were no racy London tabloids to report on royal scandals. Locals had to rely upon whispers and gossip. After the fire at Whitehall Palace in 1698, St. James's Palace became the principal London home of the monarch until the move to Buckingham Palace in 1762. Queen Anne, who reigned from 1702 to 1714, was born at St. James's Palace. The second daughter of James II, she was the last of the Stuarts. Although she gave birth to 17 children, the longest survivor lived just 11 years.

Royal mistresses were hustled into and out of St. James's Palace as frequently as royal deliveries of tea and biscuits. Some of the mistresses were installed more or less permanently in the palace itself, at least until they fell into disfavor, as they so often did.

Barbara Villiers, another mistress of Charles II, became the Countess of Castlemaine and Duchess of Cleveland. Two roads around the palace were named for her: Cleveland Street and Cleveland Row. Although Pepys looked favorably

You can get to Hampton Court by bus, train, boat, or car. London Transport buses no. 111, 131, 216, 267, and 461 make the trip, as do Green Line Coaches (ask at the nearest London Country Bus office for routes 715, 716, 718, and 726). Frequent trains from Waterloo Station (Network Southeast) go to Hampton Court Station. Boat service is offered to and from Kingston, Richmond, and Westminster.

KEW

Kew is 9 miles southwest of central London, near Richmond.

✪ Royal Botanic Gardens, Kew Gardens

Kew, Surrey. ☎ **0181/940-1171.** Admission £4 ($6.30) adults, £2 ($3.15) students and senior citizens, £1.50 ($2.35) children, £10 ($15.80) family ticket. Mon–Sat 9:30am–4pm (Apr–Oct, to 6:30pm); Sun and public holidays 9:30am–8pm. Closed Jan 1, Dec 25.

These are among the best-known botanic gardens in Europe and offer thousands of varieties of plants. But Kew is no mere pleasure garden—rather, it's essentially a vast scientific research center that happens to be beautiful. A pagoda, erected in 1761–62, represents the "flowering" of chinoiserie. The Visitor Centre at Victoria Gate houses an exhibit telling the story of Kew, as well as a bookshop where guides to the garden are available.

upon Gwyn, he found Villiers "the curse of the nation." When Charles took a wife, Villiers—called "the fairest and lewdest of the royal concubines"—became lady-in-waiting to the new queen. Villiers even had the power to replace statesmen who did not meet with her favor.

Charles was perhaps outmatched by his womanizing brother, James II (1633–1701), who as Duke of York had at least seven "royal concubines." Even Charles found his brother amazing, perhaps like Prince Charles today commenting on the conquests of his brother, "Randy Andy," back in the 1980s. King Charles II once remarked of his brother: "I do not believe there are two men who love women more than I do, but my brother, devout as he is, loves them more."

One of the most famous mistresses of James II was Arabella Churchill, sister of the first duke of Marlborough. She bore him four children, and he installed her in a house at 21 St. James's Square. But when the royal cad grew bored, he evicted her and turned the property over to Catherine, daughter of Sir Charles Sedley, the playwright better known as a "rake." Catherine became the "Countess of Dorchester," and one of their children, also called Catherine, became the "Duchess of Buckingham." Called "the king's bastard daughter," this Catherine lives on as a wax effigy at Westminster Abbey along with more "legitimate" offsprings.

The notorious "house of James II's concubines" no longer exists. It was rebuilt and incorporated into the property at 20 St. James's Square. In the early part of the 20th century, it became the girlhood home of Queen Elizabeth, the Queen Mother. From all reports, she chased away memories of the "naughty ladies" who brought sex, passion, and children to the Stuarts.

The Queen Mother, who has witnessed most of the major events of the 20th century, has led a life—evocative of Caesar's wife—that is "above reproach."

The gardens, on a 300-acre site, encompass lakes, greenhouses, walks, garden pavilions, and museums, together with fine examples of the architecture of Sir William Chambers. No matter what season you visit Kew, there's always something to see, beginning with the first spring flowers and lasting through the winter, when the Heath Garden is at its best. Among the 50,000 plant species are notable collections of arum lilies, ferns, orchids, aquatic plants, cacti, mountain plants, palms, and tropical water lilies.

The least expensive and most convenient way to visit the gardens is to take the District line tube to Kew Gardens on the south bank of the Thames. The most romantic way to come in summer is via a steamer from Westminster Bridge to Kew Pier.

Kew Palace

Kew Gardens, Kew, Surrey. ☎ **0181/940-3321.** Admission £1.50 ($2.35) adults, 90p ($1.40) students and senior citizens, 80p ($1.25) children. Apr–Sept daily 11am–5:30pm.

Much interest focuses on the red-brick palace (dubbed the Dutch House), a former residence of King George III and Queen Charlotte. Now a museum, it was built in 1631 and houses memorabilia of the reign of George III, along with a royal collection of furniture and paintings. It is reached by walking to the northern tip of the Broad Walk.

Queen Charlotte's Cottage

Kew Gardens, Kew, Surrey. ☎ **0181/940-1171.** Admission £1 ($1.60) adults, children, students and senior citizens. Apr–Sept Sat–Sun and bank holidays 11am–5:30pm.

Built in 1771, this cottage is half-timbered and thatched; George III is believed to have been the architect. The house has been restored to its original splendor in great detail, including the original Hogarth prints that hung on the downstairs walls.

Kew Bridge Steam Museum

Green Dragon Lane, Brentford, Middlesex. ☎ **0181/568-4757.** Admission on steam days, £3.25 ($5.15) adults, £1.80 ($2.85) children; on other days, £2 ($3.15) adults, £1 ($1.60) children. Steam exhibits, Sat–Sun and Mon holidays 11am–5pm; static exhibition, Mon–Fri 11am–5pm.

This museum houses what is probably the world's largest collection of steam-powered beam engines. These were used in the Victorian era and up to the 1940s to pump London's water, and one engine can pump 700 gallons per stroke. There are seven restored engines that are steamed on weekends, plus other unrestored engines, a steam railway, a waterwheel, and a working forge. The museum has a tearoom and bookshop, plus free parking for cars.

The museum is north of Kew Bridge, under the tower, a 10-minute walk from Kew Gardens. You can reach it by a British Rail train from Waterloo Station to Kew Bridge Station; by bus no. 65, 237, 267, or 391 (no. 7 on Sunday); or by tube to Gunnersbury or South Ealing, and then by bus.

GREENWICH

Greenwich Mean Time is the basis of standard time throughout most of the world, the zero point used in the reckoning of terrestrial longitudes since 1884. But Greenwich is also home of the Royal Naval College, the National Maritime Museum, and the Old Royal Observatory. In dry dock at Greenwich Pier is the clipper ship *Cutty Sark,* as well as Sir Francis Chichester's *Gipsy Moth IV.*

About 4 miles from the City, Greenwich is reached by a number of methods, and part of the fun of making the jaunt is getting there. Ideally, you'll arrive by boat, as Henry VIII preferred to do on one of his hunting expeditions. In summer, launches depart at regular intervals from the pier at Charing Cross, Tower Bridge, or Westminster. The boats leave daily for Greenwich about every half hour from 10am to 7pm (times are approximate, depending on the tides). Bus no. 1 runs from Trafalgar Square to Greenwich; bus no. 188 goes from Euston through Waterloo to Greenwich. From Charing Cross Station, the British Rail train takes 15 minutes to reach Greenwich, and there is now the new Docklands Light Railway, running from Tower Gateway to Island Gardens on the Isle of Dogs. A short walk under the Thames through a foot tunnel brings you out in Greenwich opposite the *Cutty Sark.*

WHAT TO SEE & DO

On Saturday and Sunday in Greenwich, there are arts, crafts, and antique markets. Ask at the Tourist Information Centre, 46 Greenwich Church St. (☎ 0181/858-6376), open daily from 10:15am to 4:45pm, about guided walking tours and other activities in town.

Cutty Sark

Cutty Sark Gardens, King William Walk, Greenwich Pier, SE10. ☎ **0181/858-3445.** Admission £3.25 ($5.15) adults, £2.25 ($3.55) children. Apr–Oct Mon–Sat 10am–6pm, Sun noon–6pm; winter Mon–Sat 10am–5pm, Sun noon–5pm.

Unquestionably, the last of the great clippers holds the most interest here; it has been seen by millions. At the spot where the vessel is now berthed stood the 19th-century Ship Inn, where Victorians came for whitebait dinners. Ordered built by Capt. Jock Willis ("Old White Hat"), the clipper was launched in 1869 to sail the China tea-trade route. It was named after the witch Nannie in Robert Burns's "Tam o' Shanter" (note the figurehead). Yielding to the more efficient steamers, the *Cutty Sark* later was converted to a wool-carrying clipper and plied the route between Australia and England. Before its retirement in 1954, it had had many owners, and even various names.

Gipsy Moth IV

Cutty Sark Gardens, King William Walk, Greenwich Pier, SE10. ☎ **0181/858-3445.** Admission 50p (80¢) adults, 25p (40¢) children under 16. Apr–Oct Mon–Sat 10am–6pm, Sun noon–6pm. Closed Nov–Mar.

Next to the clipper—and looking like a sardine beside a shark—lies the equally famous *Gipsy Moth IV.* This was the ridiculously tiny sailing craft in which Sir Francis Chichester circumnavigated the globe—solo! You can go on board and marvel at the minuteness of the vessel in which the gray-haired old sea dog made his incredible 119-day journey. His chief worry—or so he claimed—was running out of ale before he reached land.

Royal Naval College

King William Walk, Greenwich, SE10. ☎ **0181/858-2154.** Admission free. Fri–Wed 2:30–5pm (last entrance 4:30pm). Closed some public holidays (days are published in the daily papers).

This college grew up on the site of the Tudor palace in Greenwich where Henry VIII and Elizabeth I were born. William and Mary commissioned Wren to design the present buildings in 1695 to house naval pensioners, and these became the Royal Naval College in 1873. The buildings are baroque masterpieces; the Painted Hall (by Thornhill from 1708 to 1727) and the chapel are outstanding.

National Maritime Museum

Romney Rd., Greenwich, SE10. ☎ **0181/858-4422.** Admission £5.50 ($8.70) adults; £4.50 ($7.10) students and senior citizens; £3 ($4.75) children (5 to 16). Apr–Sept Mon–Sat 10am–5pm, Sun noon–5pm; Oct–Mar Mon–Sat 10am–5pm, Sun 2–5pm. Closed Dec 24–26.

Built around Inigo Jones's 17th-century Palladian Queen's House, this museum portrays Britain's maritime heritage. Actual craft, marine paintings, ship models, and scientific instruments are displayed, including the uniform coat that Lord Nelson wore at the Battle of Trafalgar. Other treasures include the chronometer (or sea watch) used by Captain Cook when he made his Pacific explorations in the 1770s.

The Old Royal Observatory, Greenwich Park (☎ 0181/858-4422), part of the museum, is also worth exploring. Sir Christopher Wren was the architect; in fact, he was interested in astronomy even before he became famous. The observatory overlooks Greenwich and the Maritime Museum from a park laid out to the design of Le Nôtre, the French landscaper. Here you can stand at 0° longitude, as the Greenwich Meridian, or prime meridian, marks the first of the globe's north-south divisions. See also the big red time-ball used in olden days by ships sailing down the river from London to set their timepieces by. There's a fascinating bewilderment of astronomical-and-navigational instruments; time and travel become more realistic after a visit here.

Where to Dine

Cutty Sark Tavern

Ballast Quay, off Lassell St., Greenwich, SE10 ☎ **0181/858-3146.** Pub Snacks £2.75–£8 ($4.35–$12.65). AE, DC, MC, V. Mon–Sat 11am–11pm; Sun noon–3pm and 7–10:30pm. Food daily noon–2:30pm. ENGLISH.

With plenty of local color, this English riverside tavern is one of the most historic pubs in the environs of London, established in 1698. Today it's a preferred watering hole for a bevy of pop-music stars who live in the area. There is sometimes live music on Tuesday night. Pub snacks are served in the bar, and at lunch you can order hot main dishes from a changing menu likely to offer typical fare such as fresh pasta with wild mushrooms, spicy poached mussels and clams, pasta and tomato soup, organic pork sausages served hotdog style, braised rabbit with a mustard sauce, or grilled red snapper with a hot pepper sauce.

Trafalgar Tavern

Park Row, Greenwich, SE10 ☎ **0181/858-2437.** Reservations recommended for restaurant. Pub snacks and appetizers £2.75–£4.50 ($4.35–$7.10); main courses £3.75–£9.25 ($5.95–$14.60). MC, V. Apr–Sept daily 11am–3:30pm and 6–11pm; Oct–Mar daily 11am–11pm. ENGLISH.

Trafalgar Tavern, a 2-minute walk north of Greenwich Pier, overlooks the Thames at Greenwich and is surrounded by many attractions; directly opposite the tavern is the Royal Naval College. Ringed with nautical paintings and engravings, lots of heavy dark wood, and brass artifacts, the restaurant invites you to enjoy traditional English specialties that go well with the 18th-century naval memorabilia. Try the steak-and-kidney pie, one of the succulent steaks, or perhaps chateaubriand. Pheasant and venison are also on the menu. You can also order daily specials, with freshly prepared vegetables. In the rear is a separate restaurant section specializing in fish. The full menu is available during opening hours.

Runnymede

Two miles outside Windsor is the 188-acre meadow on the south side of the Thames, in Surrey, where King John put his seal on the Great Charter. Today Runnymede is also the site of the John F. Kennedy Memorial, an acre of English ground given to the United States by the people of Britain. The memorial, a large block of white stone, is hard to see from the road. The pagoda that you can see from the road was placed there by the American Bar Association to acknowledge the fact that American law stems from the English system.

The historic site, to which there is free access all year, lies on the Thames, half a mile west of Runnymede Bridge on the south side of the A308. If you're taking the M25, exit at Junction 13. The nearest rail connection is at Egham, half a mile away. For bus information for the surrounding area, call 0181/668-7261.

Syon Park

Syon Park lies in Brentford, Middlesex, 9 miles from Piccadilly Circus, on 5 acres of the duke of Northumberland's Thames-side estate. It is one of the most beautiful spots in all of Great Britain; there's always something in bloom. Called "The Showplace of the Nation in a Great English Garden," Syon Park was opened to the public in 1968. A nation of green-thumbed gardeners is dazzled here, and the park is also educational, showing amateurs how to get the most out of their small gardens. The vast flower- and plant-studded acreage betrays the influence of Capability Brown, who laid out the grounds in the 18th century.

Particular highlights include a 6-acre rose garden, a butterfly house, and the great conservatory, one of the earliest and most famous buildings of its type, built in 1822–29. There's a quarter-mile-long ornamental lake studded with water lilies and silhouetted by cypresses and willows and even a gardening supermarket. The gardens also include a miniature steam railway that costs an additional £1 ($1.60) for adults or 50p (80¢) for children. Syon is also the site of the first botanical garden in England, created by the father of English botany, Dr. William Turner in 1548. Trees include a 200-year-old Chinese juniper, an Afghan ash, Indian bean trees, and liquidambars.

On the grounds is **Syon House,** built in 1431, the original structure incorporated into the duke of Northumberland's present home. The house was later remade to the specifications of the first duke of Northumberland in 1762–69. The battlemented facade is that of the original Tudor mansion, but the interior is from the 18th century design of Robert Adam. Basil Taylor said of the interior feeling: "You're almost in the middle of a jewel box." In the Middle Ages, Syon was a monastery, later suppressed by Henry VIII. Catherine Howard, the king's fifth wife, was imprisoned in the house before her scheduled beheading in 1542.

The gardens are open all year (except Christmas and Boxing Day). The gates open at 10am and close at 6pm; in winter (after October 31), the gates close at 5pm. Admission is £2.25 ($3.55) for adults and £1.75 ($2.75) for children, students, and senior citizens.

The house is open only on Saturday and Sunday from 11am to 5pm (last entrance at 4:15pm). A combined ticket to the house and gardens costs £5.50 ($8.70) for adults and £4 ($6.30) for children, students, and senior citizens. For more information, phone 0181/560-0881. Syon Park lies 2 miles west of Kew Bridge (the road is signposted from the A315/310 at Busch Corner). By public transport, from Waterloo Station in London, take British Rail to Kew Bridge Station. From there, catch bus no. 237 or 267 to the pedestrian entrance to Syon House. It's faster, however, to take the tube to Gunnersbury, then bus 237 or 267.

Thorpe Park

One of Europe's leading family leisure parks, Thorpe Park, Staines Road, Chertsey, Surrey (☎ 0193/256-9393), lies only 21 miles from central London on the A320 between Staines and Chertsey, with easy access from Junctions 11 and 13 on the M25. The entrance fee of £11.25 ($17.80) for adults and £10.25 ($16.20) for children under 14 includes all rides, shows, attractions, and exhibits. Additional charges are made only for coin-operated amusements. Just a few of the favorite rides and shows are Loggers Leap, Thunder River, the Family Tea Cup Ride, Cinema 180, and the Palladium Theatre, as well as the Flying Fish, an outdoor roller coaster, Carousel Kingdom, an undercover entertainment area, and the U.K.'s first four-lane water slide. Newer attractions include Miss Hippo's Fungal Safari and Mr. Rabbit's Tropical Travels along with a U.S. stunt dive team show called Conica Splashtacular. Free transport is provided around the 500 acres by railway and water bus.

Guests can picnic on the grounds or patronize one of the restaurants or fast-food areas. The park is open daily from March 26 through October from 10am to 5pm. The nearest main-line station is Staines, from Waterloo Station in London. Many bus services also operate directly from Victoria Coach Station in London to Thorpe Park.

✪ Woburn Abbey

Few tourists visiting Bedfordshire miss the Georgian mansion of Woburn Abbey, Woburn, Bedfordshire MK43 0TP (☎ 0152/529-0666), the seat of the dukes of Bedford for more than three centuries. It is located 44 miles north of London. The much-publicized 18th-century estate is signposted half a mile from the village of Woburn, which itself lies 13 miles southwest of Bedford. Its state apartments are rich in furniture, porcelain, tapestries, silver, and a valuable art collection, including paintings by van Dyck, Holbein, Rembrandt, Gainsborough, and Reynolds. A series of paintings by Canaletto, showing his continuing views of Venice, grace the walls of the Canaletto Room, an intimate dining room. (Prince Philip said the duke's collection was superior to the Canalettos at Windsor—but Her Royal Highness quickly corrected him.) Of all the paintings, one of the most notable from a historical point of view is the *Armada Portrait* of Elizabeth I. Her hand rests on the globe, as Philip's invincible armada perishes in the background.

Queen Victoria and Prince Albert visited Woburn Abbey in 1841; Victoria's Dressing Room displays a fine collection of 17th-century paintings from the Netherlands. Among the oddities and treasures at Woburn Abbey are a Grotto of Shells, a Sèvres dinner service (gift of Louis XV), and a chamber devoted to memorabilia of "The Flying Duchess." Wife of the 11th duke of Bedford, she was a remarkable woman who disappeared on a solo flight in 1937 (the same year as Amelia Earhart). The duchess, however, was 72 years old at the time.

In the 1950s the present duke of Bedford opened Woburn Abbey to the public to pay off his debt of millions of pounds in inheritance taxes. In 1974 he turned the estate over to his son and daughter-in-law, the Marquess and Marchioness of Tavistock, who reluctantly took on the business of running the 75-room mansion. And what a business it is, drawing hundreds of thousands of visitors a year and employing more than 300 people to staff the shops and grounds.

Today Woburn Abbey is surrounded by a 3,000-acre deer park that includes the famous Père David deer herd, originally from China and saved from extinction at Woburn. The Woburn Safari Park has lions, tigers, giraffes, camels, monkeys, Przewalski horses, bongos, elephants, and other animals.

The house and park are open only on Saturday and Sunday from January 1 to March 26; visiting times for the house are 11am to 4pm (till 5pm on Sunday and bank holidays). From March 27 to December 31, the house can be visited on Monday through Saturday from 11am to 5pm. The park is open on Monday through Saturday from 10am to 4pm and on Sunday from 10am to 5pm. Admission is £6.50 ($10.25) for adults and £2.50 ($3.95) for children.

Light meals are available at the Flying Duchess Pavilion Coffee Shop.

In summer, travel agents can book you on organized coach tours out of London. Otherwise, motorists take the M1 (motorway) north to Junction 12 or 13, where Woburn Abbey directions are signposted.

Hughenden Manor

In Buckinghamshire, sits Hughenden Manor, High Wycombe, Buckinghamshire HP14 4LA, a country manor that not only gives us insight into the age of Victoria but also acquaints us with a remarkable man. In Benjamin Disraeli we meet one of the most enigmatic figures of 19th-century England. At age 21 Dizzy published anonymously his five-volume novel *Vivian Grey*. Then he went on to other things and in 1839 married an older widow for her money, though they apparently developed a most harmonious relationship. He entered politics in 1837 and continued writing novels; his later ones met with more acclaim.

☯ In Their Footsteps

Oscar Wilde (1854–1900) Born in Dublin, this Irish poet, novelist, and dramatist was noted for his epigrammatic wit. Eccentric in taste and dress, he served 2 years in prison on a conviction of homosexuality before retreating—bankrupted and disgraced—to Paris, where he died.

Accomplishments: Best remembered for his plays, Wilde was a genius of the English theater, as exemplified by *The Importance of Being Earnest* and *Lady Windermere's Fan*. His *The Picture of Dorian Gray* became in its time a notorious novel. **Favorite Haunts:** Café Royale in London; various boy brothels. Residences: In London: 1 Tite St., SW3; 34 Tite St., SW3; and 10–11 St. James's St., SW1. **Resting Place:** Père-Lachaise (Paris).

In 1848 Disraeli acquired Hughenden Manor, a country house that befitted his fast-rising political and social position. He served briefly as prime minister in 1868, but his political fame rests on his stewardship as prime minister from 1874 to 1880. He became Queen Victoria's friend—and in 1877 she paid him a rare honor by visiting him at Hughenden. In 1876 Disraeli became the earl of Beaconsfield: he had arrived, but his wife had died, and he was to die in 1881. Instead of being buried at Westminster Abbey, he preferred the simple little graveyard of Hughenden Church.

Today Hughenden houses an odd assortment of memorabilia, including a lock of Disraeli's hair, letters from Victoria, autographed books, and a portrait of Lord Byron, known to Disraeli's father.

If you're driving to Hughenden Manor on the way to Oxford, continue north of High Wycombe on the A4128 for about 1½ miles. If you're relying on public transportation from London, take coach no. 711 to High Wycombe, then board a Beeline bus (High Wycombe–Aylesbury no. 323 or 324). The manor house and garden are open April to October, Wednesday through Saturday from 2 to 6pm and on Sunday and bank holidays from noon to 6pm; in early March, on Saturday and Sunday only, from 2 to 6pm. It's closed from November to the end of March and on Good Friday. Admission is £3.60 ($5.70) for adults, £1.80 ($2.85) for children. For more information, call 0149/452-8051.

○ Hatfield House

West of Hertford, Hatfield House, Hatfield, Hertfordshire AL9 5NQ (☎ **0170/726-2823**), is one of the great English country houses. Only the banqueting hall of the original Tudor palace remains; the remainder is Jacobean.

Hatfield was much a part of the lives of both Henry VIII and his daughter Elizabeth I. In the old palace, built in the 15th century, Elizabeth romped and played as a child. Although Henry was married to her mother, Anne Boleyn, at the time of Elizabeth's birth, the marriage was later nullified (Anne lost her head and Elizabeth her legitimacy). Henry also used to stash away his oldest daughter, Mary Tudor, at Hatfield. But when Mary became Queen of England and set about earning the dubious distinction of "Bloody Mary," she found Elizabeth a problem. For a while she kept her in the Tower of London but eventually let her return to Hatfield. In 1558, while at Hatfield, Elizabeth learned of her succession to the throne of England.

The Jacobean house that exists today has much antique furniture, tapestries, and paintings, as well as three often-reproduced portraits, including the ermine and rainbow portraits of Elizabeth I. The great hall is suitably medieval, complete with a minstrel's gallery. One of the rarest exhibits is a pair of silk stockings, said to have been worn by Elizabeth herself, the first woman in England to don such apparel. The park and the gardens are also worth exploring. Luncheons and teas are available from 11am to 5pm in the converted coach house in the old palace yard.

Hatfield is open from March 25 to the second Sunday in October, Tuesday through Saturday from noon to 4pm, on Sunday from 1:30 to 5pm, and on bank holiday Mondays from 11am to 5pm; it's closed Good Friday. Admission is £5 ($7.90) for adults, £3.20 ($5.05) for children. The house is across from the station in Hatfield. From London, take the fast trains from King's Cross or Moorgate.

Elizabethan banquets are staged in the banqueting hall of The Old Palace Tuesday and Thursday through Saturday, with much gaiety and music. Guests are invited to drink in an anteroom, then join the long tables for a feast of five courses with continuous entertainment from a group of Elizabethan players, minstrels, and jesters. Wine is included in the cost of the meal, but you're expected to pay for your before-dinner drinks yourself. The best way to get there from London for the feast is to book a coach tour for an inclusive fee starting at £40.50 ($64). The Evan Evans agency has tours leaving from Mount Royal Hotel, Cockspur St., and Herbrand St. in London. The coach returns to London after midnight. If you get there under your own steam, the cost is £25.75 ($40.70) on Tuesday and Thursday, £26.75 ($42.25) on Friday, and £27.75 ($43.85) on Saturday. For reservations, call 0170/726-2055.

OFFBEAT LONDON

Chelsea Physic Garden, 66 Royal Hospital Rd., SW3 (☎ 0171/352-5646). Founded in 1673 by the Worshipful Society of Apothecaries, this is the second-oldest surviving botanical garden in England. Sir Hans Sloane, doctor to George II, required the apothecaries of the Empire to discover 50 plant species a year for presentation to the Royal Society. The aim was to grow plants for medicinal study, and plant specimens and even trees arrived by barge. Many plants grew in English soil for the first time. Cotton seeds from this garden were shipped to the new colony of Georgia to launch an industry. You can wander about the 4-acre garden, which includes England's earliest rock garden, viewing the collection. In 1983, the gardens were opened to the public. Some 7,000 plants still grow here—everything from the pomegranate to the Willow Pattern tree. Even an exotic cork oak can be viewed. Hours are Wednesday through Sunday from 2 to 5pm, late March through October. Tube: Sloane Square.

Vidal Sassoon School of Hairdressing, 56 Davies Mews, W1 (☎ 0171/629-4635). At this internationally famous school of Sassoony, you can be made over. Depending on what you choose to pay, you may have the services of a mere stylist or you can command "the creative team" (if you would like to resemble either Demi Moore or Tom Cruise—or perhaps both). Precision cutting and innovative styling—no shaggy perms—are the hallmarks of this frighteningly trendy place. Hours are Monday through Friday from 10am to 3pm. Some appointments can run up to three hours or more. Tube: Bond Street.

The Voice Box, Level 5, Royal Festival Hall, SE1 (☎ 0171/921-0906). Part of London's creatively fertile Arts Centre Project, this is a venue for readings of prose and poetry as set by the organization's Literature Department. The readings are performed by celebrated writers and are generally held in the evenings around 7:30pm. Attendance at the readings costs from £3.50–£6 ($5.55–$9.50), and for students £2–£3 ($3.15–$4.75). For information about the readers, as well as a complete listing of schedules, you can obtain a free copy of a brochure *Literature Quarterly.* Next door is the Poetry Library (☎ 0171/921-0943), which houses the largest collection of 20th-century poetry in Britain. You can also find periodicals of poetry, audio and video recordings, and a bulletin board with information about workshops and contests. Although membership is free, you must bring an ID with your current address on it. Hours are from 11am to 8pm daily. Tube: Waterloo.

London College of Fashion, 20 John Princess St., W1 (☎ 0171/514-7400). Feeling unstylish? At this school, you can pamper yourself without overtaxing your wallet. The most expensive treatment costs £5 ($7.90), which covers the cost of the products used. The students in the beauty-therapy department perform facials, body wraps, electrical massages, and cathiodermie, as well as a long list of other self-indulgent goodies. Hours are Monday through Friday from 9am to 8pm, with the last treatment scheduled at 5pm. Some appointments can take three hours or more. Tube: Oxford Circus.

Porchester Baths, Queensway, W2 (☎ 0171/792-3980). Looking for a re-minder of the (relatively recent) past, when bathtime was considered a rare and not-very-frequent event? The Porchester Baths were constructed in 1929 in marble and gold and have been hailed as the art deco masterpiece of London bathhouses. In the Porchester Centre, you will find a swimming pool, dry-heat saunas, and a steamy Turkish bath. For a visit of up to three hours, you're charged £15.40 ($24.35). It's women's day on Tuesday, Thursday, and Friday, and men only on Monday, Wednesday, and Saturday. Hours are from 10am to 10pm. On Sunday, it's women only from 10am to 4pm, and mixed couples from 4 to 10pm. No nudity is allowed. Tube: Bayswater.

College of Psychic Studies, 16 Queensbury Place, SW7 (☎ 0171/589-3292). London has been the home of some of the most noteworthy eccentrics in Europe, and many of them are deeply interested in psychic phenomena. This college focuses on every aspect of spiritualism, stressing psychic development and healing. On Thursday evenings, you can visit the healing clinic for a half hour session, free, but donations are welcomed. If you would like a sitting with a "sensitive," also a half hour, the cost ranges from £17–£31 ($26.85–$49). On the weekends, personal workshops are held for psychic development. Hours are Monday through Thurs-day 10am to 7:30pm, and on Friday 10am to 4:30pm. The college is closed the last two weeks of August. Tube: South Kensington.

7

London Shopping & After Dark

When Prussian Field Marshal Blücher, Wellington's stout ally at Waterloo, first laid eyes on London, he allegedly slapped his thigh and exclaimed, "Herr Gott, what a city to plunder!"

He was gazing at what, for the early 19th-century, was an overwhelming number of shops and stores. Since those days, other cities have approached London's level as shopping centers, but none has ever surpassed it.

And when night falls, the pickings are equally rich, since London has one of the most varied spectrums of after-dark diversions of any city in the world.

1 The Shopping Scene

London displays an enormous variety of wares. You can pick up bargains ranging from a still-functioning hurdy-gurdy to a replica of the crown jewels. For the best buys, search out new styles in clothing, as well as traditional and well-tailored men's and women's suits, small antiques and curios, woolens, tweeds, tartans, rare books, Liberty silks, Burberrys, English china, silver, even arms and armor—to name just a few.

London stores keep fairly uniform hours, usually shorter than their American counterparts. Most stores are open Monday through Saturday from 9am to 5:30pm, with late shopping on Wednesday or Thursday to 7 or 8pm; however, many central shops close at about 1pm on Saturday. In the East End, around Aldgate and Whitechapel, many shops are open on Sunday from 9am to 2pm. There are a few all-night stores, mainly in the Bayswater section, and shops seldom close for lunch.

Bargains—that magic word in every traveler's dictionary—are everywhere, but they are likely to be limited by customs regulations. See "Customs" in Chapter 2 for more information.

Many London shops will help you beat the whopping value-added tax (VAT) levied on much of England's merchandise. By presenting your passport, you can frequently purchase goods tax free, but only if you have your purchase sent directly to your home address or to the plane you're taking back.

The huge purchase taxes imposed on so-called luxury goods are responsible for the extremely high cost of items such as wine, spirits, tobacco, cigarettes, and gasoline.

Owing to limited baggage space on most commercial aircraft, many shoppers ask to have goods shipped from London to their homes in the U.S., Canada, Australia, or elsewhere. Mail + Pack, 343-543 Latimer Road, London W10 (☎ 0171/287-3301), specializes in packing small to medium-size consignments, and it can also arrange to ship antiques and a wide range of collectibles. Rates include all packing charges, customs documentation, and home delivery. It's usually less expensive to take your purchases directly to the company's headquarters. However, the company can also arrange to pick up your goods, for a surcharge, at your London hotel or at the store where you made the purchase.

SHOPPING AREAS

London's retail stores tend to cluster in certain areas, a holdover from the era when each guild or craft had its own street, so you can often head in a certain direction to find a certain type of merchandise. The following is a very rough outline of the main shopping districts (not including the "Specialty Shopping Streets," which I will detail below) to help you get started.

Regent Street   Curving down elegantly from Oxford Circus to Piccadilly Circus, this stylish thoroughfare is crammed with fashionable stores, selling everything from silks to silverware. It has both department stores and boutiques, but the accent is on the medium-size establishment in the upper-medium price range. Tube: Oxford Circus or Piccadilly Circus.

Oxford Street   The main shopping artery of London, Oxford Street runs from St. Giles Circus to Marble Arch and is an endless, uninspiring but utility-crammed row of stores, stores, and more stores. It accounts for six of London's major department stores, as well as just about every kind of retailing establishment imaginable. Tube: Tottenham Court Road.

Piccadilly   Unlike the circus, Piccadilly Street is distinctly in the upper bracket, specializing in automobile showrooms, travel offices, art galleries, plus London's poshest grocery store, Fortnum & Mason. Tube: Piccadilly Circus.

Bond Street   Divided into New and Old, Bond Street connects Piccadilly and Oxford Street and is synonymous with the luxury trade. Here are found the very finest–and most expensive–of tailors, hatters, milliners, cobblers, and antiques dealers. Tube: Bond Street.

Knightsbridge   Together with Kensington and Brompton Roads, this forms an extremely svelte shopping district south of Hyde Park. It's patronized for furniture, antiques, jewelry, and Harrods department store. Tube: Knightsbridge.

The Strand   Stately, broad, and dignified, the Strand runs from Trafalgar Square into Fleet Street. It's lined with hotels, theaters, and specialty stores that you could spend a whole day peeking into. Tube: Charing Cross or Aldwych (weekdays only).

Kensington High Street   This has been called "the Oxford Street of West London." Stretching for about $1^1/2$ miles, it includes many shops. You'll also find lots of stores on the side streets, such as Earl's Court Road and Abingdon Road; Thackeray and Victoria streets retain something of the old village atmosphere. From Kensington High Street, you can walk up Kensington Church Street, which, like Portobello Road, is one of the city's main shopping avenues, selling everything from antique furniture to impressionist paintings. Tube: High Street Kensington.

SPECIALTY SHOPPING STREETS

If you think London has unique department stores, wait until you see its equally unique shopping streets.

Carnaby Street   Just off Regent Street is the legendary Carnaby Street. Alas, it no longer dominates the world of fashion as it did in the '60s, but it's still visited by the young, especially punkers, and some of its shops display claptrap and quick-quid merchandise. However, for value, style, and imagination, the Chelsea (King's Road) and Kensington boutiques have left Carnaby far behind. Tube: Oxford Circus.

King's Road   The formerly villagelike main street of Chelsea starts at Sloane Square with Peter Jones's classy department store and meanders on for a mile until it reaches a swank new shop-filled complex, Chelsea Harbour. Until 1830 this was actually a king's private road, running from the palaces at Whitehall or St. James's to the country places at Hampton Court, Richmond, and Chelsea. (Queen Victoria ended that when she became the first sovereign to live at Buckingham Palace in 1837.)

The leap of King's Road to the "mod throne" in the late '60s came with the advent of designer Mary Quant. Fashion boutiques, including the famous "Granny Takes a Trip" (it had half a motor car crashing through its window), once lined the boulevard.

Today the street is still crowded with young people and it can still lay claim to being outrageous. More and more in the 1990s, King's Road is a lineup of markets and "multistores," large or small conglomerations of in- and outdoor stands, stalls, and booths fulfilling all sorts of functions within one building or enclosure. They spring up so fast that it's impossible to keep track of them, but few thorough shopping strolls in London can afford to ignore King's Road. Tube: Sloane Square.

Saint Christopher's Place   One of London's most interesting and little-known (to the foreign visitor) shopping streets is Saint Christopher's Place, W1. It lies just off Oxford Street: Walk down Oxford from Selfridges toward Oxford Circus, ducking north along Gees Court across Barrett Street. There you will be surrounded by antiques markets and good shops for women's clothing and accessories. Tube: Bond Street.

Beauchamp Place   Beauchamp Place (pronounced "Bee-cham"), one of London's top shopping streets, is a block off Brompton Road, near Harrods department store. The *International Herald Tribune* called it "a higgledy-piggledy of old-fashioned and trendy, quaint and with-it, expensive and cheap." Whatever you're looking for—from a pâté de marcassin to a carved pine mantelpiece—you are likely to find it here. It's pure fun, even if you don't buy anything. Tube: Knightsbridge.

Princes Arcade   If you like "one-stop" shopping, you may be drawn to the restored Princes Arcade, which was opened by Edward VII in 1883, when he was Prince of Wales. Between Jermyn Street and Piccadilly, in the heart of London, the arcade has wrought-iron lamps that light your way as you search through some 20 bow-fronted shops, looking for that special curio—maybe a 16th-century nightcap or a pair of shoes made by people who have been satisfying royal tastes since 1847. Small signs hanging from metal rods indicate the kind of merchandise a particular store sells. Tube: Piccadilly Circus.

Burlington Arcade   Next door to the Royal Academy of Arts, the Burlington Arcade, W1, was built in 1819 by Lord George Cavendish. The bawdy Londoners of those days threw rubbish over his garden wall, particularly oyster shells, so he built the arcade as a deterrent. Today you can leisurely browse through the antiques and bric-a-brac in the 38 shops housed in this ancient monument, which is protected by Her Majesty.

The arcade has been popular with Londoners for years. Author Mary Ann Evans—alias George Eliot—met the journalist George Lewes in Jeff's Bookshop, and they were lovers until he died in 1878. In his 1879 guide to London, Charles Dickens compared the arcade and its double row of shops to "a Parisian passage."

If you linger here until 5:30pm, you can watch the beadles (the last of London's top-hatted policemen and Britain's oldest police force) ceremoniously put in place the iron grilles that block off the arcade until 9am the next morning, when they just as ceremoniously remove them, marking the start of a new business day. Also at 5:30pm, a hand bell, called the Burlington Bell, is sounded, signaling the end of trading. Tube: Piccadilly Circus.

ESPECIALLY FOR KIDS

Children's Book Centre
237 Kensington High St., W8. ☎ **0171/937-7497.** Mon–Sat 9:30am–6:30pm, Tues to 6pm, Thurs to 7pm. Tube: High Street Kensington.

This is the best place to go for children's books—it has thousands of titles. Fiction is arranged according to age, up to the 14 or 16 age group. It also sells videos and toys for children.

Hamleys
188–196 Regent St., W1. ☎ **0171/734-3161.** Mon–Wed 10am–6:30pm, Thurs 10am–8pm, Fri 10am–7pm, Sat 9:30am–7pm, Sun noon–6pm. Tube: Oxford Circus.

This is an Ali Baba's cave of toys and games, with merchandise ranging from electronic games and Star Wars robots on the ground floor to toys for all age groups on other floors.

2 Shopping A to Z

ANTIQUES

Alfie's Antique Market
13–25 Church St., NW8. ☎ **0171/723-6066.** Tues–Sat 10am–6pm. Tube: Marylebone or Edgware Road.

This is the biggest and one of the best-stocked conglomerates of antiques dealers in London, all crammed into the premises of what was built before 1880 as a department store. Named after the father of the present owner—an antiques dealer in London's East End before the war—it contains more than 370 stalls, showrooms, and workshops scattered over 35,000 square feet of floorspace.

Antiquarius Antiques Centre
131–141 King's Rd., SW3. ☎ **0171/351-5353.** Mon–Sat 10am–6pm. Tube: Sloane Square.

Antiquarius echoes the artistic diversity of the street on which it is located. More than 150 stall holders offer specialized merchandise, such as antique and period jewelry, porcelain, silver, antique books, boxes, clocks, prints, and paintings, with an occasional piece of antique furniture. You'll also find a lot of art deco items.

Chelsea Antiques Market

245–253 King's Rd., SW3. ☎ **0171/352-1720.** Mon–Sat 10am–6pm. Tube: Sloane Square.

Sheltered in a rambling old building, this market offers endless browsing possibilities for the curio addict. About one-third of the market is given over to old or rare books. You're likely to run across Staffordshire dogs, shaving mugs, Edwardian buckles and clasps, ivory-handled razors, old velours and lace gowns, wooden tea caddies, antique pocket watches, wormy Tudoresque chests, silver snuffboxes, grandfather clocks, and jewelry of all periods.

Chenil Galleries

181–183 King's Rd., SW3. ☎ **0171/351-5353.** Mon–Sat 10am–6pm. Tube: Sloane Square or South Kensington.

Built in 1905 as studio and exhibition space for artists, this building has functioned since 1979 as the headquarters of about 30 different antiques dealers. Each focuses on a different style of art object, and some carry limited but carefully chosen carpets, porcelain, dolls, furniture, and paintings. Although it operates under the same management as the above-mentioned Antiquarius Antiques Centre, its ambience is calmer, quieter, slow paced, and deliberately genteel.

Grays and Grays

In the Mews Antique Markets, 58 Davies St. and 1–7 Davies Mews, W1. ☎ **0171/629-7034.** Mon–Fri 10am–6pm. Tube: Bond Street.

Just south of Oxford Street and opposite the Bond Street tube station, you'll find Grays and Grays in a triangle formed by Davies Street, South Molton Lane, and Davies Mews. The two old buildings have been converted into walk-in stands with independent dealers. The term "antique" here covers items from oil paintings to, say, the 1894 edition of the *Encyclopaedia Britannica*. Also sold here are exquisite antique jewelry, silver, gold, maps and prints, bronzes and ivories, arms and armor, Victorian and Edwardian toys, furniture, antique lace, scientific instruments, crafting tools, and Chinese, Persian, and Islamic pottery, porcelain, miniatures, and antiquities. There is an engraver and an exchange bureau, plus a café in each building.

Mall Antiques Arcade

At Camden Passage, Islington, N1. Tues, Thurs, Fri 10am–5pm, Wed 7:30am–5pm, Sat 9am–6pm. Tube: Angel.

Here you'll find one of Britain's greatest concentrations of antiques businesses. About 35 dealers, specializing in fine furniture, porcelain, and silver, are housed in individual shop units. There is no central phone.

ARTS & CRAFTS

On Sunday morning along Bayswater Road, pictures, collages, and craft items are hung on the railings along the edge of Hyde Park and Kensington Gardens—for more than a mile. If the weather is right, start at Marble Arch and walk and walk, shopping or just sightseeing as you go along. Along Piccadilly, you'll see much of the same thing by walking along the railings of Green Park on a Saturday afternoon.

Crafts Council

44A Pentonville Rd., Islington, N1. ☎ **0171/278-7700.** Tues–Sat 11am–6pm, Sun 2–6pm. Tube: Angel.

This is the national body for promoting contemporary crafts. Here you can discover some of today's most creative work at the Crafts Council Gallery, Britain's largest crafts gallery. There is also a shop selling craft objects and publications, a picture library, a reference library, and a café.

BOOKS

W.& G. Foyle Ltd.

113–119 Charing Cross Rd., WC2. ☎ **0171/439-8501.** Mon–Wed, Fri–Sat 9am–6pm, Thurs 9am–7pm. Tube: Tottenham Court Road.

Claiming to be the world's largest bookstore, W. & G. Foyle has an impressive array of hardcovers and paperbacks. The shop also sells travel maps, records, videotapes, and sheet music.

Hatchards Ltd.

187 Piccadilly, W1. ☎ **0171/439-9921.** Mon–Fri 9am–6pm, Sat 9:30am–6pm, and Sun 11am–5pm. Tube: Piccadilly Circus or Green Park.

On the south side of Piccadilly, Hatchards is one of the oldest and most famous bookshops in the world. It is a landmark for the tourist, a paradise for the browser and the book collector, and a British institution for account holders and mail-order customers throughout the world. In 1797 John Hatchard, having acquired 15 years' experience in the book trade, opened the store. Hatchards has traditionally served the royal families of Europe and is now one of only 12 establishments to hold all four royal warrants. Among early customers were Queen Charlotte, wife of George III, and Queen Adelaide, wife of William IV. It is filled with books ranging from popular fiction to specialized reference. There are shelves of guidebooks, atlases, cookbooks, paperbacks, plus puzzle books to occupy you on train and plane trips.

Stanfords

12–14 Long Acre, WC2. ☎ **0171/836-1321.** Mon–Sat 10am–6pm, Tues–Fri 9am–7pm. Tube: Leicester Square or Covent Garden.

Established in 1852, this is not only the world's largest map shop, but also the best travel-book store in London (naturally, it carries a complete selection of the Frommer guides, in case you're going on to another country after England).

BRASS RUBBING

London Brass Rubbing Centre

At St. Martin-in-the-Fields Church, Trafalgar Sq., WC2. ☎ **0171/930-9306.** Mon–Sat 10am–6pm, Sun noon–6pm. Tube: Charing Cross.

The center is in the big, brick-vaulted 1730s crypt, alongside the Café-in-the-Crypt, a bookshop, and an art gallery. The center has 88 exact copies of bronze portraits ready for use. Paper, rubbing materials, and instructions on how to begin are furnished, and classical music is played for visitors' enjoyment as they proceed. The charges range from £1.50 ($2.35) for a small copy to £11.50 ($18.15) for the largest, a life-size Crusader knight.

There is also a gift area, where you can buy brass-rubbing kits for children, budget-priced ready-made rubbings, Celtic jewelry, miniature brasses, medieval panels, and model knights. To make brass rubbings in countryside churches, you must obtain permission from the parish of your choice. Once you have received written permission, the center offers instructions and sells the necessary materials.

London Brass Rubbing Centre

At All Hallows by the Tower, Byward St., EC3. ☎ **0171/481-2928.** Mon–Fri 11am–4pm, Sat 11am–4pm, Sun 1–4pm. Tube: Tower Hill.

The brass-rubbing center at this fascinating church, next door to the Tower, has a crypt museum, Roman remains, and traces of early London, including a Saxon wall predating the Tower. Samuel Pepys, the famed diarist, climbed to the spire of this church to watch the raging fire of London in 1666. Material and instructions are supplied; the charges range from £1.50 ($2.35) to £11.50 ($18.15) for the largest.

CHINA

Thomas Goode

19 S. Audley St., W1. ☎ **0171/499-2823.** Mon–Sat 10am–6pm. Tube: Bond Street or Green Park.

Established in 1827, 10 years before Queen Victoria came to the throne, this is perhaps the most famous china and glass shop in the world, with three royal warrants; it has Minton majolica elephants gracing its front windows. The main entrance, with its famous mechanical doors, leads you to the china, glass, and silverware displayed in the 14 showrooms. A Thomas Goode catalog is available.

Lawleys

154 Regent St., W1. ☎ **0171/734-3184.** Mon, Wed, Fri 9:30am–6pm, Tues 10am–6pm, Thurs 9:30am–7pm. Tube: Piccadilly Circus or Oxford Circus.

A wide range of English bone china, as well as crystal and giftware, is sold here at this store which was founded in the 1930s. It maintains one of the largest inventories of porcelain in Britain, scattered over two floors of its large premises. The firm specializes in Royal Doulton, Minton, Royal Crown Derby, Wedgwood, and Aynsley china; Lladró figures; David Winter Cottages; Border Fine Arts; and other famous giftware ranges. They also sell cutlery.

The Glasshouse

21 St. Albans Place, N1. ☎ **0171/359-8162.** Tues–Fri 10am–6pm, Sat 11am–5pm. Tube: Angel.

Not only can visitors buy beautiful glass here, but they can also watch the craftspeople producing glass works of art in the workshop. Glass can be made to a shopper's own designs.

CHOCOLATE

Charbonnel et Walker Ltd.

1 Royal Arcade, 28 Old Bond St., W1. ☎ **0171/491-0939.** Mon–Fri 9:30am–5pm, Sat 10am–5pm. Tube: Green Park.

Here you'll find what may be the finest chocolate in the world. The staff of this bowfronted shop, on the corner of the Royal Arcade off Old Bond Street, will send messages spelled out on the chocolates themselves. The prices are determined by weight. Create your own box of candy or select one of their ready-made presentation boxes.

Prestat

14 Princes Arcade, SW1. ☎ **0171/629-4838.** Mon–Sat 9:30am–5:30pm. Tube: Piccadilly Circus.

Prestat is chocolate maker "to Her Majesty the Queen by appointment." Why not take home a box of assorted Napoléon truffles? Or a wide assortment of other flavors may tempt you: coffee-flavored chocolate, mint-flavored chocolate, or chocolate-coated brandy cherries. All boxes are elegantly gift wrapped.

CLOCKS

Strike One Islington Limited

48 Balcombe St., NW1. ☎ **0171/224-9719.** By appointment only. Tube: Baker Street.

This store sells clocks, music boxes, and barometers. Strike One clearly dates and prices each old clock—from Victorian dial clocks to early English long-case time-pieces—and every purchase is guaranteed worldwide for a year against faulty workmanship. Strike One specializes in Act of Parliament clocks. It also issues an illustrated catalog, which is mailed internationally to all serious clock collectors. On top of that, the firm undertakes to locate any clock a customer might request if no suitable example is in stock.

CONTEMPORARY ART

Berkeley Square Gallery

23A Bruton St., W1. ☎ **0171/493-7939.** Mon–Fri 10am–6pm, Sat 10am–2pm. Tube: Green Park.

Established in 1987 this busy gallery sells 19th- and 20th-century graphics by modern masters, including Francis Bacon, Matisse, Chagall, Picasso, Braque, David Hockney and sculpture by Lynn Chadwick. The gallery is considered innovative and creative even within the competitive world of London art galleries.

COVENT GARDEN ENTERPRISES

An impressive array of shops, pubs, and other attractions can be found in the Central Market Building at Covent Garden. For the shops listed below, take the tube, of course, to Covent Garden.

Apple Market

Covent Garden Piazza, WC2. ☎ **0171/836-9136.** Tues–Sat 10am–5pm. Antiques sold 7am–5pm (go early). Arts & Crafts sold alternate Sun 10am–5pm.

A fun, bustling place, the Apple Market almost qualifies as street entertainment and is filled with traders selling . . . well, everything. Much is what the English call "collectible nostalgia." You'll have to sift through some of the worthless items to find the genuinely worthy ones, such as brass door knockers. Be sure to keep your resistance up as you wander; some of the vendors are mighty persuasive.

Contemporary Applied Arts

43 Earlham St., WC2. ☎ **0171/836-6993.** Mon–Wed, Fri, Sat 10am–6pm, Thurs 10am–7pm.

This association of craftspeople encourages both traditional and progressive contemporary artwork. The galleries at the center house a diverse retail display that includes glass, ceramics, textiles, wood, furniture, jewelry, and metalwork all created by outstanding artisans currently producing in the country. There is also a program of special exhibitions that focuses on innovations in the crafts; these are solo or small-group shows from the membership. Many of Britain's best-established makers, as well as promising, lesser-known ones, are represented in this association.

Jubilee Market

Covent Garden Piazza, WC2. Mon–Sat 9am–5pm.

At this small open-air general market, antiques are sold on Monday, crafts on Saturday, and various other items on other days by dozens of independent dealers who arrive early to set up their stalls.

Naturally British

13 New Row (by Covent Garden), WC2. ☎ **0171/240-0551.** Mon–Sat 11am–7pm, Sun noon–5pm.

This shop has a traditional British ambience with old wooden floors and antique furniture. A wide range of English, Welsh, and Scottish goods is sold, including toys, clothes, ceramics, jewelry, and food. Many items can be made to order, including rocking horses, painted christening spoons, and furniture.

Neal Street East

5 Neal St., WC2. ☎ **0171/240-0135.** Mon–Wed 11am–7pm; Thurs–Sat 10am–7pm; Sun, bank holidays noon–6pm.

In this vast shop devoted to giftware from around the world, you can find dried and silk flowers, pottery, baskets, chinoiserie, toys, calligraphy, modern and antique clothing, textiles, and ethnic jewelry. There is also an extensive china and glass department and bookshop.

Neal's Yard

Off Neal St., WC2.

Behind the warehouse off Neal Street runs a narrow road leading to Neal's Yard, a mews of warehouses that retain some of the old London atmosphere. The open warehouses display vegetables, health foods, fresh-baked breads, cakes, sandwiches, and, in an immaculate dairy, the largest variety of flavored cream cheeses you are ever likely to encounter.

The Tea House

15A Neal St., WC2. ☎ **0171/240-7539.** Mon–Sat 10am–7pm, Sun, national holidays, noon–6pm.

This shop sells everything associated with tea, tea drinking, and teatime. It boasts more than 70 quality teas and tisanes, including whole-fruit blends, the best tea of China (gunpowder, jasmine with flowers), India (Assam leaf, choice Darjeeling), Japan (Genmaicha green), and Sri Lanka (pure Ceylon), plus such longtime favorite English blended teas as Earl Grey. The shop also offers novelty teapots and mugs, among other items.

DEPARTMENT STORES

Daks Simpson Piccadilly

203 Piccadilly, W1. ☎ **0171/734-2002.** Mon–Sat 9am–6pm. Tube: Piccadilly Circus.

Simpson Piccadilly, which opened in 1936 as the international home of DAKS clothing and accessories for men and women, also offers distinctive designer clothing from famous names suitable for every conceivable occasion. Simpson also offers jewelry from Christian Dior, cosmetics from Estee Lauder, chocolates by Leonidas, and a wide selection of gifts. The store has a good restaurant that offers traditional English food; an English breakfast is served from 10:15 to 11:30am; lunch from noon to 2:30pm; afternoon tea from 2:30 to 6:15pm; the Sushi Bar is open from noon to 2:30pm. For light meals, try the Gallery Wine Bar, overlooking Jermyn Street.

Harrods

87–135 Brompton Rd., Knightsbridge, SW1. ☎ **0171/730-1234.** Mon–Tues, Sat 10am–6pm, Wed–Friday 10am–7pm. Tube: Knightsbridge.

As firmly entrenched in English life as Buckingham Palace and the Ascot Races, Harrods is an elaborate emporium, at times as fascinating as a museum. In a magazine article about Harrods, a salesperson called it "more of a sort of way of life than a shop." The store underwent refurbishment to restore it to the elegance and luxury of the 1920s and '30s.

Aside from the fashion department (including high-level tailoring), you'll find such incongruous sections as a cathedral-ceilinged and arcaded meat market. Harrods has everything: men's custom-tailored suits, tweed overcoats, cashmere or lamb's-wool sweaters for both men and women, hand-stitched traveling bags, raincoats, mohair jackets, English porcelain such as Royal Doulton and Wedgwood, scarves of handwoven Irish wool, a perfumery department, "lifetime" leather suitcases, and pianos.

You have a choice of 16 restaurants and bars at Harrods. One of the highlights for visitors is the Food Halls. Harrods began as a grocer in 1849, and groceries are still the heart of the business. Among other offerings, Harrods has 500 different cheeses, 130 different types of bread, along with exotic fruits and vegetables, game, flowers, confectionery items, whatever. The motto might be: "If you can eat or drink it, you'll find it at Harrods." In the basement you'll find Harrods Bank, a theater-booking service, a Travel Bureau, and Harrods Shop with a range of souvenirs, including the famous green-and-gold tote bags.

The whole fifth floor is devoted to sports and leisure, with all of the equipment and costumes you need for participating in everything from tennis to polo, from horseback riding to angling. The Toy Kingdom is on the fourth floor, as well as the children's wear departments. The whole floor has everything a child could need, even hairdressing.

Liberty Public Limited Company
214–220 Regent St., W1. ☎ **0171/734-1234.** Mon, Tues, Fri, Sat 9:30am–6pm; Wed 10am–6pm; Thurs 9:30am–7:30pm. Tube: Oxford Circus.

Renowned worldwide for selling high-quality, stylish merchandise in charming surroundings, this chain has its flagship store on Regent Street, with six floors of fashion, fabrics, china, and home furnishings. The personal "corner shop" service is staffed with helpful and informed assistants. In addition to the famous Liberty Print fashion fabrics, furnishing fabrics, scarves, ties, luggage, and gifts, the shop sells well-designed high-quality merchandise from all over the world. The company also has branches around England, including one at Heathrow Airport Terminal 3.

Marks & Spencer
458 Oxford St., W1. ☎ **0171/935-7954.** Mon–Wed, Sat 9am–7pm, Thurs, Fri 9am–8pm. Tube: Marble Arch.

Situated 3 blocks from Marble Arch, Marks & Spencer is Britain's leading retailer. The store offers a wide variety of clothing for men, women, and children, along with many other items, including household furnishings. An extensive food section in the basement sells both basic and luxury items. Facilities and services for the tourist include tax-free shopping, an exchange bureau, and cash-dispensing machines on all floors that take all major credit cards, such as American Express, Visa, and MasterCard.

Peter Jones
Sloane Sq., SW1. ☎ **0171/730-3434.** Mon, Tues, Thurs, Fri, Sat 9:30am–6pm; Wed 9:30am–7pm. Tube: Sloane Square. Bus 11, 19, 22, 137, 211, 249, 319, 609, or C1.

Founded in 1877 and rebuilt in 1936, Peter Jones is well known for its fashions and for its household departments, including china, glass, perfumery, soft furnishings, and linens. The store also displays a constantly changing selection of antiques. On the ground floor you face an abundance of gift ideas, ranging from framed pictures to small objets d'art. The store also has a coffee shop and a first-class licensed restaurant, both offering extensive views over London rooftops.

Selfridges

400 Oxford St., W1. ☎ **0171/629-1234.** Mon–Wed, Fri, Sat 9:30am–7pm, Thurs 9:30am–8pm. Tube: Bond Street or Marble Arch.

Much more economical than Harrods, Selfridges is one of the biggest department stores in Europe, with more than 500 divisions, selling everything from artificial flowers to groceries. The specialty shops are particularly enticing, with good buys in Irish linen, Wedgwood, leather goods, silver-painted goblets, and cashmere and woolen scarves. There's also the Miss Selfridge Boutique for young women. To help you travel light, the Export Bureau will air-freight your purchases to anywhere in the world, completely tax free. In the basement Services Arcade, the London Tourist Board will help you find your way around London's sights with plenty of maps, tips, and advice.

FASHION

Austin Reed

103–113 Regent St., W1. ☎ **0171/734-6789.** Mon–Wed, Fri, Sat 9:30am–6pm, Thurs 9:30am–7pm. Tube: Piccadilly Circus.

Austin Reed is known for quality clothing. The suits of Chester Barrie, for example, are said to fit like bespoke (custom-tailored) models. The store always has a wide variety of top-notch jackets and suits, both from its own line as well as such designer names as Hugo Boss. Men can outfit themselves from dressing gowns to overcoats. The entire first floor is devoted to women's clothing, including carefully selected suits, separates, coats, shirts, knitwear, and accessories. There's an original 1930s art deco barber shop in the basement which still has a loyal following; call for an appointment.

Thomas Pink

85 Jermyn St., SW1. ☎ **0171/930-6364.** Mon–Fri 9:30am–6pm, Sat 9:30am–5:30pm. Tube: Green Park.

These Jermyn Street shirtmakers, named after an 18th-century Mayfair tailor, gave the world the expressions "Hunting pink" and "In the pink." They have an excellent reputation for well-made cotton shirts for both men and women. The shirts are made of the finest twofold pure cotton poplin, coming in a wide range of patterns, plain colors, stripes, or checks. Some patterns are classic; others are constantly changing with unusual designs. All are generously cut with extra-long tails and finished with a choice of double cuffs or single-button cuffs.

MEN'S FASHION

The selection of menswear in England is perhaps the finest in the world and ranges from Savile Row (at celestial prices) to bargain-basement wear. Your best buys are in ready-to-wear, not the superexpensive tailored clothing.

Aquascutum

100 Regent St., W1. ☎ **0171/734-6090.** Mon–Wed, Fri 9:30am–6pm, Thurs 9:30am–7pm, Sat 9:30am–6:30pm. Tube: Piccadilly Circus.

The popular *Time Out* said that this shop is "about as quintessentially British as you'll get this side of Savile Row, and it's a popular stop-off for American tourists wanting to look more British than the Brits." On four floors, the classic shop sells high-quality British and imported clothing for men and women who want the classic look. It also offers leisure wear. On the third floor is the Seasons Café.

Burtons West One

379 Oxford St. W1. ☎ **0171/495-6282.** Mon–Wed, Fri 10am–7pm, Thurs 10am–8pm, Sat 9am–6:30pm. Tube: Bond Street.

The new look in Burtons fashion is represented here at their flagship store. Incorporating "all lifestyles," its menswear ranges from casual to formal, with competitive prices.

Gieves & Hawkes

1 Savile Row, W1. ☎ **0171/434-2001.** Mon–Wed, Fri, Sat 9am–6pm, Thurs 9am–7pm. Tube: Piccadilly Circus or Green Park.

Despite Gieves & Hawkes's prestigious address on Savile Row and a list of clients that includes the Prince of Wales, the prices here are not the lethal tariffs of other stores along this street. It's expensive, but you get good quality, as befits its reputation as a supplier to the British Royal Navy since the days of Lord Nelson. Cotton shirts, silk ties, Shetland sweaters, and exceptional suits—both ready-to-wear and custom-made—are sold.

Harrods

87–135 Brompton Rd., Knightsbridge, SW1. ☎ **0171/730-1234.** Tube: Knightsbridge.

Harrods is a worthy choice for just about everything (see "Department Stores," above). Don't overlook its men's store, which has a large array of high-quality ready-to-wear suits and all the accessories, including shoes, knitwear, socks, shirts, and pajamas.

Hilditch & Key

37 and 73 Jermyn St., SW1. ☎ **0171/930-5336.** Mon–Sat 9:30–5:30pm. Tube: Green Park or Piccadilly Circus.

Perhaps the finest name in men's shirts, Hilditch & Key has been in business since 1899. There are two shops on this street, at no. 37 and no. 73. Hilditch also has an outstanding tie collection.

WOMEN'S FASHION

For raincoats, see Burberry's under "Raincoats," below, which also has a selection of other coats for women, along with scarves and handbags. For sporting wear, refer to Lillywhites under "Sporting Goods," below. Listed under "Department Stores," DAKS Simpson Piccadilly, once exclusively a men's store, now offers a variety of fashions for women. And of course, you must preview the fashions at the world's most famous department store, Harrods, listed above under "Department Stores." The following are a few suggestions, but of course there are hundreds of women's clothing stores in all parts of town.

Bradley's

85 Knightsbridge, SW1. ☎ **0171/235-2902.** Mon, Tues, Thurs, Fri 9:30am–6pm, Wed 9:30am–7pm, Sat 10am–6pm. Tube: Knightsbridge.

Bradley's is the best-known lingerie store in London. Even some members of the royal family shop here. Bradley's fits "all sizes" in silk, cotton, lace, polycotton, whatever. You'll love the fluffy slippers, and its satin or silk nightgowns will make you feel like Myrna Loy enticing William Powell in the old "Thin Man" flicks.

The Changing Room

10A Gees Court, St. Christopher's Place, W1. ☎ **0171/408-1596.** Mon–Wed, Fri, Sat 10:30am–6:30pm, Thurs 10:30am–7:30pm. Tube: Bond Street.

This small but well-staffed shop stocks the clothing and accessories of at least a dozen designers, including Betty Jackson, Issey Mikaye, Helen Story, and Ally Capellino. The establishment's expertise lies in its ability to coordinate items from different lines to create unique fashion statements for all types of women in all kinds of situations. It also sells scarves by Georgina von Etzdorf and clothing from a handful of other manufacturers you might or might not have heard about. The Changing Room maintains a second location near Covent Garden, at Thomas Neal's Warehouse, Shorts Gardens, WC2 (☎ 0171/379-4158).

Fenwick of Bond Street

63 New Bond St., W1. ☎ **0171/629-9161.** Mon–Sat 9:30am–6pm. Tube: Bond Street.

Fenwick is a stylish fashion store that offers an excellent collection of women's wear, ranging from moderately priced ready-to-wear items to designer fashions. A wide range of lingerie (in all price ranges) is also sold here. The store dates from 1891.

Hyper-Hyper

26–40 Kensington High St., W8. ☎ **0171/938-4343.** Mon–Wed, Fri, Sat 10am–6pm, Thurs 10am–7pm. Tube: High Street Kensington.

Showcasing young and talented British fashion designers since 1983, Hyper-Hyper displays the work of nearly 70 designers at all times. From sportswear to evening-wear, with plenty of accessories thrown in, including shoes, Hyper-Hyper will thrill and intrigue. Menswear is also sold here.

Laura Ashley

256–258 Regent St., W1. ☎ **0171/437-9760.** Mon–Tues 10am–6:30pm, Thurs 10am–8pm, Wed, Fri 10am–7pm., Sat 9:30am–7pm. Tube: Oxford Circus.

This is the main headquarters and largest branch of a company that taught the world about the aesthetics of the peaches-and-clotted-cream English country look. On its premises, you'll find flower-print Victorian dresses; easy-to-wear jersey and knitwear clothing for women; belts; handbags; furniture; curtains; and fabric-by-the-yard. This is one of more than 150 branches of what is now a worldwide company, still managed in part by members of the late Laura Ashley's family.

Pandora

16–22 Cheval Place, SW7. ☎ **0171/589-5289.** Mon–Sat 10am–6pm. Tube: Knightsbridge.

A London institution since it was first established in the 1940's, Pandora is located in fashionable Knightsbridge, a stone's throw from Harrods. The store carries dozens of hand-me-down designer dresses. Several times a week, chauffeurs drive up with bundles from the anonymous gentry of England that are likely to include dresses, jackets, suits, and gowns that fashionable women would like to sell. Entire generations of London women have clothed themselves at this store. One woman, voted best dressed at Ascot several years ago, was wearing a secondhand dress acquired at Pandora's. The identities of the owners are strictly guarded, but many buyers are thrilled with the thought of wearing a royal hand-me-down. Prices are generally one-third to one-half their retail value. Chanel, Anne Klein, and Valentino are among the designers represented. Outfits are no more than two seasons old.

CHILDREN'S FASHION

The best buys—in both quality and price—are generally found at the leading department stores.

Selfridges

400 Oxford St., W1. ☎ **0171/629-1234.** Mon–Wed, Fri, Sat 9:30am–7pm, Thurs to 8pm. Tube: Bond Street or Marble Arch.

Clothing for both babies and children can be found on the third floor. There's also a baby-changing area there.

FOOD

Fortnum & Mason Ltd.

181 Piccadilly, W1. ☎ **0171/734-8040.** Mon–Sat 9:30am–6pm. Tube: Piccadilly Circus or Green Park.

Fortnum & Mason is no mere grocery store—it has been a British tradition since 1707. Down the street from the Ritz, it draws the carriage trade, those from Mayfair or Belgravia who come seeking such tinned treasures as pâté de foie gras or boar's head. Today this store exemplifies the elegance and style one would expect from an establishment with two royal warrants. Enter the doors and be transported to another world of deep-red carpets, crystal chandeliers, spiraling wooden staircases, and unobtrusive, tailcoated assistants.

The grocery department is renowned for its impressive selection of the finest foods from around the world—the best champagne, the most scrumptious Belgian chocolates, and succulent Scottish smoked salmon. You might choose one of their wicker baskets of exclusive foods to have shipped home, perhaps through their telephone and mail-order service. You can wander through the other four floors and inspect the bone china and crystal cut glass, perhaps find the perfect present in the leather or stationery department, or reflect on the changing history of furniture, paintings, and ornaments in the antiques department. Dining choices include Patio & Buttery, St. James's Restaurant, and the Fountain Restaurant.

IRISH WARE

IRISH SHOP

14 King St., WC2. ☎ **0171/379-3625.** Mon–Sat 10am–7pm, Sun noon–6pm. Tube: Covent Garden.

For more than 25 years this small family business has been selling a wide variety of articles shipped directly from Ireland. The staff will be happy to welcome you and answer any questions on the selection of out-of-the-ordinary tweeds, traditional linens, hand-knit Aran fisher's sweaters, and Celtic jewelry. Merchandise includes Belleek and Royal Tara china, tapes of Irish music, souvenirs, and gift items. Waterford crystal in all styles and types is a specialty.

JEWELRY

Asprey & Company

165–169 New Bond Street, W1. ☎ **0171/493-6767.** Mon–Fri 9am–5:30pm, Sat 10am–5pm. Tube: Green Park.

It's as well-entrenched a name in luxury gift items as anything you're likely to find within Britain, with a clientele that includes the likes of the Sultan of Brunei and Queen Elizabeth. (Some of her jewelry comes from here.) Don't come with the idea of going slumming: There are about 14 different departments scattered over four floors of a dignified Victorian building whose decor was originally installed in 1841. The emporium itself dates from 1781. You'll find antiques, porcelain, leather goods, crystal, clocks, and enough unusual objects of dignified elegance to stock an English country house. Some of the jewelry sells for up to $8 million; a worthy selection of engagement rings cost around $5,000 each, and some utilitarian objects go for around £10 ($15.80) each. Looking for something for someone who has everything? Try a gilded toothbrush, an engraved swizzle stick, or any of a wide assortment of whiskey flasks.

Sanford Brothers Ltd.

3 Holborn Bars, Old Elizabeth Houses, EC1. ☎ **0171/405-2352.** Mon–Fri 10am–4:30pm. Tube: Chancery Lane.

A family firm, Sanford Brothers Ltd. has been in business since 1923. It sells all manner of jewelry, both modern and Victorian; silver of all kinds; and a fine selection of clocks and watches. The Old Elizabethan buildings that house the shop are among the sights of old London.

MAPS

Map House

54 Beauchamp Place, SW3. ☎ **0171/589-4325.** Mon–Fri 9:45am–5:45pm, Sat 10:30am–5pm. Tube: Knightsbridge.

An ideal place to find an offbeat souvenir of your visit to London, the Map House was established in 1907 at the height of the Edwardian Age. It sells antique maps and engravings, as well as items from a vast selection of old prints of London and England, both originals and reproductions. An original engraving, guaranteed to be more than a century old, can cost as little as £5 ($7.90), although some rare and/or historic items sell for an extravagant £50,000 ($79,000).

MUSIC

Virgin Megastore

14–16 Oxford St., W1. ☎ **0171/631-1234.** Mon, Wed–Sat 9:30am–8pm, Tues 10am–8pm, Sun noon–6pm. Tube: Tottenham Court Rd.

If a record's just been released—and if it's worth hearing in the first place—chances are this store carries it. It's like a giant "grocery store" of records, and you can hear the release on a headphone before making a purchase. Even the rock stars themselves come here on occasion to pick up new releases. A large selection of classical and jazz recordings is also sold. In between choosing your favorites, you can enjoy a coffee at the café or perhaps purchase a ticket from the Virgin Atlantic ticket office. Another Megastore is at 527 Oxford St., W1 (☎ 071/491-8582).

Tower Records

1 Piccadilly Circus, W1. ☎ **0171/439-2500.** Mon–Sat 9am–midnight, Sun noon–9:30pm. Tube: Piccadilly Circus.

Attracting throngs from a neighborhood whose pedestrian traffic is almost overwhelming, this store claims to be the largest tape, record, and CD store in Europe. Sprawling over four floors, it's practically a tourist attraction in its own right, an icon of the changes sweeping over the entertainment and information industries. In addition to copies of most of the musical expressions ever recorded, it inventories everything on the cutting edge of information technology, including interactive hardware and software for CD-ROM, computers, and laser disks. Its collection of books and periodicals includes most of Britain's magazines. There's also an impressive collection of travel guides and maps.

NOTIONS

Floris
89 Jermyn St., SW1. ☎ **0171/930-2885.** Mon–Fri 9:30am–5:30pm, Sat 10am–5pm. Tube: Piccadilly Circus.

A variety of toilet articles and fragrances is found in the floor-to-ceiling mahogany cabinets that line Floris's walls, considered architectural curiosities in their own right. The walls were installed relatively late in the establishment's history (that is, 1851), long after the shop had received its royal warrants as suppliers of toilet articles to the royal family. The business was established in 1730 by a Minorcan entrepreneur, Juan Floris, who brought from his Mediterranean home a technique for extracting fragrances from local flowers. Fashionable residents of St. James's flocked to the shop to purchase his soaps, perfumes, and grooming aids. Today, you can still buy essences of flowers grown in English gardens, including stephanotis, lily of the valley, and lavender.

Penhaligon's
41 Wellington St., WC2. ☎ **0171/836-2150.** Mon–Sat 10am–6pm. Tube: Covent Garden.

A Victorian perfumery established in 1870, Penhaligon's holds royal warrants to HRH the Duke of Edinburgh and HRH the Prince of Wales. It offers a large selection of perfumes, aftershaves, soaps, and bath oils for women and men, and the antique silver perfume bottles make perfect gifts.

PHILATELY

The Museum Shop
National Postal Museum, King Edward Building, King Edward St., EC1. ☎ **0171/239-5420.** Mon–Fri 9:30am–4:30pm. Tube: St. Paul's.

Previously described as a sightseeing attraction (see "Museums" in Chapter 6), this complex also houses The Museum Shop. On sale are postcards, NPM ties, a selection of model vehicles (including a 1950s clockwork toy van), and letter boxes, along with various publications, including *Postal Reform & The Penny Black: A New Appreciation.*

POSTERS

London Transport Museum Shop
Covent Garden, The Piazza, WC2. ☎ **0171/379-6344.** Daily 10am–6pm. Closed Christmas Day and December 26. Tube: Covent Garden.

This unique shop carries a wide selection of posters, books, cards, T-shirts, and other souvenir items. The London Underground maps can be purchased here, as well as massive pictorial posters as seen at tube stations.

RAINCOATS

Burberry's
18-22 Haymarket, SW1. ☎ **0171/930-3343.** Mon–Sat 10am–6pm, Thurs to 7pm. Tube: Piccadilly Circus.

The word *Burberry* has been synonymous with raincoats ever since King Edward VII publicly ordered his valet to "bring my Burberry" when the skies threatened rain. Its circa-1912 Haymarket store connects three lavishly stocked floors to an oak-lined staircase upon which have trod some of the biggest names in politics, the stage, and the screen. An impeccably trained staff sells the famous raincoat, along with a collection of excellent men's shirts, sportswear, knitwear, and accessories. Women's raincoats are also available. Don't think you'll find anything cheap at this world-famous retailer; you'll get prestige and quality. But sometimes there are sales.

SHOES

Charles Jourdan

39–43 Brompton Rd., SW3. ☎ **0171/581-3333.** Mon–Sat 10am–6:30pm. Tube: Knightsbridge.

Charles Jourdan, a France-based chain, offers a wide variety of men's and women's shoes in a store with more square footage than any other upscale shoe boutique in London. The inventory reflects sober good taste and style and includes designs by Lagerfeld and Michelle Perry for Jourdan. Also available are bags, handbags, and a boutique-style collection of clothing for men and women. Most of the merchandise is made in France, Italy, or Spain.

Church's

143 Brompton Rd., SW3. ☎ **0171/589-9136.** Mon–Sat 9am–7pm. Tube: Knightsbridge.

Well-made shoes, the status symbol of well-heeled executives in financial districts around the world, have been turned out by these famous shoemakers since 1873. Today, nicely outfitted English gents often prefer to stamp around London in their Church's shoes. These are said to be recognizable to every London maitre d'hotel, who have always been suspected of appraising the wealth of their clients by their footwear. Always a bastion of English tradition, Church's has gradually changed with the tides of style and now offers a limited selection of more modern designs along with traditional wing tips. There is also a fashionable selection of shoes for women. This branch, though not the largest in terms of floor space, probably has the largest inventory of the company's products of any store in the world. Incidentally, it is a few steps away from Harrods.

Lilley & Skinners

360 Oxford St., W1. ☎ **0171/629-6381.** Mon–Wed, Fri, Sat 10am–6:30pm, Thurs 10am–8pm. Tube: Bond Street.

Lilley & Skinners is the largest shoe store in Europe, displaying many different brands of shoes over three floors of showrooms staffed by an army of salespeople. It specializes in not particularly glamorous names and offers good value and a wide selection of difficult to find sizes.

Natural Shoe Store

21 Neal St., WC2. ☎ **0171/836-5254.** Mon, Tues, Sat 10am–6pm, Wed–Fri to 7pm, Sun noon–5:30pm. Tube: Covent Garden.

Shoes for both men and women are stocked in this shop, which also does shoe repairs. The selection includes all comfort and quality footwear—from Birkenstock to the best of the British classics.

SHOPPING MALLS

Whiteleys of Bayswater

Queensway, W2. ☎ **0171/229-8844.** Mon–Sat 10am–8pm, Sun noon–6pm. Tube: Bayswater or Queensway.

Once, this was a store that gave Harrods some competition, but it eventually went belly-up. It occupies its former premises in an Edwardian mall; the chief tenant here is a branch of Marks & Spencer, but there are also 70 to 80 other shops, mostly specialty outlets. On the top floor is an array of some 10 restaurants, cafés and bars. There's also an eight-screen movie theater.

SILVER

London Silver Vaults

Chancery Lane, WC2. ☎ **0171/242-5506.** Mon–Fri 9:30am–5:30pm, Sat 9:30am–12:30pm. Tube: Chancery Lane.

Established in 1882, these are the largest silver vaults in the world. You can shop in vault after vault for that special treasure.

SPORTING GOODS

Lillywhites Ltd.

24–36 Lower Regent St., Piccadilly Circus, SW1. ☎ **0171/915-4000.** Mon, Wed–Fri 9:30am–7pm; Saturday 9:30am–6pm. Tube: Piccadilly Circus.

Established in 1863, Lillywhites offers everything connected with sports, together with fashionable leisure wear for both men and women. This is Europe's biggest sports store and has floor after floor of sports clothing, equipment, and footwear.

STREET MARKETS

Street markets have played an important role in London, and I recommend them not only for bric-a-brac but also for a low-cost adventure. In fact, you don't have to buy a thing; but be warned—some of the stall keepers are mighty persistent. Here are the best ones:

BERWICK STREET MARKET   This may be the only street market in the world that is flanked by two rows of strip clubs, porno stores, and adult-movie dens; however, don't let that put you off. This array of stalls and booths sells probably the best and cheapest fruit and vegetables in town, as well as ancient records that may turn out to be collector's items, tapes, books, and old magazines. The market is open Monday through Saturday 8am to 5pm. Tube: Oxford Circus or Tottenham Court Road.

LEATHER LANE   At this lively market, open Monday through Saturday from 11am to 5pm, you'll find a nice variety of items for sale: fruit, vegetables, books, men's shirts and sweaters, and women's clothing. There are no try-ons at this outdoor market, so you have to inspect the size of the clothing carefully. Tube: Chancery Lane.

NEW CALEDONIAN MARKET   This is commonly known as the Bermondsey Market, owing to its location at Bermondsey Square, SE1, at the corner of Long Lane and Bermondsey Street; the extreme east end of the market is at Tower Bridge Road. This is one of Europe's outstanding street markets in size and quality of goods offered. The stalls are well known, and many dealers come into London from the country. The market is held on Friday from 7am until noon, and the most serious bargain hunters get here early; antiques plus other items are generally lower in price here than they are at Portobello Road and the other street markets, but bargains are gone by 9am. Tube: London Bridge, then bus 78 or walk down Bermondsey Street.

PETTICOAT LANE   On Sunday between 9am and 2pm (go before noon), throngs of shoppers join the crowds on Petticoat Lane (also known as Middlesex Street, E1), where you can buy inferior clothing, food, and plenty of junk. Despite the street's reputation, many readers have found that a Sunday morning trip here is no longer worth the effort. The area is surrounded by a maze of lanes that begin at the Liverpool Street Station on the Bishopsgate side. Tube: Liverpool Street, Aldgate, or Aldgate East.

PORTOBELLO ROAD MARKET   A magnet for collectors of virtually everything, Portobello Market, Portobello Road, W11, is mainly a Saturday happening from 6am (it's best to go early) to 5pm. The name came from Admiral Vernon's capture of a Caribbean city, Puerto Bello, in 1739. A farm once stood here, but by the 1860s a market had emerged. Once known mainly for fruit and vegetables (still sold, incidentally, throughout the week), Portobello in the past four decades became synonymous with antiques (but don't take the stall holder's word for it). You can also browse around for jewelry, weapons (modern and antique), toys, kitchenware, scientific instruments, china, books, movie posters, magazines long defunct, watches, pens, music boxes, whatever.

The market is divided into three major sections, including the most crowded, which is the southern antiques section, running between Colville Road and Chepstow Villas. The greatest concentration of pickpockets is in this area, so be duly warned. The second section (and the oldest part) is the "fruit and veg" market, which lies between Westway and Colville Road. In the third and final section, Londoners operate a flea market, selling bric-a-brac and lots of secondhand goods.

In addition to stalls, many permanent shops are located both on and off Portobello Road—mostly between Westway and Colville Road—and can be visited throughout the week. From many of the stores, the serious collector can pick up a copy of a helpful official guide, *Saturday Antique Market: Portobello Road & Westbourne Grove,* published by the Portobello Antique Dealers Association. It lists where to find what, ranging from music boxes to militaria, from lace to 19th-century photographs. The serious collector can visit any of the 90-odd antiques and art shops during the week when the temporary market is closed.

Many art galleries can also be found in and around the area, such as on Kensington Park Road, Blenheim Crescent, and in the fruit and vegetable section of Portobello Road. Tube: Ladbroke Grove or Notting Hill Gate.

TRAVEL CENTER

British Airways Travel Department Store
156 Regent St., W1. ☎ **0171/434-4700.** Mon–Fri 9:30am–6pm, Sat 10am–4:30pm. Tube: Piccadilly Circus or Oxford Circus.

The retail flagship of British Airways, housed on three floors, offers not only worldwide travel and ticketing, but also a wide range of services and shops—including a travel clinic for immunization and a drugstore selling first-aid kits and travel medication. There's also an exchange bureau, plus a passport and visa service, as well as a theater-booking desk. The ground floor offers luggage, guidebooks, maps, and other quality goods, plus travel accessories, and a coffee shop serving teas, coffee, and pastries. Other services include a change machine, photobooth, phones, toilets, public fax, and photocopying facilities. Passengers with hand baggage only can check in here for a BA flight.

WOOLENS

Berk

46 Burlington Arcade, W1. ☎ **0171/493-0028.** Mon–Fri 9am–5:30pm, Sat 9am–5pm. Tube: Piccadilly Circus.

Berk, the cashmere specialist, is one of those irresistible "fancy shops" for which London is famous. To shelter your precious cashmere from the elements, the shop also carries Burberry's raincoats, golf jackets and caps, and rain hats. All this is displayed in the Burlington Arcade, an attraction in its own right.

British Designer Knitwear Group

2–6 Quadrant Arcade, 80 Regent St., W1. ☎ **0171/439-4659.** Mon, Wed, Fri 10am–6pm; Thurs, Sat 10am–7pm. Tube: Piccadilly Circus.

For woolens from all over the British Islands, including the Shetlands in Scotland, this is one of the city's best-recommended outlets. It even offers Irish pullovers from the fog-shrouded Aran Islands. The woolens are handmade, and often, many of the designers are well known. Some of the woolens will make you look like the "tweedy" English, if that is your desire; others are higher fashion.

Scotch House

84–86 Regent St., W1. ☎ **0171/734-5966.** Mon–Wed 10am–6pm, Thurs 10am–7pm, Fri 10am–6:30pm, Sat 9am–6:30pm. Tube: Piccadilly Circus.

Scotch House is renowned for its comprehensive selection of top-quality cashmere and wool knitwear for both men and women. Also available is a wide range of tartan garments and accessories, as well as Scottish tweed classics. The children's collection covers ages 2 to 13 and also offers excellent value and quality.

Westaway & Westaway

Opposite the British Museum, 62–65 Great Russell St., WC1. ☎ **0171/405-4479.** Mon–Sat 9am–5:30pm, Sun 11am–6pm. Tube: Tottenham Court Road.

A visit here is a substitute for a shopping trip to Scotland. They stock an enormous range of kilts, scarves, waistcoats, capes, dressing gowns, and rugs in authentic clan tartans. What's more, they are knowledgeable about minutely intricate clan symbols. They also sell superb—and untartaned—cashmere, camel's hair, and Shetland knitwear, along with Harris tweed jackets, Burberry raincoats, and cashmere overcoats for men. Another branch is at 92–93 Great Russell St., WC1.

3 After Dark

Nowhere else but in London will you find a panorama of legitimate theaters, operas, concerts, nightclubs, folk-music cafés, and ballrooms—along with vaudeville at Victorian music halls, striptease joints, and gambling clubs. Your choices are countless—from the dives of Soho to the elegant jazz clubs—and so much depends on your taste, pocketbook, and even the time of year.

THE ENTERTAINMENT SCENE   About 90% of London's bright lights burn in the area roughly defined as the West End. The core of this region is Piccadilly Circus, with Coventry Street running down to Leicester Square. To the north lies Soho, chockablock with entertainment in various hues of scarlet. To the east is the theater land of Covent Garden, to the south Trafalgar Square, and to the west the fashionable and expensive night world of Mayfair.

INFORMATION   Ask a newsstand dealer for a copy of *Time Out* or *Where*, both of which contain listings of theaters and nightclubs.

THE PERFORMING ARTS
THEATER

In London, you'll have a chance to see the world-renowned English theater on its home ground. You may want to spend a classical evening at the National Theatre, catch up on that Broadway musical you missed in the United States, or scout out a new play—perhaps next year's big Stateside hit. Matinees are on Wednesday (Thursday at some theaters) and on Saturday. It's impossible to describe all of London's theaters in this space, so below are listed just a few from the treasure trove.

RESERVATIONS   Several evenings at the London theater are an essential part of a trip to Britain for many people. If you want to see specific shows—especially hit ones—purchase your tickets in advance. The most recommended method is to purchase your ticket from the theater's box office. Many theaters will accept bookings by telephone if you give your name and credit-card number when you call; then all you have to do is go to the theater before the performance to collect your tickets, which will be sold at the theater price. If you don't show up they charge your account anyway. A few theaters will even reserve tickets for the gallery—the cheapest seats.

TICKET AGENTS   You can also make theater reservations through ticket agents. Before going through a ticket agent, it's wise to call the theater directly to see if any tickets are available at the regular price. In the case of hit shows, only brokers may be able to get you a seat, but you'll pay for the privilege.

Under a British voluntary code, ticket brokers should disclose the face value of a ticket as well as their fee. But since the requirement is voluntary, many brokers don't bother to disclose this information. Their markup is usually 20% to 25%, but spot checks in London have revealed markups as high as 80% of the face value of the ticket.

With offices in London and the United States, Keith Prowse/First Call can reserve tickets for hit shows weeks or even months in advance. In the United States, contact them at Suite 1000, 234 W. 44th St. New York, NY 10036 (☎ 212/398-1430 or toll free 800/669-8687). In London their number is 0171/836-9001. The fee for booking a ticket in the USA is 28%; in London, it's 20% to 25%.

One of the most reliable ticket agents is British Airways, which has some of the best seats available for London productions (including musicals), Stratford-upon-Avon, and the Edinburgh Festival. The reservation service is only available to BA customers. For information and reservations, call toll free 800/AIRWAYS in the United States or Canada.

Visitors interested in ordering theater tickets days, weeks, or months in advance can contact Edwards & Edwards at the Palace Theatre, Shaftesbury Avenue, W1A 4EU (☎ 0171/734-4555), or at 12 Lower Regent St., SW1 (☎ 0171/839-3952). Tickets to almost anything in London can be arranged in advance by telephone (a personal visit is seldom necessary). Tickets will be mailed or delivered to the box office of any particular theater, usually after imposing a service charge of about 10% to 20%.

Some North Americans prefer to order tickets for London plays through Edwards & Edwards's New York office, 1 Times Square Plaza, New York, NY

Major Concert & Performance Halls

The following is a quick-reference list of major performance spaces in London, with box office telephone numbers. Details are provided in the listings below.

Barbican Centre (☎ 0171/638-8891)
London Coliseum (☎ 0171/632-8300)
London Palladium (☎ 0171/494-5100)
Royal Albert Hall (☎ 0171/589-8212)
Royal National Theatre (☎ 0171/928-2252)
Royal Opera House (☎ 0171/240-1200)
South Bank Centre, including Royal Festival Hall (☎ 0171/928-8800)

10036 (☎ 212/944-0290 in New York City or toll free 800/223-6108 from elsewhere in the U.S.). In some cases, if they're available, tickets to certain London theaters can be preordered using a credit card. A service charge is added to the final bill.

GALLERY & DISCOUNT TICKETS   London theater tickets are priced quite reasonably when compared with those in the United States. Prices vary greatly depending on the seat—from £8.50 to £35 ($12.80 to $52.50). Sometimes gallery seats (the cheapest) are sold only on the day of the performance, so you'll have to head to the box office early in the day and return an hour before the performance to queue up, since they're not reserved seats.

Discounted tickets are sometimes offered—but usually not to long-running plays on their last legs or to new "dogs," which you may not want to see anyway. Reduced tickets are more likely to be available for matinees—Wednesday or Thursday and Saturday. A really hot musical—or "bomb" to the Brits—in its early life almost never offers discounted tickets.

Warning: Beware of scalpers who hang out in front of theaters with hit shows. There are many reports of scalpers selling forged tickets, and their prices are outrageous.

Old Vic
Waterloo Rd., SE1. ☎ **0171/928-2651** or 0171/928-7616 (box office). Plays, £6–£20 ($9.50–$31.60); musicals, £9–£22 ($14.20–$34.80). Tube: Waterloo.

The old Vic is a 175-year-old theater whose facade and much of the interior have been restored to their original early 19th-century style, but most of the modernization is behind the scenes. The proscenium arch has been moved back, the stage has tripled in size, and more seats and stage boxes have been added. Fully air-conditioned and equipped with three bars, it presents short seasons of varied plays, and several subscription offerings have been introduced.

Open Air
Inner Circle, Regent's Park, NW1. ☎ **0171/486-2431.** Tickets £7.50–£17.50 ($11.85–$27.65). May 26–Sept 10, daily at 8pm, plus Wed, Thurs, Sat 2:30pm. Tube: Baker Street.

This outdoor theater is right in the center of Regent's Park. The setting is idyllic, and the longest theater bar in London provides both food and drink. Presentations are mainly Shakespeare, usually in period costume, and both seating and acoustics are excellent. If it rains, you're given tickets for another performance.

Royal Court Theatre

Sloane Sq., SW1. ☎ **0171/730-1745.** Tickets, Mon (all seats), £5 ($7.90); Tues–Sat, £5–£18 ($7.90–$28.45), Sat matinees, 5–£15 ($7.90–$23.70) downstairs. Mon–Sat 7:30pm, plus Sat 3:30pm. Tube: Sloane Square.

The English Stage Company has operated this theater for more than 40 years, with an emphasis on new playwrights. John Osborne got his start here with the 1956 production of *Look Back in Anger.* Also on the premises is Theatre Upstairs, a studio theater devoted to new and experimental works.

Royal National Theatre

South Bank, SE1. ☎ **0171/928-2252.** Tickets, £8.50–£22 ($13.40–$34.80); midweek matinees, Saturday matinees, and previews cheaper. Mon–Sat 10am–11pm. Tube: Waterloo, Embankment, or Charing Cross.

Occupying a prime site on the South Bank of the River Thames is the flagship of British theater, the Royal National Theatre. Winner of more than 200 top drama awards since its opening in 1976, and home to one of the world's greatest stage companies, the National houses not one but three theaters. The largest, named after Lord Laurence Olivier, is the Olivier, with 1,200 seats and a style reminiscent of the Greek amphitheater with its fan-shaped open stage. The more traditional proscenium-arch auditorium, the Lyttelton, seats 900 people, while the Cottesloe is a small box-shaped studio theater with flexible seating and staging, with space for up to 400 people. Across its three stages the National presents a repertoire of the finest in world theater from classic drama to award-winning new plays, and from comedy to musicals to shows for young people.

The National is also a full-time theater center which is open to everyone, with or without a ticket. The National features three bookshops, free foyer exhibitions and live music, backstage tours, short early evening events when theater professionals discuss their work, two restaurants, seven bars, a coffee bar, and three buffets, plus riverside walks and terraces.

Royal Shakespeare Company (RSC)

Barbican Centre, Silk St., Barbican, EC2. ☎ **0171/638-8891** (box office). Barbican Theatre, £7–£24 ($11.10–$37.90); The Pit, £12–£15 ($19–$23.70) matinees, £15–£16 ($23.70–$25.30) evening performances. Tube: Barbican or Moorgate.

One of the world's finest theater companies is based in Stratford-upon-Avon and here at the Barbican Centre. The central core of the company's work remains the plays of William Shakespeare, but it also presents a wide-ranging program of three different productions each week in the Barbican Theatre—the 1,200-seat main auditorium, which has excellent sight lines throughout, thanks to a raked orchestra—and the Pit, the small studio space where much of the company's new writing is presented.

In recent years, the RSC has had great success in transferring its hit shows, such as *Les Misérables* and *Les Liaisons Dangereuses,* to West End theaters, while continuing its diverse repertoire both in London and Stratford.

Sadler's Wells Theatre

Rosebery Ave., EC1. ☎ **0171/278-8916.** Tickets, £5–£40 ($7.90–$63.20). Tube: Angel.

A theater has stood here since 1683, on the site of a well that was once known for the healing powers of its waters. Once the home of the famed Sadler's Wells Ballet, which moved to Covent Garden to become the Royal Ballet, the theater today is a showcase for British and foreign modern ballet and modern dance

Central London Theaters

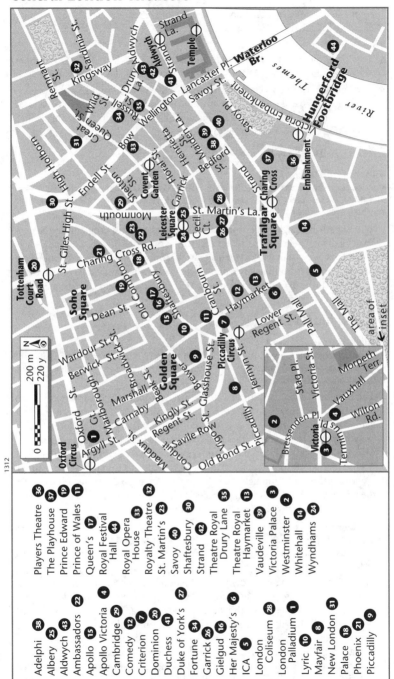

Tube Station ⊖

companies and international opera. The box office sells tickets Monday through Saturday from 10am to 8:30pm.

Young Vic

66 The Cut, Waterloo, SE1. ☎ **0171/928-6363.** Tickets, £8–£18 ($12.65–$28.45) adults, £5–£6.50 ($7.90–$10.25) students and children. Performances 7:30pm. Tube: Waterloo.

The Young Vic presents classical and modern plays in the round for theatergoers of all ages and backgrounds, with an emphasis on attracting young people aged 16 to 25. Recent productions have included Shakespeare, Ibsen, Arthur Miller, and specially commissioned plays for young people.

GILBERT AND SULLIVAN

Gilbert and Sullivan Evenings

Mansion House at Grim's Dyke, Old Redding, Harrow Weald, Middlesex HA3 6SH. ☎ **0181/ 954-4227.** Tickets £36 ($56.90) per person including dinner. Every other Sunday at 8pm in winter; each Sunday at 8pm rest of the year.

The English Heritage Singers present Gilbert and Sullivan programs in the context of a dinner event. You arrive for cocktails in the Library Bar of the house where Gilbert once lived and worked on his charming operettas. Sullivan once visited the premises. A full Edwardian-style dinner is served, with costumed performances of the most beloved of Gilbert and Sullivan songs both during and after the meal. You can request your favorite G&S melodies.

OPERA & BALLET

English National Opera

London Coliseum, St. Martin's Lane, WC2. ☎ **0171/632-8300** for reservations. Tickets, £8–£12 ($12.65–$18.95) balcony, £10–£48 ($15.80–$75.85) upper dress circle or stalls. Tube: Charing Cross or Leicester Square.

The London Coliseum, built in 1904 as a variety theater and converted into an opera house in 1968, is London's largest and most splendid theater. The English National Opera is one of the two national opera companies and performs a wide range of works, from great classics to Gilbert and Sullivan to new and experimental works, staged with flair and imagination, and with every performance in English. A repertory of 18 to 20 productions is presented 5 or 6 nights a week for 11 months of the year. Although the balcony seats are cheaper, many visitors prefer the Upper Circle or Dress Circle. About 100 discount balcony tickets are sold on the day of performance from 10am during the opera season (Aug–June).

Royal Opera House

Bow St., WC2 (Box Office, 48 Floral St., WC2). ☎ **0171/304-4000.** Tickets, £2–£64 ($3.15–$101.10) ballet, £4–£133 ($6.30–$210.10) opera. Mon-Sat 10am to 8pm. Tube: Covent Garden.

This classical building is on the northeast corner of Covent Garden, which was London's first square, laid out by Inigo Jones as a residential piazza. Until a few years ago the whole area was a thriving fruit and vegetable market, originally started by nuns selling surplus stocks from their convent garden. In the 16th century the section became fashionable to live in, and soon became one of the centers of London nightlife. The first theater was built on the present site in 1732. The existing opera house, one of the most beautiful theaters in Europe, was constructed in 1858 and is now the home of The Royal Opera and The Royal Ballet, leading international companies. Newspapers give full details of performances.

CONCERT & MULTIPURPOSE HALLS

Barbican Centre

Silk St., The Barbican, EC2. ☎ **0171/638-8891**. Tickets, £6–£30 ($9.50–$47.40). Daily 9am–8pm. Tube: Barbican or Moorgate.

Considered the largest art and exhibition center in western Europe, the Barbican was created to make a perfect setting in which to enjoy good music and theater from comfortable, roomy seats. The theater is the London home of the Royal Shakespeare Company (see description above), and the Concert Hall is the permanent home of the London Symphony Orchestra and host to visiting orchestras and performers.

In addition to the hall and theater, the Barbican Centre has The Pit, a studio theater; Barbican Art Gallery, a showcase for the visual arts; the Concourse Gallery and foyer exhibition spaces; Cinemas One and Two, which show recently released mainstream films; Barbican Library, a general lending library that also places a strong emphasis on the arts; a Conservatory, one of London's largest plant houses; and three restaurants as well as bars.

Kenwood Lakeside Concerts

Kenwood, Hampstead Heath. ☎ **0181/348-1286**. Tickets, £10–£15 ($15.80–$23.70) adults; £8–£12 ($12.65–$18.95) for students and over 60. Every summer Saturday at 7:30pm mid-June to early September. Tube: Golders Green or Archway, then bus no. 210

On the north side of Hampstead Heath, these concerts have been a British tradition for some 50 years. Laser shows and firework displays enliven an otherwise dignified cultural scene. Music drifts across the lake from the performance bandshell.

London Palladium

Argyll St., W1. ☎ **0171/494-5100**. Tickets range from £10–£30 ($15.80–$47.40), depending on show. Closed Sunday. Tube: Oxford Circus.

It's hard to encapsulate the prestige of this show-business legend in a paragraph. Performers from Britain, Europe, and America consider that they have "arrived" when they've appeared here. The highlight of the season is the Royal Command Performance, held before the queen, which includes an introduction of the artists to Her Majesty.

In days of yore, the Palladium has starred Frank Sinatra, Shirley MacLaine, Andy Williams, Perry Como, Julie Andrews, Tom Jones, Sammy Davis, Jr., and so on.

Royal Albert Hall

Kensington Gore, SW7. ☎ **0171/589-8212**. Tickets, £8–£120 ($12.65–$189.60), depending on the event. Tube: South Kensington, Kensington High Street or Knightsbridge.

Opened in 1871 and dedicated to the memory of Queen Victoria's consort, Prince Albert, this building encircles one of the world's most famous auditoriums with a seating capacity of 5,200. Since 1941, the hall has been the setting for the BBC Henry Wood Promenade Concerts ("The Proms"), a concert series that lasts for eight weeks between mid-July and mid-September. (The Proms has been a British tradition since 1895.) Although most of the audience occupies reserved seats, true aficionados usually opt for standing room in the orchestra pit for close-up views of the musicians performing on stage. The programs are considered outstanding, and often present newly commissioned works for the first time. The last night of The Proms is the most traditional, as such rousing favorites as "Jerusalem" or

"Land of Hope and Glory" echo through the hall. For tickets call Ticketmaster at 0171/379-4444 instead of Royal Albert Hall directly. Sporting events such as boxing also figure strongly here. For Royal Albert Hall 24-hour events information, call 01891/500292, a service updated daily. Ticket availability is also given. Rates for calling this number range from 36p to 48p (60¢ to 80¢) a minute.

South Bank Centre, Royal Festival Hall

At South Bank, SE1. ☎ **0171/928-8800.** Tickets, £5–£35 ($7.90–$55.30); credit cards accepted (AE, DC, MC, V). Box office 10am to 9pm. Tube: Waterloo or Embankment.

In the aftermath of World War II, London's musical focus shifted to a uniquely specialized complex of buildings that were erected between 1951 and 1964 on the site of a bombed-out 18th-century brewery. Out of the industrial wastelands on the rarely visited south side of the Thames, across Waterloo Bridge from more glamorous neighborhoods of London, rose three of the most comfortable and acoustically perfect concert halls in the world. They include Royal Festival Hall, Queen Elizabeth Hall, and the Purcell Room. Within their precincts, more than 1,200 performances a year are presented, including classical music, ballet, jazz, popular classics, pop and contemporary dance. The center also accommodates the internationally famous Hayward Gallery whose exhibitions include both contemporary and historical art. Recent exhibitions have included Andy Warhol, Renoir, Jasper Johns, Leonardo da Vinci, Le Corbusier, and Salvador Dali.

The Royal Festival Hall is open from 10am every day and offers an extensive range of things to see and do. There are free exhibitions in the foyers and free lunchtime music from 12:30pm. The Poetry Library is open from 11am to 8pm, as well as shops that provide a wide selection of books, records, and crafts.

The Festival Buffet offers a wide variety of food at reasonable prices, and there are numerous bars throughout the foyers. The People's Palace offers lunch and dinner and offers a spectacular view of the Thames. Reservations are recommended by calling 0171/921-0800.

Wigmore Hall

36 Wigmore St., W1. ☎ **0171/935-2141.** £4–£35 ($6.30–$55.30). Tube: Bond Street or Oxford Circus.

An intimate auditorium, Wigmore Hall is where you'll hear excellent recitals and concerts. There are regular series of song recitals, piano, and chamber music, along with early music and baroque concerts. A free list of the month's programs is available from the hall. Performances are given nightly, plus Sunday Morning Coffee Concerts and additional concerts on Sunday at 4 or 7pm.

THE CLUB & MUSIC SCENE

Midnight divides the world of bright lights like a curtain. This "midnight curtain" prevents you from just dropping into a place for a nightcap—you must order something to eat when you have an alcoholic drink after 11pm. The midnight curtain doesn't exempt you from a cover charge—frequently disguised as a membership fee. After hours, you can still enjoy a stage show, take a spin on the dance floor, and try your luck at a gaming table. And you can devour a five-course meal while drinking yourself into oblivion.

About this front-door mumbo jumbo that passes as membership enrollment: what it amounts to is so-called temporary membership, which satisfies the letter—if not the spirit—of the law and allows you to get in without delay. In many cases, the temporary membership is deducted from the cost of dinner, but there is no hard-and-fast rule.

At this point, I'd better add a word for the benefit of male travelers. London's club world is full of "hostesses." These ladies intend to get you to buy things—from drinks to dolls to cigarettes—which can shoot up your tab far beyond what you budgeted to spend. Recognized meeting places for the young—like discos and ballrooms—do not employ hostesses.

NIGHTCLUBS & CABARETS

Camden Palace

1A Camden High St., NW1. ☎ **0171/387-0428.** Cover £4 ($6.30) Tues–Wed, £10 ($15.80) Fri–Sat. Tues, Wed 9pm–2:30am, Fri 9pm–4am, Sat 9pm–6am. Closed Mon, Thurs, Sun. Tube: Camden Town or Mornington Crescent.

Camden Palace is housed inside what was originally a theater built around 1910. It draws an over-18 crowd who flock there in various costumes and energy levels according to the night of the week. Since it offers a rotating style of music, it's best to phone in advance to see if that evening's musical genre appeals to your taste. Styles range from rhythm and blues to what young rock experts call "boilerhouse," "garage music," "acid funk," "hip-hop," and "twist & shout." A live band performs only on Tuesday. There's a restaurant if you get the munchies, and a pint of lager goes for £2.40 ($3.80).

The Green Room at the Cafe Royal

68 Regent St., W1. ☎ **0171/437-9090.** £48 ($75.85) 3-course dinner without wine; £20 ($31.60) cover charge for show without dinner. Reservations are important. Drinks £4 ($6.30) each. Dinner 7pm Tues–Sat, followed by 60- to 90-minute show beginning at 9:15 or 9:30pm. Tube: Piccadilly Circus.

Although it's a relative newcomer to London's nightlife scene, this cabaret has already become a much-talked-about force among world-class entertainers and their fans. Set one floor above street level, in a sober and modern function room poised amid the gilded and frescoed premises of the Café Royal, the establishment offers a changing cast of such entertainers as Helen Shapiro, Barbara Dickson, Buddy Greco, and Blossom Deary. Many visitors opt for dinner before the show begins; others arrive just for the entertainment.

L'Hirondelle

99–101 Regent St., W1. ☎ **0171/734-6666.** £10 ($15.80) cover charge for nondiners, plus £5 ($7.90) cover charge added to first drink. Three-course dinner £32.50 ($51.35) Mon–Sat 8:30pm–3:30am. Tube: Piccadilly Circus.

L'Hirondelle stands in the heart of the West End and puts on some of the most lavish floor shows in town. What's more, you can dine, drink, and dance without taking out a "temporary membership." Neither is there an entrance fee. The shows are really full-scale revues and go on at 11pm and 1am. Dancing to one of the few live bands in London is from 10pm. Dancing-dining partners are available.

Tiddy Dols

55 Shepherd Market, Mayfair, W1. ☎ **0171/499-2357.** Dinner £19.95 ($29.90), includes cover charge. Café/wine bar open Mon–Sat noon–midnight, Sun noon–11pm. Tube: Green Park.

Housed in nine small atmospheric Georgian houses that were built around 1741, Tiddy Dols is named after the famous gingerbread baker and eccentric. Guests come to Tiddy Dols to enjoy such dishes as jugged hare, cock-a-leekie, plum pudding, and the original gingerbread of Tiddy Dol. While dining, they are entertained with madrigals, Noël Coward, Gilbert and Sullivan music, and music-hall songs. In summer, there is a large pavement café with parasols and a view of the "village" of Shepherd Market; in winter there are open fires. Dancing is restricted to special evenings.

COMEDY CLUB

The Comedy Store

Coventry St. and Oxendon, off Piccadilly Circus, SW1. ☎ **01426/914433** for a recorded message. Cover £8 ($12.60) Mon–Fri; £10 ($15.80) Sat; £9 ($14.20) Sun. Shows Sun–Thurs 8pm, Fri, Sat 8pm and midnight. Tube: Leicester Square or Piccadilly Circus.

This is London's most visible showcase for both established and emerging comic talent, set in the heart of the city's nighttime district. Even if the performers are unfamiliar to you, you will still enjoy the spontaneity of live British comedy. Visitors must be over 18 years of age. There is no particular dress code at this place, and many clients wear jeans. Reservations are accepted through Ticketmaster at 0171/344-4444, and the club opens 1½ hours before each show.

ROCK

Marquee

105 Charing Cross Rd., WC2. ☎ **0171/437-6603.** Cover £5–£10 ($7.90–$15.80), depending on the performer. Sun, Mon, Wed 7–11pm; Tues, Thurs 7–10:15pm, 11pm–3am; Fri 7–10:15pm, 11pm–4am; Sat 7–10:15pm, 11pm–6am. Tube: Leicester Square or Tottenham Court Road.

Marquee is considered one of the best-known centers for rock in the world. Its reputation goes back to the 1950s and another location, but it remains forever young, in touch with the sounds of the future. Famous groups such as the Rolling Stones played at the Marquee long before their names spread beyond the shores of England. You don't have to be a member—you just pay at the door. Live bands perform daily from 7pm to midnight. Many well-known musicians frequent the place regularly on their nights off. The club occupies a building that was once a cinema.

The Rock Garden

6–7 The Piazza, Covent Garden, WC2. ☎ **0171/836-4052.** The Venue, Cover £5 ($7.90); diners enter free. Venue open Mon–Fri 8pm–3am, Sat 4–10pm, Sun 7:30pm–midnight. Tube: Covent Garden; night buses from neighboring Trafalgar Square.

Long-established as a site for the presentation of a wide array of electronic and rock-and-roll bands, this establishment maintains a bar and a stage in the cellar and a restaurant on the street level. The cellar area, known as The Venue, has hosted such names as Dire Straits, Police, and U2 before they became more famous (and more expensive). Today, acts vary widely, incorporating the up-and-coming rock-related talents to Europe as well as, quite simply, some bands you might never hear from ever again. In the restaurant, meals, costing from £12 ($19), include T-bone steaks, chili, salads, and hamburgers. The restaurant is open Monday through Thursday and on Sunday from noon to midnight and on Friday and Saturday from noon to 1am.

JAZZ & BLUES

The Blue Note

1 Hoxton Sq., N1. ☎ **0171/729-2476.** Cover £4–£10 ($6.30–$15.80). Club Mon–Sat 10pm–3am, Sun 1pm–midnight. Drinks from £3 ($4.75). Tube: Old St.

Formerly operating under the name "The Bass Clef," this club is located in a brick-fronted building that functioned as an important hospital in the early 20th century. It presents performances that range from traditional jazz, such as the music of Jessica Williams, all the way to contemporary hip-hop and funk. There is a restaurant on the premises serving café-style fare with meals priced at from £5 ($7.90) each. Open: Restaurant daily noon–11pm. Call for show times.

The Bull's Head

373 Lonsdale Rd., Barnes, SW13. ☎ **0181/876-5241.** Cover £2–£8 ($3.15–$12.65). Mon–Sat 11am–11pm; Sun noon–10:30pm. Tube to Hammersmith, then bus 9A to Barnes Bridge, then retrace the path of the bus for some 200 yards on foot; or take Hounslow Look train from Waterloo Station and get off at Barnes Bridge Station, then walk 5 minutes to club.

The Bull's Head has presented live modern jazz concerts every night of the week for more than 30 years. One of the oldest hostelries in the area, it was a staging post in the mid-19th century where travelers on their way to Hampton Court and beyond could eat, drink, and rest while the coach horses were changed. Today the place is known for its jazz, performed by musicians from all over the world. Jazz concerts are presented on Sunday from noon to 10:30pm. Monday through Saturday, you can hear music from 8 to 11pm. You can order food at the Carvery in the Saloon Bar daily or dine in the 17th-century Stable Restaurant. Main dishes in the Carvery cost £3.50 ($5.55). In the restored stables, the cook specializes in steak, fish, and other traditional fare; meals cost £8 ($12.65) and up. Food hours in the Carvery are lunch only, served daily from noon to 3pm; whereas the Stable serves daily from 7pm till around midnight. Wine by the glass costs from £1.75 ($2.75).

100 Club

100 Oxford St., W1. ☎ **0171/636-0933.** Cover Fri £7 ($11.05) for everybody; Sat £7 ($11.05) members, £8 ($12.65) nonmembers; Sun £5 ($7.90) members, £6 ($9.50) non-members. Mon, Fri 8:30pm–3am, Sat 7:30pm–1am, Sun 7:30–11:30pm. Tube: Tottenham Court Road or Oxford Circus.

Although less plush and cheaper, the 100 Club is considered a serious rival of the above among many dedicated jazz gourmets. Its cavalcade of bands includes the best British jazz musicians, as well as many touring Americans. Drinks start at £1.80 ($2.85).

Pizza Express

10 Dean St., W1. ☎ **0171/437-9595.** Cover £6–£9 ($9.50–$14.20). Mon–Sat 8:30pm–1am; Sun noon–midnight. Tube: Tottenham Court Road.

Although this seems an unlikely venue for a night club, it offers some of the best jazz in London. While enjoying a thin-crust Italian pizza (the ordering of food is compulsory), you can hear either the local band or a hot group that's visiting, often from the U.S. Darkly lit, the club has cool jazz and hot food from the pizza oven. Sometimes it's important to reserve, as this place fills up quickly.

Ronnie Scott's

47 Frith St., W1. ☎ **0171/439-0747.** Cover Mon–Thurs £12 ($18.95); Fri–Sat £14 ($22.10). Mon–Sat 8:30pm–3am. Tube: Tottenham Court Road or Leicester Square.

Mention the word "jazz" in London and people immediately think of Ronnie Scott's, long the citadel of modern jazz in Europe where the best English and American groups are booked. Featured on almost every bill is an American band, often with a top-notch singer. It's in the heart of Soho, a 10-minute walk from Piccadilly Circus via Shaftesbury Avenue, and worth an entire evening. Not only can you saturate yourself in the best of jazz, you get reasonably priced drinks and dinners as well. There are three separate areas: the Main Room, the Upstairs Room, and the Downstairs Bar. You don't have to be a member, although you can join if you wish. If you have a student ID you are granted entrance Monday through Thursday for £7 ($11.05). In the Main Room you can either stand at the bar to watch the show or sit at a table, where you can order dinner. The Downstairs Bar is more intimate, a quiet rendezvous where you can meet and talk with the regulars, often some of the world's most talented musicians. The Upstairs Room is separate and it has a disco called the Club Latino. Drinks begin at £2.10 ($3.30); a half pint of beer, £1.10 ($1.75).

DANCE CLUBS & DISCOS

Diva 2

43 Thurloe St., SW7. ☎ **0171/584-2000.** No cover. Tube: Kensington.

This place combines a first-class Italian restaurant with a carefully controlled disco. So that diners can converse in normal tones, the flashing lights and electronic music of the disco are separated from the dining area by thick sheets of glass. Full meals, costing from £25 ($39.50), include an array of Neapolitan-inspired dishes. Only clients of the restaurant are allowed into the disco, which prevents hordes of late-night revelers from cramming into the place when the regular pubs close. Drinks from £2.30 ($3.65); beer, at £2 ($3.16). Open Monday through Saturday 7:30pm to 3am. Mid-May to September, Sunday noon to 10pm.

Equinox

Leicester Square, WC2. ☎ **0171/437-1446.** Cover £5–£10 ($7.90–$15.80), depending on night. Tube: Leicester Square.

Built in 1992 on the site of a dance emporium (the London Empire) that witnessed the changing styles of social dancing since the 1700s, the Equinox has established itself as a firm favorite among London nightlifers. It has nine bars, the largest dance floor in London, and a restaurant modeled along the lines of an American diner from the 1950s. With the exception of "rave" music, virtually every kind of dance music is featured here, including dance hall, pop, rock and roll, garage, and Latin. The setting is lavishly illuminated with one of Europe's largest lighting rigs, and the crowd is as varied as London itself. Open Monday through Saturday 9pm to 3:30am. Mid–May to September, Sunday noon to 10pm.

Hippodrome

Leicester Sq., WC2. ☎ **0171/437-4311.** Cover £2–£10 ($3.15–$15.80). Tube: Leicester Square.

Here you will find one of London's greatest discos, an enormous place where light and sound beam in on you from all directions. Revolving speakers even descend from the roof to deafen you in patches, and you can watch yourself on closed-circuit video. Golden Scan lights are a spectacular treat. There are six bars, together with an à la carte balcony restaurant. Lasers and a hydraulically controlled stage for visiting international performers are only part of the attraction of this place. Drinks run £3 ($4.75) and up. Open Monday through Saturday 9pm to 3:30am.

Smollensky's on The Strand

105 The Strand, WC2. ☎ **0171/497-2101.** No cover except £3.50 ($5.55) for live music. Tube: Charing Cross or Embankment.

This American eatery and drinking bar is a cousin of Smollensky's Balloon at 1 Dover St. (see "The Bar Scene," below, for my recommendation). At the Strand location, there is dancing on Thursday, Friday, and Saturday nights. On Sunday nights there is a special live jazz session, in association with Jazz F.M., an English radio station devoted to jazz. Many visit just for drinks, ordering everything from house cocktails to classic cocktails to deluxe cocktails. Beer costs from £2.40 ($3.80), drinks from £2.95 ($4.65). Meals, ranging from barbecue loin of pork to corn-fed chicken, average £20 ($31.60). Open Monday through Wednesday noon to midnight, Thursday through Saturday noon to 12:30am, Sunday noon to 3:30pm and 6:30 to 10:30pm.

Stringfellows

16–19 Upper St. Martin's Lane, WC2. ☎ **0171/240-5534.** Cover £3–£15 ($4.75–$23.70), depending on the night. Tube: Leicester Square.

This is considered one of the relatively elegant staples on London's nighttime landscape, with a widely varied clientele and lots of velvet and glossy accessories. In theory, it's a members-only club, but—and only at the discretion of management—nonmembers may be admitted. Its disco has a glass dance floor and a dazzling sound-and-light system. On the premises is a restaurant suitable for late-night suppers and two different drinking areas, one slightly less formal than the other. Open Monday through Saturday 9pm to 3:30am; dancing Monday through Saturday 11pm to 1:30am. Beer £2.50 to £3.25 ($3.95 to $5.15), drinks £3.25 ($4.90) and up.

Wag Club

35 Wardour St., W1. ☎ **0171/437-5534.** No cover. Tube: Piccadilly Circus or Leicester Square.

This popular dance club is found behind an innocuous-looking brick facade in one of London's busiest nightlife centers. The club is situated on two floors, one decorated with Celtic designs in gold with colorful renditions of medieval tarot cards. The lower floor has been redecorated in bright primary colors, with huge black-and-white canvasses evocative of Franz Klein. White fur fabric sculptures adorn the walls and advanced modern lighting illuminates a floor of dancers. The music policy—live bands, recorded music, whatever—changes every night. Beer costs £2 ($3.15). Open Tuesday through Thursday 10:30pm to 3:30am and Friday and Saturday 10:30pm to 5:30am.

GAY & LESBIAN CLUBS

The most reliable source of information on gay clubs and activities is the Gay Switchboard (☎ 0171/837-7324). The staff runs a 24-hour service for information on places and activities catering to homosexual men and women. See also "Gay Bars," below in this chapter.

Heaven

The Arches, Craven St., WC2. ☎ **0171/839-3852.** Cover £5–£9 ($7.90–$14.20). Tube: Charing Cross or Embankment.

A London landmark, established by the same investors who brought the world Virgin Atlantic Airlines, this club is set within the vaulted cellars of Charing Cross Railway Station. Painted black inside, and reminiscent of a very large air-raid shelter, Heaven is one of the biggest and best-established gay venues in Great Britain. It's divided into at least four distinctly different areas, each of these connected by a labyrinth of catwalks, stairs, and hallways. Its design allows for different activities to occur simultaneously within the club at the same time. It features different "theme nights," where, depending on the night of the week, gay men, gay women, or for-the-most-part heterosexual people seem to predominate. Call before you go to learn the latest format. Open Tuesday through Saturday from 10:30pm to 3:30am, Sunday 9pm to 1am.

Madame Jo Jo's

8 Brewer St., W1. ☎ **0171/734-2473.** Cover £9–£12 ($14.20–$18.95). Tube: Piccadilly Circus.

Set side by side with some of Soho's most explicit girlie shows, Madame Jo Jo also presents "girls," but they're in drag. This is London's most popular transvestite show, with revues staged nightly at 12:15am and 1:15am and a popular piano bar. Drinks cost about £3 ($4.75). Open Monday through Saturday from 10pm to 3am, Sunday 2 to 8pm.

Roy's West End

11 Upper St. Martin's Lane, WC2. ☎ **0171/836-5121.** Tube: Leicester Square.

Roy's, which was originally launched on Fulham Road and now sits in the midst of London's theaterland, is the leading gay restaurant in town. It enjoys a garden-inspired setting, with a color scheme of cream and terra-cotta. Menu items include deep fried garlic mushrooms; pan-fried chicken livers cooked in Armagnac; smoked salmon with lemon and capers; a traditional English beefsteak with kidney pudding; or sliced breast of Aylesbury duckling with a red wine sauce. Most meals average from £15–£20 ($23.70–$31.60). It is open only for dinner, Monday through Saturday from 6 to 11:30pm.

Steph's

39 Dean St., W1. ☎ **0171/734-5976.** Tube: Piccadilly Circus.

Looking like a stage set for *Pink Flamingos,* Steph's is one of the most charming restaurants of Soho, near the exclusive Groucho Club. Its owner is Stephanie Cooke, a much-traveled former British schoolteacher who is today the sophisticated host of this little well-run restaurant. Her partner is Richard Thiel. A theatrical clientele, among others, is attracted to the place. The clientele is mixed—straight, gay, bi, or whatever.

You could conceivably come here just to have fun, but the food is worthy in its own right. Everything is cooked fresh, so sit back, relax, and enjoy such specialties as Snuffy's chicken, beef-and-oyster pie, or selections from the charcoal grill, including fillet steak with barbecue sauce. Steph might even suggest her own "diet"—a plate of wild Scottish smoked salmon and a bottle of champagne. The ubiquitous burger also appears on the menu, as do salads and even a vegetarian club sandwich (how fashionable can you get?). Meals begin at £16 ($25.30). Open Monday through Thursday from noon to 3pm and 5:30 to 11:30pm, Friday noon to 3pm and 5:30pm to midnight, and Saturday only from 5:30pm to midnight.

Wild About Oscar

In the Philbeach Hotel, 30–31 Philbeach Gardens, SW5. ☎ **0171/373-1244.** Tube: Earl's Court.

Catering to a mostly gay clientele, this restaurant is situated on the garden level of an interconnected pair of Victorian row houses. Decorated in blues and greens, and with portraits of Oscar Wilde (the restaurant's namesake), the establishment overlooks the brownstone's garden and offers well-prepared French cuisine, with three-course fixed-price menu costing £20 ($31.60). A two-course menu goes for £15 ($23.70). There's a small cocktail bar open only to restaurant patrons and residents of the adjoining gay hotel. Open daily for dinner only from 7 to 10:30pm.

THE BAR SCENE
PUBS, WINE BARS & BARS

American Bar

In the Savoy Hotel, The Strand, WC2. ☎ **0171/836-4343.** Tube: Charing Cross or Embankment.

At the American Bar, still one of the most sophisticated gathering places in London, the bartender is known for such special concoctions as the "Savoy Affair" and the "Prince of Wales," as well as for making the best martini in town. Monday through Saturday evenings, jazz piano music is featured. The location—near so many West End theaters—is ideal for a pre- or posttheater drink. Men should wear jackets and ties. Drinks cost from £4.50 to £8.50 ($7.10 to $13.45). Open Monday through Saturday from 11am to 3pm and 5:30 to 11pm, Sunday noon to 3pm and 7 to 10:30pm.

Bracewell's Bar

In the Park Lane Hotel, Piccadilly, W1. ☎ **0171/499-6321.** Tube: Green Park or Hyde Park Corner.

Chic, nostalgic, and elegant, it's the kind of bar where Edward VII and his stylish companion, Ms. Langtry, might have felt very much at home. Its plush, comfortable decor contains touches of Chinese lacquer, upholstered sofas, soft lighting, and an ambience like that of an elegant private club. The bar adjoins Bracewells (see Chapter 5), one of the finest hotel restaurants in London. Mixed drinks begin at £5.90 ($9.30); beer, at £2.70 ($4.25). Open Monday through Saturday from 11am to 3pm and 5:30 to 11pm and on Sunday from noon to 2:30pm and 7 to 10:30pm.

Cocktail Bar

In the Café Royal, 68 Regent St., W1. ☎ **0171/437-9090.** Tube: Piccadilly Circus.

In business since 1865, this bar was once patronized by Oscar Wilde, James Whistler, and Aubrey Beardsley. Decorated in a 19th-century rococo style, it is one of the more glamorous places in London where one can order a drink. Café Royal cocktails, including the Golden Cadillac and the Prince William, begin at £5.50 ($8.70); mixed drinks at £3 ($4.70). Nonalcoholic drinks are also served, and you can order wine by the glass from superb wine cellars. A traditional English tea, served between 3 and 5pm, costs £11 ($17.40). Open Monday through Saturday from noon to 11:30pm and on Sunday from noon to 6pm.

The Dorchester Bar

In the Dorchester, Park Lane, W1. ☎ **0171/629-8888.** Tube: Hyde Park Corner.

This is a fun and sophisticated modern hideaway on the lobby level of one of the most lavishly decorated hotels in the world. Amid its champagne-colored premises, you'll find a clientele from all over the world which shares certain assumptions about the pleasures that only taste and lots of money can buy. You can order upscale bar snacks, lunches, and suppers throughout the day and evening, including lobster cream soups, Scottish smoked salmon, fried fillet of sea bass with seasonal salads, and "fine chocolate layers with a chocolate mousse." Otherwise, the bartender can make any drink ever conceived on the planet Earth. A pianist plays suitable background music every evening after 7pm. Open Monday through Saturday from 11am to 11pm, Sunday noon to 10:30pm. Entrance is free. Drinks are priced from £5 ($7.90).

Lillie Langtry Bar

In the Cadogan Hotel, Sloane St., SW1. ☎ **0171/235-7141.** Tube: Sloane Square.

This spot epitomizes some of the charm and elegance of the Edwardian era. Lillie Langtry, actress and society beauty at the turn of the century (notorious as the mistress of Edward VII), used to live here. She became known as "Jersey Lily." The bar, next to Langtry's Restaurant, exudes a 1920s aura. Oscar Wilde was arrested on charges of sodomy here. But that unfortunate event is long forgotten, and the great playwright is honored on the drink menu with "Hock and Selzer," his favorite drink at the Cadogan, according to Sir John Betjeman's poem, "The Arrest of Oscar Wilde at the Cadogan Hotel." We'd call it a white wine spritzer today. The most popular drink is a Cadogan Cooler. An international menu is also served in the adjoining restaurant. Choices change daily but are likely to include roast rack of lamb, Scottish salmon, Dover sole, and breast of duck. On Monday through Friday, a set luncheon is offered for £16.90 ($26.70), increasing to £17.90 ($28.30). Not available on Saturday, the menu includes three courses and a half bottle of the house wine. The Cadogan set dinner costs £21.90 ($34.60). Cocktails, beginning at £4.75 ($7.50), are served daily from 11:30am to 11pm. A glass of wine costs from £2.95 ($4.65).

Rumours

33 Wellington St., WC2. ☎ **0171/836-0038.** Tube: Covent Garden.

Inspired by the kind of modern cocktail-style bar that might cater to a young and hip crowd in New York or Newport, this is the kind of place where you might expect Tom Cruise to turn up as bartender. Set behind a purple and fluorescent-pink exterior, within what functioned a century ago as a wholesale flower market, Rumours contains Gothic candlesticks, soaring columns camouflaged as palm trees, and a decor that mingles elements of 18th-century England with Miami Beach. This place is a popular watering hole for the neighborhood's young and restless, who order such frothy concoctions as strawberry homicides, little devils, corpse revivers, and double zombies. Cocktails cost from £3 to £4 ($4.75 to $6.30). Open Monday through Saturday 5 to 11pm, Sunday noon to 10:30pm.

Smollensky's Balloon

1 Dover St., W1. ☎ **0171/491-1199.** Tube: Green Park.

A basement restaurant, this American eatery and drinking bar is packed during happy hour from 5:30 to 7pm with Mayfair office workers fortifying themselves before heading home. The place has a 1930s piano bar atmosphere, with polished wood and a mirrored ceiling. Steaks and french fries are its favorite fare, although you can also order well-prepared vegetarian dishes. Meals start at £13 ($20.55); house cocktails (good measures), at £3.95 ($6.25); beer, at £2.25 ($3.55). A pianist/singer entertains Monday through Saturday evenings. Open Monday through Saturday from noon to midnight and on Sunday from noon to 3pm and 4 to 7pm.

SPECIALTY BARS

Bouzouki

Elysée

13 Percy St., W1. ☎ **0171/636-4804.** Tube: Goodge Street or Tottenham Court Road.

Elysée is for *Never on Sunday* devotees who like the reverberations of bouzouki and the smashing of plates. The domain of the Karegeorgis family, it offers hearty fun at moderate tabs. You can dance nightly to the music by Greek musicians. At two different intervals (last one at 1am) a cabaret is provided, highlighted by an altogether amusing act of balancing wine glasses (I'd hate to pay the breakage bill). You can book a table on either the ground floor or the second floor, but the Roof Garden is a magnet in summer. The food is good too, including the house specialty, the classic moussaka, and the kebabs from the charcoal grill. A complete meal with wine costs £25 ($39.50), and there is a £3 ($4.75) cover charge. Open Monday through Saturday from 7pm to 4am.

Gay Bars

Brief Encounter
41 St. Martin's Lane, WC2. ☎ **0171/240-2221.** Tube: Leicester Square or Charing Cross.

This aptly named place that stands across from the duke of York's Theatre is in the very heart of West End theater land. In fact, it's the most frequented West End gay pub. Bars are on two levels, but even so it's hard to find room to stand up, much less drink. Some men are in jeans, leather, or whatever, whereas others are dressed in business suits from their stockbroker jobs in the City. Lager begins at £1.88 ($2.95). Open Monday through Saturday from noon to 11pm and on Sunday from noon to 10:30pm. In winter, the club opens at noon Monday through Saturday.

Coleherne
261 Old Brompton Rd., SW5. ☎ **0171/373-9859.** Tube: Earl's Court.

This denim-and-leather bar must be featured in every gay guide to Europe ever written, and consequently it's often jammed. Lunch and afternoon tea are served upstairs. Lager starts at £1.88 ($2.70). Open Monday through Saturday 11am to 11pm and on Sunday from noon to 3pm and 7 to 10:30pm.

The Duke of Wellington
110 Balls Pond Rd., N1. ☎ **0171/249-3729.** Tube: Highbury.

Originally built in the late 19th century as a workingman's pub, this is now one of the most popular gay bars in North London, with a higher percentage of gay women than that attracted by many of London's other gay bars. Divided into two rooms, each with its own bar and its own devoted corps of aficionados, it hosts Saturday night disco parties (free entrance) and live music at least one night a week. Its name as bandied about by patrons of this place? The Dyke of Wellington, in honor of its large number of lesbian fans. Open Monday through Saturday noon to midnight, Sunday noon to 11pm. Pint of lager from £1.85 ($2.90).

The Fridge
Town Hall Parade, Brixton Hill, SW2. ☎ **0171/326-5100.** Cover: £3-£9 ($4.75-$14.20), depending on the scheduled event. Tube: Brixton.

Situated within a 15-minute tube ride from central London, this club is one of the most popular dance and music clubs in London. Open only 3 or 4 nights a week, and catering each night to specific groups of clients, it's young, trendy, and features a well-engineered sound system with up-to-date music. On the premises are two bars (one on street level, another on a balcony upstairs), and a restaurant. Tuesdays and Saturdays are most heavily patronized by gays (mostly men), Thursdays and Fridays are favored by persons of unknown sexuality, who would probably respond, if asked, that they were straight. It's a good idea to phone before setting out for this place, as its venue might change even during the lifetime of this edition. Open Tuesday from 10pm to 3am and Thursday through Saturday 9pm to 3am.

Halfway to Heaven

7 Duncannon St., WC2. ☎ **0171/930-8312.** Tube: Charing Cross or Embankment.

Housed within a century-old structure whose beamed ceiling might remind you of a setting in a novel by Charles Dickens, this is perhaps the least frenetic gay bar in the Trafalgar Square neighborhood. Remarkable for crossing many generational lines, it welcomes a clientele aged from 18 to 65, none of whom seem particularly interested in the changing fashions of what's currently trendy or not. Open Monday through Saturday from noon to 11pm, Sunday noon to 10:30pm. Lager costs from £1.86 ($2.95).

79CXR

79 Charing Cross Rd., W1. ☎ **0171/439-7250.** No cover. Tube: Leicester Square.

Named after an abbreviation for the street where it is located (Charing Cross Road, near Leicester Square), this long, high-ceilinged bar has a clientele that is almost overwhelmingly gay and mostly male. There's no disco, no food service, and no entertainment, but something about the place evokes a sense of camaraderie and fun. A balcony runs along the edges of the high-ceilinged room, looking down over the hubbub below. Open Monday through Saturday noon to 1am; Sunday 7pm to midnight. Lager £1.85 ($2.90) per pint.

MORE ENTERTAINMENT

CASINOS

London was a gambling metropolis long before anyone had ever heard of Monte Carlo and when "pre-Bugsy" Las Vegas was an anonymous sandpile in the desert.

Queen Victoria's reign changed all that, as usual by jumping to the other extreme. For more than a century, games of chance were so rigorously outlawed that no bartender dared to keep a dice cup on the counter.

However, according to the 1960 "Betting and Gaming Act," gambling was again permitted in "bona fide clubs" by members and their guests.

There are at least 25 of them in the West End alone, with many more scattered throughout the suburbs. But I cannot make specific recommendations. Under a new law, casinos aren't allowed to advertise, which in this context would mean appearing in a guidebook. It isn't illegal to gamble, only to advertise a gambling establishment. Most hall porters can tell you where you can gamble in London.

You will be required to become a member of your chosen club, and then you must wait 24 hours before you can play at the tables . . . and then it must be strictly for cash. The most common games are roulette, blackjack, punto banco, and baccarat.

MOVIES

MGM Cinema

Panton St., off Leicester Sq., SW1. ☎ **0171/930-0631.** Tickets, £3–£6 ($4.75–$9.50). Tube: Leicester Square or Piccadilly Circus.

This streamlined, black-and-white block houses four superb theaters under one roof. They share one sleekly plush lobby, but each runs a separate program, always including at least one European film, along with the latest releases, often from the United States.

National Film Theatre
South Bank, Waterloo, SE1. ☎ **0171/928-3232.** 40p (65¢) daily membership, £4.35 ($6.85) screenings with membership. Tube: Waterloo.

This cinema is in the South Bank complex. More than 2,000 films a year from all over the world are shown here, including features, shorts, animation, and documentaries.

Odeon Leicester Square and Odeon Mezzanine
Leicester Sq., SW1. ☎ 0**1426/915-683.** Tickets, £7–£9 ($11.05–$14.20). Tube: Leicester Square.

The Odeon is another major London film theater, with one main screen and a 290-seat mezzanine complex comprising another five screens. All screens feature the latest international releases.

Museum of the Moving Image (MOMI)
Underneath Waterloo Bridge, SE1. ☎ **0171/401-2636.** Admission £5.50 ($8.70) adults, £4 ($6.30) children and senior citizens, £4.70 ($7.45) students, £16 ($25.30) family tickets. Tube: Waterloo or Embankment.

MOMI is also part of the South Bank complex. Tracing the history of the development of cinema and television, it takes the visitor on an incredible journey from cinema's earliest experiments to modern animation, from Charlie Chaplin to the operation of a TV studio. There are artifacts to handle, buttons to push, and a cast of actors to tell visitors more. Allow 2 hours for a visit. Open daily from 10am to 6pm (last admission 5pm).

STRIP SHOWS
Soho has many strip shows, sometimes two in one building. Along Frith Street, Greek Street, Old Compton Street, Brewer Street, Windmill Street, Dean and Wardour Streets, and the little courts and alleys in between, the disrobing establishments jostle cheek by jowl. Big ones and small ones, fancy and dingy, elaborate and primitive, they all sport outside photos of the inside attractions, gloriously exotic names, and bellowing speakers to draw your attention.

Raymond Revuebar
Walker's Court, Brewer St., W1. ☎ **0171/734-1593.** Cover £19.50 ($30.80). Tube: Piccadilly Circus.

The Revuebar dates from 1958. Proprietor Paul Raymond is considered the doyen of strip society and his young, beautiful, handpicked strippers are among the best in Europe. This strip theater occupies the much-restored premises of a Victorian dance hall, with a decor of flaming red velvet. There are two bars, which allow clients to take their drinks to their seats. Whiskey costs £2.50 ($3.95) for a large measure. The club presents two shows nightly: at 8 and 10pm.

Stork Club
99 Regent St., W1. ☎ **0171/734-3686.** Three-course dinner and show, £35 ($55.30). Tube: Piccadilly Circus.

This first-class nightclub incorporates good food, a Las Vegas–style cabaret with a lineup of attractive dancers who don't believe in overdressing, and an ambience noted for its good taste and theatrical flair. Located near the corner of Swallow Street in the upscale heart of Mayfair, it welcomes diners and drinkers to a royal blue-and-peach-colored decor of art deco inspiration. Two shows are staged nightly, one at 11:45pm and another at 1am. Foreign visitors who don't want dinner can sit at the bar and pay a £10 ($15.80) cover charge to see the show. Drinks begin at £4 ($6.30). Open Monday through Saturday from 8:30pm to 3:30am.

8

Windsor & Oxford

The historical Thames Valley and Chiltern Hills lie so close to London that they can easily be reached by automobile, train, or Green Line coach. In fact, you can explore this area during the day and return to London in time to see a West End show.

The most-visited historic site in England is Windsor Castle, 21 miles west of London, one of the most famous castles in Europe and the most popular day trip for visitors venturing out of London for the first time.

Certainly your principal reason for visiting Oxfordshire is to explore the university city of Oxford, about an hour's ride from London by car or train. But Oxford is not the only attraction in the county; the shire is a land of great mansions, old churches of widely varying architectural styles, and rolling farmland.

In a sense, Oxfordshire is a kind of buffer zone between the easy living in the southern towns and the industrialized cities of the heartland. Southeast are the chalky Chilterns, and in the west you'll be moving toward the wool towns of the Cotswolds. The upper Thames winds its way across the southern parts of the county.

A DRIVING TOUR

Day 1   Leave London and head 21 miles west to Windsor where you can explore Windsor Castle and spend the night. Windsor can also be used as a base for exploring Savill Garden.

Day 2   Head northwest to Cookham, immortalized by the artist Sir Stanley Spencer, and continue to the west until you reach Henley-on-Thames. From here you can visit the Elizabethan manor house of Mapledurham, which is reached by car from the A4074 Oxford–Reading road. Henley-on-Thames also makes a good base for visiting the Wellington Ducal Estate at Stratfield Saye, near Reading. Spend the night in Henley.

Day 3   Head for Oxford for the night, going northwest and passing through Dorchester, a lovely little Thames-side town, with an ancient abbey, containing cloisters, gardens, and a church from 1170 with medieval windows. The American Friends of the Abbey restored the east window in 1966 in memory of Sir Winston Churchill. Explore Dorchester with its thatched cottages, ancient inns, and timbered houses.

What's Special About Windsor & Oxford

Great Towns/Villages
- Oxford, one of the world's greatest universities and a seat of learning since the 12th century.
- Windsor, site of the castle founded by William the Conqueror (ca. 1070), the world's largest inhabited castle.
- Henley-on-Thames, a small town and resort at the foothills of the Chilterns, famed for its High Street and Royal Regatta.

Castles
- Windsor Castle, steeped in royal associations, where the royal family spends Christmas.
- Blenheim Palace, majestic palace of the duke of Marlborough at Woodstock, with decorative work by Grinling Gibbons; Churchill was born here.

Architectural Highlights
- St. George's Chapel, Windsor Castle, a notable example of Perpendicular architecture and rich vaulting, with several royal tombs.
- New College, Oxford, founded in 1379 by William of Wykeham; its initial quadrangle formed the architectural design for other colleges.

☕ **TAKE A BREAK**   George Hotel, High Street (☎ **01865/340404**) dates back some five centuries. One of the oldest inns in England, it overlooks Dorchester Abbey. This former coaching inn offers both a restaurant and a garden.

From Dorchester, take A415 west toward Oxford, stopping off at Abingdon which grew up around an abbey dating from the 7th century. After a look around, continue north to Oxford.

Day 4   Explore the colleges at Oxford in the morning and in the afternoon drive to Woodstock, 8 miles northwest of Oxford, to explore Blenheim Palace. Either stay in Woodstock or return to Oxford for the night.

1 Windsor

21 miles W of London

Windsor, the site of England's greatest castle and its most famous boys' school, was called "Windlesore" by the ancient Britons, who derived the name from winding shore—so noticeable as you walk along the Thames here.

ESSENTIALS
GETTING THERE
By Train   The train from Waterloo or Paddington Station in London (☎ **0171/262-6767**) makes the trip in 30 minutes. There are more than a dozen trains per day, and the cost is £5 ($7.90).

By Bus   Green Line coaches (☎ **0171/668-7261**) no. 700, 701, 702, and 718 from Hyde Park Corner in London take about 1½ hours. A same-day round-trip costs £4.35 to £5.50 ($6.85 to $8.70).

By Car   Take M4 west from London.

VISITOR INFORMATION

The **telephone area code** is 01753. A **Tourist Information Centre** is located across from Windsor Castle on High Street (☎ **01753/852010**). There's also an information booth in the tourist center at Windsor Coach Park.

WHAT TO SEE & DO

The bus will drop you near the Town Guildhall, to which Wren applied the finishing touches. It's only a short walk up Castle Hill to the top sights.

CASTLE SIGHTS

✪ Windsor Castle

Castle Hill. ☎ **01753/868286.** Admission £9 ($14.20) adults, £6.50 ($10.25) students and senior citizens, £5 ($7.90) children 16 and under. Mar–Oct, daily 10am–5pm; Nov–Feb, daily 10am–4pm. Ticket sales cease about one hour before closing; last admissions are 15 minutes before closing. Closed periods in Apr, June, and Dec when the royal family is in residence.

When William the Conqueror ordered a castle built on this spot, he began a legend and a link with English sovereignty that has known many vicissitudes: King John cooled his heels at Windsor while waiting to put his signature on the Magna Carta at nearby Runnymede; Charles I was imprisoned here before losing his head; Queen Bess did some renovations; Victoria mourned her beloved Albert, who died at the castle in 1861; the royal family rode out much of World War II behind its sheltering walls; and when Queen Elizabeth II is in residence, the royal standard flies.

The apartments display many works of art, porcelain, armor, furniture, three Verrio ceilings, and several 17th-century Gibbons carvings. Several works by Rubens adorn the King's Drawing Room and in the relatively small King's Dressing Room is a Dürer, along with Rembrandt's portrait of his mother, and Van Dyck's triple portrait of Charles I. Of the apartments, the grand reception room, with its Gobelin tapestries, is the most spectacular.

In November 1992, a fire swept through part of Windsor Castle, severely damaging it. The castle has since reopened, but until the restoration has been completed in 1998 visitors can't see all the rooms formerly open to the public.

The Windsor changing of the guard is a much more exciting and moving experience, in my opinion, than the London exercises. In Windsor when the court is in residence, the guard marches through town, stopping the traffic as it wheels into the castle to the tune of a full regimental band; when the queen is not there, a drum-and-pipe band is mustered. From May to August, the ceremony takes place Monday through Saturday at 11am. In winter, the guard is changed every 48 hours Monday through Saturday. It's best to call the number listed above to find out which days the ceremony will take place. In fact, it's always advisable to call ahead and check what's open before visiting. The castle is in the town center.

Queen Mary's Doll's House

Windsor Castle. ☎ **01753/831118.** Admission £1 ($1.60). Open same days and hours as Windsor Castle (see above).

A palace in perfect miniature, the Doll's House was given to Queen Mary in 1923 as a symbol of national goodwill. The house, designed by Sir Edwin Lutyens, was created on a scale of 1 to 12. It took 3 years to complete and involved the work of 1,500 tradesmen and artists. Every item is a miniature masterpiece; each room is exquisitely furnished and every item is made exactly to scale. Working elevators stop on every floor, and there is running water in all five bathrooms. There's electric lighting throughout the house.

○ St. George's Chapel

The Cloisters, Windsor Castle. ☎ **01753/865538.** Admission included in admission to Windsor Castle. Mon–Sat 10am–4pm, Sun 2–3:45 or 4pm (call first to check hours). Closed during services, Jan, and a few days in mid-June.

A gem of the Perpendicular style, this chapel shares the distinction with Westminster Abbey of being a pantheon of English monarchs (Victoria is a notable exception). The present St. George's was founded in the late 15th century by Edward IV on the site of the original Chapel of the Order of the Garter (Edward III, 1348). You first enter the nave, which has fan vaulting (a remarkable achievement in English architecture) and contains the tomb of George V and Queen Mary, designed by Sir William Reid Dick. Off the nave in the Urswick Chapel, the Princess Charlotte memorial provides an ironic touch; if she had survived childbirth in 1817, she—and not her cousin Victoria—would have ruled the British Empire. In the aisle are tombs of George VI and Edward IV. The Edward IV "Quire," with its imaginatively carved 15th-century choir stalls (crowned by lacy canopies and Knights of the Garter banners), evokes the pomp and pageantry of medieval days. In the center is a flat tomb, containing the vault of the beheaded Charles I, along with Henry VIII and his third wife, Jane Seymour. Finally, you may want to inspect the Prince Albert Memorial Chapel, reflecting the opulent tastes of the Victorian era.

Historical note: Queen Victoria died on January 22, 1901, and was buried beside her beloved Prince Albert in a mausoleum at Frogmore (a private estate), a mile from Windsor. The prince consort died in December 1861. The house, gardens, and mausoleum are open May 3–4 and May 17 from 10:30am to 7pm and the mausoleum is also open on May 24. The admission price is £1.50 ($2.35). The grounds are only open for group bookings in September. Call 01753/868286 ext. 2235 for more details.

OTHER SIGHTS

The **town of Windsor** is largely Victorian, with lots of brick buildings and a few remnants of Georgian architecture. In and around the castle are two cobblestone streets, Church and Market, which have antiques shops, silversmiths, and pubs. One shop on Church Street was supposedly occupied by Nell Gwynne, who needed to be within call of Charles II's chambers. After lunch or tea, you may want to stroll along the 3-mile, aptly named Long Walk.

On Sunday, there are often polo matches in **Windsor Great Park**—and at Ham Common—and you may see Prince Charles playing and Prince Philip serving as umpire. The queen often watches. The queen goes riding in the park and on Sunday attends a little church near the Royal Lodge. Traditionally, she prefers to drive herself there, later returning to the castle for Sunday lunch. For more information, call 01753/434212.

TOURS

BUS TOURS   Guide Friday (☎ **01753/855755** for information and reservations) runs the best bus tours in Windsor, carefully tailored on a "come and go as you please" basis which is enormously appealing. Tours generally depart 7 days a week between 11:15am and 5pm opposite the main entrance to Windsor Castle on Castle Hill. Tours run only between March 25 and October 30 daily.

Tours cover a distance of 9 miles and incorporate the best sights of Windsor, Eton, and Datchet (Datchet is a charming English village 4 miles east of Windsor, which lies at the end of a road loaded with sights and history). Tours are conducted in open-top buses, and if no one gets off the bus, the tour takes an hour. However, the tours are designed to allow visitors to get on and off at will anywhere along the way, so they can become a full-day outing.

Tours cost £5 ($7.90) for adults, £1.50 ($2.35) for children 5 to 12, free for children 4 and under. No credit cards.

BOAT TOURS Tours depart from the main embarkation point along The Promenade, Barry Avenue, for a 35-minute ride to Boveney Lock. The cost is £2.40 ($3.80) for adults, half price for children. However, you can also take a 2-hour tour through the Boveney Lock and up past stately private riverside homes, the Bray Film Studios, Queens Eyot, and Monkey Island, all for a cost of £4.60 ($7.25) for adults, half price for children. Finally, you can take a 35-minute tour from Runnymede on board the *Lucy Fisher*, a replica of a Victorian paddle steamer. You pass Magna Carta Island, among other sights. The cost is £2.40 ($3.80) for adults, half price for children. In addition, a range of longer tours is also offered. The boats offer light refreshments and have a licensed bar. The decks are covered in case of an unexpected shower. Tours are operated by **French Brothers Ltd.,** Clewer Boathouse, Clewer Court Road, Windsor (☎ **01753/851900**).

WHERE TO STAY

You may choose to make Windsor your base for London sightseeing. Trains leave London as late as 10:30 or 11pm, so it's quite easy to attend an early theater performance and have dinner before returning to Windsor for the night.

Warning: During the Ascot races and Windsor Horse Show, reservations are necessary far in advance.

MODERATE

The Castle Hotel

18 High St., Windsor, Berkshire SL4 1LJ. ☎ **01753/851011,** or 800/225-5843 in the U.S. and Canada. Fax 01753/830244. 103 rms, 1 suite. TV TEL. £99 ($156.40) single; £120–£160 ($189.60–$252.80) double; £180 ($284.40) suite. Breakfast £10.50 ($16.60) extra. AE, DC, MC, V. Free parking.

Near Windsor Castle, on the main street, is this solid and long-established hotel with a dignified Georgian facade. It was originally built in the 15th century to shelter the hundreds of workers laboring on the town's foundations and royal buildings. By the 17th century it had changed its name from the Mermaid to the Castle and profited from the heavy stagecoach traffic that often deposited visitors at its doorstep. In 1986 the Spanish royal entourage was housed in 17 of its best rooms; Princess Anne has dropped in for breakfast; and the duke of Edinburgh has been a guest speaker at several functions. Centuries ago the grounds behind the hotel served as the stable yard for Windsor Castle, but now they're used for a modern bedroom wing.

✪ Sir Christopher Wren's House Hotel

Thames St., Windsor, Berkshire SL4 1PX. ☎ **01753/860172.** 39 rms, 1 suite. TV TEL. Mon–Thurs, £99.50–£109.50 ($157.20–$173.00) single; £119.50–£129.50 ($188.80–$204.60) double; £139.50 ($220.40) suite. English breakfast £8.50 ($13.45) extra. Fri–Sun (including breakfast), £39.50–£99 ($62.40–$156.40) single or double; suite £99 ($156.40). AE, DC, MC, V. Free parking.

Designed by Christopher Wren in 1676 as his own home, this former town house, between Eton and Windsor, just a 3-minute walk from the castle, occupies a prime position on the Thames, its gardens overlooking swans and boats. The central hall is impressive, with a Queen Anne black marble refectory table. Wren's oak-paneled former study is equipped with his Empire desk, a fireplace, and shield-back Hepplewhite chairs. The bay-windowed main drawing room, decorated with mirrors, sconces, and a formal marble fireplace, opens onto a garden and a riverside flagstone terrace for after-dinner coffee and drinks. Some of the bedrooms have fine old furniture, and all are equipped with trouser presses. Several overlook the river. Room 2, which was Sir Christopher Wren's bedroom, is said to be haunted. Open to nonresidents, the hotel restaurant, the Orangerie, is recommended below.

INEXPENSIVE

Royal Adelaide Hotel

46 Kings Rd., Windsor, Berkshire SL4 2AG. ☎ **01753/863916.** Fax 01753/830682. 41 rms. TV TEL. £57.50 ($90.85) single; £67.50 ($106.65) double. Rates include English breakfast. AE, DC, MC, V. Free parking.

This interesting Georgian building is opposite the famous Long Walk leading to Windsor Castle, 5 minutes away. It was named for Queen Adelaide, who visited the premises during her reign, thereby dubbing it "royal." All the well-furnished bedrooms, which vary in size, have trouser presses, hairdryers, radios, alarm clocks, and hot-beverage facilities. A fixed-priced dinner is available at £14.50 ($22.90) for three courses. The cuisine is both English and French.

Ye Harte & Garter Hotel

31 High St., Windsor, Berkshire SL4 1PH. ☎ **01753/863426.** Fax 01753/830527. 40 rms with bath. TV TEL. £39.95 ($63.10) single; £43.95–£49.95 ($69.45–$78.90) double; £180 ($284.40) suite. Rates include breakfast. AE, DC, MC, V.

On Castle Hill opposite Windsor Castle, the old Garter Inn, named for the Knights of the Garter, was the setting for scenes in Shakespeare's *Merry Wives of Windsor*. The Garter burned down in the 1800s and was rebuilt as part of one hostelry that included the Hart. From the front bedrooms you can watch the guards marching up High Street every morning on their way to change the guard at the castle. The rooms are equipped with trouser presses, hot-beverage equipment, and other amenities. You can dine in the Country Grill Restaurant, and the hotel's café (known as "The Bar") serves teas and coffees in addition to liquor and beer.

A NEARBY PLACE TO STAY

Expensive

✪ The Oakley Court Hotel

Windsor Rd., Water Oakley, Windsor, Berkshire SL4 5UR. ☎ **01628/74141.** Fax 01628/37011. 82 rms, 10 suites. MINIBAR TV TEL. £135–£141 ($213.30–$222.80) single; £155–£187 ($244.90–$295.45) double; £255–£375 ($402.90–$592.50) suite. English breakfast £14 ($22.10) extra. AE, DC, MC, V. Free parking. Take the river road, A308, 3 miles from Windsor toward Maidenhead.

Built beside the Thames by a Victorian industrialist as his showcase home, this establishment has thick stone walls, jutting gables, and bristling turrets that would lend themselves to the filming of a horror movie. (That's exactly what crews of cinematographers did during an uninhabited period in the 1960s and 1970s. The resulting films included *Rocky Horror Picture Show,* Hammer's *Dracula,* and several highly forgettable made-for-TV romances.) Today, the mansion functions as a comfortable and well-accessorized hotel. Although the grandest of the public rooms are in the main house, most of the accommodations are in a pair of modern wings that ramble through the estate's 35 acres of well-tended parks and gardens. There's a relatively formal restaurant, the Oakleaf (recommended separately), and an informal tavern, Boaters Brasserie, which opens at noontime for lunch and dinner every day except Sunday. The platters of food begin at around £5.50 ($8.70) each. You can rent a boat for punting on the Thames, stroll through the gardens, arrive easily at Heathrow (a 20-minute drive), or order room service 24 hours a day.

WHERE TO DINE

Many visitors prefer to dine in Eton across the bridge. Most of the restaurants and fast-food places along the main street of Windsor, in front of the castle, serve dreary food.

MODERATE

The Orangerie

In Sir Christopher Wren's House Hotel, Thames St. ☎ **01753/861354.** Main courses £9.95–£25.75 ($15.70–$40.70); set menu £12.75 ($20.15). AE, DC, MC, V. Daily noon–2:30pm and 6:30–10:30pm. CONTINENTAL.

Already recommended as a hotel, this building, a 3-minute walk from the castle, boasts the most elegant and charming restaurant in Windsor, with garden terraces and a conservatory. The dining room is designed a bit like a greenhouse, with cabriole-legged furniture, lots of chintz, and views of the garden through tall French windows. At dinner a pianist entertains. Specialties include fresh swordfish with sun-dried tomato and cucumber relish and jerk seasoning. In summer, guests can dine in the garden on an Italian terrace beside the Thames.

A NEARBY PLACE TO DINE
Moderate

✪ Oak Leaf Restaurant

In the Oakley Court Hotel, Windsor Rd., Water Oakley. ☎ **01753/74141.** Reservations recommended. Main courses £9.25–£18.50 ($14.60–$29.25); fixed-price meal £26 ($41.10) at lunch, £30 ($47.40) at dinner. AE, DC, MC, V. Daily 12:30–1:45pm and 7:30–9:45pm. Take the river road, A308, 3 miles from Windsor toward Maidenhead. CONTINENTAL.

In the elegant Victorian core of a previously recommended hotel, this restaurant serves a clientele which has included Prince Charles, Prince Philip, and many of the affluent residents of Windsor and its surrounding townships. Menu choices include such dishes as roast sea bass with saffron mash and a sweet-pepper and black-olive dressing; grilled calf's liver with bacon; fillet of Scottish beef with pâté of wild mushrooms, potatoes, and a red-wine shallot sauce; and breast of duck with creamed parsnip, prune, and Armagnac chutney.

EASY EXCURSIONS
ETON

To visit Eton, home of what is arguably the most famous public school (Americans would call it a private school) in the world, you can take a train from Paddington Station, go by car, or take the Green Line bus to Windsor. By car, take the M4 motorway to Exit 5 to go straight to Eton. However, parking is likely to be a problem, so we advise turning off M4 at Exit 6 to Windsor; you can park there and take an easy stroll past Windsor Castle and across the Thames bridge.

Follow Eton High Street to the college. (From Windsor Castle's ramparts, you can look down on the river and on the famous playing fields of Eton.)

What to See & Do

Eton College (☎ **01753/671177**) was founded by an adolescent boy himself, Henry VI, in 1440. Some of England's greatest men, notably the duke of Wellington, have played on these fields. Twenty prime ministers were educated here, as well as such literary figures as George Orwell, Aldous Huxley, Ian Fleming, and Percy Bysshe Shelley, who, during his years at Eton (from 1804 to 1810), was called "Mad Shelley" or "Shelley the Atheist" by his fellow pupils. If it's open, take a look at the Perpendicular chapel, with its 15th-century paintings and reconstructed fan vaulting.

The history of Eton College since its inception in 1440 is depicted in the **Museum of Eton Life,** Eton College (☎ **01753/671177**), located in vaulted wine cellars under College Hall, which were originally the storehouse for use of the college's masters. The displays, ranging from formal to extremely informal, include a turn-of-the-century boy's room, schoolbooks, sports trophies, canes used by senior boys to apply punishment they felt needful to their juniors, and birch sticks used by masters for the same purpose. Also to be seen are letters written home by students describing day-to-day life at the school, as well as samples of the numerous magazines produced by students over the centuries, known as ephemera because of the changing writers and ideas. Many of the items to be seen were provided by Old Etonians.

Admission to the school and museum costs £2.30 ($3.65) for adults and £1.60 ($2.55)for children. Otherwise, you can take guided tours for £3.40 ($5.35) for adults or £2.80 ($4.40) for children. Eton College is open from April 1 until October 8 daily from 2 to 5pm (last admission at 4:30pm). During holidays it's open from 10:30am to 4:30pm. However, it may close for special events.

Where to Dine: Moderate

Antico

42 High St. ☎ **01753/863977.** Reservations strongly recommended. Main courses £9–£13 ($14.20–$20.55). AE, DC, MC, V. Mon–Fri 12:30–2:30pm and 7–10pm, Sat 7–10pm. Closed bank holidays. ITALIAN.

Considered the finest Italian restaurant in town, this establishment serves Mediterranean food in a formal setting. People have been dining here for 200 years, although not from an Italian menu. In a traditional English setting, dating from 1787, and decorated with artifacts of bygone days, the restaurant has definitely turned to Italy for its cuisine. On your way to the tiny bar you pass a cold table, displaying an array of hors d'oeuvres, fresh fish, and cold meats. There's a wide choice of fish dishes, such as grilled fresh sardines, Dover sole, or calamari. Beef fillet is a favorite dish. Desserts from the trolley are offered.

House on the Bridge

71 High St. ☎ **01753/860914.** Reservations recommended. Main courses £10.95–£17.95 ($17.30–$28.35); fixed-price meal £15.75 ($24.90) at lunch, £24.95 ($39.40) at dinner. AE, DC, MC, V. Daily noon–2:30pm and 6–11pm. ENGLISH/INTERNATIONAL.

This restaurant is charmingly housed in a red-brick and terra-cotta Victorian building, adjacent to the bridge and beside the river at the edge of Eton. Near the handful of outdoor tables is an almost vertical garden whose plants cascade into the Thames. Among the well-prepared main dishes are crispy duckling with Calvados and Seville oranges, chicken suprême flavored with tarragon and served with mushrooms, and chateaubriand. Some specialties such as roast rack of herb-flavored lamb are served only for two diners. Desserts include flambées and crêpes Suzette.

Eton Wine Bar

82–83 High St. ☎ 01753/854921. Reservations recommended. Main courses £5.95–£10.95 ($9.40–$17.30). AE, DC, MC, V. Mon–Sat noon–2:30pm and 6–11pm, Sun noon–2:45pm and 7–10:30pm. FRENCH/ENGLISH/CONTINENTAL.

Just across the bridge from Windsor, this charming place located on the main street among the antiques shops features pinewood tables and old church pews and chairs, and there's a glassed-in conservatory out back. You might begin with one of the well-prepared soups such as carrot and orange or cream of asparagus and leek. Main dishes include English pies and steaks and at least two vegetarian dishes, such as mushroom-and-asparagus cream fettuccine or spinach-and-tomato terrine.

SAVILL GARDEN

Savill Garden, Wick Lane, Englefield Green, Egham, Surrey (☎ 01753/860222), is in Windsor Great Park and is signposted from Windsor, Egham, and Ascot. Started in 1932, the 35-acre garden is considered one of the finest of its type in the northern hemisphere. The display starts in spring with rhododendrons, camellias, and daffodils beneath the trees; then throughout the summer there are spectacular displays of flowers and shrubs presented in a natural and wild state. It's open daily all year (except at Christmas) from 10am to 6pm (to 4pm in winter); admission is £3.30 ($5.20)for adults, free for children 15 and under. It's located 5 miles from Windsor along A30; turn off at Wick Road and follow the signs to the gardens. The nearest rail station is at Egham; from there you'll need to take a taxi a distance of 3 miles. There's a licensed, self-service restaurant on the premises.

Adjoining the Savill Garden are the **Valley Gardens,** full of shrubs and trees in a series of wooded natural valleys running down to the water. It's open daily throughout the year. Entrance to the gardens is free, although parking your car costs £2.60 ($4.10) per vehicle.

2 Ascot

28 miles W of London

While following the royal buckhounds through Windsor Forest, Queen Anne decided to have a racecourse on Ascot Heath. The first race meeting at Ascot, which is directly south of Windsor at the southern end of Windsor Great Park, was inaugurated in 1711. Since then, the Ascot Racecourse has been a symbol of high society as pictures of the royal family, including the queen and Prince Philip, have been flashed around the world. Nowadays, instead of Queen Anne, you are likely to see Princess Anne, an avid horsewoman.

ESSENTIALS

GETTING THERE

By Train   Trains travel between Waterloo in London and Ascot Station, which is about 10 minutes from the racecourse. Service is about every 30 minutes during the day (trip time: 30 min.).

By Bus   Frequent bus departures from London's Victoria Coach Station.

By Car   From Windsor, take A332 west.

VISITOR INFORMATION

The **telephone area code** is 01344.

WHAT TO SEE & DO

The ✪ **Ascot Racecourse,** High Street (☎ **01344/22211**), the largest and probably the most prestigious racecourse in the country, is open throughout the year, though no races are held during March. Visitors are sold tickets for space in one of three distinctly different observation areas, known locally as "enclosures." These include the Members' Enclosure, which during the Royal Meeting (4 days in June) is known as the Royal Enclosure. Also available are Tattersall's Enclosure, largest of the three; and the Silver Ring, which does not enjoy direct access to the paddocks and has traditionally been the site of most of Ascot's budget seating. Except during the Royal Meeting, newcomers can usually secure viewing space in the Member's Enclosure, but only if they phone ahead to confirm that space is available. Tickets costs £5 to £25 ($7.90 to $39.50), depending on the race, the season, and the enclosure you request. Children 15 and under are admitted free if accompanied by an adult. Although the highlight of the Ascot social season is the above-mentioned Royal Meeting (or Royal Week), when many women wear fancy hats and white gloves, there is excellent racing on Diamond Day (fourth Saturday in July) and during the Festival at Ascot (last Saturday and Sunday in September), when the prize money usually exceeds £1 million per event.

Advance bookings for guaranteed seating in the most desirable areas during the most popular races can be arranged beginning January 1 every year. Write for tickets to the Secretary's Office, Ascot Racecourse, Ascot, Berkshire SL5 7JN. For admission to the Royal Enclosure, write to Her Majesty's Representative, Ascot Office, St. James's Palace, London SW1 (☎ **0171/930-9882**). First-timers usually have difficulty being admitted to the Royal Enclosure, since their application must be endorsed by someone who has been admitted to the Royal Enclosure at least eight times before.

WHERE TO STAY & DINE

EXPENSIVE

✪ The Royal Berkshire

London Rd., Sunninghill, Ascot, Berkshire SL5 OPP. ☎ **01344/23322.** Fax 01344/27100. 57 rms, 6 suites. TV TEL. £120 ($189.60) single; £165 ($260.70) double; £205–£405 ($323.90–$639.90) suite. AE, DC, MC, V. Breakfast £14 ($22.10) extra. Free parking. Take A322 2 miles northeast of Ascot.

The interior of this elegant hotel does justice to its history. Built of russet-colored bricks in Queen Anne style in 1705, it housed the Churchill family for many years. Harmonious color schemes and well-chosen furnishings set a stylish tone in the bedrooms, which are divided between the main house and an annex that's also furnished in good taste and with style. Many people visit only for a meal in the Stateroom Restaurant, which overlooks the lawns and gardens of the hotel. The food, some of the finest in the area, is prepared with quality ingredients and often with artistic flair. Set luncheons are featured for £22.15 ($35) and set dinners for £32.50 ($51.35). There's a good à la carte menu that changes frequently and offers a range of contemporary English dishes. Meals are served daily from 12:30 to 2:30pm and 7:15 to 9:30pm.

MODERATE

Berystede Country House Hotel

Bagshot Rd., Sunninghill Ascot, Berkshire SL5 9JH. ☎ **01344/23311.** Fax 01344/872301. 85 rms, 6 suites. TV TEL. £95 ($150.10) single; £115 ($181.70) double; from £160 ($252.80) suite. Breakfast £10.50 ($16.60) extra. AE, DC, MC, V. Free parking. Take the A330 1½ miles south of Ascot.

This hotel is a Victorian fantasy of medieval towers, half-timbering, steeply pitched roofs, and a landscaped garden. The entrance hall incorporates a huge stone fireplace which, if the weather's cool enough, might be blazing. The bedrooms, with their high ceilings and chintz, evoke the aura of a private country house. The suite boasts mahogany reproductions of 18th-century antiques. Fixed-price lunches cost £15.50 ($24.50); fixed-price dinners, £21 ($33.20). The rooms all have bath and hot beverage-making facilities.

INEXPENSIVE

Brockenhurst

Brockenhurst Rd., South Ascot, Berkshire SL5 9HA. ☎ **01344/21912.** Fax 01344/873252. 11 rms. TV TEL. Mon–Thurs, £75 ($118.50) single; £85 ($134.30) double. Fri–Sun, £65 ($102.70) single; £75 ($118.50) double. Rates include continental breakfast. English breakfast £5 ($7.90) extra. AE, DC, MC, V. Free parking.

A small, tastefully refurbished 1905 Edwardian hotel of charm and distinction, Brockenhurst is conveniently situated near shops and the train station. The most expensive rooms are called "executive" and include whirlpool baths, trouser presses, and hairdryers. The hotel has a bar and offers a room-service menu. The owners serve mainly a French cuisine, and, if given 24 hours' notice, will try to prepare a meal of your choice, costing £20 ($31.60) and up.

3 Henley-on-Thames

35 miles W of London

At the eastern edge of Oxfordshire, Henley-on-Thames, a small town and resort on the river at the foothills of the Chilterns, is the headquarters of the Royal Regatta held annually in late June and early July. The regatta is the number-one event among European oarspeople and dates back to the first years of Victoria's reign.

The Elizabethan buildings, the tearooms, and the inns along the town's High Street live up to one's conception of what an English country town should look like. Cardinal Wolsey is said to have ordered the building of the tower of the Perpendicular and Decorated parish church.

Henley-on-Thames is an excellent stopover en route to Oxford. However, readers on the most limited of budgets will appreciate the much less expensive lodgings in Oxford; the fashionable inns of Henley-on-Thames (Charles I slept here) are far from cheap.

ESSENTIALS

GETTING THERE

By Train   Trains depart from London's Paddington Station but require a change at the junction in Twyford. More than 20 trains make the journey daily, requiring about an hour for the total trip.

By Bus   About 10 buses depart every day from London's Victoria Coach Station for Henley. Although no changes or transfers are required, bus travel is actually slower (about 1³/₄ hr.) than the train because of the multiple stops along the way. There is no Sunday service in winter.

By Car   From London, take M4 toward Reading, to Junction 819, then drive northwest on A4130.

VISITOR INFORMATION

The **telephone area code** is 01491. A **Tourist Information Centre** is at Town Hall, Market Place (☎ **01491/578034**).

SPECIAL EVENTS

The **Henley Royal Regatta** (July 3, 6, and 7) is one of the country's premier racing events. If you want a closeup view from the Stewards' Enclosure, you'll need a guest badge, which is obtainable through a member only. In other words, you have to know someone, but admission to the Regatta Enclosure is open to all. Information is available from the Secretary, Henley Royal Regatta, Henley-on-Thames, Oxfordshire RG9 2LY (☎ **01491/572153**).

WHERE TO STAY & DINE

During the Royal Regatta, rooms are difficult to secure unless you've made reservations months in advance.

INEXPENSIVE

Red Lion Hotel

Hart St., Henley-on-Thames, Oxfordshire RG9 2AR. ☎ **01491/572161.** Fax 01491/410039. 26 rms, 23 with bath (some with tube, some with shower). TV TEL. £43 ($67.95) single without bath, £70 ($110.60) single with bath; £83 ($131.15) double with bath, £95 ($150.10) deluxe double with bath. Breakfast £5.75–£8.75 ($9.10–$13.85) extra. AE, MC, V. Free parking.

This 16th-century ivy-covered, red-brick coaching inn near Henley Bridge used to keep a bedchamber ready for the duke of Marlborough, who would stop here on his way to Blenheim. The guest list reads like a hall of fame—Johnson and Boswell, and even George IV, who, it is said, consumed 14 mutton chops one night. Most of the well-furnished bedrooms overlook the Thames. The hotel also offers laundry service.

The last dinner is served at 10pm, but 24-hour room service is provided. Guests congregate in the low-beamed lounge and take meals in the Riverside Restaurant, where à la carte dinners average £26 ($41.10).

A NEARBY PLACE TO STAY & DINE

Stonor Arms

Stonor, near Henley-on-Thames, Oxfordshire RG9 6HE. ☎ **01491/638863.** Fax 01491/638863. 8 rms, 1 suite. TV TEL. £82.50 ($130.35) single; £92.50 ($146.15) double; £137.50 ($217.25) suite. Rates include breakfast. AE, MC, V.

For the finest dining in the area, as well as accommodations, savvy guests leave Henley-on-Thames and head to the village of Stonor, 4 miles north by A423 on B480. The village pub dates from the 1700s. Chef-owner Stephen Frost, backed up by a hard-working and talented staff, prepares such fine food he often attracts people from London. For those who wish to stay over, a wing of bedrooms is handsomely furnished, often with antiques. Cots for children can be added to most rooms.

In the more formal Stonor Restaurant, only dinner is served, costing £29.50 ($46.60) for a fixed-price menu. Service is Monday through Saturday from 7 to 9:30pm. Blades, the less expensive choice, charges £15.05 to £25.30 ($23.80 to $39.95) for meals which are served daily from noon to 2pm and 7 to 9:30pm. Blades occupies two conservatories and offers such dishes as pork prawn with mustard dressing to pan-fried pigeon breasts with braised lentils. In the Stonor, the menu is mainly English, but with some French and Italian influences. Main dishes change nightly but are likely to include loin of rabbit stuffed with prunes, pan-fried breast of duckling with an apple purée, or lamb shanks with leek polenta. Fresh produce is used whenever possible, and the fish is brought in from Cornwall. Outdoor dining in summer is possible.

EASY EXCURSIONS

MAPLEDURHAM HOUSE ON THE THAMES   The Elizabethan mansion home of the Blount family (☎ 01734/7233450) lies beside the Thames in the unspoiled village of Mapledurham and is accessible by car from the A4074 Oxford–Reading road. A much more romantic way of reaching the lovely old house is to take the boat that leaves the promenade next to Caversham Bridge at 2pm on Saturday, Sunday, and bank holidays from Easter to September; from the end of July to the beginning of September the boat runs daily. The journey upstream takes about 40 minutes, and the boat leaves Mapledurham again at 5pm for the return trip to Caversham. This gives you plenty of time to walk through the house and see the Elizabethan ceilings and the great oak staircase, as well as the portraits of the two beautiful sisters with whom the poet Alexander Pope, a frequent visitor here, fell in love. The family chapel, built in 1789, is a fine example of modern gothic architecture. Cream teas with homemade cakes are available at the house, costing £2.50 ($3.95). On the grounds, the last working water mill on the Thames still produces flour.

The house is open Easter to September, on Saturday, Sunday, and public holidays from 2:30 to 5pm; the entrance charge is £3 ($4.75) for adults and £1.50 ($2.35) for children 5 to 14. The mill is open only from Easter to September on Saturday, Sunday, and public holidays from 1 to 5pm; admission is £2.50 ($3.95) for adults and £1.25 ($2) for children. A combination ticket for the house and mill is £4 ($6.30) for adults and £2 ($3.15) for children 5 to 14.

The round-trip boat ride from Caversham costs £3.20 ($5.05) for adults, £2.10 ($3.30) for children. Further details about the boat can be obtained from **D & T Scenics Ltd.,** Pipers Island, Bridge Street, Caversham Bridge, Reading (☎ 01734/481088).

THE WELLINGTON DUCAL ESTATE   This trip to **Stratfield Saye House,** Stratfield Saye, Reading, Berkshire RG7 2BT (☎ 01256/882882), 7 miles south of Reading on A33 to Basingstoke, takes you a little farther afield. It has been the home of the dukes of Wellington since 1817, when the 17th-century house was bought for the Iron Duke to celebrate his victory over Napoleon at the Battle of Waterloo. A grateful Parliament granted a large sum of money for its purchase. Many memories of the first duke remain in the house, including his billiard table, battle spoils, and pictures. The funeral carriage that since 1860 had rested in St. Paul's Cathedral crypt is on display. In the gardens is the grave of Copenhagen, the charger ridden to battle at Waterloo by the first duke. There are also extensive pleasure grounds together with a licensed restaurant and gift shop.

A short drive away, and under the same administration, is **Wellington Country Park** (☎ 01734/326444), used by many local residents as a place to bring their children for picnics, pedestrian rambles, and exercise. Although most of the allure derives from the park's lake, its waterfowl, and its miles of well-maintained walking paths, the park also encompasses the National Dairy Museum, where you can see the relics of 150 years of dairying; a riding school; a miniature steam railway; a deer park; and the Thames Valley Time Trail, a walk-through series of exhibits related to the geology of the region and the dinosaurs that once inhabited it.

Stratfield Saye is open from May to the last Sunday in September, Saturday through Thursday from 11:30am to 4pm. Admission costs £4.50 ($7.10) for adults and £2.25 ($3.55) for children 5 to 15. Wellington Country Park is open March to October, daily from 10am to 5:30pm; the rest of the year, Saturday and Sunday from 10am to dusk. Admission costs £3 ($4.75) for adults and £1.50 ($2.40) for children 5 to 15. Children 4 and under enter free. A combination ticket for the house and the park costs £6 ($9.50) for adults and £3 ($4.75) for children.

4 Oxford

54 miles NW of London, 54 miles SE of Coventry

A walk down the long sweep of The High, one of the most striking streets in England; a mug of cider in one of the old student pubs; the sound of May Day dawn when choristers sing in Latin from Magdalen Tower; the Great Tom bell from Tom Tower, whose 101 peals traditionally signal the closing of the college gates; towers and spires rising majestically; the barges on the upper reaches of the Thames; nude swimming at Parson's Pleasure; the roar of a cannon launching the bumping races; a tiny, dusty bookstall where you can pick up a valuable first edition—all that is Oxford, home of one of the greatest universities in the world, and also an industrial center of a large automobile business.

At any time of the year you can enjoy a tour of the colleges, many of which represent a peak in England's architectural kingdom, as well as a valley of Victorian contributions. The Oxford Information Centre (see below) offers guided walking tours daily throughout the year. Just don't mention the other place (Cambridge) and you shouldn't have any trouble.

The city predates the university—in fact, it was a Saxon town in the early part of the 10th century. By the 12th century, Oxford was growing in reputation as a seat of learning, at the expense of Paris, and the first colleges were founded in the 13th century. The story of Oxford is filled with conflicts too complex and detailed to elaborate here. Suffice it to say, the relationship between town and gown wasn't as peaceful as it is today. Riots often flared, and both sides were guilty of abuses. Nowadays, the young people of Oxford take out their aggressiveness in sporting competitions.

Ultimately, the test of a great university lies in the caliber of the people it turns out. Oxford can name-drop a mouthful: Roger Bacon, Sir Walter Raleigh, John Donne, Sir Christopher Wren, Samuel Johnson, Edward Gibbon, William Penn, John Wesley, William Pitt, Matthew Arnold, Lewis Carroll, Arnold Toynbee, Harold Macmillan, Graham Greene, A. E. Housman, T. E. Lawrence, and many others.

Impressions

Beautiful City! so venerable, so lovely, so unravaged by the fierce intellectual life of our century, so serene!

There are our young barbarians, all at play! And yet, steeped in sentiment as she lies, spreading her gardens to the moonlight, and whispering from her towers the last enchantments of the Middle Age, who will deny that Oxford, by her ineffable charm, keeps ever calling us nearer to the true goal of all of us, to the ideal, to perfection,— to beauty, in a word, which is only truth seen from another side?—nearest, perhaps, than all the science of Tübingen. Adorable dreamer, whose heart has been so romantic! who has given thyself so prodigally, given thyself to sides and to heroes not mine, only never to the Philistines! home of lost causes, and forsaken beliefs, and unpopular names, and impossible loyalties!

—Matthew Arnold (1822–88), *Essays in Criticism*

ESSENTIALS
GETTING THERE

By Train   Trains from Paddington Station (☎ 01712/262-6767) reach Oxford in 1¼ hours. Service is every hour. A cheap, same-day round-trip ticket costs £12.40 ($19.60).

By Bus   The X90 London Express departs from Victoria Station (☎ 0171/730-0202) for the Oxford Bus Station daily. Coaches usually leave about every 20 minutes during the day, taking 1¾ hours. A same-day round-trip ticket costs £7 ($11.05).

By Car   Take M40 west from London and just follow the signs.

ORIENTATION

Traffic and parking are a disaster in Oxford, and not just during rush hours. However, there are four large **"Park and Ride" parking lots** on the north, south, east, and west of the city's ring road, all well marked. Parking is free at all times, but from 9:30am on, and all day Saturday, you pay about 75p ($1.20) for a bus ride into the city, which drops you off at St. Aldate's Cornmarket or Queen Street to see the city center. The buses run every 8 to 10 minutes in each direction. There is no service on Sunday. The parking lots are on the Woodstock road near the Peartree traffic circle, on the Botley road toward Farringdon, on the Abingdon road in the southeast, and on A40 toward London.

VISITOR INFORMATION

The **telephone area code** is 01865. The **Oxford Information Centre** is at Gloucester Green, opposite the bus station (☎ 01865/726871). The center sells a comprehensive range of maps, brochures, souvenir items, as well as the famous Oxford University T-shirt. It's open Monday through Saturday from 9:30am to 5pm and Sunday from 10am to 3:30pm.

The best way to get a running commentary on the important sightseeing attractions is to go to the Oxford Information Centre. **Two-hour walking tours** through the city and the major colleges leave daily in the morning and afternoon and cost £3.20 ($5.05) for adults and £2 ($3.15) for children; the tours do not include New College or Christ Church.

WHAT TO SEE & DO
SEEING OXFORD UNIVERSITY

Many Americans arriving at Oxford ask: "Where's the campus?" If a local shows amusement when answering, it's because Oxford University is, in fact, made up of 35 colleges. To tour all of these would be a formidable task. It's best to focus on just a handful of the better known colleges.

A Word of Warning: The main business of a university, is, of course, to educate—and this function at Oxford has been severely interfered with by the number of visitors who disturb the academic work of the university. So, unfortunately, visiting is restricted to certain hours and small groups of six or fewer. Furthermore, there are areas where visitors are not allowed at all, but the tourist office will be happy to advise you when and where you may "take in" the sights of this great institution.

OVERVIEW   For a bird's-eye view of the city and colleges, climb **Carfax Tower,** located in the center of the city. This is the one with the clock and figures that strike the quarter hours. Carfax Tower is all that remains from St. Martin's Church, where William Shakespeare once stood as godfather for William Davenant, who also became a successful playwright. A church stood on this site from 1032 until 1896. The tower used to be higher, but after 1340 it was lowered, following complaints from the university to Edward III that townspeople threw stones and fired arrows at students during town-and-gown disputes. Admission is £1.20 ($1.90) for adults, 60p (95¢) for children. The tower is open from Easter to October, daily from 10am to 6pm. For information, call 01865/792653.

The Oxford Story, 6 Broad St. (☎ **01865/790055**), helps the visitor understand the complexities of Oxford University. Insight into the structure of the colleges and a look at some of the architectural and historical features that might otherwise be missed are highlighted. Visitors are also filled in on the general background of the colleges and the deeds of some of the famous people who have passed through its portals. The audiovisual presentation is given daily from 10am to 4:30pm, with an admission charge of £6 ($9.50) for adults and £3.25 ($5.15) for children.

✪ **CHRIST CHURCH**   Begun by Cardinal Wolsey as Cardinal College in 1525, Christ Church (☎ **01865/276499**), known as the House, was founded by Henry VIII in 1546. Facing St. Aldate's Street, Christ Church has the largest quadrangle of any college in Oxford.

Tom Tower houses Great Tom, the 18,000-pound bell referred to earlier. It rings at 9:05pm nightly, signaling the closing of the college gates. The 101 times it peals originally signified the number of students in residence at the time of the founding of the college. Although the student body has grown significantly, Oxford traditions live on forever. There are some interesting portraits in the 16th-century great hall, including works by Gainsborough and Reynolds. Prime ministers are pictured, since Christ Church was the training ground for 13 prime ministers. There's a separate picture gallery.

The college chapel was built over a period of centuries, beginning in the 12th century. (Incidentally, it's not only the college chapel, but also the cathedral of the diocese of Oxford.) The cathedral's most distinguishing features are its Norman pillars and the vaulting of the choir, dating from the 15th century. In the center of the great quadrangle is a statue of Mercury mounted in the center of a fish pond.

The college and cathedral can be visited from 9am to 6pm. The entrance fee is £3 ($4.75) for adults and £2 ($3.15) for children.

MAGDALEN COLLEGE Pronounced "*Maud*-lin," Magdalen College, High Street (☎ 01865/276000), was founded in 1458 by William of Waynflete, bishop of Winchester and later chancellor of England. Its alumni range from Wolsey to Wilde. Opposite the botanic garden, the oldest in England, is the bell tower, where the choristers sing in Latin at dawn on May Day. The reflection of the 15th-century tower is cast in the waters of the Cherwell below. On a not-so-happy day, Charles I—his days numbered—watched the oncoming Roundheads from this tower. Visit the 15th-century chapel, in spite of many of its latter-day trappings. Ask when the hall and other places of special interest are open. The grounds of Magdalen are the most extensive of any Oxford college; there's even a deer park. You can visit from Easter to September, daily from noon to 6pm; off-season, daily from 2 to 6pm. Admission costs £1.50 ($2.35), but it's charged only from Easter to September.

MERTON COLLEGE Founded in 1264, Merton College, Merton Street (☎ 01865/276310), is among the three oldest colleges at the university. It stands near Corpus Christi College on Merton Street, the sole survivor of Oxford's medieval cobbled streets. Merton College is noted for its library, built between 1371 and 1379 and said to be the oldest college library in England. There was once a tradition of keeping some of its most valuable books chained. Now only one book is so secured, to show what the custom was like. One of the treasures of the library is an astrolabe (an astronomical instrument used for measuring the altitude of the sun and stars) thought to have belonged to Chaucer. You pay £1 ($1.60) to visit the ancient library, as well as the Max Beerbohm Room (the satirical English caricaturist who died in 1956). The library and college are open Monday through Friday from 2 to 4pm and Saturday and Sunday from 10am to 4pm. It's closed for one week at Easter and at Christmas.

A favorite pastime is to take **Addison's Walk** through the water meadows. The stroll is so named after a former alumnus, Joseph Addison, the 18th-century essayist and playwright noted for his contributions to the *The Spectator* and *The Tatler.*

UNIVERSITY COLLEGE University College, High Street (☎ 01865/276602), is the oldest one at Oxford and dates back to 1249, when money was donated by an ecclesiastic, William of Durham (the old claim that the real founder was Alfred the Great is more fanciful). The original structures have all disappeared, and what remains today represents essentially the architecture of the 17th century, with subsequent additions in Victoria's day as well as in more recent times. For example, the Goodhart Quadrangle was added as late as 1962. The college's most famous alumnus, Shelley, was "sent down" for his part in collaborating on a pamphlet on atheism. However, all is forgiven today, as the romantic poet is honored by a memorial erected in 1894. The hall and chapel of University College can be visited daily during vacations from 2 to 4pm for a charge of £1.50 ($2.35) for adults, 60p (95¢) for children.

NEW COLLEGE New College, New College Lane, off Queen's Lane (☎ 01865/279555), was founded in 1379 by William of Wykeham, bishop of Winchester and later lord chancellor of England. His college at Winchester supplied a constant stream of students. The first quadrangle, dating from before the end of the 14th century, was the initial quadrangle to be built in Oxford and formed the architectural design for the other colleges. In the antechapel is Sir Jacob Epstein's remarkable modern sculpture of *Lazarus* and a fine El Greco painting of St. James. One of the treasures of the college is a crosier (pastoral staff of a bishop) belonging to the founding father. In the garden, you can see the remains of the old city wall and the mound. The college (entered at New College Lane) can be visited Easter to September, daily from 11:30am to 5pm; off-season, daily from 2 to 5pm. Admission is £1 ($1.60) from Easter to September, free off-season.

PUNTING—A LOCAL SPORT

At **Punt Station,** Cherwell Boathouse, Bardwell Road (☎ **01865/515978**), you can rent a punt (flat-bottom boat maneuvered by a long pole and a small oar) for £6 to £8 ($9.50 to $12.65) per hour, plus a £30 to £40 ($47.40 to $63.20) deposit. Similar charges are made for punt rentals at Magdalen Bridge Boathouse. Punts are rented from March to mid-June and late August to October, daily from 10am until dusk; from mid-June to late August, when a larger inventory of punts is available, daily from 10am to 10pm.

SHOPPING

Golden Cross, an arcade of first-class shops and boutiques, lies between Cornmarket Street and the Covered Market (or between High Street and Market Street). Parts of the arcade date from the 12th century. Many buildings remain from the medieval era, along with some 15th- and 17th-century structures. The market also has a reputation as the Covent Garden of Oxford, where live entertainment takes place on Saturday mornings in summer. In the arcade shops you'll find a wide selection of merchandise, including handmade Belgian chocolates, specialty gifts, clothing for both women and men, and luxury leather goods.

WHERE TO STAY

Accommodations in Oxford are limited, though the addition of motels on the outskirts has aided the plight of those who require modern amenities. Recently, some of the more stalwart candidates in the city center have been refurbished. In addition, motorists may want to consider country houses or small B&Bs on the outskirts of town; they offer the best living in Oxford if you don't mind commuting. Bedrooms, albeit expensive ones, are also provided at the Bath Place Hotel and Le Manoir aux Quat' Saisons (recommended under "Where to Dine," below).

The **Oxford Information Centre,** Gloucester Green, opposite the bus station (☎ **01865/726871**), operates a year-round room-booking service for a fee of £2.50 ($3.95), plus a refundable deposit. If you'd like to seek lodgings on your own, the center has a list of accommodations, maps, and guidebooks.

EXPENSIVE

✪ **Old Parsonage Hotel**

1 Banbury Rd., Oxford OX2 6NN. ☎ **01865/310210.** Fax 01865/311262. 26 rms, 4 suites. MINIBAR TV TEL. £105 ($165.90) single; £140 ($221.20) double; £195 ($308.10) suite. Rates include English breakfast. AE, DC, MC, V. Free parking. Bus 7.

This massively renovated hotel near St. Giles Church and Keble College is so old (1660) it looks like an extension of one of the ancient colleges. Originally a 13th-century hospital named Bethleen, it was restored in the early 17th century. Oscar Wilde once lived here for a time and is famed for the remark, "Either this wallpaper goes, or I do." In the 20th century a modern wing was added, and in 1990 it was completely renovated and made into a first-rate hotel. The bedrooms are individually designed, with such amenities as a remote-control radio and hairdryer. The marble bathrooms are air-conditioned, with their own phone extensions. All the suites and some bedrooms have sofa beds. The bedrooms open onto the private gardens, and 10 of them are on the ground floor. The Parsonage Bar serves everything from cappuccino to mixed drinks. Here, in lieu of a restaurant, you can order from a well-prepared menu of continental and English food from 7am until "late at night." There's also 24-hour room service.

The Randolph

Beaumont St., Oxford, Oxfordshire OX1 2LN. ☎ **01865/247481**, or 800/225-5843 in the U.S. and Canada. Fax 01865/791678. 101 rms, 8 suites. TV TEL. £95–£120 ($150.10–$189.60) single; £120–£160 ($189.60–$252.80) double; £180–£380 ($284.40–$600.40) suite. Breakfast £11.50 ($18.15) extra. AE, DC, MC, V. Free parking. Bus 7.

For more than a century the Randolph has been overlooking St. Giles, the Ashmolean Museum, and the Cornmarket. The lounges, although modernized, are still cavernous enough for dozens of separate conversational groupings. The furnishings are traditional, and all rooms have a private bath, hairdryer, and hot beverage-making facilities.

The hotel's Spires Restaurant presents both a time-tested English and a modern cuisine in a high-ceilinged Victorian dining room. An à la carte dinner costs about £35 ($55.30) per person, while a fixed-price dinner goes for £25 ($39.50). The restaurant serves daily: lunch from 12:30 to 2pm and dinner from 7 to 10pm. There's also a wine bar with an entrance off the street, serving from 11am to 11pm Monday though Saturday. The hotel's Chapters Bar has a tradition-laden atmosphere. The drink list offers everything from "textbook classics" to "epilogue."

MODERATE

Eastgate Hotel

23 Merton St., The High, Oxford, Oxfordshire, OX1 4BE. ☎ **01865/248244**, or 800/225-5843 in the U.S. and Canada. Fax 01865/791681. 42 rms, 1 suite. TV TEL. £90 ($142.20) single; £105 ($165.90) double; £130 ($205.40) suite. Breakfast £5.95–$8.50 ($9.40–$13.45) extra. AE, DC, MC, V. Free parking. Bus 7.

The Eastgate, built on the site of a 1600s structure, stands opposite the ancient Examination Halls, within walking distance of Oxford colleges and the city center. Recently refurbished, it offers modern facilities while retaining somewhat the atmosphere of an English country house. All rooms have radios as well as hot-beverage-making equipment. The Shires Restaurant offers a selection of roasts and traditional English fare, complemented by a choice of wines. A three-course table d'hôte is priced at £17.95 ($28.35).

Oxford Moat House

Godstow Rd., Wolvercote Roundabout, Oxford, Oxfordshire OX2 8AL. ☎ **01865/59933.** Fax 01865/310259. 151 rms, 4 suites. TV TEL. £95 ($150.10) single; £115 ($181.70) double; £195 ($308.10) suite. English breakfast £9.50 ($15) extra. AE, DC, MC, V. Free parking. Closed Dec 24–Jan 2. Bus 60.

This hostelry is one of the Queens Moat Houses group, incorporating the principles of motel design, with an emphasis on spacious, glassed-in areas and streamlined bedrooms. Generally patronized by motorists, it's located at the northern edge of Oxford 2 miles from the center, hidden from the traffic at the junction of A40 and A34. Each room features a radio, video, and trouser press. The Moat

Oxford

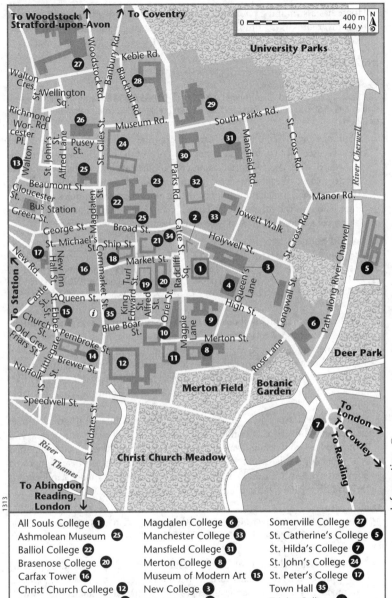

College	No.	College	No.	College	No.
All Souls College	1	Magdalen College	6	Somerville College	27
Ashmolean Museum	25	Manchester College	33	St. Catherine's College	5
Balliol College	22	Mansfield College	31	St. Hilda's College	7
Brasenose College	20	Merton College	8	St. John's College	24
Carfax Tower	16	Museum of Modern Art	15	St. Peter's College	17
Christ Church College	12	New College	3	Town Hall	35
Corpus Christi College	11	Oriel College	10	Trinity College	23
Exeter College	21	Pembroke College	14	University College	9
Hertford College	2	Queen's College	4	University Museum	29
Jesus College	18	Regent's Park College	26	Wadham College	32
Keble College	28	Rhodes House	30	Worcester College	13
Lincoln College	19	Sheldonian Theatre	34		

House has a swimming pool, squash courts, a sauna, a solarium, and a snooker (billiards) room. Its Oxford Blue Restaurant serves an English menu, with a fixed-price meal reasonably priced at £16.50 ($26.05).

INEXPENSIVE

⑤ Adams Guest House

302 Banbury Rd., Oxford, Oxfordshire OX2 7ED. ☎ **01865/56118.** 6 rms. TV. £25 ($39.50) single; £38 ($60.05) double. Rates include English breakfast. No credit cards. Bus 7, 20, 21, or 22.

In Summertown, $1^1/_4$ miles from Oxford, opposite Radio Oxford, is the Adams Guest House, operated by John Strange; it's one of the best B&Bs in the northern Oxford area. The comfortable and cozy rooms have private showers and tea or coffee makers. Breakfast is served in a dining room decorated in old-world style. Mr. Strange will provide touring tips. A bus runs every few minutes to the city center. Close to the Adams Guest House are a bank, seven restaurants, shops, a post office, a swimming pool, a bike-rental shop, and a launderette.

Cotswold Lodge Hotel

66A Banbury Rd., Oxford, Oxfordshire OX2 6JP. ☎ **01865/512121.** Fax 01865/512490. 50 rms. TV TEL. Mon–Thurs, £75 ($118.50) single; £97.50 ($154.05) double; £112.50 ($177.75) triple. Fri–Sun, £65 ($102.70) single; £87.50 ($138.25) double; £102.50 ($161.95) triple. Rates include English breakfast. AE, DC, MC, V. Free parking. To get here, see the directions below.

This Victorian building is about half a mile from the city center. The bedrooms have been refurbished to a good standard, with such amenities as hairdryer, color TV, phone, and tea- or coffee-making equipment. Drinks are offered in a bar with a log fire, and the restaurant serves a wide range of food, everything from simple bar snacks to elegant candlelit dinners. A table d'hôte lunch costs £12.50 ($19.75), and a table d'hôte dinner goes for £17.50 ($27.65). Room service is available 24 hours.

To get here, leave M40 at Junction 8 for Oxford and follow A40. About 1 mile after passing through a set of traffic lights at the Park and Ride parking area, you come to a large roundabout (traffic circle); go right here, taking the exit signposted A40. In about 3 miles you reach another roundabout; turn left here, signposted Summertown City Center. This is Banbury Road; the hotel is about 2 miles down the road on the left-hand side at the corner of Norham Road.

Dial House

25 London Rd., Headington, Oxford, Oxfordshire OX3 7RE. ☎ **01865/69944.** 8 rms. TV. £35–£40 ($55.30–$63.20) single; £45–£50 ($71.10–$79) double. No credit cards. Free parking. Bus 7, 7A, 20, 21, or 22.

Two miles east of the heart of Oxford, beside the main highway leading to London, is this country-style house originally built between 1924 and 1927. Graced with mock Tudor half-timbering and a prominent blue-faced sundial (from which it derives its name), it has cozy and recently renovated bedrooms, each equipped with tea-making facilities and hairdryers. No smoking is permitted in the bedrooms, although smoking is allowed in a small guest lounge. The owners, Julie and Tony Lamb, serve only breakfast in their bright dining room.

Tilbury Lodge Private Hotel

5 Tilbury Lane, Eynsham Rd., Botley, Oxford, Oxfordshire OX2 9NB. ☎ **01865/862138.** Fax 01865/863700. 10 rms. TV TEL. £40 ($63.20) single; £60 ($94.80) double, £80

($126.40) double with four-poster. Rates include English breakfast. MC, V. Free parking. Bus 42, 45, 45A, 45B, or 109.

On a quiet country lane about 2 miles west of the center of Oxford, this small hotel is less than a mile from the railway station. Eddie and Eileen Trafford accommodate guests in their well-furnished and comfortable bedrooms. The most expensive room has a four-poster bed. The guesthouse also has a Jacuzzi and welcomes children. If you don't arrive by car, Eddie can pick you up at the train station; alternatively, a bus can take visitors to Botley, an area of Oxford.

Welcome Lodge

Peartree Roundabout, Woodstock Rd., Oxford, Oxfordshire OX2 8JZ. ☎ **01865/54301,** or 800/225-5843 in the U.S. and Canada. Fax 01865/513474. 95 rms. TV TEL. Mon–Thurs, £49.50 ($78.20) single or double. Fri–Sun, £39.50 ($62.40) single or double. Rates include English breakfast. AE, DC, MC, V. Free parking. Park and Ride bus, with frequent trips from downtown Oxford to a public parking lot nearby.

Located 3 miles north of Oxford, near the beginning of the A34 highway leading away from town, this large commercial hotel is suitable for motorists who want to be within easy reach of the university and the shopping districts of Oxford. Situated near a large bus stop, the hotel is easy to spot because of the international flags fluttering in the breezes. Its lower-level bedrooms open onto private terraces. The furnishings are in the typical motel style, with compact, built-in necessities. Each room has a picture-window wall, individually controlled heating, and tea-making facilities. Dining choices include the Lodgekeepers Restaurant and bar, the Little Chef Grill, the Granary Self-Service Restaurant, and a family shop.

NEARBY PLACES TO STAY

Moderate

Studley Priory Hotel

Main St., Horton-cum-Studley, Oxfordshire OX33 1AZ. ☎ **01865/351203,** or 800/ 437-2687 in the U.S. and Canada. Fax 01865/351613. 18 rms, 1 suite. TV TEL. £88 ($139.05) single; £98–£150 ($154.85–$237) double; £225 ($355.50) suite. Rates include English breakfast. AE, DC, MC, V. Free parking. For directions to this hotel, see below.

The Studley Priory Hotel may be remembered by those who saw the movie *A Man for All Seasons.* The former Benedictine priory, a hotel since 1961, was used in background shots as the private residence of Sir Thomas More. It's a stunning example of Elizabethan architecture, although it originally dates from the 12th century. Located on 13 acres of wooded grounds and occupied for around 300 years by the Croke family, the manor is only 7 miles from Oxford. It's built of stone in the manorial style, with large halls, long bedroom wings, and gables with mullioned windows. The rooms are very large and the furnishings tasteful. Room service is provided all day. Even if you're not staying over, you may want to visit for lunch or dinner. A three-course set Sunday lunch costs £19.50 ($30.80); à la carte meals range from £22.50 to £29.75 ($35.55 to $47).

Getting here is a bit complicated—so be armed with a good map when you strike out from Oxford. From Oxford, drive to the end of Banbury Road. At the traffic circle, take the third exit (toward London). Go approximately $3^{1}/_{2}$ miles. At the next traffic circle, take the first exit (signposted Horton-cum-Studley) and travel $4^{1}/_{2}$ miles. Go through the estate and stay on the same road until you come to "staggered crossroads." Go straight across, signposted HORTON-CUM-STUDLEY $2^{1}/_{2}$ MILES. This road will bring you straight into the village, and the hotel is at the top of the hill on the right-hand side.

Weston Manor

Weston-on-the-Green, Oxfordshire OX6 8QL. ☎ **01869/350621**. Fax 01869/350901. 34 rms, 3 suites. TV TEL. £80–£85 ($126.40–$134.30) single; £105–£110 ($165.90–$173.80) double; from £125 ($197.50) suite. Rates include English breakfast. AE, DC, MC, V. Free parking. Drive 6 miles north of Oxford on A34.

Ideal as a center for touring the district (Blenheim Palace is only 5 miles away), the manor, owned and run by the Osborn family, has existed since the 11th century; portions of the present building date from the 14th and 16th centuries. The estate was an abbey until abbeys were abolished by Henry VIII. Of course, there are ghosts: Mad Maude, the naughty nun who was burned at the stake for her "indecent and immoral" behavior, returns to haunt the Oak Bedrooms. Prince Rupert, during the English Civil War, hid from Cromwell's soldiers in one of the fireplaces, eventually escaping in drag as the "maiden of the milk bucket."

The reception lounge is dominated by a Tudor fireplace and a long refectory table. Most of the bedrooms are spacious, furnished with antiques (often fourposters), old dressing tables, and chests. The Great Hall is one of the most beautiful dining rooms in England, with an open-rafter and beamed ceiling, the lower portion solidly paneled with a rare example of linen fold. There's a minstrels' gallery and a large wrought-iron chandelier. The English food is first rate. A la carte meals average £25 ($39.50), and the big Sunday lunch costs £15 ($23.70). In warm weather, you can enjoy an open-air swimming pool surrounded by gardens.

WHERE TO DINE
VERY EXPENSIVE

✪ Le Manoir aux Quat' Saisons

Great Milton, Oxfordshire OX44 7PD. ☎ **01844/278881**. Fax 01844/278847. Reservations required. Main courses £30–£33 ($47.40–$52.15); lunch *menu du jour* £29.50–£36.50 ($46.60–$57.65); lunch or dinner *menu gourmand* £65 ($102.70). AE, DC, MC, V. Daily 11:45am–2:30pm and 6:15–10:30pm. Take Exit 7 off M40 and head along A329 toward Wallingford; look carefully for signs for Great American Milton Manor around a mile later. FRENCH.

Some 12 miles southeast of Oxford, Le Manoir aux Quat' Saisons enjoys a reputation for offering the finest cuisine in the Midlands. The gray- and honey-colored stone manor house was originally built by a Norman nobleman in the early 1300s, and over the years attracted many famous visitors. The connection with France has been masterfully revived by the Gallic owner and chef, Raymond Blanc. His reputation for comfort and cuisine attracts guests from as far away as London— gastronomes who regard the 1-hour trek as a delicious excuse for a day in the country.

The main focus of the establishment is a pair of beamed-ceiling dining rooms whose mullioned windows offer views of the garden. You can enjoy such specialties as quail eggs, spinach, parmesan, and black truffle ravioli in a poultry jus and meunière butter and swiss chard; a mousse of Jerusalem artichokes with a vegetable fumet scented with chevril; grilled fillet of turbot with red-wine butter and beurre blanc garnished with deep-fried vegetables; braised boned oxtail filled with shallots and wild mushrooms in a Hermitage red-wine sauce with purée of parsnips; and roast wild partridge with its juices and émincé of onion with thyme and black currants. After-dinner coffee is served beside the fire in the lounge. If you call, they'll give you travel directions.

The gabled house was built in the 1500s and improved and enlarged in 1908. An outdoor swimming pool, still in use, was added much later. Inside,

19 luxurious bedrooms, each decorated boudoir style with lots of flowery draperies, ruffled canopies, radio, color TV, phone, private bath, springtime colors, and high-quality antique reproductions, cost £175 to £375 ($276.50 to $592.50), double occupancy.

MODERATE

Bath Place Hotel

4–5 Bath Place (at Holywell St.), Oxford OX1 3SU. ☎ **01865/791812.** Fax 01865/791834. Reservations recommended. Main courses £16.50–£21.50 ($26.05–$33.95); eight-course fixed-price dinner £49.50 ($78.20). AE, MC, V. Tues 7–10pm, Wed–Sat noon–2:30pm and 7–10pm, Sun noon–2:30pm. Bus 7. MEDITERRANEAN.

Composed of four 17th–century cottages that were joined into an interconnected whole, this establishment has been well known since 1989 as a haven for sophisticated cuisine. Since it also houses 10 cozy bedrooms upstairs, it operates something like a French *restaurant avec chambres,* where diners can head directly upstairs after an evening meal, thus avoiding the need to drive off the premises after food and wine. The menu, which changes about every month, reflects a pleasing mixture of Mediterranean cuisines, with heavy emphasis on French. Menu choices might include salmon and scallop ravioli served on a bed of braised endive with grilled scallops and an olive oil emulsion of basil, saffron, Noilly port, olives, and tomatoes; a warm salad of woodpigeon breasts, orange and tomato dressed with walnut oil, and a sauce made with pan juices, raspberry vinegar, and orange juice; grilled fillet of Cornish sea bass with charcoal-grilled provençal vegetables and a saffron-butter sauce; Scottish beef sirloin with bordelaise sauce and a confit of shallots and garlic; and seafood tagliatelle, lightly grilled served with homemade pasta and beurre blanc sauce.

Each of the upstairs bedrooms features a TV and telephone. With breakfast included, singles cost £70 to £85 ($110.60 to $134.30); doubles, £85 to £125 ($134.30 to $197.50).

Cherwell Boathouse Restaurant

Bardwell Rd. ☎ **01865/52746.** Reservations recommended. Main courses £8–£12 ($12.65–$18.95); fixed-price dinner from £17.50 ($27.65); set lunch £16.50 ($26.05). AE, DC, MC, V. Tues 6–11:30pm, Wed–Sat noon–2pm and 6–11:30pm, Sun noon–2pm. Closed Dec 24–30. Banbury Road bus. ENGLISH/FRENCH.

This virtual Oxford landmark on the River Cherwell is owned by Anthony Verdin, who is assisted by a young crew. A fixed-price menu is offered and the cooks change the menu every 2 weeks to take advantage of the availability of fresh vegetables, fish, and meat. There is a very reasonable, even exciting, wine list. Children are charged half price. In summer, the restaurant also serves on the terrace. Before dinner, you can try "punting" on the Cherwell; punts are rented on the other side of the boat house.

Elizabeth

82 St. Aldate's St. ☎ **01865/242230.** Reservations recommended. Main courses £13.25–£17.75 ($20.95–$28.05); fixed-price lunch £15 ($23.70). AE, DC, MC, V. Tues–Sun 12:30–2:30pm and 6:30–11pm. Closed Easter weekend and Christmas week. Bus 7. FRENCH/CONTINENTAL.

Despite the portraits of Elizabeth II that hang near the entrance, this restaurant is named after its original owner, a matriarch who founded the place in this stone-sided house in the 1930s. Today, you're likely to find a well-trained staff from

Spain, who serve beautifully presented dishes in the French style. The larger of the two dining rooms displays reproductions of paintings by Goya and Velázquez and exudes a restrained kind of dignity; the smaller room is devoted to *Alice in Wonderland* designs inspired by Lewis Carroll. Menu choices might include chicken royale; a range of Scottish steaks; grilled salmon, Dover sole, and sea bass, served in white-wine or lemon-butter sauce; Basque pipérade; duck with orange sauce; and roast rack of lamb with gratin dauphinois.

15 North Parade

15 North Parade Ave. ☎ **01865/513773.** Reservations recommended. Main courses £9–£11.75 ($14.20–$18.55); fixed-price meal £10–£13.75 ($15.80–$21.75) at lunch, £15 ($23.70) at dinner. MC, V. Tues–Sat noon–2pm and 7–10:30pm, Sun noon–2pm. Bus 7. INTERNATIONAL.

Located close to Banbury Road, and popular with the town's academic community, this restaurant has won the respect of residents and foreign visitors alike. In an environment of faded blue-green walls, mirrors, and minimalist design, you can enjoy such dishes as parsnip, carrot, and tomato soup; charcoal-grilled chicken with flagelot beans and marjoram; roast guinea fowl; and charcoal-grilled rib of pork with spicy salsa sauce.

INEXPENSIVE

Al-Shami

25 Walton Crescent. ☎ **01865/310066.** Reservations recommended. Main courses £5.75–£12 ($9.10–$18.95); fixed-price menu £15 ($23.70). No credit cards. Daily noon–midnight. Bus 7. LEBANESE.

Ideal for meals all afternoon and late into the evening, this Lebanese restaurant has awakened the sleepy taste buds of Oxford. Before it opened, the only choice you had after the theater were Chinese and Indian restaurants. Many diners don't go beyond the appetizers, since they comprise more than 35 delectable hot-and-cold selections—everything from felafel to a salad made with lamb's brains. Charcoal-grilled chopped lamb, chicken, or beef constitute most of the main-dish selections. In between, guests nibble on uncut raw vegetables such as fresh tomatoes. Desserts are chosen from the trolley. Vegetarian meals are also available.

ⓢ Munchy Munchy

6 Park End St. ☎ **01865/245710.** Reservations recommended. Main courses £4.50–£8 ($7.10–$12.65). MC, V. Tues–Sat noon–2pm and 5:30–10pm, Sun noon–2pm. Closed 2 weeks in Sept and 2 weeks in Dec. Bus 52. SOUTHEAST ASIAN/INDONESIAN.

Some Oxford students, who frequent this restaurant near the station, claim that it offers the best food value in the city. Main dishes depend on what's available in the marketplace, and there are no appetizers. Ethel Ow is adept at herbs and seasoning, and often uses fresh fruit creatively, as reflected in such dishes as king prawns sautéed with tumeric, coriander, and a purée of apricots. Indonesian and Malaysian dishes are popular. Sometimes, especially on Friday and Saturday, long lines form at the door. Children 5 and under are not permitted on Friday and Saturday evenings.

PUBS

The Bear Inn

Alfred St. ☎ **01865/721783.** Reservations not accepted. Snacks and bar meals £1.85–£4.75 ($2.90–$7.50). No credit cards. Mon–Sat noon–11pm, Sun noon–3pm and 7–10:30pm. Bus 2A or 2B. ENGLISH.

A short block from The High, overlooking the north side of Christ Church College, this is the village pub and an Oxford tradition. Its swinging inn sign depicts the bear and ragged staff, old insignia of the earls of Warwick, who were among the early patrons. Built in the 13th century, the inn has been known to many famous Oxford students and residents. Over the years it has been mentioned time and time again in English literature.

The Bear has served a useful purpose in breaking down social barriers, bringing a wide variety of people together in a relaxed way. You might talk with a raja from India, a university don, a titled gentleman—and the latest in a line of owners that goes back more than 700 years. Some former owners developed an astonishing habit: clipping neckties. Around the lounge bar you'll see the remains of thousands of ties, which have been labeled with their owners' names. For those of you who want to leave something behind, a thin strip from the bottom of your tie will be cut off (with your permission, of course). After this initiation, you may want to join in some of the informal songfests of the undergraduates.

The Trout Inn

195 Godstow Rd., Wolvercote. ☎ **01865/54485.** Main courses £6.95–£29.50 ($11–$46.60); pub snacks £3.95–£6 ($6.25–$9.50). AE, DC, MC, V. Restaurant, daily noon–3pm and 7–10pm. Pub, daily 11am–11pm. Bus 520 or 521 to Wolvercote; then walk half a mile. ENGLISH.

Some $2^1/_2$ miles north of Oxford and hidden away from visitors and townspeople, the Trout is a private world where you can get ale and beer—and standard fare. Have your drink in one of the historic rooms, with their settles, brass, and old prints, or go out in sunny weather to sit on a stone wall. On the grounds are peacocks, ducks, swans, and herons that live in and around the river and an adjacent weir pool; they'll join you if you're handing out crumbs. Take an arched stone bridge, stone terraces, architecture with wildly pitched roofs and gables, add the Thames River, and you have the Trout. The Stable Bar, the original 12th-century part, complements the inn's relatively new 16th-century bars. Daily specials are featured, and there's a cold snack bar. Hot meals are served all day in the restaurant; salads are featured in summer, and there are grills in winter. As its name implies, the inn serves trout, prepared in six different ways, plus a dish you're not likely to find elsewhere in Britain: beef Godstow, fillet steak cooked in bacon and served with a black-currant sauce. Although the pub is open all day Sunday, no liquor is served from 3 to 6pm. On your way there and back, look for the view of Oxford from the bridge.

The Turf Tavern

4 Bath Place (off Holywell St.). ☎ **01865/243235.** Reservations not accepted. Main dishes all £4.85 ($7.65). MC, V. Mon–Sat 11am–11pm, Sun noon–3pm and 7–10:30pm. Bus 52. ENGLISH.

This 13th-century tavern lies on a very narrow passageway near the Bodleian Library. Thomas Hardy used the place as the setting for *Jude the Obscure*. It was "the local" of Burton and Taylor when they were in Oxford many years ago making a film, and today's patrons might include Kris Kristofferson and John Hurt, as well as a healthy sampling of the university's students and faculty. During his student days at Oxford, the future U.S. president, Bill Clinton, was a frequent visitor here. Before and after his election, private investigators and journalists came to the pub trying to glean favorable or unfavorable anecdotes about the U.S. leader. At night, the nearby old tower of New College and part of the old city wall are floodlit, and during warm weather you can choose a table in any of the three separate gardens that radiate outward from the pub's central core. For wintertime warmth, braziers are lighted in the courtyard and in the gardens.

A separate food counter, set behind a glass case, displays the day's fare. (If you're hungry, present yourself to the employee behind the case, and carry your food back to your table.) Menu choices include salads, soups, sandwiches, and platters of such traditional dishes as English beef pie, roast chicken, lasagne, and mutton. Local ales (including one named Headbanger, with a relatively high alcohol content) are served, as well as a range of wines. The pub is reached via St. Helen's Passage, which stretches between Holywell Street and New College Lane. (You'll probably get lost, but any student worth his beer can direct you.)

5 Woodstock (Blenheim Palace)

8 miles NW of Oxford, 62 miles NW of London

The small country town of Woodstock, the birthplace in 1330 of the Black Prince, ill-fated son of King Edward III, lies on the edge of the Cotswolds. Some of the stone houses here were constructed when Woodstock was the site of a royal palace. This palace had so suffered the ravages of time that its remains were demolished when Blenheim Palace was built. Woodstock was once the seat of a flourishing glove industry.

ESSENTIALS
GETTING THERE

By Train   Take the train to Oxford (see above).

By Bus   The Gloucester Green bus (no. 20) leaves Oxford about every 30 minutes during the day (trip time: 36 min.) Call 01865/711312 for details.

By Car   Take A44 from Oxford.

VISITOR INFORMATION

The **telephone area code** is 01993. The **Tourist Information Centre** is on Hensington Road (☎ **01993/811038**).

SEEING THE PALACE

This extravagant baroque ✪ **Blenheim Palace** (☎ **01993/811091**) regards itself as England's answer to Versailles. Blenheim is the home of the 11th duke of Marlborough, a descendant of John Churchill, the first duke, who was an on-again, off-again favorite of Queen Anne's. In his day (1650–1722), the first duke became the supreme military figure in Europe. Fighting on the Danube near a village named Blenheim, Churchill defeated the forces of Louis XIV, and the lavish palace of Blenheim was built for the duke as a gift from the queen. It was designed by Sir John Vanbrugh, who was also the architect of Castle Howard; the landscaping was created by Capability Brown.

The palace is loaded with riches: antiques, porcelain, oil paintings, tapestries, and chinoiserie. North Americans know Blenheim as the birthplace of Sir Winston Churchill. His birth room is included in the palace tour, as is the Churchill exhibition, four rooms of letters, books, photographs, and other relics. Today the former prime minister lies buried in Bladon Churchyard, near the palace.

Blenheim Palace is open from mid-March to October, daily from 10:30am to 4:45pm. Admission costs £7 ($11.05) for adults, £3.50 ($5.55) for children 5 to 15.

WHERE TO STAY & DINE
MODERATE

✪ The Bear Hotel

Park St., Woodstock, Oxfordshire OX20 1SZ. ☎ **01993/811511,** or 800/225-5843 in the U.S. and Canada. Fax 01993/813380. 41 rms, 3 suites. TV TEL. £95 ($150.10) single; £115 ($181.70) double; £180 ($284.40) suite. Breakfast £5.95–£8.95 ($9.40–$14.15) extra. AE, DC, MC, V. Free parking.

Reputed to be one of the six oldest coaching inns in England, dating from the 16th century, the half-stone structure is located in the center of Woodstock. Look for the signs in front with the picture of a huge brown bear. History surrounds you here, even such relatively recent history as the hiding away here of Richard Burton and Elizabeth Taylor, although an even more recent client was Richard Branson. These celebrities stayed in the Marlboro suite, an attractively decorated sitting room with a minibar, plus a bedroom and bath. One of the chambers of the hotel is haunted, legend says. Modern amenities are combined with antiques in the bedrooms, which have hairdryers, trouser presses, and private baths. Blazing hearth fires are found throughout the hotel when the days and nights are cool. You can relax in the big, black-beamed bar or the comfortable lounge for drinks and enjoy traditional dishes in the dining room. If you stay 2 consecutive nights over a Friday to Sunday period, single or double occupancy costs £84 ($132.70) including dinner on both nights. Otherwise, a table d'hôte lunch costs £14.95 to £16.95 ($23.60 to $26.80), with a table d'hôte dinner priced at £25.95 ($41).

Feathers

Market St., Woodstock, Oxfordshire OX20 1SX. ☎ **01993/812291.** Fax 01993/813158. 14 rms, 3 suites. TV TEL. £75 ($118.50) single; £99–£150 ($156.40–$237) double; £185 ($292.30) suite. Rates include continental breakfast. AE, DC, MC, V. Free parking.

Feathers dates from the 17th century and has been an inn since the 18th century. The bedrooms in this beautifully furnished hotel just a short walk from Blenheim Palace are individually decorated and have private baths. The two lounges have wood fires. One boasts fine china and valuable old books; the other is oak-paneled with sturdy beams. A multitude of stuffed birds (from which the house took its name) adorn the bar; from there you can go into the delightful garden in the courtyard.

The food at Feathers is of high quality. Whether you're here for lunch or for a candlelit dinner, you're sure to enjoy the well-prepared dishes. In summer, you can have a light lunch or afternoon tea in the courtyard garden. Lunch is served daily from 12:30 to 2:15pm; dinner, daily from 7:30 to 9:30pm. Fixed-price lunches and dinners cost £21.50 to £26.50 ($33.95 to $41.85).

9 Kent & Surrey

Lying to the south and southeast of London are the shires (counties) of Kent and Surrey—both fascinating areas within easy commuting distance of the capital. Of all the tourist centers, Canterbury in Kent is of foremost interest.

Once the ancient Anglo-Saxon kingdom of Kent, this county is on the fringes of London yet is far removed in spirit and scenery. Since the days of the Tudors, cherry blossoms have enlivened the fertile landscape. Not only orchards, but hop fields abound, and conical oasthouses with kilns for drying hops dot the rolling countryside. Both the hops and orchards have earned Kent the title of garden of England—and in England, the competition's rough.

Kent suffered severe destruction during World War II, since it was the alley over which the Luftwaffe flew in its blitz of London. But in spite of much devastation, it's still filled with interesting old towns, mansions, and castles. The county is also rich in Dickensian associations—in fact, Kent is sometimes known as Dickens Country. His family once lived near the naval dockyard at Chatham.

Long before William the Conqueror marched his pillaging Normans across its chalky North Downs, Surrey was important to the Saxons. In fact, early Saxon kings were once crowned at what is now Kingston-on-Thames (their Coronation Stone is still preserved near the guildhall).

More recently, this tiny county has for some time been in danger of being gobbled up by the expansion of London and turned into a sprawling suburb. But although the area bordering the capital is densely populated, Surrey still retains much unspoiled countryside, largely because its many heaths and commons form undesirable land for postwar suburban houses. Essentially, Surrey is a county of commuters (Alfred Lord Tennyson was among the first), since someone employed in the city can travel to the remotest corner of Surrey from London in about 45 minutes to an hour.

A DRIVING TOUR

Day 1   Head east from London for an overnight stay at Royal Tunbridge Wells. En route visit Chartwell, former home of Winston

What's Special About Kent & Surrey

Great Towns/Villages
- Canterbury, a cathedral city and the headquarters of the Anglican church, a center of international pilgrimage.
- Dover, Britain's historic "gateway" to continental Europe, famed for its white cliffs.

Castles
- Knole, one of the largest private houses of England, a great example of pure English Tudor architecture.
- Hever Castle, dating from the end of the 13th century, a gift from Henry VIII to the "great Flanders mare," Anne of Cleves.
- Penshurst Place, a magnificent English gothic mansion, one of the outstanding country houses of Britain.
- Leeds Castle, near Maidstone, dating from A.D. 857, and once called "the loveliest castle in the world."
- Dover Castle, whose keep was built at the command of Henry II in the 12th century.

Gardens
- Chilham Castle Gardens, landscaped by Capability Brown on former royal property 6 miles west of Canterbury.

Historic Home
- Chartwell House, former country home of Sir Winston Churchill, with much memorabilia.

Churchill, and also Knole, one of the largest private estates in England, an example of the English Tudor style of architecture.

Day 2   Before going to Canterbury the next morning, visit Penhurst Place, one of the outstanding country homes in Britain, 6 miles west of Tonbridge (not to be confused with Tunbridge Wells). Later in the day explore Hever Castle and Gardens, dating from 1270, former childhood home of Anne Boleyn, one of the wives of Henry VIII. Arrive in Canterbury in the late afternoon and plan to spend the night.

Day 3   From Canterbury, continue south along the A2 to the seaport of Dover, Britain's historic gateway to the Continent. Dover has few attractions, since it suffered heavily during World War II bombardments. After seeing its white cliffs and its castle, you might want to press on to another destination. If you anchor at Maidstone, 36 miles from London, you'll be in a position to explore Leeds Castle the following morning.

☕ **TAKE A BREAK**   A good place to anchor for the night is Grangemoor, 4–8 St. Michael's Rd. (off Tonbridge Road), Maidstone, Kent ME16 8BS (☎ **0622/677623;** fax 0622/678246). This family-run hotel offers 12 well-equipped bedrooms, renting for £30 ($47.40) single and £52 ($82.15) double. It's located in a tranquil residential area, although close to the center of Maidstone. A Tudor-style bar and restaurant are also available, with meals costing £12 ($18.95) and up.

Day 4   Visit Leeds Castle in the morning. Around midday head west to visit Surrey (albeit briefly), passing first through Dorking, 26 miles south of London. Three miles northwest of the town stands Polesden Lacey (see below). Spend the night in one of the local inns such as Forte Crest Hotel.

1 Canterbury

56 miles SE of London

Under the arch of the ancient West Gate journeyed Chaucer's knight, solicitor, nun, squire, parson, merchant, miller, and others—spinning tales. They were bound for the shrine of Thomas à Becket, archbishop of Canterbury, who was slain by four knights of Henry II on December 29, 1170. (The king later walked barefoot from Harbledown to the tomb of his former friend, where he allowed himself to be flogged in penance.) The shrine was finally torn down in 1538 by Henry VIII, as part of his campaign to destroy the monasteries and graven images. Canterbury, by then, had already become a fixed attraction. The medieval Kentish city on the River Stour is the ecclesiastical capital of England. The city was once completely walled, and many traces of its old fortifications remain. Canterbury was inhabited centuries before the birth of Jesus Christ. Julius Caesar arrived on the Kent coast in 54 B.C., but Roman occupation didn't begin until much later. Although its most famous incident was the murder of Becket, the medieval city witnessed other major events in English history, including Bloody Mary's order to burn nearly 40 victims at the stake. Richard the Lion-Hearted returned this way from crusading, and Charles II passed through on the way to claim his crown.

ESSENTIALS
GETTING THERE

By Train   By train from Victoria, Charing Cross, Waterloo, or London Bridge Station, the journey takes $1\frac{1}{2}$ hours. There is frequent service.

By Bus   The bus from Victoria Coach Station takes 2 to 3 hours. Buses leave twice daily.

By Car   From London, take A2, then M2. Canterbury is signposted all the way. The city center is closed to cars, but it's only a short walk from several parking areas to the cathedral.

VISITOR INFORMATION

The **telephone area code** is 01227. The **Visitors Information Centre** is at 34 St. Margaret's St. (☎ **01227/766567**), near St. Margaret's Church.

WHAT TO SEE & DO

From Easter to early November, daily guided tours of Canterbury are organized by the **Guild of Guides,** Arnett House, Hawks Lane (☎ **01227/459779**), costing £2.50 ($3.95) for adults and £1.80 ($2.85) for students and children 13 and over. Don't go to the office to take the tours; rather, meet at the Visitors Information Centre at 34 St. Margaret's St., in a pedestrian zone near the cathedral, daily (including Sunday) at 2pm. From the end of May to mid-September, there's also a tour at 11am Monday through Saturday.

From just below the Weavers House, boats leave for half-hour **trips on the river** with a commentary on the history of the buildings you pass. Umbrellas are provided to protect you against inclement weather.

✪ Canterbury Cathedral

11 The Precincts. ☎ **01227/762862.** Admission £2 ($3.20) adults, £1 ($1.60) children. Guided tours (based on demand) £2.80 ($4.40) adults, £1 ($1.60) children 12 and under. Easter–Oct, daily 8:30am–7pm; Nov–Apr, Mon–Fri 8:30am–4pm, Sat 6:30am–1pm.

The foundation of this splendid cathedral dates back to the coming of the first archbishop, Augustine, from Rome in A.D. 597, but the earliest part of the present building is the great romanesque crypt built circa 1100. The monastic "quire" erected on top of this at the same time was destroyed by fire in 1174, only 4 years after the murder of Thomas à Becket on a dark December evening in the northwest transept, still one of the most famous places of pilgrimage in Europe. The destroyed "quire" was immediately replaced by a magnificent early gothic one, the first major expression of that architectural style in England. Its architects were the Frenchman, William of Sens, and "English" William, who took Sens's place after the Frenchman was crippled in an accident in 1178 that later proved fatal.

The cathedral is noteworthy for its medieval tombs of royal personages, such as King Henry IV and Edward the Black Prince, as well as numerous archbishops. To the later Middle Ages belong the great 14th-century nave and the famous central "Bell Harry Tower." The cathedral stands on spacious precincts amid the remains of the buildings of the monastery—cloisters, chapter house, and Norman water tower, which have survived intact from Henry VIII's dissolution to the present day.

Becket's shrine was destroyed by the Tudor king, but the site of that tomb is in Trinity Chapel, near the high altar. The saint is said to have worked miracles, and the cathedral has some rare stained glass depicting those feats. Perhaps the most miraculous event is that the windows escaped Henry VIII's agents of destruction as well as Hitler's bombs. The windows were removed as a precaution at the beginning of the war. During the war, a large area of Canterbury was flattened, but the main body of the church was unharmed. However, the cathedral library was damaged during a German air raid in 1942. The replacement windows of the cathedral were blown in, which proved the wisdom of having the medieval glass safely stored away. East of the Trinity Chapel is "Becket's Crown," where there's a chapel dedicated to the "Martyrs and Saints of Our Own Time." St. Augustine's Chair, one of the symbols of the authority of the archbishop of Canterbury, stands behind the high altar.

The Canterbury Tales

23 St. Margaret's St. ☎ **01227/454888.** Admission £4.50 ($7.10) adults, £3.75 ($5.95) students, £3.25 ($5.15) children 4–15. Daily 9:30am–5:30pm.

One of the most visited museums in town re-creates the pilgrimages of Chaucerian England through a series of medieval tableaux. Visitors are given headsets with earphones, which relate much-edited oral recitations of Chaucer's *Canterbury Tales* and the murder of St. Thomas à Becket, which occurred in the nearby cathedral. A tour of all exhibits takes about 45 minutes and is conducted in several languages, including, of course, English. Audiovisual aids bring famous characters to life, and stories of jealousy, pride, avarice, and love are recounted. The exhibits are located off the High Street, near the cathedral.

WHERE TO STAY

Before you can begin any serious exploring, you'll need to find a hotel. You have several possibilities, both in the city and on the outskirts, ranging from craggy

The Canterbury Tale

A pilgrimage from London to the cathedral city of Canterbury was and is one of the major goals of many visitors venturing outside London. The trail was blazed—at least in fiction—by Geoffrey Chaucer, who was born in London some time between 1340 and 1345 and who died in London in 1400. Although he wrote other works, he is remembered chiefly today for his *The Canterbury Tales*, which he started around 1387 but which was left unfinished upon his death.

It is essentially 23 stories of a group of pilgrims assembled at the Tabard Inn in Southwark in London. Chaucer had praise for the now-demolished Tabard ("the chambres and the stables weren wyde").

Chaucer's own life would almost have been a tale to have been included in his rollicking series of often bawdy stories. A London comptroller of petty customs, he was elected to Parliament in 1386. But his life suffered several misfortunes until he was rescued by pensions from both Richard II and Henry IV.

The journey of the pilgrims from London to Canterbury was to visit the tomb of Thomas à Becket, which was demolished in 1538. The trail of the pilgrims, at least according to the gospel of Chaucer, was along the Old Kent Road. In the poem the pilgrims cast lots to decide who will begin the storytelling to pass the time, the honor falling to the Knight.

The city of Rochester is mentioned in the Prologue to "The Monk's Tale." Sidyngborne, coming at the end of "The Wife of Bath's Prologue," is a reference to the town of Sittingbourne. At Ospringe, 45 miles from London, stands one of the few buildings that has survived on the old pilgrims' route—the Maison Dieu, under protection from English Heritage and open to the public. The last topographical reference in Chaucer's unfinished poem was in the Prologue to "The Manciple's Tale":

> *a litel toun*
> *Which that ycleped is Bobbe-up-and-down,*
> *Under the Blee, by Caunterbury waye.*

This, it is believed, was a reference to Harbledown, which stands on the outskirts of Canterbury and in the Middle Ages was noted for its hospital of St. Nicholas, a leper foundation.

Elizabethan houses of historic interest to modern studio-type bedrooms with private baths.

MODERATE

Chaucer Hotel

63 Ivy Lane (off Lower Bridge St.), Canterbury, Kent CT1 1TU. ☎ **01227/464427,** or 800/ 225-5843 in the U.S. and Canada. Fax 01227/450397. 42 rms. £60 ($94.80) single; £80 ($126.40) double. Breakfast £8.50 ($13.45) extra. AE, DC, MC, V. Free parking.

On a historic street, the Chaucer Hotel is within a few minutes' walk of the cathedral and the Micawber house made famous in *David Copperfield*. Originally it was a Georgian house, although it was extensively rebuilt following World War

Kent, Surrey & the Sussexes

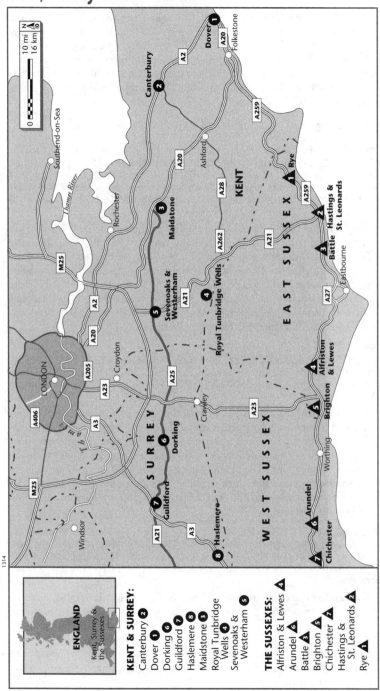

II bomb damage. Your comfortably furnished room will lie at the end of a labyrinth of stairs, narrow hallways, and doors. (The hotel staff will carry your luggage and park your car.) Don't overlook the possibility of a drink in the Pilgrim's Bar, with its Regency mantelpieces and French windows open to outdoor terraces in summer. The hotel also has a nice restaurant, the Geoffrey Chaucer, serving English meals until 9:30pm, and it provides 24-hour room service. A table d'hôte dinner costs £16.95 ($26.80).

INEXPENSIVE

Cathedral Gate Hotel

36 Burgate, Canterbury, Kent CT1 2HA. ☎ **01227/464381.** Fax 01227/462800. 23 rms, some with shower only, 10 with bath. TV TEL. £25 ($39.50) single without bath, £34 ($53.70) single with shower only; £45 ($71.10) double without bath, £37.50–£54 ($59.25–$85.30) double with bath. Rates include continental breakfast. AE, DC, MC, V. Parking £1.50 ($2.35).

The Cathedral Gate is for modern-day pilgrims who want to rest their bones at an inn shouldering up to the cathedral's gateway. Built in 1438, adjoining Christchurch Gate and overlooking the Buttermarket, the hotel offers views of the cathedral. In 1620 this former hospice became one of the earliest of the fashionable coffeehouses and teahouses of England, and the interior reveals many little architectural details of the 17th century. The rooms are comfortably furnished, and afternoon tea and supper are served. An in-house bar is licensed to serve residents. The hotel is a 10-minute walk from the train station.

County Hotel

High St., Canterbury, Kent CT1 2RX. ☎ **01227/766266.** Fax 01227/451512. 72 rms, 1 suite. TV TEL. £65–£71 ($102.70–$112.20) single; £72–£95 ($113.75–$150.10) double; £170 ($268.60) suite. Breakfast £5.50–£8.50 ($8.70–$13.45) extra. AE, DC, MC, V. Parking £3 ($4.75).

This place has been a hotel since the closing years of Victoria's reign, with a recorded history going back to the end of the 12th century. The bedrooms are equipped with tea and coffee makers and radios. Some are period rooms with either Georgian or Tudor four-poster beds. For fine dining, go to Sully's Restaurant, the hotel's fully air-conditioned dining room (see "Where to Dine," below). For snacks, vegetarian specialties, salads, and hot dishes, the coffee shop may be your best bet. There's also the Tudor Bar, where you can have an apéritif or after-dinner libations.

⑤ Ebury Hotel

65–67 New Dover Rd., Canterbury, Kent CT1 3DX. ☎ **01227/768433.** Fax 01227/459187. 15 rms. TV TEL. £41 ($64.80) single; £59.50–£62 ($94–$97.95) double. Rates include English breakfast. AE, MC, V. Free parking. Closed Dec 14–Jan 14. Follow the signs to A2, Dover Road.

Acclaimed as one of the finest B&B hotels in Canterbury, this gabled Victorian house stands at the edge of the city. Built 150 years ago, it's composed of two separate houses that were joined several years ago. It's important to reserve here, since this owner-operated hotel is quite popular. Its accommodations are well furnished, roomy, and pleasantly decorated. The hotel has a heated, indoor swimming pool and spa, as well as a spacious lounge and a licensed restaurant serving good meals prepared with fresh vegetables.

Falstaff Hotel

8–10 St. Dunstan's St., Canterbury, Kent CT2 8AF. ☎ **01227/462138.** Fax 01227/463525. 24 rms. TV TEL. £68 ($107.45) single or double. Breakfast £4.50–£7.50 ($7.10–$11.85) extra. AE, DC, MC, V. Free parking.

Despite the comfortable modernity of its bedrooms, which were refurbished in 1994, this hotel was established in 1403 as a coaching inn. Located 400 yards from the West Station, the Falstaff is a classic Canterbury hostelry which retains its flagstone-covered courtyard and its sense of history. The bedrooms are small but cozy, well maintained, and neatly organized. The hotel also operates as a well-recommended restaurant, where meals range from £10 to £20 ($15.80 to $31.60).

✪ Howfield Manor

Chartham Hatch, Canterbury, Kent CT4 7HQ. ☎ **01227/738294.** Fax 01227/731535. 13 rms, 1 suite. TV TEL. £62.50 ($98.75) single; £82.50 ($130.35) double; £95 ($150.10) four-poster. Rates include English breakfast. AE, MC, V. Free parking. Take the A28 3¼ miles from Canterbury.

The oldest section of this brick manor house, which dates from 1181, is now used as a restaurant called the Old Well. An ancient well remains from when it was built as a chapel for an Augustinian priory. Set on 5 acres of rolling meadows, the house offers tastefully furnished bedrooms with such amenities as alarm clocks, trouser presses, and hairdryers. Drinks are served from Priory Bar and can be taken into the warm, comfortable lounge. The hotel's restaurant is one of the best in Canterbury. A table d'hôte costs £18.95 ($29.95).

Slatters

St. Margaret's St., Canterbury, Kent CT1 2TR. ☎ **01227/463271.** Fax 01227/764117. 31 rms. TV TEL. £49.50 ($78.20) single; £54.50 ($86.10) double. Rates include English breakfast. AE, DC, MC, V. Free parking.

In the heart of Canterbury, 200 yards from the cathedral, this building is historic but the bedrooms are motel-like. Most of them convert into sitting areas during the day, with armchairs. Each room is furnished with radio, trouser press, hairdryer, and a welcome tray with tea- or coffee-making facilities. The fully licensed French restaurant serves a table d'hôte dinner. Bar snacks are also available at lunchtime.

✪ Three Tuns Inn

24 Watling St. (just off Castle Street), Canterbury, Kent CT1 2UD. ☎ **01227/767371.** Fax 01227/785962. 5 rms. TV TEL. £30.95 ($48.90) single; £34.95 ($55.20) double. Rates include English breakfast. AE, DC, MC, V. Free parking.

In the center of town, this old-fashioned inn derives most of its business from its exceptionally busy pub. However, many readers appreciate the handful of antique bedrooms upstairs, which impart a feeling of old-world charm. The inn occupies a fine 15th-century building on the site of an ancient Roman theater. William and Mary, who later became king and queen of England, stopped here in 1679, and you can follow their example, even going so far as to stay in the same room. Today, that room is attractively furnished and has a four-poster bed. The pub downstairs serves a buffet-style "tavern fare" lunch Monday through Saturday from noon to 2pm and Sunday from noon to 3pm. You choose from a row of steaming hot plates, paying £4.25 ($6.70) for a platter. The spillover from the pub gravitates into a side room, the Chapel Restaurant, where illegal Catholic masses were held during the Civil War. It still has the entrance to a secret passageway that allowed the celebrants to leave quickly in case of danger.

WHERE TO DINE
MODERATE

Duck Inn

Pett Bottom, near Bridge. ☎ **01227/830354.** Reservations recommended. Main courses £3.95–£11.95 ($6.25–$18.90); two-course fixed-price lunch (Mon–Fri) £7.50 ($11.85); three-course fixed-price dinner £10 ($15.80). AE, DC, MC, V. Drive 5 miles outside Canterbury near the village of Bridge on the road to Dover. ENGLISH.

Once called the Woodsmen Arms, this restaurant became known as the Duck Inn because of its low door. As patrons would enter the establishment, the clientele would shout "duck"; thus the name evolved. Set in the Pett Bottom valley in a 16th-century structure, this restaurant offers traditional English fare. Although there are bar and restaurant areas, diners can have their meals served to them throughout the establishment, including outdoors in the English country garden during the summer season. The menu posted on two chalkboards changes weekly, although a few standard English favorites remain on a permanent basis. You can start with one of the homemade soups such as country vegetable or celery and Stilton. For your main course, the menu may include game pies (in season) or mussels marinara, and some duck preparation is always on the menu. For a finish, try one of the local favorites, the homemade date pudding with toffee sauce. For James Bond fans this restaurant will be of particular interest. According to the film, *You Only Live Twice*, 007 grew up next door to the Duck Inn.

Sully's

In the County Hotel, High St. ☎ **01227/766266.** Reservations recommended. Main courses £14–£17 ($22.10–$26.85); set lunch £13.50 ($21.35) for two courses, £16 ($25.30) for three courses; set dinner £17 ($26.85) for two courses, £19.50 ($30.80) for three courses. AE, DC, MC, V. Daily 12:30–2:20pm and 7–10pm. ENGLISH/CONTINENTAL.

The most distinguished restaurant in Canterbury is located in its most distinguished hotel (see "Where to Stay," above). The seating and comfort level are first-rate, and both visitors and locals (the latter usually celebrating some special occasion) frequent this establishment. Considering the quality of the ingredients, the menu offers good value. You can always count on a selection of plain, traditional English dishes, but try one of the more imaginatively conceived platters instead. There's a respectable wine list.

Tuo e Mio

16 The Borough. ☎ **01227/761471.** Reservations recommended, especially at lunch. Main courses £6–£12.50 ($9.50–$19.75). AE, DC, MC, V. Tues 7–10:45pm, Wed–Sun noon–2:30pm and 7–10:45pm. Closed the last two weeks in Aug and the last two weeks in Feb. ITALIAN.

Tuo e Mio is a bastion of zesty Italian cookery, the finest in town in its category. Signor R. P. M. Greggio, known locally as Raphael, sets the style and plans the menu at his casual bistro. Some dishes are standard, including the pastas, beef, and veal found on most Italian menus, but the daily specials have a certain flair, based on the fresh and good-quality ingredients available on any given day. Try the fish dishes, including skate, which is regularly featured. A selection of reasonably priced Italian wines accompanies your food selection. The dining room is a respectable, conservative bastion of white walls, white napery, white-coated waiters, and time-blackened ceiling beams.

2 Dover

76 miles SE of London, 84 miles NE of Brighton

One of the ancient Cinque Ports, Dover is famed for its white cliffs. In Victoria's day, it basked in popularity as a seaside resort, but today it's known as a port for cross-Channel car and passenger traffic between England and France (notably Calais). Dover was one of England's most vulnerable and easy-to-hit targets during World War II; repeated bombings destroyed much of its harbor. Dover has gained increasing importance since the opening of the Channel Tunnel (Chunnel) in 1994. Today more than ever you're likely to see many French families *en vacances*. For some of those families, Dover will represent their only glimpse of England.

ESSENTIALS
GETTING THERE

By Train Frequent trains run between Victoria Station or Charing Cross Station in London and Dover daily from 5am to 10pm. Arrivals in Dover are at Priory Station, off Folkestone Road. During the day two trains per hour depart Canterbury East Station heading for Dover.

By Bus Frequent buses throughout the day leave from London's Victoria Coach Station bound for Dover. The local bus station is on Pencester Road (☎ 01304/ 240024). There is also frequent daily service between Canterbury and Dover.

By Car From London, head first to Canterbury (see above), then continue along A2 southeast until you reach Dover, on the coast.

VISITOR INFORMATION

The **telephone area code** for Dover is 01304. The **Tourist Information Centre** is on Townwall Street (☎ **01304/205108**).

WHAT TO SEE & DO

Dover Castle

Castle Hill. ☎ **01304/201628.** Admission £5.50 ($8.70) adults, £2.80 ($4.40) children. Apr–Sept, daily 10am–6pm; Oct–Mar, daily 10am–4pm. Bus 90 bound for Deal.

Rising nearly 400 feet above the port is one of the oldest and best-known castles in England. Its keep was built at the command of Becket's fair-weather friend, Henry II, in the 12th century. The ancient castle was called back to active duty as late as World War II. The "Pharos" on the grounds is a lighthouse built by the Romans in the first half of the 1st century. The Romans first landed at nearby Deal in 54 B.C., but after 6 months they departed and didn't return until nearly 100

Impressions

The sea is calm tonight.
The tide is full, the moon lies fair
Upon the straits;—on the French coast the light
Gleams and is gone; the cliffs of England stand
Glimmering and vast, out in the tranquil bay.

—Matthew Arnold, "Dover Beach," 1867

years later, in A.D. 43, when they stayed and occupied the country for 400 years. The castle houses a military museum and a film center, and the restaurant is open all year.

Hellfire Corner

Dover Castle, Castle Hill. ☎ **01304/201628.** Admission free with castle admission (see above). Open same days and hours as the castle (see above). Bus 90 bound for Deal.

These secret tunnels were used during the evacuation of Dunkirk in 1940 and the Battle of Britain. Some 200 feet below ground, they were the headquarters of Operation Dynamo, which saw the evacuation of more than 300,000 troops from Dunkirk. For years they were on the top-secret list, but now can be explored on a guided tour. They were originally excavated to house cannons to be used (if necessary) against an invasion by Napoleon.

Roman Painted House

New St. ☎ **01304/203279.** Admission £1.50 ($2.35) adults, 50p (80¢) children. Apr–Oct, daily 10am–5:30pm.

This 1,800-year-old Roman structure—called Britain's "buried Pompeii"—has exceptionally well preserved walls and an under-floor heating system. It's famous for its unique Bacchic murals and has won four national awards for presentation. You'll find it in the town center near Market Square.

WHERE TO STAY
INEXPENSIVE

The Churchill

Waterloo Crescent, Dover, Kent CT17 9BP. ☎ **01304/203633.** Fax 01304/216320. 54 rms, all with bath (tub or shower). TV TEL. £49 ($77.40) single; £69 ($109) double; £85 ($134.30) triple or quad. Rates include English breakfast. AE, DC, MC, V. Free parking.

Dover's most consistently reliable hotel is composed of an interconnected row of town houses built to overlook the English Channel in the 1830s. After World War I the premises were transformed into a hotel, and in 1994 it was completely refurbished after being acquired by the Henley Lodge hotel chain. There's a rambling seafront balcony, a glass-enclosed front veranda, and bedrooms that are comfortable and tranquil, each with a radio, satellite TV, and hot-beverage facilities. The restaurant, Winston's, serves an international menu with a table d'hôte at £14.95 ($23.60). Lunch is served daily from 12:30 to 2pm and dinner from 7:30 to 9:15pm. The hotel lies close to the eastern and western docks and the Hoverport for travel to and from France and Belgium.

The County Hotel

Townwall St., Dover, Kent CT16 1SZ. ☎ **01304/203270.** Fax 01304/213230. 79 rms, all with bath (tub or shower). TV TEL. £65 ($102.70) single; £69–£76 ($109–$120.10) double or twin. Breakfast £8.95 ($14.15) extra. AE, DC, MC, V. Free parking.

In the center of town, just a few minutes away from the train station, the seafront, and the international ferry terminal and Hoverport, this hotel features rooms with queen-size beds, radios, in-house movies, and hairdryers. On the premises are an indoor heated swimming pool and Braid's Restaurant, with a carvery and salad bar, plus coffee-shop facilities and an English-style bar. Room service from 10am to 8pm and laundry service are available.

WHERE TO DINE
INEXPENSIVE

Britannia
41 Townwall St. ☎ **01304/203248.** Reservations recommended for the restaurant. Main courses £4.75–£7.95 ($7.50–$12.55). AE, DC, MC, V. Restaurant, daily 6–9:30pm. Pub, Mon–Sat 11am–11pm, Sun noon–2:30pm and 7–10:30pm. INTERNATIONAL.

If you gravitate to typically English, pub-style meals, try this restaurant, whose windows overlook the ferry terminal and the many ships arriving from Calais and Boulogne. Its well-maintained facade has a bow window, with lots of gilt and brass nautical accents. The popular pub is on the ground floor and the restaurant on the upper level. Try a prawn cocktail or a pâté for an appetizer, followed by rump steak or a mixed grill. A selection of vegetarian dishes is also offered. Dover sole is a specialty.

Topo Gigio
1–2 King St. ☎ **01304/201048.** Reservations recommended. Pizzas £3.95–£6.10 ($6.25–$9.65); main courses £5–£10.45 ($7.90–$16.50). MC, V. Mon–Thurs noon–2:30pm and 6:30–10:30pm, Fri–Sat noon–2:30pm and 6:30–11pm, Sun noon–2:30pm. ITALIAN.

Established in 1991 by an Italian entrepreneur from Vicenza, this restaurant was named after the most famous cartoon character in Italy, Topo Gigio, a lookalike for Mickey Mouse. Located a short walk from Dover's market square, in a setting accented with brick arches and a wood-burning pizza oven, it serves 15 types of pastas, 16 types of pizzas, and a varied choice of steak, chicken, veal, and fish dishes prepared in the Italian style or in virtually any way you request. The restaurant's staff and clientele tend to be animated and energetic, which might make an outing here lighthearted and fun.

3 Westerham & Sevenoaks

Westerham: 20 miles SE of London
Sevenoaks: 26 miles SE of London

ESSENTIALS
GETTING THERE

By Train   Trains run daily from London's Victoria Station to both Westerham and Sevenoaks. Taxis wait at the station.

By Car   Head east along M25, taking the exit to Westerham where B2026 leads to Chartwell (the road is signposted).

WESTERHAM

The Westerham area abounds in homes of famous men, which have now been preserved as museums and memorials. Chartwell, where Sir Winston Churchill lived for many years, displays personal mementos, his own paintings, and gifts from people around the world. On the lake at Chartwell swim black swans. Down House is where Darwin wrote his still-controversial *On the Origin of Species*. Here you can amble down the scientist's "Thinking Path." Quebec House, the boyhood home of General Wolfe, and Squerryes Court are of particular interest to Canadians.

WHAT TO SEE & DO

Chartwell (Churchill's home)

Off B2026. ☎ **01732/866368.** House only (Mar and Nov), £2.50 ($3.95); house and garden, £4.50 ($7.10); gardens only, £2 ($3.15); Churchill's studio, 50p (80¢). Children enter for half price. Apr–Oct, Tues–Thurs noon–5pm, Sat–Sun 11am–4:30pm; Mar and Nov (house only), Wed and Sat–Sun 11am–4pm. Drive 2 miles south of Westerham on B2026 and follow the signs.

Chartwell was the late prime minister's home from 1922 and is now a museum. Not as grand as Blenheim Palace where Sir Winston was born in 1874, the rooms of Chartwell remain as the Conservative politician left them; they include maps, documents, photographs, pictures, and other personal mementos. Two rooms display a selection of gifts that the prime minister received from people all over the world. There is also a selection of many of his well-known uniforms. Terraced gardens descend toward the lake, where you'll find black swans swimming. Many of Churchill's paintings are displayed in a garden studio. A restaurant on the grounds serves from 10:30am to 5pm on days when the house is open.

Quebec House

Quebec Sq. ☎ **01959/562206.** Admission £2 ($3.15) adults, £1 ($1.60) children. Apr–Oct, Sun–Wed and Fri 2–6pm. Take B2026 to the junction of Edenbridge and Sevenoaks roads (A25 and B2026).

This square, red-brick gabled house is the boyhood home of Gen. James Wolfe, who led the English in their victory over the French in the battle for Québec. Wolfe was born in Westerham on January 2, 1727, and lived here until he was 11 years old. A National Trust property, Quebec House contains an exhibition about the capture of Québec and memorabilia associated with the military hero.

Squerryes Court

Off A25. ☎ **01959/562345.** House and grounds, £3.50 ($5.55) adults, £3.20 ($5.05) senior citizens and students, £1.60 ($2.40) children; grounds only, £2 ($3.15) adults, £1.80 ($2.85) senior citizens and students, £1 ($1.60) children. House and grounds, Mar, Sun 2–6pm; Apr–Sept, Wed, Sat–Sun, and bank holidays 2–6pm. Take A25 just west of Westerham and follow the signs.

Built in 1681 and owned by the Warde family for 250 years, this still-occupied manor house has—besides a fine collection of paintings, tapestries, and furniture—pictures and relics of General Wolfe's family. The military hero received his commission on the grounds of the house—the spot is marked by a cenotaph.

In Nearby Downe

Down House (Darwin's home)

Luxted Rd., Downe, Orpington. ☎ **01689/859119.** Admission £2.50 ($3.95) adults, £1.50 ($2.35) senior citizens and students, £1 ($1.60) children 5–15, free for children 4 and under. Mar–Dec 15, Wed–Sun 1–6pm. Closed Dec 16–Feb. From Westerham, get on A233 and drive 5¹/₂ miles south of Bromley to the village of Downe. From London's Victoria Station, take a daily train to Bromley South, then go by bus no. 146 (Mon–Sat only) to Downe; Down House lies a quarter mile southeast of the village of Downe along Luxted Road.

The famous naturalist/evolutionary theorist lived here from 1842 until his death in 1882. The drawing room and old study have been restored to the way they were when Charles Darwin was working on his famous—and still-controversial—book *On the Origin of Species*, first published in 1859. The museum also includes collections and memorabilia from Darwin's voyage on the HMS *Beagle*. There's also a room dedicated to his famous grandfather, Dr. Erasmus Darwin, and a modest exhibit on evolution is in the new study, the last room to be added to the house. An important feature of the museum is the garden, which retains original landscaping and a glass house, beyond which lies the Sand Walk or "Thinking Path," where Darwin took his daily solitary walk.

SEVENOAKS

The architecture enthusiast will find the Sevenoaks area a veritable treasure trove. In nearby Knole (just 1¹/₂ miles away), you'll find one of the finest examples of Tudor architecture, the palace of Knole. The ancient home of Ightham Mote is well worth a visit to see its Great Hall; you'll cross a stone bridge over a moat to its central courtyard.

WHAT TO SEE & DO

✪ Knole

At the south end of the town of Knole, east of A225, opposite St. Nicholas Church. ☎ **01732/450608.** House, £4 ($6.30) adults, £2 ($3.15) children. House, Apr–Oct, Wed, Fri, Sat–Sun and bank holiday Mon 11am–5pm; Thurs 2–5pm. Gardens, May–Sept, the first Wed of the month. Park, daily to pedestrians; open to cars when the house is open. Frequent train service is available from London (about every 30 min.) to Sevenoaks, and then you can take a taxi or walk the remaining 1¹/₂ miles to Knole.

Begun in the mid-15th century by Thomas Bourchier, archbishop of Canterbury, Knole is one of the largest private houses in England and is considered one of the finest examples of pure English Tudor-style architecture. It's set in a 1,000-acre deer park, 5 miles north of Tonbridge, at the Tonbridge end of the town of Sevenoaks. (Don't confuse Tonbridge with Tunbridge Wells.) Virginia Woolf, often a guest of the Sackvilles, used Knole as the setting for her novel *Orlando*.

Henry VIII liberated the former archbishop's palace from the church in 1537. He spent considerable sums of money on Knole, but there is little record of his spending much time here after extracting the place from the reluctant Archbishop Cranmer; history records one visit only, in 1541. It was then a royal palace until Queen Elizabeth I granted it to Thomas Sackville, first earl of Dorset, whose descendants have lived here ever since. The Great Hall and the Brown Gallery are Bourchier rooms, early 15th century, both much altered by the first earl, who made other additions in about 1603. The earl was also responsible for the Great Painted Staircase. The house covers 7 acres and has 365 rooms, 52 staircases, and seven courts. The elaborate paneling and plasterwork provide a background for the 17th- and 18th-century tapestries and rugs, Elizabethan and Jacobean furniture, and the collection of family portraits. The building was given to the National Trust in 1946.

Ightham Mote

Ivy Hatch, Sevenoaks. ☎ **01732/810378.** Admission £4 ($6.30) adults, £2 ($3.15) children. Apr–Oct, Mon and Wed–Fri noon–5pm, Sun 11am–5pm. Closed Nov–Mar. Drive 6 miles east of Sevenoaks on A227 to the small village of Ivy Hatch; the estate is 2¹/₂ miles south of Ightham; it's also signposted from A25.

This National Trust property is well worth a stop if you're in the area visiting other stately homes and castles. Dating from 1340, it was extensively remodeled in the early 16th century, and the Tudor chapel with its painted ceiling, the timbered outer wall, and the ornate chimneys reflect that period. A stone bridge crosses the moat and leads into the central courtyard overlooked by the magnificent windows of the Great Hall. The rest of the house is built around the courtyard. From the Great Hall, a Jacobean staircase leads to the old chapel on the first floor, where you go through the solarium, with an oriel window, to the Tudor chapel.

Unlike many other ancient houses in England that have been occupied by the same family for centuries, Ightham Mote passed from owner to owner, with each family leaving its mark on the place. When the last private owner, an American who was responsible for a lot of the restoration, died, he bequeathed the house to the National Trust.

4 Royal Tunbridge Wells

36 miles SE of London, 33 miles NE of Brighton

Dudley Lord North, courtier to James I, is credited with the accidental discovery in 1606 of the mineral spring that led to the creation of a fashionable resort. Over the years the "Chalybeate Spring" became known for its curative properties and was considered the answer for everything from too many days of wine and roses to failing sexual prowess. It's still possible to "take the water" today.

The spa resort reached its peak in the mid-18th century under the foppish patronage of "Beau" Nash (1674–1761), a dandy and final arbiter on how to act, what to say, and even what to wear (for example, he got men to remove their boots in favor of stockings).

Tunbridge Wells continued to enjoy a prime spa reputation through to the reign of Queen Victoria, who used to vacaation here as a child, and in 1909 Tunbridge Wells received its Royal status.

ESSENTIALS
GETTING THERE

By Train Two to three trains per hour leave London's Charing Cross Station during the day bound for Hastings, but going via the town center of Royal Tunbridge Wells (trip time: 50 min.).

By Bus There are no direct bus links with Gatwick Airport or London. However, there is hourly service during the day between Brighton and Royal Tunbridge Wells (call 01634/832666 for the bus schedule). You can purchase tickets aboard the bus.

By Car After reaching the ring road around London, from whichever part of London you're in, continue east along M25, cutting southeast at the exit for A21 to Hastings.

VISITOR INFORMATION

The **telephone area code** is 01892. The **Tourist Information Centre,** Old Fishmarket, The Pantiles (☎ **01892/515675**), provides a full accommodations list and offers a room-reservations service.

WHAT TO SEE & DO

The most remarkable feature of Royal Tunbridge Wells is **The Pantiles,** a colonnaded walkway for shoppers, tea drinkers, and diners, built near the wells. The area boasts many other interesting and charming spots which can be viewed on a walk around the town, and a wide variety of entertainment is presented at the Assembly Hall and Trinity Arts Centre.

Canadians touring in the area may want to seek out the grave of the founder of their country's capital. **Lt. Col. John By** of the Royal Engineers (1779–1836) died at Shernfold Park in Frant, East Sussex, near Tunbridge Wells, and is buried in the churchyard there. His principal claim to fame is that he established the city of Ottawa and built the Rideau Canal.

Within easy touring distance from Royal Tunbridge Wells are a number of castles, gardens, and stately homes, all with their own history and beauty; for example, Sissinghurst Castle, the home of novelist Vita Sackville-West, and Chartwell, former home of Sir Winston Churchill.

WHERE TO STAY
MODERATE

The Spa Hotel

Mount Ephraim, Royal Tunbridge Wells, Kent TN4 8XJ. ☎ **01892/520331.** Fax 01892/510575. 76 rms. TV TEL. £69–£84 ($109–$132.70) single; £84–£110 ($132.70–$173.80) double. Breakfast £8.50 ($13.45) extra. AE, DC, MC, V. Free parking. From The Pantiles, take Major Yorke Road.

Standing on 14 acres, this building dates back to 1766; once a private home, it was converted to a hotel in 1880. This is the kind of place where many guests check in for long stays. Facilities include a beauty salon, hair studio, dance studio, half-mile jogging track, a sauna, a solarium, tennis courts, and an indoor swimming pool. The Chandelier Restaurant serves a combination English and French cuisine. Fixed-price meals cost £14 to £19 ($22.10 to $30).

INEXPENSIVE

Russell

80 London Rd., Royal Tunbridge Wells, Kent TN1 1DZ. ☎ **01892/544833,** or 800/832-2957 in the U.S. Fax 01892/515846. 21 rms, 5 suites. TV TEL. £64 ($101.10) single; £82 ($129.55) double; £92 ($145.35) suite. Rates include English breakfast. Discounts are usually offered during periods of low occupancy. AE, DC, MC, V. Free parking.

One of the best-recommended hotels at the spa is the Russell, which is composed of three row houses (each built in 1875) that were joined and transformed into a hotel in 1920. (At the time the hotel's name was the Victoria, although 4 years later someone changed it to the Russell, but no one remembers why.) Owned and managed by tactful members of the Wilkinson family, the hotel overlooks Tunbridge Wells's Common (central square), a short walk from the main shopping district. The in-house restaurant serves fixed-price meals at £16.50 ($26.05) each.

WHERE TO DINE
MODERATE

✪ Thackeray's House

85 London Rd. (at the corner of Mount Ephraim Rd.). ☎ **01892/511921.** Reservations required. Main courses £12.50–£17.50 ($19.75–$27.65); fixed-price midweek dinner (Tues–Thurs) £22.50 ($35.55); four-course dinner £42 ($66.35); two-course lunch £10 ($15.80). MC, V. Tues–Sat 12:30–2:30pm and 7–10pm, Sun 12:30–2:30pm. ENGLISH/FRENCH.

Thackeray's serves the finest food in Royal Tunbridge Wells. You get a little history here as well, since this second-oldest house in the spa was once inhabited by novelist William Makepeace Thackeray. He wrote *Tunbridge Toys* here. The house dates from about 1660. Bruce Wass, the owner-chef, worked at one of my favorite restaurants in London, Odin's, before coming here to set up his own place. He has created an elegant atmosphere, backed by attentive service, for his specialties.

Care goes into all his dishes, and many have flair, including an occasional salad of preserved duck with quail's eggs. He reaches perfection with such dishes as roast monkfish with saffron, tomatoes, and capers or peppered fillet of venison with port sauce. For dessert, he is most often cited for his chocolate Armagnac loaf, which may be served with a coffee sauce.

EASY EXCURSIONS

✪ Penshurst Place

At Penshurst, near Tonbridge. ☎ **01892/870307.** Admission to house and grounds, £4.95 ($7.80) adults, £2.75 ($4.35) children. Apr–Oct 1 daily and Sat–Sun in Mar and Oct. House noon–5:30pm; grounds 11am–6pm.

This stately home 6 miles west of Tonbridge is one of the outstanding country houses in Britain. In 1338, Sir John de Pulteney, four times lord mayor of London, built the manor house whose Great Hall still forms the heart of Penshurst— after more than 600 years. The boy king, Edward VI, presented the house to Sir William Sidney, and it has remained in that family ever since. It was the birthplace in 1554 of Sir Philip Sidney, the soldier-poet. In the first half of the 17th century Penshurst was known as a center of literature and attracted such personages as Ben Jonson, who was inspired by the estate to write one of his greatest poems. Today it's the home of the second viscount de l'Isle. The Nether Gallery, below the Long Gallery, which has a suite of ebony-and-ivory furniture from Goa, houses the Sidney family collection of armor. Visitors can also view the splendid state dining room. In the Stable Wing is an interesting toy museum.

On the grounds are nature and farm trails plus an adventure playground for children.

✪ Hever Castle and Gardens

Off B2026, between Sevenoaks and East Grinstead. ☎ **01732/865224.** Castle and gardens, £5.70 ($9) adults, £4.90 ($7.75) seniors citizens and students, £2.90 ($4.60) children 5–16, free for children 4 and under; family ticket (two adults, two children) £14.30 ($22.60). Gardens only, £4.30 ($6.80) adults, £3.80 ($6) senior citizens and students, £2.50 ($3.95) children 5–16, free for children 4 and under; £11.10 ($17.55) family ticket. Mar 14–Nov 5, gardens, daily 11am–6pm (last entry at 5pm); castle, daily noon–6pm. For further information, call the Hever Castle Estate Office. Follow the signs northwest of Royal Tunbridge; it's 3 miles southeast of Edenbridge, midway between Sevenoaks and East Grinstead, and 20 minutes from Exit 6 of M25.

Hever Castle dates back to 1270 when the massive gate house, the outer walls, and the moat were first constructed. Some 200 years later the Bullen (or Boleyn) family added a comfortable Tudor dwelling house inside the walls. Hever Castle was the childhood home of Anne Boleyn, the second wife of Henry VIII and mother of Queen Elizabeth I. The castle holds many memories of her.

In 1903 William Waldorf Astor acquired the estate and invested time, money, and imagination in restoring the castle, building the "Tudor Village," and creating the gardens and lakes. The Astor family's contribution to Hever's rich history can be appreciated through the collections of furniture, paintings, and objets d'art and through the quality of workmanship employed, particularly in the wood carving and plasterwork.

The gardens at Hever Castle were created between 1904 and 1908. They have now reached their maturity and are a blaze of color throughout most of the year.

The spectacular Italian Garden contains statuary and sculpture dating from Roman to Renaissance times. William Waldorf Astor acquired these items in Italy and brought them to Hever where they form a magnificent sight among the displays of shrubs and climbing and herbaceous plants. The formal gardens include a walled Rose Garden, fine topiary work, and a maze. There's a 35-acre lake and throughout the gardens there are streams, cascades, and fountains.

5 Maidstone

36 miles SE of London, 64 miles NE of Brighton

ESSENTIALS

GETTING THERE

By Train   Trains run frequently from London's Victoria Station to Maidstone.

By Bus   Buses run weekdays from London's Victoria Coach Station to Maidstone.

By Car   From London's ring road, continue east along M26 and M20.

VISITOR INFORMATION

The **telephone area code** is 01622. The **Tourist Information Centre** is at The Gatehouse, Palace Gardens, Mill Street (☎ **01622/673581**).

LEEDS CASTLE

Once described by Lord Conway as the loveliest castle in the world, ✪ **Leeds Castle,** Maidstone, Kent ME17 1PL (☎ **01622/765400**), dates from A.D. 857. Originally built of wood, it was rebuilt in 1119 in its present stone structure on two small islands in the middle of the lake; it was an almost impregnable fortress before the importation of gunpowder. Henry VIII converted it to a royal palace.

The castle has strong links with America through the sixth Lord Fairfax who, as well as owning the castle, owned 5 million acres in Virginia and was a close friend and mentor of the young George Washington. The last private owner, the Hon. Lady Baillie, who restored the castle with a superb collection of fine art, furniture, and tapestries, bequeathed it to the Leeds Castle Foundation. Since then, **royal apartments,** known as "Les Chambres de la Reine" (the queen's chambers), in the Gloriette, the oldest part of the castle, have been open to the public. The Gloriette, the last stronghold against attack, dates from Norman and Plantagenet times, with later additions by Henry VIII.

Within the surrounding parkland is a **wildwood garden and duckery** where rare swans, geese, and ducks can be seen. The redesigned aviaries contain a superb collection of birds, including parakeets and cockatoos. Dogs are not allowed here, but dog lovers will enjoy the **Dog Collar Museum** at the gate house, with a unique collection of collars dating from the Middle Ages. A nine-hole golf course is open to the public. The **Culpepper Garden** is a delightful English country flower garden. Beyond are the castle greenhouses, with the maze centered on a beautiful underground grotto and the vineyard recorded in the *Domesday Book.* It is once again producing Leeds Castle English white wine.

From March to October, the park is open daily from 10am to 5pm; the castle, daily from 11am to 5:30pm. From November to February, the park is open daily from 10am to 3pm; the castle, daily from 10:15am to 3:30pm. The castle and grounds are closed on the last Saturday in June and the first Saturday in July prior to open-air concerts. Admission to the castle and grounds is £7.50 ($11.85) for adults and £5 ($7.90) for children. Students and senior citizens pay £6 ($9.50). Car parking is free, with a free ride on a fully accessible minibus available for those who cannot manage the half-mile-or-so walk from the parking area to the castle.

Snacks, salads, cream teas, and hot meals are offered daily at a number of places on the estate, including Fairfax Hall, a restored 17th-century tithe barn, and the Terrace Restaurant which provides a full range of hot and cold meals.

Kentish Evenings are presented in Fairfax Hall most Saturdays throughout the year (except in August), starting at 7pm with a cocktail reception, then a private guided tour of the castle. Guests feast on smoked salmon mousse, followed by broth and roast beef carved at the table, plus seasonal vegetables. The meal is rounded off by dessert, cheese, and coffee. A half bottle of wine is included in the overall price of £37 ($58.45) per person. During the meal, musicians play appropriate music for the surroundings and the occasion. Advance reservations are required, made by calling the castle. Kentish Evenings finish at 12:30am. Participants in Kentish Evenings are advised to arrange nearby overnight accommodations.

If you are not driving during your trip, British Rail and several London-based bus-tour operators offer inclusive day excursions to Leeds Castle. The castle is 4 miles east of Maidstone at the junction of the A20 and the M20 London–Folkestone roads.

6 Dorking

26 miles S of London

This town, birthplace of Lord Laurence Olivier, lies on the Mole River at the foot of the North Downs. Within easy reach are some of the most scenic spots in the shire, including Silent Pool, Box Hill, and Leith Hill.

Three miles to the northwest and 1½ miles south of Great Bookham, off the A246 Leatherhead–Guildford road, stands **Polesden Lacey** (☎ **01372/452048**), a former Regency villa built in 1824. It houses the Greville collection of antiques, paintings, and tapestries. In the early part of this century it was enlarged to become a comfortable Edwardian country house when it was the home of a celebrated hostess, Mrs. Ronald Greville, who frequently entertained royalty from 1906 to 1939. The estate consists of 1,000 acres, and the 18th-century garden is filled with herbaceous borders, a rose garden, and beech walks.

The grounds are open daily throughout the year from 11am to dusk. The house is open in March only on Saturday and Sunday from 1:30 to 4:30pm; April to October, Wednesday through Sunday from 1:30 to 5:30pm, except on bank holiday Mondays and the Sundays preceding the holiday, when the hours are from 11am to 5:30pm. Admission to the grounds is £2.50 ($3.95) for adults and entrance to the house is £3 ($4.75); children under 17 are charged half price and children 4 and under enter free. A licensed restaurant on the grounds is open from 11am on the days the house can be visited.

ESSENTIALS
GETTING THERE

By Train   There is frequent daily train service from London's Victoria Station to Dorking (trip time: 35 min.).

By Bus   Green Line buses (no. 714) leave from London's Victoria Coach Station daily, heading for Kingston with a stop at Dorking (trip time: 1 hr.).

By Car   Take A24 south from London.

VISITOR INFORMATION

The **telephone area code** is 01306.

WHERE TO STAY & DINE

INEXPENSIVE

Burford Bridge Hotel

Box Hill, Dorking, Surrey RH5 6BX. ☎ **01306/884561,** or 800/225-5843 in the U.S. and Canada. Fax 01306/880386. 48 rms. TV TEL. £85 ($134.30) single or double Mon–Thurs, £65 ($102.70) Fri–Sun. Breakfast £6.25–£8.95 ($9.90–$14.15) extra. AE, DC, MC, V. Parking £1 ($1.60). Take the A24 1¹/₂ miles north of Dorking.

The Burford Bridge Hotel offers stylish living in a rural town from which a train will zip you into London in less than half an hour. At the foot of the beautiful Box Hill, the hotel has many historical associations. Lord Nelson was a frequent patron, and Keats completed "Endymion" here in 1817. Wordsworth and Robert Louis Stevenson also visited the hotel occasionally. You get the best of both the old and the new here, including a tithe barn (ca. 1600) as well as a large bedroom.

The restaurant serves good English food, and a bar opens onto a flowered patio with a fountain. Meals begin at £15.50 ($24.50). In summer, you can enjoy the garden swimming pool and frequent barbecues.

White Horse Hotel

High St., Dorking, Surrey, RH4 1BE. ☎ **01306/88138,** or 800/225-5843 in the U.S. and Canada. Fax 01306/887241. 68 rms. TV TEL. £75 ($118.50) single or double Mon–Thurs, £45–£55 ($71.10–$86.90) Fri–Sun. Breakfast £5.95–£8.95 ($9.40–$14.15) extra. AE, DC, MC, V. Free parking.

Just 10 miles from Gatwick Airport you can dine or lodge at a hotel that is supposed to have been the home of the "Marquis of Granby" in the *Pickwick Papers.* At least Dickens was known to have frequented the bar parlor. All the well-furnished rooms have radio and beverage facilities. Some are in a modern annex. Often called "the most interesting house in Dorking," the inn has a restaurant as well as a Pickwick Bar that offers a table d'hôte dinner for £17.95 ($28.35). The hotel also has a rose garden and can arrange a temporary membership in a nearby sports club with its own swimming pool.

7 Guildford

33 miles SW of London

The guildhall in this country town on the Wey River has an ornamental projecting clock that dates from 1683, and Charles Dickens considered High Street, which slopes to the river, one of the most beautiful in England.

Lying 2¹/₂ miles southwest of the city, **Loseley House,** Loseley Park, Guildford (☎ **01483/304440**), a beautiful and historic Elizabethan mansion visited by Queen Elizabeth I, James I, and Queen Mary, has been featured on TV and in five films. Its works of art include paneling from Henry VIII's Nonsuch Palace, period furniture, a unique carved chalk chimneypiece, magnificent ceilings, and cushions made by the first Queen Elizabeth. The mansion is open from the beginning of

May to the end of September, Wednesday through Saturday from 2 to 5pm, charging £3.50 ($5.55) for adults and £2 ($3.15) for children. Lunches and teas are served in the 17th-century tithe barn from 11am to 5pm, and you can tour the farm and visit the farm shop.

ESSENTIALS
GETTING THERE

By Train   The train departs from London's Waterloo Station (trip time: 40 min.).

By Bus   National Express operates buses from London's Victoria Coach Station daily, with a stopover at Guildford on its runs from London to Portsmouth. It's usually more convenient to take the train.

By Car   From London, head south along A3.

VISITOR INFORMATION

The **telephone area code** is 01483. The **Tourist Information Centre** is at 14 Tunsgate (☎ **01483/444333**).

WHERE TO STAY & DINE
MODERATE

Forte Crest Hotel
Egerton Rd., Guildford, Surrey GU2 5XZ. ☎ **01483/574444**, or 800/225–5843 in the U.S. and Canada. Fax 01483/302690. 109 rms, 2 suites. MINIBAR TV TEL. £109 ($172.20) single or double; £149 ($235.40) suite. Breakfast £4.95–£10.95 ($7.80–$17.30) extra. AE, DC, MC, V. Free parking. Head about 2 miles southwest of the center of Guildford, just off A3.

In this 1987 hostelry, surrounded by landscaped grounds, a feeling of heritage is conveyed by natural red elm joinery, polished brass fittings, and marble floors. The bedrooms incorporate both living and sleeping areas, and all are equipped with radios and hot-beverage facilities. The needs of disabled guests have been taken into consideration.

If a guest stays a minimum of 2 nights during a period ranging from Friday through Sunday, half board costs £75 ($118.50) per person daily, based on double occupancy.

The hotel has an in-house brasserie that serves French and English food at reasonable prices. There's also a health and fitness club with an indoor heated swimming pool and a sun terrace.

A NEARBY PLACE TO STAY
Inexpensive

✪ Inn on the Lake
Ockford Rd., Godalming, Surrey GU7 1RH. ☎ **01483/415575.** Fax 01483/860445. 17 rms. TV TEL. £75–£85 ($118.50–$134.30) double. Rates include English breakfast. AE, DC, MC, V. Free parking. From Guildford, take A3100 south for 3 miles.

This haven of landscaped gardens with ducks drowsing on pools beside the lake is only 3 miles from Guildford. The rooms, each a double, are decorated with pretty country prints and simple furniture, all with a tea and coffee maker and radio. Excellent snacks are served in a real old-world bar, where some of the timbers date from Tudor times. In summer, barbecues are held in the garden. For more substantial dinners, fixed-price menus are offered at £14.50 ($22.90) and £17.50 ($27.65) plus à la carte with a varied selection of grills, English favorites, and continental dishes. The house was listed in the *Domesday Book* and has Tudor, Georgian, and Victorian associations. A postwar addition blends more or less gracefully into the complex.

EASY EXCURSIONS

One of the great gardens of England, **Wisley Garden,** Wisley, Woking (☎ **01483/224234**), is situated in Wisley near Ripley just off M25 (Junction 10) on the A3 London–Portsmouth road. Every season of the year, this 250-acre garden has a profusion of flowers and shrubs, ranging from the alpine meadow carpeted with wild daffodils in spring, Battleston Hill brilliant with rhododendrons in early summer, the heather garden's colorful foliage in the fall, and a riot of exotic plants in the glasshouses in winter. Recent developments include model gardens and a landscaped orchid house. This garden is the site of a laboratory where botanists, plant pathologists, and an entomologist experiment and assist amateur gardeners. There's a large gift shop with a wide range of gardening books and a licensed restaurant and cafeteria. Open all year, Monday through Saturday from 10am to 7pm (or sunset if earlier). Admission is £4.75 ($7.50) for adults, £1.75 ($2.75) for children 6 to 16, free for children 5 and under.

8 Haslemere

42 miles SW of London, 37 miles NW of Brighton

In this quiet, sleepy town, early English musical instruments are made by hand and an annual music festival (see below) is the town's main drawing card. Over the years, the Dolmetsch family has been responsible for the acclaim that has come to this otherwise unheralded little Surrey town, which lies in the midst of some of the shire's finest scenery.

ESSENTIALS

GETTING THERE

By Train   Haslemere is an hour's train ride from Waterloo Station in London.

By Bus   There is no bus service from London to Haslemere because the train service is so excellent. Once in Haslemere, local buses connect the town to such nearby villages as Farnham and Grayshott.

By Car   From Guildford (see above), continue south on A3100, going via Godalming and branching onto A286.

VISITOR INFORMATION

The **telephone area code** is 01428.

THE FESTIVAL

In the center of Haslemere rises one of Surrey's most visible theaters, **Haslemere Hall,** Bridge Road, Haslemere, Surrey GU27 2AS (☎ **01428/642161**). Throughout the year, it presents concerts, musical comedies, and serious drama whose program changes about every month. (One recent highlight was an amateur production of *Camelot* with a cast of talented locals called the Haslemere Players.) Throughout the year, someone will usually be on hand to sell tickets and answer questions Monday through Friday from 9am to 1pm and Saturday from 9am to noon.

Despite Haslemere Hall's ongoing program of cultural events, one of Surrey's musical highlights occurs for 6 days in mid-July, when the ✪ **Haslemere Festival** attracts music aficionados from throughout Europe. At that time, a world-famous musicologist, Dr. Carl Dolmetsch, CBE, accompanied by three generations of his family and friends, presents a program of 16th-, 17th-, and 18th-century chamber music. The music, including obscure pieces culled from the extensive family archives, is produced on harpsichords, violas da gamba, recorders, violins, and lutes that either date from those centuries or are reproductions faithfully crafted by the Dolmetsch family in their Haslemere workshops. During the festival, matinees begin at 3:15pm, evening performances at 7:15pm. One of the oldest music festivals in Britain, the tradition was established in 1925 by musical legend Arnold Dolmetsch and has continued with fierce determination every year since, even through the darkest days of World War II. Tickets usually range from £5.50 to £9.50 ($8.70 to $15), depending on seat location and event.

Well-intentioned musicians and music lovers are allowed to visit the Dolmetsch workshops, set on the village outskirts, by phoning ahead for a mutually convenient time of arrival. You should not construe your trip as an outing to a museum, but rather as a visit to an arts-conscious factory of international renown where musical instruments are manufactured to centuries-old standards. For information, contact **Dolmetsch Musical Instruments,** B.R.I., Blackdown, Haslemere, Surrey, GU27 3AY (☎ **01428/643235**).

WHERE TO STAY
MODERATE

✪ Lythe Hill Hotel
Petworth Rd., Haslemere, Surrey GU27 3BQ. ☎ **01428/651251**, or 800/323-5463 in the U.S. Fax 01428/644131. 22 rms, 18 suites. TV TEL. £84 ($132.70) single; £95 ($150.10) double; £110–£150 ($173.80–$237) suite. Breakfast £8 ($12.65) extra. AE, MC, V. Free parking. Take B2131 1¹/₂ miles east from Haslemere.

This 14th-century farmhouse of historic interest on the outskirts of Haslemere is situated on 20 acres of parkland overlooking National Trust woodlands—just an hour from London, Heathrow, and Gatwick. Across the courtyard is the main hotel, with luxuriously appointed bedrooms and suites, as well as an English restaurant. In the black-and-white–timbered farmhouse are five elegant period units with marble-tile baths. One has a four-poster bed dated 1614.

Downstairs in the farmhouse is the renowned, oak-beamed and paneled Auberge de France Restaurant, offering a classic French cuisine served by candlelight on polished oak tables. Specialties include turbot, fresh Scottish salmon, tournedos de boeuf, and a cellar of fine wines. Dinner costs around £30 ($47.40). Open from 7:30 to 9:45pm Tuesday through Sunday, and on Sunday from noon to 2pm for lunch as well.

WHERE TO DINE
MODERATE

Fleur de Sel
23–27 Lower St. ☎ **01428/651462.** Reservations required. Fixed-price lunch £12.50 ($19.75) for two courses, £16.50 ($26.05) for three courses; fixed-price dinner £21 ($33.20)

for two courses, £26 ($41.10) for three courses. AE, MC, V. Tues–Fri noon–2pm and 7–10pm, Sat 7–10pm, Sun noon–2pm. FRENCH.

Michele and Bernadette Perraud bought this restaurant, formerly Morel's, in 1994. Although the restaurant has changed hands, the food is still classically French. This main-street establishment, created from a row of terraced cottages, is bright and furnished in modern overtones, but there's nothing about the decor that detracts from the cuisine.

Formerly head chef at the Michelin three-star restaurant, the Waterside Inn in Bray, M. Perraud changes the menu seasonally and offers nightly specials. For starters, the menu may include a puff pastry case filled with asparagus in a creamy tomato sauce or pasta parcels filled with lobster. The main courses may feature a breast of chicken stuffed with prawns and citrus fruits, roast crispy duck in a honey-and-ginger sauce, or fillets of Scottish salmon with a tomato-and-basil sauce. To finish, try the crème brûlée or a concoction of chocolate biscuits, chocolate, and coffee mousse with pistachio sauce.

10 The Sussexes

If King Harold hadn't loved Sussex so much, the course of English history might have been changed forever. Had the brave Saxon waited longer in the north, he could have marshaled more adequate reinforcements before striking south to meet the Normans. But Duke William's soldiers were ravaging the countryside he knew so well, and Harold rushed down to counter them.

Harold's enthusiasm for Sussex is understandable. The landscape rises and falls like waves. The county is known for its downlands and tree-thickened weald, from which came the timbers to build England's mighty fleet in days gone by. The shires lie south of London and Surrey, bordering Kent in the east, Hampshire in the west, and opening directly onto the sometimes sunny seaside-town–dotted English Channel.

Like the other sections in the vulnerable south of England, Sussex witnessed some of the most important moments in the country's history. Apart from the Norman landings at Hastings, the most life-changing transformation occurred in the 19th century, as middle-class Victorians flocked to the seashore, pumping new spirit into Eastbourne, Worthing, Brighton, even old Hastings. The cult of the saltwater worshipers flourished, and still does to this day. Although Eastbourne and Worthing are much frequented by the English, we'd place them several fathoms below Brighton and Hastings, which are much more suitable if you're seeking a vacation by the sea.

The old towns and villages of Sussex, particularly Rye and Winchelsea, are far more intriguing than the seaside resorts. No Sussex village is lovelier than Alfriston (and the innkeepers know it, too), Arundel is noted for its castle, and the cathedral city of Chichester is a mecca for theater buffs. Traditionally, and for purposes of government (and this book), Sussex is divided into East Sussex and West Sussex.

A DRIVING TOUR

Day 1   Drive down from London or take the train to the ancient seaport of Rye on the Sussex coast. Anchor into one of the historic inns, perhaps the Mermaid. At some point during the day visit the

---

What's Special About the Sussexes

Great Towns/Villages
- Rye, former Cinque Port, considered one of England's best-preserved medieval villages.
- Alfriston, ancient town in the Cuckmere Valley and a former smugglers' haunt.
- Brighton, first and largest seaside resort in the southeast, with its famed Royal Pavilion.

Castles
- Arundel Castle, ancestral home of the dukes of Norfolk, with an exceptional collection of paintings in this Georgian town.
- Hastings Castle, first of the Norman castles built in England (ca. 1067).
- Battle Abbey, the setting for the Battle of Hastings in 1066.

Ace Attractions
- The Royal Pavilion at Brighton, a John Nash version of an Indian Moghul's palace.
- The Hastings Embroidery, a commemorative needlework tracing 900 years of English history.

Literary Shrines
- Bateman's, northwest of Battle, home of Rudyard Kipling and filled with mementos of English days of empire in India.
- Monks House, outside Lewes, a National Trust property, home to Virginia and Leonard Woolf from 1919 to Leonard's death in 1969.

---

adjoining village of Winchelsea, which, like Rye, was an ancient Cinque Port. Winchelsea lies 3 miles farther along A259.

Day 2 Head west from Rye along A259, which meets the coast at Hastings and adjoining St. Leonards. After visiting the ruins of Hastings Castle, head to the small town of Battle, 6 miles inland, for a look at Battle Abbey. Anchor somewhere in the area for the night.

Day 3 The next morning continue west along the coast, passing through the seaside town of Eastbourne, which grew up in the mid-1880s, a development ordered by William Cavendish, the seventh duke of Devonshire. It has a 3-mile-long seafront and a largely shingle beach. From Eastbourne, take A2021 north to Polegate, heading west until the turnoff south along a secondary south to Alfriston. This is one of the prettiest villages of England. Spend the night (see below for more details).

Day 4 In the morning drive north until you reach A27 going west to Lewes. Spend the morning exploring this town and have lunch. In the early afternoon drive southwest along A27 to the resort of Brighton ("London by the Sea") for the night. Try to arrive in time to see the Royal Pavilion. If you're too late, see it in the morning before departing Brighton.

Day 5 Continue west along A27 to Arundel and see its castle; have lunch there. In the afternoon complete the final lap of the journey, going along A17 to Chichester where, it is hoped, you can arrange your schedule to see a performance at its famed theater.

1 Rye

62 miles SE of London

"Nothing more recent than a Cavalier's Cloak, Hat and Ruffles should be seen in the streets of Rye," said Louis Jennings. This ancient town, formerly an island, was flourishing in the 13th century. Rye, near the English Channel, and neighboring Winchelsea were once part of the "Antient" Cinque Port Confederation. Rye in its early days was a smuggling center, its residents sneaking in contraband from the marshes to stash away in little nooks.

But the sea receded from Rye, leaving it perched like a giant whale out of water, 2 miles from the Channel. Its narrow cobblestone streets twist and turn like a labyrinth, jumbled along them buildings whose sagging roofs and crooked chimneys indicate the town's medieval origins. The old town's entrance is **Land Gate,** where a single lane of traffic passes between massive, 40-foot-high stone towers. The parapet of the gate has holes through which boiling oil used to be poured on unwelcome visitors, such as French raiding parties.

Attacked several times by French fleets, Rye was practically razed in 1377. But it rebuilt itself sufficiently, decking itself out in the Elizabethan style, so that Queen Elizabeth I, during her visit in 1573, bestowed upon the town the distinction of Royal Rye. This has long been considered a special place and over the years has attracted the famous, such as novelist Henry James.

Today the town has lots of sites of architectural interest, notably the mid-12th-century **St. Mary's Parish Church,** Church Square (☎ **01797/224935**), with its 16th-century clock flanked by two gilded cherubs, known as Quarter Boys because of their striking of the bells on the quarter hour. The church is often referred to as "the Cathedral of East Sussex" because of its size and beauty. If you're courageous, you can climb a set of wooden stairs and ladders to the bell tower of the church, from which an impressive view is afforded. It's open June to September, daily from 9am to 6pm; off-season, daily from 9am to dusk. Contributions are appreciated to enter the church. Admission to the tower costs £1.60 ($2.55) for adults and 80p ($1.25) for children.

ESSENTIALS
GETTING THERE

By Train   From London, the Southern Region Line offers trains south from Charing Cross or Cannon Street Station, with a change at Ashford, before continuing on to Rye. You can also go via Tunbridge Wells with a change in Hastings. Trains run every hour during the day, arriving at the Rye Train Station off Cinque Ports Street (trip time: $1^1/_2$ to 2 hr.).

By Bus   You need to take the train to get to Rye, but once you're there you'll find buses departing for many destinations, including Hastings. Schedules of the various bus companies are posted on signs in the parking lot. For bus connections information in the surrounding area, call 01634/832666.

By Car   From London, take M25, M26, and M20 east to Maidstone, going southeast along A20 to Ashford. At Ashford, continue south on A2070.

VISITOR INFORMATION

The **telephone area code** is 01797. The **Tourist Information Centre** is at The Strand Quay (☎ **01797/226696**).

WHAT TO SEE & DO

Lamb House

West St. (at the top of Mermaid St.). ☎ **01797/224982.** Admission £2 ($3.15) adults and children. Apr–Oct, Wed and Sat 2–6pm. Closed Nov–Mar.

Henry James lived at Lamb House from 1898 to 1916. There are many James mementos in the house, which is set in a walled garden. Its former owner rushed off to join the gold rush in North America but perished in the Klondike, and James was able to buy the freehold for a modest £2,000. Some of his well-known books were written here. In *English Hours*, James wrote: "There is not much room in the pavilion, but there is room for the hard-pressed table and tilted chair—there is room for a novelist and his friends."

Rye Castle Museum

Gungarden. ☎ **01797/226728.** Admission £1.50 ($2.35) adults, £1 ($1.60) students and senior citizens, 50p (80¢) children. Apr–Oct, daily 10:30am–5:30pm; Nov–Mar, Sat–Sun 11:30am–4pm.

This stone fortification was constructed about 1250 by King Henry III to defend the coast against attack by the French. For 300 years it was the town jail but has long since been converted into a museum. A wealth of local and Cinque Ports history comes alive here, along with the saga of Romney Marsh and its legendary smugglers.

A NEARBY ATTRACTION

The neighboring Cinque Confederation port to Rye, **Winchelsea** has also witnessed the water's ebb. It traces its history back to Edward I and has experienced many dramatic moments, such as sacking by the French. In the words of one 19th-century writer, Winchelsea is "a sunny dream of centuries ago." The finest sight of this dignified residential town is a badly damaged 14th-century church containing a number of remarkable tombs.

On the outskirts of Winchelsea, you can visit **Smallhythe Place,** Smallhythe, near Tenterden (☎ **01580/762334**), for 30 years the country house of Dame Ellen Terry, the English actress acclaimed for her Shakespearean roles who had a long theatrical association with Sir Henry Irving; she died in the house in 1928. This timber-framed structure, known as a "continuous-jetty house," was built in the first half of the 16th century and is filled with Terry memorabilia. An Elizabethan barn, adapted as a theater in 1929, is open to view on most days. The house is on B2082 near Tenterden, about 6 miles north of Rye, and is open April to October, Saturday through Wednesday from 2 to 6pm. Adults pay £2.50 ($3.95) admission; children, £1.30 ($2.05). Take bus no. 312 from Tenterden or Rye.

WHERE TO STAY

Some of the best rooms in Rye are at the Old Vicarage in East Street; see "Where to Dine," below.

MODERATE

The George

High St., Rye, East Sussex TN31 7JP. ☎ **01797/222114,** or 800/225-5843 in the U.S. and Canada. Fax 01797/224065. 22 rms. TV TEL. Mon–Thurs, £70 ($110.60) single; £75 ($118.50) double. Breakfast £9.25 ($14.60) extra. Fri–Sun (minimum of 2 nights required), £54 ($85.30) per person daily, including half board. AE, DC, MC, V. Free parking.

This coaching inn has a 400-year history. In the 18th century it drew a diverse clientele: some traveling by horse-drawn carriage, others by boat, between London and France. This is one of the most charming small inns in the region, with half-timbered architecture. Some of the timbers may be from the wreck of an English ship broken up in Rye Harbour after the defeat of the Spanish Armada.

The Georgian ballroom is complete with a minstrel's gallery. The hotel also has an old-fashioned restaurant and at least two blazing fireplaces in cold weather. A three-course fixed-price dinner costs £15.95 ($25.20).

⊖ Holloway House

High St., Rye, East Sussex TN31 7JF. ☎ **01797/224748.** 7 rms. TV TEL. Sun–Thurs, £39–£60 ($61.60–$94.80) single; £50–£90 ($79–$142.20) double. Fri–Sat, £70–£90 ($110.60–$142.20) single or double. Rates include English breakfast. Midweek breaks (any 2 nights or more, Sun–Thurs), £25 ($39.50) per person, including breakfast. MC, V.

Winner of several awards for the beauty of its small front garden and the quality of its restoration, this charming house was originally built in 1568 above a much older vaulted cellar. (Local historians think that the cellar was the foundation of a prominent medieval inn, the White Vine, which is frequently mentioned in historical archives.) Restored from an almost derelict shell in 1987 by Sheila Brown, the capable owner, it carefully maintains the Georgian detailing of the formal public rooms and the Tudor-style wall and ceiling beams of the antique bedrooms. An in-house restaurant, strictly separated into smoking and no-smoking sections, serves evening meals priced from around £10 ($15.80) each.

Hope Anchor Hotel

Watchbell St., Rye, East Sussex TN31 7HA. ☎ **01797/222216.** Fax 01797/223796. 12 rms, 10 with bath. TV. £36 ($56.90) single without bath, £40 ($63.20) single with bath; £50 ($79) and up double without or with bath. Rates include English breakfast. MC, V. Free parking.

At the end of a cobblestone street on a hill dominating the town stands this 17th-century hostelry, which enjoys panoramic views of the surrounding countryside and overlooks the Strand Quay where yachts can be seen at their moorings. Oak beams and open fires in winter make this a most inviting place to spend a few days. The bedrooms are comfortable, all with hot-beverage facilities. Two feature four-poster beds and have recently been refurbished.

Bar meals are served at lunch and in the evening, and the Hope Anchor Restaurant offers an English cuisine, featuring fresh fish caught locally. A dinner in the restaurant costs £15 ($23.70).

✪ Mermaid Inn

Mermaid St. (between West St. and the Strand), Rye, East Sussex TN31 7EU. ☎ **01797/223065.** Fax 01797/225069. 28 rms, 27 with bath. TV TEL. £44 ($69.50) single or double without bath, £58 ($91.65) single or double with bath. Rates include English breakfast. AE, DC, MC, V. Free parking.

The Mermaid Inn is one of the most famous of the old smugglers' inns of England, known to that band of cut-throats, the real-life Hawkhurst Gang, as well as to Russell Thorndike's fictional character, Dr. Syn. One of the present rooms, in fact, is called Dr. Syn's Bedchamber, and is connected by a secret staircase—set in the thickness of the wall—to the bar. The most sought-after rooms are in the building overlooking the cobblestone street. All rooms have a private bath except for two, a single and one double. Five have four-poster beds.

When Elizabeth came to Rye and the Mermaid in 1573, the inn had already been operating nearly 150 years. A covered carriageway leads to the parking area.

In the center of the hotel is a courtyard, where you'll see a pedestal fountain with water flowing down on the heads of water lilies.

INEXPENSIVE

⑤ Durrant House Hotel
Market St. (off High St.), Rye, East Sussex TN31 3LA. ☎ **01797/223182.** 9 rms, 7 with bath; 1 suite. TV. £39 ($61.60) single or double without bath; £46 ($72.70) single or double with bath; £70 ($110.60) suite. Rates include English breakfast. MC, V. Free parking.

This beautiful Georgian house is set on a quiet residential street at the end of Market Street. Exemplifying its charm and character, the hotel has a cozy lounge with an arched, brick fireplace and, across the hall, a residents' bar. Over the years it has attracted many famous people. In more recent times, the renowned artist Paul Nash lived next door until his death in 1946; in fact, his celebrated view, as seen in his painting *View of the Rother*, can be enjoyed from the River Room of the hotel. The house is named for a previous owner, Sir William Durrant, a friend of the duke of Wellington, who bought it in the 18th century. At one time the house was used as a relay station for carrier pigeons; these birds brought news of the victory at Waterloo. The Durrant House Restaurant serves a traditional English cuisine, specializing in seafood. French and Italian specialties are also served. A five-course table d'hôte menu costs £23.50 ($37.15) and includes a bottle of wine.

WHERE TO DINE
MODERATE

Flushing Inn
4 Market St. ☎ **01797/223292.** Reservations required. Fixed-price meal £19 ($30) at lunch, £19–£23.50 ($30–$37.15) at dinner. AE, DC, MC, V. Mon noon–2pm, Wed–Sun noon–2pm and 6:45–9pm. Closed first 2 weeks in Jan. SEAFOOD/ENGLISH.

In a 16th-century inn on a cobblestone street near Rye Parish Church, the Flushing Inn has preserved the best of the past, including a wall-size fresco in the restaurant dating from 1544 and depicting a menagerie of birds and heraldic beasts. A rear dining room overlooks a carefully tended flower garden. A special feature is the Sea Food Lounge Bar, where sandwiches and plates of seafood are available for £2 to £12 ($3.15 to $18.95). Besides these lunches and dinners, gastronomic evenings are held at regular intervals between October and April. For one of these specialty meals, including your apéritif, wine, and after-dinner brandy, you pay £48 ($75.85) per person. Fine-wine evenings cost £60 to £68 ($94.80 to $107.45). The Flushing Inn has been run by the Mann family since 1960, with the second generation now fully active in the business.

The Landgate Bistro
5–6 Landgate. ☎ **01797/222829.** Reservations required. Main courses £7.90–£11.90 ($12.50–$18.80); fixed-price menu (Tues–Thurs) £14.90 ($23.55). AE, DC, MC, V. Tues–Fri 7–9:30pm, Sat 7–10pm. MODERN BRITISH.

Much appreciated by clients who sometimes travel from other parts of Sussex for an evening meal here, this restaurant occupies a pair of interconnected Georgian shops whose exteriors are covered with what locals refer to as "mathematical tiles" (18th-century simulated brick applied over stucco facades to save money). Inside, Toni Ferguson-Lees and her partner, Nick Parkin, prepare savory versions of modern British cuisine which changes with the seasons. Depending on the inspiration of the chefs, menu choices might include braised squid with white wine, tomatoes, and garlic; grilled Dover sole; pigeon breast with a stock and red-wine sauce; and noisettes of English lamb with tomato-basil sauce.

INEXPENSIVE

The Old Vicarage in East Street

East St., Rye, East Sussex TN31 7JY. ☎ **01797/225131.** Reservations usually required. Main courses £8.90–£11.80 ($14.05–$18.65); three-course fixed-price dinner £12.95 ($20.45). DC, MC, V. Daily 6:45–9pm. Closed Jan and 1 week in Nov. FRENCH/INTERNATIONAL.

Once the Georgian vicarage for St. Mary's Church, this charming establishment off High Street was converted into a French-style *restaurant avec chambres* in 1979. Although the owners, Sarah and Bill Foster, maintain four beautifully decorated bedrooms upstairs, the establishment is best known for its elegant restaurant. After an apéritif in the cocktail bar, dinner guests proceed into the blue-and-white dining room, where, within sight of a carved fireplace, they enjoy a selection of dishes from the classic French and international cuisine. The menu changes monthly to make the most of the best in local fish and meat. A typical meal listing might include homemade onion soup, fish bisque, puff pastry stuffed with pine nuts and spinach with a homemade tomato sauce, garlic mussels, steak-and-mushroom pie, pasta with mixed herbs, garlic, and cheese, followed by desserts such as vacherin aux fruits and a selection of unusual homemade desserts.

Each of the bedrooms is suitable for one or two people and, with breakfast included, rents for £28 to £42 ($44.25 to $66.35) daily per person. Units feature private baths, color TVs, phones, and a carefully assembled kind of panache. Do not confuse this establishment with a nearby B&B called the Old Vicarage.

2 Hastings & St. Leonards

63 miles SE of London. 45 miles SW of Dover

The world has seen bigger battles, but few are as well remembered as the Battle of Hastings in 1066. When William, duke of Normandy, landed on the Sussex coast and lured King Harold (already fighting Vikings in Yorkshire) southward to defeat, the destiny of the English-speaking people was changed forever. The actual battle occurred at what is now Battle Abbey (9 miles away), but the Norman duke used Hastings as his base of operations.

Linked by a 3-mile promenade along the sea, Hastings and St. Leonards were given a considerable boost in the 19th century by Queen Victoria, who visited several times. Neither town enjoys such royal patronage today; rather, they do a thriving business with the English on vacation. Hastings and St. Leonards have the usual shops and English sea-resort amusements.

ESSENTIALS
GETTING THERE

By Train   Daily trains run from London's Victoria Station or Charing Cross to Hastings hourly. Trip time is 1¹/₂ to 2 hours, depending on the train.

By Bus   Hastings is linked by bus to Maidstone, Folkestone, and Eastbourne, which has direct service with scheduled departures. National Express operates regular daily service from London's Victoria Coach Station.

By Car   From the M25 ring road around London, head southeast to the coast and Hastings on A21.

VISITOR INFORMATION

The **telephone area code** is 01424. The **Tourist Information Centre** is at 4 Robertson Terrace (☎ **01424/718888**).

WHAT TO SEE & DO

Hastings Castle

Castle Hill Rd., West Hill. ☎ **01424/718888.** Admission £2.50 ($3.95) adults, £1.75 ($2.75) children. Apr–Sept, daily 10am–5:30pm; Oct–Mar, daily 11am–3:30pm. Take the West Cliff Railway from George Street to the castle for 60p (95¢), 40p (65¢) for children.

In ruins now, the first of the Norman castles built in England sprouted on a western hill overlooking Hastings, around 1067. Precious little is left to remind us of the days when proud knights, imbued with a spirit of pomp and spectacle, wore bonnets and girdles. The fortress was defortified by King John in 1216 and later served as a church. Owned by the Pelham dynasty from the latter 16th century to modern times, the ruins have been turned over to Hastings. There is now an audiovisual presentation of the castle's history, including the famous battle of 1066. From the mount, you'll have a good view of the coast and promenade.

✪ Hastings Embroidery

Town Hall, Queen's Rd. ☎ **01424/718888.** Admission £1.25 ($2) adults, 75p ($1.20) children. May–Sept, Mon–Fri 10am–4:30pm; Oct–Apr, Mon–Fri 11:30am–3pm.

A commemorative work, the Hastings Embroidery is a remarkable achievement that traces 900 years of English history through needlework. First exhibited in 1966, the 27 panels, 243 feet in length, depict 81 historic scenes, including some of the nation's greatest moments and legends: the murder of Thomas aà Becket, King John signing the Magna Carta, the Black Plague, Chaucer's pilgrims going to Canterbury, the Battle of Agincourt with the victorious Henry V, the War of the Roses, the Little Princes in the Tower, Bloody Mary's reign, Drake's *Golden Hind*, the arrival of Philip II's ill-fated Armada, Guy Fawkes's gunpowder plot, the sailing of the *Mayflower*, the disastrous plague of 1665, the great London fire of 1666, Nelson at Trafalgar, the Battle of Waterloo, the Battle of Britain, and the D-day landings at Normandy. Also exhibited is a scale model of the battlefield at Battle, with William's inch-high men doing in Harold's model soldiers.

Smugglers Adventure

St. Clements Caves, West Hill. ☎ **01424/422964.** Admission £3.80 ($6) adults, £2.50 ($3.95) children, £10.95 ($17.30) family. Easter–Sept, daily 10am–5:30pm; Oct–Easter, daily 11am–4:30pm. Take the West Cliff Railway from George Street to West Hill for 60p (95¢) adults, 40p (65¢) for children.

Here you can descend into the once-secret underground haunts of the smugglers of Hastings. In these chambers, where the smugglers stashed their booty away from Customs authorities, you can see an exhibition and museum and a video in a theater and take a subterranean adventure walk with 50 life-size figures, along with dramatic sound and lighting effects.

WHERE TO STAY

INEXPENSIVE

Beauport Park Hotel

Battle Rd. (A2100), Hastings, East Sussex TN38 8EA. ☎ **01424/851222** or 800/528-1234 in the U.S. and Canada. Fax 01424/852465. 21 rms, 2 suites. TV TEL. £65 ($102.70) single; £85 ($134.30) double; £90–£95 ($142.20–$150.10) suite. Rates include English breakfast.

Weekend breaks (for 2 nights, including half board), Apr–Oct, £218 ($344.45) double; Nov–Mar, £238 ($376.05) double. AE, DC, MC, V. Free parking. Head 3¹/₂ miles northwest of Hastings, at the junction of A2100 and B2159. Bus 4 or 5 from Hastings.

Originally the private estate of General Murray, former governor of Québec (who had previously served under General Wolfe), the building was destroyed by fire in 1923 and reconstructed in the old style. It's surrounded by beautiful gardens (the Italian-style grounds in the rear feature statuary and flowering shrubbery). The living room and lounge are tastefully furnished, and the French windows in the dining room open onto the parklike rear.

The hotel offers a well-prepared and handsomely served cuisine. Some of the produce comes from the hotel's own gardens. A fixed-price lunch is served at £15 ($23.70), with many choices available. The fixed-price dinner is £18 ($28.45), again with a wide selection.

The Royal Victoria

Marina, St. Leonards, Hastings, East Sussex TN38 OBD. ☎ **01424/445544**. Fax 01424/721995. 42 rms, 10 suites. MINIBAR TV TEL. Mon–Tues, £65 ($102.70) single; £75 ($118.50) double. Fri–Sun, £36 ($56.90) single; £50 ($79) double. Daily, £80 ($126.40) suite. Rates include English breakfast. AE, DC, MC, V. Free parking.

This seafront hotel, constructed in 1828, has the most impressive architecture of any establishment in town and offers the best accommodation in Hastings or St. Leonards. Since a complete refurbishing in 1988, the Royal Victoria has returned to its premier position. Attractively furnished and decorated, the hotel offers some of the best food in its restaurant, which accepts nonresidents who reserve. Bar snacks ranging from sandwiches to steaks cost £1.95 to £6.50 ($3.10 to $10.25), and a fixed-price dinner goes for £15 ($23.70). Service is daily from noon to 2pm and 7 to 9:30pm.

WHERE TO DINE
MODERATE

Röser's

64 Eversfield Place. ☎ **01424/712218**. Reservations required. Main courses £10.95–£16.95 ($17.30–$26.80); fixed-price meal £15.95 ($25.20) at lunch, £19.95 ($31.50) at dinner (Tues–Fri). AE, DC, MC, V. Tues–Fri noon–2pm and 7–10pm, Sat 7–10pm. Closed first 2 weeks in Jan and last week in Aug. FRENCH.

This is a pleasant surprise in what is often considered one of the gastronomic wastelands of southern England. Set in a brick-fronted Victorian row house very similar to each of its neighbors opposite the pier, the restaurant is a showcase for the cuisine of Gerald Röser. Menu choices change about every 3 weeks but might include seared Scottish scallops with saffron sauce and charcoal-grilled vegetables; fresh, locally caught sea bass served Mediterranean-style with olive oil, lemon juice, and capers; and, in season, wild boar chop with lentil sauce. Service is first-rate.

3 Battle

55 miles SE of London, 34 miles NE of Brighton

Seven miles from Hastings, in the heart of the Sussex countryside, is the old market town of Battle, famed in history as the setting for the Battle of Hastings in 1066. King Harold, last of the Saxon kings, encircled by his housecarls, fought bravely, not only for his kingdom but for his life. He was killed by William, duke of

Normandy, and his body was dismembered. To commemorate the victory, William the Conqueror founded **Battle Abbey** at the south end of Battle High Street (☎ 01424/773792); some of the construction stone was shipped from his own lands at Caen in northern France.

During the dissolution of the monasteries from 1538 to 1539 by King Henry VIII, the church of the abbey was largely destroyed. Some buildings and ruins, however, remain in what Tennyson called "O Garden, blossoming out of English blood." The principal building still standing is the Abbot's House, which is leased to a private school for boys and girls and is open to the general public only during summer holidays. Of architectural interest is the gate house, which has octagonal towers and stands at the top of the Market Square. All of the north Precinct Mall is still standing, and one of the most interesting sights of the ruins is the ancient Dorter Range, where the monks once slept.

The town of Battle grew up around the abbey; even though it has remained a medieval market town, many of the old half-timbered buildings regrettably have lost much of their original character because of stucco plastering carried out by past generations.

The abbey is open April to September, daily from 10am to 6pm; October to March, daily from 10am to 4pm. Admission is £3.50 ($5.55) for adults and £1.75 ($2.75) for children. The abbey is located a 5-minute walk from the train station.

ESSENTIALS
GETTING THERE

By Train   The train station at Battle is a stop on the London–Hastings rail link, with departures from both Charing Cross and Victoria stations in London. For more information, call 0171/620-5555. Trip time: 1 hour, 20 minutes.

By Bus   It's best to go from London to Battle by train. However, if you're in Rye or Hastings in summer, you can take one of several frequent buses that run to Battle. For information and schedules, call 01345/581457.

By Car   From M25 (the ring road around London), cut south to Sevenoaks and continue along A21 to Battle via A2100.

VISITOR INFORMATION

The **telephone area code** is 01424. The **Tourist Information Centre** is at 88 High St. (☎ 01424/773721).

WHERE TO STAY & DINE
MODERATE

✪ Netherfield Place

Netherfield Rd., Battle, East Sussex TN33 9PU. ☎ **01424/774455** or 800/828-5572 in the U.S. Fax 01424/774024. 14 rms. TV TEL. £55–£75 ($86.90–$118.50) single; £100–£130 ($158–$205.40) double. Rates include English breakfast. AE, DC, MC, V. Free parking. Closed Dec 15–Jan 15. Take the A2100 1³/₄ miles northwest of Battle.

Built in 1924 on 30 acres of parkland, this is by far the best place to stay. The symmetrical wings of this brick-fronted Georgian mansion extend toward flowering gardens on all sides. Once you pass beneath the cornices of the entrance you'll discover a world of plush upholstery, comfortable bedrooms, and sun-flooded panoramas.

You can enjoy tea or a drink in the glassed-in lounge overlooking the trees outside. The international cuisine is both good and carefully served, prepared with fresh, wholesome produce. Fresh fruit and vegetables come from the hotel's garden. Dinners cost £26 ($41.10).

INEXPENSIVE

George Hotel

23 High St., Battle, East Sussex TN33 OEA. ☎ **01424/774466.** Fax 01424/774853. 22 rms. TV TEL. Mon–Thurs, £50 ($79) single; £65 ($102.70) double. Fri–Sun, £28 ($44.25) single or double. Rates include breakfast. AE, DC, MC, V. Free parking.

Although there has been some kind of inn on this site for more than 600 years, the hotel that stands here today dates from 1739. Much renovated since then, the George combines modern comfort in a historic building. The owners offer well-furnished rooms with private bath and hot-beverage facilities.

The hotel has a comfortable bar, with a full snack menu. Open log fires make the place cozy in winter. The spacious restaurant, the George, features English and continental dishes. Lunch and dinner begin at £11 ($17.40).

4 Alfriston & Lewes

60 miles S of London

Nestled on the Cuckmere River, **Alfriston** is one of the most beautiful villages of England and has several old inns. High Street, with its old market cross, looks like one's idea of what an English village should be. Some of the old houses still have hidden chambers where smugglers stored their loot.

The village lies northeast of Seaford on the English Channel, in the vicinity of the resort of Eastbourne and the modern port of Newhaven. During the day, Alfriston is likely to be overrun by coach tours (it's that lovely, and that popular).

Only about a dozen miles away along A27 toward Brighton, **Lewes,** an ancient Sussex town centered in the South Downs, is worth exploring. Since the home of the Glyndebourne Opera is only 5 miles to the east, the accommodations of Lewes are difficult to reserve during the Glyndebourne Opera Festival. The town has many historical associations, listing such residents as Thomas Paine, who lived at Bull House, on High Street, now a restaurant.

ESSENTIALS
GETTING THERE

By Train   Rail service is available from London's Victoria Station and London Bridge Station heading for Lewes. One train per hour makes the trip during the day (trip time: $1^1/4$ hr.). Trains are more frequent during rush hours. There is no rail service to Alfriston.

By Bus   Buses run daily to Lewes from London's Victoria Coach Station, although there are many, many stops along the way (trip time: 3 hr.)—it's better to take the train. Once in Lewes, you can connect with a bus run by the Southdown Bus Company that will take you from Lewes to Alfriston in 30 minutes. The bus station at Lewes is on East Street in the center of town.

By Car   Head east along M25 (the London ring road), cutting south on A26 via East Grinstead to Lewes. Once at Lewes, follow A27 east to the signposted turnoff for the village of Alfriston.

Puck of Pook's Hill

"Heaven looked after it in the dissolute times of mid-Victorian restoration and caused the vicar to send his bailiff to live in it for 40 years, and he lived in peaceful filth and left everything as he found it."

Rudyard Kipling was writing of Bateman's, the 17th-century ironmaster's house in the village of Burwash, on A265, some 27 miles northeast of Brighton, close to the border with Kent.

Born in Bombay, India, in 1865, Kipling loved the countryside of Sussex, and the book that best expressed his feelings for the shire is *Puck of Pook's Hill* (1906). The following year he was to win the Nobel Prize for literature. He lived at Bateman until his death in 1936. His widow was to die 3 years later at the dawn of World War II, and she left the house to the National Trust.

Kipling is known mainly for his adventure stories, such as *The Light That Failed* (1890), *The Jungle Book* (1894), and *Captains Courageous* (1897). He is also remembered for his tales concerning India, including *Kim* (1901). He lived in America after his marriage to Caroline Balestier in 1892. But by 1896 he had returned to the south of England, occupying a house at Rottingdean, a little village on the Sussex Downs, 4 miles east of Brighton. Here he wrote the famous line: "What should they know of England who only England know?" In a steam-driven motor car, Kipling and Caroline set out to explore Sussex, of which they were especially fond. Although the population of Rottingdean was only that of a small village, they decided at some point that it had become too crowded. In their motor car one day they spotted Bateman's, which was to become a final home for both of them. "It is a good and peaceable place standing in terraced lawns nigh to a walled garden of old red brick, and two fat-headed oasthouses with red brick stomachs, and an aged silver-grey dovecot on top," Kipling wrote.

The Burwash city fathers invited Kipling to unveil a memorial to the slain of World War I, and he agreed. It's in the center of town at the church. Kipling said that visitors should "remember the sacrifice." Both the church and an inn across the way appear in the section of *Puck of Pook's Hill* called "Hal o' the Draft." The famed writer and son of Anglo-Indian parents died in London and was given an impressive funeral before burial in the Poets' Corner at Westminster Abbey.

VISITOR INFORMATION

The **telephone area code** for Alfriston is 01323; the **area code** for Lewes is 01273. The **Tourist Information Centre** is in Lewes at 187 High St. (☎ **01273/483448**).

WHAT TO SEE & DO
IN ALFRISTON

Drusilla's Park, 1 mile outside Alfriston off A27 (☎ **01323/870656**), has won awards. It's not large but is fascinating nonetheless, with a flamingo lake, Japanese garden, and unusual breeds of some domestic animals, among other attractions. Children are especially delighted, as there's a playland covering more than an acre. The park is open daily from 10am to 5pm (until 4pm in winter), charging £5.50 ($8.70) for adults, £4.75 ($7.50) for children 3 to 12 (free for children 2 and under). It's closed December 24–26.

IN LEWES

The half-timbered **Anne of Cleves House,** 52 Southover High St. (☎ **01273/ 474610**), was part of Anne of Cleves's divorce settlement from Henry VIII, but Anne never lived in the house and there's no proof that she ever visited Lewes. Today the house is a Museum of Local History and is cared for by the Sussex Archaeological Society. The museum has a furnished bedroom and kitchen and displays of furniture, local history of the Wealden iron industry, and other local crafts. Admission is £1.90 ($3) for adults, 80P ($1.25) for children. It's open April to October, Monday through Saturday from 10am to 5pm and Sunday from 2 to 5pm. Take bus no. 123.

Lewes, of course, grew up around its Norman **castle.** Adjacent to the castle is the **Museum of Sussex Archaeology,** 169 High St. (☎ **01273/486290**). A 20-minute audiovisual show is also presented. A joint admission ticket to both the castle and the museum costs £2.90 ($4.60) for adults, £1.50 ($2.35) for children. Both sites can be visited April to October, Monday through Saturday from 10am to 5:30pm and Sunday from 11am to 5:30pm; other months, Monday through Saturday from 10am to dusk and Sunday from 11am to dusk. Take bus no. 27, 28, 121, 122, 166, 728, or 729.

KIPLING'S HOME IN SUSSEX

Rudyard Kipling (1865–1936), the British writer famous for stories about the days of empire in India, lived his last 34 years (1902–36) at **Bateman's,** a country house northwest of Battle and half a mile south of Burwash, on A265, the Lewes–Etchingham road (☎ **01435/882302**). The sandstone house, built in 1634, was bequeathed, together with its contents and 300 acres of land, to the National Trust by Kipling's widow. The interior is filled with Asian rugs, antique bronzes, and other mementos the writer collected in India and elsewhere. Kipling's library is among the points of interest. The house and gardens are open only April to October, Saturday through Wednesday from 11am to 5pm. Admission usually costs £4 ($6.30) for adults and £2 ($3.15) for children.

WHERE TO STAY

IN ALFRISTON

Moderate

Star Inn

High St., Alfriston, East Sussex BN26 5TA. ☎ **01323/870495** or 800/435-4542 in the U.S. Fax 01323/870922. 35 rms. TV TEL. £75 ($118.50) single; £87.50 ($138.25) double. Breakfast £8.50 ($13.45) extra. AE, DC, MC, V. Free parking.

The Star Inn occupies a building dating from 1450, although it was originally founded in the 1200s, perhaps to house pilgrims en route to Chichester and the shrine of St. Richard. In the center of the village, its carved front still unchanged, it boasts an overhanging second story of black-and-white timbers and bay windows. The lounges are on several levels, a forest of old timbers. Out back is a motel wing, with studio rooms. All units have radios, heating, and built-in wardrobe. A three-course dinner is priced at £17.95 ($28.35).

White Lodge Country House Hotel

Sloe Lane, Alfriston, East Sussex BN26 5UR. ☎ **01323/870265.** Fax 01323/870284. 17 rms. TV TEL. £50 ($79) single; £80–£110 ($126.40–$173.80) double. Rates include English breakfast. AE. MC, V. Free parking. Bus Southdown no. 712.

This converted private home, a 5-minute walk from the town center off A27, is now one of the most opulently furnished hotels in the region, run by the original owners. It's situated amid 5 acres of gardens. The public rooms are outfitted like French salons, with carved 18th- and 19th-century antiques, many of them gilded. Bronze statues inspired by classical Greek myths are placed about. Each of the beautifully furnished bedrooms has a color TV, trouser press, hairdryer, lots of tasseled curtains, and countryside views.

The daytime dining room is French, with Louis XV furniture centered around a chiseled fireplace of violet-tinged marble. Dinner is served below the reception area in an Edwardian room. A four-course lunch, served daily from 12:15 to 1:45pm, goes for £11.75 ($18.55); a four-course dinner, served from 7:15 to 9:45pm, costs £16.95 ($26.80). Menu specialties include smoked salmon, grilled lemon sole, and, in season, marinated venison.

IN LEWES
Moderate
Shelleys Hotel
High St., Lewes, East Sussex BN7 1XS. ☎ **01273/472361.** Fax 01273/483152. 17 rms, 2 suites. TV TEL. £85 ($134.30) single; £110–£130 ($173.80–$205.40) double; from £150 ($237) suite. AE, DC, MC, V. Free parking.

This 1526 manor house was owned by the earl of Dorset before it was sold to the Shelley family, distant relatives of the famous poet. Radical changes were made to the architecture in the 18th century. Nowadays, the standards of the management are reflected in the fine antiques, the bowls of flowers, the paintings and prints, the well-kept gardens, and most important, the staff. In the rear is a sun terrace and lawn for tea and drinks; horse chestnuts and copper beech shade the grounds. The central hall is enhanced by Ionic columns, a domed ceiling, and the family coat of arms. The bay windows of the front drawing room open onto the rear gardens, and the lounge is paneled. The bedrooms are personal, individually furnished, usually spacious, and most comfortable. Room 11 has a 16th-century frieze of bacchanalian figures and a design of entwining grapes and flowers. You can order meals in-house, beginning at £13.50 ($21.35) for lunch or £18 ($28.45) for dinner.

WHERE TO DINE
IN ALFRISTON
Moderate
✪ Moonrakers
High St. ☎ **01323/870472.** Reservations recommended. Main courses £8.50–£14.50 ($13.45–$22.90); fixed-price menus £12.95–£15.95 ($20.45–$25.20). AE, MC, V. May–Sept, Mon–Sat 7–10pm; Oct–Apr, Tues–Sat 7–10pm. Closed Jan 20–Feb 13. ENGLISH.

The welcome is warm at this charming 16th-century restaurant with old beams, an inglenook fireplace, a well-prepared cuisine, and a convenient location in the heart of town. Norman Gillies, the owner, supervises a staff that prepares such dishes as salmon in puff pastry with prawn and creamy vermouth stuffing; roast lamb with a garlic-and-herb crust; and a dessert specialty of sticky toffee pudding. Open only for dinner, the restaurant has a comprehensive wine list and a polite staff. Logs burn brightly in the fireplace in winter, and in summer there's a flowering patio for outside dining. The two dining rooms are reserved, respectively, for smokers and nonsmokers.

IN LEWES
Inexpensive
Pailin

20 Station St. ☎ **01273/473906.** Reservations recommended. Main courses £4.25–£6.50 ($6.70–$10.25); fixed-price lunch or dinner £13 ($20.55). AE, DC, MC, V. Mon–Sat noon–2:30pm and 6:30–10:30pm, Sun 6:30–10:30pm. Closed Nov 5 and Dec 25–26. THAI.

The spicy hot cuisine of Bangkok and central Thailand has come to Lewes. Prices are moderate, and the cuisine is well flavored, with fresh ingredients. Begin perhaps with the lemon-chicken soup with lemongrass, typical of Thai cuisine, and follow with a crab-and-prawn "hot pot." A special favorite with local residents is the barbecued chicken which has been carefully marinated. It's served with a sweet-and-sour plum sauce—quite hot but delectable. Many dishes are flavored with a sweet-and-sour sauce. Vegetarian meals are served, and children are also welcomed and given small portions at reduced prices.

EASY EXCURSIONS

RODMELL   This small downland village lies midway between Lewes and the port of Newhaven on C7. Its chief claim to fame is **Monks House,** a National Trust property that was bought by Virginia and Leonard Woolf in 1919 and was their home until his death in 1969. Virginia wrote of the profusion of fruit and vegetables produced by the garden and of the open-water meadows looking out on the downs. Much of the house was furnished and decorated by Virginia's sister, Vanessa Bell, and the artist Duncan Grant. The house has extremely limited visiting hours: from the first Saturday in April until the last Wednesday in October, and then only on Wednesday and Saturday from 2 to 5:30pm. Admission is £2 ($3.15); free for children 4 and under. More information is available by calling the headquarters of the National Trust in East Sussex (☎ **01892/890651**).

Rodmell also has a 12th-century church, a working farm, and a tiny Victorian school still in use. Take Southdown bus no. 123 from the Lewes rail station.

BLUEBELL RAILWAY   This all-steam railway starts at Sheffield Park Station near Uckfield in East Sussex (☎ **01825/722730**) on A275 between East Grinstead and Lewes. The name is taken from the spring flowers that grow alongside the track, running from Sheffield Park to Kingscote. It's a delight for railway buffs, with locomotives dating from the 1870s through the 1950s, when British Railways ended steam operations. You can visit locomotive sheds and a small museum, then later patronize the bookshop or have lunch in a large buffet, bar, and restaurant complex. The round-trip is 1¹/₂ hours as the train wanders through a typical English countryside. The cost is £7 ($11.05) for adults, £3.70 ($5.85) for children, with a family ticket going for £19 ($30). Trains run Saturday and Sunday throughout the year and daily from May to September.

5 Brighton

52 miles S of London

Brighton was one of the first of the great seaside resorts of Europe. The village on the sea from which the present town grew was named Brighthelmstone, and the English eventually shortened it to Brighton. The original swinger who was to shape so much of its destiny arrived in 1783—the prince of Wales; his presence and patronage gave immediate status to the seaside town.

Fashionable dandies from London, including Beau Brummell, turned up. The construction business boomed, as Brighton blossomed with charming and attractive town houses and well-planned squares and crescents. From the Prince Regent's title came the voguish word "Regency," which was to characterize an era, but more specifically refers to the period between 1811 and 1820. Under Victoria, and despite the fact that she cut off her presence, Brighton continued to flourish.

Alas, earlier in this century, as the English began to discover more glamorous spots on the Continent, Brighton lost much of its old *joie de vivre*. It became labeled as "tatty," featuring the usual run of fun-fair-type English seaside amusements. However, that state of affairs long ago changed, owing largely to the huge numbers of Londoners who moved in (some of whom now commute); the invasion has made Brighton increasingly lighthearted and sophisticated. For instance, a beach east of town attracts nude bathers—Britain's first such venture.

ESSENTIALS
GETTING THERE
By Train   London's favorite seaside resort lies on the Sussex coast. Fast trains— 41 a day—leave from Victoria or London Bridge Station (trip time: 55 min.).

By Bus   Buses from Victoria Coach Station take around 2 hours.

By Car   M23 (signposted from central London) leads to A23, which takes you into Brighton.

VISITOR INFORMATION
The **telephone area code** is 01273. At the **Tourist Information Centre,** 10 Bartholomew Sq. (☎ **01273/323755**), opposite the town hall, you can make hotel reservations, reserve tickets for National Express coaches, and pick up a list of current events.

WHAT TO SEE & DO
The Lanes, a closely knit section of alleyways off North Street in Brighton (many of the present shops were formerly fisher's cottages), were frequented in Victoria's day by style-setting curio and antique collectors. Some are still there, although they now share space with boutiques.

✪ The Royal Pavilion
☎ **01273/603005.** Admission £3.85 ($6.10) adults, £2.85 ($4.50) senior citizens and students, £2.25 ($3.55) children 5–15, free for children 4 and under. Oct–Apr, daily 10am–5pm; May–Sept, daily 10am–6pm. Closed Dec 25–26. Bus 1, 2, 3, 5, or 6.

Among the royal residences of Europe, the Royal Pavilion at Brighton, a John Nash version of an Indian Moghul's palace, is unique. Ornate and exotic, it has been subjected over the years to the most devastating wit of English satirists and pundits; but today we can examine it more objectively as one of the

Impressions

A clean Naples with genteel lazzaroni— . . .
Brighton that always looks so brisk, gay, and gaudy,
like a harlequin's jacket— . . . .
　　　　　　　—William Makepeace Thackeray, *Vanity Fair* (1847–48)

outstanding examples of the orientalizing tendencies of the romantic movement in England.

The pavilion was built in 1787 by Henry Holland, but it no more resembled its present appearance than a caterpillar does a butterfly. By the time Nash had transformed it from a simple classical villa into an Orientalist fantasy, the Prince Regent had become King George IV, and the king and one of his mistresses, Lady Conyngham, lived in the palace until 1827.

A decade passed before Victoria, then queen, arrived in Brighton. Although she was to bring Albert and the children on a number of occasions, the monarch and Brighton just didn't mix. The very air of the resort seemed too flippant for her. By 1845, Victoria began packing, and the royal furniture was carted off. Its tenants gone, the pavilion was in serious peril of being torn down, but by a narrow vote, Brightonians agreed to purchase it. Gradually it was restored to its former splendor, enhanced in no small part by the return of much of its original furniture on loan by the present tenant at Buckingham Palace.

Of exceptional interest is the domed **Banqueting Room,** with a chandelier of bronze dragons supporting lilylike glass globes. In the great kitchen, with its old revolving spits, is a collection of Wellington's pots and pans, his *batterie de cuisine*, from his town house at Hyde Park Corner. In the **State Apartments,** particularly the domed salon, dragons wink at you, serpents entwine, lacquered doors shine. The Music Room, with its scalloped ceiling, is a fantasy of water lilies, flying dragons, reptilian paintings, bamboo, silk, and satin.

In the second-floor **gallery,** look for Nash's views of the pavilion in its elegant heyday. Other attractions include **Queen Victoria's Apartments,** beautifully re-created, and the impressively restored **South Galleries,** breakfast rooms for George IV's guests. Refreshments are available in the Queen Adelaide Tea Room, which has a balcony overlooking the Royal Pavilion Gardens.

WHERE TO STAY
VERY EXPENSIVE

✪ The Grand

Kings Rd., Brighton, East Sussex BN2 1FW. ☎ **01273/321188.** Fax 01273/202694. 192 rms, 8 suites. A/C TV TEL. £130 ($205.40) single; £165–£230 ($260.70–$363.40) double; from £460 ($726.80) suite. Rates include English breakfast. AE, DC, MC, V. Parking £10 ($15.80). Bus 1, 2, or 3.

This is the premier hotel of Brighton. The original Grand was constructed in 1864, and it entertained some of the most eminent Victorians and Edwardians. This landmark was massively damaged in a 1984 terrorist attack on Margaret Thatcher and key figures in the British government. Several colleagues were killed, Mrs. Thatcher narrowly escaped, and entire sections of the hotel looked as if they had been hit by an air raid. That gave its present owners, De Vere Hotels, the challenge to create a new Grand, and frankly, the new one is better than the old. It's the most elegant Georgian re-creation in town.

You enter via a glassed-in conservatory and register in a grandiose public room, with soaring ceilings and elaborate moldings. The hotel has plushly comfortable furniture in traditional tastes with well-chosen accessories. The rooms, of a very high standard, are generally spacious with many amenities, including private baths, radios, hospitality trays, trouser presses, and hairdryers. The sea-view rooms have minibars. There are also units designed for "lady executives," as well as "romantic rooms" with double whirlpool baths. Some accommodations are equipped with additional facilities for the disabled. Subject to availability during certain slow seasons, anyone who stays 2 nights or more can choose a half-board arrangement costing £70 ($110.60) in a single and £84 to £129 ($132.70 to $203.80) in a double.

Dining/Entertainment: Both British and continental cuisine are served in the King's Restaurant, with superb ingredients handled by the kitchen staff. The restaurant serves set menus throughout the week for £24 ($37.90), followed by a Saturday-night dinner-dance with live music costing £28 ($44.25) per person. The Victoria Bar is an elegant rendezvous, and Midnight Blues is considered the most sophisticated club at the resort.

Services: 24–hour room service, laundry, babysitting.

Facilities: Hobden's Health Spa (complete with spa pool, steam room, sauna, solarium, and massage and exercise arena), hairdressing salon, beautician.

EXPENSIVE

Brighton Metropole

106 King's Rd., Brighton, East Sussex BN1 2FU. ☎ **01273/775432.** Fax 01273/207764. 312 rms, 16 suites. TV TEL. £125 ($197.50) single; £165 ($260.70) double; £370–£490 ($584.60–$774.20) suite. Weekend breaks (2-night minimum) £70 ($110.60) single; £108 ($170.65) double. Rates include English breakfast. AE, DC, MC, V. Parking £12 ($18.95). Bus 1, 2, or 3.

Originally built in 1889, with a small portion of its bedrooms housed in a post-war addition, the Brighton Metropole is the largest hotel in Brighton and one of the top three or four hotels at the resort. Centrally located on the seafront, it offers recently refurbished, conservatively comfortable bedrooms with private baths and showers, radios, in-house movies, hairdryers, trouser presses, and beverage-making facilities.

On the premises is a leisure club, including an indoor swimming pool, plus an array of dining and drinking facilities, among them the Arundel and Windsor restaurants, the Canon Pub, and the Metro Night Club.

Brighton Thistle Hotel

King's Rd., Brighton, East Sussex BN1 2GS. ☎ **01273/206700,** or 800/44-UTELL in the U.S. Fax 01273/820692. 199 rms, 5 suites. TV TEL. Mon–Thurs, £120 ($189.60) single; £140 ($221.20) double; £275 ($434.50) suite. Fri–Sun, £69 ($109) single; £98 ($154.85) double; £198 ($312.85) suite. AE, DC, MC, V. Free parking. Bus 1, 2, or 3.

This hotel is one of the finest accommodations in the south of England. Rising from the seafront, it has been stylishly and rather luxuriously designed for maximum comfort. Guests wander at leisure through an array of tastefully furnished public rooms.

Dining/Entertainment: Its restaurant, La Noblesse, is outstanding and merits a separate recommendation (see "Where to Dine," below). The Promenade restaurant, overlooking the sea, has an imaginative and well-planned menu. Nonresidents can enjoy meals in the restaurants Monday through Saturday from noon to 2pm and 7 to 11pm. There's also a coffee shop that remains open until 11pm and a bar.

Services: 24-hour room service, laundry, babysitting.

Facilities: The hotel is perhaps the best equipped in the town, certainly for the athletic, with a gym and an indoor swimming pool, plus a solarium and sauna.

MODERATE

🌑 Topps Hotel

17 Regency Sq., Brighton, East Sussex BN1 2FG. ☎ **01273/729334.** Fax 01273/203679. 15 rms. MINIBAR TV TEL. £45 ($71.10) single; £79–£99 ($124.80–$156.40) double. Rates include English breakfast. AE, DC, MC, V. Parking £5 ($7.90). Closed Christmas. Bus 1, 2, 3, 5, or 6.

Flower boxes fill the windows of this cream-colored town house, whose owners, Paul and Pauline Collins, have devoted years to upgrading it. The hotel enjoys a diagonal view of the sea from its position beside the sloping lawn of Regency Square. Each of the differently shaped and individually furnished accommodations has a radio and a trouser press. A small restaurant in the basement serves dinners to guests who reserve by giving the room number.

INEXPENSIVE

Old Ship Hotel

King's Rd., Brighton, East Sussex BN1 1NR. ☎ **01273/329001.** Fax 01273/820718. 146 rms, 6 suites. TV TEL. £80–£90 ($126.40–$142.20) single; £105–£115 ($165.90–$181.70) double; from £99 ($156.40) suite for two. Rates include English breakfast. Weekend breaks (2-night minimum, including dinner and free parking) £35 ($55.30) single; £49.50 ($78.20) double. AE, DC, MC, V. Parking £12 ($18.95). Bus 1, 2, or 3.

Centrally situated on the seafront, the Old Ship boasts a paneled interior, comfortable sea-view lounges, an oak-paneled bar, and a spacious sea-facing restaurant, the Great Escape, that, naturally, specializes in seafood. A well-organized kitchen serves nicely prepared meals with selections from an impressive wine list. In 1651 the owner of an inn on this site saved the life of King Charles II by spiriting him away in his ship. Laundry, babysitting, and 24-hour room service are available.

Paskins Hotel

19 Charlotte St., Brighton, East Sussex BN2 1AG. ☎ **01273/601203.** Fax 01273/621973. 20 rms, 16 with bath. TV TEL. £20 ($31.60) single without bath, £25 ($39.50) single with bath; £35 ($55.30) double without bath, £40–£55 ($63.20–$86.90) double with bath. Rates include English breakfast. Children 10 and under sharing with two adults charged £10 ($15.80). AE, DC, MC, V. Free parking. Bus 7 or 52.

This well-run small hotel owned by Michael and Sue Paskins is only a short walk from the Palace Pier and Royal Pavilion. The rates depend on the plumbing and furnishings; the most expensive units are fitted with four-poster beds. The hotel is licensed and provides bar food most evenings; it's also surrounded by lots of restaurants.

🌑 Regency Hotel

28 Regency Sq., Brighton, East Sussex BN1 2FH. ☎ **01273/202690.** Fax 01273/220438. 12 rms, 10 with bath (tub or shower); 1 suite. TV TEL. £32 ($50.55) single without bath, £38 ($60.05) single with shower; £56 ($88.50) double without bath, £65 ($102.70) double with shower; £90 ($142.20) Regency suite with bath. Rates include English breakfast. AE, DC, MC, V. Parking £9 ($14.20). Bus 1, 2, 3, 5, or 6.

This typical Regency town house was built in 1820 with bow windows, a canopied balcony, and a porticoed entrance. The property was once the home of Jane, dowager duchess of Marlborough, and great-grandmother of Sir Winston Churchill. This landmark building features fine cornices, paneled doors, and a fireplace. It was skillfully converted into a family-managed hotel with a licensed bar and modern comforts. Each bedroom has a direct-dial phone, color TV, and hairdryer, and many rooms enjoy window views across the square and out to the sea. The Regency Suite has a half-tester bed (1840) and antique furniture, along with a huge bow window dressed with ceiling-to-floor swagged curtains and a balcony facing the sea and West Pier. Gail and Ambrose Simons welcome guests from all over the world.

⊙ Twenty-One Hotel

21 Charlotte St., Marine Parade, Brighton, East Sussex BN2 1AG. ☎ **01273/686450.** 6 rms. TV TEL. £46–£68 ($72.70–$107.45) double. Rates include English breakfast. AE, MC, V. Bus 7 or 52.

One of the most sophisticated—perhaps the most sophisticated—of the smaller hotels of Brighton, this early Victorian white house is a block from the sea. Janet and David Power rent attractive and well-furnished bedrooms with hot-beverage facilities, hairdryers, TVs, and direct-dial phones. A basement-level garden unit opens directly onto an ivy-clad courtyard.

Dinner is available, with a minimum notice of 24 hours. A set three-course meal is served for £15.95 ($25.20) Tuesday through Saturday. Possible main courses are breast of duck with cherry brandy and orange sauce or breast of chicken with a mustard-and-cream sauce. A good selection of wines is available.

IN NEARBY HOVE

Inexpensive

Courtlands Hotel

21–27 The Drive, Hove, East Sussex BN3 3JE. ☎ **01273/731055.** Fax 01273/328295. 54 rms, 1 suite. TV TEL. £38 ($60.05) single; £60 ($94.80) double or suite. Rates include English breakfast. AE, DC, MC, V. Free parking. Bus 52.

The Courtlands, a mile west of the center, is 400 yards from the sea, opening onto the wide thoroughfare known as "The Drive." It's a comfortable Victorian building, recently modernized. In the complex are five particularly agreeable rooms with minibars in a pair of outlying cottages. The bedrooms are spacious and harmonious. Since the one suite is the same price as a double, it's usually chosen first.

This traditional hotel has more than adequate facilities, including the Golden Dolphin lounge bar and a dining room opening onto gardens. A nice cuisine, both international and English, is assured. The hotel has a solarium and a heated swimming pool.

The Dudley

Lansdowns Place, Hove, Brighton, East Sussex BN3 1HQ. ☎ **01273/736266.** Fax 01273/729802. 60 rms. TV TEL. £60 ($94.80) single; £70 ($110.60) double. Breakfast £8.50 ($13.45) extra. AE, DC, MC, V. Free parking. Bus 52.

Near the seafront in Hove, the Dudley is just a few blocks from the resort's bronze statue of Queen Victoria. Going up marble steps, you register beneath crystal chandeliers and within view of 18th-century antiques and oil portraits of Edwardian-era debutantes. The large, high-ceilinged public rooms emphasize the deeply comfortable chairs, the thick cove moldings, and the chandeliers. The bedrooms offer TVs, coffee-making equipment, direct-dial phones, tall windows, and conservatively stylish furniture.

You must pass through a bar to reach the entrance to the dining room, which offers a good British cuisine. A three-course dinner costs £15.95 ($25.20). Laundry, babysitting, and 24-hour room service are available.

Sackville Hotel

189 Kingsway, Hove, Brighton, East Sussex BN3 4GU. ☎ **01273/736292.** Fax 01273/205759. 44 rms, 2 suites. TV TEL. Mon–Thurs, £55 ($86.90) single; £70 ($110.60) double. Fri–Sun, £37.50 ($59.25) single; £60 ($94.80) double (minimum 3 nights). Suite (daily) £85 ($134.30). Rates include English breakfast. AE, DC, MC, V. Free parking. Bus 52.

Its lime- and cream-colored neobaroque facade was built across the road from the beach in 1902. Today, in a comfortably updated form, the Sackville welcomes visitors with high-ceilinged bedrooms featuring big windows, sea views, and an assortment of Queen Anne furnishings. All units have terraces.

A large ground-floor dining room offers a warm, masculine formality, with views of the sea and good service and food. An adjacent bar, Winston's, is filled with photographs of Churchill in war and peace.

WHERE TO DINE
MODERATE
China Garden

88 Preston St. (in the center off Western Rd.). ☎ **01273/325124.** Reservations recommended. Main courses £10–£20 ($15.80–$31.60); fixed-price menu £15.50–£29.95 ($24.50–$47.30). AE, DC, MC, V. Daily noon–11:30pm. Closed Dec 25–26. CHINESE.

The Beijing and Canton menu at China Garden is large and satisfying. Dim sum (a popular luncheon choice) is offered only until 4pm. Try such dishes as chicken with lemon sauce, crispy sliced pork Szechuan style, or roast duck with pancakes, spring onions, cucumber, and duck sauce.

English's Oyster Bar and Seafood Restaurant

29–31 East St. ☎ **01273/327980.** Reservations recommended. Main courses £8–£25.95 ($12.65–$41); fixed-price menus £5.95–£9.95 ($9.40–$15.70). AE, DC, MC, V. Mon–Sat noon–10:15pm, Sun 12:30–9:30pm. SEAFOOD.

This popular seafood restaurant is in a trio of very old fisherman's cottages that were interconnected when the establishment was founded at the turn of the century. Owned and operated by the same family since the end of World War II, it sits behind a nostalgic brass-trimmed facade in the center of town near Brighton's bus station. For years, diners have enjoyed such selections as native oysters on the half shell, hot seafood en croûte with lobster sauce, fried Dover sole, and fresh, locally caught plaice. Throughout, the place seems infused with a sense of turn-of-the-century Britain caught up in the diverting ritual of heading south to Brighton to enjoy the sea. In summer guests can dine al fresco on the terrace.

La Marinade

77 St. George's Rd., Kemp Town. ☎ **01273/600992.** Reservations recommended. Main courses £9.95–£16.95 ($15.70–$26.80); fixed-price meal £10.75–£12.75 ($17–$20.15) at lunch, £15.50–£17.50 ($24.50–$27.65) at dinner. AE, MC, V. Tues–Fri noon–2pm and 7–10pm, Sat 7–10pm, Sun noon–2pm. FRENCH.

The cuisine here, inspired by the regions of Normandy and Brittany, shows a certain subtle preparation. You get a nice range of sensitively cooked dishes, where care has been taken to preserve natural flavors. The white-butter sauce, for example, on our recently sampled fish dish was just as good as that served in the Loire Valley. La Marinade is off King's Cliff along the seafront.

Langan's Bistro

1 Paston Place (near the waterfront off King's Cliff). ☎ **01273/606933.** Reservations required. Main courses £13.95–£14.95 ($22.05–$23.60); fixed-price three-course lunch

£14.50 ($22.90). AE, DC, MC, V. Tues–Fri 12:30–2:15pm and 7:30–10:15pm, Sat 7:30–10:15pm, Sun 12:30–2:15pm. Closed 2 weeks in Aug. FRENCH.

This is the latest—and most welcome—branch of this minichain of restaurants, which gained fame in London. The venture onto the Brighton scene has improved the restaurant lineup here considerably. A meal at Brighton's version of Langan's is not unlike a meal across the Channel in France.

The menu is wisely limited, but it's based on the freshest of ingredients available at the market. You might, for example, begin with a salad made from warm scallops, then follow with grilled turbot with langoustine coulis or roast lamb served with a tomato-and-garlic confit. Vegetarian dishes are also available. Desserts are often sumptuous, as reflected by a crème brûlée flavored with apple and cinnamon.

✪ La Noblesse

In the Brighton Thistle Hotel, King's Rd. ☎ 01273/206700. Reservations required. Fixed-price meal £16.50 ($26.05) at lunch, £23 ($36.35) at dinner, £38 ($60.05) menu gourmand. AE, DC, MC, V. Mon–Fri noon–2:30pm and 7–9:30pm, Sat 7–9:30pm. CLASSIC CONTINENTAL.

This is the flagship restaurant of this previously recommended hotel (see "Where to Stay," above). The chefs are in fine form, as reflected in their menu. The elegant surroundings in pink, blue, and brass form a proper backdrop for this "night out on the town" choice for Brighton. A continental staff is perfectly trained, serving such dishes as broiled fillet of beef topped with wild mushrooms and a tarragon-and-cream sauce; braised oxtail stuffed with fresh herbs and celeriac and served with potato purée, tomatoes, and basil; and pan-fried calf's liver with an orange-and-Dubonnet sauce. The sauces are generally excellent, cooked to bring out natural flavors. Vegetarian meals are also available, including baby ratatouille on a bed of fresh spinach pasta with deep-fried choux paste and vegetable quenelles in a chevril-and-basil sauce.

Old Ship Hotel Restaurant

In the Old Ship Hotel, King's Rd. ☎ 01273/329001. Reservations recommended. Main courses £8–£16 ($12.65–$25.30); fixed-price three-course meal £10.50 ($16.60) at lunch, £18 ($28.45) at dinner. AE, DC, MC, V. Daily 12:30–2pm and 7–9:30pm. Bus 1, 2, or 3. ENGLISH.

A long-enduring favorite, the Old Ship Restaurant in the center of town on the seafront enjoys an ideal location, with premises opening onto the waterfront. Whenever possible, locally caught fish appears on the menu. Try such dishes as pan-fried pork loin with saffron rice or grilled fillet of turbot with a lemon-and-butter sauce. Vegetables, which accompany the main dishes, are always fresh and cooked "new style." Sometimes local dishes such as turkey from Sussex appear on the menu, but with a French sauce. The wine list is excellent. Stop in the adjoining pub for a before- or after-dinner drink.

6 Arundel

58 miles SW of London, 21 miles W of Brighton

This small town in West Sussex nestles at the foot of one of England's most spectacular castles. The town was once an Arun River port, and its residents enjoyed the prosperity of considerable trade and commerce. However, today the harbor traffic has been replaced with buses filled with tourists.

ESSENTIALS
GETTING THERE

By Train Trains leave hourly during the day from London's Victoria Station (trip time: $1^1/_4$ hr.).

By Bus Most bus connections are through Littlehampton, opening onto the English Channel west of Brighton. From Littlehampton, you can leave the coastal road by taking bus no. 11, which runs between Littlehampton and Arundel hourly during the day.

By Car From London, follow the signs to Gatwick Airport and from there head south toward the coast along A29.

VISITOR INFORMATION

The **telephone area code** is 01903. The **Tourist Information Centre** is at 61 High St. (☎ **01903/882268**).

WHAT TO SEE & DO

✪ Arundel Castle

Mill Rd. ☎ **01903/883136.** Admission £5 ($7.90) adults, £3.50 ($5.55) children 5–15, free for children 4 and under. Apr–Oct, Sun–Fri noon–5pm. Closed Nov–Mar.

The ancestral home of the dukes of Norfolk is a much-restored mansion of considerable importance. Its legend is associated with some of the great families of England—the Fitzalans and the powerful Howards of Norfolk.

Arundel Castle has suffered destruction over the years, particularly during the Civil War, when Cromwell's troops stormed its walls, perhaps in retaliation for the 14th earl of Arundel's (Thomas Howard) sizable contribution to Charles I. In the early 18th century the castle virtually had to be rebuilt, and in late Victorian times it was remodeled and extensively restored again. Today it's filled with a nice collection of antiques, along with an assortment of paintings by old masters, such as van Dyck and Gainsborough.

Surrounding the castle, in the center off High Street, is a 1,100-acre park (scenic highlight: Swanbourne Lake).

Arundel Cathedral

London Rd. ☎ **01903/882297.** Admission free, but donations appreciated. June–Sept, daily 9am–6pm; Oct–May, daily 9am–dusk. From the town center, continue west from High Street.

A Roman Catholic cathedral, the Cathedral of Our Lady and St. Philip Howard stands at the highest point in town. It was constructed for the 15th duke of Norfolk by A. J. Hansom, who invented the Hansom taxi. However, it was not consecrated as a cathedral until 1965. The interior includes the shrine of St. Philip Howard, featuring Sussex wrought ironwork.

Arundel Toy and Military Museum

At "Doll's House," 23 High St. ☎ **01903/882908.** Admission £1.25 ($2) adults, £1 ($1.60) children and senior citizens, £4 ($6.30) family. Easter–Oct, daily 10:45am–5pm; Nov–Apr, Sat–Sun 10:45am–5pm.

In a Georgian cottage in the heart of historic Arundel, this museum displays a vast and intriguing family collection spanning many generations of old toys and games, small militaria, dolls, dollhouses, tin toys, musical toys, famous stuffed bears, Britain's animals and model soldiers, arks, boats, rocking horses, crested military models, an eggcup collection, and other curiosities. The museum is opposite Treasure House Antiques and Collectors Market.

Brass Rubbing Centre / Heritage of Arundel Museum

61 High St. ☎ **01903/882268.** Admission free. May to mid–Oct, Tues–Sat 10:30am–4:30 or 5pm. Closed mid-Oct–Apr.

Both attractions are located in the same stone-sided house as the town's tourist office. The **Brass Rubbing Centre** is in the cellar, where a collection of movable plaques and gravestones, each of historic and artistic interest, awaits the chalk and heavy paper of those who would like to trace their forms. You're charged according to the stone you choose to copy, usually about £2.50 ($3.95) per item.

On the street level, adjacent to the rooms housing the tourist information office, is the **Heritage of Arundel Museum.** It displays postcards, memorabilia, antique costumes, and historic documents relating to the history of Arundel and its famous castle.

WHERE TO STAY

INEXPENSIVE

Norfolk Arms

22 High St., Arundel, West Sussex BN18 9AD. ☎ **01903/882101.** Fax 01903/884275. 34 rms. TV TEL. £39.95 ($63.10) single; £79.90 ($126.25) double. AE, DC, MC, V. Rates include breakfast. Free parking.

A former coaching inn, the Norfolk Arms is on the main street just a short walk from the castle. The lounges and dining room are in the typically English country-inn style—not ostentatious but unquestionably comfortable. The hotel has been restored with many modern amenities blending with the old architecture. The bedrooms are handsomely maintained and furnished, each with personal touches.

In the restaurant you can order good English food, with set lunches costing £6.95 to £9.50 ($11 to $15). When available, fresh local produce is offered. You can also order set dinners for £15.95 to £19.50 ($25.20 to $30.80), which include many traditional English dishes.

IN NEARBY AMBERLEY

Expensive

❍ Amberley Castle Hotel

Amberley, near Arundel, West Sussex BN18 9ND. ☎ **01798/831992,** or 800/525-4800 in the U.S. Fax 01798/831998. 14 rms. TV TEL. £95–£225 ($150.10–$355.50) single, twin, or double. AE, DC, MC, V. Rates include English breakfast. Free parking. Take B2139 north of Arundel; the hotel is 1¹/₂ miles southwest of Amberley.

The best place for food and lodging is near the village of Amberley. Joy and Martin Cummings have operated this deluxe establishment since 1988, in a 14th-century castle with sections dating from the 12th century. From the battlements you'll have views of weald and downland. Elizabeth I herself once held the lease on this castle (1588–1603), and Cromwell's forces attacked it during the Civil War. Charles II visited the castle on two occasions. Each of the sumptuous rooms, all doubles, is named after a castle in Sussex, and each has a private Jacuzzi bath as well as a video library.

Dining/Entertainment: Nonresidents who reserve can attend the 12th-century Queen's Room Restaurant, the finest dining room in the area. Service is under a barrel-vaulted ceiling with lancet windows and the food is classic French and traditional English. Service is daily from 7 to 10pm, with meals costing from £25.50 ($40.30) on the table d'hôte, from £45 ($71.10) if ordered à la carte.

WHERE TO DINE
INEXPENSIVE
China Palace

67 High St. ☎ **01903/883702.** Reservations recommended on weekends. Main courses £5.80–£8 ($9.20–$12.65); fixed-price three-course dinner for two £31 ($49). AE, DC, MC, V. Daily noon–2:15pm and 6pm–midnight. CHINESE.

The most prominent Chinese restaurant in the region has an elaborately carved 17th-century ceiling imported by a former owner long ago from a palace in Italy. The interior decorations include the artfully draped sails from a Chinese junk. Its painted stone building is located across the road from the crenellated fortifications surrounding Arundel's castle. The Peking and Szechuan cuisine includes such classic dishes as Peking duck, crispy lamb, king prawns Kung Po, and lobster with fresh ginger and spring onions.

Winchester Bistro and Bar

25 Tarrant St. ☎ **01903/882222.** Reservations recommended. Main courses £3.95–£8.95 ($6.25–$14.15). MC, V. Apr–Sept, Mon–Sat 11am–11pm, Sun noon–3pm and 7–10:30pm; Oct–Mar, Mon–Sat 11am–3pm and 6–11pm, Sun noon–3pm and 7–10:30pm. BRITISH.

Located in the center of town near the castle, this establishment offers hearty fare at reasonable prices. The overall theme here is motor-racing, with photographs of historic racing cars that have competed at Goodwood such as a 1920s Mercedes. The pictures were donated by Lord March, John Cooper, and Sir John Brougham. You can often find several members of the racing set enjoying a cocktail or a bite to eat in the dining room. The menu changes weekly and may include prime beef and guinea fowl stew with herb dumplings, grilled lamb cutlets with rosemary, steak-and-kidney pie with spring vegetables, poached wild salmon with hollandaise, and Scottish beef with melted Stilton. The menu includes bistro fare—soups, salads, and pastas such as garlic, cheese, onion, and mushroom. The building that houses this establishment was originally constructed in the 18th century and converted from a chemist's shop (pharmacy) in the 1960s.

7 Chichester

69 miles SW of London, 31 miles W of Brighton

According to one newspaper, Chichester might have been just a market town if the Chichester Festival Theatre had not been established in its midst. One of the oldest Roman cities in England, Chichester draws a crowd from all over the world for its theater presentations.

Only a 5-minute walk from the Chichester Cathedral and the old Market Cross, the 1,400-seat theater, with its apron stage, stands on the edge of Oaklands Park. It opened in 1962 (first director: Lord Laurence Olivier), and its reputation has grown steadily, pumping new vigor and life into the former walled city, although originally many irate locals felt the city money could have been better spent on a swimming pool instead of a theater.

ESSENTIALS
GETTING THERE

By Train   Trains depart for Chichester from London's Victoria Station once every hour during the day (trip time: 1½ hr.). However, if you visit Chichester to attend the theater, plan to stay over—the last train back to London is at 9pm.

By Bus   Buses to Chichester leave from London's Victoria Coach Station four times per day.

By Car   From London's ring road, head south on A3, turning onto A286 for the final approach to Chichester.

VISITOR INFORMATION

The **telephone area code** is 01243. The **Tourist Information Centre** is at 29A South St. (☎ **01243/775888**).

WHAT TO SEE & DO
CHICHESTER FESTIVAL THEATRE & MINERVA STUDIO THEATRE

The ✪ **Chichester Festival Theatre** offers plays and musicals during the summer season (May to September) and in the winter and spring months orchestras, jazz, opera, theater, ballet, and a Christmas show for the entire family. Matinee performances begin at 2:30pm and evening performances at 7:30pm, except first nights, which begin at 7pm, and Friday and Saturday when they begin at 8pm.

The **Minerva** is a studio theater that offers one of the most adventurous programs during the year in the south and houses a theater restaurant (☎ **01243/782219**), society club room, and shop. Performances here begin at 2:45 and 7:45pm.

Theater reservations made over the telephone will be held for a maximum of 4 days (call 01243/781312). It's better to mail inquiries and checks to the Box Office, Chichester Festival Theatre, Oaklands Park, Chichester, West Sussex PO19 4AP. MasterCard, Visa, and American Express are accepted. Season ticket prices range from £9.50 to £22.50 ($15 to $35.55). Unreserved seats, sold only on the day of performance, cost £6.50 to £7.50 ($10.25 to $11.85).

EASY EXCURSIONS

FISHBOURNE   A worthwhile sight only 1½ miles from Chichester is the remains of the **Roman Palace,** Salthill Road, Salthill (☎ **01243/785859**), the largest Roman residence yet discovered in Britain. Built around A.D. 75 in villa style, it has many mosaic-floored rooms and even an underfloor heating system. The gardens have been restored to their original 1st-century plan. The story of the site is told both by an audiovisual program and by text in the museum. There is a cafeteria.

The museum charges £3.50 ($5.55) for adults, £1.60 ($2.50) for children, or £8.70 ($13.75) for a family ticket. From December to February it's open only on Sunday from 10am to 4pm; the rest of the year it's open daily: in March and November from 10am to 4pm, April to October from 10am to 5pm (to 6pm in August). The museum is situated to the north of A259, off Salthill Road, and signposted from Fishbourne. Parking is free. Buses stop regularly at the bottom of Salthill Road, and the museum is within a 5–minute walk of British Rail's station at Fishbourne.

OLD BOSHAM   Bosham, 4 miles west of Chichester on A259, is one of the most charming villages in West Sussex and is primarily a sailing resort, linked by good bus service to Chichester. It was the site where Christianity was first established on the Sussex coast. The Danish king Canute made it one of the seats of his North Sea empire, and it was the site of a manor (now gone) of the last of England's Saxon kings, Harold, who sailed from here to France on a journey that finally culminated in the invasion of England by William the Conqueror in 1066.

Bosham's little **church** was depicted in the Bayeux Tapestry. Its graveyard overlooks the boats, and the church is filled with ship models and relics, showing the villagers' link to the sea. A daughter of King Canute is buried inside. Near the harbor, it is reached by a narrow lane.

WEALD & DOWNLAND OPEN AIR MUSEUM   In the beautiful Sussex countryside at Singleton, 6 miles north of Chichester on A286 (the London road), historic buildings that have been saved from destruction are being reconstructed on a 40-acre downland site. The structures show the development of traditional building from medieval times to the 19th century in the weald and downland area of southeast England.

Exhibits include a Tudor market hall, a medieval farmstead and other houses dating from the 14th to the 17th century, a working water mill producing stone-ground flour, a blacksmith's forge, plumbers' and carpenters' workshops, a toll cottage, a 17th-century treadwheel, agricultural buildings including thatched barns and an 18th-century granary, a charcoal burner's camp, and a 19th-century village school.

The museum is open March to October, daily from 11am to 6pm; November to February, Wednesday, Saturday, and Sunday from 11am to 4pm. Admission is £4.20 ($6.65) for adults and £2.10 ($3.30) for children. A family ticket costs £11 ($17.40). For further information, call 01243/811348. Take bus no 260 from Chichester.

WHERE TO STAY
MODERATE

The Dolphin & Anchor
West St., Chichester, West Sussex PO19 1QE. ☎ **01243/785121**, or 800/225-5843 in the U.S. and Canada. Fax 01243/533408. 49 rms. TV TEL. £60 ($94.80) single; £85 ($134.30) double. Breakfast £6.25–£8.75 ($9.90–$13.85) extra. AE, DC, MC, V. Free parking.

Two old inns joined together, right at the historic 15th-century Market Cross and opposite the Chichester Cathedral, the Dolphin & Anchor is in the center off South Street, a 10-minute walk from the Festival Theatre. The setting blends 19th-century architectural features, including an old coaching entrance, with 20th-century comforts.

There are lounges, bars, the Whig and Tory Restaurant, and the Roussillon Bar, which serves light meals and grills until 8pm.

INEXPENSIVE

Ship Hotel
North St., Chichester, West Sussex PO19 1NH. ☎ **01243/778000.** Fax 01243/788000. 37 rms. TV TEL. £46 ($72.70) single; £67 ($105.85) double or twin. Rates include English breakfast. AE, DC, MC, V. Free parking.

One of the classic Georgian buildings of the city, the Ship is only a few minutes' walk from the cathedral, the Chichester Festival Theatre, and many fine antiques shops. It was built as a private house in 1790 for Adm. Sir George Murray (one of Nelson's commanders) and still retains an air of elegance and comfort. A grand Adam staircase leads from the main entrance to the bedrooms, which are all named after historic ships. Hornblower's Lounge, relatively formal with its own fireplace and rows of books, is an elegant place for a drink. Murray's Restaurant offers good value for the money and features a special four-course dinner menu every evening for £15.50 ($24.50).

PLACES TO STAY NEARBY
Moderate
✪ Millstream Hotel
Bosham Lane, Bosham, Chichester, West Sussex PO18 8HL. ☎ **01243/573234.** Fax 01243/573459. 29 rms. TV TEL. £59 ($93.20) single; £101 ($159.60) double. Rates include English breakfast. AE, DC, MC, V. Free parking. Take the road to the village of Bosham and its harbor, off A27. Bus: Bosham bus from Chichester.

The Millstream was originally built in the 1700s to provide food and accommodation for the people and horses who traveled through Sussex from other parts of England. Located 5 miles south of Chichester, the hotel is in the hamlet of Bosham, which is frequently visited because of the legendary beauty of its harbor. Behind a facade of weathered yellow bricks, the hotel features blazing fireplaces, a sense of history, and a recently redecorated and upgraded collection of bedrooms, each with floral-patterned wallpaper and conservative furniture. On the premises is a cocktail bar and an adjacent restaurant, where you can order such dishes as moules marinières (mussels) and roast Sussex lamb with fresh herbs. Dinner begins at £17.25 ($27.25); lunch, at £12.75 ($20.15).

✪ The Spread Eagle Hotel
South St., Midhurst, West Sussex GU29 9NH. ☎ **01730/816911.** Fax 01730/815668. 41 rms, 1 suite. TV TEL. £69 ($109) single; £79–£110 ($124.80–$173.80) double; £155 ($244.90) suite. Rates include continental breakfast. AE, DC, MC, V. Free parking. Midhurst bus from Chichester.

The 1430 inn and the market town of Midhurst are so steeped in history that the room you sleep in and the pavement you walk on have a thousand tales to tell. The rooms have beams, small mullioned windows, and unexpected corners, and five of them are equipped with four-poster beds.

Dinner is served in the dining hall, lit by candles that flicker on the gleaming tables. In the winter, log fires blaze. Meals cost £25 ($39.50) and up. The lounge with its timbered ceiling is where Elizabeth I and her court might have sat to watch festivities in the Market Square outside. The eagle in the lounge is the actual one from the back of Hermann Göring's chair in the Reichstag. It was acquired for its apt illustration of the hotel's name.

WHERE TO DINE
MODERATE
Commeça
67 Broyle Rd. ☎ **01243/788724.** Reservations required. Main courses £9.60–£12.30 ($15.15–$19.45). MC, V. Tues–Fri 12:15–2pm and 6–10pm, Sat 6–10pm, Sun 12:15–2pm. FRENCH.

This is the best French restaurant in town—in fact, the best restaurant, period. The decor is unpretentious, with a certain French Provincial quality. The chef is French, as a look at the menu offerings will reveal. Try feuilleté of salmon with chives, sole Commeça, perhaps fillet of beef with a Dijon mustard sauce. Good-quality ingredients are used. You'll find Commeça just a 5-minute walk from the center.

IN NEARBY CHILGROVE

Moderate

White Horse

1 High St., Chilgrove. ☎ **01243/535219.** Reservations required. Main courses £11.50–£17.50 ($18.15–$27.65); fixed-price lunch £17.50 ($27.65) for three courses, £23 ($36.35) for four courses. AE, MC, V. Tues–Sat noon–3pm and 6–10pm. Closed Feb, the last week in Oct, and Dec 25–26. Head 6¹/₂ miles north of Chichester on B2141 to Petersfield. ENGLISH/ FRENCH.

The wine cellar at this informally elegant country restaurant is one of the most comprehensive in Britain. This is partly because of the careful attention the owners pay to the details of their 18th-century inn, whose patina has been burnished every day since it was first built in 1765. The trio of dining rooms features old beams and lots of hardwood; close attention has been given to the gleaming silver table settings. Menu choices include roast breast of pheasant on a bed of celeriac purée, cold lobster, and roast lamb in a reduced sauce.

Hampshire & Dorset 11

This countryside is reminiscent of scenes from Burke's *Landed Gentry,* from fireplaces where stacks of logs burn to wicker baskets of apples freshly brought in from the orchard. Old village houses, now hotels, have a charming quality. Beyond the pear trees, on the crest of a hill, you'll find the ruins of a Roman camp. A village pub, with two rows of kegs filled with varieties of cider, is where the hunt gathers.

You're in Hampshire and Dorset, two shires jealously guarded by the English, both of which protect their special rural treasures. Everybody knows of Southampton and Bournemouth, but less known is the hilly countryside farther inland. You can travel through endless lanes and discover tiny villages and thatched cottages untouched by the industrial invasion.

The area is rich in legend and in literary and historical associations. Here Jane Austen and Thomas Hardy wrote and set their novels. Here, too, King Arthur held court at the Round Table. And from here sailed such famous ships as the *Mayflower,* Lord Nelson's *Victory,* the D-day invasion flotilla, and the *QE2.*

HAMPSHIRE This is the country Jane Austen wrote of—firmly middle class, largely agricultural, its inhabitants doggedly convinced that Hampshire is the greatest place on earth. Austen wrote six novels, including *Pride and Prejudice* and *Sense and Sensibility,* that earned her a permanent place among the great 19th-century writers. Her books provide an insight into the manners and mores of the English who soon established a powerful empire. Although the details of the life she described have now largely faded, the general mood and spirit of the Hampshire she depicted remains.

Hampshire encompasses the South Downs, the Isle of Wight (Victoria's favorite retreat), and the naval city of Portsmouth. The more than 90,000 acres of the New Forest were preserved by William the Conqueror as a private hunting ground. William lost two of his sons in the New Forest—one killed by an animal, the other by an arrow. Today it's a vast woodland and heath, ideal for walking and exploring.

What's Special About Hampshire & Dorset

Great Towns/Villages
- Winchester, the ancient capital of England, with a cathedral built by William the Conqueror.
- Portsmouth, the premier port of the south (the first dock was built in 1194); home to HMS *Victory*, Nelson's flagship.
- Lyme Regis, with its famed Cobb, a favorite of Jane Austen and a setting for *The French Lieutenant's Woman.*

Literary Shrines
- Chawton Cottage, where novelist Jane Austen lived.
- Thomas Hardy's Cottage at Higher Bockhampton.

Buildings
- Beaulieu Abbey, Lord Montagu's estate west of Southampton, a sumptuous private home from 1538 surrounded by gardens.
- Osborne House, Queen Victoria's most cherished residence, where she died on January 22, 1901.
- Broadlands, an elegant Palladian house on the River Test, former home of the late Lord Mountbatten.
- Winchester Cathedral, dating from 1079, the longest medieval cathedral in Britain.

Beaches
- Bournemouth, the premier seaside resort of Dorset, set among pines with sandy beaches and fine coastal views.
- Chesil Beach, a 20-mile-long wall-like bank of shingle running from Abbotsbury to the Isle of Portland— great for beachcombing.

Natural Spectacles
- The New Forest, 145 square miles of heath and woodland, once the hunting ground of Norman kings.

Although Hampshire is filled with many places of interest, for our purposes we've concentrated on two major areas: Southampton for convenience of transportation and accommodations and Winchester for history.

DORSET   This is Thomas Hardy country. Some of the towns and villages in Dorset, although altered considerably, are still recognizable from his descriptions. "The last of the great Victorians," as he was called, died in 1928 at age 88. His tomb is in a position of honor in Westminster Abbey.

One of England's smallest shires, Dorset encompasses the old seaport of Poole in the east and Lyme Regis in the west (known to Jane Austen). Dorset is a southwestern county and borders the English Channel. It's known for its cows, and Dorset butter is served at many an afternoon tea. This is mainly a land of farms and pastures, with plenty of sandy heaths and chalky downs.

The most prominent tourist center of Dorset is the Victorian seaside resort of Bournemouth. If you don't anchor there, you might also try a number of Dorset's other seaports, villages, and country towns; we mostly stick to the areas along the impressive coastline. Dorset, as the vacation-wise English might tell you, is a budget traveler's friend.

A DRIVING TOUR

Day 1 Arrive in Portsmouth for a full day's sightseeing agenda, including visits to the Mary Rose, the HMS Victory, the Royal Naval Museum, and Charles Dickens's Birthplace museum. If time remains, visit the D-Day Museum. Stay overnight in Portsmouth or adjoining Southsea.

Day 2 Take A27 west for a morning's visit to Southampton and have lunch there. A short visit will do, as there isn't too much of interest to tourists there. Eight miles northwest of Southampton in Romsey (on A32), visit Broadlands in the afternoon, the home of the late Earl Mountbatten who was assassinated in 1979. After a visit, continue north for the night to Winchester.

Day 3 Devote the day to exploring the New Forest, encompassing some 92,000 acres. Cut southwest, passing through Romsey again before heading for such centers as Lyndhurst or Brockenhurst (either one of which you could investigate for an overnight stopover). Visit Beaulieu Abbey and Buckler's Hard. You might also consider an overnight stay in Buckler's Hard at Master Builders House Hotel. The well-heeled traveler can journey west to New Milton, which lies to the east of Bournemouth, to spend the night at the Chewton Glen Hotel, which offers the finest food and accommodations in the area.

Day 4 From the port of Lymington, west of Beaulieu and south of Brockenhurst, journey to the Isle of Wight for an overnight stay, arriving in time for lunch and an afternoon visit to Osborne House, former vacation retreat of Queen Victoria.

☕ **TAKE A BREAK** Winterbourne, via Bonchurch Shute, Isle of Wight PO38 1PU (☎ **01983/852535**), is a hotel surrounded by gardens opening onto views of the sea. It also has a restaurant serving good food, with meals beginning at £15.50 ($24.50). The novelist Charles Dickens lived here in 1849, pronouncing it "the prettiest place I ever saw in my life, at home or abroad." Obviously an overstatement, but this place is a winner, nonetheless.

Day 5 After a morning drive around the Isle of Wight, return to the mainland and continue west along A337 to Bournemouth, the major resort of the south, for the night.

Day 6 After leaving Bournemouth, continue driving along the coast for an exploration of Dorset, passing through Wareham, Wool, and finally Dorchester for an overnight stop.

Day 7 In the morning go west along A35, passing Bridport until you reach Lyme Regis where you can spend the night. This was the setting for the film *The French Lieutenant's Woman.*

1 Portsmouth & Southsea

75 miles SW of London, 19 miles SE of Southampton

Virginia, New Hampshire, even Ohio, may have a Portsmouth, but the forerunner of them all is the old port and naval base on the Hampshire coast. German bombers in World War II leveled the city, hitting about nine-tenths of its buildings. But the seaport was rebuilt admirably.

Its maritime associations are known around the world. From Sally Port, the most interesting district in the Old Town, countless naval heroes have embarked to fight England's battles. That was certainly true on June 6, 1944, when Allied troops set sail to invade occupied France.

Southsea, adjoining Portsmouth, is a popular seaside resort with fine sands, gardens, bright lights, and a host of vacation attractions. Many historic monuments can be seen along the stretches of open space, where you can walk on the Clarence Esplanade and look out on the Solent and view the busy shipping activities of Portsmouth harbor.

ESSENTIALS
GETTING THERE

By Train Trains from London's Waterloo Station stop at Portsmouth and Southsea Station frequently throughout the day (trip time: 2 hr.).

By Bus National Express coaches operating out of London's Victoria Coach Station make the run to Portsmouth and Southsea every 2 hours during the day (trip time: 2 hr., 20 min.).

By Car From London's ring road, drive south on A3.

VISITOR INFORMATION

The **telephone area code** is 01705. The **Tourist Information Centre** is at The Hard in Portsmouth (☎ **01705/826722**).

WHAT TO SEE & DO

You might want to begin your tour on the Southsea front, where you can see a number of **naval monuments.** These include the big anchor from Nelson's ship *Victory,* plus a commemoration of the officers and men of HMS *Shannon* for heroism in the Indian Mutiny. An obelisk with a naval crown honors the memory of the crew of HMS *Chesapeake,* and a massive column, the Royal Naval Memorial, honors those lost at sea in the two world wars. A shaft is also dedicated to men killed in the Crimean War. There are also commemorations of those who fell victim to yellow fever in Queen Victoria's service in Sierra Leone and Jamaica.

The **Southsea Common,** between the coast and houses of the area, known in the 13th century as Froddington Heath and used for army bivouacs, is a picnic and play area today. Walks can be taken along Ladies' Mile if you want to be away from the common's tennis courts, skateboard and roller-skating rinks, and other activities.

✪ The *Mary Rose* Ship Hall and Exhibition

College Rd., Portsmouth Naval Base. ☎ **01705/750521.** Admission £4.95 ($7.80) adults, £4.45 ($7.05) senior citizens, £2.95 ($4.65) children and students. Daily 10am–5:30pm. Closed Dec 25. Use the entrance to the Portsmouth Naval Base through Victory Gate and follow the signs.

The *Mary Rose,* flagship of the fleet of King Henry VIII's wooden men-of-war, sank in the Solent in 1545 in full view of the king. In 1982 the heir to the throne, Charles, prince of Wales, watched the *Mary Rose* break the water's surface after more than four centuries on the ocean floor, not exactly shipshape and Bristol fashion but surprisingly well preserved nonetheless. Now the remains are on view, but the hull must be kept permanently wet.

The hull and the more than 20,000 items brought up by divers constitute one of the major archeological discoveries in England in many years. Among the artifacts on permanent exhibit are the almost-complete equipment of the ship's barber-surgeon, with cabin saws, knives, ointments, and plaster all ready for use; long bows and arrows, some still in shooting order; carpenters' tools; leather jackets; and some fine lace and silk. Close to the Ship Hall is the *Mary Rose* Exhibition, where

Hampshire & Dorset

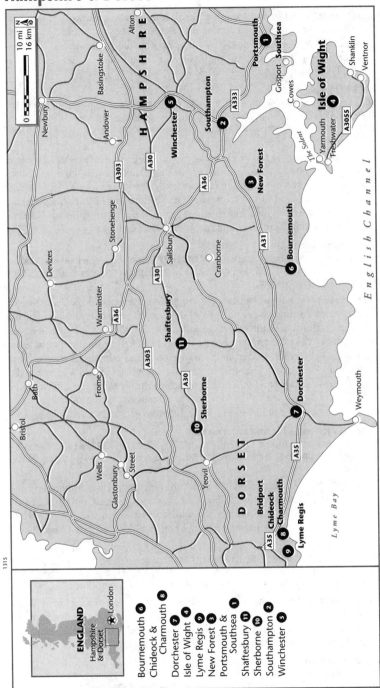

1315

ENGLAND
Hampshire & Dorset
★ London

Bournemouth **6**
Chideock &
  Charmouth **8**
Dorchester **7**
Isle of Wight **4**
Lyme Regis **9**
New Forest **3**
Portsmouth &
  Southsea **1**
Shaftesbury **11**
Sherborne **10**
Southampton **2**
Winchester **5**

artifacts recovered from the ship are stored. It features an audiovisual theater and a spectacular two-deck reconstruction of a segment of the ship, including the original guns. A display with sound effects recalls the sinking of the vessel.

For more information, write the *Mary Rose* Trust, College Road, H.M. Naval Base, Portsmouth, Hampshire PO1 3LX.

HMS *Victory*

No. 2 Dry Dock, in Portsmouth Naval Base. ☎ **01705/839766.** Admission £4.95 ($7.80) adults, £4.45 ($7.05) senior citizens, £2.95 ($4.65) children. Mar–Oct, daily 10am–5:30pm; Nov–Feb, daily 10am–5pm. Closed Dec 25. Use the entrance to the Portsmouth Naval Base through Victory Gate.

Of major interest is Lord Nelson's flagship, a 104-gun, first-rate ship. Although it first saw action in 1778, it earned its fame on October 21, 1805, in the Battle of Trafalgar when the English scored a victory over the combined Spanish and French fleets. It was in this battle that Lord Nelson lost his life. The flagship, after being taken to Gibraltar for repairs, returned to Portsmouth with Nelson's body on board (he was later buried at St. Paul's in London).

Royal Naval Museum

In the dockyard, Portsmouth Naval Base. ☎ **01705/733060.** Admission free with ticket for HMS *Victory;* otherwise, £2.65 ($4.20) adults, £2.10 ($3.30) senior citizens, £1.65 ($2.60) children. Daily 10am–5:30pm.

The museum is next to Nelson's flagship, HMS *Victory,* and the *Mary Rose* in the heart of Portsmouth's historic naval dockyard. The only museum in Britain devoted exclusively to the general history of the Royal Navy, it houses relics of Nelson and his associates, together with unique collections of ship models, naval ceramics, figureheads, medals, uniforms, weapons, and other naval memorabilia. Special displays feature "The Rise of the Royal Navy" and "HMS *Victory* and the Campaign of Trafalgar." Other exhibits include the Victorian navy, the navy in the 20th century, the modern navy, and representations of the sailor in popular art and culture. The museum complex includes a buffet and souvenir shop.

Charles Dickens's Birthplace Museum

393 Old Commercial Rd., off Mile End Rd. (M275). ☎ **01705/827261.** Admission £1 ($1.60) adults, 60p (95¢) students, free for children 12 and under. Apr–Sept, daily 11am–5pm. Closed Oct–Mar.

The small terrace house of 1804 in which the famous novelist was born on February 7, 1812, and lived for a short time, has been restored and furnished to illustrate the middle-class taste of the southwestern counties of the early 19th century. The museum is near the center of Portsmouth off Kingston Road.

Southsea Castle

Clarence Esplanade, Southsea. ☎ **01705/827261.** Admission £1.50 ($2.35) adults, £1.20 ($1.90) senior citizens, 90p ($1.40) students and children 13–18, free for children 12 and under. Mar–Oct, daily 10am–5pm; Nov–Feb, Sat–Sun 10am–4:30pm. Closed Dec 24–26.

A fortress built of stones from Beaulieu Abbey in 1545 as part of King Henry VIII's coastal defense plan, the castle is now a museum. Exhibits trace the development of Portsmouth as a military stronghold, as well as naval history and the archaeology of the area. The castle is in the center of Southsea near the D-Day Museum.

D-Day Museum

Clarence Esplanade, Southsea. ☎ **01705/827261.** Admission £3.60 ($5.70) adults, £2.20 ($3.50) children and students, £9.40 ($14.85) family of four. Daily 10am–5pm. Closed Dec 24–26.

Right next door to Southsea Castle, this museum—devoted to the Normandy landings—displays the Overlord Embroidery, which shows the complete story of Operation Overlord. The appliquéed embroidery, believed to be the largest of its kind (272 feet long and 3 feet high), was designed by Sandra Lawrence and took 20 women of the Royal School of Needlework 5 years to complete. There's a special audiovisual program with displays, including reconstructions of various stages of the mission with models and maps. You'll see a Sherman tank in working order, Jeeps, field guns, and even a DUKW (popularly called a Duck), that incredibly useful amphibious truck that operated on land and sea. The museum is on the seafront at Southsea.

Portchester Castle

Near Farnham. ☎ **01705/378291.** Admission £2 ($3.15) adults, £1.90 ($3) seniors, £1.30 ($2.05) children 5–16, free for children 4 and under. Apr–Sept, daily 10am–6pm; Oct–Mar, daily 10am–4pm. Lies on the south side of Portchester off A27 (between Portsmouth and Southampton).

On a spit of land on the northern side of Portsmouth Harbour are the remains of this castle, plus a Norman church. Built in the late 12th century by King Henry II, the castle is set inside the impressive walls of a 3rd-century Roman fort built as a defense against Saxon pirates, when this was the northwestern frontier of the declining Roman Empire. By the end of the 14th century, Richard II had modernized the castle and had made it a secure small palace. Among the ruins are the hall, kitchen, and great chamber of this palace. Portchester was popular with medieval kings, who stayed here when they visited Portsmouth. The last official use of the castle was as a prison for French seamen during the Napoleonic Wars.

Royal Navy Submarine Museum

Haslar Jetty Rd., Gosport. ☎ **01705/529217.** Admission £3.50 ($5.55) adults, £2.50 ($3.95) children and senior citizens. Apr–Oct, daily 10am–4:30pm; Nov–Mar, daily 10am–3:30pm. Closed Christmas week. Bus 9. Ferry: From The Hard in Portsmouth to Gosport.

Cross Portsmouth Harbour by one of the ferries that bustle back and forth all day to Gosport. Some departures go directly from the station pontoon to HMS *Alliance* for a visit to the submarine museum, which traces the history of underwater warfare and life from the earliest days to the present nuclear age and contains excellent models, dioramas, medals, and displays from all ages. There's also as much about submariners themselves as about the steel tubes in which they make their homes, and although the museum focuses on English boats, it includes much of international interest.

The principal exhibit is HMS *Alliance,* and after a brief audiovisual presentation, visitors are guided through the boat by ex-submariners. Midget submarines, not all of them English, including an X-craft, can be seen outside the museum. Also on display is HM *Torpedo Boat No. 1,* better known as *Holland I,* launched in 1901, which sank under tow to the breaker's yard in 1913 and was salvaged in 1982.

WHERE TO STAY
INEXPENSIVE

Hospitality Inn

South Parade, Southsea, Portsmouth, Hampshire PO4 ORN. ☎ **01705/731281.** Fax 01705/817572. 113 rms, 2 suites. TV TEL. £66 ($104.30) single; £72 ($113.75) double; £125 ($197.50) suite. Rates include English breakfast. AE, DC, MC, V. Free parking. Southsea bus.

The balconied Victorian facade of this hotel directly east of Southside Common rises above the boulevard running beside the sea. Restored by its owners, the hotel's interior decor, depending on the room, ranges from contemporary to full-curtained traditional. Each of the bedrooms has been renovated with built-in furniture and equipped with such extras as a trouser press and tea-making facilities. A restaurant serves dinner for £14.95 ($23.60) and up.

Portsmouth Marriott

North Harbour, Cosham, Portsmouth, Hampshire PO6 4SH. ☎ **01705/383151**, or 800/228-9290 in the U.S. and Canada. Fax 01705/388701. 168 rms, 2 suites. TV TEL. £65–£90 ($102.70–$142.20) single; £75–£90 ($118.50–$142.20) double; £145 ($229.10) suite. English breakfast £3.50–£10.25 ($5.55–$16.20) extra. AE, DC, MC, V. Free parking. Bus: Take the bus marked COSHAM from Portsmouth's center.

Located 2 miles southeast of Portsmouth's center, a short walk from the ferry-boat terminal for ships arriving from Le Havre and Cherbourg in France, this seven-story building towers above everything in its district. Originally built as a Holiday Inn in 1980, it was acquired by Marriott in 1992. Some of the public areas are sheltered by a steel-and-glass domelike structure known as the "Holidome," whose big windows create an effect resembling that of a greenhouse or conservatory. The bedrooms are clean, comfortable, and modern, with tiled bathrooms and such electronic amenities as video movies. There's a cocktail lounge and a restaurant that serves lunch and dinner.

In Nearby Wickham
Moderate

✪ The Old House Hotel

The Square, Wickham, Fareham, Hampshire PO17 5JG. ☎ **01329/833049**. Fax 01329/833672. 12 rms. TV TEL. £65 ($102.70) single; £75 ($118.50) double. Breakfast £6–£9 ($9.50–$14.20) extra. AE, DC, MC, V. Free parking. Head 9 miles from Portsmouth, at the junction of B2177 and A32, or 2 miles north of the M27 motorway linking Brighton through Portsmouth to Bournemouth. Bus 69 from Fareham.

A handsome early Georgian (1715) house, thought to have been the first of its architectural type in the village, the Old House is surrounded by low, medieval timber structures around the square. The paneled Georgian rooms on the ground and first floors of the hotel contrast with the beamed bedrooms on the upper floors, once the servants' quarters. All nine bedrooms have period furniture, many pieces original antiques; an additional three rooms, in an annex 50 yards from the main property in a building dating from the 16th century, enjoy all the facilities of the main hotel, including private baths.

The restaurant occupies what was once a timber-frame outbuilding with stables, adjacent to a garden overlooking the Meon River; it serves French provincial cuisine.

WHERE TO DINE
INEXPENSIVE

Bistro Montparnasse

103 Palmerston Rd., Southsea. ☎ **01705/816754**. Reservations required Sat. Main courses £10.80–£14.80 ($17.05–$23.40). AE, MC, V. Tues–Sat 7–10pm. Closed 2 weeks in Jan (dates vary). Follow the signs to the D-Day Museum, and at the museum turn left and go to the next intersection; the restaurant is on the right. Southsea bus. BRITISH/FRENCH.

Generally conceded to serve the best food in the area, this bistro offers background music to get you in the mood for a well-rounded selection of dishes served in a welcoming atmosphere. Fresh produce is delicately prepared. The cooking is familiar fare, and fresh fish—caught locally—is also served. Although the menu changes, you might try such dishes as confit of pork with Spätzle and a beer sauce, peppered fillet of beef with shallot-and-port jus, escalope of salmon baked with fennel and ginger, and a vegetarian dish such as spinach, pinenut, and olive tart with caramelized-onion sauce. For the finish, try the chocolate-amaretto trifle with macaroons or baked ricotta and raisin crêpes with apricot sauce.

2 Southampton

87 miles SW of London, 161 miles E of Plymouth

To many North Americans, England's number-one passenger port, home base for the *QE2,* is the gateway to Britain. Southampton is a city of wide boulevards, parks, and shopping centers. During World War II, some 31.5 million men set out from here (in World War I, more than twice that number).

Its supremacy as a port dates from Saxon times, when the Danish conqueror, Canute, was proclaimed king here in 1017. Southampton was especially important to the Normans and helped them keep in touch with their homeland. Its denizens were responsible for bringing in the bubonic plague, which wiped out a quarter of the English population in the mid-14th century. On the Western Esplanade is a memorial tower to the Pilgrims, who set out on their voyage to the New World from Southampton on August 15, 1620. Both the *Mayflower* and the *Speedwell* sailed from here but were forced by storm damages to put in at Plymouth, where the *Speedwell* was abandoned. The memorial is a tall column with an iron basket on top—the type used as a beacon before lighthouses.

If you're spending time in Southampton between ships, you may want to explore some of the major sights of Hampshire near the port—the New Forest, Winchester, the Isle of Wight, and Bournemouth in neighboring Dorset.

ESSENTIALS
GETTING THERE

By Plane There's a small airport outside Southampton, but it's used mainly for flights to the Channel Islands. For information, call 01703/629600.

By Train British Rail serves the south, with departures from London's Waterloo Station several times daily (trip time: 66 min.).

By Bus National Express operates hourly departures from London's Victoria Coach Station, heading for Southampton (trip time: 2¹/₂ hr.).

By Car Take M3 southwest from London.

VISITOR INFORMATION

The **telephone area code** is 01703. The **Tourist Information Centre** is at 9 Civic Centre Rd. (☎ **01703/221106**).

WHAT TO SEE & DO

In addition to the tours and museums listed below, **Ocean Village** and the **town quay** on Southampton's waterfront are bustling with activity and are filled with shops, restaurants, and entertainment possibilities.

TOURS

Southampton has a long and varied history, as witnessed by the Roman settlement at Bitterne, the Saxon port of Hamwic, and the Norman town with town walls, most of which still stand. City tourist guides offer a wide range of free guided walks and regular city bus tours. Free guided walks of the medieval town are offered throughout the year on Sunday and Monday at 10:30am and June to September twice daily at 10:30am and 2:30pm. Tours start at Bargate. For details of various boat or bus trips that might be offered at the time of your visit, check with the tourist office (see above).

MUSEUMS

Tudor House Museum

Bugle St., St. Michael's Sq. ☎ **01703/332513.** Admission free. Tues–Fri 10am–noon and 1–5pm, Sat 10am–noon and 1–4pm, Sun 2–5pm. This museum will be closed from the end of Sept. 1996 for about 2 years for renovations. Bus 2, 6, 8, or 13.

The museum is housed in a late medieval timber-framed house with a banqueting hall furnished in a 16th-century style. It features exhibitions of Georgian, Victorian, and Edwardian domestic and social life and also sponsors temporary shows. Its garden, based on 16th-century texts and illustrations, is unique in southern England and has 50 species of herbs and flowers.

Museum of Archaeology

God's House Tower, Winkle St. ☎ **01703/632493.** Admission £1.50 ($2.35) adults, 75p ($1.20) children and senior citizens. Tues–Fri 10am–noon and 1–5pm, Sat 10am–noon and 1–4pm, Sun 2–5pm. Bus 2, 6, 8, or 13.

Housed in part of the town's 15th-century defenses, the exhibitions here trace the history and portray the daily life of the Roman, Saxon, and medieval eras. The lives of the inhabitants are depicted in exhibitions.

Southampton Maritime Museum

The Wool House, Town Quay. ☎ **01703/632493.** Admission free. Tues–Fri 10am–1pm and 2–5pm, Sat 10am–1pm and 2–4pm, Sun 2–5pm. Bus 2, 6, 8, or 13.

This museum is housed in an impressive 14th-century stone warehouse with a magnificent timber ceiling. Its exhibits trace the history of Southampton, including a model of the docks as they looked at their peak in the 1930s. Also displayed are artifacts from some of the great ocean liners whose home port was Southampton.

WHERE TO STAY

Finding an accommodation right in Southampton isn't as important as it used to be. Very few ships now arrive, and the places to stay just outside the city are, in the main, superior to what you'll find in the city itself. For accommodations in the area, refer to the "New Forest" section, below. However, we'll provide some accommodation listings for those who, for transportation or other reasons, may want to stay in the city center.

INEXPENSIVE

Dolphin Hotel

35 High St., Southampton, Hampshire SO14 2HN. ☎ **01703/339955,** or 800/225-5843 in the U.S. and Canada. Fax 01703/333650. 71 rms, 2 suites. TV TEL. £50 ($79) single; £60

($94.80) double; £80 ($126.40) suite. AE, DC, MC, V. Breakfast £5.95–£8.50 ($9.40–$13.45) extra. Free parking. Bus 2, 6, or 8.

This bow-windowed Georgian coaching house on the main street, dating back to the 13th century, was Jane Austen's choice, and Thackeray's when he was writing *Pendennis*. Even Queen Victoria came in her horse-drawn carriage. It's in the center of the city, approached through an arched entrance over which rests a coat of arms of William IV and Queen Adelaide. The bedrooms vary widely in size, but are generally spacious and well furnished. The open staircase holds a rare collection of naval uniform prints.

English meals at the Thackery Restaurant are quite good, with a table d'hôte dinner beginning at £15.95 ($25.20). Drinks are served in the Nelson Bar. The hotel has health and fitness facilities.

Forte Post House
Herbert Walker Ave., Southampton, Hampshire SO15 1HJ. ☎ **01703/330777**, or 800/ 225-5843 in the U.S. and Canada. Fax 01703/332510. 128 rms. TV TEL. £56–£69.50 ($88.50–$109.80) single or double Sun–Thurs, £43–£57.50 ($67.95–$90.85) Fri–Sat. AE, DC, MC, V. Breakfast £5.50–£7.95 ($8.70–$12.55) extra. Free parking. Bus 2, 6, or 8.

This 10-floor high-rise across from Mayflower Park was built near the new docks to overlook the harbor, but is only 5 minutes away from the city center. You can unload your luggage under a sheltered drive and walk into the reception area. The rooms are handsome and spacious, with fine built-in pieces, private baths, and picture-window walls.

Among the facilities of the hotel are a heated, open-air swimming pool and a residents' lounge with color TV. The Trader Bar adjacent to the restaurant offers an intimate atmosphere.

Polygon Hotel
Cumberland Place, Southampton, Hampshire SO15 4WQ. ☎ **01703/330055**, or 800/ 225-5843 in the U.S. and Canada. Fax 01703/332435. 87 rms, 3 suites. TV TEL. £47 ($74.25) single; £55 ($86.90) double; £70 ($110.60) suite. AE, DC, MC, V. Breakfast £6.95–£8.50 ($11–$13.45) extra. Free parking. Bus 2, 6, or 8.

This is the oldest and most historic hotel in Southampton, bearing the name of the Polygon district in which it sits. Originally built during the 17th century, it was expanded first by the Victorians, and then by its owners just prior to World War II. The present hotel retains many of its Victorian details, despite many modernizations and refurbishments. Some of the bedrooms were refurbished in 1994. All accommodations feature conservatively traditional furniture, country house-style curtains, radios, and hot-beverage facilities. Many offer views over Watts Park and Southampton's Civic Centre. There's a plushly upholstered bar and a dignified restaurant, Chandlers, where full meals begin at £15 ($23.70) each.

Southampton Moat House
119 Highfield Lane, Portswood, Southampton, Hampshire SO17 1AQ. ☎ **01703/559555**. Fax 01703/583910. 66 rms. TV TEL. Mon–Thurs, £55 ($86.90) single; £65 ($102.70) double. Fri–Sun, £39.50 ($62.40) single; £44.50 ($70.30) double. Breakfast £5.95–£7.95 ($9.40– $12.55) extra. AE, DC, MC, V. Free parking. Bus 11 or 13.

In a residential area on the northern outskirts of the city, this modern hotel off Portswood Road, a member of Queens Moat Houses group, offers comfortable accommodations with private baths and efficient service. Its restaurant, Hamilton's, serves an à la carte menu with dinner costing about £14 ($22.10) and comple-mented by a comprehensive wine list.

WHERE TO DINE
MODERATE
Porter's

Town Quay Rd. ☎ **01703/221159.** Reservations recommended for the restaurant; not necessary for the Brasserie. Main courses £7–£25 ($11.05–$39.50); glass of wine from £2.50 ($3.95). AE, DC, MC, V. Mon–Sat 11am–3pm and 6:30–11:30pm (last order). Bus 2, 6, or 8. SEAFOOD.

Considered the best restaurant in town, Porter's was designed by Scottish-born architect John Geddes as a warehouse and boat yard. At the time, the sea came up to its foundations and boats could unload their cargoes directly into its cavernous interior. Today, although the exterior is rustic and weathered, its interior is stylishly decorated in shades of rose and turquoise, with French Regency accessories. The restaurant has a wine cellar with 600-year-old walls, once part of the medieval wall that ringed Southampton. Meals feature preparations of mussels, lobster, trout, plaice, and oysters, with a changing array of specialties that might include salmon with a leek, chive, and seafood sauce; mussel-and-bacon chowder with croûtons; grilled Dover sole; and such meat dishes as fillet of beef and Stilton with port sauce and sautéed Black Angus peppered steak.

In 1992 the restaurant added an informal wine bar and Brasserie, much favored by local businesspeople at lunch and by relatively informal diners in the evening. It features less formal versions of the food served in the nearby restaurant.

INEXPENSIVE
La Margherita

4–6 Commercial Rd. ☎ **01703/333390.** Main courses £4.90–£11.50 ($7.75–$18.15); pastas and pizzas £5.20–£6.20 ($8.20–$9.80). AE, MC, V. Mon–Sat noon–2pm and 6:30–11:15pm, Sun 6–11pm. Bus 7, 9, or 10. ITALIAN.

Popular with young people and families, this restaurant offers pizza and pasta, as well as veal, poultry, beef, and fish. It has one of the most extensive menus in town, beginning with a wide selection of appetizers, ranging from a medley of antipasti to Parma ham and melon. Look for the catch of the day, which might be shark steak prepared Sicilian style or red mullet. Trout Mafiosa is one of the most amusing selections. Several vegetarian dishes are offered, including pastas, pizzas, even vegetable burgers. An English sirloin is always available, and you can also order half a fresh chicken in a deviled sauce. The dessert specialty is Claire Francis coupe (raspberry sorbet and black currants, with fruits, cream, and liqueur). You can order wine by the glass and end your meal with a strong espresso.

AN EASY EXCURSION

Eight miles northwest of Southampton in Romsey on A31 stands ✪ **Broadlands** (☎ 01794/516878), the home of the late Earl Mountbatten of Burma, who was assassinated in 1979. Lord Mountbatten, who has been called "the last war hero," lent the house to his nephew, Prince Philip, and Princess Elizabeth as a honeymoon haven in 1947, and in 1981 Prince Charles and Lady Diana spent the first nights of their honeymoon here.

Broadlands is owned by Lord Romsey, Lord Mountbatten's eldest grandson, who has created a fine exhibition and audiovisual show that depicts the highlights of his grandfather's brilliant career as a sailor and statesman. The house, originally linked to Romsey Abbey, was purchased by Lord Palmerston in 1736 and was later transformed into an elegant Palladian mansion by Capability Brown and Henry Holland. Brown landscaped the parkland and grounds and made the river (the Test) the main object of pleasure. The house and riverside lawns are open July to October only, daily from 10am to 4pm. Admission is £5 ($7.90) for adults, £3.50 ($5.55) for children 12 to 16, and free for children 11 and under.

3 The New Forest

95 miles SW of London, 10 miles W of Southampton

Encompassing about 92,000 acres, the New Forest is a large tract created by William the Conqueror, who laid out the limits of this then-private hunting preserve. Successful poachers faced the executioner if they were caught, and those who hunted but missed had their hands severed.

Henry VIII loved to hunt deer in the New Forest, but he also saw an opportunity to build up the British naval fleet by supplying oak and other hard timbers to the boat yards at Buckler's Hard on the Beaulieu River. Today you can visit the old shipyards and also the museum with its fine models of men-of-war, pictures of the old yard, and dioramas showing the building of these ships, their construction, and their launching. It took 2,000 trees to build one man-of-war.

Nowadays, a motorway cuts through the area, and the once-thick forest has groves of oak trees separated by wide tracts of common land that's grazed by ponies and cows, hummocked with heather and gorse, and frequented by rabbits. But away from the main roads, where signs warn of wild ponies and deer, you'll find a private world of peace and quiet.

ESSENTIALS
GETTING THERE

By Train   Go to Southampton (see above), where rail connections can be made to a few centers in the New Forest, depending on where you're going. Where the train leaves off, bus connections are possible to all the towns and many villages.

By Bus   Southampton and Lymington have the best bus connections to New Forest villages.

By Car   Head west from Southampton on A35.

VISITOR INFORMATION

The **telephone area code** depends on the town or village (see individual write-ups). The information office is at the **New Forest Visitor Centre,** Main Car Park, Lyndhurst (☎ 01703/282269).

WHAT TO SEE & DO

✪ Beaulieu Abbey–Palace House

Beaulieu, on B3056 in the New Forest. ☎ **0590/612345.** Admission £7.75 ($12.25) adults, £6.25 ($9.90) senior citizens and students, £5.25 ($8.30) children 4–16, free for children 3 and under; £24 ($37.90) family (two adults and up to four children). Easter–Sept, daily 10am–6pm; Oct–Easter, daily 10am–5pm. Closed Dec 25. Buses run from the Lymington bus station Mon–Sat; Sun you'll need a taxi or private car.

The abbey and house, as well as the National Motor Museum, are on the property of Lord Montagu of Beaulieu (pronounced *Bew*-ley), at Beaulieu, 5 miles southeast of Lyndhurst and 14 miles west of Southampton. A Cistercian abbey was founded on this spot in 1204 and the ruins can be explored today. The Palace

House was the great gate house of the abbey before it was converted into a private residence in 1538 and is surrounded by gardens.

On the grounds, the **National Motor Museum,** one of the best and most comprehensive motor museums in the world, with more than 250 vehicles, is open to the public. It traces the story of motoring from 1895 to the present. Famous autos include four land-speed record holders, among them Donald Campbell's *Bluebird.* The collection was built around Lord Montagu's family collection of vintage cars. A special feature is called "Wheels." In a darkened environment, visitors can travel in specially designed "pods," each of which carries up to two adults and one child along a silent electric track. They move at a predetermined but variable speed, and each pod is capable of rotating almost 360°. This provides a means by which the visitor is introduced to a variety of displays spanning 100 years of motor development. Sound-and-visual effects are integrated into individual displays. In one sequence, visitors experience the thrill of being involved in a Grand Prix race. For further information, contact the visitor reception manager, John Montagu Building (☎ **01590/612345**).

Maritime Museum

Buckler's Hard. ☎ **01590/616203.** Admission £2.75 ($4.35) adults, £2.20 ($3.50) students and senior citizens, £1.85 ($2.90) children; £7.50 ($11.85) family. Mar–May, daily 10am–6pm; June–Sept, daily 10am–9pm; Oct–Feb, daily 10am–4:30pm.

Buckler's Hard, a historic 18th-century village 2¹/₂ miles from Beaulieu on the banks of the River Beaulieu, is where ships for Nelson's fleet were built, including the admiral's favorite, *Agamemnon,* as well as *Eurylus* and *Swiftsure.* The Maritime Museum reflects the shipbuilding history of the village. Its displays include shipbuilding at Buckler's Hard; Henry Adams, master shipbuilder; Nelson's favorite ship; Buckler's Hard and Trafalgar; and models of Sir Francis Chichester's yachts and items of his equipment. The cottage exhibits are a recreation of 18th-century life in Buckler's Hard. Here you can stroll through the New Inn of 1793 and a shipwright's cottage of the same period or look in on the family of a poor laborer at home. All these displays include village residents and visitors of the late 18th century. The walk back to Beaulieu, 2¹/₂ miles along the riverbank, is well marked through the woodlands. During the summer, you can take a half-hour cruise on the River Beaulieu in the present *Swiftsure,* an all-weather catamaran cruiser.

WHERE TO STAY
In New Milton
Very Expensive

✪ Chewton Glen Hotel

Christchurch Rd., New Milton, Hampshire BH25 6QS. ☎ **01425/275341.** Fax 01425/272310. 37 rms, 20 suites. TV TEL. £185–£350 ($292.30–$553) double; from £285 ($450.30) suite. Breakfast £9.50–£14.50 ($15–$22.90) extra. AE, DC, MC, V. Free parking. After leaving the village of Walkford, follow signs off A35 (New Milton–Christchurch road), through parkland.

A gracious country house on the fringe of the New Forest, Chewton Glen is within easy reach of Southampton and Bournemouth. In the old house, the magnificent staircase leads to well-furnished chambers, each a double, opening onto views over the spacious grounds. In the new wing, you find yourself on the ground level with French doors opening onto your own private patio. Here the decor is in muted colors, the rooms named for the heroes of novels written by Captain Marryat (author of *The Children of the New Forest*). Everywhere log fires burn and fresh flowers add fragrance. The garden sweeps down to a stream and then to rhododendron woods.

Dining/Entertainment: In the dining room, the standards of cooking and presentation are high. Particular emphasis is placed on fresh ingredients. The chef favors a modern cuisine, complemented by excellent sauces and velvety smooth desserts. The fixed-price meal of three courses is changed daily. A fixed-price lunch is £23.50 ($37.15), going up to £25 ($39.50) on Sunday. A fixed-price dinner costs £40 ($63.20).

Services: 24-hour room service, valet and laundry service.

Facilities: Open-air heated swimming pool and an indoor swimming pool, two indoor tennis courts, nine-hole golf course, health club, sauna, Jacuzzi.

IN LYNDHURST
Moderate

Crown Hotel
9 High St., Lyndhurst, Hampshire SO45 7NF. ☎ **01703/282922,** or 800/528-1234 in the U.S. and Canada. Fax 01703/282751. 39 rms, 1 suite. MINIBAR TV TEL. £59 ($93.20) single; £89 ($140.60) double; £121 ($191.20) suite. Rates include English breakfast. AE, DC, MC, V. Free parking. Exit the M27 motorway at Junction 1 and drive 3 miles due south. Bus 56 or 56A.

Although the present building is only 100 years old, there has been a hostelry here on the main street of the New Forest village of Lyndhurst, opposite the church with its tall spire, for centuries. The rooms are comfortable and traditionally furnished.

Much local produce is used in the dining room, including venison. The food is not only good but reasonable in price. A fixed-price lunch or dinner begins at £16 ($25.30), and there are also à la carte selections. Sunday lunch is well patron- · ized by the local people. The hotel also does substantial bar meals.

Inexpensive

Ⓢ Lyndhurst Park Hotel
68 High St., Lyndhurst, Hampshire SO43 7NL. ☎ **01703/283923.** Fax 01703/283019. 59 rms. TV TEL. £49.95 ($78.90) single; £79.90 ($126.25) double.Rates include English breakfast. AE, DC, MC, V. Free parking. Bus 56 or 56A.

A large Georgian country house set on 5 acres of beautiful gardens, this hotel boasts an outdoor heated swimming pool and an all-weather tennis court. The bedrooms all have radio alarms, tea and coffee makers, hairdryers, and trouser presses. There is a bar, plus an oak-paneled restaurant, where a wide selection of dishes is offered at lunch and dinner. A four-course dinner with coffee will cost £16.50 to £19.50 ($26.05 to $30.80).

IN BROCKENHURST
Moderate

Balmer Lawn Hotel
Lyndhurst Rd., Brockenhurst, Hampshire SO42 7ZB. ☎ **01590/623116.** Fax 01590/ 623864. 55 rms. TV TEL. £55 ($86.90) single; £90 ($142.20) double. Rates include English breakfast. AE, DC, MC, V. Free parking. Take A337 (Lyndhurst–Lymington road) about half a mile outside Brockenhurst.

This hotel was originally built as a modest private home during the 17th century and was later enlarged into an imposing hunting lodge. During World War II, it functioned as a military hospital, staffed with nurses and white-coated doctors. (Within the past decade, significant numbers of overnight guests here have spotted the ghost of one of these doctors with his stethoscope still roaming the hotel's first floor.) The hotel has a pleasant and humorous staff (who refer to the ghost as "Dr. Eric"), a woodland location about 10 minutes' walk from Brockenhurst's center, a bar, and well-prepared meals. These include informal bar snacks at lunchtime and more formal restaurant meals at night. Lunches begin at £8.50 ($13.45); dinners, at £16.95 ($26.80).

Carey's Manor

Lyndhurst Rd., Brockenhurst, Hampshire SO42 7RH. ☎ **01590/623551.** Fax 01590/622799. 78 rms, 1 suite. TV TEL. £69 ($109) single; £109–£129 ($172.20–$203.80) double; £159 ($251.20) suite. Rates include English breakfast. AE, DC, MC, V. Free parking. From the center, head toward Lyndhurst on A337.

This manor house dates back to Charles II, who used to come here when Carey's was a hunting lodge. Greatly expanded in 1888, the building became a country hotel in the 1930s. Much improved in recent years, it's better than ever now. The old house is still filled with character, as exemplified by its mellow, timeworn paneling and carved oak staircase. Each bedroom, whether in the restored main building or in the garden wing, has a private bath with tub or shower, radio, hairdryer, and trouser press. The hotel also serves good food—a modern British and French cuisine. A table d'hôte luncheon costs £11.95 ($18.90) and a table d'hôte dinner goes for £19.95 ($31.50). Carey's is ideal as a resort, with an indoor swimming pool, gym, solarium, and sauna, all on 5 acres of landscaped grounds. It's about a 90-minute drive from London.

New Park Manor

Lyndhurst Rd., Brockenhurst, Hampshire SO42 7QH. ☎ **01590/623467.** Fax 01590/622268. 21 rms, 3 suites. TV TEL. £85 ($134.30) single; £150 ($237) double; £170 ($268.60) suite for two. Rates include half board. AE, MC, V. Free parking. Head 2 miles north off A337 (Lyndhurst–Brockenhurst road) past a 500-year-old thatched lodge.

This former royal hunting lodge, dating from the days of William the Conqueror and a favorite of Charles II, is the only hotel in the New Forest itself. Though it's now a modern country hotel, the original rooms have been preserved, including such features as beams and open log fires. The owners have installed central heating throughout. Each room is comfortable and well kept. Included in the tariff is the use of a swimming pool in a sheltered corner of the garden (heated in summer) and a hard tennis court. Riding from the hotel's stables is available.

The candlelit restaurant, with its log fire, specializes in flambé cookery. The chef often uses fresh garden produce, which is complemented by a good wine list. A table d'hôte meal costs £27.50 ($43.45).

In Beaulieu / Buckler's Hard

Moderate

Master Builders House Hotel

Buckler's Hard, Beaulieu, Hampshire SO42 7XB. ☎ **01590/616253.** Fax 01590/616297. 23 rms. TV TEL. £45 ($71.10) single; £90 ($142.20) double. With half board (2-night minimum required), £70 ($110.60) single; £120 ($189.60) double. Rates include English breakfast. AE, MC, V. Free parking.

About $2^1/2$ miles south of Beaulieu, in the historic maritime village of Buckler's Hard, this 17th-century red-brick building was once the home of master ship-builder Henry Adams. Responsible for many of the wooden hulls that later domi-nated the seaways of the world, Adams incorporated many of his shipbuilding techniques into the construction of this lovely old house. Views from some of the bedrooms overlook the grass-covered slipways which, centuries ago, were used to ease newly built ocean vessels into the calm waters of the nearby river.

Most of the hotel's comfortable and conservatively decorated accommodations are in a modern wing, built after World War II. The hotel's historic core is de-voted to the Yachtsman Buffet Bar and to the Restaurant. There, near wide win-dows overlooking the busy river, fixed-price meals cost £12.50 to £30 ($19.75 to $47.40).

Montagu Arms

Palace Lane, Beaulieu, Hampshire, SO42 7ZL. ☎ **01590/612324.** Fax 01590/612188. 21 rms, 3 suites. TV TEL. £69.90 ($110.45) single; £98.90–£109.90 ($156.25–$173.65) double; £139.90 ($221.05) suite. Rates include English breakfast. AE, DC, MC, V. Free parking.

The core of this historic coaching inn was built in the 1700s to supply food and drink to the teams of laborers who hauled salt from the nearby marshes to other parts of England. Over the years, the establishment's name changed from the Ship Inn to the George Inn, in honor of the then king of England. Around 1925 a new wing was added and the name changed to the Montagu Arms. Today, the oldest part of the inn is its pub, which continues to serve food and ale to a clientele who appreciate its well-oiled patina and sense of history. One of the prides of the es-tablishment is a walled garden, whose periphery was built with stones salvaged from Beaulieu Abbey after it was demolished by Henry VIII. Equally important is the hexagonal column supporting a fountain in the hotel's central courtyard— one of six salvaged, according to legend, from the ruined abbey's nave. On the pre-mises is an oak-beamed and paneled dining room, serving fixed-price lunches for £14.95 ($23.60) and fixed-price dinners for £23.90 ($37.75). The bedrooms are immaculate and modernized, with conservative and comfortable furnishings.

WHERE TO DINE
MODERATE

Le Poussin

The Courtyard, at the rear of 49–55 Brookley Rd., Brockenhurst. ☎ **01590/23063.** Reser-vations recommended. Lunch £10 ($15.80) for two courses, £15 ($23.70) for three courses; dinner £20 ($31.60) for two courses, £25 ($39.50) for three courses. MC, V. Wed–Sat noon–2pm and 7–10pm, Sun noon–2pm. Closed 2 weeks in Jan and 1 week in Sept. GAME/FISH.

Le Poussin is located in what was originally a 19th-century stable and workshop for an itinerant craftsman known as a tinker. To reach it, pass beneath the arched alleyway (located midway between nos. 49 and 55 Brookley Rd.) and enter the stylishly simple premises directed by English-born chef Alexander Aitken and his wife, Caroline.

Amid a decor accented with framed 19th-century poems and illustrations cel-ebrating, in one form or another, the gastronomic pleasures of poultry, the staff will offer an array of fish and game dishes whose ingredients usually come fresh from the nearby New Forest. In season, you'll find several different versions of venison, the most visible of which is called "Fruits of the New Forest." (It consists of individually cooked portions of pigeon, wild rabbit, hare, and venison, encased in puff pastry and served with game sauce.) Your meal might begin with a *pithivier* of lobster (a dome-shaped puff pastry traditionally prepared as a dessert but in this case served as an appetizer and filled with chunks of lobster encased in a lobster mousse). Dessert choices change with the season but will usually include a festival of wild strawberries served with an elder-flower sorbet.

4 The Isle of Wight

91 miles SW of London, 4 miles S of Southampton

The Isle of Wight is known for its sandy beaches and its ports, favored by the yachting set. The island has long attracted such literary figures as Alfred, Lord Tennyson and Charles Dickens. Tennyson wrote his beloved poem "Crossing the Bar" en route across the Solent from Lymington to Yarmouth.

The Isle of Wight is compact in size, measuring 23 miles from east to west, 13 miles from north to south. **Ryde** is the railhead for the island's transportation system. **Yarmouth** is something else—a busy little harbor providing a mooring for yachts and also for one of the lifeboats in the Solent area.

Cowes is the premier port for yachting in Britain. Henry VIII ordered the castle built here, but it's now the headquarters of the Royal Yacht Squadron. The seafront, the Prince's Green, and the high cliff road are worth exploring. Hovercraft are built in the town, which is also the home and birthplace of the well-known maritime photographer Beken of Cowes. It's almost *de rigueur* to wear oilskins and wellies, leaving a wet trail behind you.

Newport, a bustling market town in the heart of the island, is the capital and has long been a favorite of British royalty. Along the southeast coast are the twin resorts of **Sandown,** with its new pier complex and theater, and **Shanklin,** at the southern end of Sandown Bay, which has held the British annual sunshine record more times than any other resort. Keats once lived in Shanklin's Old Village. Farther along the coast, **Ventnor** is called the "Madeira of England" because it rises from the sea in a series of steep hills.

On the west coast are the many-colored sand cliffs of **Alum Bay.** The Needles, three giant chalk rocks, and the Needles Lighthouse, are the farther features of interest at this end of the island. If you want to stay at the western end of Wight, consider **Freshwater Bay.**

ESSENTIALS
GETTING THERE

By Train   There's a direct train from London's Waterloo Station to Portsmouth that deposits travelers directly at the pier for a ferry crossing to the Isle of Wight; ferries are timed to meet train arrivals. Travel time from London to the arrival point of Ryde on the Isle of Wight (including ferry-crossing time) is 2 hours. One train per hour departs during the day from London to Portsmouth.

By Car   Drive to Southampton (see above) and take the ferry, or leave Southampton and head west along A35, cutting south on A337 toward Lymington on the coast where the ferry crossing to Yarmouth (Isle of Wight) is shorter than the trip from Southampton.

By Ferry   A car-ferry from the Town Quay in Southampton goes to East Cowes (Isle of Wight). The fare for a car and its passengers varies slightly according to its size, but the average round-trip fare is £38 ($60.05) for a crossing that takes about an hour each way, depending on the weather.

More popular with train travelers is the passenger-only high-speed ferryboat (a double-hulled catamaran) that travels between Southampton and West Cowes. Its price is £8.80 ($13.90) for adults and £4.40 ($6.95) for children, round-trip; trip time is around 25 minutes. Another passenger ferry operates between Portsmouth and Ryde, taking 20 minutes and costing £8.70 ($13.75) for adults and £4.35 ($6.85) for children, round-trip. Daytime departures leave every 30 minutes in summer and every 60 minutes in winter. A final option involves a Hovercraft that travels from Southsea (Portsmouth's neighbor) to Ryde, charging £8.90 ($14.05) for adults and £4.45 ($7.05) for children. For information on departure times and schedules, call the tourist office in Shanklin (see below) or 01983/293383 for car-ferries and 01983/811000 for passenger ferries.

GETTING AROUND

Visitors can explore the Isle of Wight just for the day on an "Around the Island Rover" bus trip. Tickets may be purchased on the bus, and you can board or leave the bus at any stop on the island. The price of a Day Rover is £4.50 ($7.10) for adults and £2.25 ($3.55) for children. It also entitles you to passage on the island's only railway, which runs from the dock at Ryde to the center of Shanklin, a distance of 8 miles. For further information, call the Newport Bus Station (☎ **01983/523831**).

VISITOR INFORMATION

The **telephone area code** is 01983. The **information office** is at 67 High St., Shanklin (☎ **01983/862942**).

WHAT TO SEE & DO

✪ Osborne House

A mile southeast of East Cowes. ☎ **01983/200022.** Admission £5.80 ($9.15) adults, £4.40 ($6.95) senior citizens, £2.90 ($4.60) children. Apr–Sept, daily 10am–6pm; Oct, daily 10am–5pm. Closed Nov–Mar. Bus 4 or 5.

Queen Victoria's most cherished residence, a mile southeast of East Cowes, was built at her own expense. Prince Albert, with his characteristic thoroughness, contributed to many aspects of the design of the Italian-inspired mansion, which stands amid lush gardens, right outside the village of Whippingham. The rooms have remained as Victoria knew them, right down to the French piano she used to play and all the cozy clutter of her sitting room. Grief-stricken at the death of Albert in 1861, she asked that Osborne House be kept as it was, and so it has been. Even the turquoise scent bottles he gave her, decorated with cupids and cherubs, are still in place. It was in her bedroom at Osborne House that the queen died on January 22, 1901.

Carisbrooke Castle

Carisbrooke, 1¼ miles southwest of Newport. ☎ **01983/522107.** Castle and museum £3.50 ($5.55) adults, £2.75 ($4.35) children. Apr–Oct, daily 10am–6pm; Nov–Mar, Mon–Sat 10am–4pm. Bus 91A.

This fine medieval castle lies in the center of the Isle of Wight and is considered one of the island's most recommendable side trips. During one of the most turbulent periods of English history, Charles I was imprisoned here, far from his former seat of power in London, by Cromwell's Roundheads in 1647. On the castle premises is a 16th-century Well House, where during periods of siege, donkeys took turns treading a large wooden wheel connected to a rope that hauled up

---

🕐 In Their Footsteps

Queen Victoria (1819–1901)   The woman who sat on the British throne longer than any other monarch and who became the empress of India. Ruling over the "golden age" of the British Empire, she lent her name to the Victorian era and was the mother of the future King Edward VII. She married her cousin, Prince Albert of Saxe-Coburg-Gotha, in 1840.

Accomplishments: She was a powerful monarch, influencing British imperial policies as well as the morals that permeated her era. She liked Disraeli's policies, but not those of the Liberal Gladstone. Most of the empire, certainly Great Britain, admired and respected her to the end. **Favorite Residences:** Osborne House on the Isle of Wight and her "beloved" Balmoral in Scotland. **Resting Place:** Frogmore (a private estate) near Windsor.

---

buckets of water from a well. Accessible from the castle's courtyard is a museum (☎ **01983/523112**) with exhibits relating to the social history of the Isle of Wight and about 20 items related to the history of Charles I's imprisonment.

WHERE TO STAY
IN RYDE
Inexpensive

🕐 Biskra House Beach Hotel
17 St. Thomas's St., Ryde, Isle of Wight PO33 2DC. ☎ **01983/567913.** Fax 01983/616976. 9 rms. MINIBAR TV TEL. £31.50–£35 ($49.75–$55.30) single; £47.50–£57.50 ($75.05–$90.85) double. Rates include English breakfast. MC, V. Free parking.

You'll find some of the best dining on the island at Biskra House, which also offers rooms. The rooms are furnished in a comfortable, slightly old-fashioned way, with tea- or coffee-making facilities and hairdryers. The most expensive double room in the house has a private balcony with views over the Solent where occupants gather to watch sunsets.

Giuseppe's Cellar Restaurant is Italian, serving full meals daily from 7 to 9:30pm, costing £16 ($25.30) and up per person. The Clipper Bar Restaurant opens onto gardens fronting the beach and serves lunch from noon to 2pm.

Hotel Ryde Castle
The Esplanade, Ryde, Isle of Wight PO33 1JA. ☎ **01983/563755.** Fax 01983/568925. 22 suites. TV TEL. £45 ($71.10) suite for one; £55.50 ($87.70) suite for two. Rates include English breakfast. AE, DC, MC, V. Free parking. Bus 1 or 1A.

This historic seafront castle looking out on the Solent makes a fine base for exploring the island. The castle, dating from the 16th century, has been added to over the centuries. Illustrious occupants have included the grandson of Queen Victoria and Field Marshall Montgomery prior to the D-Day landings. With its crenellated ivy-clad exterior and its well-kept public rooms, the hotel attracts families as well as solo visitors. The comfortable suites have radios, hairdryers, and tea- or coffee-making equipment; double suites have four-poster beds. Both table d'hôte and à la carte meals are offered in the hotel dining room, where full use is made of fresh fish caught locally and island farm products. Meals cost £13 ($20.55), and up, and the bar/lounge offers a wide range of inexpensive snacks for lunch.

IN SHANKLIN
Inexpensive
Bourne Hall Country Hotel

Luccombe Rd., Shanklin, Isle of Wight PO37 6RR. ☎ **01983/862820.** Fax 01983/865138.
30 rms. TV TEL. £35.45–£43 ($56–$67.95) single; £65–£82 ($102.70–$129.55) double. Rates
include English breakfast. AE, DC, MC, V. Free parking. Bus 12A.

Many visitors prefer to base themselves at Shanklin because of its old village,
with its thatched cottages and the Chine, two of the leading attractions on the
island. At Bourne Hall they receive a warm welcome from the owners, who have
one of the best-equipped hotels in the area, complete with two swimming pools,
a sauna, a solarium, and a Jacuzzi. Each room is well furnished and comfortably
maintained.

ⓢ Luccombe Chine House

Luccombe Chine, Shanklin, Isle of Wight PO37 6RH. ☎ **01983/862037.** 6 rms. TV. £27–
£36 ($42.65–$56.90) per person. Rates include English breakfast. MC, V. Free parking. Closed
Dec–Jan. Take A3055 (Shanklin–Ventnor road) to the signposted private driveway. Bus 12A.

The Luccombe Chine House is situated on some 10 acres of grounds opening
onto Luccombe Bay. Each room is immaculately kept and well furnished, with
hot-beverage facilities and hairdryer; all have four-poster beds. It's a good base from
which to explore the Isle of Wight. The food is also good, with meals beginning
at £12 ($18.95).

IN SANDOWN
Inexpensive
St. Catherine's Hotel

1 Winchester Park Rd., Sandown, Isle of Wight PO36 8HJ. ☎ **01983/402392.** Fax 01983/
402392. 20 rms. TV TEL. £22.50 ($35.55) single; £45 ($71.10) double. Rates include English
breakfast. DC, MC, V. Free parking. Bus 16 from Ryde.

Just a few minutes' walk from Sandown's sandy beach, leisure center, and pier
complex, with its sun lounges and theater, St. Catherine's was built in 1860 of
creamy Purbeck stone and white trim for the dean of Winchester College. A
modern extension was added for streamlined and sunny bedrooms. The brightly
redecorated lounge has matching draperies at the wide bay windows. There are card
tables and a small library of books. Adjacent is a cozy, fully stocked bar and
a spacious, comfortable dining room, serving high-quality English food, with a
meal costing £9.50 ($15). The bedrooms have duvets, white furniture, and built-
in headboards.

IN CHALE
Inexpensive
Clarendon Hotel and Wight Mouse Inn

Newport Rd. (B3399; 50 yards off Military Rd.), Chale, Isle of Wight PO38 2HA. ☎ **01983/
730431.** 12 rms, 2 suites. TV. £74.03 ($116.95) single; £89.30–£96.36 ($141.10–$152.25)
double. Rates include half board. DC, MC, V. Free parking.

This old coaching inn lies on the most southerly part of the island, where the
vegetation is almost tropical. From here, you have views over the Channel to the
mainland coast. The Clarendon is a cheerful place to spend the night. Some
of the rooms are beautifully furnished with antiques, and all have tea and coffee
makers. Children are most welcome here.

The meals are ample, with many fresh ingredients. In the pub, the Wight Mouse Inn, open all day every day for hot meals and drinks, they serve a large selection of beers, including real ales, and 365 scotch whiskies (one for every day of the year), in addition to the more usual drinks. Live entertainment is provided nightly year round. Traditional English dishes are served in the more formal Clarendon Restaurant.

WHERE TO DINE
MODERATE

The Cottage
8 Eastcliff Rd., Shanklin Old Village. ☎ **01983/862504.** Reservations recommended. Main courses £12.95 ($20.45); fixed-price lunch £8.85 ($14). AE, DC, MC, V. Tues–Sat noon–2pm and 7:30–9:45pm. Closed Feb and Oct to mid-Nov. ENGLISH/FRENCH.

Established in 1973, this restaurant is in a 200-year-old stone-sided cottage that's set among thatch-covered buildings in the center of Shanklin. Inside, two floors of pink and blue dining rooms have lace tablecloths and heavy oaken beams. Fixed-price lunches feature such dishes as chicken sautéed in cream or a roast of the day (pork, lamb, or beef) served with new potatoes and two vegetables. Though most lunchtime diners opt for the fixed-price lunch, tempting à la carte dishes are available at both lunch and dinner. Neil Graham supervises a menu that might include sea trout poached and served in a mousseline sauce with wild rice cooked in Darjeling tea or fillets of beef served on a pink peppercorn and cream sauce.

Adjacent to the restaurant, at no. 4 Eastcliff Rd. (same phone), is a gift shop under the same management which sells a mostly English collection of high-quality gifts. These include porcelain, carved mahogany, umbrellas, and designer gifts from such names as Sanderson.

5 Winchester

72 miles SW of London, 12 miles N of Southampton

The most historic city in all of Hampshire, Winchester is big on legends—it's associated with King Arthur and the Knights of the Round Table. In the Great Hall, all that remains of Winchester Castle, a round oak table, with space for King Arthur and his 24 knights, is attached to the wall. But all that spells undocumented romance. What is known, however, is that when the Saxons ruled the ancient kingdom of Wessex, Winchester was the capital. The city is also linked with King Alfred, who is believed to have been crowned here and is honored today by a statue. The Danish conqueror, Canute, came this way too, as did the king he ousted, Ethelred the Unready (Canute got his wife, Emma, in the bargain). The city is the seat of the well-known Winchester College, whose founding father was the bishop of Winchester, William of Wykeham. Established in 1382, it's reputed to be the oldest public (private) secondary school in England. Traditions are strong in Winchester. You can still go to St. Cross Hospital—dating from the 12th century—now an almshouse. There you'll get ye olde pilgrim's dole of ale and bread (and if there's no bread, you can eat cake). You must arrive, however, on a weekday before 11am. Winchester is essentially a market town; it's on the downs on the Itchen River.

ESSENTIALS
GETTING THERE

By Train   From London's Waterloo Station there is frequent daily train service to Winchester (trip time: 1 hr.).

By Bus   National Express buses leaving from London's Victoria Coach Station depart every 2 hours for Winchester during the day (trip time: 2 hr.).

By Car   From Southampton, drive north on A335; from London, take the M3 motorway southwest.

VISITOR INFORMATION

The **telephone area code** is 01962. The **Tourist Information Centre** is at the Winchester Guildhall, The Broadway (☎ **01962/840500**).

WHAT TO SEE & DO

For centuries, ✪ **Winchester Cathedral,** The Square (☎ **01962/853137**), has been one of the great churches of England. The present building, the longest medieval cathedral in Britain, dates from 1079, and its Norman heritage is still in evidence. When a Saxon church stood on this spot, St. Swithun, bishop of Winchester and tutor to young King Alfred, suggested modestly that he be buried outside. When he was later buried inside, it rained for 40 days. The legend lives on: Just ask a resident of Winchester what will happen if it rains on St. Swithun's Day, July 15, and you'll get a prediction of rain for 40 days.

In the present building, the nave with its two aisles is most impressive, as are the chantries, the reredos (late 15th century), and the elaborately carved choir stalls. Of the chantries, that of William of Wykeham, founder of Winchester College, is perhaps the most visited (it's found in the south aisle of the nave). The cathedral also has a number of other tombs, notably those of Jane Austen and Izaak Walton (exponent of the merits of the pastoral life in *The Compleat Angler*). The latter's tomb is to be found in the Prior Silkestede's Chapel in the South Transept. Jane Austen's grave is marked with a commemorative plaque. At Winchester Cathedral there are chests containing the bones of many Saxon kings and the remains of the Viking conqueror, Canute, and his wife, Emma, in the presbytery. The son of William the Conqueror, William Rufus (who reigned as William II), is also buried at the cathedral. There are free guided tours April to October, Monday through Saturday at 11am, 12:30pm, 2pm, and 3pm.

The crypt is flooded during winter months, but part of it may be seen from a viewing platform. When it's not flooded, there are regular tours, Monday through Saturday at 10:30am and 2:30pm. The cathedral library and the Triforium Gallery are open from Easter to October on Monday from 2 to 4:30pm and Tuesday through Saturday from 10:30am to 1pm and 2 to 4:30pm; from November to Easter, on Saturday from 10:30am to 4pm. The library houses Bishop Morley's 17th-century book collection and an exhibition room contains the 12th-century Winchester Bible. The Triforium shows sculpture, woodwork, and metalwork from 11 centuries and affords magnificent views over the rest of the cathedral. Admission to the library and Triforium Gallery is £1.50 ($2.35) for adults and 50p (80¢) for children. No admission fee is charged for the cathedral, but a donation of £2 ($3.15) is suggested. A Visitors' Centre was opened in 1993 by Queen Elizabeth II and the duke of Edinburgh; it comprises a cathedral refectory and a shop. The refectory offers homemade food ranging from light snacks to three-course lunches, and the shop sells an array of gifts and souvenirs. There is no admission charge.

WHERE TO STAY

EXPENSIVE

✪ Lainston House

Sparsholt, Winchester, Hampshire SO21 2LT. ☎ **01962/863588.** Fax 01962/776672. 35 rms, 3 suites. MINIBAR TV TEL. £95 ($150.10) single; £125–£225 ($197.50–$355.50) double; £245 ($387.10) suite. Breakfast £8–£10 ($12.65–$15.80) extra. AE, DC, MC, V. Free parking. Take A272 3^1/$_2$ miles northwest of Winchester.

The beauty of this fine, restored William and Mary red-brick manor house strikes visitors as they approach via a long, curving, tree-lined drive. It's situated on 63 acres of rolling land, linked with the name Lainston in the *Domesday Book* of 1086. Inside the stately house, elegance is the keynote, with Delft-tile fireplaces, oak-and-cedar paneling, molding, and cornices of the original owners preserved, set off with period pieces. The largest and most elegant rooms are in the main house, with traditional English furnishings and color-coordinated decors. Other rooms, less spacious but also comfortable and harmoniously furnished, are in a nearby annex built in 1990.

In either of the two dining rooms, you can order such French and English specialties as roast partridge or roast loin of lamb rolled with a herb stuffing. Dinners cost £30 to £40 ($47.40 to $63.20).

MODERATE

Royal Hotel

St. Peter St., Winchester, Hampshire SO23 8BS. ☎ **01962/840840,** or 800/528-1234 in the U.S. Fax 01962/841582. 75 rms, 3 suites. TV TEL. £75 ($118.50) single; £85 ($134.30) double; £105 ($165.90) suite. Breakfast £6.50 ($9.80) extra. AE, DC, MC, V. Free parking.

This fine old privately owned hotel was built at the end of the 17th century as a private house. It has a modern extension overlooking gardens. All rooms have traditional English styling. For 50 years it was used by nuns from Brussels as a convent before being turned into a hotel—when it soon became the center of the city's social life. It's only a few minutes' walk from the cathedral, yet still enjoys a secluded position. Best of all is the garden hidden behind high walls. Meals are served in a small, formal dining room with a view of the private garden, where a fixed-price dinner costs £19 ($30). Shoe cleaning, valet service, and 24-hour room service constitute some of the amenities.

INEXPENSIVE

⑤ Stratton House

Stratton Rd., St. Giles Hill, Winchester, Hampshire SO23 8JQ. ☎ **01962/863919.** Fax 01962/842095. 10 rms, 7 with bath. TV. £24 ($37.90) single without bath, £35–£40 ($55.30–$63.20) single with bath; £44–£48 ($69.50–$75.85) double without bath. Rates include English breakfast. No credit cards. Free parking. Closed Dec 24–Jan 1. Free pickup available from the train or bus station.

This lovely old Victorian house (ca. 1890) is situated on an acre of St. Giles Hill, overlooking the city. It's about a 5- to 10-minute walk from the center. All the comfortably furnished bedrooms have TVs and hot-beverage facilities. A three-course evening meal can be arranged for £7 ($11.05). There is ample parking in a private courtyard.

✪ Wykeham Arms

75 Kingsgate St., Winchester, Hampshire SO23 9PE. ☎ **01962/853834.** Fax 01962/
854411. 7 rms. MINIBAR TV TEL. £62.50 ($93.80) single; £72.50 ($108.80) double. Rates
include English breakfast. AE, MC, V. Free parking.

This is one of the most enduring recommendations in Winchester, known to almost everyone in town for its food and bar facilities. It lies behind a 200-year-old
brick facade in the historic center of town, near the cathedral. The bedrooms are
comfortably and traditionally furnished with antiques or reproductions and such
lighthearted touches as fresh flowers and baskets of potpourri.

Most of the establishment's income and prestige derive from its paneled pub and
restaurant, where carefully flavored food is served in historic surroundings. Lunches
(served Monday through Saturday from noon to 2:30pm) are informal affairs
where pub snacks and platters are served after clients place their orders at the bar.
Sandwiches, ploughman's lunches, and such platters as Thai chicken with rice and
chutney are priced at £3.50 to £6 ($5.55 to $9.50). Evening meals (served Monday through Saturday from 6:30 to 8:45pm) are more elaborate, with waitresses
taking orders directly at the tables. Main dishes, priced at £11 to £13 ($17.40
to $20.55), are more elegant than you might have imagined. They include, for
example, Wykeham's cottage pie served with crusted bread, creamy chicken casserole with rice, fish cakes served with a spicy tomato sauce, and such vegetarian
dishes as ratatouille and vegetable quiches.

WHERE TO DINE
MODERATE

Nine the Square

9 Great Minster St. ☎ **01962/864004.** Reservations recommended. Main courses £4.95–
£14.95 ($7.80–$23.60). AE, MC, V. Mon–Sat noon–2:30pm and 7–10:30pm. CONTINENTAL.

One of the assets of this establishment is its enviable view of Winchester Cathedral. Diners may either head upstairs to the comfortably formal restaurant or
remain at street level where dining tables are scattered within view of a sometimes-
crowded stand-up bar and the preferred drinks seem to be glasses of a wide array
of European wines.

Menu items are identical on both floors of the establishment. There are at least
four kinds of freshly made pastas, including saffron spaghetti with carbonara sauce;
mushroom and ricotta cheese crêpes; breast of chicken Stroganoff with saffron rice;
brodetto, an Italian fish casserole; steamed salmon with rhubarb; and charcoal-
grilled pigeon with an onion-and-Cassis confit.

INEXPENSIVE

⑤ Elizabethan Restaurant

18 Jewry St. ☎ **01962/853566.** Reservations recommended. Main courses £7.50–£14.95
($11.85–$23.60); fixed-price lunch and early-evening menu £9.50 ($15). AE, DC, MC, V.
Daily noon–2:30pm and 6–10:30pm. ENGLISH/FRENCH.

In the atmosphere of another century, a 3-minute walk north of the center,
the Elizabethan offers an opportunity to dine under hand-hewn beams by candlelight. The street-level bar is for drinks and lunch snacks, costing £1.45 to
£4.60 ($2.30 to $7.25), while the more formal dining room is one floor above. The
restaurant sits in the upper reaches of the village, in a building originally dating
from 1509. Well run, the kitchen offers an excellent English cuisine with many

---

Impressions

Our Chawton Home, how much we find
Already in it to our mind;
And how convinced, that when complete
It will all other houses beat
That ever have been made or mended,
With rooms concise or rooms distended.

—Jane Austen, 1809

French-inspired dishes. Try, for example, poached salmon with a white-wine and cream sauce, chicken dijonnaise, or veal marsala. A tourist menu costs only £9.50 ($14.30) for three courses. A la carte dinners cost £15 to £16 ($23.70 to $25.30).

AN EASY EXCURSION

If you love Jane Austen, you might want to make a trip to see **Chawton Cottage,** Jane Austen's house, in Chawton, 1 mile southwest of Alton off A31 and B3006 (☎ **01420/83262**). The location is 15 miles east of Winchester; the cottage is signposted at Chawton. Born in 1775, Jane Austen was the daughter of the Oxford-educated rector, the Rev. Mr. George Austen, a typical Hampshire country gentleman, who had lots of charm but little money. In keeping with a custom of the time, the Austens gave their third son, Edward, to a wealthy, childless family connection, Thomas Knight. As Knight's heir, it was Edward who let his mother and sisters live in the house.

Visitors can see the surroundings in which the novelist spent the last $7^1/2$ years of her life, her most productive period. In the unpretentious but pleasant cottage, you can see the table on which Jane Austen penned new versions of three of her books and wrote three more, including *Emma.* You can also see the rector's George III mahogany bookcase and a silhouette likeness of the Reverend Austen presenting his son to the Knights. It was in this cottage that Jane Austen became ill in 1816 with what would have been diagnosed by the middle of the 19th century as Addison's disease.

There's an attractive garden in which visitors are invited to have picnics and an old bake house with Austen's donkey cart. Visitors can also browse through a bookshop with both new and secondhand books. The home is open from 11am to 4:30pm: daily April to October; Wednesday through Sunday in March, November, and December; and Saturday and Sunday in January and February. Admission is £2 ($3.15) for adults, 50p (80¢) for children 8 to 18. It's closed Christmas Day and Boxing Day (December 26).

6 Bournemouth

104 miles SW of London, 15 miles W of the Isle of Wight

The south-coast resort at the doorstep of the New Forest didn't just happen: It was carefully planned and executed—a true city in a garden. Flower-filled, park-dotted Bournemouth is filled with much architecture inherited from those arbiters of taste, Victoria and her son, Edward. (The resort was discovered back in Victoria's day, when seabathing became an institution.) Bournemouth's most distinguished feature is its chines (narrow, shrub-filled, steep-sided ravines) along the coastline.

It is estimated that of Bournemouth's nearly 12,000 acres, about one-sixth is composed of green parks and flower beds, such as the Pavilion Rock Garden, which amblers pass through day and night. The total effect, especially in spring, is striking and helps explain Bournemouth's continuing popularity with the garden-loving English.

Bournemouth, along with Poole and Christchurch, forms the largest urban area in the south of England. It makes a good base for exploring a historically rich part of England; on its outskirts are the New Forest, Salisbury, Winchester, and the Isle of Wight. It also has some 20,000 students attending the various schools or colleges, who explore, in their off-hours, places made famous by such poets and artists as Shelley, Beardsley, and Turner.

The resort's amusements are varied. At the Pavilion Theatre, for example, you can see West End–type productions from London. The Bournemouth Symphony Orchestra is justly famous in Europe. And there's the usual run of golf courses, band concerts, variety shows, and dancing. The real walkers might strike out at Hengistbury Head and make their way past sandy beaches, the Boscombe and Bournemouth piers—all the way to Alum Chine, a distance of 6 miles.

ESSENTIALS
GETTING THERE

By Train An express train from Waterloo Station takes 2 hours. There is frequent service throughout the day.

By Bus Buses leave London's Waterloo Station every 2 hours during the day, heading for Bournemouth (trip time: 2¹/₂ hr.).

By Car Take M3 southwest from London to Winchester, then A31 and A338 south to Bournemouth.

VISITOR INFORMATION

The **telephone area code** is 01202. The **information office** is at Westover Road (☎ 01202/789789).

WHERE TO STAY
EXPENSIVE

Carlton Hotel

Meyrick Rd., East Overcliff, Bournemouth, Dorset BH1 3DN. ☎ **01202/552011.** Fax 01202/299573. 64 rms, 6 suites. TV TEL. £95 ($150.10) single; £120 ($189.60) double; from £160 ($252.80) suite. Rates include English breakfast. AE, DC, MC, V. Free parking.

Better defined as a vacation resort than as an ordinary hotel, the Carlton sits atop a seaside cliff lined with private homes and other hotels. Many of the better rooms are quite spacious, offering king-size beds, along with armchairs and writing desks. All bathrooms are contemporary, with a number of amenities (including both a bathtub and a shower) and a bidet. The Carlton boasts a luxury restaurant and cocktail bar, elegant lounges, a boutique, a swimming pool, and a health and beauty spa. There, a sudsy whirlpool, a gymnasium, sauna, Jacuzzi, tanning beds, and a trained staff contribute to healthy vacations. Lunch goes for £15.50 ($24.50), and dinner costs £23.50 ($37.15). Laundry and 24-hour room service are available.

MODERATE

✪ Langtry Manor Hotel

26 Derby Rd. (north of Christchurch Rd., A35), East Cliff, Bournemouth, Dorset BH1 3QB. ☎ **01202/553887.** Fax 01202/290550. 23 rms, 3 suites. MINIBAR TV TEL. £59.50 ($94) single occupancy of a double room; £99–£119 ($156.40–$188) double; £139–£159 ($219.60–$251.20) suite for two. Rates include English breakfast. AE, DC, MC, V. Free parking.

The Red House, as it was originally called, was built in 1877 for Lillie Langtry, the famous Jersey Lily, as a gift from Edward VII to his favorite mistress. The house contains all sorts of reminders of its illustrious inhabitants, including initials scratched on a windowpane and carvings on a beam of the entrance hall. On the half-landing is the peephole through which the prince could scrutinize the assembled company before coming down to dine, and one of the fireplaces bears his initials. The bedrooms, each a double, range from ordinary twins to the Lillie Langtry Suite, Lillie's own room, with a four-poster bed and a double heart-shaped bathtub; or you can rent the Edward VII Suite, furnished as it was when His Royal Highness lived in this spacious room. The huge carved-oak fireplace has hand-painted tiles depicting scenes from Shakespeare. The four-poster bed is genuine Jacobean. One-night stays in four-poster rooms and suites carry a weekend supplement of £40 ($63.20) per person.

The owner has furnished the hotel in the Edwardian style. There is no menu; the dishes are just produced for inspection. A three-course dinner begins at £19.25 ($30.40) Sunday through Friday. On Saturday night an Edwardian banquet, costing £15 ($23.70), is presented with the staff in period dress.

Norfolk Royale Hotel

Richmond Hill, Bournemouth, Dorset BH2 6EN. ☎ **01202/551521.** Fax 01202/299729. 88 rms, 7 suites. MINIBAR TV TEL. £90 ($142.20) single; £120 ($189.60) double; £175 ($276.50) suite. Breakfast £4.75–£8.75 ($7.50–$13.85) extra. AE, DC, MC, V. Free parking.

One of the oldest prestige hotels of the resort, a few blocks from the seafront and the central shopping area, underwent a major £5-million renovation program, restoring it to its former Edwardian elegance. Disregarding what lies on its periphery, it's like a country estate, with a formal entrance and a rear garden and fountain shaded by trees. The public rooms are geared to holiday guests, with two bars. The rooms and suites have been luxuriously appointed with the traditional styles of the Edwardian period blending with modern comforts such as private baths, phones, and TVs. Among the special features of the hotel are the swimming pool covered with a glass dome and the Orangery restaurant set in the terraced gardens. Meals cost £18.50 ($29.25) and up.

✪ Royal Bath Hotel

Bath Rd., Bournemouth, Dorset BH1 2EW. ☎ **01202/555555.** Fax 01202/554158. 124 rms, 7 suites. TV TEL. £95 ($150.10) single; £120–£160 ($189.60–$252.80) double; £280 ($442.40) suite. Rates include English breakfast. AE, DC, MC, V. Parking £5 ($7.90).

This early Victorian version of a French château, with towers and bay windows looking out over the bay and Purbeck Hill, opened on June 28, 1838, the very day of Victoria's coronation. After the adolescent prince of Wales (later—a long time later—Edward VII) stayed here, the hotel added "Royal" to its name. Over the years it has attracted everybody from Oscar Wilde to Rudolf Nureyev and the great prime minister, Disraeli. Each luxuriously furnished bedroom has a private bath and the larger rooms have sitting areas.

The hotel has two restaurants: the Garden Restaurant and Oscar's (see our separate recommendation in "Where to Dine," below). The table d'hôte dinner at the Garden Restaurant is £23 ($36.35), and a fixed-price lunch, served Sunday only, is £16.50 ($26.05). The resident band plays for a dinner-dance Saturday evenings. For health enthusiasts, there's a sauna, as well as Swedish massages and special diets. Amid its 3 acres of clifftop gardens is a heated swimming pool.

Swallow Highcliff Hotel

105 St. Michael's Rd., West Cliff, Bournemouth, Dorset BH2 5DU. ☎ **01202/557702.** Fax 01202/292734. 146 rms, 8 suites. MINIBAR TV TEL. £90 ($142.20) single; £120 ($189.60) double; £195 ($308.10) suite. Rates include English breakfast. AE, DC, MC, V. Free parking.

The high-ceilinged interior of this 1888 cliffside hotel has been tastefully renovated into a subtly updated format, retaining most of the elegant ceiling moldings but replacing the antiques with conservatively modern counterparts. Many of the bedrooms have beautiful views of the sea. The bedrooms, each well furnished and maintained, are either in the main building or in coastguard cottages built in 1912. The hotel premises offer a heated swimming pool, tennis court, sauna, solarium, putting green, and games room. An elegant restaurant serves well-prepared food in a grand manner, with formal service. Dinners cost £17.95 ($28.35).

IN NEARBY POOLE
Moderate

The Mansion House

7–11 Thames St., Poole, Dorset BH15 1JN. ☎ **01202/685666.** Fax 01202/665709. 27 rms, 1 suite. TV TEL. Mon–Thurs, £75 ($118.50) single; £110 ($173.80) double; £150 ($237) suite. Fri–Sun, £52 ($82.15) single; £85 ($134.30) double; £130 ($205.40) suite. Rates include English breakfast. AE, DC, MC, V. Free parking.

The Mansion House, 4 miles west of Bournemouth, was built more than 200 years ago by an English entrepreneur engaged in cod fishing off the coast of Newfoundland. The neoclassical detailing and fan-shaped windows that pierce the red brick of the establishment's facade are the pride and well-maintained joy of the owners.

A pair of bars are decorated with formal and rustic decors. An upstairs lounge and the graciously furnished bedrooms provide plenty of quiet, well-decorated corners for relaxation. Excellent modern English cuisine is served, costing £11.50 to £14 ($18.15 to $22.10) for a fixed-price lunch, £19.50 ($30.80) for a fixed-price dinner.

WHERE TO DINE
EXPENSIVE

Oscar's

In the Royal Bath Hotel, Bath Rd. ☎ **01202/555555.** Reservations required. Main courses £16–£18 ($25.30–$28.45); fixed-price meal £15.50 ($24.50) at lunch, £28.50 ($45.05) at dinner. AE, DC, MC, V. Mon–Sat 12:30–2:15pm and 7:30–10:15pm. FRENCH.

Sporting Oscar Wilde mementos, this restaurant is located cliffside, offering panoramic views of the sea. The French chef, Gérard Puigdellivol, presents à la carte dishes as well as fixed-price menus. The appetizers might include a salad of warm sliced duck breast with seasonal greens, dressed with a spiced honey-and-sherry vinaigrette; cream of mushroom soup topped with a nutmeg-scented sabayon; or Oriental beef, marinated and cooked with Eastern spices with fresh spinach leaves. Main courses are likely to include a nage of scallops, tiger prawns, and salmon bound with a cardomon- and corriander-infused butter; tournedos of beef fillet served with a rich red-wine sauce and garnished with sautéed mushrooms, spinach purée, and a potato fritter; or farmhouse chicken fricasée with a delicate velvet sauce and garnished with asparagus spears. To finish, try the iced rum-and-raisin parfait served in a tuille with a light banana nage or chocolate-and-caramel millefeuille, crisp layers of chocolate puff pastry filled with a caramel cream.

MODERATE

✪ Sophisticats

43 Charminster Rd. ☎ **01202/291019.** Reservations required. Main courses £10.50–£12.95 ($16.60–$20.45). No credit cards. Tues–Sat 7–10pm. Closed 2 weeks in Feb and 2 weeks in Nov. FRENCH/INTERNATIONAL.

Among the leading restaurants at this south-coast resort, Sophisticats is worth a repeat visit. In a shopping section, about 1¹/₂ miles north of Bournemouth, Sophisticats tempts its diners with its excellent fresh fish, and you can order any number of veal and beef dishes (sometimes the latter will be prepared in the Indonesian style). Appetizers are filled with flavor and texture, and a highly desirable finish to a meal is a dessert soufflé (but let the waiter know in time).

EASY EXCURSIONS
KINGSTON LACY

An imposing 17th-century mansion, Kingston Lacy, at Wimborne Minster, on B3082 (Wimborne–Blandford road), 1¹/₂ miles west of Wimborne (☎ **01202/883402**), was the home for more than 300 years of the Bankes family, who had as guests such distinguished persons as King Edward VII, Kaiser Wilhelm, Thomas Hardy, George V, and Wellington. The house displays a magnificent collection of artworks by such masters as Rubens, Titian, and van Dyck. There's also an important collection of Egyptian artifacts.

The present house was built to replace Corfe Castle, the Bankes' family's home that was destroyed in the Civil War. During her husband's absence while performing duties as chief justice to King Charles I, Lady Bankes led the defense of the castle, withstanding two sieges before being forced to surrender to Cromwell's forces in 1646 because of the actions of a treacherous follower. The keys of Corfe Castle hang in the library at Kingston Lacy.

The house, set on 250 acres of wooded park, is open only from April to October, Saturday through Wednesday from noon to 5:30pm; the park is open from 11:30am to 6pm. Admission to the house, garden, and park is £5.50 ($8.70) for adults, £2.70 ($4.25) for children. Admission to the garden is £2.20 ($3.50) for adults, £1.10 ($1.75) for children.

WAREHAM

This historic little town on the Frome River 2 miles west of Bournemouth is a good center for touring the South Dorset coast and the Purbeck Hills. It has the remains of early Anglo-Saxon and Roman town walls, plus the Saxon church of St. Martin, with its effigy of T. E. Lawrence (Lawrence of Arabia), who died in a

Impressions

The real framework, the place which his spirit will never cease to haunt.
                                                                    —E. M. Forster, on Clouds Hill

Lawrence of Arabia

T. E. Lawrence (1888–1935) hated the name "Lawrence of Arabia," and he probably would have been mortified, embarrassed, and repulsed by the movie of that name (in which he was portrayed by Peter O'Toole) which did more than anything else—including his fascinating career—to make him a legend.

This soldier and author of a much-rewritten memoir, *Seven Pillars of Wisdom*, preferred anonymity and sought to hide behind various aliases. For example, in 1922 he enlisted in the RAF under the alias of "John Hume Ross," but was found out by the press. As a member of the Tank Corps, he was known as "T. E. Shaw" when he was posted to Bovington Camp, between Wareham and Dorchester in South Dorset. It was near Bovington Camp and Clouds Hill (his small home) that he died in a motorcycle accident following his discharge. Sir Winston Churchill attended the funeral.

Lawrence was also an archaeologist. His exploits in that field while on an expedition to Syria (1911–1914) resulted in his book *Crusader Castles*, which earned him early fame. In World War I he was attached to General Wingate's staff with the Hejaz expeditionary force (1917) and to General Allenby's staff (1918). Lawrence was a leader of the Arab revolt against the Turks (1917–1918), which is recounted in his memoirs. One commentator said Lawrence was "one of the few romantic legends to have emerged from a most unromantic war."

In spite of all his military exploits, Lawrence loathed army life and was planning to open a small printing press shortly before he died. Although he wanted to attract as little attention as possible to himself, he could hardly have imagined the great fame that lay ahead of him.

motorcycle crash in 1935. His former home, **Clouds Hill** (☎ **01985/843600**), lies 7 miles west of Wareham (1 mile north of Bovington Camp) and is extremely small. It's open only April to October, on Wednesday, Thursday, Friday, and Sunday from 2 to 5pm. Admission is £2.20 ($3.50), free for children 4 and under.

Aficionados of Lawrence and/or military history should probably also head for the **Tank Museum,** in the village and army base of Bovington Camp (☎ **01929/403463**), an installation maintained by the British military. Among the dozens of rare and historic armed vehicles are exhibitions and memorabilia on the life of T. E. Lawrence. Admission is £5 ($7.90) for adults and £3 ($4.75) for children 5 to 16. It's open daily from 10am to 4:30pm (last admission).

WHERE TO STAY & DINE: MODERATE

✪ The Priory Hotel
Church Green, Wareham, Dorset BH20 4ND. ☎ **01929/552772.** Fax 01929/554519. 15 rms, 4 suites. TV TEL. £80–£105 ($126.40–$165.90) single; £90–£160 ($142.20–$252.80) double; £185 ($292.30) suite. Rates include English breakfast. AE, DC, MC, V. Free parking.

Beside the River Frome and near the village church, this hotel has a well-tended garden adorned by graceful trees. Inside, a warmly paneled bar and a sumptuous lounge filled with antiques open onto views of the lawn. The bedrooms are tastefully furnished with antiques and complementary textiles and have many extras. In the hotel's restaurant, dishes are cooked to order, and every effort is made to use the abundant local produce. The headwaiter will always advise of daily specials.

The hotel is noted for its outstanding restaurant. Set lunches cost £12.95 ($20.45) for two courses, £14.95 ($23.60) for three courses. Fixed-price dinners range from £24.50 to £28.50 ($38.70 to $45.05).

7 Dorchester

120 miles SW of London, 27 miles W of Bournemouth

Thomas Hardy, in his 1886 novel *The Mayor of Casterbridge,* gave Dorchester literary fame. Actually, Dorchester was notable even in Roman times, when Maumbury Rings, considered the best Roman amphitheater in Britain, was filled with the sounds of 12,000 spectators screaming for the blood of the gladiators. Dorchester, a county seat, was the setting of another bloodletting, the "Bloody Assize" of 1685, when Judge Jeffreys condemned to death the supporters of the duke of Monmouth's rebellion against James II.

ESSENTIALS
GETTING THERE
By Train   Trains run from London's Waterloo Station during the day at the rate of one per hour (trip time: 2¹/₂ hr.).

By Bus   Several National Express coaches a day depart from London's Waterloo Station heading for Dorchester (trip time: 3 hr.). In Dorchester, Grove Trading Estate (☎ **01305/262992**), sells tickets both for National Express buses for London and for local buses.

By Car   From London, take M3 southwest, but near the end take A30 toward Salisbury, where you connect with A354 for the final approach to Dorchester.

VISITOR INFORMATION
The **telephone area code** is 01305. The **Tourist Information Centre** is at Unit ll, Antelope Walk. (☎ **01305/267992**).

WHAT TO SEE & DO
IN TOWN

Dorset County Museum
High West St. (next to St. Peter's Church). ☎ **01305/262735**. Admission £2.35 ($3.70) adults, £1.20 ($1.90) children 5–16 and senior citizens, free for children 4 and under. July–Aug, daily 10am–5pm; Sept–June, Mon–Sat 10am–5pm.

Impressions

Casterbridge [Dorchester] was the complement of the rural life around: not its urban opposite. Bees and butterflies in the cornfields at the top of the town, who desired to get to the meads at the bottom, took no circuitous course, but flew straight down High Street without any apparent consciousness that they were traversing strange latitudes. And in autumn airy spheres of thistledown floated into the same street, lodged upon the shop fronts, blew into drains, and innumerable tawny and yellow leaves skimmed along the pavement, and stole through people's doorways into their passages with a hesitating scratch on the floor, like the skirts of timid visitors.

—Thomas Hardy, *The Mayor of Casterbridge* (1886)

This museum has a gallery devoted to memorabilia of Thomas Hardy's life. In addition, you'll find an archeological gallery with displays and finds from Maiden Castle, Britain's largest Iron Age hill fort, plus galleries on the geology, local history, and natural history of Dorset.

IN NEARBY HIGHER BOCKHAMPTON

Hardy's Cottage

Higher Bockhampton. ☎ **01305/262366.** Admission £2.50 ($3.95). Apr–Oct, Fri–Wed 11am–6pm or dusk. Closed Nov–Mar.

Thomas Hardy was born in 1840 at Higher Bockhampton, 3 miles northeast of Dorchester and half a mile south of Blandford Road (A35). His home, now a National Trust property, may be visited by appointment. You approach the cottage on foot—it's a 10-minute walk after parking your vehicle in the space provided in the wood. Write in advance to Hardy's Cottage, Higher Bockhampton, Dorchester, Dorset DT2 8QJ, England, or call the number above.

Athelhampton House & Gardens

On A35, 1 mile east of Puddletown. ☎ **01305/848363.** Admission £4.20 ($6.65) adults, £1.50 ($2.35) children. July–Aug, Mon–Fri noon–5pm; Mar 27–June and Sept–Oct 30, Tues–Thurs and Sun noon–5pm. Take the Dorchester–Bournemouth road (A35) east of Dorchester for 5 miles.

This is one of England's great medieval houses and considered to be the most beautiful and historic in the south. Thomas Hardy mentioned the place in some of his writings but called it Athelhall. It was begun during the reign of Edward IV on the legendary site of King Athelstan's palace. A family home for more than 500 years, it's noted for its 15th-century Great Hall, Tudor great chamber, state bedroom, and King's Room. The house is on 10 acres of formal and landscaped gardens, with a 15th-century dovecote, river gardens, fish ponds, fountains, and rare trees. It's a mile east of Puddletown.

In 1992, the same year as the fire at Windsor Castle, a dozen of the house's rooms were damaged by an accidental fire caused by faulty wiring in the attic. However, skilled craftspeople restored all the magnificent interiors.

WHERE TO STAY & DINE

IN DORCHESTER

Inexpensive

Kings Arms Hotel

30 High East St., Dorchester, Dorset DT1 1HF. ☎ **01305/265353.** Fax 01305/260269. 31 rms, 2 suites. TV TEL. Mon–Thurs, £39.50 ($62.40) single; £79 ($124.80) double. Fri–Sun, £32.50 ($51.35) single; £65 ($102.70) double. Daily (including bottle of champagne and breakfast), £99 ($156.40) suite for two. Breakfast £3.45–£4.45 ($5.45–$7.05) extra. AE, DC, MC, V. Free parking.

In business for more than three centuries, the Kings Arms has great bow windows above the porch and a swinging sign hanging over the road, a legacy of its days as a coaching inn. An archway leads to the courtyard and parking area at the back of the hotel. All the rooms have been refurbished and have radios and hot-beverage facilities. A pub-style food emporium is also on the premises, dispensing platters-cum-bar-snacks priced at £2.75 to £15 ($4.35 to $23.70).

Impressions

It was a long low cottage with a hipped roof of thatch, having dormer windows breaking up into the eaves, a chimney standing in the middle of the ridge and another at each end. The window-shutters were not yet closed, and the fire- and candle-light within radiated forth upon the thick bushes of box and laurestinus growing in clumps outside, and upon the bare boughs of several codlin-trees hanging about in various distorted shapes, the result of earlier training as espaliers combined with careless climbing into their boughs in later years. The walls of the dwelling were for the most part covered with creepers, though these were rather beaten back from the doorway—a feature which was worn and scratched by much passing in and out, giving it by day the appearance of an old keyhole.

—Thomas Hardy, *Under the Greenwood Tree* (1872)

IN NEARBY EVERSHOT
Very Expensive

✪ Summer Lodge
Summer Lane, Evershot, Dorset DT2 0JR. ☎ **01935/83424.** Fax 01935/83005. 17 rms. TV TEL. £140 ($221.20) single; £205–£295 ($323.90–$466.10) double. Rates include English breakfast, afternoon tea, and four-course dinner. AE, DC, MC, V. Free parking. Head north from Dorchester on A37.

In this country-house hotel 15 miles north of Dorchester, the resident owners, Nigel and Margaret Corbett, provide care, courtesy, and comfort. Once home to the heirs of the earls of Ilchester, the country house, in the village of Evershot, stands on 4 acres of secluded gardens. Evershot appears as Evershed in *Tess of the D'Urbervilles*, and author Thomas Hardy designed a wing of the house. In this relaxed, informal atmosphere, the bedrooms have views either of the garden or over the village rooftops to the fields beyond. Although centrally heated, the hotel offers log fires in winter. Guests sit around the fire getting to know each other in a convivial atmosphere.

The chefs specialize in properly prepared traditional English dishes, placing the emphasis on home-grown and local produce. In addition to the dining room with its French windows, opening onto a terrace, the Corbetts have a bar, plus a heated outdoor pool and an all-weather tennis court.

IN NEARBY CHEDINGTON
Expensive

Chedington Court
Chedington, near Beaminster, Dorset DT8 3HY. ☎ **01935/891265.** Fax 01935/891442. 10 rms. TV TEL. £82–£102 ($129.55–$161.15) single; £144–£184 ($227.50–$290.70) double. Rates include half board. AE, DC, MC, V. Free parking. Drive 4¹/₂ miles southeast of Crewkerne, just off A356, to Winyard's Gap.

The Village of Chedington, 17 miles from Dorchester, is known to mapmakers and geographers as the source of two of England's famous rivers, the Axe and the Parrett. The legendary King Alfred is said to have found solace in this countryside from the pressures of ruling his kingdom. This Jacobean manor house—situated on 10 acres of terraces, gardens, and lawns—features mullioned windows, boldly angled gables, and steep slate roofs. The manor was converted into a 10-room hotel in 1981 by the establishment's owners, Philip and Hilary Chapman. Much of the style and some of the grandeur of the Victorians have been preserved. There's a glassed-in conservatory laden with mimosa. The bedrooms are individually furnished, sometimes with antiques, canopied beds, and fireplaces, along with some elegant accessories. One contains satinwood furniture that once adorned a suite aboard the *Queen Mary.*

The fresh and flavorful meals served in the dining room from 7 to 9pm are a high point of the day. Each is carefully prepared and presented in a room with a view over the garden. The hotel has its own 18-hole, par-74 golf course nearby.

In Nearby Lower Bockhampton

Moderate

Yalbury Cottage Country House Hotel and Restaurant

Lower Bockhampton, near Dorchester, Dorset DT2 8PZ. ☎ **01305/262382.** Fax 01305/266412. 8 rms. TV TEL. £54–£57 ($85.30–$90.05) single; £88–£94 ($139.05–$148.50) double. Rates include half board. MC, V. Free parking. Head 2 miles east of Dorchester (A35) and watch for signs to Lower Bockhampton.

This thatch-roofed cottage with inglenooks and beamed ceilings is in a small country village within walking distance of Thomas Hardy's cottage and Stinsford Church, where his heart is buried. The comfortably furnished and equipped bedrooms overlook the gardens or fields beyond, reflecting a mood of tranquillity. The bedrooms have all pinewood furniture in the English cottage style. Each has hot-beverage facilities, hairdryer, and other small touches for guests' added comfort.

The restaurant is open, evening only, for both residents and nonresidents. Well-flavored sauces and lightly cooked fresh vegetables enhance traditional English and continental dishes. The dining room is open to nonresidents; it costs £17.50 ($27.65) for a table d'hôte dinner.

8 Chideock & Charmouth

157 miles SW of London, 1 mile W of Bridport

Chideock is a charming village hamlet of thatched houses with a dairy farm in the center. About a mile from the coast, it's a gem of a place for overnight stopovers, and even better for longer stays. The countryside, with its rolling hills, may tempt you to go exploring.

On Lyme Bay, Charmouth, like Chideock, is another winner. A village of Georgian houses and thatched cottages, Charmouth provides some of the most dramatic coastal scenery in West Dorset. The village is west of Golden Cap, which, according to the adventurers who measure such things, is the highest cliff along the coast of southern England.

ESSENTIALS

Getting There

By Train   The nearest connection is Dorchester (see above).

By Bus   Buses run frequently throughout the day west from both Dorchester and Bridport.

By Car   From Bridport, continue west along A35.

VISITOR INFORMATION

The **telephone area code** for Chideock and Charmouth is 01297.

WHERE TO STAY & DINE
IN CHIDEOCK
Inexpensive

⊛ Chideock House Hotel

Main St., Chideock, Dorset DT6 6JN. ☎ **01297/489242.** 9 rms, 8 with bath. £25 ($39.50) single without bath, £30 ($47.40) single with bath; £50 ($79) double with bath. Rates include English breakfast. MC, V. Free parking. Bus 31 from Bridport.

In a village of winners, this 15th-century thatched house is perhaps the prettiest. The house was used by the Roundheads in 1645, and the ghosts of the village martyrs still haunt the house since their trial was held here. The resident owners are Anna and George Dunn. Located near the road, with a protective stone wall, the house has a garden in back, and a driveway leads to a large parking area. The beamed lounge has two fireplaces, one an Adam fireplace with a wood-burning blaze on cool days. All the bedrooms have hot-beverage facilities. The restaurant, serving both French and English cuisine, offers a £12.50 ($19.75) table d'hôte dinner Monday through Saturday from 7 to 9pm. On Sunday, only lunch is offered, costing £8.95 ($14.15) for a fixed-price menu served from noon to 2pm.

IN CHARMOUTH
Moderate
White House

2 Hillside, The Street, Charmouth, Dorset DT6 6PJ. ☎ **01297/560411.** Fax 01297/560702. 7 rms, 3 suites (all with bath or shower), 1 suite. TV TEL. £41–£48.50 ($64.80–$76.65) single; £72–£77 ($113.75–$121.65) double; £86–£92 ($135.90–$145.35) suite. Rates include English breakfast. AE, DC, MC, V. Free parking. Closed Dec. Bus 31 from Bridport.

The White House is a Georgian home, with much of its period architecture, including bow doors, well preserved. It's tastefully furnished in a traditional style in keeping with the character of the house. John and Mollie Balfour took this place, constructed in 1827, and turned it into a most comfortable place at which to stay. Each of their handsomely furnished bedrooms has hot-beverage facilities. Bar lunches are available during the day; at night home-cooked dishes, with a selection of carefully chosen wines, are offered. West Country regional dishes are featured, including, for example, Dorset honeyed duckling. Dinners begin at £18.50 ($29.25).

9 Lyme Regis

160 miles SW of London, 25 miles W of Dorchester

On Lyme Bay near the Devonshire border, the resort of Lyme Regis is one of the most attractive centers along the south coast. For those who shun big, commercial holiday centers, Lyme Regis is ideal—it's the true English coastal town with a highly praised mild climate. Sea gulls fly overhead; the streets are steep and winding; walks along Cobb Beach are brisk and stimulating; the views, particularly of the craft in the harbor, are so photogenic that John Fowles, a longtime resident of the town, selected it as the site for the 1980 filming of his novel *The French Lieutenant's Woman*. During its heyday, the town was a major seaport. (The duke of Monmouth landed here on return from his exile in Holland in 1685, followed by an unsuccessful attempt to overthrow the regime of his father, Charles II.) Later, Lyme developed into a small spa, including among its clientele Jane Austen. She wrote her final novel, *Persuasion* (published posthumously and based partly on the town's life), after staying here in 1803 and 1804.

Today, one of the town's most visible spokespersons is Richard J. Fox, three-time winner of Britain's cherished Town Crier Award. Famed for his declamatory delivery of official (and sometimes irreverent) proclamations, he followed a 1,000-year-old tradition of newscasting. Dressed as Thomas Payne, a dragoon who died in Lyme Regis in 1644 during the Civil War, Mr. Fox leads visitors on a 2-hour walk around the town every Tuesday at 3pm, beginning at Guildhall, mentioned below. No reservations are necessary, and the price is £1.20 ($1.90) for adults and 80p ($1.25) for children. He can be reached on the premises of **Country Stocks,** 53 Broad St. (☎ **01297/443568**). This shop sells such wares as sweets, antiques, and gifts and is open daily from 10am to 5pm.

Another famous building is **The Guildhall,** Bridge Street (call the tourist office), whose Mary and John Wing (built in 1620) houses the completed sections of an enormous tapestry woven by local women. Depicting Britain's colonization of North America, it's composed of a series of 11- by 4-foot sections, each of which took a team of local women 11 months to weave. Admission is free, but if anyone wants to add a stitch to the final tapestry as a kind of charitable donation, it costs £1 ($1.60). It's open Monday through Friday from 10am to 4pm.

The surrounding area is a fascinating place for botanists and zoologists because of the predominance of blue lias, a sedimentary rock well suited to the formation of fossils. In 1810 Mary Anning (at the age of 11) discovered one of the first articulated ichthyosaur skeletons. She went on to become one of the first professional fossilists in England. Books outlining walks in the area and the regions where fossils can be studied are available at the local information bureau, mentioned above.

ESSENTIALS
GETTING THERE

By Train   Take the London–Exeter train, getting off at Axminster and continuing the rest of the way by bus.

By Bus   Bus no. 31 runs from Axminster to Lyme Regis at the rate of one coach per hour during the day. There's also National Express bus service (no. 705) that runs daily in summer at 9:50am from Exeter to Lyme Regis, taking $1^3/4$ hours.

By Car   From Bridport, continue west along A35, cutting south to the coast at the junction with A3070.

VISITOR INFORMATION

The **telephone area code** for Lyme Regis is 01297. The **Tourist Information Centre** is at Guildhall Cottage, Church Street (☎ **01297/442138**).

WHERE TO STAY & DINE
INEXPENSIVE

Alexandra Hotel

Pound St., Lyme Regis, Dorset DT7 3HZ. ☎ **01297/442010.** Fax 01297/443229. 27 rms. TV TEL. £45 ($71.10) single; £75–£105 ($118.50–$165.90) double. Rates include English breakfast. AE, DC, MC, V. Free parking.

Built in 1735, this hotel, situated on a hill about 5 minutes from the center of town, was originally the home of the dowager Countess Poulett and was later owned by the duke de Stacpoole. But by the turn of the century it had reverted from an aristocratic address to a hotel with well-furnished bedrooms. Today it has been discreetly modernized but with an awareness of its original character; it has 1½ acres of garden. Both table d'hôte and à la carte meals are offered in the hotel's excellent dining room, with dinner from £15 ($23.70).

⑤ Kersbrook Hotel and Restaurant

Pound Rd., Lyme Regis, Dorset DT7 3HX. ☎ 01297/442596. 8 rms. £55–£65 ($86.90–$102.70) single; £100–£110 ($158–$173.80) double. Rates include half board. AE, MC, V. Free parking. Closed Dec–Jan.

Built of stone in 1790 and crowned by a thatch roof, the Kersbrook sits on a ledge above the village, which provides a panoramic view of the coast, on 1½ acres of gardens landscaped according to the original 18th-century plans. The public rooms have been refurnished with antique furniture, re-creating old-world charm yet with modern facilities. Mr. and Mrs. Eric Hall Stephenson are the resident proprietors.

The hotel is justifiably proud of its pink, candlelit restaurant, serving table d'hôte and à la carte meals daily from 7:30 to 9:30pm, with an extensive wine list. The chef is known as an artist in the kitchen. A traditional Old English and French cuisine is served, with dinner costing £16.50 ($26.05)and up and a set lunch going for £7.95 to £8.95 ($12.55 to $14.15).

Royal Lion

Broad St., Lyme Regis, Dorset DT7 3QF. ☎ 01297/445622. Fax 01297/445859. 30 rms. TV TEL. £33–£35 ($52.15–$55.30) single; £66–£70 ($104.30–$110.60) double. Rates include English breakfast. AE, DC, MC, V. Free parking.

This hotel was built in 1610 as a coaching inn, growing throughout the years to incorporate oak-paneled bars, lounges, and comfortably up-to-date bedrooms. Situated in the center of town on a hillside climbing up from the sea, the hotel features country-inspired furnishings and such venerable antiques as the canopied bed that was used regularly by Edward VII when he was prince of Wales. On the premises is an indoor swimming pool, a Jacuzzi, a minigym, a cocktail lounge, and a pub. Bar snacks are dispensed daily from noon to 2pm, priced at £1.95 ($3.10) to £5.30 ($8.35). Evenings, the restaurant serves à la carte and fixed-price meals beginning at £14.25 ($22.50) per person every night from 7:30 to 9pm (last orders).

10 Shaftesbury

100 miles SW of London, 29 miles NE of Dorchester

The origins of this typical Dorsetshire market town date back to the 9th century when King Alfred founded the abbey and made his daughter the first abbess. King Edward the Martyr was buried here, and King Canute died in the abbey but was buried in Winchester. Little now remains of the abbey, but the ruins are beautifully laid out. The museum adjoining St. Peter's Church at the top of Gold Hill provides a good idea of what the ancient Saxon hilltop town was like.

Today, ancient cottages with thatched roofs and tiny paned windows line the steep cobbled streets and modern stores compete with the outdoor market on High Street and the cattle market off Christy's Lane. The town is an excellent center from which to visit Hardy Country (it appears as Shaston in *Jude the Obscure*), Stourhead Gardens, and Longleat House.

ESSENTIALS
GETTING THERE

By Train   There is no direct access. Take the Exeter train leaving from London's Waterloo Station to Gillingham in Dorset, where a 4-mile bus or taxi ride to Shaftesbury awaits you. Trains from London run every 2 hours.

By Bus   Connections are possible from London's Victoria Coach Station once a day. There are also two or three daily connections from Bristol, Bath, Bournemouth, and Salisbury.

By Car   Head west from London on M3, continuing along A303 until the final approach by A350.

VISITOR INFORMATION

The **telephone area code** is 01747. The **Tourist Information Centre,** at 8 Bell St. (☎ **01747/853514**), is open daily from April to October, but Saturday only from November to March.

WHERE TO STAY & DINE
IN SHAFTESBURY
Moderate

Royal Chase Hotel
Royal Chase Roundabout, Shaftesbury, Dorset SP7 8DB. ☎ **01747/853355.** Fax 01747/851969. 34 rms. TV TEL. £49.50 ($78.20) single; £87.40 ($138.10) double. Rates include English breakfast. AE, DC, MC, V. Free parking.

This was once a button-making factory and later a monastery, but now it's a delightfully informal hotel at the junction of A30 and A350. Early-morning tea and a newspaper are complimentary. The bedrooms are comfortably furnished and well equipped. The hotel offers an indoor swimming pool and a Turkish steam room.

A meal in the elegant Byzant Restaurant, which begins at £19.90 ($29.90), includes several regional dishes such as local trout, seasonal game, and venison marinated in sherry. Dinner is served nightly from 7 to 9:30pm. A more informal restaurant, the Country Restaurant, serves light meals, snacks, and children's favorites throughout the day. They serve Thomas Hardy's Ale, featured in the *Guinness Book of Records* as the strongest beer available in a bottle. Even for less fanatical drinkers, the bar, dominated by an open-kitchen range and decorated with Dorsetshire bygones, is an attraction. There are traditional bar games, shove ha'penny, and table skittles at which to pitch your skill.

IN NEARBY STURMINSTER NEWTON
Moderate

✪ Plumber Manor
Hazelbury Bryan Rd. (off A357), Sturminster Newton, Dorset DT10 2AF. ☎ **01258/472507.** Fax 01258/473370. 16 rms. TV TEL. £65–£75 ($102.70–$118.50) single; £84–£115 ($132.70–$181.70) double. Rates include English breakfast. AE, DC, MC, V. Free parking. Closed Feb.

This Jacobean manor house, on 600 acres of farmland less than 2 miles southwest of Sturminster Newton, has been lived in by the Prideaux-Brune family since the early 17th century. The present inhabitants, Richard Prideaux-Brune and his wife, Alison, open the lovely old place to guests. Downstairs, a large hall from which the staircase rises is decorated with family portraits. A comfortable lounge is furnished with antiques. There's a bar to serve the restaurant, made up of three connecting dining rooms where guests can sample the excellent cooking of Brian Prideaux-Brune, Richard's brother. Upstairs, a gallery leads to some of the bedrooms, opening onto views over the gardens and the countryside. The others, in a long, low stone barn across the courtyard from the stable block (large umbrellas are provided to make the crossing if necessary), are well designed, with wide window seats, views over the gardens, and well-chosen furnishings. Three-course dinners, which range from £20 to £25 ($31.60 to $39.50) per person, are from a series of menus offering choices in each category. Try the English lamb or roast pheasant in port sauce. All main courses are served with fresh vegetables. Plumber Manor has a family atmosphere, with the Prideaux-Brunes treating their clientele as houseguests.

AN EASY EXCURSION

The ruined 14th-century English Heritage castle has a lakeside setting on the landscaped grounds of New Wardour Castle, a 1776 Palladian mansion that is now a private home. **Old Wardour Castle** (☎ **01747/870487**), built in 1392 by Lord Lovel, was acquired in 1547 by the Arundell family and modernized in 1578. After being besieged during the Civil War, however, it was abandoned. Today it houses displays on the war sieges and the landscape, as well as an architectural exhibition. It lies 1¹/₂ miles north of A30 going west out of Salisbury, 2 miles southwest of Tisbury. Admission is £1.50 ($2.35) for adults, 85p ($1.35) for children 5 to 16, free for children 3 and under. It's open from April to September, daily from 10am to 6pm; in October, daily from 10am to 4pm; and November to March, Wednesday through Sunday from 10am to 4pm.

Three miles west of Wardour is a privately owned manor house, **Hook Manor,** which North Americans might like to know was built by Cecil Calvert, the second Lord Baltimore, the staunchly Catholic cofounder of Maryland. Today, the city of Annapolis, Maryland, has a historic center known as the Wardour District, whose name derives from the famous nearby castle. Wardour, translated from the Celtic, means "defensive riverbank." Wardour Castle and the surrounding district remained Catholic throughout the Cromwellian Wars, its peerage abandoned by the largely Protestant monarchists later on in English history.

11 Sherborne

128 miles SW of London, 19 miles NW of Dorchester

A little gem of a town, with well-preserved medieval, Tudor, Stuart, and Georgian buildings, Sherborne is in the heart of Dorset, surrounded by wooded hills, valleys, and chalk downs. It was here that Sir Walter Raleigh lived before his fall from fortune.

ESSENTIALS
GETTING THERE

By Train   Frequent trains throughout the day depart from London's Waterloo Station (trip time: 2 hr.).

By Bus   There is one National Express coach departure daily from London's Victoria Coach Station.

By Car   Take M3 west from London, continuing southwest on 303 and B3145.

VISITOR INFORMATION

The **telephone area code** is 01935. The **Tourist Information Centre** is on Digby Road (☎ **01935/815341**).

WHAT TO SEE & DO

In addition to the attractions listed below, you can go to **Cerne Abbas,** a village south of Sherborne, to see the Pitchmarket, where Thomas and Maria Washington, uncle and aunt of America's George Washington, once lived.

Sherborne Old Castle

Castleton, off A30, half a mile east of Sherborne. ☎ **01935/812730.** Admission £1.30 ($2.05) adults, £1 ($1.60) senior citizens and students, 70p ($1.10) children 5–16, free for children 4 and under. Apr–Sept, daily 10am–1pm and 2–6pm; Oct, daily 10am–1pm and 2–4pm; Nov–Mar, Wed–Sun 10am–1pm and 2–4pm. Closed Jan 1 and Dec 24–26. Follow the signs 1 mile east from the town center.

The castle was built in the early 12th century by the powerful Bishop Roger de Caen, but it was seized by the Crown at about the time of King Henry I's death in 1135 and Stephen's troubled accession to the throne. The castle was given to Sir Walter Raleigh by Queen Elizabeth I. The gallant knight built Sherborne Lodge in the deer park close by (now privately owned). The buildings were mostly destroyed in the Civil War, but you can still see a gate house, some graceful arcades, and decorative windows.

Sherborne Castle

Cheap St. (off New Road a mile east of the center). ☎ **01935/813182.** Castle and grounds, £3.60 ($5.70) adults, £1.80 ($2.85) children; grounds only, £1.50 ($2.35) adults, 80p ($1.25) children. Easter–Sept, Thurs, Sat–Sun, and bank holidays 12:30–5pm.

Sir Walter Raleigh built this castle in 1594, when he decided that it would not be feasible to restore the old castle to suit his needs. This Elizabethan residence was a square mansion, to which later owners added four Jacobean wings to make it more palatial. After King James I had Raleigh imprisoned in the Tower of London, the monarch gave the castle to a favorite Scot, Robert Carr, and banished the Raleighs from their home. In 1617 it became the property of Sir John Digby, first earl of Bristol, and has been the Digby family home ever since. The mansion was enlarged by Sir John in 1625, and in the 18th century the formal Elizabethan gardens and fountains of the Raleighs were altered by Capability Brown, who created a serpentine lake between the two castles. The 20 acres of lawns and pleasure grounds around the 50-acre lake are open to the public. In the house are fine furniture, china, and paintings by Gainsborough, Lely, Reynolds, Kneller, and van Dyck, among others.

Sherborne Abbey

Abbey Close. ☎ **01935/812452.** Admission free but donations for upkeep welcomed. Apr–Sept, daily 10am–6pm; Oct–Mar, daily 9am–4pm.

One of the great churches of England, this abbey was founded in 705 as the Cathedral of the Saxon Bishops of Wessex. In the late 10th century it became a Benedictine monastery, and since the Reformation it has been a parish church. It's famous for its fan-vaulted roof, added by Abbot Ramsam at the end of the 15th century; this was the first fan vault of wide span erected in England. Inside are many fine monuments, including Purbeck marble effigies of medieval abbots as well as Elizabethan "four-poster" and canopied tombs. The baroque statue of the earl of Bristol stands between his two wives and dates from 1698. A public school occupies the abbey's surviving medieval monastic buildings and was the setting for a novel by Alec Waugh, *The Loom of Youth*, and for the MGM classic film *Goodbye, Mr. Chips*, starring Robert Donat. The most recent film shot here was Terence Rattigan's *The Browning Version*, starring Albert Finney.

WHERE TO STAY & DINE
MODERATE

Eastbury Hotel

Long St., Sherborne, Dorset DT9 3BY. ☎ **01935/813131.** Fax 01935/817296. 15 rms. TV TEL. £45 ($71.10) single; £65–£80 ($102.70–$126.40) double. Rates include English breakfast. AE, DC, MC, V. Free parking.

This Georgian town-house hotel is situated in its own walled garden near the 8th-century abbey and Sherborne's two castles. Built in 1740 during the reign of George II, it has a traditional ambience, with its own library of antiquarian books. Beautifully restored, it still maintains its 18th-century character. The best fresh English produce is served in the dining room, which has an extensive wine list. Meals begin at £13.50 ($21.35).

INEXPENSIVE

Sherborne Hotel

Horsecastles Lane, Sherborne, Dorset DT9 6BB. ☎ **01935/813191.** Fax 01935/816493. 59 rms. TV TEL. £59.50 ($94) single or double Mon–Thurs, £29–£38 ($45.80–$60.05) Fri–Sun (including English breakfast). English breakfast £6.95 ($11) extra. AE, DC, MC, V. Free parking.

Built of red brick in 1969, near the A30 road and about a mile west of Sherborne's center, this hotel was designed in a two-story low-rise format near a school and a scattering of factories and houses. Although popular with business travelers, it's more elegant than a typical roadside hotel, with more amenities than might be expected and easy access to Sherborne's historic center. The bedrooms are conservatively modern, each with satellite TV. There's a bar on the premises, and Castles Restaurant, where fixed-price dinners cost £16.95 ($26.80) and à la carte lunches begin at around £6.50 ($10.25). The staff is efficient and helpful.

The great patchwork quilt area of southwest England, part of the "West Countree," abounds in cliffside farms, rolling hills, foreboding moors, semitropical plants, and fishing villages that provide some of the finest scenery in England. The British approach sunny Devon with the same kind of excitement one would normally reserve for hopping over to the Continent. Especially along the coastline—the English Riviera—the names of the seaports, villages, and resorts have been synonymous with holidays in the sun: Torquay, Clovelly, Lynton-Lynmouth.

It's easy to involve yourself in West Country life. You can pony trek across moor and woodland, past streams and sheep-dotted fields, or stop at local pubs to soak up atmosphere and ale.

Devon is a land of jagged coasts—the red cliffs in the south face the English Channel. In South Devon, the coast from which Drake and Raleigh set sail, the tranquil life prevails, and on the bay-studded coastline of North Devon, pirates and smugglers found haven. The heather-clad uplands of Exmoor, with red deer, extend into North Devon from Somerset—a perfect setting for an English mystery. Much of the district is already known to those who have read Victorian novelist R. D. Blackmore's romance of the West Country, *Lorna Doone.* Aside from the shores, many of the scenic highlights are in the two national parks: Dartmoor in the south, Exmoor in the north.

Almost every hamlet is geared to accommodate tourists. However, many small towns and fishing villages don't allow cars to enter; these towns have parking areas on the outskirts, but this can involve a long walk to reach the center of the harbor area. From mid-July to mid-September the most popular villages are quite crowded, and you should have a reservation since the number of hotels is limited. Perhaps your oddly shaped bedroom will be in a barton (farm) mentioned in the *Domesday Book,* or in a thatched cottage.

Devon General and Western National Bus Lines combine to offer a discounted **"Key West Ticket."** Adults, for example, can enjoy unlimited use of the lines at these rates: £12.95 ($20.45) for 3 days, £21.95 ($34.70) for 7 days, or 1 month for £81 ($128). For families (two adults and two children 13 and under), there's only a 3-day ticket at £29.95 ($47.30) or a 7-day ticket at £43.95 ($69.45). You can plan your journeys from the maps and timetables available at any Western National/Devon General office when you purchase

---

What's Special About Devon

Beaches
- The English Riviera, 22 miles of Devonshire coastline and 18 beaches, with Torquay at the center—even palm trees grow here.

Great Towns/Villages
- Exeter, a university city rebuilt after the 1940s bombings around its venerable cathedral, with notable waterfront buildings.
- Plymouth, the largest city in Devon and a major port and sea base, from which the Pilgrims set sail on the *Mayflower* for the New World.
- Torquay, Devon's premier seaside resort, which grew from a small fishing village—it's set against a backdrop of colorful cliffs and beaches.
- Clovelly, cascading down a mountainside, considered by many the most charming village in England.

Natural Spectacles
- Dartmoor National Park, northeast of Plymouth, a landscape of gorges and moors filled with gorse and purple heather, and home of the Dartmoor pony.

Buildings
- Exeter Cathedral, dating from Saxon times and built in the "decorated" style of the 13th and 14th centuries.
- Buckland Abbey, near Yelverton, the former home of the dashing Sir Francis Drake, hero to the English, "pirate" to the Spanish.

Film Location
- Powderham Castle, outside Exeter, backdrop for *Remains of the Day* (1993), starring Anthony Hopkins and Emma Thompson.

---

your ticket. Further information may be obtained from Devon General Ltd., Paris Street, Exeter, Devon EX1 2JP (☎ **01392/42771**).

A DRIVING TOUR

Day 1   Begin in Exeter, 201 miles southwest of London, and visit its cathedral, one of the most famous in the West Country, and its other attractions such as the Guildhall, St. Nicholas Priory, and the Underground Passages. In the afternoon explore Powderham Castle at Powderham, where *Remains of the Day* was filmed, and return to Exeter for the night.

Day 2   The whole day can be spent exploring Dartmoor, one of Britain's most famed national parks. Here you can visit the Museum of Dartmoor Life, go horseback riding, or take walking tours. The best centers for spending the night are Ashburton, Lydford, and Two Bridges.

Day 3   Head for Chagford, which is only 13 miles west of Exeter, visiting Castle Drogo and Sir Francis Drake's House. This little town has some of the best places to stay in Devon, notably the Gidleigh Park Hotel, although it offers far cheaper digs than that. Many writers have holed up here to complete a book, such as *Brideshead Revisited*.

Day 4   Continue south toward the English Channel, visiting Totnes in the morning and proceeding to Torquay for the night. Along with Paignton and Brixham, Torquay is the center of what is called the English Riviera. It doesn't have the rural charm that people come to Devon for, but it's a change of pace and lets you see "English life as uniquely experienced at its seaside resorts." Stay overnight there.

Day 5   Continue southwest for a morning visit to Dartmouth. Perhaps you'll have lunch there before descending on Plymouth for the night. In Plymouth you'll want to explore the Barbican with its mass of narrow streets and various other attractions that will consume the rest of your day.

⬤ **TAKE A BREAK**   The Plymouth Arts Centre Restaurant, 38 Looe St., Plymouth (☎ **01752/660060**), offers one of the most filling and downhome meals in town. Prices range from £2 to £4 ($3.15 to $6.30), and it's also ideal for a snack. You can even see a movie downstairs if you'd like. Food service is Monday from 10am to 2pm, Tuesday through Saturday from 10am to 8pm, and Sunday from 5:30 to 7:30pm.

Day 6   At this point, and if you have time, you can visit Cornwall (see Chapter 13). However, to continue your exploration of Devon, cut north across the county through some of the most beautiful rural scenery in England, reaching the village of Clovelly for lunch, where you can dine at one of its quaint old inns. Then continue east for an overnight stay at the twin resorts of Lynton or Lynmouth, which lie at the doorway to Exmoor National Park.

1 Exeter

201 miles SW of London, 46 miles NE of Plymouth

The county town of Devonshire, on the banks of the river Exe, Exeter was a Roman city founded in the 1st century A.D. Two centuries later it was encircled by a mighty stone wall, traces of which remain today. Conquerors and would-be conquerors, especially Vikings, stormed the fortress in later centuries; none was more notable than William the Conqueror. Irked at Exeter's refusal to capitulate (perhaps also because it sheltered Gytha, mother of the slain Harold), the Norman duke brought Exeter to its knees on short notice.

Under the Tudors the city grew and prospered. Sir Walter Raleigh and Sir Francis Drake were two of the striking figures who strolled through Exeter's streets. In May 1942 the Germans bombed Exeter, destroying many of the city's architectural treasures. Exeter was rebuilt, but the new, impersonal-looking shops and offices can't replace the Georgian crescents and the black-and-white–timbered buildings with their plastered walls. Fortunately, much was spared.

ESSENTIALS
GETTING THERE

By Plane   Exeter Airport (☎ **01392/367433**) serves the southwest, offering both charter and scheduled flights. Lying 5 miles east of the historic center of Exeter, the airport has a modern terminal with excellent facilities, including taxis, car rentals, bars, a food buffet, an exchange bureau, and shops. It has scheduled flights to Belfast, Jersey, Cork, Dublin, and the Isles of Scilly among other connections. There are no direct flights to London.

By Train Trains from London's Paddington Station depart every hour during the day (trip time: $2^1/_2$ hr.). Trains also run once an hour during the day between Exeter and Plymouth (trip time: $1^1/_4$ hr.).

By Bus A National Express coach departs from London's Victoria Coach Station every 30 minutes during the day (trip time: 4 hr.). You can also take bus no. 38 or 39 between Plymouth and Exeter. During the day two coaches depart per hour (trip time: 1 hr.).

By Car From London, take M4 west, cutting south to Exeter on M5 (junction near Bristol).

VISITOR INFORMATION

The **telephone area code** is 01392. The **Tourist Information Centre** is at the Civic Centre, Paris Street (☎ **01392/265700**).

WHAT TO SEE & DO

Just off "The High," at the top of Castle Street, stands an impressive **Norman Gate House** from William the Conqueror's Castle. Although only the house and walls survive, the view from here and the surrounding gardens is panoramic.

IN TOWN

✪ Exeter Cathedral

1 The Cloisters. ☎ **01392/55573**. Admission free, though a donation of £2 ($3.15) is requested of adults. Mon–Fri 7:15am–6:15pm, Sat–Sun 8:30am–6:30pm.

The Roman II Augusta Legion made its camp on the site where the Cathedral Church of Saint Peter now stands in Exeter. It has been occupied by Britons, Saxons, Danes, and Normans. The English Saint Boniface, who converted northern Germany to Christianity, was trained here in 690. Bishop Leofric was installed here as bishop for Devon and Cornwall in 1050 by Edward the Confessor. The conqueror's nephew, Bishop Warelwast, began building the present cathedral about 1112, and the twin Norman towers still stand. Between the towers runs the longest uninterrupted true gothic vault in the world, at a height of 66 feet and to a length of 300 feet. This was completed in 1369 and is the finest existing example of decorated gothic architecture, featuring rare tierceron arches, large matching windows, and decorated corbels and bosses. The Puritans destroyed the cathedral Cloisters in 1650 and a German bomb destroyed the twin Chapels of St. James and St. Thomas in May 1942. Now restored, it's one of the prettiest churches anywhere. Its famous choir sings evensong every day except Wednesday.

Exeter Guildhall

High St. ☎ **01392/265500**. Admission free. Easter–Oct, Mon–Fri 10:30am–1pm and 2–4pm, Sat 10:30am–1pm; Nov–Easter, Mon–Fri 10:30am–1pm and 2–4pm, alternate Sats 10:30am–1pm.

This colonnaded building on the main street is regarded as the oldest municipal building in the kingdom—the earliest reference to the guildhall is in a deed from 1160. The Tudor front that straddles the pavement was added in 1593. Inside you'll find a fine display of silver, plus a number of paintings, including one of Henrietta Anne, daughter of Charles I (born in Exeter in 1644). The ancient hall is paneled in oak.

Devon

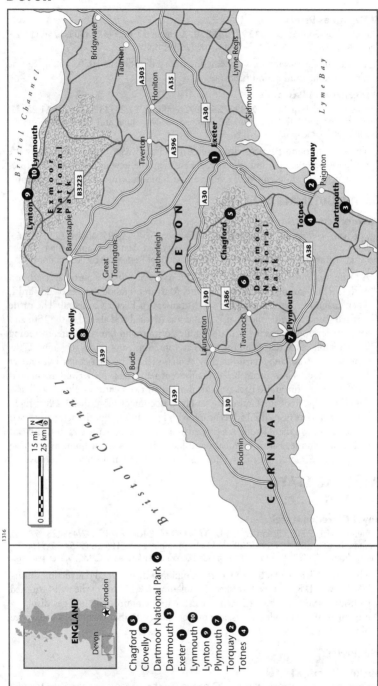

St. Nicholas Priory

The Mint, off Fore St. ☎ **01392/265858.** Admission £1.25 ($2) adults, 75p ($1.20) children. Easter–Oct, Mon–Sat 1–5pm. Closed Nov–Easter.

This is the guest wing of a Benedictine priory founded in 1070. You'll see fine plaster ceilings and period furniture.

Underground Passages

Boots Corner, off High St. ☎ **01392/265887.** Admission £2.25 ($3.55) adults, £1.25 ($2) children. Apr and July–Sept, Mon–Sat 10am–5pm; May–June and Oct–Easter, Tues–Fri 2–5pm, Sat 10am–5pm.

The Underground Passages, accessible from High Street, were built to carry the medieval water supply into the city. By entering the new underground interpretation center, visitors can view a video and exhibition before taking a guided tour.

ON THE OUTSKIRTS OF EXETER

Powderham Castle

Powderham, Kenton. ☎ **0626/890243.** Admission £4.40 ($6.95) adults, £2.95 ($4.65) children 5–17, free for children 4 and under. Easter–Oct, Sun–Fri 10am–5:30pm. Closed Nov–Easter. Take the A379 Dawlish road 8 miles south of Exeter; the castle is signposted.

A castle was built here in the late 14th century by Sir Philip Courtenay, sixth son of the second earl of Devon, and his wife, Margaret, granddaughter of Edward I. Their magnificent tomb is in the south transept of Exeter Cathedral. The castle suffered damage during the Civil War and was restored and altered in the 18th and 19th centuries. The castle has many family portraits and fine furniture, including a remarkable clock that plays full tunes at 4pm, 8pm, and midnight, some 17th-century tapestries, and a chair used by William III for his first council of state at Newton Abbot. The staircase hall contains some remarkable plasterwork set in bold relief against a turquoise background, more than two centuries old, as well as a detailed pedigree of the Courtenay family, a document more than 12 feet high. The chapel dates from the 15th century, with hand-hewn roof timbers and carved pew ends. Powderham Castle is a private house occupied by the countess and earl of Devon, who let Ismail Merchant and James Ivory use their home as a setting for the film *Remains of the Day*, with Anthony Hopkins and Emma Thompson.

WHERE TO STAY
MODERATE

Royal Clarence Hotel

Cathedral Yard, Exeter, Devon EX1 1HD. ☎ **01392/58464.** Fax 01392/439423. 52 rms, 4 suites. TV TEL. £82–£89.50 ($129.55–$141.40) single; £98–£105.50 ($154.85–$166.70) double; from £135 ($213.30) suite. Rates include English breakfast. AE, DC, MC, V. Free parking.

The Royal Clarence Hotel is a Georgian building that escaped destruction during World War II. Recently refurbished, it's full of history. Many of the well-furnished bedrooms overlook the 14th-century cathedral. Comfortable lounges display a mixture of antiques, gilt mirrors, and modern pieces. In the restaurant, a fixed-price dinner costs £15 ($23.70). You can also order à la carte.

INEXPENSIVE

Buckerell Lodge Hotel

Topsham Rd., Exeter, Devon EX2 4SQ. ☎ **01392/52451,** or 800/528-1234 in the U.S. and Canada. Fax 01392/412114. 52 rms. TV TEL. £35 ($55.30) single; £75 ($118.50) double.

English breakfast £8.95 ($14.15) extra. AE, DC, MC, V. Free parking. Take B3182 1 mile southeast, off Junction 30 of M5. Bus K, T, or R.

Buckerell Lodge is perhaps the finest place to stay in the area. The origins of the house go back to the 12th century, but it has been altered and changed beyond recognition over the years. The exterior is a symmetrical and severely dignified building with a Regency feel to it; it's pierced with bay windows. The entire building was renovated in stages between 1992 and 1994. Often a choice of commercial travelers, it's also a tourist favorite, especially in summer. The look today is Regency, and the bedrooms are well decorated and nicely equipped and come in a range of styles and sizes.

On the premises, Raffles Restaurant is one of the finer dining choices in the area. Taking its name from the famed hotel in Singapore, it specializes in fresh fish, game, steaks, and poultry, and there's always something for the vegetarian. Both a table d'hôte and an à la carte menu are featured. Fixed-price lunches, served daily from noon to 2pm, cost £14.50 ($22.90), with a table d'hôte evening dinner, offered daily from 7:30 to 9:30pm, going for £19.95 ($31.50).

Devon Hotel

Exeter Bypass, Matford, Exeter, Devon EX2 8XU. ☎ **01392/59268.** Fax 01392/413142. 41 rms. TV TEL. Mon–Thurs, £47 ($74.25) single; £59 ($93.20) double. Fri–Sun, £40 ($63.20) single; £50 ($79) double. Rates include English breakfast. AE, DC, MC, V. Free parking.

The Devon Motel lies on the outskirts of the city at the western sector of the bypass on A38. It's convenient to the airport and as a stopping-off point for those headed for the West Country. Inside, all is compact and built-in, with a picture window overlooking the meadows beyond. On the premises are a restaurant and bars. An à la carte dinner begins at £11 ($17.40) and a four-course table d'hôte dinner costs £14 ($22.10).

Rougemont Hotel

Queens St. (opposite the central train station), Exeter, Devon EX4 3SP. ☎ **01392/54982.** Fax 01392/420928. 88 rms, 2 suites. TV TEL. £73 ($115.35) single; £83 ($131.15) double; £95–£120 ($150.10–$189.60) suite. Rates include English breakfast. AE, DC, MC, V. Free parking.

The Rougemont Hotel is imbued with a stylish flair that none of its competitors provides. Fairly recently, this great, old-fashioned Victorian hotel underwent renovations. Its neoclassical architecture is a background for the contemporary furnishings. Much of the comfort and tasteful decor are found in the bedrooms. A fixed-price dinner costs £16.95 ($26.80). Guests gather in the Adam-style Drake's Bar for drinks. A good stock of wine comes from the cellar, which, incidentally, was once a debtors' prison.

✪ St. Olaves Court Hotel

Mary Arches St. (off High St.), Exeter, Devon EX4 3AZ. ☎ **01392/217736,** or 800/ 544-9993 in the U.S. Fax 01392/413054. 15 rms. TV TEL. Mon–Thurs, £65–£75 ($102.70–$118.50) single; £80–£90 ($126.40-$142.20) double. Fri–Sun, £50 ($79) single; £60 ($94.80) double. Rates include continental breakfast. AE, DC, MC, V. Free parking.

The St. Olaves Court Hotel is such a favorite that it's almost considered a special address. A Georgian mansion, it is situated in the center of Exeter, having been constructed as a home by a rich merchant, circa 1830. The location is ideal, within a short walk of the cathedral—you can hear the church bells. The house has been discreetly furnished, in part with antiques. Each of the bedrooms has been individually decorated and has such amenities as hot-beverage facilities and radios. A trouser press, hairdryer, and what the English call a "hospitality tray" are found in every room, some of which are equipped with Jacuzzis.

The hotel also features an excellent English cuisine in its Golsworthy Restaurant, serving meals until 9:30pm (see our separate recommendation in "Where to Dine," below).

White Hart Hotel

65–66 South St., Exeter, Devon EX1 1EE. ☎ **01392/79897.** Fax 01392/50159. 60 rms. TV TEL. Mon–Thurs, £54.50 ($86.10) single; £78 ($123.25) double. Fri–Sun, £38 ($60.05) single; £48 ($75.85) double. Rates include English breakfast. AE, DC, MC, V. Free parking.

The White Hart Hotel, in the center of town, a coaching inn in the 17th and 18th centuries, is one of the oldest inns in the city. It is said that Cromwell stabled his horses here. The hotel is a mass of polished wood, slate floors, oak beams, and gleaming brass and copper. The bedrooms, which combine old and new, are equipped with bathtubs or showers. Guests are housed in either the old wing or a more modern one. Some units are considered deluxe.

Hostler's Dining Room, the hotel's main restaurant, serves breakfast and dinner only, plus a Sunday lunch with all the trimmings; the latter features fixed-price menus ranging from £6.95 to £9.75 ($11 to $15.40). The hotel has a wine cellar, which supplies the Ale & Port House (a bar with waiter service where you can feast on traditional English fare), plus the well-known Bottlescreu Bills wine bar, which offers beefsteak-and-oyster pie or, in summer, barbecued steak in the wine garden. You may want to patronize the bar even if you're not a guest. It's open Monday through Saturday from 11am to 11pm and Sunday from noon to 3pm and 7 to 10:30pm.

IN NEARBY BICKLEIGH

Perhaps the finest way to enjoy the cathedral city of Exeter, especially if you have a car, is to stay on the outskirts, 10 to 19 miles from the heart of the city. In the Exe Valley, 4 miles south of Tiverton and 10 miles north of Exeter, lies Bickleigh, a hamlet with a river, an arched stone bridge, a mill pond, and thatch-roofed cottages—the epitome of English charm, one of the finest spots in all of Devon.

Inexpensive

✪ Bickleigh Cottage Country Hotel

Bickleigh Bridge, Bickleigh, Devon EX16 8RJ. ☎ **01884/855230.** 9 rms. £28.50 ($45.05) single; £45 ($71.10) double. Rates include English breakfast. MC, V. Free parking. Closed Nov–Mar. Bus 55 from Exeter.

This is a thatched, 17th-century hotel with a riverside garden leading down to the much-photographed Bickleigh Bridge. Add to this image swans and ducks gliding by. Inside, the rooms are cozy with oak beams and old fireplaces. Mr. and Mrs. Stuart Cochrane, the owners, provide good and nourishing meals. The raspberries and gooseberries come fresh from the garden and are topped with generous portions of Devonshire cream. Dinner is priced from £10.50 ($16.60).

WHERE TO DINE
MODERATE

✪ Golsworthy Restaurant

In the St. Olaves Court Hotel, Mary Arches St. ☎ **01392/217736.** Reservations recommended. Main courses £12.50–£18.50 ($19.75–$29.25); fixed-price "light lunch" £10.50

($16.60); fixed-price lunch or dinner £13.50 ($21.35). AE, DC, MC, V. Sun–Fri noon–2pm and 6:30–9:30pm, Sat 6:30–9:30pm. CONTINENTAL.

Acknowledged as the finest restaurant in Exeter, this establishment is in a previously recommended hotel originally built as the home of a merchant (James Golsworthy) and later served briefly as a nunnery. Guests enjoy a before-dinner drink in a paneled bar that overlooks a verdant garden. The cuisine, which reflects the sophisticated Europeanized palate of the congenial owners, might include breast of wood pigeon served on a purée of lentils and a port-scented jus; pan-fried fillet of sea trout with herbed nut brown butter and fresh lemon; oven-roasted rack of Devon lamb with a rosemary-and-potato rösti and a madeira jus; salmon soufflé with mixed salad greens and a lemon-and-chive oil; baked breast of chicken filled with mushrooms and tarragon encased in puff pastry and served with glazed shallots; and pan-fried ribeye of beef with smoked ham and potato and mushroom gnocchi. Any of these might be followed by a salad of Stilton cheese with walnuts or a dark-chocolate tort with vanilla crème anglaise and orange salad.

INEXPENSIVE

Coolings Wine Bar

11 Gandy St. ☎ **01392/434184.** Soup £1.95 ($3.10); main courses £3.95–£4.95 ($6.25–$7.80); glass of wine from £1.75 ($2.75). MC, V. Mon–Sat 11am–11pm. Bus N. ENGLISH.

Situated in a Victorian building on a short, cobblestone street that intersects Exeter's High Street near the center of town is this beckoning place with beams, checkered tablecloths, and tables that spill over into the cellar. Wine by the glass includes many dozens of vintages from throughout Europe. The food, prepared on the premises, includes a plentiful selection of meats, pies, and quiches, as well as such changing specialties as chicken Waldorf and sugar-baked ham, braised beef and daily roasts, such as turkey, each served with freshly prepared salads. Hot platters are listed on a chalkboard, along with the featured wine of the day. Liquor is served daily Monday through Saturday from 11am to 11pm; however, the full menu is available only at lunch—noon to 2:30pm. After that, a more limited menu, mainly pub snacks, is served throughout the afternoon and evening. The menu is changed almost daily.

The Ship Inn

St. Martin's Lane. ☎ **01392/72040.** Reservations recommended. Restaurant, main courses £5.75–£11.95 ($9.10–$18.90). Pub, platters £2.50–£5.75 ($3.95–$9.10). MC, V. Restaurant, Mon–Sat noon–3pm and 6–9:30pm. Pub, Mon–Sat 11am–3pm, Sun noon–2pm (drinks, Mon–Sat 11am–11pm, Sun noon–3pm and 7–10:30pm). ENGLISH.

The Ship Inn was often visited by Sir Francis Drake, Sir Walter Raleigh, and Sir John Hawkins. Of it Drake wrote: "Next to mine own shippe, I do most love that old 'Shippe' in Exon, a tavern in Fyssh Street, as the people call it, or as the clergie will have it, St. Martin's Lane." The pub still provides tankards of real ale, lager, and stout, and is still loved by both young and old. A large selection of snacks is offered in the bar every day, while the restaurant upstairs provides more substantial English fare. At either lunch or dinner, you can order from a wide selection including French onion soup, whole grilled lemon sole, and five different steaks. The price of the main courses includes vegetables, a roll, and butter. Portions are large, as in Elizabethan times.

2 Dartmoor National Park

213 miles SW of London, 13 miles W of Exeter

This national park lies northeast of Plymouth, stretching from Tavistock and Okehampton on the west to near Exeter in the east, a granite mass that sometimes rises to a height of 2,000 feet above sea level. The landscape offers vistas of gorges with rushing water, gorse, and purple heather ranged over by Dartmoor ponies—a foreboding landscape for the experienced walker only.

Some 13 miles west from Exeter, the peaceful little town of **Moretonhampstead,** perched on the edge of Dartmoor, makes a good center. Moretonhampstead contains an old market cross and several 17th-century colonnaded almshouses.

The much-visited Dartmoor village of **Widecombe-in-the-Moor** is only 7 miles from Moretonhampstead. The fame of the village of Widecombe-in-the-Moor stems from an old folk song about Tom Pearce and his gray mare, listing the men who were supposed to be on their way to Widecombe Fair when they met with disaster: Bill Brewer, Jan Stewer, Peter Gurney, Peter Davy, Daniel Whiddon, Harry Hawke, and Old Uncle Tom Cobley. Widecombe also has a parish church worth visiting. Called the **Cathedral of the Moor,** with a roster of vicars beginning in 1253, the house of worship in a green valley is surrounded by legends. When the building was restored, a wall plate was found bearing the badge of Richard II (1377–99), the figure of a white hart.

In Dartmoor, you'll find 500 miles of footpaths and bridleways and more than 90,000 acres of common land with public access. The country is rough, and on the high moor you should always make sure you have good maps, a compass, and suitable clothing and shoes.

ESSENTIALS

GETTING THERE

By Train   Take the train down from London to Exeter (see above), then depend on local buses to connect you with the various villages of Dartmoor.

By Bus   Transmoor Link, a public transport bus service, usually operates throughout the summer and is an ideal way to get onto the moor. Information on the Transmoor Link and on the bus link between various towns and villages on Dartmoor is available from the Transport Co-ordination Centre (☎ 01392/382800).

By Car   Exeter is the most easily reached "gateway" by highway. From Exeter, continue west on B3212 to such centers of Dartmoor as Easton, Chagford, Moretonhampstead, and North Bovey. From these centers, tiny roads—often not really big enough for two cars—cut deeper into the moor.

VISITOR INFORMATION

See the individual recommendations for phone area codes. Accommodation information is operated by the **Dartmoor Tourist Association,** Duchy Building, Princetown, Yelverton, Devon PL20 6QF (☎ 01822/890567). Local information centers will also provide a list of accommodations.

WHAT TO SEE & DO

The Dartmoor National Park Authority (DNPA) runs **guided walks** of varying difficulty, ranging from 1¹/₂ to 6 hours for a trek of some 9 to 12 miles. All you have to do is turn up suitably clad at your selected starting point. Details are available from DNP information centers or from the **Dartmoor National Park Authority Headquarters,** Parke, Haytor Road, Bovey Tracey, Devon TQ13 9JQ (☎ **01626/832093**). The charge for walks is £1.50 to £3 ($2.35 to $4.75).

Throughout the area are stables where you can arrange for a day's trek across the moors. For ✪ **horseback riding** on Dartmoor there are too many establishments to list. All are licensed, and you are accompanied by an experienced rider/guide. The moor can be dangerous since sudden fogs descend without warning on treacherous marshlands. Prices are around £6 ($9.50) per hour, £13 ($20.55) for a half day, and £22 ($34.75) for a full day. Most riding stables are listed in a useful free publication, *The Dartmoor Visitor,* which also provides details on guided walks,

---

Frommer's Nature Notes

The surprising part about the moors near Dartmouth is that they exist at all, and haven't been swallowed up in a labyrinth of housing development. Set just 15 miles inland from the sea, and the largest open space in the southwest of England, they're a world removed from the beach-going playland of the British Riviera, which follows the coastline between nearby Plymouth and Torquay. Isolated and vaguely hypnotic, the moors are renowned as the setting for Sir Arthur Conan Doyle's *Hound of the Baskervilles,* and known as one of the most dramatically lonely settings in England.

Bleak, and fertile only in some sections, they're inhabited by the ghosts of tragic lovers and jilted ladies who haunt the region. About a third of Dartmoor is privately owned by Prince Charles; the remainder belongs mostly to the British government. Regardless of its exact ownership, the region is as rich in myth and legend as anywhere else in Britain. Crisscrossed with about 500 miles of bridle paths and hiking trails, and covering about 360 square miles (180 of which comprise the Dartmoor National Park), the moors rest on a granite base with numerous rocky outcroppings.

If you're a trekker, avoid the sometimes-dangerous marshes in the low-lying sections, and don't take the region's hazards lightly: The moors have punished trekkers who venture into their rugged recesses without a compass or adequate food and clothing. There is virtually no shelter of any kind away from the main roads, and the weather (especially fog and driving rain) is unpredictable. Adding to the danger is the fact that sections along the moor's northern edge are used by the British military as firing ranges. (Fortunately, these are clearly marked.)

Something about the windblown expanses of heather, gorse, bramble, and vines seems to amplify the fragile emotions of romantic heroes and heroines into obsessions rich with implications in British literature, including *Lorna Doone.*

There are few specific places to visit while crossing the moors. The towns are small and not particularly noteworthy—they can generally all be visited in one day. Examples include Ottery St. Mary (famous as the birthplace of Coleridge), South Molton, Chagford Tavistock, and Grimspount (which inspired the setting for the above-mentioned *Hound of the Baskervilles*).

Most travelers approach the moors from either Plymouth or Exeter. Smaller hamlets on the park's perimeter include Yelverton, Princetown, Postbridge, Moretonhampstead, and Steps Bridge.

places to go, accommodations, local events, and articles about the national park. *The Dartmoor Visitor* is obtainable from DNP information centers and tourist information centers or by mail. Send an International Reply Coupon to the DNPA headquarters (address above).

The market town of Okehampton owes its existence to the Norman castle built by Baldwin de Bryonis, sheriff of Devon, under orders from his uncle, William the Conqueror, in 1068, just 2 years after the Conquest. The Courtenay family lived there for many generations until Henry VIII beheaded one of them and dismantled the castle in 1538. The **Museum of Dartmoor Life,** at the Dartmoor Centre, 3 West St., Okehampton (☎ **01837/52295**), is housed in an old mill with a water wheel and is part of the Dartmoor Centre, a group of attractions around an old courtyard. Also here are working craft studios, a Victorian Cottage Tea Room, and a Dartmoor National Park information center. Museum displays cover all aspects of Dartmoor's history from prehistoric times, including geology, industries, living conditions, crafts, farm tools and machinery, and some old vehicles—a Devon box wagon of 1875, a 1922 Bullnose Morris motorcar, a 1937 motorcycle. There's a reconstructed cider press, a blacksmithy, and a tourist information center. The museum is open only from Easter to October, Monday through Saturday from 10am to 5pm (daily from June to September). Admission is £1.60 ($2.55) for adults, 85p ($1.35) for children.

WHERE TO STAY & DINE
In Ashburton
Moderate

Holne Chase Hotel
Two Bridges Rd., Ashburton, near Newton Abbot, Devon TQ13 7NS. ☎ **01364/471.** Fax 01364/453. 14 rms, 2 suites. TV TEL. £50–£65 ($79–$102.70) single; £90–£100 ($142.20–$158) double; £115 ($181.70) suite. Rates include English breakfast. Discount packages available. AE, DC, MC, V. Free parking.

The Holne Chase Hotel is a white-gabled country house, 3 miles northwest of the center of town, within sight of trout- and salmon-fishing waters. You can catch your lunch and take it back to the kitchen to be cooked. Although the mood of the moor predominates, Holne Chase is surrounded by trees, lawns, and pastures, a perfect setting for walks along the Dart. It's off the main Ashburton–Princetown road, between the Holne Bridge and New Bridge. Every bedroom in the house is named after a tributary of the River Dart.

The house is furnished in period style, a refurbished bar also being done in the style of the rest of the hotel. The cooking combines the best of English fare with specialty dishes that are made all the better whenever produce from the gardens or fresh fish from the Dart River and Torquay are used. Devon beef and lamb are also featured. The old cellars hold a nice selection of wine. A fixed-price lunch costs £14.50 ($22.90), and a fixed-price dinner goes for £21 ($33.20).

In Lydford
Inexpensive

⑤ The Castle Inn
Lydford, near Okehampton, Devon EX20 4BH. ☎ **01822/820241.** Fax 01822/820454. 7 rms, 5 with bath; 1 suite. £28.75 ($45.45) single without bath; £38.75 ($61.25) single with bath; £42.50 ($67.15) double without bath, £52.50 ($82.95) double with bath; £57.50

($90.85) suite for two. Special Country Breaks (any 2 nights): £83.20–£166.40 ($131.45–$262.90), including half board. AE, DC, MC, V. Free parking.

The Castle Inn is a 16th-century structure next to Lydford Castle, 1 mile off A386 midway between Okehampton and Tavistock. The inn, with its pink facade and row of rose trellises, is the hub of the village. The owners have maintained the character of the commodious rustic lounge with its collection of old furniture and accessories. One room, called the "Snug," has a group of high-backed oak settles arranged in a circle.

In the Foresters' Bar, meals are served from 11am to 3pm daily. The cost depends on your choice of a main course. Bar snacks are available as well. Lunches are bar meals priced at £3.50 to £10.95 ($5.55 to $17.30) each. Dinners include the bar meals described above, but also offer more elaborate restaurant fare at £14.95 ($23.60) for a three-course table d'hôte dinner, with an à la carte main course priced at £8.95 to £13.95 ($14.15 to $22.05). Dinner is available daily from 6 to 11pm. The bedrooms are not large but are well planned and attractively furnished, often with mahogany and marble Victorian pieces.

IN TWO BRIDGES
Inexpensive

⑤ Cherrybrook Hotel
Two Bridges, Yelverton, Devon PL20 6SP. ☎ **01822/88260.** 7 rms, all with shower only. TV. £25 ($39.50) single; £50 ($79) double. Rates include English breakfast. No credit cards. Free parking. Closed Dec 22–Jan 2.

The Cherrybrook Hotel, on B3212 between Postbridge and Two Bridges, is a small family-run hotel in the center of the Dartmoor National Park, on the high moor but within easy driving distance of Exeter and Plymouth. It was built in the early 19th century by a friend of the Prince Regent who received permission to enclose a large area of the Dartmoor forest for farming. Part of the farm was later leased to a gunpowder-manufacturing company, whose remains can still be seen. The lounge and bar with their beamed ceiling and slate floors are a reminder of those times. Andy and Margaret Duncan rent comfortably furnished and well-maintained rooms. You can also dine here, paying £14 ($22.10) for a four-course dinner and coffee.

3 Chagford

218 miles SW of London, 13 miles W of Exeter, 20 miles NW of Torquay, 6 miles NE of Postbridge

Six hundred feet above sea level, Chagford is an ancient Stannary Town; with moors all around, it's a good base for you to explore North Dartmoor. Chagford overlooks the Teign River in its deep valley and is itself overlooked by the high granite tors. There's good fishing in the Teign. From Chagford, the most popular excursion is to Postbridge, a village with a prehistoric clapper bridge.

ESSENTIALS
GETTING THERE

By Train   Go to Exeter, then take a local bus to Chagford.

By Bus   From Exeter, take the Transmoor Link National Express bus no. 82.

By Car   From Exeter, drive west on A30, then south on A382 to Chagford.

VISITOR INFORMATION

The **telephone area code** is 01647.

WHAT TO SEE & DO

Castle Drogo

In the hamlet of Drewsteignton. ☎ **01647/433306.** Castle and grounds, £4.60 ($7.25) adults, £2.30 ($3.65) children; grounds only, £2 ($3.15) adults, £1 ($1.60) children. Castle, Apr–Oct, Sat–Thurs 11am–5pm (closed Nov–Mar); grounds, daily 10:30am–5:30pm. Take A30 and follow the signs; the castle is 4 miles northeast of Chagford and 6 miles south of the Exeter–Okehampton road (A30).

This massive granite castle was designed and built between 1910 and 1930 by the architect Sir Edwin Lutyens for his client, Julius Drewe. Founder of a nationwide chain of grocery stores, Drewe named his castle after an alleged ancestor, Count Drogo de Teign, who was awarded land in this region by William the Conqueror after the Norman conquest of 1066. Located 17 miles west of Exeter, the castle occupies a bleak but dramatic position high above the River Teign, with views sweeping out over the moors. The tour covers an elegant series of formal rooms designed in the best tradition of the Edwardian age, including drawing rooms, dining rooms, salons, a gun room with a vaulted ceiling, and a garden. There are two restaurants on the premises, both with waitress service, and a tearoom where tea, pastries, and snacks are served buffet style.

✪ Sir Francis Drake's House

Buckland Abbey, Yelverton. ☎ **01822/853607.** Admission £4 ($6.30) adults, £2 ($3.15) children. Apr–Oct, Fri–Wed 10:30am–5:30pm; Nov–Mar, Sat–Sun 2–5pm. Go 3 miles west of Yelverton off A386.

Constructed in 1278, Sir Francis Drake's House was originally a Cistercian monastery. The monastery was dissolved in 1539 and became the country seat of sailors Sir Richard Grenville and, later, Sir Francis Drake. The house remained in the Drake family until 1946, when the abbey and grounds were given to the National Trust. The abbey is now a museum and houses exhibits including Drake's drum, banners, and other artifacts. Light snacks are available daily.

WHERE TO STAY & DINE

VERY EXPENSIVE

✪ Gidleigh Park Hotel

Gidleigh Rd. (2 miles outside town), Chagford, Devon TQ13 8HH. ☎ **01647/432367.** Fax 01647/432574. 14 rms, 1 cottage. TV TEL. £210–£330 ($331.80–$521.40) single; £260–£375 ($410.80–$592.50) double; £410 ($647.80) cottage for two. Rates include English breakfast, morning tea, newspaper, dinner, service, and tax. AE, DC, MC, V. Free parking. To get here, see the directions below.

A visit to this Tudor-style hotel, a Relais & Châteaux, is highly recommended. Its American owners, Kay and Paul Henderson, have renovated and refurnished the house with flair and imagination. In a park of 40 acres, large beech and oak trees abound. Inside, the oak-paneled public rooms and the open log fires invite a return to yesterday. The windows open onto views of the garden and the Teign Valley, with Dartmoor lying beyond. Most of the bedrooms are on the second floor and are reached by a grand staircase; all have a private bath. The hotel has a three-room thatched cottage with two bathrooms across the river, 350 yards from the hotel, that's available for two, three, or four people.

Excellent meals are served in an oak-paneled dining room; nonguests are charged £50 to £55 ($79 to $86.90). The menu is changed daily, and only the best and freshest products are used. Dining here has been called a memorable experience. In fact, this restaurant has been called "one of the best in the West Country," and its wine list has received numerous awards.

To get here from Chagford Square, turn right onto Mill Street at Lloyds Bank. After 200 yards, turn right and go down the hill to the crossroads. Cross straight over onto Holy Street, following the lane passing Holy Street Manor on your right and shifting into low gear to negotiate two sharp bends on a steep hill. Over Leigh Bridge, make a sharp right turn into Gidleigh Park. A half-mile drive will bring you to the hotel.

INEXPENSIVE

⑤ Easton Court Hotel

Easton Cross, Chagford, Devon TQ13 8JL. ☎ **01647/433469.** Fax 01647/433469. 8 rms. TV TEL. £42 ($66.35) single; £84 ($132.70) double. Rates include English breakfast. AE, MC, V. Free parking. Closed Jan. Take A382 1¹/₂ miles northeast of Chagford. Bus 359 from Exeter.

Ever since it was established as a hotel in the 1920s by an American, Carolyn Cobb, this Tudor house has been known to discerning visitors, including many literary and theatrical celebrities. Alec Waugh wrote *Thirteen Such Years* and Patrick Leigh Fermor penned *The Traveller's Tree* here. But it's best known as the place where Evelyn Waugh wrote *Brideshead Revisited.* The guestbook reads like a *Who's Who* of yesteryear: Robert Donat, Margaret Mead, Ralph Richardson, C. P. Snow, Richard Widmark, John Steinbeck. The atmosphere here is consistent with one's preconceived impression of a country place in England: an ancient stone house with a thatched roof, heavy oak beams, an inglenook where log fires burn in cold weather, and a high-walled flower garden. The bedrooms are snug and comfortable, accommodating 15 guests at a time. British and international dishes are served, including coq au vin, steak-and-mushroom pie, and curried prawns. Meals, available to nonresidents who reserve, cost £22 ($34.75) and up.

Great Tree Hotel

Sandy Park, Chagford, Devon TQ13 8JS. ☎ **01647/432491.** Fax 01647/432562. 11 rms. TV TEL. £50–£61 ($79–$96.40) single; £79–£98 ($124.80–$154.85) double. Rates include English breakfast. AE, DC, MC, V. Free parking. Take A30 to the traffic circle at Whiddon Down and drive 2 miles south on A382.

Formerly an old hunting lodge, the Great Tree Hotel is a comfortable country house located on 25 acres of private grounds. The bedrooms are country style, with radios and tea and coffee makers. Beverly and Nigel Eaton-Gray, the proprietors, offer a five-course dinner prepared, insofar as possible, with home-grown produce; the cost is £19.95 ($31.50). English and continental meals are served in their Whitewater Restaurant. There are bar snacks at lunch and Devonshire cream teas on the terrace or by the log fire in winter.

4 Torquay

223 miles SW of London, 23 miles SE of Exeter

In 1968, the towns of Torquay, Paignton, and Brixham joined to form "The English Riviera" as part of a plan to turn the area into one of the super three-in-one resorts of Europe. The area today—the birthplace of mystery writer Agatha Christie—opens onto 22 miles of coastline and 18 beaches.

Torquay is set against a backdrop of the red cliffs of Devon, with many sheltered pebbly coves. With its parks and gardens, including numerous subtropical plants and palm trees, it's often compared to the Mediterranean. At night, concerts, productions from the West End (the D'Oyly Carte Opera appears occasionally at the Princess Theatre), vaudeville shows, and ballroom dancing keep the vacationers—and many honeymooners—entertained.

ESSENTIALS
GETTING THERE

By Plane   The nearest connection is Exeter Airport (see above), 40 minutes away.

By Train   Frequent trains run throughout the day from London's Paddington Station to Torquay (trip time: 2¹/₂ hr.).

By Bus   National Express coach links from London's Victoria Coach Station leave every 2 hours during the day for Torquay.

By Car   From Exeter (see above), head west on A38, veering south at the junction with A380.

VISITOR INFORMATION

The **telephone area code** is 01803. The **Tourist Information Centre** is at Vaughan Parade (☎ **01803/297428**).

WHERE TO STAY
MODERATE

Homers

Warren Rd., Torquay, Devon TQ2 5TN. ☎ **01803/213456**. Fax 01803/213458. 14 rms, 1 suite. TV TEL. May–Oct, £42 ($66.35) single; £60 ($94.80) double; £98 ($154.85) suite. Nov–Apr, £42 ($66.35) single; £50 ($79) double; £80 ($126.40) suite. Rates include half board. AE, DC, MC, V. Free parking. Turn left from the Sea Front along the front (inside lane) straight up the hill; Warren Road is on the right (it's a very tight turn by St. Luke's Church).

The solid Victorian walls of this house were originally built in the 1850s as the summer vacation home of a Yorkshire-based mining magnate. In 1994, new owners Gerald Clarke and Guy Mansell began a gradual renovation of each of the bedrooms, leaving many family antiques in place along with nostalgically old-fashioned homey touches. Set near the top of steeply inclined gardens overlooking Tor Bay, the hotel has a restaurant, Les Ambassadeurs. There, evening meals, made with fresh ingredients, begin at around £14.75 ($23.30) each.

✪ The Imperial

Park Hill Rd., Torquay, Devon TQ1 2DG. ☎ **01803/294301**, or 800/225-5843 in the U.S. and Canada. Fax 01803/298293. 150 rms, 17 suites. MINIBAR TV TEL. £80–£130 ($126.40–$205.40) single; £100–£150 ($158–$237) double; from £200 ($316) suite. Rates include English breakfast, use of sporting facilities, and dancing in the ballroom Mon–Sat. AE, DC, MC, V. Garage parking £5 ($7.90); free parking lot.

This leading five-star hotel in the West Country dates from the 1860s. It sits on 5¹/₂ acres of subtropical gardens opening onto rocky cliffs, with views of the Channel. Inside is a world of soaring ceilings, marble columns, and ornate plasterwork—enough to make a former visitor, Edward VII, feel at home. Each of the bedrooms enjoys lots of well-ordered space, traditional furniture, a private bath, and a radio. Each accommodation has a private balcony suspended high above a view that encompasses offshore islands with black rocks and sheer sides.

The elegant Regatta Restaurant serves either table d'hôte at £32 ($50.55) or à la carte, of both British and international dishes, supplemented by a fine wine list. Service is daily from 12:30 to 2:30pm for lunch. If you go for dinner (served from 7 to 9:30pm), it's important to reserve a table.

Palace Hotel

Babbacombe Rd., Babbacombe, Torquay, Devon TQ1 3TG. ☎ **01803/200200.** Fax 01803/299899. 134 rms, 6 suites. TV TEL. £50–£60 ($79–$94.80) single; £90–£110 ($142.20–$173.80) double; £160–£200 ($252.80–$316) suite for two. Rates include English breakfast. AE, DC, MC, V. Parking £5 ($7.90). From the center take B3199 east. Bus 32.

This Victorian hotel was built when life was experienced on a grand scale, reflected by the spacious public rooms with their molded ceilings and columns. With all its many improvements in recent years, the hotel should be able to enter the next century in a premier position. A four-star hotel, it is luxurious in appointments and facilities. Its public facilities, in fact, are the most impressive in Torquay, with both in- and outdoor swimming pools along with in- and outdoor tennis courts, two indoor squash courts, even a nine-hole golf course. All its bedrooms are well furnished. The hotel occupies 25 choice acres of real estate in Torquay, sweeping down to Anstey's Cove.

INEXPENSIVE

ⓢ Palm Court Hotel

Sea Front, Torquay, Devon TQ2 5HD. ☎ **01803/294881.** Fax 01803/211199. 64 rms, 62 with bath. TV TEL. £19–£33.50 ($30–$52.95) single with bath; £17–£31 ($26.85–$49) double without bath, £38–£65 ($60.05–$102.70) double with bath. Rates include English breakfast. Half board £26–£43 ($41.10–$67.95) per person. DC, MC, V. Parking £3 ($4.75).

The Palm Court Hotel, facing south onto the esplanade overlooking Torquay, offers style and good living. The original row of Regency-era houses were joined together to form a hotel in the 1920s. Two lounges are wood-paneled with leaded-glass windows. In the dining room is a minstrels' gallery. There are two up-to-date bars and the Sands Restaurant, open all day. All rooms have been modernized and are equipped with hot-beverage facilities and central heating. Each single has a private bath, although two doubles are without bath. With garden chairs and tables on the sun terrace outside the restaurant, the Palm Court becomes a social center. At night the colored floodlighting around the bay evokes a Riviera atmosphere.

IN NEARBY MAIDENCOMBE

Expensive

Orestone Manor

Rockhouse Lane, Maidencombe, Torquay, Devon TQ1 4SX. ☎ **01803/328098.** Fax 01803/328336. 18 rms. TV TEL. £50–£125 ($79–$197.50) single; £90–£180 ($142.20–$284.40) double. Rates include English breakfast. Winter discounts available. AC, DC, MC, V. Free parking. Closed Jan. Drive 3¹/₂ miles north of Torquay on B3199.

Orestone Manor lies in a small village north of Torquay. Sometimes the best way to enjoy a bustling seaside resort is from afar, nestling in a country home. Orestone Manor provides such an opportunity from February to December. In one of the loveliest valleys in South Devon, this gabled manor house, constructed in the early

19th century as a private home, enjoys a tranquil rural setting, situated on 2 acres of well-landscaped gardens. The bedrooms are handsomely and comfortably furnished and offer beverage-making facilities. If payment is either by American Express or Diner's Club cards, a 3% penalty is assessed. Tasty bar lunches are provided Monday through Saturday, and a fixed-price dinner, correctly prepared and using fresh ingredients, is £25.50 ($40.30).

WHERE TO DINE
MODERATE

⑤ Remy's

3 Croft Rd. ☎ **01803/292359.** Reservations required. Fixed-price menu £13.85 ($21.90). MC, V. Tues–Sat 7:15–9:30pm. From the Sea Front, head north on Shedden Hill. Bus 32. FRENCH.

Considered by some the finest independent dining spot in town, Remy's serves food at reasonable prices, offering a fixed-price menu of three courses which changes daily. Owner and chef de cuisine Remy Bopp, of France, sets great store by his raw ingredients, whether they be fresh fish from a local fisherman or vegetables from the market. Everything is homemade, including bread, ice cream, sorbet, and pastries. Food-wise guests can also enjoy his carefully selected group of French wines.

A RESTAURANT WITH B&B: INEXPENSIVE

⑤ Mulberry Room

1 Scarborough Rd., Torquay, Devon TQ2 5UJ. ☎ **01803/213639.** Reservations required for dinner. Main courses £5–£7.50 ($7.90–$11.85); fixed-price lunch £5.95 ($9.40) for two courses, £7.95 ($12.55) for three courses. No credit cards. Wed–Sat noon–2pm and 7:30–9:30pm, Sun noon–2pm. From the Sea Front, turn up Belgrave Road; Scarborough Road is the first right. Bus 32. ENGLISH.

Lesley Cooper is an inspired cook, and she'll feed you well in her little dining room, seating some two dozen diners at midday. The restaurant is situated in the dining area of one of Torquay's Victorian villas, facing a patio of plants and flowers, with outside tables for summer lunches and afternoon teas. The vegetarian will find comfort here, while regular diners can feast on her baked lamb, honey-roasted chicken, or grilled natural fried fillets of sole with tartar sauce. Traditional roasts draw the Sunday crowds. The choice is wisely limited so that everything served will be fresh.

You can even stay here in one of three bedrooms, each comfortably furnished and well kept, with private bath. B&B charges range from £21 to £25 ($33.20 to $39.50) per person daily, making it one of the bargains of the resort.

5 Totnes

224 miles SW of London, 12 miles NW of Dartmouth

One of the oldest towns in the West Country, the ancient borough of Totnes rests quietly in the past, seemingly content to let the Torquay area remain in the vanguard of the building boom. On the River Dart, upstream from Dartmouth, Totnes is so totally removed in character from Torquay that the two towns could be in different countries. Totnes has several historic buildings, notably the ruins of a Norman castle, an ancient guildhall, and the 15th-century Church of St. Mary, constructed of red sandstone. In the Middle Ages the old cloth town was encircled by walls, and the North Gate serves as a reminder of that period.

ESSENTIALS
GETTING THERE

By Train   Totnes is on the main London–Plymouth line. Trains leave London's Paddington Station frequently throughout the day.

By Bus   Totnes is served locally by the Western National and Devon General bus companies (☎ **01752/222666** in Plymouth for information about individual routings).

By Boat   Many visitors approach Totnes by river steamer from Dartmouth. Contact Dart Pleasure Craft, River Link (☎ **01803/834488**), for information.

By Car   From Torquay, head west on A385.

VISITOR INFORMATION

The **telephone area code** is 01803. The year-round **Tourist Information Centre** is at the Plains (☎ **01803/863168**).

WHERE TO STAY
INEXPENSIVE

Royal Seven Stars

The Plains, Totnes, South Devon TQ9 5DD. ☎ **01803/862125.** Fax 01803/862125. 18 rms, 12 with bath. TV TEL. £40 ($63.20) single without bath, £51.50 ($81.35) single with bath; £54 ($85.30) double without bath, £59.50 ($94) double with bath. Rates include English breakfast. DC, MC, V. Free parking.

A historic former coaching inn in the center of town, the Royal Seven Stars largely dates back to 1660. The hotel has an interesting porch over its entrance and overlooks a square in the town center, near the banks of the River Dart. The interior courtyard, once used for horses and carriages, is now enclosed in glass, with an old pine staircase. With antiques and paintings, the hotel's own heraldic shield, hand-carved chests, and a grandfather clock, the courtyard forms an inviting entrance to the inn. The bedrooms have been modernized and have built-in furniture. Each has comfortable beds and hot-beverage facilities. Some rooms have four-poster beds.

A buffet bar is open for lunch all year as well as for supper May to September. A three-course lunch or four-course dinner can be enjoyed in the Brutus Room, open all year. Lunch costs £8.50 ($13.45), and dinner, £16.50 ($26.05).

IN NEARBY STOKE GABRIEL

Inexpensive

⑨ Gabriel Court Hotel

Stoke Gabriel, near Totnes, South Devon TQ9 6SF. ☎ **01803/782206.** Fax 01803/782333. 19 rms, 3 family rms. TV TEL. £48–£54 ($75.85–$85.30) single; £77 ($121.65) double; £105 ($165.90) family room for three. Rates include English breakfast. AE, DC, MC, V. Free parking. Those arriving via A38 should leave it at Buckfastleigh, taking A384 to Totnes, then A385 to Paignton; approximately 1 mile out of Totnes, turn right at the sign to Stoke Gabriel.

The Gabriel Court was a manor house owned by the same family from 1487 to 1928, when it was converted into a hotel. Michael and Eryl Beacom, the proprietors, offer good value and hospitality. The hotel overlooks a pretty village on the banks of the River Dart, standing in a terraced Elizabethan garden, with a heated swimming pool and a lawn tennis court. The 3-acre site is the setting for the white-painted house, which offers well-furnished, comfortable bedrooms. Each of these is in a modern extension which was converted from a hayloft.

The Gabriel Court enjoys a reputation for its well-cooked English food, enhanced by fruit and vegetables from its own garden, as well as trout and salmon from the Dart. The hotel has a bar, and in winter log fires make the restful lounges cozy retreats.

IN NEARBY DARTINGTON

Inexpensive

Cott Inn

Dartington, near Totnes (on the old Ashburton–Totnes turnpike), South Devon TQ9 6HE. ☎ **01803/863777.** Fax 01803/866629. 6 rms. TV TEL. £45 ($71.10) single; £50 ($79) double. Rates include English breakfast. AE, DC, MC, V. Free parking. Bus X80 travels from Totnes to Dartington, but most people take a taxi for the 1¹/₂-mile journey.

Built in 1320, this hotel is the second-oldest inn in England. It's a low, rambling two-story building of stone, cob, and plaster, with a thatched roof and 3-foot-thick walls. The owners rent low-ceilinged double rooms upstairs, with modern conveniences, including hot and cold running water. The inn is a gathering place for the people of Dartington, and you'll feel the pulse of English country life. In winter, log fires keep the lounge and bar snug. You'll surely be intrigued with the tavern, where you can also order a meal. A buffet is laid out at lunchtime, priced according to your choice of dish. The à la carte dinners feature local produce prepared in interesting ways; scallops, duck, steak, or fresh salmon may be available. Even if you're not staying over, you might want to drop by the pub (five beers are on draft). Pub hours are Monday through Saturday from 11am to 2:30pm and 5:30 to 11pm and Sunday from noon to 3pm and 7 to 10:30pm.

WHERE TO DINE

INEXPENSIVE

The Elbow Room

6 North St. ☎ **01803/863480.** Reservations required. Main courses £8.95–£11.95 ($14.15–$18.90); fixed-price three-course dinner £12.95 ($20.45). AE, DC, MC, V. Tues–Sat noon–2pm and 7–9:30pm. INTERNATIONAL.

An intimate rendezvous for diners, the Elbow Room is in a converted one-time cider press and adjoining cottage in the center adjacent to the Castle Car Park. The original 300-year-old stone walls have been retained and the decor matched to them, providing a unique atmosphere. Roger and Vona Savin offer a standard of food and service that attracts gourmets. Mrs. Savin combines technical skill with inspiration and a flair for the unusual in the selection, preparation, and presentation of her appetizers, main courses, and homemade desserts. Main courses include fresh vegetables. The menu is restricted to a maximum of 10 offerings and may include such dishes as fillet of beef with an English mustard-and-sherry sauce, roast loin of lamb with a herb crust and rosemary, halibut baked in a tomato-and-cream sauce, or beef Stroganoff. The lunch menu offers a selection of roasts. Mr. Savin presides over the restaurant with charm and expertise.

There are also accommodations—a double room and a twin-bedded room with private bath (tub or shower), plus two singles without bath. The single rate is £19.50 ($30.80), rising to £22.50 ($35.55) per person in a double, which includes either an English or continental breakfast.

6 Dartmouth

236 miles SW of London, 35 miles SE of Exeter

At the mouth of the Dart River, this ancient seaport is the home of the Royal Naval College. Traditionally linked to England's maritime greatness, Dartmouth sent out the young midshipmen who saw to it that "Britannia ruled the waves." You can take a river steamer up the Dart to Totnes (book at the kiosk at the harbor); the scenery along the way is panoramic, as the Dart is Devon's most beautiful river.

Dartmouth's 15th-century castle was built during the reign of Edward IV. The town's most noted architectural feature is the Butterwalk, which lies below Tudor houses. The Flemish influence in some of the houses is pronounced.

ESSENTIALS
GETTING THERE

By Train   Dartmouth is not easily reached by public transport. Trains run to Totnes (see above) and Paignton.

By Bus   There is one bus a day from Totnes to Dartmouth.

By Car   From Exeter, take A38 southwest, cutting southeast to Totnes on A381; then follow A381 to the junction with B3207.

By Boat   There are riverboats making the 10-mile run from Totnes to Dartmouth, but these depend on the tide and operate only from Easter to the end of October. See Totnes, above, for details on obtaining boat schedules.

VISITOR INFORMATION

The **telephone area code** is 01803. The **Tourist Information Centre** is at the Engine House, Mayors Avenue (☎ **01803/834224**).

WHERE TO STAY
MODERATE

Dart Marina Hotel

Sandquay, Dartmouth, Devon TQ6 9PH. ☎ **01803/832580,** or 800/225-5843 in the U.S. and Canada. Fax 01803/835040. 33 rms, 2 suites. TV TEL. £43–£53 ($67.95–$83.75) single; £86–£106 ($135.90–$167.50) double; £100–£120 ($158–$189.60) suite for two. Rates include half board. AE, DC, MC, V. Free parking.

This hotel is an ocher-walled establishment at the edge of its own marina, within a 3-minute walk from the center of town. It was originally built as a clubhouse for local yachting enthusiasts late in the 19th century, and was then enlarged and transformed into a hotel just before World War II. The bar and each of the bedrooms affords a view of yachts bobbing at anchor in the Dart River, and about 14 of the bedrooms have private balconies. The bedrooms are conservative and comfortable, with radios and coffee-making facilities.

INEXPENSIVE

Royal Castle Hotel

11 The Quay, Dartmouth, Devon TQ6 9PS. ☎ **01803/833033.** Fax 01803/835445. 25 rms. TV TEL. £50 ($79) single; £80–£115 ($126.40–$181.70) double. Rates include English breakfast. MC, V. Free parking.

A coaching inn since 1639, the Royal Castle Hotel has hosted Sir Francis Drake, Queen Victoria, Charles II, and Edward VII (bedrooms named after them commemorate their visits). Horse-drawn carriages (as late as 1910) dispatched passengers in a carriageway, now an enclosed reception hall. The glassed-in courtyard, with its winding wooden staircase, has the original coaching horn and a set of 20 antique spring bells connected to the bedrooms. Many of the rooms open off the covered courtyard and the rambling corridors display antiques. All units have been recently restored and have central heating and private baths. Some are air-conditioned and three units offer a Jacuzzi, which carries a £10 ($15.80) supplement.

The meals, taken in the restaurant under a beautiful Adam ceiling, are excellent, in the best English tradition. Dinner costs £15.95 to £20.25 ($25.20 to $32). A favorite place to settle in is the Galleon Bar, once two old kitchens, with double fireplaces and large hand-hewn beams said to have been salvaged from Spanish Armada ships. There's another pub-style bar, with settles, that's popular with the locals. Guests lounge on the second floor in a room with a bay window overlooking the harbor.

WHERE TO DINE
EXPENSIVE

✪ The Carved Angel

2 South Embankment. ☎ **01803/832465.** Reservations required. Main courses £19.50–£24.50 ($30.80–$38.70); three-course fixed-price meals £29 ($45.80) at lunch Tues–Sat and £35 ($55.30) Sun, £45 ($71.10) at dinner. No credit cards. Tues–Sat 12:30–1:45pm and 7:30–9:30pm, Sun 12:30–1:45pm. Closed Jan–Feb 15. CONTINENTAL.

Considered the best restaurant in town, the Carved Angel serves specialties that tend to be more akin to the creative cuisine of the Continent than to the traditional cookery of England. Co-owners Nick Coiley and Joyce Molyneux welcome visitors to their stylishly simple riverside restaurant, whose kitchen is partially screened from the dining room by plants. This building was formerly a Victorian storefront. The restaurant is behind a half-timbered, heavily carved facade that rises opposite the harbor. Inside, a central statue of a carved angel is ringed with a decor of neutral colors. Typical dishes include fish soup provençal, Dart salmon in pastry with currants and ginger, and, for dessert, hot lemon-and-coconut soufflé with homemade ice cream.

MODERATE

Horn of Plenty

In the Tamar View House, Gulworthy, Tavistock, Devon PL19 8JD. ☎ **01822/832528.** Reservations required. Fixed-price meals £17.50 ($27.65) at lunch, £28.50 ($45.05) at dinner, AE, MC, V. Mon 7–9:30pm, Tues–Sun noon–2pm and 7–9:30pm. Closed Dec 25. Drive 3 miles west of Tavistock on A390. INTERNATIONAL.

As you drive from Tavistock to Callington, you'll see a small sign pointing north along a leafy drive to the solid Regency house where the owners operate what the French call a *restaurant avec chambres*. It was built by the duke of Bedford in the early 1800s as a private home. After a day of touring the country, guests enjoy well-prepared dinners, which might include fillet of beef, grilled local salmon in a white-wine sauce on a bed of potatoes and fresh herbs, or roast partridge with game chips and red-currant jelly. On Monday evening a three-course dinner is offered for £18.50 ($29.25). Even though all meals are fixed-price arrangements, there is a choice of foods in each category.

You can stay in one of the spacious, warm, and elegant bedrooms (seven in all) that have been installed over the old stables of the house. With a continental breakfast included, singles range from £68 to £80 ($107.45 to $126.40) while doubles go for £88 to £98 ($139.05 to $154.85). All accommodations have color TVs, hot-beverage facilities, phones, and well-stocked minibars.

7 Plymouth

242 miles SW of London, 161 miles SW of Southampton

The historic seaport of Plymouth is more romantic in legend than in reality. But this was not always so—during World War II, the blitzed area of greater Plymouth lost at least 75,000 buildings. The heart of present-day Plymouth, including the municipal civic center on the Royal Parade, has been entirely rebuilt; however, the way it was rebuilt is the subject of much controversy.

For the old part of town, you must go to the Elizabethan section, known as the Barbican, and walk along the quay in the footsteps of Sir Francis Drake (once the mayor of Plymouth) and other Elizabethan seafarers, such as Sir John Hawkins, English naval commander and slave trader. It was from here in 1577 that Drake set sail on his round-the-world voyage.

Of special interest to visitors from the United States is the final departure point of the Pilgrims in 1620, the already-mentioned Barbican. The two ships, *Mayflower* and *Speedwell*, that sailed from Southampton in August of that year put into Plymouth after they suffered storm damage. Here the *Speedwell* was abandoned as unseaworthy and the *Mayflower* made the trip to the New World alone. The Memorial Gateway to the Waterside on the Barbican marks the place, tradition says, from which the Pilgrims' ship sailed.

ESSENTIALS
GETTING THERE
By Plane   Plymouth Airport lies 4 miles from the center of the city. Brymon Airways has direct service from the London airports at Heathrow and Gatwick to Plymouth. For service, call Brymon (☎ **01752/707023**).

By Train   Frequent trains run from London's Paddington Station to Plymouth in 3 to 3$^1/_2$ hours, depending on the train.

By Bus   National Express has frequent daily bus service between London's Victoria Coach Station and Plymouth (trip time: 4$^1/_2$ hr.).

By Car   From London, take M4 west to the junction with M5 going south to Exeter. From Exeter, head southwest on A38 to Plymouth.

VISITOR INFORMATION
The **telephone area code** is 01752. The **Tourist Information Centre** is at the Island House, The Barbican (☎ **01752/264849**).

WHAT TO SEE & DO
The **Barbican** is a mass of narrow streets, old houses, and quayside shops selling antiques, brasswork, old prints, and books. Fishing boats still unload their catch

at the wharves, and passenger-carrying ferryboats run short harbor cruises. A trip includes views of Drake's Island in the sound, the dockyards, naval vessels, and the Hoe from the water. A cruise of Plymouth Harbour costs £3 ($4.75) for adults and £1.50 ($2.35) for children. Departures are February to November, with cruises leaving every half hour from 10:30am to 3pm daily. These Plymouth Boat Cruises are booked at the Phoenix Wharf, The Barbican (☎ **01752/822797**).

White Lane Gallery

1 White Lane, The Barbican. ☎ **01752/221450.** Admission free. Mon noon–4pm, Tues–Sat 10am–5pm. Bus 39.

This gallery specializes in contemporary art and crafts, with changing exhibitions of paintings and ceramics. It also has three resident craftspeople, including a potter, furniture maker, and silk painter. It's a 5-minute walk from the town center in Plymouth's historic Barbican, near the *Mayflower* Steps.

Plymouth Gin Distillery

Black Friars Distillery, 60 Southside St. ☎ **01752/667062.** Admission £1.75 ($2.75) adults, 95p ($1.50) children 10–18, free for children 9 and under. Easter–Sept, Mon–Sat 10:30am–4pm. Closed Oct–Easter. Bus 54.

Plymouth Gin has been produced here for 200 years on a historic site that dates back to a Dominican monastery built in 1425. There are public guided tours. A Plymouth Gin Shop is on the premises. The gin distillery is adjacent to a historic monument, now part of the Distillery Beefeater Restaurant. These premises, one of Plymouth's oldest surviving buildings, were where the Pilgrims met prior to sailing for the New World.

Prysten House

Finewell St. ☎ **01752/661414.** Admission 60p (95¢) adults, 30p (45¢) children. Easter–Oct, Mon–Sat 10am–4pm. Closed Nov–Easter.

Built in 1490 as a town house close to St. Andrew's Church, it is now a church house and working museum. Rebuilt in the 1930s with American help, it displays a model of Plymouth in 1620 and tapestries depicting the colonization of America. At the entrance is the gravestone of the captain of the U.S. brig *Argus*, who died on August 15, 1813, after a battle in the English Channel.

WHERE TO STAY

MODERATE

Duke of Cornwall Hotel

Millbay Rd., Plymouth, Devon PL1 3LG. ☎ **01752/266256.** Fax 01752/600062. 70 rms. TV TEL. £69.50 ($109.80) single; £79.50 ($125.60) double. Rates include English breakfast. AE, DC, MC, V. Free parking.

The Duke of Cornwall Hotel is a Victorian gothic building that survived World War II bombings. Constructed in 1863, it was regarded by Sir John Betjeman as the finest example of Victorian architecture in Plymouth. The refurbished bedrooms all have radios, hairdryers, trouser presses, and coffee-making facilities. Some rooms have antique four-poster beds.

The hotel dining room is of an elegant contemporary style with a circular ceiling supporting a fine chandelier. Lunch begins at £16.95 ($26.80); dinner, at £18 ($28.45).

Plymouth Moat House Hotel

Armada Way, Plymouth, Devon PL1 2HJ. ☎ **01752/662866.** Fax 01752/673816. 199 rms, 13 suites. A/C TV TEL. £64.50–£69.50 ($101.90–$109.80) single; £74.50–£79.50 ($117.70–$125.60) double; £89.50–£99.50 ($141.40–$157.20) suite. English breakfast £9.50 ($15) extra. AE, DC, MC, V. Free parking.

One of the most distinguished hotels in the West Country, overlooking the harbor and the Hoe, the Plymouth Moat House rises like a midget high-rise. The good-sized rooms are well furnished with long double beds and have wide picture windows and tea and coffee facilities, trouser presses, and hairdryers. Babysitting is available. A covered swimming pool is on the grounds, and there's a sauna and sun terrace as well, with garden tables set up for poolside refreshments.

In the Blue Riband Restaurant, with its panoramic sea views, both à la carte and a table d'hôte menu are served. Meals average £15.50 to £18.50 ($24.50 to $29.25). Seafood is a specialty, some of the catch brought fresh each day from the Barbican.

INEXPENSIVE

⑤ Astor Hotel

14–22 Elliott St., The Hoe, Plymouth, Devon PL1 2PS. ☎ **01752/225511.** Fax 01752/251994. 55 rms. TV TEL. Mar–Oct, £55 ($86.90) single; £69 ($109) double. Nov–Feb, £35 ($55.30) single; £40 ($63.20) double. Rates include English breakfast. AE, DC, MC, V. Free parking overnight, £2 ($3.15) daytime parking nearby.

The hotel building was originally constructed during the Victorian era as the private home of a prosperous sea captain. In 1987 it underwent a major restoration, and today it has comfortable bedrooms, each with radio and coffee-making facilities. The hotel is situated near the Hoe on a street lined with 19th-century buildings. On the premises are well-decorated public lounges and a cozy and accommodating bar—open to residents and nonresidents alike—separated from the reception desk by a fan-shaped trio of glass doors. Three-course fixed-price meals in the hotel's restaurant cost £8.50 ($13.45) at lunch and £15 ($23.70) at dinner. Otherwise, less expensive bar snacks, priced at £3 to £6 ($4.75 to $9.50) per platter, can be ordered over the countertop of the bar.

Forte Post House

Cliff Rd., The Hoe, Plymouth, Devon PL1 3DL. ☎ **01752/662828,** or 800/225-5843 in the U.S. and Canada. Fax 01752/660974. 106 rms. TV TEL. £56 ($88.50) single or double Sun–Thurs, £43 ($67.95) Fri–Sat. Breakfast £5.50–£7.95 ($8.70–$12.55) extra. AE, DC, MC, V. Free parking.

The hotel is situated on a hilltop above the bay. The nine-story hotel was constructed in 1970, its clientele divided equally between tourists and business travelers. The hotel has well-furnished rooms, all but a dozen of which face the sea. Each unit has a radio, minibar, iron, and coffee maker.

On the premises is a pub, the Traders Bar, with a separate entrance, along with a free-form, heated outdoor pool (open daily May to September) and a restaurant with wide-angle views of the sea. Meals cost £16 ($25.30) and up.

⑤ Novotel Plymouth

270 Plymouth Rd., Marsh Mills Roundabout, Plymouth, Devon PL6 8NH. ☎ **01752/221422,** or 800/221-4542 in the U.S. Fax 01752/221422. 100 rms. A/C TV TEL. Mon–Thurs, £42.50 ($67.15) single or double. Breakfast £7.50 ($11.85) extra. Fri–Sat (including

breakfast), £45 ($71.10) single or double. AE, DC, MC, V. Two children 15 or under stay free in parents' room. Free parking. Bus 21 or 22.

The Novotel Plymouth, a 10-minute drive from the center beside the A38, is suitable for motorists, especially those with children. With landscaped gardens and plenty of parking, it offers an ample number of soundproofed bedrooms. Two children under 16 sharing a room with their parents also receive free breakfast. There's a swimming pool and a children's play area. A grill restaurant is open daily from 6am to midnight. Meals begin at £12.50 ($19.75).

WHERE TO DINE
MODERATE

✪ Chez Nous

13 Frankfort Gate. ☎ **01752/266793.** Reservations required. Main courses £17–£36 ($26.85–$56.90); fixed-price dinner £28.50 ($45.05). AE, DC, MC, V. Tues–Sat 12:30–2pm and 7–10:30pm. Closed first 3 weeks in Feb and Sept. FRENCH.

The most distinguished restaurant in Plymouth is Chez Nous, situated directly off Western Approach. Owner and chef Jacques Marchal borrows heavily from the past, but also expresses his creative talent. His type of cooking is called *la cuisine spontanée*—using fresh produce that changes with the seasons. Chez Nous is quite pretty and cozy, situated in a shopping complex. Look for the specials of the day on the chalkboard menu. Accompanied by a classic and rather elegant wine list, the food is likely to include such dishes as scallops steamed with ginger, bouillabaisse, and duck breast on a bed of lentils. Fish, generally, is the preferred main dish to order here. Desserts and appetizers are also prepared with care. Fresh, quality ingredients are a hallmark of the cuisine.

Green Lanterns

31 New St., The Barbican. ☎ **01752/660852.** Reservations recommended for dinner. Main courses £4.25–£5.50 ($6.70–$8.70) at lunch, £10.45–£14.55 ($16.50–$23) at dinner. AE, MC, V. Mon–Sat 11:45am–2:15pm and 6:30–10:45pm. Bus 54. ENGLISH.

A 16th-century eating house on a Tudor street, the Green Lanterns lies 200 yards from the *Mayflower* Steps. The lunch menu offers a selection of grills, chicken, and fish—all served with vegetables. The kitchen also features chalkboard specials such as Lancashire hot pot. Several unusual dishes are featured on the dinner menu such as goose breast in breadcrumbs, wild duck (teal), and venison in red wine. Chicken, beef, turkey, plaice, and mackerel are also available—all served with vegetables. Family owned, the Green Lanterns is run by Simon Grinter, who knows that tourists like the Elizabethan atmosphere, traditional English fare, and personal service. The restaurant is near the municipally owned Elizabethan House.

8 Clovelly

240 miles SW of London, 11 miles SW of Bideford

This is the most charming of all Devon villages and one of the main attractions of the West Country. Starting at a great height, the village cascades down the mountainside, with its narrow, cobblestone High Street that makes travel by car impossible—you park your car at the top and make the trip on foot; supplies are carried down by donkeys. Every step of the way provides views of tiny cottages, with their terraces of flowers lining the main street. The village fleet is sheltered at the stone quay at the bottom.

Tips: To avoid the tourist crowd, stay out of Clovelly from around 11am until teatime. Visit nearby villages during the middle of the day when the congestion here is at its height. Also, to avoid the climb back up the slippery incline, go to the rear of the Red Lion Inn and queue up for a Land Rover. In summer the line is often long, but considering the alternative, it's worth the wait.

ESSENTIALS
GETTING THERE

By Train From London's Paddington Station, trains depart for Exeter frequently. At Exeter, passengers transfer to a train headed for the end destination of Barnstable. Travel time from Exeter to Barnstable is 1 1/4 hours. From Barnstable, passengers transfer to Clovelly by bus.

By Bus From Barnstable, about one bus per hour, operated by either the Red Bus Company or the Filers Bus Company, goes to Bideford (trip time: 40 min.). At Bideford, connecting buses (with no more than a 10-minute wait between the arrival and the departure) continue on for the 30-minute drive to Clovelly. Two Land Rovers make continuous round-trips to the Red Lion Inn from the top of the hill, costing 70p ($1.10) per person each way.

By Car From London, head west on M4, cutting south at the junction with M5. At the junction near Bridgwater, continue west along A39 toward Lynton. A39 runs all the way to the signposted turnoff for Clovelly.

VISITOR INFORMATION

The **telephone area code** is 01237. For information, go to the **Clovelly Visitor Centre** (☎ **01237/431781**), where you'll pay £1.80 ($2.85) for the cost of parking, use of facilities, entrance to the village, and an audiovisual theater admission, offering a multiprojector show tracing the story of Clovelly back to 2,000 B.C.

WHERE TO STAY
INEXPENSIVE

ⓢ New Inn
High St., Clovelly, North Devon EX39 5SY. ☎ **01237/431303.** Fax 01237/431636. 20 rms, 5 with bath. £19.50 ($30.80) single without bath; £24 ($37.90) single with bath; £39 ($61.60) double without bath; £48 ($75.85) double with bath. Rates include English breakfast. AE, DC, MC, V.

About halfway down High Street is the village pub, a good meeting place at sundown. It offers the best lodgings in the village, in two buildings on opposite sides of the steep street (but only a 12-foot leap between their balconies). Five of the bedrooms are furnished with TV and phone.

This little country inn is also recommended for meals in the oak-beamed dining room. The local fare, including Devonshire cream, is featured whenever possible. Locally caught lobsters are also prepared by the chef. Motorists can park in the lot at the entrance to the town. It's advisable to pack an overnight case, since the luggage has to be carried down (but is returned to the top by donkey).

Red Lion
The Quay, Clovelly, Devon EX39 5TF. ☎ **01237/431237.** Fax 01237/431044. 12 rms. TV TEL. £39 ($61.60) single; £63 ($99.55) double. Rates include English breakfast. MC, V.

At the bottom of the steep cobbled street, right on the stone seawall of the little harbor, the Red Lion occupies the jewel position in the village. Rising three

Impressions

There was no road in it, there was no wheeled vehicle in it, there was not a level yard in it. From the sea-beach to the cliff-top two irregular rows of white houses, placed opposite to one another, and twisting here and there, and there and here, rose, like the sides of a long succession of stages of crooked ladders, and you climbed up the village or climbed down the village by the staves between, some six feet wide or so, and made of sharp irregular stones.

—Charles Dickens, *A Message from the Sea* (1860)

stories with gables and a courtyard, it's actually an unspoiled country inn, where life centers around an antique pub and village inhabitants, including sea captains, who gather to satisfy their thirst over pints of ale. Most of the bedrooms look out directly to the sea, and all of them have hot and cold running water and adequate furnishing. Dinner is available in the sea-view dining room for £15.75 ($24.90), with a choice of 12 main dishes, three to four of which are always fresh local fish, and then a selection from the dessert trolley. The manager suggests that the Red Lion is not suitable for children under 7 years of age.

A NEARBY PLACE TO STAY & DINE

Halmpstone Manor

Chittlehampton Rd., Bishop's Tawton, Barnstaple, North Devon EX32 OEA. ☎ **01271/ 830826.** 5 rms. TV TEL. £65 ($102.70) single; £100–£130 ($158–$205.40) double. Rates include English breakfast. AE, DC, MC, V. Free parking.

In the countryside, this manor house lies near Bishop's Tawton, 2³/₄ miles south of Barnstaple by A39 on A377 (Barnstaple itself is 40 miles northwest of Exeter and 222 miles west of London). This functioning farm is operated by Charles and Jane Stanbury. Originally built in the 11th century as a manor house with 22 rooms, the structure has diminished in size because of two fires that occurred in the 15th and 16th centuries. The edifice was rebuilt in 1701 in its present form with 15th-century paneling located in the dining room and high ceilings in the four-poster bedrooms. Family heirlooms are scattered throughout, and all the rooms have hot-beverage facilities and trouser presses.

For a period of time, Mrs. Stanbury worked temporarily at the prestigious restaurant Le Gavroche in London and brings some of that experience to her dining table. She offers a menu based on French and modern English fare made with fresh local ingredients, including dishes such as fillet of Devonshire beef in red-wine sauce with caramelized shallots and spring lamb encased in a herb-brioche crust glazed with port. For a finish, try the sticky toffee pudding with butterscotch sauce or the Cornish cheese made with a crust of stinging nettles called yarg, the cheesemaker's last name spelled backward. A six-course dinner costs £25 ($39.50) for residents and £30 ($47.40) for nonresidents.

9 Lynton-Lynmouth

206 miles W of London, 59 miles NW of Exeter

The north coast of Devon is set off dramatically in Lynton, a village some 500 feet high, which is a good center for exploring the Doone Valley and that part of Exmoor that overflows into the shire from neighboring Somerset. The Valley of the Rocks, west of Lynton, offers the most panoramic scenery.

Lynton is linked to its twin, Lynmouth, about 500 feet below, near the edge of the sea, by one of the most celebrated railways in Devon. It covers the differences in distance and altitude by means of a complicated network of cables and pulleys, allowing cars to travel up and down the face of the rocky cliff. The length of the track is 862 feet with a gradient of 1 inch, which gives a vertical height of approximately 500 feet. The two passenger cars are linked together with two steel cables, and the operation of the lift is on the counterbalance system, which is simply explained as a pair of scales where one side, when weighted by water ballast, pulls the other up.

The East Lyn and West Lyn rivers meet in Lynmouth, a popular resort with the British. For a panoramic view of the rugged coastline, you can walk on a path halfway between the towns that runs along the cliff. From Lynton, or rather from Hollerday Hill, you can look out onto Lynmouth Bay, Countisbury Foreland, and Woody Bays in the west.

ESSENTIALS
GETTING THERE

By Train   The resort is rather remote, and the local tourist office recommends that you rent a car. However, local daily trains from Exeter arrive at Barnstable.

By Bus   From Barnstable, bus service is provided to Lynton at a frequency of one about every 2 hours.

By Car   Take M4 west from London to the junction with M5, then head south to the junction with A39. Continue west on A39 to Lynton-Lynmouth.

VISITOR INFORMATION

The **telephone area code** for Lynton-Lynmouth is 01598. The **Tourist Information Centre** is at the Town Hall, Lee Road (☎ **01598/752225**).

WHERE TO STAY & DINE
INEXPENSIVE

Bath Hotel

Sea Front, Lynmouth, North Devon EX35 6EL. ☎ **01598/752238.** 24 rms. TV TEL. £32 ($50.55) single; £54–£74 ($85.30–$116.90) double. Rates include English breakfast. AE, DC, MC, V. Free parking. Closed Nov–Feb and weekdays in Mar.

Despite this hotel's functional appearance, its small, almost-obliterated core dates from the 16th century. Most of what a visitor will see, however, is a solidly built, peach-colored structure that dates from after World War II, set in a prominent position between the busy coastal road and the towering cliffs. All but a few of the comfortably furnished bedrooms offer views over the water. Well-prepared fixed-price meals are served in the hotel's restaurant for between £15.50 and £25 ($24.50 and $39.50). Each of these includes choices for vegetarians; lobster is one of the specialties.

☉ Hewitt's Hotel and Restaurant

The Hoe, North Walk, Lynton, Devon EX35 6HJ. ☎ **01598/752293.** Fax 01598/752489. 10 rms. TV TEL. £42–£45 ($66.35–$71.10) single; £84–£90 ($132.70–$142.20) double. Rates include English breakfast. MC, V. Free parking.

Hewitt's Hotel and Restaurant is named for Sir Thomas Hewitt, who helped construct the funicular railway that links the twin resorts. In the 1860s he also built a home for himself, and that place today is one of the most successful little inns in Lynton. Situated on some 24 acres, it opens onto beautiful vistas of Lynmouth Bay (best enjoyed while seated on a sunny terrace). The old house is filled with architectural character, as exemplified by its grand staircase, time-mellowed paneling, antiques, and stained-glass windows. All rooms are well furnished and comfortably appointed, with sea views; some are provided with private balconies. The hotel is "for all seasons" and has a country-house atmosphere. It has been described as a "perfect Agatha Christie set."

The quality of the bar lunches is far above average, and dinner is among the best served at the resort. In fact, it's reason enough to stay here, and you won't be overcharged either since meals begin at £19.50 ($30.80). A medley of British and continental dishes is served.

⑤ Rising Sun Hotel

The Harbour, Lynmouth, North Devon EX35 6EQ. ☎ **01598/753223.** Fax 01598/743480. 16 rms, 1 cottage. TV TEL. £39.50–£44.50 ($62.40–$70.30) single; £79–£89 ($124.80–$140.60) double; £118 ($186.45) Shelley's Cottage for two. Rates include English breakfast. AE, DC, MC, V. Free parking.

The Rising Sun Hotel is a thatched inn right at the end of the quay at the mouth of the Lyn River. Not only is the harbor life spread before you, but you can bask in the wonder and warmth of an inn that has been in business for more than 600 years. All the bedrooms, with crazy levels and sloping ceilings, offer views of the water, the changing tides, and bobbing boats. It's a lovely old place, where the staircase is so narrow and twisting that it requires care to negotiate. The ceilings are low and the floorboards creak. Behind the inn, halfway up the cliff, is a tiny garden bright with flowers in summer, where you can sit and gaze out over the thatched roofs to the sea. The owner has refurbished the place and added more rooms by joining two adjacent properties, and he has rooms available nearby in Shelley's Cottage, where the poet honeymooned in 1812. R. D. Blackmore wrote part of *Lorna Doone* while staying at the hotel. Two of the rooms have four-poster beds. It's a delight to dine at the Rising Sun since everything is 101% British in the dining room, with its deeply set window and fireplace. See the original 14th-century fireplace in the bar.

Tors Hotel

Lynmouth, Lynton, North Devon EX35 6NA. ☎ **01598/753236.** Fax 01598/752544. 35 rms. TV TEL. £37–£77 ($58.45–$121.65) single; £64–£94 ($101.10–$148.50) double. Rates include English breakfast. AE, DC, MC, V. Free parking. Closed Jan–Feb.

Set high on a cliff, the Tors Hotel opens onto a view of the coastline and the bay of Lynmouth. It was built in 1895 in the fashion of a Swiss château, with more than 40 gables, Tyrolean balconies jutting out to capture the sun (or the moon), black-and-white–timbered wings, and some 30 chimneys. Surrounding the hotel are a terrace and a heated swimming pool. The interior has been modernized, and much attention has been lavished on the comfortable bedrooms. A fixed-price lunch costs £12 ($18.95), and a fixed-price dinner goes for £17 ($26.85).

Cornwall 13

The ancient duchy of Cornwall is in the extreme southwestern part of England, often called "the toe." This peninsula is a virtual island—culturally if not geographically. Encircled by coastline, it abounds in rugged cliffs, hidden bays, fishing villages, sandy beaches, and sheltered coves where smuggling was once rampant. Although many of the little seaports with hillside cottages resemble towns along the Mediterranean, Cornwall retains its own distinctive flavor.

The Celtic-Iberian origin of the Cornish people is apparent in superstition, folklore, and fairy tales. When Cornish people speak of King Arthur and his Knights of the Round Table, they're not just handing out a line to tourists. To them, Arthur and his knights really existed, roaming around Tintagel Castle, now in ruins.

The ancient land had its own language until about 250 years ago, and some of the old words (*pol* for pool, *tre* for house) still survive. The Cornish dialect is more easily understood by the Welsh than by those who speak the Queen's English.

We suggest berthing at one of the smaller fishing villages, such as East or West Looe, Polperro, Mousehole, or Portloe—where you'll experience the true charm of the duchy. Many of the villages, such as St. Ives, are artists' colonies. Except for St. Ives and Port Isaac, some of the most interesting places lie on the southern coast, often called the Cornish Riviera, which strikes many foreign visitors as being the most intriguing. However, the north coast has its own peculiar charm as well.

A DRIVING TOUR

Day 1   After leaving Plymouth (see Devon, Chapter 12), continue west into Cornwall, cutting south of B3253 leading to the old fishing villages of Looe and Polperro. Either one would make an ideal stopover, and you'll have time to take at least part of the 4¹/₂-mile cliff walk from Looe to Polperro.

Day 2   From Polperro, continue west to the old seaport of Fowey, which rises by terraces above the Fowey Harbour. It's known for its regatta in the late summer. Armed with a good road map, you can go west from Fowey but in the direction of St. Mawes (take A3078 for the final lap of the trip). Stay overnight there.

What's Special About Cornwall

Beaches
- A majestic coastline—both north and south—studded with fishing villages and hidden coves for swimming, with Penzance and St. Ives the major meccas.

Great Towns/Villages
- Penzance, a granite resort and fishing port on Mount's Bay, with a Victorian promenade.
- St. Ives, an old fishing port and artists' colony, with a good surfing beach.
- Mousehole, considered the most charming old fishing port in Cornwall, filled with twisting lanes and granite cottages.

Natural Spectacles
- Isles of Scilly, 27 miles off the Cornish coast, with only 5 islands inhabited out of more than 100.
- Land's End, where England comes to an end, 9 miles west of Penzance.

Castles
- Tintagel Castle, on a wild stretch of the Atlantic coast, the legendary castle of King Arthur, Lancelot, and Merlin.
- St. Michael's Mount, off the coast of Penzance, which is part medieval, part 17th century.

Gardens
- Abbey Gardens of Tresco on the Isles of Scilly, 735 acres with 5,000 species of plants from some 100 countries.

Day 3   From St. Mawes, cross over to the port of Falmouth for a morning's visit. The old seaport was once the seat of piracy. See Pendennis Castle and perhaps have lunch in the area at one of the old pubs, such as King's Head on the corner of Church St. Climb. After leaving Falmouth, you can spend the afternoon exploring the Lizard Peninsula between Falmouth and Penzance. Lizard Point is the most southerly prong of England. Continue west along the coast to Penzance for the night.

☕ **TAKE A BREAK**   The Nelson Bar, in the Union Hotel on Chapel Street (☎ **01736//62319**), is known for its robust pub grub and collection of Nelsoniana. It's the spot where the admiral's death at Trafalgar was first revealed to the English people. Watch for daily specials. Food is served daily from noon to 2pm and 6:30 to 9pm.

Day 4   In Penzance the following morning, visit the castle on St. Michael's Mount. Drive south along the coast, stopping for lunch at Mousehole before continuing on to Land's End at the southern tip of England. After leaving Land's End, continue along the northwestern coast of Cornwall to the artist's colony at St. Ives for an overnight stop.

Day 5   In the morning visit the Tate Gallery and the Barbara Hepworth Museum and Garden before going on to Port Isaac, on the northern coast, for the night. Pay a side visit to Tintagel Castle, popularly known as King Arthur's Castle.

1 Looe

20 miles W of Plymouth, 264 miles SW of London

The ancient twin towns of East and West Looe are connected by a seven-arched stone bridge that spans the river. Houses on the hills are stacked one on top of the other in terrace fashion. In both fishing villages you can find good accommodations.

Fishing and sailing are two of the major sports, and the sandy coves, as well as East Looe Beach, are spots for seabathing. Beyond the towns are cliff paths and downs worth a ramble. Looe is noted for its shark fishing, but you may prefer simply walking the narrow, crooked medieval streets of East Looe, with its old harbor and 17th-century guildhall.

ESSENTIALS
GETTING THERE

By Train   Daily trains run from Plymouth, and rail connections can also be made from Exeter (Devon) and Bristol (Avon).

By Bus   Local bus companies have various routings from Plymouth into Looe. Ask at the tourist office in Plymouth for a schedule (see Chapter 12).

By Car   From Plymouth, take A38 west, then B3253.

VISITOR INFORMATION

The **telephone area code** is 01503. The **Tourist Information Centre** (summer only) is at the Guildhall, Fore Street (☎ **01503/262072**).

WHERE TO STAY & DINE
MODERATE

Hannafore Point Hotel

Marine Dr., Hannafore, West Looe, Cornwall PL13 2PH. ☎ **01503/263273.** Fax 01503/263272. 37 rms. TV TEL. £45–£54.50 ($71.10–$86.10) per person, single or double occupancy. Rates include half board. DC, MC, V. Free parking.

This rambling, gabled structure commands a fine view of the harbor—you can see miles of Cornish coastline and one of the most beautiful bays in England. Hannafore Point is in the main center for shark and deep-sea fishing and is ideal for exploring either Cornwall or parts of Devon.

In addition to the older bay-windowed rooms, newer sections have picture windows for viewing the harbor and St. George's Island. The entrance opens onto several levels of comfortable lounges and bars, with cantilevered stairs and balconies. The hotel has an elevator, and there's a comprehensive activity center with an indoor pool on the premises. Most of the front bedrooms have balconies, and each has a radio and hot-beverage facilities. The panoramic view adds to the pleasure of dining in the Headland Restaurant, where fresh ingredients are used

Impressions

There is in the Cornish character, smouldering beneath the surface, ever ready to ignite, a fiery independence, a stubborn pride.
—Daphne du Maurier, *Vanishing Cornwall* (1967)

in the fine Cornish and French cuisine. A table d'hôte meal in the restaurant costs £14.95 ($23.60) per person. The hotel also has a health club with a sauna.

INEXPENSIVE

Commonwood Manor Hotel

St. Martin's Rd. (the main Plymouth–Looe road, B3253), East Looe, Cornwall PL13 1LP. ☎ **01503/262929.** 11 rms, 1 suite. TV TEL. £37 ($58.45) single; £62–£70 ($97.95–$110.60) double; £93–£105 ($146.95–$165.90) suite. Rates include English breakfast. AE, MC, V. Free parking. Closed Nov–Mar.

A family-operated, country-house hotel on the edge of town at the entrance to Looe, about a 12-minute walk from the harbor and the center of the resort, Commonwood Manor stands on a wooded hillside surrounded by 3 acres of private grounds that open onto the Looe River Valley, with a heated swimming pool. Guests receive a warm welcome and are shown to one of the well-furnished and comfortably appointed bedrooms.

The meals are good, prepared with fresh ingredients, and dinners cost £11.50 to £14.50 ($18.15 to $22.90).

ⓢ Fieldhead Hotel

Portuan Rd., Hannafore, West Looe, Cornwall PL13 2DR. ☎ **01503/262689.** Fax 01503/264114. 14 rms. MINIBAR TV TEL. £35 ($55.30) single; £70 ($110.60) double. Rates include English breakfast. AE, MC, V. Free parking. Closed Jan.

Originally built in 1896 as a private home, and now one of the best hotels in the area, the Fieldhead is situated on 2 acres of gardens, with a heated, outdoor swimming pool, and commands a view of the sea. The rooms have a high standard of traditional furnishings, with beverage-making facilities and radio. Most of them also open onto views of Looe Bay. Sea views are also possible from the hotel's restaurant, where flowers and candles on the tables add a festive note for the home-cooked English and continental cuisine. A five-course meal costs £14.50 ($22.90) and up.

Talland Bay Hotel

Talland-by-Looe, Cornwall PL13 2JB. ☎ **01503/72667.** Fax 01503/72940. 20 rms. TV TEL. £40–£70 ($63.20–$110.60) single; £80–£140 ($126.40–$221.20) double. Rates include continental breakfast. AE, DC, MC, V. Free parking. Closed Jan. Take A387 4 miles southwest of Looe.

A country house dating from the 16th century, situated on $2^1/2$ acres, this hotel is the domain of Barry and Annie Rosier, who will direct you to local beaches and the croquet lawn. Its rectangular swimming pool is ringed with flagstones and a semitropical garden. Views from the tastefully furnished bedrooms include the sea and rocky coastline. Some of the bedrooms are in an annex.

The food is the best in the area, featuring excellently prepared seafood. Even if you aren't staying here, you may want to reserve a table. Table d'hôte meals cost £20 ($31.60) per person. A popular buffet lunch is served by the pool in summer. The restaurant is open for lunch Monday through Saturday from 12:30 to 2pm and Sunday from 12:45 to 1:30pm; for dinner, daily from 7:30 to 9pm.

IN NEARBY ST. KEYNE

Inexpensive

The Old Rectory Country House Hotel

Duloe Rd., St. Keyne, near Liskeard, Cornwall PL14 4RL. ☎ **01579/342617.** 8 rms. TV. £25–£30 ($39.50–$47.40) single; £45–£50 ($71.10–$79) double. Rates include English

Cornwall

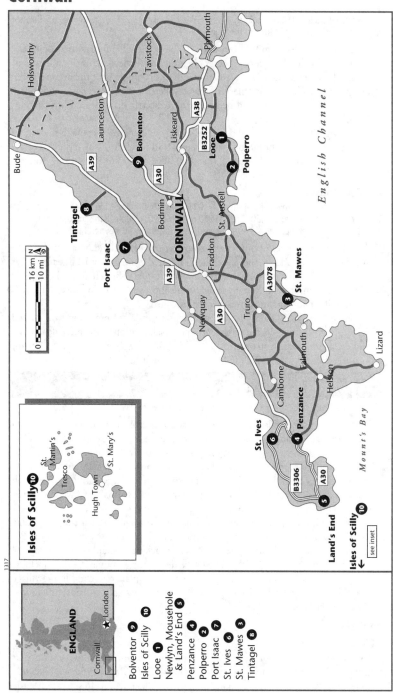

Bolventor **9**
Isles of Scilly **10**
Looe **1**
Newlyn, Mousehole & Land's End **5**
Penzance **4**
Polperro **2**
Port Isaac **7**
St. Ives **6**
St. Mawes **3**
Tintagel **8**

ENGLAND
Cornwall
London

Isles of Scilly **10**
St. Martin's
Tresco
St. Mary's
Hugh Town

English Channel

Plymouth
Holsworthy
Tavistock
Launceston
Bolventor **9**
Liskeard
Bude
A39
A38
B3252
Looe **1**
2
Polperro
A30
St. Austell
Bodmin
CORNWALL
Tintagel **8**
Port Isaac **7**
Fraddon
St. Mawes
A39
A3078
3
Newquay
A30
Truro
Falmouth
Lizard
Cambone
Helston
St. Ives **6**
Penzance **4**
Land's End
B3306
A30
5
Isles of Scilly **10**
see inset
Mount's Bay

breakfast. DC, MC, V. Free parking. From Liskeard, take B3254 to St. Keyne, go through St. Keyne, and make a left turn at the sign.

Peacefully secluded 5 miles from Looe in the beautiful countryside of southeast Cornwall, the hotel overlooks 3 acres of gardens with views across the valley. The owners have raised the hotel to a high standard to complement the original architecture, with paneled doors, marble fireplaces, Persian rugs, velvet sofas, and crystal. All the comfortably furnished bedrooms have electric blankets and hot-beverage facilities.

An English and continental cuisine is served on Wedgwood china in the elegant dining room where home-prepared meals and a selection of table wines are offered. The cost is £12.50 ($19.75) and up. The restaurant is open only to hotel guests.

✪ Well House

St. Keyne, Liskeard, Cornwall PL14 4RN. ☎ **01579/342001.** Fax 01579/343891. 7 rms. TV TEL. £60 ($94.80) single; £67.50–£105 ($106.65–$165.90) double. Rates include continental breakfast. MC, V. Free parking. From Liskeard, take B3254 to St. Keyne, 3 miles away.

Well House is another of those *restaurants avec chambres* found occasionally in the West Country, and it's one of the best. Located 3 miles from Liskeard, it has 5 acres of gardens opening onto vistas of the Looe Valley. It offers beautifully furnished bedrooms, with many thoughtful extras, such as fresh flowers. There is a swimming pool and an all-weather tennis court.

Guests flock here mainly for the cuisine, served daily from noon to 2pm and 7:15 to 9pm. Set menus are offered at both lunch or dinner, the price depending on how many courses you order: £19.95 ($31.50) for two courses, £24.95 ($39.40) for three courses, and £29.70 ($46.95) for four courses.

2 Polperro

271 miles SW of London, 6 miles SW of Looe, 26 miles W of Plymouth

This ancient fishing village is reached by a steep descent from the top of a hill from the main road leading to Polperro. You can take the 4$^1/_2$-mile cliff walk from Looe to Polperro, but the less adventurous will want to drive. However, in July and August motorists are forbidden to take cars into town unless they are booked at a hotel, in order to prevent traffic bottlenecks. There's a large parking area, which charges according to the length of your stay. For those unable to walk, a horse-drawn bus will take visitors to the town center.

Polperro is one of the handsomest villages in Cornwall, and parts of it resemble the 17th century. The village is surrounded by cliffs, and a stream called the Pol runs through it. The heart of the village is its much-photographed, much-painted fishing harbor, where the pilchard boats, loaded to the gunwales, used to dock. At one time it was estimated that nearly every man, woman, and child in the village spent time salting down pilchards for the winter or smuggling. Today the tourist trade has replaced contraband.

ESSENTIALS
GETTING THERE

By Train Most visitors arrive by car, but the nearest main-line station is at Liskeard, less than 4 hours from London's Paddington Station, with a branch line to Looe (see above). Taxis meet incoming trains to take visitors to the various little villages in the area.

By Bus   Local bus services are possible from Liskeard or Looe.

By Car   Take A387 southwest from Looe.

VISITOR INFORMATION

The **telephone area code** is 01503. There is no local information office. Ask at Looe (see above—summer only).

WHERE TO STAY

In and around Polperro, you'll find a number of quite good and colorful cottages, houses, small hotels, and inns that receive paying guests.

INEXPENSIVE

Claremont

Fore St., Polperro, Cornwall PL13 2RG. ☎ **01503/272241.** Fax 01503/272241. 12 rms. TV TEL. £24.75–£30.75 ($39.10–$48.60) single; £39–£60 ($61.60–$94.80) double. Rates include English breakfast. AE, MC, V. Free parking.

This 17th-century cottage with postwar additions lies behind a white facade on the main street leading to the village center. It sits above the village, offering a view over its rooftops. Service and access to the owners of this pleasant hotel are probably the most compelling reasons to check in. The bedrooms are all comfortably furnished.

The owners serve genuine French cooking daily from 7 to 9pm, a dinner costing £10.95 ($17.30) and up.

Lanhael House

Langreek Rd., Polperro, Cornwall PL13 2PW. ☎ **01503/72428.** Fax 01503/73077. 5 rms, 3 with bath (tub or shower). TV. £23 ($36.35) single without bath; £35 ($55.30) double without bath, £38 ($60.05) double with bath. Rates include English breakfast. No credit cards. Closed mid-Oct to Apr.

One of the best moderately priced accommodations at the resort, Lanhael House, situated off the road to Fowey, dates from the 17th century. Today it has many amenities, including a swimming pool and a terrace to capture the sun of the Cornish coast. The bedrooms are comfortable and attractively furnished, each with tea- or coffee-making equipment. An evening meal can be provided if arrangements are made in advance.

IN NEARBY PELYNT & LANREATH

If you find the busy activity of the two little harbors of Looe and Polperro too much for you, the pace of the nearby communities of Pelynt and Lanreath may be just right. The sleepy little village of Pelynt is just 3 miles north of Polperro. Peaceful Lanreath lies just 6 miles away from Polperro off the road to West Looe. Most visitors take a car or taxi from the Looe train station. The two places listed here number among England's major inns of character.

Inexpensive

Jubilee Inn

Jubilee Hill, Pelynt, near Looe, Cornwall PL13 2JZ. ☎ **01503/220312.** Fax 01503/220920. 9 rms. TV TEL. £33–£35 ($52.15–$55.30) single; £56–£60 ($88.50–$94.80) double. Rates include English breakfast. V. Free parking.

Built in the 16th century, this inn takes its name from Queen Victoria's Jubilee celebration, when it underwent restoration. It's a comment on, rather than a monument to, the past. The location is 4 miles from Looe and 3 miles from Polperro. The lounge has a hooded fireplace, with a raised hearth, Windsor armchairs, antique porcelain, and copper bowls filled with flowers cut from the garden behind the building. A glass-enclosed circular staircase takes you to the bedrooms. Fitting onto the outside, the winding stairway has been built to serve as a combined tower and hothouse. All but the three newest bedrooms have excellent 19th-century furnishings.

The dining room is elegantly Victorian, with mahogany chairs and tables. Vegetables come fresh from the inn's own garden. Both lunch and dinner are served in the bar, where bar snacks cost £3.30 to £10 ($5.20 to $15.80) per platter, or in the dignified dining room. There, à la carte meals cost around £15 to £25 ($23.70 to $39.50) each.

⑤ Punch Bowl Inn

Lanreath, near Looe, Cornwall PL13 2NX. ☎ **01503/220218.** Fax 01503/220218. 14 rms. TV. £20–£25 ($31.60–$39.50) per person, single or double occupancy. Rates include English breakfast. MC, V. Free parking. From Polperro, take B3359 north.

First licensed in 1620, the Punch Bowl has since served as a courthouse, coaching inn, and rendezvous for smugglers. Today its old fireplaces and high-backed settles, as well as its bedrooms (some with four-posters), provide hospitality. There's a modern lounge, TV room, and air-conditioned cocktail bar.

Even if you're not stopping over, you may sample the fare or drinks in one of the kitchens (actually bars—they're among the few "kitchens" licensed in Britain as "bars"). In the Stable Restaurant, with its Tudor beams and fireplace, you order à la carte, from a bowl of soup to steak. Meals begin at £15 ($23.70). Food is served from 6 to 11pm daily.

WHERE TO DINE
INEXPENSIVE

✿ The Kitchen

Fish na Bridge. ☎ **01503/72780.** Reservations required. Main courses £8.50–£12 ($13.45–$18.95). MC, V. Apr–Oct, Wed–Mon 7–9:30pm; off-season, Fri–Sat 7–9:30pm. Closed Nov–Easter. SEAFOOD.

This pink cottage about halfway down to the harbor from the parking area was once a wagon builder's shop; it's now a restaurant run by Vanessa and Ian Bateson (Vanessa makes all the desserts and bakes the bread). It offers good English cookery, with everything homemade from the best fresh ingredients available. The menu changes seasonally and prominently features local fresh fish. Typical dishes include Fowey sea trout with lemon-and-herb butter and breast of duckling with blueberry-and-Drambuie sauce. Many vegetarian dishes are offered as main courses.

Nelson's Restaurant

Saxon Bridge. ☎ **01503/72366.** Reservations required. Main courses £5.50–£14 ($8.70–$22.10); three-course table d'hôte lunch or dinner £10.95 ($17.30). AE, MC, V. Tues and Sat 7–9:45pm, Wed–Fri and Sun noon–1:45pm and 7–9:45pm. Closed mid-Jan to mid-Feb. SEAFOOD.

Situated in the lower reaches of Polperro, near the spot where the local river meets the sea, this is the only structure in town specifically built as a restaurant. Established in 1937, with a recent reincarnation from Peter and Betty Nelson, it features succulent preparations of regional fish that arrive fresh from local fishing boats. The menu specialties change with the availability of local ingredients, but usually include Dover sole Nelson, carpetbagger's steak (stuffed with scallops and prawns), turbot with an oyster-cream sauce, lobster, and several preparations of mussels and fresh crab. The decor is nautical, with lots of ships' wheels, diving helmets, and seafaring paraphernalia.

3 St. Mawes

300 miles SW of London, 2 miles E of Falmouth, 18 miles S of Truro

Overlooking the mouth of the Fal River, St. Mawes is often compared to a port on the French Riviera—it's sheltered from northern winds, and subtropical plants can grow here. From the town quay, you can take a boat to Frenchman's Creek and Helford River, as well as other places. St. Mawes is noted for its sailing, boating, fishing, and yachting, and half a dozen sandy coves lie within 15 minutes by car from the port. The town, built on the Roseland Peninsula, makes for interesting walks, with its colorful cottages and sheltered harbor. On Castle Point, Henry VIII ordered the construction of St. Mawes Castle.

ESSENTIALS
GETTING THERE

By Train   Trains leave from London's Paddington Station for Truro several times a day, requiring $4^1/_2$ hours for the trip. Passengers transfer at Truro to one of the two buses that make the 45-minute bus trip from Truro to St. Mawes. It's much easier and better to take a taxi from either Truro or, even more advantageous, from the village of St. Austell, which is the train stop before Truro.

By Bus   Buses depart from London's Victoria Coach Station several times a day for Truro, requiring 6 hours for the trip. Most visitors prefer the train.

By Car   To reach St. Mawes, turn left off A390 (the main road along the southern coast of Cornwall), at a junction 4 miles past St. Austell, onto the Tregony road, which will take you into St. Mawes.

By Ferry   There's a ferry traveling to St. Mawes from both Falmouth and Truro, but schedules are erratic, varying with the tides and the weather conditions.

VISITOR INFORMATION

The **telephone area code** is 01326.

WHERE TO STAY & DINE
MODERATE

The Idle Rocks

Tredenham Rd., St. Mawes, Cornwall TR2 5AN. ☎ **01326/270771.** Fax 01326/270062. 24 rms. TV TEL. July–Sept, £55–£71 ($86.90–$112.20) per person, single or double occupancy; Oct–June, £49–£66 ($77.40–$104.30) per person, single or double occupancy. Rates include half board. AE, MC, V. Free parking.

This solid old building right on the seawall sports gaily colored umbrellas and tables all along the terrace. The establishment was originally built in the 19th century as a storage shed for boats, then expanded into a hotel shortly after World War II. Water laps at the wall, and the site opens onto views over the river and the constant traffic of sailing boats and dinghies. The bar serves tasty lunch snacks, including fresh seafood caught locally. Most of the bedrooms have sea or river views, and they're equipped with central heating, hot-beverage facilities, radios, intercoms, and private baths with tubs or showers. The 15 units in the main hotel building charge higher rates; there are 9 more rooms in a relatively modern, stone-sided annex. Golf is available at the Truro Golf Club at reduced greens fees.

✪ The Tresanton

27 Lower Castle Rd., St. Mawes, Cornwall TR2 5DR. ☎ **01326/270544.** Fax 01326/270002. 22 rms, 2 suite. TV TEL. £63 ($99.55) single; £90–£116 ($142.20–$183.30) double; £92 ($145.35) per person suite. Rates include half board. MC, V. Free parking. Closed Oct 31–Dec 23 and Jan–Mar 1. Follow the road along the harbor to St. Mawes Castle; the hotel is 250 yards from the castle.

This hotel is composed of what were originally three 18th- and 19th-century private houses, one beside the road and the other halfway up the hill (the third building houses the hotel's genial staff). The largest of the three buildings is situated away from the traffic and has spacious veranda terraces, with lots of places to sit outside among the many flowers, looking across the bay. One reader wrote: "It's quite simply the most charming and delightful hotel I have ever stayed in." The bedrooms are fresh and bright, furnished for the most part in the French country-house manner, and are stocked with sewing kits, tissues, and books; all have a private bath and face the sea. The lounge has an open fireplace and comfortable chairs.

The dining room, also overlooking the sea, has attractive murals and a decor designed to carry the eye from the house to the sun terraces, the subtropical gardens, and the sea beyond. The menu wisely emphasizes fish dishes and serves à la carte dinners for around £14 ($22.10) each.

INEXPENSIVE

The Rising Sun

The Square, St. Mawes, Cornwall TR2 5DJ. ☎ **01326/270233.** 11 rms. TV TEL. £37 ($58.45) per person, single or double. Rates include English breakfast. AE, MC, V. Free parking.

Converted from a quartet of 17th-century fishing cottages, with a flower-draped flagstone terrace out front, this colorful seafront inn in the center of town oozes charm. Known as one of Cornwall's best inns and owned by the St. Austell Breweries, it uses some of its ground floor as one of St. Mawes's busiest pubs. This is a rustically appealing place with stone accents, a fireplace, and bar snacks priced at £2.25 to £8.95 ($3.55 to $14.15). The inn's restaurant—a dignified room adjacent to the pub—has a reputation for good food, and you might want to patronize it even if you don't stay at the hotel. Table d'hôte meals begin at £16.95 ($26.80) each and feature a variety of fish dishes. The inn's bedrooms are functional and cozy, and each is equipped with tea- and coffee-making facilities, color TV, and phone.

4 Penzance

280 miles SW of London, 77 miles SW of Plymouth

This little harbor town, which Gilbert and Sullivan made famous, is at the end of the Cornish Riviera. It's noted for its moderate climate (it's one of the first towns in England to blossom with spring flowers), and summer throngs descend for fishing, sailing, and swimming. Overlooking Mount's Bay, Penzance is graced in places with subtropical plants, including palm trees.

Those pirates in *The Pirates of Penzance* were not entirely fictional. The town was raided by Barbary pirates, destroyed in part by Cromwell's troops, sacked and burned by the Spaniards, and bombed by the Germans. In spite of its turbulent past, it offers tranquil resort living today.

The most westerly town in England, Penzance makes a good base for exploring Land's End, the Lizard peninsula, St. Michael's Mount, the old fishing ports and artists' colonies of St. Ives, Newlyn, and Mousehole—even the Isles of Scilly.

ESSENTIALS
GETTING THERE

By Train   Ten express trains depart daily from Paddington Station in London for Penzance (trip time: 5^1/$_2$ hr.).

By Bus   The *Rapide*, run by National Express from Victoria Coach Station in London (☎ **0171/730-0202**), costs £33.50 ($52.95) for the one-way trip from London, which takes about 8 hours. The buses have toilets and reclining seats, and a hostess dispenses coffee, tea, and sandwiches.

By Car   Drive southwest across Cornwall on A30 all the way to Penzance.

VISITOR INFORMATION

The **telephone area code** is 01736. The **Tourist Information Centre** is on Station Road (☎ **01736/62207**).

WHAT TO SEE & DO

✪ Castle

On St. Michael's Mount, Mount's Bay. ☎ **01736/710507.** Admission £3.20 ($5.05) adults, £1.60 ($2.55) children. Apr–Oct, Mon–Fri 10:30am–4:45pm; Nov–Mar, Mon, Wed, and Fri by conducted tour which only leaves at 11am, noon, 2pm, and 3pm, weather and tide permitting. Bus 20, 21, or 22 from Penzance to Marazion, the town opposite St. Michael's Mount.

Rising about 250 feet from the sea, St. Michael's Mount is topped by a part-medieval, part-17th-century castle; it's 3 miles east of Penzance and is reached at low tide by a causeway. At high tide the mount becomes an island, reached only by motor launch from Marazion. A Benedictine monastery, the gift of Edward the Confessor, stood on this spot in the 11th century. The castle now has a collection of armor and antique furniture. In winter, you can go over only when the causeway is dry. There's a tea garden on the island, as well as a National Trust restaurant, both open in summer. The steps up to the castle are steep and rough, so wear sturdy shoes. To avoid disappointment, it's a good idea to call the number listed above to learn the state of the tides, especially during the cooler months.

Minack Theatre

Porthcurno. ☎ **01736/810694.** Theater tickets £5 ($7.90). Tour tickets £1.50 ($2.35). Exhibition hall, Easter–Oct 30, daily 10am–5:30pm. Performances, end of May to mid-Sept, matinees at 2pm, evening shows at 8pm. Leave Penzance on A30 heading toward Land's End; after 3 miles, bear left onto B3283 and follow the signs to Porthcurno.

Considered one of the most unusual theaters in southern England, this open-air amphitheater was cut from the side of a rocky Cornish hill near the village of Porthcurno, 9 miles southwest of Penzance. Its by-now-legendary creator was Rowena Cade, an arts enthusiast and noted eccentric, who began the theater after World War I by physically carting off much of the granite from her chosen hillside. On the premises is an exhibition hall that showcases a permanent record of her life and accomplishments. She died a very old woman in the 1980s, confident of the enduring appeal of her theater to visitors from around the world.

Up to 750 visitors at a time can sit directly on grass- or rock-covered ledges, sometimes on cushions if they're available, within sight lines of both the actors and a sweeping view out over the ocean. Experienced theatergoers sometimes bring raincoats for protection against the occasional drizzle. Theatrical events are staged by repertory theater companies that travel throughout Britain, and are likely to include everything from Shakespeare to musical comedy.

WHERE TO STAY
MODERATE
Abbey Hotel
Abbey St., Penzance, Cornwall TR18 4AR ☎ **01736/66906.** Fax 01736/51163. 6 rms, 1 suite. TV. £65 ($102.70) single; £80–£120 ($126.40–$189.60) double; £130 ($205.40) suite. Rates include English breakfast. AE, MC, V. Free parking.

Charming and small-scale, this hotel occupies a stone-sided house that was erected in 1660 on the site of a 12th-century abbey which was demolished by Henry VIII. It's located on a narrow side street on raised terraces that overlook the panorama of Penzance Harbour. Behind the hotel is a medieval walled garden that was part of the original abbey. The bedrooms are stylishly furnished with English country-house flair. The owners, Michael and Jean Cox, bring vitality, style, and charm to the hotel business. Mrs. Cox is the former international model Jean Shrimpton.

On the premises is a restaurant, where herbs from the above-mentioned garden flavor some of the food. Sample dinner dishes include homemade soups, mackerel pâté, fresh local fish, and some kind of roast joint. Everything is fresh and delicately cooked, usually as part of fixed-price dinners costing £22.50 ($35.55).

INEXPENSIVE

⑤ The Georgian House
20 Chapel St., Penzance, Cornwall TR18 4AW. ☎ **01736/65664.** 12 rms, 6 with bath (tub or shower). TV TEL. £18.50 ($29.25) single without bath, £25 ($39.50) single with bath; £34 ($53.70) double without bath, £42 ($66.35) double with bath. Rates include English breakfast. AE, MC, V. Free parking.

This former home of the mayors of Penzance, reputedly haunted by the ghost of a Mrs. Baines, who owned it hundreds of years ago, has been completely renovated into an intimate hotel, whose bright, cozy rooms all have hot- and cold-water basins and tea and coffee makers. The house is centrally heated, with a comfortable reading lounge, a licensed bar with a nautical motif, and an intimate dining room, where good Cornish meals are served from April to October. The house accepts guests all year.

Tarbert Hotel
11 Clarence St., Penzance, Cornwall TR18 2NU. ☎ **01736/63758.** Fax 01736/331336. 12 rms. TV TEL. £25.50–£38 ($40.30–$60.05) single; £46–£71 ($72.70–$112.20) double. Rates include English breakfast. AE, MC, V. Closed Dec 23–Jan 26.

The dignified granite-and-stucco walls of this once-private house were built in the 1830s by a predecessor of Harrods department store, which operated a sideline business of home construction. (The present owners state that it was the home of a local merchant sea captain who is believed to have perished at sea between 1839 and 1841.) It lies about 2 minutes' walk northwest of the town center. Some of the bedrooms retain their original high ceilings and elaborate cove moldings, and each is equipped with a tea-making facility and comfortable furniture.

Frommer's Nature Notes

Much of Cornwall includes some of the most evocatively barren landscape in Britain; it's composed of gray rocks, weathered headlands jutting seaward, and very few trees. The weather alternates between bright sunshine and the impenetrable fogs for which the edges of the English Channel are famous.

The land and seascapes provide welcome relief for the many British urbanites who come for trekking excursions around the Cornish peninsula's coastline. The government maintains a clearly signposted coastal path more than 600 miles long that skirts the edge of the sea, following the tortured coastline from Minehead (in Somerset, near Dunster) to Poole (in Dorset, near Bournemouth). En route, the path goes through some of the least developed regions of southern England, including hundreds of acres of privately owned land as well as the northern border of the Exmoor National Park. Throughout there is an ancient sense of Celtic mysticism and existential loneliness. Low-lying gorse, lichens, and heathers characterize the vegetation. In marked contrast to the windblown uplands, verdant subtropical vegetation grows in the tidal estuaries of the Fowey, Fal, Helford, and Tamar rivers.

Your choices for exploring the coasts of Cornwall and Devon (and parts of Somerset and Dorset as well) are numeous. A full circumnavigation of the southwestern peninsula on the coastal path would take four to six weeks of hard trekking; although the route is sometimes arduous, no special equipment other than sturdy shoes, good stamina, and waterproof clothing is required. It might also be worthwhile to consult a locally researched guidebook, the *Sou'West Way Associations' Complete Guide to the Coastal Path,* which can be ordered from the Sou'West Way Association, 1 Orchard Dr., Kingskerswell, Newton Abbot, Devon TQ12 5DG (☎ **01803/873061**) for £3.99 ($6.30).

Recognizing that most trekkers have only a day or at most a week for their treks across Cornwall, the book divides the 600-mile coastal path into segments, rates them for degrees of interest and difficulty, and lists a network of recommended pubs, bed-and-breakfast hotels, inns, and campgrounds en route. The organization can also procure guides who will accompany groups of hikers across the Cornish moors for special lectures and sightseeing.

Be aware that the evocative loneliness of the Cornish moors might be marred by hundreds of other trekkers during Britain's school holidays. If possible, schedule your visit for relatively quiet periods, and remember that the weather between late October and early May includes substantial amounts of rain, fog, and wind.

A restaurant, specializing in fresh seafood brought in by local fishing boats, serves fixed-price evening meals from 7 to 9pm every night, priced from £12.50 ($19.75) each. During the day bar lunches are served to residents, and there's also a licensed bar with an extensive wine list and draft beer. Menu choices are likely to include salmon steak in a white-wine sauce with cucumbers and prawns; poached halibut steak with tomatoes, basil, and spring onion; duckling breast with an apricot-and-brandy sauce; or a whole red mullet with lemon-balm butter. A vegetarian menu is also offered, including such dishes as nutty broccoli and sweet corn flan or pasta shells with mixed vegetables in a spicy tomato sauce topped with cheese and baked.

WHERE TO DINE
MODERATE

Harris's Restaurant

46 New St. ☎ **01736/64408.** Reservations recommended. Main courses £9.50–£15.50 ($15–$24.50). AE, MC, V. Mon 7–10pm, Tues–Sat noon–1:45pm and 7–10pm. Closed Nov. FRENCH/ENGLISH.

Down a narrow cobblestone street off Market Jew Street, opposite Lloyds Bank, this warm, candlelit place has a relaxed atmosphere. Light lunches, served upstairs, include crab Florentine, lobster salad, and salmon crêpes. Dinner is more elaborate, offering breast of duckling in a port-wine sauce, fillet steak with a red-wine and wild-mushroom sauce, and lamb with crab-apple jelly and rosemary.

INEXPENSIVE

Turk's Head

49 Chapel St. ☎ **01736/63093.** Main courses £3.95–£8.95 ($6.25–$14.15); bar snacks from £1.50 ($2.35). MC, V. Mon–Sat 11am–2:30pm and 5:30–10pm, Sun noon–2:30pm and 7–10:30pm (bar, Mon–Sat 11am–3pm and 5:30–11pm, Sun noon–3pm and 7–10:30pm). From the rail station, turn left just past Lloyd's Bank. ENGLISH.

Dating from 1233, this inn is reputed to be the oldest in Penzance. It serves the finest food of any pub in town, far superior to its chief rival, the nearby Admiral Benbow. In summer, drinkers overflow into the garden. Inside, the inn is decorated in a mellow style, as befits its age, with flatirons and other artifacts hanging from its timeworn beams. Meals include fishermen's pie, local seafood, and chicken curry, and prime quality steaks including rib eye. See the chalkboards for the daily specials.

5 Isles of Scilly

27 miles WSW of Land's End

Several miles off the Cornish coast, the Scilly Isles are warmed by the Gulf Stream to the point where semitropical plants thrive. Some winters never see signs of frost. Culturally linked more to Cornwall than to France, they're known as the first landfall most oceangoing passengers see on ocean journeys from North America and figured prominently in the myths and legends of the ancient Greeks and Romans.

There are five inhabited and more than 100 uninhabited islands in the group. Some are only a few square miles, while others, such as the largest, St. Mary's, encompass some 30 square miles. Three of these islands—Tresco, St. Mary's, and St. Agnes–attract visitors from the mainland. Early flowers are the main export and tourism the main industry.

The Isles of Scilly were known to the early Greeks and the Romans, and in Celtic legend they were inhabited entirely by holy men. There are more ancient burial mounds on these islands than anywhere else in southern England, and artifacts have clearly established that people lived here more than 4,000 years ago. Today there's little left of this long history for the visitor to see.

St. Mary's is the capital, with about seven-eighths of the total population of all the islands, and it's here that the ship from the mainland docks at Hugh Town. However, if you'd like to make this a day visit, we recommend the helicopter flight from Penzance to Tresco, the neighboring island, where you can enjoy a day's walk through the 735 acres, mostly occupied by the Abbey Gardens.

ESSENTIALS
GETTING THERE

By Plane or Helicopter   Isles of Scilly Skybus Ltd. (☎ **01736/62009**) operates between two and eight flights per day, depending on the season, between Penzance's Land's End Airport and Hugh Town on St. Mary's Island. Flight time on the eight-passenger fixed-wing planes is 20 minutes each way. The round-trip fare is £50 ($79) for same-day return, and £48 ($75.85) if you plan to stay over for the night.

    There's also a helicopter service maintained by British International Helicopters at the Penzance Heliport Eastern Green (☎ **01736/63871**), which operates, weather permitting, 2 to 12 daily helicopter flights between Penzance and both St. Mary's and the less populated island of Tresco. Flight time is 20 minutes from Penzance to either island. A same-day round-trip fare is £55 ($86.90), rising to £82 ($129.55) if you spend a night or more on the island. A bus, whose timing coincides with the departure of each helicopter flight, runs to the heliport from the railway station in Penzance for a cost of £1.50 ($2.35) per person each way.

By Rail   The rail line ends in Penzance (see above).

By Ship   Slower but perhaps more romantic, you can travel via the Isles of Scilly Steamship Co. Ltd., Quay Street, Penzance (☎ **01736/62009**), which offers daily runs between Penzance and the Scillies from April to October. The trip from Penzance to Hugh Town, St. Mary's, takes 2 hours 40 minutes, with continuing service on to Tresco. Steamships depart Monday through Friday at 9:15am, returning from St. Mary's at 4:30pm. Saturday schedules vary according to the time of year, sometimes with two sailings a day. In winter, service is much more limited. A same-day round-trip ticket from Penzance to St. Mary's costs £29 ($45.80) for adults, £15 ($23.70) for children 14 and under. An onward ticket from St. Mary's to Tresco costs an additional £6 ($9.50).

VISITOR INFORMATION

The **telephone area code** is 01720. For information about Tresco's boat schedules, possible changes in hours and prices at the Abbey Gardens, and other matters, call 0720/22849. **St. Mary's Tourist Information Office** is at Porthcressa Bank, St. Mary's (☎ **01720/422536**).

TRESCO

No cars or motorbikes are allowed on Tresco, but bikes can be rented by the day; the hotels use a special wagon towed by a farm tractor to transport guests and luggage from the harbor.

    The ✪ **Abbey Gardens** are the most outstanding feature of Tresco, started by Augustus Smith in the mid-1830s. When he began his work, the area was a barren hillside, a fact visitors now find hard to believe.

    The gardens are a nature-lover's dream, with more than 5,000 species of plants from some 100 different countries. The old abbey, or priory, now in ruins, is said to have been founded by Benedictine monks in the 11th century, although some historians date it from 964. Of special interest in the gardens is Valhalla, a collection of nearly 60 figureheads from ships wrecked around the islands; the gaily painted figures from the past have a rather eerie quality, each one a ghost with a different story to tell. The gardens are open daily from 10am to 4pm. Admission is £4 ($6.30) for adults, free for children 13 and under.

After a visit to the gardens, take a walk through the fields, along paths, and across dunes thick with heather. Flowers, birds, shells, and fish are abundant. Birds are so unafraid that they land within a foot or so of you and feed happily. You can call 01720/422849 for information about the abbey.

WHERE TO STAY
Expensive
✪ Island Hotel

Old Grimsby, Tresco, Isles of Scilly, Cornwall TR24 0PU. ☎ **01720/422883.** Fax 01720/ 423008. 38 rms, 2 suites. TV TEL. £60–£93 ($94.80–$146.95) per person, single or double. Rates include half board. AE, MC, V. Closed late Oct to early Mar.

This is considered the finest hotel in the Scillies, located at Old Grimsby near the northeastern shore of Tresco. It was established in 1960, when a late 19th-century stone cottage was enlarged with conservatory-style windows and a series of long and low extensions. Today the plant-filled interior provides a feeling not unlike what you might experience in the Caribbean, with water views and lots of inside greenery. Some rooms overlook the sea, others face inland, and all were renovated in 1990. All are comfortably furnished with easy chairs and storage spaces. The hotel is noted for its subtropical garden. Nonresidents pay around £28 ($44.25) for a five-course evening meal.

Moderate
New Inn

Tresco, Isles of Scilly, Cornwall TR24 0QQ. ☎ **01720/422844.** Fax 01720/422807. 12 rms. TEL. £48–£65 ($75.85–$102.70) per person, single or double occupancy, depending on the season. Rates include half board. AE, DC, MC, V.

Composed of an interconnected row of 19th-century fisher's cottages and shops, much enlarged since its transformation into a hotel, this establishment is situated at the center of the island, beside its unnamed main road. Much of its income derives from its status as a pub, which offers an outdoor area for those who'd like to picnic or drink a glass of ale. Inside, the bar is a meeting place for locals and visitors alike. Lunch snacks are available, and a bar meal costs £5 ($7.90) and up for two courses. Fixed-price dinners cost £13.50 to £18.50 ($21.35 to $29.25) and are served nightly between 7:30 and 8:30pm. The pictures in the bar show many of the ships that sank or foundered around the islands in the past, as well as some of the gigs used in pilotage, rescue, smuggling, and pillage. The inn has a heated outdoor swimming pool.

ST. MARY'S
GETTING AROUND

Cars are available but hardly necessary. The **Island Bus Service** has a basic charge of £2 ($3.15) from one island point to another; children ride for half fare.

Bicycles are one of the most practical means of transport. **Buccabu Bicycle Rentals,** Porthcressa, St. Mary's (☎ 01720/422289), is the larger of the island's two bike rental outfits. They stock "shopper's cycles" with three speeds, "hybrid" bikes with 6 to 12 speeds, and 18-speed mountain bikes. All are available at prices that range from £3.50 to £4.50 ($5.55 to $7.10) daily. A sum of £5 to £10 ($7.90 to $15.80) is required for a deposit, depending on the length of the bike rental.

WHAT TO SEE & DO

The **Isles of Scilly Museum,** on Church Street in St. Mary's (☎ **01720/422337**), illustrates the history of the Scillies from 2500 B.C. with drawings, artifacts from wrecked ships, and assorted relics discovered on the islands. It's open April to October, daily from 10am to noon and 1:30 to 4:30pm, and May to September, also daily from 7:30 to 9pm; off-season, only on Wednesday from 2 to 4pm. Admission is 75p ($1.20) for adults, 10p (15¢) for children.

WHERE TO STAY

Moderate

Star Castle Hotel

The Garrison, St. Mary's, Isles of Scilly TR21 0JA. ☎ **01720/422317**. Fax 01720/422343. 30 rms. TV TEL. £48–£75 ($75.85–$118.50) per person. Rates include half board. DC, MC, V. Free parking. Closed mid-Oct to mid-Mar.

This hotel was originally built as a castle in 1593, in the shape of an eight-pointed star, to defend the Isles of Scilly against Spanish attacks in retaliation for the 1588 defeat of the armada. Owing to the original building's purpose, the hotel has views out to sea as well as over the town and the harbor. The great kitchen has a huge fireplace where a whole ox could be roasted. A young prince of Wales (later King Charles II) took shelter here in 1643 when he was being hunted by Cromwell and his parliamentary forces. In 1933 another prince of Wales officiated at the opening of the castle as a hotel—the man who succeeded to the throne as King Edward VIII but was never crowned.

The 18 bedrooms in the garden annex are extra-large units, each with a bath and each opening directly onto the gardens. Eight double rooms and five single rooms are in the castle. There's a glass-covered, heated swimming pool, and the garden has many sheltered places for you to relax. Lunches tend to be simple pub-style platters, and orders are accepted in the cellar bar. Dinners are more elaborate, and most of the vegetables come from the hotel's large gardens. Nonresidents are charged £17.95 ($28.35) for a four-course dinner. If you pay with a credit or charge card, expect a 3% surcharge to be added to your bill.

Inexpensive

⑤ Carnwethers Country House

Pelistry Bay, St. Mary's, Isles of Scilly, Cornwall TR21 0NX. ☎ **01720/422415**. 10 rms. £33–£48 ($52.15–$75.85) per person. Rates include half board. No credit cards. Closed Oct–May.

Pelistry Bay, a secluded part of St. Mary's island northeast of the airport, has a well-sheltered sandy beach, and this modernized farmhouse stands here on top of a hill looking out to fields, beach, and the sea. You can walk at low tide across to the nearby uninhabited island of Tolls. The guesthouse rooms are spotless, warm, and comfortable. The main lounge is in two parts, one for conversation and reading, the other with a library filled with books about the island.

At dinner a limited choice of traditional English fare is offered. Dinner, served at 6:30pm, includes fresh local produce and home-grown vegetables. Breakfast is a substantial meal, the marmalade being a particular pride of the house. There's a well-stocked bar. The house has its own grounds and a croquet lawn. A heated outdoor swimming pool is in operation from May to September. Sauna and a games room are also available.

6 Newlyn, Mousehole & Land's End

Newlyn: 1 mile S of Penzance
Mousehole: 3 miles S of Penzance, 2 miles S of Newlyn
Land's End: 9 miles W of Penzance

ESSENTIALS
GETTING THERE

By Train   From London, journey first to Penzance (see above), then take a local bus for the rest of the journey.

By Bus   From Penzance, take bus A to Mousehole and bus no. 1 to Land's End. There is frequent service throughout the day.

By Car   After reaching Penzance, drive south on B3315.

VISITOR INFORMATION

The **telephone area code** is 01736.

NEWLYN

From Penzance, a promenade leads to Newlyn, another fishing village of infinite charm on Mount's Bay. In fact, its much-painted harbor seems to have more fishing craft than that of Penzance. The late Stanhope Forbes founded an art school in Newlyn, and in the past few years the village has achieved a growing reputation for its artists' colony, attracting both serious painters and Sunday sketchers. From Penzance, the old fishing cottages and crooked lanes of Newlyn are reached by bus.

WHERE TO STAY & DINE
Moderate

Higher Faugan Hotel

Chywoone Hill, Newlyn, Penzance, Cornwall TR18 5NS. ☎ **01736/62076.** Fax 01736/ 51648. 11 rms. TV TEL. £38–£45 ($60.05–$71.10) single; £76–£94 ($120.10–$148.50) double. Rates include English breakfast. Children under 12 stay free in parents' room. AE, DC, MC, V. Free parking. Take B3315 three-quarters of a mile south of Penzance.

The structure was built in 1904 by painter Alexander Stanhope Forbes, whose work is now in demand, as is that of his wife, Elizabeth Adela Forbes, and many other artists from the "Newlyn" school. The spacious building's granite walls, big windows, and steep roofs are surrounded by 10 acres of lawn, garden, and woodland, all of which can be covered on foot by adventurous visitors. Amenities include a heated outdoor swimming pool, a putting green, a hard tennis court, a billiards room, and a dining room serving beautifully prepared English and continental specialties. The rooms are traditionally furnished and well maintained.

MOUSEHOLE

The Cornish fishing village of Mousehole attracts hordes of tourists, who, fortunately, haven't changed it too much. The cottages still sit close to the harbor wall; the fishers still bring in the day's catch; the salts sit around smoking tobacco, talking about the good old days; and the lanes are as narrow as ever. About the most exciting thing to happen here was the arrival in the late 16th century of the Spanish galleons, whose sailors sacked and burned the village. In a sheltered cove of Mount's Bay, Mousehole (pronounced *Mou*-sel) today has developed as the nucleus of an artists' colony.

WHERE TO STAY & DINE
Inexpensive
Carn Du Hotel
Raginnis Hill, Mousehole, Cornwall TR19 6SS. ☎ **01736/731233.** 7 rms. TV. £50–£60 ($79–$94.80) double. Rates include English breakfast. AE, MC, V. Free parking. Take B3315 from Newlyn past the village of Sheffield (1½ miles) and bear left toward Castallack; after a few hundred yards, turn left to Mousehole, indicated by a sign; coming down the hill, the Carn Du is on the left facing the sea.

Twin bay windows gaze over the top of the village onto the harbor with its bobbing fishing vessels. The hotel's bedrooms (all doubles or twins) offer radios and much comfort. The owners will arrange sporting options for active vacationers but won't mind if you prefer to sit and relax.

The meals, going for £14.95 ($23.60), are straightforward and fresh, usually accompanied by a bottle of wine from the cellars. You might precede your meal with a drink in one of the lounges.

The Lobster Pot
Mousehole, Cornwall TR19 6QX. ☎ **01736/731251.** Fax 01736/731140. 25 rms, 22 with bath (tub or shower). TV TEL. June–Sept, £25 ($39.50) per person single or double without bath, £42–£51 ($66.35–$80.60) per person single or double with bath. Feb–May and Oct–Dec, £21 ($33.20) per person single or double without bath, £35–£45 ($55.30–$71.10) single or double with bath. Rates include English breakfast. MC, V. Closed Jan.

Tasteful, nostalgic, and charming, this little hotel is housed in four adjacent former fishers' cottages near the water's edge of Mousehole. In addition to the main hotel, guests are housed in Clipper House, Gull's Cry, or Harbour's Edge. Seven of the bedrooms open onto sea views across the harbor and Mount's Bay beyond. The bedrooms are comfortably furnished, with such amenities as tea or coffee makers, color TV, direct-dial phone, trouser press, hairdryer, and razor points. Families are especially welcomed.

Even if you're not a resident, the Lobster Pot is one of the best dining choices in town. A fixed-price dinner costs £15.50 ($24.50), or you can order à la carte, especially if you want to partake of the chef's specialty, freshly caught lobster (when available). It can be prepared virtually any way you want: steamed, grilled, Newburg, or Thermidor. Crab, sole, and salmon are also featured.

In Nearby Lamorna Cove: Moderate
Lamorna Cove Hotel
Lamorna Cove, Penzance, Cornwall TR19 6XH. ☎ **01736/731411.** 12 rms, 4 suites. TV TEL. £29.50–£34.50 ($46.60–$54.50) per person. Rates include English breakfast. MC, V. Free parking. Take a taxi from Penzance.

Situated near one of the most perfect coves in Cornwall, only 5 miles south of Penzance but seemingly inaccessible down a winding, narrow road, this hotel was skillfully terraced—after months of blasting—into a series of rocky ledges that drop down to the sea. Originally built as a chapel for Cornish miners, with a bell tower that has been saved despite numerous enlargements and improvements, the hotel offers a rocky garden that clings to the cliff sides and surrounds a small swimming pool and a sun terrace overlooking the sea. The bedrooms are comfortable and cozy with sea views. Nearby, a long and narrow dining room runs the length of the building, and a public lounge is furnished with comfortable chairs, centered around a wintertime log fire, with many pictures and antiques.

If you don't have time to stay at the hotel, stop in for one of its well-recommended meals. Bar snacks cost £3.50 to £11.50 ($5.55 to $18.15), and a full meal in the restaurant begins at around £17.50 ($27.65).

LAND'S END

Craggy Land's End is where England comes to an end. America's coast is 3,291 miles west of the rugged rocks that tumble into the sea beneath Land's End. Some enjoyable cliff walks and spectacular views are available here.

WHERE TO STAY & DINE

Moderate

State House Hotel

Land's End, Sennen, Cornwall TR19 7AA. ☎ **01736/871844.** Fax 01736/871599. 33 rms. TV TEL. £34.50–£60 ($54.50–$94.80) per person. Rates include English breakfast. AE, MC, V. Free parking.

Situated behind a white facade in a complex of buildings rising from the rugged landscape at the very tip of England, at the end of the main A30 road, this hotel has a panoramic clifftop position, exposed to the wind and sea spray. The rooms are attractively furnished and well maintained. Each unit is a double.

Much of the hotel's business comes from the many day visitors who stop by for a snack or cup of coffee in one of the three eating areas. Bar meals are served daily from noon to 2pm, and a cafeteria remains open all day. In the evening, more formal meals are served, mostly to residents, who pay about £21 ($33.20) for an à la carte dinner.

7 St. Ives

319 miles SW of London, 21 miles NE of Land's End, 10 miles NE of Penzance

This north-coast fishing village, with its sandy beaches, is England's most famous artists' colony. It's a village of narrow streets and well-kept cottages. The artists settled in many years ago and have integrated with the fishers and their families.

The artists' colony has been established long enough to have developed several schools or "splits," and they almost never overlap—except in a pub where the artists hang out, or where classes are held. The old battle continues between the followers of the representational and the devotees of the abstract in art, with each group recruiting young artists all the time. In addition, there are the potters, weavers, and other craftspeople—all working, exhibiting, and selling in this area.

A word of warning: St. Ives becomes virtually impossible to visit in August, when you're likely to be trampled underfoot by busloads of tourists, mostly the English themselves. However, in spring and early fall the pace is much more relaxed, and a visitor can have the true experience of the art colony.

ESSENTIALS

GETTING THERE

By Train   There is frequent service throughout the day between London's Paddington Station and the rail terminal at St. Ives (trip time: 5¹/₂ hr.).

By Bus   Several coaches a day run from London's Victoria Coach Station to St. Ives (trip time: 7 hr.).

By Car   Take A30 across Cornwall, driving northwest at the junction with B3306, leading to St. Ives on the coast.

During the summer months many of the streets in the center of town are closed to vehicles. You may want to leave your car in the Lelant Saltings Car Park, 3 miles from St. Ives on A3074, and take the regular train service into town, an 11-minute journey. Departures are every half hour. It's free to all car passengers and drivers, and the parking charge is £6 to £8 ($9.50 to $12.65) per day. You can also use the large Trenwith Car Park, close to the town center, for £1 ($1.60) and then walk down to the shops and harbor or take a bus costing 30p (45¢) per person.

VISITOR INFORMATION

The **telephone area code** is 01736. The **Tourist Information Centre** is at the Guildhall, Street-an-Pol (☎ **01736/796297**).

WHAT TO SEE & DO

✪ Tate Gallery

Portmeor Beach. ☎ **01736/796226.** Admission £3.50 ($5.55) per adult, including one child under 11; £2 ($3.15) senior citizens and students 11 or older. Apr–Oct, Mon, Wed, and Fri–Sat 11am–7pm; Tues and Thurs 11am–9pm; Sun 11am–5pm; bank holidays 11am–5pm. Nov–Mar, Tues–Sun 11am–5pm. Closed Dec 24–25.

This branch of London's famous Tate Gallery exhibits changing groups of work from the Tate Gallery's preeminent collection of St. Ives painting and sculpture, dating from about 1925 to 1975. The gallery is administered jointly with the Barbara Hepworth Museum (see below). The collection includes examples of works by artists associated with St. Ives, including Alfred Wallis, Ben Nicholson, Barbara Hepworth, Naum Gabo, Peter Lanyon, Terry Frost, Patrick Heron, and Roger Hilton. All the artists whose works are shown here had a decisive effect on the development of painting in the U.K. in the second half of the 20th century. About 100 works are on display at all times.

The museum occupies a spectacular site overlooking Portmeor Beach, close to the home of Alfred Wallis and to the studios used by many of the St. Ives artists. The museum is a three-story building, backing directly onto the cliff face and exploiting the dramatic sea views offered by the site.

Barbara Hepworth Museum and Garden

Barnoon Hill. ☎ **01736/796226.** Admission £1.50 ($2.35) adults, 75p ($1.20) children. Apr–Oct, Mon–Sat 11am–7pm, Sun 11am–5pm, bank holidays 11am–5pm; Nov–Mar, Tues–Sun 11am–5pm.

Dame Barbara Hepworth lived at Trewyn from 1949 until her death in 1975 at the age of 72. In her will she asked that her working studio be turned into a museum where visitors for years to come could see where she lived and created her world-famed sculpture. Today the museum and garden are virtually just as she left them. On display are about 47 sculptures and drawings, covering the period from 1928 to 1974, as well as photographs, documents, and other Hepworth memorabilia. You can also visit her workshops, housing a selection of tools and some unfinished carvings. The museum is administered jointly with the Tate Gallery (see above).

WHERE TO STAY
MODERATE

⑤ Garrack Hotel

Burthallan Lane, Higher Ayr, St. Ives, Cornwall TR26 3AA. ☎ **01736/796199.** Fax 01736/798955. 18 rms. TV TEL. £37.50–£55.50 ($59.25–$87.70) per person. Rates include English breakfast. AE, DC, MC, V. Free parking. Take B3306 to the outskirts of St. Ives; after passing a gas station on the left, take the third road left toward Portmeor Beach and Ayr (there's a red telephone kiosk at the fork) and after 200 yards look for the hotel sign. Frequent minibus service.

This vine-covered little hotel, once a private home, commands a panoramic view of St. Ives and Portmeor Beach from its 2-acre knoll at the head of a narrow lane. It's one of the friendliest and most efficiently run small, medium-priced hotels on the entire coast, with every room furnished in a warm, homelike manner. The atmosphere in the living room is inviting, with a log-burning fireplace, antiques, and comfortable chairs.

The Garrack belongs to Mr. and Mrs. Kilby, who are proud of their meals (see our dining recommendation, below). The Leisure building has been completely rebuilt. In addition to the swimming pool and its integral Jacuzzi-type whirlpool spa, there are a sauna, solarium, changing rooms, and exercise equipment. A small bar overlooks the bay. On a patio you can sunbathe. There is a launderette.

Pedn-Olva Hotel

The Warren, St. Ives, Cornwall TR26 2EA. ☎ **01736/796222.** Fax 01736/797710. 35 rms. £35 ($55.30) per person, single or double. Rates include English breakfast. Half board £42.50 ($67.15) per person. MC, V. Parking £2.50 ($3.95).

You'll pass through the lobby to the lounges and restaurant before coming to the panoramic view over the bay that's the outstanding feature of this establishment, which was originally built in the 1870s as the home of the paymaster for the local mines, then transformed into a hotel in the 1930s. The bedrooms are well furnished and maintained in modern style. There are sun terraces with lounges and umbrellas and a swimming pool for those who don't want to walk down the rocky path to Porthminster Beach. If you crave solitude, however, scramble down the rocks to sunbathe just above the gentle rise and fall of the sea. A dinner costs £13 ($20.55) and up.

Porthminster Hotel

The Terrace, St. Ives, Cornwall TR26 2BN. ☎ **01736/795221.** Fax 01736/797043. 46 rms. TV TEL. £52–£64 ($82.15–$101.10) single; £104–£128 ($164.30–$202.25) double. Rates include half board. AE, DC, V. Free parking.

This leading Cornish Riviera resort stands on the main road into town amid a beautiful garden and within easy walking distance of Porthminster Beach. Large and imposing, the Porthminster is a traditional choice for visitors to St. Ives. With its staunchly Victorian architecture from 1894, it's warm and inviting. The bedrooms are spacious and well furnished. Facilities include a sun lounge, a solarium, and a sauna, as well as a swimming pool that sees action from June to September. Bar lunches go for £8 ($12.65), with dinners costing £17 ($26.85) and up if you're not on the half-board plan.

WHERE TO DINE
INEXPENSIVE

⑤ Oliver's Restaurant

In the Garrack Hotel, Burthallan Lane, Higher Ayr. ☎ **01736/796199.** Reservations recommended. Fixed-price dinner £16.50 ($26.05). AE, DC, MC, V. Daily 7–8:30pm. To get here, see the Garrack Hotel in "Where to Stay," above. Frequent minibus service. ENGLISH/INTERNATIONAL.

The dining room at the Garrack Hotel, the domain of Mr. and Mrs. Kilby, produces an excellent cuisine and, whenever possible, uses fresh ingredients from their own garden. The hotel dining room, open to nonresidents, offers a set dinner, plus a cold buffet or snacks at the bar. The menu features some of the finest of English dishes, such as roast shoulder of lamb with mint sauce, John Dory fillets with cucumber relish, and a wide sampling of continental fare, such as fillet of salmon hollandaise and pork medallions with a French mustard sauce. Live lobsters swim in the Kilbys' seawater tank—until they're removed for preparation and cooking to order. Of course, if you order cold lobster salad, a little prior notice is required. Cheese and dessert trolleys are at your service.

8 Port Isaac

266 miles SW of London, 14 miles SW of Tintagel, 9 miles N of Wadebridge

Port Isaac remains the most unspoiled fishing village on the north Cornish coastline, in spite of large numbers of summer visitors. By all means wander through its winding, narrow lanes, gazing at the whitewashed fishing cottages with their rainbow trims.

ESSENTIALS
GETTING THERE

By Train   Bodmin is the nearest railway station. It lies on the main line from London (Paddington Station) to Penzance (about a 4- or 4^1/$_2$-hour trip), and many hotels will send a car to pick up guests at the Bodmin station. If you reject the idea of a taxi and insist on taking a bus from Bodmin, you must change buses at Wadebridge, and connections are not good. Driving time from Bodmin to Port Isaac is 40 minutes.

By Bus   A bus to Wadebridge goes to Port Isaac about six times a day. It's maintained by the Prout Brothers Bus Co. Wadebridge is a local bus junction to many other places in the rest of England.

By Car   From London, take M4 west, then drive south on M5. Head west again at the junction with A39, continuing to the junction with B3267, which you follow until you reach the signposted cutoff for Port Isaac.

VISITOR INFORMATION

The **telephone area code** is 01208.

WHERE TO STAY & DINE
MODERATE

✪ Port Gaverne Hotel

Port Gaverne, Port Isaac, Cornwall PL29 3SQ. ☎ **01208/880244.** Fax 01208/880151. 19 rms. TV TEL. £53–£57 ($83.75–$90.05) single; £86–£94 ($135.90–$148.50) double. Rates include English breakfast. AE, DC, MC, V. Free parking. Closed early Jan to mid-Feb.

Built in the 17th century as a coastal inn for fishermen who needed a rest from their seagoing labors, the Port Gaverne, half a mile east of Port Isaac, today caters to vacationing families and couples. The bedrooms are well furnished with traditional styling and each has a radio. The hotel boasts a sheltered cove for boating and swimming, and can arrange shark fishing, pony trekking, and country hikes. Its painted facade is draped with vines, and inside you'll find a duo of comfortably atmospheric bars for relaxing beside a fireplace (one of them is a modified baking oven). Clusters of antiques, stained glass, and early photographs of Cornwall add sometimes bittersweet grace notes.

Dinners are served by candlelight and include locally caught lobster, fish, or crab in season, as well as locally raised lamb and beef. Bar snacks are also available, and dinners cost £15 to £22 ($23.70 to $34.75).

INEXPENSIVE

ⓢ Slipway Hotel

The Harbour Front, Port Isaac, Cornwall PL29 3RH. ☎ **01208/880264.** 10 rms, 5 with bath. TEL. £19–£24 ($30–$37.90) single without bath; £38–£48 ($60.05–$75.85) double without bath, £52–£65 ($82.15–$102.70) double with bath. Rates include English breakfast. AE, DC, MC, V. Free parking. Closed Feb.

Originally built in 1527, with major additions in the early 1700s, this waterside building has seen more uses than any other structure in town, serving as everything from fishing cottages to the headquarters of the first bank here. Once the building was a lifeboat station for rescuing sailors stranded on stormy seas. The bedrooms are comfortable and cozy.

Despite the allure of the accommodations, this hotel is best known for its restaurant, where ultra-fresh seafood is a constant favorite. Its main dining room contains a minstrel's gallery and lies adjacent to a popular bar known to virtually everyone in town. At lunch, only bar snacks, priced at £2.50 to £6.50 ($3.95 to $10.25), are served. Dinner, beginning at £18 ($28.45) per person, is more elaborate, featuring fish imported directly from the nets of local fisherfolk. Menu choices include grilled fillets of turbot served with miniature shrimp and portugaise sauce, and one of the most elaborate seafood platters in town.

9   Tintagel

264 miles SW of London, 49 miles NW of Plymouth

On a wild stretch of the Atlantic coast, Tintagel is forever linked with the legends of King Arthur, Lancelot, and Merlin. If you become excited by tales of Knights of the Round Table, you can go to Camelford, 5 miles inland from Tintagel. The town has claims to being Camelot.

ESSENTIALS

GETTING THERE

By Train   The nearest railway station is in Bodmin, which lies on the main rail line from London to Penzance. From Bodmin, you'll have to drive or take a taxi for 30 minutes to get to Tintagel (there's no bus service from Bodmin to Tintagel).

By Bus   If you insist on taking the bus, passengers usually travel from London to Plymouth by bus or by train. In Plymouth, the bus and rail stations are almost adjacent to one another. One bus a day travels from Plymouth to Tintagel, at 4:20pm, but it takes twice the time (2 hr.) required for a private car (which only takes about 50 minutes) since the bus stops at dozens of small hamlets along the way.

By Car   From Exeter, head across Cornwall on A30, continuing west at the junction with A395. From this highway, various secondary roads lead to Tintagel.

VISITOR INFORMATION

The **telephone area code** is 01840.

WHAT TO SEE & DO

Tintagel Castle

Half a mile northwest of Tintagel. ☎ **01840/770328.** Admission £2.20 ($3.50) adults, £1.70 ($2.70) students and senior citizens, £1.10 ($1.75) children. Good Fri–Sept, daily 10am–6pm; Oct–Maundy Thurs, Tues–Sun 10am–4pm.

These 13th-century ruins of a castle—built on the foundations of a Celtic monastery from the 6th century—are popularly known as King Arthur's Castle. They stand 300 feet above the sea on a rocky promontory, and to get to them you must take a long, steep, tortuous walk from the parking lot. In summer, many visitors make the ascent to Arthur's Lair, up 100 rock-cut steps. You can also visit Merlin's Cave at low tide.

Old Post Office

3–4 Tintagel Center. ☎ **01208/4281.** Admission £2 ($3.15) adults, £1 ($1.60) children. Apr–Sept, daily 11am–5:30pm; Oct, daily 11am–4:45pm. Closed Nov–Mar.

This National Trust property was once a 14th-century manor, but since the 19th century it has had a genuine Victorian post room.

WHERE TO STAY & DINE

INEXPENSIVE

Bossiney House Hotel

Bossiney Rd., Bossiney, Tintagel, Cornwall PL34 0AX. ☎ **01840/770240.** Fax 01840/770501. 19 rms. £29–£31 ($45.80–$49) single; £48–£52 ($75.85–$82.15) double. Rates include English breakfast. AE, MC, V. Free parking. Closed Nov–Mar. Take B3263 half a mile northeast of Tintagel.

The hotel, in its inviting location, is comfortable. It has a TV lounge and a well-stocked bar/lounge with a fine view of the surrounding meadows marching right up to the tops of the cliff as well as the wide expanse of lawn with a putting green. A big English breakfast and other well-prepared meals are served in the dining room, which offers a panoramic view out over the lawns. A set dinner costs £10 ($15.80). On the grounds is a Scandinavian log chalet with a heated swimming pool, a sauna, and a solarium. The bedrooms have streamlined modern styling.

⊗ Old Borough House

Bossiney, Tintagel, Cornwall PL34 0AY. ☎ **01840/770475.** 6 rms, 2 with bath. £16.50 ($26.05) single without bath, £19.50 ($30.80) single with bath; £33 ($52.15) double without bath, £39 ($61.60) double with bath. Rates include English breakfast. No credit cards. Walk north from the ruins of Tintagel Castle for 10 minutes.

Run by the Rayner family, this Cornish house has thick stone walls, small windows, low ceiling beams, and an illustrious history dating back to 1558. Most of what stands today was completed in the late 1600s, when it served as the residence for the mayor of Bossiney, the hamlet in which it's situated. (Bossiney was the seat from which Sir Francis Drake was elected for a brief period to the English Parliament.) The accommodations are cozy, low-ceilinged, antique, and very comfortable. There's a sitting room with a TV for guest use, and, if advance notice is given, evening meals are available for £10 ($15.80).

Trebrea Lodge

Trenale, near Tintagel, Cornwall PL34 0HR. ☎ **01840/770410.** Fax 01840/770092. 7 rms. TV TEL. £42–£52.50 ($66.35–$82.95) single; £70–£80 ($110.60–$126.40) double. Rates include English breakfast. MC, V. Free parking. From Tintagel, take the Boscastle road and turn right at the Roman Catholic church; make another right at the top of the lane.

Although its origins date back more than 600 years, Trebea Lodge reflects the charm of a small Cornish manor house of the Georgian period. The public rooms are all furnished with antiques, as are the bedrooms, one of which boasts a grand four-poster bed. All bedrooms have a private bath (tub or shower), color TV, direct-dial phone, and tea or coffee maker. The rooms open onto uninterrupted views over the countryside to the Atlantic Ocean. A table d'hôte menu, costing £16 ($25.30), is served in an oak-paneled dining room where all the food is prepared by Sean Devlin, one of the owners, using fresh local ingredients to produce both traditional English and continental dishes.

10　Bolventor

260 miles SW of London, 20 miles E of Newquay

This village east of Tintagel near Launceston is often visited by the fans of Daphne du Maurier since this was the setting for her novel *Jamaica Inn* (see below). The inn is named for the Caribbean island where the one-time owner of the inn had become prosperous from his sugar plantation there. Opposite the inn, a small road leads to Dozmary Pool where the "waves wap and the winds wan" into which Sir Bedivere threw Excalibur at King Arthur's behest.

ESSENTIALS
GETTING THERE

By Train　Trains whose final destination is Penzance leave London's Paddington Station, pass through Plymouth, then (several stations later) stop at Liskeard and then at Bodmin. Either of these stations lies close enough to Bolventor so that a taxi could be rented for the 20-minute ride on to Bolventor.

By Bus　There are no buses going to Bolventor.

By Car　Take A30 across Cornwall to Launceston and follow the signs.

VISITOR INFORMATION

The **telephone area code** is 01566.

WHERE TO STAY & DINE
INEXPENSIVE

Jamaica Inn

Bolventor, Launceston, Cornwall, PL15 7TS. ☎ **01566/86250.** 6 rms. TV. £25–£35 ($39.50–$55.30) single; £35–£60 ($55.30–$94.80) double. Rates include English breakfast. MC, V. Free parking. The inn is on A30 between Bodmin and Launceston.

This long, low building was built in 1547 as a coaching inn. Today it has a room dedicated to the memory of Daphne du Maurier and her novel *Jamaica Inn* (filmed by Alfred Hitchcock). The bedrooms include one four-poster room. The hotel has a bar (open all day) and a grill restaurant (open only in the evening). Snacks are available daily from 10am to 10pm.

Wiltshire, Somerset & Avon 14

For our final look at the "West Countree," we move now into Wiltshire, Somerset, and Avon, the most antiquity-rich shires of England. When we reach this area of pastoral woodland, London seems far removed.

When you cross into **Wiltshire,** you'll be entering a country of chalky, grassy uplands and rolling plains. Much of the shire is agricultural, and a large part is devoted to pastureland. Wiltshire produces an abundance of England's dairy products and is noted for sheep raising. Here you'll traverse Salisbury Plain, Vale of Pewsey, and Marlborough Downs (the latter making up the greater part of the landmass).

Most people agree that the West Country, a loose geographical term, begins at Salisbury, with its early English cathedral. Nearby is Stonehenge, England's oldest prehistoric monument. Both Stonehenge and Salisbury are in Wiltshire.

The western shire of **Somerset** has some of the most beautiful scenery in England. The undulating limestone hills of Mendip and the irresistible Quantocks are especially lovely in spring and fall. Somerset opens onto the Bristol Channel, with Minehead its chief resort.

Somerset is rich in legend and history, with particularly fanciful associations with King Arthur and Queen Guinevere, Camelot, and Alfred the Great. Its villages are noted for the tall towers of their parish churches.

You may find yourself in a vine-covered old inn, talking with the regulars, or you'll discover a large estate in the woods surrounded by bridle paths and sheep walks (Somerset was once a great wool center); or maybe you'll settle down in a 16th-century thatched stone farmhouse set in the midst of orchards in a vale. By the way, Somerset is reputed to have the best cider anywhere.

Avon encompasses the territory around the old port of Bristol, an area that used to be in Somerset. The old Roman city of Bath is a major point of interest.

A DRIVING TOUR

Day 1   From London, head to Salisbury, 90 miles to the southwest. You'll arrive in plenty of time for lunch (make it the Haunch of

What's Special About Wiltshire, Somerset & Avon

Great Towns/Villages
- Bath, a Georgian spa city beside the river Avon, known for its abbey and spa waters.
- Glastonbury, with its famed abbey, a country town with many religious and historical links—associated with the legends of King Arthur.

Ancient Monuments
- Stonehenge, a huge circle of lintels and megalithic pillars, 3,500 to 5,000 years old—the most important prehistoric monument in Britain.
- Old Sarum, outside Salisbury, the remains of an Iron Age fortification.

Buildings
- Glastonbury Abbey, the oldest Christian foundation and once the most important abbey in England.
- Wells Cathedral, one of the best examples of the early English style of architecture, known for the medieval sculpture of its west front.
- Salisbury Cathedral, just as painted by John Constable, with its 404-foot pinnacle, the tallest in England.

Natural Spectacle
- Exmoor National Park, once the English royal hunting preserve, stretching for 265 square miles on the north coast of Devon and Somerset.

Palace
- Wilton House, at Wilton, the magnificent home of the earl of Pembroke, with 17th-century staterooms by Inigo Jones.

Venison). In the afternoon explore Salisbury Cathedral and other attractions and walk around the town.

Day 2   While still based in Salisbury, spend the following day exploring the most important sights in the environs, including Old Sarum and Wilton House and definitely Stonehenge. Return to Salisbury for the evening but dine at Silver Plough 5 miles to the east (an old farmhouse).

Day 3   In the morning drive northwest to Glastonbury and explore the ruins of Glastonbury Abbey.

TAKE A BREAK   The Assembly Rooms, off High Street in Glastonbury (☎ **01458/834677**), is the community center of Glastonbury, with a café open Tuesday through Sunday at 10am (closing hours vary). It serves vegetarian food, drinks, and inexpensive desserts.

In the afternoon drive northeast to Wells along A39 for the night, perhaps arriving in time to see its cathedral.

Day 4   In the morning explore Wookey Hole Caves & Paper Mill and the Cheddar Show Caves at Cheddar Gorge nearby. Then drive to Bath for the afternoon, in time to visit its Pump Room and Roman Baths.

Day 5   While still based in Bath, explore Bath Abbey in the morning and visit the American Museum in the afternoon. Bath should be seen, not simply for its individual attractions, but for the architectural interest of the whole. Walk around and explore as many of its streets and crescents as possible.

Day 6   In the afternoon drive to Avebury, one of the largest prehistoric sights of Europe (see below).

Day 7   Drive the short distance 13 miles northwest of Bath for an oversight stay in Bristol. Take an official guided walking tour and visit Bristol Cathedral, SS *Great Britain,* and other attractions, dining that night at Harvey's.

1 Salisbury

90 miles SW of London, 53 miles SE of Bristol

Long before you've even entered Salisbury, the spire of Salisbury Cathedral will come into view—just as John Constable painted it so many times. The 404-foot pinnacle of the early English and Gothic cathedral is the tallest in England.
Salisbury, or New Sarum, lies in the valley of the Avon River, and is a fine base for touring such sights as Stonehenge. Filled with Tudor inns and tearooms, it is known to readers of Thomas Hardy as Melchester and to fans of Anthony Trollope as Barchester.

ESSENTIALS
GETTING THERE

By Train   A Network Express train departs hourly from Waterloo Station in London bound for Salisbury (trip time: 2 hr.), and Sprinter trains make a speedy journey from Portsmouth, Bristol, and South Wales, likewise departing hourly. There is also direct rail service from Exeter, Plymouth, Brighton, and Reading.

By Bus   Five National Express buses per day run from London Monday through Friday. On Saturday and Sunday four buses depart Victoria Coach Station heading for Salisbury (trip time: 2 1/2 hr.).

By Car   From London, head west on M3 to the end of the run, continuing the rest of the way on A30.

VISITOR INFORMATION

The **telephone area code** is 01722. The **Tourist Information Centre** is at Fish Row (☎ **01722/334956**).

WHAT TO SEE & DO

✪ Salisbury Cathedral

The Close. ☎ **01722/328726.** Cathedral £2 ($3.15); chapter house 30p (45¢). May–Aug daily 8:30am–8:30pm; Sept–Apr daily 8:30am–6:30pm.

You can search all of England, but you'll find no better example of the early English, or pointed, style than Salisbury Cathedral. Construction was begun as early as 1220 and took 38 years to complete; this was considered rather fast in those days since it was customary for a cathedral building to require at least three centuries. The soaring spire was completed at the end of the 13th century. Despite an ill-conceived attempt at renovation in the 18th century, the architectural integrity of the cathedral has been retained.

The cathedral's 13th-century octagonal chapter house (note the fine sculpture), which is especially attractive, possesses one of the four surviving original texts of the Magna Carta, along with treasures from the diocese of Salisbury and manuscripts and artifacts belonging to the cathedral. The cloisters enhance the beauty of the cathedral, and the exceptionally large close, with at least 75 buildings in its compound (some from the early 18th century and others predating that), sets off the cathedral most effectively.

Brass Rubbing Centre

Cathedral Cloisters. ☎ **01722/328726.** Admission free. Mid-June to mid-Sept Mon–Sat 10am–6pm, Sun 11:15am–4pm.

Here you can choose from a variety of exact replicas molded perfectly from the original brasses: local medieval and Tudor knights and ladies, famous historical faces, even Celtic designs. A helpful staff will guide you. The £3 ($4.75) average charge made for each rubbing includes materials and instruction. You can also buy ready-made rubbings and historical gift items.

Mompesson House

Cathedral Close. ☎ **01722/335659.** Admission £3 ($4.75) adults, £1.50 ($2.35) children. Apr–Oct Sat–Wed noon–5:30pm.

This is one of the most distinguished houses in the area. Built by Charles Mompesson in 1701, while he was a member of Parliament for Old Sarum, it is a beautiful example of the Queen Anne style, well known for its fine plasterwork ceilings and paneling. There is also a collection of 18th-century drinking glasses. Visitors can wander through a garden and later order a snack in the garden tearoom.

The Royal Gloucestershire, Berkshire and Wiltshire Regiment (Salisbury) Museum-Redcoats in the Wardrobe

The Wardrobe, 58 The Close, Salisbury, Wiltshire. ☎ **01722/414536.** Admission £1.80 ($2.85) adults; £1 ($1.60) children. Feb–Mar and Nov Mon–Fri 10am–4:30pm; Apr–Oct daily 10am–4:30pm.

The elegant house in which the museum's collections are displayed dates from 1254 and contains exhibits covering three centuries of military history. Visitors can relax in the garden leading to the River Avon (with views made famous by Constable) and enjoy homemade fare from the Redcoats Tea Rooms.

WHERE TO STAY

IN SALISBURY

Moderate

Red Lion Hotel

4 Milford St., Salisbury, Wiltshire SP1 2AN. ☎ **01722/323334.** Fax 01722/325756. 54 rms, 2 suites. TV TEL. £79–£89 ($124.80–$140.60) double; £94 ($148.50) suite. Rates include English breakfast. Breakfast £4.50–£8 ($7.10–$12.65) extra. AE, DC, MC, V. Free parking.

Since the 1300s the Red Lion has been accommodating wayfarers who rumbled in stagecoaches from London across the Salisbury Plain to the West Country. Cross under its arch into a courtyard with a hanging, much-photographed creeper, a red lion, and a half-timbered facade, and you'll be transported back to an earlier era. However, the Red Lion has stayed abreast of the times, even installing an elevator. Each comfortable bedroom also has a radio, hot-beverage facilities, and hair dryer. The most expensive rooms feature a four-poster bed.

Many patronize the hotel for its continental and English cuisine. A set lunch costs £8 ($12.65) for two courses and £10.25 ($16.20) for three courses. A three-course dinner goes for £15.50 ($24.50). The restaurant has a wattle-and-daub wall dating from 1230, and the antique-filled hotel is also noted for its clocks, including a skeleton organ clock in the reception hall. Meals are served daily from noon to 2pm and 7 to 8:45pm.

✪ The Rose and Crown

Harnham Rd., Salisbury, Wiltshire SP2 8JQ. ☎ **01722/327908** or 01800/289330 in England. Fax 01722/339816. 27 rms, 1 suite. TV TEL. £113.75–£128.75 ($179.75–$203.45) double; £158.75 ($250.85) suite. Rates include English breakfast. AE, DC, MC, V. Free parking. Take A3094 1¹/₂ miles from the center of town.

This half-timbered, 13th-century gem stands with its feet almost in the river Avon, and beyond the water you can see the tall spire of the cathedral. You can easily walk over the arched stone bridge to the center of Salisbury from here in 10 minutes or so. The lawns and gardens between the inn and the river are shaded by old trees, and chairs are set out so you can enjoy the view and count the swans. The inn, part of the Queens Moat House Hotels chain, has both a new and an old wing. The new wing is modern, but to me the old wing is more appealing, with its sloping ceilings and antique fireplaces and furniture. Each bedroom has a radio and hot-beverage facilities, hair dryer, and trouser press.

You can dine on English fare while overlooking the river. A luncheon goes for £12.50 ($19.75) and a dinner costs £16.50 ($26.05). Across the courtyard are two taverns. Guests have the choice of either of two bars with oak beams and log fires.

White Hart

1 St. John St., Salisbury, Wiltshire SP1 2SD. ☎ **01722/327476.** Fax 01722/412761. 58 rms. TV TEL. £95–£120 ($150.10–$189.60) double. Breakfast £5.95–£8.50 ($9.40–$13.45) extra. AE, DC, MC, V. Free parking.

Combining the best of old and new, the White Hart has been a Salisbury landmark since Georgian times. Its classic facade is intact, with tall columns crowning a life-size effigy of a hart. The older accommodations are traditional, and a new section has been added in the rear, opening onto a large parking area—like a motel. New-wing units are tastefully conceived and decorated. You can enjoy a before-dinner drink in Spires Bar, followed by a meal in the Shire's Restaurant for £16.95 ($26.80).

Inexpensive

⑤ Grasmere House

70 Harnham Rd., Salisbury, Wiltshire SP2 9JN. ☎ **01722/338388.** Fax 01722/333710. 20 rms. TV TEL. £70–£95 ($110.60–$150.10) double. Rates include English breakfast. AE, DC, MC, V. Free parking. Take A3094 1¹/₂ miles from the center of town.

Grasmere stands near the confluence of the Nadder and Avon rivers on 1¹/₂ acres of grounds. Constructed in 1896 for Salisbury merchants, the house still suggests a family home. Architectural features were retained as much as possible, including a "calling box" for servants in the dining room. Three of the luxurious bedrooms overlook the cathedral. The house also operates a good restaurant, popular with locals and residents alike, where lunch or dinner costs from £15 ($23.70) per person. Steaks are a specialty, served in any number of ways, ranging from flambéed to au poivre.

The King's Arms Hotel

9–11 St. Johns St., Salisbury, Wiltshire SP1 2SB. ☎ **01722/327629.** Fax 01722/414246. 15 rms (all with bath or shower). TV TEL. £60–£78 ($94.80–$123.25) double. Rates include English breakfast. AE, DC, MC, V. Free parking.

You'll recognize this former coaching inn in black-and-white Tudor style by its leaded-glass windows, an old pub sign out front, and a covered entrance for alighting coach passengers. It is unsophisticated without being self-consciously so. A special feature is the William and Mary four-poster room. The other bedrooms are cozy and well kept, with traditional styling. No one seems to know the age of the inn, although it's generally acknowledged that it was built before the cathedral. Conspirators helping Charles II flee to France were thought to have met here in the mid-17th century. The hotel features a good restaurant, called Pippins, old oak beams, the original ironwork, a priest's hiding hole, and an Elizabethan fireplace. Enjoy a pint of ale in the oak-beamed pub, as you sit in a high-backed settle, warming yourself in front of the open fire.

⊛ The New Inn

39–47 New St., Salisbury, Wiltshire SP1 2PH. ☎ **01722/327679.** 8 rms. TV TEL. £45–£65 ($71.10–$102.70) double. Rates include English breakfast. AE, DC, MC, V. Free parking.

This upscale B&B is one of the finest in Salisbury but, despite its name, it isn't new at all. It's a 15th-century building whose walled garden backs up to the cathedral close wall. The bedrooms are cozy, heavily beamed, and evocative of an earlier century. The center of the inn is the serving bar, which is a common center for three outer rooms: one, a tiny sitting area; another, a tavern with high-backed settles and a fireplace; and the third, a lounge. Food and drink are available to nonresidents. In the pub, appetizers range from £2.25–£5 ($3.55–$7.90), with main courses costing from £5–£10 ($7.90–$15.80). Adjacent to the main building, The Old House Restaurant, with Victorian decor, offers set lunches and four-course dinners costing from £15.95 to £20.95 ($25.20 to $33.10).

IN NEARBY DINTON

Moderate

✪ Howard's House

Teffont Evias, near Salisbury, Wiltshire SP3 5RJ. ☎ **01722/716392.** Fax 01722/716820. 9 rms. TV TEL. £107.50 ($169.85) double. Rates include English breakfast. AE, MC, V. Free parking. Take A36 and A30 west of Salisbury for 10¹/₂ miles; it's on B3089.

On a lane opposite the Black Horse, this partial 17th-century dower house stands in a medieval hamlet. It has been turned into one of the most appealing small hotels and restaurants in the area. The Ford and Firmin families combined their talent and money to convert this building into an exceptional accommodation. The bedrooms are carefully furnished, and much attention was given to the decoration and comfort of the place. For example, lots of towels are provided.

Even if you don't stay here, consider stopping by for a meal (but call to reserve a table first). Dinner is served nightly from 7:30 to 10pm, costing about £27 ($42.65) for an à la carte meal. There are ample choices on the fixed-price menu. Try such dishes as grilled sirloin steak with a pepper ragoût and horseradish Béarnaise or roast cod with an herb crust, capers, and an olive oil dressing. Chilled mango mousse with marinated strawberries makes a splendid dessert. A fixed-price lunch for £17.50 ($27.65) is also served on Sunday from 12:30 to 2:30pm. The hotel has attractive gardens, and on chilly nights log fires burn.

WHERE TO DINE

INEXPENSIVE

Harper's Restaurant

7–9 Ox Row, Market Sq. ☎ **01722/333118.** Reservations recommended. Main courses £8.50–£10.90 ($13.45–$17.20); 3-course fixed-price meals £7.70 ($12.15) at lunch, £13.50

Wiltshire, Somerset & Avon

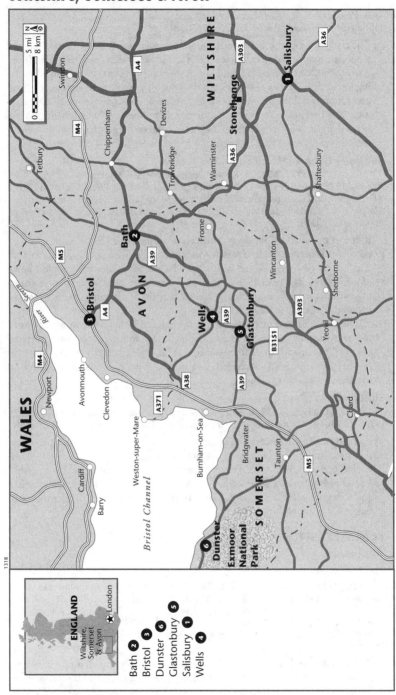

($21.35) at dinner. AE, DC, MC, V. Mon–Sat noon–2pm; dinner Mon–Sat 6:30–10pm, Sun (Spring bank holiday–Oct) 6:30–9:30pm. ENGLISH.

The chef-owner of this place prides himself on specializing in "real food," home-made, uncomplicated, and wholesome. The pleasantly decorated restaurant is on the second floor of a red-brick building at the back side of Salisbury's largest parking lot, in the center of town. Within the same all-purpose dining room, you can order from two different menus, one featuring cost-conscious bistro-style platters, including beefsteak casserole with "herbey dumplings." A longer menu, listing items that take a bit more time to prepare, includes all-vegetarian pasta diavolo or spareribs with french fries and rice.

Salisbury Haunch of Venison

1 Minster St. ☎ **01722/322024.** Reservations recommended. Main courses £5.95–£11.95 ($9.40–$18.90); bar platters for lunches, light suppers, and snacks £4.50–£8 ($7.10–$12.65). AE, DC, MC, V. Lunch daily noon–2pm; dinner Mon–Sat 7–10:30pm. Pub, Mon–Sat 11am–11pm, Sun noon–3pm and 7–10:30pm. Closed on Christmas–Easter and Mon–Wed for dinner. ENGLISH.

Right in the heart of Salisbury, this creaky-timbered, 1320 chophouse serves excellent dishes, especially English roasts and grills. Stick to its specialties and you'll rarely go wrong. Diners with more adventurous palates will sample a bowl of game soup. The pièce de résistance of the inn is its local New Forest haunch of venison, gin and juniper berries. For a bargain lunch, enjoy the bar snacks, including game pie made with venison.

The centuries have given a gleam to the oak furnishings, and years of polishing have worn down the brass. Twisting steps lead to tiny, cozy rooms (there is one small room with space for about four to sit, where you can saturate yourself in the best of England's yesterdays and todays). Two windows of the barroom overlook St. Thomas's cloisters.

Sunflowers

2–4 Ivy St. ☎ **01722/333948.** Reservations recommended. Main courses £3.25–£5.50 ($5.15–$8.70). MC, V. Lunch Mon–Sat 10am–3pm; dinner Thur–Sat 6:30–9:30pm. VEGETARIAN.

Formerly called Crustaceans, this restaurant, owned by Chris Walker, specializes in vegetarian cuisine. Dishes may include vegetable ragoût, salad niçoise, or an Indian pancake filled with spiced potatoes and cauliflower served with dahl. For a finish the menu offers such specialties as a hazelnut and apricot meringue, and a tart of apples and custard. Wine, lagers, beer, and cider are offered at this nonsmoking establishment.

In Nearby Pitton

Inexpensive

Silver Plough

White Hill, Pitton, near Salisbury. ☎ **01722/72266.** Reservations recommended. Main courses £7.50–£11.50 ($11.85–$18.15); bar platters £4.50–£6 ($7.10–$9.50). AE, DC, MC, V. Restaurant, lunch daily noon–2:30pm; dinner Mon–Sat 7–10pm, Sun 7–9pm. Pub, Mon–Sat 11am–3pm and 6–11pm, Sun noon–3pm and 7–10:30pm. Closed on Dec 25–26 and Jan 1. Take A30 5 miles east of Salisbury; it's at the southern end of the hamlet of Pitton. ENGLISH.

Built as a stone-sided farmhouse 150 years ago, the Silver Plough is now a charming and accommodating country pub with an attached restaurant. Specializing in fish and game dishes, it contains heavily beamed ceilings hung with tankards, coach horns, and other country-inspired memorabilia. Snacks available in the bar include, among others, ratatouille au gratin and grilled sardines with garlic butter and freshly baked bread. In the somewhat more formal dining room, the chef prepares such dishes as fresh Dorset mussels in a white wine, garlic, and cream sauce, sliced breast of duck in cracked pepper or orange sauce, and roast guinea fowl in a sharp strawberry sauce. The Silver Plough has known many famous visitors, but apart from displaying a signed letter from Queen Victoria thanking the women of England for their concern after the death of her husband, Albert, the management prefers to stick to its quiet, country atmosphere and to concentrate on making its guests feel at home.

EASY EXCURSIONS

✪ Old Sarum

Castle Road, 2 miles north of Salisbury off A345. ☎ **01722/335398.** Admission £1.50 ($2.35) for adults, 80p ($1.25) for children. Apr–Sept daily 10am to 6pm; other times daily from 10am to 4pm. Bus nos. 3, 5, 6, 7, 8, and 9 run every 20 minutes during the day from the Salisbury bus station.

Old Sarum, is believed to have been an Iron Age fortification. The earthworks were known to the Romans as Sorbiodunum. Much later Saxons also used the fortification. The Normans built a cathedral and a castle here in what was then a Middle Ages walled town. Parts of the old cathedral were taken down to build the city of New Sarum (Salisbury).

✪ Wilton House

2¹/₂ miles west of Salisbury on A30. ☎ **01722/743115.** Admission £5.75 ($9.10) adults, £3.75 ($5.95); children 5–15, under 5 free. Grounds only admission £2.75 ($4.35) adults; £1.75 ($2.75) children. Apr–Oct 11am–6pm daily. Last admission is 5pm.

In the town of Wilton is one of England's great country estates, the home of the earls of Pembroke. Wilton House dates from the 16th century, but has undergone numerous alterations, most recently in Victoria's day. It is noted for its 17th-century staterooms by the celebrated architect Inigo Jones. Many famous personages have either lived at or visited Wilton. It is also believed that Shakespeare's troupe entertained here. Preparations for the D-day landings at Normandy were laid out here by Eisenhower and his advisers, with only the silent Van Dyck paintings in the Double Cube room as witnesses.

The house is filled with beautifully maintained furnishings and displays world-class art, including paintings by Sir Anthony Van Dyck, Rubens, Brueghel, and Reynolds. A dynamic film introduced and narrated by Anna Massey brings to life the history of the family since 1544, the year they were granted the land by Henry VIII. You then visit a reconstructed Tudor kitchen and Victorian laundry plus "The Wareham Bears," a unique collection of some 200 miniature dressed teddy bears.

Growing on the 21-acre estate are giant Cedars of Lebanon, the oldest of which were planted in 1630. The Palladian Bridge was built in 1737 by the ninth earl of Pembroke and Roger Morris. There are rose and water gardens, riverside and woodland walks, and a huge adventure playground for children. Guides assist in the principal staterooms.

✪ Stonehenge

At the junction of A303 and A344/A360. ☎ **01980/623108.** Admission £3 ($4.75) adults; £1.50 ($2.35) children; £2.30 ($3.65) for students. Apr–May, Sept–Oct 8, daily 9:30am–6pm;

June daily 9:30am–7pm; July–Aug daily 9am–7pm; Oct 9–15 daily 9am–5pm; Oct 16–Mar daily 9:30am–4pm. Bus: STONEHENGE

Two miles west of Amesbury and about 9 miles north of Salisbury is the renowned Stonehenge, Stone Circle, believed to be anywhere from 3,500 to 5,000 years old. This huge circle of lintels and megalithic pillars is the most important prehistoric monument in Britain.

Some visitors are disappointed when they see that Stonehenge is nothing more than concentric circles of stones. Perhaps they do not understand that Stonehenge represents an amazing engineering feat since many of the boulders, the bluestones in particular, were moved many miles (perhaps from southern Wales) to this site.

The widely held view of the 18th- and 19-century romantics that Stonehenge was the work of the Druids is without foundation. The boulders, many weighing several tons, are believed to have predated the arrival in Britain of the Celtic cult. Recent excavations continue to bring new evidence to bear on the origin and purpose of Stonehenge. Controversy surrounds the prehistoric site especially since the publication of *Stonehenge Decoded* by Gerald S. Hawkins and John B. White, which maintains that Stonehenge was an astronomical observatory—that is, a Neolithic "computing machine" capable of predicting eclipses.

Your ticket permits you to go inside the fence surrounding the site that protects the stones from vandals and souvenir hunters. You can go all the way up to a short rope barrier about 50 feet from the stones.

Nether Wallop

12 miles from Stonehenge, 8 miles from Salisbury, and 10 miles from Winchester on a country road between A343 and A30.

East of Salisbury is the little village of Nether Wallop (not to be confused with Over Wallop or Middle Wallop in the same vicinity). Aficionados of television's "Mystery" series about Agatha Christie's Miss Marple will be interested in this village, used as Miss Christie's fictitious St. Mary Mead, home of Miss Marple. Visitors to Nether Wallop can easily identify the sites in many of the TV movies.

2 Dunster

3 miles SE of Minehead, 184 miles W of London

The village of Dunster in Somerset is near the eastern edge of Exmoor National Park. It grew up around the original Dunster Castle, constructed as a fortress for the de Mohun family, whose progenitor came to England with William the Conqueror. The village, about 4 miles from the Cistercian monastery at Cleeve, has an ancient priory church and dovecote, a 17th-century gabled yarn market, and little cobbled streets dotted with whitewashed cottages.

ESSENTIALS
GETTING THERE

By Train   The best rail link is to Minehead via Taunton, which is easily reached on the main London-Penzance line from Paddington Station in London. From Minehead you have to take a taxi or coach to reach Dunster.

By Bus   At Taunton, you can take one of the seven Southern National coaches (no. 28), leaving hourly Monday through Saturday; there is only one bus on Sunday. Trip time is 1 hour and 10 minutes. Buses (no. 38 or 39) from Minehead stop in Dunster Village at the rate of one per hour, but only from June to September. Off-season visitors must take a taxi.

By Car   From London, head west along M4, cutting south at the junction with M5 until you reach the junction with A39 going west to Minehead. Before your final approach to Minehead, cut south to Dunster along A396.

VISITOR INFORMATION

The **telephone area code** is 01643. Dunster doesn't have an official tourist office, but an **Exmoor National Park Visitor Centre** is found at Dunster Steep (☎ **01643/821835**), 2 miles east of Minehead. It's open April to mid-November, from 10am to 5pm.

WHAT TO SEE & DO

✪ Dunster Castle

On A396 (just off A39), Dunster. ☎ **01643/821314.** Castle and grounds, £4.80 ($7.60) adults, £2.40 ($3.80) children; grounds only, £2.70 ($4.25) adults, £1.30 ($2.05) children. Castle Apr–Oct Sat–Wed 11am–5pm; grounds daily 10am–5pm. Bus 38 or 39 from Minehead.

The castle is on a tor (high hill), from which you can see Bristol Channel, and it stands on the site of a Norman castle granted to William de Mohun of Normandy by William the Conqueror shortly after the conquest of England. The 13th-century gateway built by the de Mohuns is all that remains of the original fortress. In 1376 the castle and its lands were bought by Lady Elizabeth Luttrell and belonged to her family until given to the National Trust in 1976, together with 30 acres of surrounding parkland. The first castle was largely demolished during the Civil War, and the present Dunster Castle is a Jacobean house built in the lower ward of the original fortifications in 1620, then rebuilt in 1870 to look like a castle. From the terraced walks and gardens you'll have good views of Exmoor and the Quantock Hills.

Some of the outstanding artifacts within are the 17th-century panels of embossed painted and gilded leather depicting the story of Antony and Cleopatra, and a remarkable allegorical 16th-century portrait of Sir John Luttrell shown wading naked through the sea with a female figure of peace and a wrecked ship in the background. The 17th-century plasterwork ceilings of the dining room and the finely carved staircase balustrade of cavorting huntsmen, hounds, and stags are also noteworthy.

WHERE TO STAY & DINE

MODERATE

Luttrell Arms

32-36 High St., Dunster, Somerset TA24 6SG. ☎ **01643/821555** or 800/225-5843 in the U.S. and Canada. Fax 01643/821567. 27 rms (all with bath or shower). TV TEL. £95–£110 ($150.10–$173.80) double. Breakfast £8.50 ($13.45) extra. AE, DC, MC, V.

On the site of what has been a hostelry for weary travelers for more than 600 years, this hotel is the outgrowth of a guesthouse the Cistercian abbots at Cleeve had built in the village of Dunster. It was named for the Luttrell lords of the manor, who bought Dunster Castle and the property attached to it in the 14th century. It has, of course, been provided with the amenities expected by modern travelers, but from its stone porch to the 15th-century Gothic hall with hammer-bean roof (now divided) it still retains a feeling of antiquity. The bedrooms are comfortably appointed and attractively decorated in keeping with the hotel's long history; four of them have four-poster beds.

A lounge is upstairs, while downstairs you can enjoy a drink in the timbered Tudor bar, with its large inglenook fireplace. This was once the kitchen of the hostelry. A meal in the dining room, costing £17.95 ($28.35) can be ordered from a varied menu. Depending on the season, you might choose guinea fowl or baked sugared ham with Somerset cider sauce. Bar food is also offered. A fixed-price Sunday lunch goes for £10.95 ($17.30).

A NEARBY PLACE TO STAY

Cordon Mill

Vellow, Williton, Somerset, TA4 4LS. ☎ **01984/6565522.** Fax 01984/656197. 6 rms. TV TEL. £50–£60 ($79–$94.80) double. Rates include English breakfast. MC, V. Free parking.

Situated on an arable 200-acre farm, 5 miles northeast of Dunster, this guesthouse, a former water mill, sports a 100-year-old waterwheel made by the local ironworks. The wheel was a replacement for the original after it collapsed. The former miller would mill corn for the locals and teach the others the craft. Daphne and Richard Criddle own this establishment, offering patrons homestyle food and accommodations. The individually decorated rooms are equipped with television, telephone, tea and coffee facilities, and private bath or shower. Mrs. Criddle serves English fare, including venison, roast lamb, and pheasant. All the food is homemade and may include a few French-inspired dishes "when the inspiration strikes."

EASY EXCURSIONS

Combe Sydenham Hall

Monksilver. ☎ **01984/656284.** £4 ($6.30) adults, £1.50 ($2.35) children. Easter–Oct, Country Park Sun–Fri 10am–5pm; courtroom and gardens Mon–Fri 1:30–4pm; tearoom and shop Sun–Fri 10am–5pm, Sat 11am–2pm. Drive 5 miles south of Watchet on the B3188 road between Monksilver and Elsworthy.

This hall was the home of Elizabeth Sydenham, wife of Sir Francis Drake, and it stands on the ruins of monastic buildings that were associated with nearby Cleeve Abbey. Here you can see a cannonball that legend says halted the wedding of Lady Elizabeth to a rival suitor in 1585. The gardens include Lady Elizabeth's Walk, which circles ponds originally laid out when the knight was courting his bride-to-be. The valley ponds fed by springwater are full of rainbow trout (ask about getting fly-fishing instruction). Woodland walks are possible to Long Meadow with its host of wildflowers. Also to be seen are a deserted hamlet, whose population reputedly was wiped out by the Black Death, and a historic corn mill. In the hall's tearoom, smoked trout and pâté are produced on oak chips, as in days of yore, and there are a shop, working bakery, and car park.

Incidentally, it was from Watchet, a few miles east of Minehead along the coast, that Coleridge's Ancient Mariner sailed.

Coleridge Cottage

35 Lime St., Nether Stowey, near Bridgwater. ☎ **01278/732662.** £1.50 ($2.35) adults, 80p ($1.25) children. April 2–Oct 3 Tues–Thurs and Sun 2–5pm.

The hamlet of Nether Stowey is on A39, north of Taunton across the Quantock Hills to the east of Exmoor. The cottage is at the west end of Nether Stowey on the south side of A39 and 8 miles west of Bridgwater. Here you can visit the home of Samuel Taylor Coleridge where he wrote "The Rime of the Ancient Mariner." During his 1797–1800 sojourn here, he and his friends, William Wordsworth and

Frommer's Nature Notes

Straddling the border between Somerset and Devon, along the northern coast of England's southwest peninsula, is **Exmoor National Park,** a deliberately undeveloped plateau whose lonely moors are generally located at least 1,200 feet above sea level. One of the most cherished national parks in Britain, it includes the wooded valleys of the rivers Exe and Barle, the Brendon Hills, a sweeping stretch of rocky coastline, and such sleepy but charming villages as **Culbone, Selworthy, Minehead,** and **Allerford.** Bisected by a network of heavily eroded channels for brooks and streams, the park is distinctive for its lichen-covered rocks, gray-green grasses, gorse, and heather. The moors reach their highest point at Dunkery Beacon, at 1,707 feet above sea level.

Although it's one of the smallest national parks in Britain, aficionados praise it for a coastline which many believe is the most beautiful in England. Softly contoured, without the dramatic peaks and valleys of other national parks, the terrain is composed mostly of weathered sandstone resting on a primeval foundation of slate. Although noteworthy for its absence of trees, the terrain encompasses a limited handful of very old oak groves which are studied by forestry experts for their growth patterns.

On clear days, the coast of South Wales, 20 miles away, can be spotted across the estuary of the Bristol Channel. The wildlife that thrives on the park's rain-soaked terrain includes a breed of wild ponies (the Exmoor pony) whose bloodlines can be traced back to ancient species.

The region's most famous literary references are based on R. D. Blackmoor's novel *Lorna Doone* (1869), whose protagonists hid from 17th-century bailiffs within Exmoor's sheltering hills. ("The land lies softly. . . ." is a line from that book which evocatively describes the gentle contours of Exmoor's softly undulating surfaces.) The region's most widely publicized (unsolved) murder prompted local authorities to drain Pinkery Pond in 1906, in hopes of finding a body (but it was never found).

Despite the region's lack of trees, much of the park's terrain was classified as a Royal Forest and hunting preserve during the Middle Ages. (Part of the explanation for its low population density is the soil's relative infertility.) In 1819, the British government abandoned all attempts to maintain the district as a royal hunting preserve. Although the park's borders were opened to settlement and investment, it remained sparsely settled until 1954, when it was added to Britain's network of National Parks. Today, development programs of all kinds are rigidly restricted; although there are more than 600 miles of walking trails within the confines of the park, most visitors stay on the coastal trail that winds around the bays and inlets of England's southwestern peninsula.

Both the park's administrative headquarters and its visitor center are located within a pair of 19th-century houses in the hamlet of Dulverton, in Somerset, near the park's eastern edge. A program of walking tours is offered to anyone who's interested, at least five times a week. Themes include Woodland Walks, Moorland Walks, Bird Watching Excursions, and Deer Spottings. Most of the tours last from four to six hours, and all are priced at a modest £1 ($1.60) or £2 ($3.15) each. Wear sturdy shoes and raingear. For information about the park and its tours, contact the Exmoor National Park's Visitor Center, Dulverton, Somerset TA22 9HL (☎ 01398/323665).

sister Dorothy, enjoyed exploring the Quantock woods. The parlor and reading room of his National Trust property are open to visitors.

3   Glastonbury

136 miles SW of London, 26 miles S of Bristol, 6 miles SW of Wells

Glastonbury may be one of the oldest inhabited sites in Britain. Excavations have revealed Iron Age lakeside villages on its periphery, and some of the discoveries dug up may be viewed in a little museum on the High Street. After the destruction of its once-great abbey, the town lost prestige; today it is a market town. The ancient gatehouse entry to the abbey is a museum, and its principal exhibit is a scale model of the abbey and its community buildings as they stood in 1539, at the time of the dissolution.

ESSENTIALS
GETTING THERE

By Train   Go to Taunton, which is on the London–Penzance line leaving frequently from London's Paddington Station; at Taunton, proceed the rest of the way by bus. Or leave London's Paddington Station for Bristol Temple Meads, and go the rest of the way by Badgerline bus no. 376.

By Bus   From Taunton, take the Southern National bus (no. 17) to Glastonbury Monday through Saturday. There are one to three departures per day (trip time: 1 hr.). A Badgerline bus (no. 376) runs from Bristol via Wells to Glastonbury every hour Monday through Saturday; on Sunday, the schedule is reduced to every 2 hours. Trip time is 1 1/2 hours. For information about bus schedules of Badgerline, call 01934/621201; for data about Southern National, call 01823/272033. One National Express bus a day (no. 402) leaves London's Victoria Coach Station at 5:30pm and arrives in Glastonbury at 9:40pm.

By Car   Take M4 west from London, then cut south on A4 going via Bath to Glastonbury.

VISITOR INFORMATION

The **telephone area code** is 01458. The **Tourist Information Centre** is at The Tribunal, 9 High St. (☎ **01458/832954**).

WHAT TO SEE & DO

✪ Glastonbury Abbey

Abbey Gatehouse. ☎ **01458/832267**. Admission £2 ($3.15) adults, £1 ($1.60) children under 16. Daily 9:30am–6pm or dusk.

What was once one of the wealthiest and most prestigious monasteries in England is no more than a ruined sanctuary today, but it provides Glastonbury's claim to historical greatness, an assertion augmented by legendary links to such figures as Joseph of Arimathea, King Arthur, Queen Guinevere, and St. Patrick.

It is said that Joseph of Arimathea journeyed to what was then the Isle of Avalon, with the Holy Grail in his possession. According to tradition, he buried the chalice at the foot of the conical Glastonbury Tor and a stream of blood burst forth. You can scale this more than 500-foot-high hill today, on which rests a 15th-century tower.

Joseph, so it goes, erected a church of wattle in Glastonbury. (The town, in fact, may have had the oldest church in England, as excavations have shown.) And at one point the saint is said to have leaned against his staff, which was immediately transformed into a fully blossoming tree; a cutting alleged to have survived from the Holy Thorn can be seen on the abbey grounds today—it blooms at Christmastime. Some historians have traced this particular story back to Tudor times.

The most famous link—popularized for Arthurian fans in the Victorian era by Tennyson—concerns the burial of King Arthur and Queen Guinevere on the abbey grounds. In 1191 the monks dug up the skeletons of two bodies on the south side of the lady chapel, said to be those of the king and queen. In 1278, in the presence of Edward I, the bodies were removed and transferred to a black marble tomb in the choir. Both the burial spot and the shrine are marked today.

A large Benedictine Abbey of St. Mary grew out of the early wattle church. St. Dunstan, who was born nearby, was the abbot in the 10th century and later became archbishop of Canterbury. Edmund, Edgar, and Edmund "Ironside," three early English kings, were buried at the abbey.

In 1184 a fire destroyed most of the abbey and its vast treasures. It was eventually rebuilt, after much difficulty, only to be dissolved by Henry VIII. Its last abbot, Richard Whiting, was hanged at Glastonbury Tor. Like the Roman forum, the abbey was used as a stone quarry for years.

Today you can visit the ruins of the chapel, linked by an early English "Galilee" to the nave of the abbey. The best-preserved building on the grounds is a 14th-century octagonal Abbot's Kitchen, where oxen were once roasted whole to feed the wealthier pilgrims.

Somerset Rural Life Museum

Abbey Farm, Chilkwell St., Glastonbury. ☎ **01458/831197.** Admission £1.50 ($2.35) adults, 40p (65¢) children. Easter–Oct Mon–Fri 10am–5pm, Sat–Sun 2–6pm; Nov–Mar Mon–Fri 10am–5pm, Sat 11am–4pm.

The history of the Somerset countryside since the early 19th century is exemplified in this museum based in the abbey farm. The centerpiece of the museum is the abbey barn, built around 1370. The magnificent timbered room, stone tiles, and sculptural details (including the head of Edward III) make it special. There is also a Victorian farmhouse comprising exhibits that illustrate farming in Somerset during the "horse age" as well as domestic and social life in Victorian times. In summer, there are demonstrations of buttermaking, weaving, basketwork, and many other traditional craft and farming activities, which are rapidly disappearing. There is a museum shop and tearoom.

Impressions

Out of this lake, which filled the center of a beautiful plain, embellished with groupes of beeches and elms, and fed with sheep, issued a river, that, for several miles, was seen to meander through an amazing variety of meadows and woods, till it emptied itself into the sea; with a large arm of which, and an island beyond it, the prospect was closed. On the right of the valley opened another of less extent, adorned with several villages, and terminated by one of the towers of an old ruined abbey, grown over with ivy, and part of the front, which remained still entire.

—Henry Fielding, *The History of Tom Jones, A Foundling* (1749)

WHERE TO STAY
INEXPENSIVE

The George & Pilgrims

1 High St., Glastonbury, Somerset BA6 9DP. ☎ **01458/831146.** Fax 01458/832252.
13 rms. TV TEL. £65–£75 ($102.70–$118.50) double. Rates include English breakfast.
AE, DC, MC, V.

One of the few pre-Reformation hostelries still left in England, this inn once
offered hospitality to Glastonbury pilgrims; now it accepts modern travelers. In
the center of town, the inn has a facade that looks like a medieval castle, with
stone-mullioned windows with leaded glass. Some of the bedrooms were formerly
monks' cells; others have four-posters, veritable carved monuments of oak. You
may be given the Henry VIII Room, from which the king watched the burning
of the abbey in 1539.

The building's original kitchen now functions as a bar, where patrons drink
beneath the span of old oaken beams. Nearby is a brasserie, specializing in English
and continental food (see "Where to Dine", below).

Number 3 Hotel

3 Magdalene St., Glastonbury, Somerset BA6 9EW. ☎ **01458/832129.** 6 rms. TV TEL. £65
($102.70) double. Rates include continental breakfast. MC, V. Free parking. Closed Jan–Feb.

John and Ann Tynan have operated this small family property, adjoining the
Glastonbury ruins, since the mid-1980s. The couple closed the on-site restaurant
so Mrs. Tynan, a chiropractor, could devote her time to administering massage and
aromatherapy to guests. Housed in a Georgian structure, the six double rooms are
all tastefully and individually decorated, including television, telephone, hot
beverage facilities, and private bath or shower.

WHERE TO DINE
MODERATE

The Brasserie

In the George & Pilgrims Hotel, 1 High St. ☎ **01458/831146.** Reservations recommended.
Main courses £4.95–£8.25 ($7.80–$13.05); fixed-price three-course meal £9.50 ($15).
AE, MC, V. Lunch daily noon–2:30pm; dinner Sun–Thurs 7–9:30pm, Fri–Sat 7–10pm.
ENGLISH/CONTINENTAL.

Housed in the George & Pilgrims Hotel, this restaurant offers a table d'hôte menu
that changes daily, as well as an à la carte menu with the chef's special of the
day posted on blackboards. A la carte dishes may include peppered soup; warm
avocado and walnuts in a light Stilton sauce; gammon steak topped with poached
egg and pineapple; suprême of chicken marinated in white wine, lemon, and herbs;
and vegetarian choices such as broccoli and cream cheese bake or vegetable
Stroganoff with a timbale of saffron and wild rice. Desserts are varied, including
treacle sponge with custard or white chocolate fudge cake served hot or cold.

4 Wells

21 miles SW of Bath, 123 miles SW of London

To the south of the Mendip Hills, the cathedral town of Wells is a medieval gem.
Wells was a vital link in the Saxon kingdom of Wessex—that is to say, it was
important in England long before the arrival of William the Conqueror. Once the
seat of a bishopric, it was eventually toppled from its ecclesiastical hegemony by

the rival city of Bath. But the subsequent loss of prestige has paid off handsomely for Wells today: After experiencing the pinnacle of prestige, it fell into a slumber—hence, much of its old look remains. Wells was named after wells in the town, which were often visited by pilgrims to Glastonbury in the hope that their gout could be eased by its supposedly curative waters.

ESSENTIALS
GETTING THERE
By Train   Take the train to Bath (see below) and continue the rest of the way by bus.

By Bus   Wells has good bus connections with its surrounding towns and cities. Badgerline bus no. 175 links Wells with Bath. Departures are every hour Monday through Saturday and every 2 hours on Sunday. Both no. 376 and 378 buses run between Bristol and Glastonbury every hour Monday through Saturday and every 2 hours on Sunday.

By Car   Take M4 west from London, cutting south on A4 toward Bath and continuing along A39 into Wells.

VISITOR INFORMATION
The **telephone area code** is 01749. The **Tourist Information Centre** is at the Town Hall, Market Place (☎ **01749/672552**).

WHAT TO SEE & DO
Begun in the 12th century, **Wells Cathedral** (☎ **01749/674483**), in the center of town, is a well-preserved example of the early English style of architecture. The medieval sculpture (six tiers of hundreds of statues recently restored) of its west front is without equal. The western facade was completed in the mid-13th century. The landmark central tower was erected in the 14th century, with the fan vaulting attached later. The inverted arches were added to strengthen the top-heavy structure.

Much of the stained glass dates from the 14th century. The fan-vaulted lady chapel, also from the 14th century, is in the Decorated style. To the north is the vaulted chapter house, built in the 13th century and recently restored. Look also for a medieval astronomical clock in the north transept. There is no charge to enter the cathedral; however, visitors are asked to make voluntary donations of £2.50 ($3.95) for adults, 75p ($1.20) or students and children. The Cloister Restaurant and Cathedral Shop are adjacent to the cathedral.

After a visit to the cathedral, walk along its cloisters to the moat-surrounded **Bishop's Palace.** The Great Hall, built in the 13th century, is in ruins. Finally, the street known as the **Vicars' Close** is one of the most beautifully preserved streets in Europe. The cathedral is usually open daily from 7:15am to 6pm or until dusk in summer.

WHERE TO STAY
MODERATE

The Swan Hotel

11 Sadler St., Wells, Somerset BA5 2RX. ☎ **01749/678877** or 800/528-1234 in the U.S. and Canada. Fax 01749/677647. 38 rms. TV TEL. £83.50–£91 ($131.95–$143.80) double. Rates include English breakfast. AE, DC, MC, V. Free parking.

Set behind a stucco facade on one of the town's main arteries, this place was originally built in the 15th century as a coaching inn. It faces the west front of Wells Cathedral. Several of the well-furnished bedrooms are equipped with four-poster beds. The spacious and elegant public rooms stretch out to the left and right of the entrance as you enter. Both ends have a blazing and baronial fireplace, beamed ceilings, and paneling. The Swan Hotel Restaurant is recommended separately (see below).

INEXPENSIVE

⑤ Star Hotel

18 High St., Wells, Somerset BA5 2SQ. ☎ **01749/673055.** Fax 01749/672654. 12 rms (all with bath or shower). TV. £50–£65 ($79–$102.70) double. Rates include continental breakfast. AE, DC, MC, V. Free parking.

The Star had its origins sometime in the 16th century, but is most closely associated with the great coaching era, though the hotel front was restored in the Georgian period. The cobbled carriageway, still preserved, leads to the dining room—once the stables. The hotel bedrooms have been modernized, yet retain their old charm. Copper and brass are extensively used for decoration, and several original stone walls and timbers have been exposed. The inn has a reputation for good food; an à la carte dinner costs £15 ($23.70).

WHERE TO DINE
MODERATE

Swan Hotel Restaurant

In the Swan Hotel, 11 Sadler St. ☎ **01749/678877.** Reservations recommended. Fixed-price lunch £12.50 ($19.75); fixed-price dinner £16.50 ($26.05). AE, DC, MC, V. Lunch daily noon–2:30pm; dinner daily 7–9:30pm. TRADITIONAL ENGLISH.

Owned and operated by this previously recommended hotel, this restaurant is decorated in a traditional English style. It offers table d'hôte meals, a class English repertoire of dishes. Begin perhaps with the chef's homemade pâté, then follow with grilled lamb cutlets, roast Somerset chicken with bacon, or roast duckling with applesauce. All dishes are served with potatoes and fresh vegetables. Wine is sold by the glass.

AN EASY EXCURSION

Easily reached by heading west out of Wells, the **Caves of Mendip** are two exciting natural sightseeing attractions in Somerset—the great caves of Cheddar and Wookey Hole.

Wookey Hole Caves & Paper Mill

Wookey Hole, near Wells. ☎ **01749/672243.** 2-hour tour £6 ($9.50) adults, £3.50 ($5.55) children 16 and under; £16 ($25.30) family ticket. Apr–Oct daily 9:30am–5:30pm; Nov–Mar daily 10:30am–4:30pm. Free parking. Closed Dec 17–25. Follow the signs from the center of Wells for 2 miles. Bus 172 from Wells.

Just 2 miles from Wells, you'll first come to the source of the Axe River. In the first chamber of the caves, as legend has it, is the Witch of Wookey turned to stone. These caves are believed to have been inhabited by prehistoric people at least 60,000 years ago. A tunnel opened in 1975 leads to the chambers unknown in early times and previously accessible only to divers.

Leaving the caves, you follow a canal path to the mill, where paper has been made by hand since the 17th century. Here you can watch the best-quality paper being made by skilled workers according to the tradition of their ancient craft. Also in the mill is a "Fairground Memories" exhibition, a colorful assembly of relics from the world's fairgrounds, and an Edwardian Penny Pier Arcade where new pennies can be exchanged for old ones with which to play the original machines. Other attractions include the Magical Mirror Maze, an enclosed passage of multiple image mirrors, and Movie Mania, celebrating a century of films.

Visitors can use the self-service restaurant and picnic area.

Cheddar Show Caves

Cheddar Gorge. ☎ **01934/742343.** Admission £6 ($9.50) adults, £4 ($6.30) children 5–15; 4 and under free. Easter–Sept daily 10am–5:30pm; Oct–Easter daily 10:30am–4:30pm. Closed Dec 24–25. From A38, cut onto A371 to Cheddar village.

A short distance from Bath, Bristol, and Wells is the village of Cheddar, home of Cheddar cheese. It lies at the foot of Cheddar Gorge, within which are the Cheddar Caves, underground caverns with impressive formations. The caves are more than a million years old, including Gough's Cave, with its cathedrallike caverns, and Cox's Cave, with its calcite sculptures and brilliant colors. The Crystal Quest is a dark walk "fantasy adventure" taking you deep underground, and in the Cheddar Gorge Heritage Centre is displayed a 9,000-year-old skeleton. You can also climb Jacob's Ladder for cliff-top walks and Pavey's Lookout Tower for views over Somerset—on a clear day you may even see Wales. Adults and children over 12 years of age can book an Adventure Caving expedition, which includes overalls, helmets, and lamps. Other attractions include local craftspeople at work, ranging from the glassblower to the sweet maker, plus the Cheddar Cheese & Cider Depot, Gough's Shop, and Gough's Tea-Room.

Chewton Cheese Dairy

Priory Farm, Chewton Mendip. ☎ **01761/241666.** Admission £2 ($3.15) adults, £1.50 ($2.35) senior citizens, £1 ($1.60) children 5–15; 4 and under free. Daily 9am–4:30pm. Head 6 miles north of Wells on the A39 Bristol-Wells road.

The dairy is owned by Lord Chewton, and visitors are welcome to watch through the viewing window in the restaurant as the traditional cheese-making process is carried out most mornings. A video presentation is also featured. The best time to visit the dairy is between noon and 2:30pm. Although the dairy is open on Sunday and Thursday, there are no cheese-making demonstrations then. You can purchase a "truckle" (or wheel) of mature Cheddar to send home. The restaurant offers coffee, snacks, farmhouse lunches, and cream teas. Guided tours are offered April through October.

5 Bath

115 miles W of London, 13 miles SE of Bristol

Avon encompasses the territory around the old port of Bristol, an area that used to be in Somerset. In 1702 Queen Anne made the trek from London to the mineral springs of Bath, thereby launching a fad that was to make the city the most celebrated spa in England.

The most famous personage connected with Bath's popularity was the 18th-century dandy Beau Nash. The master of ceremonies of Bath, Nash cut a striking figure as he made his way across the city, with all the plumage of a bird of paradise. This polished arbiter of taste and manners made dueling déclassé. While dispensing (at a price) trinkets to the courtiers and aspirant gentlemen of his day, Beau was carted around in a sedan chair.

The 18th-century architects John Wood the Elder and his son provided a proper backdrop for Nash's considerable social talents. These architects designed a city of stone from the nearby hills, a feat so substantial and lasting that Bath today is the most harmoniously laid-out city in England. During Georgian times, this city on a bend of the Avon River was to attract a following among leading political and literary figures, such as Dickens, Thackeray, Nelson, and Pitt. Canadians may already know that General Wolfe lived on Trim Street, and Australians may want to visit the house at 19 Bennett St. where their founding father, Admiral Phillip, lived. Even Henry Fielding came this way, observing in *Tom Jones* that the ladies of Bath "endeavour to appear as ugly as possible in the morning, in order to set off that beauty which they intend to show you in the evening."

Bath has had two lives. Long before its Queen Anne, Georgian, and Victorian popularity, it was known to the Romans as Aquae Sulis. The foreign legions founded their baths here (which may be visited today) to ease their rheumatism in the curative mineral springs.

Remarkable restoration and careful planning have ensured that Bath retains its handsome look today. The city suffered devastating destruction from the infamous Baedeker air raids of 1942, when Luftwaffe pilots seemed more intent on bombing historical buildings than in hitting any military target.

SPECIAL EVENTS   Bath's graceful Georgian architecture provides the setting for one of Europe's most prestigious international festivals of music and the arts. For 17 days in late May and early June each year the city is filled with more than 1,000 performers. The **Bath International Music Festival** focuses on classical music, jazz, new music, and the contemporary visual arts, with orchestras, soloists, and artists from all over the world. In addition to the main music and art program, there is all the best in walks, tours, and talks, plus free street entertainment and a free Festival Club in Bath's famous Pump Room. Full details can be obtained from The Bath Festivals Booking Office, Linley House, 1 Pierrepont Place, Bath BA1 1JY (☎ 01225/463362).

ESSENTIALS
GETTING THERE
By Train   Trains leave London's Paddington Station bound for Bath at the rate of one every hour during the day (trip time: 70–90 min.).

By Bus   One National Express coach leaves London's Victoria Coach Station every 2 hours during the day (trip time: 2¹/₂ hr.). Coaches also leave Bristol bound for Bath (trip time: 50 min.).

By Car   Drive west on M4 to the junction with A4, on which you continue west to Bath.

VISITOR INFORMATION
The **telephone area code** is 01225. The **Bath Tourist Information Centre** is at Abbey Chambers, Abbey Churchyard (☎ **01225/462831**), opposite the Roman Baths.

WHAT TO SEE & DO
In addition to the attractions listed below, you may want to visit some of the buildings, crescents, and squares in town. The **North Parade** (where Goldsmith lived) and the **South Parade** (where English novelist and diarist Frances Burney

once resided) represent harmony, and are the work of John Wood the Elder. The younger Wood, on the other hand, designed the **Royal Crescent,** an elegant half-moon row of town houses copied by Astor architects for their colonnade in New York City in the 1830s. **Queen Square** is one of the most beautiful—Jane Austen and Wordsworth used to live here, though not together—showing off quite well the work of Wood the Elder. Also of interest is **The Circus,** built in 1754, as well as the shop-lined **Pulteney Bridge,** designed by Robert Adam and often compared to the Ponte Vecchio of Florence.

✪ Bath Abbey

Orange Grove. ☎ **01225/422462.** Admission free; donation requested £1 ($1.60). Heritage Vaults £2 ($3.15) adults, £1 ($1.60) students, children, and senior citizens. Abbey Apr–Oct Mon–Sat 9am–6pm; Nov–Mar, Mon–Sat 9am–4:30pm; year-round, Sun 1–2:30pm and 4:30–5:30pm. Heritage Vaults, Mon–Sat 10am–4pm.

Built on the site of a much larger Norman cathedral, the present-day abbey is a fine example of the late perpendicular style. When Queen Elizabeth I came to Bath in 1574, she ordered a national fund to be set up to restore the abbey. The west front is the sculptural embodiment of a Jacob's Ladder dream of a 15th-century bishop. When you go inside and see its many windows, you'll understand why the abbey is called the "Lantern of the West." Note the superb fan vaulting, with its scalloped effect. Beau Nash was buried in the nave and is honored by a simple monument totally out of keeping with his flamboyant character. In 1994 the Bath Abbey Heritage Vaults opened on the south side of the abbey. This is a subterranean exhibition, tracing the history of Christianity at the abbey site since Saxon times.

✪ Pump Room and Roman Baths

Abbey Churchyard. ☎ **01225/477776,** ext. 2785. Admission £5 ($7.90) adults, £3 ($4.75) children. Apr–Sept, daily 9am–6pm; Oct–Mar, Mon–Sat 9:30am–5pm, Sun 10am–5pm. Evenings in Aug 8–10pm.

Founded in A.D. 75 by the Romans, the baths were dedicated to the goddess Sulis Minerva; in their day they were an engineering feat. Even today they're considered among the finest Roman remains in the country, and are still fed by Britain's most famous hot-spring water. After centuries of decay, the original baths were rediscovered during Queen Victoria's reign. The site of the Temple of Sulis Minerva has been excavated and is now open to view. The museum displays many interesting objects from Victorian and recent digs (look for the head of Minerva). Coffee, lunch, and tea, usually with music from the Pump Room Trio, can be enjoyed in the 18th-century pump room, overlooking the hot springs. There's also a drinking fountain with hot mineral water.

Impressions

The Circus is a pretty bauble, contrived for show, and looks like Vespasian's amphitheater turned outside in. If we consider it in point of magnificence, the great number of small doors belonging to the separate houses, the inconsiderable height of the different orders, the affected ornaments of the architrave, which are both childish and misplaced, and the areas projecting into the street, surrounded with iron rails, destroy a good part of its effect upon the eye; and perhaps we shall find it still more defective, if we view it in the light of convenience.

—Tobias Smollett (1721–1771)

Theatre Royal

Sawclose. ☎ **01225/448844.** Tickets, £7–£23 ($11.05-$36.35). Box office Mon–Sat 10am–8pm. Shows Mon–Wed at 7:30pm, Thurs–Sat at 8pm. Wed matinees throughout the year at 2:30pm. Sat matinees in winter at 2:30pm. For credit-card bookings, call 01225/448861.

Theatre Royal, located next to the new Seven Dials development, was restored in 1982 and refurbished with plush seats, red carpets, and a painted proscenium arch and ceiling; some now believe it is the most beautiful theater in Britain. It has 940 seats, with a small pit and grand tiers rising to the upper circle. Beneath the theater, reached from the back of the stalls or by a side door, are the theater vaults, where you will find a bar in one with stone walls. The next vault has a restaurant.

The theater publishes a list of forthcoming events; its repertoire includes, among other offerings, West End shows.

No. 1 Royal Crescent

1 Royal Crescent. ☎ **01225/428126.** £3.50 ($5.55) adults, £2.50 ($3.95) children; family ticket £8 ($12.65). Mar–Oct Tues–Sun 10:30am–5pm, Nov to mid-Dec Tues–Sun 10:30am–4pm (last admission 30 minutes before closing). Closed Good Friday.

The interior of this Bath town house has been redecorated and furnished by the Bath Preservation Trust to look as it might have toward the end of the 18th century. The house is located at one end of Bath's most magnificent crescent, west of the Circus.

The American Museum

Claverton Manor, Bathwick Hill. ☎ **01225/460503.** Admission £5 ($7.90) adults, £2.50 ($3.95) children. Late Mar to late Oct, Tues–Sun 2–5pm. Bus 18.

Some 2¹/₂ miles outside Bath, you can get an idea of what life was like in America prior to the mid-1800s. It was the first American museum established outside the United States. In a Greek Revival house (Claverton Manor) designed by a Georgian architect, the museum sits proudly on extensive grounds high above the Avon valley. Among the authentic exhibits—shipped over from the States—are a New Mexico room, a Conestoga wagon, an early American beehive oven (try gingerbread baked from the recipe of George Washington's mother), the dining room of a New York town house of the early 19th century, and (on the grounds) a copy of Washington's flower garden at Mount Vernon. There is a permanent exhibition in the New Gallery of the Dallas Pratt Collection of Historical Maps, as well as seasonal exhibitions, and there is an American arboretum on the grounds.

WHERE TO STAY
EXPENSIVE

Bath Spa Hotel

Sydney Rd., Bath, Avon BA2 6JF. ☎ **01225/444424.** Fax 01225/444006. 90 rms, 8 suites. MINIBAR TV TEL. £129–£219 ($203.80–$346) double; £219 ($346) suite for two. Breakfast £13.50 ($21.35) extra. AE, DC, MC, V. Free parking. East of the city off A36.

This restored 19th-century mansion is a 10-minute walk from the center of Bath. Behind a facade of Bath stone, it lies at the end of a tree-lined drive on 7 acres of landscaped grounds, with a Victorian grotto and a Grecian temple. Winston Churchill visited when it was the headquarters of the Admiralty in World War II. In its long history, it had served many purposes (once a hostel for nurses) before being returned to its original grandeur. The drawing room of what was once an English general's house (he served in India) is today restored. It is representative of the new style of the hotel, which uses log fireplaces, elaborate moldings, oak paneling, and staircases to create country-house charm. The rooms are handsomely furnished with the best of English furniture and well-chosen and coordinated fabrics. Most of them are spacious.

Dining/Entertainment: The former owner called his home Vellore House, which is now the name of the restaurant where continental cuisine is served. You're given immaculate service and superb food and wine at a cost of £35 ($55.30) for a fixed-price dinner served from 7 to 10pm daily. A second restaurant, the Alfresco Restaurant, is also popular, offering a Mediterranean-style menu. In summer, guests can dine outside in an informal garden with a fountain.

Services: 24-hour room service, valet and laundry service, beauty treatments, hairdressing salon.

Facilities: Indoor swimming pool, gymnasium, tennis court, sauna and whirlpool bath, croquet lawn, children's nursery.

Fountain House

9–11 Fountain Buildings, Lansdown Rd., Bath, Avon BA1 5DV. ☎ **01225/338622.** Fax 01225/445855. 14 suites. MINIBAR TV TEL. £120–£168 ($189.60–$265.45) one-bedroom suite for two people; £168–£202 ($265.45–$319.15) two-bedroom suite for four people. Rates include continental breakfast. AE, DC, MC, V. Parking £11.75 ($18.55).

The three buildings that comprise this hotel are a trio of Georgian neoclassic, natural stone-fronted structures dating from 1735. British entrepreneur Robin Bryan created an all-suite hotel that has been favorably compared to the most prestigious in England. Each suite is decorated with original or reproduction antiques, lots of color-coordinated chintz, at least one bedroom, a sitting room, private bath, and all the electronic equipment you'd expect in such an elegant hotel. The hotel stands within 100 yards of Milsom Street, the city's main shopping and historic thoroughfare. It doesn't serve a formal breakfast. Instead, the breakfast food is delivered in a basket to the door and guests prepare their own breakfast at their own pace.

✪ The Priory Hotel

Weston Rd., Bath, Avon BA1 2XT. ☎ **01225/331922.** Fax 01225/448276. 21 rms. TV TEL. £155 ($244.90) standard double; £195 ($308.10) deluxe room for two. Rates include English breakfast. AE, DC, MC, V. Free parking.

Converted from one of Bath's Georgian houses in 1969, The Priory is situated on 2 acres of formal and award-winning gardens with manicured lawns and flower beds, a swimming pool, and a croquet lawn. The bedrooms are individually decorated and furnished with antiques; my personal favorite is Clivia (all rooms are named after flowers or shrubs), a nicely appointed duplex in a circular turret.

The restaurant consists of three separate dining rooms, one in a small salon in the original building; the others have views over the garden. The menu is varied and reflects seasonal availability. Grouse, partridge, hare, and venison are served in season in several recipes, as is the succulent best end of lamb roasted with herb-flavored bread crumbs. A three-course dinner is offered for £32 ($50.55). Lunch ranges from £13 ($20.55) to £23 ($36.35), and on Sunday traditional roasted meats are featured.

✪ Queensberry Hotel

Russell St., Bath, Avon BA1 2QF. ☎ **01225/447928** or 800/323-5463 in the U.S. Fax 01225/446065. 22 rms. TV TEL. £98–£164 ($154.85–$259.10) double. Rates include continental breakfast. AE, MC, V. Parking 50p (80¢) per hour.

Much of the beauty of this place derives from the many original fireplaces, ornate ceilings, and antiques, which the creators of the property, Stephen and Penny Ross, have preserved. Each of three interconnected town houses that form this hotel was constructed in the early Georgian era. Today each bedroom has antique furniture and carefully chosen upholstery, in keeping with the character of the house. Open since 1988, the Queensberry has become one of Bath's most important hotels.

At the hotel you can dine at the Olive Tree, offering a contemporary English cuisine. See separate recommendation in "Where to Dine," below.

Royal Crescent Hotel

16 Royal Crescent, Bath, Avon BA1 2LS. ☎ **01225/319090** or 800/457-6000 in the U.S. Fax 01225/339401. 28 rms, 14 suites. TV TEL. £165–£205 ($260.70–$323.90) double; £275–£375 ($434.50–$592.50) suite. Breakfast £8–£11 ($12.65–$17.40) extra. AE, DC, MC, V. Free parking.

A special place, standing proudly in the center of the famed Royal Crescent, the Georgian colonnade of town houses was designed by John Wood the Younger in 1767. Long regarded as Bath's premier hotel, it has attracted the rich and famous. Crystal chandeliers, period furniture, and paintings add to the rich adornment. The bedrooms, including the Jane Austen Suite, are often lavishly furnished with such amenities as four-poster beds and Jacuzzi baths. Each bedroom is not only individually designed, but also offers such comforts as a trouser press, hair dryer, bathrobes, bottled mineral water, remote-control TV, direct-dial phone, fruit plates, and other special touches. Excellent English cuisine is served in the Dower House Restaurant. Reservations are essential for rooms or meals. A fixed-price lunch, served daily from 12:30 to 2pm, costs £14.50 ($22.90) for two courses or £18.50 ($29.25) for three courses. A table d'hôte dinner, offered nightly from 7 to 9:30pm, goes for £33.50 ($52.95).

MODERATE

Francis Hotel

Queen Sq., Bath, Avon BA1 2HH. ☎ **01225/424257** or 800/225-5843 in the U.S. and Canada. Fax 01225/319715. 90 rms, 3 suites. TV TEL. £75 ($118.50) single; £95 ($150.10) double; £120 ($189.60) triple; £120–£170 ($189.60–$268.60) suite. English breakfast £9.25 ($14.60) extra. AE, DC, MC, V. Free parking.

An integral part of Queen Square, the first major development of John Wood the Elder, architect and creator of Bath's most prestigious buildings, the Francis is an example of 18th-century taste. Originally consisting of six private residences dating from 1729, the Francis was opened as a private hotel by Emily Francis in 1884 and has offered guests first-class service for more than 100 years. Many of the well-furnished and traditionally styled bedrooms overlook Queen Square—named in honor of George II's consort, Caroline. The public rooms feature shell-shaped niches, moldings, some 18th-century antiques, a cocktail bar, and the Edgar Restaurant, which offers a wide array of both British and international food; a fixed-price meal costs £17.95 ($28.35).

Lansdown Grove Hotel

Lansdown Rd., Bath, Avon, BA1 5EH. ☎ **01225/315891.** Fax 01225/448092. 44 rms (all with bath or shower). TV TEL £55 ($86.90) single; £85 ($134.30) double. Rates include English breakfast. AE, DC, MC, V. Free parking.

A well-run hotel outside the center of the city, the Lansdown Grove is situated on the south-facing slopes with good views. Its drawing room is informal, with flowering chintz draperies, a large gilt-and-marble console, and comfortable armchairs. The well-furnished bedrooms all have hair dryers and trouser presses.

It's a pleasure to eat in the sunny dining room, with its bay window that opens onto the garden. Before-dinner drinks are available in the cocktail bar.

INEXPENSIVE

Apsley House Hotel

141 Newbridge Hill, Bath, Avon BA1 3PT. ☎ **01225/336966.** Fax 01225/425462. 5 rms, 2 suites (all with bath or shower). TV TEL £45 ($71.10) single; £55 ($86.90) double; £75–£85 ($118.50–$134.30) suite. Rates include a continental breakfast. DC, MC, V. Free parking. Take A4 to Upper Bristol Rd. and fork right at the traffic signals into Newbridge Hill.

This charming and stately building, just a mile west of the center of Bath, dates back to 1830—the reign of William IV. It's set in its own gardens, with a square tower, arched windows, and a walled garden with south views. In 1994 new owners refurbished the hotel, filling it with country-house chintzes and a collection of antiques borrowed from the showrooms of an antiques store they own. (Some of the furniture in the hotel is for sale; inquire further about the details.) The bedrooms are comfortably furnished and filled with fine fabrics and attractive accessories.

Dukes' Hotel

53–54 Great Pulteney St., Bath, Avon BA2 4DN. ☎ **01225/463512.** Fax 01225/483733. 22 rms. TV TEL. £45–£60 ($71.10–$94.80) single; £55–£75 ($86.90–$118.50) double; £65–£80 ($102.70–$126.40) family rm. Rates include English breakfast. AE, MC, V. Free parking. Bus 18.

A short walk from the heart of Bath, this building dates from 1780 but has been completely restored and rather elegantly furnished and modernized, both in its public rooms and its bedrooms. Many of the original Georgian features, including cornices and moldings, have been retained. Amenities include electric trouser presses and hair dryers. Guests can relax in a refined drawing room or patronize the cozy bar. A traditional English menu is also offered, costing £15.50 ($24.50) for a three-course meal.

⑤ Laura Place Hotel

3 Laura Place, Great Pulteney St., Bath, Avon BA2 4BH. ☎ **01225/463815.** Fax 01225/310222. 8 rms (all with bath or shower). TEL. £50 ($79) single; £62–£85 ($97.95–$134.30) double. Rates include English breakfast. AE, MC, V. Free parking. Bus 18 or 19.

Built the year of the French Revolution (1789), this hotel has won a civic award for the restoration of its stone facade. Set on a corner of a residential street overlooking a public fountain, it lies within a 2-minute walk of the Roman Baths and Bath Abbey. The hotel has been skillfully decorated with antique furniture and fabrics evocative of the 18th century.

Number Ninety Three

93 Wells Rd., Bath, Avon BA2 3AN. ☎ **01225/317977.** 4 rms. TV £19–£35 ($30–$55.30) single; £38–£47 ($60.05–$74.25) double. Rates include English breakfast. AE, MC, V. Bus 3, 13, 14, 17, 23, or 33.

This well-run guesthouse is a traditional B&B, British style: small but immaculately kept and well maintained. Its owner is a mine of local information. The elegant Victorian house serves a traditional English breakfast, and it is within easy walking distance from the city center, rail and National Bus stations. Evening meals are available by prior arrangement. Parking can be difficult in Bath, but the hotel will advise.

Pratt's Hotel

South Parade, Bath, Avon BA2 4AB. ☎ **01225/460441.** Fax 01225/448807. 46 rms. TV TEL. £49.95 ($78.90) single; £79.90 ($126.25) double. Rates include English breakfast. Children under 15 sharing a room with two adults stay free. AE, DC, MC, V. Parking £5.40 ($8.55).

Once the home of Sir Walter Scott, Pratt's is conveniently located for sightseeing and has functioned as a hotel since 1791. Several elegant terraced Georgian town houses were joined together to make a comfortable hotel with warm, cheerful lounges, a bar, and a high-ceilinged dining room. The attractive cuisine is served in the dining room, where a fixed-price dinner costs £14.75 ($23.30).

ⓈSydney Gardens Hotel

Sydney Rd., Bath, Avon BA2 6NT. ☎ **01225/464818.** 6 rms. TV TEL. £59 ($93.20) single; £69 ($109) double. Rates include English breakfast. MC, V. Free parking.

This spot is reminiscent of the letters of Jane Austen, who wrote to friends about the long walks she enjoyed in Sydney Gardens, a public park just outside the city center. In 1852 an Italianate Victorian villa was constructed here of gray stone on a lot immediately adjacent to the gardens. Three rooms have twin beds and the other three have 5-foot-wide double beds. Each accommodation is individually decorated with an English country-house charm. Amenities include radio alarm clocks, hair dryers, and beverage-making facilities. No meals other than breakfast are served, since the center of town with many restaurants is within a 10-minute walk. There's also a footpath running beside a canal for an additional pedestrian adventure. No smoking is allowed.

IN NEARBY HINTON CHARTERHOUSE

Moderate

Homewood Park

Hinton Charterhouse, Bath, Avon BA3 6BB. ☎ **01225/723731.** Fax 01225/723820. 15 rms. £95–£160 ($150.10–$252.80) double. Rates include English breakfast. AE, DC, MC, V. Free parking. Take A36 (Bath–Warminster road) 6 miles south of Bath.

This small, family-run hotel, set on 10 acres of grounds, was built in the 18th century and enlarged in the 19th. Overlooking the Limpley Stoke Valley, it's a large Victorian house with grounds adjoining the 13th-century ruin of Hinton Priory. You can play tennis and croquet in the garden. Riding and golfing are available nearby, and beautiful walks in the Limpley Stoke Valley lure guests. Each of the bedrooms is luxuriously decorated, with exceptional color-coordinated fabrics, and each is furnished with taste and charm. Most of the rooms overlook the gardens and grounds or offer views of the valley.

Most visitors come here for the cuisine, served in a dining room facing south, overlooking the gardens. The French and English cooking is prepared with skill and flair, and you should expect to spend from £29.50 ($46.60) for dinner.

IN NEARBY STON EASTON

Expensive

✪ Ston Easton Park

Ston Easton, Somerset BA3 4DF. ☎ **01761/241631.** Fax 01761/241377. 26 rms. TV. £160–£320 ($252.80–$505.60) double. Children under 7 not accepted. Rates include continental breakfast. AE, DC, MC, V. Free parking.

From the moment you pass a group of stone outbuildings and the century-old beeches of the 30-acre park—just up the road from Farrington Gurney—you know you've come to a very special place. The mansion was created in the mid-1700s from the shell of an existing Elizabethan house, and in 1793 Sir Humphry Repton designed the landscape. In 1977, after many years of neglect, Peter and Christine Smedley acquired the property and poured money, love, and labor into its restoration. Now it's one of the great country hotels of England. A pair of carved mahogany staircases ringed with ornate plaster detailing might be considered works of sculpture. The sheer volume of antiques filling the place is staggering. There's a manorial library, as well as a drawing room suitable for a diplomatic reception. The tasteful bedrooms are filled with flowers, plus upholstery and antiques.

A sunflower-colored formal dining room displays museum-quality oil portraits, grandeur, and exquisite attention to detail. The chef prepares superb food, offering imaginative menus. A lunch costs £26 ($41.10), and a dinner goes for £38.50 ($60.85). Guests who return early from sightseeing enjoy tea on the terrace at the front of the hotel.

IN NEARBY HUNSTRETE

Expensive

Hunstrete House

Hunstrete, Chelwood, near Bristol, Avon BS18 4NS. ☎ **01761/490490.** Fax 01761/490732. 21 rms, 2 suites. TV TEL. £145–£165 ($229.10–$260.70) double; £195–£215 ($308.10–$339.70) suite. Half board £135 ($213.30) single; £195–£215 ($308.10–$339.70) double; £260 ($410.80) suite. Rates include English breakfast. MC, V. Free parking. Take A4 about 4 miles west of Bath, then A368 another 4¹/₂ miles toward Weston-super-Mare.

This fine Georgian house, a Relais & Châteaux, is situated on 92 acres of private parkland. The existence of the village of Hunstrete was first recorded in 936 when King Athelstan passed through on his way to the abbey in Glastonbury. Six units are in the Courtyard House, attached to the main structure and overlooking a paved courtyard with its Italian fountain and flower-filled tubs. Swallow Cottage, which adjoins the main house, has its own private sitting room, double bedroom, and bath. Units in the main house are individually decorated and furnished in attractive colors. There is a heated swimming pool in a sheltered corner of the walled garden.

Part of the pleasure of staying at Hunstrete is the contemporary and classic cuisine. If priced independently of accommodations, a fixed-price lunch costs £15 ($23.70) for three courses, and a fixed-price dinner goes for £29.50 ($46.60) for three courses.

WHERE TO DINE

MODERATE

The Hole in the Wall

16 George St. ☎ **01225/425242.** Reservations recommended. Main courses £12 ($18.95). Fixed-price three-course meal £19.50 ($30.80). AE, MC, V. Lunch Mon–Fri noon–2pm; dinner Mon–Sat 6–11pm. MODERN ENGLISH/FRENCH.

After a brief, unsuccessful interlude as an Italian restaurant, this much-renovated Georgian town house reopened in 1994 as the rebirth of an establishment which was among the most famous restaurants in Britain during the 1970s. Its owners are Gunna and Christopher Chown, whose successful restaurant in Wales has already received critical acclaim from many sources. The pair of interconnected dining rooms are accented with polished copper pots, darkened ceiling beams, whitewashed walls, and a large fireplace. The menu choices change frequently, according to the inspiration of the chef and the availability of ingredients, but they might include a warm salad of monkfish with Parma ham and exotic mushrooms; summer mushroom cutlet; braised lamb shank with roasted potatoes, garlic, and tomatoes; braised pork tenderloin wrapped in bacon with a brandy cider, and applesauce; and chocolate sorbet along with various warm and cold puddings. The house that accommodates the restaurant, incidentally, was built of honey-colored Bath stone around 1790.

⊗ The Moon and Sixpence

6A Broad St. ☎ **01225/460962.** Reservations recommended. Main courses £8.50–£11.95 ($13.45–$18.90; fixed-price dinner £14.95–£18.95 ($23.60–$29.95); fixed-price lunch £13.50 ($21.35); lunch buffet in the wine bar £5.50 ($8.70). AE, MC, V. Lunch daily noon–2:30pm; dinner daily 5:30–10:30pm. INTERNATIONAL.

One of the leading restaurants and wine bars of Bath, the Moon and Sixpence occupies a stone structure east of Queen Square, with an extended conservatory and sheltered patio. Situated just off Broad Street, it has a cobbled passageway that leads you past a fountain into its courtyard.

At lunch a large cold buffet with a selection of hot dishes is featured in the wine bar section. In the upstairs restaurant overlooking the bar, full service is offered. Main courses are likely to include such dishes as fillet of lamb with caramelized garlic or médaillons of beef fillet with a bacon, red wine, and shallot sauce. Look for the daily specials on the continental menu.

The Olive Tree

In the Queensberry Hotel, Russel St. ☎ **01225/447928.** Reservations recommended. Main courses £12.75–£14 ($20.15–$22.10); three-course fixed-price lunch £11.50 ($18.15); three-course fixed-price dinner £18 ($28.45). AE, MC, V. Lunch Mon–Sat noon–2pm; dinner Mon–Sat 7–10:30pm and Sun 7–9:30pm. MODERN ENGLISH/MEDITERRANEAN.

In the basement of this previously recommended hotel, Stephen and Penny Ross operate one of the most sophisticated little restaurants in Bath with a white-tile floor and black wood chairs. Stephen uses the best of local produce, with an emphasis on freshness. The menu is changed to reflect the season, with game and fish being the specialties. You might begin with a Provençale fish soup with rouille and croûtons or eggplant and mozzarella fritters with a sweet red pepper sauce, unless the grilled scallops with noodles and pine nuts tempts you instead. Then you could go on to try grilled calf's liver with compote of apples, sauternes, and muscat or the breast of pheasant flavored with apple and ginger. Stephen is also known for his desserts, which are likely to include such treats as a hot chocolate soufflé or an apricot and almond tart.

Popjoy's Restaurant

Sawclose. ☎ **01225/460494.** Reservations recommended. Main courses £7.95–£10.95 ($12.55–$17.30); three-course fixed-price lunch £5.20 ($8.20); three-course fixed-price dinner £12.75 ($20.15). AE, DC, MC, V. Lunch Tues–Sat noon–2pm; dinner Tues–Wed 6–9:30pm and Thurs–Sat 6–10pm. FRENCH/INTERNATIONAL.

Owned by Malcom Burr, this restaurant is named after Bath's most famous couple of the English Regency, Beau Nash and his mistress, Julianna Popjoy. Two dining rooms are located on separate floors of the circa 1720 Georgian home where the couple entertained their friends and one another and established the fashions of the day. Patrons dine within a setting of reds and grays with oak tables and chairs.

Menu choices may include a terrine of duck and chicken liver wrapped in bacon with a tomato coulis; watercress and potato soup; sautéed lamb kidneys with crispy smoked bacon; braised lamb shoulder with a sage and garlic stuffing; tagliatelle with leeks and cream sauce; grilled sirloin steak glazed with parsley butter; or breaded chicken with banana and spiced coconut cream.

INEXPENSIVE

Beaujolais

5 Chapel Row, Queen Sq. ☎ **01225/423417.** Reservations recommended. Lunch main courses £5.80–£8.80 ($9.15–$13.90); dinner appetizers £3–£4.50 ($4.75–$7.10); dinner main courses £10.50–£14 ($16.60–$22.10). MC, V. Lunch Mon–Sat noon–2pm; dinner Mon–Sat 7–11pm. FRENCH.

This is perhaps the best-known bistro in Bath, maintaining its old habitués but also attracting new admirers every year. Established in 1973, it is the oldest restaurant in Bath under its original ownership. Diners are drawn to the good, honest cookery and the decent value. One area of the restaurant is reserved for nonsmokers. The disabled (wheelchair access), children (special helpings), and vegetarians will all find comfort here. The house wines are modestly priced from £8.90 ($14.05) per bottle. Begin with a salad made with goat cheese and warm spinach leaves, followed perhaps with a delectable onion-flavored veal chop, a cassoulet, or a côte de boeuf.

Woods

9–13 Alfred St. ☎ **01225/314812.** Reservations recommended. Main courses £11.45 ($18.10); fixed-price lunches £5–£12 ($7.90–$18.95); fixed-price dinners £10–£12 ($15.80–$18.95). AE, MC, V. Lunch Mon–Sat noon–2:30pm; Sun noon–4pm; dinner Mon–Sat 6–10:30pm. Closed Dec 25–26. ENGLISH/FRENCH/ORIENTAL.

Named after John Wood the Younger, architect of Bath's famous Assembly Room, which lies across the street, this restaurant is housed within a Georgian building that functioned for many years as an emporium for food and clothing. Today, the restaurant is run by horse-racing enthusiast David Price and his French-born wife, Claude. A fixed-price menu is printed on paper, whereas the seasonal array of à la carte items are chalked onto a frequently changing blackboard. Menu selections might include pear and parsnip soup; smoked chicken salad with Stilton and avocado; pan-fried cod roe; Derbyshire black pudding; and breast of chicken with tomatoes, mushrooms, red wine, and tarragon.

EASY EXCURSIONS
✪ LONGLEAT HOUSE

Between Bath and Salisbury, Longleat House, Warminster, in Wiltshire (☎ 01985/844400), owned by the seventh marquess of Bath, lies 4 miles southwest of Warminster and 4¹/₂ miles southeast of Frome on A362. The first view of this magnificent Elizabethan house, built in the early Renaissance style, is romantic enough, but the wealth of paintings and furnishings in its lofty rooms is enough to dazzle.

From the Elizabethan Great Hall to the library, the state rooms, and the grand staircase, the house is filled with variety. The state dining room is full of silver and plate, and fine tapestries and paintings adorn the walls in profusion. The library represents the finest private collection in the country. The Victorian kitchens are open, offering a glimpse of life below the stairs in a well-ordered country home. Various exhibitions are mounted in the stable yard. Events are staged frequently on the grounds, and the Safari Park has a vast array of animals in open parklands, including Britain's only white tiger.

The Maze, the largest in the world, was added to the attractions by Lord Weymouth. It has more than 1¹/₂ miles of paths. The first part is comparatively easy, but the second part is rather complicated.

Admission to Longleat House is £4.80 ($7.60) for adults, £3 ($4.75)for children; admission to Safari Park, £5.50 ($8.70) for adults, £4 ($6.30) for children. Special exhibitions and rides require separate admission tickets. Passport tickets for all Longleat's attractions cost £11 ($17.40) for adults and £9 ($14.20) for children, including admission to the Butterfly Garden, Simulator Dr. Who Exhibition, Postman Pat's Village, Adventure Castle, and more. It's open from mid-March to September, daily from 10am to 6pm; October to Easter, daily from 10am to 4pm. The park is open mid-March to October, daily from 10am to 6pm (last cars are admitted at 5:30pm or sunset).

STOURHEAD

After Longleat, you can drive 6 miles down B3092 to Stourton, a village just off the highway, 3 miles northwest of Mere (A303). A Palladian house, Stourhead (☎ 01747/840348) was built in the 18th century by the banking family of Hoare. The magnificent gardens, which blended art and nature, became known as *le jardin anglais*. Set around an artificial lake, the grounds are decorated with temples, bridges, islands, and grottoes, as well as statuary.

The gardens are open daily from 8am to 7pm (or until dusk), costing £4.20 ($6.65) for adults and £2.20 ($3.50) for children from March through October. Off-season tickets cost £3.20 ($5.05) for adults and £1.60 ($2.55) for children. The house is open from March 26 through October 30 Saturday through Wednesday from noon to 5:30pm, costing £4.20 ($6.65) for adults and £2.20 ($3.50) for children.

AVEBURY

One of the largest prehistoric sites in Europe, Avebury lies on the Kennet River 7 miles west of Marlborough. Unlike Stonehenge, visitors can walk around the 28-acre site at Avebury, winding in and out of the circle of more than 100 stones, some weighing up to 50 tons. The stones are made of sarsen, a sandstone found in Wiltshire. Inside this large circle are two smaller ones, each with about 30 stones standing upright. Native Neolithic tribes are believed to have built these circles.

Avebury is on A361 between Swindon and Devizes and a mile from the A4 London-Bath road. The closest rail station is at Swindon, some 12 miles away, which is served by the main rail line from London to Bath. A limited bus service (no. 49) runs from Swindon to Devizes through Avebury.

What to See and Do

Avebury Museum
Avebury. ☎ **01672/539250.** Admission £1.50 ($2.35) adults, 80p ($1.25) children. Apr–Oct, daily 10am–6pm; Nov–Mar daily 10am–4pm.

Founded by Alexander Keiller, this museum houses one of Britain's most important archaeological collections. It began with Keiller's material from excavations at Windmill Hill and Avebury, and now includes artifacts from other prehistoric digs at West Kennet, Long Barrow, Silbury Hill, West Kennet Avenue, and the Sanctuary.

The Great Barn Museum of Wiltshire Rural Life

Avebury. ☎ **01672/539555.** Admission 95p ($1.50) adults, 50p (80¢) children. Mid-Mar to Oct, daily 10am–5:30pm; Nov to mid-Mar, Sat–Sun 11am–4:30pm.

Housed in a 17th-century thatched barn is a center for the display and interpretation of Wiltshire life during the last three centuries. There are displays on cheese making, blacksmithing, thatching, sheep and shepherds, the wheelwright, and other rural crafts, as well as local geology and domestic life.

Where to Dine: Inexpensive

Stones Restaurant

High St. ☎ **01672/539514.** Reservations not accepted. Soup £2.50 ($3.95); lunch buffet £5.25 ($8.30); afternoon cream teas £3.25 ($5.15). No credit cards. Apr–Oct, daily 10am–6pm (hot food noon–2:30pm); Nov–Mar, Sat–Sun 10am–5pm. INTERNATIONAL.

This restaurant has been a hit ever since it was opened in 1984 within a converted Victorian stable block by two archaeologists, Dr. Hilary Howard and her husband, Michael Pitts. They specialize in freshly made food grown organically without artificial additives, which is prepared in original ways and sold at reasonable prices. Their array of luncheon hot platters, which changes every day, might include spiced chili with fried peppers served with a mixture of wild, tamargue, and white rice, French beans with a spiced tomato sauce, and avocado and sour cream relish; celery, apple, and Gruyère roast with a rich mushroom sauce served with a gratin of carrots and leeks, and paprika roasted potatoes; or the mason's lunch (two cheeses, hand-churned butter, an apple, and homemade bread, pickles, and crackers). Pastries, coffee, fruit juices, bottled beer, cold quiche, snacks, and an array of Welsh and English cheeses are available throughout the day. Especially attractive is the midafternoon cream tea served with whole-wheat scones and clotted cream imported from Cornwall. The owners travel abroad every winter, bringing back their culinary inspirations from Asia and the Pacific.

6 Bristol

13 miles NW of Bath, 120 miles W of London

Bristol, the largest city in the West Country, is just across the Bristol Channel from Wales and is a good center for touring western Britain. This historic inland port is linked to the sea by 7 miles of the navigable Avon River. Bristol has long been rich in seafaring traditions and has many links with the early colonization of America. In fact, some claim that the new continent was named after a Bristol town clerk, Richard Ameryke. In 1497, John Cabot sailed from Bristol, which led to the discovery of the northern half of the New World.

ESSENTIALS

GETTING THERE

By Plane   Bristol Airport (☎ 01275/474444) is conveniently situated beside the main A38 road, just over 7 miles from the city center.

By Train   Rail services to and from the area are among the fastest and most efficient in Britain. British Rail runs very frequent services from London's Paddington Station to each of Bristol's two main stations: Temple Meads in the center of Bristol, and Parkway on the city's northern outskirts (trip time: 1½ hr.).

By Bus National Express buses depart every hour during the day from London's Victoria Coach Station (trip time: 2½ hr.).

By Car Head west from London on M4.

VISITOR INFORMATION

The **telephone area code** is 0117. The **Tourist Information Centre** is at St. Nicholas Church, St. Nicholas St. (☎ **0117/260767**).

WHAT TO SEE & DO

Guided walking tours are conducted in summer and last about 1½ hours. The tours depart from Neptune's Statue on Saturday at 2:30pm and on Thursday at 7pm. Guided tours are also conducted through Clifton, a suburb of Bristol, which has more Georgian houses than Bath.

SS *Great Britain*

City Docks, Great Western Dock. ☎ **0117/9260680.** Admission £3.40 ($5.40) adults, £2.30 ($3.65) children. Apr–Oct, daily 10am–6pm; Nov–Mar, daily 10am–5pm. Bus 511 from city center, a rather long haul.

In Bristol, the world's first iron steamship and luxury liner has been partially restored to its 1843 appearance, although it's still a long way from earning its old title of a "floating palace." This vessel, which weighs 3,443 tons, was designed by Isambard Brunel, a Victorian engineer.

Incidentally, in 1831 (at the age of 25), Brunel began a Bristol landmark, Suspension Bridge, over the 250-foot-deep Avon Gorge at Clifton.

Bristol Cathedral

College Green. ☎ **0117/9264879.** Admission free; donation requested £2 ($3.15). Daily 8am–6pm. Bus 8 or 9.

Construction of the cathedral, once an Augustinian abbey, was begun in the 12th century, and the central tower was added in 1466. The chapter house and gate house are good examples of late Norman architecture, and the choir is magnificent. The cathedral's interior was singled out for praise by Sir John Betjeman, the late poet laureate.

St. Mary Redcliffe

10 Redcliffe Way. ☎ **0117/9291487.** July-Aug, daily 8am–8pm; Oct–June, daily 8am–5pm. Bus 20, 21, or 22.

The parish church of St. Mary Redcliffe is one of the finest examples of Gothic architecture in England. Queen Elizabeth I on her visit in 1574 is reported to have described it as "the fairest, goodliest and most famous parish church in England," and Thomas Chatterton, the boy poet, called it "the pride of Bristol and the western land." The American Chapel houses the tomb and armor of Adm. Sir William Penn, father of the founder of Pennsylvania.

Theatre Royal

King St. ☎ **0117/9493993.** Tickets, £5–£17 ($7.50–$25.50). Any City Centre bus.

Built in 1766, this is now the oldest working playhouse in the U.K. It is the home of the Bristol Old Vic. Backstage tours leave from the foyer. Tours Fri–Sat at noon; £2 ($3.15) adults, £1.50 ($2.35) children and students under 19. Call the box office for the current schedule.

WHERE TO STAY
MODERATE

Hilton National Bristol

Redcliffe Way, Bristol, Avon BS1 6NJ. ☎ **0117/9260041** or 800/445-8667 in the U.S. and Canada. Fax 0117/9230089. 193 rms, 8 suites. MINIBAR TV TEL. £89 ($140.60) double; £150 ($237) suite. Breakfast £10.50 ($16.60) extra. AE, DC, MC, V. Free parking. Bus 1 or 2.

Situated conveniently amid the commercial bustle of the center of town, this modern hotel offers an imaginative decor. Many bedrooms are outfitted in pastels, and all have private baths, radios, in-house video, and tea and coffee makers.

Its split-level restaurant, The Kiln, is located inside the brick-lined walls of a former 16th-century glass kiln refurbished in the style of a French brasserie, and offers English and French specialties. Dinner begins at £15.50 ($24.50).

Bristol Marriott

Lower Castle St., Bristol, Avon BS1 3AD. ☎ **0117/9294281** or 800/228-9290 in the U.S. and Canada. Fax 0117/9225838. 279 rms, 10 suites. A/C TV TEL. Mon–Thurs £80–£105 ($126.40–$165.90) double; £170 ($268.60) suite; Fri–Sun £69 ($109) double; £120 ($189.60) suite. Rates include English breakfast. AE, DC, MC, V. Free parking. Bus 8 or 9.

Rising 10 stories from the heart of town, at the edge of Castle Park, this comfortably modern hotel is one of Bristol's tallest buildings. Built in 1973, and managed (but not owned) by Marriott, it attracts many business travelers as well as goodly numbers of foreign tourists. Bedrooms are conservatively modern, comfortable, and monochromatic, and public areas are stylish and spacious—all in the upscale traditions of the well-recommended Marriott chain. The more elegant of the hotel's two restaurants is The Château, serving fixed-price meals from £20 ($31.60) each. Less formal is The Brasserie, where platters of British and continental food range from £5 ($7.90) to £14 ($22.10) each. On the premises is a heated indoor swimming pool and full leisure facilities, including a fully equipped gymnasium.

Grand Hotel

Broad St., Bristol, Avon BS1 2EL. ☎ **0117/9291645.** Fax 0117/9227619. 179 rms, 8 suites. TV TEL. £110 ($173.80) double; £125–£145 ($197.50–$229.10) suite. Breakfast £10 ($15.80) extra. Discounts (minimum of 2 consecutive nights Fri–Sun): £45 ($71.10) single; £90 ($142.20) double, including half board. AE, DC, MC, V. Bus 8 or 9.

This Victorian grand hotel sits on a street in the commercial heart of town. The architectural detailing that led to its reputation as one of the most noteworthy hotels in town includes rows of fan-shaped windows, intricate exterior corniches, lavishly ornate crystal chandeliers, two bars (one in a nautical mode), and a pair of comfortable restaurants, including the Brass Nails, which serves good food. A fixed-price dinner of £17.50 ($27.65) is offered in the Brass Nails, whereas The White Lion is less formal and less expensive. Bedrooms are traditionally furnished and well maintained and three-fourths of them contain a minibar. After numerous renovations, the hotel bedrooms are more conservatively modern than the public rooms, which still retain much of their Victorian detailing.

WHERE TO DINE
MODERATE

✪ Harvey's Restaurant

12A Denmark St. ☎ **0117/9275034.** Required reservations. Main courses £17–£20 ($26.85–$31.60); fixed-price lunch £16 ($25.30); fixed-price dinner £29 ($45.80). AE, DC, MC, V. Lunch Mon–Fri noon–1:45pm; dinner Mon–Sat 7–10:45pm. BRITISH.

Harvey's Restaurant is situated in medieval cellars that have belonged to Harvey's of Bristol, famous for Harvey's Bristol Cream sherry, since 1796. Today, Harvey's is one of the top restaurants in Bristol and the West Country, serving contemporary British food based upon classical methods. The philosophy of chef-manager Ramon Farthing is to respect the natural flavor of every ingredient, however humble or exotic, with a constant reappraisal of cooking methods and presentation. The à la carte selections are complemented by an extensive wine list, with the red wines of Bordeaux a specialty.

The rest of the historic cellars accommodate Harvey's Wine Museum, with collections of English 18th-century drinking glasses, antique decanters, corkscrews, bottles, silverware, and furniture. The museum is open daily, and there are regular guided tours with tutored tastings. It is usually possible for restaurant customers to browse in the museum prior to lunch or dinner.

✪ Lettonie

9 Druid Hill, Stoke Bishop. ☎ **0117/9686456.** Reservations required. Fixed-price lunch £17.95 ($28.35); fixed-price dinner £34.50 ($54.50). AE, MC, V. Lunch Tues–Sat noon–2pm; dinner Tues–Sat 7–9:30pm. Closed 2 weeks in August, 2 weeks at Christmas. Bus 40. FRENCH.

One of Bristol's most celebrated restaurants lies 4 miles northeast of the city center, on the far side of the residential suburb of Clifton Down. Set within a 1930s-era building, it seats only 24 diners who sometimes reserve 10 days or more in advance. (Inspired by the national origins of his parents, the restaurant's owner and chef, Martin Blunos, named his restaurant after the Latvian word for Latvia, Lettonie.) Assisted by his wife, Sian, the chef prepares such dishes as scrambled duck eggs with Sevruga caviar and blini pancakes (this is accompanied by a glass of iced vodka); tortellini of pike with crayfish sauce; braised stuffed pig's trotters with Madeira sauce, goat's cheese ravioli with celery and lemon-butter sauce; and a dessert of apricots prepared five ways. Each table setting is individually decorated with flowers, antique silver, and the owners' personal memorabilia.

⑤ Michael's

129 Hotwell Rd., Bristol, Avon BS8 4RU. ☎ **0117/9276190.** Reservations required for Sat dinner. 2-course fixed-price menus £9.95 ($15.70) at lunch, £12.95–£17.95 ($20.45–$28.35) at dinner. MC, V. Lunch Sun only noon–3pm; dinner Mon–Sat 7–11pm. Take A370 west; then turn north and go over the suspension bridge. FRENCH/MODERN ENGLISH.

This charming and well-patronized restaurant is near Clifton on a highway leading toward the Avon Gorge. In its pleasant bar, decorated like an Edwardian parlor, an open fire burns. The dining room is also bright and inviting. The fixed-price menus are imaginative and change according to the availability of seasonal produce. The service is informal and enthusiastic. Always call for a table. There's no smoking in the dining room. If you want a cigarette, stick to the bar.

EASY EXCURSIONS
THORNBURY

Twelve miles north of Bristol, Thornbury is known for its castle (now a hotel; see below). Many of the crenellations and towers were built in 1511 as the last defensible castle ever constructed in England. Its owner was beheaded by Henry VIII for certain words spoken in haste. Henry confiscated the lands and, to celebrate, stayed here for 10 days with Anne Boleyn in 1535. Later, Mary Tudor spent 3 years of her adolescence here.

Where to Stay and Dine: Moderate

✪ Thornbury Castle

Thornbury, near Bristol, Avon BS12 1HH. ☎ **01454/281182.** Fax 01454/416188. 18 rms, 1 suite. TV TEL. £105–£200 ($165.90–$316) double; £200 ($316) suite. Rates include continental breakfast. AE, DC, MC, V. Free parking. From Bristol, approach Thornbury on B4061; continue downhill to the monumental water pump, bear left, and continue for 300 yards.

A genuine Tudor castle (built in 1511) and once owned by Henry VIII, it is surrounded by trees and thick stone walls. The rooms are superbly fitted with fine furniture and many amenities; eight have four-posters.

French and English dishes highlight the menus at the hotel's three dining rooms. A three-course lunch begins at £18.50 ($29.25) per person and is served from noon to 2pm daily. A three-course dinner, from £33 ($52.15) per person, is served from 7 to 9:30pm daily. Although the menu changes, some of the regular offerings include: grilled fillet of red mullet served with Balsamic vegetables and a warm lemon vinaigrette or pan-fried fillet of Angus beef with a garlic and shallot sauce with a panache of vegetables presented on savoy cabbage.

15 Cotswolds

The Cotswolds, a stretch of limestone hills sometimes covered by grass and many barren plateaus known as wolds, is a pastoral land dotted by ancient villages and deep wooded ravines. This bucolic scene in the middle of southwest England, about a two-hour drive west of London, is found mainly in Gloucestershire, with portions in Oxfordshire, Wiltshire, and Worcestershire. The wolds or plateaus led to this area's being given the name Cotswold, Old English for "God's high open land."

Cotswold lambs used to produce so much wool that they made their owners very rich—wealth they invested in some of the finest domestic architecture in Europe, made out of honey-brown Cotswold stone. The wool-rich gentry didn't neglect their church contributions either. Often the simplest of villages will have a church that in style and architectural detail seems far beyond the means of the hamlet.

If possible, try to explore the area by car. That way, you can spend hours viewing the land of winding goat paths, rolling hills, and sleepy hamlets, with names such as Stow-on-the-Wold, Wotton-under-Edge, Moreton-in-Marsh, Old Sodbury, Chipping Campden, Shipton-under-Wychwood, Upper and Lower Swell, and Upper and Lower Slaughter, often called "the Slaughters."

A DRIVING TOUR

Day 1 Motorists take M4 from London to Gloucestershire for a tour of the Cotswolds. At Exit 20, take M5 north to enter the area, beginning at the old spa of Cheltenham, 99 miles northwest of London. Once there, stroll its Promenade and visit such attractions as its Pittville Pump Room. Plan an overnight stay.

Day 2 Detour south from Cheltenham along A46 to Painswick, one of the most enchanting towns in the Cotswolds. There is no one major attraction—it's the model Cotswold village itself that is of interest, as you'll note as you stroll about. Consider a luncheon stopover. In the afternoon continue south to Stroud, then take A419 east to Cirencester, the "unofficial capital of the Cotswolds." Its attractions can be visited in an afternoon. Stay overnight there.

What's Special About the Cotswolds

Great Towns/Villages
- Broadway, called "the show village of England," with 16th-century stone houses and cottages.
- Painswick, considered by some the prettiest village in England, with a 15th-century parish church.
- Bibury, vying with Painswick for the title of England's prettiest village; noted for its 15th-century Arlington Row of cottages.
- Stow-on-the-Wold, an attractive Cotswold wool town with a large marketplace and some fine old houses.

Architectural Highlights
- The High Street of Broadway, representing some of the finest domestic architecture in Britain, with honey-colored stone buildings.
- The High Street of Chipping Campden—historian G. M. Trevelyan called it "the most beautiful village street now left in the island."

Museum
- Corinium Museum, Cirencester, containing one of the finest collections of Roman antiquities in Britain.

Spa Retreat
- Cheltenham, one of England's most fashionable spas, with Regency architecture of ironwork, balconies, and verandas; its Promenade is called "the most beautiful thoroughfare in England."

Especially for Kids
- Birdland, Bourton-on-the-Water, a garden set on 8$^1/_2$ acres with some 1,200 birds of 361 different species.

TAKE A BREAK   Tatyan's, 27 Castle Street in Cirencester (☎ 01285/653529), is one of the best places for a meal, featuring an array of Peking, Hunan, and Szechuan specialties. The menu is large (nearly a dozen prawn dishes, for example). A set lunch goes for £8.50 ($13.45), with a table d'hôte dinner ranging from £11.50 to £14 ($18.15 to $22.10). Lunch is daily from noon to 2pm and dinner daily from 6 to 10:30pm. Closed for Sunday lunch in summer, all day Sunday in winter.

Day 3   From Cirencester, take the A433 northeast to Burford, which is considered the gateway to the Cotswolds for many. Explore this old market town and visit some of its many antique shops. After a look-see take the A424 northwest until you come to a secondary road cutting west to Bourton-on-the-Water. There you can visit Birdland and see the Cotswold Countryside Collection lying off the A40 between Burford and Cheltenham at Northleach. In the later afternoon take the A429 north to Stow-on-the-Wold for an overnight stopover.

Day 4   In the morning take the walking tour (see "A Great Cotswold Ramble," below) west of Stow-on-the-Wold, beginning in Upper Slaughter. Have lunch in the area. After lunch drive north on A429 for a visit to Moreton-in-Marsh, one of the best-known towns in the Cotswolds. Spend the night there.

Day 5   Take secondary roads northwest to Chipping Campden and explore its High Street. You can do that and still be in Broadway to the west for lunch. Broadway is the premier tourist mecca of the Cotswolds, and you'll want not only to spend the night there but also to schedule as much time as you have left wandering this old town with its shops and inns. There's something of interest around every corner.

1 Tetbury

113 miles W of London, 27 miles NE of Bristol

In the rolling Cotswolds, Tetbury never used to be in the mainstream of tourism like Oxford or Stratford-upon-Avon; however, after a famous royal man and his lovely bride took up residence at the Macmillan place, a Georgian building on nearly 350 acres, Tetbury began drawing crowds from all over the world. Prince Charles could be seen riding horses, and perhaps tourists could spot Princess Di shopping in the village. The nine-bedroom Windsor mansion, Highgrove, lies just outside town on the way to Westonbirt Arboretum. It cannot be seen from the road. Princess Di is no longer in residence, although Prince Charles is. He's often seen around Tetbury today with his neighbor and friend, Camilla Parker-Bowles.

The town has a 17th-century market hall and a lot of antiques shops, as well as boutiques. Its inns, even before royalty moved in, were not cheap, and the prices certainly have not dropped since that time.

ESSENTIALS
GETTING THERE

By Train   There is no direct service from London. Frequent daily trains run from London's Paddington Station to Kemble, 7 miles east of Tetbury. There is adequate bus service between Kemble and Tetbury.

By Bus   National Express buses leave from London's Victoria Coach Station with direct service to Cirencester, 10 miles northeast of Tetbury. From Cirencester, several buses a day run to Tetbury.

By Car   From London, take M40 northwest to Oxford, continuing along A40 to the junction with A429. Drive south to Cirencester, where you connect with A433 southwest into Tetbury.

VISITOR INFORMATION

The **telephone area code** is 01666. The **Tourist Information Centre** is in The Old Court House, 63 Long St. (☎ **01666/503552**); it's open only March through October.

WHERE TO STAY
MODERATE

✪ Calcot Manor

Calcot, Near Tetbury, Gloucestershire GL8 8YJ. ☎ **01666/890391** or **800/987-7433** in the U.S. Fax 01666/890394. 20 rms. TV TEL. £87–£125 ($137.45–$197.50) double. Rates include early morning tea and continental breakfast. AE, DC, MC, V. Free parking. Take A4135 3¹/₂ miles west of Tetbury.

The Cotswolds

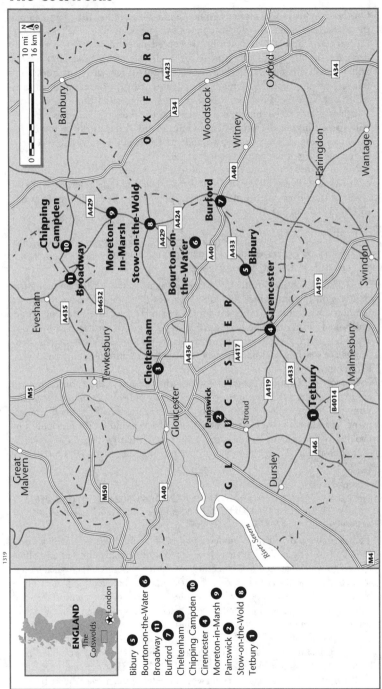

On the grounds of this former farmhouse is a 14th-century tithe barn, among the oldest in Britain. The thick stone walls of the main house shelter a flowering terrace where tea and drinks are served in good weather. Tastefully decorated public rooms mix touches of modernism with clusters of flowers and English antiques. The bedrooms are furnished with antiques, rich fabrics, private baths, and modern conveniences; four are equipped with whirlpool baths, and one has a four-poster bed. In 1994 the owners added four new rooms set within an old granary on the property; each has comfortable furnishings and child-listening equipment. Views from many of the rooms encompass a sweep of lawn and the Cotswold countryside. Facilities include an open-air swimming pool.

Meals are relaxing, with continental touches gathered from the proprietors' catering experience in Switzerland and France. The food is the finest served in the area, featuring fixed-price menus. Dinner, daily from 7:30 to 9:30pm, costs £22 to £26 ($34.75 to $41.10).

✪ The Close

8 Long St., Tetbury, Gloucestershire GL8 8AQ. ☎ **01666/502272.** Fax 01666/504401. 15 rms. TV TEL. £85 ($134.30) single; £95–£150 ($150.10–$237) double. Rates include English breakfast. AE, DC, MC, V. Free parking.

The Close, which dates from 1596, takes its name from a Cistercian monastery that was on this site. Once the home of a wealthy Cotswold wool merchant, the house was built of honey-brown Cotswold stone, with gables and stone-mullioned windows. The ecclesiastical-type windows in the rear overlook a garden with a reflecting pool, a haven for doves. Most of the bedrooms are spacious and handsomely furnished with antiques; all have private bathrooms.

Inside, you'll find a Georgian room with a domed ceiling (once an open courtyard), where before-dinner drinks are served and you can peruse the menu. Dining is in one of two rooms. Candlelight on winter evenings, floral arrangements, sparkling silver and glass are the perfect background for the fine food. The cooking is superb, and an à la carte menu offers specialty dishes. A fixed-price dinner costs £25.25 ($39.90) and up per person. A set lunch goes for £18.50 ($29.25).

The Snooty Fox

Market Place, Tetbury, Gloucestershire GL8 8DD. ☎ **01666/502436.** Fax 01666/503479. 12 rms. TV TEL. £60–£76 ($94.80–$120.10) single; £80–£130 ($126.40–$205.40) double. Rates include continental breakfast. AE, DC, MC, V.

This desirable hotel in the commercial heart of Tetbury was originally a 16th-century coaching inn. The Victorians added a high front porch under which flowers grow in what used to be watering troughs for horses. A stone-walled lounge with comfortable chairs and a Gothic fireplace opens off the reception area. Three bedrooms have antique beds with canopies, and the rest are comfortably and tastefully furnished in a more modern style. Each room is equipped with radio, hair dryer, trouser press, and hot-beverage facilities.

There's a popular bar inside, with an amusing caricature of a Snooty Fox in full riding regalia, and one of the most elegant restaurants in town. A table d'hôte lunch costs £13.50 to £14.50 ($21.35 to $22.90), and a table d'hôte dinner is £18 ($28.45). In warm weather, tables are set at the edge of the market square beneath the 19th-century iron overhang.

2 Cirencester & Painswick

CIRENCESTER

89 miles W of London, 16 miles S of Cheltenham, 17 miles SE of Gloucester, 36 miles W of Oxford

Don't worry about how to pronounce the name of the town. There's disagreement even among the English. Say "Siren-cess-ter" and you won't be too far off. Cirencester is often considered the unofficial capital of the Cotswolds, probably a throwback to its reputation in the Middle Ages, when it flourished as the center of the great Cotswold wool industry. In Roman Britain, five roads converged on Cirencester, which was called Corinium in those days. In size, it ranked second only to London. Today it is chiefly a market town and a good base for touring.

ESSENTIALS
GETTING THERE

By Train Because Cirencester has no railway station of its own, passengers usually get off at the nearby town of Kemble, 4 miles to the southwest. Trains depart several times a day from London's Paddington Station for Kemble (trip time: 80 min.). Passengers sometimes (but not always) must transfer trains at Swindon. From Kemble, a bus travels to Cirencester four to five times a day.

By Bus National Express buses leave from London's Victoria Coach Station with direct service to Cirencester.

By Car From London, take M40 northwest to Oxford, continuing along A40 to the junction with the A429. Drive south on the A429 to Cirencester.

VISITOR INFORMATION

The **telephone area code** is 01285. The **Tourist Information Centre** is at Corn Hall, Market Place (☎ **01285/654180**).

WHAT TO SEE & DO

Corinium Museum

Park St. ☎ **01285/655611.** Admission £1.50 ($2.35) adults, 75p ($1.20) children. Mon–Sat 10am–5pm, Sun 2–5pm. Closed Mon in winter.

The museum houses one of the finest collections of archaeological remains from the Roman occupation, found locally in and around Cirencester. Mosaic pavements found here on Dyer Street in 1849 and other mosaics are the most important exhibits. Provincial Roman sculpture, including such figures as Minerva and Mercury, pottery, and artifacts salvaged from long-decayed buildings, provide a link with the remote civilization that once flourished here. The museum has been completely modernized to include full-scale reconstructions and special exhibitions on local history and conservation.

Cirencester Parish Church

Market Place. ☎ **01285/653142.** Admission free; donations invited. Mon–Fri 9:30am–4:30pm, Sun 12:30–6pm.

Dating back to Norman times and Henry I is the Church of John the Baptist, overlooking the Market Place in the town center. (Actually, a church may have stood on this spot in Saxon times.) In size, the Cirencester church appears to be a cathedral—not a mere parish church. The present building represents a variety of styles, largely perpendicular, as in the early-15th-century tower. Among the treasures inside are a 15th-century pulpit and a silver-gilt cup given to Queen Anne Boleyn two years before her execution.

WHERE TO STAY & DINE
INEXPENSIVE

The Fleece Resort Hotel

Market Place, Cirencester, Gloucestershire GL7 2NZ. ☎ **01285/658507.** Fax 01285/651017. 28 rms, 2 suites. TV TEL. Sun–Thurs £77 ($121.65) double; £92 ($145.35) suite. English breakfast £4.50 ($7.10) extra. Fri–Sat (including English breakfast): £42.50 ($67.15) double; £70 ($110.60) suite. AE, DC, MC, V. Free parking.

Its half-timbered facade hints at its origins as an Elizabethan coaching inn. Later it was enlarged by the Georgians and has had many modernizations. On warm days its flowering courtyard offers one of the most pleasant dining spots in town. Inside, a handful of open fireplaces warm the beamed interior whenever it's chilly. The comfortably modern bedrooms feature old-fashioned hints of yesteryear, such as quilted bedcoverings, and there are modern radio and coffee-making facilities.

The staff prepares French-inspired dinners. Dinner is served in a formal dining room, where fixed-price menus cost £12.95 ($20.45) for three courses. A la carte lunches are offered in the Shepherd's Bar, where platters range from £4.95 to £6.95 ($7.80 to $11).

Stratton House Hotel

Gloucester Rd., Cirencester, Gloucestershire GL7 2LE. ☎ **01285/651761.** Fax 01285/640024. 41 rms (all with bath or shower). TV TEL. £72–£85 ($113.75–$134.30) double. Rates include English breakfast. AE, DC, MC, V. Free parking. Take A417 1¼ miles northwest of Cirencester.

Built in several stages throughout the 18th century, with a discreetly designed modern wing added in the 1990s, this is an inviting and comfortable country house whose design is part Jacobean and part Georgian. It is surrounded by beautiful grounds with a walled garden and herbaceous borders. The large and well-furnished bedrooms have hair dryers and trouser presses. Two-thirds of the rooms are in the modern wing—designer-decorated, with coordinated colors and an aura evoking a traditional private English country house. In the dining and drawing rooms, some fine antique furniture and oil paintings may be seen. At dinner there is a choice of British dishes costing £15.75 to £18 ($24.90 to $28.45) for a fixed-price menu. There is a timbered-beam bar, and in winter log fires blaze in this bar and in the main hall.

IN NEARBY PURTON: MODERATE

The Pear Tree at Purton

Church End, Purton, near Swindon, Wiltshire SN5 9ED. ☎ **01793/772100.** Fax 01793/772369. 18 rms, 2 suites. TV TEL. £80–£100 ($126.40–$158) single or double; from £120 ($189.60) suite. Rates include English breakfast. AE, DC, MC, V. Free parking. Closed Dec 26–30.

This English country hotel/restaurant, three miles from Junction 16 of M4 and five miles from Swindon, offers well-furnished, individually decorated rooms (equipped with hair dryers, trouser presses, and free sherry and mineral water) that open onto views of the garden and countryside. Each accommodation—three with four-poster beds—is named after a famous Purtonian, such as Anne Hyde, mother of Queen Mary and Queen Anne. The Cotswold stone house was formerly the vicarage for the twin-towered parish Church of St. Mary; set in 7^1/$_2$ acres, it looks out over a traditional Victorian garden and toward the source of the Thames.

The owners, Francis and Anne Young, run the best restaurant in the area. The cuisine is inspired by France, although the recipes and cooking are distinctly English. The best seasonal produce is featured, including local beef, lamb, and pork. Seafood is brought fresh from Devon, and many of the herbs used to flavor the dishes come from the establishment's own garden. Dining is in an attractive conservatory, and service is daily from noon to 2:30pm and 7 to 9:30pm (until 10pm on Friday and Saturday). A fixed-price lunch goes for £17.50 ($27.65), and a fixed-price dinner costs £27.50 ($43.45). Reservations are necessary.

PAINSWICK

4 miles N of Stroud, 107 miles W of London, 10 miles SW of Cheltenham

The sleepy little town of Painswick is considered a model village. All its houses, although erected at different periods, blend harmoniously because the builders used only Cotswold stone as their building material. The one distinctive feature on the Painswick skyline is the spire of its 15th-century parish church. It's also known for its annual Clipping Feast (when the congregation joins hands and circles around the church as if it were a maypole, singing hymns as they do). Ancient tombstones dot the churchyard.

ESSENTIALS
GETTING THERE

By Train   The nearest railway station is at Stroud, 3 miles away. Trains depart from London's Paddington Station several times a day, sometimes (but not always) requiring a change of train at Swindon (trip time: 90–120 min., depending on the train). From Stroud, buses run to Painswick, some as frequently as once every hour. There are also many taxis waiting at the Stroud railway station.

By Bus   Buses depart from Bath in the direction of Cheltenham on Wednesday and Saturday, stopping in Painswick (and many other small towns) along the way. The train is really much more convenient.

By Car   From Cirencester (see above), continue west along A419 to Stroud; then head north on A46 to Cheltenham.

VISITOR INFORMATION

The **telephone area code** is 01452. The summer-only **Tourist Information Centre** is at the Painswick Library, Stroud Road (☎ 01452/813552).

WHERE TO STAY
MODERATE

✪ Painswick Hotel

Kemps Lane, Painswick, Gloucestershire GL6 6YB. ☎ **01452/812160.** Fax 01452/814059. 20 rms. TV TEL. £88–£130 ($139.05–$205.40) double. Rates include English breakfast. AE, MC, V. Free parking.

Completely refurbished, this beautiful Georgian house behind the Painswick parish church, with an 18th-century facade, was once a vicarage and is encircled by terraces of formal gardens. Many readers have reported it to be the highlight of their Cotswold tour. In rooms, cuisine, and service, it merits a major detour from wherever else you were going. The hotel has high standards of cuisine and service in its half-paneled dining room, where meals cost £19.50 ($30.80) for two courses, £23.50 ($37.15) for three courses, and £27.50 ($43.45) for four courses. The bedrooms are comfortably and attractively furnished.

⊖ Thorne

Friday St., Painswick, Gloucestershire GL6 6QJ. ☎ **01452/812476.** Fax 01452/812912. 2 rms. TV. £42–£44 ($66.35–$69.50) per person. Rates include half board, wine, and cocktails. No credit cards. Free parking. Free transfers from the rail station.

Before Columbus sailed on his quest for a new route to China, there was a market hall in Painswick, supported by stone pillars. In Shakespeare's time, Gloucestershire stonemasons turned the hall into one of the most beautiful houses in the town. Today, right in the middle of Painswick, that market hall is the home of Barbara Blatchley. This handsome, beautifully appointed, centrally heated house has only two twin guest rooms. A qualified "Blue Badge Guide," Barbara will arrange trips to Bath, Stratford-upon-Avon, Oxford, and Stonehenge.

Meals are served in the beam-ceilinged dining room, where two of the market pillars dating from 1400 are part of the wall. Top-quality farm produce and fresh vegetables are used in meal preparation. If you arrive at the railway station in Stroud, Barbara will arrange to have you picked up at no extra charge.

WHERE TO DINE
MODERATE

The Country Elephant

New St. ☎ **01452/813564.** Reservations required. Main courses £12.25–£16 ($19.35–$25.30). DC, MC, V. Wed–Sun (morning coffee) 10:30am–noon; noon–2pm; afternoon tea (Apr–Aug only) 2:30–5pm; 7–10pm. INTERNATIONAL.

Housed in a centrally located building crafted from Cotswold stone, this excellent restaurant serves some of the most imaginative (and finest) food in town. Owned by John Rees, it boasts walls dating from the 14th century (in the kitchens) and the 17th century (in the dining rooms). Many guests enjoy a predinner drink near the open fireplace of the heavily beamed bar. Robert Rees, the young head chef, trained at Le Gavroche in London and spent five subsequent years in Bath at the Royal Crescent Hotel, The Bath Spa Hotel, and The Circus Restaurant. His cuisine is excellent and served in comfortable and relaxed surroundings, including a summer garden. Begin perhaps with a chilled confit of spicy duck with a pine-nut dressing or else *feuillete* of chicken livers and spinach with Madeira and morel jus. For a main course, try the roast suprême of corn-fed chicken with a wild rice pilaf or else sautéed pigeon breasts with button onions, spicy lentils, bacon, and lardons. Desserts might include crème caramel or a selection of British cheese.

3 Cheltenham

99 miles NW of London, 9 miles NE of Gloucester, 43 miles W of Oxford

In a sheltered area between the Cotswolds and the Severn Vale, a mineral spring was discovered by chance. Legend has it that the Cheltenham villagers noticed pigeons drinking from a spring and observed how healthy they were—which is why the pigeon has been incorporated into the town's crest.

Always seeking a new spa, George III arrived in 1788 and launched the town. The duke of Wellington came to ease his liver disorder. Even Lord Byron came this way, proposing marriage to Miss Millbanke.

Cheltenham is one of England's most fashionable spas. It is also the winner of a contest, "Beautiful Britain in Bloom," and many visitors come here just to see its gardens from spring to autumn.

The architecture is mainly Regency, with lots of ironwork, balconies, and verandas. Attractive parks and open spaces of greenery make the town especially inviting. The main street, the Promenade, has been called "the most beautiful thoroughfare in Britain." Rather similar are such thoroughfares as Lansdowne Place and Montpellier Parade. The design for the dome of the Rotunda was based on the Pantheon in Rome. Montpellier Walk, with its shops separated by caryatids, is one of the most interesting shopping centers in England.

ESSENTIALS
GETTING THERE

By Train Twenty-one trains from London's Paddington Station arrive daily (trip time: 2 hr., 15 min. often involving a change of trains at Bristol or Swindon). Trains between Cheltenham and Bristol take only an hour, with continuing service to Bath.

By Bus National Express offers nine buses daily from London's Victoria Coach Station to Cheltenham (trip time: 2 hr., 35 min.).

By Car From London, head northwest on M40 to Oxford, continuing along A40 to Cheltenham.

VISITOR INFORMATION

The **telephone area code** is 01242. The **Tourist Information Centre** is at 77 Promenade (☎ **01242/522878**).

SPECIAL EVENTS

The **International Festival of Music** and the **Festival of Literature** take place each year in July and October, respectively, and attract internationally acclaimed performers and orchestras.

WHAT TO SEE & DO

Escorted coach tours of the Cotswolds are scheduled every Tuesday, Thursday, and Sunday from June through December; for details, call the information center listed above.

Pittville Pump Room

East Approach Dr., Pittville Park. ☎ **01242/523852** for the Pump Room, **01242/512470** for the Gallery of Fashion. Pump Room, free; gallery, £1.50 ($2.35) adults, 50p (80¢) children, students, and senior citizens. Pump Room, May–Sept, daily 10am–4:30pm; Oct–Apr, Tues–Sat 11am–4pm. Gallery of Fashion, May 29–Sept 30, Tues–Sat 11am–4:20pm, Sun and bank holiday Mon 11am–4:20pm. From the center take Portland St. and Evesham Rd.

Cheltenham Waters are the only natural, consumable alkaline waters in Great Britain, and are still taken at one of the spa's finest Regency buildings. On Sundays from the end of May until the end of September, the Pittville Pump Room is open for a host of activities, including Sunday lunch, afternoon cream teas, live classical music, landau carriage rides around the city, and brass bands playing in Pittville Park—it's real traditional England. The Gallery of Fashion, also located in the pump room, depicts the social history of Cheltenham Spa. Memorabilia include photographs and prints of the U.S. Army when it was stationed at Pittville in the 1940s.

Cheltenham Art Gallery & Museum

Clarence St. ☎ **01242/237431.** Admission free. Mon–Sat 10am–5:20pm.

This gallery houses one of the foremost collections of the arts-and-crafts movement, notably the fine furniture of William Morris and his followers. One section is devoted to Edward Wilson, Cheltenham's native son who died with Captain Scott in the Antarctic in 1912. The gallery is located near Royal Crescent and the Coach Station.

Everyman Theatre

Regent St. ☎ **01242/572573.** Admission £6–£16.50 ($9.50–$26.05), depending on the event. Box office, Mon–Sat 10am–8pm. Closed June 25–July 28.

Cheltenham is the cultural center of the Cotswolds, a role that it maintains at least in part due to the presence of Everyman Theatre. Designed in the 1890s as an opera house by the leading theater architect of Victorian England, Frank Matcham, it retains its ornate cornices, sculpted ceilings, and plush velvets despite extensive renovations to its stage and lighting facilities. Small (658 seats) and charming, it produces at least two major musicals and about a half-dozen dramatic pieces every year. Examples of last season's works included *The House of Mirth* and *Madame Butterfly*, as well as a selection of British comedies performed by the local repertory company.

WHERE TO STAY
EXPENSIVE

✪ Greenway

Shurdington, near Cheltenham, Gloucestershire GL51 5UG. ☎ **01242/862352** or 800/543-4135 in the U.S. Fax 01242/862780. 19 rms. TV TEL. £130–£185 ($205.40–$292.30) double. Rates include English breakfast. AE, DC, MC, V. Free parking. Take A46 less than 4 miles southwest of Cheltenham.

An elegant and beautifully furnished Cotswold country house in a garden setting, this is an ivy-clad Cotswold showpiece. Restored with sensitivity and decorated and furnished to a high standard, Greenway rents rooms in both its main house and a converted coach house, all with private bath or shower. Original paintings and antiques abound throughout the hotel. On a chilly day, open fires beckon. Guests are assured of comfort here.

Dining/Entertainment: The dining room is elegantly appointed with an extension added in the Victorian conservatory style. The cooking is superb, using quality produce and good, fresh ingredients that are handled deftly. Lunch is served from 12:30 to 2pm Sunday through Friday, and dinner is from 7:30 to 9:30pm Monday through Saturday; on Sunday, at 7:30pm only. A two-course set lunch costs £15 ($23.70), with a three-course set lunch going for £17 ($26.85). A la carte dinners begin at £27.50 ($43.45). Service is formal, on target, and polite, all at the same time.

MODERATE

Hotel de la Bere and Country Club

Southam, Cheltenham, Gloucestershire GL52 3NH. ☎ **01242/237771** or 800/225-5843 in the U.S. and Canada. Fax 01242/236016. 57 rms. TV TEL. Sun–Thurs £80–£95 ($126.40–$150.10) double; Fri–Sat £70–£95 ($110.60–$150.10) double. Half-board (2-night minimum required) £60 ($94.80) per person. AE, DC, MC, V. Free parking. Take B4632 3 miles north-east of town.

The building on this property dates from 1500. Constructed of Cotswold stone, it stands near the Cheltenham racecourse. Owned by the De la Bere family for three centuries, it was converted into a hotel in 1972, and every effort has been made to ensure that the original charm of the building still remains. Five of the rooms boast double four-poster beds, and all have hot-beverage facilities and private baths; they are tastefully decorated and furnished to preserve their individual charm and character.

The restaurant, the Elizabethan Room, and the Royalist Room are all paneled in oak, and there is also a Great Hall, complete with minstrel's gallery. The menu is impressive, and there are some interesting first courses. The hotel restaurant doesn't serve lunch except on Sunday; dinner, however, is offered nightly, costing £18 ($28.45) for a fixed-price meal or else from £22 ($34.75) à la carte.

Hotel on the Park

Evesham Rd., Cheltenham, Gloucestershire GL52 2AH. ☎ **01242/518898.** Fax 01242/511526. 9 rms, 3 suites. TV TEL. £89 ($140.60) double; £109 ($172.20) suite. Rates include English breakfast. AE, DC, MC, V. Free parking.

Opened in 1991 in what was formerly the private villa of a local building contractor in the 1830s, this is the most-talked-about hotel in town. It is located among similar terraced buildings in the once-prominent village of Pittville Spa, a half mile north of the town center of Cheltenham. Owned and operated by Darryl and Lesley-Anne Gregory, who undertook most of the Regency-inspired interior design, it has received several awards since its opening. Each bedroom is named after one or another prominent 19th-century visitor who came here shortly after the villa was built. Comfortable and high-ceilinged, the bedrooms have stylish accessories and a tasteful assortment of antique and reproduction furniture. The hotel dining room, called The Restaurant, is in the classic Regency style, offering both à la carte and set menus. A fixed-price lunch goes for £14.95 ($23.60), with a set dinner going for £19.50 ($30.80).

Queen's Hotel

Promenade, Cheltenham, Gloucestershire GL50 1NN. ☎ **01242/514724** or 800/225-5843 in the U.S. and Canada. Fax 01242/224145. 74 rms. TV TEL. £90–£130 ($142.20–$205.40) double. Breakfast £9.50 ($15) extra. AE, DC, MC, V. Free parking.

At the head of the Regency Promenade, this hotel looks down on the Imperial Gardens. Architecturally it is imposing, built in 1838 in the style of Rome's temple of Capitoline Jupiter. The distinguished interior boasts a Regency decor and an unusually fine staircase. The attractively furnished bedrooms at the back are quieter, and all have a private bath. Everything is well furnished, although decidedly old-fashioned. Fixed-price lunches range from £14 to £16 ($22.10 to $25.30), and a fixed-price dinner costs £26 ($41.10).

WHERE TO DINE
MODERATE

Le Champignon Sauvage

24–26 Suffolk Rd. ☎ **01242/573449.** Reservations required. 3-course fixed-price lunch £17.50 ($27.65); 3-course fixed-price dinner (Mon–Fri) £18.50–£22.50 ($29.25–$35.55); 3- to 4-course fixed-price dinners (Mon–Sat) £29.50–£33 ($46.60–$52.15). AE, MC, V. Mon–Fri 12:30–1:30pm; Mon–Sat 7:30–9:15pm. FRENCH/ENGLISH.

This is one of the leading restaurants of this old spa. David Everitt-Matthias, a chef of considerable talent, wisely limits the selection of dishes every evening for better quality control. Some evenings he allows his imagination to roam a bit, so dining here is always a surprise, a pleasant one usually. You might begin, for example, with such dishes as rabbit ravioli in a sauce studded with parsnips and assorted nuts or even braised ox cheek resting on "melted" split peas. Main courses are likely to include salmon smoked in goose fat, smoked haddock with mousse and ratatouille, or boned leg of guinea fowl stuffed with wild mushrooms. A selection of freshly made desserts is also featured, ranging from pears poached in red wine and spices to an iced honey and apricot terrine.

✪ Epicurean

81 The Promenade. ☎ **01242/222466.** Reservations required. Lunch fixed-price menus £15–£20 ($23.70–$31.60); dinner fixed-price menus £37 ($58.45); £55 ($86.90) seven courses. AE, DC, MC, V. Tues–Sun 12:30–2pm; Mon–Sat 7–10:30pm. Closed 2 weeks in Jan, 1 week Aug. CONTINENTAL/BRITISH.

In a terrace building opening onto the most fashionable street of this spa, this is the town's premier resort. Patrick and Claire McDonald operate a second-floor restaurant that is formal and elegant, plus a basement Café Bar open Monday through Saturday from 11am to 11pm and a ground floor bistro where two can dine for £40 to £50 ($63.20 to $79), including wine and service.

But it is the Epicurean Restaurant that attracts the serious diner. The cooking is British with strong continental overtones. We've always called the cuisine "elegant but uncluttered." Fixed-price formats offer a choice of about five or six dishes with each course. You might begin with a risotto of wild mushrooms flavored with white truffles or roasted foie gras with shallots. Main dishes are likely to range from salmon with spinach or chicken and scallops with sauterne sauce. Previous dishes have included a ravioli of fish with celeriac pancakes, or even stuffed pigs' trotters. For dyed-in-the-wool Anglophiles there is sometimes a fillet of beef served with clapshot and haggis. Desserts might include a trifle made of winter fruits (that is, dried fruits) in aspic or perhaps a soufflé or a delectable bread-and-butter pudding.

4 Bibury

86 miles W of London, 30 miles W of Oxford, 26 miles E of Gloucester

On the road from Burford to Cirencester, Bibury is one of the loveliest spots in the Cotswolds. In fact, the utopian romancer of Victoria's day, poet William Morris, called it England's most beautiful village. On the banks of the tiny Coln River, Bibury is noted for Arlington Row, a group of 15th-century gabled cottages, its biggest and most-photographed attraction, which is protected by the National Trust.

ESSENTIALS
GETTING THERE

By Train   About five trains per day depart from London's Paddington Station for Kemble (trip time: 1 hr., 10 min.). Some of these will require a rapid change of train in Swindon (just across the tracks to another waiting train). From Kemble, 13 miles south of Bibury, there are no buses, but most hoteliers will arrange for a car to meet guests if you make arrangements in advance.

By Bus   From London's Victoria Coach Station, you can take one of the five daily buses that depart for Cirencester, 7 miles from Bibury. There are no buses into Bibury, but, once again, local hotels will send a car, and taxis are available.

By Car   Take M4 from London, getting off at Exit 15 toward Cirencester. Then, take A33 (on some maps this is still designated as B4425) to Bibury.

VISITOR INFORMATION

The **telephone area code** is 01285.

WHERE TO STAY & DINE
EXPENSIVE

The Swan

Bibury, Gloucestershire GL7 5NW. ☎ **01285/740695.** Fax 01285/740473. 17 rms, 1 suite. TV TEL. £140–£185 ($221.20–$292.30) double; £210 ($331.80) suite. Rates include English breakfast. AE, DC, MC, V. Free parking.

Well-managed, upscale, and discreet, this hotel and restaurant originated as a riverside cottage in the 1300s, was greatly expanded throughout the centuries, and received its latest enlargement and refurbishment in 1991. Alex and Liz Furtek, the establishment's owners, outfitted parts of the interior in a cozily overstuffed mode reminiscent of the years during World War II. There's an elegant bar trimmed in oak; many of the accessories of a rustically elegant English country life; wood-burning fireplaces; and murals showing groups of well-wishers during the hotel's most recent renovations. An automatic "pianola" (player piano) provides music from a position in the lobby. The bedrooms are each outfitted with antique furniture and an individualized decor of charm and taste.

On the premises is an informal brasserie, with outdoor seating within the hotel's courtyard. This is open daily from 10am to 10pm for coffee, drinks, snacks, and platters of food. There's also a more formal restaurant with crystal chandeliers and heavy damask curtains. Specializing in modern British food, it's open only for dinner every night from 7:30 to 9:30pm, and for lunch every Sunday from 12:30 to 2pm. The restaurant serves fixed-price five-course menus for £35 ($55.30) per person; there are many choices within each menu category. Food items change frequently, but might include a tartare of avocado with crabmeat; Bibury trout from the nearby river, prepared several different ways; panfried scallops with ginger; roasted monkfish with leek-tarragon sauce and crevettes; and such desserts as a terrine of yellow peaches in a sangría jelly served with caramelized orange sauce.

INEXPENSIVE

✪ Bibury Court Hotel

Bibury, Gloucestershire GL7 5NT. ☎ **01285/740337.** Fax 01285/740660. 20 rms (19 with bath), 1 suite. TV TEL. £70–£78 ($110.60–$123.25) double with bath; £97 ($153.25) suite. Rates include continental breakfast. AE, DC, MC, V. Free parking.

This Jacobean manor house was built by Sir Thomas Sackville in 1633 (parts of it date from Tudor times). You enter the 8 acres of grounds through a large gateway, and the lawn extends to the Coln River. The house was privately owned until it was turned into a hotel in 1968. The structure is built of Cotswold stone, with many gables, huge chimneys, leaded-glass stone-mullioned windows, and a formal graveled entryway. Inside, there are many country manor furnishings and antiques, as well as an open stone log-burning fireplace. Many of the rooms have four-poster beds, original oak paneling, and antiques. Meals are quite special, with dinners priced from £20 ($31.60). Lunchtime bar meals begin at £5.50 ($8.70). After tea and biscuits in the drawing room, walk across the lawn along the river where you'll find a little church.

5 Burford

76 miles NW of London, 20 miles W of Oxford

In Oxfordshire is Burford, an unspoiled medieval town built of Cotswold stone that serves as a gateway to the Cotswolds and is largely famous for its nearly Norman church (ca. 1116) and its High Street lined with coaching inns. Oliver Cromwell passed this way, as (in a happier day) did Charles II and his mistress, Nell Gwynne. Burford was one of the last of the great wool centers, the industry bleating out its last breath as late as Victoria's day. You may want to photograph the bridge across the Windrush River where Queen Elizabeth I once stood. Burford is definitely equipped for tourists, as the antiques shops along the High will testify.

Visitors come to Minster Lovell because of Minster Lovell Hall (☎ 01993/775315), which dates from the 1400s but which lies in ruins. The medieval dovecote with nesting boxes survives. An early Lovell is said to have hidden in the moated manor house and subsequently starved to death after a battle in the area. The legend of the mistletoe bough originated in the village by the Windrush River. Minster Lovell is mainly built of Cotswold stone, with thatch or stone-slate roofs. It's a pity that there is a forest of TV antennas, but the place is still attractive to photographers. Admission is £1.50 ($2.35) for adults, 50p (80¢) for children. It's open from Good Friday to September, from 10am to 6pm, Thursday through Sunday only. Minster Lovell lies $2^1/_2$ miles west of Witney. To reach Minster Lovell from Burford, take A40 to Oxford, cutting northwest along the secondary road signposted to Minster Lovell.

ESSENTIALS
GETTING THERE

By Train   The nearest station is at Oxford. Many trains depart from London to Oxford every day (trip time: 45 min.). From Oxford, passengers walk a very short distance to the entrance of the Taylor Institute, from which about three or four buses per day make the 30-minute run to Burford.

By Bus   A National Express coach runs from London's Victoria Coach Station to Burford several times a day, with many stops along the way (trip time: 2 hr.).

By Car   From Oxford, head west on A40 to Burford.

VISITOR INFORMATION

The **telephone area code** is 01993. The **Tourist Information Centre** is at the Old Brewery, Sheep Street (☎ **01993/823558**).

WHERE TO STAY & DINE
EXPENSIVE

✪ Bay Tree Hotel

12–14 Sheep St., Burford, Oxfordshire OX18 6LW. ☎ **01993/822791.** Fax 01993/823008. 20 rms, 3 suites. TV TEL. £105–£185 ($165.90–$292.30) double; £145–£185 ($229.10–$292.30) suite. Rates include English breakfast. AE, DC, MC, V. Free parking.

The house was built for Sir Lawrence Tanfield, the unpopular lord chief baron of the Exchequer to Elizabeth I, definitely not noted for his hospitality. But time has erased his unfortunate memory, and the splendor of this Cotswold manor house remains, even more so after a major overhaul. The house has oak-paneled rooms with stone fireplaces, where logs burn in chilly weather. There is a high-beamed hall with a minstrel's gallery. Room after room is furnished tastefully and individually decorated. The 20th-century comforts have been discreetly installed, and the beds are a far cry from the old rope-bottom contraptions of the days of Queen Elizabeth I. Try to get one of the rooms overlooking the terraced gardens at the rear of the house. The hotel has a country-style bar, The Woolsack, offering guests and visitors a choice of light meals at lunchtime and in the evening. The head chef is well known for his tempting menus, with dishes based on local and seasonal produce. The 65-seat oak-beamed restaurant, which overlooks the gardens, retains all of its original charm. Fixed-price lunches begin at £11.95 to £13.50 ($18.90 to $21.35); fixed-price dinners cost £22.50 ($35.55). The delightful conservatory is now the residents' lounge.

MODERATE

Golden Pheasant Hotel

91 High St., Burford, Oxfordshire OX18 4QA. ☎ **01993/823223.** Fax 01993/822621. 12 rms (all with bath or shower). TV TEL. £72–£92 ($113.75–$145.35) double; £5 ($7.90) per person supplement on Fri–Sat nights. Rates include continental or English breakfast. AE, DC, MC, V. Free parking.

On the main street, the Golden Pheasant has the oldest set of property deeds surviving in Burford. In the 1400s it was the home of a prosperous wool merchant, but it began serving food and drink in the 1730s when it was used both to brew and serve beer. Like many of its neighbors, the Golden Pheasaant is capped with a slate roof and fronted with light gray, hand-chiseled stones. Inside, within view of dozens of old beams and a blazing fireplace, a candlelit restaurant serves both French and English specialties, with à la carte dinners costing £15 to £20 ($23.70 to $31.60). The rooms are comfortable and cozy; one has a four-poster bed.

INEXPENSIVE

Lamb Inn

Sheep St., Burford, Oxfordshire OX18 4LR. ☎ **01993/823155.** Fax 01993/822228. 15 rms. TV TEL. £85–£95 ($134.30–$150.10) double. Rates include English breakfast. MC, V.

This thoroughly Cotswold house was solidly built in 1430 with thick stones, mullioned and leaded windows, many chimneys and gables, and a slate roof now mossy with age. It opens onto a stone-paved rear garden, with a rose-lined walk and a shaded lawn. The bedrooms are a mixture of today's comforts, such as good beds and plentiful hot water, and antiques. The public living rooms have heavy oak beams, stone floors, window seats, Oriental rugs, and fine antiques (Chippendale, Tudor, Adam, Georgian, Jacobean).

In the drinking lounge, a special beer, made in an adjoining brewery, is served. Light lunches and snacks are served in the bars and lounges or in the garden in summer. Dinner as well as a traditional Sunday lunch are offered in the beamed dining room with a garden view. Dinners begin at £20 ($31.60). If you're dining here in the right season, you can feast on treats of the rivers or forest, such as salmon, trout, and wild boar. A well-tended Sunday lunch costs £17.50 ($27.65).

6 Bourton-on-the-Water

85 miles NW of London, 36 miles NW of Oxford

In this scenic Cotswold village, you may feel like Gulliver voyaging to Lilliput. Bourton-on-the-Water lies on the banks of the tiny Windrush River. Its mellow stone houses, its village greens on the banks of the water, and its bridges have earned it the title of the Venice of the Cotswolds. But that label tends to obscure its true charm.

ESSENTIALS
GETTING THERE

By Train   Trains go from Paddington Station in London to nearby Moreton-in-Marsh (trip time: 2 hr.). From Moreton-in-Marsh, Pulhams Bus Company runs buses for the 15-minute (6-mile) journey on to Bourton-on-the-Water. Other cities with train service into London include Cheltenham or Kingham, and both of those, while somewhat more distant, also have bus connections into Bourton-on-the-Water.

By Bus   National Express coaches, from Victoria Coach Station in London, travel to both Cheltenham and Stow-on-the-Wold. From either of those towns, Pulhams Bus Company operates about four buses per day into Bourton-on-the-Water.

By Car   From Oxford, head west on A40, until you reach the junction with A429 (Fosse Way). Take it northeast to Bourton-on-the-Water.

VISITOR INFORMATION

The **telephone area code** is 01451.

WHAT TO SEE & DO

Old New Inn

High St. ☎ **01451/820467.** Admission £1.30 ($2.05) adults, 90p ($1.40) children. Daily 9:30am–6pm or dusk.

To see Lilliput, you need to visit this inn on the main street. In the garden is a near-perfect and most realistic model village.

Birdland

Rissington Rd. ☎ **01451/820480.** Admission £3 ($4.75) for adults, £1.50 ($2.35) for children 4–14, free for those under 3. Mar–Oct, daily 10am–6pm; Nov–Feb, daily 10am–4pm.

Established in 1958 on $8^{1}/_{2}$ acres of field and forests about a mile east of Bourton-on-the-Water, on the banks of Windrush River, this is a handsomely designed homage to the ornithological splendors of the world. It houses about 1,200 birds representing 361 species. Included is the largest and most varied collection of penguins in any zoo, with glass-walled tanks that allow observers to appreciate their agile underwater movements. There's also an enviable collection of hummingbirds. Many of the birds here are on exhibition for the first time. Birdland provides a picnic area and a children's playground in a wooded copse.

A NEARBY ATTRACTION

Cotswold Countryside Collection

Fosse Way, Northleach, Cheltenham (Cotswold District Council). ☎ **01451/860715.** Admission £1.50 ($2.35) adults, 75p ($1.20) children, £3.75 ($5.95) family ticket. Apr–Oct, Mon–Sat 10am–5pm, Sun 2–5pm.

Opened in 1981, this museum of rural life displays is located off A40 between Burford and Cheltenham. You can see the Lloyd-Baker collection of agricultural history, including wagons, horse-drawn implements, and tools, as well as a seasons-of-the-year display. A Cotswold gallery records the social history of the area. Below Stairs is an exhibition of laundry, dairy, and kitchen implements. The museum was once a house of correction, and its history is displayed in the reconstructed cell block and courtroom.

WHERE TO STAY & DINE
INEXPENSIVE

Chester House Hotel and Motel

Victoria St., Bourton-on-the-Water, Cheltenham, Gloucestershire GL54 2BU. ☎ **01451/ 820286.** Fax 01451/820471. 23 rms (all with bath or shower). TV TEL. £78.50 ($124.05) double. Rates include buffet breakfast. AE, DC, MC, V. Free parking. Closed Dec to mid-Feb.

This weathered, 300-year-old, Cotswold-stone house built on the banks of the Windrush River is conveniently located in the center of town. It blends an old building with a row of stables converted into a hotel with comfortable bedrooms. The hotel also has an intimate bar and a stone-walled restaurant with a full restaurant license for serving drinks. Diners are served a reliable English cuisine, including Cotswold lamb. Meals begin at £18.95 ($29.95).

The Old Manse Hotel

Victoria St., Bourton-on-the-Water, Cheltenham, Gloucestershire GL54 2BX. ☎ **01451/ 820082.** Fax 01451/810381. 12 rms (all with bath or shower). TV TEL. Sun–Thurs £61–£82 ($96.40–$129.55) double; £105 ($165.90) suite. Fri–Sat £75–£98 ($118.50–$154.85) double; £125 ($197.50) suite. Single occupancy of double room £15 ($23.70) surcharge. Rates include English breakfast. MC, V. Free parking.

An architectural gem reminiscent of the setting of Nathaniel Hawthorne's *Mosses from an Old Manse,* this hotel in the center of town is by the slow-moving river that wanders through the village green. Built of Cotswold stone in 1748, with chimneys, dormers, and small-paned windows, it has been modernized inside. The bedrooms have recently been refurbished to a high standard. Dining is a treat in the Secret Garden, serving dinner Monday through Saturday from 6 to 9pm and Sunday from 7 to 9pm. Typical dishes include such appetizers as homemade venison sausage or sautéed breast of pigeon, followed by Dover sole, stuffed Bibury trout, and roast English lamb. Sometimes roast pheasant is featured, and grilled steaks are always offered.

☉ Old New Inn

High St., Bourton-on-the-Water, Cheltenham, Gloucestershire GL54 2AF. ☎ **01451/ 820467.** Fax 01451/810236. 17 rms (6 with bath). TV. £52 ($82.15) double without bath; £64 ($101.10) double with bath. Rates include English breakfast. MC, V. Free parking.

Old New Inn can lay claim to being the landmark hostelry in the village. On the main street, overlooking the river, it's a good example of Queen Anne design (the miniature model village in its garden was referred to earlier). Hungry or tired travelers are drawn to the old-fashioned comforts and cuisine of this most English inn. The rooms are comfortable, with homelike furnishings and soft beds.

Nonresidents are also welcome here for meals, with lunches at £10 ($15.80) and dinner from £15 ($23.70). You may want to spend an evening in the pub lounge playing darts or chatting with the villagers.

EN ROUTE TO STOW-ON-THE-WOLD

Midway between Bourton-on-the-Water and Stow-on-the-Wold are the twin villages of Upper and Lower Slaughter. (Don't be put off by the names—these are two of the prettiest villages in the Cotswolds. Actually the name "Slaughter" is a corruption of "de Sclotre," the name of the original Norman landowner.) The houses are constructed of honey-colored Cotswold stone, and a stream meanders right through the street, providing a home for the ducks that wander freely about, begging scraps from kindly visitors. In Upper Slaughter you can visit a fine example of a 17th-century Cotswold manor house.

WHERE TO STAY & DINE
VERY EXPENSIVE

✪ Lower Slaughter Manor

Lower Slaughter, near Cheltenham, Gloucestershire GL54 2HP. ☎ **01451/820456.** Fax 01451/822150. 14 rms, 2 suites. TV TEL. £180–£275 ($284.40–$434.50) double; £290 ($458.20) suite for two. Children over 10 years of age accepted. Rates include half board. AE, MC, V. Free parking. Take A429 turnoff at the sign for The Slaughters, and drive ¹/₂ mile; manor is on right as you enter the village.

Built in 1658, Lower Slaughter Manor was owned by Sir George Whitmore, high sheriff of Gloucestershire. It remained in the same family until 1964 when it was sold as a private residence. Now converted into one of the showplace hotels of the Cotswolds, it is owned by Audrey and Peter Marks. Standing on its own private grounds, it has beautifully proportioned reception rooms and tastefully furnished bedrooms, some with four-poster beds.

Dining/Entertainment: The restaurant has received accolades for its old and traditional recipes prepared in a modern manner. A typical dinner menu might include such appetizers as a terrine of foie gras and chicken or a salad of panfried marinated quail, followed by roast breast of Lunesdale duckling, gray-leg partridge roasted with wild mushrooms, or even pigs' trotters "our way." Grilled Dover sole is regularly featured, as is fillet of Scottish beef. The wine list offers some 300 selections, including fine Burgundy wines, as well as Bordeaux and California wines.

Services: Room service.

Facilities: Indoor heated swimming pool, sauna, all-weather tennis court, croquet lawn.

MODERATE

✪ Lords of the Manor Hotel

Upper Slaughter, near Cheltenham, Gloucestershire GL54 2JD. ☎ **01451/820243** or 800/322-2408 in the U.S. Fax 01451/820696. 29 rms. TV TEL. £115–£140 ($181.70–$221.20) standard double; £190 ($300.20) four-poster rm. Rates include English breakfast. AE, DC, MC, V. Free parking. Take A429 18 miles north of Cheltenham.

A 17th-century house set on several acres of rolling fields, the Lords of the Manor has gardens with a stream featuring brown trout. Modernized in its amenities, the hotel has successfully maintained the quiet country-house atmosphere of 300 years ago. Half the bedrooms are in a sympathetically converted old barn and granary, and many have views of the Cotswold hills; all have private baths.

The walls in the lounge bar are hung with family portraits of the original lords of the manor. Another bar overlooks the garden, and chintz and antiques are everywhere. The country atmosphere is carried into the dining room as well, with its antiques and mullioned windows. The well-prepared dishes are all fresh and home cooked. Table d'hôte lunches cost £14.95 ($23.60) for two courses, £17.95 ($28.35) for three courses; table d'hôte dinners go for £33.50 ($52.95) for three courses. The cooking is modern English with some French influence.

The Great Cotswold Ramble

A walking tour between the villages of Upper and Lower Slaughter, with an optional extension to Bourton-on-the-Water, is considered one of the most memorable in England. It's 1 mile each way between the Slaughters, or 2½ miles from Upper Slaughter to Bourton-on-the-Water. This walk could take between two and four hours.

The names of the villages of Upper and Lower Slaughter are so unusual, and their architecture so charming, that you're likely to remember your ambulatory experience many years later. Also worthwhile is the fact that by striking out on foot, you can avoid at least some of the roadway traffic which taxes the nerves and goodwill of local residents during peak season. En route, you're likely to glimpse the waterfowl that inhabit the rivers, streams, and millponds that criss-cross this much-praised and very desirable region of Britain.

Fortunately for trekkers with only a few hours to spare, there's a well-worn footpath (Warden's Way) that meanders beside the edge of the swift-moving river. Originating in Upper Slaughter (where its start is marked at the town's central car park), the path beckons all kinds of nature enthusiasts to its well-trod borders. En route, you will see sheep grazing in meadows, antique houses crafted from honey-colored local stone, stately trees arching over ancient millponds, and footbridges that have endured centuries of foot traffic and rain.

Don't think for a moment that the rivers of this region (including the Eye, Colne, Diklar, and Windrush) are sluggish, slow-moving streams: Between Upper and Lower Slaughter, the water literally rushes down the incline, powering a historic mill that you'll find on the northwestern edge of Lower Slaughter. In quiet eddies, you'll see ample numbers of waterfowl and birds, including wild ducks, gray wagtails, mute swans, coots, and Canadian geese. You could follow this route in reverse, although since parking is more plentiful in Upper Slaughter than in Lower Slaughter, it's probably more convenient to begin in the former town.

After admiring the historic houses of Lower Slaughter, you might opt for a meal or drink within the 17th-century premises of the separately recommended Lower Slaughter Manor which is quite close to the edge of Warden's Way.

Most visitors prefer to end their outdoor ramble here, retracing their steps upstream to the carpark at Upper Slaughter where they left their cars. Others, however, want to continue their walk for another 1½ miles to Bourton-on-the-Water. (Warden's Way continues to Bourton-on-the-Water and is signposted along the way.)

To extend your trip, follow Warden's Way across the A429 highway, which is identified by locals as Fosse Way. (The road follows the route of an ancient Roman footpath.) Your path will leave the river's edge and strike out across cattle pastures in a southerly direction. Most of the distance from Lower Slaughter to Bourton-on-the-Water is tarmac-covered; it's closed to motor traffic, but ideal for trekkers or cyclists. Watch for bird life en route, and remember that you're legally required to close each of the several gates that stretch across the footpath.

Warden's Way will introduce you to Bourton-on-the-Water through the hamlet's northern edges. The first landmark you'll see will be the tower of St. Lawrence's Anglican Church. From the base of the church, walk south along The Avenue (one of the hamlet's main streets) and end your Cotswold ramble on the Village Green, directly in front of the War Memorial.

7 Stow-on-the-Wold

9 miles SE of Broadway, 10 miles S of Chipping Campden, 4 miles S of Moreton-in-Marsh, 21 miles S of Stratford-upon-Avon

Stow-on-the-Wold is an unspoiled Cotswold market town, in spite of the busloads of tourists who stop off en route to Broadway and Chipping Campden. The town is the loftiest in the Cotswolds, built on a wold (rolling hill) about 800 feet above sea level. In its open market square you can still see the stocks where offenders in the past were jeered at and punished by the townspeople, who threw rotten eggs at them. The final battle between the Roundheads and the Royalists took place in Stow-on-the-Wold. The town, which is really like a village, is used by many as a base for exploring the Cotswold wool towns, as well as Stratford-upon-Avon.

ESSENTIALS
GETTING THERE

By Train   From London, take a train to Moreton-in-Marsh (see below) from London's Paddington Station, a service that runs several times a day. From Moreton-in-Marsh, continue by a Pulhams bus for the ten-minute ride to Stow-on-the-Wold.

By Bus   National Express coaches also run daily from London's Victoria Coach Station to Moreton-in-Marsh, where a Pulhams Bus Company coach goes the rest of the way to Stow-on-the-Wold. Several Pulhams coaches also run daily to Stow-on-the-Wold from Cheltenham.

By Car   From Oxford, take A40 west to the junction with A424, near Burford. Head northwest along A424 to Stow-on-the-Wold.

VISITOR INFORMATION

The **telephone area code** is 01451. The **Tourist Information Centre** is at Hollis House, The Square (☎ **01451/831082**).

WHERE TO STAY & DINE
EXPENSIVE

The Grapevine Hotel

Sheep St., Stow-on-the-Wold, Cheltenham, Gloucestershire GL54 1AU. ☎ **01451/830344** or 800/528-1234 in the U.S. and Canada. Fax 01451/832278. 23 rms (all with bath or shower). TV TEL. £54–£74 ($85.30–$116.90) per person. Rates include breakfast. "Bargain Breaks" (2-night minimum): £47–£77 ($74.25–$121.65) per person, including half board. AE, DC, MC, V. Free parking. Closed Dec 24–Jan 10.

The Grapevine, facing the village green, mixes urban sophistication with reasonable prices, rural charm, and intimacy. Known for both its hotel and its restaurant, this is one of the most innovative and charming places to stay in this much-visited village. It was named after the ancient vine whose tendrils shade and shelter the beautiful conservatory restaurant. Each bedroom has tasteful furnishings, radio, hair dryer, and a tea and coffee maker. Six rooms have a minibar.

The reading room, comfortable lounge, and cozy bar with Victorian accessories create a warm ambience for tea, bar snacks, or dinner. Full meals feature English, French, and Italian cuisine and are served from 7 to 9:30pm daily. Bar snacks are served at midday. The hotel has won an AA Rosette for its cuisine. Dinners are more elaborate, beginning at £18.45 ($29.15) for a fixed-price menu, and including perhaps turkey scallops with white-wine sauce, beef fillet topped with Stilton, or, for the vegetarian, garlic mushroom mille-feuilles.

MODERATE

Fosse Manor Hotel

Fosse Way, Stow-on-the-Wold, Cheltenham, Gloucestershire GL54 1JX. ☎ **01451/830354.** Fax 01451/832486. 20 rms (all with bath or shower), 2 suites. TV TEL. £98 ($154.85) double; £140 ($221.20) suite. Rates include English breakfast. "Bargain Breaks" (2-night minimum required): £55–£63 ($86.90–$99.55) per person, including half board. AE, DC, MC, V. Free parking. Take A429 1¼ miles south of Stow-on-the-Wold.

The hotel lies near the site of an ancient Roman road that used to bisect England, its stone walls and neo-Gothic gables almost concealed by strands of ivy. From some of the high stone-sided windows you can enjoy a view of a landscaped garden with a sunken lily pond, flagstone walks, and an old-fashioned sundial. Inside, the interior is conservatively modernized with such touches as a padded and upholstered bar and a dining room where dinners cost £17.50 ($27.65). The bedrooms are homelike, with matching fabrics and wallpaper, and two of the rooms are favorites of honeymooners.

✪ Wyck Hill House

Burford Rd., Stow-on-the-Wold, Cheltenham, Gloucestershire GL54 1HY. ☎ **01451/ 831936.** Fax 01451/832243. 30 rms, 3 suites. TV TEL. £108–£150 ($170.65–$237) double; £180 ($284.40) suite. Rates include English breakfast. AE, DC, MC, V. Free parking. Drive 2½ miles south of Stow-on-the-Wold on A424.

Wyck Hill House dates from 1720 when its stone walls were begun as a manor house. One wing of the manor house, it was discovered in the course of recent restoration, rested on the foundations of a Roman villa. Today, Wyck Hill House is one of the most sophisticated country hotels in the region, located on 100 acres of grounds and gardens. The opulent interior adheres to 18th-century authenticity with room after room leading to paneled libraries and Adam sitting rooms. The well-furnished bedrooms are in the main hotel, in the coach-house annex, or in the orangery.

Excellent food is also served, with a two-course lunch costing £11.50 ($18.15) and a three-course lunch going for £13 ($20.55). Dinners are à la carte, averaging £30 ($47.40) per meal.

INEXPENSIVE

✪ Stow Lodge Hotel

The Square, Stow-on-the-Wold, Cheltenham Gloucestershire GL54 1AB. ☎ **01451/830485.** 20 rms. TV. £73-£81 ($115.35-$128) double. Rates include English breakfast. AE, DC. Free parking.

Stow Lodge dominates the marketplace, but is set back far enough to maintain its aloofness. Its gardens, honeysuckle growing over the stone walls, diamond-shaped windows, gables, and many chimneys capture the best of country living, while letting you anchor right into the heart of town. The ample, well-furnished no-smoking bedrooms have radios, central heating, and hot-beverage facilities. Arrange to have your afternoon tea out back by the flower garden. The owners discovered an old (ca. 1770) open stone fireplace in their lounge and offer log fires as an added attraction. A la carte dinners, costing from £15 ($23.70), are served daily from 7 to 8:45pm and are likely to feature poached salmon steak, grilled local trout, various steaks, and roast duckling with a choice of sauces.

IN NEARBY LOWER SWELL
Expensive

The Old Farmhouse Hotel

Lower Swell, Stow-on-the-Wold, Cheltenham, Gloucestershire GL54 1LF. ☎ **01451/ 830232.** Fax 01451/870962. 13 rms (11 with bath), 1 suite. TV TEL. £41–£50 ($64.80–$79) per person double without bath; £65–£75 ($102.70–$118.50) per person double with bath; £88–£95 ($139.05–$150.10) per person suite. Rates include half board. MC, V. Free parking. Closed Jan 1–14. Take B4068 1¼ miles west of Stow-on-the-Wold.

This small, intimate hotel in the heart of the Cotswolds was converted from a 16th-century farmhouse. The hotel has been completely refurbished and the original fireplaces restored, once again blazing with log fires.

The relaxed atmosphere, together with excellent food and wine, has made this a popular stop for visitors, so reserving a room before your arrival is strongly recommended. Two accommodations under the eaves share a bath, and all units are different because of the building's farmhouse origin. Each accommodation is a double. Dinner is served daily from 7pm, with last orders taken at 9pm. The table d'hôte menu is changed daily, costing £17.50 ($27.65) for four courses and coffee. The hotel has a secluded walled garden and ample private parking.

8 Moreton-in-Marsh

83 miles NW of London, 4 miles N of Stow-on-the-Wold, 7 miles S of Chipping Campden, 17 miles S of Stratford-upon-Avon

Moreton-in-Marsh is an important center for rail passengers headed for the Cotswolds because it's near many villages of interest. Incidentally, don't take the name "Moreton-in-Marsh" too literally. "Marsh" derives from an old word meaning "border." Look for the 17th-century market hall and the old curfew tower, and then walk down the High (the main street), where Roman legions trudged centuries ago. The town once lay on the ancient Fosse Way.

ESSENTIALS
GETTING THERE

By Train   From London's Paddington Station, British Rail provides daily service to Moreton-in-Marsh (trip time: 1 hr., 50 min.).

By Bus   National Express coaches run from London's Victoria Coach Station to Moreton-in-Marsh daily.

By Car   From Stow-on-the-Wold (see above), take A429 north.

VISITOR INFORMATION

The **telephone area code** is 01608. The nearest tourist office is at Stow-on-the-Wold (see above).

WHERE TO STAY
MODERATE

Manor House Hotel

High St., Moreton-in-Marsh, Gloucestershire GL56 0LJ. ☎ **01608/650501** or 800/876-9480 in the U.S. Fax 01608/651481. 39 rms (all with bath or shower), 1 suite. TV TEL. £85–£90

($134.30–$142.20) double; £120 ($189.60) suite. Rates include English breakfast. AE, DC, MC, V. Free parking.

The Manor House comes complete with its own ghost, a priest's hiding hole, a secret passage, and a moot room used centuries ago by local merchants to settle arguments over wool exchanges. On the main street, it's a formal yet gracious house, and its rear portions reveal varying architectural periods of design. Here, the vine-covered walls protect the garden. Inside are many living rooms, one especially intimate with leather chairs and a fireplace-within-a-fireplace, ideal for drinks and the exchange of "bump-in-the-night" stories. The hotel has a heated indoor pool, a spa bath, and a sauna. The bedrooms are tastefully furnished, often with antiques or fine reproductions. Many have fine old desks set in front of window ledges, with a view of the garden and ornamental pond.

A favorite nook is the bar, with its garden view through leaded Gothic windows. Evening meals in the two-level dining room are candlelit. A table d'hôte lunch goes for £9.50 ($15), and dinner is £19.50 ($30.80).

INEXPENSIVE

Redesdale Arms

High St., Moreton-in-Marsh, Gloucestershire GL56 0AW. ☎ **01608/650308.** Fax 01608/651843. 15 rms, 2 suites. TV TEL. £39.50 ($62.40) single or double; £60 ($94.80) suite. English breakfast £4.95 ($7.80) extra. AE, MC, V. Free parking.

This is one of the largest and best-preserved coaching inns in Gloucestershire. Originally established around 1774 as the Unicorn Hotel, it functioned around 1840 as an important link in the Bath-to-Lincoln stagecoach routes, offering food and accommodations to both humans and horses during the arduous journey. In 1891, it was renamed in honor of Baron Redesdale, donor of Moreton's unusual town hall, which still stands a few steps away.

Since then, the inn has been considerably upgraded, with modernized and comfortably furnished bedrooms, but much of the old-fashioned charm remains intact. Guests gravitate to the bar, where drinks are served in front of a six-foot-high stone fireplace. During nice weather, tables are set up in a sheltered courtyard.

The inn is especially well known for its meals and its English and French cuisine. A two-course lunch or dinner ranges from £10 to £15 ($15.80 to $23.70), with bar snacks priced from £2.25 to £6.50 ($3.55 to $10.25).

☺ The White Hart Royal Hotel

High St., Moreton-in-Marsh, Gloucestershire GL56 0BA. ☎ **01608/650731.** Fax 01608/650880. 19 rms. TV TEL. £80 ($126.40) double. Rates include English breakfast. AE, DC, MC, V. Free parking.

A mellow old Cotswold inn once graced by Charles I (in 1644), the White Hart provides modern amenities without compromising the personality of yesteryear. The well-furnished bedrooms all have hot and cold running water, innerspring mattresses, and a few antiques intermixed with basic 20th-century pieces. The bar is built of irregular Cotswold stone. You can enjoy drinks in front of the ten-foot open fireplace. Lunches are informal affairs served in the hotel's pub, where platters priced from £3.50 to £9.50 ($5.55 to $15) are featured. Dinners are more elaborate sitdown events, with four-course table d'hôte menus priced at £15 ($23.70) each. The hotel passed from ownership by one of Britain's largest chains, the Forte Group, into private hands in 1992.

WHERE TO DINE

After long years of slumber, the restaurant picture in Moreton-in-Marsh has awakened—in fact, the town is now known as "the dining center of the Cotswolds." That reputation is based entirely on the two restaurants previewed below.

MODERATE

Annie's

3 Oxford St. ☎ **01608/651981.** Reservations recommended. Main courses £15–£18 ($23.70–$28.45); Sun lunch £17.50 ($27.65). AE, DC, MC, V. Sun noon–2pm; Mon–Sat 7–10pm. Closed 3 weeks in late Jan. ENGLISH/FRENCH COUNTRY COOKING.

Situated in the heart of town, on a side street that merges with Fosse Way (the old Roman road), lies a stone-sided three-story house whose walls range from 300 to 400 years of age. Here David and Anne Ellis prepare ample portions of English and French country cuisine which have won an enthusiastic response from weekending Londoners escaping from their careers in television and the West End theater district.

Specialties include a warm salad of panfried pigeon breast on a bed of greens with panfried mushrooms, bacon, and warm balsamic vinaigrette; a feuilleté of smoked haddock lined with spinach in a Stilton-flavored cream sauce; saddle of venison with a port wine and juniperberry sauce served with a phyllo parcel and puréed vegetables; fillet of lamb with a sauce of young leeks and pink peppercorns; and a gourmet version of steak-and-kidney pie. Desserts include a brown-sugar meringue filled with rose-petal cream and tropical fruits and such perennial English favorites as treacle tart and spotted dick.

✪ Marsh Goose

High St. ☎ **01608/652111.** Reservations recommended. Lunch main courses £10–£13 ($15.80–$20.55); 3-course fixed-price lunch £13.50 ($21.35); 4-course fixed-price dinner £23 ($36.35). AE, MC, V. Tues–Sun 12:30–2:30pm; Tues–Sat 7:30–9:45pm. MODERN BRITISH.

Despite its unique allure and country-house elegance, this is very much an outpost of young and sophisticated Londoners seeking temporary respite in a tranquil area. The premises were formerly the stables for a coaching inn; then they served as a shoe shop until their recent transformation. Today, you'll dine amid exposed Cotswold stone, a medley of neutral colors, and many of the accessories of the English country life.

The unusual cuisine is modern British, with goodly doses of Caribbean style thrown in. Examples include a curried parsnip soup; calves' liver with mangoes and Dubonnet sauce; breast of roasted guinea fowl with a creamy mustard sauce and prunes wrapped in bacon; and a suprême of salmon with mussels and a saffron-flavored cream sauce. The most talked-about dessert is a black-coffee jelly in a brownie-snap basket with butterscotch sauce and clotted cream. There's an exceptionally cozy bar area with ceiling beams and an open fireplace for before-dinner drinks.

9 Broadway

15 miles SW of Stratford-upon-Avon, 93 miles NW of London, 15 miles NE of Cheltenham

Many of the prime attractions of the Cotswolds, as well as Shakespeare country, lie within easy reach of Broadway, which is near Evesham at the southern tip of Hereford and Worcester. The best-known Cotswold village, Broadway has a wide and beautiful High Street flanked with honey-colored stone buildings, remarkable for their harmony of style and design. Overlooking the Vale of Evesham, it's a major stopover for bus tours and is mobbed in summer; however, it manages to retain its charm in spite of the invasion.

ESSENTIALS
GETTING THERE

By Train Connections are possible from London's Paddington Station via Oxford. The nearest railway stations are at Moreton-in-Marsh (seven miles away) or at Evesham (five miles away). Frequent buses arrive from Evesham, but one has to take a taxi from Moreton.

By Bus From London's Victoria Coach Station, one coach daily runs to Broadway, taking $2^1/_2$ hours.

By Car From Oxford, head west on A40, then A434 to Woodstock, Chipping Norton, and Moreton-in-Marsh.

VISITOR INFORMATION

The **telephone area code** is 01386. The **Tourist Information Centre** is at 1 Cotswold Court (☎ **01386/852937**), open March through December only.

WHERE TO STAY
VERY EXPENSIVE

✪ Buckland Manor

Buckland, near Broadway, Gloucestershire WR12 7LY. ☎ **01386/852626.** Fax 01386/853557. 13 rms. TV TEL. £160–£325 ($252.80–$513.50) double. Children under 12 not accepted. Rates include early morning tea and English breakfast. AE, MC, V. Free parking. Take B4632 about 2 miles south of Broadway, into Gloucestershire.

This imposing slate-roofed manor house is ringed with fences of Cotswold stone, green lawns, lambs, and daffodils. Its jutting chimneys rise a few steps from the Buckland church, with its darkened stone tower. The core of the manor house was erected in the 13th century, with wings added in succeeding centuries, especially the 19th century. The Oak Room, with a four-poster bed and burnished paneling, occupies what used to be a private library. In each of the rooms, leaded windows overlook gardens and grazing land with Highland cattle and Jacob sheep. Even the oversize bathrooms each contain at least one antique, as well as carpeting and modern plumbing. French-inspired meals, served in the elegant dining room with a baronial fireplace, cost £30 ($47.40) and up. Meals are served to nonresidents as well as residents. Service is daily from noon to 2pm and 7:30 to 9pm.

EXPENSIVE

✪ Lygon Arms

High St., Broadway, Hereford and Worcester WR12 7DU. ☎ **01386/852255.** Fax 01386/858611. 60 rms, 5 suites. TV TEL. £140–£150 ($221.20–$237) double; from £215 ($339.70) suite. VAT extra. Rates include continental breakfast. AE, DC, MC, V. Free parking.

This many-gabled structure, its mullioned windows looking right out on the road in the center of town, basks in its reputation as one of the greatest old English inns. In the rear it opens onto a private garden, with 3 acres of lawns, trees, and borders of flowers, stone walls with roses, and nooks for tea or sherry. The oldest portions date from 1532 or earlier, but builders many times since have made their additions. King Charles I reputedly drank with his friends in one of the oak-lined chambers, and later, his enemy Oliver Cromwell slept here the night before the Battle of Worcester. Today an earlier century is evoked by the almost over-whelmingly charming cluster of antique-laden public rooms. These include cavernous fireplaces, smoke-stained paneling, 18th-century pieces, and polished brass. Many but not all the rooms are in the antique style; a new wing offers a more 20th-century environment. Each room is furnished with a radio, hair dryer, and trouser press.

Dining/Entertainment: You dine in the oak-paneled Great Hall, with a Tudor fireplace, a vaulted ceiling, and a minstrels' gallery. Meals range from £32 ($50.55).

Services: 24-hour room service, laundry service.

Facilities: A country club adjoins the old inn. The club building was created from an 18th-century abattoir; formerly owned by pie makers, it was also the site of the only butchery in England run by a clergyman. Many health and leisure facilities are available here, including a large swimming pool and a sauna.

MODERATE

Collin House Hotel and Restaurant

Collin Lane, Broadway, Hereford and Worcester WR12 7PB. ☎ **01386/858354.** 7 rms. £88–£99 ($139.05–$156.40) double. Rates include English breakfast. MC, V. Free parking. From Broadway, follow the signs to Evesham before turning right onto Collin Lane; the hotel is a mile west of Broadway off A44.

This 16th-century Cotswold stone farmhouse has been transformed into a hotel sitting on a country lane amid eight acres of gardens and orchards. The cozy bed-rooms are named for flowers that grow here in profusion. Large structural timbers, tasteful wallpaper, private baths, and mullioned windows make them attractive; Wild Rose, with its sloped ceiling, is probably the most romantic.

Traditional English food, flavorfully and freshly prepared, is served in the evening by candlelight in a room with stone-rimmed windows and ceiling beams. Lunch is served daily from noon to 2:30pm, either in the bar (inexpensively) or in the more formal dining room where a four-course fixed-price menu goes for £15 ($23.70). Dinner is served nightly from 7 to 9pm, costing from £16 to £24 ($25.30 to $37.90).

Dormy House

Willersey Hill, Broadway, Hereford and Worcester WR12 7LF. ☎ **01386/852711.** Fax 01386/858636. 46 rms, 3 suites. TV TEL. £120–£145 ($189.60–$229.10) double; £155 ($244.90) suite. Rates include English breakfast. AE, DC, MC, V. Free parking. Closed Dec 24–28. Take A44 2 miles southeast of Broadway.

This manor house high on a hill above the village boasts views in all directions. Its panoramic position has made it a favorite place for those who desire a meal, afternoon tea, or lodgings. Halfway between Broadway and Chipping Campden, it was created from a sheep farm. The owners transformed it, furnishing the 17th-century farmhouse with a few antiques, good soft beds, and full central heating; they also extended these amenities to an old adjoining timbered barn, which they converted into studio rooms, with open-beamed ceilings. Bowls of fresh flowers adorn tables and alcoves throughout the hotel.

The establishment serves an excellent cuisine. A table d'hôte luncheon costs £15 ($23.70) for two courses or £17 ($26.85) for three courses. A fixed-price dinner goes for £26.50 ($41.85). The cellar houses a superb selection of wines. Bar meals range from £6.50 ($10.25).

INEXPENSIVE

Broadway Hotel

The Green, Broadway, Hereford and Worcester WR12 7AA. ☎ **01386/852401.** Fax 01386/
853879. 19 rms (all with bath or shower). TV TEL. £60–£74 ($94.80–$116.90) double. Rates
include English breakfast. AE, DC, MC, V. Free parking.

Right on the village green, perhaps one of the most colorful places in Broadway,
is this converted 15th-century house, formerly used by the abbots of Pershore,
combining the half-timbered look of the Vale of Evesham with the stone of the
Cotswolds. While keeping its old-world charm, the hotel has been modernized and
converted to provide comforts. All the pleasantly furnished rooms have hot-
beverage facilities and central heating. One of the rooms with full private bath has
a four-poster bed. The cooking is fine, the service personal, the dining room
attractive. The comfortable cocktail bar is well stocked. Locals claim that the best
luncheon stopover in Broadway, if you're keeping an eye on costs, is the bar at this
hotel. Lunches are served daily from noon to 2pm, with bar platters priced from
£3.50 to £6 ($5.55 to $9.50). Dinner in the main dining room is served daily,
featuring English specialties such as fish, duckling, or venison. A table d'hôte
three-course meal costs £16 ($25.30), whereas à la carte main courses range from
£9.50 to £15 ($15 to $23.70).

WHERE TO DINE
MODERATE

Hunter's Lodge Restaurant

48 High St. ☎ **01386/853247.** Reservations recommended. Main courses £11.25–£14.50
($17.80–$22.90); fixed-price menu £18.50 ($29.25). AE, DC, MC, V. Sat–Sun 12:30–1:45pm;
Thurs–Sat 7:30–9:45pm. CONTINENTAL.

Housed in a building that dates back to 1650, this restaurant sits back from the
main street of town, surrounded by lawns, flower beds, and shady trees. The stone
gables are partially covered with ivy, the windows are deep set with mullions and
leaded panes, and the formal entrance has a small foyer furnished with antiques.
The English-Swiss owners prepare an array of dishes that might include mushroom
Stroganoff in a sour-cream sauce, a salad of king prawns with bacon, boned and
roasted quail in a cider-cream sauce, monkfish with courgettes (zucchini) and
herbs, a vegetable strudel with yogurt dressing, grilled salmon with tomatoes and
ginger, and a deviled rack of lamb with mustard glaze and an herb-flavored crust.
The establishment's most popular dessert is an almond meringue with an apricot
sauce.

10 Chipping Campden

36 miles NW of Oxford, 12 miles S of Stratford-upon-Avon, 93 miles NW of London

The English, regardless of how often they visit the Cotswolds, are attracted in great
numbers to this town, once an important wool center. Off the main road, it's easily accessible to major points of interest, and double-decker buses frequently run
through here on their way to Oxford or Stratford-upon-Avon.

On the northern edge of the Cotswolds above the Vale of Evesham, Campden,
a Saxon settlement, was recorded in the *Domesday Book.* In medieval times, rich
merchants built homes of Cotswold stone along its model High Street, described

by historian G. M. Trevelyan as "the most beautiful village street now left in the island." The houses have been so well preserved that Chipping Campden to this day remains a gem of the Middle Ages. Its church dates from the 15th century, and its old market hall is the loveliest in the Cotswolds. Look, also, for its alms-houses, which, along with the market hall, were built by a great wool merchant, Sir Baptist Hicks, whose tomb is in the church.

ESSENTIALS
GETTING THERE

By Train   Trains depart from London's Paddington Station for Moreton-in-Marsh (trip time: 90 to 120 minutes). At Moreton-in-Marsh, a bus operated by Barry's Coaches travels the seven miles to Chipping Campden only two days a week. Most visitors get a taxi at Moreton-in-Marsh to go to Chipping Campden.
By Bus   The largest and most important nearby bus depot is Cheltenham, which receives service several times a day from London's Victoria Coach Station. From Cheltenham, however, bus service (again by Barry's Coaches) is infrequent and uncertain, departing at the most only three times per week.
By Car   From Oxford, take A40 west to the junction with A424, which you take northwest, passing by Stow-on-the-Wold. The route becomes A44 until you reach the junction with B4081, which you take northeast to Chipping Campden.

VISITOR INFORMATION

The **telephone area code** is 01386. The summer-only **Tourist Information Centre** is at Woolstaplers Hall Museum, High Street (☎ **01386/840101**).

WHERE TO STAY & DINE
EXPENSIVE

✪ Cotswold House Hotel
The Square, Chipping Campden, Gloucestershire GL55 6AN. ☎ **01386/840330.** Fax 01386/840310. 15 rms. TV TEL. £105 ($165.90) double; £190 ($300.20) four-poster room. Rates include breakfast. AE, DC, V. Free parking.

A stately, formal Regency house dating from 1800, right in the heart of the village, opposite the old wool market, Cotswold House sits amid 1¹/₂ acres of tended, walled garden with shaded seating. Note the fine winding Regency staircase in the reception hall. The bedrooms are furnished with themes ranging from Gothic to French to military, with many others included along the way.

You can dine in the restaurant, which serves first-class English and French food in a formal, elegant room, or in Greenstocks Brasserie, open daily from 9:30am to the last orders at 10pm. Here light dishes and meals are served.

MODERATE

Noel Arms Hotel
High St., Chipping Campden, Gloucestershire GL55 6AT. ☎ **01386/840317** or 800/528-1234 in the U.S. and Canada. Fax 01386/841136. 26 rms. TV TEL. £80–£90 ($126.40–$142.20) double. Children up to 10 stay free in parents' room. Rates include English breakfast. AE, DC, MC, V. Free parking.

This old coaching inn has been famous in the Cotswolds since the 14th century. In 1651 Charles II rested here after his defeat at the Battle of Worcester. Today, Chipping Campden's oldest inn is still going strong. Tradition is kept alive in the decor, with fine antiques, muskets, swords, and shields. There's a private sitting room for residents, but you may prefer the lounge with its 12-foot-wide fireplace. Twelve of the bedrooms date back to the 14th century; the others, comfortably furnished and well appointed, are housed in a modern wing built of Cotswold stone.

The oak-paneled Gainsborough Restaurant offers an extensive menu, with an international wine list. A three-course set dinner costs £17.75 ($28.05). The three-course Sunday lunch costs £10.95 ($17.30) and is well attended, both by locals and visitors. Typical English dishes such as venison and mushroom pie or roast prime sirloin of beef with Yorkshire pudding are featured. During the week bar snacks cost from £1.95 to £6 ($3.10 to $9.50). The hotel's tavern always attracts a crowd that enjoys its real ales, malt whiskies, open fires, and Cotswold stone walls.

INEXPENSIVE

⑤ Kings Arms Hotel

The Square, Chipping Campden, Gloucestershire GL55 6AW. ☎ **01386/840256.** 15 rms. TV TEL. £60 ($94.80) double. Rates include English breakfast. MC, V. Free parking.

Dating from the late 1600s, with many renovations since, this partly Georgian building stands in the center of town and has its own garden, from which come many of the fresh vegetables used in its meals. All the accommodations are well tended, pleasantly furnished, and spotlessly clean.

The inn enjoys a good reputation for its cooking. Bar meals are served in the pub, or else you can dine more formally, enjoying a fixed-price dinner for £12.50 to £14.50 ($19.75 to $22.90) or a fixed-price Sunday lunch for £9.50 ($15).

IN NEARBY CHARINGWORTH

Expensive

✪ Charingworth Manor Hotel

Charingworth, near Chipping Campden, Gloucestershire GL55 6NS. ☎ **01386/593353** or 800/525-4800 in the U.S. Fax 01386/593555. 24 rms. TV TEL. £115–180 ($181.70–$284.40) double. AE, DC, MC, V. Free parking. Take B4035 3¹/4 miles east of Chipping Campden.

A manor has stood on this spot since the time of the *Domesday Book.* The present Tudor-Jacobean house, in honey-colored stone with slate roofs, has 55 acres of grounds; in the 1930s it was host to such illustrious guests as T. S. Eliot. The old-world charm of the place has been preserved, in spite of modernization; log fires and well-chosen antiques create a delightful country-house ambience. Each room is individually decorated and luxuriously furnished, both in its use of antiques and English fabrics. Amenities include a hair dryer, trouser press, and room safe. Many of the period rooms have four-poster beds. Guests can also wander through a well-manicured garden.

Dining/Entertainment: Lunch is offered for £8.50 to £17.50 ($13.45 to $27.65); there's also a fixed-price dinner for £29.50 ($46.60) in the elegant restaurant of the hotel, which is situated under low-ceiling beams. Excellent ingredients are deftly handled in the kitchen to create a French and English menu. Game is often featured. The wine list is carefully chosen. Lunch is served daily from noon to 2pm and dinner daily from 7 to 9:30pm.

Services: 24-hour room service, laundry service.

Facilities: A Leisure Spa opened in 1992 consisting of a luxurious indoor heated pool built in Romanesque style, a sauna, steam room, solarium, and billiards room. There is also an all-weather tennis court on the grounds.

16 Stratford-upon-Avon & Warwick

Shakespeare Country in the heart of England is, after London, the district most visited by North Americans. Many who don't recognize the county name, Warwickshire, know its foremost tourist town, Stratford-upon-Avon, birthplace of England's greatest writer. Other places that attract overseas visitors include Warwick and Kenilworth castles, as well as Coventry Cathedral.

The county and its neighboring shires form a land of industrial cities, green fields, and market towns dotted with buildings, a few of which have changed little since Shakespeare's time.

A DRIVING TOUR

Day 1   Stratford-upon-Avon is most often visited from London. Motorists from London take the M40 toward Oxford, continuing along A34 to reach Stratford, hometown of William Shakespeare. To see just the major sights, you'll need to spend at least two nights here. After lunch in a typical tavern, you can see several of the major literary pilgrimage centers in the afternoon.

Day 2   While still based at Stratford, visit Ragley Hall in the morning and George Washington's ancestral home, Sulgrave Manor—both of which can be viewed in a day. Take in as much Shakes-pearean theater as you can upon your return to Stratford.

Day 3   You can stay in Stratford for your final night and visit Warwick on a day trip, or else transfer to Warwick and check into a local hotel (not as good as those in Stratford). Visit Warwick Castle in the morning and explore the ruins of Kenilworth Castle in the early afternoon before a late-afternoon visit to Coventry Cathedral.

1 Stratford-upon-Avon

91 miles NW of London, 40 miles NW of Oxford, 8 miles S of Warwick

Tourism is responsible for the large amount of traffic to this market town on the Avon River. Actor David Garrick really launched the shrine in 1769 when he organized the first of the Bard's commemorative birthday celebrations. William Shakespeare, of course, was born in Stratford-upon-Avon. Little is known about his early life, and many of the stories connected with Shakespeare's days in

---

What's Special About Stratford-upon-Avon & Warwick

Castles
- Warwick Castle, between Stratford and Coventry, regarded as England's finest medieval castle.
- Kenilworth Castle, in magnificent ruins, the setting of Sir Walter Scott's romance *Kenilworth.*

Literary Shrines
- Shakespeare's Birthplace, Stratford, where the Bard was born on April 23, 1564.
- Anne Hathaway's Cottage, a mile from Stratford, a wattle-and-daub cottage where Anne Hathaway lived before marrying Shakespeare.

Buildings
- Ragley Hall, built in 1680 outside Stratford, home of the marquess of Hertford, and restored to its original look.
- Coventry Cathedral, consecrated in 1962, designed by Sir Basil Spence in a modern style that was opposed by traditional architectural devotees.

Theatrical Event
- Attending a performance at the Royal Shakespeare Theatre on the River Avon in Stratford.

Stratford are largely fanciful, invented to amuse and entertain the vast number of literary fans who make the pilgrimage.

Another magnet for tourists today is the Royal Shakespeare Theatre, where Britain's foremost actors perform during a long season that lasts from early April until late January. Stratford-upon-Avon is also a good center for trips to Warwick Castle, Kenilworth Castle, Sulgrave Manor (ancestral home of George Washington), and Coventry Cathedral.

ESSENTIALS
GETTING THERE

By Train   Frequent trains from Paddington Station take 2¼ hours. Call 0171/ 262-6767 for schedules. Standard round-trip tickets cost £22.50 ($35.55).

By "Road & Rail Link"   This Shakespeare Connection by train and bus is a sure way to attend the Royal Shakespeare Theatre and return to London on the same day. It leaves from London's Euston Station (☎ 0171/387-7070) Monday through Friday at 9:15am, 10:45am, and 4:55pm. (There's also a late-evening departure at 9:45pm, although that would, obviously, not permit you to attend a play the same evening.) Saturday departures from Euston are at 9:05am, 10:35am, 5:05pm, and 9:35pm; and Sunday departures from Euston are at 9:45am and 5:45pm. If you want to explore London during the day and then attend an evening performance at one of the theaters that night, the best train to catch is the one at 5:05pm Monday to Saturday. Travel is by train to Coventry, then bus to Stratford. Returns to London are scheduled to coincide with the end of theater performances, with departures at 11:15pm. The "Road & Rail Link" is operated by British Rail and Guide Friday. The Guide Friday office in Stratford is at Civic Hall, 14 Rother St. (☎ 01789/294466). The fare from Euston Station to Stratford costs £25 ($39.50) for a one-way ticket or £29 ($45.80) for a round-trip ticket valid for three months. Ask for a Shakespeare Connection ticket at London's Euston Station or at any British Rail London Travel Centre. Holders of BritRail passes who use the service ride the train free and then pay the bus fare to Stratford from Coventry, which costs £6.50 ($10.25) one-way or £8.50 ($13.45) round-trip.

When you arrange your Shakespeare Connection ticket, the ticket vendor at Euston Station can simultaneously sell you tickets for Guide Friday tours of Stratford, admission tickets to the five sites within Stratford's Shakespeare Trust, and add-on extension visits from Stratford to Warwick Castle.

By Bus   Eight National Express (☎ 0171/730-0202) coaches a day leave from Victoria Station, with a trip time of 3¼ hours. A single-day round trip ticket costs £13 ($20.55).

By Car   Take M40 toward Oxford and continue to Stratford-upon-Avon on A34.

VISITOR INFORMATION

The **telephone area code** is 01789. The **Tourist Information Centre,** Bridgefoot (☎ **01789/293127**), will provide any details you might wish about the Shakespeare properties. It's open March to October on Monday through Saturday from 9am to 6pm, on Sunday from 11am to 5pm. From November to February, it's open on Monday through Friday from 9am to 5pm.

To contact Shakespeare Birthplace Trust, which administers many of the attractions, send a self-addressed envelope and International Reply Coupon to the Director, the Shakespeare Centre, Henley Street, Stratford-upon-Avon, Warwickshire CV37 6QW (☎ 01789/204016).

WHAT TO SEE & DO
THE THEATER

✪ **The Royal Shakespeare Company** has a major showcase in Stratford-upon Avon, the Royal Shakespeare Theatre, Waterside, Stratford-upon-Avon CV37 6BB (☎ **01789/295623**), on the banks of the Avon. Seating 1,500 patrons, the theater has a season that runs from early April until late January. The company has some of the finest actors on the British stage. In an average season, five Shakespearean plays are staged.

Usually, you'll need reservations. There are two successive booking periods, each one opening about two months in advance. You can pick these up from a North American or an English travel agent. If you wait until your arrival in Stratford, it may be too late to get a good seat. Tickets can be booked through New York agents Edwards and Edwards or Keith Prowse (who will add a service charge) or direct with the theater box office with payment by major credit card. Call the box office at the number listed above. The box office is open Monday through Saturday from 9am to 8pm, although it closes at 6pm on days when there are no performances. The price of seats usually ranges from £6 to £42 ($9.50 to $66.35) . A small number of tickets are always held for sale on the day of a performance. You can make a credit-card reservation and pick up your ticket on the day it is to be used, but you can't cancel once your reservation is made unless 2 full weeks of advance notice is given.

Stratford-upon-Avon

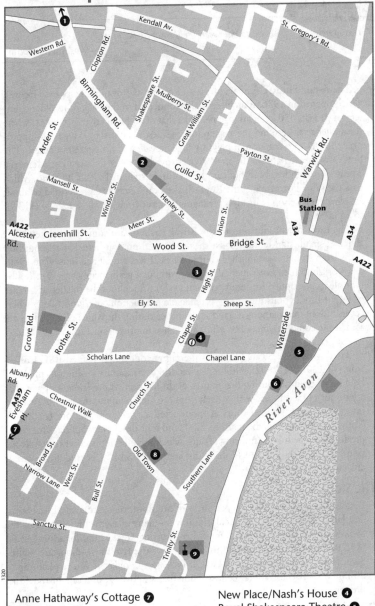

Anne Hathaway's Cottage ❼
Hall's Croft ❽
Harvard House ❸
Holy Trinity Church ❾
Mary Arden's House and the
   Shakespeare Countryside Museum ❶

New Place/Nash's House ❹
Royal Shakespeare Theatre ❺
Shakespeare's Birthplace ❷
Swan Theatre ❻

It is something, I thought, to have seen the dust of Shakespeare.
—Washington Irving

The **Swan Theatre** (same address and phone as Royal Shakespeare Theatre), which opened in 1986, is architecturally connected to the back of its older counterpart. It seats 430 in an arrangement like that of an Elizabethan playhouse, where the audience sits around the stage on three sides. (The design is especially appropriate for the presentation of plays by Shakespeare and his contemporaries.) The Swan was erected after a fire in 1926 destroyed an older theater (The Memorial Theatre), which had been built in the Victorian style in 1879. The Swan, which uses the same box office as the Royal Shakespeare, presents a repertoire of about six plays each season, with tickets ranging in price from £8.70 to £28.50 ($13.75 to $45.05).

The most recent addition to the Royal Shakespeare complex is **The Other Place,** a small, starkly minimalist theater located on Southern Lane, about 300 yards from its better-established counterparts. It was redesigned in the late 1980s as a workshop (i.e., experimental) theater without a permanent stage; seats can be radically repositioned (or removed completely) throughout the theater. Examples of recent productions include a "promenade production" of *Julius Caesar* where actors moved freely among a stand-up audience during the whole play. Tickets are sold at the complex's main box office and range in price from £13 to £19 ($20.55 to $30) each.

Based within the Swan Theatre is the rather confusingly named **RSC Collection** (☎ 01789/412602). Although a handful of temporary exhibitions might be held on its premises during the lifetime of this edition, at presstime it operated as a base for guided tours, with a lively running commentary, through the world-famous theaters. Guided tours are conducted at 1:30 and 5:30pm (excluding Thursday and Sunday, the matinee days), and four times every Sunday afternoon, production schedules permitting. Tours, which include stopovers at the organizations' souvenir shop, cost £4 ($6.30) for adults, £3 ($4.75) for students or senior citizens.

THE SIGHTS

Besides the attractions on the periphery of Stratford, there are many Elizabethan and Jacobean buildings in this colorful town—many of them administered by the Shakespeare Birthplace Trust. One ticket—costing £8 ($12.65) for adults, £3.60 ($5.70) for children—will permit you to visit the five most important sights. Seniors and students pay £7 ($11.05). Pick up the ticket if you're planning to do much sightseeing (obtainable at your first stopover at any one of the Trust properties).

✪ Shakespeare's Birthplace

Henley St. ☎ **01789/204016.** Admission £2.75 ($4.35) adults, £1.30 ($2.05) children. Mar 20–Oct 19, Mon–Sat 9am–5:30pm; Sun 9:30am–5:30pm; off-season, Mon–Sat 9:30am–4pm; Sun 10am–4pm. Closed Jan 1, Good Friday, and Dec 24–26.

The son of a glover and whittawer (leather worker), the Bard was born on St. George's day (April 23) in 1564 and died 52 years later on the same day. Filled with Shakespeare memorabilia, including a portrait and furnishings of the

The Mysterious Bard

Nathaniel Hawthorne, the American author and one of millions of visitors to Stratford-upon-Avon over the years, noted in *Our Old Home* (1863) that upon seeing some Shakespeare exhibits he was "conscious of not the slightest emotion . . . nor any quickening of the imagination." That is hardly the case with most visitors.

Even as far back as 1756, the Rev. Francis Gastrell, owner of the Bard's last home, was beseiged by pilgrims wanting to see a mulberry tree Shakespeare had planted. The pastor chopped it down, which led to a local riot. One neighbor purchased the fallen tree and made a fortune selling chips from it. These chips are said to have mysteriously grown into full trees when planted all over England. Not since chips from Christ's crucifixion cross have such souvenir relics been so eagerly sought.

When the fabled actor David Garrick arrived in Stratford in 1769 for a three-day Shakespeare festival (the first), the town was launched into its role as a place of pilgrimage for literary fans, or even for those who have never seen a Shakespearean play. The festival didn't please all: one disgruntled visitor claimed, "I was charged nine guineas for six hours' sleep and two shillings for asking a country bumpkin what time it was."

In spite of all the fuss made over him, William Shakespeare the man remains a mystery. Each year some scholarly new work appears that attempts to explain the life of the Bard, although evidence about him remains sketchy. One of the latest of these titles is *Shakespeare: The Evidence: Unlocking the Mysteries of the Man and His Work,* by Ian Wilson (St. Martin's, 1994). In this book Wilson alleges that John Shakespeare, a glover and father of William, was a secret member of the Catholic undergound, and also that William himself harbored Catholic sympathies. Part of the hypothesis for this is a "spiritualized" last will—believed to be that of John Shakespeare—discovered in 1757, although quickly lost to history. It is known that William purchased Blackfriars Gatehouse, a clandestine Catholic gathering place, in 1613.

In this rather intriguing book, Wilson alleges that Ferdinando Stanley (Lord Stranges) was Shakespeare's mystery patron behind his *Henry VI/Richard II* tetralogy. At Stanley's court, young Will could have observed political intrigue and courtly behavior, information that he later incorporated into his plays. That would be one explanation for how an actor of modest circumstances would know as much about court life as he did. However, there is little evidence to support this conclusion, in spite of Wilson's indefatigable sleuthing in the Elizabethan world.

Although Shakespeare is held in high esteem today, that wasn't the case in his lifetime. In the late 16th century, theater was strictly low-brow entertainment, second only to watching an execution by hanging.

In London, versions of *Hamlet, Othello, King Lear,* and *Macbeth* were performed in the midst of brothels and prostitute "Winchester geese" (so called because the bishop of Winchester owned the land on which these whorehouses stood). The Lord Mayor of London had no jurisdiction at the Globe Theatre in London's Southwark district, which became the cradle of English drama until the original theater burned down in 1613. A prop cannon shot an ember into its thatched roof during a performance of *Henry VIII.*

writer's time, the Trust property is a half-timbered structure, dating from the first part of the 16th century. The house was bought by public donors in 1847 and preserved as a national shrine. You can visit the oak-beamed living room, the bedroom where Shakespeare was probably born, a fully equipped kitchen of the period (look for the "babyminder"), and a Shakespeare Museum, illustrating his life and times. Later, you can walk through the garden. It's estimated that some 660,000 visitors pass through the house annually. Next door to the birthplace is the modern **Shakespeare Centre,** built to commemorate the 400th anniversary of the Bard's birth. It serves both as the administrative headquarters of the Birthplace Trust and as a library and study center. An extension of the original center, which opened in 1981, includes a visitors' center, which acts as a reception area for all those coming to the birthplace. It's in the town center near the post office close to Union Street.

✪ Anne Hathaway's Cottage

Cottage Lane, Shottery. ☎ 01789/292100. Admission £2.30 ($3.65) adults, £1.10 ($1.75) children. Mar 20–Oct 19, Mon–Sat 9am–5:30pm, Sun 9:30am–5:30pm; off-season, Mon–Sat 9:30am–4pm, Sun 10am–4pm. Closed Jan 1, Good Friday, and Dec 24–26. You can walk across the meadow to Shottery from Evesham Place in Stratford (pathway marked), or take a bus from Bridge St.

In the hamlet of Shottery 1 mile from Stratford-upon-Avon is the thatched, wattle-and-daub cottage where Anne Hathaway lived before her marriage to Shakespeare. It's the most interesting and seemingly the most photographed of the Trust properties. The Hathaways were yeoman farmers, and the cottage provides a rare insight into the life of a family of Shakespeare's day. Shakespeare married her when he was only 18 years old, and she much older. Many of the original furnishings, including the courting settle and utensils, are preserved inside the house, which was occupied by descendants of Shakespeare's wife's family until 1892. After a visit to the house, you'll want to linger in the garden and orchard.

New Place/Nash's House

Chapel St. ☎ 01789/292325. Admission £1.90 ($3) adults, 90p ($1.40) children. Mar 20–Oct, Mon–Sat 9:30am–5pm; Sun 10am–5pm; off-season Mon–Sat 10am–4pm; Sun 10:30–4pm. Closed Jan 1, and Dec 24–26. Walk west down High St.; Chapel St. is a continuation of High St.

This is where Shakespeare retired in 1610, a prosperous man as judged by the standards of his day. He died here six years later, at the age of 52. Regrettably, only the site of his former home remains today, since the house was torn down. You enter the gardens through Nash's House (Thomas Nash married Elizabeth Hall, a granddaughter of the poet). Nash's House has 16th-century period rooms and an exhibition illustrating the history of Stratford. The popular Knott Garden adjoins the site and represents the style of a fashionable Elizabethan garden. New Place has its own great garden, which once belonged to Shakespeare. Here, the Bard planted a mulberry tree, so popular with latter-day visitors to Stratford that the cantankerous owner of the garden chopped it down. The mulberry tree that grows there today is said to have been planted from a cutting of the original tree.

Mary Arden's House and the Shakespeare Countryside Museum

Wilmcote. ☎ 01789/293455. Admission £3.20 ($5.05) adults, £1.40 ($2.20) children. Mar 20–Oct 19, Mon–Sat 9:30am–5pm, Sun 10am–5pm; off-season, Mon–Sat 10am–4pm, Sun 10:30–4pm. Closed Jan 1, Good Friday, and Dec 24–26. Take the A34 (Birmingham) road for 3 1/2 miles.

This Tudor farmstead, with its old stone dovecote and various outbuildings, was the girlhood home of Shakespeare's mother. It's situated at Wilmcote, 3¹/₂ miles from Stratford. The house contains rare pieces of country furniture and domestic utensils. In the barns, stable, cowshed, and farmyard you'll find an extensive collection of farming implements illustrating life and work in the local countryside from Shakespeare's time to the present.

Visitors also see the neighboring Glebe Farm, whose interior evokes farm life in late Victorian and Edwardian times. Light refreshments are available, and there is a picnic area.

Hall's Croft

Old Town. ☎ **01789/292107.** Admission £1.90 ($3) adults, 90p ($1.40) children. Mar 20–Oct 19, Mon–Sat 9:30am–5pm; Sun 10am–5pm; off-season Mon–Sat 10am–4pm; Sun 10:30–4pm. Closed Jan 1, and Dec 24–26. To reach Hall's Croft, walk west from High St., which becomes Chapel St. and Church St. At the intersection with Old Town, go left.

This house is on Old Town street, not far from the parish church, Holy Trinity. It was here that Shakespeare's daughter Susanna probably lived with her husband, Dr. John Hall. Hall's Croft is an outstanding Tudor house with a beautiful walled garden, furnished in the style of a middle-class home of the time. Dr. Hall was widely respected and he built up a large medical practice in the area. Exhibits illustrating the theory and practice of medicine in Dr. Hall's time are on view. Visitors to the house are welcome to use the adjoining Hall's Croft Club, which serves morning coffee, lunch, and afternoon tea.

Holy Trinity Church

Old Town. ☎ **01789/266316.** Church, free; Shakespeare's tomb, 50p (80¢) adults, 30p (45¢) students. Mar–Oct, Mon–Sat 8:30am–6pm, Sun 2–5pm; Nov–Feb, Mon–Sat 8:30am–4pm, Sun 2–5pm. Continue past the Royal Shakespeare Theatre with the river on your left; the church is reached after a 4-minute walk.

In an attractive setting near the Avon River is the parish church where Shakespeare is buried ("and curst be he who moves my bones"). The Parish Register records his baptism in 1564 and burial in 1616 (copies of the original). The church has been described as one of the most beautiful parish churches in England.

Harvard House

High St. ☎ **01789/204507.** Admission £1.25 ($2) adults, 50p (80¢) students and children. May 22–Sept 24, daily 10am–4pm. Closed Sept 25–May 21.

Harvard House is a fine example of an Elizabethan town house. Rebuilt in 1596, it was once the home of Katherine Rogers, mother of John Harvard, founder of Harvard College. In 1909 the house was purchased by a Chicago millionaire, Edward Morris, who presented it as a gift to the American university. It's the most ornate house in Stratford. The rooms are filled with period furniture, and

---

Impressions

After we had seen Shakespeare's tomb and birthplace, we went back to the inn there, where we slept that night, and I recollect that all night long I dreamt of nothing but a black gentleman, at full length, in plaster-of-Paris, with a lay-down collar tied with two tassels, leaning against a post and thinking; and when I woke in the morning and described him to Mr. Nickleby, he said it was Shakespeare just as he had been when he was alive, which was very curious indeed.

—Charles Dickens, *Nicholas Nickleby*

the floors are made of local flagstone. Look for the Bible Chair, used for hiding the Bible during the days of Tudor persecution.

The Royal Shakespeare Theatre Summer House

Avonbank Gardens. ☎ **01789/297671.** Admission free. Apr–Sept, daily 10am–6pm; Oct, daily 11am–4pm.

This is a brass-rubbing center, where medieval and Tudor brasses illustrate the knights and ladies, scholars, merchants, and priests of a bygone era. The Stratford collection includes a large assortment of exact replicas of brasses. Entrance is free, but visitors are charged depending on which brass they choose to rub. According to size, the cost ranges from 95p ($1.50) to make a rubbing of a small brass, to a maximum of £15.95 ($25.20) for a rubbing of the largest, a seven-foot behemoth that takes an enthusiast a full day to complete. The price includes all the necessary paper and waxes, and a demonstration of the methodology of rubbing.

TOURS

Guided tours of Stratford-upon-Avon leave from the Guide Friday Tourism Center, Civic Hall, Rother Street (☎ 01789/294466), daily. In summer, departures of open-top double-decker buses take place every 15 minutes from 9:30am to 5:30pm. You can take a one-hour ride without stops, or you can get off at any or all of the town's five Shakespeare's Properties. Anne Hathaway's Cottage and Mary Arden's House are the two likely stops to make outside the town center. Although the bus stops are clearly marked along their historic route, the most logical starting point is on the sidewalk in front of the Pen & Parchment Pub, at Bridgefoot, at the bottom of Bridge Street. Tour tickets are valid all day so you can hop on and off the buses wherever you want. The price for these tours is £7 ($11.05) for adults or £2 ($3.15) for children under 12, and £4.50 ($7.10) for senior citizens or students.

NEARBY ATTRACTIONS

Ragley Hall

Alcester. ☎ **01789/762090.** Admission to house, garden, and park, £4.50 ($7.10) adults, £4 ($6.30) senior citizens, £3 ($4.75) children. Easter–Sept, Tues–Thurs and Sat–Sun, house 11am–5pm; gardens 10am–6pm. Closed Oct–Easter. Since there is no suitable bus service, visitors arrive by car. Ragley Hall is located on A435 to Evesham, about 1¹/₂ miles west of the town of Alcester. There is easy access from the main motorway network, including M40 from London, some 100 miles away.

A magnificent 115-room Palladian country house, Ragley Hall, built in 1680, is the home of the Earl and Countess of Yarmouth. It's located near Alcester, 9 miles from Stratford-upon-Avon. The house has been restored and appears much as it did during the early 1700s. Great pains have been taken to duplicate colors and, in some cases, the original wallpaper patterns. The pictures, furniture, and works of art that fill the vast and spacious rooms represent ten generations of collecting by the Seymour family. Ragley Hall may be a private home, but it has a museumlike quality, and many of its artifacts have great historical importance. Perhaps the most spectacular attraction is the lavishly painted south staircase hall. Muralist Graham Rust painted a modern trompe l'oeil work depicting the Temptation.

Coventry

Coventry, 19 miles north of Stratford-upon-Avon, has long been noted in legend as the ancient market town through which Lady Godiva took her famous ride—

giving rise to a new expression in English, *Peeping Tom.* The veracity of the Lady Godiva story is hard to ascertain. It's been suggested that the good lady never appeared nude in town, but was the victim of scandalmongers. Coventry today is a Midlands industrial city. The city was partially destroyed during the Blitz in the early 1940s, but the restoration is miraculous.

✪ Coventry Cathedral

Priory Row, Coventry. ☎ **01203/227597.** Admission to cathedral, free, but suggested donation £2 ($3.15); tower, £1 ($1.60) adults, 80p ($1.25) children; visitor center, £1.25 ($2), 75p ($1.20) children 6–16. June–Sept, daily 9:30am–6pm; Oct–May, daily 9:30am–4:30pm. Local buses from Stratford-upon-Avon run north to Coventry every 30 minutes during the day.

Sir Basil Spence's controversial cathedral (consecrated in 1962) is the city's main attraction. The cathedral is on the same site as the 14th-century perpendicular building, and you can visit the original tower. Many locals maintain that the structure is more likely to be appreciated by the foreign visitor, since the Britisher is more attached to traditional cathedral design. Some visitors consider the restored sight as one of the most poignant and religiously evocative modern churches in the world.

Outside is Sir Jacob Epstein's bronze masterpiece, *St. Michael Slaying the Devil.* Inside, the outstanding feature is the 70-foot-high altar tapestry by Graham Sutherland, said to be the largest in the world. The floor-to-ceiling abstract stained-glass windows are the work of the Royal College of Art. The West Screen (an entire wall of stained glass installed during the 1950s) is quite interesting, with its engraved glass depicting rows of stylized saints and prophets with angels flying around among them.

In the undercroft of the cathedral is a visitor center, where a 20-minute documentary film, the Spirit of Coventry, is shown more or less continually. Also within the visitor center is the Walkway of Holograms, whose otherwise plain walls are accented with three-dimensional images of the stations of the cross created with reflective light. One of the most evocative objects within the collection of artifacts is a charred cross wired together by local workmen from burning timbers which crashed to the cathedral's floor during the bombing. An audiovisual exhibit on the city and church includes the fact that 450 aircraft dropped 40,000 firebombs on the city in one day.

After visiting the cathedral, you may want to have tea in Fraters Restaurant nearby.

✪ Sulgrave Manor

Manor Rd., Sulgrave, Banbury. ☎ **01295/760205.** Admission £3 ($4.75) adults, £1.50 ($2.35) children 5–16, free for children under 5. Apr–Sept, Mon, Tues, Thurs, and Fri 2–5:30pm; Sat–Sun 10:30am–1pm and 2–5:30pm. Closed Dec–Feb (except for some special weekends in December—call for data which varies annually). You'll need a car. From Stratford-upon-Avon, take A422 via Banbury (whose famous cross entered nursery rhyme fame) and continue to Brackley; 6 miles from Brackley, leave A422 and join B4525, which goes to the tiny village of Sulgrave. Signs will lead you to Sulgrave Manor.

American visitors especially will be interested in this small mid-16th-century Tudor manor. As a part of Henry VIII's plan to dissolve the monasteries, he sold the priory-owned manor in 1539 to Lawrence Washington, who had been mayor of Northampton; George Washington was a direct descendant of Lawrence (seven generations removed). The Washington family occupied Sulgrave for more than a century, but in 1656, Col. John Washington left for the New World.

In 1914 the manor was purchased by a group of English people in honor of the friendship between Britain and America. Over the years, major restoration has taken place, with an eye toward returning it as much as possible to its original state. Beginning with a large donation in 1927, the Colonial Dames have been largely responsible for raising the money. From both sides of the Atlantic, the appropriate furnishings were donated, including a number of portraits—even a Gilbert Stuart original of the first president. On the main doorway is the Washington family coat of arms—two bars and a trio of mullets—which is believed to have been the inspiration for the "Stars and Stripes."

WHERE TO STAY
IN STRATFORD-UPON-AVON

During the long theater season, you may run into difficulty if you arrive without a reservation. However, you can go to the Tourist Information Centre, Bridgefoot, Stratford-upon-Avon, Warwickshire, CV37 6GW (☎ 01789/293127). See "Essentials," above. A staff person who is experienced in finding accommodations for travelers in all budget categories will try to book a room for you in your desired price range. The fee for room reservations is 10% of the first night's stay (bed-and-breakfast charges only). It's also possible to reserve accommodations if you write well in advance. If you do write, be sure to specify the price range and the number of beds required. The booking charge is £3.50 ($5.55).

Expensive
Welcombe Hotel

Warwick Rd., Stratford-upon-Avon, Warwickshire CV37 0NR. ☎ **01789/295252.** Fax 01789/414666. 67 rms, 9 suites. TV TEL. £150 ($237) double; £175–£225 ($276.50–$355.50) suite. Rates include English breakfast. AE, DC, MC, V. Free parking. Take A439 1¹/₂ miles northeast of the town center.

One of England's great Jacobean country houses, this hotel is a ten-minute ride from the heart of Stratford-upon-Avon. The home once belonged to Sir Archibald Flower, the philanthropic brewer who helped create the Shakespeare Memorial Theatre. Converted into a hotel, it is surrounded by 157 acres of grounds and has a formal entrance on Warwick Road, a winding driveway leading to the main hall. Guests gather for afternoon tea or drinks on the rear terrace, with its Italian-style garden and steps leading down to flower beds. The public rooms are heroic in size, with high mullioned windows providing views of the park. The bedrooms—some big enough for tennis matches—have pleasant furnishings.

Dining/Entertainment: The hotel's restaurant offers table d'hôte or à la carte menus. A fixed-price lunch goes for £18.50 ($29.25), with a fixed-price dinner costing £27.50 ($43.45).

Services: 24-hour room service, laundry service.

Facilities: 18-hole 6,202-yard golf course, tennis courts, putting green.

Moderate
Alveston Manor Hotel

Clopton Bridge, Stratford-upon-Avon, Warwickshire CV37 7HP. ☎ **01789/204581** or 800/225-5843 in the U.S. and Canada. Fax 01789/414095. 103 rms, 3 suites. TV TEL. £105–£135 ($165.90–$213.30) double; £165 ($260.70) suite. Breakfast £6.50–£9.75 ($10.25–$15.40) extra. AE, DC, MC, V. Free parking.

This black-and-white timbered manor is perfect for theatergoers—it's just a two-minute walk from the Avon off B4066. It has a wealth of chimneys and gables, and everything from an Elizabethan gazebo to Queen Anne windows. Mentioned in the *Domesday Book,* the building predates the arrival of William the Conqueror. The rooms in the manor house will appeal to those who appreciate old slanted floors, overhead beams, and antique furnishings. Some triples or quads are available in the modern section, which is connected by a covered walk through the rear garden. The rooms here have built-in pieces and a color-coordinated decor. The lounges are in the manor; there's a view of the centuries-old tree at the top of the garden—said to have been the background for the first presentation of *A Midsummer Night's Dream.* In the main living room, with its linen-fold paneling, logs burn in the Tudor fireplace.

Meals are served in the softly lit Manor Restaurant amid oak beams and leaded-glass windows. A fixed-price dinner costs £23.50 ($37.15).

Dukes

Payton St., Stratford-upon-Avon, Warwickshire CV37 6UA. ☎ **01789/269300.** Fax 01789/414700. 22 rms (all with bath or shower). TV TEL. £67–£105 ($105.85–$165.90) double. Rates include English breakfast. AE, DC, MC, V. Free parking.

Located in the center of Stratford north of Guild Street, this little charmer was formed when two Georgian town houses were united and restored. The family-operated inn has a large garden and is close to Shakespeare's birthplace. The public areas and bedrooms are attractive, having been restored to an impressive degree of comfort and coziness. The furniture is tasteful, much of it antique. Dukes also serves a good English and continental cuisine, with meals costing £18 ($28.45) and up.

Falcon

Chapel St., Stratford-upon-Avon, Warwickshire CV37 6HA. ☎ **01789/205777.** Fax 01789/414260. 72 rms, 1 suite. TV TEL. £99 ($156.40) double; £100 ($158) suite. Breakfast £6.50–£9.50 ($10.25–$15) extra. AE, DC, MC, V. Free parking.

The Falcon is a blending of the very old and the very new. At the rear of a black-and-white timbered inn, licensed a quarter of a century after Shakespeare's death, is a 1970 bedroom extension, joined by a glass-covered passageway. In the heart of Stratford, the inn faces the Guild Chapel and the New Place Gardens. You arrive at the rear portion to unload luggage, just as horse-drawn coaches once dispatched their passengers. The bedrooms in the mellowed part have oak beams, diamond leaded-glass windows, some antique furnishings, and good reproductions. Each room includes a radio, electric trouser press, and hot-beverage facilities.

The lounges are comfortable—some of the finest in the Midlands. In the intimate Merlin Lounge is an open copper-hooded fireplace where coal and log fires are kept burning under beams salvaged from old ships (the walls are a good example of wattle and daub, typical of Shakespeare's day). The Oak Bar is a forest of weathered beams, and on either side of the stone fireplace is the paneling removed from the poet's last home, New Place. A fixed-price dinner costs £16 ($25.30), and a fixed-price Sunday lunch goes for £9.50 ($15). However, most other lunches are à la carte, costing around £15 ($23.70), unless patrons prefer to eat in the bar, where platters range from £4 to £10 ($6.30 to $15.80).

Grosvenor House Hotel

12–14 Warwick Rd., Stratford-upon-Avon, Warwickshire CV37 6YT. ☎ **01789/269213.** Fax 01789/266087. 64 rms (all with bath or shower). TV TEL. £95 ($150.10) double. Rates include English or continental breakfast. DC, MC, V. Free parking in large hotel lot.

A pair of Georgian town houses, built in 1832 and 1843, respectively, were joined together to form this hotel. Situated in the center of town, with lawns and gardens to the rear, it is a short stroll from the intersection of Bridge Street and Water-side, allowing easy access to the Avon River, Bancroft Gardens, and the Royal Shakespeare Theatre. All bedrooms have radios as well as tea and coffee makers. The informal bar (open until midnight) and terrace offer relaxation before or after you lunch or dine in the large restaurant, whose floor-to-ceiling windows face the gardens.

Moat House International

Bridgefoot, Stratford-upon-Avon, Warwickshire CV37 6YR. ☎ **01789/414411.** Fax 01789/298589. 245 rms, 2 suites. TV TEL. £125 ($197.50) double; £190 ($300.20) suite. Breakfast £9.50 ($15) extra. AE, DC, MC, V. Free parking.

A four-star hotel, the Moat House International stands on 5 acres of landscaped lawns on the banks of the River Avon near Clopton Bridge. It is one of the flag-ships of Queens Moat Houses, a British hotel chain, and was built in the early 1970s and last renovated in 1995. Every bedroom has a high standard of comfort. Amenities include bathrooms with generous shelf space, large mirrors, and hair dryer. There is 24-hour room service, a laundry service, and a leisure complex that includes a swimming pool.

The hotel restaurant features a British and continental menu, and the Riverside Restaurant offers a carvery of hot and cold roasts, costing £15.50 ($24.50). You can drink in the Tavern Pub and in the Actors Nightspot, a disco open only on Friday and Saturday from 9pm to 2am. Hotel residents enter free; nonresidents pay a £4.50 ($7.10) entrance fee.

Shakespeare

Chapel St., Stratford-upon-Avon, Warwickshire CV37 6ER. ☎ **01789/294771** or 800/225-5843 in the U.S. and Canada. Fax 01789/415411. 63 rms, 4 suites. TV TEL. £115 ($181.70) double; £140–£150 ($221.20–$237) suite. Breakfast £9.50 ($15) extra. AE, DC, MC, V. Free parking.

Filled with historical associations, the original core of this hotel, which dates from the 1400s, has seen many additions in its long life. It's been called both the Four Gables Hotel and the Five Gables Hotel. In the 1700s a demure facade of Regency brick was added to conceal the intricate timber framing, but in the 1880s, with a rash of Shakespearean revivals, the hotel was restored to its original Tudor look. Residents relax in the post-and-timber-studded public rooms, within sight of fireplaces and playbills from 19th-century productions of Shakespeare's plays.

The bedrooms are named in honor of noteworthy actors, Shakespeare's plays, or Shakespearean characters. The oldest are capped with hewn timbers, and all have modern comforts. Even the newer accommodations are at least 40 to 50 years old and have rose and thistle patterns carved into many of their exposed timbers. The rooms are equipped with hair dryers. There is 24-hour room service and laundry service.

The hotel restaurant, David Garrick, serves well-prepared lunches and dinners. Set lunches are served for £16.95 ($26.80), with a table d'hôte dinner going for £25.95 ($41).

White Swan

Rother St., Stratford-upon-Avon, Warwickshire CV37 6NH. ☎ **01789/297022** or 800/225-5843 in the U.S. and Canada. Fax 01789/268773. 35 rms, 2 suites. TV TEL. £85 ($134.30) double; £100 ($158) suite. Breakfast £8.50 ($13.45) extra. AE, DC, MC, V. Free parking.

This cozy, intimate hotel is one of the most atmospheric in Stratford and is, in fact, considered the oldest building there. It was in business for more than 100 years before Shakespeare appeared on the scene. The gabled medieval front would present the Bard with no surprises, but the modern comforts inside would surely astonish him, even though many of the rooms have been preserved. Paintings dating from 1550 hang on the lounge walls. All the bedrooms are well appointed; the amenities include a radio, trouser press, and hair dryer. The hostelry has a spacious restaurant where good food is served. The oak-beamed bar is a popular meeting place (see "Pubs" below).

Inexpensive

The Arden Thistle Hotel

44 Waterside, Stratford-upon-Avon, Warwickshire CV37 6BA. ☎ **01789/294949.** Fax 01789/415874. 63 rms. TV TEL. £90 ($142.20) double. Breakfast £6.50–£8.50 ($10.25–$13.45) extra. AE, DC, MC, V. Free parking.

Across the street from the main entrance of the Royal Shakespeare and Swan theatres, this hotel's interior was completely refurbished in 1993 after it was purchased by the Thistle chain. Its red-brick main section dates from the Regency period, although over the years a handful of adjacent buildings were included and a modern extension was added. Today, the interior has a well-upholstered lounge and bar; a dining room (Bards) with bay windows; a covered garden terrace; and comfortable bedrooms with hot-beverage facilities. A fixed-price dinner in the restaurant costs £17.95 ($28.35).

Forte Post House

Bridgefoot, Stratford-upon-Avon, Warwickshire CV37 7LT. ☎ **01789/266761** or 800/225-5843 in the U.S. and Canada. Fax 01789/414547. 60 rms. TV TEL. £56 ($88.50) single or double. English breakfast £7.95 ($12.55) extra. AE, DC, MC, V. Free parking.

An 18th-century Georgian facade with tall, narrow windows fronts this hotel, which looks out over the swans of Avon near Clopton Bridge. The complex is surrounded by gardens on a low, flat area beside a canal, a five-minute drive south of the Royal Shakespeare Theatre leading toward Oxford. The bedrooms are comfortably modern and filled with tasteful furnishings; most are located in a modern, red-brick extension. Amenities include a radio and hot-beverage facilities.

The River Bar offers a view of the planting outside. The Swan Nest Restaurant serves food in a room lined with early 19th-century paintings. A la carte dinners cost around £17.50 ($27.65).

Sequoia House

51–53 Shipston Rd., Stratford-upon-Avon, Warwickshire CV37 7LN. ☎ **01789/268852.** Fax 01789/414559. 24 rms (20 with bath or shower). TV TEL. £39 ($61.60) double without bath, £69 ($109) double with bath. Rates include English breakfast. AE, DC, MC, V. Free parking.

This privately run hotel has its own beautiful garden on three-quarters of an acre across the Avon, conveniently located for visiting the major Shakespeare properties of the National Trust. It's also within easy walking distance of the theater. In fact, the hotel is just across the Avon River opposite the theater. Renovation has vastly improved the house, which was created from two late Victorian buildings. Today it offers rooms with beverage-making equipment and hot and cold running water. Guests gather in a lounge that has a licensed bar and an open Victorian fireplace. The hotel also has a private parking area.

⑤ Stratford House

18 Sheep St., Stratford-upon-Avon, Warwickshire CV37 6EF. ☎ **01789/268288.** Fax 01789/295580. 10 rms (all with bath or shower), 1 family rm. TV TEL. £78–£88 ($123.25–$139.05)

double; £120 ($189.60) suite. Rates include English breakfast. AE, DC, MC, V. Parking £3 ($4.75).

This Georgian house stands 100 yards from the River Avon and the Royal Shakespeare Theatre. The staff of this small hotel extends a warm welcome to North American guests. The house is furnished tastefully and with style, somewhat like a private home, with books and pictures along with a scattering of antiques. Everything is spotlessly maintained. There is a walled courtyard on the side with flowering plants. All bedrooms have tea and coffee makers. Both hotel guests and outsiders can dine in the garden restaurant, Shepherd's, recommended separately (see "Where to Dine," below).

ⓢ Stratheden Hotel

5 Chapel St., Stratford-upon-Avon, Warwickshire CV37 6EP. ☎ **01789/297119.** Fax 01789/ 297119. 9 rms. TV TEL. £48–£56 ($75.85–$88.50) double. Rates include English breakfast. MC, V.

Tucked away in a desirable position on a plot of land that was first mentioned in a property deed in 1333, a short walk north of the Royal Shakespeare Theatre, is the Stratheden Hotel. Built in 1673 (and today the oldest-remaining brick building in the town center), it has a tiny rear garden and top-floor rooms with slanted, beamed ceilings. Under the ownership of the Wells family for the past quarter century, it has improved in both decor and comfort with the addition of fresh paint, new curtains, and good beds. The glass cupboard in the entry hallway holds family heirlooms and collector's items. The dining room, with a bay window, has an overscale sideboard that once belonged to the "insanely vain" Marie Corelli, an eccentric novelist, poet, and mystic, and a favorite author of Queen Victoria. The Victorian novelist (1855–1924) was noted for her passion for pastoral settings and objets d'art. You can see an example of her taste: a massive mahogany tester bed in Room 4.

ⓢ Victoria Spa Lodge

Bishopton Lane, Stratford-upon-Avon, Warwickshire CV37 9QY. ☎ **01789/267985.** Fax 01789/204728. 7 rms. TV. £39–£50 ($61.60–$79) single or double. Rates include English breakfast. MC, V. Free parking.

Overlooking Stratford Canal, 1¹/₂ miles north of the town center where A3400 intersects A46, this lodge was originally a spa. Opened in 1837, the year Queen Victoria ascended to the throne, it was the first establishment to be given her name. The queen's eldest daughter, Princess Vicky, stayed here when it was a spa. Once it was the home of the famous cartoonist, Bruce Bairnsfather. Accommodating hosts Paul and Dreen Tozer offer tastefully decorated and comfortable bedrooms with such amenities as color TV, radio alarms, and hair dryer. A full English breakfast is offered or a vegetarian alternative. Breakfast is served in a cheerful antique-furnished dining room. Pleasant walks are possible along the path to Stratford.

IN NEARBY ALDERMINSTER

Expensive

✪ Ettington Park Hotel

Alderminster, near Stratford-upon-Avon, Warwickshire CV37 8BS. ☎ **01789/450123.** Fax 01789/450472. 39 rms, 9 suites. TV TEL. £145 ($229.10) double; £180 ($284.40) suite. Rates include English breakfast. AE, DC, MC, V. Free parking. Drive on A3400 toward Oxford.

This Victorian Gothic mansion is one of the most sumptuous retreats in Shakespeare Country. It opened as a hotel in 1985, but has a history that spans more than nine centuries. The land is a legacy of the Shirley family, whose 12th-century burial chapel stands near the hotel. Like a grand private home, the hotel boasts baronial fireplaces, a conservatory, and a charming staff. The Adam ceilings, stone carvings, and ornate staircases have all been beautifully restored. A new wing, assembled with the same stone and neo-Gothic carving of the original house, stretches toward a Renaissance-style arbor entwined with vines. The giant sequoias, ancient yews, and cedars are surrounded by lawns and terraced gardens, whose flowers and ferns cascade toward a rock-lined stream. The bedrooms conjure memories of another era, yet the most modern comforts are concealed behind antique facades.

Dining/Entertainment: In the dining room, the Shirley family crest is inlaid in hundreds of marquetry depictions in the carved and burnished paneling. The cuisine is a medley of English and French specialties, a fixed-price dinner costing £28 ($44.25).

Services: 24-hour room service, laundry.

Facilities: Jacuzzi, indoor swimming pool, sauna, tennis.

IN NEARBY WILMCOTE

⑤ Swan House Hotel
The Green, Wilmcote, Stratford-upon-Avon, Warwickshire CV37 9XJ. ☎ **01789/267030.** Fax 01789/204875. 12 rms (all with bath or shower). TV. £55–£66 ($86.90–$104.30) double. Rates include English breakfast. AE, MC, V. Free parking. Take A3400 3^1/$_2$ miles northwest of Stratford.

Shakespeare's mother, Mary Arden, lived in this tiny village where you'll find the tranquil Swan House. Actually an upgraded village pub-hotel, it offers not only appealing and well-furnished bedrooms at moderate prices, but also good meals. Amenities include hot-beverage makers, and a four-poster bed is available.

Homemade hot and cold bar snacks and meals are served in the popular beamed bar with an open fire and the original well. The bar offers four real ales at lunch and in the evening. Guests can eat outdoors in the large garden with a sun terrace in summer.

WHERE TO DINE
MODERATE

The Box Tree Restaurant
In the Royal Shakespeare Theatre, Waterside. ☎ **01789/293226.** Reservations required. Matinee lunch £15.50 ($24.50); dinner £23.50 ($37.15). AE, MC, V. Thurs–Sat noon–2:30pm, Mon–Sat 5:45pm–midnight. FRENCH/ITALIAN/ENGLISH.

This restaurant is in the best location in town—right in the theater itself—with glass walls providing an unobstructed view of the Avon and its swans. During intermission there is a snack feast of smoked salmon and champagne. After each evening's performance you can dine by flickering candlelight. There's a special phone for reservations in the theater lobby. Many dishes are definitely old English (apple and parsnip soup); others reflect a continental touch, such as fried polenta with fillets of pigeon and bacon. For your main course, you might select Dover sole, salmi of wild boar, pheasant suprême, or roast loin of pork. Homemade desserts are likely to include crème brûlée, an old-time favorite at The Box Tree.

Giovanni
8 Ely St. ☎ **01789/297999.** Reservations required. Main courses £6.90–£13.80 ($10.90–$21.80). MC, V. Mon–Sat noon–2pm and 6–11:30pm. ITALIAN.

Actors favor this intimate restaurant housed in a yellow-brick cottage with an Italianate facade. The trattoria includes a cocktail lounge with antiques. The classic Italian menu begins with minestrone and includes such pasta dishes as lasagne and cannelloni, as well as offerings like escalope piemontese and scampi Provençale. A good Italian dessert is the zabaglione, although it is prepared for two or more diners. A selection of excellent continental ices is also featured, including everything from Italian cassata to *mela stregata*.

Liaison

1 Shakespeare Street. ☎ **01789/293400.** Reservations recommended. Main courses £12.50–£15.75 ($19.75–$24.90). Set lunch £12.50 ($19.75); set dinner £19.50 ($30.80). AE, DC, MC, V. Mon–Fri noon–2:30pm; Mon–Sat 6–10:30pm. MODERN BRITISH.

Situated conveniently close to Shakespeare's birthplace (within a three-minute walk), in the heart of Stratford, this restaurant occupies the high-ceilinged premises of what was formerly a Methodist chapel built in 1854. (Until 1993, it also functioned for a brief period as an automobile museum.) Menu choices are modern and elegant, loosely based on traditional British cuisine, with creative input from contemporary sources. Examples include a lobster club sandwich, a trio of salmon (comprising portions of marinated salmon, tartare of salmon, and poached fillet of salmon), an old-fashioned confit of duckling, and a traditional version of bread and butter pudding.

Shepherd's Garden Restaurant

In the Stratford House Hotel, 18 Sheep St. ☎ **01789/268288.** Reservations recommended. Lunch platters £4.95–£5.95 ($7.80–$9.40). Dinner main courses £7.50–£10.95 ($11.85–$17.30). AE, DC, MC, V. Mon–Sat 10am–6pm and 5:45–9:15pm. ENGLISH/FRENCH.

Light and airy, this restaurant has a skylit conservatory look and a loyal clientele of local residents who drop by for simple lunches and for more elaborate dinners. Lunches are within a lounge-style setting which spills out during nice weather onto a walled outdoor patio. Evening meals are accented with cascading vines and potted plants—a suitable setting for the dinners served to many of the directors and actors from the nearby theaters. Cuisine is English and French, and might include a terrine of salmon and scallops; grilled goat's cheese with marinated peppers; chicken livers pan-fried in whiskey; fillets of chicken with herbs; and boeuf bourguignonne. Vegetarian main courses are likely to include macaroni with cheese and leeks, and a fricassé of wild mushrooms.

INEXPENSIVE

⑤ Hussain's

6A Chapel St. ☎ **01789/267506.** Reservations recommended. Main courses £5.75–£10.95 ($9.10–$17.30). AE, DC, MC, V. Daily noon–2pm and 5:15–11:45pm. INDIAN.

Dining here has been compared to a visit to a private Indian home. The restaurant has many admirers—some consider it one of the brighter spots on the culinary landscape. At least it pleased actor Ben Kingsley. The owner has chosen a well-trained, alert staff, who welcome guests, advising them about special dishes. Against a setting of pink crushed-velvet paneling, you can select from an array of northern India dishes. Herbs and spices are blended imaginatively in the kitchen to impart a distinctive flavor. Many tandoori dishes are offered, along with various curries with lamb or prawn. Hussain's is across from the Shakespeare Hotel and historic New Place.

⑤ The Box Tree/The River Terrace Restaurant

In the Royal Shakespeare Theatre, Waterside. ☎ **01789/293226.** Reservations required. At Box Tree, set lunch or dinner £23.50 ($37.15). At River Terrace, main courses £6.50–£7 ($10.25–$11.05). AE, MC, V accepted at Box Tree; no credit cards at the River Terrace. Box Tree, Thurs and Sat noon–2pm; daily 5:45–11:30pm. River Terrace, Mon–Sat 10:30am–9:30pm; Sun 10:30am–5pm. Closed one week in Feb. ENGLISH.

This pair of restaurants satisfies the hunger pangs of actors, directors, stage hands, and members of the audience. The more formal of the two venues is the Box Tree, where English meals are served with style by a polite and hardworking staff. Less formal is the River Terrace, whose view extends over the back of the theater as far as the River Avon. In its own way, the River Terrace is probably the most arts-oriented self-service restaurant in Britain, site of welcome doses of caffeine and salad offered to some of the best Shakespearean actors around. Menu choices include typical English and pasta dishes, baked ham, and vegetarian dishes, as well as morning coffee and afternoon tea.

The Opposition

13 Sheep Street. ☎ **01789/269980.** Reservations recommended. Main courses £5.50–£12.50 ($8.70–$19.75). MC, V. Mon–Sat noon–2pm; daily 5:30–11pm. INTERNATIONAL.

Located in the heart of Stratford, within a 16th-century building whose twin dining rooms are both sheathed with exposed timbers and old bricks, this is a refreshingly unpretentious restaurant with a high turnover of loyal clients. Its name has nothing to do with Parliamentary or governmental processes, as many English residents think. Instead, the present owners kept a name that dates back to sibling rivalry between its original founder (a woman) and her brother who owned a competing restaurant (The Opposition) next door. Morning coffee, tea cakes, and croissants are sold Monday to Saturday from 11am to noon, but most people appreciate the place for a meal. Menu choices include chicken (cooked with spinach, stuffed with mango and curry, or prepared Cajun-style); salmon (either grilled or poached and served with hollandaise); and grilled sirloin or fillet of beef. In case you wondered what Banoffi pie is (a specialty here), it's made with toffee, bananas, biscuits, and whipped cream.

PUBS

The Black Swan (also known as the Dirty Duck)

Waterside. ☎ **01789/297312.** Reservations required. Main courses £6–£14 ($9.50–$22.10); bar snacks £1–£3.65 ($1.60–$5.75); pint of ale £1.80 ($2.85). MC, V (restaurant only). Pub, Mon–Sat 11am–11pm, Sun noon–3pm and 7–10:30pm. Restaurant, Tues–Sun noon–2pm; Mon–Sat 6–11:30pm. ENGLISH.

Affectionately known as the Dirty Duck, this has been a popular hangout for Stratford players since the 18th century. The wall is lined with auto-graphed photos of its patrons, some of long ago such as Lord Olivier. The front lounge and bar crackles with intense conversation. In the spring and fall an open fire blazes. In the Dirty Duck Grill Room, typical English grills, among other dishes, are featured. You'll be faced with a choice of a dozen appetizers, most of which would make a meal in themselves. Main dishes include braised kidneys or oxtails, roast chicken, or honey-roasted duck. In fair weather you can have drinks in the front garden and watch the swans on the Avon glide by.

The Garrick Inn

25 High St. ☎ **01789/292186.** Reservations not accepted. Main courses £5–£9 ($7.90–$14.20). MC, V. Meals daily noon–8:30pm. Pub, Mon–Sat 11am–11pm, Sun noon–3pm and 7–10:30pm. ENGLISH.

This black-and-white timbered Elizabethan pub from 1595 near Harvard House has an unpretentious charm. It's named after David Garrick, one of England's greatest actors. The front bar is decorated with tapestry-covered settles, an old oak refectory table, and an open fireplace which attracts the locals. The black bar has a circular fireplace with a copper hood and mementos of the triumphs of the English stage. The pub is open on Sunday from 3 to 7pm, but only to those dining here. The specialty is homemade pies such as steak and ale, steak and kidney, or chicken and mushroom.

The White Swan

Rother St. ☎ **01789/297022.** Reservations recommended. Bar snacks £2–£6 ($3.15–$9.50); 3-course fixed-price dinner £16.95 ($26.80). AE, DC, MC, V. Morning coffee daily 10am–noon; self-service bar snacks daily noon–2pm; afternoon tea daily 2–5pm; dinner Mon–Thurs 6–9pm, Fri–Sat 6–9:30pm, Sun 7–9pm. ENGLISH.

This is one of the most atmospheric pubs in Stratford-upon-Avon, in the oldest building in town (see the hotel of the same name recommendation in "Where to Stay," above). Once you step inside, you're drawn into a world of cushioned leather armchairs, old oak settles, oak paneling, and fireplaces. Despite the fact that everyone seems to be looking for her, Emma Thompson has never been sighted in this historic pub. You're much more likely, however, to meet a worthy cross-section of amiable drinkers who revel in a setting once enjoyed by Will Shakespeare himself when it was known as the Kings Head. At lunch you can partake of the hot dishes of the day, along with fresh salads and sandwiches.

2 Warwick

92 miles NW of London, 8 miles NE of Stratford-upon-Avon

Most visitors come to this town just to see Warwick Castle. Then they're off on their next adventure, usually to the ruins of Kenilworth Castle (see below). But the historic center of medieval Warwick has a lot more to offer.

In 1694 a fire swept through the heart of Warwick, destroying large parts of the town, but a number of Elizabethan and medieval buildings still survive, along with some fine Georgian structures from a later date. (Very few traces of the town walls remain, except the East and West Gates.) Warwick cites Ethelfleda, daughter of Alfred the Great, as its founder. But most of its history is associated with the earls of Warwick, a title created by the son of William the Conqueror in 1088. The story of those earls—the Beaumonts, the Beauchamps (such figures as "Kingmaker" Richard Neville)—makes for an exciting episode in English history.

ESSENTIALS

GETTING THERE

By Train   Trains run frequently between Stratford-upon-Avon and Warwick.

By Bus   One Midland Red bus per hour (no. 18 or X16) departs Stratford-upon-Avon during the day (trip time: 15–20 min.).

By Car   You can approach Warwick via A46 from Stratford-upon-Avon.

VISITOR INFORMATION

The **telephone area code** is 01926. The **Tourist Information Centre** is at The Court House, Jury Street (☎ **01926/492212**).

WHAT TO SEE & DO

✪ Warwick Castle

Castle Hill. ☎ **01926/408000.** Admission £8.25 ($13.05) adults, £4.25 ($6.70) children 4–16, £5.95 ($9.40) senior citizens, £6.25 ($9.90) students. Free for children 3 and under. Daily 10am–6pm. Closed Christmas Day.

Perched on a rocky cliff above the Avon in the town center, this stately late-17th-century-style mansion is surrounded by a magnificent 14th-century fortress. The importance of the site has long been recognized. The first significant fortifications at Warwick were built by Ethelfleda, daughter of Alfred the Great, in 915. Two years after the Norman Conquest in 1068, William the Conqueror ordered the construction of a motte and baily castle. The castle mound is all that remains today of the Norman castle, as this was sacked by Simon de Montfort in the Barons' War of 1264.

The Beauchamp family, the most illustrious medieval earls of Warwick, are responsible for the appearance of the castle today, and much of the external structure remains unchanged from the mid-14th century. When the castle was granted to Sir Fulke Greville by James I in 1604, he spent £20,000 (an enormous sum in those days) converting the existing castle buildings into a luxurious mansion. The Grevilles have held the earl of Warwick title since 1759, when it passed from the Rich family.

The staterooms and Great Hall house fine collections of paintings, furniture, arms, and armor. The armory, dungeon, torture chamber, ghost tower, clock tower, and Guy's tower create a vivid picture of the castle's turbulent past and its important role in the history of England.

The private apartments of Lord Brooke and his family, who in recent years sold the castle to Tussaud's Group, are open to visitors. They house a display of a carefully reconstructed Royal Weekend House Party of 1898. The major rooms contain wax portraits of important figures of the time: young Winston Churchill; the duchess of Devonshire; Winston's widowed mother, Jennie; and Clara Butt, the celebrated singer, along with the earl and countess of Warwick and their family. In the Kenilworth bedroom, the Prince of Wales, later King Edward VII, reads a letter, and in the red bedroom the duchess of Marlborough prepares for her bath. Among the most lifelike of the figures is a little uniformed maid who is bending over a bathtub into which water is running to test the temperature. Surrounded by gardens, lawns, and woodland, where peacocks roam freely, and skirted by the Avon, Warwick Castle was described by Sir Walter Scott in 1828 as "that fairest monument of ancient and chivalrous splendor which yet remains uninjured by time."

Visitors can also see the Victorian rose garden, a re-creation of an original design from 1868 by Robert Marnock. The original garden had fallen into disrepair, and a tennis court was built on the site. In 1980, however, it was decided to restore the garden and, as luck would have it, Marnock's original plans were discovered in the county records office. Close by the rose garden is a Victorian alpine rockery and water garden. The romantic castle is host to various colorful pageants.

St. Mary's Church

Warwick Parish Office, Old Sq. ☎ **01926/400771.** Admission free; donations accepted. Apr–Sept, 10am–6pm; Oct–Mar 10am–4pm. All buses to Warwick stop at Old Square.

Destroyed in part by the fire of 1694, this church with its rebuilt battlemented tower and nave is considered among the finest examples of late 17th- and early 18th-century architecture. The Beauchamp Chapel, spared from the flames, encases the Purbeck marble tomb of Richard Beauchamp, a well-known earl of Warwick who died in 1439 and is commemorated by a gilded bronze effigy. The most powerful man in the kingdom, not excepting Henry V, Beauchamp has a tomb considered one of the finest remaining examples of perpendicular-Gothic style from the mid-15th century. The tomb of Robert Dudley, earl of Leicester, a favorite of Elizabeth I, is against the north wall. The perpendicular-Gothic choir dates from the 14th century, and the Norman crypt and the chapter house are from the 11th century.

Lord Leycester Hospital

High St. ☎ **01926/491422.** Admission £2 ($3.15) adults, £1 ($1.60) children. Easter–Oct, Tues–Sun 10am–5pm; Nov–Easter, Tues–Sun 10am–4pm.

At the West Gate, this group of half-timbered almshouses was also spared from the great fire. The buildings were erected about 1400, and the hospital was founded in 1571 by Robert Dudley, earl of Leicester, as a home for old soldiers. It's in use by ex-service personnel and their spouses today. On top of the West Gate is the attractive little chapel of St. James, dating from the 12th century but renovated many times since.

Warwick Doll Museum

Oken's House, Castle St. ☎ **01926/495546.** Admission £1 ($1.60) adults, 70p ($1.10) children. Easter–Sept, daily 10am–5pm; Oct–Easter, Sat–Sun 10am–4pm.

One of the most charming Elizabethan buildings in Warwick houses this doll museum, near St. Mary's Church. Founded in 1955, its seven rooms display an extensive collection of dolls in wood, wax, and porcelain. Off Jury Street in the center, the house once belonged to Thomas Oken, a great benefactor of Warwick.

Warwickshire Museum

Market Hall, The Market Place. ☎ **01926/412500.** Admission free. Mon–Sat 10am–5:30pm, Sun (May–Sept) 2–5pm. From Jury St. in the center, take a right onto Swan St., which leads to the museum.

This museum was established in 1836 to house a collection of geological remains, fossils, and an exhibit of amphibians from the Triassic period. There are also displays illustrating the history, archaeology, and natural history of the county, including the famous Sheldon tapestry map.

St. John's House Museum

St. John's. ☎ **01926/412021.** Admission free. Oct–Apr, Tues–Sat 10am–12:30pm and 1:30–5:30pm; May–Sept, Tues–Sat 10am–12:30pm and 1:30–5:30pm, Sun 2:30–5pm.

At Coten End, not far from the castle gates, is this early 17th-century house with exhibits on Victorian domestic life. A schoolroom is furnished with original 19th-century school furniture and equipment. During the school term, Warwickshire children, dressed in period costumes, can be seen learning Victorian-style lessons. Groups of children also use the Victorian parlor and the kitchen. Since it's impossible to display more than a small number of items at a time, a study room is available where you can see objects from the reserve collections. The costume collection is a particularly fine one, and visitors can study the drawings and photos that make up the costume catalog. These facilities are available by appointment only. Upstairs is a military museum, tracing the history of the Royal Warwickshire Regiment from 1674 to the present day. For more information or for an appointment to use the study room, telephone the Keeper of Social History at the number above. St. John's House is at the crossroads of the main Warwick-Leamington road (A425/A429) and the Coventry road (A429).

WHERE TO STAY

Many people prefer to stay in Warwick and commute to Stratford-upon-Avon.

MODERATE

Hilton National Warwick/Stratford

Warwick Bypass (A429 Warwick Rd.), Warwick, Warwickshire CV34 6RE. ☎ **01926/499555** or 800/445-8667 in the U.S. and Canada. Fax 01926/410020. 161 rms, 20 junior suites. TV TEL. £90 ($142.20) single or double; £105 ($165.90) suite. English breakfast £10.25 ($16.20) extra. AE, DC, MC, V. Free parking. Take A429 2 miles north of Warwick (7 miles north of Stratford-upon-Avon).

This Hilton is at the elbow junction of a network of highways, making it popular with commercial travelers. It has a hutch-style, low-slung modern design of earth-colored brick, and a series of interconnected bars, lounges, and public areas, as well as a heated indoor swimming pool. The establishment hosts many conferences and sales meetings for local companies. Foreign visitors find that its standardized comfort and easy-to-find location make it a good base for touring Warwick and the surrounding regions. The rooms are well furnished, and there is 24-hour room service. The hotel's Sonnetts Restaurant offers a three-course carvery lunch at £11.95 ($18.90) and a three-course carvery dinner at £17.50 ($27.65).

INEXPENSIVE

Lord Leycester Hotel (Calotels)

17 Jury St., Warwick, Warwickshire CV34 4EJ. ☎ **01926/491481.** Fax 01926/491561. 52 rms (all with bath or shower). TV TEL. £69.50 ($109.80) double; Fri–Sun £60 ($94.80) double. Rates include English breakfast. AE, DC, MC, V. Free parking.

In 1726 this manor house belonged to Lord Archer of Umberslade. Years later it was converted into an inn under the sign of the three tuns (wine casks); still later, it once again became a private residence. In 1926 it was finally turned into a hotel. Each comfortable bedroom is equipped with a radio and hot-beverage maker. A small à la carte English menu is offered in the dining room, or you can have snacks in Alexander's Bar. Meals begin at £11.25 ($17.80). There is a large parking lot at the rear of the hotel, within walking distance of the castle and other historic buildings of Warwick.

⑤ Tudor House Inn & Restaurant

90–92 West St., Warwick, Warwickshire CV34 6AW. ☎ **01926/495447.** Fax 01926/492948. 11 rms (8 with bath or shower). TV TEL. £54 ($85.30) double with bath. Rates include English breakfast. AE, DC, MC, V. Free parking. 1/2 mile south on A429, opposite the main car park for Warwick Castle.

At the edge of town is a black-and-white timbered inn built in 1472. It's one of the few buildings to escape the fire that destroyed High Street in 1694. Off the central hall are two large rooms, each of which could be the setting for an Elizabethan play. All bedrooms have washbasins, and two have doors only four feet high. In the corner of the lounge is an open turning staircase. Bar snacks range from £1.50 to £10 ($2.35 to $15.80), and in the restaurant main courses cost from £5 to £12 ($7.90 to $18.95) each. Tudor House is on the main road from Stratford-upon-Avon leading to Warwick Castle.

WHERE TO DINE
INEXPENSIVE

Nicolini's Bistro

18 Jury St. ☎ **01926/495817.** Reservations recommended. Main courses £8.75–£15.50 ($13.85–$24.50). AE, DC, MC, V. Mon–Sat noon–2pm and 6–10:30pm. ITALIAN.

Established in 1979, this restaurant features an appealing blend of the cuisines from northern and central Italy. Lynne and Nicky, as they are known locally, welcome you into their pleasant restaurant decorated with greenery. Check out the crisp salads and luscious desserts. You're faced with an array of appetizers, including king prawns cooked in garlic butter or Nicky's polenta served with a napoletana sauce and baked in the oven. Pastas such as lasagne can be ordered either as an appetizer or a main course. Main courses include daily specialties, as well as such standard Italian fare as pork marsala or veal milanese. The restaurant is located in the center of town near the castle.

3 Kenilworth

5 miles N of Warwick, 13 miles N of Stratford-upon-Avon, 102 miles NW of London

The major attraction here is **Kenilworth Castle,** Kenilworth (☎ 52078), which at one time had walls that enclosed an area of 7 acres, but is now in magnificent ruins. It is the subject of Sir Walter Scott's romance *Kenilworth.* In 1957 Lord Kenilworth presented the decaying castle to England, and limited restoration has since been carried out.

The castle was built by Geoffrey de Clinton, a lieutenant of Henry I. Caesar's Tower, with its 16-foot-thick walls, is all that remains of the original castle. Edward II was forced to abdicate at Kenilworth in 1327, before being carried off to Berkeley Castle in Gloucestershire, where he was undoubtedly murdered. In 1563 Elizabeth I gave the castle to her favorite, Robert Dudley, earl of Leicester. The earl built the gate house, which the queen visited on several occasions. After the Civil War, the Roundheads were responsible for breaching the outer walls and towers and blowing up the north wall of the keep. This was the only damage inflicted following the earl of Monmouth's plea that it be "Slighted with as little spoil to the dwellinghouse as might be."

Admission is £1.85 ($2.90) for adults, £1 ($1.60) for children 5 to 16 (under 4, free). Seniors pay £1.50 ($2.35). From Good Friday to the end of September, the castle is open daily from 10am to 6pm; in other months, daily from 10am to 4pm. The castle is closed January 1 and December 24 to 26.

ESSENTIALS
GETTING THERE

By Train   From London (both Paddington and Euston stations) InterCity train lines make frequent and fast connections to either Coventry or Stratford-upon-Avon, from which Midland Red Line buses make regular connections into Kenilworth.

By Bus   Midland Red Line buses run frequently from either Stratford-upon-Avon or Coventry.

By Car   From Warwick (see above), drive to Kenilworth on A46, toward Coventry.

VISITOR INFORMATION

The **telephone area code** is 01926. The **Tourist Information Centre** is at the Kenilworth Library, 11 Smalley Place (☎ **01926/52595**).

WHERE TO STAY
INEXPENSIVE

⊛ Clarendon House Hotel

6–8 Old High St., Kenilworth, Warwickshire CV8 1LZ. ☎ **01926/57668.** Fax 01926/50669. 31 rms (all with bath or shower). TV TEL. £65 ($102.70) double. Rates include English breakfast. MC, V. Free parking.

A family-run hotel and restaurant, the Clarendon House is in the old part of Kenilworth. The oak tree around which the original alehouse was built in 1430 is still supporting the roof of the building today. The present owners welcome guests to spend the night in one of the tastefully decorated rooms.

Before the evening meal, guests gather in the timbered and oak-paneled Royalist Retreat Bar and lounges. The hotel's Cromwell's Bistro restaurant is housed in what was once the inn stable. The oddly timbered room is decorated with antique maps and armor, constant reminders that a Cromwellian garrison once stayed at the inn during a siege of Kenilworth Castle. In season you could dine on such specialties as jugged hare, pheasant georgienne (marinated in Madeira wine with oranges, grapes, and walnuts), grouse, or mallard (wild duck cooked in red wine, mushrooms, and fines herbes). Lunch at this establishment is always in the form of bar meals, priced from £1.50 to £5.50 ($2.35 to $8.70). Bar lunches are served Monday through Saturday from noon to 1:45pm. At Sunday lunch, a fixed-price menu is offered for £9.50 ($15) for three courses. A la carte meals, served in the more formal restaurant, range from £20 to £22 ($31.60 to $34.75), and service is from 7 to 9:30pm Sunday through Thursday and from 7 to 10pm on Friday and Saturday.

WHERE TO DINE
MODERATE

Restaurant Bosquet

97A Warwick Rd. ☎ **01926/52463.** Reservations required. Main courses £14.50–£15.50 ($22.90–$24.50); fixed-price dinners £21 ($33.20). AE, MC, V. Tues–Sat 7–9pm. Closed last 3 weeks in August. FRENCH.

This narrow, stone-fronted town house from the late Victorian age is a culinary oasis in Kenilworth. It's owned and operated by French-born Bernard Lignier (who does the cooking) and his English wife, Jane, who supervises the dining room. The à la carte menu changes with the seasons and might include such French-inspired food as terrine of wild duck with foie gras and truffles, saddle of venison with mandarin oranges and juniper berries; saddle of lamb coated with truffles, and a dessert specialty known as an *assiette* of chocolates.

East Anglia: Cambridgeshire, Essex, Suffolk & Norfolk

The four counties of East Anglia—Essex, Suffolk, Norfolk, and Cambridgeshire—are essentially bucolic. East Anglia was an ancient Anglo-Saxon kingdom dominated by the Danes. Beginning in the 12th century, its cloth industry brought it prosperity, which is apparent today in the impressive spires of some of its churches. In part, it's a land of heaths, fens, marshes, and "broads" in Norfolk. Cambridge is the most-visited city in East Anglia, but don't ignore Suffolk and Essex—Constable Country—with some of the finest landscapes in England. Norwich, the seat of the dukes of Norfolk, is less popular, but those who do venture toward the North Sea will be rewarded.

CAMBRIDGESHIRE

Most visitors gravitate toward Cambridge, the center of Cambridgeshire, but those with more time may want to visit some of the county itself, especially the cathedral city of Ely. Cambridgeshire is in large part an agricultural region, with some distinct geographic features, including the black peat soil of the Fens, a district crisscrossed by dikes and drainage ditches. Many old villages and market towns abound, including Peterborough, which sits on the divide between the flat Fens and the "wolds" of the East Midlands. Birdwatchers, fishing enthusiasts, walkers, and cyclists are all drawn to the area.

Many famous figures in English history came from this land, including Oliver Cromwell (1699–1758), the Lord Protector during the English Civil War.

ESSEX

Even though it's close to London and industrialized in places, Essex is a land of rolling fields with unspoiled rural areas and villages. Most motorists pass through it on the way to Cambridge. In the east there are many seaside towns and villages.

The major city is Colchester, in the east, known for its oysters and roses. Fifty miles from London, it was the first Roman city in Britain and is the oldest-recorded town in the kingdom. Parts of its Roman fortifications remain. A Norman castle has been turned into a museum, housing a fine collection of Roman-British artifacts. Among the former residents of Colchester were King Cole, subject of the nursery rhyme, and Cunobelinus, the warrior king, Shakespeare's Cymbeline.

What's Special About East Anglia

Great Towns/Villages
- Cambridge, one of the world's oldest and greatest universities, on the River Cam with 31 colleges.
- Thaxted, a "classic" East Anglia small town with outstanding buildings, dominated by a hilltop medieval church.
- Long Melford, one of Suffolk's loveliest villages, remarkable for the length of its High Street.
- Lavenham, the showplace of Suffolk small towns, a symphony of color-washed buildings.

Castle
- Sandringham, the country home of British monarchs since the days of King Edward VII.

Architectural Highlights
- King's College Chapel, Cambridge, founded by the adolescent Henry VI in 1441; Henry James called it "the most beautiful in England."
- Audley End House, outside Saffron Walden, a Jacobean mansion, considered the finest in East Anglia.

Cathedrals
- Ely Cathedral, dating from 1081, a handsome example of the perpendicular style.
- Norwich Cathedral, dating from 1096, with two-story cloisters—the only one of its type in England.

However, since Colchester is not on the route of most visitors, I have focused instead on tiny villages in the western part of Essex, including Saffron Walden and Thaxted, which represent the best part of the shire. You can explore all of East Anglia quite easily on your way to Cambridge or on your return trip to London. They lie roughly 25 to 30 miles south of Cambridge.

SUFFOLK

The easternmost county of England, Suffolk is a refuge for artists, just as it was in the day of its famous native sons, Constable and Gainsborough. Through them, many of the Suffolk landscapes have been preserved on canvas.

A fast train can make it from London to East Suffolk in approximately 1½ hours. Still, its fishing villages, dozens of flint churches, historic homes, and national monuments remain far removed from mainstream tourism in England.

The major towns of Suffolk are Bury St. Edmunds, the capital of West Suffolk, and Ipswich in the east, a port city on the Orwell River. But to capture the true charm of Suffolk, you must explore its little market towns and villages. Beginning at the Essex border, we'll head toward the North Sea, highlighting the most scenic villages as we move eastward across the shire.

NORFOLK

Bounded by the North Sea, Norfolk is the biggest of the East Anglian counties. It's a low-lying area, with fens, heaths, and salt marshes. An occasional dike or windmill makes you think you're in the Netherlands. One feature of Norfolk is its network of Broads—miles and miles of lagoons, shallow in part, connected by streams. Summer sports people flock to Norfolk to hire boats for sailing or fishing.

From Norwich itself, Wroxham, capital of the Broads, is easily reached, only eight miles to the northeast. Motorboats regularly leave from this resort, taking parties on short trips. Some of the best scenery of the Broads is to be found on the periphery of Wroxham.

A DRIVING TOUR

Day 1   From London, drive north to Cambridge on M11. The distance is only 55 miles and you'll arrive in time for lunch. Visit the most interesting colleges in the afternoon, especially King's College, and plan to spend the night there. Also see the Fitzwilliam Museum. If possible, work in a punting trip along the River Cam.

☕ **TAKE A BREAK**   King's Pantry, King's Parade, across from King's College (☎ 01223/321551), is a cellar whole-food and vegetarian establishment with fewer than a dozen tables. A three-course lunch goes for only £6.95 ($11); if you're around for dinner, the set price is only £11 ($17.40). Hours are Monday through Saturday from 8am to 5pm and 6 to 9:30pm; Sunday, 8am to 6pm.

Day 2   After an overnight stay in Cambridge, drive along A10 the next morning to visit Ely and its cathedral. Then dip south again for an overnight stay in either Thaxted or Saffron Walden on B1383, and visit Audley End House.

Day 3   From Thaxted or Saffron Walden, head east, enjoying a luncheon stopover in Long Melford before visiting Lavenham for an overnight stay. If it's in your budget range, stay at the Swan.

Day 4   Visit Sandringham Castle, north of Norwich, but make Norwich your overnight stopover. It has a range of accommodations in all price ranges, and as the capital of East Anglia is a worthy destination itself. Visit both Norwich Cathedral and Norwich Castle if time permits.

☕ **TAKE A BREAK**   The Mecca, 5 Orford Hill, off Bell Avenue (☎ 01603/614829), in Norwich, is the town's best deli; it also includes a tea shop and a vegetarian restaurant—all on different floors. Hours are Monday through Saturday from 8:30am to 5:30pm. After visiting the cathedral, drop by for afternoon tea which is served from 2:30pm.

1 Cambridge

55 miles N of London, 80 miles NE of Oxford

Cambridge is a college of images: the Bridge of Sighs; spires and turrets; drooping willows that witness much punting; dusty secondhand bookshops; carol singing on Christmas Eve in King's College Chapel; dancing until sunrise at the May balls; the sound of Elizabethan madrigals; narrow lanes where Darwin, Newton, and Cromwell once walked; the "Backs," where the lawns of the colleges sweep down to the Cam River; the tattered black robe of a hurrying upperclassman flying in the wind.

Impressions

Next morning went with H.M. [his mentor, Horace Moule, son of the Vicar of Fordington] to King's Chapel early. M. opened the great West doors to show the interior vista: we got upon the roof where we could see Ely Cathedral gleaming in the distant sunlight. A never-to-be-forgotten morning. H.M. saw me off for London. His last smile.

—Thomas Hardy

The university city of Cambridge, along with Oxford, is one of the ancient seats of learning in Britain. The city on the banks of the Cam River is also the county town of Cambridgeshire. In many ways the stories of Oxford and Cambridge are similar—particularly the age-old conflict between town and gown. But beyond the campus, Oxford has a thriving, high-tech industry.

There is much to explore in Cambridge—so give yourself time to wander, even aimlessly. For those who are pressed, I'll offer more specific direction.

There are many historic buildings in the city center, all within walking distance, including Great St. Mary's Church (from which the original Westminster chimes come), St. Benet's Church, the Round Church, the Fitzwilliam Museum (one of the largest and finest provincial museums), the Folk Museum, and the modern Kettles Yard Art Gallery.

For more insight into the life and times of Cambridge, both town and gown, join one of the guided tours from the Cambridge Tourist Information Centre (see address below). The center has a wide range of information, including data on public transportation in the area and on different sightseeing attractions.

TOURIST SERVICES   A tourist reception center for Cambridge and Cambridgeshire is operated by **Guide Friday Ltd.** at Cambridge Railway Station (☎ 01223/362444). The center, on the concourse of the railway station, sells brochures and maps. Also available is a full range of tourist services, including accommodations booking. In summer the center is open daily from 9am to 6:30pm; it closes at 3pm in winter. Guided tours of Cambridge leave the center daily. In summer, aboard open-top, double-decker buses, there are departures every 15 minutes from 9:45am to 6pm; in winter, there are hourly departures. The tour can be a one-hour ride or you can get off at any of the many stops, such as King's College Chapel or the American Cemetery, then rejoin the tour whenever you wish. Tickets are valid all day for you to hop on and off the buses. The price of the tour is £6.50 ($10.25) for adults, £4.50 ($7.10) for senior citizens and students, and £2 ($3.15) for children 5 to 15 (no charge for kids 4 or under).

ESSENTIALS
GETTING THERE

By Train   Trains depart frequently from Liverpool Street Station and King's Cross Station, arriving an hour later. For inquiries in London, call 0171/9385100; or in Cambridge 01223/311999. An off-peak same-day roundtrip is £12.80 ($20.20). A peak-time same-day roundtrip is £14.50 ($22.90). An off-peak longer stay roundtrip (up to 5-day period) is £17.50 ($27.65).

By Bus   National Express coaches run hourly between London's Victoria Coach Station, arriving at Drummer Street Station in Cambridge (trip time: 2 hr.). A one-way or same-day roundtrip costs £8.50 ($13.45).

By Car   Head north from London on M11.

VISITOR INFORMATION

The **telephone area code** is 01223.

Orientation   The center of Cambridge is made for pedestrians, so park your car at one of the many car parks (they get more expensive as you approach the city center) and take the opportunity to visit some of the colleges spread throughout the city. Follow the courtyards through to the "Backs" (the college lawns) and walk through to Trinity (where Prince Charles studied) and St. John's Colleges, including the Bridge of Sighs.

Information   The **Cambridge Tourist Information Centre,** Wheeler Street (☎ **01223/322640**), is in back of the Guildhall.

Bicycling   The most popular way of getting around in Cambridge, next to walking, is bicycling. **Geoff's Bike Hire,** 65 Devonshire Rd. (☎ 01223/365629), has bicycles for rent for £6 ($9.50) per day or £15 ($23.70) per week. A deposit of £25 ($39.50) is required. Open Monday through Saturday from 9am to 5:30pm, and in summer also on Sunday from 9am to 5:30pm.

If you're using a bike just within town (and provided that one is available), you can get one free. The **Community Bicycle Scheme** offers a fleet of 500 brightly painted green bikes available free from 26 "bike parks," requiring no deposit. When you're through, you're requested to leave the bike at the nearest bike park destination. The tourist office will provide more details.

WHAT TO SEE & DO
CAMBRIDGE UNIVERSITY

Oxford University predates Cambridge, but by the early 13th century scholars began coming here too. Eventually, Cambridge won partial recognition from Henry III, rising or falling with the approval of subsequent English monarchs. Cambridge consists of 31 colleges for both men and women. Colleges are closed for exams from mid-April until the end of June.

A word of warning: Unfortunately, because of the disturbances caused by the influx of tourists to the university, Cambridge has had to limit visitors, or even exclude them altogether, from various parts of the university. In some cases, a small entry fee will be charged. Small groups of up to six people are generally admitted with no problem, and you can inquire from the local tourist office about visiting hours.

The following listing is only a sample of some of the more interesting colleges. If you're planning to stop in Cambridge for a long time, you might also want to visit: **Magdalene College,** on Magdalene Street, founded in 1542; **Pembroke College,** on Trumpington Street, founded in 1347; **Christ's College,** on St. Andrew's Street, founded in 1505; and **Corpus Christi College,** on Trumpington Street, which dates from 1352.

✪ **KING'S COLLEGE**   The adolescent Henry VI founded King's College on King's Parade (☎ **01223/350411**) in 1441. Most of its buildings today are from the 19th century. The perpendicular **King's College Chapel,** dating from the Middle Ages, is its crowning glory and one of the architectural gems of England. The chapel, owing to the chaotic vicissitudes of English kings, wasn't completed until the early years of the 16th century.

Its most characteristic features are the magnificent fan vaulting—all of stone—and the great windows, most of which were fashioned by Flemish artisans between

East Anglia

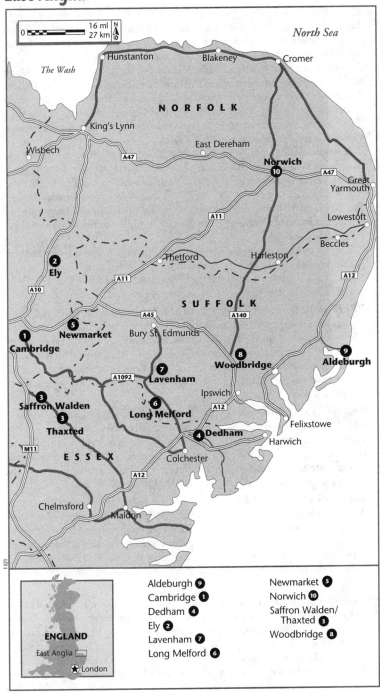

16 ml
27 km

The Wash

North Sea

Hunstanton
Blakeney
Cromer

N O R F O L K

King's Lynn

Wisbech

East Dereham

A47

Norwich
10

A47

Great
Yarmouth

Lowestoft

Beccles

Ely
2

A10

A11

Thetford

Harleston

A12

S U F F O L K

A45

A140

Newmarket
5

Bury St. Edmunds

A11

Cambridge
1

A1092

Lavenham
7

Woodbridge
8

Aldeburgh
9

Saffron Walden
3

Long Melford
6

Ipswich

Thaxted
3

A12

Dedham
4

Felixstowe

M11

E S S E X

Colchester

Harwich

A12

Chelmsford

Maldon

1321

Aldeburgh **9**
Cambridge **1**
Dedham **4**
Ely **2**
Lavenham **7**
Long Melford **6**

Newmarket **5**
Norwich **10**
Saffron Walden/
Thaxted **3**
Woodbridge **8**

ENGLAND

East Anglia

★ London

1517 and 1531 (the west window, however, dates from the late Victorian period). The stained glass, in hues of red, blue, and amber, portray biblical scenes. The long range of the windows, from the first on the north side at the west end, all the way around the back of the chapel to the first on the south side, depicts the Birth of the Virgin; the Annunciation; the Birth of Christ; the Life, Ministry, and Death of Christ; the Resurrection; the Ascension; the Acts of the Apostles; and the Assumption. The upper range contains Old Testament parallels to these New Testament stories. The chapel also houses *The Adoration of the Magi* by Rubens. The rood screen is from the early 16th century. Henry James called King's College Chapel "the most beautiful in England."

It is open during vacation time Monday to Saturday, 9:30am to 4:30pm, and on Sunday from 10am to 4:30pm. During the term the public is welcome to attend choral services, which are at 5:30pm Tuesday to Saturday and at 10:30am and 3:30pm Sunday. During the term the chapel is open to visitors Monday through Saturday from 9:30am to 3:15pm and on Sunday from 1:15 to 2:15pm and 5 to 5:30pm; it is closed December 26 to January 3. It may be closed at other times for recording sessions.

There is an exhibition in the seven northern side chapels showing why and how the chapel was built. To visit the college and chapel, including the exhibition, costs £2 ($3.15) for adults, £1 ($1.60) for students and children 12 to 17. Those under 12 are admitted free.

PETERHOUSE   This college (☎ 01223/338200) on Trumpington Street attracts visitors largely because it's the oldest Cambridge college, founded in 1284. The founder was Hugh de Balsham, the bishop of Ely. Of the original buildings, only the hall remains, but this was restored in the 19th century and now boasts stained-glass windows by William Morris. Old Court, constructed in the 15th century, was renovated in 1754; the chapel dates from 1632. Ask permission to enter at the porter's lodge.

TRINITY COLLEGE   On Trinity Street, Trinity College (not to be confused with Trinity Hall) is the largest college in Cambridge. It was founded in 1546 by Henry VIII, who consolidated a number of smaller colleges that had existed on the site. The courtyard is the most spacious in Cambridge, built when Thomas Nevile was master. Sir Christopher Wren designed the library. For admission to the college, apply at the porter's lodge, or call **01223/338400** for information.

EMMANUEL COLLEGE   On St. Andrew's Street, Emmanuel (☎ 01223/334233) was founded in 1584 by Sir Walter Mildmay, a chancellor of the exchequer to Elizabeth I. It's of interest to Harvard students since John Harvard, founder of that university, studied here. You can take a nice stroll around its attractive gardens. You might even visit the chapel designed by Sir Christopher Wren and consecrated in 1677. Both the chapel and college are open daily from 9:30am to 12:15pm and 2 to 6pm.

QUEENS' COLLEGE   On Queens' Lane, Queens' College (☎ 01223/335511) is thought by some to be the loveliest of Cambridge's colleges. Dating back to 1448, it was founded by two English queens, one the wife of Henry VI, the other the wife of Edward IV. Its second cloister is the most interesting, flanked by the early 16th-century half-timbered President's Lodge. Admission is £1 ($1.60), and a short printed guide is issued. Normally, individual visitors are

Cambridge

admitted daily from 1:45 to 4:30pm, but during July, August, and September the college is also open to visitors daily from 10:15am to 12:45pm. Entry and exit is by the old porter's lodge in Queens' Lane only. The old hall and chapel are usually open to the public when not in use.

ST. JOHN'S COLLEGE On St. John's Street, the college (☎ **01223/338600**) was founded in 1511 by Lady Margaret Beaufort, mother of Henry VII. A few years earlier she had founded Christ's College. Before her intervention, an old monk-run hospital had stood on the site of St. John's. The impressive gateway bears the Tudor coat of arms, and Second Court is a fine example of late Tudor brickwork. But its best-known feature is the Bridge of Sighs crossing the Cam, built in the 19th century, patterned after the bridge in Venice. It connects the older part of the college with New Court, a Gothic revival on the opposite bank from which there is an outstanding view of the famous "Backs." The Bridge of Sighs is closed to visitors but can be seen from the neighboring Kitchen Bridge. Wordsworth was an alumnus of St. John's College. The college is open daily from 10:30am to 5:30pm March to October. Admission is £1.50 ($2.35) for adults and 75p ($1.20) for children. Visitors are welcome to attend choral services in the chapel.

OTHER SIGHTS

The Fitzwilliam Museum

Trumpington St., near Peterhouse. ☎ **01223/332900.** Admission free. Tues–Sat 10am–5pm, Sun 2:15–5pm. Guided tours, Sun 2:30pm. Closed Jan 1, Good Friday, and Dec 24–31.

This museum was the gift of the Viscount Fitzwilliam, who in 1816 gave Cambridge University his paintings and rare books—along with £100,000 to build the house in which to display them. Other gifts have since been bequeathed to the museum, and now it's one of the finest in England. The collection has also been beefed up by loans and purchases. It's noted for its porcelain, old prints, antiquities, and oils (17th-century Italian, including Titian, Veronese, and Tintoretto; Rubens; Van Dyck; French impressionists; and a superb collection of 18th- and 19th-century British paintings). Up to 20 temporary exhibitions are presented every year. A gallery for Japanese prints opened in 1992.

Great St. Mary's

King's Parade. ☎ **01223/350914.** Admission £1.20 ($1.90) adults, 30p (45¢) children. Daily 9am–5pm.

The university church was built on the site of an 11th-century church, but the present building dates largely from 1478. It was closely associated with events of the Reformation. The cloth that covered the hearse of King Henry VII is on display in the church. There is a fine view of Cambridge from the top of the tower.

TOURS

The person to know if you're in the Cambridge area is Mrs. Isobel Bryant, who operates **Heritage Tours** from her 200-year-old home, Manor Cottage, Swaffham Prior CB5 0JZ (☎ 01638/741440). An expert on the region, she will arrange tours starting from your hotel or Cambridge railway station to Lavenham with its thatched and timbered houses, to the fine medieval churches of the Suffolk villages, to Ely Cathedral, or to one of the nearby grand mansions with their many treasures. The charge of £90 ($142.20) is for the day for up to three or £100

($158) for four passengers and all travel expenses, including the service of the driver/guide. Lunch in a village pub and admission fees add £5 ($7.90) per person.

Mrs. Bryant also offers walking tours around the Cambridge colleges; they cost £30 ($47.40) for a family-size party and last about two hours. Another tour is offered of Newmarket, the center of England's horse-racing. For a group of 12 or more, a whole-day tour costs £15 ($23.70) per person; a half-day tour goes for £8 ($12.65) per person. A shorter tour can be arranged for individuals or a family group.

PUNTING

Punting on the Cam is a traditional pursuit of students and visitors to Cambridge. Downstream, you pass along the "backs" or ivy-covered rear views of the colleges, with their lush gardens sweeping down to the Cam. Upriver, you can go to a distance of about two miles to Grantchester, immortalized by Rupert Brooke (author of the sonnet, "The Soldier"), perhaps best known for the verse cited on the following page.

Stop in at "The Green Man" (see "Pubs" below). Literary types flock to Grantchester, which can be reached both by punting and or by taking the path following the River Granta for less than an hour to Grantchester Meadows. The town lies about a mile from the meadows. When the town clock stopped for repairs in 1985, its hands were left frozen "for all time" at ten to three in honor of Brooke's famed verse.

To reach Grantchester or else just to go punting along the "Backs" of the colleges, you maneuver in a wood-built, flat-bottomed boat—somewhat like a Venetian gondola. The punt is, in fact, called the gondola of England. A pole about 15 feet long is used to propel the craft. The river's floor is muddy, and many a student has lost his punt in the riverbed shaded by the willows. People sprawled along the banks of the Cam on a summer day are waiting to judge and ridicule you as you maneuver the punt. If your pole gets stuck, it's better to leave it sticking in the mud instead of risking a plunge into the river.

Scudamore's Boatyards, Granta Place (☎ **01223/359750**), by the Anchor Pub, has been in business since 1910. All craft rent for £6 ($9.50) per hour on weekdays, £8 ($12.65) per hour on weekends, including punts, canoes, and rowboats. A £30 ($47.40) deposit, payable in cash or with credit card, is required. There is a maximum of six persons per punt. They are open from March to late September or October, depending on the weather, and every morning from 9am until dusk, depending on the weather and number of clients.

The **Cambridge Punt Company,** working out of The Anchor Pub, Silver Street (☎ **01223/327280**), is well recommended for its 45-minute rowboat tours. A guide (usually a Cambridge student) appropriately dressed in a boater (straw hat) and a blazer will both row and give running commentary to groups of between one and six persons. Tours cost £5 ($7.90) for adults, £2.50 ($3.95) for children 5 to 12. Kids 4 and under free. The boats are moored near the base of the Anchor Pub. Spokespersons for the company maintain a dialogue with the Anchor's service staff, any of whom can call a guide over to your table. Furthermore, if you want to row yourself along the Cam, "unchauffeured," boats rent for £6 ($9.50) per hour during the week, £8 ($12.65) per hour on weekends. The company is open daily from mid-March to late October, 10am to 7pm, although if it rains or if the winds get too high, everyone packs up and goes home. In July and August the hours are 9am to dusk.

WHERE TO STAY
EXPENSIVE

The Garden House Hotel

Granta Place, Mill Lane, Cambridge, Cambridgeshire CB2 1RT. ☎ **01223/63421.** Fax 01223/316605. 111 rms, 7 suites. MINIBAR TV TEL. £129–£175 ($203.80–$276.50) double; £295 ($466.10) suite. Breakfast £11.95 ($18.90) extra. AE, DC, MC, V. Free parking.

This modern hotel is situated between the riverbank and a cobblestone street in the oldest part of town, a short stroll from the principal colleges. Next door is a boatyard where you can rent punts. The hotel has a series of outdoor terraces where drinks and afternoon tea are served in nice weather. The earth-tone brick and stained-wood exterior harmonizes with the wall coverings in the bar and lounge, where visitors can relax on comfortable sofas and chairs. The well-furnished bedrooms are equipped with radios, soundproof windows, hot-beverage facilities, and hair dryers. Most rooms have balconies and river views.

The hotel's Le Jardin Restaurant, which overlooks the river and gardens, offers fixed-price and à la carte menus, including vegetarian meals, at lunch and dinner. A three-course fixed-price menu costs £22 ($34.75). The Riverside Lounge provides a selection of hot and cold light meals, accompanied in the evening by piano music. When the weather permits, the Cocktail Bar serves drinks on the terrace and lawn. The hotel has ample parking.

MODERATE

Gonville Hotel

Gonville Place, Cambridge, Cambridgeshire CB1 1LY. ☎ **01223/66611** or 800/528-1234 in the U.S. and Canada. Fax 01223/315470. 62 rms. TV TEL. £89.50 ($141.40) double. Rates include English breakfast. AE, DC, MC, V. Free parking.

Only a five-minute walk from the center of town, this comfortable hotel and its grounds are opposite Parker's Piece. It's not unlike a country house—ivy covered, with shade trees and a formal car entry. In 1973 it was gutted and rebuilt as a commercial hotel, in hopes of attracting businesspeople as well as tourists in summer. The rooms are comfortable and furnished in a modern style. There is central heating throughout and air-conditioning in the restaurant. A fixed-price lunch costs £12 ($18.95); dinner, £15 ($23.70). You can also order à la carte.

University Arms Hotel

Regent St., Cambridge, Cambridgeshire CB2 1AD. ☎ **01223/351241.** Fax 01223/315256. 115 rms, 1 suite. TV TEL. £110–£115 ($173.80–$181.70) double; £150 ($237) suite. Rates include English breakfast. AE, DC, MC, V. Free parking. Bus 1.

Built in 1834, this hotel maintains much of its antique charm and many of its original architectural features despite discreet modernization over the years. Near the city center and the university, this traditional hotel offers tastefully decorated bedrooms with central heating, electric-razor outlets, and a radio. Most overlook Parker's Piece, where one of England's greatest cricketers, Sir Jack Hobbs, learned to play. The Octagon Lounge, with its stained-glass domed ceiling and open log

Impressions

"Stands the Church clock at ten to three? And is there honey still for tea?"
—Rupert Brooke (1912)

fire, is a popular place to meet for tea. The spacious oak-paneled restaurant features both table d'hôte and à la carte menus. Dinner costs £17 ($26.85) and up.

Tip: The hotel porter can arrange a guided tour of the city for you.

INEXPENSIVE

Arundel Hotel

53 Chesterton Rd., Cambridge, Cambridgeshire CB4 3AN. ☎ **01223/67701.** Fax 01223/67221. 105 rms. TV TEL. £53–£77 ($83.75–$121.65) double. Rates include continental breakfast. AE, DC, MC, V. Free parking. Bus 3 or 5.

Occupying one of the most desirable sites of Cambridge, this hotel (until recently) consisted of six identical Victorian row houses—each fronted with the same dark-yellow local bricks—which were interconnected many years ago to form a coherent whole. In 1994, after two additional row houses were purchased from the university, the hotel was enlarged, upgraded, and expanded into the well-maintained hostelry you'll see today. Rooms that overlook the River Cam and Jesus Green cost more than those facing the other way; and because there's no elevator, rooms on lower floors cost more than those near the roof. Regardless of their location, all accommodations are clean, simple, and comfortable. There's a bar and restaurant (see "Where to Dine," below) on the premises and a garden with outdoor tables for warm-weather drinking. A coin-operated launderette is on the premises.

Cambridgeshire Moat House

Huntingdon Rd., Bar Hill, Cambridge, Cambridgeshire CB3 8EU. ☎ **01954/780555.** Fax 01954/780010. 100 rms. TV TEL. £75 ($118.50) single or double. English breakfast £9.50 ($15) extra. AE, DC, MC, V. Free parking. Take A604 5½ miles northwest of the town center.

Although this hotel caters to many visitors headed for the monuments of Cambridge, it also does a healthy business as a resort hotel for sports enthusiasts. Set in an isolated spot in the open countryside, it's surrounded by a verdant golf course. Built around 1977, it has conservatively modern public rooms, comfortable bedrooms with views of the acreage outside, and sports facilities which include a heated indoor swimming pool, sauna, three squash courts, two outdoor tennis courts, a helipad, putting green, and an 18-hole championship golf course charging greens fees ranging from £12.50 to £15 ($19.75 to $23.70). The bedrooms, each comfortably furnished, are equipped with radios, hair dryers, trouser presses, and hot-beverage facilities. The restaurant offers both table d'hôte and à la carte menus. Table d'hôte dinners cost £17 ($26.85). Meals are also served daily in the bar.

Post House Hotel

Lakeview, Bridge Rd., Lakeview Bridge, Impington, Cambridge, Cambridgeshire CB4 4PH. ☎ **01223/237000** or 800/225-5843 in the U.S. and Canada. Fax 01223/233426. 118 rms. TV TEL. Sun–Thurs £59.50 ($94) single or double; Fri–Sat £41.50–£57.50 ($65.55–$90.85) single or double. Breakfast £5.50–£7.95 ($8.70–$12.55) extra. AE, DC, MC, V. Free parking. Drive 2 miles north of Cambridge on B1049 (Histon Rd.) to the A45 intersection. Bus 104.

Located a short walk from a small artificial lake, with bedrooms overlooking the lake, this modern two-story hotel was vaguely influenced by the designs of nearby country houses. There's a grassy courtyard partially enclosed by the hotel's wings, and peak-ceilinged public rooms furnished with scattered clusters of sofas and chairs. The bedrooms have large windows with pleasant views and baths. Facilities include a heated indoor swimming pool, Jacuzzi, sauna, and lobby bar. The hotel restaurant, the Churchill, has mahogany paneling and reproductions of paintings created by Sir Winston Churchill.

⑤ Regent Hotel

41 Regent St., Cambridge, Cambridgeshire CB2 1AB. ☎ **01223/351470.** Fax 01223/ 566562. 26 rms. TV TEL. £73.50 ($116.15) double. Rates include English breakfast. AE, DC, MC, V.

This is one of the nicest of the reasonably priced small hotels in Cambridge. Right in the city center, overlooking Parker's Piece, the house was built in the 1840s as the original site of Newham College. When the college outgrew its quarters, the building became a hotel. The attractive, comfortable bedrooms have radios, hair dryers, and trouser presses. There's a cocktail bar on the street level, and the restaurant serves Italian specialties.

WHERE TO DINE
MODERATE

✪ Arundel House Restaurant

In the Arundel Hotel, 53 Chesterton Rd. ☎ **01223/67701.** Reservations recommended. Main courses £7.50–£13.50 ($11.85–$21.35); 2-course fixed-price lunch £8.75 ($13.85); 3-course fixed-price lunch £9.95 ($15.70); Sun lunch £10.25 ($16.20); 3-course fixed-price dinner £14.95 ($23.60). AE, DC, MC, V. Daily noon–2:30pm and 6:30–9:30pm. Bus No. 3 or 5. FRENCH/BRITISH/VEGETARIAN.

One of the best and most acclaimed restaurants in Cambridge is in this 105-bedroom hotel on Chesterton Road, occupying a site overlooking the River Cam and Jesus Green. The location is a short walk from the city center. Winner of many awards, the cuisine is noted not only for its excellence and use of fresh produce, but also for its good value. The decor is warmly inviting with Sanderson curtains, Louis XV–style upholstered chairs, and spacious tables. The menu changes frequently, and you dine both à la carte or on the set menu. There is also a children's menu where the maximum price is £2 ($3.15). Perhaps you'll begin with a country game soup (venison, pheasant, hare, and rabbit) or a creamy fish soup. Fish choices are likely to include trout or salmon; or else try English lamb steak cooked with calvados, roast pheasant, or fillet steak.

Midsummer House

Midsummer Common. ☎ **01223/69299.** Reservations required. 2-course lunch £17 ($26.85); 3-course lunch £23 ($36.35); Sun lunch £25 ($39.50); 2-course fixed price dinner £20 ($31.60); 3-course fixed price dinner £32 ($50.55); 4-course fixed price dinner £38 ($60.05); Sat dinner £30–£36 ($47.40–$56.90). AE, MC, V. Tues–Fri and Sun 12:30–2pm; Tues–Sat 7–9:30pm. FRENCH.

Located near the River Cam, the Midsummer House is one of the dining discoveries of Cambridge. It is situated within the Edwardian-era cottage that once housed the groundskeeper for Midsummer Common, the largest of central Cambridge's several verdant squares. The preferred dining area is in an elegant conservatory, but you can also find a smartly laid table upstairs. The fixed-price menus are wisely limited, and quality control is much in evidence here. The chef/patron, Hans Schweitzer, knows the French school, except that every dish seems to bear his own special imprint—and that's quite good. Attired in funereal black, the waiters will come to your assistance as you peruse the menu for the freshest or most exciting selection on any given day. Specialties include *délice* of salmon, foie gras, terrine of summer vegetables, *carré* of lamb in jus, fillet of turbot wrapped in a "pig's veil" (the membrane from a pig's stomach), salmon and turbot in puff pastry, and a *mille-feuille* of sweetbreads and kidneys.

✪ Twenty Two

22 Chesterton Rd. ☎ **01223/351880.** Reservations required. Fixed-price menu £19.95 ($31.50). AE, MC, V. Tues–Sat 7:30–9:30pm. ENGLISH/CONTINENTAL.

Who would expect to find one of the best restaurants in Cambridge in this quiet residential and hotel district? In the vicinity of Jesus Green, it has up until now been an address jealously guarded by the locals who "don't want tourists to spoil it." It's an exponent of the best of contemporary English and continental cookery, relying on the freshest ingredients in any season. The fixed-price menu is always changing, but it is based on fresh produce from the market. Owners David Carter and Louise Crompton use time-tested recipes along with their own inspirations. Typical dishes include pigeon terrine brandy basket or fillet of pork with prunes, followed by homemade ice cream.

INEXPENSIVE

✪ Browns

23 Trumpington St. ☎ **01223/461655.** Reservations not necessary. Main courses £5.95–£11 ($9.40–$17.40). AE, MC, V. Mon–Sat 11am–11:30pm, Sun noon–11:30pm. Bus 2. ENGLISH/CONTINENTAL.

Long a favorite at Oxford, it also became a sensation at Cambridge some time ago. With a neoclassical colonnade in front, it has all the grandeur of the Edwardian era. It was actually built in 1914 as the outpatient department of a hospital dedicated to Edward VII. Today it's the most lighthearted place for dining in the city, with wicker chairs, high ceilings, pre–World War I woodwork, and a long bar covered with bottles of wine. The extensive bill of fare includes various renditions of spaghetti, fresh salads, several selections of meat and fish (from charcoal-grilled leg of lamb with rosemary to fresh fish in season), hot sandwiches, and the chef's daily specials posted on a blackboard. If you drop by in the afternoon, you can also order thick milk shakes or natural fruit juices. In fair weather, outdoor seating is provided. The location is five minutes from King's College and opposite the Fitzwilliam Museum.

Charlie Chan

14 Regent St. ☎ **01223/61763.** Reservations recommended. Main courses £8–£14 ($12.65–$22.10); fixed-price menus £10–£20 ($15.80–$31.60). AE, MC, V. Daily noon–2:15pm and 6–11:15pm. CHINESE.

Most people agree that this is the finest Chinese restaurant in Cambridge, and in my experience, Charlie Chan is reliable and capable in spite of its large selection of dishes. It's a long corridorlike restaurant, with pristine decor and tile floors. Most of the dishes are inspired by the traditional cuisine of Beijing. The specialties we've most enjoyed include an aromatic and crispy duck, lemon chicken, and prawn with garlic and ginger. It's best to go with a party—that way you can sample many different dishes. It's located on a busy commercial street.

PUBS

Cambridge Arms

4 King St. ☎ **01223/359650.** Reservations not accepted. Bar snacks from £2.60–£4 ($4.10–$6.30). AE, V. Mon–Sat noon–7pm, Sun noon–3pm. Pub, Mon–Sat 11am–11pm, Sun noon–3pm and 7–10:30pm. ENGLISH.

This bustling, no-nonsense pub in the center of town has plenty of atmosphere and dispenses endless platters of food to clients who order it over the bar's countertop. Menu possibilities include the chef's daily specials, grilled steaks, lasagne, and an array of both hot and cold dishes. Also on site is a Victorian-style coffee shop open Monday through Saturday from 11am to 5pm. From late May until the first of November, it is also open Sunday from 11am to 5pm.

The Green Man

59 High St., Grantchester. ☎ **01223/841178.** Reservations not necessary. Lunch main courses £4–£8 ($6.30–$12.65); fixed price dinner £9.95 ($15.70). AE, MC, V. Daily noon–2:30pm and 6–9pm. Pub, Mon–Sat 11am–11pm; Sun noon–10:30pm (no liquor 3–7pm). Bus 118 from Cambridge. ENGLISH.

Named in honor of Robin Hood, this 400-year-old inn is perhaps the most popular pub for outings from Cambridge. It's located on A604, 2 miles south of Cambridge in the hamlet of Grantchester. The village was made famous by Rupert Brooke, the Edwardian-era poet best known for his sonnet "The Soldier." Grantchester is considered one of the shire's most beautiful villages, with an old church and gardens leading down to a series of peaceful meadows. Even if you've never heard of Brooke, you might enjoy spending a late afternoon here, wandering through the old church and then heading, as everybody does, to the Green Man. In winter you'll be welcomed with a crackling fire, but in summer you might want to retreat to the beer garden in back. From there, you can stroll to the edge of the River Cam. Place your food order at the counter, after which an employee will carry the food to your table. Menu choices include steak-and-Guinness pie, steak-and-mushroom pie, lasagne, and a seven-inch Yorkshire pudding.

2 Ely

70 miles NE of London, 16 miles NE of Cambridge

The top attraction in the fen country, outside of Cambridge, is Ely Cathedral. Ely used to be known as the Isle of Ely, until the surrounding marshes and meres were drained. The last stronghold of Saxon England, Ely was defended by Hereward the Wake, until his capitulation to the Normans in 1071.

ESSENTIALS
GETTING THERE

By Train   Ely is a major railway junction served by express trains to Cambridge. Service is frequent from London's Liverpool Street Station.

By Bus   Frequent buses run between Cambridge and Ely.

By Car   From Cambridge, take A10 north.

VISITOR INFORMATION

The **telephone area code** is 01353. The **Tourist Information Centre** is at Oliver Cromwell's House, 29 St. Mary's St. (☎ **01353/662062**).

WHAT TO SEE & DO

✪ Ely Cathedral

The College. ☎ **01353/667735.** Admission £2.80 ($4.40) adults, £2 ($3.15) senior citizens, students, children 12–16. Free for children under 12. Apr–Oct, daily 7am–7pm; Nov–Mar, Mon–Sat 7:30am–6pm, Sun 7:30am–5pm.

The near-legendary founder of the cathedral was Etheldreda, the wife of a Northumbrian king who established a monastery on the spot in 673. The present structure dates from 1081. Visible for miles around, the landmark octagonal lantern is the crowning glory of the cathedral. Erected in 1322, following the collapse of the old tower, it represents a remarkable engineering achievement. Four hundred tons of lead and wood hang in space, held there by timbers reaching to the eight pillars.

You enter the cathedral through the Galilee West Door, a good example of the early English style of architecture. The lantern tower and the Octagon are the most notable features inside, but visit the lady chapel too. Although its decor has deteriorated over the centuries, it's still a handsome example of the perpendicular style, having been completed in the mid-14th century. The entry fee goes to help preserve the cathedral.

Ely Museum

28C High St. ☎ **01353/666655.** Admission £1 ($1.60) adults, 50p (80¢) children 6–16, free for children 5 and under. Tues–Sun 10:30am–1pm and 2:15–5pm.

Artifacts from the area are displayed here, including a rare collection of 17th-century Ely trade tokens. A gallery presents old films of Ely and the surrounding fen land.

NEARBY ATTRACTIONS

Grimes Graves

On B1107, 2³/₄ miles northeast of Brandon, Norfolkshire. ☎ **01842/810656.** Admission £1.30 ($2.05) adults; £1 ($1.60) students and senior citizens; 70p ($1.10) children 5–15; free for children 4 and under. Apr–Oct, daily 10am–6pm; Nov–Mar, Wed–Sun 10am–4pm.

This is considered the largest and best-preserved group of Neolithic flint mines in Britain, and probably produced the cutting edges of spears, arrows, and knives for prehistoric tribes throughout the region. Because of its isolated location within sparsely populated, fir-wooded countryside, it's easy to imagine yourself transported back through the millennia. Most visitors arrive by taking A134 for 7 miles northwest of Thetford, then transferring to B1107.

A guardian will meet you near the well-signposted parking lot. After determining that you are not physically impaired in any way, he or she will open one or several of the mine shafts, each of which requires a descent down an almost-vertical 30-foot ladder. (A visit is not recommended for very young children, the elderly, or the infirm.) Since the tunnel and shaft have been restored and reinforced, it's now possible to see where work took place during Neolithic times. Though not essential, many archaeologists, professional and amateur, bring their own flashlights with them. The mines, incidentally, are situated close to the military bases that housed thousands of American air force personnel during World War II.

Imperial War Museum

Duxford Airfield, on A505, at Junction 10 of M11. ☎ **01223/835000.** Admission £6 ($9.50) adults, £3 ($4.75) children. Mid-Mar to Oct, daily 10am–6pm; Nov to mid-Mar, daily 10am–4pm. Closed Dec 24–26. Take M11 to Junction 10, 8 miles south of Cambridge. Bus: Cambus no. 103 from Drummer Street Station in Cambridge.

In this former Battle of Britain station and U.S. Eighth Air Force base in World War II, you'll find a huge collection of historic civil and military aircraft from both world wars, including the only B-29 Superfortress in Europe. Other exhibits include midget submarines, tanks, and a variety of field artillery pieces, as well as a historical display on the U.S. Eighth Air Force. Additional charges are imposed for special events, and parking is free.

WHERE TO STAY
INEXPENSIVE

Lamb Hotel

2 Lynn Rd., Ely, Cambridgeshire CB7 4EJ. ☎ **01353/663574.** Fax 01353/666350. 32 rms. TV TEL. £60 ($94.80) double. Rates include English breakfast. AE, DC, MC, V. Bus 109.

Right in the center of town, this hotel is a former coaching inn. In the shadow of the cathedral, this Queens Moat House hotel offers renovated bedrooms with private baths or showers and hot-beverage facilities. In the 1400s this place was known as the "Holy Lambe," a stopping-off spot for wayfarers, often pilgrims, passing through East Anglia. Fixed-price dinners cost £14.50 ($22.90).

WHERE TO DINE
MODERATE

✪ The Old Fire Engine House

25 St. Mary's St. ☎ **01353/662582.** Reservations required. Main courses £10.95–£13.50 ($17.30–$21.35). MC, V. Daily 12:30–2pm; Mon–Sat 7:30–9pm (last entry). Bus 109. ENGLISH.

Opposite St. Mary's Church is one of the finer restaurants in East Anglia. It's worth making a special trip to this converted fire station in a walled garden, within a building complex that includes an art gallery. Soups are served in huge bowls, accompanied by coarse-grained crusty bread. Main dishes include duck with orange sauce, jugged hare, steak-and-kidney pie, baked stuffed pike, casserole of rabbit, and pigeon with bacon and black olives. Desserts include fruit pie and cream, although I'd recommend the syllabub, made with cream and liquor. In summer you can dine outside in the garden or even order a cream tea. The restaurant is owned and in large part run by Ann Jarnan, who still finds time to talk to customers.

3 Saffron Walden/Thaxted

43 miles NE of London, 15 miles SE of Cambridge

In the northern corner of Essex, a short drive from Thaxted, is the ancient market town of Walden, renamed Saffron Walden because of the fields of autumn crocus that used to grow around it. Despite its proximity to London, it isn't disturbed by heavy tourist traffic. Residents of Cambridge escape to this old borough for weekends.

Many houses in Saffron Walden are distinctive in that the 16th- and 17th-century builders faced their houses with parget—a kind of plasterwork (sometimes made with cow dung) used for ornamental facades. There are many 15th- and 16th-century timber-framed houses with pargeting, as well as the 14th-century Sun Inn, and the perpendicular-style Church of Saffron Walden, the largest in Essex. Saffron Walden is one of the few market towns in England that still has its original medieval street pattern.

ESSENTIALS
GETTING THERE

By Train   Trains leave London's Liverpool Street Station in the direction of Cambridge several times a day. Two or three stations before Cambridge, passengers should get off in the hamlet of Audley End, 8 miles north of Thaxted and

1 mile from Saffron Walden. There is a bus from Audley End, but it meanders around so much that most visitors prefer to take a taxi instead.

By Bus Cambus no. 122 leaves Cambridge Monday through Saturday at 12:15pm, 2:40pm, and 5:35pm, heading for Saffron Walden. Cambus no. 9 departs only Sunday every 1½ hours between 10am to 6pm. The last bus back on Sunday departs Saffron Walden at 7:10pm. National Express buses leave London's Victoria Coach Station several times a day and stop at Saffron Walden, six miles north of Thaxted. From there, about three (at most) buses head on to Thaxted. However, most visitors find it easier to take a taxi.

By Car From Cambridge, take A1301 southeast, connecting with B184 (also southeast) into Saffron Walden and the adjoining village of Thaxted.

VISITOR INFORMATION

The **telephone area code** is 01799 for Saffron Walden and 01371 for Thaxted. The **Tourist Information Centre** is at 1 Market Sq. (☎ **01799/510444**), in Saffron Walden.

WHAT TO SEE & DO IN SAFFRON WALDEN

One mile west of Saffron Walden (on B1383) is **Audley End House** (☎ 01799/ 522842), considered one of the finest mansions in East Anglia. This Jacobean house, begun by Thomas Howard, treasurer to the king, in 1605, was built on the foundation of a monastery. James I is reported to have said, "Audley End is too large for a king, though it might do for a lord treasurer." Among the house's outstanding features is an impressive Great Hall with an early 17th-century screen at the north end, considered one of the most beautiful ornamental screens in England. The rooms decorated by Robert Adam feature fine furniture and works of art. Among the attractions are a "Gothick" chapel and a charming Victorian ladies' sitting room. The park surrounding the house was landscaped by Capability Brown. It has a lovely rose garden, a river and cascade, and a picnic area. In the stables, built at the same time as the mansion, is a collection of agricultural machinery, as well as a Victorian coach, old wagons, and the estate fire wagon. From April 1 until the end of September, the house and grounds are open Wednesday through Sunday. Hours are daily from 1 to 6pm. Admission is £5.50 ($8.70) for adults, £4.10 ($6.50) for students and senior citizens, and £2.80 ($4.40) for children 5 to 16. Under 5 free.

The location is 1¼ miles (a 20-minute walk) from Audley End Station, where trains arrive from Cambridge.

WHERE TO STAY & DINE
INEXPENSIVE

The Saffron Hotel

10–18 High St., Saffron Walden, Essex CB10 1AY. ☎ **01799/522676.** Fax 01799/513979. 17 rms. TV TEL. £60–£80 ($94.80–$126.40) double. Rates include English breakfast. MC, V. Free parking.

In the center of this Cromwellian market town stands The Saffron Hotel, dating from the 16th century. The hotel combines modern comforts with old-world charm, as reflected in its individually designed and decorated rooms. Amenities include tea and coffee makers and central heating. Most rooms overlook High Street or the inner courtyard with its patio garden. Stories abound in the area about The Saffron Hotel ghost.

The hotel's restaurant, which is well known locally, is decorated in the Regency style. Dining is by candlelight in an area overlooking a floodlit patio garden. A fixed-price lunch costs £13.50 ($21.35) and a fixed-price dinner goes for £19 ($30), each consisting of three courses. Lunch is served Sunday through Friday from noon to 2pm and dinner Monday through Saturday from 7:30 to 9:30pm. A traditional bar features a range of local real ales, 30 malt whiskies, and a tempting array of inexpensive meals costing from £4.50 to £9 ($7.10 to $14.20). Look for the photographs of local airfields in World War II.

AN EXCURSION TO THAXTED

Sitting on the crest of a hill 43 miles north of London, the Saxon town of Thaxted has the most beautiful small church in England, whose graceful spire can be seen for miles around. Its belfry has special chimes that call parishioners to church services. Dating back to 1340, the church is a nearly perfect example of religious architecture. Thaxted also has a number of well-preserved Elizabethan houses.

WHERE TO STAY & DINE
Moderate
Whitehall

Church End, Broxted, Essex CM6 2BZ. ☎ **01279/850603.** Fax 01279/850385. 25 rms. TV TEL. £105–£155 ($165.90–$244.90) double. Rates include English breakfast. AE, DC, MC, V. Free parking. Take B1052 about 4 miles southwest of Thaxted.

This hotel lies adjacent to the village church of Broxted, with a garden behind it and lots of open land nearby. In the 18th century this property was attached to almost 28,000 acres of prime farmland. By the 1900s the countess of Warwick, then its mistress, entertained King Edward VII within these baronial walls. Today, in an elegantly simplified format, guests are still entertained more or less royally. Some bedrooms are uniquely furnished in 18th-century style; all have thoughtful extras and views of the 300-year-old yew trees in the ancient walled garden. Half of the rooms lie within a modern wing that was added in 1985. In the new wing, the rooms are conservatively traditional, with country-house accessories and English styling. A medieval brew house with a soaring ceiling is the setting for specialties prepared with fresh ingredients. Fixed-price menus cost £27.50 ($43.45) for two courses, £34 ($53.70) for three courses, and £37.50 ($59.25) for a six-course "menu surprise."

4 Dedham

63 miles NE of London, 8 miles NE of Colchester

Remember Constable's *Vale of Dedham*? In this little Essex village on the Stour River you're in the heart of Constable Country. Flatford Mill is only a mile farther down the river. The village, with its Tudor, Georgian, and Regency houses, is set in the midst of the water meadows of the Stour. Constable painted its church and tower. Dedham is right on the Essex-Suffolk border and makes a good center for exploring both North Essex and the Suffolk border country.

ESSENTIALS
GETTING THERE

By Train　Trains depart every 20 minutes from London's Liverpool Street Station for the 50-minute ride to Colchester. From Colchester, it's possible to take a taxi from the railway station to the bus station, then board a bus run by the Eastern National Bus Company for the 5-mile trip to Dedham. (Buses leave about once an hour.) Most people take a taxi from Colchester directly to Dedham.

By Bus   National Express buses depart from London's Victoria Coach Station for Colchester, where you have the choice of taking either another bus or a taxi to Dedham.

By Car   From the London ring road, branch northeast on A12 to Colchester, turning off at East Bergholt onto a small secondary road leading east to Dedham.

VISITOR INFORMATION

The **telephone area code** is 01206.

WHAT TO SEE & DO

Less than a mile from the village center is **Castle House,** East Lane (☎ 322127), home of Sir Alfred Munnings, president of the Royal Academy (1944–49) and painter extraordinaire of racehorses and other animals. The house and studio, which have sketches and other works, are open from early May to early October, on Sunday, Wednesday, and bank holidays (plus Thursday and Saturday during August) from 2 to 5pm. Admission is £2 ($3.15) for adults, 25p (40¢) for children.

The English landscape painter John Constable (1776–1837) was born at East Bergholt, directly north of Dedham. Near the village is **Flatford Mill,** East Bergholt (☎ 01206/298283), subject of one of his most renowned works. The mill, in a scenic setting, was given to the National Trust in 1943, and has since been leased to the Field Studies Council for use as a residential center.

Short courses are offered on all aspects of the countryside and the environment. None of the buildings have exhibits, nor are they open to the general public, but students of all ages are welcome to attend the courses. The fee includes accommodation, meals, and tuition. Write to Director of Studies, Field Studies Council, Flatford Mill Field Centre, East Bergholt, Colchester, Essex CO7 6UL.

WHERE TO STAY
MODERATE

✪ Maison Talbooth

Stratford Rd., Dedham, Colchester, Essex CO7 6HN. ☎ **01206/322367.** Fax 01206/322752. 10 suites. MINIBAR TV TEL. £105–£140 ($165.90–$221.20) double. Breakfast £7.50 ($11.85) extra. MC, V. Free parking. Take Stratford Rd. half a mile west of the town center.

This small and exclusive hotel is located in a handsomely restored Victorian country house. Accommodations here consist of spacious suites distinctively furnished by one of England's best-known decorators. High-fashion colors abound, antiques are mixed discreetly with reproductions, and the original architectural beauty has been preserved. A superluxury suite has a sunken bath and a draped bed. Each suite has its own theme. When you arrive, you're welcomed and brought to your suite, where fresh flowers, fruit, and a private bar are standard.

INEXPENSIVE

Dedham Hall/Fountain House Restaurant

Brook St., Dedham CO7 6AD. ☎ **01206/323027.** 6 rms. TV. £49–£57 ($77.40–$90.05) double. Rates include English breakfast. MC, V. Free parking.

Situated three minutes by foot east of the center of town, this well-managed hotel has flourished since its adoption by Jim and Wendy Sarton in 1991. Set on 5 acres of grazing land whose centerpiece is a pond favored by geese and wild swans, it consists of a 400-year-old brick-sided cottage linked to a 200-year-old home of stately proportions. The older section is reserved for the breakfast room, a bar, and a sitting room for residents of the six second-floor bedrooms. Accommodations are cozy, comfortable, and clean, with tea-making facilities. A cluster of three converted barns provide accommodations for many artists who congregate here several times throughout the year for painting seminars and art workshops.

A goodly portion of the establishment's income comes from the Fountain House restaurant, which moved here from a different location two miles away when the Sartons took over in 1991. Beneath beamed ceilings, near a logwood fire, you can enjoy fixed-price lunches for £16.50 ($26.05) and fixed-price dinners for £18.50 ($29.25). There's a wide selection of dishes with all-fresh ingredients and an abundance of natural flavors. Examples include scrambled eggs with smoked salmon, and grilled Dover sole with butter sauce. The preferred dessert is a chocolate fondue. Advance reservations are advisable.

WHERE TO DINE
MODERATE

✪ Le Talbooth

Gun Hill. ☎ **01206/323150.** Reservations required. Main courses £13–£18 ($20.55–$28.45); fixed-price lunch £19.95 ($31.50). AE, MC, V. Daily noon–2pm and 7–9pm. ENGLISH/FRENCH.

A hand-hewn, half-timbered weaver's house is the setting for this restaurant standing amid beautiful gardens on the banks of the River Stour in Constable Country. Le Talbooth was featured in Constable's *Vale of Dedham*. You descend a sloping driveway leading past flowering terraces. A well-mannered staff will usher you to a low-ceilinged bar for an apéritif. Taller guests are cautioned to beware of low ceiling beams, which add an atmospheric touch from another era. Owner Gerald Milsom has brought a high standard of cooking to this rustically elegant place, where a well-chosen wine list complements the good food. An à la carte menu changes six times a year, and special dishes change daily, reflecting the best produce available at the market. Main dishes are likely to range from garlic-studded Scottish beef fillet to roast Barbary duck.

5 Newmarket

62 miles NE of London, 13 miles NE of Cambridge

This old Suffolk town has been famous as a racing center since the time of James I. Visitors can see Nell Gwynne's House, but mainly they come to visit Britain's first and only equestrian museum.

ESSENTIALS
GETTING THERE

By Train　Trains depart from London's Liverpool Street Station every 45 to 60 minutes for Cambridge. In Cambridge, passengers change trains and head in the direction of Mildenhall. Three stops later, they arrive at Newmarket.

By Bus   About eight National Express buses depart from London's Victoria Coach Station for Norwich every day, stopping at Stratford, Stansted, and (finally) Newmarket along the way.

By Car   From Cambridge, head east on A133.

VISITOR INFORMATION

The **telephone area code** is 01638.

WHAT TO SEE & DO

National Horseracing Museum

99 High St. ☎ **01638/667333**. Admission £3.30 ($5.20) adults, £1 ($1.60) children, £2 ($3.15) senior citizens. Apr–Nov, Tues–Sat 10am–5pm, Sun noon–4pm. Closed Dec–Mar; Mon except bank holidays and Mon in July–Aug.

This museum is housed in the old subscription rooms, early 19th-century rooms used for placing and settling bets. Visitors will be able to see the history of horse racing over a 300-year period. There are fine paintings of famous horses, paintings on loan from Queen Elizabeth II, and copies of old parliamentary acts governing races. There is also a replica of a weighing-in room. A continuous 53-minute audiovisual presentation shows races and racehorses.

To make history come alive for the museum visitor, they also offer equine tours of this historic town. Guides take you to watch morning gallops on the heath where you'll see bronzes of horses from the past and other points of interest. An optional tour of a famous training establishment is offered, plus a visit to the Jockey Club rooms, known for its fine collection of paintings. Reservations are necessary, but the tour, which lasts a whole morning, is conducted April to October. The museum is closed from December to March, but those with a special interest in seeing it during those months can telephone.

The National Stud

July Race Course. ☎ **01638/663464**. Admission £3.50 ($5.55) adults, £2.50 ($3.95) children and senior citizens. Mar 27–Sept 30. Guided tours are at 11:15am and 2:30pm Mon–Fri, 11:15am on Sat, and 2:30pm Sun. Closed Oct–Mar 26.

Next to Newmarket's July Race Course, 2 miles southwest of the town, is the place for those who wish to see some of the world's finest horses, as well as watch a working Thoroughbred breeding stud in operation. A tour lasting about 75 minutes lets you see many mares and foals, plus top-class stallions. Reservations for tours must be made at the National Stud office or by phoning the number given above.

WHERE TO STAY & DINE
MODERATE

Swynford Paddocks

Six Mile Bottom, Cambridgeshire CB8 0UE, Tel. **01638/570234**. Fax 01638/570283. 15 rms (all with bath or shower). TV TEL. £107 ($169.05) double. Rates include English breakfast. AE, DC, MC, V. Free parking. Take A1304 6 miles southwest of Newmarket.

This well-appointed country house, one of the finest in the area, is situated on a 60-acre stud farm surrounded by beautiful grounds. Once a favorite retreat of Lord Byron, it has since been converted into a first-class hotel and restaurant (it is open to nonresidents, but you should call first). Many guests use it as a base for exploring not only Newmarket but Cambridge. The attractive bedrooms are handsomely furnished. The rates are expensive, but you get a lot of quality here. The restaurant serves a first-rate English and French cuisine, with dinners beginning at £22.95 ($36.25).

INEXPENSIVE

Heath Court Hotel

Moulton Rd., Newmarket, Suffolk CB8 8DY. ☎ **01638/667171.** Fax 01638/666533. 47 rms (all with bath or shower), 1 suite. TV TEL. Mon–Thurs £70–£90 ($110.60–$142.20) double; Fri–Sun £65–£75 ($102.70–$118.50) double. Suites £120 ($189.60) all week. Extra bed £20 ($31.60). Rates include English breakfast. AE, DC, MC, V. Free parking.

The town's best inn, a member of Queen's Moat Houses, is near The Gallops (the exercise area for the stables at the Newmarket Heath racetrack), about a five-minute walk from the center of town. Built in the mid-1970s in a two-story format of red brick, it's a favorite of the English horse-racing world and is often fully booked during certain periods of the racing season. It is decorated in an appropriate country-elegant style in its public rooms, including oil portraits of horses and souvenirs of the racing life in its bar and restaurant. The bedrooms are well appointed, conservatively modern, and comfortable. Bertie's Brasserie is the main eatery of the hotel, an informal restaurant serving an English and continental menu, ranging from pink-roasted knuckle of lamb to paella, including Newmarket bangers and mash.

6 Long Melford

61 miles NE of London, 34 miles SE of Cambridge

Long Melford has been famous since the days of the early cloth makers. Like Lavenham, it attained prestige and importance during the Middle Ages. Of the old buildings remaining, the village church is often called "one of the glories of the shire." Along its 3-mile-long High Street—said to boast the highest concentration of antiques shops in Europe—are many private homes erected by wealthy wool merchants of yore. Of special interest are Long Melford's two stately homes.

ESSENTIALS

GETTING THERE

By Train   From London's Liverpool Street Station, trains run toward Ipswich and on to Marks Tey. There you can take a shuttle train going back and forth between that junction and Sudbury. From the town of Sudbury, it's a 3-mile taxi ride to Long Melford.

By Bus   From Cambridge, take a bus (maintained by Chambers Bus Company) to Bury St. Edmunds, then change buses for the final ride into Long Melford. Chambers runs these buses about once an hour throughout the day and early evening.

By Car   From Newmarket (see above), continue east on A45 to Bury St. Edmunds, but cut south on A134 (toward Sudbury) to Long Melford.

VISITOR INFORMATION

The **telephone area code** is 01787. There is a **Tourist Information** office at St. Stephens Church, St. Stephens Lane (☎ **01473/258070**) at Ipswich, 24 miles away.

WHAT TO SEE & DO

Melford Hall

On the east side of A134, Long Melford. ☎ **01787/880286.** Admission £3.50 ($5.55) adults, £1.75 ($2.75) children.May–Sept, Wed–Thurs, Sat–Sun, and bank holiday Mon 2–5:30pm; Apr and Oct, Sat–Sun and bank holiday Mon 2–5:30pm. Closed Nov–Mar.

Standing in Long Melford on the east side of A134 is the ancestral home of Beatrix Potter, who often visited. Jemima Puddleduck still occupies a chair in one of the bedrooms upstairs, and some of her other figures are on display. The house, built between 1554 and 1578, has paintings, fine furniture, and Chinese porcelain. The gardens alone are considered worthy of a visit.

Kentwell Hall

On A134 between Sudbury and Bury St. Edmunds. ☎ **01787/310207.** Admission £7.50 ($11.85) adults, £6.50 ($10.25) senior citizens, £5.50 ($8.70) children. Apr 7–June 16 and Oct, Sun only noon–5pm; July 17–Sept 30, daily noon–5pm. The entrance is north of the green in Long Melford on the west side of A134, about half a mile north of Melford Hall.

At the end of an avenue of linden trees, the red-brick Tudor mansion surrounded by a broad moat has been restored by its owners, barrister Patrick Phillips and his wife. A 15th-century moat house, interconnecting gardens, a brick-paved maze, and a costume display are of interest, and there are also rare-breed farm animals to be seen. Two gate houses are constructed in 16th-century style. The hall hosts regular re-creations of Tudor domestic life, including the well-known annual events for the weeks June 16 to July 14 and lesser events over holiday weekends.

WHERE TO STAY
INEXPENSIVE

Black Lion Hotel

The Green, Long Melford, Suffolk CO10 9DN. ☎ **01787/312356.** Fax 01787/374557. 8 rms, 1 suite. TV TEL. £65–£75 ($102.70–$118.50) double; £85 ($134.30) suite. Rates include continental or English breakfast. AE, MC, V. Free parking.

Since the 1100s, there has been some type of inn on this spot. Fourteenth-century documents mention it as the spot where drinks were dispensed to revolutionaries during one of the peasants' revolts. The present building dates from the early 1800s; it has been richly restored by its present owners. It overlooks one of the loveliest village greens in Suffolk. Each of the individually decorated bedrooms features a tea- and coffee-making facility. An added bonus is the hotel's well-patronized Countrymen restaurant, which offers excellent food and a well-chosen wine list. Fixed-price meals cost £13.25 ($20.95) at lunchtime and £18.75 ($29.65) at dinner. Bar lunches are served for £3.25 ($5.15) and up.

✪ Bull Hotel

Hall St., Long Melford, Sudbury, Suffolk CO10 9JG. ☎ **01787/378494** or 800/225-5843 in the U.S. and Canada. Fax 01787/880307. 23 rms (all with bath or shower), 2 suites. TV TEL. £85 ($134.30) double; £100–£110 ($158–$173.80) suite. Breakfast £5.95–£8.50 ($9.40–$13.45) extra. Discounts (2-night minimum): Mon–Thurs, £54 ($85.30) per person, single or double; Fri–Sun, £62 ($97.95) per person, single or double, including half board. AE, DC, MC, V. Free parking.

Here is an opportunity to experience life in one of the great old inns of East Anglia. Built by a wool merchant in 1540, this hotel is probably Long Melford's finest and best-preserved building. Improvements have been made and the interior has been modernized. Incorporated into the general hotel is a medieval weavers' gallery and the open hearth with Elizabethan brickwork. The bedrooms are a mix of old and new. The Cordell Restaurant is the outstanding part of the Bull, with its high-beamed ceilings, trestle tables, and handmade chairs, as well as a 10-foot fireplace. English and continental cuisine are served; you may want to consider a dining stop-over even if you're not staying here. A fixed-price dinner goes for £17.95 ($28.35). In both the restaurant and bar, lunch is served daily from noon to 2pm and dinner from 7 to 9pm. Menu choices are likely to include sweet pickled herring with dill sauce, poached fillet of plaice with white wine and mushroom sauce, grilled rump steak with a whole-grain mustard sauce, and such vegetarian dishes as baked avocado with a tomato-and-basil sauce.

WHERE TO DINE
MODERATE

Chimneys
Hall St. ☎ **01787/379806.** Reservations required. Main courses £14.50–£20.50 ($22.90–$32.40); fixed price lunch £15.50 ($24.50). AE, MC, V. Daily noon–2pm; Mon–Sat 7–9pm. BRITISH.

Founded in a historic building in the 1920s, this is the best-established and most venerable restaurant in town. The building where it is housed was erected in the 16th century and retains its original dark-stained oaken beams and mellow brick walls in the dining room. In back there is a walled garden. The establishment offers fixed-price menus with a wide choice of foods within every menu category, each influenced by the best aspects of modern British cuisine. If it's featured, try ravioli stuffed with smoked Scottish salmon or perhaps a wild-mushroom soup given added zest by herbs and a dash of Madeira. For a main course, sample such fare as breast of guinea fowl with cabbage and bacon.

INEXPENSIVE

✪ Scutchers Bistro
Westgate St. ☎ **01787/310200.** Reservations recommended. Main courses £6–£10 ($9.50–$15.80). AE, MC, V. Mon–Sat noon–2pm and 7–9:30pm. BRITISH.

Since its establishment in 1991, this upscale bistro has earned favorable recommendations from many diners throughout Suffolk. It's housed on the premises of The Scutchers Arms, which most local residents considered their favorite pub until the new owners painted its facade a bright yellow and covered its heavily beamed interior with vivid Mediterranean colors. Menu choices change daily and are described on both printed cards and blackboards. Your meal might include smoked haddock and prawn cake with crunchy vegetables; sautéed tiger prawns with mushrooms, bacon, and garlic; steamed scallops with asparagus and lemon-flavored hollandaise; warm smoked salmon on a couscous salad; and a very English version of steamed fruit pudding with custard. The building that houses this establishment, incidentally, was erected in stages between the 1600s and the 1800s and was named after the workers (scutchers) who in olden days rendered flax into linen.

7 Lavenham

66 miles NE of London, 35 miles SE of Cambridge

Once a great wool center, Lavenham is considered a typical East Anglian village. It features a number of half-timbered Tudor houses washed in the characteristic Suffolk pink. The prosperity of the town in the days of wool manufacture is apparent in the guildhall, on the triangular main "square," built from wool-trading profits. Inside are exhibits on the textile industry of Lavenham, showing how yarn was spun, then "dyed in the wool" with woad (the plant used by the ancient Picts to dye themselves blue), and following on to the weaving process. There is also a display showing how half-timbered houses were constructed.

The Church of St. Peter and St. Paul, at the edge of Lavenham, has interesting carvings on the misericords and the chancel screen, as well as ornate tombs. This is one of the "wool churches" of the area, built by pious merchants in the perpendicular style with a landmark tower.

ESSENTIALS
GETTING THERE

By Train Board a train at London's North Street Station to Colchester. These depart at least once an hour, sometimes even more often. There, connect to the town of Sudbury (connections are good; only very short delays between trains). At Sudbury, there are about nine daily buses making the short run to Lavenham. These buses are maintained by Beeston's Coaches, Ltd. Total trip time from London is between 2 and $2^1/_2$ hours.

By Car From Bury St. Edmunds, continue south on A134 toward Long Melford (see above), but at the junction with A1141 cut southeast to Lavenham.

VISITOR INFORMATION

The **telephone area code** is 01787. The **Tourist Information Centre** is on Lady Street (☎ **01787/248207**). It is open Easter until the end of September.

WHERE TO STAY
MODERATE

✪ The Swan

High St., Lavenham, Sudbury, Suffolk CO10 9QA. ☎ **01787/247477** or 800/225-5843 in the U.S. and Canada. Fax 01787/248286. 44 rms, 3 suites. MINIBAR TV TEL. £110 ($173.80) double; £125 ($197.50) suite. English breakfast £8.95 ($14.15) extra. AE, DC, MC, V. Free parking.

Linked to the Middle Ages, this lavishly timbered inn is one of the oldest and best-preserved buildings in this relatively unmarred village. Its success has necessitated incorporating an adjoining ancient wool hall, which provides a high-ceilinged and timbered guesthouse and raftered, second-story bedrooms opening onto a tiny cloistered garden. The bedrooms vary in size, according to the eccentricities of the architecture. Most have beamed ceilings and a mixture of traditional pieces that blend well with the old. The more expensive rooms feature four-poster beds. There are nearly enough lounges for guests to try a different one every night of the week.

The Garden Bar opens onto yet another garden, with old stone walls and flower beds. Londoners often visit on weekends for dinner and chamber-music concerts, which are performed from September to March. Meals in the two-story-high dining room, where you sit on leather-and-oak chairs with brass studs, have their own drama. Even if you're not spending the night, you can sample the three-course lunch priced at £14.95 ($23.60). Evening table d'hôte dinners go for £21.95 ($34.70). During World War II, Allied pilots (who made the Swan their second home) carved their signatures into the bar, a longish room with a timbered ceiling and a fine weapons collection.

WHERE TO DINE
INEXPENSIVE

✪ The Great House

Market Place, Lavenham, Sudbury, Suffolk CO10 9QZ. ☎ **01787/247431.** Reservations recommended. Main courses £13–£16 ($20.55–$25.30); fixed-price meals £16.95 ($26.80) at dinner (Tues–Fri). MC, V. FRENCH.

With its Georgian facade and location near the marketplace, The Great House is the finest place to dine. The interior is also attractively decorated, with Laura Ashley prints, an inglenook, and old oak beams. The owner, Régis Crépy, is also the chef de cuisine. He is assisted by his wife, Martine. He is an inventive cook, as reflected by such dishes as marinated smoked salmon with cucumber purée and sour cream, sauté of sweetbreads with a wild-mushroom sauce, and médaillons of lamb fillet in lime sauce. The least expensive way to dine here is to order the fixed-price lunch.

The house also rents four elegantly decorated bedrooms (suites, actually) for £68 to £78 ($107.45 to $123.25) for a double. An English breakfast is included in the rates, and the rooms have private baths or showers, TVs, and phones.

8 Woodbridge & Aldeburgh

Woodbridge: 81 miles NE of London, 47 miles S of Norwich Aldeburgh: 97 miles NE of London, 41 miles SE of Norwich

The market town of Woodbridge is also a yachting center, situated on the Deben River. Its best-known, most famous resident was Edward FitzGerald, Victorian poet and translator of the "Rubaiyat of Omar Khayyam." The poet died in 1883 and was buried some four miles away at Boulge.

Woodbridge is a good base for exploring the East Suffolk coastline, particularly the small resort of Aldeburgh, noted for its moot hall.

Bordering on the North Sea, Aldeburgh is a favorite resort of educated travelers, and it attracts many Dutch, who make the sea crossing via Harwich and Felixstowe, now major entry ports for traffic from the Continent. It was the home of Benjamin Britten (1913–76), renowned composer of the operas *Peter Grimes* and *Billy Budd,* as well as many orchestral works. Many of his compositions were first performed at the **Aldeburgh Festival,** which he founded in 1946. The festival takes place in June, featuring internationally known performers. There are other concerts and events throughout the year. Write or call the tourist office for details. The Snape Maltings Concert Hall nearby is generally regarded as one of the more successful among the smaller British concert halls; it also houses the Britten-Pears School of Advanced Musical Studies, established in 1973.

The town dates from Roman times, and has long been known as a small port for North Sea fisheries. There are two golf courses, one at Aldeburgh and another at Thorpeness, two miles away. A yacht club is situated on the River Alde nine miles from the river's mouth. There are also two bird sanctuaries nearby, Minsmere and Havergate Island. Both are famous for their water fowl, and they are managed by the Royal Society for the Protection of Birds.

Constructed on a shelf of land at the sea level, the High (or main) street runs parallel to the often-turbulent waterfront. A cliff face rises some 55 feet above the main street. A major attraction is the 16th-century **Moot Hall Museum,** Market Cross Place, Aldeburgh (☎ **01728/453295**). The hall dates from the time of Henry VIII, but its tall twin chimneys are later additions. The timber-frame structure displays old maps, prints, and Anglo-Saxon burial urns, as well as other items of historical interest. It is open July and August daily from 10:30am to 12:30pm and 2:30 to 5pm; it is also open Easter to June and in September daily from 2:30 to 5pm. Admission is 45p (70¢) for adults, free for children.

Aldeburgh is also the site of the nation's northernmost martello tower, erected to protect the coast from a feared invasion by Napoléon.

ESSENTIALS
GETTING THERE

By Train Aldeburgh doesn't have a rail station. Trains leave either London's Victoria Station or Liverpool Street Station (depending on the schedule) about six per day in the direction of the line's last stop, Lowestoft. Six stops after Ipswich, the train will stop in the hamlet of Saxmundham. From Saxmundham, there are about a half dozen buses traveling the 6 miles to Aldeburgh. These tend to be daytime (not nighttime) buses. Instead, visitors often hire a taxi at Saxmundham for the trip on to Aldeburgh. Woodbridge, larger and busier than Aldeburgh, has a railway station. The same line described above (to Lowestoft) stops at Woodbridge, which lies two stops after Ipswich.

By Bus A National Express coach departs once a day from London's Victoria Coach Station for Great Yarmouth and passes through Aldeburgh (and also through Woodbridge) en route. Travel time to Aldeburgh is woefully long (4^1/$_4$ hr.) because it visits every country town and virtually every narrow lane along the way.

Note that Aldeburgh and Woodbridge lie 15 miles from one another and are served frequently with bus no. 80/81, operated by the Eastern Counties Bus Company.

Many visitors reach both towns by taking the bus from Ipswich; there are about half a dozen each day, operated by the Eastern Counties Bus Company.

By Car From London's ring road, A12 runs northeast to Ipswich. From Ipswich, continue northeast on A12 to Woodbridge or stay on the road until you reach the junction with A1094, at which point you can head east to the North Sea and Aldeburgh at the end of the line.

VISITOR INFORMATION

The **telephone area code** for Aldeburgh is 01728 and for Woodbridge it's 01394. The **Tourist Information Centre** is at the Cinema, High Street (☎ **01728/453637**), in Aldeburgh, open May through October.

WHERE TO STAY & DINE
NEAR WOODBRIDGE
Moderate

✪ Seckford Hall

On A12, Woodbridge, Suffolk IP13 6NU. ☎ **01394/385678.** Fax 01394/380610. 27 rms, 7 suites. TV TEL. £105–£120 ($165.90–$189.60) double; £148 ($233.85) suite. AE, DC, MC, V. Free parking. Take A12 1^1/$_4$ miles southwest of Woodbridge.

This ivy-covered brick estate captures the spirit of the days of Henry VIII and his strong-willed daughter Elizabeth (the latter may have held court here) with its crow-stepped gables, mullioned windows, and ornate chimneys—pure Tudor. It was built in 1530 by Sir Thomas Seckford, a member of one of Suffolk's first families. You enter through a heavy, studded Tudor door into a flagstone hallway with antiques. The butler will show you to your bedroom. Many rooms have four-poster beds, and one of the four-posters is a monumental 1587 specimen. Owners Mr. and Mrs. Michael Bunn will see to it that your stay is like a house party. Facilities include a heated indoor swimming pool.

If you arrive before sundown, you may want to stroll through a portion of the 34-acre gardens, which include a rose garden, herbaceous borders, and greenhouses.

At the bottom of the garden is an ornamental lake, complete with weeping willows and paddling ducks. At 4pm you can enjoy a complete tea in the Great Hall. Sip your brew slowly as you enjoy the atmosphere of heavy beams and a stone fireplace. Your chair may be Queen Anne, your table Elizabethan. Dinner will be announced by the butler. Good English meals are served in a setting of linen-fold paneling and Chippendale and Hepplewhite chairs. After-dinner coffee and brandy are featured in the Tudor Bar. (Nonresidents can stop by for dinner, which is à la carte; it's best to phone first.) A fixed-price lunch costs £13 ($20.55), with à la carte dinners priced from £25 ($39.50). Seckford Hall is 1 1/2 miles from the Woodbridge rail station.

IN ALDEBURGH
Moderate
Wentworth Hotel

Wentworth Rd., Aldeburgh, Suffolk IP15 5BD. ☎ **01728/452312.** Fax 01728/454343. 38 rms (35 with bath). TV TEL. £84–£106 ($132.70–$167.50) double with bath. Rates include English breakfast. AE, DC, MC, V. Free parking. Closed Dec 27–Jan 10.

A traditional country-house hotel with tall chimneys and gables, the Wentworth overlooks the sea. Built in the early 19th century as a private residence, it was converted into a hotel around 1900. Many rooms have lovely views. Since 1920, the Pritt family has welcomed the world to their hotel, including Sir Benjamin Britten and the novelist E. M. Forster. In summer tables are placed outside so guests can enjoy the sun, but in winter the open fires in the lounges, even the cozy bar, are a welcome sight. Many come here just to enjoy the good food and wine. Bar lunches range from £6 ($9.50), with a table d'hôte dinner costing £11.50 ($18.15) Sunday through Friday, rising to £17.50 ($27.65) on Saturday. In 1994, the management completely gutted a 19th-century building across the road from the main house, converting it into a comfortable, seven-room annex. The standards there match those of the main house.

Inexpensive
Brudenell Hotel

The Parade, Aldeburgh, Suffolk IP15 5BU. ☎ **01728/452071** or 800/225-5843 in the U.S. and Canada. Fax 01728/454082. 47 rms. TV TEL. £75–£90 ($118.50–$142.20) double. English breakfast £8.95 ($14.15) extra. AE, DC, MC, V. Free parking.

Located on the waterfront, this hotel was built at the beginning of the 20th century. It has been remodeled and redecorated to achieve a pleasant interior. Many of the bedrooms face the sea, and each has a radio, tea and coffee makers, central heating, and comfortable beds. The dining room, with an all-glass wall overlooking the coast, is an ideal spot for a three-course luncheon costing £11.95 ($18.90). Dinner goes for £17.50 ($27.65).

9 Norwich

109 miles NE of London, 20 miles W of the North Sea

Norwich still holds to its claim as the capital of East Anglia. As the county town of Norfolk, Norwich is, despite its partial industrialization, a charming and historic city. It's the most important shopping center in East Anglia and has a lot to offer in the way of hotels and entertainment. In addition to its cathedral, it has more than 30 medieval parish churches built of flint.

There are many interesting hotels in the narrow streets and alleyways; there is also a big open-air market, busy every weekday, where fruit, flowers, vegetables, and other goods are sold from stalls with colored canvas roofs.

ESSENTIALS
GETTING THERE

By Train   There is hourly service from London's Liverpool Street Station (trip time: 1 hr., 50 min.).

By Bus   National Express buses depart London's Victoria Coach Station once each hour (trip time: 3 hr.).

By Car   From London's ring road, head north toward Cambridge on M11, but turn northeast at the junction with A11, which will take you all the way to Norwich.

VISITOR INFORMATION

The **telephone area code** is 01603. There is a **Tourist Information Centre** at The Guildhall, Goal Hill (☎ **01603/666071**).

WHAT TO SEE & DO

✪ Norwich Cathedral
62 The Close. ☎ **01603/764385.** Admission to cathedral free; treasury 50p (80¢). Oct–May, daily 7:30am–6pm; June–Sept, daily 7:30am–7pm.

Principally of Norman design, the cathedral dates from 1096. It is noted primarily for its long nave, with its lofty columns. Its spire, built in the late perpendicular style, rises 315 feet; together with the keep of the castle, it forms a significant landmark on the Norwich skyline. On the vaulted ceiling are more than 300 bosses (knoblike ornamental projections) depicting biblical scenes. The impressive choir stalls with the handsome misericords date from the 15th century. Edith Cavell—"Patriotism is not enough"—an English nurse executed by the Germans during World War I, is buried on the cathedral's Life's Green. The quadrangular cloisters, which date back to the 13th century, are the largest monastic cloisters in England.

The cathedral visitors' center includes a refreshment area and an exhibition and film room with tape/slide shows about the cathedral. Inquire at the information desk about guided tours. A short walk from the cathedral will take you to Tombland, one of the most interesting old squares in Norwich.

Impressions

"Yes, there it spreads from north to south, with its venerable houses, its numerous gardens, its thrice twelve churches, its mighty mound, which, if tradition speaks true, was raised by human hands to serve as the grave heap of an old heathen king, who sits deep within it, with his sword in his hand and his gold and silver treasures about him. There is an old grey castle on top of that mighty mound; and yonder, rising three hundred feet above the soil, from among those noble forest trees, behold that old norman master-work, that cloud-encircled cathedral spire around which a garrulous army of rooks and choughs continually wheel their flight. Now, who can wonder that the children of that fine old city are proud of her, and offer up prayers for her prosperity."

—George Borrow (1816)

Norwich Castle (Norfolk Museums Service)

Castle Meadow. ☎ **01603/223624.** Admission £2.20 ($3.50) adults, £1 ($1.60) children. Museum, Apr–Sept, Mon–Sat 10am–5pm, Sun 2–5pm.

In the center of Norwich, on a partly artificial mound, sits the castle, formerly the county jail. Its huge 12th-century Norman keep and the later prison buildings are used as a civic museum and headquarters of the countywide Norfolk Museums Service. There are guided tours of the battlements and dungeons throughout the day.

The museum's art exhibits include an impressive collection of pictures by artists of the Norwich School, the most distinguished of whom were John Crome (b. 1768) and John Sell Cotman (b. 1782). The castle museum also has the best collection of British ceramic teapots in the world and unrivaled collections of Lowestoft porcelain and Norwich silver. Rare prehistoric gold jewelry and other archaeological finds help to illustrate Norfolk's wealth and importance and the life of its people. A set of dioramas shows Norfolk wildlife in its natural setting. You can also visit a geology gallery. The cafeteria is open Monday through Saturday from 10am to 4:30pm, Sunday 2 to 4:30pm.

Sainsbury Centre for Visual Arts

University of East Anglia, Earlham Rd. ☎ **01603/456060.** Admission £1 ($1.60) adults, 50p (80¢) children and students. Tues–Sun noon–5pm. Bus 23, 26, or 27 from Castle Meadow.

The center was the gift in 1973 of Sir Robert and Lady Sainsbury, who contributed their private collection to the University of East Anglia, three miles west of Norwich on Earlham Road. Together with their son David, they gave an endowment to provide a building to house the collection. The center, designed by Foster Associates, was opened in 1978, and since then the building has won many national and international awards. Features of the structure are its flexibility, allowing solid and glass areas to be interchanged, and the superb quality of light, which permit optimum viewing of works of art. Special exhibitions are often presented in the 1991 Crescent Wing extension.

The Sainsbury Collection is one of the foremost in the country, including modern, ancient, classical, and ethnographic art. Its most prominent works are those by Francis Bacon, Alberto Giacometti, and Henry Moore. There's a regular program of special exhibitions. The restaurant on the premises offers a self-service buffet Monday through Friday from 10:30am to 2pm and a carvery service from 12:30 to 2pm. A conservatory coffee bar serves light lunches and refreshments Tuesday through Sunday from noon to 4:30pm.

The Mustard Shop

3 Bridewell Alley. ☎ **01603/627889.** Admission free. Mon–Sat 9:30am–5pm.

The Victorian-style Mustard Shop displays a wealth of mahogany and shining brass. The standard of service and pace of life reflect the personality and courtesy of a bygone age. The Mustard Museum features exhibits on the history of the Colman Company and the making of mustard, its properties and origins. There are old advertisements, as well as packages and "tins." You can browse in the shop, selecting whichever mustards you prefer. Really hot, English-type mustards are sold, as well as the continental blends. Besides mustards, the shop sells aprons, tea towels, chopping boards, pottery mustard pots, and mugs.

Second Air Division Memorial Library

Bethel St. ☎ **01603/215206.** Admission free. Daily 10am–5pm.

A memorial room honoring the Second Air Division of the Eighth United States Army Air Force is part of the central library. The library staff will assist veterans who wish to visit their old air bases in East Anglia. At the library, one can find pertinent books, audiovisual materials, and records of the various bomber groups.

WHERE TO STAY
MODERATE
Maids Head Hotel

Palace St., Tombland, Norwich, Norfolk NR3 1LB. ☎ **01603/761111.** Fax 01603/613688. 80 rms (all with bath or shower), 7 suites. TV TEL. £80 ($126.40) double; £138–£145 ($218.05–$229.10) suite. Rates include English breakfast. AE, DC, MC, V. Free parking.

In business since 1272, the Maids Head claims to be the oldest continuously operated hotel in the United Kingdom. Located in the oldest part of the city, next to Norwich Cathedral, the hotel has two architectural styles: Elizabethan and Georgian. The Georgian section has a prim white entry and small-paned windows. The bedrooms are supplied with bowls of fresh fruit and newspapers; and traditional services, such as shoe cleaning, breakfast in bed, and afternoon cream teas, are offered. The four-poster Queen Elizabeth I Suite (where the Tudor monarch allegedly once slept) is much sought after. Breakfast and lunch are served in an indoor/outdoor restaurant called the Courtyard Carvery. There, a fixed-price lunch costs £9.95 ($15.70), and tea, coffee, and sandwiches are served every day to non-residents from 9am to 5:30pm. Dinner is more elaborate—it is usually served amid the Georgian-era paneling of the Minstrel Room. There, à la carte dinners cost from £13 ($20.55) to around £15 ($23.70) per person.

INEXPENSIVE
Forte Post House Hotel

Ipswich Rd., Norwich, Norfolk NR4 6EP. ☎ **01603/456431** or 800/225-5843 in the U.S. and Canada. Fax 01603/506400. 113 rms. MINIBAR TV TEL. Sun–Thurs £56 ($88.50) single or double; Fri–Sat £43 ($67.95) single or double. Breakfast £5.50–£7.95 ($8.70–$12.55) extra. AE, DC, MC, V. Free parking. Take A140 (Ipswich road) 2 miles from city center and 1 mile from A11 (London road).

Situated on a sloping hillside about 2 miles from the city center, this red-brick building offers comfortably contemporary accommodations for business travelers and tourists. Many of the bedrooms feature sitting areas with sofas and armchairs and soothingly monochromatic color schemes. On the premises there is Trader's Restaurant and Bar as well as an activity center with an indoor pool, gym, solarium, and sauna.

Hotel Nelson

121 Prince of Wales Rd., Norwich, NR1 1DX. ☎ **01603/760260.** Fax 01603/620008. 126 rms, 6 suites. TV TEL. £86.50–£93.50 ($136.70–$147.75) double; £99.50 ($157.20) suite. Rates include English breakfast. AE, DC, MC, V. Free parking.

This modern four-story hotel is located by the water, near Thorpe Station and Foundry Bridge. Each of the bedrooms provides a view of either the river or a pleasant courtyard. A nautical theme prevails in most of the public rooms. One of the restaurants, the Quarterdeck, brings back memories of Norwich's most famous son, Horatio, Admiral Lord Nelson. This restaurant offers fast, cheerful service and a choice of dishes such as Cromer fish pie or beef-and-beer casserole with mushrooms and noodles. It's open daily from 10:30am for coffee and drinks, from noon to 2pm for lunch, and from 5:30 to 10:30pm for informal dinners, beginning at £13.50 ($21.35). Facilities include a swimming pool, sauna, and a gym.

ⓢ Jarvis Lansdowne Hotel

116 Thorpe Rd., Norwich, Norfolk NR1 1RU. ☎ **01603/620302.** Fax 01603/761706. 45 rms. TV TEL. Mon–Thurs, £65 ($102.70) double. Fri–Sun, £31.50 ($49.75) per person, single or double. Breakfast £6–£8.50 ($9.50–$13.45) extra. AE, DC, MC, V. Free parking. Take Thorpe Rd. ¹/₂ mile east of city center.

This hotel was originally constructed in the 18th century as a residence for the local lord mayor.

Guests enjoy many modern conveniences, as well as high standards of service and atmosphere. The refurbished bedrooms are situated in the main building, as well as in two semidetached cottages. The cottages have bay windows and wooden beams as well as a private garden. The reception area's chandeliers light the way up the elegant staircase to the restaurant, where a fixed-price lunch costs £9.95 ($15.70) and a fixed-price dinner goes for £13.50 ($21.35).

WHERE TO DINE
MODERATE

Adlard's

79 Upper St. Giles St. ☎ **01603/633522.** Reservations required. Lunch £13.50 ($21.35) for 2 courses, £16.50 ($26.05) for 3 courses; dinner £31 ($49) for 3 courses, £34 ($53.70) for 4 courses. MC, V. Tues–Sat 12:30–1:45pm; Mon–Sat 7:30–10:30pm. BRITISH.

Chef and owner David Adlard is clearly the culinary star of Norwich. The stylish dining room has a clean crisp decor of green and white, with candlelit tables and a collection of paintings. David and his wife, Mary, see to it that service is correct in every way, but also relaxed enough to make diners comfortable. The chef specializes in modern British cookery, bringing his own interpretation to every dish. These are likely to include poached salmon suprême with a chive-flavored butter sauce, rosette of lamb with an artichoke mousse, or pheasant with a game mousse accompanied by Madeira sauce.

Brasted's

8–10 St. Andrews Hill. ☎ **01603/625949.** Reservations required. Main courses £9.50–£14.75 ($15–$23.30); fixed-price lunches £8.50–£15 ($13.45–$23.70). MC, V. Mon–Fri noon–2pm; Mon–Sat 7–10pm. ENGLISH/FRENCH.

Within an easy stroll of both the cathedral and the castle, Brasted's is housed in a lovely home in the oldest part of Norwich. After exploring the two major sights of Norwich, you can come here to sample the savory cooking of John Brasted, for whom the restaurant is named. The owner and chef de cuisine, Mr. Brasted knows how to combine the best of yesterday with modern cooking techniques and innovations. As you enjoy the rather flamboyant interior, you can peruse the menu. You'll probably settle for one of the fresh fish dishes of East Anglia. Other dishes, including vegetables and desserts, seem equally well prepared.

Greens Seafood Restaurant

82 Upper St. Giles St. ☎ **01603/623733.** Reservations recommended. Main courses £8–£16 ($12.65–$25.30). Set-price lunches £12.50–£15 ($19.75–$23.70); set-price dinners £20–£24 ($31.60–$37.90). MC, V. Tues–Fri 12:15–2:15pm; Tues–Sat 7–10:45pm, Mon 7–10:45pm June–Aug. SEAFOOD.

Located in a much-altered 18th-century building, which functioned long ago as a bank, this restaurant's interior is painted green in honor of its name. Surrounded by sepia-toned engravings of the seafaring life, you'll enjoy the best and freshest fish in the region. Menu choices include both intricate and complicated preparations of fresh seafood influenced by classic European traditions, as well as a wide selection of less complicated grilled fish served with a variety of sauces.

Examples of this restaurant's "classic menu" include ravioli stuffed with a purée of scallops and served with bean sprouts, oyster mushrooms, and a coriander/ginger sauce; smoked goose-breast salad served with a leg of goose cooked *en confit;* and fillet of sea bass with scallop mousse, served with tarragon-cream sauce and crayfish tails. The list of grilled fish includes skate, salmon, sea bass, turbot, sole, and many others served with herb butter, white wine and garlic, or hollandaise, according to your preference. A live pianist provides music throughout about half of each of the dinner hours. The owner and chef is Dennis Crompton.

Marco's

17 Pottergate. ☎ **01603/624044.** Reservations required. Main courses £12.50–£16.50 ($19.75–$26.05). Fixed-price lunch £14 ($22.10). AE, DC, MC, V. Tues–Sat 12:30–2pm and Tues–Sat 7:30–10pm. NORTHERN ITALIAN.

Located in a Regency house, a two-minute walk from Market Place, this is the premier Italian restaurant of Norwich. By no means should you imagine that this is the kind of place where Chianti bottles hang from the ceiling and troubadours serenade clients in the style of Naples. Instead, you'll find one of the smallest dining rooms in town (only six tables) decorated with elegant cove moldings, the building's original marble fireplace, and soothing tones of buttermilk, gold, and black. Although smoking is not allowed in the dining room, a comfortable bar/lounge decorated in the Chinese style (in honor of another Italian named Marco, Marco Polo) permits guests to congregate before or after dinner for drinks and cigarettes. Try such dishes as baked saddle of lamb with a red currant, mint and orange sauce, or else chicken breast with slices of Parma ham served with a Marsala sauce. A fish specialty from Genoa—a *buridda*—combines monkfish, seabass, and king prawns, flavored with garlic, wine, herbs, and tomato.

EXCURSIONS FROM NORWICH

Blickling Hall

Blickling, near Aylsham. ☎ **01263/733084.** House and gardens, Mon–Sat £4.90 ($7.75) adults, £2.40 ($3.80) children; Sun and bank holiday Mon £5.50 ($8.70) adults, £2.75 ($4.35) children. Gardens only, £3.50 ($5.55) adults, £1.60 ($2.55) children. Apr–Oct, Tues–Wed and Fri–Sun 1–5pm (gardens, shop, and restaurant noon–5pm). Blickling Hall lies 14 miles north of the city of Norwich, 1½ miles west of Aylsham on B1354; take A140 toward Cromer and follow the signs.

A long drive, bordered by massive yew hedges that frame your first view of this old house, leads you to Blickling Hall. A great Jacobean house built in the early 17th century, it is perhaps one of the finest examples of such architecture in the country. The long gallery has an elaborate 17th-century ceiling, and the Peter the Great Room, decorated later, has a fine tapestry on the wall. The house is set in ornamental parkland with a formal garden and an orangery. Meals and snacks are available.

✪ Sandringham

Sandringham, 8 miles northeast of King's Lynn (off A149). ☎ **01553/772675.** House, grounds, and museum £4 ($6.30) adults, £3 ($4.75) senior citizens, £2 ($3.15) children. Grounds and museum: £3 ($4.75) adults, £2.50 ($3.95) senior citizens, £1.50 ($2.35) children. Easter–Oct 2, daily 11am–4:45pm, Sun noon–4:45pm. Closed July 19–Aug 4. Directions: See below.

Some 110 miles northeast of London, Sandringham has been the country home of four generations of British monarchs, ever since the Prince of Wales (later King Edward VII) purchased it in 1861. The son of Queen Victoria, along with his Danish wife, Princess Alexandra, rebuilt the house, situated on 7,000 acres of grounds, and in time it became a popular meeting place for British society. The red-brick and stone Victorian-Tudor mansion consists of more than 200 rooms, and in recent years some of the rooms have been opened to the public, including two drawing rooms, the ballroom, and a dining room. Sandringham is now among the many British royal residences that can be visited by the public, and its atmosphere of a well-loved family home is a contrast to the formal splendor of Buckingham Palace. Guests can also view a loft salon with a minstrel's gallery used as a sitting room by the royal family and full of photographs and mementos. A **Land Train,** designed and built on the estate, makes it easy for visitors to reach Sandringham House which sits at the heart of 60 acres of beautiful grounds. Although the vast majority of people coming to Sandringham enjoy walking through the grounds and across the impressive lawns, some of the more elderly, disabled, or frail find it too tiring. The Land Train, with its covered carriages and room for wheelchairs, makes their visits more comfortable but can be used by anyone.

Sandringham Museum holds a wealth of rare items relating to the history of the Royal Family at Sandringham. Displays tell the story of the monarchs who have owned the estate since 1862. Visitors can see the big game trophies in settings that include a safari trail.

Sandringham is 50 miles east of Norwich and 8 miles northeast of King's Lynn (off A149). King's Lynn is the end of the main train route from London's Liverpool Street Station that goes via Cambridge and Ely. Trains to King's Lynn arrive from London once every 2 hours (trip time: 2¹/₂ hr.). From Cambridge, the train ride takes only 1 hour. Buses from both Cambridge and Norwich run to King's Lynn, where you can catch bus no. 411 to take you the rest of the way to Sandringham.

The Northwest 18

The great industrial shadow of the 19th century cast such a darkness over England's northwest that the area has been relatively neglected by foreign visitors. At best, most Americans rush through it heading for the glories of the Lake District and Scotland.

However, the northwest, in spite of its industry and bleak commercial area, has much beauty for the tourist who is willing to seek it out. Manchester, Lancaster, Morecambe, and Southport—to name only a few—are all interesting cities, and much of the countryside is beautiful and is filled with inns, restaurants, and pubs, along with many sightseeing attractions.

We will concentrate, however, on only two of its more popular cities—Chester and Liverpool, followed by the most interesting towns and villages of the Lake District, such as Windermere.

Cheshire, the county in which Chester lies, is world renowned for its cheese. This low-lying northwestern county is largely agricultural and, bordering Wales, it has had a turbulent history: The towns and villages of Cheshire offer a good base for touring North Wales, the most beautiful part of that little country.

Liverpool, former home of the Beatles, has done much in recent years to revitalize its tourist industry, especially since the restoration of its waterfront, which today houses many museums and exhibitions. An extension of London's Tate Gallery also opened there in 1988, with a collection of modern art.

One of England's most popular summer retreats in Queen Victoria's day was the Lake District. In its time the district has lured such writers as Samuel Taylor Coleridge; Charlotte Brontë; Charles Lamb; Percy Bysshe Shelley; John Keats; Alfred, Lord Tennyson; and Matthew Arnold.

The Lake District, called a "miniature Switzerland," is actually quite small, measuring about 35 miles wide. Most of the district is in Cumbria, although it begins in the northern part of Lancashire.

Driving in the wilds of this northwestern shire is fine for a start. But the best activity is walking, which is an art best practiced here with a crooked stick. There is a great deal of rain and heavy mist, and sunny days are few. When the mist starts to fall, try to be near an inn or pub, where you can drop by and warm yourself beside an open fireplace. You'll be carried back to the good old days, since many places in Cumbria have valiantly resisted change.

What's Special About the Northwest

Great Towns/Villages
- Chester, a Roman and medieval walled city, famed for its Rows (galleried arcades reached by steps from the street).
- Liverpool, the home of the Beatles, a major 18th-century port for the trade of sugar and enslaved persons.
- Windermere, major center for England's most beautiful lake and best resort for a Lake District base.

Natural Spectacles
- Scafell Pike, rising to a height of 3,210 feet, the tallest peak in England.
- Lake Windermere, the grandest of lakes, a recreational center in summer, attracting boaters.

Literary Shrines
- Rydal Mount, outside Ambleside, home of William Wordsworth from 1813 until his death in 1850.
- Brantwood, home of John Ruskin, the poet, artist, and towering figure of the Victorian age.

Cathedral
- Cathedral Church of Christ, Liverpool, the last Gothic cathedral erected worldwide and the fifth-largest cathedral in the world.

Museum
- Tate Gallery, Liverpool, housing a noted collection of 20th-century art.

The far-northwestern part of the shire, bordering Scotland, used to be called Cumberland. Now part of Cumbria, it is generally divided geographically into a trio of segments: the Pennines, dominating the eastern sector (loftiest point at Cross Fell, nearly 3,000 feet high); the Valley of Eden; and the lakes and secluded valleys of the west, by far the most interesting. The area, so beautifully described by the romantic Lake Poets, enjoys many literary associations.

The largest town is Carlisle in the north—a possible base for explorations to Hadrian's Wall. Built in the 2nd century A.D. by the Romans, the 75-mile wall stretches from Wallsend in the east to Bowness on the Solway. Brockhole National Park Centre, between Ambleside and Windermere, is well worth a visit.

A DRIVING TOUR

Day 1   From London, take M1 and M6 and head north to Chester (the M6 continues north, with cutoffs to various villages and towns in the Lake District). If you leave London early enough, you can arrive in Chester, 207 miles northwest of London in time for a walk along The Rows, a double-decker layer of shops. Stay overnight in Chester.

Day 2   In the morning explore Chester Cathedral and Chester zoo, 2 miles north of the center, then continue north along the signposted route to Liverpool for the night. Arrive in time for lunch and visit both its cathedrals (see below) and Tate Gallery Liverpool. Spend the night there.

☕ **TAKE A BREAK** La Grande Bouffe, 48A Castle Street in Liverpool (☎ 0151/236-3375), is a basement restaurant which is mostly self-service for lunches served Monday through Friday from noon to 3pm. The steamed monkfish à la niçoise places you on the French Riviera, but homemade black pudding returns you squarely to the northwest of England. Dinners are also served Tuesday through Saturday from 6 to 10:30pm.

Day 3 In the morning visit the Merseyside Maritime Museum before heading to the Lake District (along M6), arriving in Windermere for a stay of two nights.

Day 4 In the morning explore the Windermere Steamboat Museum and go for a boat ride on the lake. In the afternoon visit Rydal Mount, the home of William Wordsworth, 1 1/2 miles north of Ambleside. Return to Windermere for the night.

Day 5 Transfer to Grasmere and visit Dove Cottage and the Wordsworth Museum in the morning. In the afternoon explore Hawkshead and Coniston, stopping in at Brantwood, former home of John Ruskin. Return to Grasmere for the night.

Day 6 For a final look at the Lake District, go to Keswick, 22 miles northwest of Windermere for the night. This will allow you to explore Derwentwater, one of the loveliest lakes in the district. In the afternoon, drive to Ullwater, 26 miles southeast of Keswick, to view this seven-mile expanse of water, the second largest lake in the district, where Wordsworth first saw those daffodils he was later to make immortal in poetry.

1 Chester

207 miles NW of London, 19 miles S of Liverpool, 91 miles NW of Birmingham

Chester is ancient, having been founded by a Roman legion on the Dee River in the 1st century A.D. It reached its pinnacle as a bustling port in the 13th and 14th centuries but declined following the gradual silting up of the river. The upstart Liverpudlians captured the sea-trafficking business. While other walls of medieval cities of England were either torn down or badly fragmented, Chester still has 2 miles of fortified city walls intact.

The main entrance into Chester is Eastgate, which dates only from the 18th century. Within the walls are half-timbered houses and shops; of course, not all of them date from Tudor days. Chester is unusual in that some of its builders used black-and-white timbered facades even during the Georgian and Victorian eras.

The Rows are double-decker layers of shops, one tier on the street level, the others stacked on top and connected by a footway. The upper tier is like a continuous galleried balcony—rain is never a problem. Shopping upstairs is much more adventurous than down on the street. Thriving establishments operate in this traffic-free paradise: tobacco shops, restaurants, department stores, china shops, jewelers, and antiques dealers. For the best look take a walk on arcaded Watergate Street.

At the junction of Watergate, Northgate, and Bridge streets, at noon and 3pm Tuesday through Saturday, April to September, at the City Cross, the town crier issues his news (local stuff on sales, exhibitions, and attractions in the city) to the accompaniment of a hand bell. Eastgate Street is now a pedestrian way, and musicians often perform for your pleasure beside St. Peter's Church and the Town Cross.

ESSENTIALS
GETTING THERE

By Train   About 21 trains per day from London's Euston Station depart every hour for Chester (trip time: 3 hr.). Trains also run every 30 minutes between Liverpool and Chester (trip time: 45 min.).

By Bus   One National Express bus every hour runs between Birmingham and Chester (trip time: 2 hr.). The same bus line also offers service between Liverpool and Chester. It's also possible to catch a National Express coach from London's Victoria Coach Station to Chester.

By Car   From London, head north on M1, crossing onto M6 at the junction near Coventry. Continue northwest to the junction with A54, which leads west to Chester.

VISITOR INFORMATION

The **telephone area code** is 01244. The **Tourist Information Centre** is at the Town Hall, Northgate Street (☎ **01244/318356**), and offers a hotel-reservation service as well as information. Arrangements can also be made for coach tours or walking tours of Chester (including a ghost hunter tour).

WHAT TO SEE & DO

In a big Victorian building opposite the Roman amphitheater, the largest uncovered amphitheater in Britain, the **Chester Visitor Centre,** Vicars Lane (☎ **01244/351609**), offers a number of services to visitors. A visit to a life-size Victorian street complete with sounds and smells helps your appreciation of and orientation to Chester. The center has a gift shop and a licensed restaurant serving meals and snacks. Admission is free, and the center is open daily from 9am to 6pm and to 5pm in winter. Guided walking tours of the city depart daily.

In the center of town, you'll see the much-photographed Eastgate clock. Climb the nearby stairs to the top of the **city wall.** You can walk along the wall looking down on Chester. Passing through centuries of English history, you'll go by a cricket field, see the River Dee, formerly a major trade artery, and get a look at many 18th-century buildings. The wall also goes past some Roman ruins, and it's possible to leave the walkway to explore them. The walk is charming and free.

Chester Cathedral
St. Werburgh St. ☎ **01244/324756.** Admission free. Daily 7am–6:30pm.

The present building, founded in 1092 as a Benedictine abbey, was made an Anglican cathedral church in 1541. Many architectural restorations were carried out in the 19th century, but older parts have been preserved. Notable features include the fine range of monastic buildings, particularly the cloisters and refectory, the chapter house, and the superb medieval wood carving in the quire (especially for misericords). Also worth seeing are the long south transept with its various chapels, the consistory court, and the medieval roof bosses in the lady chapel. A freestanding bell tower, the first to be built in England since the Reformation, was completed in 1975 and may be seen southeast of the main building. Facilities include a refectory, a gift shop, and an audiovisual presentation.

Chester Zoo
Off A41, Upton-by-Chester, 2 miles north of the center. ☎ **01244/380280.** Admission £7 ($11.05) adults; £4.50 ($7.10) children 3–15. Monorail £1 ($1.60) adults, 80p ($1.25)

The Northwest

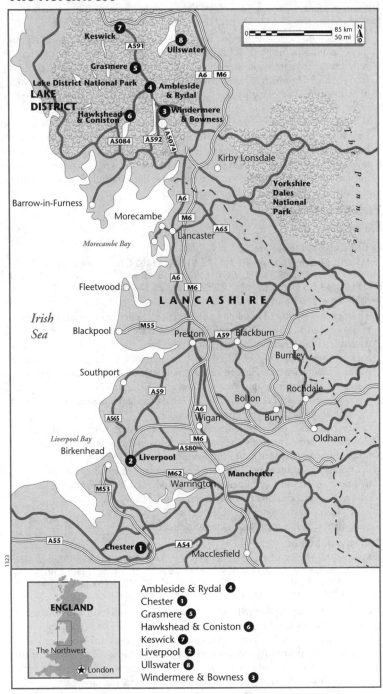

Keswick ⑦
Ullswater ⑧
A591
Grasmere ⑤
A6 M6
Lake District National Park
LAKE DISTRICT
Ambleside & Rydal ④
Hawkshead & Coniston ⑥
Windermere & Bowness ③
A5084 A592 A5074

Barrow-in-Furness

Kirby Lonsdale

Yorkshire Dales National Park

A6

Morecambe

M6

A65

Lancaster

Morecambe Bay

The Pennines

Fleetwood

A6

M6

LANCASHIRE

Irish Sea

Blackpool

M55

Preston

A59 Blackburn

Burnley

Southport

A59

Rochdale

Bolton

A565

A6

Wigan

Bury

Oldham

Liverpool Bay

M6

Birkenhead

A580

② **Liverpool**

M62

Manchester

Warrington

M53

M55

A55

Chester ①

A54

Macclesfield

0 ──────── 85 km / 50 mi

N

1323

ENGLAND

The Northwest

★ London

Ambleside & Rydal ④
Chester ①
Grasmere ⑤
Hawkshead & Coniston ⑥
Keswick ⑦
Liverpool ②
Ullswater ⑧
Windermere & Bowness ③

children. Free for kids under 3. Daily 10am–3:30 to 5:30pm, depending on season (last admission). Closed Dec 25. From Chester's center, head north along Liverpool Rd.

Established in 1934, Chester Zoo is the largest and most comprehensive repository of animals in the north of England; it is also the site of some of the most carefully manicured gardens in the region. Many rare and endangered species breed freely in a setting which is particularly renowned for the most successful colonies of chimpanzees and orangutans in Europe. The 110 acres of gardens feature unusual shrubs, rare trees, and warm-weather displays of carpet bedding with as many as 160,000 plants that are timed to bloom simultaneously. The water bus, a popular observation aid which operates exclusively in summer, allows you to observe hundreds of water birds that make their home on the park's lake. There's also a monorail facility which stops at the extreme eastern and western ends of the zoo, making visits less tiring. Year-round restaurants include the fully licensed Oakfield Restaurant and the Jubilee self-service cafeteria.

WHERE TO STAY
EXPENSIVE

✪ Chester Grosvenor Hotel

Eastgate St., Chester, Cheshire CH1 1DE. ☎ **01244/324024.** Fax 01244/313246. 76 rms, 11 suites. A/C MINIBAR TV TEL. £170–£190 ($268.60–$300.20) double; £270–£370 ($426.60–$584.60) suite. Breakfast £7.75–£9.95 ($12.25–$15.70) extra. AE, DC, MC, V. Free parking.

This fine, half-timbered building in the heart of Chester is one of the most luxurious hotels in northern England. Its reputation is well deserved. It is owned and named after the family of the dukes of Westminster, and its origin can be traced back to the reign of Queen Elizabeth I. Started as a Tudor inn, it became a political headquarters in Hanoverian days, was later transformed into a glittering mecca for the Regency and Victorian set, and continued to be a social center during the Edwardian era. Prince Albert visited here, and more recent guests have included Princess Diana and Prince Rainier.

The high-ceilinged, marble-floored foyer of the hotel, with its 200-year-old chandelier, carved wooden staircase, and antiques, sets the tone. The large, well-furnished bedrooms have radios and hair dryers.

Dining/Entertainment: This grand hotel has the finest drinking and dining facilities in the county. Its formal restaurant, Arkle, and its more informal La Brasserie will be reviewed later (see "Where to Dine," below).

Services: 24-hour room service, laundry.

Facilities: Sauna, gym, solarium, business center.

✪ Crabwall Manor

Parkgate Rd., Mollington, Chester, Cheshire CH1 6NE. ☎ **01244/851666** or 800/525-4800 in the U.S. and Canada. Fax 01244/851400. 42 rms, 6 suites. TV TEL. £135 ($213.30) double; £155 ($244.90) suite. Rates include English breakfast. AE, DC, MC, V. Free parking. Take A540 2¹/₄ miles northwest of Chester. Bus 22 or 23.

Chester's only country-house hotel, Crabwall Manor traces its origins back to the 16th century. Most of the present building, however, dates from the early 1800s. Standing amid 11 acres of private grounds and gardens, the capably managed hotel rents well-furnished bedrooms, each with a private bath or shower. Most of the rooms are quite large and show a certain flair in their decoration, and the bathrooms are first class, with bidets and separate showers for the most part.

The finest of contemporary English and French dishes are offered in a conservatory restaurant overlooking the gardens. Nonresidents are also welcome to enjoy the harmonious flavors, the subtle sauces, and the well-chosen meat, fowl, and fish that are served daily from 12:30 to 2pm and 7 to 9:30pm. The restaurant menu is à la carte, with three-course menus starting as low as £25 ($39.50) per head.

MODERATE

Mollington Banastre
Parkgate Rd., Chester, Cheshire CH1 6NN. ☎ **01244/851471** or 800/528-1234 in the U.S. and Canada. Fax 01244/851165. 62 rms, 2 suites. TV TEL. £90–£95 ($142.20–$150.10) double; £95 ($150.10) family rm (2 adults and up to 4 children); £134 ($211.70) suite for 2. Rates include English breakfast. AE, DC, MC, V. Free parking. Take A540 2 miles northwest of the center of Chester.

This Victorian mansion has been successfully converted into one of the leading country-house hotels in Cheshire. It's affiliated with the Best Western reservation system. A gabled house, it offers a health and leisure complex, along with a duo of restaurants and well-furnished bedrooms, each with private bath.

Rowton Hall Hotel
Whitchurch Rd., Rowton, Chester, Cheshire CH3 6AD. ☎ **01244/335262.** Fax 01244/335464. 42 rms, 1 suite. TV TEL. £88–£126 ($139.05–$199.10) double; £125–£219 ($197.50–$346) suite. Rates include English breakfast. AE, DC, MC, V. Free parking. Take A41 2 miles from the center of Chester.

Two miles from Chester, this stately home offers overnight accommodations for motorists. The gracious house, built in 1779 with a wing added later, has an eight-acre garden, with a formal driveway entrance. Rowton Hall has comfortable traditional and contemporary furnishings. All bedrooms, which have private baths, are attractively and comfortably furnished. The good English meals are served in an oak-paneled dining room with a Tudor fireplace. A special feature is the hotel's swimming pool, plus its gym offering a workout with your own personal trainer as well as remedial messages. Aerobic classes are also conducted. The hotel stands on the site of the Battle of Rowton Moor, which was fought in 1643 between the Roundheads and the Cavaliers.

INEXPENSIVE

Blossoms Hotel
St. John's St., Chester, Cheshire CH1 1HL. ☎ **01244/323186** or 800/225-5843 in the U.S. and Canada. Fax 01244/346433. 61 rms, 3 suites. TV TEL. £80 ($126.40) double; £100 ($158) suite. Breakfast £8.75 ($13.85) extra. AE, DC, MC, V. Free parking.

Blossoms Hotel has been in business since the mid-17th century, though the present structure was rebuilt late in Victoria's day. Each of the traditionally furnished bedrooms is equipped with central heating, and all have private baths, radios, and coffee makers. The old open staircase in the reception room sets the tone of the hotel.

Dinner is served in the Brooks Restaurant from 7 to 9:45pm daily, offering both a table d'hôte dinner at £17.95 ($28.35) and an à la carte menu. These are available for lunch as well as dinner. The Snooty Fox, a traditional English pub with a hunting decor, is open for lunch Monday through Saturday from 11am to 2:30pm.

WHERE TO DINE
MODERATE

✿ Arkle Restaurant

In the Chester Grosvenor Hotel, Eastgate St. ☎ **01244/324024.** Reservations required. Main courses £18–£26 ($28.45–$41.10); fixed-price lunch £18–£22.50 ($28.45–$35.55); fixed-price "menu gourmand" £37 ($58.45). AE, DC, MC, V. Tues–Sat noon–2:30pm; Mon–Sat 7–10:30pm. BRITISH/CONTINENTAL.

In this part of England, the premier restaurant is the Arkle, which is located in the Chester Grosvenor Hotel (see "Where to Stay," above). The 45-seat formal, gourmet restaurant has a superb chef de cuisine and a talented 40-strong team preparing the finest food with the freshest ingredients.

Here you get modern British and continental dishes prepared with subtle touches and a certain lightness, as reflected by the sauces and the cooking of meats and vegetables. You're likely to be served such main courses as roasted local sea bass with scallions and basil oil; fillet of beef on a bed of flaked oxtail topped with foie gras and roasted bay vegetables; roast loin of lamb on cannelloni on a bed of braised cabbage; or locally caught poached turbot with oysters and asparagus tips with fresh morels and sorrel. Desserts are equally luscious and tempting. The Arkle has an award-winning cheese selection and unique breads (a choice of at least six daily) and cheese biscuits are homemade.

❸ La Brasserie

In the Chester Grosvenor Hotel, Eastgate St. ☎ **01244/324024.** Reservations not necessary. Main courses £6.25–£18 ($9.90–$28.45). AE, DC, MC, V. Daily 6:30am–11pm. ENGLISH/FRENCH.

This restaurant is in the same building as the prestigious Chester Grosvenor Hotel; it is perhaps the best all-around dining choice in Chester, not only for convenience but also for price and quality. In a delightful art nouveau setting, the Brasserie offers an extensive à la carte menu to suit most tastes and pocketbooks. Main dishes are likely to include grilled fillet of haddock with creamed leeks, char-grilled calf's liver and bacon, Grosvenor sausages with crushed garlic potatoes and onion gray, and other hearty brasserie food.

INEXPENSIVE

Garden House Restaurant

1 Rufus Court, Northgate St. ☎ **01244/313251.** Reservations recommended. Main courses £10.50–£13.75 ($16.60–$21.75). AE, DC, MC, V. Mon–Sat noon–2pm and 6:30–9:30pm. INTERNATIONAL.

The renovation of the building that houses this restaurant (and also the food served within it) has won several civic awards. It's located within a complex of Georgian buildings originally designed as an archbishop's palace and later occupied by the city's hangman. You can dine on either of two levels which are interconnected with a sweeping Georgian staircase lined with oil portraits and silver candelabrum. (Upstairs is generally considered more formal and elegant than downstairs.) During nice weather, additional tables are set in the large outdoor garden, overlooking pieces of sculpture strategically placed amid the shrubbery.

Menu choices include a risotto of wild and long grain rice cooked in chicken stock and threaded with chicken, all on a bed of Parma ham; fresh mussels steamed in their shells with leeks, onions, garlic, carrots, and parsley bound in a cream and white wine sauce; pan-fried fillets of beef topped with pâté and coated with a brandy Dijon mustard sauce; pan-fried pork wrapped in Parma ham laid on port wine sauce and garnished with a basket of sweet onion confit; and roasted médaillons of monkfish topped with black pepper and garlic with roasted capsicum sauce. A wide range of vegetarian dishes is also offered, including a mixture of eggplant and cheese flavored with oriental spices and wrapped in a phyllo pastry parcel laid on a tomato and basil sauce, or vegetable cheesecake, a selection of vegetables bound in cottage and curd cheese based and surrounded with a cucumber and dry vermouth sauce.

AN EASY EXCURSION TO NANTWICH

Fifteen miles southeast of Chester, this old market town on the Weaver River is particularly outstanding because of its black-and-white timbered houses. The best known, Churche's Mansion, is a dining recommendation.

WHERE TO STAY
Moderate

✪ Rookery Hall

Main Rd., Worleston, near Nantwich, Cheshire CW5 6DQ. ☎ **01270/610016.** Fax 01270/ 626027. 45 rms, 5 suites. TV TEL. £150 ($237) double; from £190 ($300.20) suite. Rates include English breakfast. AE, DC, MC, V. Free parking. Take A51 2$^{1}/_{2}$ miles north of Nantwich.

With its striking Italianate facade and massive proportions, this structure would appear at home in the Loire Valley in France. More château than manor house, it was built in 1815 but radically altered in 1860 into the High Victorian design that stands today. Guests are welcomed to the handsomely furnished bedrooms, each with comfortable amenities.

While you enjoy panoramic views of the surrounding countryside, you can sample well-prepared food, a combination of English dishes and modern French cuisine. The lavishly paneled dining room is a suitable setting for meals based on traditional English cookery with a modern twist. Dinners begin at £28.50 ($45.05). The restaurant at the hotel has received many awards for its food and service. All dishes are freshly prepared and cooked to order. Meat and fish dishes are cooked lightly to preserve their natural flavors, and the freshest vegetables are prepared to retain their natural crispness. You might begin with a hot oak-smoked salmon with crab and ginger beignets, then follow with a fillet of beef with roast parsnip purée, onion marmalade, and celeriac or Lancashire chicken with coriander tagliatelle and ginger shallot sauce.

WHERE TO DINE
Moderate

Churche's Mansion Restaurant

150 Hospital St. ☎ **01270/625933.** Reservations recommended. 2-course fixed-price lunch £12.50 ($19.75); 3-course fixed-price lunch £15.50 ($24.50); 4-course fixed-price dinner £24 ($37.90). DC, MC, V. Morning coffee daily 10–11:45am; Tues–Sat noon–2:30pm and 7–9:30pm. Closed Jan. Take A534 half a mile east of the center, to the junction with A52. ENGLISH.

Churche's Mansion lies in Nantwich at the junction of Newcastle Road and the Chester bypass. Many years ago, the late Dr. and Mrs. E. C. Myott learned that this historic home had been advertised for sale in America and asked the town council to step in and save it. Outbidding the American syndicate that wanted to transport it to the United States, they sought out the mysteries of the house: a window in the side wall, inlaid initials, a Tudor well in the garden, and a long-ago love knot with a central heart (a token of Richard Churche's affection for his young wife). At lunch you are likely to be served a terrine of smoked and marinated salmon with a mustard and dill sauce; char-grilled fillet of sirloin with parsley butter and baked tomatoes stuffed with red pesto; or a risotto with grilled wild mushrooms. At dinner the chef is likely to prepare such typical dishes as roast duck with orange carrots and a sweet herb sauce; steamed salmon with shallots, red wine dressing, and deep-fried vegetables; or a cassoulet with dumplings and a bean mixture with a spicy sauce and herbed crumbs.

2 Liverpool

219 miles NW of London, 103 miles NW of Birmingham, 35 miles W of Manchester

Liverpool, with its famous waterfront on the River Mersey, is a great shipping port and industrial center that gave the world such famous figures as the fictional Fannie Hill and the Beatles. King John launched it on its road to glory when he granted it a charter in 1207. Before that, it had been a tiny 12th-century fishing village, but it quickly became a port for shipping men and materials to Ireland. In the 18th century its port grew to prominence as a result of the sugar, spice, and tobacco trade with the Americans. By the time Victoria came to the throne, Liverpool had become Britain's biggest commercial seaport. Recent refurbishing of the Albert Dock, establishment of a Maritime Museum, and the converting of warehouses into little stores similar to those in Ghirardelli Square in San Francisco have made this an up-and-coming area once again, with many attractions for visitors.

Liverpudlians are proud of their city, with its new hotels, two cathedrals, shopping and entertainment complexes, and parks and open spaces (2,400 acres in and around the city). Liverpool's main shopping street, Church, is traffic free.

ESSENTIALS
GETTING THERE

By Plane Liverpool has its own airport, Spoke (☎ **0151/486-8877**), which has frequent daily flights from many parts of the United Kingdom, including London, the Isle of Man, and Ireland.

By Train Express trains from London's Euston Station arrive frequently at Liverpool (trip time: 2¼ hr.). There is also frequent service from Manchester (trip time: 1 hr.).

By Bus National Express buses from London's Victoria Coach Station depart every 2 hours (trip time: 4¼ hr.). Buses also arrive every hour from Manchester (trip time: 1 hr.).

By Car From London, head northwest on M1, until it links with M6. Continue northwest on M6 until you reach the junction with M62 heading west to Liverpool.

VISITOR INFORMATION

The **telephone area code** is 0151. The **Tourist Information Centre** is at the Atlantic Pavilion, Albert Dock (☎ **0151/708-8854**). There is also a Tourist Information Centre in the City Centre: Merseyside Welcome Centre, Clayton Square (☎ **0151/709-3631**).

Liverpool

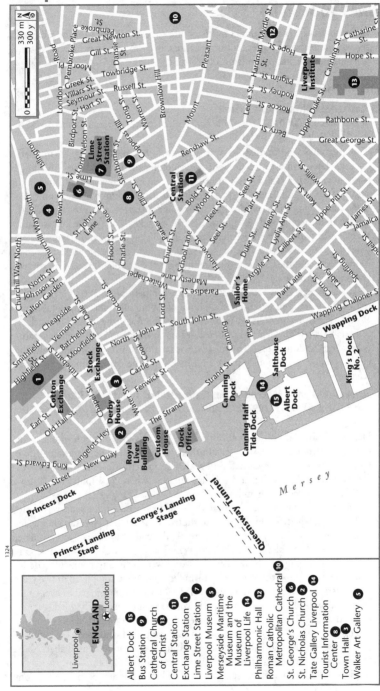

Albert Dock **15**
Bus Station **9**
Cathedral Church of Christ **13**
Central Station **11**
Exchange Station **1**
Lime Street Station **7**
Liverpool Museum **5**
Merseyside Maritime Museum and the Museum of Liverpool Life **14**
Philharmonic Hall **12**
Roman Catholic Metropolitan Cathedral **10**
St. George's Church **6**
St. Nicholas Church **2**
Tate Gallery Liverpool **14**
Tourist Information Center **8**
Town Hall **3**
Walker Art Gallery **5**

WHAT TO SEE & DO

Liverpool has a wealth of things for the visitor to see and enjoy—major cathedrals, restored waterfront glories, cultural centers, even the places where the Beatles began their meteoric rise to fame and fortune.

THE CATHEDRALS

✪ Cathedral Church of Christ

Saint James Mount. ☎ **0151/7096271.** Admission to cathedral, free; tower, £1.50 ($2.35) adults, £1 ($1.60) children. Daily 8am–6pm.

The great new Anglican edifice was begun in 1904 and was largely completed 74 years later. On a rocky eminence overlooking the River Mersey, this might possibly be the last Gothic-style cathedral to be built worldwide. Dedicated in the presence of Queen Elizabeth II in 1978, it is the largest church in the country and is the fifth largest in the world: Its vaulting under the tower is 175 feet high, the highest in the world, and its length—619 feet—makes it one of the longest cathedrals in the world. The organ has nearly 10,000 pipes, the most found in any church. The tower houses the highest (219 feet) and the heaviest (31 tons) bells in the world, and the Gothic arches are the highest ever built. From the tower, you can see to North Wales.

The architect, Giles Scott, after winning a competition in 1903 for this building's design, went on to rebuild the House of Commons, gutted by bombs, after World War II. He personally laid the last stone on the highest tower pinnacle.

In 1984 a Visitor Centre and Refectory was opened, and its dominant feature is an aerial sculpture of 12 huge sails, with a ship's bell, clock, and light that changes color on an hourly basis. Full meals may be enjoyed in the charming refectory.

✪ Roman Catholic Metropolitan Cathedral of Christ the King

Mount Pleasant. ☎ **0151/709-9222.** Admission free. Daily 8am–6pm (closes 5pm Sun in winter).

Half a mile away from the Anglican cathedral stands the Roman Catholic cathedral—the two are joined by a road called Hope Street. The sectarian strife of earlier generations has ended, and a change in attitude, called by some the "Mersey Miracle," was illustrated clearly in 1982 when Pope John Paul II drove along Hope Street to pray in both cathedrals.

The construction of the cathedral, designed by Sir Edwin Lutyens, was started in 1930, but when World War II interrupted in 1939, not even the granite and brick vaulting of the crypt was complete. At the end of the war it was estimated that the cost of completing the structure as Lutyens had designed it would be some £27 million. Architects throughout the world were invited to compete to design a more realistic project to cost about £1 million and to be completed in five years. Sir Frederick Gibberd won the competition and was commissioned to oversee the construction of the circular cathedral in concrete and glass, pitched like a tent at one end of the piazza that covered all the original site, crypt included.

Between 1962 and 1967 construction was completed, and today the cathedral provides seating for more than 2,000, all within 50 feet of the central altar. Above the altar rises a multicolored glass lantern weighing 2,000 tons and rising to a height of 290 feet. Called a "space age" cathedral, it has a bookshop, a tearoom, and tour guides.

SIGHTS ON THE WATERFRONT

A fun thing to do is to take the famous Mersey Ferry that travels from the Pier Head to both Woodside and Seacombe. Service operates daily from early morning to early evening throughout the year. Special cruises operate throughout the summer including trips along the Manchester Ship Canal. For more information, contact the **Mersey Ferries,** Victoria Place, Seacombe, Wallasey (☎ 6301030).

Albert Dock

Albert Dock Co. Ltd. ☎ **0151/708-8854.** Admission free. Shops, daily 10am–6pm. Bars and restaurants, daily 10am–11pm. Bus "Albert Dock Shuttle" from the city center.

Built of brick, stone, and cast iron, this showpiece development on Liverpool's waterfront opened in 1846, saw a long period of decline, and has been renovated and refurbished so that it's now England's largest Grade 1 Listed Building, a designation for landmark buildings. The dockland warehouses now house quality shops, restaurants, cafés, an English pub, and a cellar wine bar. One pavilion encompasses the main building of the Merseyside Maritime Museum (see below) and another is the home of the Tate Gallery Liverpool, the National Collection of modern art in the north of England (see below). Parking is available.

✪ Merseyside Maritime Museum and the Museum of Liverpool Life

Albert Dock. ☎ **0151/207-0001.** Admission £3.75 ($5.95) adults, £1.90 ($3) children, senior citizens, and students. Mon–Sat 10am–5:30pm; Sun noon–5:30pm. Bus "Albert Dock Shuttle" from city center.

Set in the historic heart of Liverpool's waterfront, this museum provides a unique blend of floating exhibits, craft demonstrations, working displays, and special events. In addition to restored waterfront buildings, exhibitions present the story of mass emigration through Liverpool in the last century, shipbuilding on Merseyside, and the Battle of the Atlantic Gallery. The Liverpool Life Museum explores the history of Liverpool, its people and their contribution to national life. "Anything to Declare," the National Museum of H. M. Customs & Excise, tells the story of customs. You can also see a restored pier master's house and a working cooperage. A fine restaurant, a coffee shop, a waterfront café, gift shops, and ample parking space are among the facilities. There is wheelchair access and toilet facilities for the disabled visitor.

✪ Tate Gallery Liverpool

Albert Dock. ☎ **0151/709-3223.** Admission free except for special exhibitions, £2.50 ($3.95) adults; £1 ($1.60) children. Tues–Sun 10am–6pm. Bus "Albert Dock Shuttle" from the city center.

Opened in 1988, this museum displays much of the national collection of 20th-century art, complemented by changing art exhibitions of international standing. For example, in 1994, there was an exhibition of the sculpture of Barbara Hepworth.

✪ Walker Art Gallery

William Brown St. ☎ **0151/207-0001.** Admission free. Daily 10am–5pm.

One of Europe's finest art galleries offers an outstanding collection of European art from 1300 to the present day. The gallery is especially rich in European Old Masters, Victorian and Pre-Raphaelite works, and contemporary British art. It also has an award-winning sculpture gallery, featuring works from the 18th and 19th centuries. Seek out, in particular, Simone Martini's *Jesus Discovered in the Temple* and Salvator Rosa's *Landscape with Hermit*. Rembrandt is on show, as is an enticing

Nymph of the Fountain by Cranach. Naturally, the work of British artists is stronger, ranging from *Horse Frightened by a Lion* by Stubbs to *Snowdon from Llan Nantlle* by Richard Wilson. Among the Pre-Raphaelites is Ford Madox Brown's *Coat of Many Colours* and narrative paintings such as *When Did You Last See Your Father?* by W.R. Yeames. French Impressionists include the works of Monet, Seurat, and Degas, among others. Modern British paintings include works by Lucian Freud and Stanley Spencer.

Liverpool Museum

William Brown St. ☎ **0151/207-0001.** Admission free. Daily 10am–5pm.

One of Britain's finest museums features collections from all over the world—from the earliest beginnings with giant dinosaurs through centuries of great art and inventions. The Natural History Centre allows a visitor to use microscopes and video cameras to learn about the natural world. Living displays from the vivarium and aquarium form a large part of the collections, and a planetarium features daily programs covering modern space exploration—an armchair tour toward the beginning of the universe and the far-flung reaches of the cosmos.

WHERE THE BEATLES BEGAN

Whether or not they're Beatles fans, most visitors who come to Liverpool want to take a look at where Beatlemania began. Mathew Street is the heart of Beatle land, and **Cavern Walks** (☎ **0151/236-9082**) is a shopping development and tour service built on the site of the former Cavern Club, where the Beatles performed almost 300 times. John Doubleday's statue of the group is in the central piazza of the Cavern complex, surrounded by shops and restaurants. The outside of Cavern Walks was decorated by Cynthia Lennon, John's first wife. Another statue of John, Paul, George, and Ringo, this one by Liverpool sculptor Arthur Dooley, is opposite the building facade.

Farther along Mathew Street is the **John Lennon Memorial Club** and the **Beatles Shop,** 31 Mathew St. (☎ **0151/236-8066**), open Monday through Saturday from 9:30am to 5:30pm, plus Sunday March through December from 10:30am to 4pm. Around the corner on Stanley Street is a statue of Eleanor Rigby, seated on a bench.

WHERE TO STAY
MODERATE

Atlantic Tower

30 Chapel St., Liverpool, Merseyside L3 9RE. ☎ **0151/227-4444** or 800/847-4358 in the U.S. Fax 0151/236-3973. 210 rms, 6 suites. A/C TV TEL. £88–£98 ($139.05–$154.85) double; £165 ($260.70) suite. Breakfast £6.95–£8.95 ($11–$14.15) extra. AE, DC, MC, V. Free parking.

Showcased in a high-rise that evokes the bow of a great luxury liner, the Atlantic Tower is considered one of the two or three top hotels in the city. You check into a spacious lobby and are shown to one of the well-furnished bedrooms, each with private bath or shower. Many of the bedrooms provide views of the River Mersey, and a minibar can be requested. You can dine in the Stateroom Restaurant, enjoying drinks in a bar that resembles a Pullman coach.

Britannia Adelphi Hotel

Ranalagh Place, Liverpool, Merseyside L3 5UL. ☎ **0151/709-7200.** Fax 0151/708-0743. 374 rms, 17 suites. TV TEL. Mon–Thurs, £87 ($137.45) double; £95–£120 ($150.10–$189.60) suite. Fri–Sun £48 ($75.85) double; £75–£85 ($118.50–$134.30) suite. Breakfast £5.75–£8.95 ($9.10–$14.15) extra. AE, DC, MC, V. Parking £4–£8 ($6.30–$12.65).

This "grand hotel" of Liverpool, built in 1914, is known for its fine rooms and good cuisine. Past the elegant entrance, you enter a world of marble corridors, molded ceilings, and dark polished wood. However, these traditional features are complemented by a range of modern amenities since the hotel has been completely refurbished. Each well-furnished and attractively appointed bedroom has a private bath or shower. Facilities include three restaurants, four bars, a disco/wine bar, hair and beauty salons, and a health club with swimming pool, gym, solarium, and Jacuzzi. There is garage space for 100 cars.

Liverpool Moat House

Paradise St., Liverpool, Merseyside O1 8JD. ☎ **0151/709-0181.** Fax 0151/709-2706. 244 rms, 7 suites. A/C TV TEL. Mon–Thurs £95 ($150.10) single or double; £190–£235 ($300.20–$371.30) suite. English breakfast £8.50 ($13.45) extra. Fri–Sun (including English breakfast) £70 ($110.60) double; £165–£210 ($260.70–$331.80) suite. AE, DC, MC, V. Free parking.

In the opinion of some, this is Liverpool's leading hotel. Located in the center of the city, it's one of the most comfortable, efficient hotels in Merseyside. The bedrooms are spread across eight floors, and each has a private bath or shower. Typically favored by businesspeople, the hotel also lures sightseers drawn to the attractions of "new Liverpool." The hotel's facilities include a solarium, gym, indoor swimming pool, and garden. Its coffee shop stays open until 10:30pm for late arrivals. It also offers the Garden Restaurant serving British and French dishes, with a set menu costing £16.25 ($25.70).

✪ Trials

56–62 Castle St., Liverpool, Merseyside O2 7LQ. ☎ **0151/227-1021.** Fax 0151/236-0110. 20 suites. MINIBAR TV TEL. Mon–Thurs £95 ($150.10) double. Fri–Sun £70 ($110.60) double. Breakfast £6–£7.50 ($9.50–$11.85) extra. AE, DC, MC, V. Parking £6 ($9.50).

Trials is a leading hotel in Liverpool, although it's small and offers only suites. Rather luxurious, this hotel with charm and character was created in 1986 from a centrally located Victorian structure that had once been a bank. Now beautifully converted, this hotel is often the choice of discriminating visitors to this ccity. The plush accommodations are split-level and have Jacuzzis, private baths or showers, trouser presses, and hair dryers. Trials Restaurant serves breakfast only while the Trials Bar serves lunch Monday through Friday from noon to 2pm, costing £1.75 to £3.95 ($2.75 to $6.25). The hotel has 24-hour room service.

WHERE TO DINE
MODERATE

Armadillo

31 Mathew St. ☎ **0151/236-4123.** Reservations required. Lunch main courses £6.95 ($11); Dinner main courses £12.95–£14.95 ($20.45–$23.60). AE, MC, V. Mon–Sat noon–3pm; Tues–Sat 5–10:30pm. MODERN BRITISH.

One of the leading restaurants in Liverpool not associated with a hotel, this restaurant is housed within the solid stone walls of a converted Victorian warehouse, across the street from the site of the famous Cavern, where the Beatles got their start. The cuisine includes such dishes as linguine with crab, spiced chickpeas with basmati rice and yogurt, fennel and salmon broth, and spring lamb cutlets with an apricot stuffing and rosemary jus. With a conservative modern decor and big windows, this restaurant seems to be near the top of everybody's list of favorites in Liverpool.

✪ Jenny's Seafood Restaurant

Old Ropery, Fenwich St. ☎ **0151/236-0332.** Reservations required. Main courses £6–£30 ($9.50–$47.40); fixed-price lunch or dinner £16.95 ($26.80). AE, MC, V. Mon–Fri noon–2:15pm; Tues–Sat 7–10pm. Closed August 15–31 and 2 weeks at Christmas. SEAFOOD.

In either this location, or or a former one nearby, this restaurant has been a Liverpool staple for as long as anyone can remember and was named after a long-ago manager whose personality lingered on for many years after her death. You'll find it near the harbor, in a big white Victorian building on a cul-de-sac at the lower end of Fenwich Street. Small, cozy, and select, it serves an array of fresh seafood which might include grilled Dover sole in Newburgh sauce or in white wine, prawn, and mushroom sauce; at least three different preparations of sea bass, including one baked in a salt crust; monkfish, flounder, prawns, and North Atlantic lobsters.

INEXPENSIVE

⑤ Far East

27–35 Berry St. ☎ **0151/709-3141.** Reservations required. Main courses £3.20–£9.50 ($5.05–$15); fixed-price meals £5.50–£6.30 ($8.70–$9.95) at lunch, £9.90–£18.50 ($15.65–$29.25) at dinner. AE, DC, MC, V. Mon–Thurs noon–11:30pm; Fri–Sat noon–1am; Sun noon–11pm. CANTONESE.

Far East is considered the finest Chinese restaurant in town. Liverpool is famous for its Chinese restaurants, which is not surprising since the city has one of the largest Chinese populations in Europe and its own "Chinatown." Here you might enjoy a dim sum lunch, later returning in the evening for more haute Chinese fare. You face a bewildering array of Cantonese specialties, including chili-flavored large prawns. The chefs also do marvelous things with duck. However, you're likely to get carried away with the à la carte specialties and spend at least £15 ($23.70).

3 Windermere & Bowness

274 miles NW of London, 10 miles NW of Kendal, 55 miles N of Liverpool

The largest lake in England is Windermere, whose shores wash up against the town of Bowness (or Bowness-on-Windermere), with Windermere close by. Both resorts lie on the eastern shore of the lake. A ferry service connects Hawkshead and Bowness. Windermere, the resort, is the end of the railway line.

From either town, you can climb Orrest Head in less than an hour for a panoramic view of England's Lakeland. From that vantage point, you can even see **Scafell Pike,** rising to a height of 3,210 feet—the peak pinnacle in all of England.

The twin resorts of Windermere and Bowness are separated by 1¹⁄₂ miles. The rail station is at Windermere. To go to Bowness and its pier (from which you can catch a ferry across the lake), turn left from the rail terminal and cross the center of Windermere until you reach New Road. This eventually changes its name to

Impressions

The two views we have had of it are of the most noble tenderness—they can never fade away—they make one forget the divisions of life; age, youth, poverty and riches; and refine one's sensual vision into a sort of north star which can never cease to be open lidded and stedfast over the wonders of the great power.

—John Keats on Lake Windermere (1818)

Lake Road before it approaches the outskirts of Bowness. It's about a 20-minute walk downhill. The CMS Lakeland Experience bus also runs from the Windermere Station to Bowness every 20 minutes.

ESSENTIALS
GETTING THERE

By Train Trains to Windermere meet with the main line at Oxenholme for connections both north to Scotland and south to London. Information about rail services in the area can be obtained by calling the Oxenholme Railway Station (☎ 01539/720397). Frequent connections are possible throughout the day.

By Bus The National Express bus link, originating at London's Victoria Coach Station, serves Windermere, with good connections also to Preston, Manchester, and Birmingham. Local buses to various villages and towns in the Lake District (see below) are operated mainly by Cumberland Motor Services (CMS) and go to Kendal, Ambleside, Grasmere, and Keswick. Information on various routings within the Lake District can be secured by calling the White Haven Bus Station (☎ 01946/63222).

By Car Head north from London, as if going toward Liverpool (see above), but stay on M6 until you reach the A685 junction heading west to Kendal. From Kendal, A591 continues west to Windermere.

By Ferry There are boat cruises from Bowness, 1¹/₂ miles from Windermere, in summer. These are operated by the Bowness Bay Boating Company (☎ 015395/31188 for information). There's also a ferry service from Bowness across the lake to the western shore.

VISITOR INFORMATION

The **telephone area code** for Windermere and Bowness is 015394. The **Tourist Information Centre** at Windermere is on Victoria Street (☎ 015394/46499), and the **Tourist Information Centre** at Bowness is a summer-only office at The Glebe (☎ 015394/42895).

WINDERMERE

There is regular steamer service around Windermere, the largest of the lakes, about 10¹/₂ miles long. It's also possible to take a steamer on Coniston Water, a small lake that Wordsworth called "a broken spoke sticking in the rim." Coniston Water is a smaller and less heavily traveled lake than Windermere. Ullswater, a lake measuring 7¹/₂ miles long, used to be called "Ulfr's Water." It is second in size to Lake Windermere and can also be crossed by lake steamer.

  Windermere Steamboat Museum, Rayrigg Road, Windermere (☎ 015394/45565), houses probably the finest collection of steamboats in the world. Important examples of these elegant Victorian and Edwardian steamboats have been preserved in working order.

  The steamboats are exhibited in a unique wet dock where they are moored in their natural lakeside setting. The fine display of touring and racing motorboats in the dry dock links the heyday of steam with some of the most famous names of powerboat racing and record-breaking attempts on Windermere, including Sir Henry Segrave's world water speed record set in 1930.

  All the boats have intriguing stories, including the veteran S.L. *Dolly,* built around 1850 and probably the oldest mechanically driven boat in the world. The vessel was raised from the lake bed of Ullswater in 1962 and, following restoration, ran for 10 years with her original boiler. *Dolly* is still steamed on special occasions.

The wet dock also houses the Chris-Craft speedboat *Jane* dating from 1938. In the dry dock is the first glider to take off from the water (1943), and the record-breaking hydroplane *Miss Windermere IV.* There is also Beatrix Potter's rowing boat and the sailing dinghy *Amazon* from Arthur Ransome's classic story "Swallows and Amazons."

Also displayed is the *Esperance,* an iron-hulled steam yacht built for a local industrialist, Henry William Schneider, in 1869, and the S.S. *Raven* built in 1871 to carry everything from coal and timber to farm produce and beer to the scattered communities around the lake when the only alternative would have been to transport these goods by horse and cart over very poor roads.

The museum is open daily from Easter to the end of October, charging an admission of £2.80 ($4.40) for adults and £1.40 ($2.20) for children. The S.L. *Osprey* (1902) is steamed most days and visitors can make a 50-minute trip on the lake, where tea or coffee will be made using the Windermere steam kettle and served by the crew.

ORGANIZED TOURS   Windermere is a starting point for many interesting tours in the Lake District area. To provide a true appreciation of the Lake District and its many attractions, try **Mountain Goat Holidays and Tours,** Victoria Street, Windermere (☎ **015394/45161**). Begun in 1972, it has become firmly established in the Lake District for touring or walking holidays. They also specialize in planning and operating tailor-made group holidays and tours to meet a customer's exact requirements. These tours include trips to the Northern Lakes, Grasmere, Keswick, Buttermere, and Honister Pass, with a visit to Wordsworth's home in Grasmere and Rydal Mount. Mountain Goat also runs daily minicoach tours that take you to many of the otherwise-inaccessible spots of the area. The cost is from £20 ($31.60) per person for full-day tours and £12 to £14 ($18.95 to $22.10) for half-day tours. Write for a brochure.

WHERE TO STAY
Expensive

ⓢ **Holbeck Ghyll**
Holbeck Lane, Windermere, Cumbria LA23 1LU. ☎ **015394/32375.** Fax 015394/34743.
14 rms. TV TEL. £60–£100 ($94.80–$158) per person. Rates include English breakfast and 5-course dinner. Children under 17 half price when sharing their parents' room. MC, V. Free parking. On A591 3¹/₄ miles northwest of the town center.

Perhaps the most enchanting place to stay in the area, this country-house hotel was once a 19th-century hunting lodge owned by Lord Lonsdale, one of the richest men in Britain. It still has a wealth of oak paneling and stained glass. Overlooking Lake Windermere, this hotel offers not only the highest standards in decor, food, and service, but excellent value for money. An inglenook fireplace welcomes visitors, as do the resident owners, David and Patricia Nicholson. Each bedroom is beautifully maintained and has a special decor in the English chintz and Laura Ashley tradition. The property also includes woods with walking paths, streams, ponds, and an all-weather tennis court.

The hotel also operates one of the finest restaurants in the Lake District, where a five-course menu costs £29 ($45.80) for nonresidents. The menu changes every

Frommer's Nature Notes

Despite the reverence with which the English treat their country's Lake District, it required an act of Parliament in 1951 to protect its natural beauty. Sprawling over almost 900 square miles of hills, much-eroded mountains, forests, and lakes, the Lake District National Park is the largest, and (with 14 million visitors a year) one of the most popular national parks in the U.K.—a kind of Yellowstone National Park of the British Isles.

Its scenery and literary references (Wordsworth, Beatrix Potter, John Ruskin, Samuel Taylor Coleridge, and Hugh Walpole were among its most ardent fans) add an academic gloss to one of the most idealized regions of Britain. More recent (broadly televised) fame came to the park in the 1950s, when boat racing champion Colin Campbell died tragically when his speedboat (*Bluebird*) exploded on Coniston Water while he tried to break the world's speedboat record.

Alas, the park's popularity is now one of its major drawbacks, attracting weekend escapists like a magnet, especially in summertime and during bank holiday weekends. During mild weather in midsummer, such stone-built towns as Windermere, Keswick, and Ambleside are likely to be among the most crowded towns of their size in England. In compensation, however, great efforts are made to maintain the well-defined footpaths that radiate in a network throughout the district. Rigid building codes manage to accommodate the district's corps of full-time residents and the scores of tourist-industry service facilites, while preserving the purity of a landscape that incorporates more than 100 lakes and countless numbers of grazing sheep.

Tourist information offices within the park are richly stocked with maps and suggestions for several dozen bracing rambles. Suitable examples include a 4-mile circumnavigation around the town of Windermere, a long (7-mile) or short (3½-mile) hike between Embleside and Grasmere; or a boat ride from Windermere to the southern edge of the town's lake, followed by a trek northward along the lake's scenic western shore.

Regardless of the itinerary you select, you'll spot frequent green-and-white signs (or their older equivalents in varnished pine with Adirondack-style routed letters) announcing "footpath to . . ."

Be aware before you go that the Lake District receives more rainfall than any other district of England, and that sturdy walking shoes and raingear are almost essential. Hiking after dark is not recommended under any circumstances.

Any tourist information office within the park can provide you with leaflets describing treks through the park. The Windermere Tourist Information Centre, Victoria Street, Windermere, Cumbria OLA23 1AD (☎ **015394/46499**) is especially helpful. Additional information about the park and its three scalable peaks (Scafell Pike, Skiddaw, and Helvellyn, none of which rises more than 3,200 feet above sea level), can be obtained from the Park Management and Visitors' Services, National Park Office, Brockhole, Windermere, Cumbria LA23 1LJ England (☎ **015394/46601**).

day and is never repeated. It's likely to include, as an appetizer, a warm tartlet of creamy Roquefort cheese and walnuts set on slices of beef tomato with crisp endives, black olives, baby corn, and basil in a balsamic dressing, following by a suprême of chicken poached in white wine with shallots and fresh tarragon, served on a sauté of leeks with wild mushrooms and cream sauce or pork tenderloin studded with garlic and topped with a crust of whole grain mustard and herbs, set on braised red cabbage with crisp crackling, a duchess potato, and a cream sauce made from the cooking liquor.

✪ Miller Howe Hotel

Rayrigg Rd., Windermere, Cumbria LA23 1EY. ☎ **015394/42536.** Fax 015394/45664. 13 rms. TV TEL. £70–£125 ($110.60–$197.50) per person per night. Rates include English breakfast and 4-course dinner. Surcharge of 12.5% is added for staff gratuities on all accounts. AE, DC, MC, V. Free parking. Closed mid-Dec to mid-Mar. On the A592 between Windermere and Bowness.

An international clientele comes to this inn, which bears the unique imprint of its creator, former actor John Tovey. At the beginning of the 1970s he chose a country estate overlooking Lake Windermere (with views of the Langdale Pikes), and converted it to provide stylish accommodations and an exquisite cuisine. The house was built in 1916 in the Edwardian style, sitting on $4^{1}/_{2}$ acres of statue-dotted garden and parkland. His large, graciously furnished rooms have names (not numbers) and he treats guests as if they were invited to a house party. Each room is supplied with binoculars to help guests fully enjoy the view; there are even copies of *Punch* from the 1890s. Each room also has a private bath or shower. Antiques are scattered lavishly throughout the house.

Dining/Entertainment: Dinner at Miller Howe is worth the drive up from London. Cris Blaydes, who has been "trained" in the Miller Howe Manner, has been with the kitchen staff since 1983; in 1994 Tovey decided to let him develop new, lighter dishes during the weekly test cooking sessions. The results went beyond the owner's expectations and led to the appointment of Mr. Blaydes as head chef. He uses hot and cold vinaigrettes rather than rich cream sauces, cutting out many of the cluttery garnishes and getting back to basics. Even if you can't stay overnight, at least consider a meal here, for which you must reserve. The fixed-price dinner (four courses) will cost £26 ($41.10) per person, including coffee. Regional dishes using local produce are a special feature. You might try pan-fried loin of Lakeland lamb marinated in Dijon mustard, red wine, rosemary, and garlic on a fresh rhubarb, ginger, and cumin purée with roasted garlic; seared breast of Lunesdale duckling with garlic, wild mushrooms, pesto, and spring onion with a heavily reduced port wine sauce; and roast local guinea fowl marinated in red wine, juniper, and herbs with sage, onion, and bread sauce along with a rich Madeira gravy. Men must wear coats and ties in the dining room. Dinners are served nightly, with seating at everyone's respective tables between 7:30 and 8pm. Lunches are simple fixed-price meals which include several kinds of quiche, seasonal salad, a dessert pudding of the day, and a glass of wine, the total of which is priced at £12.50 ($19.75).

Moderate

Cedar Manor

Ambleside Rd., Windermere, Cumbria LA23 1AX. ☎ **015394/43192.** Fax 015394/45970. 12 rms. TV TEL. £72–£82 ($113.75–$129.55) double. Rates include half board. MC, V. Free parking. Take A591 (Kendal-Ambleside road).

One of the most desirable country-house hotels in the area is Cedar Manor. Originally built in 1860, with gables and chimneys, it was the summer getaway home for a wealthy industrialist from Manchester. But since those times it has been converted into a small hotel of exceptional merit. Each of the well-furnished bed-rooms is equipped with a private bath or shower. A cedar tree, perhaps from India, has grown in the garden for some two centuries, and from that tree the hotel takes its name. Meals are good and wholesome. Typical dishes include roast leg of lamb, fresh Scottish salmon steak, and roast leg of pork.

Langdale Chase Hotel
On A591, Windermere, Cumbria LA23 1LW. ☎ **015394/32201.** Fax 015394/32604. 32 rms. TV TEL. £88–£136 ($139.05–$214.90) double. Rates include English breakfast. AE, DC, MC, V. Free parking. A591 2 miles north of Windermere, toward Ambleside. Bus 55.

A great, old, lakeside house built for grandeur, this hotel is comparable to a villa on Lake Como, Italy. The story goes back to 1930 when the dynamic Ms. Dalzell and her mother took over the country estate, with its handsomely landscaped gardens, and decided to accept paying guests while retaining an uncommercial house-party atmosphere. Waterskiing, rowing, lake bathing, tennis, croquet on the grounds, and fishing attract the sports minded. The bedrooms have excellent furniture and private baths. The interior of the Victorian stone château, with its many gables, balconies, large mullioned windows, and terraces, is a treasure house of antiques. The main lounge hall looks like a setting for one of those English drawing-room comedies. The house was built in part with bits and pieces salvaged from the destruction of a nearby abbey and castle—hence, the ecclesiastical paneling. On the walls are distinctive paintings, mostly Italian primitives, although one is alleged to be a Van Dyck.

The dining room ranks among the finest in the Lake District—with guests selecting tables that are good vantage points for lake viewing. The cuisine is highly personal, mostly liberated English fare, supported by a fine wine list. Open to non-residents, the dining room charges from £14.50 ($22.90) for a fixed-price lunch, £23.50 ($37.15) for a fixed-price dinner. A la carte menus are also offered.

Quarry Garth Country House
Troutbeck Bridge, Windermere, Cumbria LA23 1LF. ☎ **015394/88282.** Fax 015394/46584. 10 rms. TV TEL. £55 ($86.90) per person. Rates include half board. AE, DC, MC, V. Free parking. 2 miles northwest on A591.

A hotel of character, this country house is really the home of Huw and Lynne Phillips, who like an "unstuffy" atmosphere but who run the place with efficiency and precision. Set on eight well-maintained acres, the hotel has leaded, mullioned windows and a terrace. With its gardens, woods, and banks of wild flowers, it is a good spot for a holiday of peace and tranquility.

The bedrooms are attractively furnished in traditional English styling, each with a private bath offering big, fluffy towels. Amenities include hair dryers, direct-dial phones, color TV, radio, and coffee-making equipment. The menu features classic English dishes such as kidney and wild mushroom pie with dark ale, along with selections from the Continent. Fresh local produce is used whenever possible. Nonresidents who'd like to have dinner here can call for a reservation, paying £21 ($33.20) for a table d'hôte dinner.

WHERE TO DINE
Moderate

✪ Roger's
4 High St., Windermere. ☎ **015394/44954.** Reservations required. Main courses £5.50–£11.50 ($8.70–$18.15); fixed-price dinner £15.75 ($24.90). AE, DC, MC, V. Mon–Sat 7–9:30pm. ENGLISH/INTERNATIONAL.

The stellar French dining room of Cumbria, Roger's carries the name of its skilled chef de cuisine, Roger Pergl-Wilson. For almost a decade he has been going strong at this location (a part of England where restaurants seem to have a high mortality rate). That means he's doing something right. You can judge for yourself.

A table d'hôte dinner is a superb value, but you're most likely to be tempted to order à la carte. Homegrown ingredients go into the cookery whenever possible. Regardless, everything tastes fresh here, as care goes not only into the preparation but also into the presentation, which is polite and efficient without being overly formal. Deer from the field, salmon from the rivers, char from Lake Windermere, and quail from the air—everything seems deftly handled here.

BOWNESS

Directly south of Windermere, a satellite resort, Bowness, also opens onto Lake Windermere. It's an attractive old town, with lots of interesting architecture, much of it dating back to Queen Victoria's day. This has been an important center for boating and fishing for a long time, and you can rent boats of all descriptions to explore the lake.

WHERE TO STAY

Moderate

⑤ Lindeth Fell Hotel

Lyth Valley Rd., along the A5074, Bowness-on-Windermere, Cumbria LA23 3JP. ☎ **015394/ 43286.** Fax 015394/47455. 14 rms (all with bath or shower). TV TEL. £99–£118 ($156.40–$186.45) double. Rates include half board. MC, V. Free parking. Closed Nov 16–Mar 14. Take A5074 1 mile south of Bowness.

High above the town and the lake is a traditional large Lakeland house built of stone and brick in 1907, with many of its rooms overlooking the handsome gardens and the lake. The owners, the Kennedys, run the place more like a country house than a hotel, achieving an atmosphere of comfort in pleasingly furnished surroundings. The cooking is supervised by Diana Kennedy and a resident chef, with local produce used whenever possible to prepare a variety of Lakeland and traditional English dishes, including noisettes of border lamb with mint and onion purée and poached Scottish salmon with chive and lemon butter sauce. In pursuit of the country-house atmosphere, the Kennedys offer tennis, croquet, and putting on the lawn, as well as a private tarn for fishing. All bedrooms have beverage-making facilities. It's open from March 15 to mid-November.

Inexpensive

⑤ Lindeth Howe

Longtail Hill, Storrs Park, Bowness-on-Windermere, Cumbria LA23 3JF. ☎ **015394/45759.** Fax 015394/46368. 15 rms (all with bath or shower). TV. £60 ($94.80) double. Rates include continental or English breakfast. MC, V. Free parking. Take B5284 south.

This is a country house in a scenic position above Lake Windermere, with six acres of grounds. The house, part stone and part red brick with a roof of green Westmoreland slate, was built for a wealthy mill owner in 1879, but its most famous owner was Beatrix Potter, who installed her mother here while she lived across the lake at Sawrey. The present owners, Eileen and Clive Baxter, have furnished it in fine style. Most of the bedrooms have lake views. They are comfortably furnished, with in-house movies, beverage-making facilities, and central heating. Four rooms have handsome four-poster beds. There are no singles. The dining room has two deep bay windows overlooking the lake. The lounge features a brick fireplace with a solid oak mantel set in an oak-framed inglenook. The hotel has a sauna and solarium.

4 Ambleside & Rydal

278 miles NW of London, 14 miles NW of Kendal, 4 miles N of Windermere

An idyllic retreat, Ambleside is one of the major centers of the Lake District, attracting pony trekkers, fell hikers, and rock scalers. The charms are here all year, even in late autumn, when it's fashionable to sport a mackintosh. Ambleside is perched at the top of Lake Windermere. Just a small village and not filled with attractions, Ambleside is used primarily as a refueling stop or overnight stopover for those exploring the Lake District.

Between Ambleside and Wordsworth's former retreat at Grasmere is Rydal, a small village on one of the smallest lakes, Rydal Water. The village of Rydal is noted for its sheep-dog trials at the end of summer. The location is $1^{1}/_{2}$ miles north of Ambleside on A591.

ESSENTIALS
GETTING THERE
By Train   Go to Windermere (see above); then continue the rest of the way by bus.

By Bus   Cumberland Motor Services (CMS) has hourly bus service from Grasmere and Keswick (see below) and from Windermere. All these buses into Ambleside are labeled either no. 555 or no. 557.

By Car   From Windermere (see above), continue northwest on A591.

VISITOR INFORMATION
The **telephone area code** is 015394. The summer-only **Tourist Information Centre** is at Old Courthouse, Church Street, in Ambleside (☎ **015394/32582**). It is open throughout the year, although in winter is open Friday and Saturday only.

WHAT TO SEE & DO
✪ **Rydal Mount,** off A591, $1^{1}/_{2}$ miles north of Ambleside (☎ **015394/33002**), was the home of William Wordsworth from 1813 until his death in 1850. Part of the house was built as a farmer's lake cottage around 1575. A descendant of Wordsworth's now owns the property, which displays numerous portraits, furniture, and family possessions as well as mementos and books of the poet. The $4^{1}/_{2}$-acre garden, landscaped by Wordsworth, is filled with rare trees, shrubs, and other features of interest. The house is open daily: 9:30am to 5pm from March to October, 10am to 4pm from November to February (closed Tuesday in winter). Admission is £2.50 ($3.95) for adults, £1 ($1.60) for children 5 to 16. Free for kids 4 and under.

WHERE TO STAY & DINE
IN AMBLESIDE
Expensive

Nanny Brow Hotel
Clappersgate, Ambleside, Cumbria LA22 9NF. ☎ **015394/32036.** Fax 015394/32450. 11 rms, 7 suites. MINIBAR TV TEL. £60–£70 ($94.80–$110.60) per person single or double;

£75–£80 ($118.50–$126.40) per person suite for two. AE, DC, MC, V. Free parking. On A593 about 1 mile west of Ambleside.

Situated on a hill, this former private home, built in 1904, has been turned into one of the most successful hotels in the Ambleside area. The Tudor-style gabled house is reached via a steep tree-flanked drive. Once you arrive, you find a country-house setting with a lovely sitting room with intricate cove moldings and, if the weather merits it, a log fire. The rooms are in both the main house and a garden wing, the latter offering first-rate accommodations (some of the suites have half-tester beds). The food is well prepared, using fresh ingredients. Nonresidents who'd like to dine here pay £20 ($31.60) for a four-course dinner or £22 ($34.75) for a six-course dinner. Other facilities include a solarium and a whirlpool bath.

Wateredge Hotel

Borrans Rd., Waterhead, Ambleside, Cumbria LA22 0EP. ☎ **015394/32332.** Fax 015394/32332. 23 rms. TV TEL. £120–£162 ($189.60–$255.95) double. Rates include half board. AE, DC, MC, V. Free parking. Closed mid-Dec to early Feb. On A591 1 mile south of Ambleside.

The center of this hotel was formed long ago from two 17th-century fishing cottages. Wateredge was, in fact, listed as a lodging house as early as 1873, and further additions were made in the early 1900s. Situated in beautiful gardens overlooking Lake Windermere, the hotel also serves some of the best food in the area. Public rooms have many little nooks for reading and conversation, and there is also a cozy bar. However, on sunny days guests prefer to laze in one of the chairs on the lawn. The rooms vary in size and appointments; some are spacious, others much smaller.

Dining/Entertainment: A six-course fixed-price dinner costs about £25.90 ($40.90) for nonresidents, and is offered nightly from 7 to 8:30pm. If hotel guests don't take all the tables, nonresidents can join the dining party. Fresh produce is used, and the quality of cooking is high. In winter a log fire will greet you.

Moderate

⑨ Kirkstone Foot

Kirkstone Pass Rd., Ambleside, Cumbria LA22 9EH. ☎ **015394/32232.** 30 rms. TV TEL. £79–£110 ($124.80–$173.80) double. Rates include English breakfast. MC, V. Free parking. Closed Jan. Take Rydal Rd. north, turning right onto Kirkstone Pass Rd.

The facilities of this 17th-century manor house have been expanded with the construction of several slate-roofed and self-catering apartments in the surrounding parklike grounds. The original building is encircled by a well-tended lawn, while the interior is cozily furnished with overstuffed chairs and English paneling. The comfortable accommodations, 15 in the main house and 15 in the outlying units, are tastefully decorated in a cozy family style.

The restaurant offers home-cooked English meals. Fresh produce is used whenever possible. A five-course dinner costs £19.95 ($31.50) for nonresidents.

⑨ Riverside Hotel

Near Rothay Bridge, Under Loughrigg, Ambleside, Cumbria LA22 9LJ. ☎ **015394/32395.** Fax 015394/32395. 10 rms. TV TEL. £88–£96 ($139.05–$151.70) double. Rates include half board. MC, V. Free parking. Closed Nov–Feb. Directions: See below.

Secluded on a quiet lane, this small country hotel was formed by combining three adjoining houses dating to the 1820s. Located on the riverside, the hotel has the solid slate-block walls and slate roof common to Cumbria and, despite its peaceful location, lies within a few minutes' walk from the center of Ambleside. It's owned by Jim and Jean Hainey, who accommodate guests and provide good meals priced at £18 ($28.45) for nonresidents who phone ahead. Each of the simple but comfortable bedrooms is furnished with a radio, hair dryer, and central heating.

To get here, approaching Ambleside from Windermere on A591, take the left fork at Waterhead toward Coniston. Follow the Coniston Road for about a mile until you come to the junction at Rothay Bridge. Turn left across the bridge and then immediately make a sharp right along the small lane signposted Under Loughrigg.

✪ Rothay Manor

Rothay Bridge, Ambleside, Cumbria LA22 0EH. ☎ **015394/33605.** Fax 015394/33607. 15 rms, 3 suites. TV TEL. £113–£128 ($178.55–$202.25) double; £156–£234 ($246.50–$369.70) suite. Rates include English breakfast. AE, DC, MC, V. Free parking. Take A593 half a mile south of Ambleside.

At this spot, which is reminiscent of a French country inn, the star is the cuisine, along with a dedicated chef in the kitchen, well-selected French wines, and comfortable, centrally heated bedrooms and suites. Each of the individually decorated units has a bath and shower, and most have shuttered French doors opening onto a sun balcony and offering a mountain view. Throughout the estate you'll find an eclectic combination of antiques (some Georgian blended harmoniously with Victorian), flowers, and enticing armchairs.

The manor is also a restaurant open to nonresidents. The spacious dining room is decked with antique tables and chairs. The flawless appointments include fine crystal, silver, and china. Buffet lunches are served from 12:30 to 2pm every day except Sunday when a traditional Sunday lunch is featured, always with a whole sirloin of roast beef with Yorkshire pudding, among other dishes, and perhaps wild mallard duck breast sautéed in herb-flavored butter. Dinners, from 7:45 till 9:30pm, are more ambitious, costing £22 ($34.75) for two courses, £25 ($39.50) for three courses, and £28 ($44.25) for five courses.

Inexpensive

Riverside Lodge Country House

Near Rothay Bridge, Ambleside, Cumbria LA22 0EH. ☎ **015394/34208.** 5 rms. TV. £23–£27.50 ($36.35–$43.45) per person per night. Rates include continental breakfast. MC, V. Free parking. Take A593 from Ambleside, which crosses Rothay Bridge.

This early Georgian house is set on a riverbank, a short walk from the town center, near the foot of Loughrigg Fell, on three acres of grounds. The property is run by Alan and Gillian Rhone and it's featured in the book *Famous Lakeland Homes* by Kathleen Eyres. Bonnie Prince Charlie rested here in 1745. The lodge has some beamed ceilings and offers well-furnished bedrooms, some with river views. Each room is a double. Enjoy a drink in the intimate lounge with its open fire before going into the breakfast room overlooking the river.

IN RYDAL
Inexpensive

Glen Rothay Hotel

On A591, Rydal, Ambleside, Cumbria LA22 9LR. ☎ **015394/32524.** 9 rms (all with bath or shower), 2 suites. TV TEL. £50–£66 ($79–$104.30) double; from £116 ($183.30) suite for two. Rates include English breakfast. AE, DC, MC, V. Free parking. On A591 1¹/₂ miles northwest of Ambleside.

Built in the 17th century as a wayfarer's inn, this hotel adjoins Dora's Field, immortalized by Wordsworth. Set back from the highway, it has a stucco-and-flagstone facade added by Victorians. Inside, the place has been modernized, but original details remain, including beamed ceilings and paneling. There is a popular street-level pub, plus a more formal cocktail lounge, with a fireplace and comfortable armchairs, as well as a dining room serving solid English food. A table d'hôte meal costs £10 ($15.80) for residents and £14.95 ($23.60) for non-residents. The comfortable bedrooms upstairs have private baths or showers, central heating, and coffee makers, and a few offer four-poster beds.

5 Grasmere

282 miles NW of London, 18 miles NW of Kendal, 43 miles S of Carlisle

On a lake that bears its name, Grasmere was the home of Wordsworth from 1799 to 1808. He called this area "the loveliest spot that man hath ever known." The nature poet lived with his sister, Dorothy (the writer and diarist) at **Dove Cottage,** which is now a museum administered by the Wordsworth Trust. Wordsworth, who followed Southey as poet laureate, died in the spring of 1850 and was buried in the graveyard of the village church at Grasmere. Another tenant of Dove Cottage was Thomas De Quincey (*Confessions of an English Opium Eater*). For a combined ticket costing £4 ($6.30) for adults, £2 ($3.15) for children, you can visit both Dove Cottage and adjoining **Wordsworth Museum.** They're both on A591 directly south of the village of Grasmere on the road to Kendal. The Wordsworth Museum houses manuscripts, paintings, and memorabilia. There are also various special exhibitions throughout the year, exploring the art and literature of English romanticism. The property is open daily from 9:30am to 5:30pm; closed from Dec 24 to 26 and January 8 to February 4. For further information, call 015394/35544 or 015394/35268 for Dove Cottage Restaurant information.

ESSENTIALS
GETTING THERE

By Train Go to Windermere (see above) and continue the rest of the way by bus.

By Bus Cumberland Motor Services (CMS) runs hourly bus service to Grasmere from Keswick (see below) and Windermere (see above). Buses running in either direction are marked no. 555 or no. 557.

By Car From Windermere (see above), continue northwest along A591.

VISITOR INFORMATION

The **telephone area code** is 015394. The summer-only **Tourist Information Centre** is on Red Bank Road (☎ **015394/35245**).

Impressions

. . . Had never seen so humble a ménage: and, contrasting the dignity of the man with this honourable poverty, and his courageous avowal of it, his utter absence of all effort to disguise the simple truth of the case, I felt my admiration increase to the uttermost by all I saw.

—Thomas De Quincey (1807) on Dove Cottage

WHERE TO STAY & DINE
VERY EXPENSIVE

✪ Michael's Nook

Quarter mile east of A591, Grasmere, Cumbria LA22 9RP. ☎ **015394/35496** or 800/544-9941 in the U.S. Fax 015394/35765. 14 rms, 2 suites. TV TEL. £160–£280 ($252.80–$442.40) double; £350–£390 ($553–$616.20) suite. Rates include English breakfast and dinner. AE, DC, MC, V. Free parking. Turn off A591 at Swan Hotel, ¹/₂ mile northeast of Grasmere.

This country-house hotel, once a private residence, is situated on its own secluded 3-acre garden. A Lakeland home of stone (honoring a hill shepherd, Michael, subject of a Wordsworth poem), it is adorned with much fine mahogany woodwork and paneling, especially its elegant staircase. Throughout the house, owned by Grasmere antiques dealer Reg Gifford and his wife, Elizabeth, are many fine antiques, enhanced by the glow of log fires or vases of flowers. Amenities include hair dryers and sandalwood sachets in drawers; one room has a four-poster bed. During some peak weekends, a minimum three-night stay is requested, but shorter bookings are accommodated whenever possible.

Dining/Entertainment: Only about 20 people can be served in the intimate dining room, which accepts reservations from nonresidents for both lunch and dinner. Additional seating is available in the Oak Room. Meals are carefully prepared, with menus changing daily. You might choose poached prawns or sautéed calves' liver in shallot-and-vinegar sauce. Lunch is priced at £27.50 ($43.45) and is served at 12:30pm daily; dinner, at 7:30pm daily, costs £38 ($60.05) for nonresidents. In summer, dinner sittings on Saturday are at 7 and 9pm.

EXPENSIVE

White Moss House

On A594, Rydal Water, Grasmere, Cumbria LA22 9SE. ☎ **015394/35295**. 5 rms, 1 cottage. TV TEL. £140 ($221.20) double; cottage £174 ($274.90) for two, £348 ($549.85) for four. Rates include half board. MC, V. Free parking. Closed Nov–Feb. On A591 1¹/₂ miles south of town.

This old Lakeland cottage, once owned by Wordsworth, overlooks the lake and the fells. You'll be welcomed here by Peter and Susan Dixon, who will pamper you with morning tea in bed, turn down your bedcovers at night, and cater to your culinary preferences. The rooms are comfortably furnished and well heated in nippy weather. Since there are only five double accommodations, advance booking is essential. All units have radios, trouser presses, hair dryers, and such bathroom amenities as soap, shampoo, and herbal bath salts. There's also Brockstone, their cottage annex, a five-minute drive along the road, where two, three, or four guests can be accommodated in utter peace.

Dining/Entertainment: Dinner is a leisurely affair beginning at 8pm. You're served five courses, which might include roast of lamb with an orange and red-currant sauce or quail with a chicken and brown-rice stuffing. For dessert, hope that Mrs. Beeton's chocolate pudding is featured. Dinner begins at £27.50 ($43.45) for nonresidents, and you must reserve a table early.

MODERATE

Swan Hotel

On A591, Grasmere, Cumbria LA22 9RF. ☎ **015394/35551** or 800/225-5843 in the U.S. and Canada. Fax 015394/35741. 36 rms. TV TEL. £90–£100 ($142.20–$158) double. English breakfast £8.75 ($13.85) extra. AE, DC, MC, V. Free parking.

Following a renovation, only the shell of this 1650 building remains. Many of the bedrooms are in a modern wing, added in 1975, that fits gracefully onto the building's older core. The hotel is located 400 yards outside Grasmere, beside the road leading to Keswick. Sir Walter Scott used to slip in for a secret drink early in the morning, and Wordsworth mentioned the place in "The Waggoner." In fact, the poet's wooden chair is in one of the rooms. The restaurant serves daily from noon to 2pm and 7 to 9pm, providing both table d'hôte and à la carte meals. A three-course table d'hôte lunch costs £11.25 ($17.80), and a three-course table d'hôte dinner goes for £17.95 ($28.35).

Wordsworth Hotel

Stock Lane, Grasmere, Cumbria LA22 9SW. ☎ **015394/35592.** Fax 015394/35765. 37 rms, 2 suites. TV TEL. £110–£150 ($173.80–$237) double; from £190 ($300.20) suite. Rates include English breakfast. AE, DC, MC, V. Free parking. Turn left on A591 at the Grasmere Village sign and follow the road past the church, over the bridge, and around an S-bend; the Wordsworth is on the right.

Reg Gifford of Michael's Nook Country House Hotel owns this hostelry in the heart of the village, situated in a 3-acre garden. An old stone Lakeland house (once the hunting lodge of the earl of Cadogan), the Wordsworth has been completely refurbished to provide luxuriously appointed bedrooms with views of the fells, as well as modern baths, radios, and trouser presses. Three rooms have a four-poster bed. The original master bedroom has a Victorian bathroom, with a brass towel rail and polished pipes and taps. There is 24-hour room service, laundry service, a large swimming pool, sauna, and minigym.

There are several lounges, with comfortable armchairs. A buffet lunch is served in the cocktail lounge, including the chef's hot dish of the day. A fixed-price four-course dinner in the Prelude Restaurant at £29.50 ($46.60) is likely to include a light fruit or vegetable appetizer, soup, fish or meat course, dessert or cheese, and coffee and petit fours. The cuisine is in the modern English style. Meals are served Sunday through Thursday from 12:30 to 2pm and 7 to 9 pm and to 9:30pm on Friday and Saturday.

INEXPENSIVE

⊗ Red Lion Hotel

Red Lion Sq., Grasmere, Cumbria LA22 9SS. ☎ **015934/35456.** Fax 015394/35579. 35 rms (all with bath or shower). TV TEL. £33.50–£43.50 ($52.95–$68.75) per person per night. Rates include English breakfast. AE, DC, MC, V. Free parking.

This 200-year-old coaching inn is only a short stroll from Wordsworth's Dove Cottage, and it's assumed that the poet often stopped here for a meal, drink, or to warm himself by the fire. Recently refurbished, the hotel offers comfortably furnished bedrooms with private baths. Enjoy a drink or lunch in the airy surroundings of the Easdale Bar, or try the Lamb Inn and Buttery for a more traditional pub atmosphere. In the dining room, you'll be served some of the finest fare in the district; a fixed-price meal starts at £16.50 ($26.05), or you can order à la carte.

6 Hawkshead & Coniston

263 miles NW of London, 52 miles S of Carlisle, 19 miles NW of Kendal

Discover for yourself the village of Hawkshead, with its 15th-century grammar school where Wordsworth went to school for eight years (he carved his name on a desk that is still there). Near Hawkshead, in the vicinity of Esthwaite Water, is the 17th-century Hill Top Farm, former home of author Beatrix Potter.

At Coniston, 4 miles west of Hawkshead, you can visit the village famously associated with John Ruskin. Coniston is a good base for rock climbing. The Coniston "Old Man" towers in the background at 2,633 feet, giving mountain climbers one of the finest views of the Lake District.

ESSENTIALS

GETTING THERE

By Train   Go first to Windermere (see above) and proceed the rest of the way by bus.

By Bus   Cumberland Motor Services (CMS) runs buses from Windermere to Hawkshead and Coniston, three per day Monday through Saturday and two per day on Sunday. Take either bus no. 505 or no. 515 from Windermere.

By Car   From Windermere, proceed north on A591 to Ambleside, cutting southwest on B5285 to Hawkshead.

By Ferry   The Bowness Bay Boating Company (☎ **015394/31188**) in summer operates a ferry service from Bowness, directly south of Windermere, to Hawkshead. It reduces driving time considerably.

VISITOR INFORMATION

The **telephone area code** for Hawkshead and Coniston is 015394. The **Tourist Information Centre** is at Hawkshead at the Main Car Park (☎ **015394/36525**). It's open only in summer.

WHAT TO SEE & DO

Brantwood

Coniston. ☎ **015394/41396**. Admission £3.25 ($5.15) adults, free for children; nature walk, £1 ($1.60) adults, free for children. Mid-Mar to mid-Nov, daily 11am–5:30pm; mid-Nov to mid-Mar, daily 11am–4pm.

John Ruskin, poet, artist, and critic, was one of the great figures of the Victorian age and a prophet of social reform, inspiring such diverse men as Proust, Frank Lloyd Wright, and Gandhi. He moved to his home, Brantwood, on the east side of Coniston Water, in 1872 and lived there until his death in 1900. The house today is open for visitors to view much Ruskiniana, including some 200 pictures by him. Also displayed are his coach and boat, the *Jumping Jenny*. A video program tells the story of Ruskin's life and work.

An exhibition illustrating the work of W. J. Linton is laid out in his old printing room. Linton was born in England in 1812 and died at New Haven, Connecticut, in 1897. Well known as a wood engraver and for his private press, he lived at Brantwood, where he set up his printing business in 1853. He published *The English Republic,* a newspaper and review, before sailing to America in 1866, where he set up his printing press in 1870. The house is owned and managed by the Education Trust, a self-supporting registered charity. Part of the 250-acre estate is open as a nature trail.

The Brantwood stables, designed by Ruskin, have been converted into a tearoom and restaurant, the Jumping Jenny. Also in the stable building is the Lakeland Guild Craft Gallery, which follows the Ruskin tradition of encouraging contemporary craft work of the finest quality.

Literary fans may want to pay a pilgrimage to the graveyard of the village church, where Ruskin was buried; his family turned down the invitation to have him interred at Westminster Abbey.

John Ruskin Museum

Yewdale Rd., Coniston Village. ☎ **015394/41387.** Admission £2 ($3.16) adults, £1 ($1.58) children. Easter–Oct, daily 10am–1pm and 2–4pm. Closed Nov–Easter.

At this institute, in the center of the village, you can see Ruskin's personal possessions and mementos, pictures by him and his friends, letters, and a collection of mineral rocks he collected.

WHERE TO STAY
IN HAWKSHEAD
Inexpensive

Highfield House

Hawkshead Hill, Hawkshead, Ambleside, Cumbria LA22 OPN. ☎ **015394/36344.** Fax 015394/36793. 11 rms. TV. £62–£69 ($97.95–$109) double. Rates include English breakfast. MC, V. Free parking.

This solidly built stone-sided house sits proudly on the side of a hill that enjoys sweeping views over the Lake District (at least on clear days) for a distance of up to 12 miles. Constructed around 1870, it is situated three-quarters of a mile east of Hawkshead Village (on the road leading to Coniston), surrounded by 2½ acres of its own land. Operated by members of the Bennett family, it has cozy bedrooms, either with pastel colors or wallpaper inspired by the turn-of-the-century designs of William Morris. A four-course dinner is always available for £16 ($25.30) per person, but advance notice is recommended.

IN CONISTON
Inexpensive

Coniston Sun Hotel

Brow Hill, Coniston, Cumbria LA21 8HQ. ☎ **015394/41248.** 11 rms (all with bath or shower). TV TEL. £60 ($94.80) double. Rates include English breakfast. MC, V. Free parking.

This is the most popular, traditional, and attractive pub, restaurant, and hotel in this Lakeland village. In reality it's a country-house hotel of much character, dating from 1902, although the inn attached to it is from the 16th century. Situated on its own beautiful grounds above the village, 150 yards from the town center off A593, it lies at the foot of the Coniston "Old Man." Donald Campbell established his headquarters here during his attempt to break the world water-speed record. Each of the bedrooms is decorated with style and flair, and two of them have four-posters. Fresh local produce is used whenever possible in the candlelit restaurant. Log fires take the chill off a winter evening, and guests relax informally in the lounge, which is like a library. Many sports can be arranged.

WHERE TO DINE
IN HAWKSHEAD

Grizedale Lodge

Grizedale, Hawkshead, Cumbria LA22 0QL. ☎ **015394/36532.** Reservations recommended. Bar lunches from £6 ($9.50); fixed-price dinner £18.95 ($29.95). MC, V. Tues–Sun

12:30 1:45pm; daily 7–8pm. Closed Jan 2–Feb 14. From Hawkshead take Newby Bridge Road for about 500 yards, then turn right (signposted GRIZEDALE & FOREST PARK CENTER) and follow this road for 2 miles. ENGLISH/FRENCH.

The best place for food in the area is this country *restaurant avec chambres,* which was built in 1902 as a hunting lodge for the chairman of the Cunard Line. Many people come here just to dine because the cuisine is top-notch. During the day guests order bar lunches, but at night they can enjoy a memorable five-course meal in a tranquil setting. Service is personable.

Mr. and Mrs. Elson offer nine handsomely furnished bedrooms for guests, each with a private bath and TV. For half board, charges are £37.50 ($59.25) in a single, up to £70 ($110.60) in a double.

7 Keswick

22 miles NW of Windermere, 294 miles NW of London, 31 miles NW of Kendal

Keswick opens onto Derwentwater, one of the loveliest lakes in the district. It makes a good center for exploring the northern half of Lake District National Park. The small town has two landscaped parks, and above the town is a historic Stone Circle thought to be some 4,000 years old.

St. Kentigern's Church dates from 553, and a weekly market held in the center of Keswick can be traced back to a charter granted in the 13th century. It's a short walk to the classic viewing point—Friar's Crag—on Derwentwater. The walk will also take you past boat landings with launches that operate regular tours around the lake.

Around Derwentwater there are many places with literary associations that evoke memories of Wordsworth, Robert Southey (poet laureate), Coleridge, and Hugh Walpole. Several of Beatrix Potter's stories were based at Keswick. The town also has a professional repertory theater that schedules performances in the summer. There is a modern swimming pool, plus an 18-hole golf course at the foot of the mountains four miles away.

Close at hand are villages and lakes, including Borrowdale, Buttermere, and Bassenthwaite, while the open country of "John Peel" fame is to the north of the 3,053-foot Skiddaw.

ESSENTIALS
GETTING THERE

By Train   Go first to Windermere (see above) and proceed the rest of the way by bus.

By Bus   Cumberland Motor Services (CMS) has a regular service from Windermere and Grasmere (bus no. 555).

By Car   From Windermere, drive northwest on A591.

Impressions

The first thing which I remember, as an event in life, was being taken by my nurse to the brow of friar's crag on Derwentwater; the intense joy, mingled with awe, that I had in looking through the hollows in the mossy roots, over the crag, into the dark lake, has associated itself more or less with all twining roots of trees ever since.
　　　　　　　　　　　　　　　　　　　　　　　　　　　　　　　　—John Ruskin

VISITOR INFORMATION

The **telephone area code** is 017687. The **Tourist Information Centre** is at Moot Hall, Market Square (☎ **017687/72645**).

WHERE TO STAY & DINE
IN KESWICK
Inexpensive
Brundholme Country House

Brundholme Rd., Keswick, Cumbria CA12 4NL. ☎ **017687/74495.** Fax 017687/73536. 11 rms. TV TEL. £40–£50 ($63.20–$79) double. Rates include English breakfast. MC, V. Free parking. Closed late Nov–Feb 14. At the A66 Keswick roundabout, turn left toward Brundholme.

Coleridge wrote that this Regency villa (restored and opened as a choice hotel in 1988) was "in a delicious situation." He was referring to the views over Keswick to the enveloping hills. Wordsworth was also known to visit this house above the River Greta. Owner Ian Charlton is also the chef de cuisine. The well-chosen staff is one of the most helpful in the area. Some of the comfortable, well-furnished bedrooms are quite large. The hotel also has a garden.

This country-house hotel is known mainly for its French and English cuisine, using, whenever possible, local produce such as char (a succulent fish found in Lake Windermere) or trout from Borrowdale. The local game from Cumberland is reputedly the best in England. Try such specialties as homemade soups, jugged hare, and Cumberland ham. Meals are served daily from 12:30 to 1:30pm and 7:30 to 8:30pm. Dinner costs around £25 ($39.50).

Grange Country House

Manor Brow, Ambleside Rd., Keswick, Cumbria CA12 4BA. ☎ **017687/72500.** 10 rms. TV TEL. £60–£74 ($94.80–$116.90) double. Rates include English breakfast. MC, V. Free parking. Closed Nov to mid-Mar. On the southeast side of Keswick overlooking the town just off A591.

A tranquil retreat, this charming hotel and its gardens are situated on a hilltop. The hotel, which dates from the 1800s, is furnished in part with antiques. Guests enjoy the crackling log fires in chilly weather. Many of the attractively furnished, well-kept rooms open onto beautiful views of the Lakeland hills. The hotel, run by Jane and Duncan Miller, also offers a first-rate cuisine. Guests can dine here for £17.50 ($27.65) in the evening.

⑤ Skiddaw Hotel

Market Square, Keswick, Cumbria CA12 5BN. ☎ **017687/72071.** Fax 017687/74850. 40 rms. TV TEL. £59–£61 ($93.20–$96.40) double. English breakfast £6 ($9.50) extra. AE, MC, V. Free parking.

This hotel has an impressive facade and entrance marquee built right onto the sidewalk in the heart of Keswick at the market square. The owners have refurbished the interior, retaining the best features, which they have combined with modern facilities. The bedrooms, which are compact and eye-catching, have hot-beverage-making facilities.

Guests gather in the lounge or the popular cocktail bar with an art nouveau ambience. The meals feature well-prepared English and continental cuisine, available à la carte all day. In addition, a chef's special, such as Lancashire hot pot, is offered at lunch. Dinner costs £16 ($25.30). There is a wide selection of wines.

IN NEARBY BASSENTHWAITE LAKE
Moderate
✪ Armathwaite Hall Hotel

Bassenthwaite Lake, Keswick, Cumbria CA12 4RE. ☎ **017687/76551.** Fax 017687/76220. 39 rms, 4 studio suites. TV TEL. £100–£164 ($158–$259.10) double; £120–£190 ($189.60–$300.20) suite. Rates include English breakfast. AE, DC, MC, V. Free parking. B5291 1¹/₂ miles west of Bassenthwaite, or 7 miles northwest of Keswick.

Rich in history, this hotel was originally built in the 1300s as a house for Benedictine nuns. During the Middle Ages it was plundered frequently, leaving the sisters wretchedly poor. By the 17th century a series of wealthy landowners had completed the severe Gothic design of its stately facade, and in 1844 an architecturally compatible series of wings were added. In the 1930s it was converted into a hotel, and Sir Hugh Walpole, who once stayed here, found it "a house of perfect and irresistible charm." Ringed with almost 400 acres of woodland (some of it bordering the lake), the place offers a magnificent entrance hall filled with hunting trophies and sheathed with expensive paneling. A Victorian billiard room is lined with old engravings, and a first-class restaurant offers a view of the lake. A three-course fixed-price lunch costs £13.95 ($22.05), and a six-course fixed-price dinner goes for £28.95 ($45.75). An indoor swimming pool is ringed with stone walls and sheltered from the rain by a roof of wooden trusses. Each of the handsomely furnished bedrooms comes with a private bath and radio. The hotel also provides the finest equestrian center in the area.

In 1993, the hotel's owners added a small but diverting attraction on its premises, a minizoo featuring unusual breeds of both barnyard and wild animals. Located within a ten-minute walk of the hotel, Trotters & Friends, Coalbeck Farm, Bassenthwaite, is open daily from 10am to 5pm (last admission). Its collection includes potbellied pigs, llamas, goats, rabbits, and owls. Adults pay £2.50 ($3.95); children age 3 to 14 £1.80 ($2.85). Kids 2 and under enter free.

IN NEARBY BORROWDALE
Expensive
Stakis Lodore Swiss Hotel

Borrowdale Rd. (B5289), Borrowdale, Keswick, Cumbria CA12 5UX. ☎ **017687/77285.** Fax 017687/77343. 68 rms, 2 suites. MINIBAR TV TEL. £95 ($150.10) double; from £170 ($268.60) suite. Winter discounts available. Breakfast £6.75–£8.50 ($10.65–$13.45) extra. AE, DC, MC, V. Parking indoor parking £4 ($6.30); outdoors, free. B5289 3¹/₂ miles south of Keswick.

Since 1987, the Stakis hotel chain has run this hostelry that overlooks Derwentwater, amid fields where cows graze. With its spike-capped mansard tower, symmetrical gables, and balcony-embellished stone facade, it resembles a hotel you might find in the foothills of Lake Geneva. Ironically, the family name of the Swiss owners who built this place in the 19th century was England. The old tradition of good rooms, good food, and service continues today. The interior has been modernized, and each of the well-furnished bedrooms has a hair dryer, private bath, radio, and coffee maker.

Dining/Entertainment: The food is exceptional for the area, with a fixed-price dinner costing £20.50 ($32.40) for nonresidents. Dishes include roast topside of English beef with Yorkshire pudding, Morecambe Bay shrimp, and plaice sautéed in butter. Call for a reservation, especially at dinner. Meals are served from 12:30 to 2pm and 7:30 to 9:15pm daily.

Services: 24-hour room service, laundry.
Facilities: Indoor swimming pool, garden.

Inexpensive

Borrowdale Hotel

Borrowdale Rd. (B5289), Borrowdale, Keswick, Cumbria CA12 5UY. ☎ **017687/77224.** Fax 017687/77338. 34 rms. TV TEL. £40–£59 ($63.20–$93.20) per person, single or double. Rates include English breakfast. MC, V. Free parking. B5289 3¹/₂ miles south of Keswick.

When the weather is inclement, log fires welcome guests in this Lakeland stone building (originally a coaching inn) circa 1866. The rooms are comfortable and many have fine views. All have private baths or showers, toilets, radios, intercom units, and hair dryers. Some traditional four-poster beds are available.

The main attraction here is the restaurant. A traditional English lunch on Sunday costs £10.50 ($16.60). During the rest of the week, bar lunches with a choice of 20 main courses cost in the £6 ($9.50) range. The six-course dinner, consisting of appetizer, main course, and dessert, each with a choice of at least six different dishes, starts at £18.50 ($29.25). Cuisine from all parts of the globe is offered, and the menu changes daily. If you would like to have the daily roast, the chef will carve it at your table from a silver trolley.

8 Ullswater

296 miles NW of London, 26 miles SE of Keswick

A 7-mile expanse of water, stretching from Pooley Bridge to Patterdale, Ullswater is the second-largest lake in the district. Incidentally, it was on the shores of Ullswater that Wordsworth saw his "host of golden daffodils." While housed in the area, it's easy to explore several places of archaeological interest, such as Hadrian's Wall, east of Carlisle, or Long Meg stone circle near Penrith.

ESSENTIALS
GETTING THERE

By Train   Penrith is the region's main rail junction. About three trains from London's Euston Station arrive daily in Penrith—usually a change of trains isn't necessary. Once in Penrith, passengers usually take a taxi to Ullswater.

By Bus   From June 24 to September 29, two buses operated by Cumberland Motor Services begin in Carlisle and end in Bowness-on-Windermere. They stop at the Penrith Rail Station, where passengers must take a taxi to Ullswater.

By Car   From Penrith, drive southeast on B5320.

VISITOR INFORMATION

The **telephone area code** is 017684. The summer-only **Tourist Information Centre** for the lake is at The Square, Pooley Bridge (☎ **017684/86530**).

WHERE TO STAY & DINE
VERY EXPENSIVE

✪ Sharrow Bay Country House Hotel

Howtown Rd., Lake Ullswater, near Penrith, Cumbria CA10 2LZ. ☎ **017684/86301.** Fax 017684/86349. 22 rms, 6 suites. TV TEL. £260–£310 ($410.80–$489.80) double; £310 ($489.80) suite for 2. Rates include English breakfast. No credit cards. Free parking. Howtown Rd. 2 miles south of Pooley Bridge.

Impressions

We saw a few daffodils close to the water side. We fancied that the lake had floated the seeds ashore and that the little colony had so sprung up. But as we went along there were more and yet more and at last under the boughs of the trees, we saw that there was a long belt of them along the shore, about the breadth of a country turnpike road. I never saw daffodils so beautiful. . . .

—Dorothy Wordsworth (1802)

This country-house hotel has been a Relais & Châteaux since 1954, making it the oldest member of that prestigious group in Britain. It's an unusual Victorian house, which had been a private home until it was purchased by Francis Coulson in 1948. Realizing its potential, he began restoration work on the structure, with its low angled roof and wide eaves, sleeping on the floor while the work was in progress. Three years later he was joined by Brian Sack, and together they turned Sharrow into one of England's finest eating places. This was also the first country-house hotel to be created in Great Britain with only five rooms at the beginning. The hotel offers antique-filled bedrooms, 16 of which are in the gate house and cottages. Each of the individually decorated bedroooms is named after one or another of the glamorous (and often famous) women who have swept in and out of the lives of this establishment's articulate owners. Some of the rooms have a minibar, and some offer views of the lakes, trees, or Martindale Fells.

Dining/Entertainment: The six-course £40.75 ($64.40) fixed-price menu offers a formidable list of choices, all of them made with ultrafresh ingredients and superb vegetables. About a dozen appetizers always include the chef's specialty, mousseline of fresh salmon with hollandaise sauce. Main courses make the best of homegrown ingredients. Menu items might include honey-glazed roast breast of Lunesdale duckling with a confit of onions, ginger and coriander in a pastry parcel, orange segments, and a spicy sauce, and, in season, a wide array of game dishes. The dessert selections are among the best you'll find anywhere in northwest England, including a white chocolate and raspberry mousse with raspberry sauce, crème brûlée with macerated strawberries, and a selection of real English puddings of which the chefs are justifiably proud. The service and management team here are especially efficient and sensitive to travelers' needs.

If you're motoring through the area, call ahead and make a reservation for the £30.75 ($48.60) fixed-price luncheon or for the elegant afternoon tea, priced at £11.75 ($18.55). Meals are served from 1 to 1:45pm and from 8 to 8:45pm daily, with afternoon tea prepared anytime between 4 and 6:30pm. Note carefully that this place is extremely popular and famous throughout England, as much for its aura of genteel elegance as for its beauty. Advance calls are strongly recommended if you intend to visit.

19

The Northeast

The northeast of England is rich in attractions, with its most visited cities, Lincoln and York, lying on the "cathedral circuit."

Lincoln is the largest city of Lincolnshire, bordered on one side by the North Sea. Of all England's counties (or shires) of the East Midlands, Lincolnshire is the most interesting to visit. Within Lincolnshire, other than the cathedral city of Lincoln, the most interesting section is Holland.

Located in the southeast, Holland is a land known for its fields of tulips, marshes, and fens, as well as windmills reminiscent of the Netherlands. Tourists, particularly North Americans, generally cross the tulip fields and pass by the busy port of Boston before making the swing north to Lincoln, which is inland.

Yorkshire, known to readers of *Wuthering Heights* and *All Creatures Great and Small,* embraces both the moors of North Yorkshire and the dales. With the radical changing of the old county boundaries, the shire is now divided into North Yorkshire (the most interesting from the tourist's point of view), West Yorkshire, South Yorkshire, and Humberside.

Away from the cities and towns that still carry the taint of the Industrial Revolution, the beauty is wild and remote and is characterized by limestone crags, caverns along the Pennines, mountainous uplands, rolling hills, chalk land wolds, heather-covered moorlands, broad vales, and tumbling streams.

Yorkshire offers not only the beauty of its inland scenery, but also its 100 miles of shoreline, with rocky headlands, cliffs, and sandy bays, rock pools, sheltered coves, fishing villages, bird sanctuaries, former smugglers' dens, and yachting havens, which is definitely worth a visit.

Across this vast region came the Romans, the Anglo-Saxons, the Vikings, the monks of the Middle Ages, kings of England, lords of the manor, craftspeople, hill farmers, and wool growers, all leaving their own mark. You can still see Roman roads and pavements, great abbeys and castles, stately homes, open-air museums, and craft centers, along with parish churches, old villages, and cathedrals. In fact, Yorkshire's battle-scarred castles, Gothic abbeys, and great country manor houses (from all periods) are unrivaled anywhere in Britain.

Northumbria is made up of the counties of Northumberland, Cleveland, and Durham. Tyne and Wear is one of the more recently

What's Special About the Northeast

Great Towns/Villages
- Lincoln, ancient city dominated by a towering 11th-century cathedral with triple towers.
- York, Roman walled city nearly 2,000 years old, with many medieval buildings.

Cathedrals
- York Minster, with a history spanning some 800 years; noted for its 100 stained-glass windows.
- Lincoln Cathedral, dating from the 12th century, with a tower rising 271 feet, the second tallest in England.

Literary Shrine
- Haworth, where the Brontës lived.

Natural Spectacles
- Yorkshire Dales, some 700 square miles of water-carved wonderland preserved as a national park.
- Yorkshire Moors, heather-covered moorland; the 553-square-mile parkland borders the North Sea.

Ancient Monument
- Hadrian's Wall, built by conquering Romans, once considered a wonder of the Western world.

Building
- Castle Howard, near Malton in North Yorkshire, with lakes, fountains, and extensive gardens, was the main setting for the *Brideshead Revisited* TV miniseries.

created counties, and has Newcastle upon Tyne as its center. The Saxons who came to northern England centuries ago carved out this kingdom, which at the time stretched from the Firth of Forth in Scotland to the banks of the Humber in Yorkshire. Vast tracts of that ancient kingdom remain natural and unspoiled. Again, this slice of England has more than its share of industrial towns, but as a visitor, you should set out to explore the wild hills and open spaces and cross the dales of the eastern Pennines.

The whole area evokes ancient battles and bloody border raids. Space limitations prevent a proper discussion of this area, which is often overlooked by the rushed North American visitor. However, you should venture into the area at least to see Hadrian's Wall, a Roman structure that was considered one of the wonders of the Western world. The finest stretch of the wall lies within the Northumberland National Park, between the stony North Tyne River and the county boundary at Gilsland.

A DRIVING TOUR

Day 1   Although one of the more remote parts of England, the northeast is relatively easy to reach from London or points in the south. Motorists can take the M1 from London to the "doorway" to the area, the cathedral city of Lincoln, 140

The Northeast

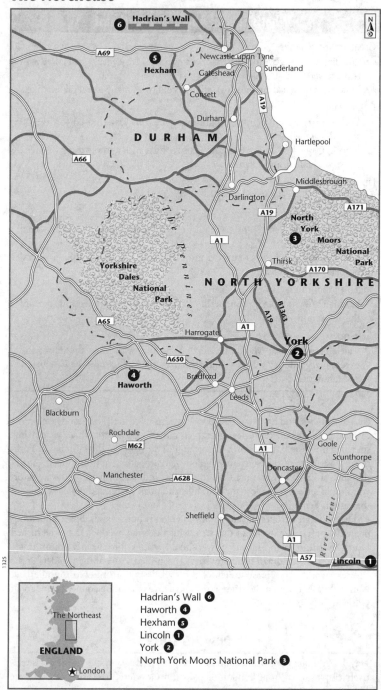

Hadrian's Wall **6**

A69

5
Hexham

Newcastle upon Tyne

Gateshead · Sunderland

Consett

A19

Durham

D U R H A M

Hartlepool

A66

Middlesbrough

A171

Darlington

A19

**North
York**

A1

3

Moors

**National
Park**

Thirsk

A170

N O R T H   Y O R K S H I R E

**Yorkshire
Dales
National
Park**

The Pennines

B1363

A19

A65

Harrogate

A1

York
2

A650

Bradford

4
Haworth

Leeds

Blackburn

Rochdale

M62

Goole

Scunthorpe

Manchester

A628

Doncaster

Sheffield

A1

River Trent

A57

Lincoln **1**

N

The Northeast

ENGLAND

★ London

Hadrian's Wall **6**
Haworth **4**
Hexham **5**
Lincoln **1**
York **2**
North York Moors National Park **3**

1325

miles north of London. There they can visit Lincoln Cathedral and other attractions and stay overnight there. The White Hart Hotel is recommended, although there are far cheaper lodgings (see below).

Days 2-4　Continue north to York, a distance of 82 miles, and spend the night there. You'll arrive in time for lunch and can visit such premier attractions as York Minster and York Castle Museum. If possible, take an organized walking tour (see below). At night visit such typical pubs as The Black Swan and perhaps have dinner at Melton's Restaurant.

☕ **TAKE A BREAK**　Oscar's Wine Bar & Bistro, 8A Little Stonegate in York (☎ 01904/652002), offers heaping plates of meats and salads, attracting a young crowd (often because of the inexpensive beer). There's a courtyard and a large menu. Jazz and blues are performed on Monday nights. Hours are Monday through Saturday from 11am to 11pm, Sunday noon to 3pm and 7 to 10:30pm.

Spend days 3 and 4 making easy excursions from York—notably Castle Howard, the fabled 18th century palace of the northeast, as well as Fountains Abbey & Studley Royal, lying 4 miles southwest of Ripon. The final day can be spent driving through the Yorkshire Dales National Park, using Hawes as a base and refueling stop.

Day 5　Head west of York to Haworth in West Yorkshire, and visit the literary shrines of the Brontës, the second most visited literary pilgrimage in England (after Stratford-upon-Avon). Haworth lies 45 miles southwest of York. Spend the night at the Old White Lion Hotel and take your meals at the Weaver's Restaruant.

Day 6　Drive east toward Leeds and take the A1 north to Hexham where you can book into a hotel and spend the rest of the day exploring Hadrian's Wall.

1 Lincoln

140 miles N of London, 94 miles NW of Cambridge, 82 miles SE of York

One of the oldest cities of England, Lincoln was known to the Romans as Lindum and some of the architectural glory of the Roman Empire still stands to charm the present-day visitor. The renowned Newport Arch (the North Gate) is the last remaining arch left in Britain that still spans a principal highway.

ESSENTIALS
GETTING THERE

By Train　Trains arrive every hour during the day from London's King's Cross Station (trip time: 2 hr.) and usually require a change of trains at Newark. Trains also arrive from Cambridge, again necessitating a change at Newark.

By Bus　National Express buses from London's Victoria Coach Station service Lincoln (trip time: about 3 hr.). Once in Lincoln, local and regional buses service the county from the City Bus Station, off St. Mary's Street, opposite the train station.

By Car　From London, take M1 north until you reach the junction with A57, heading east to Lincoln.

VISITOR INFORMATION

The **telephone area code** is 01522. The **Tourist Information Centre** is at 9 Castle Hill (☎ **01522/529828**).

WHAT TO SEE & DO

One of the most visited attractions in Lincoln, **Greyfriars City and County Museum,** will be closed for repairs until 1997.

Museum of Lincolnshire Life

Burton Rd. ☎ **01522/528448.** Admission £1.20 ($1.90) adults, 60p (95¢) children. May–Sept, daily 10am–5:30pm; Oct–Apr, Mon–Sat 10am–5:30pm, Sun 2–5:30pm.

This is the largest museum of social history in the region, housed in what was originally built as an army barracks in 1857. Situated within a short walk north of the city center, it houses displays ranging from a Victorian schoolroom to a collection of locally built steam engines.

✪ Lincoln Cathedral

Minster Yard. ☎ **01522/544544.** Admission is suggested donation £2.50 ($3.95) adults, £1 ($1.60) senior citizens, students, and children. Cathedral, May–Aug, Mon–Sat, 7:15am–8pm, Sun, 7:15am–6pm; Sept–Nov, Mon–Sat, 7:15am–6pm, Sun, 7:15am–5pm. Coffee shop, Mon–Sat, 10am–4:30pm. Closed Sun.

No other English cathedral dominates its surroundings as does Lincoln's. Visible from up to 30 miles away, the central tower is 271 feet high, which makes it the second tallest in England. Lincoln's central tower once carried a huge spire, which, prior to heavy gale damage in 1549, made it the tallest in the world at 525 feet. Construction on the original Norman cathedral was begun in 1072, and it was consecrated 20 years later. It sustained a major fire and, in 1185, an earthquake. Only the central portion of the West Front and lower halves of the western towers survive from this period. The present cathedral is Gothic style, particularly the early English and decorated periods. The nave is 13th century, but the black font of Tournai marble originates from the 12th century. In the Great North Transept is a rose medallion window known as the Dean's Eye. Opposite it, in the Great South Transept, is its cousin, the Bishop's Eye. East of the high altar is the Angel Choir, consecrated in 1280, and so called after the sculpted angels high on the walls. The exquisite wood carving in St. Hugh's Choir dates from the 14th century. Lincoln's roof bosses, dating from the 13th and 14th centuries, are handsome, and a mirror trolley assists visitors in their appreciation of these features, which are some 70 feet above the floor. Oak bosses are in the cloister.

In the Seamen's Chapel (Great North Transept) is a window commemorating Lincolnshire-born Capt. John Smith, one of the pioneers of early settlement in America and the first governor of Virginia. The library and north walk of the cloister were built in 1674 to designs by Sir Christopher Wren. In the Treasury is fine silver plate from the churches of the diocese.

WHERE TO STAY
MODERATE

✪ White Hart Hotel

Bailgate, Lincoln, Lincolnshire LN1 3AR. ☎ **01522/526222** or 800/225-5843 in the U.S. Canada. Fax 01522/531798. 35 rms, 13 suites. TV TEL. £100–£115 ($158–$181.70) double; £135–£160 ($213.30–$252.80) suite. English breakfast £6.50–£9.25 ($10.25–$14.60) extra. AE, DC, MC, V. Free parking. Bus 1A.

Since Richard II visited this region shortly before this hotel was constructed (and probably stayed at an inn on the site), the White Hart is named after his emblem.

Lincoln

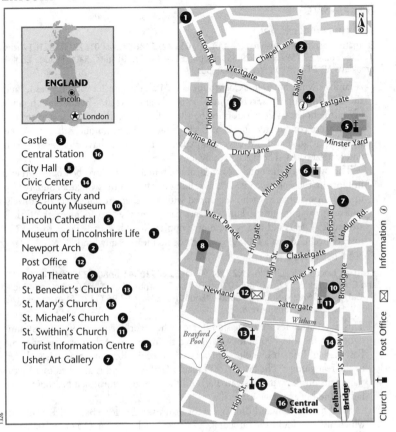

ENGLAND
Lincoln
London

Castle **3**
Central Station **16**
City Hall **8**
Civic Center **14**
Greyfriars City and
    County Museum **10**
Lincoln Cathedral **5**
Museum of Lincolnshire Life **1**
Newport Arch **2**
Post Office **12**
Royal Theatre **9**
St. Benedict's Church **13**
St. Mary's Church **15**
St. Michael's Church **6**
St. Swithin's Church **11**
Tourist Information Centre **4**
Usher Art Gallery **7**

A letter written in 1460 by a London woman who paid sixpence for her room complains that her bed was lumpy. The facade covering the inn dates from the 1700s when it was a luxurious private home. Its life as a modern hotel began in 1913 when the live-in owners started accepting paying guests, but only if they came with ironclad references. The hotel also bears the honor of having hosted several meetings between Churchill and Eisenhower in the darkest days of World War II. Other guests have included David Lloyd George, Edward VIII, and Baroness Margaret Thatcher.

Once through a revolving mahogany door, you enter a large and finely proportioned lounge filled with fine antiques, rare and unusual clocks, and display cabinets of rare silver, glass, and porcelain. The Georgian main dining room has elegant furnishings and well-prepared lunches and dinners. Each of the accommodations has some antique furniture, a well-accessorized bath, and views of the old city. To reach your room, you negotiate a labyrinth of narrow halls and stairways. The White Hart is surrounded by ancient cobblestone streets usually reserved for pedestrians. The cathedral and the oldest part of Lincoln are only a short walk from the doorstep.

INEXPENSIVE

⑤ D'isney Place Hotel

Eastgate, Lincoln, Lincolnshire LN2 4AA. ☎ **01522/538881.** Fax 01522/511321. 17 rms, 1 suite. £62–£82 ($97.95–$129.55) double; £124 ($195.90) suite. Rates include English breakfast. AE, DC, MC, V. Free parking. Bus 1A or 8.

A family-owned hotel, it is close to the cathedral, the minster yard, the castle, and the Bailgate shops. It was built in 1735 and later enlarged. The southern boundary of the house gardens is formed by the wall of the cathedral close and towers, which were constructed in 1285. Each of the rooms is uniquely decorated and includes a radio and hot-beverage makers. Some units have four-poster beds and Jacuzzi baths. There is a parking lot.

The owners of the hotel also control the rentals of five two-bedroom cottages in Lincoln, each of which is within walking distance of the cathedral. Suitable for up to four occupants, each is equipped with a kitchenette, all sheets and towels, and serviceable furniture. Four cottages date from the Victorian era, the fifth is around 250 years old and is the most popular. Weekly rentals range from £220 to £260 ($347.60 to $410.80) and include no meals of any kind.

Forte Post House Hotel

Eastgate, Lincoln, Lincolnshire LN2 1PN. ☎ **01522/520341** or 800/225-5843 in the U.S. and Canada. Fax 01522/510780. 70 rms. TV TEL. Sun–Thurs, £56 ($88.50) single or double; Fri–Sat, £43 ($67.95) single or double. English breakfast £7.95 ($12.55) extra. AE, DC, MC, V. Free parking. Bus 1A or 8.

This hotel occupies a historic site: In fact, when workmen were digging its foundations in the mid-1960s, they discovered the remnants of the north tower of the East Gate of Roman Lincoln. A preserved part of the Roman city wall is included in the rear garden. The hotel faces Lincoln Cathedral and is attached to a Victorian mansion (now the Eastgate Bar). All the recently refurbished bedrooms have radios and hot-beverage makers.

Breakfast, lunch, and dinner are served in the Trader's Bar and Restaurant, which also overlooks the cathedral. A la carte lunches go for £15 ($23.70), and à la carte dinners cost from £18 ($28.45).

⑤ Grand Hotel

St. Mary's St., Lincoln, Lincolnshire LN5 7EP. ☎ **01522/524211.** Fax 01522/537661. 48 rms. TV TEL. £52.50–£58 ($82.95–$91.65) double. Rates include English breakfast. AE, DC, MC, V. Free parking. Bus 1A or 8.

In the mid-1930s, two hotels were combined into the Grand, which, in spite of its name, is not glamorous, but solid, stable, clean, and welcoming. This extensively remodeled hotel has suitable amenities and a cooperative staff. The bedrooms are compact, with many built-in features and coordinated colors. The Grand is easy to spot just opposite the bus depot and near the rail station. The West bar and the lounges are streamlined, but the Tudor bar pays homage to the past. The food is a top-notch bargain, in both price and taste. From 7 to 8:30pm, a four-course table d'hôte dinner is offered for £12 ($18.95). The food is not only good and typically English, but the portions are ample. You can also lunch at the Grand daily from noon to 2pm. A buttery is open daily from 11am to 10pm.

WHERE TO DINE
MODERATE
Jews House Restaurant

The Jews House, 15 The Strait. ☎ **01522/524851.** Reservations required. Main courses £11.95–£14.95 ($18.90–$23.60); fixed-price lunch £10.95 ($17.30), fixed-price dinner £19.95 ($31.50). AE, DC, MC, V. Tues–Sat noon–2pm; Mon–Sat 7–9:30pm. Bus 1A or 8. CONTINENTAL.

Originally built around 1150, this stone-fronted building is said by local historians to be the oldest lived-in house in Europe. The dining room has a low-beamed ceiling, a cast-iron fireplace, and an array of medieval features. Two of the massive ceiling beams are known to date from the construction of the original house. Seating only about 28 diners, the establishment is run by chef-proprietor Richard Gibbs and his wife, Sally. The menu features stylish dishes that change weekly according to market ingredients and the inspiration of the chef. Examples include grilled goat cheese served on a bed of fresh spinach with croutons and bacon, grilled mussels in their half-shells slathered with a hazelnut-butter sauce, roast rack of lamb with a basil and pine-nut crust, and such fish dishes as steamed turbot with a fennel and fresh tomato sauce.

Wig & Mitre

29 Steep Hill. ☎ **01522/535190.** Reservations recommended. Main courses £5–£13.95 ($7.90–$22.05); English breakfast £5 ($7.90); sandwiches £2.95–£5.75 ($4.65–$9.10). AE, DC, MC, V. Daily 8am–midnight. Bus 1A or 8. INTERNATIONAL.

This is not only one of the best pubs in old Lincoln, but its bill of fare is superior to that found in most restaurants. Sitting on the aptly named Steep Hill near the cathedral, redolent of an Old English atmosphere, the establishment operates somewhat like a café-brasserie. The main restaurant, behind the drinking section on the second floor, has oak timbers, Victorian armchairs, and settees. The 14th-century pub, which has been substantially restored over the years, also has a summer beer garden. If the restaurant is full, all dishes can be served in the bar downstairs. Blackboard specials change daily, and you are likely to be offered roast rack of lamb resting on onion-and-sage purée, fricassée of guinea fowl, and roast duck suprême garnished with pink grapefruit. A favorite dessert is chocolate roulade.

2 York

203 miles N of London, 26 miles NE of Leeds, 88 miles N of Nottingham

Few cities in England are as rich in history as York. It is still encircled by its 13th- and 14th-century city walls—about 2½ miles long—with four gates. One of these, Micklegate, once grimly greeted visitors coming up from the south with the heads of traitors. To this day, you can walk on the footpath of the medieval walls.

The crowning achievement of York is its minster, or cathedral, which makes the city an ecclesiastical center equaled only by Canterbury. In spite of this, York is one of the most overlooked cities on the cathedral circuit. Perhaps foreign visitors are intimidated by the feeling that the great city of northeastern England is too far north. Actually, it lies about 203 miles north of London on the Ouse River and can easily be tied in with a motor trip to Edinburgh. Or, after visiting Cambridge, a motorist can make a swing through a too-often-neglected cathedral circuit: Ely, Lincoln, York, and Ripon.

There was a Roman York (Hadrian came this way), then a Saxon York, a Danish York, a Norman York (William the Conqueror slept here), a medieval York, a Georgian York, and a Victorian York (the center of a flourishing rail business). Today a large amount of 18th-century York remains, including Richard Boyle's restored Assembly Rooms.

At some point in your exploration, you may want to visit the Shambles; once the meat-butchering center of York, it dates back before the Norman Conquest. This messy business has given way, but the ancient street survives and is filled with jewelry stores, cafés, and buildings that huddle so closely together that you can practically stand in the middle of the pavement, arms outstretched, and touch the houses on both sides of the street.

Recently interest has focused on discoveries of the Viking era, from 867 to 1066, when the city was known as Jorvik, the Viking capital and a major Scandinavian trade center (see below).

Incidentally, the suffix "gate" used for streets and sites in York derives from the Scandinavian word for "street"—a historical reminder of the earlier Viking period.

ESSENTIALS
GETTING THERE

By Plane   British Midland flights arrive at Leeds/Bradford Airport, a 50-minute flight from London's Heathrow Airport. Connecting buses at the airport take you east and the rest of the distance to York.

By Train   From London's King's Cross Station, York-bound trains leave every 10 minutes (trip time: 2 hr.).

By Bus   Four National Express buses depart daily from London's Victoria Coach Station for York (trip time: 4¹/₂ hr.).

By Car   From London, head north on M1, cutting northeast below Leeds at the junction with A64, heading east to York.

VISITOR INFORMATION

The **telephone area code** is 01904. The **Tourist Information Centre** is at De Grey Rooms, Exhibition Square (☎ **01904/621756**).

WHAT TO SEE & DO

To get to know York, start at York Minster and walk down past Youngs Hotel, the reputed birthplace of Guy Fawkes. Turn right onto Stonegate, a pedestrian area with old shops, a 12th-century house on the right, and some old coffeehouses. Continue across Davygate into St. Helen's Square to see the guildhall and Mansion House, then go left onto Coney Street and take a right onto Lower Ousegate.

At the beginning of Ouse Bridge, take the steps down to King's Staith, with a pub on the left for refreshment, before you continue onto South Esplanade and St. George's Gardens beside the river. At the bridge, join the road again and turn left. In front of you stand the Castle Museum, the Assize Courts, and Clifford's Tower. Walk up Tower Street and Clifford Street to Nessgate. Turn right onto

York

Barley Hall **8**

Clifford's Tower **11**

Guildhall **3**

Jorvik Viking Centre **10**

Mansion House **4**

Merchant Adventurers' Hall **9**

National Railway Museum **1**

St. William's College **7**

Treasurer's House **5**

York Castle Museum **12**

York Minster **6**

Yorkshire Museum **2**

High Ousegate and continue across Parliament Street to the beginning of the Shambles on the left.

Walk up the Shambles past the attractive shops and ancient buildings to Kings Square, then bear right onto Goodramgate. Walk down Goodramgate and, at the end, cross Deangate onto College Street with St. William's College on the right. At the end, a narrow road leads to the Treasurer's House.

You're now behind the east end of the minster. Walk around to the west end and then up Bootham Bar, through the city gate, and turn left into Exhibition Square. The art gallery is on the right, the tourist information center to the left, and, beside it, York's Theatre Royal. Continue down St. Leonard's Street to the crossroads and turn right onto Museum Street. Cross the river and go right to join part of the old medieval wall, which you follow all the way to Skeldergate Bridge. Then follow the river's course upstream again to the center of York.

✪ York Minster

Deangate. ☎ **01904/624426.** Chapter house, £1.50 ($2.35) adults, 60p (95¢) children; crypt, 60p (95¢) adults, 30p (45¢) children; foundations and treasury, £1.80 ($2.85) adults, 70p ($1.10) children; tower, £2 ($3.15) adults, £1 ($1.60) children. Chapter house, foundations and treasury, and tower, Mon–Sat 10am–6pm, Sun 1–6pm (closing time in winter 4:30pm). Crypt, Mon–Fri 10am–4:30pm, Sat 10am–3:30pm, Sun 1–3:30pm.

One of the great cathedrals of the world, York Minster traces its origins back to the early 7th century; the present building, however, dates from the 13th century and stands at the converging point of several streets: Deangate, Duncombe Place, Minster Yard, and Petergate.

Like the cathedral at Lincoln, York Minster is characterized by three towers built in the 15th century. The central tower is lantern-shaped in the perpendicular style and from the top of the tower on a clear day there are panoramic views of York and the Vale of York. It is a steep climb up a stone spiral staircase and not recommended for the very elderly, very young, or anyone with a heart condition or breathing difficulties.

Perhaps the most memorable distinguishing characteristic of the cathedral is its stained glass from the Middle Ages—in glorious Angelico blues, ruby reds, forest greens, and honey-colored ambers. See especially the Great East Window, the work of a 15th-century Coventry-based glass painter. In the north transept is an architectural gem of the mid-13th century—the Five Sisters Window with its five lancets in grisaille glass. The late 15th-century choir screen has an impressive lineup of historical figures—everybody from William the Conqueror to the overthrown Henry VI.

At a reception desk near the entrance to the minster, groups can arrange a guide, if one is available. Conducted tours are free but donations toward the upkeep of the cathedral are requested.

Impressions

The external appearance of an old cathedral cannot be but displeasing to the eye of every man, who has any idea of the propriety of proportion, even though he may be ignorant of architecture as a science; and the long slender spire puts one in mind of a criminal impaled, with a sharp stake rising up through his shoulder.

—Tobias Smollett (1721–1771)

Treasurer's House

Minster Yard. ☎ **01904/624247**. Admission £3 ($4.75) adults, £1.50 ($2.35) children. Apr–Oct, daily 10:30am–5pm (last entry 4:30pm).

The Treasurer's House stands on a site where a continuous succession of buildings has stood since Roman times. The main part of the house, built in 1620, was refurbished by Yorkshire industrialist Frank Green at the turn of the century; he used this elegant town house to display his collection of 17th- and 18th-century furniture, glass, and china. An audiovisual program and exhibit explain the work of the medieval treasures and the subsequent fascinating history of the house. It has an attractive small garden in the shadow of York Minster. Some summer evenings you can enjoy coffee by candlelight in the Great Hall. An attractive licensed restaurant, where Yorkshire specialties are served, is open the same hours as the house.

✪ York Castle Museum

Eye of York off Tower St. ☎ **01904/653611**. Admission £4.20 ($6.65) adults, £2.90 ($4.60) children. Apr–Oct, Mon–Sat 9:30am–5:30pm, Sun 10am–5:30pm; Nov–Mar, Mon–Sat 9:30am–4pm, Sun 10am–4pm.

On the site of York's Castle, this is one of the finest folk museums in the country. Its unique feature is a re-creation of a Victorian cobbled street, Kirkgate, named for the museum's founder, Dr. John Kirk. He acquired his large collection while visiting his patients in rural Yorkshire at the beginning of this century. The period rooms range from a neoclassical Georgian dining room through an overstuffed and heavily adorned Victorian parlor to the 1953 sitting room with a brand-new television set purchased to watch the coronation of Elizabeth II. In the Debtors' Prison, former prison cells display craft workshops. There is also a superb collection of arms and armor. In the Costume Gallery, displays are changed regularly to reflect the collection's variety. Half Moon Court is an Edwardian street, with a gypsy caravan and a pub (sorry, the bar's closed!). During the summer, you can visit a watermill on the bank of the River Foss. It's recommended that you allow at least two hours for a visit to this museum.

National Railway Museum

Leeman Rd. ☎ **01904/621261**. Admission £4.20 ($6.65) adults, £2.10 ($3.30) children. Mon–Sat 10am–6pm, Sun 11am–6pm. Closed Dec 24–26.

This was the first national museum to be built outside London, and it has attracted millions of visitors since it opened in 1975. Adapted from an original steam-locomotive depot, the museum gives visitors a chance to see how Queen Victoria traveled in luxury and to look under and inside steam locomotives. In addition, there's a collection of railway memorabilia, including an early 19th-century clock and penny machine for purchasing tickets on the railway platform. More than 40 locomotives are on display. One, the *Agenoria*, dates from 1829 and is a contemporary of Stephenson's well-known *Rocket*. Of several royal coaches, the most interesting is Queen Victoria's Royal Saloon; it's like a small hotel, with polished wood, silk, brocade, and silver accessories.

Jorvik Viking Centre

Coppergate. ☎ **01904/643211**. Admission £4.25 ($6.70) adults, £2.50 ($3.95) children; £3.15 ($5) senior citizens and students. Apr–Oct, daily 9am–7pm; Nov–Mar, daily 9am–5:30pm.

This Viking city, discovered many feet below present ground level, was reconstructed as it stood in 948. In a "time car," you travel back through the ages to

1067, when Normans sacked the city, and then ride slowly through the street market peopled by faithfully modeled Vikings. You also go through a house where a family lived and down to the river to see the ship chandlers at work and a Norwegian cargo ship unloading. At the end of the ride, you pass through the Finds Hut, where thousands of artifacts are displayed. The time car departs at regular intervals.

Theatre Royal

St. Leonard's Place. ☎ **01904/623568.** Tickets, gallery seats £5 ($7.90), dress circle seats £13 ($20.55). Evening shows, daily at 7:30pm or 8pm; matinees, Wed at 2:30pm, Sat at 4pm. Closed Mar 18–May 19.

This old, traditional theater building has modern additions to house the box office, bars, and restaurant. It's worth inquiring about the current production, as the Royal Shakespeare Company includes York in its tours; the Arts Council presents dance, drama, and opera; and visiting celebrities appear in classics. There is also an excellent resident repertory company.

AN ORGANIZED WALKING TOUR

The best way to see York is to go to Exhibition Square (opposite the Tourist Information Center), where a volunteer guide will take you on a free 1 1/2-hour walking tour of the city. You'll learn about history and lore through numerous intriguing stories. Tours are given April through October, daily at 10:15am and 2:15pm, plus 7pm from June to August; from November to March, a daily tour is given at 10:15am. Groups can book by prior arrangements by writing Assn. of Vol. Guides, De Grey Rooms, Exhibition Square, York YO1 2HB.

WHERE TO STAY
EXPENSIVE

✪ Middlethorpe Hall Hotel

Bishopthorpe Rd., York, North Yorkshire YO2 1QB. ☎ **01904/641241** or 800/260-8338 in the U.S. Fax 01904/620176. 23 rms, 7 suites. TV TEL. £120–£170 ($189.60–$268.60) double; £199 ($314.40) suite. Breakfast £7.45–£10.50 ($11.75–$16.60) extra. AE, MC, V. Free parking. A64 1 1/2 miles south of York.

Set on a 26-acre park, this hotel is located on the outskirts of York, near the racecourse. Built in 1699, the stately, red-brick, William and Mary country house had fallen into disrepair as a nightclub before it was purchased by Historic House Hotels and beautifully restored, both inside and out. Fresh flowers are displayed profusely and lots of antiques provide the ambience of a classic manor house. As befits such a house, there is an elegant drawing room as well as a library. The rooms, which are individually decorated, are divided between the main house and restored outbuildings. Guests find in their room such niceties as homemade cookies and bottles of mineral water, as well as bathrobes.

Dining/Entertainment: Meals are served in two restaurants, one oak-paneled and one a grill room. A choice of either international or English traditional meals is offered, a table d'hôte dinner costing £33.95 to £36.95 ($53.65 to $58.40) for three to four courses.

MODERATE

Abbots Mews Hotel

6 Marygate Lane, Bootham, York, North Yorkshire YO3 7DE. ☎ **01904/634866.** Fax 01904/612848. 50 rms. TV TEL. £78–£92 ($123.25–$145.35) double. Rates include English

breakfast. AE, DC, MC, V. Free parking. Bootham west from the cathedral, then left onto Marygate; Marygate Lane is off Marygate.

The setting here, as the name suggests, is a mews. What was at one time a 19th-century Victorian coach house with stables is now a highly recommended hotel and restaurant, the latter serving international food. The rooms are comfortably furnished, with both modern and traditional styling. The hotel is also well located—close to the historic district. Good food is served here as well—you can order dinner until 9:30pm. Meals begin at £20 ($31.60).

✪ Bilbrough Manor

Bilbrough, near York, North Yorkshire YO2 3PH. ☎ **01937/834002.** Fax 01937/834724. 14 rms, 1 suite. TV TEL. £85–£135 ($134.30–$213.30) double; £150 ($237) suite. Rates include English breakfast. AE, DC, MC, V. Free parking. Closed Dec 25–30. 5 miles southwest of York on A1036.

One of the loveliest places to stay—or dine—in the vicinity of York is this hotel near the village church. The imposing neo-Gothic walls and multiple chimneys were built in 1901 as a replacement for a dilapidated manor house. However, its foundations go back to the 13th century.

The sumptuous public rooms have paneling and baronial fireplaces, along with deep chintz-covered sofas. Each of the individually furnished bedrooms is elegant and unique, with many thoughtful amenities, including a hair dryer and trouser press.

Even if you don't spend the night, you might want to dine here, sampling superb viands the chef offers in the modern French and British tradition. The carefully prepared meals are served with flourish on Wedgwood dinnerware in a historic paneled dining room. The menu changes frequently, but fresh, quality ingredients are always used. Meals are served daily from noon to 1:45pm and 7 to 9:30pm. Dinner costs £20 to £30 ($31.60 to $47.40) for two to four courses; table d'hôte luncheons go for £20 ($31.60). Always call for a reservation.

Dean Court Hotel

Duncombe Place, York, North Yorkshire YO1 2EF. ☎ **01904/625082** or 800/528-1234 in the U.S. Fax 01904/620305. 40 rms. TV TEL. £105 ($165.90) double. Rates include English breakfast. AE, DC, MC, V. Free parking.

This 1850 building lies right beneath the towers of the minster. This privately owned hotel was originally constructed to provide housing for the clergy of York Minster and then converted to a hotel after World War I. All the well-furnished rooms have bathtubs or showers and radios. The owner has done a lot to bring the facilities up to today's standards. Snacks are served in a coffee lounge from 10am to 6pm. The restaurant serves both a traditional English and an international cuisine, offered daily from 12:30 to 2pm and 7 to 9:30pm.

The Judges Lodging

9 Lendal, York, North Yorkshire YO1 2AQ. ☎ **01904/638733.** Fax 01904/679947. 13 rms. TV TEL. £89.50–£115 ($141.40–$181.70) double. Rates include English breakfast. AE, DC, MC, V. Free parking.

The earliest historical fact about this charming house is that it was the home of a certain Dr. Wintringham in 1710. At the beginning of the 19th century it is listed as having been a judges' lodging, used when they traveled north from the London Inns of Justice. You'll be greeted by the receptionist, who will register your name and then lead you to a circular wooden staircase, the only one of its type in the United Kingdom. All bedrooms have private baths or showers and some have four-poster beds. If you want to spoil yourself, you can book the large Prince Albert room, a twin-bedded room with three large windows overlooking the minster (Prince Albert actually slept in the room once). Each room has a different decor and is named accordingly. One is known as the Queen Mother Room.

There are two dining rooms; in each, candles flicker and the carefully trained staff attends to your every need. A table d'hôte dinner costs £12.45 ($19.65) and up. All meat, fish, and vegetables are fresh. Down in the old cellars—where they found bits of Roman pottery, antique pieces of glass, and other relics of the house's varied past—there is a cocktail bar, open to the public.

Viking Hotel

North St., York, North Yorkshire YO1 1JF. ☎ **01904/659822.** Fax 01904/641793. 188 rms, 2 suites. TV TEL. £110 ($173.80) double; £150 ($237) suite. English breakfast £9.50 ($15) extra. AE, DC, MC, V. Parking £5 ($7.90).

Within the ancient city walls, this modern hotel overlooks the River Ouse. Built in the 1970s, the hotel is today the largest in York. The attractions of York are only a short walk away. The well-furnished and modern bedrooms, many with views looking toward the minster, have trouser presses, hair dryers, and hot-beverage makers.

The hotel's two restaurants offer a variety of dining. In both restaurants, the Regatta and the Carvery, fixed-price lunches cost £9.50 ($15), with fixed-price dinners going for £14.50 ($22.90). Each establishment has a bar and offers a welcoming atmosphere.

INEXPENSIVE

⑤ Beechwood Close Hotel

19 Shipton Rd., Clifton, York, North Yorkshire YO3 6RE. ☎ **01904/658378.** Fax 01904/647124. 14 rms. TV TEL. £70 ($110.60) double. Rates include English breakfast. AE, DC, MC, V. Free parking. A19 north of the city.

Beechwood is a large house surrounded by trees, a garden with a putting green, and a parking area. Mr. and Mrs. Blythe run the small hotel, which offers comfortable bedrooms with central heating and hot-beverage makers. Good dinners or bar meals are served in the dining room overlooking the garden. A three-course table d'hôte meal costs £13.50 ($21.35). The hotel is a 15-minute walk to the minster, either by road or along the river.

⑤ Cottage Hotel

3 Clifton Green, York, North Yorkshire YO3 6LH. ☎ ☎ **01904/643711.** Fax 01904/611230. 19 rms. TV TEL. £60 ($94.80) double. Rates include English breakfast. AE, DC, MC, V. Free parking.

About a 10-minute walk north of York Minster, this hotel comprises two refurbished and extended Victorian houses overlooking the village green of Clifton. The hotel offers cozy bedrooms with simple furnishings and hot-beverage makers. Some 400-year-old timbers rescued from the demolition of a medieval building in one of the city's historic streets (Micklegate) grace the restaurant and bar, which does a thriving business in its own right. Among the beverages served there are two kinds of hand-pulled real ale. The hotel provides parking for its guests.

Heworth Court

76–78 Heworth Green, York, North Yorkshire YO3 7TQ. ☎ **01904/425156.** Fax 01904/415290. 26 rms. TV TEL. £76 ($120.10) double. Rates include English breakfast. AE, DC, MC, V. Free parking. A1036 to the east side of the city.

Of York's reasonably priced accommodations, this establishment is a 10- to 15-minute walk east of the center. It is a three-story red-brick Victorian structure, although many of its bedrooms are located in a modern extension added during the

1980s. The rooms are agreeably furnished and some open onto the courtyard. The hotel also offers a commendable cuisine; you can order dinner until 9:30pm. Meals cost £16.95 ($26.80) and up.

Hudson's Hotel

60 Bootham, York, North Yorkshire YO3 7BZ. ☎ **01904/621267.** Fax 01904/654719. 30 rms. TV TEL. £75–£95 ($118.50–$150.10) double; £90 ($142.35) triple. Rates include English breakfast. AE, DC, MC, V. Free parking.

Just a short walk from the minster, this hotel offers personal service. The owner converted two Victorian houses into the main hotel building in 1981 and later added an extension in the Victorian style. All accommodations are comfortably furnished and have tea and coffee makers. Hudson's has its own large parking lot. Both bar food and an English/French menu are offered, with fixed-price meals starting at £14 ($22.10).

Mount Royale Hotel

119 The Mount, York, North Yorkshire YO2 2DA. ☎ **01904/628856.** Fax 01904/611171. 17 rms, 6 suites. TV TEL. £75–£85 ($118.50–$134.30) double; £110 ($173.80) suite. Rates include English breakfast. AE, DC, MC, V. Free parking.

A short walk west of York's city walls, in a neighborhood known as The Mount, this hotel is the personal statement of two generations of the Oxtaby family. They work hard to create an amicable ambience and homelike atmosphere. The main house was built as a private home in 1833, although several years ago the owners skillfully merged the walls of a neighboring house of the same era into the original core to enlarge the premises. Accommodations and public rooms are carefully furnished with both antiques and modern pieces. Each bedroom has a bath, and some have private terraces leading into the garden. Room service, laundry, and a swimming pool are available.

The restaurant's menu features roast joints with interesting accompaniments. The extensive fixed-price menu, costing £26.50 ($41.85), carries supplements for such items as fresh out-of-season asparagus or strawberries. Justifiably popular with locals, the restaurant requires advance reservations. The dining room opens onto an attractive garden.

WHERE TO DINE

MODERATE

☺ Ivy Restaurant

In the Grange Hotel, Clifton, York, North Yorkshire YO3 6AA. ☎ **01904/644744.** Fax 01904/612453. Reservations required. Main courses £10.50–£14.50 ($16.60–$22.90); fixed-price lunch £13 ($20.55). AE, DC, MC, V. Sun–Fri 12:30–2:30pm; daily 7–10:15pm. FRENCH/ENGLISH.

In a Regency town house that's also a hotel of 30 rooms (see below), Christopher Falcus is the chef at this exceptionally good restaurant. The setting is that of a typically English country-house hotel, and there is both the main restaurant The Ivy and the Brasserie for your dining pleasure.

Vegetarians will find dishes to their liking, but meat and seafood reign supreme. The menu depends on the season and availability. However, you're likely to be tempted with fresh Scottish salmon. The menu is changed frequently but typical main courses are likely to feature roast fillet of sea bass on cream celeriac with red wine and truffle or lamb shank braised with tomatoes and garlic and served with smoked eggplant tortellini.

The Grange also rents well-furnished and comfortable bedrooms, costing from £90 ($142.20) for a single and £98 to £170 ($154.85 to $268.60) for a double, including breakfast. There is adequate parking and wheelchair access.

19 Grape Lane

19 Grape Lane. ☎ **01904/636366.** Reservations recommended for dinner. Main courses £8.95–£13.50 ($14.15–$21.35). MC, V. Tues–Sat noon–1:45pm; Tues–Fri 6:00–9:00pm, Sat 6–10pm. Closed first 2 weeks in Feb and last 2 weeks in Sept. ENGLISH.

In the heart of York, this restaurant occupies two floors of a timbered building with a wealth of its original features. With such a name, you expect a very British restaurant and you get that, but with a very contemporary touch. You might begin with monkfish salad with toasted pine kernels or fettuccine with salmon. This is followed by such main dishes as breast of guinea fowl or médaillons of hare with field mushrooms. The menus are wisely limited, so that every dish will be fresh. The wine list is ever growing, and service is thoughtful and considerate. The location is on a cobbled lane off Petergate.

INEXPENSIVE

⑤ Kites

13 Grape Lane. ☎ **01904/641750.** Reservations required. Main courses £7.95–£13.95 ($12.55–$22.05). MC, V. Sat noon–1:45pm; Mon–Sat 6:30–10:30pm. INTERNATIONAL.

About a five-minute walk from the minster, this restaurant is in the heart of York, on a small street near Stonegate. To reach it, walk up a narrow staircase to the second floor. This is a simple York bistro where the food is good and the atmosphere and service unpretentious. Kites's many devotees are attracted to its eclectic brand of cookery that's international in scope. For example, one recipe might have been a dish served in the Middle Ages in England (perhaps with adaptations), while another might come from Thailand. Kites features its own game sausages and serves such unusual dishes as duck livers with beetroot or beef fillet with chestnuts, pickled walnuts, and figs wrapped in pastry. Fondues, fresh salads, and herbs are part of the cuisine here. Vegetarian meals are also served.

✪ Melton's Restaurant

7 Scarcroft Rd. ☎ **01904/634341.** Reservations required. Main courses £9–£13.80 ($14.20–$21.80); fixed-price menu (Mon–Thurs) £19.50 ($30.80). MC, V. Tues–Sun noon–2pm; Mon–Sat 5:30–10pm. Closed Aug 31–Sept 7 and Dec 22–Jan 11. CONTINENTAL.

Some local food critics claim that Michael and Lucy Hjort serve the finest food in York. The location of their small place is approximately a mile from the heart of the city on a Victorian terrace. Mr. Hjort trained with the famous Roux brothers of Le Gavroche in London but he doesn't charge their astronomical prices. His cuisine reflects his own imprint, both in his choice of dishes and in the fresh ingredients.

In what has always been known as a sleepy culinary backwater of England, the city of York, the Hjorts have created some local excitement. Their menu changes frequently, based on the season and the chef's inspiration, but is likely to include such dishes as peppered roast rib of beef with beetroot pasta, rack of lamb with herbs, or sea bass with baked fennel in the style of the French Riviera. Vegetarian meals are also available, and families with children are welcome.

PUBS

The Black Swan

Peaseholme Green. ☎ **01904/625236.** Reservations not necessary. Main courses £3.75–£4.50 ($5.95–$7.10); beer from £1.50 ($2.35). MC, V. Mon–Sat 11am–11pm, Sun noon–3pm and 7–10:30pm. Food daily 11:30am–2:30pm. ENGLISH.

The Black Swan is a fine, timbered, frame house that was once the home of the lord mayor of York in 1417; the mother of Gen. James Wolfe of Quebec also lived here. One of the oldest inns in the city, it offers pub meals, which can be enjoyed in front of a log fire in a brick inglenook. Food consists of sandwiches, homemade soups, and Yorkshire puddings filled with beef stew. Bed and breakfast is available at £25 ($39.50) per person. There are two double rooms with private bath, plus one single and one twin with shared bath.

Kings Arms Public House

King's Staith. ☎ **01904/659435.** Reservations not accepted. Main courses £3.50–£6 ($5.55–$9.50); beer £1.35 ($2.15). No credit cards. Mon–Fri 11:30am–2:30pm, Sat 11:30am–2pm, Sun noon–2pm. ENGLISH.

Situated at the base of the Ouse Bridge, a few steps from the edge of the river, this 16th-century pub is boisterous and fun. A historic monument in its own right, it's filled with charm and character and has the ceiling beams, paneling, and weathered brickwork you'd expect. A board records various disastrous flood levels, the most recent of which inundated the place in 1991. In summer, rows of outdoor tables are placed beside the river. Your hosts serve a full range of draft and bottled beers, the most popular of which (Samuel Smith's) is still brewed in Tadcaster, only ten miles away. Place your lunch food order at the counter for bar snacks, which could include burgers, homemade curries, soups, and steak-and-kidney pie. No dinner is served.

Ye Olde Starre Inne

40 Stonegate. ☎ **01904/623063.** Reservations not accepted. Main courses £3.50–£4.95 ($5.55–$7.80). AE, DC, MC, V. Mon–Sat 11:30am–3pm, Sun noon–2:30pm; Mon–Thurs 5:30–8pm. Pub, Mon–Thurs 11am–11pm, Fri–Sat 11am–3:30pm and 7–11pm, Sun noon–3pm and 7–10:30pm. ENGLISH.

On a pedestrian street in the heart of Old York, this pub dates back to 1644 and is York's oldest licensed pub. Some inn (of one kind or another) might have stood on this spot since 900. In a pub said to be haunted by an old woman, a little girl, and a cat, you enter into an atmosphere of cast-iron tables, an open fireplace, oak Victorian settles, and time-blackened beams. In addition to standard alcoholic beverages, the pub offers an array of such English staples as steak-and-kidney pie, several different hot pots, lasagne, and platters of roast beef with Yorkshire pudding. A recent addition to the Scottish and Newcastle Brewery chain of pubs and restaurants, the establishment offers two outdoor courtyards which guests can enjoy during nice weather.

EASY EXCURSIONS FROM YORK

✪ Castle Howard

In its dramatic setting of lakes, fountains, and extensive gardens, Castle Howard, at Malton in North Yorkshire (☎ **01653/648444**), the 18th-century palace designed by Sir John Vanbrugh, is undoubtedly the finest private residence in Yorkshire. The principal location for the TV miniseries *Brideshead Revisited*, this was the first major achievement of the architect who later created the lavish Blenheim Palace near Oxford. The Yorkshire palace was begun in 1699 for the third earl of Carlisle, Charles Howard. The striking facade is topped by a painted and gilded dome, which reaches more than 80 feet into the air. The interior boasts a 192-foot-long gallery, as well as a chapel with magnificent stained-glass windows by the 19th-century artist Sir Edward Burne-Jones. Besides the collections of antique furniture, porcelains, and sculpture, the castle has many important paintings, including a portrait of Henry VIII by Holbein and works by Rubens, Reynolds, and Gainsborough.

The seemingly endless grounds around the palace also offer the visitor some memorable sights, including the domed Temple of the Four Winds, by Vanbrugh and the richly designed family mausoleum by Hawksmoor. There are two rose gardens, one with old-fashioned roses, the other featuring modern creations.

Castle Howard is open to the public daily from mid-March to late October: The grounds are open from 10am to 5pm; the house, from 11am to 5pm, with last admission at 4:30pm. Admission is £6 ($9.50) for adults, £3 ($4.75) for children. You can enjoy sandwiches, hot dishes, and wines in the self-service cafeteria. It lies 15 miles northeast of York, 3 miles off A64.

Yorktour, Tower Street, York (☎ **01904/645151**), provides a daily coach service to Castle Howard from Easter to October.

Harewood House & Bird Garden

At the junction of A61 and A659, midway between Leeds and Harrogate, stands Harewood House, Harewood, West Yorkshire (☎ **01532/886225**), the home of the earl and countess of Harewood, one of England's great 18th-century houses, which has always been owned by the Lascelles family. The fine Adam interior has superb ceilings and plasterwork and furniture made especially for Harewood by Chippendale. There are also important collections of English and Italian paintings and Sèvres and Chinese porcelain.

The gardens, designed by Capability Brown, include terraces, lakeside and woodland walks, and a 4$^1/_2$-acre bird garden with exotic species from all over the world, including penguins, macaws, flamingos, and snowy owls, as well as a tropical rain-forest exhibit. Other facilities include shops, a restaurant, and cafeteria. Parking is free, and there is a picnic area, plus an adventure playground for the children.

Admission to Harewood and its grounds is £5.95 ($9.40) for adults and £5 ($7.90) senior citizens; £3 ($4.75) children 15 and under. The house, bird garden, and adventure playground are open Easter to October, daily from 10am to 5pm. The location is seven miles south of Harrogate, eight miles north of Leeds on the Leeds-Harrogate road (at the junction of A61/A659) at Harewood Village; five miles from A1 at Wetherby, and 22 miles west of York. From York, head west along B1224 toward Wetherby and follow the signs to Harewood from there.

✪ Fountains Abbey & Studley Royal

At Fountains, 4 miles southwest of Ripon off B6265, stands Fountains Abbey and Studley Royal, Fountains (☎ **01765/608888**), on the banks of the Silver Skell. The abbey was founded by Cistercian monks in 1132 and is the largest monastic ruin in Britain. In 1987 it was awarded World Heritage status. The ruins provide the focal point of the 18th-century landscape garden at Studley Royal, one of the few surviving examples of a Georgian green garden. It's known for its water gardens, ornamental temples, follies, and vistas. The garden is bounded at its northern edge by a lake and 400 acres of deer park.

It is open January through March daily 10am to 5pm; April through September, daily 10am to 7pm; and October through December daily 10am to 5pm. It is closed December 24 to 25 and Friday in November and January. Admission is £4 ($6.30) adults, £2 ($3.15) for children.

It's best to visit the site by private car, although it can be reached from York by public transportation. From York, take bus no. 143 leaving from the York Hall Station to Ripon, 23 miles to the northwest (A59, A1, and B6265 lead to Ripon). From Ripon, it will be necessary to take a taxi 4 miles to the southwest, although some prefer to go on foot, as it's a scenic walk.

Hawes

About 65 miles northwest of York, on A684, Hawes is the natural center of Yorkshire Dales National Park. On the Pennine Way, it's England's highest market town and the capital of Wensleydale, which is famous for its cheese. There are rail connections from York taking you to Garsdale, which is 5 miles from Hawes. From Garsdale, bus connections will take you into Hawes.

The **Dales Countryside Museum,** Station Yard (the old train station; ☎ 01969/667494), traces folk life in the area of the Upper Dales, a story of 10,000 years of human history. Peat cutting and cheese making, among other occupations, are depicted. The museum is open April through October daily from 10am to 5pm. Winter opening hours are not fixed; you'll have to check locally. Admission is £1.50 ($2.35) adults, 75p ($1.20) children, students, and senior citizens.

Hawes is a good center for exploring the **Yorkshire Dales National Park,** some 700 square miles of water-carved country.

In the dales you'll find dramatic white limestone crags, roads and fields bordered by dry-stone walls, fast-running rivers, isolated sheep farms, and clusters of sandstone cottages—all hallmarks of the impressive Yorkshire Dales.

Malhamdale receives more visitors annually than any dale in Yorkshire. Two of the most interesting historic attractions are the 12th-century ruins of Bolton Priory and the 14th-century Castle Bolton, to the north in Wensleydale.

Richmond, the most frequently copied town name in the world, stands at the head of the dales and, like Hawes, makes a good center for touring the surrounding countryside.

WHERE TO STAY AND DINE: EXPENSIVE

Simonstone Hall

Hawes, North Yorkshire DL8 3LY. ☎ **01969/667255.** Fax 01969/667741. 10 rms. TV. £48–£73 ($75.85–$115.35) per person. Rates include half board. AE, DC, MC, V. Free parking.

Constructed in 1733, this building has been restored and converted into a comfortable family-run, country-house hotel offering spacious bedrooms, each a double. It's the former home of the earls of Wharncliffe and is located in a rural but not isolated area 1¹/₂ miles north of Hawes on the road signposted to Muker. The place once attracted such guests as Lillie Langtry and Disraeli. Owners Mr. and Mrs. J. R. Jeffryes are happy to have guests relax in the large, south-facing, paneled drawing rooms, which have comfortable antique furnishings.

You can have drinks in the Tawny Owl Bar and enjoy good food in the hotel's dining room. Nonresidents can enjoy home-cooked bar meals or order a two-course dinner for £15 ($23.70) or a four-course dinner for £20.25 ($32). Dinner can be complemented with good wines from the extensive cellar.

3   North York Moors National Park

The moors, on the other side of the Vale of York, have a wild beauty all their own, quite different from that of the dales. This rather barren moorland blossoms in summer with purple heather. Bounded on the east by the North Sea, it embraces a 554-square-mile area, which England has turned into a national park. For information before you go, especially good maps, contact **North York Moors National Park,** The Old Vicarage, Bondgate, Helmsley, York YO6 5BP (☎ **01439/ 770657**).

Bounded by the Cleveland and Hambleton hills, the moors are dotted with early burial grounds and ancient stone crosses. At Kilburn a white horse can be seen hewn out of the hillside.

Pickering and Northallerton, both market towns, serve as gateways to the moors. Cleveland Way National Trail, stretching for 110 miles, encircles the national park; two regional routes, 35-mile Esk Valley Walk and 40-mile Tabular Hills Walk, offer the best views of the area.

The isolation and the beauty of the landscape attracted the founders of three great abbeys: Rievaulx near Helmsley, Byland Abbey near the village of Wass, and Ampleforth Abbey near Coxwold, one of the most attractive villages in the moors. The Cistercian Rievaulx and Byland abbeys are in ruins, but the Benedictine Ampleforth still functions as a monastery and well-known Roman Catholic boys' school. Although many of its buildings date from the 19th and 20th centuries, they contain earlier artifacts.

Along the eastern boundary of the park, North Yorkshire's 45-mile coastline shelters such traditional seaside resorts as Filey, Whitby, and Scarborough, the latter claiming to be the oldest seaside spa in Britain, located supposedly on the site of a Roman signaling station. The spa was founded in 1622, when mineral springs with medicinal properties were discovered. In the 19th century its Grand Hotel, a Victorian structure, was acclaimed the best in Europe. The Norman castle on the big cliffs overlooks the twin bays.

You can drive through the moorland while based in York, but if you'd like to be closer to the moors, there are places to stay, notably Thirsk (see below).

THIRSK AND NEARBY

This old market town in the Vale of Mowbray, 24 miles north of York, on A19, is near the western fringe of the park. It has a fine parish church, but what makes it such a popular stopover is its association with the late James Herriot, author of *All Creatures Great and Small.* Mr. Herriot used to practice veterinary medicine in Thirsk.

WHERE TO STAY

Inexpensive

⑤ Brook House

Ingramgate, Thirsk, North Yorkshire YO7 1DD. ☎ **01845/522240.** Fax 01845/523133. 3 rms (none with bath). TV. £16 ($25.30) per person. Rates include English breakfast. Discount available for children. No credit cards. Free parking.

This large, brown-brick Victorian house, originally built in 1887, is situated on two acres of land and overlooks the Barbeck Brook (which flows through its front yard) and the open countryside. Despite its peace and isolation, the town's Market Square is only a three-minute walk away. Mrs. Margaret McLauchlan, the owner, is charming and kind and has even been known to do a batch of washing for guests at no extra cost (but we can't promise that). She serves a good Yorkshire breakfast, hearty and filling, plus an English tea in the afternoon. Tea-making facilities are also available for the guests, and the spacious and comfortable living room has color TV. The house is centrally heated, and in the guests' drawing room there is an open log fire in cool weather. There is ample parking for cars. The experience of knowing John and Margaret McLauchlan and enjoying their hospitality will remain long in your memory.

Note: The modern brick-sided bungalow set adjacent to Brook House's driveway also accepts overnight guests, but it is *not* associated in any way with the McLauchlan family or its enterprises.

⑤ St. James House

36 The Green, Thirsk, North Yorkshire YO7 1AQ. ☎ **01845/524120.** 4 rms (2 with bath or shower). TV. £32 ($50.55) double without bath, £40 ($63.20) double with bath. Rates include English breakfast. No credit cards. Free parking. Closed Nov–Mar.

This lovely three-story, 18th-century Georgian brick house on the village green is near the former maternity home where James Herriot's children were born. The guesthouse, operated by Mrs. Liz Ogleby, is tastefully furnished with some antiques. The attractive bedrooms (each a double) have such touches as good bone china to use with the hot-beverage facilities.

✪ Shepphard's Hotel, Restaurant & Bistro

Front St., Sowerby, near Thirsk, North Yorkshire YO7 1JF. ☎ **01845/5236555.** Fax 01845/524720. 12 rms (11 with bath). TV. £40 ($63.20) double without bath; double with bath £50–£80 ($79–$126.40); £84 ($132.70) four-poster room. Rates include English breakfast. MC, V. Free parking. Take the A19 half a mile south of Thirsk.

The late James Herriot treated his last horse on these premises, but now the Shepphard family has turned the complex into one of the finest lodging choices in the area. This family-run concern operates out of an old stable block and granary (now restaurant and bistro, with well-furnished bedrooms overhead). A country atmosphere prevails with pine furniture, and the decor often consists of nailed horse brasses on the beams. Many guests request the "fat bedroom," so named because of its outsize double bed. All the buildings in the complex are grouped around a cobbled courtyard.

Of course, many visitors come here just for the dining facilities. The restaurant has been operating out of the old stables since 1982. In 1990 a garden-room bistro was opened in the granary; the courtyard was covered over to make an atrium. Guests dine informally by candlelight in a setting of potted plants and palms.

The restaurant is open year round, and fresh local produce is used whenever possible. Breakfast is served daily from 8:30 to 9am, lunch from noon to 2pm, and dinner from 7 to 9:30pm. Mr. Herriot used to entertain his American publisher here. Main-course dishes, served with a choice of fresh vegetables, are likely to include chicken breast in a mushroom, cream, and brandy sauce; or suprême of duckling lighly grilled and fanned over a kumquat glaze. Fillet of Moors lamb is oven roasted with rosemary.

4 Haworth

45 miles SW of York, 21 miles W of Leeds

Famous as the home of the Brontës, this village is in West Yorkshire, a county that might easily be overlooked otherwise. On the high moor of the Pennines, it's the most visited literary shrine in England after Stratford-upon-Avon. Anne Brontë wrote two novels, *The Tenant of Wildfell Hall* and *Agnes Grey;* Charlotte wrote two masterpieces, *Jane Eyre* and *Villette,* which depicted her experiences as a teacher; and Emily is the author of *Wuthering Heights,* a novel of passion and haunting melancholy. Charlotte and Emily are buried in the family vault under the Church of St. Michael, and the parsonage where they lived has been preserved as the **Brontë Parsonage Museum,** Church Street (☎ **01535/642323**), which houses their furniture, personal treasures, pictures, books, and manuscripts. It may be visited April to September, daily from 10am to 5pm; October to March, daily from 11am to 4:30pm. It's closed from January 15 to February 9 and at Christmas. Admission is £3.60 ($5.70) for adults and £1.10 ($1.75) for children. A family ticket, good for two adults and three children, costs £8.30 ($13.10).

ESSENTIALS
GETTING THERE

By Train   To reach Haworth by rail, catch the train from Leeds to Keighley. Leeds has rail connections to York if you're arriving from there. At Keighley, board a privately run train—the Keighley and Worth Valley Railway—for the trip to Haworth. Some five to seven trains per day run between Keighley and Haworth in July and August. From March to June as well as in September and October, seven trains per day make the trip. For information, call 01535/647777.

By Bus   Yorkshire Rider, a private company, offers bus service between Hebden Bridge (which has rail links to Leeds and York) and Haworth. Bus no. 500 makes the trip between Hebden Bridge and Haworth from June through September only, four trips per day Sunday through Friday and one on Saturday. For information, call 01274/732237.

By Car   From York, head west toward Leeds on A64 approaching the A6120 Ring Road to Shipley; then take A650 to Keighley, and finally link up with the B6142 south to Haworth.

VISITOR INFORMATION

The **telephone area code** is 01535. The **Tourist Information Centre,** is at 2–4 West Lane in Haworth (☎ **01535/642329**).

WHERE TO STAY
INEXPENSIVE

Ⓢ Old White Lion Hotel

6 West Lane, Haworth near Keighley, West Yorkshire BD22 8DU. ☎ **01535/642313.** Fax 01535/646222. 14 rms. TV TEL. £46–£50 ($72.70–$79) double. Rates include English breakfast. AE, DC, MC, V. Free parking. Bus 664 or 665.

At the top of a cobblestone street, this hotel was built around 1700 with a solid stone roof. It's almost next door to the church where the Reverend Brontë preached, as well as the parsonage where the family lived. Paul and Christopher Bradford welcome visitors from all over the world to their warm, cheerful, and

Though I knew I looked a poor creature, and in many respects actually was so, nature had given me a voice that could make itself heard, if lifted in excitement or deepened by emotion.

—Charlotte Brontë

comfortable hotel. The bedrooms are attractively furnished. Although full of old-world charm, all rooms are completely up-to-date.

Meals featuring fresh vegetables cost £11 to £12.50 ($17.40 to $19.75) for a table d'hôte in the evenings. Bar snacks include the usual favorites—ploughman's lunch, hot pies, fish, and sandwiches.

WHERE TO DINE
INEXPENSIVE

Weaver's Restaurant
15 West Lane. ☎ **01535/643822.** Reservations recommended. Main courses £6.95–£13.95 ($11–$22.05); fixed-price lunch or dinner £11.95 ($18.90) for three courses. AE, DC, MC, V. (Oct–Mar only) Sun noon–1:30pm; Tues–Sat 7–9:30pm. BRITISH.

The best restaurant in the Brontë hometown, this spot once housed weavers. British to the core, it not only has an inviting atmosphere but it serves excellent food made with fresh ingredients. Jane and Colin Rushworth are quite talented in the kitchen. Lunch is served in the winter only. Dinners might include such classic dishes as Yorkshire pudding with gravy. If available, try one of the Gressingham ducks, which are widely praised in the United Kingdom for the quality of their meat. For dessert, you might select a Yorkshire cheese or one of the homemade delicacies. The style of the place is informal. The restaurant is likely to be closed for vacation for a certain period each summer, so call in advance to check.

5 Hexham & Hadrian's Wall

304 miles N of London, 37 miles E of Carlisle, 21 miles W of Newcastle upon Tyne

Above the Tyne River, this historic old market town has narrow streets, an old market square, a fine abbey church, and a moot hall. It makes a good base for exploring Hadrian's Wall (see below) and the Roman supply base of Corstopitum at Corbridge-on-Tyne, the ancient capital of Northumberland. The tourist office (see below), has lots of information on the wall for walkers, drivers, campers, and picnickers.

The **Abbey Church of St. Wilfrid** is full of ancient relics. The Saxon font, the misericord carvings on the choir stalls, Acca's Cross, and St. Wilfrid's chair are well worth seeing.

ESSENTIALS
GETTING THERE

By Train Take one of the many daily trains from London's King's Cross Station to Newcastle upon Tyne. At Newcastle, change trains and take one in the direction of Carlisle. The fifth or sixth (depending on the schedule) stop after Newcastle will be Hexham. Hexham lies 14 miles southeast of Hadrian's Wall. Visitors who are primarily interested in the wall (rather than in Hexham) should get off the Carlisle-bound train at the second stop (Bardon Mill) or at the third stop (Haltwhistle), which are 4 miles and 2¹/₂ miles, respectively, from the wall. At either of these hamlets, you can take a taxi to whichever part of the wall you care to visit. Taxis line up readily at the railway station in Hexham, but less often at the hamlets. If you get off at one of the above-mentioned hamlets and don't see a taxi, call ☎ 01434/344272 and a local taxi will come to get you. Many visitors ask their taxi drivers to return at a prearranged time (which they gladly do) to pick them up after their excursion on the windy ridges near the wall.

By Bus   Once again, bus passengers headed for Hexham from both York and London will need to transfer at Newcastle upon Tyne to a Northumbria Bus Lines coach which heads for Carlisle every hour or so throughout the day. The bus follows the same route as the above-mentioned train line, stopping in the hamlets mentioned above (and also in Hexham).

By Car   From Newcastle upon Tyne, head west on A69 until you see the cutoff south to Hexham.

VISITOR INFORMATION

The **telephone area code** is 01434. The **Tourist Information Centre** at Hexham is at the Manor Office, Hallgate (☎ **01434/605225**).

WHAT TO SEE & DO

✪ Hadrian's Wall

Hadrian's Wall, which extends for 73 miles across the north of England, from the North Sea to the Irish Sea, is particularly interesting for a stretch of 10 miles west of Housesteads, which lies 2³/₄ miles northeast of Bardon Mill on B6318. Only the lower courses of the wall have been preserved intact; the rest were reconstructed in the 19th century using original stones. From the wall, there are incomparable views north to the Cheviot Hills along the Scottish border and south to the Durham moors.

The wall was built in A.D. 122 after the visit of the emperor Hadrian, who was inspecting far frontiers of the Roman Empire and wanted to construct a dramatic line between the empire and the barbarians. Legionnaires were ordered to build a wall across the width of the island of Britain, stretching 73¹/₂ miles, beginning at the North Sea and ending at the Irish Sea.

The wall is a major Roman attraction in Europe. The western end can be reached from Carlisle, which also has an interesting museum of Roman artifacts; the eastern end can be reached from Newcastle upon Tyne (where some remains can be seen on the city outskirts; there's also a nice museum at the university).

Along the wall are several Roman forts, the most important of which is **Housestead Fort and Museum** (☎ **01434/344363**), called *Vercovicium* by the Romans. It lies three miles northeast of Bardon Mill on B6318. This substantially excavated fort, on a dramatic site, contains the only visible example of a Roman hospital in Britain. Admission is £2 ($3.15) for adults, £1 ($1.60) for children. It's open April through September, daily from 10am to 6pm; October through March, daily 10am to 4pm. Closed December 25 to 26 and January 1.

Just west of Housesteads, **Vindolanda** (☎ **01434/344277**) is another well-preserved fort south of the wall. It is located on a minor road 1¹/₄ miles southeast of Twice Brewed off the B6318. There is also an excavated civilian settlement outside the fort with an interesting museum of artifacts of everyday Roman life. Admission is £3.25 ($5.15) for adults, £2 ($3.15) for children. It's open daily

February through October 10am to 5pm. In July and August, the site remains open until 6:30pm.

Near Vindolanda at the garrison fort at Carvoran, close to the village of Greenhead, the **Roman Army Museum** (☎ **01697/747485**) traces the growth and influence of Rome from its early beginnings to the development and expansion of the empire, with special emphasis on the role of the Roman army and the garrisons of Hadrian's Wall. A barracks room depicts basic army living conditions. Realistic life-size figures make this a strikingly visual museum experience. Admission is £2.50 ($3.95) for adults, £1.50 ($2.35) for children. It's open March to September, daily from 10am to 5:30pm; in October, daily from 10am to 5pm. It's located at the junction of A69 and B6318, 18 miles west of Hexham.

Within easy walking distance of the Roman Army Museum is one of the most imposing and high-standing sections of Hadrian's Wall, Walltown Crags, where the height of the wall and magnificent views to north and south are impressive.

Visiting the Wall

From July 24 to September 5, the Tynedale Council and the Northumberland National Park run a bus service departing daily from a point near the railway station in Hexham at 10am, noon, 2pm, and 4pm—except on Sunday when the only departure is at 11:50am. The bus visits every important site along the wall, then turns around in the village of Haltwhistle and returns to Hexham. The cost is £4.75 ($7.50) for an all-day ticket. Many visitors take one bus out, then return on a subsequent bus 2, 4, or 6 hours later. Every Sunday a national park warden leads a 2¹/₂-hour walking tour of the wall, in connection with the bus service. The Hexham tourist office (see above) will provide further details.

NEARBY PLACES TO STAY & DINE
MODERATE

George Hotel
Chollerford, Humshaugh, near Hexham, Northumberland NE46 4EW. ☎ **01434/681611.** Fax 01434/681727. 46 rms. MINIBAR TV TEL. £110 ($173.80) double. Rates include English breakfast. AE, DC, MC, V. Free parking. Take A6079 5 miles north from Hexham.

Standing on the banks of the Tyne, this creeper-covered country hotel has gardens leading to the riverbank. It's a convenient base for visiting Hadrian's Wall. The hotel dates from the 18th century, when the original structure was built of Roman stone. It has been extensively refurbished to a high standard, with conference facilities and a leisure club. All bedrooms are comfortably furnished and equipped with such amenities as minibars with fresh milk daily for the beverage-making equipment, an iron and ironing board, hair dryer, TV, and radio.

The Fisherman's Bar is where locals gather for a traditional pub welcome and bar snacks served at lunch. A fixed-price buffet luncheon in the Riverside Restaurant begins at £13.50 ($21.35); dinner, at £19.50 ($30.80). An à la carte menu is also available, complemented by a large wine list.

Langley Castle Hotel
Langley-on-Tyne, Hexham, Northumberland NE47 5LU. ☎ **01434/688888.** Fax 01434/684019. 8 rms, 1 suite. TV TEL. £95–£125 ($150.10–$197.50) double or suite. Rates include English breakfast. AE, DC, MC, V. Free parking. From Hexham, go west on A69 to Haydon Bridge, then head south on A686 for 2 miles.

To experience a stately home, we recommend this hotel located on 10 acres of woodland at the edge of Northumberland National Park, southwest of Haydon Bridge and about 7 miles west of Hexham. It's the only medieval fortified castle

Frommer's Nature Notes

Until the establishment of the Northumberland National Park following World War II, most of its territory was involved in the endless border wars betweeen England and Scotland. Today, the park comprises almost 400 square miles of the least populated area in England, and is noted for its rugged landscape and associations with the country's ancient Roman invaders.

Touching on the border with Scotland, the park covers some of the most tortured geology in England—the Cheviot Hills—whose surfaces have been wrinkled by volcanic pressures, inundated with sea water, scoured and gouged by glaciers, silted over by rivers, and thrust upward in one of the most geologically complicated series of natural events anywhere. Much of the heather-sheathed terrain here is used for sheep grazing; woolly balls of fluff adorn hillsides ravaged by high winds and frequent rain.

The park manages to incorporate both the remains of Hadrian's Wall, one of the most impressive classical ruins of northern Europe, and the meandering course of the Pennine Way. Considered one of the most challenging hiking paths in Britain, the Pennine Way comprises about 150 miles of rugged terrain stretching through the northwestern corner of England. About 40 of those miles are within the boundaries of the park, although experienced hikers consider the Pennine Way one of many different hiking options within the region. One recommended route (which should not be attempted until first securing more detailed information from the national park headquarters, see below) stretches from Greenhead, near Haltwhistle (close to the western tip of Hadrian's Wall), across the landscape to the Hamlet of Bellingham. Less ambitious trekkers might opt to drive to Bellingham, then hike for two hours along the banks of the Tyne to the Hamlet of Riding Wood and back. The path is clearly marked and is considered one of the most worthwhile (and safest) of the local hikes. A map, priced at less than £1 ($1.60), can be purchased for these and other hiking trails at almost any local tourist office in the district. For additional information, contact the staff at the National Park Office, Northumberland National Park, Eastburn, South Park, Hexham, Northumberland, NE46 1BS, England (☎ 01434/60555).

home in England that receives paying guests. The castle, built in 1350, was largely uninhabited after being damaged in 1400 during an English-Scottish war until it was purchased in the late 19th century by Cadwallader Bates, a historian, who spent the rest of his life carefully restoring the property to its original beauty. Medieval features here include the 1350 spiral staircase, stained-glass windows, huge open fireplaces, seven-foot-thick walls, and many turrets. The luxuriously appointed bedrooms vary in size; all have radios and some have whirlpools or saunas; the rates vary according to the room's features. The hotel has an elegant drawing room, with an adjoining oak-paneled bar. Local specialties are served in the intimate restaurant, where meals cost £18.95 ($29.95) and up.

INEXPENSIVE

Anchor Hotel

John Martin St., Haydon Bridge, Northumberland NE47 6AB. ☎ **01434/684227.** Fax 01434/684586. 12 rms (10 with bath). TV TEL. £53 ($83.75) double without bath; £64

Impressions

Over the heather the wet wind blows, I've lice in my tunic and a cold in my nose.
The rain comes pattering out of the sky, I'm a Wall soldier, I don't know why.
—W. H. Auden, *Roman Wall Blues*

($101.10) double with bath. Rates include English breakfast. AE, DC, MC, V. Free parking.
A69 7 miles west of Hexham.

Ideally situated for visitors to the wall and its surroundings, between Haltwhistle (9 miles away) and Hexham (7 miles), this riverside village pub was once a coaching inn on the route from Newcastle to Carlisle. The building, which was constructed in 1700 near the edge of the North Tyne River (which still flows within a few feet of its foundations), sits in the heart of the tiny village of Haydon Bridge. The cozy bar is frequented by locals. In the country dining room, wholesome evening meals are served. A la carte dinners cost from £13 to £16 ($20.55 to $25.30). The bedrooms are comfortably furnished. Clearly, this is the most visible and most heavily patronized business in the village.

Hadrian Hotel

Wall, near Hexham, Northumberland NE46 4EE. ☎ **01434/681232.** 6 rms (4 with bath, 2 with shower but no toilet). ☎ £42 ($66.35) double with shower and sink, £49 ($77.40) double with bath. Rates include English breakfast. DC, MC, V. Free parking.

Considered an ideal hotel for stopovers along Hadrian's Wall, the Hadrian lies on the only street of the hamlet of Wall, $3^1/2$ miles north of Hexham. It's an ivy-covered 18th-century building erected of stones gathered long ago from the site of the ancient wall. The owners have carefully refurbished the place, which now has two Jacobean-style bars serving bar meals priced between £6 ($9.50) and £9 ($14.20). There is also a restaurant, serving à la carte lunches and dinners priced from £8 ($12.65) each. Each attractive bedroom is furnished with a radio alarm and hot-beverage facility. The hotel maintains a private garden for the use of its residents, and a beer garden that serves as a warm-weather extension of its pub.

Index